MICROECONOMICS

A JOURNEY THROUGH LIFE'S DECISIONS

Visit the *Microeconomics, A Journey Through Life's Decisions*
Companion Website at **www.pearsoned.co.uk/cullisjones**
to find valuable **student** learning material including:

- Extra practice and self-assessment questions with solutions
  for each chapter, to further improve your understanding.
- Annotated links to relevant economics sites on the web.

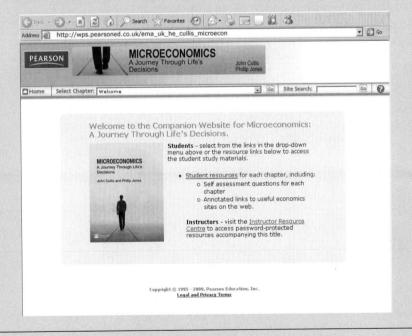

MICROECONOMICS

A JOURNEY THROUGH LIFE'S DECISIONS

John Cullis
University of Bath

Philip Jones
University of Bath

FT Prentice Hall
FINANCIAL TIMES

An imprint of **Pearson Education**
Harlow, England • London • New York • Boston • San Francisco • Toronto • Sydney • Singapore • Hong Kong
Tokyo • Seoul • Taipei • New Delhi • Cape Town • Madrid • Mexico City • Amsterdam • Munich • Paris • Milan

Pearson Education Limited
Edinburgh Gate
Harlow
Essex CM20 2JE
England

and Associated Companies throughout the world

Visit us on the World Wide Web at:
www.pearsoned.co.uk

First published 2009

ISBN: 978-0-273-71893-2

British Library Cataloguing-in-Publication Data
A catalogue record for this book is available from the British Library

Library of Congress Cataloging-in-Publication Data
A catalog record for this book is available from the Library of Congress

10   9   8   7   6   5   4   3   2   1
13   12   11   10   09

Typeset in 9/11.5 Stone Serif by 35
Printed by Ashford Colour Press Ltd., Gosport

The publisher's policy is to use paper manufactured from sustainable forests.

BRIEF CONTENTS

CONTENTS

Supporting resources

Visit www.pearsoned.co.uk/cullisjones to find valuable online resources

Companion Website for students

- Extra practice and self-assessment questions with solutions for each chapter, to further improve your understanding.
- Annotated links to relevant economics sites on the web.

For instructors

- Additional questions with answers relating to material in the text, to use in class or set for homework, testing and assessment.

Also: The Companion Website provides the following features:

- Search tool to help locate specific items of content
- E-mail results and profile tools to send results of quizzes to instructors
- Online help and support to assist with website usage and troubleshooting

For more information please contact your local Pearson Education sales representative or visit **www.pearsoned.co.uk/cullisjones**

LIST OF FIGURES

LIST OF TABLES

On awakening this morning you may have had a list of 'things to do today': help make breakfast; walk a younger brother (or sister) to school; work part-time in a local factory; go shopping; vote in a local election and write to a Member of Parliament about the conduct of United Nations in the Middle East; spend one hour volunteering in a charity-shop supporting guide dogs for the blind; deciding whether to buy insurance cover for your up-coming foreign holiday; make sure that you send a card of condolence to a bereaved cousin; considering where to go on a date to-night, etc. As you walk to college or university you might muse on the events that happened yesterday; some that were a complete surprise and others that were anticipated. Or you might spend time anticipating possible forthcoming events. In all of this, you will undoubtedly make an assessment (explicitly or implicitly) on how events and activities impact on your happiness.

This may seem a very busy day (!) but there is nothing in this list to 'raise an eyebrow'. The decisions that you are about to take and the assessments that you will make are the very essence of 'life's day to day tapestry'. If one of today's decisions is whether to read a microeconomics text, surely microeconomic theory should have something to say about life's decisions?

The time to allocate to market and non-market activity; the use of inputs in any activity; the nature of rewards; the payments to suppliers, the risks that are to be undertaken are all decisions that can be analysed by applying microeconomic theory. They all feature in the chapters of this book. The central proposition is that microeconomic theory can be applied to *all* facets of life's decisions but not that *all* facets of life's decisions can be explained by microeconomic theory.

The book is intended for students who have successfully completed a university foundation course in microeconomic theory (or its equivalent). While the objective is to highlight the 'universal' (imperialistic?) nature of microeconomic theory, the book (unlike many competing texts) does not present microeconomics as 'cut and dried'. The book does not follow a 'job done format'. Quite the reverse; on every occasion theory is challenged. The objective is to question 'received wisdom'. The book presents microeconomic theory as a debate; questioning theoretical exposition and considering future developments.

Many microeconomics texts focus only on the behaviour of consumers and producers in markets. This text encompasses this behaviour but insists that the same theory is applicable to other decisions. Many decisions are made that have a non-market orientation and a great deal of time and productive effort occurs outside the formal 'market' context. Microeconomics can be applied to a very wide variety of settings.

Blaise Pascal (1623–62), the French mathematician, physicist and religious philosopher, wrote in *Pensees*:

> 'Let no one say that I have said nothing new. . . . the arrangement of the subject is new. When we play tennis we play with the same ball but one of us places it better.'

In many ways this sentiment captures the objective of yet another microeconomic theory book. It is the arrangement that is new and it is the arrangement that is distinctive.

The text has its origins in a contract to write a book built on the theme of a 'day in the life of (and life-cycle of) *homo economicus*'. The book includes fertility economics and the economic family, through schooling and training and labour market attachment, towards involvement in the market economy. Attention is also paid to the non-market economy (as represented by the public and voluntary sectors). In later chapters microeconomics is applied to deal with decisions taken in the international economy. On one level the journey is from childhood to old age and death. On another level the journey is from the family, to neighbourhoods, to markets and to the 'global market'.

Samuels (1991) argued that it is much easier to get things published that are very close to existing publications than it is to publish something that appears to be mildly deviant. This implicit advice applies equally when attempting to publish text books. Indignant reviewers of early drafts wrote 'this is not Varian'! And of course, this was quite true; the objective was to be different. The objective was not to slavishly follow a stereotyped format. That said, the first draft was changed to accommodate reviewers and to bring the book in line with many rivals. However, much of the original structure has been retained in an attempt to publish something a little different. Fortunately for us, and hopefully you, some reviewers agreed that it would be a shame to lose everything that attempted to make this enterprise distinctive.

Part I is essentially a self-contained microeconomics course unit. Eight chapters cover the major building blocks of microeconomic theory (including risk information, insurance and uncertainty, as well as the role of time in producing fundamental commodities).

Part II comprises two chapters on the Household Economy that explain the contribution that economists (largely 'Chicago' ones) have made to this important area of individual's lives.

Part III covers the Private Economy. Two chapters deal with models of the firm (dubbed 'black box') and models that attempt to construct an internal (or institutional) content.

Part IV of the book deals with the Public Economy. One chapter focuses on the costs of financing services in the public sector. Another chapter deals with willingness to participate in collective decision-making.

Part V deals with the Voluntary Economy. The voluntary sector is analysed in the first chapter in this section of the book, while the second chapter (perhaps more cynically) questions the proposition that action deemed philanthropic is motivated by altruism.

Part VI considers the International Economy. Most economies are 'open' (in the case of the UK approximately a third of GNP is internationally traded – the foreign holiday in the opening paragraph above is an import).

Part VII concludes with the final decisions in a life time. The book sets out to illustrate microeconomics 'from the cradle to the grave' and in Part VII *homo economicus* contemplates the grave (or the 'Big Sleep').

Much of microeconomic theory is presented in a way that makes it appear unassailable; a 'Fort Knox' of 'golden' results and rules. Assumptions made, axioms adopted and proofs provided force the reader to what appears to be incontrovertible conclusions or outcomes. The objective in this book is to indicate that, both within economics and certainly outside of economics, thinkers and researchers really are not all 'singing from the same hymn sheet'. To do otherwise is a disservice to the 'richness' of post-foundation theory and the insight of academics, within and outside the economics discipline. Each chapter contains a section labelled 'Challenge' where 'other' economists' and non-economists' contributions are outlined. The intention is to make the book and the subject more vivid than we perceive others often find it. The intention is also to sharpen readers' understanding of the orthodox mainstream theorising by indicating, albeit in brief, what critics wedded to other paradigms ('ways of thinking') have to say.

The book can be used across a wide range of course units that are typical in a second/final year economics degree course. The book should be helpful for a student doing a course unit on microeconomic theory and/or course units in: the economics of social policy, public sector economics and international economics. Writing a book of this breadth necessarily incurs very many intellectual debts. After all, our claim is only that the arrangement is new! The explicit references used are, of course, detailed but we have also gained considerably from the comments of David Collard, Nipit Wongpunya and a number of anonymous publisher's referees.

Reflecting again on Pascal's remarks, whether we have placed the ball better than others or not is ultimately a judgement for the market place. Will individuals decide to buy the book when they go shopping? Will it be on economics units reading lists? When read will it enhance individuals' understanding of life's decisions? Together with our publishers we very much hope the answers to these questions are yes.

References

Pascal, B. *Pensées*, translated by W. Trotter, www.orst.edu/instruct/ph1302/tests/pascal,I-22 (1660/1999).

Samuels, W. (1991) 'Truth' and 'discourse' in the social construction of economic reality; an essay on the relation of knowledge to economic reality, *Journal of Post Keynesian Economics,* 13: 511–24.

ACKNOWLEDGEMENTS

We are grateful to the following for permission to reproduce copyright material:

Figures 4.4, 5.15, 5.17, 5.18, 6.7, 6.9, 8.5, 13.1A, 13.7, 13.14, 13.15, 14.2, 14.4, 15.5, 17.10 and 18.10 from *Public Choice and Public Finance*, 3rd edition, Oxford University Press (Cullis, J.G. and Jones, P.R. 2009), by permission of Oxford University Press; Figure 4.7 from The Common Agricultural Policy, in F. MacDonald and S. Dearden (eds) *European Economic Integration*, 3rd edition, Pearson Education (Gibbons, J. 1999); Table 4.4 from *The Costs of the Common Agricultural Policy*, Croon Helm (Buckwell, A.E., Harvey D.R., Thomson, K.L. and Parton, K.A. 1982); Table 5.1 from *Public Choice and Public Finance*, 2nd edition, Oxford University Press (Cullis, J.G. and Jones, P.R. 1998); Figure 6.12 from *The Demand and Supply of Public Goods*, Liberty Fund (Buchanan, J.M. 1968); Table 6.4 from The Coase theorem: some experimental tests, *Journal of Law and Economics*, Vol. 25, pp. 93–8, University of Chicago Press (Hoffman, E. and Spitzer, M. 1982); Figures 11.29, 11.30, 11.31 and 11.32 from Oligopsony and monopsonistic competition in labour markets, *Journal of Economic Perspectives*, Vol. 16 No. 2 Spring, pp. 155–74, American Economic Association (Bhaskar V., Manning, A. and To, T. 2002); Table 12.2 from *Economic Analysis of Property Rights*, 2nd edition, Cambridge University Press (Barzel, Y. 1997); Table 13.1 from *Public Sector Economics*, 4th edition, © 1990 Blackwell Publishing (Brown, C.V. and Jackson, P.M. 1990), reproduced with permission of Blackwell Publishing Ltd; Table 13.2 from Labour supply and taxation: a survey, *Fiscal Studies*, Vol. 13 No. 3, pp. 15–40, Institute for Fiscal Studies (Blundell. R. 1992); Table 13.3 from The end of taxation? *Public Interest*, Vol. 112 Summer, pp. 110–18, American Enterprise Institute (Payne J.L. 1993); Table 14.7 from Rent seeking, in D.C. Mueller (ed.) *Perspectives on Public Choice: A Handbook*, Cambridge University Press (Tollinson, R.D. 1997); Table 14.8 from Wolf, Charles, Jr., *Markets or Governments: Choosing between Imperfect Alternatives*, figure © 1988 Massachusetts Institute of Technology, by permission of The MIT Press; Figure 15.4 from *Altruism and Economy*, © 1978 Blackwell Publishing (Collard, D. 1978), reproduced with permission of Blackwell Publishing Ltd.; Table 15.2 from Pareto optimal redistribution, *American Economic Review*, Vol. 59, pp. 542–57, American Economic Association (Hochman, H.M. and Rodgers, J.D. 1969); Table 15.3 from The theory of crowding-out: donations, local government spending and the new federalism, in R. Magat (ed.) *Philanthropic Giving*, Oxford University Press (Steinberg, R. 1989), and The economics of charity, in N. Barr and D. Whynes (eds) *Current Issues in the Economics of Welfare*, Macmillan (Jones, A.M. and Posnett, J.W. 1993; Table 17.1 from *Modern International Economics* by Wilfred J. Ethier. Copyright © 1983 by W.W. Norton & Company, Inc. Used by permission of W.W. Norton & Company, Inc.; Table 17.4 from *Measuring the Costs of Protection in the United States* by G.C. Hufbauer and K.A. Elliott. Copyright 1994 by Peterson Institute for International Economics. Reproduced with permission of Peterson Institute for International Economics in the format Textbook via Copyright Clearance Center.

In some instances we have been unable to trace the owners of copyright material, and we would appreciate any information that would enable us to do so.

Custom publishing

Custom publishing allows academics to pick and choose content from one or more textbooks for their course and combine it into a definitive course text.

Here are some common examples of custom solutions, which have helped over 800 courses across Europe:

- different chapters from across our publishing imprints combined into one book;
- lecturer's own material combined together with textbook chapters or published in a separate booklet;
- third-party cases and articles that you are keen for your students to read as part of the course;
- any combination of the above.

The Pearson Education custom text published for your course is professionally produced and bound – just as you would expect from any Pearson Education text. Since many of our titles have online resources accompanying them we can even build a custom website that matches your course text.

If you are teaching an introductory microeconomics course, you might find Part I of this text as a self-contained unit is more appropriate for you. Similarly, if you also teach a separate public economics course, Parts IV and V may appeal to you, and for international economics, Part VI.

Custom publishing allows you to provide access to these chapters in individual volumes for your students or select your ideal combination of chapters across the text.

If, once you have had time to review this title, you feel custom publishing might benefit you and your course, please do get in contact. However minor or major the change, we can help you out.

For more details on how to make your chapter selection for your course please go to www.pearsoned.co.uk/cullisjones

You can contact us at: **www.pearsoncustom.co.uk** or via your local representative at: **www.pearsoned.co.uk/replocator**.

PART I

THE ESSENTIALS OF MICROECONOMICS

CHAPTER 1

Is microeconomics 'boring' and 'difficult'?

1.1 Introduction

Students often find microeconomic theory boring or difficult or both.[1] In this chapter an explanation of these phenomena is offered. In providing an explanation it is hoped in the remainder of the chapters to reverse the negative connotations associated with this opening chapter title. Microeconomic theory can be both interesting and accessible. But access is not free. The price to be paid is work effort; not so much in terms of more reading, more note taking and more 'highlighting' but in terms of more thinking. The process of thinking seldom yields quick results and getting to the 'promised land' (of interest and ease) requires patience, perseverance and problem solving. However, it is possible to arrive at the 'promised land' and it is hoped that these pages facilitate the journey.

Einstein told the world that time and space were not fixed characteristics of the physical universe, but rather that they were relative to the position of the observer. If this message has become easy to accept for the apparently hard physical universe, it should be that much easier to accept for the social universe. The basic point is that what you get to see, or to believe, depends on where you stand. What you get to see, or believe, depends on the underlying framework in which you are trying to fit observations. In order to understand microeconomics you have to acquire an understanding of the underlying framework in which economists attempt to interpret the world. In following this line of thought, it is clear that economics is about acquiring a mental skill (rather than studying a specific set of topics, e.g. about the business world, the stock market, the balance of payments and issues that people in general tend to identify with the subject

---

1. If evidence is required, and one early reviewer of this text thought it was, consider the following quotations: 'The reason A-level economics is not attracting students is twofold: the syllabus has not kept up with developments such as game theory and asymmetric information, and is seen as **boring**, theoretical and difficult' (La Manna 2003: 15, Emphasis added).

    Cole (1973: x) writes in the preface to his microeconomics theory text, 'Anyone who has taught economic theory has, I am sure no false impressions about the popularity of the subject. Appraisals are plentiful: It doesn't help people.' 'I can understand the words but not the graphs.' 'It tries to reduce human behaviour to quantitative terms.' 'I'll never remember how to derive a demand curve.' 'How will it help me get a job?' And, of course, '**It's boring.**' (Emphasis added.)

    More recently Varoufakis (1998: ix) in the preface to his book on the foundations of economics writes: 'This book is the result of two related personal experiences. First came the experience of learning economics as a first year student at the University of Essex back in 1978. By golly it was **boring**!' (Emphasis added.)

'economics'). Many economists are interested in economics but not in the economy. Whilst this statement is offered as an eye-catching one, it is nevertheless the case that much of microeconomic theory does not connect very directly to 'the economy' as individuals commonly perceive it. In the next section the key features in the micro-economist's view of the world are outlined as a way of substantiating the claims made above.

The style of textbooks varies. Here the intention is to provide material on micro-economics assuming the reader has successfully completed a foundational introductory first-year course in microeconomics. In trying to make the material more vivid the style adopted is akin to that of the dress-code 'smart–casual' – rather than 'formal'. It is smart in that it is hoped to provide sufficient detailed analysis so that all post-foundation-level economics can be accessed with, or from, this text. It is casual in that some of the writing has a deliberate colloquial style (to stimulate interest); indeed, where mathematical analysis is employed, this is not taken to any great degree of refinement (second-order conditions are generally ignored). It is hoped that if you stick with the material presented here and pay the price of work effort, there is a great deal to be gained (but, of course, we also want to sell the text, so 'caveat emptor'!).

1.2 'Boring boring economics!'

Why do some students find economics boring? The answer seems to lie, at least partly, in six characteristics that define the way in which students are invited to think about the world in which they live and make decisions.[2]

1.2.1 Build abstract models

Economists work by constructing economic models. The word 'model' signifies that something is not the 'real thing'. Economic models are abstractions that are meant to be useful. The idea is that progress is made by the orderly *loss* of information surrounding any problem. The objective is to abstract only the key relationships to facilitate analysis. It is clear from this that good (or bad) economic theory cannot be about realism as such. Economic theorists are not upset when they are told that they are being unrealistic. What matters is whether the model can explain, predict or offer insights with the chosen abstractions that have been judged to be key. As has been observed on a number of occasions, a map of the world on a scale 1 to 1 is totally unhelpful because you are standing on it!

Millions of people each year travel successfully around the London Underground system by using the familiar colour-coded maps that are set out for them to work with. However, these maps bear little relationship to the actual geographical structure of the network of railways that the millions of people are successfully negotiating. The coloured circles and lines are an abstraction from geographical reality and prove very helpful to people who wish to travel around London. Abstraction is required to help make a problem or explanation tractable. No claim is made that economists 'get it right' initially – or (as models are typically refined as other economists use and adapt them) – eventually! Models that are too abstract will generally fail to offer insights into any significant topic and therefore will typically be ignored. Models that are not sufficiently abstract will simply describe an issue (essentially holding a mirror up to it) and will also generally fail to offer insights into any significant topic and, therefore, be ignored. The aim is to develop

---

2. This list reflects a reordering and development of McKenzie and Tullock (1981).

models that are planted in productive ground that 'avoids the twin dangers of empty formalism and inconclusive anecdote' (to borrow a phrase from Hahn and Matthews 1965: 112).

1.2.2 Opportunity cost

Opportunity cost is a central concept in virtually all discussions in economics. 'Cost' is one of the many words typically used in economics that has a common currency as well as a specific meaning within the subject. Opportunity cost arises because the world is characterised by scarce resources (usually collected under the headings land, labour and capital and called 'the factors of production'). They are scarce relative to demand for the goods and services into which the resources can be converted via a process called 'production' (a process defined in terms of combining factors of production). The essential and fundamental point (not always recognised) is that it is impossible to have everything. If it is impossible to have everything, then choices must be made. Choices are forced and inevitable. Once a choice has been made, a cost will have necessarily been incurred. This cost is in terms of the value placed on the next-best forgone alternative at the time that a decision is made. This notion of the value placed on the next-best forgone alternative is what defines 'opportunity cost' for economists.

As this value is ultimately a conjecture (see Chapter 3), methods of identifying empirical proxies for that value are important to economic analysis. The way in which costs are identified and articulated when dealing with an economic issue should always come under careful scrutiny, as mistakes (by reference to economic theory or sleights of hand) can often be found. The reason economists seek 'opportunity costs' is that this represents the cost data that *should* influence choice. 'Opportunity costs' are often wildly at odds with visible conventional accounting data (or a list of explicit currency-denominated prices – as faced by an individual in everyday transactions). In microeconomics, the costs incurred by taking one course of action as opposed to another have a powerful impact on the course actually chosen. Other things being equal, least-cost solutions are sought as they minimise the need for sacrifice of other goods and services.

1.2.3 Rational actions

The world of microeconomics is characterised by rational actions. Individuals are acting with the objective of maximising their utility (or satisfaction). This is a strong statement and a strong postulate to adopt. It presupposes that:

(i)   individuals know what they want, i.e. know what their preferences are;
(ii) they are able to rank all alternatives available to them in terms of their expected utility to them;
(iii) they can choose the combination that will succeed in maximising their utility.

It additionally presupposes that individuals are not moving along predetermined paths but can offset environmental, biological and sociological forces (which some would claim determine what they do). In microeconomic theory, individuals are viewed as making '*real*' choices over their life.

The extent to which it is possible for them to affect the world around them will vary with intensity of preference (with respect to different goals) and their ability to command real resources. It is readily acknowledged that the world is one that is characterised by uncertainty, so that acting to maximise expected utility does not mean always succeeding in achieving that goal. Expectations can be wrong and rational individuals can lose by a choice, even though *ex ante* (looking forward) they have made the correct utility-maximising action (choice).

Furthermore, it is necessary to emphasise that economists, despite popular impression, are not obsessed with the material or (especially) the business world.[3] The apparatus of microeconomic theory is just as valid for goods that are abstract as for those that are material. Indeed, a 'good' is any positive source of utility. Economics finds it relatively easy to deal with love, hate, altruism (see Chapter 15) and other abstract feelings. 'Economics is about the things that people value' (Williams 1978: 26). Whilst other academic disciplines may claim to deal with fundamental feelings in a deeper fashion, it remains the case that they are by no means excluded from microeconomics.

1.2.4 The individual

The individual is the basic unit of analysis in microeconomic theory. It is individuals who have preferences (utility functions), make choices over alternatives and take actions. It is best to avoid, wherever possible, using the word 'society' in microeconomics. If it is used, it is important to stress that it only signifies society as being the sum of all individuals. Society is nothing more, or less, than the collection of all individuals in the world of microeconomics.

As such, microeconomic theory is said to contain a non-organic view of society – society cannot be talked about and treated as if it is an actor, as if it is an organism or entity in itself. In contrast, sociology is a subject that is built around the notion of society as an organism, as an entity, as 'a player' to use a more modern term. But this is no part of microeconomics where, to repeat, society is simply the sum of all individuals. Moreover, words like 'government' simply mean the institutions through which individuals make collective choices. Government is not an actor, not an entity with its own goals. The use of the word 'government' is meant to be a shorthand way to convey the set of institutions through which individuals work and through which individuals make collective choices or decisions.

1.2.5 Neutral or amoral stance

There is no recipe in economics about what is 'good' or 'bad'. Economists do not have a handle on any special truths about the nature of 'life, the universe and everything'. There is no recipe in economics for making a good society (collection of all individuals). Economists tend to see themselves as following a rigorous, deductive logic and demonstrate a willingness to look into the face of the devil (perhaps when others shy away). For example, in Chapter 19 economic theories of suicide are discussed. To some (especially those who have in some way been touched by it), the process of theorising about suicide must look, at best, both unnecessary and tasteless. After all, it is clear what has happened – and does anyone need academic publication so badly that they have to make this their topic!

To the economist *everything* is on the agenda, to the extent that everything is about choices made in a world characterised by uncertainty and scarce resources. With this perspective in mind almost nothing lacks an economic dimension. In short, the discipline is about analysing *how individuals behave*. The focus is individual choice. The analysis is

---

3. The writer Houellebecq (2003: 280–1) in his novel *Platform* provides some support for the case made here but does commit the mistake of seeing economics as a very narrow business-based subject. Michel, the central character, 'nurtured the theory that it was possible to decode the world . . . by reading the financial news and the stock prices'. And 'therefore forced himself to read the *Figaro* financial section daily, supplemented by even more forbidding publications like *Les Echos* or *La Tribune Desfosses*. But, 'Up to this point the only definite conclusion' he 'had categorically come to: **economics was unspeakably boring**'. (Emphasis added.)

of how changes in the economic signals, or incentives, confront and alter individual maximising behaviour.

1.2.6 Government or public-policy intervention

Government intervention is justified in neoclassical microeconomics in relation to so-called 'market failure' with the expectation that actual, as opposed to idealised, public policy can be expected to raise social welfare (see Chapters 5 and 6). Market failure comprises a series of arguments that suggest that universal perfect competition cannot always guarantee attractive results. When economists talk about attractive results, they have in mind a configuration of events that are described as 'efficient' and 'equitable'. These key concepts are reviewed below. They are central to the substance of virtually all chapters in this text. The main point here is that the benchmark form of economic organisation in microeconomics is universal perfectly competitive markets. For many, this is what a neoclassical market economy 'should' comprise.

The above is a thumbnail caricature of the mental world inhabited by individuals who think as economists. None of these six characteristics proves uncontroversial. However, all are found, implicitly or explicitly, in microeconomic analysis. Some individuals readily identify with this type of thinking, whilst others have to work harder to practise it. Putting together the highlighted headings of the characteristics that make up subsections 1.2.2 to 1.2.6 may help this latter group as it provides the following first letters:

B-uilding abstract models;
O-pportunity cost;
R-ational actions;
I-ndividuals as the unit of account;
N-eutral or amoral stance;
G-overnment intervention being justified by reference to the significant failure of markets.

In short, microeconomics *is* B O R I N G! Whilst this is a contrived mnemonic, implicit in the first chapters of many microeconomic textbooks, it serves three purposes:

(i)   First, to attempt to make clear that economists have a sense of how their subject is often perceived.
(ii) Second, to provide an aide-memoire to the economist's view of the world.[4]
(iii) Third, to offer insight on the reasons students (and others) might have found microeconomics *genuinely* boring. (You might watch people's eyes cloud over when you tell them you are an economist, shortly followed by their either making an excuse to leave you, or asking for tips about stocks and shares! – the message here is that neither response is justified when more is known about the subject.)

If the characteristics outlined are adopted then the subject is a 'golden pillow', because it never quite allows you to do what you intuitively think it ought to:

(i)   You are never invited to air your *personal prejudices*. You are, in contrast, invited to follow the logic of, and think in the context of, the restrictive and constricting framework set out above. (Your personal prejudices are permitted if you have sufficient understanding and flair to set them within the restrictive framework – a skill this text will hopefully help you acquire.)

---

4. When the material of this book has been used in lectures there have been mixed results in terms of student scores but seldom have students failed to remember the 'boring' mnemonic.

(ii) Economics offers no account of where an individual's preferences come from, rather *preferences are exogenous* (given outside the model or analysis). Of course, differences in preferences are what make people interesting – 'it wouldn't do for us all to be the same' and 'it takes all sorts to make a world' are everyday sayings that capture this. Economists have no account of the source of unusual or obsessive interests or, indeed, what are seen as ordinary ones. Furthermore, for economic theory 'to work' it appears there is a general requirement that individuals have stable preferences. If, by contrast, individuals, governed by whim and emotion, act inconsistently, the apparatus of economic theory does not help analyse behaviour. Economists doubt both that individuals really are governed by whim and emotion and that a satisfactory account of observed behaviour can be found in simply assuming that preferences must have changed for such and such to be observed (Stigler and Becker 1977).

(iii) The world of microeconomics is one of *voluntarism*. The subject is about how individuals gain from decisions to trade, broadly defined. Rational people will only voluntarily accept a change (a trade) that increases their utility or, in the limit, does not decrease it. Once this step is made and accepted as a central tenet of analysis, it can provoke a critical, niggardly and deflating view of human action. The economist's first reaction to any observed action is typically: 'What's in it for so and so?', 'What are they gaining by supporting that organisation?', 'They must be getting some kind of payback', and so on. All that may seem noble about human behaviour seems to be reduced to a narrow instrumentalism and this can seem tiresome and incorrect.

(iv) Related to trade and gains to individuals is the nature of the *changes* conceived of in economics. By and large, changes are envisaged as small – some of individual A's allocation of good X in exchange for some of individual B's allocation of good Y. The dictum on the title page of Marshall's (1891) great work *Principles of Economics* translates from the Latin to 'nature makes no leaps'. In keeping with the dictum the foundations of much neoclassical (market) analysis developed in this work is conducted in marginal – 'small change' (derivative) – terms. For such an analysis to be valid the world has to be a smooth, continuous place – hence the importance of 'no leaps' and some knowledge of 'slopes' from mathematics. In contrast, excitement is generally about big changes, revolutions and discreteness. A world of discontinuous variables ('leaps') and discord is one that approximates the view of reality many individuals perceive – witness current problems with terrorism and civil wars, which are clearly not about small voluntary changes.

In short, the analysis may appear to present an unexciting and to some unbelievable representation of the world. After all, it is conflict, human destruction and the destruction of humans that is the stuff of daily news. Human history does not seem to be the record of a world characterised by small changes and continuity! The fact that economists often clothe themselves with Marshall's dictum does not in some way make it a fundamentally correct view of the world.

(v) Related to (iv) is the use of *mathematics and statistical techniques*. If marginalist and maximising analysis is accepted then it lends itself to the use of calculus. As such, there is an entry fee to modern economics that not only includes studying the subject itself but also some mathematics as a necessary, if not sufficient, collateral input. To some critics the need for some maths is seen as unnecessary and as an excluding device. It gives the subject an uninviting feel to those not enamoured of mathematical technique. La Manna states the position forcefully: 'Mainstream economists subject themselves to scientific tests throughout the research process, from properly stated theories, testing with sophisticated statistical techniques and peer-review according to the strictest criteria. This rigorous approach may be unpopular, but it is necessary' (2003: 15).

(vi) Because it is a subject about *abstraction and deduction*, theory is transportable to any context involving individual choice. Hence, recent decades have seen so-called 'economics imperialism' on a large scale. For example, consider the application of economic theory to 'marriage', 'the family', 'racism' and 'the brain' – areas more traditionally thought to be the preserve of disciplines like psychology, sociology and social policy. While, to economists, this is a fruitful and natural extension of the framework, the fact that a very large number of economists are not directly focused on the formal economy comes as a surprise to many others (and can be resented where it seems to displace other subject disciplines).

There is a humorous, but insightful, interchange in an IEA (Institute of Economic Affairs) publication on the *Economics of Politics* (Buchanan *et al.* 1978: 88 and 92) between two professors of *economics*:

> Prof.Y:
> It is very interesting to see [Prof.] X turning into a professor of sociology. (p. 88)

> Prof.X:
> If I started to try to answer your question, I would become partly the sociologist Professor Y says I am, . . . I don't mind that: we need some good sociologists. (p. 92)

As suggested by this interchange, within the social sciences, intellectual arrogance has been associated with economists.

(vii) Linking to (v) is the effect of *model building* in making the whole subject look entirely a technical exercise and therefore uncontroversial – another word for boring! There is some truth in the argument that, once you have set up a problem in a certain way, there evolves an accepted way to solve it and a unique set of results is generated. Students with coursework suspiciously close to a particular single source often comment, 'Well, that's the *answer*, isn't it?' and/or 'The author explained it better than I could.' If this occurs it is questionable that the coursework has been set appropriately, i.e. in a way that will invite critical analysis. The aim in the pages that follow is to avoid apparent arrogance and develop an appreciation that there may be *more than one* analysis, more than one *answer*.

The aim is to invite the reader to think: to manipulate analysis and attempt their assessment, rather than simply underline or highlight *an* answer. Historically, the so-called 'social contract' philosophers argued that individuals were entitled to own land if they worked – shared their physical labour – with it. The same is true of human capital (skills, knowledge): it only becomes *yours* if you are prepared to work with it.[5]

The ultimate aim is that readers find the content to the mnemonic B.O.R.I.N.G. INTERESTING! The hope is that claims that the subject is boring will be proved false. Time devoted to the discipline of economics can be both interesting and fruitful 'but we would say that, wouldn't we?' (Note it is not claimed that it will be easy – it is work not leisure!)

Having established an underlying framework, microeconomics appears pre-set to a great extent. Once you start on a chosen route, the journey may seem rather mechanical. However, while there are all sorts of technical and analytical complexities involved in making the journey, the 'big question' is how to choose the route, i.e. how to view the world. Mainstream economic theory has so successfully charted routes that some economists

---

5. As a guide, the symptoms of beginning to acquire and own human capital are that your head starts to hurt and feel hot and concepts come into and go out of focus!

see the whole nature of microeconomics as unambiguous (see (vii) above). The mode of analysis appears to be beyond question or challenge. However, in Section 1.5 (and in all subsequent chapters) alternative (and somewhat threatening) perspectives are offered. But first, in line with point (v) above, some basic arithmetic and concepts are required to facilitate the journey. (Those familiar with basic algebra please turn to Section 1.4.)

1.3 Visualising analytical relationships: rays of hope and tangential interests

It was noted above that much of microeconomics has a mathematical base and this, for some students, is a source of difficulty. For this subset of students there is comfort – a small amount of technique can be made to go a long way. An initial investment of time and effort is required to master this 'small amount of technique'. This centres, as the sub-heading suggests, on the properties of 'rays' and 'tangents'.

Virtually all of the economics encountered in this text centres on two variables. For the moment the two variables are labelled Y and X. (Changing the labels to tell different 'stories' is part of the art of being a microeconomist.) Suppose $Y = f(X)$. This simply says that Y is a function of (depends on) X with the f indicating that the dependence is as yet unspecified in a specific way. In Figure 1.1(a) the x-axis records the value of variable X and the y-axis indicates the value Y takes at each value of X. The curve labelled TY represents the total value of Y. Microeconomics can be conducted in terms of 'totals' but for expositional reasons the average and the marginal values of Y at each value of X are usually employed. By definition in Figure 1.1(b) AY = the average value of Y (= TY/X, the total value of Y at a given X value divided by that X value). In the following exposition MY = the marginal value of $Y = \Delta TY/\Delta X$ (= the small change – indicated by the Δ symbol – in the value of total Y divided by the small change in the value of X) and this is equal to the slope of the total Y curve (TY).

Most students may have studied some trigonometry (it does not matter if you have not). When analysing triangles the key connections can be recalled by the mnemonic SOHCAHTOA (sin = opposite over hypotenuse, cos = adjacent over hypotenuse and tan = opposite over adjacent). The relevant relationship here is that $\tan \theta$ = opposite/adjacent (do not worry, you will never need to solve this explicitly, rather you simply need to use your eyes).

Using Figure 1.1 part (a) concentrate on point A_1 on TY. Suppose you need to know the average value of Y at A_1 (labelled AY_1 in Figure 1.1(b)) but only have the illustrated curve TY in front of you. From the definition of AY it is clear that its value at point A_1 is distance 0-Y_1 (= distance X_1-A_1) divided by distance 0-X_1.

Is there anything further that can be said? The answer is 'yes'. By drawing in a ray (a line) from the origin (0) to the point A_1, a triangle is completed and it can be seen that AY_1 = distance X_1-A_1' (panel (b)) = distance X_1-A_1/distance 0-X_1 = opposite/adjacent (panel (a)) = $\tan \theta_1$. For precision, if 0-Y_1 = £10 and 0-X_1 = 4 units then angle θ_1 would be 68° and $\tan 68°$ = 2.5. All this helps because it can be seen that:

(i) AY has the same value at A_3 as A_1 because $\tan \theta_1$ is common to both the triangles formed ($0,A_1,X_1$ and $0,A_3,X_3$);

(ii) by choosing other points A_0 and A_2 qualitative information about the average can be secured. At A_0 $\tan \theta_0$ becomes relevant with A_0-X_0 being the opposite and 0-X_0 the adjacent. By observation $\tan \theta_0 < \tan \theta_1$ (i.e. the angle is smaller); therefore average Y, AY_0, must be smaller than AY_1 at the value of X given by 0-X_0; hence the location of AY_0 below AY_1 in part (b) of Figure 1.1. This value AY_0 is also relevant for the point A_4 on TY and hence it is also recorded above X_4.

Point A_2 has special significance. It arises if you imagine drawing in successively steeper rays A_0, A_1 and so on until the ray just touches TY. (Any steeper rays will not touch TY.) It remains true that the average value is:

$$\frac{\text{distance } A_2\text{-}X_2}{\text{distance } 0\text{-}X_2} = \frac{\text{Opposite}}{\text{Adjacent}} = \tan \theta_2 \tag{1.1}$$

but it also is the value of $\tan \theta$ that is the largest consistent with the ray touching the curve. It tells us the maximum average value of Y occurs at a point vertically above X_2 in part (b) of Figure 1.1.

In summary, by looking at the angles of the rays formed by drawing them from the origin to the TY curve, important qualitative information about the nature of AY can be derived. It has successively higher values at X_0, X_1 and X_2 (which yields the maximum) and successively lower values beyond X_2 (witness A_3' and A_4' above X_3 and X_4 in part (b)). The AY curve must, by deduction, look like the inverted-U illustrated in part (b). Note:

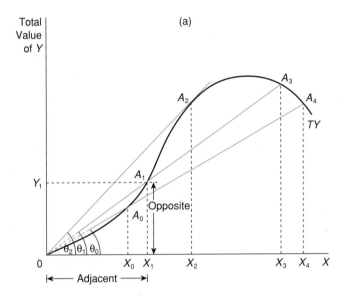

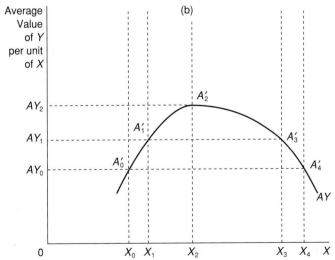

Figure 1.1
Rays and average
information

vertical distances X_0-A_0', X_1-A_1', X_2-A_2', X_3-A_3' and X_4-A_4' are the average values corresponding to A_0, A_1, A_2, A_3 and A_4 on TY (in part (a) of Figure 1.1). But, there is more.

Deducing important information on the marginal value of Y (MY) is also possible. Here the concern is more subtle: how does TY change in value as X changes in value? It is a question about taking little 'steps'. Imagine taking equal steps along the x-axis. The marginal value is the height gain in TY, or loss in TY, as each successive step is taken. The equal steps are labelled ΔX_1 to ΔX_6 in Figure 1.2(a) and (b) and the changes in TY ΔY_1 to ΔY_4 and ΔY_6. The heavily inked vertical lines indicate the TY changes. It can be seen that for ΔX_1, ΔX_2 and ΔX_3 the changes in Y (ΔY_1, ΔY_2 and ΔY_3) are getting bigger (you are

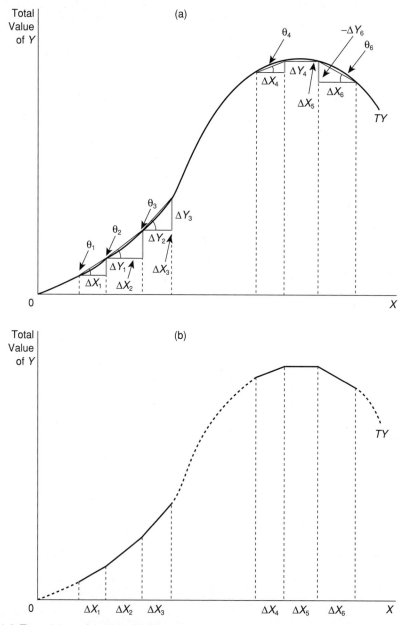

Figure 1.2 Tangents and marginal information

moving up an increasingly steep hill). For ΔX_4 the change in Y has become small ($= \Delta Y_4$) and is less than ΔY_1 (the hill is becoming less steep). ΔY_5 is missing because the step ΔX_5 involves no change in TY (you are momentarily walking on the flat). For step ΔX_6 'the road rises up to meet you'. You are going downhill and the change in TY is negative (hence $- \Delta Y_6$). Using the discussion above, the ΔYs divided by the ΔXs define tan θ in the 'little' triangles in Figure 1.2(a). The angles get successively bigger, smaller, momentarily zero, and then reverse. This says the marginal value of Y increases at an increasing rate, increases at a decreasing rate, falls to zero and becomes negative.

By making the steps in panel (a) as drawn, TY is effectively being made a series of straight-line shapes (see panel (b)). To avoid this lumpiness, or chunkiness, imagine the steps being made very, very small. The curve in panel (b) of Figure 1.2 would, to all intents and purposes, look smooth – as does Figure 1.3(a) and the tan θ's approximated

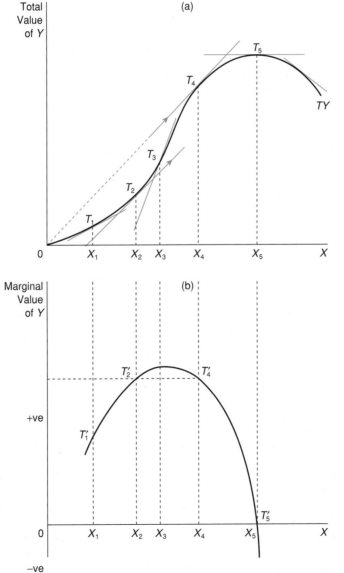

Figure 1.3
Deriving marginal
information from tangents

by the slopes of tangents to the curve (T_1, T_2, T_3, T_4 and T_5 located at X-values X_1 to X_5 respectively). T_2 is steeper than T_1 and, therefore, the marginal value is rising and T_1' at X_1 is below T_2' at X_2 in height in Figure 1.3(b). Similarly, T_3 at X_3 is associated with a greater marginal value than T_2 at X_2. T_3 is, however, special in that the tangent to the curve cuts the curve. This is known as a *point of inflection* and denotes that there is a change in the nature but not the direction of the slope taking place.

Whilst the slope of the curve remains positive up to T_5, the rate at which it increases after T_3 decreases and as an indication of this, the slope of T_4 is less than the slope of T_3. Before T_3 the rate of increase increases. Note that T_4 is parallel to T_2, indicating the marginal value at X_4 is the same as at X_2 (see T_2' and T_4' in 1.3(b)). T_3 is as steep a tangent as can be drawn to TY (and hence is a maximum value for MY). It is located above X_3 (before that MY is rising, and after it falling). T_5 is a tangent that is flat, indicating momentarily no slope and thus the marginal value at T_5' is zero. Beyond T_5 the tangents to the curve would have negative slopes like T_6 (going downhill) making it clear that the marginal values are negative beyond T_5 (see the location of T_5' in Figure 1.3(b)).

Figure 1.3(b) plots all this qualitative information about the marginal value of TY labelled MY and makes clear the information that is available from inspection of TY in Figure 1.3(a). It is possible to describe ΔTY as X changes by very small amounts (ΔX) by looking at what happens to the tangents to the curve.

With this discussion, it is possible to view Figure 1.3(a) and note that:

(i)   If successive tangents are steeper (greater positive slopes) TY is rising at an increasing rate and MY is rising and positive;

(ii)   If successive tangents are less steep (falling positive slopes) TY is rising at a decreasing rate and MY is falling but positive;

(iii) If a tangent is horizontal (a 'flat' slope) TY is stationary and MY is zero which means no changes in TY;

(iv)   If tangents fall away (negative slopes) then TY is falling but as illustrated remaining positive then MY is negative (you would be below the x-axis in Figure 1.3(b)).

What is being described here is a visual way of interpreting the first derivative of the function that describes TY. Whilst differentiation is more elegant and precise those with little or no mathematics can go a long way with the two visual rules developed above. To know about:

(a)   the *average* value – look at angles formed by successive rays from the origin to the curve;

(b)   the *marginal* value – look at the slopes of successive tangents to the curve.

Figure 1.4 allows relationships between marginal and average values to be isolated. Above X_1 the tangent to the curve T_m cuts the curve and therefore MY is at a maximum. At X_1 the angle formed by the ray 0-A_1 is θ_1 and, being less than the angle formed by T_m on the x-axis (namely θ_2), the average value is less than the marginal value at X_1. The ray 0-A_m indicates the maximum value AY can take. Given this, the peak of AY is above X_2 in Figure 1.4(b).

There is, however, an important further piece of information. The tangent to TY at A_m is T_1 and is coincident with 0-A_m; they both form the angle θ_3 on the x-axis, indicating a common tan θ value. That is, the marginal and maximum average value coincide above X_2. Given it has been established that the margin exceeds the average before X_2, the shape of TY means that MY cuts AY *from above at AY's maximum value*. Note: ray 0-A_2 forms the same angle (θ_1) as ray 0-A_1 and, therefore, the average value above X_4 must be the same at X_1 and is given by distance 0-AY' in Figure 1.4(b).

To some, all this may look a bit 'fiddly'? Unfortunately, for those who would prefer a more 'free-form' approach there is no choice (once TY is set, the shapes of AY and MY are also set – in this case as inverted 'Us' cutting each other in a precise relationship). It must

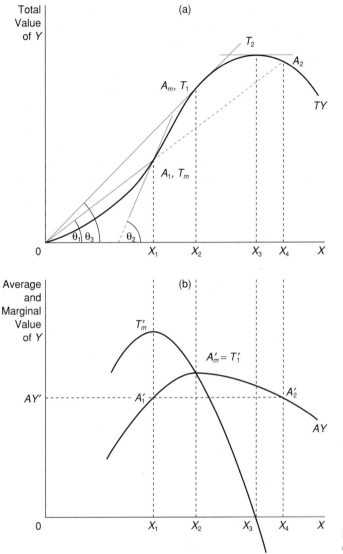

Figure 1.4
Combining average and
marginal information

be emphasised that it is the shape of *TY* that matters (different *TY*s mean different *AY*s and *MY*s, as will be clear in later chapters) and, in some respects, microeconomic theory can be reduced to the logic of relationships dictated by different shapes. Hence, it is crucial to draw any figures as accurately as information allows, not as a matter of 'fussiness' but rather because things can appear to be 'true' that cannot be 'true' if the figure is drawn inaccurately (and vice versa). 'Impossibly' drawn illustrations shout to economics examiners that candidates do not know what they are doing!

With command over the above arguments it is possible to derive some precise implications about average and marginal values from different-shaped totals and put them to 'work' on key microeconomic concepts.

Having established the notion of averages and marginals, it is easy to use them to revise the notion of *elasticity*. The elasticity of variable X with respect to variable Y (often labelled ε (epsilon) – Greek lower-case E) is defined as the proportionate change in X when there is a proportionate change in Y. It can be written as:

$$\varepsilon = \frac{\%\,\Delta X}{\%\,\Delta Y} = \frac{\Delta X/X}{\Delta Y/Y} = \frac{\Delta X.Y}{\Delta Y.X} = \frac{1}{\text{Marginal value}} \times \text{Average value} \qquad (1.2)$$

and this can also be described as $\dfrac{1}{\text{Slope}} \times$ Ray (tan of angle formed)

Elasticity is measured at a point on any curve. Observant readers will note that here we are reversing or 'inversing' the $Y = f(X)$ to take the form $X = f(Y)$. (This is because Marshall (1891) saw a demand curve as recording Quantity as a function of Price but actually plotted the 'inverse' – Price as a function of Quantity, making Quantity the independent variable, an unnecessary but conventionally adopted complication. There are some exceptions but these are not usually made by economists, e.g. Lea, Tarpy and Webley (1987)).

The series of equalities in equation (1.2) makes it clear that it is possible to deduce information about elasticity by looking at the inverse of the slope of a curve multiplied by 'ray' information, i.e. the inverse of the marginal value multiplied by the average value. Whilst the desire is to evaluate the sensitivity of variable X to variable Y proportionate (%) changes have to be considered as this results in a real or dimensionless number as the answer, i.e. the elasticity value is independent of the units in which X and Y are measured. The result is independent of whether, say, Y is measured in pence or in pounds. This is clearly an attractive property.

1.3.1 Constant elasticity cases

Using Figures 1.5(a) to 1.5(d), allows the interpretation of elasticity values. In Figure 1.5(a) the lines labelled L_1 to L_3 all emanate from the origin and, as such, a ray from the origin to the curve will be coincident with the line everywhere and only one angle can be formed, i.e. the average has a constant value. Drawing a tangent to the curve also is coincident with the line because it is a straight line. This indicates that the marginal value is also a constant and, given that the slope of the tangent is the same as that of the ray, the marginal and average values are the same for each line. Substitution of those values into equation (1.2) would always lead them to cancel out and the equation to collapse to +1. Surprisingly, L_1, L_2 and L_3 all have elasticities of +1 and equal marginal and average values. Note: L_1 would have higher equal marginal and average values than L_2, and L_2 than L_3 as the angles formed by the ray (and tangent) fall in size as you move from curve L_1 to L_2 and L_3.

Line L_4 in Figure 1.5(b) is vertical and although it exhibits many average values the tangent to the curve is very steep, i.e. infinitely steep. Now 1 divided by a very, very large number is extremely small – and in the limit is zero. Once a zero is placed in equation (1.2) the result will always be zero and a curve like L_4 has zero elasticity wherever it is located along the x-axis.

Figure 1.5(c) is the first 'curve' to be an actual curve. The curve drawn is a rectangular hyperbola which has the property that, for any x-value y-value combination on the curve, x times y has the same constant value (curves further from the origin have higher constant values). As the curve slopes down to the right (downhill) it has a negative slope and the elasticity value is everywhere –1.

In contrast, L_6 has zero slope (if tangents are drawn to the curve they are all coincident with the curve and are horizontal). Drawing in the rays would suggest falling average values as X values increase but always a positive, if small, angle would be formed. However, looking at equation (1.2) indicates that 1 divided by the marginal value would

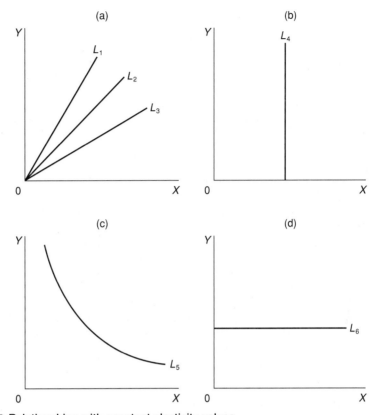

Figure 1.5 Relationships with constant elasticity values

be 1 divided by zero. This is strictly undefined but 1 divided by an extremely small number is a number that approaches infinity and the elasticity value therefore also approaches infinity. A curve such as L_6 is said to be infinitely elastic.

1.3.2 Varying elasticity cases

In Figure 1.5, curves L_1 to L_6 are unusual in that each exhibits a constant elasticity throughout its shape. What of varying elasticity?

In Figure 1.6(a) L_7 and L_8 are parallel, indicating constant and identical positive (uphill) slopes (tangents to the curve are coincident with the curve and form the same angle, θ_0, with the horizontal). However, as indicated by the dashed rays to L_7 the average value falls everywhere and given the angles formed have values that are greater than the marginal value $\tan \theta_0$. Hence 1 divided by the marginal value times the average value must always be less than +1 and such a curve is described as inelastic. It can be seen that the values fall towards zero as the value of x where the elasticity is evaluated increases.

For L_8 the average value always rises (see dashed rays to L_8) and exceeds the constant marginal value ($\tan \theta_0$) and, therefore, the elasticity value exceeds +1 everywhere and rises as the x value (where it is considered) increases.

Curve L_9 in Figure 1.6(b) features a straight line extensively used in introductory microeconomic analysis and despite its constant negative (downhill) slope exhibits all elasticity values between zero and (minus) infinity. This surprising fact can be established by noting that 1 divided by the slope is a negative constant and, therefore, it is the average value that will be influential in varying the elasticity value. Now, at point 1 the value of Y is zero and therefore Y divided by X is zero and the equation (1.2) goes to zero

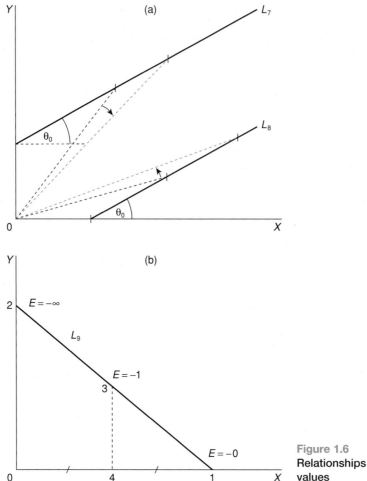

Figure 1.6
Relationships with varying elasticity values

overall. At point 2 the value of X is zero and Y divided by X is infinite and so the elasticity value at point 2 is infinite. Point 3 divides the curve into its elastic and inelastic sections; at point 3 the elasticity value is –1. For a straight-line curve this occurs at the point above half the value of the x-intercept precisely. The inverse of the slope at point 3 is distance 4-1 divided by 4-3 whereas the average value is given by 4-3 divided by 0-4. The multiplication of the terms will equal 1 when distance 0-4 equals distance 4-1. Therefore, the curve is elastic (elasticity values greater in absolute value than –1) above point 3 and inelastic (elasticity values lower in absolute value than –1) below point 3. Enough has been said to indicate how much can be gleaned from diagrams concerning elasticity values using just ray and tangency information derived from inspection alone. There is one further useful step.

1.3.3 Elasticities of substitution

A natural way to extend the concept of an elasticity is to describe the extent of the curvature of a curve via the elasticity of substitution (σ, sigma, Greek lower-case S) which is obtained by dividing the proportionate or percentage change in the slope by the proportionate or percentage change in the ray to two points on a given curve. That is, it divides the percentage change in marginal values by the percentage change in average values and, in doing so, also yields a real positive number, i.e. one that is independent of the units of measurement.

It is measured by comparing two points on a curve as the definition suggests:

$$\frac{\%\Delta \text{ in ray}}{\%\Delta \text{ in slope}} = \frac{\%\Delta\theta}{\%\Delta T} = \frac{\Delta\theta/\theta}{\Delta T/T} \tag{1.3}$$

Figures 1.7 (a) to (c) serve to illustrate some polar cases in the context of indifference curves, isoquants and social welfare functions. Recall from introductory microeconomics

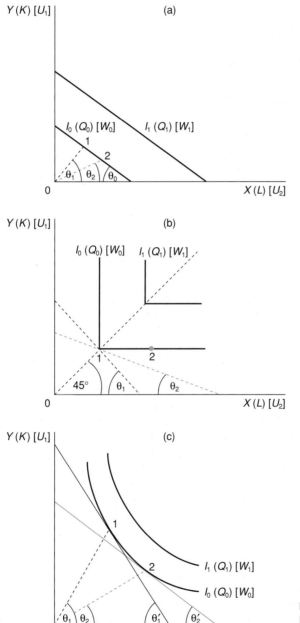

Figure 1.7
Relationships with constant elasticities of substitution

indifference curves are two-dimensional representations of (equal-utility) elements in a preference map, isoquants are two-dimensional representations of (equal-output) elements in a production function and social welfare curves are two-dimensional representations of (equal-social-welfare) elements in a social welfare function with each curve, as indicated in the brackets, representing a constant level of utility, output or social welfare. (These concepts are revised and further elaborated later.) The lettering of the axes indicates interpretation differences. If Y and X are goods (outputs) then I_0 and I_1 would be indifference curves. If (K) and (L) stand for capital and labour inputs respectively, then (Q_0) and (Q_1) would be isoquants. $[U_1]$ and $[U_2]$ are (ordinal) utility levels for individuals 1 and 2 so that $[W_0]$ and $[W_1]$ are combinations of utilities that are judged to offer equal social welfare along a given curve.

In Figure 1.7(a) goods Y and X, inputs (K) and (L) or $[U_1]$ and $[U_2]$ are perfect substitutes at a ratio determined by the angle θ_0 (formed by the tangent to the curve) whose tan value is the slope of each U, (Q) or $[W]$. As illustrated, the angle is 26.5° and the slope $\frac{1}{2}$. This value does not change with a straight line – the tangent is coincident with the curve. The rays, however, do change as you consider, say, points 1 and 2. Angle θ_1 is greater than angle θ_2 and therefore the value of the ratio Y/X (or (K/L) or $[U_1/U_2]$) rises between points 2 and 1. Given equation (1.3) the % Δ in the slope is zero and therefore the value of the elasticity of substitution can be treated as infinite, as you are dividing a number by a zero. With straight-line 'curves' $\sigma = \infty$.

In Figure 1.7(b) goods Y and X, inputs (K) and (L) or $[U_1]$ and $[U_2]$ are perfect complements at a ratio determined by the angle θ whose tan value is the slope of the ray to the corners of each U, (Q) or $[W]$. As illustrated, the angle is 45° and the slope +1. This value does not change with a set of right-angled curves, as the ray cutting the corners is the only relevant one. To stray from, say, point 1 to point 2 involves more good X ((L) or $[U_2]$) without any increase in utility (or output or social welfare) and is therefore inefficient. The tangents to the corners, however, do change as you consider, say, angles θ_1 and θ_2 but this turns out not to matter. Given equation (1.3) the % Δ in the ray is zero and therefore the value of the elasticity of substitution is zero as you are dividing zero by a number. With right-angled line 'curves' $\sigma = 0$. These two polar cases establish that the value of σ lies between zero and infinity for convex to the origin curves.

In Figure 1.7(c) goods Y and X, inputs (K) and (L) or $[U_1]$ and $[U_2]$ are substitutes at a rate determined by the changes in the angles labelled θ between points 1 and 2. As illustrated, the angles move completely in harmony with each other. This is a third special case. The special case is that of a rectangular hyperbola. If the % Δ in the ray is exactly equal to the % Δ in the slope then the equation (1.3) will always take the value 1. With rectangular hyperbola 'curves' $\sigma = 1$.

Using these special cases is useful in at least two respects:

(i)   First, intuition suggests that the flatter the curve the closer are the elements on the axes to being perfect substitutes and therefore the σ approaches ∞.

(ii) Second, a point about determinacy was made in the previous section. It is always attractive to at least begin with a precise answer to a question, especially if you think that looks more 'scientific'. Adopting special cases leads to determinacy and, by looking at extremes, it is always possible to narrow the range of outcomes possible and, at the same time, shed light on the more general cases. Many of the later chapters will make use of the 'shapes' introduced here.

There is a graphical exercise that allows the determination of the elasticity of substitution over the range of a given curve. Consider Figure 1.8 and, although the illustration is general, to lose some lettering and gain clarity assume that it is an indifference curve over goods Y and X. Recall the definition above:

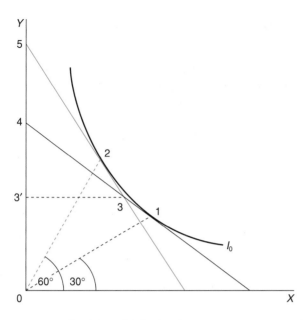

Figure 1.8
A visual interpretation of the elasticity of substitution

σ = elasticity of substitution

$$= \frac{\%\Delta \text{ in ray}}{\%\Delta \text{ in slope}} = \frac{\%\Delta\theta}{\%\Delta T} = \frac{\Delta\theta/\theta}{\Delta T/T} = \frac{\Delta(Y/X) \ / \ Y/X}{\Delta(\text{d}Y/\text{d}X) \ / \ (\text{d}Y/\text{d}X)} \tag{1.4}$$

Along the curve illustrated the changes in ray and slope are in the same direction and the resulting elasticity is therefore positive. But how positive? Draw a ray from the origin Y/X following it with another of twice that slope $2(Y/X)$ – the θ used here are 30° and 60° respectively. Next, draw in the relevant tangents to the curve at points 1 and 2 and isolate their intersection at point 3' on the y-axis by drawing a horizontal line through point 3. Now the %Δ in ray = $\Delta(Y/X) \ / \ Y/X$ = tan 30° / tan 30° = 1 by construction.

As for the Δ in slope for the straight-line tangents between points 1 and 2, this is given by the difference in ratios of distances 3'-5 / 3'-3 minus 3'-4 / 3'-3 and the %Δ in slope is given by ratios of distances (3'-5 / 3'-3 minus 3'-4 / 3'-3) / 3'-4 / 3'-3, which reduces to 5-4 / 3'-3 / 3'-4 / 3'-3 and equals the ratio 5-4 / 3'-4.

The final step is to divide %Δ in ray = 1 by %Δ in slope = (5-4 / 3'-4), yielding σ = elasticity of substitution = distance 3'-4 / distance 5-4. If distance 3'-4 = distance 5-4, then over the range illustrated, σ = elasticity of substitution = 1.

This is case (c) above. As 3'-4 < 5-4, σ = elasticity of substitution decreases in value towards special case (b) above and as 3'-4 > 5-4, σ = elasticity of substitution increases in value towards special case (a) above. If this method of 'ratio' is rehearsed it becomes a relatively easy matter to visually identify the approximate value of the elasticity of substitution of indifference curves, isoquants and social welfare curves. Intuitively, this has to be a relevant exercise whenever it is appropriate to identify the extent of a required change in quantities of goods Y and X, inputs (K) and (L) or utility levels $[U_1]$ and $[U_2]$ to hold utility, output or overall welfare constant at an initial value.

1.4 It's all in the interpretation

Table 1.1 brings some of the basic concepts of economics introduced above together with frequently encountered diagram illustrations. The point emphasised is that a given shape does not lend itself to a straightforward interpretation across the concepts of slope,

Table 1.1 Same old 'shapes' but different stories

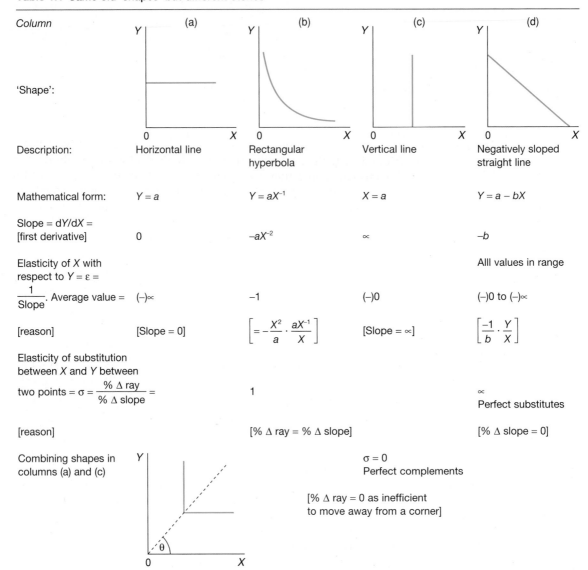

Column	(a)	(b)	(c)	(d)
'Shape':				
Description:	Horizontal line	Rectangular hyperbola	Vertical line	Negatively sloped straight line
Mathematical form:	$Y = a$	$Y = aX^{-1}$	$X = a$	$Y = a - bX$
Slope = dY/dX = [first derivative]	0	$-aX^{-2}$	∞	$-b$
Elasticity of X with respect to $Y = \varepsilon =$ $\dfrac{1}{\text{Slope}}$. Average value =	$(-)\infty$	-1	$(-)0$	All values in range $(-)0$ to $(-)\infty$
[reason]	[Slope = 0]	$\left[= -\dfrac{X^2}{a} \cdot \dfrac{aX^{-1}}{X} \right]$	[Slope = ∞]	$\left[\dfrac{-1}{b} \cdot \dfrac{Y}{X} \right]$
Elasticity of substitution between X and Y between two points = $\sigma = \dfrac{\% \Delta \text{ ray}}{\% \Delta \text{ slope}}$ =		1		∞ Perfect substitutes
[reason]		[% Δ ray = % Δ slope]		[% Δ slope = 0]
Combining shapes in columns (a) and (c)			$\sigma = 0$ Perfect complements [% Δ ray = 0 as inefficient to move away from a corner]	

elasticity and elasticity of substitution. Students, for example, frequently think a negatively sloped straight-line 'curve' (column (d)) has a constant elasticity throughout its length. Careful attention to Section 1.6 should enable the connection of concepts and 'shapes' in the table to be made without recourse to maths texts. Such connections are central to much of the analysis in later chapters as economics is an academic discipline, unlike many others, that has placed very considerable reliance on the use of diagrammatic analysis and proofs. This is not to suggest that a more rigorous mathematical approach would not be helpful or superior but rather that the simple careful observation of a diagram allows a great deal to be deduced directly.

Armed with a methodological perspective to employ and some visual quantitative skills, it is time to revise the basic concept employed in microeconomics, namely the utility-maximising rational actor.

1.5 Rationality as utility maximisation

The R and I in B-O-R-I-N-G were for 'Rational action' and 'Individual' respectively, with rationality described as an individual acting with purpose to maximise their utility or satisfaction. The full meaning of 'rational' behaviour in economics will be examined in later chapters but here it is worth emphasising that 'rational' behaviour may be far from 'obvious' and far from a 'natural' interpretation of how individuals make decisions and act.

Consider the following quotation from Hegel (cited in Knox 1952: 230): 'The rational is the highroad where everyone travels, where no one is conspicuous.' This quotation from Hegel suggests that what is rational is simply what everyone does. If the vast majority do this in such and such circumstances, then if an individual is seen to do it when such and such circumstances arise they are regarded as acting rationally. This ties the notion in with what is called 'social constructionism', which in this context would suggest that all individuals are inculcated (taught by repetition) into rational behaviour by being born into and taking part in a particular society (collection of individuals). From *this* viewpoint rational behaviour is a convention specific to particular societies or cultures. In short, there are then many 'rationalities'.

In microeconomics 'rational' behaviour is considered in more specific terms (for further discussion see Section 7.4.1). In microeconomics the starting point is to view rational behaviour as choices that are consistent with an individual's preferred course of action. Their preferred course of action is that which maximises their utility or satisfaction. The history of the notion of utility is associated with the indifference curve or utility map as a two-dimensional pictorial representation of individual preferences.

The mechanics of indifference maps were developed by Edgeworth (1881) – a famous figure in the history of economics. Whilst the mechanics have survived, Edgeworth's conception of utility generally has not. He envisaged that, with scientific progress, the level of happiness an individual was enjoying would be measurable in a cardinal fashion (like weight and height). Someone who grows from 1 to 2 metres tall is twice as tall as they were and someone who is 2.4 metres tall is twice as tall as someone else who is 1.2 metres tall. This means that height is measured on a cardinal scale that is comparable between people. The same scale 'fits all'. Or, to be more precise, the scale means the same when applied to all individuals. While height is measured in metres on a metric scale, Edgeworth coined the units, utils, for the day when measurement of an individual's level of utility became possible. If utility were measurable in this way many problems in economics would become easy (especially distributional ones which relate to equity). In these circumstances, individual A could, say, be measured to be four times as happy as individual B and action might be taken to make individual B half as happy as individual A. As it is, no one now believes that utility will ever become measurable in this cardinal fashion and therefore interpersonal (comparing individual A with B) comparisons of utility or satisfaction are ruled out. It is impossible to tell if the richest person in the world is happier than the poorest one as utility is a subjective experience that, by definition, only the individuals themselves can know about. In effect you can only have knowledge about yourself.

Given this, microeconomics is forced to work with a less strong and less informative notion of utility called 'ordinal utility'. This relies on the idea that, when faced with choices, individuals know what they prefer, i.e. they can rank all options available to them but cannot say precisely how much they prefer their first choice over their second or their second over their third etc. Fortunately, much fruitful analysis can be founded on this weaker conception of utility (as embodied in indifference curves or maps – as representations of individual preferences). Whilst preferences can be defined over individual goods, typically analysis works with combinations of goods called 'bundles' or 'baskets'.

Hirshleifer and Riley (1992) refer to utility from consequences (as opposed to individual utility over actions – see Chapter 6 below). Here an individual, A, is viewed as being in a two-good world – good X and good Y (as demonstrated in Chapter 2 this is not as restrictive as it first seems and allows the analysis to proceed in two dimensions). A basket or bundle (or 'consequence') (labelled A_1, A_2 etc. to indicate that the bundles are numbered 1, 2, etc. and the choices of a given individual A are being considered) can be defined. It is defined by a statement of how much of good X it contains per period (Q_X/t) and how much of good Y it contains per period (Q_Y/t).

1.5.1 Developing ordinal indifference curves

Indifference maps are derived by adopting and employing a series of assumptions or axioms. These are listed below:

(i)   *Completeness* says that an individual confronted with two baskets of goods A_1 and A_2 can always say one of the following three things:
   (a) they prefer A_1 to A_2 (written as $A_1 > A_2$);
   (b) they prefer A_2 to A_1 (written as A_1 inferior to A_2, i.e. $A_1 < A_2$);
   (c) they are indifferent between A_1 and A_2 (written as $A_1 \sim A_2$).
   (Note the $>$ and $<$ signs do not mean greater than and less than – after all, if you are not fond of bananas you might prefer 1 apple to 4 bananas).

(ii) *Consistency or transitivity* says that if basket of goods A_1 is preferred to basket of goods A_2 and basket of goods A_2 is preferred to basket of goods A_3 then it must be the case that basket of goods A_1 is preferred to basket of goods A_3. Not all relationships are transitive. For example, sporting relationships may not be. Bundle of players 'Man $U = A_1$' may be able to beat bundle of players 'Liverpool $= A_2$' and bundle of players 'Liverpool $= A_2$' beat bundle of players 'Arsenal $= A_3$' but bundle of players 'Arsenal $= A_3$' may be able to beat bundle of players 'Man $U = A_1$'.

(iii) *Non-satiation* says that if you wish to discuss items that are goods (positive sources of utility) then more is always preferred, i.e. you never get tired of more units per period of something that is a good to you. Of course, there are also 'bads' (negative utility sources) of which you prefer fewer units per period (more units lower your utility). There are also 'neutrals', where more units per period neither raise nor lower your utility. Different items are goods, bads or neutrals to different individuals. (For the moment goods are discussed, other preference relationships are accommodated in Chapter 2.)

(iv) *Continuity* or *substitutability* says that if two baskets of goods (A_1 and A_2) contain the same amount of two goods X and Y then $A_1 \sim A_2$ (individuals must treat identical baskets as identical[6]). If one more unit of X is added to A_1 then if non-satiation applies $A_1 > A_2$. As the name of this axiom suggests, if more Y is put into A_2 a point will come when the individual will be indifferent between A_1 and A_2 again. Once this point is reached, one more unit of Y added to A_2 will cause the individual to reverse preference so that $A_1 < A_2$. The goods have been traded off against one another, in that they have been substituted as sources of utility (so that there is continuity of preference). If one good is always preferred to another whatever the

---

6. The axiom that deals with 'identicals' in preference orderings is reflexivity. Here bundle $A_1 \geqslant A_1$ means A_1 must be preferred or indifferent to itself. As A_1 can be moved to either side of the 'preferred or indifferent to' sign, then A_1 is indifferent to itself. The attraction of this is that all bundles must belong to an indifference set – at minimum the one containing itself. Together completeness, transitivity and reflexivity guarantee any bundle can be put into one, and only one, indifference set.

quantities involved, the ordering is said to be *lexicographic* (a description based on library orderings – with books with authors' names beginning with A always coming before the Bs etc. within each classification).

(v)　*Utility maximisation* is the final axiom. It is required that the rational economic actor will always seek the highest utility possible in any choice situation. Recall, however, that it is utility as they perceive it that matters – individuals as the best judges of their own welfare – not as any other individual sees it.

The purpose of adopting axioms is to see what follows deductively or logically from them. The five axioms above allow theorists to deduce a great deal about the shape of an indifference curve and the associated map. What does an indifference curve between two goods X and Y look like?

Suppose in Figure 1.9 an individual is endowed with a bundle A_1 containing 6 units of Y and 8 units of X per period at the point labelled A_1, this will offer a given level of (subjective) utility. Points of indifference cannot be to the north-east (north and east) of point A_1. A bundle like A_2 involves 7 units of Y and 9 units of X and must offer higher utility because it contains more of both goods. Furthermore, points that involve the same quantity of good Y (X) and more X (Y) must be preferred. By the reversal of the same argument all points to the south-west (south and west) must be inferior. This indicates that points of indifference to point A_1 must lie to the north-west or south-east and indifference curves must be negatively sloped.

If Y (X) is always preferred, the *lexicographical ordering* case, then no points indifferent to point A_1 can be located (other points will be preferred or inferior). That is, points to the north (east) and north-east contain more Y (X) and must be preferred and points to the south (west) and south-west contain less Y (X) and must be inferior. The axiom of continuity matters if an indifference curve is to be located.

A second characteristic is that indifference curves cannot intersect. If they did it would violate the axiom of transitivity and non-satiation. In Figure 1.10 consider point A_1 and, in line with the above reasoning, assume that point A_2 to the north-west is on the same indifference curve, offering the individual the same level of ordinal utility. If indifference curves could cross it is feasible that the bundle defined at A_3 to the south-east offers a point of indifference to bundle A_2. However, if A_1 is indifferent to A_2 and A_2 indifferent to A_3, the axiom of transitivity says that bundle A_1 is also indifferent to bundle A_3. But this cannot be the case as bundle A_3 contains more of both good Y (4 units compared to 3 units per period) and good X (11 units compared to 9 units per period) and must be preferred on non-satiation. In this way, intersecting indifference curves can be ruled out as being inconsistent with the axioms described above.

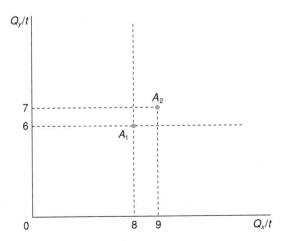

Figure 1.9
Locating points of indifference

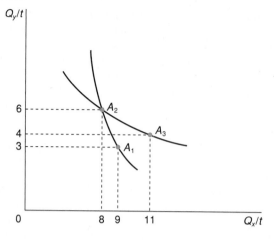

Figure 1.10
Non-intersection of indifference curves

The axiom of completeness means that all points defining bundles in Y-X space are ranked, in that they must be on one indifference curve or another. This amounts to saying that indifference curves are everywhere dense, there are no gaps and conceptually (if not physically) it is always possible to draw a third indifference curve in the gap between any two that have been illustrated.

The fourth and final characteristic developed here does not flow from the axioms but is consistent with intuition and observed behaviour. Indifference curves for goods are convex to the origin. Consider Figure 1.11 and let good X be equal slices of bread and good Y grams of cheese and consider making marginal changes to the allocation of goods. At bundle A_1 the individual has 2 slices of bread and 46 grams of cheese. The allocation of cheese is relatively plentiful to the allocation of bread, and to find a point of indifference to bundle A_1 involving the substitution of one more slice of bread for less cheese might involve the willing sacrifice of 8 grams of cheese (bundle A_2 in Figure 1.11). At bundle A_3 the individual depicted has 8 slices of bread and 7 grams of cheese and to move to a point of indifference involving the substitution of one more slice of bread the individual may only be prepared to give up one gram of the now relatively scarce cheese (bundle A_4). If this reasoning is correct, the indifference curve must be bowed, or convex,

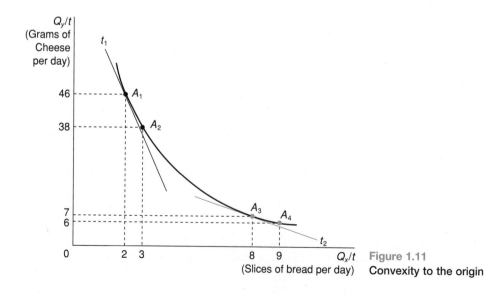

Figure 1.11
Convexity to the origin

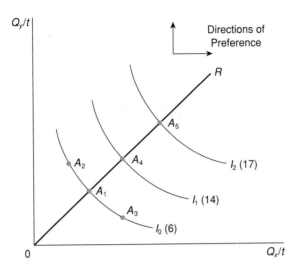

Figure 1.12
Meaning of ordinal utility

to the origin, as illustrated. This is a statement about the slope of indifference curves. Using the visual technique described above to see what is happening to the slope it is necessary to draw in successive tangents to the curve (two, t_1 and t_2, are illustrated). This indicates first that, as the tangents are downward-sloping, the curve is negatively sloped (downhill). Second, as the tangents flatten, the curve is becoming less and less steep (i.e. the slope is less and less negative). In economic terms the curve illustrated exhibits a *diminishing marginal rate of substitution* between goods X and Y – the more X you have per period the less Y it is possible to give up and still enjoy the same level of utility in your view.

The individual chooses the most desirable goods bundle according to their preference ordering. This is typically represented as a utility function (with a label for every possible commodity bundle and numbers to represent the preference ordering, the higher numbers indicating most preferred). In Figure 1.12 an indifference map between two goods for a given individual is illustrated. What meaning can be inferred from this map? Consider the ray 0-R, which is monotonically increasing (no 'downs') indicating, given it is goods that are being considered, that utility is rising along it (hence I_0, I_1 and I_2). Any bundle on the same indifference curve (I_0) must be assigned the same number, e.g. bundles A_1, A_2 and A_3 are all assigned 6 to indicate indifference. Any bundles offering higher utility, $A_5 > A_4 > A_3$ because they successively are bundles with more of both goods, must be assigned a higher number, e.g. 14 for I_1 and 17 for I_2. Now any equation that preserves the preference ordering of the bundles along that ray will do to describe utility – there is no significance to the numbers in themselves. Hence, labels I_0, I_1 and I_2 can do exactly the same work as I_6, I_{14} and I_{17} as no precise meaning can be attached to the numbers. All that is being said is that utility is the same for an individual along a given indifference curve and is higher for indifference curves further away from the origin, hence the arrows showing directions of preference.[7] This is what it means to say the utility function is ordinal. In the figure utility is defined over consequences in certain situations, so that deciding on an action means deciding on a consequence. If some scale of cardinal numbers is attached as preference labels to bundles, or consequences, any positive monotonic transformation leads to the same preference ordering, e.g. given the labels I_6, I_{14} and I_{17} adding 6 to each, subtracting 2 from each, multiplying each by 20 etc. leaves the

---

7. In some analyses indifference curves are labelled in the order of their use in a piece of analysis on the implicit assumption that everyone knows that (for goods) curves further from the origin are preferred. This practice is not followed here.

preference ordering unchanged. That is to say, if U is a satisfactory function for choices under certainty then so is $U_1 = f(U)$ as long as the first derivative $f'(U)$ of the function f used to transform U is positive.

MORE FORMAL SECTION

In terms of algebra, the utility function is depicted as follows:

$$U = U(Y,X) \tag{1.5}$$

[Utility depends on the quantities of Y and X per period]

The total differential (see Appendix 1) provides a linear approximation of what happens to U (utility) as small changes, dY and dX, are made to the quantities of Y and X per period respectively. Now, more Y (X) raises utility by an amount that is the marginal utility of Y (X), $\partial U/\partial Y$ ($\partial U/\partial X$). By definition, total utility cannot change along an indifference curve and hence the value of the total differential is constrained to be zero. In symbols:

$$dU = \partial U/\partial Y \; dY + \partial U/\partial X \; dX = 0 \tag{1.6}$$

and, by rearranging,

$$dY/dX = -\partial U/\partial X \; / \; \partial U/\partial Y \tag{1.7}$$

or

$$-dY/dX = \partial U/\partial X \; / \; \partial U/\partial Y = MRS_{xy} \tag{1.7a}$$

This says that the negative of the slope of an indifference curve (the marginal rate of substitution between X and Y) equates with the ratio of the marginal utility of X to the marginal utility of Y.

Thus far a pictorial way of representing individuals' preferences has been developed. It must be emphasised that the economist has no control over the preferences individuals have but just the ability to work with them when they have been told what they are – hence, in the absence of precise knowledge of an individual's preferences, much of theory is about exploring the properties of different cases. But what has all this to do with rationality?

To a large extent, economic rationality is simply acting consistently with respect to preferences (in order to maximise subjective utility). Economic irrationality is choosing a bundle, or consequence, that is inferior in utility terms to another that you were able to choose, i.e. not being on the highest indifference curve you could attain. Further, note the discussion so far is only about individuals' preferences – individuals looking at the menu of life, ranking alternative combinations as sources of utility to them in the absence of any consideration of income, prices, legal regulations, etc.

1.5.2 Utility maximisation with costless information in a riskless world

In many situations it is reasonable to assume that individuals know all the relevant pieces of information so that the situation is effectively one of certainty. These situations are the classic illustrations of introductory microeconomics. An individual is assumed to know their income (I) the prices of goods X and Y (P_x and P_y) and their utility function over goods X and Y represented as $U(X,Y)$. The first three pieces of information allow the formation of the budget constraint:

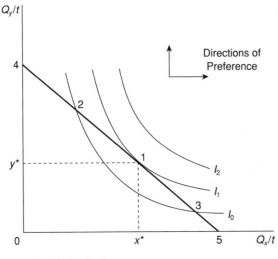

Figure 1.13
Utility maximisation with full
information in a riskless world

$$I = P_x X + P_y Y \tag{1.8}$$

which simply says that on the budget constraint the price of X times the quantity of X (labelled X) plus the price of Y times the quantity of Y sums to equal income. It is easy to plot this information on a figure in the form:

$$Y = I/P_y - (P_x/P_y) X \tag{1.9}$$

The y-axis intercept occurs where $X = 0$ and is in general I/P_y; however, if Y is the good, money – with a price of 1 (the price of £1 is £1) – the y-axis intercept (which obtains when $X = 0$) records income (point 4 in Figure 1.13 – the justification for this is further explored in Chapter 2). The x-axis intercept occurs when $Y = 0$ so that $I/P_y = (P_x/P_y) X$ and $X = I/P_x$ (the maximum number of units of good X per period that can be bought if all of income is devoted to X and its price is P_x – point 5 in Figure 1.13). The slope of the budget constraint can be seen to be $-P_x/P_y$ (up divided by along, I/P_y divided by I/P_x, or more formally, $dY/dX = -P_x/P_y$).

The location of the budget constraint prevents the individual having consumption plans that cannot be obtained. The best the individual can feasibly do is to be on the constraint. But where? This is where the knowledge of your own utility function comes in. The properties of indifference maps between two goods have been discussed above and are reflected in the three indifference curves illustrated in Figure 1.13. To settle at points other than point 1 on I_1 (e.g. points 2 and 3) involves lower utility (I_0) than can be feasibly obtained (points on I_2 offer more utility but are infeasible, being outside the budget constraint line 4-5). Therefore, the utility maximiser chooses x^* of good X and reserves y^* of income for other uses. (Note that distance y^*-4 indicates the amount of income spent on good X.) At point 1 the slopes of the indifference curve and the budget constraint are equal so it must be the case that: $MRS_{xy} = -P_x/P_y$ when utility is maximised. Also, as $MRS_{xy} = -MU_x/MU_y$, a utility maximiser must arrange expenditures such that the last penny spent on each good offers the same utility. If one good offered more utility from the marginal penny then total utility cannot be maximised and some rearrangement of expenditures is warranted. This condition can be formulated as $MU_x/P_x = MU_y/P_y$.

Simply by inspection of the so-called static consumer equilibrium in Figure 1.13 it is easy to see what factors determine the quantity of X chosen per period by an economically rational individual: the price of good X (P_x), income (I), the price of good Y (P_y), preferences or tastes (T) and the objective (O) attributed to an individual, i.e. the general arguments in the demand function of an individual should be:

$$Q_x = f(P_x, I, P_y, T, O). \tag{1.10}$$

MORE FORMAL SECTION

All of the above can be captured in a more sophisticated and concise manner using the Lagrangian multiplier technique as follows:

$$\text{Max } \mathscr{L} = U(X,Y) + \lambda(I - P_xX - P_yY) \tag{1.11}$$

The first-order conditions for a maximum are found by taking the partial derivatives with respect to X, Y and λ and setting them equal to zero.[8] This yields:

$$\partial \mathscr{L} / \partial X = \partial U / \partial X - \lambda P_x = 0 \tag{1.12}$$

$$\partial \mathscr{L} / \partial Y = \partial U / \partial Y - \lambda P_y = 0 \tag{1.13}$$

$$\partial \mathscr{L} / \partial \lambda = I - P_xX - P_yY = 0 \tag{1.14}$$

Rearranging (1.12) and (1.13) gives

$$\partial U / \partial X \bigg/ P_x = \lambda = \partial U / \partial Y \bigg/ P_y \tag{1.15}$$

$$\partial U / \partial X \bigg/ \partial U / \partial Y = MU_x / MU_y = P_x / P_y \tag{1.16}$$

which is the result identified in a more intuitive fashion above. The undetermined (uncomputed) multiplier λ can be interpreted as the shadow price on the budget constraint. As λ represents the extra utility at the margin from a one unit (£1) change in the (budget) constraint it can be interpreted as the marginal utility of income. At the optimum it can be seen as a prediction for a utility maximiser that the ratio of the marginal utility of a good to its own price will be constant for all goods and equal to λ. Whilst this presentation of the utility-maximising individual is standard, how secure are the foundations on which the presentation stands? Or, put another way: how secure is the process of the supply of knowledge that underlies a presentation like this and the very many others in subsequent chapters?

1.5.3 Duality and optimisation

One of the most quoted economics authors of the 1970s and 1980s is Diewert (e.g. 1974) whose name, amongst others, is associated with the introduction of duality results in many areas of economics. It recognises that optimising results can be obtained in two ways. The primal approach attempts to explicitly solve the optimisation problem using the direct objective function. The dual approach is a method of obtaining the same optimising results from applying partial differentiation to the indirect objective function. The natural question arises as to why we should bother with the dual if it simply gives the same results. The answer lies in a number of possible gains. The first is that it may be an easier or more convenient way of obtaining results. Second, the indirect functions often involve variables that are easier to get at empirically (e.g. prices, incomes and quantities as opposed to utility). Third, duality often provides functions and specifications of an economic problem suitable for applied econometric work. Finally, there is elegance about the dual approach that commends it in itself. Basically the structure of the thinking is:

---

8. Note the Lagrangian could have been set up:

$$\text{Max } \mathscr{L} = U(X,Y) - \lambda(P_xX + P_yY - I) \text{ and the same results would have been established.}$$

Underlying Direct Function

⇑

Indirect Function

⇓

Partial Derivatives

with the trick being the ability to appropriately specify the indirect function. In the present context of utility maximisation the primal Lagrangian approach has already been illustrated above. Below an 'easy numbers' example from Nicholson (1995) is repeated to demonstrate what is involved in the context of a specific numerical example. (For a more recent concise treatment of duality see Turkington 2007, Chapter 7.) Remember that the objective is utility maximisation.

Analysis

Theory steps:
PRIMAL (explicitly solve a direct optimisation problem)

Maximise $U(X,Y)$

Subject to $P_x X + P_y Y = I$
(solve with Lagrange)

↓

DUAL (obtain the same results from partial differentiation of the indirect objective function)
Indirect Utility Function

$U^* = V(P_x, P_y, \bar{I})$

↓

Use Roy's identity

↓

$$X = dx(P_x, P_y, I) = \frac{-\partial V / \partial P_x}{\partial V / \partial I}$$

Roy's identity: defines the optimal demand for a good (X above) as the negative of the ratio of the partial derivatives of the indirect utility function (V) with respect to the price of that particular good (P_x) and with respect to income (I).

Application steps:
Duality and the Cobb–Douglas function example

PRIMAL
Max $U(X,Y) = X^{0.5} Y^{0.5}$

subject to $I = P_x X + P_y Y$
(assume: income $I = 2$; $P_x = 0.25$ and $P_y = 1$)
Lagrangian

$$\mathcal{L} = X^{0.5} Y^{0.5} + \lambda(2 - 1Y - 0.25X)$$

For first-order conditions set partials $= 0$

DUAL-INDIRECT UTILITY FUNCTION
$U^* = U(X^*, Y^*)$
(using expressions for X^* and Y^*)
$U^* = (I/2P_x)^{0.5} (I/2P_y)^{0.5}$

$$U^* = \frac{I}{2P_x^{0.5} P_y^{0.5}} = V(P_x, P_y, I)$$

Use Roy's identity to give Marshallian demands (note money income is held constant)

→

$$\frac{\partial \mathscr{L}}{\partial X} = 0.5\, X^{-0.5}Y^{0.5} - 0.25\lambda = 0 \qquad (1.17)$$

$$X^* = \frac{-\partial V/\partial P_x}{\partial V/\partial I}$$

$$\frac{\partial \mathscr{L}}{\partial Y} = 0.5\, X^{0.5}Y^{-0.5} - \lambda = 0 \qquad (1.18)$$

$$X^* = \frac{I/4 P_x^{1.5}P_y^{0.5}}{\frac{1}{2}P_x^{0.5}P_y^{0.5}} = \frac{I}{2P_x}$$

$$\frac{\partial \mathscr{L}}{\partial \lambda} = 2 - 1Y - 0.25X = 0$$

$$X^* = 2/(2 \times 0.25) = 4$$

From (1.17)

Analogously

$$0.5\, X^{-0.5}Y^{0.5} = 0.25\lambda \qquad (1.17')$$

$$Y^* = \frac{I}{2P_y} = \frac{2}{(2 \times 1)} = 1$$

From (1.18)

$$0.5\, X^{0.5}Y^{-0.5} = \lambda \qquad (1.18')$$

Divide (1.17′) by (1.18′)

$$\frac{0.5\, X^{-0.5}Y^{0.5}}{0.5\, X^{0.5}Y^{-0.5}} = \frac{0.25\lambda}{\lambda} = \frac{1}{4} = \frac{Y}{X}$$

$$X = 4Y$$

Substitute for X in the budget constraint

$$2 = 0.25\ 4Y + 1Y$$
$$2 = 2Y$$
$$Y^* = 1\ [= I/2P_y]$$

Substitute for Y^* in the budget constraint

$$2 = 0.25\ X + 1$$
$$X^* = 4\ [= I/2P_x]$$

Direct utility $= U^* = (4)^{0.5}(1)^{0.5} = 2$

It should be evident that, if the analysis had begun with the $V(P_x,P_y,I)$, indirect utility function, a simpler procedure is facilitated. It is also worth considering the utility-maximising quantities if income and prices are changed in the same proportion. Above when $I = 2$, $P_x = 0.25$ and $P_y = 1$ the utility-maximising quantities are $X^* = 4$ and $Y^* = 1$ from the expressions $X^* = I/2P_x$ and $Y^* = I/2P_y$. Now double all prices and income so $I = 4$, $P_x = 0.5$ and $P_y = 2$. By substitution, X^* now equals $4/(2 \times 0.5) = 4$ and $Y^* = 4/(2 \times 2) = 1$. That is, the utility-maximising quantities remain unchanged. This is an important result as it indicates demand functions are homogeneous of degree zero in prices and incomes, so that if all prices and incomes are changed in the same proportion the quantity demanded is unchanged. As inflation is a rise in the general price level, including factor prices (income), it can have no impact on real choices and inflation is not a worry for microeconomic theory (and hence does not feature in micro texts). Further, note that the variables involved in the dual approach are empirically observable being income, price of good X, price of good Y, quantity purchased of good X and quantity purchased of good Y, raising the prospect that with these data and the assumption of utility-maximising behaviour, the underlying utility function can be obtained by working backwards. Hence, the direction of the arrow (upwards from indirect function to underlying direct function above). This exercise is illustrated with respect to a production function in Chapter 3 Appendix. For a discussion and application of duality in many contexts see Cornes (1992).

1.6 Challenge: Is the economic methodology plausible?

Section 1.2 on 'Boring, boring economics!' has insights for economic methodology. In an introductory economics course, individuals are generally told, feel implicitly or read explicitly about the methodology of economics. Thousands of students will have used Begg, Fischer and Dornbusch's (1991 and later editions) best-selling text and they will have read in Chapter 2 about the interconnections between models and facts in economic relationships. Facts or data are seen to be important because, first, they suggest relationships economists should explore and, second, data are used to 'test' economic hypotheses. Economic models are the product of theorising, which to be more than mere speculation must generate implications or hypotheses that relate to the 'knowable world' in a form such that they could be shown to be false. In this essentially *logical positivist* framework conventional or well-received economic theories are those that have successfully survived many attempts to falsify them. Economists are careful to not describe these theories as true; they are simply as yet unfalsified. This has a neat and attractive appeal and underlies the notion of economics as a science. However, despite this attraction many would challenge this picture of economics as a science. The point is not so much that economics is not science; rather that science is unscientific in that it does not conform to the picture commonly painted. Here, however, it is economics that is the focus. How does the body of information or stock of knowledge called microeconomics recorded in this text come to be?

One answer is provided by Samuels (1991). Samuels suggests that there are two types of people in the world: those, the majority, who demand determinacy and closedness and the minority who can tolerate ambiguity and open-endedness. The majority have a demand for certain knowledge. They want policy to be based in knowledge that is correct rather than false; they want the creation and amendment of social institutions to be based on true beliefs; and they find living in a world of uncertainty (radical indeterminacy) produces angst. Samuels, however argues that, whether individuals like it or not, certain knowledge cannot be supplied. He does this by investigating:

(i)   The process of certain knowledge supply;
(ii) The possibilities of certain knowledge supply.

1.6.1 The process of certain knowledge supply

As regards the process of certain knowledge supply, as noted above, to date most readers will have completed courses in economics that explicitly, or implicitly, have 'facts', 'hard statistics' and (as yet) unfalsified theory. This knowledge comes from evidence about the past, e.g. fossils, coins, writings, records. However, this evidence has both chance elements (what does not get destroyed, what gets discovered) and systematic bias (e.g. the evidence that survives is likely to be the record of the powerful, relatively educated, 'top' people). Second, there is the question of the interpretation of evidence. Nothing comes ready interpreted and interpretation will also have a chance element in that it depends on the personal characteristics of the interpreter. Even the most ahistorical of people must tap into their personal experience and the folklore of those around them, argues Samuels. Further systematic bias will also be present in that many interpreters want to tell 'specific' stories. For example, Tullock (1971) examines the economics of revolutions and notes the popular view is that they are about the 'good' replacing the 'bad' (which he sees as being unsustainable). If this is so, the question becomes: why has history given people this cosy picture? Elements in his answer are that: historians rely on the memoirs of the leaders of revolutions; the only effect of revolutions on historians themselves is if there are positive legacies from the past – a gain; literature about 'come and join' the revolution will be set in terms of 'higher motives' rather than base self-serving ones.

Tullock's review of the evidence on revolutions leads him to the view that they are about the rich displacing the very rich at the top of a state and not much more. In short, interpretations of the same events vary considerably.

Third, there is the question of whose ideas or whose 'schools of thought' get the limelight. In the present context it is about asking who gets to be in the economic journals and how is 'what they are saying' shaped. Here Samuels questions the notion of objectivity in the process. Armstrong (1982) provides evidence. He reports the 'letterhead effect' in which Peters and Ceci (1982) resubmitted twelve articles already published within the last three years in prestigious psychology journals. The resubmissions to the very journals that had published the articles had the same content but now apparently came from fictitious authors at a 'no-reputation' institution. Of these, three were discovered, eight rejected (none, on the grounds they said nothing new)! The 'filing cabinet effect' states that it is easier to get published material supportive of existing positions than material to the contrary. The implication is that 'out there' in thousands of separate filing cabinets is a mound of rejected articles that apparently have 'wrong data', 'wrong transformations', 'wrong theory', etc.

Next, there is the issue of replicability or, less grandly, 'checking'. Seldom is work replicated in social sciences; therefore everyone must be wary not to accept chance results. A *Journal of Money, Credit and Banking* project (see Dewald, Thursby and Anderson 1986) found that many of the published empirical results could not be reproduced and that for a small number of contributions to the journal, all of a sudden, no data could be found to check! For economists, it seems appropriate to note that the self-interest motive was observed to apply in that the errors found tended to favour the authors' views.

Allied worries were: that referees varied in their view of the competence of individuals; that there was no incentive to work on important topics and evidence that complexity and obfuscation were seen as superior to clear writing and judged better. Armstrong also reports an interesting experiment carried out by Naftulin, Ware and Donnelly (1973) in which Dr Fox (a clue in the name!), an actor, gave three almost senseless lectures to three audiences (including academics) followed by periods of questions. The lectures were generally assessed by listeners to be good or very good! Such results cast doubt on the validity of the quality of individuals' critical abilities and highlight their limitations.

Finally, there is the question of 'who wins'. With access to limelight political, historical and social factors some ideas and schools of thought are deemed winners, whilst others are marginalised. That is, academic disciplines change but not, unfortunately, as a process through which good ideas replace bad ideas as you close in on the truth. As pointed out by Samuelson (1985), Max Planck the Nobel physicist noted that no one seemed to change their mind in the face of new theories and experiments but rather people who believed one thing died, to be replaced by people who believed something else.

The message of this subsection is very clear and is that the notions of 'hard facts' and economic theory 'testing' look very fragile and doubtful the closer you get to them. Enacting the La Manna description of economics contained in his quotation on p. 8 above is a very difficult task.

1.6.2 The possibilities for certain knowledge supply

The possibilities for certain knowledge supply are heavily circumscribed by developments in epistemology (which concerns the nature and validity of knowledge) and discourse analysis. The meaning that is given to (economic) theories and statements involve the creation and deployment of language which itself is a social construct. Both lead to the notion of the 'social construction' of economic reality. With regard to the nature of economic knowledge enough has been said above to convince many that there is no objective, confirmable and replicable definition of reality and therefore there must be a willingness to accept open-endedness and methodological pluralism.

Considering discourse, theory suggests that what we all get to accept as knowledge makes sense only in the context of your underlying beginning position, i.e. it is paradigm-specific. What individuals get to 'see' in economic theory is limited by the assumptions required to produce results that are equilibrium, optimal and determinate. It must be emphasised that this line of reasoning is not that anything will do, but rather in Samuels's view, the injunction to locate and understand the grounds on which something is accepted as knowledge. Samuels writes about the credentials of your knowledge. Even having 'credentials' for your knowledge does not determine the meaning it has. Neoclassicism, Marxism etc. are intellectual constructs partly built through language.

Economics, in general, is a discursive system through which you get to see and interpret the economic model. The problem is that there are many discursive systems possible – economists are telling 'one story' among many that may be possible.

The importance of these notions about knowledge and language is that unlike the natural world, the economy is a social construction – what individuals think and believe shapes what is there. If this is accepted, economic reality is the product of and NOT the check on human thought or theorising. The so-called facts of situations are the empirical outcrop of the accepted theory and are not independent entities; people are born into and inculcated into the ways of a society that they take to be real and, by taking part in that society, shape what the next generation takes to be real.

These are powerful, and to some disturbing, thoughts. The punch line of Samuels's article is that (as students of economic knowledge) individuals have to:

(i)   accept open-endedness and ambiguity, because the alternative looks implausible;
(ii) realise that what is taken as knowledge is paradigm-specific and that there are many other stories that could be told;
(iii) accept that saying something is explainable means you can discuss it in a given paradigm.

The message is to be very uncertain about anything you think is certain, as 'doubt grows with knowledge' (Goethe, quoted in Hemenway 1988: 11).

The line of reasoning developed in this section is a call to be more vigilant about the nature of economic reasoning and evidence, not less. Individuals must be very aware of the fragility of what is being read and develop a critical facility. What makes a piece of theory work? Are the assumptions simplifying or determining? How is it being constructed? Why is it seen as accepted? And so on. To foster this process, each chapter contains material that challenges the dominant view in the same way that this section itself challenges the typical picture given to introductory students of facts, economic theory and methodology. In this section the breadth of economics is also indicated as the discussion has moved from arithmetical principles (which in the light of this section must also be viewed as social constructions that individuals, via inculcation at a young age, have become the 'certain and correct' principles of manipulation) to questions about the nature of knowledge and its construction.

1.7 Summary

This chapter has covered a variety of crucial and fundamental areas ranging through the perspective of microeconomics, some visual arithmetic techniques, utility maximisation and methodology. Readers are recommended to spend some time mastering the material here as these apparently disparate considerations are the foundations of neoclassical microeconomics. Difficulties in understanding later material and/or interpretations made will, almost certainly, trace back to this chapter. In the remaining chapters signposts back to this chapter will be provided so that, if the intellectual construct you are hopefully building shows signs of crumbling, foundational repair work can be made.

The objective in later chapters will be to emphasise that 'nothing is set in stone'. For all mainstream interpretations of theory and its construction, there are always 'wrinkles' to be found. More important, by far, however, is the knowledge that there are always 'doubters' internal and external to the discipline, trying to reinterpret it, modify it, discredit it or, more ambitiously, replace it. It is this dissent that lends dynamism to the subject and prevents the writing of further textbooks being unnecessary!

In the first part of the chapter the economists' view of the world was captured in the mnemonic BORING. Like it or not, this mnemonic is helpful when focusing on how mainstream microeconomics is constructed but the central message in this book is that these building blocks can be applied to offer INTERESTING insight when focusing on decisions that are taken from day to day.

One reason for the tag BORING was claimed to be the mathematical content of microeconomics. A substantive section of this chapter outlined some basic visual arithmetic techniques that allow the distinction between total, marginal and average values to be easily made. Also, the general concepts of elasticity and elasticity of substitution were revised and graphically simplified as a necessary prerequisite to the subsequent INTERESTING chapters.

The key concepts of rationality and utility maximisation were explored as they are central to virtually all economic discussions. The word 'constructed' was chosen carefully in the previous paragraph as the discussion of methodology introduced social constructionism. It is difficult to envisage that microeconomics unlike, say Mount Everest, would exist without people and it is people, their thoughts and inculcated values that determine what gets to be recognised as mainstream microeconomic theory. At root then, the foundations of microeconomics may well be less secure than some people, including some economists, recognise. This is in no way to attack or denigrate the subject but rather to try to offer a deeper insight. Recall the claim that is not that economics is not like science, it is that science is not like science in that, for many, especially sociologists of science, science is also a social construction.

This contribution was presented in this chapter as the first of many 'challenges' to be found in this text. The purpose of the 'challenges' is to get readers to be both aware and critical of the material presented here. Much of it is not obvious and books describing economics as the science of common sense do everyone a disservice in that they underestimate the contribution of the major economic theorists and often put students on the wrong track. Virtually all the major results of microeconomic theory are counterintuitive. Students who have not done their revision tend to write that the ideal form of economic organisation is a large single firm providing each good (monopoly), not that the ideal situation is one of duplication with many firms providing identical goods in circumstances where they feel powerless to affect the world around them (perfect competition).[9] Similarly much common sense takes people to protectionism and what is good for producers and not free trade, the microeconomic prescription (see Chapter 17).

9. It is similar to a scene in the first *Planet of the Apes* film where the Charlton Heston character explains to the friendly ape that to get more output they must keep the best produce for next year's seed. The ape laughs a great deal at this 'eat the worst and bury the best' strategy because historically they always reasoned that that it was better to eat the best and plant the worst to produce next year's crop – common sense had taken the apes the wrong way.

Appendix 1 The total differential

Given a function $Y = f(X)$ there is a way to approximate the change in Y, ΔY, when X is changed by a small amount, ΔX (the smaller ΔX the better the approximation). Consider Figure 1.14. X_1 and Y_1 is the initial point on the curve and the actual changes in X and Y are marked ΔX and ΔY. Putting a tangent T to the curve at point X_1 suggests distance V approximates ΔY so that V = Slope of T times ΔX or $V = dY/dX$ evaluated at X_1 times ΔX.

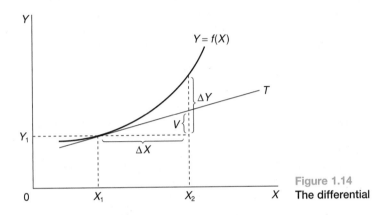

Figure 1.14
The differential

To put it in 'large change' terms, if the slope of T was $+3$ and $\Delta X = +2$, then $V = +6$. More precisely:

$$\Delta Y = dY/dX \cdot \Delta X.$$

This approximation is known as the differential of Y.

In this text the typical function has two independent variables. That is, they take the form $Y = f(Z,X)$. By extension of the argument just made, a linear approximation of the change in Y that arises as Z and X are both changed by small amounts will be given by:

$$\Delta Y = dY/dZ \cdot \Delta Z + dY/dX \cdot \Delta X$$

Tidying this up to a neater presentation as the changes are assumed to become smaller:

$$dY = \partial Y/\partial Z \cdot dZ + \partial Y/\partial X \cdot dX$$

where $\partial Y/\partial Z$ is the partial derivative of Y with respect to Z and $\partial Y/\partial X$ is the partial derivative of Y with respect to X. An interesting result obtains if dY is constrained to be zero. That is, if:

$$dY = \partial Y/\partial Z \cdot dZ + \partial Y/\partial X \cdot dX = 0,$$

$$\text{then } dZ/dX = -\partial Y/\partial X \Big/ \partial Y/\partial Z$$

The slope of a curve between Z and X (when the value of the dependent variable, here Y, is not allowed to change) is then equal to the negative of the ratio of the partial derivatives of the independent variables, a result that clearly has application to indifference curves, isoquants and social welfare curves. As will be amply demonstrated below, the partial derivatives of the independent variables have a natural economic interpretation as marginal utilities, marginal products and marginal welfare changes.

References

Armstrong, J.S. (1982) Research on scientific journals: implications for editors and authors, *Journal of Forecasting*, 83: 83–104.

Begg, D., Fischer, S. and Dornbusch, R. (1991) *Economics*, 3rd edn, London: McGraw-Hill.

Buchanan, J.M. *et al.* (1978) *The Economics of Politics*, IEA Readings No. 18.

Cole, C.L. (1973) *Microeconomics – A Contemporary Approach*, New York: Harcourt Brace Jovanovich.

Cornes, R. (1992) *Duality and Modern Economics*, Cambridge: Cambridge University Press.

Dewald, W.G., Thursby, J.G. and Anderson, R.G. (1986) Replication in economics: the *Journal of Money Credit and Banking* Project, *America Economic Review*, 76: 587–603.

Diewert, W.E. (1974) Applications of duality theory, pp. 106–71, in Intriligator, M.D. and Kendrick, D.A. (eds) *Frontiers in Quantitative Economics, Vol. II*, Amsterdam: North-Holland.

Edgeworth, F.Y. (1881) *Mathematical Psychics*, London: Kegan-Paul.

Hahn, F.H. and Matthews, R.C.O. (1965) The theory of economic growth: a survey, pp. 1–124, in *Surveys of Economic Theory, Vol. II*, London: Macmillan.

Hemenway, D. (1988) *Prices and Choices – Microeconomic Vignettes*, 2nd edn, Cambridge, Mass: Ballinger.

Hirshleifer, J. and Riley, J.G. (1992) *The Analytics of Uncertainty and Information*, Cambridge: Cambridge University Press.

Houellebecq, M. (2003) *Platform*, London: Vintage.

Knox, T.M. (1952) *Hegel's Philosophy of Right: Translated with Notes*, Oxford: Oxford University Press.

La Manna, M. (2003) Letters and opinion, *Times Higher Education Supplement*, 9 May No. 1588, p. 15.

Lea, S.E.G., Tarpy, R. and Webley, P. (1987) *A Textbook of Economic Psychology*, Cambridge: Cambridge University Press.

McKenzie, R.B. and Tullock, G. (1981) *The New World of Economics*, Homewood: Ill: R.D. Irwin.

Marshall, A. (1891) *Principles of Economics*, London: Macmillan.

Naftulin, D.H., Ware, J.E. Jr and Donnelly, F.A. (1973) The Dr Fox Lecture: a paradigm of education seduction, *Journal of Medical Education*, 48: 630–5.

Nicholson, W. (1995) *Microeconomic Theory – Basic Principles and Extensions*, Fort Worth, Tex.: Dryden.

Peters, D.P. and Ceci, S.J. (1982) Peer review practices of psychological journals: the fate of accepted, published articles, submitted again, *The Behavioral and Brain Sciences*, 5: 187–95.

Samuels, W.J. (1991) 'Truth' and 'discourse' in the social construction of economic reality: an essay on the relation of knowledge to economic reality, *Journal of Post Keynesian Economics*, 13: 511–24.

Samuelson, P.A. (1985) *Economics*, New York: McGraw-Hill.

Stigler, G. and Becker, G. (1977) De gustibus non est disputandum, *American Economic Review*, 67 (2): 76–90.

Tullock, G. (1971) The paradox of revolution, *Public Choice*, 2: 88–99.

Turkington, D.A. (2007) *Mathematical Tools for Economists*, Oxford: Blackwell.

Varoufakis, Y. (1998) *Foundations of Economics – A Beginner's Companion*, London and New York: Routledge.

Williams, A. (1978) Efficiency and welfare, pp. 25–32, in D. Black and G.P. Thomas (eds) *Providing for the Health Services*, London: Croom-Helm.

The 'clever' and 'dumb' consumer

2.1 Introduction

In a market economy individual consumers are continuously making decisions about the bundle of goods they will purchase. The economic picture of this process introduced in Chapter 1 must be extended and further elaborated if richer insights are to be made.

In Chapter 1:

(i)   Indifference curves were introduced as representations of individual preferences over 'goods';
(ii) A linear budget constraint represented income (I), P_y the price of good Y and P_x the price of good X (both assumed constant);
(iii) Static consumer equilibrium was depicted for an individual with a utility-maximising objective (O).

To extend the boundary of microeconomic analysis the first task is to develop a richer account of indifference maps and possible budget constraints.

2.2 Wider preferences and complicated constraints

In this section two questions are raised. What if good Y and/or good X are not 'goods' to an individual? What if all units of a good cannot always be purchased at one single price per unit?

2.2.1 The 'good', the 'bad' and the 'neutral'

Recapping on Chapter 1, indifference curves for goods were deduced to be negatively sloped, non-intersecting, everywhere dense and, relying on intuition, convex to the origin. The slope of the indifference curve indicates the rate at which the individual is willing to substitute one good for the other to remain at the same level of utility. This rate is called the (diminishing) Marginal Rate of Substitution between X and Y ($-dY/dX = \partial U/\partial X \,/\, \partial U/\partial Y = MU_x/MU_y = MRS_{xy}$).[1]

But as an account of preferences, the picture is incomplete. What about people for whom X (Y) is not a good? Or people who dislike both? Microeconomic theory would be poor if it could only deal with goods. Fortunately, the result in Equation (1.16) (Chapter 1) is general. Figure 2.1 illustrates the shapes of the indifference map for a whole series of possibilities other than the standard two 'goods' case of Chapter 1. These new shapes are identified when the axioms (or assumptions) adopted are relaxed in turn.

---

1. Using this subscript ordering throughout the text we follow the convention described by Ferguson and Gould (1975).

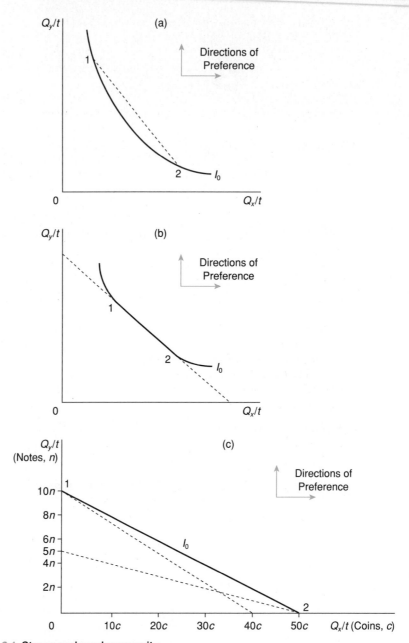

Figure 2.1 Strong and weak convexity

Strict convexity of indifference curves means that, if a straight line is used to join two points on an indifference curve between two goods (points 1 and 2 in Figure 2.1(a)), all the points on that line will be preferred to points 1 and 2. The straight line will be a linear combination of the allocations of good X and good Y at points 1 and 2. If weak convexity obtains then indifference curves can have straight-line segments (as illustrated by the segment 1-2 in Figure 2.1(b)). For the theorist, the disadvantage of this is that it is possible to lose determinacy. If the dashed budget line in Figure 2.1(b) was the relevant one, the equilibrium combination of good X and good Y is no longer unique; rather all points on segment 1-2 are equally attractive to the individual. But this can be turned into an advantage in that, for some goods, expecting an indifference curve convex to the origin would be inappropriate. Consider the case of £5 notes and £1 coins. Abstracting from the weight etc. (characteristics of notes versus coins), one should be a perfect substitute for the other at a ratio of 1 to 5.

Figure 2.1(c) is the case of Y and X as perfect substitutes at a given ratio, i.e. the slope of the indifference curve MU_x/MU_y equals a negative constant. So, if an individual has £50 cash and the Q_y/t axis is £5 notes and the Q_x/t axis is £1 coins, the constant slope of the indifference curve is $-1/5$. Given that banks and obliging individuals will exchange one £5 note for five £1 coins, the budget line is also a straight line with slope $-1/5$ (illustrated dashed). Whilst the illustration has no prediction as to how the £50 will be held, it does allow the case of perfect substitutes to be illustrated.

If, for some reason, the budget line did not have a slope of $-1/5$ a corner solution (i.e. at one of the axes) is predicted. Assume you have ten £5 notes and a bank will give only four £1 coins for a £5 note (budget slope $= -1/4$), a result at point 1 would be stable, i.e. holding all notes, as no one would want to turn them into forty £1 coins. Assume you have fifty £1 coins and a bank will give £5 notes only for ten £1 coins (budget slope $= -1/10$), a result at point 2 would be stable, i.e. holding all coins.

A further step is to replace strict convexity with concavity. This is illustrated in Figure 2.2. Concavity involves an increasingly negative marginal rate of substitution. Imposing a dashed budget constraint indicates that with two goods and increasingly negative marginal-rate-of-substitution indifference curves, a corner solution is selected over a tangency; point 1 offers higher utility than point 2 (I_1 as opposed to I_0). This provides an empirical, as opposed to an intuitive, rationale for convexity, i.e. if concavity was widespread then individuals would not be choosing variety in their utility-maximising bundles, as corner solutions would dominate. The fact that variety is chosen by the vast majority of individuals provides support for the standard-shape indifference curve between goods.

Turn now to the assumption of non-satiation (or the axiom of dominance). Weak dominance allows for more units of a good to be neutral with respect to utility. Figure 2.3(a) is the case of good X being a neutral. If MU_x is zero then the slope of the indifference curve (MU_x/MU_y) is also zero, i.e. for more units of good X to have no impact on utility (as its quantity per unit of time increases), the indifference map comprises horizontal indifference curves. Weak dominance allows points 1 and 2 to be assigned the

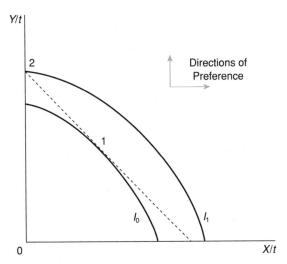

Figure 2.2
Concave indifference curves

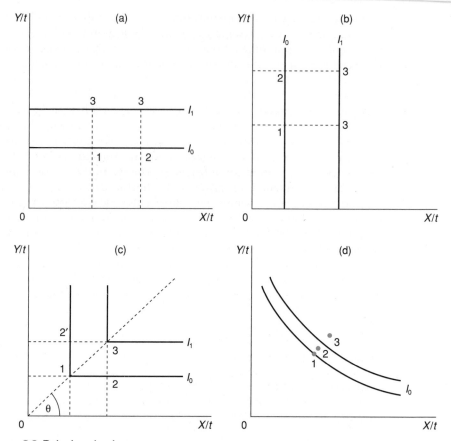

Figure 2.3 Relaxing dominance

same utility level (I_0), even though point 2 involves more units of good X per period. Note: good Y remains a good, so that increased units of Y per period increases utility (see points 3 are on I_1).

Figure 2.3(b) is the case of good Y being a neutral. If MU_y is zero then the shape of the indifference curve is a vertical line as $MU_x/MU_y = \infty$. That is, for good Y to have no impact on utility (as its quantity per unit of time increases), the indifference map comprises vertical indifference curves. Weak dominance allows points 1 and 2 to be assigned the same utility level (I_0), even though point 2 involves more units of good Y per period. Note: good X remains a good, so that increased units of Y per period increases utility (see points 3 on I_1).

Figure 2.3(c) effectively make Y and X neutrals unless they come in a certain ratio, as is the case of perfect complements. The typical example is left- and right-foot shoes. If Y/t is left-foot shoes and X/t is right-foot shoes at point 1 the individual has one of each and at point 3 the individual has two of each – and utility is correspondingly increased from I_0 to I_1. Two right-foot shoes and one left-foot shoe at point 2 has the same utility as one of each at point 1. Similarly, two left-foot shoes and one right-foot shoe at point 2′ has the same utility as one of each at point 1. Shoe shops intuitively know this: displaying only one of each pair outside their shops (safe in the knowledge that utility-maximisers cannot increase their utility by stealing the displayed shoes). The fact that points 2 and 2′ may involve a burden (i.e. decrease utility) is usually met by the assumption of free disposal, i.e. the assumption that it is costless to get rid of any unwanted units of a good.

Before dealing with 'bads' explicitly, the question of thick indifference curves is illustrated by Figure 2.3(d). The figure has two lines but one indifference curve, I_0; while point 2 has more of goods Y and X than at point 1, it is on the same indifference curve on the grounds that the individual may not perceive the increased X and Y if the changes are small. Only at point 3 is a new higher indifference level met when quantity changes are perceived.

Figure 2.4(a) illustrates a full indifference mountain that will allow the two-dimensional description of preferences to be completed. Point 1 is the top of an ordinal indifference mountain. As far as the depicted individual is concerned, this is their ideal combination of X and Y per period. Any deviation from this point has to be to a lower level of utility. Indifference 'ridge lines' are introduced. The 'vertical-ish' one joins points where the marginal utility of good X is zero and the 'horizontal-ish' one where the marginal utility of good Y is zero. Points where the individual is sated with good X and good Y are located, dividing the circular map into four quadrants. Quadrant I is the classic two-goods case, as indicated by the directions of preference. To stay on the same indifference curve with more X (Y), less Y (X) also has to be involved to counteract the positive effect on utility of more X (Y). The indifference curves are negatively sloped (decreasing at an increasing rate, i.e. getting flatter); MU_x and MU_y are both positive. In quadrant II, Y has become a bad; to stay on the same indifference curve with more Y, more X also has to be enjoyed

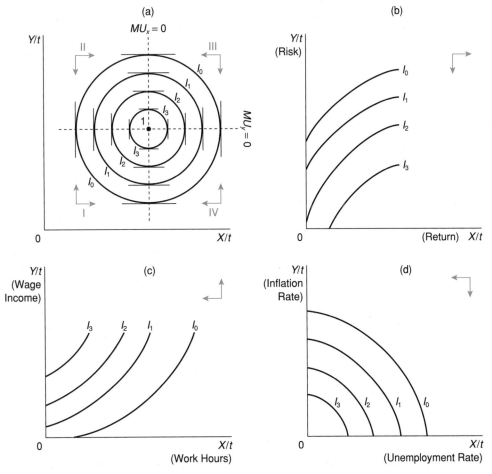

Figure 2.4 Mixed preferences

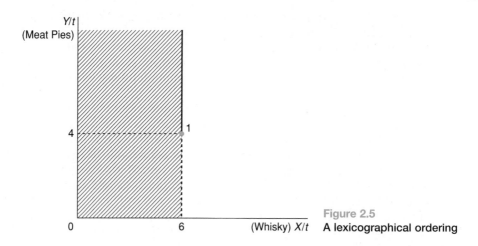

Figure 2.5
A lexicographical ordering

to counteract the negative effect on utility of more Y (MU_y negative). The indifference curves are positively sloped (increasing at a decreasing rate, i.e. getting flatter). In quadrant IV, X has become a bad; to stay on the same indifference curve with more X, more Y also has to be enjoyed to counteract the negative effect on utility of more X (MU_x negative). The indifference curves are positively sloped, increasing at an increasing rate (getting steeper). In quadrant III, X and Y have both become bads; to stay on the same indifference curve with more X (Y), less Y (X) also has to be involved to counteract the negative effect on utility of more X (Y) (MU_y and MU_x are both negative). The indifference curves are negatively sloped, decreasing at an increasing rate (getting steeper). (A general description of this diagram with the signs of the first and second derivatives is provided in Appendix 2.)

Figures 2.4(b), (c) and (d) break down the circle of indifference to illustrate maps between bad Y and good X in panel (b), between good Y and bad X in panel (c) and between bad Y and bad X in panel (d). Some labels have been added to the axes to give a feel of what types of commodities (or economic variables) might be involved.

The final assumption (or axiom) relaxed here is that of continuity, or substitutability. This involves the case of *lexicographical orderings* and has severe implications. Such orderings involve more of one good always being preferred. The individual illustrated is an alcoholic, so good X can be whisky and good Y meat pies. The individual in Figure 2.5 has an endowment of four meat pies and six bottles of whisky per period at point 1. It is impossible to find a point of indifference to point 1. The dashed line and shaded area to the left involve allocations that are unambiguously inferior to an alcoholic, in that they involve less alcohol. Allocations on the continuous line and to the right are unambiguously superior to an alcoholic in that they involve more meat pies, or more meat pies and more alcohol. If lexicographical orderings were thought to be widespread, indifference curve analysis would have little application, in that it would not be possible to draw the curves. Luckily for economic theory such preferences are both thought to be and seem rare.

2.2.2 A variety of budget constraints

In Chapter 1 a straight-line budget constraint was developed with a constant slope of $-P_x/P_y$. However, not all situations will correspond to this. A number of possibilities present themselves. A piecewise linear budget constraint arises when different quantities involve different price ratios over different ranges of the constraint. Figure 2.6(a) shows the price ratio falling as the quantity on the x-axis increases; this may correspond to

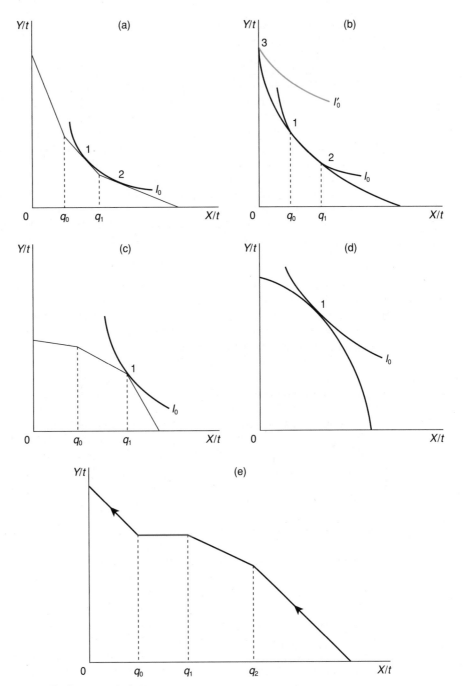

Figure 2.6 Budget constraints

second-degree price discrimination, where different blocks of units are sold at successively lower prices as quantities per period chosen rise.

A reverse picture is shown as 2.6(c) where the price ratio increases as the quantity increases. Income tax systems are typically designed so that choosing more hours of leisure per period becomes less and less costly in terms net of tax income as tax rates are typically higher on higher incomes. If price ratios alter continuously then a curvilinear budget is appropriate (see Figure 2.6(b) and (d)).

In panel (b) the price ratio is continuously falling, whereas in panel (d) it is continuously rising. Finally, in panel (e) a mixed picture is presented where the price ratio decreases, then increases somewhat and finally returns to its original level as X/t increases. For example, assume you have bought insurance for health care (good X/t). The coverage insists you buy the first 0-q_0 units at the market price ratio (a so-called deductible), the next q_0-q_1 units are fully insured and are free at the point of demand (that is $P_x = 0$ and $-P_x/P_y$ will also be zero and the budget constraint is horizontal), whereas use beyond q_1 to q_2 is at a reduced, but not free, rate (you pay part of the price of each unit a co-payment) and, finally, beyond q_2 the full market price ratio is faced once more. Clearly, quite complex budget constraints are easily created and lend a bias to the equilibria observed. Budget constraints that are convex to the origin suggest indeterminacy, see range 1-2 in panel (b) or a corner solution at point 3 in panel (b). In panel (a) the quantities associated with the range 1-2 would never be observed as an equilibrium. Concavity tends to encourage an interior equilibrium (see point 1 in panel (d) or equilibria at an interior corner at point 1 in panel (c)).

The general message that emerges from the last two subsections is that it is relatively easy to create more realistic situations but the 'price' that has to be paid for richer situations is in the loss of determinacy – there are no 'free lunches' even in theory! In the next section a straight-line budget constraint is once more employed in the context of demand curve derivation and analysis.

2.3 Deriving a demand curve

Having established that consumer efficiency requires that the slope of the indifference curve must be equated with the slope of the budget constraint, it is evident that a static equilibrium involves (see Chapter 1):

$$MRS_{xy} \equiv -dY/dX|_{u=u_0} \equiv \partial U/\partial X \big/ \partial U/\partial Y \equiv MU_x/MU_y = P_x/P_y = -dY/dX \tag{2.1}$$

or, considering the final substantive two terms,

$$MU_x/P_x = MU_y/P_y \tag{2.1a}$$

if utility is to be maximised. From the discussion in Chapter 1 it was clear the quantity of good X demanded per period by a utility maximiser was described by the function:

$$Q_x = f(P_x \mid \bar{I}, \bar{P}_y, \bar{T}, \bar{O}) \tag{2.2}$$

where

Q_x = quantity of X purchased per period of time;
P_x = price per unit of good X;
I = income (a flow measured per period);
P_y = the prices of other goods and services;
T = tastes or preferences;
O = the objective of the consumer taken to be utility maximisation. Every term beyond the vertical bar line is being held constant – hence the bars over the variables. This is the *'ceteris paribus'* – other things equal – assumption ubiquitous in economics.

Figure 2.7 repeats Figure 1.13 with the addition of two extra budget constraints (see panel (a)) built around two lower prices for good X, namely P_1 and P_2 as opposed to P_0. On the y-axis point Y_0 is MI_0, the individual's money income, divided by $P_y = 1$. Points 1, 2 and 3 are the equilibrium points as the price of good X changes. Given that a demand

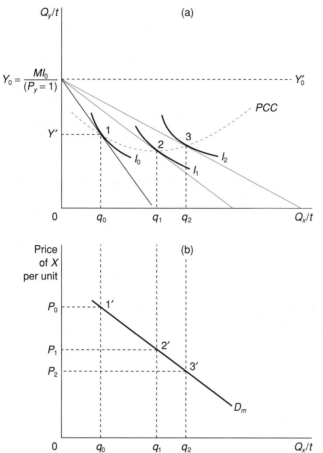

Figure 2.7
Deriving an individual's demand curve

curve plots the relationship between 'own price' and the quantity of X chosen per period, these three points can be translated to points on a demand curve for an individual for good X (see panel (b)). That is, points 1', 2' and 3' indicate the utility-maximising quantities of good X per period at prices P_0, P_1 and P_2. The demand curve here shows the quantities of good X that this individual is both willing and able to buy at each price level per unit of time other things equal (i.e. *ceteris paribus*).

This represents the most common tool employed in microeconomic analysis but it is often talked about in a casual, hand-waving way (and an experienced listener often questions the full understanding of the curve presented). To avoid falling into this category, a number of key points of appreciation must be kept in mind:

(1) The curve (described as a 'curve' even when it is a straight line) illustrates what the individual is willing and able to do; it is not about desires or needs – it is about what individuals can actually do – it comprises feasible points.

(2) The x-axis has Q_x/t on it because this is a flow context. Purchase and consumption are occurring at a rate, e.g. 10 units per week or per month. There is a supply and demand analysis for stocks measured at a point in time but this is not it (an early treatment of stock demand was provided by Wicksteed 1914).

(3) 'Other things equal' refers to the terms specified to be held constant in the function described above, i.e. I, P_y, T and O. It can also be noted that, although the individual demand function above is specified $Q_x = f(P_x \mid \ldots)$, so that quantity demanded is

the dependent variable, this relationship is plotted in inverse form, so that price is placed on the dependent-variable y-axis and Q_x/t on the independent-variable x-axis. Whilst the mathematical convention would have Q_x/t on the y-axis and P_x on the x-axis this is not generally done – following Marshall (who made such a massive contribution to the development of microeconomics that '. . . if it was good enough for him . . .').

(4) The curve illustrates the relationship between own price per unit (P_x) and Q_x/t. A change in own price generates a movement along a demand curve called an 'expansion' (a move along the curve to the right) or 'contraction' (a move along the curve to the left) of demand.

(5) A change in any of the variables held constant, i.e. those beyond the bar, causes a new demand curve to be created either bodily to the right (an increase in demand) or to the left (a decrease in demand).

(6) There are two sensible ways to interpret diagrams in economics. One is to look along a horizontal from the y-axis; in this case the curve indicates that at a price of P_2, for example, the individual will choose q_2 units per period. The second one is to look along a vertical from the x-axis; in this case the curve indicates that, at a quantity of q_2 units per period, the individual is prepared to pay a price of P_2 for that q_2th unit. Note the individual illustrated will pay more than P_2 for all the units before the q_2th one. (This point is developed below.)

(7) The concept involved here is a timeless one, in that all points on the curve are simultaneously available. It is not the case that P_1 is last month's price, P_2 the month before that and P_0 the month before the month before that. The demand curve is not a historical record of price–quantity-per-period events, rather it is an analytical device. The particular Q_x/t observed this period depends on what the current price turns out to be.

Whilst the points noted above may, at first sight, seem trivial and obvious, many students of the subject fail to fully appreciate them and their impact on the understanding of demand analysis. The picture developed above is for an isolated individual and needs to be summed with all other individuals who demand good X if a market demand curve is to be created. This summation has to be done in a specific way. Figure 2.8 illustrates the process. Panels (a) and (b) are the demand curves for two individuals; if the market only consists of these two individuals then the market demand curve is the horizontal sum of the two curves. That is, each possible price is taken and the quantities demanded per period by each individual at that price are summed. Given the two-person case, down to a price of P_0 the market demand curve is simply A's demand curve, after that B's demand is also relevant and the market curve has a kink at that point and becomes less steep below it. If price P_1 obtains, market demand will be q_M units per period, of which

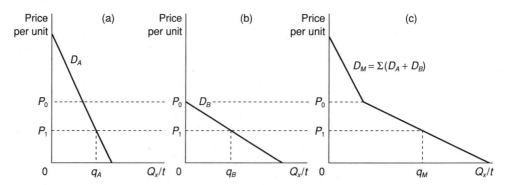

Figure 2.8 Horizontal summation and the market demand curve

q_A are purchased by individual A and q_B are purchased by individual B, and by construction q_A plus q_B will equal q_M.

When individuals C, D, E, etc. are added the lumpiness of the construct will tend to disappear, so that market demand curves are typically illustrated as straight lines sloping down to the right (the straight line assumption makes mathematical derivations and illustrations much easier).

More formally, the process indicates that if the '*ceteris paribus*' variables are unchanged the aggregate or market demand Q_{xM} for good X for a given price $\bar{P}_x$ is the sum of the quantities demanded by n individual consumers:

$$Q_{xM} = \sum_{i=1}^{n} Q_{xi} (\bar{P}_x) \quad \text{over all } \bar{P}_x \tag{2.3}$$

The underlying logic of horizontal summation is that good X is a private good, so that it is rival in consumption. That is, one person's consumption of a unit of good X stands in a rival relationship to another person's consumption of that same unit, so that each consumer must have their own units of good X if they are to enjoy the consumption benefits. Where a good is non-rival in consumption, vertical summation is appropriate (see Chapter 11). Note horizontal and vertical summation (taking each Q_x/t and summing the prices individuals are willing to pay) do not generate the same total/market construction. (It is not a case of being fussy over words.)

Two further issues centre on the interpretation of Figure 2.7(a). Joining up points of equilibrium like 1, 2 and 3 produces the price consumption curve (PCC) showing the path of consumption as the price of good X changes. Furthermore, in the construction Y_0 was described as MI_0, the individual's money income, divided by $P_y = 1$ which treats Y as the good – money – with a price of one, so that the y-axis can be interpreted as income. Distance 0-Y' is the amount of income reserved for other use and Y_0-Y' is the expenditure on good X when 0-q_0 quantity is purchased per period. Using the horizontal straight line emanating from point Y_0, that is Y_0-Y_0', it can be seen that the vertical distance between point 2 and Y_0-Y_0' is greater with P_1 than with P_0. That is, expenditure on good X has increased as price and quantity per period have risen. At point 3, price was lowered to P_2, but note the vertical distance between point 3 and Y_0-Y_0' has fallen, indicating expenditure on good X has fallen even though the quantity has risen from q_1 to q_2 per period. This observation connects to the concept of *own-price elasticity* (introduced in Chapter 1 and developed below).

Before moving on, it is important to establish that it is legitimate to view the y-axis as income. Fortunately, Hicks (1946) established this legitimacy with his 'composite commodity theorem'. The importance of the theorem is that it is possible to work in two dimensions, not only without loss of generality, but with increased understanding. The underlying reason Hicks developed can be grasped intuitively. Suppose there was a four-good budget constraint for goods R, S, T and X. It would take the form:

$$I = P_r \cdot R + P_s \cdot S + P_t \cdot T + P_x \cdot X \tag{2.4}$$

where R, S, T and X are the quantities of each good, P_r, P_s, P_t and P_x are their prices and I is income per period. This is unwieldy to deal with and the task is to reduce R, S and T to a composite commodity Y. The theorem says the quantity of the composite commodity is found by forming the total expenditure on R, S and T, dividing by the price of any one of them. The price chosen as the divisor is also the price of the composite commodity. If P_r is the chosen price then:

$$Y = (P_r/P_r) \cdot R + (P_s/P_r) \cdot S + (P_t/P_r) \cdot T \tag{2.5}$$

$$Y = R + (P_s/P_r) \cdot S + (P_t/P_r) \cdot T \tag{2.5a}$$

and the composite commodity price is P_r.

If $I = £420$ then the budget constraint might be exhausted as follows:

$$420 = 3 \cdot 20 + 6 \cdot 10 + 9 \cdot 30 + 2 \cdot 15$$

where R, S, T and X are the quantities of each good, 20, 10, 30 and 15 units respectively, P_r, P_s, P_t and P_x are their prices 3, 6, 9 and 2 respectively; then the quantity of Y is:

$$Y = 20 + (6/3) \cdot 10 + (9/3) \cdot 30 = 20 + 20 + 90 = 130 \text{ units} \quad \text{and its price} = £3.$$

Placing this information into a budget constraint yields:

$$I = 3 \cdot 130 + 2 \cdot 15 = 420.$$

To clarify, let Y be the good money and a price of 1 chosen as the divisor. In effect, the price of £1 is £1. Then the value of Y will always equal income per period not spent on good X (and when $X = 0$ on the y-axis $Y = I$). Using some less convenient numbers:

$$328 = 1 \cdot 40 + 7 \cdot 13 + 5 \cdot 33 + 2 \cdot 16 = I$$

$$Y = 40 + (7/1) \cdot 13 + (5/1) \cdot 33 = 40 + 91 + 165 = 296 \text{ units and its price} = £1$$

$$I = 1 \cdot 296 + 2 \cdot 16 = 328.$$

On a budget constraint the x-axis intercept occurs when $Y = 0$, so that for budget exhaustion $I = 328 = 2 \cdot X$ and $X = 164$. The y-axis intercept occurs when $X = 0$, so that for budget exhaustion $I = 328 = 1 \cdot Y$ and $Y = 328 = I$ and therefore the value of Y on the y-axis intercept can be treated as the value in £s of income and, when the value of the units of X is positive, the y-axis divides into the amount of income in £s reserved for other uses and the expenditure on units of good X.

To summarise: the general situation in microeconomics is one in which the analysis is concerned with the 'trade-off' between good X and all other commodities. Typically, the only price variations of interest are those for good X (movements in P_x). In these circumstances it is clearly very useful to be able to treat all other goods as a single composite commodity. Hicks established the conditions under which this was an appropriate way forward. His theorem states that, if the relative prices of a group of commodities are fixed, then for the purposes of demand analysis, they can be treated as a single composite commodity with a price given by an appropriate index of the prices of the goods. In our numerical example, the composite good, Y, became money and its price unity. Given these assumptions, the composite commodity on the Y-axis, Q_y/t, has the interpretation of the income endowment (and its allocation to total expenditure on X and the sum retained for other uses). In short, the crucial assumption in the interpretation of Q_y/t as income in money terms is that as the price of X is changed the relative prices of goods R, S and T are unchanged.

Reverting to point 1 in Figure 2.7(a) it is the case that

$$MRS_{xy} \equiv -dY/dX|_{u=u_0} \equiv \partial U/\partial X / \partial U/\partial Y \equiv MU_x/MU_y = P_x/P_y = -dY/dX \quad (2.6)$$

The definitional equivalent sign '$\equiv$' is important for precision of interpretation, as is $dY/dX|_{u=u_0}$. The second and fifth terms $-dY/dX|_{u=u_0} = P_x/P_y$ are equalised by utility maximisation and are, therefore, only true at an equilibrium point like 1 in 2.7(a). These two terms can be usefully rewritten as $P_x = -dY/dX \cdot P_y$. Looking at the right-hand side, $-dY/dX$ is the negative of a negative slope and is, therefore, a positive magnitude (showing how much Y the individual in equilibrium will willingly give up, that is dY, for a small increase in good X (dX) holding utility constant at $U = U_0$, i.e. being on I_0). Multiplying that magnitude by the value of a unit of Y, namely P_y, puts it in monetary terms. Hence, the interpretation of the right-hand side is the money value of Y purchases that the individual will give up in exchange for one more unit of good X. On the left-hand side that is equal to P_x. That is, if P_x is read off a utility constant demand curve it can be interpreted as the marginal willingness to pay for good X by a utility-maximising individual. But observation of Figure 2.7 shows that the demand curve $D_{m(I=I_0)}$ is not a utility constant demand curve, as point 1' comes from I_0, 2' from I_1 and 3' from I_2. Utility is increasing along $D_{m(I=I_0)}$. The demand curve in Figure 2.7(b) is the so-called Marshallian money income constant demand curve as $I = Y_0$ throughout its length. The interpretation just outlined raises the question of what a utility constant demand curve would look like. This question is answered below, when the impact of other demand variables has been introduced.

2.4 Demand and the *'ceteris paribus'* variables

(i)   *Changes in income* When income (now Y because of the composite commodity theorem) increases, individuals will have more money to spend on all goods and services. For *normal* goods, individuals will demand a greater quantity of good X per period (at any given price of good X). This means that in Figure 2.9 the demand curve $D(Y_1)$ – i.e. the demand curve when income is Y_1 – 'increases' to the right as income increases to Y_2. Conversely, it follows that when income falls to Y_0, individuals have less to spend and demand for good X will be lower (at any price of good X), i.e. the demand curve 'decreases' to the left.

In the case of *inferior* goods (not illustrated) the situation is the reverse. When income increases demand decreases (the demand curve shifts to the left) and when income decreases more is consumed (the demand curve shifts to the right). For example, when income falls it may be that individuals might have to supplement their diet with greater quantities of food products such as potatoes. The demand for potatoes would then increase as income falls (see the discussion of inferior goods and Giffen goods).

(ii)   *Changes in the price of other goods* (P_z): When individuals demand a particular good (e.g. good X) a choice usually has been made between good X and other goods (e.g. good Z) which are *substitutes*, for example, the choice of one brand of chocolate bar as compared with another brand of chocolate bar. If the price of good Z were to rise it is likely that (at any price of good X) more of good X would be demanded. Once again, this is consistent with a shift of the demand curve to the right. Conversely,

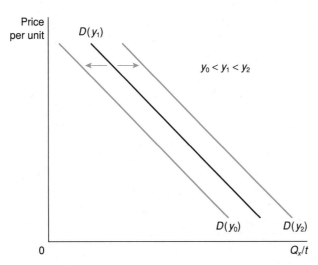

Figure 2.9
Shifts of the demand curve for a normal good

as the price of good Z falls, less is likely to be demanded of good X at any price of good X, i.e. there is a demand decrease in the shape of a shift to the left of the demand curve for good X.

As well as substitute goods, there are also *complements*. For example, when there is a fall in the price of cars there is usually an increase in the demand for petrol. When there is a fall in the price of CD players there is likely to be an increase in the demand for CDs. When good X is a complement for good, say, V, as the price of good V falls so the demand of good X is likely to increase. The demand for good X increases at any price of good X, i.e. the demand for good X increases, involving a shift to the right of the demand curve. As the price of good V increases there will be a decrease in demand of good X at any price of good X; i.e. the demand curve for good X shifts to the left.

(iii) *Change in tastes* (T): Tastes and preferences will have an important effect on demand and this is well understood by those involved in marketing and advertising. For example, if it became the height of fashion to be identified as a consumer of good X then (at any given price of good X) more will be demanded; the demand curve for good X shifts to the right. Conversely, if good X became unfashionable less will be demanded of good X (at any price of good X) and the demand curve shifts to the left.

These variables are not the only ones that will shift the demand curve for good X. For example, when considering the *market* demand curve, demographic changes may be important (e.g. an increase in population may shift the demand curve to the right – more individuals over which to conduct the horizontal sum). Also, for specific goods, specific variables may be of importance (e.g. demand for ice cream is likely to be affected by the weather). As noted above, the analytical approach throughout is to focus on the dependent variable (quantity demanded of good X per period) and one other variable (e.g. the price of good X per unit), holding constant all other variables (*ceteris paribus*). When the relationship between the dependent variable, demand, and the chosen explanatory variable is established it is then possible to consider how this relationship is affected by changes in other explanatory variables.

2.5 Demand elasticities

The elasticity concept, noted in Chapter 1, now comes to the fore. Own-price elasticity of demand measures the responsiveness of the quantity demanded of a good (Q_x/t) to a change in its price (P_x). It is defined as the percentage change in quantity of a good demanded divided by the percentage change in price. In this way (and using relationships developed in Chapter 1) the own-price elasticity of demand can be written as:

$$\varepsilon_{(P_x)} = \frac{\% \, \Delta Q_x}{\% \, \Delta P_x} = \frac{\Delta Q_x / Q_x}{\Delta P_x / P_x} = \frac{\Delta Q_x \cdot P_x}{\Delta P_x \cdot Q_x} = \frac{1}{\text{Marginal value}} \times \text{Average value}$$

and it can also be written as:

$$\frac{1}{\text{Slope of the demand curve}} \times \text{Ray (tan of angle formed to a point on the curve)}$$

or as:

$$\varepsilon_{(P_x)} = \frac{\text{percentage change in quantity demanded}}{\text{percentage change in price}} = \frac{\Delta Q_x / Q_x}{\Delta P_x / P_x} \qquad (2.6)$$

(where ε indicates an elasticity value and P_x indicates it is with respect to own price.)

If, for example, there was a 3 per cent reduction in quantity demanded of good X per period as a consequence of a 1 per cent increase in price, the price elasticity of demand is –3. While price elasticity of demand will typically be negative (because an increase in price contracts demand), it is the case that demand elasticity is high when the absolute value of price elasticity is high and conversely that price elasticity is low when the absolute value is low. This means that if demand has an elasticity of –3 demand is more elastic than if elasticity were –2. Demand is said to be 'elastic' if price elasticity of demand is more negative than –1 and 'inelastic' price elasticity of demand lies between –1 and 0. A price elasticity of –1 is often referred to as 'unit' elastic demand. As it is 'known' that own price demand elasticity can generally be predicted to be negative, the absolute value is often discussed leaving the negative sign implicit. Here, however, the negative signs are retained but the 'x' is suppressed for simplicity.

As noted in Chapter 1, an elasticity is a 'unit-free' estimate because it is formulated as a percentage. For example, if price is increased by twenty per cent this is a similar increase whether price is measured in terms of pounds, dollars or rupees. In Figure 2.10(a),

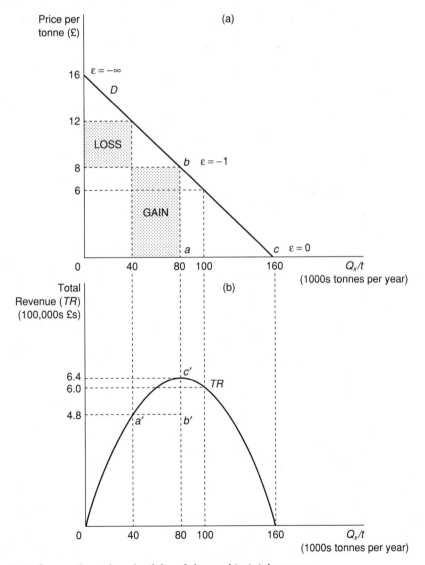

Figure 2.10 Connecting price elasticity of demand to total revenue

D depicts the relationship between quantity demanded per period (thousands of tonnes per year and price of the good price per tonne). In the example illustrated, although the slope of D is constant, price elasticity is not everywhere the same on this demand curve. Price elasticity of demand (ε) is the proportionate change in quantity demanded (dQ/Q) for a proportionate change in price (dP/P) (proportions being used as alternatives to percentages). As price elasticity of demand equals (dQ/Q) / (dP/P) and, as described in Chapter 1, this can be expressed as (dQ/dP) · (P/Q), it becomes clear that the estimate of elasticity depends not only on the slope of the line (a marginal value) but also on the price to quantity ratio (an average value) at which the estimate is taken.

Point elasticity of demand (elasticity at any point on the demand curve) therefore, changes throughout D. For example, at the x-axis intercept, point c price equals 0, so that price elasticity of demand is zero, while, when quantity equals 0 price elasticity of demand equals minus infinity.

Point elasticity of demand falls (in absolute terms) along a linear demand curve. At lower prices, it becomes inelastic. It can be shown that price elasticity of demand at the midpoint of D will equal -1. The slope of D indicates that, when price falls by £1, an extra 10,000 units are demanded. However, the slope of the line does not measure the elasticity of demand.

For different commodities the slope may vary according to the scale in which units are measured (e.g. prices in terms of pounds or dollars; quantity demanded in terms of tonnes, yards, gallons or quarts). However, price elasticity is the percentage change in quantity demanded for a percentage change in price and is a real (or dimensionless) number.

At a price of £8 (i.e. a price = distance a-b) quantity demanded (80,000 units) is 0-a. The slope of the line dP/dQ is a-b/b-c and this is the reciprocal of dQ/dP. It follows that dQ/dP. P/Q can be written as (a-c)/(a-b) · (a-b)/(0-a). Therefore, price elasticity equals a-c/ 0-a. At prices above a-b demand is price elastic (a-c > 0-a) and below it is price inelastic (a-c < 0-a).

The fact that price elasticity of demand changes at different points along a linear demand curve means that there is a distinction between *point elasticity* (elasticity at a given point on the demand curve) and what is called *arc elasticity* (elasticity measured over a small range of the curve). In Figure 2.10 if price fell from £12 to £8 it may appear appropriate to write dP/P as $-4/12$ and as quantity demanded expands from 40 thousand units to 80 thousand units dQ/Q can be written as 40/40. In this case, arc elasticity of demand would be reported as (1 divided by $-1/3$) = -3. However, for a price change measured by a move in the opposite direction dP/P could be written as 4/8 and dQ/Q as $-40/80$, so that arc elasticity appears equal to -1. The difference relates to the fact that point elasticity has changed at each point over this range of the demand curve.

One convention to deal with this difficulty – and to provide an estimate that does not depend on the direction of movement along the demand curve – is to measure arc elasticity with reference to average elasticity and average quantity. Price elasticity of demand is then said to be:

$$\frac{dQ}{^{1}/_{2}\,(Q_{1} + Q_{2})} \text{ divided by } \frac{dP}{^{1}/_{2}\,(P_{1} - P_{2})}$$

which in this case is equal to -1.67.

2.5.1 What factors determine own price elasticity of demand?

Own-price elasticity of demand depends on:

(i) *Substitutes*: If the product concerned has close substitutes it is probable that an increase in price will reduce demand substantially. When price rises, consumers have the option of easily switching expenditure to a substitute commodity. As a consequence, the narrower the definitions of any commodity (e.g. a particular brand of chocolate, rather than chocolate in general) the larger will be the elasticity of demand. The narrowness with which a good is defined will influence the number of substitutes that it has.

(ii) *Luxury or necessity:* The more that the good is a luxury good, rather than a necessity, the greater the elasticity is likely to be. Therefore, for example, estimates by Deaton (1975) show that demand for dairy produce has a low price elasticity (–0.03) as does demand for bread and cereals (–0.22). By comparison, different forms of leisure pursuits have a higher price elasticity of demand: entertainment (–1.14), expenditure abroad (–1.6) and catering (–61).

(iii) *Fraction of expenditure:* If the good is one on which individuals spend a large fraction of their budget, price elasticity of demand is likely to be greater. The demand for soap, or matches, for example, may be price-inelastic because as price changes households will not significantly adjust their demand (since they spend relatively little on the good).

(iv) *The number of uses to which a commodity may be put.* If a good can be put to quite a number of uses it is thought likely to be more elastic in demand. For example, wool can be used in producing upholstery, clothing and tapestries; a small change in price may result, therefore, in a proportionately large change in quantity demanded.

(v) *Time* will also be important; the longer the period of time under consideration the greater is the possibility that consumers may find substitutes. Short-run price elasticity is an estimate of the response over the period immediately following a price change (e.g. one year). In the long run, when individuals have had time to adjust (e.g. over five years) price elasticity of demand will be greater.

Oil, for example, may be very price-inelastic in demand over a short period of time. Over the longer term, however, households may more easily respond to changes in price. They may convert household heating arrangements (e.g. by changing to coal or electricity). They may take fewer trips in cars or they may change to more fuel-efficient cars. Thompson (1985) cites estimates of the price elasticity of demand for gasoline in the USA. In the immediate short run the quantity of gasoline could be expected to decline 1% for each 10% increase in retail prices (i.e. a price elasticity equal to –0.10). Estimates for periods of 2 to 3 years cluster in the neighbourhood of –0.25. Over 5 years the estimate is 0.49 and for 10 years it is –0.82.

2.5.2 Price elasticity and a firm's revenue

There is a link between price elasticity of demand and the responsiveness of revenue to changes in the price of the product sold. In Figure 2.10(a) the addition to revenue that a firm might expect, as a result of a price change, is dependent on the price elasticity of demand for its product. At a price of £12 the business may expect to sell 40,000 units per period with the implication that total revenue would be £480,000. If price were to fall to £8 the demand would expand to 80,000, so that total revenue would increase to £640,000. Inspection of Figure 2.10(a) shows that, if price were to fall to £6 per unit, sales would increase but now revenue would fall to £600,000. When the absolute value of the price elasticity of demand is greater than 1 it is clear that a fall in price will increase total revenue.

Marginal revenue (i.e. the addition to total revenue as the quantity sold per period increases) is positive when price elasticity of demand takes an absolute value greater than 1. Therefore, in Figure 2.10(b) an increase in quantity of a'-b' is associated with a positive increase in revenue of b'-c' (this increase in revenue being the difference between the hatched rectangles in Figure 2.10(a) marked 'gain' and 'loss'). At a price of £8 it will be apparent that successive price reductions now serve to reduce total revenue. When price elasticity of demand exceeds one (in absolute terms), marginal revenue from a price fall is positive. When price elasticity is less than one (in absolute terms), marginal revenue from a price fall is negative.

It is possible to define total revenue (TR) as $P(Q) \cdot Q$, so that positive marginal revenue (MR) can be defined as the first derivative of total revenue with respect to quantity per period:

$$MR = \frac{dTR}{dQ} = P + Q\frac{dP}{dQ} > 0 \tag{2.7}$$

and rearranging,

$$MR = \frac{dTR}{dQ} = P\left(1 + \frac{Q\ dP}{P\ dQ}\right) > 0 \tag{2.7a}$$

As the final term in the brackets is the inverse of the own-price elasticity:

$$1/[\varepsilon_{(P_x)}] = \frac{Q\ dP}{P\ dQ}$$

when marginal revenue is positive:

$$\varepsilon_{(P_x)} < -1 \tag{2.7b}$$

(or greater than one if absolute values are being discussed).

If $\varepsilon_{(P_x)} = -1$, substituting this into Equation (2.7a) reveals that $MR = 0$.

2.5.3 Applications of price elasticity of demand

But to what use can these elasticity values be put? Economics texts are full of lessons that can be drawn from elasticity values. Three examples are provided below.

(i) *The lesson of misplaced concern*

When farmers experience bad harvests there is frequently concern for the farming community. However, it is often at the very time that harvests are poor (e.g. when there is drought and bad weather) that farm incomes are at their highest. The paradox is that when output is down (e.g. because of droughts), and the media report the 'desperate' state of farmers, farm incomes are typically better than usual.

How can this paradox be explained? In Figure 2.11 the demand curve D is shown for an agricultural good X. If, at the time of harvest, supply of the good is abundant, supply for the agricultural good is shown by $0\text{-}q_2$ and this supply price is $0\text{-}P_1$. However, if there was a drought and the harvest was poor, supply might fall to $0\text{-}q_1$. While farmers may be disgruntled at the impact of weather on agricultural output, the lower output means that the price of the good would rise to $0\text{-}P_2$. The price elasticity of demand will be important when assessing how this will affect the income of farmers. In Figure 2.11 these changes occur on the price-inelastic range of the demand curve D. It follows that when price increases, farmers' revenue increases. In Figure 2.11 revenue has risen from $0\text{-}P_1\text{-}1\text{-}q_2$ to $0\text{-}P_2\text{-}2\text{-}q_1$. As area $P_1\text{-}P_2\text{-}2\text{-}3$ is greater than area $q_1\text{-}3\text{-}1\text{-}q_2$, revenue for farmers has increased. It is because demand for agricultural produce is price inelastic that, when there are shortages, farm income increases and, when harvests are plentiful, farm income is lower (see Nicholson 1997).

The analysis of price elasticity explains a relationship that on first sight might appear counter-intuitive. Concern for the farming community is likely to increase in response to evidence that harvests have suffered because of bad weather. However, if farm prices rise so can income, so predicting what happens relies on awareness, here, of price-inelastic demand. (It seems – *no* clouds means a silver lining!)

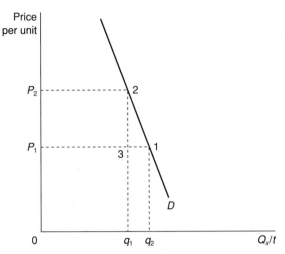

Figure 2.11
Farm income: a paradox?

(ii) *The lesson of not giving up too soon*

Varian (1999) reports research by Carter *et al.* (1987) that focused on case study analysis of the effectiveness of trade unions. The case is the action in 1979 of the United Farm Workers against lettuce growers in California. The strike appeared effective; it was supported by workers and reduced production by almost one-half.

Once again, outcome cannot be assessed without taking price elasticity of demand into consideration. In terms of impact on production the strike seemed effective but in terms of impact on employers it was disappointing. The reduction in output meant that there was an increase in the price of lettuce (price rose by nearly 400 per cent). The result was that there was an almost doubling of profits!

The distinction between the short run and long run was important. At that time, most of the lettuce consumed in the US during winter months was grown at this location. When supply was so drastically reduced in one season, there was no time to replace it with lettuce grown elsewhere. If the trade union strike had persisted for several seasons other supply sources would have been found. This would reduce the price of lettuce back towards the norm. Ironically, the strike may then have had greater effect!

(iii) *The lesson of increasing export revenues*

Begg *et al.* (2003) refer to an account in the *Economist* magazine (30 July 1994). This reported that the 1995 Brazilian coffee harvest would not be the expected 26.5 million bags but, because of a frost in 1994, might be as little as 15.7 million bags. As a result coffee prices more than doubled in real terms. Speculators realised that, with price inelasticity, a shortage would drive up price significantly. A comparison of 1993 and 1995 revealed that Brazilian export revenue from coffee increased despite the bad harvest. (In Chapter 17 more will be said of price elasticity when considering whether or not countries should set import or export taxes to increase their welfare.)

2.5.4 Income elasticity of demand and cross-price elasticity of demand

Elasticity simply refers to the responsiveness of one variable with respect to changes in another. Returning to the demand function described in Equation (2.1), it can be seen that the other factors listed will have an effect on quantity demanded per period. Perhaps one of the most general of these other factors is income. Income elasticity of demand can be defined as:

$$\varepsilon(I) = \frac{\% \, \Delta Q_x}{\% \, \Delta I} = \frac{\Delta Q_x / Q_x}{\Delta I / I} = \frac{\Delta Q_x \cdot I}{\Delta I \cdot Q_x} = \frac{1}{\text{Marginal value}} \times \text{Average value}$$

It can be written as:

$$\frac{1}{\text{Slope of the Engel curve}} \times \text{Ray (tan of angle formed to a point on the curve)}$$

or as:

$$\varepsilon(I) = \frac{\text{percentage change in quantity demanded}}{\text{percentage change in income}} = \frac{\Delta Q / Q}{\Delta I / I} \qquad (2.8)$$

(where ε indicates an elasticity value and I indicates it is with respect to income).

Figure 2.12 illustrates how Engel curves (labelled EC) are generated from consumer equilibrium diagrams. Parallel shifts in the budget (in panels (a), (b) and (c)) indicate the effects of increases in income. Points of equilibrium are found at tangencies with successively higher indifference curves (I_0, I_1, I_2) at points 1, 2 and 3. Joining tangency points

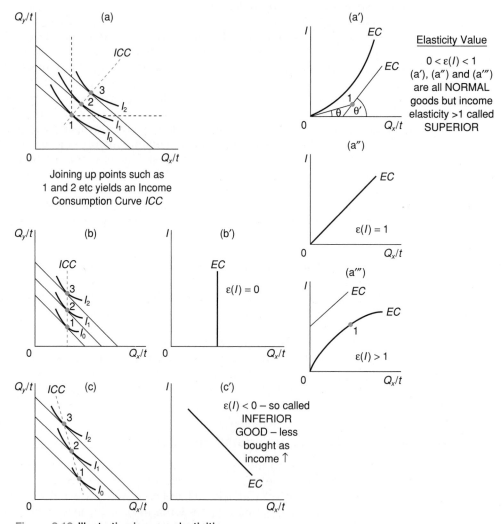

Figure 2.12 **Illustrating income elasticities**

gives the income consumption curve (labelled *ICC*). Plotting the value of income (*I*) on the *y*-axis in Figure 2.12 panels (a′), (a″), (a‴), (b′) and (c′) against equilibrium quantities of *X* per period gives Engel curves showing the relationship between income and chosen equilibrium quantities of *X* per period consistent with the elasticity description above. The income elasticity values associated with each Engel curve 'shape' are indicated in Figure 2.12.

Some examples will help illustrate the concept and its meaning. If income elasticity of beer is 0.88, then when income goes up by 1%, the quantity consumed increases by 0.88% (see Figure 2.12 panel (a′)). Use of the ray–tangent observation rule can be seen in action by considering point 1 in Figure 2.12 (a′). The angle formed by the ray is θ and gives the average value as $\tan \theta$. The angle formed by the tangent to point 1 is θ' and gives the marginal value as $\tan \theta'$. Visually $\theta' > \theta$ and therefore $\tan\theta/\tan\theta' < 1$. If income elasticity is 1.38 then when income increases by 1% the quantity of wine consumed increases by 1.38% (see Figure 2.12 panel (a‴) and confirm your understanding of the ray–tangent observation rule with respect to point 1). It follows that if income were to fall, then consumption of wine would fall accordingly.

If a good has a positive income elasticity the good is referred to as a *normal* good. Most goods are normal goods (see Figure 2.12 panels (a′), (a″) and (a‴)). A good is a normal good if income elasticity is greater than, or equal to, zero: $\varepsilon(I) \geq 0$. For example, Bordley and McDonald (1993) estimated that the income elasticity of demand for motor cars was 1.6.

Some goods have negative income elasticities ($\varepsilon(I) < 0$) (see Figure 2.12 panel (c′)) and these are referred to as *inferior* goods. Examples of inferior goods are food products such as potatoes – foods that the poor consume as a large portion of their diet. However, some goods which might be regarded, by some, as inferior may be regarded by others as superior. Willis (1973) estimated the income elasticity for the number of children in a family. He found that children are an inferior good (income elasticity = –0.18) when the family has average income and the wife has little education. By contrast, children proved to be a normal good for families in which the wife is well educated. The case of zero income elasticity is illustrated in Figure 2.12 panels (b) and (b′) as rising income has no effect on the equilibrium quantity of *X* chosen.

In just the same way as price elasticity may differ with price, so income elasticity for demand may vary with income. For example, potatoes may be a normal good at very low income levels (as income increases more potatoes may be consumed). However, as income increases potatoes may become an inferior good (as income increases individuals may introduce other items such as buns and cakes into their diet and the demand for potatoes may decrease).

Cross-price elasticity records the percentage change in quantity demanded of one good (e.g. good *X*) as a result of a percentage change in the price of another good (e.g. *Y*)

$$\varepsilon(P_y) = \frac{\% \,\Delta Q_x}{\% \,\Delta P_y} = \frac{\Delta Q_x/Q_x}{\Delta P_y/P_y} = \frac{\Delta Q_x \cdot P_y}{\Delta P_y \cdot Q_x} = \frac{1}{\text{Marginal value}} \times \text{Average value}$$

It can be written as:

$$\frac{1}{\text{Slope of the cross-price demand curve}} \times \frac{\text{Ray (tan of angle formed to a point on}}{\text{the curve)}}$$

or as:

$$\varepsilon(P_y) = \frac{\text{percentage change in quantity demanded of good } X}{\text{percentage change in price of good } Y} = \frac{\Delta Q_X/Q_X}{\Delta P_y/P_y} \qquad (2.9)$$

(where ε indicates an elasticity value and P_y indicates it is with respect to the price of another good).

Figure 2.13 illustrates how cross-price demand curves (labelled $D(P_y)$) are generated from consumer equilibrium diagrams. Upward swivelling of the budget constraints, with the x-axis intercept fixed in panels (a), (b) and (c), indicate the effects of decreases in the price of good Y. Points of equilibrium are found at tangencies with successively higher indifference curves (I_0, I_1, I_2) at points 1, 2 and 3. Joining tangency points gives the cross-price consumption curve (labelled $CPCC$). Plotting the value of P_y on the y-axis in Figure 2.13 panels (a'), (b') and (c') against equilibrium quantities of X per period gives cross-price demand curves – showing the relationship between the price of good Y and chosen equilibrium quantities of X per period, consistent with the elasticity description above. The cross-price elasticity values associated with each cross-price demand curve 'shape' are indicated in Figure 2.13.

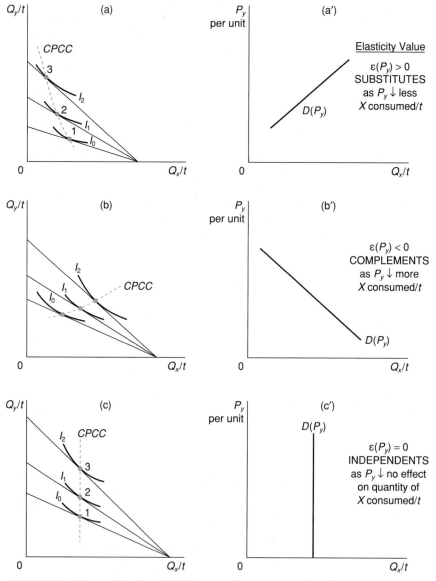

Figure 2.13 Illustrating cross-price elasticities

When goods are substitutes the cross-price elasticity of demand will be positive (when the price of one good decreases the quantity demanded per period of the substitute good also decreases). When goods are complements the cross-price elasticity of demand will be negative (when the price of one good decreases the quantity demanded per period of a complement will increase).

In principle, taste or preference elasticity could be developed but given the great difficulty of quantifying tastes this is an absentee from the list of demand elasticities. Having considered some applications of the demand elasticity concepts it is now time to return to the role of the demand curve in welfare analysis.

2.6 Consumer surplus: compensating and equivalent variations

Holding utility constant is one way of defining real income constant. After all, what can be more fundamental than holding your subjective level of utility constant? In the next sections it is this interpretation of real income constant that is central. It is denoted by the achievement of a given level of utility, $U = U_0$, associated with indifference curve I_0.

2.6.1 Income and substitution effects

The economic change modelled in Figures 2.14(i) to 2.14(iii) is a fall in price of good X from P_0 to P_1. In terms of Figure 2.14(i) with P_0 in operation point 1 on I_0 is the initial

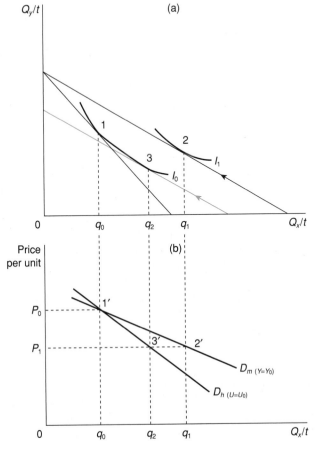

Figure 2.14(i)
Normal good case

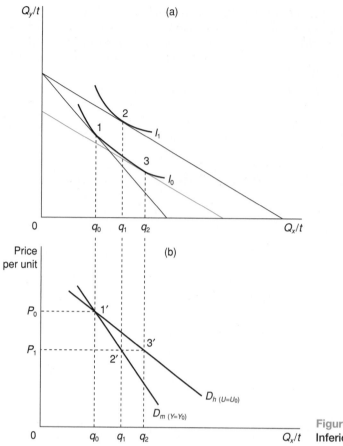

Figure 2.14(ii)   Inferior good case

equilibrium with q_0 the chosen (utility-maximising) quantity of X per period. Allowing the price of good X to fall to P_1 in Figure 2.14(i)(a) causes point 2 to be the new utility-maximising equilibrium (with q_1 the new quantity).

As discussed above, there is a difference between a real-income constant situation and the Marshallian demand curve. It is now possible to be more precise about what it is. In Figure 2.14(i)(b) points 1′ and 2′ corresponding to points 1 and 2 in panel (a) are points on the Marshallian money income-constant demand curve, labelled $D_{m(Y=Y0)}$ − Y for income – in panel (b). The price effect has moved quantity from q_0 to q_1. To isolate the real-income-constant demand curve, a compensating variation in income is required. The exercise is one of reducing income at the new price ratio until the initial utility level $U = U_0$ is once again secured on I_0. Move the new budget constraint to the left in a parallel fashion until it is tangential to I_0 (here at point 3 with q_2). Point 3 in panel (a) dictates point 3′ in panel (b) so that 1′ and 3′ are points on the, so-called, Hicksian (see Hicks 1946) real income constant demand curve labelled $D_{h(U=U0)}$.

In Figure 2.14(i) the income effect is positive, having moved quantity chosen from q_2 to q_1. In this case good X is said to be normal as individuals buy more of it as income rises. The substitution effect from q_0 to q_2 may appear positive (reflecting a response to a change in relative prices real income constant – $U = U_0$), but this is a positive response to a fall in price (i.e. the full effect is negative). For a price fall the Marshallian demand curve for a normal good tracks to the right from point 1′ (i.e. outside the Hicksian one).

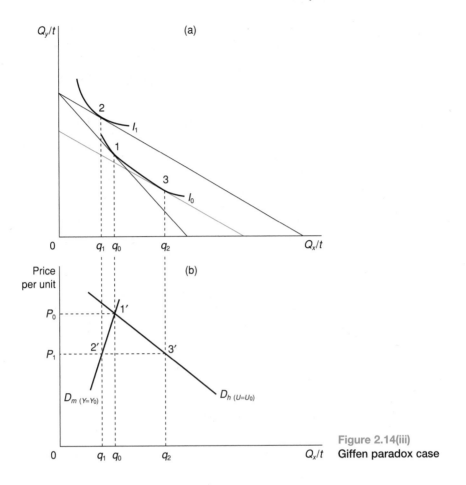

Figure 2.14(iii)
Giffen paradox case

In terms of Figure 2.14(ii) – with P_0 in operation – point 1 on I_0 is the initial equilib-rium with q_0 the chosen quantity of X. Allowing the price of good X to fall to P_1 in Figure 2.14(ii) panel (a) means that point 2 is the new utility-maximising equilibrium (with q_1 the new quantity). In Figure 2.14(ii)(b) points 1′ and 2′ corresponding to points 1 and 2 in panel (a) are points on the Marshallian money-income-constant demand curve, labelled $D_{m(Y=Y0)}$ in panel (b). The price effect has moved quantity from q_0 to q_1. To isolate the real-income-constant demand curve a compensating variation in income is again required. Moving the new budget constraint to the left in a parallel fashion until it is tangential to I_0 (here at point 3 with q_2 the associated quantity) again serves to separate the substitution and income effects. Point 3 in panel (a) dictates point 3′ in panel (b) so that 1′ and 3′ are points on the Hicksian real income-constant demand curve $D_{h(U=U0)}$. In Figure 2.14(ii) the income effect is negative, having moved quantity chosen from q_2 to q_1. In this case, good X is said to be inferior as individuals buy less of it as income rises. The substitution effect from q_0 to q_2 is positive, reflecting a response to a change in relative prices, real income constant ($U = U_0$). For a price fall the Marshallian demand curve for an inferior good tracks to the right from point 1′ (i.e. inside the Hicksian one).

In terms of Figure 2.14(iii) – with P_0 in operation – point 1 on I_0 is the initial equilib-rium with q_0 the chosen quantity of X. Allowing the price of good X to fall to P_1 in Figure 2.14(iii) panel (a) causes point 2 to be the new utility-maximising equilibrium with q_1 the new quantity. In Figure 2.14(iii)(b) points 1' and 2' corresponding to points 1 and 2 in panel (a) are points on the Marshallian, money-income-constant demand curve labelled $D_{m(Y=Y0)}$ in panel (b). The price effect has moved quantity from q_0 to q_1 and is negative, i.e. a price fall has caused the quantity chosen to fall! A positively sloping Marshallian demand curve is possible in the circumstance that the negative income effect outweighs the positive substitution effect of a price fall. To isolate the real-income-constant demand curve, a compensating variation in income is again required. Moving the new budget constraint to the left in a parallel fashion until it is tangential to I_0 (here at point 3 with q_2 the associated quantity) again serves to separate the substitution and income effects. Point 3 in panel (a) dictates point 3' in panel (b), so that 1' and 3' are points on the Hicksian real-income-constant demand curve $D_{h(U=U_0)}$. In Figure 2.14(iii) the income effect is negative and so strong (having moved quantity chosen from q_2 to q_1) quantity has fallen from the original level, q_0.

In this case, good X is said to conform to the *Giffen paradox* as individuals buy less of it as price falls (and real income rises). The Giffen paradox is associated with the English statistician and economist who observed that potato consumption actually rose in 19th-century Ireland as the price of potatoes rose. Switching to the construction here, a fall in the price of potatoes (carbohydrate is an inferior food source) produces a negative income effect on quantity. This is so large that it outweighs the positive substitution effect of the lower price (individuals are said to be switching to meat as protein is a superior food source). The substitution effect from q_0 to q_2 is positive reflecting a response to a change in relative prices, real income constant ($U = U_0$). For a price fall the Marshallian demand curve tracks to the left from point 1' (i.e. inside the Hicksian one).

Marshall introduced the concept of *consumer surplus* as the difference between willingness to pay and actual payment as a measure of the welfare gain of consuming a good. An easy way to see this is to use the quasi-linear utility function where $U = U(X) + Y$ and the first- and second-order derivatives are respectively $u' > 0$ and $u'' < 0$. That is, the marginal utility of X is positive but falls as successive units of X are consumed. If $U = X^{1/2} + Y$ then $dU/dX = \frac{1}{2}X^{-1/2}$ and $d^2U/dX^2 = -\frac{1}{4}X^{-3/2}$ and utility is linear in terms of Y (= income).

This specification makes indifference curves vertically displaced parallel versions of each other, so that parallel movements in the income constraint (a pure income effect) leaves the quantity of X chosen per period unchanged. (The vertical income consumption curve (*ICC*) indicating zero income elasticity as in Figure 2.12(b).) In short, the quasi-linear indifference map generates no income effect on X.

Figure 2.15 illustrates the case. Y_0 is the composite commodity (sometimes described as 'Hicks–Allen money income'), that is, $Y_0 = I_0 / P_y(= 1)$ and the market price of good X is P_1, making, as noted above, Y_0/P_1 the x-axis intercept. A utility-maximising individual finds equilibrium at point 1 on I_1, choosing q_0 of good X. The question posed is how much would this individual pay rather than consume zero units of good X? I_0 cuts the y-axis = zero units of X at point 2 in panel (a). As drawn, the individual is indifferent between points 2 and 3 (point 2 is Y_0 and no units of X and point 3 is Y_1 and q_0 units of X) and therefore would pay as much as distance 3-4 for q_0 of good X. In the market the individual is paying only distance 1-4 (labelled *EXP* for expenditure) so that distance 1-3 measures consumer surplus (*CS*). In panel (b) a demand curve illustration of this is provided. With P_0 in panel (a) the budget constraint would run from Y_0 to the x-axis intercept at Y_0/P_0. With equilibrium at a corner at point 2, zero X is chosen and the y-axis intercept in panel (b) is set. At P_1, q_0 is chosen. The depicted individual would pay trapezoid 0-P_0-$1'$-q_0 for q_0 of X but actually has an expenditure on X of 0-P_1-$1'$-q_0. Therefore triangle P_1-P_0-$1'$ corresponds to Marshall's (1920) definition of consumer surplus.

Chapter 2 The 'clever' and 'dumb' consumer

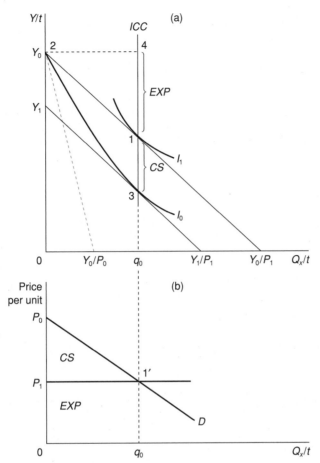

Figure 2.15
The quasi-linear utility function and consumer surplus

More formal treatment

It is evident that consumer surplus is the difference between the maximum the individual would have been willing to pay for units bought per period and the actual
payment made for those units. Putting the demand function in inverse form $P = f(Q)$
and using Figure 2.15(b) makes the relevant price per unit P_1 and quantity per period
q_0. So that, as described above, triangle P_1-P_0-$1'$ corresponds to the definition of consumer surplus. In terms of the definite integral consumer surplus (CS) is:

$$CS = \int_0^{q_0} [f(Q) - P_1] \, dQ = \int_0^{q_0} f(Q) \, dQ - \int_0^{q_0} P_1 \, dQ = \int_0^{q_0} f(Q) \, dQ - P_1 q_0 \qquad (2.10)$$

Whilst this is a more formal way of saying consumer's surplus is the area under the
demand curve up to q_0 (0-P_0-$1'$-q_0) minus expenditure on q_0 of the good (0-P_1-$1'$-q_0),
it must be remembered the analysis began with a special utility function. Netting out
the income effect via the use of a quasi-linear indifference map is, however, restrictive. It suggests there is a unique measure of the consumer surplus change from a
price change (by looking at the relevant area under the demand curve labelled D in
Figure 2.15) but this is not always the case.

2.6.2 Duality and optimisation once more

It is now possible to extend the use of the duality concept used in Chapter 1. Initially the right-hand column of the following outline remains as in Chapter 1 but a left-hand column has been added.

Analysis

The left-hand column recognises that, if U^* is the maximum utility obtainable given $P_xX + P_yY \leq \bar{I}$. That is, $\bar{I}$ is the minimum expenditure (E^*) to achieve U^* given P_x and P_y captured in the indirect utility function $U^* = V(P_x,P_y,I)$. The expenditure function defines the inverse relationship $E^* = E(P_x,P_y,U^*)$. That is, $E(P_x,P_y,U^*) = \bar{I}$ iff $U^* = V(P_x,P_y,\bar{I})$.

PRIMAL (explicitly solve a direct optimisation problem)

Maximise $U(X,Y)$	Minimise $E(X,Y)$
Subject to $P_xX + P_yY \leq I$	Subject to $U^* = U(X,Y)$
(solve with Lagrange)	(solve with Lagrange)
$\downarrow$	$\downarrow$

DUAL (obtain the same results from partial differentiation of the indirect objective function)

Indirect Utility Function $\qquad\qquad\qquad\qquad$ Expenditure Function

$U^* = V(P_x,P_y,\bar{I}) \qquad\qquad \Leftrightarrow \qquad\qquad E^* = E(P_x,P_y,U^*)$

$\qquad\qquad\qquad\qquad\qquad$ INVERSES

$\qquad\downarrow \qquad\qquad\qquad\qquad\qquad\qquad\qquad\qquad\qquad \downarrow$

Roy's Identity $\qquad\qquad\qquad\qquad\qquad\qquad\qquad$ Shephard's Lemma

$\qquad\downarrow \qquad\qquad\qquad\qquad\qquad\qquad\qquad\qquad\qquad \downarrow$

Marshallian Demand $\qquad\qquad\qquad\qquad\qquad$ Compensated Demand

$$X = d_x(P_x,P_y,I) = -\frac{\partial V/\partial P_x}{\partial V/\partial I} \qquad\qquad X = h_x(P_x,P_y,U) = \frac{\partial E}{\partial P_x}$$

(compensated on utility = U^*
i.e. constant real income)

Shephard's Lemma: first-order differentiation of the expenditure function (E) with respect to an output price (P_x) yields the expenditure-minimising demand function (X) for the output corresponding to that output price.

Using the expenditure function should give exactly the same results as the indirect utility function in Chapter 1 refer back to p. 31.

PRIMAL $\qquad\qquad\qquad\qquad\qquad\qquad$ DUAL-EXPENDITURE FUNCTION

Min $E = P_x X + P_y Y$
s.t. $U^* = X^{0.5}Y^{0.5}$ $\qquad\qquad [U^* = 2] \quad E(P_x,P_y,U^*) = E^* = 2U^*P_x^{0.5}P_y^{0.5}$

Lagrangian
$\mathcal{L} = P_x X + P_y Y + \lambda(U^* - X^{0.5}Y^{0.5})$

$\dfrac{\partial \mathcal{L}}{\partial X} = P_x - 0.5X^{-0.5}Y^{0.5} = 0 \qquad$ (1) $\quad$ Use Shephard's Lemma to give compensated demands

$\dfrac{\partial \mathcal{L}}{\partial Y} = P_y - 0.5\, X^{0.5}Y^{-0.5} = 0 \qquad$ (2) $\quad X^* = \dfrac{\partial E}{\partial P_x} = \dfrac{U^* P_y^{0.5}}{P_x^{0.5}} = \dfrac{2\sqrt{1}}{\sqrt{0.25}} = \dfrac{2}{0.5} = 4$

$\dfrac{\partial \mathcal{L}}{\partial \lambda} = (U^* - X^{0.5}Y^{0.5}) = 0 \qquad\qquad Y^* = \dfrac{\partial E}{\partial P_y} = \dfrac{U^* P_x^{0.5}}{P_y^{0.5}} = \dfrac{2\sqrt{0.25}}{\sqrt{1}} = \dfrac{2 \times 0.5}{1} = 1$

Using (1) and (2),

$$\frac{P_y}{P_x} = \frac{0.5X^{0.5}Y^{-0.5}}{0.5X^{-0.5}Y^{0.5}} = \frac{X}{Y}$$

or

$$P_x X = P_y Y$$
$$E = P_x X^* + P_y Y^* = 2P_x X^*$$

So that

$$X^* = \frac{E}{2P_x} \text{ and } Y^* = \frac{E}{2P_y}$$

the utility target requires

$$U^* = (X^*)^{0.5}(Y^*)^{0.5} = (E/2P_x)^{0.5} (E/2P_y)^{0.5}$$

$$U^* = \frac{E}{2Px^{0.5}Py^{0.5}}$$

$$E = 2U^* P_x^{0.5} P_y^{0.5} = 2 \times 2 \times (0.25)^{0.5}(1)^{0.5}$$
$$E = 2$$

Given,

Indirect Utility Function		Expenditure Function
$U^* = V(P_x, P_y, \bar{I})$	$\Leftrightarrow$	$E^* = E(P_x, p_y, U^*)$
	INVERSES	

Expenditure E^* will take the same value as $\bar{I}$

It should be possible to derive the indirect utility function from the expenditure function. Using the example above:

$$E(P_x, P_y, U^*) = E^* = 2U^* P_x^{0.5} P_y^{0.5} \qquad \text{Expenditure Function}$$
Write $\qquad I = 2U^* P_x^{0.5} P_y^{0.5}$
giving $\qquad U^* = I / 2 P_x^{0.5} P_y^{0.5}$
i.e. $V(P_x, P_y, \bar{I}) = I / 2P_x^{0.5} P_y^{0.5} \qquad \text{Indirect Utility Function}$
$E(P_x, P_y, U^*) = \bar{I}$ iff $U^* = V(P_x, P_y, \bar{I})$

The next question posed is why it might be important to differentiate different types of demand curve.

2.6.3 Compensating and equivalent variations

It was revealed above that P_x could be used as a measure of the marginal willingness to pay for good X provided it was read off a real income-constant demand curve. A Marshallian demand curve therefore needs to be replaced by a real income-constant compensated demand curve. This is the Hicksian demand curve derived above. Looking back at Figures 2.14(i) to (iii) it can be seen the Hicksian demand curves are always negatively sloped as they rely on the substitution effect and therefore relative price changes alone. They are central to the analysis of consumer welfare. In this section the economic change under consideration is a fall in the price of good X that is assumed to be normal so that the income effect is positive. The question posed is: 'how might the welfare change resulting from a lower price of X be measured?' In Figure 2.16(a) the price change

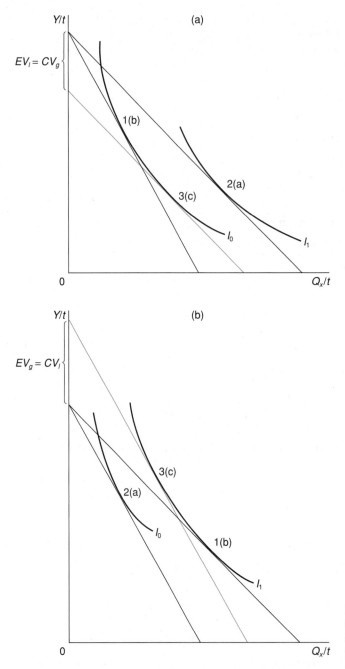

Figure 2.16
Compensating and
equivalent variations for a
price change

increases the individual's utility level from that associated with I_0 to I_1. The movement
from point 1 on I_0 to 2 on I_1 indicates how the individual has responded to the price fall.
A measure of the welfare gain, as felt by the individual, would be the maximum they
would pay rather than forgo the change (a gain). The compensating variation in income
is the exercise that reveals this sum. The CV_g (compensating variation for a gain) involves
taking as much income off the individual as possible, at the new price ratio, but still
allowing them to achieve the utility level I_0. Move the budget constraint backwards in a
parallel fashion so that it is tangential to I_0 at point 3, then the compensation variation
in income equals CV_g on the y-axis in panel (a).

Figure 2.16(b) shows the price of the good X rising. The individual moves from point 1 on I_1 to point 2 on I_0, i.e. a lower utility level. The compensating variation for a loss is defined as the minimum sum the individual is willing to accept to put up with the utility loss. It equals the addition to income at the new price ratio that just allows the individual to secure utility level I_1 once more. In panel (b) this sum is marked as CV_l. This treatment of measuring gains and losses implies a property right (ownership) assignment. The individual has a property right over the position they enjoyed before the good (or bad) economic change (the utility level associated with point 1). This is an *ex-ante* (looking-forward) approach. Measuring consumer surplus gains and losses from a price change, however, can be done in another way.

The literature includes equivalent variations (EV) where the property right is about the individuals after the economic change has occurred. This is an *ex-post* – looking-backwards – approach. It is about making the world with the price change the reference point. Using g for a gain and l for loss:

EV_g = the minimum sum the individual would accept rather than forgo the price fall;

EV_l = the maximum the individual would pay in order to avoid the price rise.

Fortunately the same figures can be used to illustrate that:

$$CV_g = EV_l$$

$$CV_l = EV_g$$

In Figure 2.16(a) for a price rise (a loss), the individual would move from (a) on I_1 to (b) on I_0. Making I_0 the reference point, the maximum payment the individual would make to avoid the new price ratio taking place is the required backward shift in the budget constraint at the old price ratio (allowing the individual to achieve the utility level I_0). This involves the variation in income that moves the individual from point (a) to point (c) on I_0 and, in income terms, is EV_l ($= CV_g$) on the y-axis.

In Figure 2.16(b) for a price fall (a gain), the individual would move from (a) on I_0 to (b) on I_1. Making I_1 the reference point the minimum payment the individual would make to avoid the new price ratio taking place is the required forward shift in the budget constraint at the old price ratio that allows the individual to achieve the utility level I_1. This involves the variation in income that moves the individual from point (a) to point (c) on I_1 and, in income terms, is EV_g ($= CV_l$) on the y-axis. Hence there is a symmetry to the concepts.

As can be gleaned from the illustrations that make up Figure 2.16, there is a direct connection between compensating and equivalent variations and demand curves. However, typically what economists draw is the Marshallian money-income-constant demand curve but, for welfare analysis, it is the real-income-constant demand curves that are relevant. In Figure 2.17 the various concepts are connected for the price fall of a normal good. Allow the price of X to fall from P_0 to P_1 with money income constant; a price fall means that real income is rising, as witnessed by the ability to get on higher levels of utility. That is, moving from point 1 and q_0 in panel (a) on I_0 to point 2 in panel (a) on I_1 with quantity q_1. In Figure 2.17(a) points 1 and 2 correspond to 1′ and 2′ in panel (b) and are two points on the Marshallian money-income-constant demand curve labelled $D_{m(Y=Y_0)}$. The concepts of CV and EV are related to a real-income-constant situation (being built around a given indifference curve). Therefore, the concept requires you to have a real-income-constant demand curve. As CV is built around *ex-ante* utility, I_0 is the relevant curve and 1 with q_0 and 3 with q_2 are the relevant points once real income has been held constant by removing CV_g. Points 1′ and 3′ are on the Hicksian real-income-constant demand curve when utility is held constant at the level associated with I_0, namely U_0, hence the label $D_{h(U=U_0)}$ in panel (b). As EV is built around *ex-post* utility, I_1 is

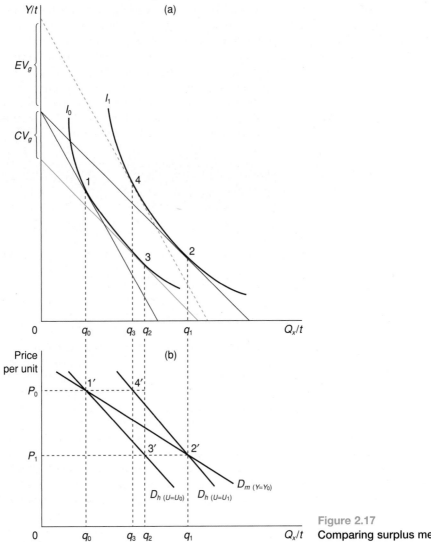

Figure 2.17 Comparing surplus measures

the relevant curve and 2 with q_1 and 4 with q_3 are the relevant points once real income has been held constant by adding EV_g. Points 2′ and 4′ are on the Hicksian real-income-constant demand curve when utility is held constant at the level associated with I_1, namely U_1. Hence the label $D_{h(U=U_1)}$ in panel (b). It must now be possible to tie the measures of welfare gain from a price fall of good X from P_0 to P_1 to areas under the demand curves.

$$P_0\text{-}1'\text{-}2'\text{-}P_1 = \text{Marshallian CS gain (medium)}$$

$$P_0\text{-}1'\text{-}3'\text{-}P_1 = CV_g \text{ (smallest)}$$

$$P_0\text{-}4'\text{-}2'\text{-}P_1 = EV_g \text{ (biggest)}$$

Key then to the use of real-constant-demand curves is that CV and EV are translated to areas under the compensated curves. The vertical distances in panel (a) equal the trapezoids in panel (b). Measures of welfare in neoclassical economics are made with respect to real-income-constant demand curves.

If income effects are small, different demand curves do not appear to matter (what a lot of work for very little!). If income effects are large then any evaluative study will be affected by the measure chosen to represent consumer surplus (or welfare gain) of an economic change. Even when income effects are small it is best not to be dismissive. In Chapter 19 consumer surplus measures are used to value human life so that what appears to be an academic debate over a small difference will translate to life and death consequences for some! Whilst compensated curves are relevant for welfare evaluation, what are the other factors that affect the use of compensated and uncompensated demand curves? (The latter involve only a substitution effect in predicting quantities chosen.) If:

1. real income rises, e.g. if technology or the resource endowment of an economy improves (lower marginal costs), then the uncompensated demand curve is relevant;
2. real income is constant, e.g. if a tax rises and at the same time another tax is reduced or transfers increased or a public-sector project is undertaken then the compensated demand curve is relevant.

Different concepts have their different uses and the skill is in deciding which is appropriate and when.

2.7 Applying the concept of consumer surplus: pricing at EuroDisney

Before applying the above concepts it is useful to summarise the argument so far. Consumer surplus is the difference between the price that the consumer would be willing to pay rather than go without a good (or service) and the price that the consumer does actually pay. It can be estimated by reference to the demand curve. It is the very existence of this surplus that makes market purchases attractive to individuals (but often they are vulnerable to producers who seek to remove some or all of that surplus).

To illustrate an application of this concept (and producer motivation), consider the pricing policy used for entrance to a theme park such as EuroDisney (Oi 1971; Dobson *et al.* 1989). Often, theme parks price by one admission charge which then allows customers access to all attractions (rides) within the theme park. Why?

Assume, initially, that all customers are identical and that the demand curve is linear and shown as D_1 in Figure 2.18(a). The marginal cost of a ride on an attraction at EuroDisney is assumed to be zero. The demand curve shows that, at no charge, 20 rides are demanded per period. By comparison, at a price of £8 there is a demand for zero rides. With reference to D_1, at a price of £4 per ride 10 rides are demanded. If consumers were charged £4 per ride this would yield revenue of £40. Consumer surplus would then be shown as the triangle £4-£8-*a*, which has a value of £20 (= 5 × £4).

However, if there were one admission charge and no charge per ride consumer surplus would be the triangle above the horizontal quantity axis, i.e. triangle 0-£8-20 whose value is £80 (= 10 × £8). If EuroDisney were to charge an entrance fee and allow rides at no charge, the most that a consumer would pay on entrance to the theme park would be the sum represented by this larger triangle, namely, £80.

An admission fee with rides available at no charge appears a better pricing policy than free entry and rides at £4 per ride. However, there is always the alternative of charging an entrance fee *and* a price of £4 per ride. In these circumstances the highest entrance fee that might be charged is equal to the triangle above the price of £4 and this is equal to £20. Revenue per customer (with this pricing strategy) would equal the entrance fee of £20 plus the revenue from rides which is £40, yielding a total revenue of £60. The reason that EuroDisney would simply charge an admission fee is that revenue would be equal to £80.

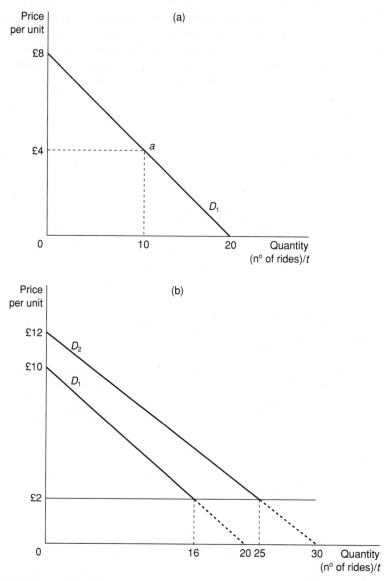

Figure 2.18 **Pricing at EuroDisney**

The analysis shows why admission charges might prove a revenue-maximising strategy. However, the analysis is sensitive to the assumption that all individuals are identical. Figure 2.18(b) identifies two different demand curves D_1 and D_2. In 1992/93 EuroDisney made a loss of £614 million (Dobson *et al.* 1998). Its response was to lower the entrance fee! What sense does this make?

In Figure 2.18(b) there are two types of customer whose demand curves are D_1 and D_2. Individual 1 takes 20 rides at a zero price (and no rides at a price of £10). Individual 2 takes 30 rides at a zero price (and no rides at a price of £12). EuroDisney charges the same price for all customers and this means that it focuses on the consumer surplus of individual 2, charging an entrance fee equal to £180. At this admission charge individual 1 is not a customer. The most that individual 1 will pay is £100. By lowering the entrance charge to £100 EuroDisney increases revenue. The lower entrance charge attracts more customers. (Also the lower entrance charge means that individual 2 retains some consumer surplus – equal to £80.) When account is taken of the difference between consumers, the strategy of reducing the entrance fee is not so surprising.

While the example illustrates how consumer surplus sheds insight on a surprising response, the outcome described here is not necessarily the revenue-maximising strategy. The adoption of a two-part tariff may, instead, prove the best response when individuals are not identical.[2]

2.8 Challenge: How secure is conventional consumer theory?

The previous sections of this chapter have laid down the accepted standard conventional neoclassical theory of consumer behaviour, much of which will be familiar to readers from introductory economics courses. Economists have, however, reacted to this basic approach in many ways. These challenges have been to (i) increase the strength of the foundations of the theory, (ii) increase its level of sophistication, or more fundamentally (iii) to deny its relevance. The next three subsections provide examples of each type of response.

2.8.1 Revealed preference – strengthening foundations

Many economists have sought to elaborate consumer theory and/or make its foundations more secure. Revealed preference, developed by Samuelson (1965), is about making indifference curve analysis more secure by basing it on individual choices made in different price–income situations. If an individual chooses one bundle of goods over any other bundle that could have been afforded then the individual is revealed to prefer the first bundle over any other bundles that could have been purchased. To develop the theory of revealed preference, begin by considering consumer choice over two goods X and Y.

In Figure 2.19, the line $B_0\text{-}B_0'$ represents the budget line. Choices such as bundles at points 1 or 2 would exhaust the consumer's budget but a bundle such as 3 could be bought with a lower expenditure $B\text{-}B'$ (represented by the dashed line in Figure 2.19). Suppose the consumer actually chooses bundle 1. Assuming the individual acts rationally, then no other affordable combination of the two goods would give more utility (notice the connection of rationality with utility maximisation – see Chapter 1). It may be concluded that bundle 1 is 'revealed preferred' to all other choices in $0\text{-}B_0\text{-}B_0'$. More specifically, bundle 1 is revealed preferred to bundles 2 and 3 (bundle 3 has less of both X and Y than bundle 1). Both these alternatives could have been purchased by the individual, but were not. Note: point 1 is inferior to a point like 4, which contains more of both goods or the same amount of one good and more of the other along the lines $A\text{-}1\text{-}A'$. Points of indifference to 1 must lie in the shaded area.

Revealed preference analysis cuts down on the zone of indifference by adding another budget constraint $B_1\text{-}B_1'$ through point 1. In Figure 2.20 segment $1\text{-}B_1'$ cannot be revealed preferred as it was an affordable option when $B_0\text{-}B_0'$ applied. However, a point like 5 can be chosen with points in the area $C\text{-}5\text{-}C'$ being preferred to 5 on the same reasoning as above. If budget line $B_2\text{-}B_2'$ is also introduced through point 1, a point like 6 might be

2. In Figure 2.18(b) assume that price for rides is charged at £2 per ride. The consumer surplus for individual 1 is given by the area above this price, i.e. a triangle equal to £64. If the entrance charge is £64 and the price per ride is £2 then, as individual 1 takes 16 rides, individual 1's total expenditure is £64 + £32 = £96. The revenue from individual 2 is £64 + £50 (as individual 2 takes 25 rides at £2 per ride). Total revenue is £210 which is greater than £200 if there were only an admission fee. With two types of customers EuroDisney might increase its revenue by charging an entrance fee plus tickets for rides (i.e. a two-part tariff).

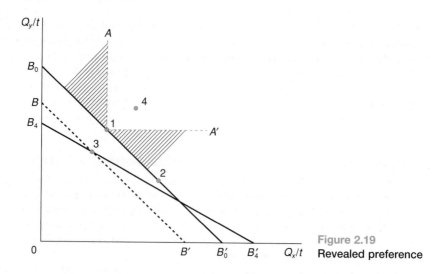

Figure 2.19
Revealed preference

revealed preferred and area *D*-6-*D′* being preferred to 6, also on the same reasoning as above. Points of indifference to 1 must now lie in a reduced shaded area as 5 and 6 are revealed preferred to point 1.

It is easy to imagine if many budget constraints are put in through point 1 the points preferred to 1 like 5 and 6 will increase, defining the upper bound of an indifference curve labelled *I*. But B_0-B_0', at the moment, remains as the lower bound. To chip away at this it is necessary to consider a point revealed inferior to point 1, say point 2. Now imagine rotating a budget constraint with point 2 at its centre until point 2 is revealed preferred. If that constraint is B_3-B_3' then 2 is revealed preferred to all points in the cross-hatched area and, given 1 is preferred to 2, this area is also inferior to 1 and cannot include a point of indifference to 1. A budget line through a point like 7 would also isolate a triangle of inferiority. Again, if many, many budget constraints are placed to select a bundle on B_0-B_0' inferior to 1 the lower bound of indifference can be located.

Whilst this theory establishes that an indifference map could be constructed from behavioural choices, the empirical process would clearly be empirically demanding. This is not to imply revealed preference has no role. Burton and Young (1990) use it to try to establish whether changing patterns of UK meat consumption from 1960 to 1987 could be consistent with relative price and income changes alone as opposed to preference changes.

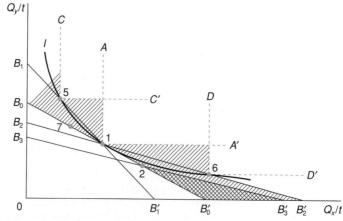

Figure 2.20 Forming an indifference curve

The theory implies a simple consistency condition on consumer choice: if, for two bundles 1 and 3, 1 is revealed preferred to 3, then 3 cannot be revealed preferred to 1. The implication of this is that bundle 3 will only be chosen when bundle 1 is not within the attainable set of alternatives. Again, referring to Figure 2.19, if line B_0-B_0' represents the budget line, the consumer chooses bundle 1. Now, suppose that relative prices change in such a way that the new budget line is the line B_4-B_4', and in this case bundle 3 is chosen. Bundle 1 is chosen when 3 is available (3 lies within the set of choices given the budget line B_0-B_0') and 3 is chosen when 1 is unattainable with the given budget set B_4-B_4' (1 is outside the budget set). So, these choices accord with the, so-called, weak consistency condition.

This condition can also be expressed in terms of expenditure. For bundle 1 to be revealed preferred to 3, the expenditure on 1 must be at least as great as expenditure on 3, as 3 must be in the budget set. For 3 to be chosen subsequently, 1 must involve a greater expenditure at the price ratio then obtaining. That is, 1 must be outside the budget constraint. If choice is between only two commodity bundles and the consumer's choices satisfy this simple consistency condition; then the choices are consistent with the hypothesis that the consumer acts 'as if' maximising utility with constant preferences.

Note that the consistency condition is a testable hypothesis about consumer behaviour. It would be violated if 1 was chosen when 3 could have been chosen and 3 was chosen when 1 could have been chosen. An example of a violation of the weak consistency condition is also illustrated in Figure 2.21. Here, 1' is selected when the budget line is B_0-B_0' and 2' is selected when the budget line is B_1-B_1'. Hence, when 1' is selected 2' is a bundle that is an affordable alternative, and when 2' is chosen, 1' is an affordable alternative.

The consistency condition could be violated if either the individual is not choosing the utility-maximising bundle available or if the individual's preferences have changed. Either case is not attractive to neoclassical microeconomics, as the former undercuts the driving motivation that makes the theory 'work' and the latter is frowned upon as an explanation of choices, as any economic event could be justified by the words: 'obviously preferences have changed'.

So far, only the case of two goods has been considered and the choice between two bundles. In practice, there are many more commodities and to check the consistency of consumer behaviour whole sequences of choices would need examination. The theory suggests a second stronger condition, concerning the consistency of consumer behaviour when confronted by a sequence of choices. The strong condition states that (for

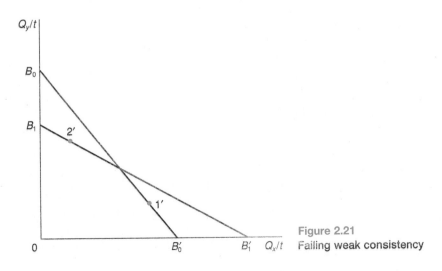

Figure 2.21
Failing weak consistency

three bundles 1, 2 and 3), if 1 is revealed preferred to 2 and 2 is revealed preferred to 3, then bundle 3 cannot be revealed preferred to bundle 1. In fact, the weak consistency condition is just a special case of the strong condition when the number of commodity bundles is two.

For any number of commodities and commodity bundles, if consumer choices satisfy the strong condition, then they are consistent with the hypothesis that the consumer acts as if maximising utility, with stable preferences, as neoclassical demand theory suggests. Hence, if no violations to this condition (cast in terms of expenditures on each bundle are uncovered in the data), it should be possible to find an empirical demand system that fully explains consumption patterns in terms of relative price and income changes alone. There is no need to invoke preference changes.

The data on meat consumption in Britain over the period 1960–87 turned out to be consistent with the conditions of revealed preference theory. This, of course, does not prove that preference changes did not occur over the period, as there is always the possibility that changes in preferences have occurred undetected. What can be said is that the data are not inconsistent with revealed preference and stable preferences.

2.8.2 The characteristics approach – greater sophistication

Lancaster (1966) is the economist who has become associated with the characteristics approach to consumer analysis. In this approach attributes of products are the objects over which consumers have preferences. The approach has a number of distinctive implications that relate to: (i) discrete switching at the individual level; (ii) consumer and producer 'production' of attributes; (iii) price and quantity moving together; and (iv) advertising. Key elements in the analysis are introduced below.

To make matters simple, initially consider a commodity that only has two attributes and a consumer who has already decided how much to spend on this commodity. In Figure 2.22, characteristic 1 is on the y-axis and characteristic 2 on the x-axis. A ray from the origin shows (in its angle) the fixed combinations of each characteristic embodied in each brand of the commodity you intend to purchase. Given the rays and cost per unit of attribute the fixed budget constraint dictates how far along each ray the individual with a fixed budget can go. (Note this has most resonance in a context in which household budgets are set sequentially, as in the transactions costs approach below, i.e. a food budget is determined, a luxuries budget, a savings and investment budget, etc.) These points are 1, 2 and 3 along the brand rays. Imposing a conventional indifference map for

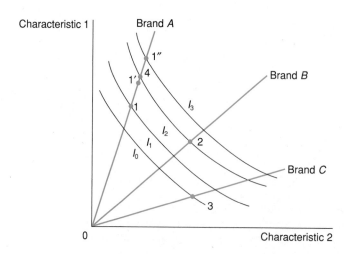

Figure 2.22
Lancaster's characteristics approach

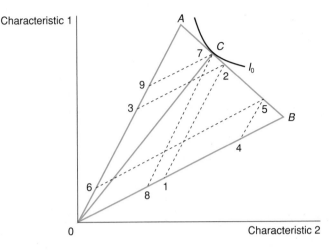

Figure 2.23
Completing the parallelogram and consumer brand creation

two characteristics in the figure indicates the utility-maximising choice is Brand B at point 2 on I_2. Point 1 is on I_1 and point 3 is only on I_0.

Now the discrete switching implication at the level of the individual can be seen. So far the world has been one of marginal adjustments in response to a change of economic stimulus. If the price of Brand A falls then point 1 migrates north-west along the Brand A ray. If the price fall only shifts point 1, as far as 1', then nothing happens. It is only after point 4 that utility maximisation indicates a change of purchase pattern. For example, if a price change makes point 1" attainable the individual depicted will completely switch from Brand B to Brand A, moving to 1" on I_3. Although this is a discrete change at the level of the individual, at the market level this may resemble a continuous marginal adjustment as different people have different preference maps and therefore trigger points of brand shift.

Consumer and producer production of attributes is consistent with Becker's (1965) view that consumers are just as much 'producers' as producers. Depending on the nature of the characteristics involved it may be possible to mix them. Figure 2.23 indicates two brand rays which are line vectors labelled A and B. If the characteristics they embody can continuously be mixed, the possibilities are contained in the sum of the two line vectors, which is achieved by 'completing the parallelogram'. If 0-B and 0-A represent maximum attainable quantities of A and B what are the maximum combinations they generate? If 0-1 of B is purchased and 0-3 is the amount of A obtainable with the remaining part of the budget then the sum of the two is found by drawing in a line parallel to 0-3 emanating from point 1 of equal length to 0-3, i.e. line 1-2. It follows that point 2 is one point on the sum of the two vectors and 0-3-2-1 forms a parallelogram.

Distances 0-1 and 0-3 show how much of B and A are used in the brand respectively. If 0-4 of B is purchased and 0-6 is the amount of A obtainable with the remaining part of the budget, then the sum of the two is found by drawing in a line parallel to 0-6 emanating from point 4 of equal length to 0-6, i.e. line 4-5. Point 5 is also one point on the sum of the two vectors and 0-6-5-4 forms a parallelogram. Distances 0-4 and 0-6 show how much of B and A are used in the brand respectively. It is easy to verify that by repeating the process many, many times a continuous line between A and B will be generated so that the consumer may make their own brand to maximise their utility. Here, this is shown at point 7, with 'personal' brand C made up of 0-8 of B and 0-9 of A – affording the utility level I_0. In Figure 2.24, four brand rays are introduced 0-A, 0-B, 0-C and 0-D. Summing them produces the continuous characteristics combinations frontier A-B-C-D. Note the A-C combination is dominated by the frontier, as is A-D. Section C-D has a

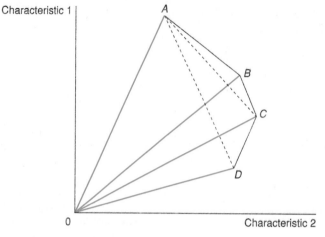

Figure 2.24
Characteristics combinations frontier

positive slope and would never be chosen by any individual for whom characteristics 1 and 2 are 'goods'.

However, it may be the case that producers can produce brands at lower cost, either because of technical knowledge or technological advantages, e.g. static increasing returns to scale may arise in the case of literal mixing because of area–volume relationships – if you double the sides of a container you more than double its volume. Reverting to Figure 2.23, producers (once they recognise C is demanded) may be able to displace consumer production, by offering to do it at lower cost – moving the consumer to the north-west of point 7 and utility level I_0 for a given outlay. Completing the parallelogram assumes combining A and B is costless in itself. *Ex-post* response by producers may be displaced by market research to lead, or anticipate, new brands. Market research considerations, plus the fact that the various rays and combinations are labelled 'brands', takes the discussion much closer to the world of commerce and firms offering many brands. This indicates why Lancaster's work is typically afforded more space in business economics.

Price changes alter the shape of the characteristics combination frontier. In Figure 2.25, rays A, B and C are reproduced. A sharp fall in the price of A moves point A to A' and turns the frontier from concavity to the origin to linearity as segments A-B and C-D are dominated. Given the implied linear consumption technologies, an income increase moves A, B and C in proportion along their rays, shifting the frontier out in a proportional fashion to A", B' and C'.

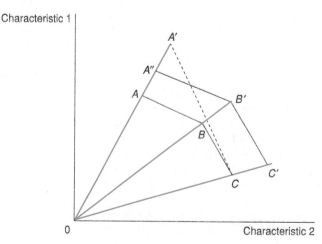

Figure 2.25
Price and income changes

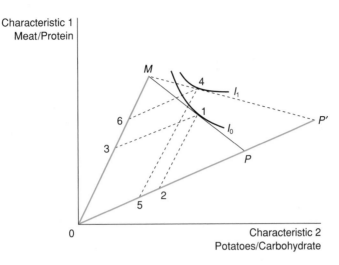

Figure 2.26
The Giffen paradox once more

The Giffen paradox (of both falling price and quantity demanded) arises much more commonly in the characteristics approach. In Figure 2.26, characteristic 1 is meat or protein intake and 2 is potatoes or carbohydrate intake to fit in with the discussion of Section 2.6.1. With initial prices and budget allocation to food, in the form of meat and potatoes, 0-M meat is available and 0-P potatoes, with the utility-maximising meal being point 1 on I_0 (with 0-2 potato and 0-3 meat). A fall in the price of potatoes now moves P to P' and M-P' becomes the characteristics combination frontier, so that utility is maximised at point 4 on I_1 with 0-5 < 0-2 of potatoes and 0-6 > 0-3 of meat. The price of potatoes has fallen along with their quantity consumed.

Whilst the characteristics approach is, to many minds, a step towards consumer reality, other economists have gone further down the road to realism.

2.8.3 Prospect theory and the dumb consumer – increasing relevance

Many economics texts seem to have the title *Economics – the Science of Common Sense*. Unfortunately, this appears not to be the case; for if it was, it would be much easier to teach! Much of economics is counter-intuitive (as in the elasticity lessons above). Increasingly, it is accepted as a reflection of a body of results of cognitive psychology (psychology of 'decision making, thinking' and how the brain works) and experimental economics that the 'common sense' people display is not that of economic rationality. Instead, it proves *anomalous* behaviour (though that behaviour is, nonetheless, systematic).

For example, introductory economics texts argue that sunk costs (expenditures on a durable specific factor input that has no obvious alternative use and, therefore, little resale value) cannot affect marginal cost and influence choice. Suppose that £15 has been expended on a project in the past and a further £5 is required to complete the project, in a context where £8 is the expected benefit. The question arises as to whether to complete the project. The typical response is to say the costs are £15 plus £5 = £20 and the benefits only £8 so that the project should not be completed. However, if the £15 is a sunk cost (and therefore must be treated as a bygone), the marginal cost to complete the project is £5 and the marginal benefit is £8. Therefore, it is efficient to complete the project. The first £15 is 'spilt milk' – irrelevant to the decision. Given this, the message is 'not to cry over spilt milk'. So why do 'dumb' people do this (either literally or figuratively)?

This question suggests the need for a theory that offers a role to sunk costs. Prospect theory developed by Kahneman and Tversky (1979) can do this. Generally, prospect theory indicates that:

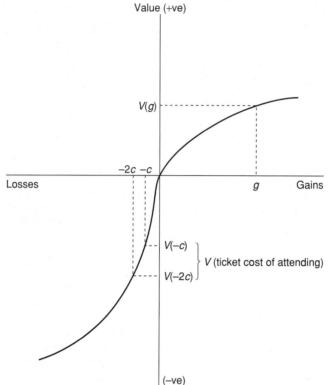

Figure 2.27
The value function and sunk costs

(i) probabilities are replaced by decision weights (see Chapter 19);
(ii) the utility function is replaced with a value function.

Considering (ii), how can it give a role to sunk costs?

Kahneman and Tversky offer, as a central construct, the value function defined over changes in income or wealth, illustrated as Figure 2.27. It has a particular shape, increasing at a decreasing rate in the +ve, +ve quadrant and decreasing at a decreasing rate in the −ve, −ve quadrant. However, the curve is not symmetrical about the x-axis, being steeper in the −ve, −ve quadrant. (If this was a utility function it would indicate risk aversion for gains and risk-loving for losses – see Chapter 7.) The implication is: the absolute value assigned to, say, a £100 gain is less than the absolute value assigned to £100 loss, $v(£100) < v(−£100)$ in absolute terms in Figure 2.27. Why should this matter?

In one of Kahneman and Tversky's experiments, two groups of respondents were asked to consider a question similar to the following:

You have been given a concert ticket in London (you are in Bath some 100 miles away). On the day of the concert the weather is very bad, making travel to London very difficult. Do you think:

A. There is a greater than 50% chance you would still go.
B. There is a less than 50% chance you would still go.

You have paid £40 for a concert ticket in London (you are in Bath some 100 miles away). On the day of the concert the weather is very bad, making travel to London very difficult. Do you think:

A. There is a greater than 50% chance you would still go.
B. There is a less than 50% chance you would still go.

The difference in the questions is the expenditure of £40 on a ticket that has already been made (a sunk expenditure that nothing can be done about on the day). Yet individuals who have notionally paid for a ticket differentially respond that: 'There is a greater than 50% chance I would still go.' That is, the sunk cost must be doing some work in individuals' decision making (encouraging them to go to the concert). To explore this, imagine those with free tickets are made indifferent as to whether to go or not – so that:

$$v(g) + v(-c) = 0,$$

where

g = the benefit from the concert;
c = all the costs involved in travelling to the concert.

Reference to the value function to assign value to these expenditures (in a process called 'coding') indicates that g is considerably greater than the absolute value of c for $v(g) = v(-c)$ (see Figure 2.27). The question is how the decision is transformed by the presence of the £40 ticket expenditure. For individuals who purchased a ticket, going to the concert or not involves the value calculation:

If go: $v(g) + v[-(c + £40)]$ compared to   If don't go: $v(-£40)$.

Given the assumptions, the g and c values cannot have an impact on the decision. It then must be a case of how the –£40 is assigned value. Again, for simplicity assume c = £40 = ticket price. In the 'not go' case its impact is measured from the origin as $v(-c)$. In the 'go' case $v(g)$, the gain is subtracted from the c cost and the ticket price integrated with it. The ticket cost, when integrated with $-c$, is assigned less value, as it is arising on a shallower part of the loss curve (compare $v(-c)$ with $v(-2c)$). Choosing to go induces less net value loss [equal to distance v (ticket cost attending)] in Figure 2.27 than not going [$v(-c)$]. The impact of integrating the –£40 ticket cost on value is to push the loss-minimising individual to go to the concert. The sunk cost has affected the decision in the way indicated by the experimental results.

Defenders of neoclassical theory see conventional utility theory as close enough an approximation to actual choices for it to be reliable in practical applications. They argue that a considerable amount of anomalous behaviour is not observed and that, in laboratory testing of economic theory, participants lack the 'correct' motivation. In short, they see neoclassical theory as being applied in 'evolved' settings, where similar decisions are repeated. But the experimental evidence remains very strong and behavioural economics is increasingly popular with many economists (being seen as more realistic, reflecting an array of partially analysed, yet systematic, heuristic responses).

Different economists want economics to do different things. Consider Table 2.1 in which two perspectives are described.

Table 2.1 **Contrasting views of theory**

Features	Mainstream neoclassical microeconomic theorising	Behavioural economics theorising
1. Methodology	Deductive	Inductive
2. Results	Prescriptive	Descriptive
3. Breadth of application	Sophisticated minority	Dumb majority
4. Rational thinking errors	Rare and eradicated	Common and systematic
5. Need for consumer protection	Minimal	Significant
6. Illustration	Neoclassical consumer theory	Thaler's transactions utility theory

Thaler (1980, 1994), having rehearsed the Kahneman–Tversky value function in the way described above, sets about building a consumer theory consistent with the features described under behavioural economics above. Being inductive means moving from observations and data on actual behaviour to later theorising, or generalising, about what individuals are doing. Thaler suggests individuals conform to his two-stage transactions utility approach by following a purchase evaluation stage and subsequently a decision making stage.

In the evaluation stage, two types of utility are weighed up. The first is acquisition utility, which is very close to the concept of consumer surplus explored above. A value for acquisition utility comes from comparing the actual price outlaid ($-p$) with a money sum p' which makes the individual indifferent between being given the good Z free and receiving that sum. Given this, acquisition utility would generally be coded as $v(p' - p)$. The second is transactions utility, which assigns a value to the trade itself by comparing the price outlay with the so-called reference price (p^*) for the good Z. This reference price is seen as a fair price and in general is expected to reflect the costs of production. Hence, transactions utility is represented as $v(-p{:}-p^*)$.

Total utility is the sum of the two utility sources and, in general form, the purchase evaluation device gives total utility (W) as:

$$W(Z,p,p^*) = v(p',-p) + \beta v(-p{:}-p^*) \tag{2.11}$$

which indicates the value of buying good Z at price p with reference price p^*.

The coefficient β can take several values: $\beta = 0$ effectively reduces the equation back to neoclassical theory; $\beta > 0$ means transaction utility applies and $\beta > 1$ is seen as representing the chronic bargain hunter as transactions utility is given more than proportionate weight.

The second is the decision-making stage, where decisions are made sequentially. 'Real-world' individuals fear their own lack of self-control (leading them into debt) and seek to guard against it. The way to do this is to set a local temporal budget constraint, e.g. a week, or more typically a month, as many are paid monthly. Individuals do not 'income-smooth' (equalising the marginal utility of income at the end of each time period, as utility maximisation would suggest), because they do not trust themselves to 'pay back' appropriately. Additionally, individuals have 'mental accounts', so that each good is considered for purchase in a different category or account, e.g. food account, holiday account, education account. These accounts may, in some instances, be literal, e.g. the rent envelope. A key matter is that there is no fungibility between these accounts. That is, a dollar in the holiday account cannot be moved and spent as a dollar in the food account. Solow (1987) notes 'We [economists] think of wealth as fungible. We think a dollar is a dollar. Why don't *they*?' Evidence suggests that the allocation of savings differs according to which 'mental account' income is attributed (i.e. to a 'current income account', to an 'asset account' or to a 'future income account'. Winnett and Lewis (1995) identify 'mental accounting schemas'; the use of income depends on the distinction between liquidity, windfall/regular and capital/labour income. In a study of household saving they discovered that 'all income from capital is classified as non-spendable' (p. 441).

The final step involves an individual buying the set of purchases such that it maximises $\Sigma W(Z,p,p^*)$ subject to the income constraint $\Sigma(p_i,Z_i) \leq I$ where I stands for income and there are i goods categories. This is an integer programming problem whose solution is to evaluate purchases as they arise and purchase good Z at price p, if and only if, $W(Z,p,p^*)/p \geq k_{it}$ where k_{it} is the budget constraint for category i in time period t. Although this may look like $MU_x/P_x = MU_y/P_y = \lambda$, here the k_{it}s vary over the goods categories and time periods because this is not global optimisation as in neoclassical theory. Luxury goods tend to have high k's and more 'worthy' goods low k's. This inductive theorising (the theory in part was based on family interview data) should ring a bell as a description of how consumer decisions are actually made.

However, whilst at first sight this may seem a radical departure from conventional theory, note that individuals code to maximise value (cf. maximising utility) and have to act *as if* they can solve an integer programming[3] problem (cf. Lagrange multiplier for constrained utility maximisation). Coding to maximise value is called 'hedonic coding' and provides insights into how individuals may make systematic errors and need protecting from themselves. The basic rules of coding can be gleaned from observation of the shape of the value function. Gains should be segregated (coded separately); coding two £5 presents separately generates more value than a single £10 present, as it introduces a flatter part of the value function for the second £5. Losses should be integrated (coded together); coding two £5 bills separately generates more negative value than a single £10 bill, as the £10 bill introduces a flatter part of the value function for the second £5 (less negative value than coding from the origin). Credit card bills exploit this coding mechanism. Mixed gains and losses that cancel to an overall gain should be integrated to take advantage of the steep part of the value function for gains. Mixed gains and losses that cancel to an overall large loss should be segregated to take advantage of the steep part of the value function for gains, as opposed to the flat part of the value function for losses. Consider coding a £6000 loss and a £40 gain in a segregated way on Figure 2.27 compared to an integrated coding of a £5960 loss. Mixed gains and losses, which cancel to an overall small loss, should be integrated to avoid the steep part of the value function for losses as opposed to the less steep part of the value function for gains. Consider coding a £12 loss and a £10 gain in a segregated way on Figure 2.27 compared to an integrated coding of a £2 loss. In the segregated coding the common element of £10 would be assigned much greater negative value (−£2 to −£12) than the offsetting £10 gain (0 to +£10). Marketing managers have been adept at using hedonic coding to their advantage for years. Increasingly, however, public officials like tax officers have learned to increase tax compliance by framing payments in a coding-friendly way.

For those convinced by prospect theory and associated theorising, its rejection by mainstream economists illustrates their unwillingness to be moved by evidence about the world that does not fit conventional neoclassical theoretical presuppositions. In this way, the subject is brought back to the relationship between theory and evidence introduced in Chapter 1.

2.9 Summary

This chapter has covered a great deal of material fundamental to a good understanding of post-foundational microeconomic theory.

- The 'Chapter 1 picture' of the utility-maximiser has been enhanced by indicating how the range of preferences, illustrated by indifference maps, can be extended and how non-linear budget constraints can be accommodated.
- The derivation of an individual's demand curve for a good X was explained and its reliance on an indifference map, exhibiting a diminishing marginal rate of substitution, was apparent. Horizontal summation was used to construct a market demand curve.
- The role of the *ceteris paribus* assumptions in the demand function was illustrated along with different demand elasticity concepts.

---

3. Integer programming is a special case of mathematical programming in which the solution variables are required, as the name suggests, to take integer values.

- Income and substitution effects were isolated and their connection to compensating and equivalent variations as measures of welfare change explored.
- Applications of demand elasticities and consumer surplus showed how economic concepts have day-to-day relevance. In the final section of the chapter 'challenges' to strengthen, expand and displace conventional neoclassical consumer theory were provided in the form of revealed preference, the characteristics approach and prospect theory respectively.

Virtually all the concepts introduced in this chapter reappear in later chapters, so that time devoted to getting to grips with the material of this chapter will pay off in terms of ease of later understanding.

Appendix 2 Signing derivatives

This appendix provides in Figure 2.28 the signs of the first and second derivatives associated with a set of circular shapes. It is presented for variables V_1 and V_2 because it has general application throughout economics. For example, if indifference curve are relevant V_1 would be output X/t and V_2 output Y/t, whereas for isoquants V_1 would be input labour (L/t) and V_2 input capital (K/t).

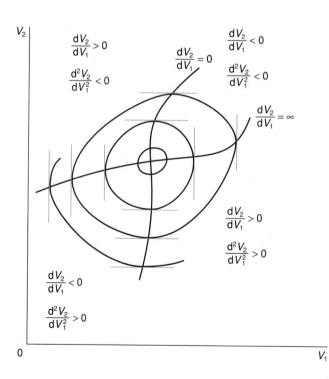

Figure 2.28
A surface showing areas of positively and negatively sloped curves plus 'ridge lines'

References

Becker, G.S. (1965) Theory of allocation of time, *Economic Journal*, 75: 493–517.

Begg, D., Fisher, S. and Dornbusch, R. (2003) *Economics*, 7th edn, Maidenhead: McGraw-Hill.

Bordley, R.F. and McDonald, J.B. (1993) Estimating aggregate income elasticities from the population income-share elasticity, *Journal of Business and Economic Statistics*, 11 (2): 653–83.

Burton, M. and Young, T. (1990) Meat consumption: have tastes changed? *Economic Review*, 8 (2): 7–10.

Carter, C. *et al.* (1987) Agricultural labor strikes and farmers' incomes, *Economic Inquiry*, 25: 121–33.

Deaton, A. (1975) The measurement of income and price elasticities, *European Economic Review*, 6 (3): 261–73.

Dobson, S., Maddala, G.S. and Miller, E. (1989) *Microeconomics*, Maidenhead: McGraw-Hill.

Ferguson, C.E. and Gould, J.P. (1975) *Microeconomic Theory*, Illinois: Irwin.

Hicks, J.R. (1946) *Value and Capital*, 2nd edn, London: Oxford University Press.

Kahneman, D. and Tversky, A. (1979) Prospect theory: an analysis of decision under risk, *Econometrica*, 47: 263–91.

Lancaster, K. (1966) A new approach to consumer theory, *Journal of Political Economy*, 74 (2): 132–57.

Marshall, A. (1920) *Principles of Economics*, 8th edn, London: Macmilllan.

Nicholson, W. (1997) *Intermediate Microeconomics and its Applications*, 7th edn, Fort Worth: Dryden Press.

Oi, W.Y. (1971) A Disneyland dilemma in two part tariffs for a Mickey Mouse monopoly, *Quarterly Journal of Economics*, 85 (1): 77–96.

Samuelson, P.A. (1965) *Foundations of Economic Analysis*, Cambridge, Mass.: Harvard University Press.

Solow, R. (1987) Comments on 'How much (or little) life cycle is there in micro data? The cases of the United States and Japan', pp. 224–8 in R. Dornbusch, S. Fischer, and J. Bossons, *Macroeconomics and Finance*, Cambridge, Mass.: MIT Press.

Thaler, R.H. (1980) Toward a positive theory of consumer choice, *Journal of Economic Behavior and Organization*, 1: 39–60.

Thaler, R.H. (1994) *Quasi Rational Economics*. New York: Russell Sage Foundation.

Thompson, Jr, A.A. (1985) *Economics of the Firm: Theory and Practice*, 4th edn, Englewood Cliffs, NJ: Prentice-Hall.

Varian, H.R. (1999) *Intermediate Microeconomics: a Modern Approach*, 5th edn, New York: W. W. Norton.

Wicksteed, P.H. (1914) The scope and method of political economy, *Economic Journal*, 24: 1–23.

Willis, R.J. (1973) A new approach to the economic theory of fertility behavior, *Journal of Political Economy*, 81 (2) (part 2): S14–S64.

Winnett, A. and Lewis, A. (1995) Household accounts, mental accounts and savings behaviour: some old economics rediscovered? *Journal of Economic Psychology*, 16: 431–48.

CHAPTER 3

The 'black box' competitor

3.1 Introduction

On reaching second-level microeconomics many students claim that they have not 'done' the theory of the firm. Part of this response is doubtless the self-serving hope that the lecturer will, once again, repeat material at an introductory level. However, a more genuine reason is that the neoclassical theory of the firm does not really correspond very closely to the image individuals have in their heads of firms. The perception is of firms as places where there are workers, executive types; there are tea urns, cafeterias; there are works days out and, perhaps most of all, these days, banks of computers. In short, there are many activities going on which involve people. Yet, in the theory of the firm in neoclassical economics there are no frictions; there are no people as such, merely a set of lines on diagrams and a set of equations that dictate outcomes (after a certain number of assumptions have been made). Hence, the 'black box' epithet found in the chapter heading.

At the outset, it is worth noting two further reasons why the theory of the firm is not what individuals imagine firms to be. First, the theory of the firm, at this level, does not embrace uncertainty in any meaningful sense (and certainly not in a fundamental sense). Everything tends to be known (whereas uncertainty and risk are surely everywhere). Second, the theory of the firm does not, at any point, analyse the processes by which resources are allocated. In this way, the popular imagination of what the firm 'looks like' tends to be lost from view. Wiseman (1989) introduces these two points as part of a strong critique of the ' "standardised" economic theory of the competitive economy' (p. 146) and, therefore, its relevance to anything much. However, before rejecting the 'standard' model, a reasonable understanding of its workings seems a logical prerequisite.

Against this critical background, what does the theory of the firm do? The first claim that can be made is that it describes equilibrium states, the second is that it develops comparative alternative equilibrium states (known as 'comparative static analysis'). It indicates what happens if you make a change in one of the variables held constant in analysis and poses the question: what new equilibrium arises as a consequence? The tasks of this chapter are to explain the foundations of this analysis, to justify this level of abstraction and to show why it is important.

The theory of the firm, generally, discusses four major market forms. These are:

(1) perfect competition;
(2) monopoly;
(3) monopolistic competition;
(4) oligopoly.

Forms (2), (3) and (4) are all forms of imperfect competition.

A good understanding of perfect competition is vital because it is *the* theoretical benchmark against which economists appraise other economic arrangements. It is not that economists think (in any sense) that it exists out there (although there may be some markets where the conditions required are approximated). It is essentially a fictional economy in which arrangements are ideal for consumers. It is the market form that corresponds completely to consumer sovereignty. To make any piece of theory 'work' in economics, a set of assumptions is required. An essential starting point for all the market forms, which are discussed in detail in later chapters, is an understanding of cost structures and where they come from. The next section explains the derivation of the classic U-shaped cost curves that are generally present in many market forms.

3.2 From production functions to cost curves

The derivation of the standard 'U-shaped' costs curve is vital to the understanding of a great deal of economics and, therefore, requires particular attention. The derivation requires a number of steps, moving from representing the physical process of production of any good X to converting that physical information to a common numeraire – money terms. Production occurs when the factors of production are combined with each other. The factors of production are commonly collected under the three, all-encompassing, headings of land, labour (L below) and capital (K below), so that entrepreneurship can be subsumed under 'labour' and raw materials can be subsumed under 'land'.

At the outset, the key distinction made in economics between the long and the short run needs to be emphasised. These periods do not correspond to calendar time, rather it is about the time (in the context of a particular process) that is required to make adjustments. As a matter of definition, the short run defines a time period where there is at least one factor of production that is fixed in quantity (i.e. that factor cannot be altered). The long run is the time period where, by definition, all factors of production can be varied. The calendar periods these definitions correspond to depend entirely on the process under discussion. In some processes it may be possible to adjust all factors in a matter of weeks, in others it may take years.

At the end of this section the objective is to understand the nature of the long-run and short-run cost functions. Symbolically:

$$\text{Long-run total cost function} = TC = f(Q_x, T_c, P_f) \tag{3.1}$$

where:

TC = total cost;
Q_x = output level of a good X;
T_c = technology;
P_f = factor prices (rent, wages and the rental price of capital).

$$\text{Short-run total cost function} = TC = f(Q_x, T_c, P_f \mid \bar{K}) \tag{3.2}$$

As in Chapter 2, a bar over a variable indicates it is fixed in quantity exogenously. This is further emphasised by the vertical line visually isolating some variables as being outside the analysis at this stage. Here, capital, K, is viewed as fixed, reflecting the plausible assumption that it is the factory building, or a specialised piece of machinery that is most difficult to alter in quantity quickly. It needs to be recognised that the processes described below are anonymous in that the factors could equally be interchanged – the theory is independent of the labels.

As it is necessary to develop the theory on a page in two dimensions – before your very eyes – one factor of production has to be left aside (the alternative would be many very awkward diagrams or a more mathematical treatment). The analysis here follows the standard process of dropping land – it is as if all processes use the same raw material inputs. The cost of lost generality is compensated for by greater simplicity. This leaves labour as the factor that can be varied in the short run. Again, this is thought plausible in that overtime hours can be worked, extra shifts organised and more workers employed.

At this level of theory, cost curve relationships are central as they connect quantities of output of X per period with different cost concepts, other things equal – hence the bars and vertical lines below.

Symbolically:

$$\text{Long-run total cost curves} = TC = f(Q_x \mid \bar{T}_c, \bar{P}_f) \tag{3.3}$$

$$\text{Short-run total cost curves} = TC = f(Q_x \mid \bar{T}_c, \bar{P}_f, \bar{K}) \tag{3.4}$$

3.2.1 Production functions as representations of technology

A production function is a mathematical relationship that relates the *maximum* quantity of output that can be obtained from any stated input combination. In symbols:

$$Q_x = Q_x(K, L) \tag{3.5}$$

Typically, the production function will be an equation. However, if a visual representation is required (as it is here), it is illustrated as an isoquant map. An isoquant is the parallel construct in production theory to indifference curves in consumption theory. A single isoquant, say $\overline{Q_0}$, records all combinations of quantities of capital (K) and labour (L) per period that give a stated quantity of output. Because along $\overline{Q_0}$ there is no change in output, the total differential is constrained to equal zero. That is, by definition $dQ = 0$:

$$dQ = (\partial Q/\partial K)dK + (\partial Q/\partial L)dL = 0 \tag{3.6}$$

Therefore, by rearranging Equation (3.6) it can be seen that the slope of the isoquant is:

$$-dK/dL = \partial Q/\partial L \, \big/ \, \partial Q/\partial K = MP_l/MP_k = MRTS_{KL} \tag{3.7}$$

In words, the marginal product of labour (MP_l) divided by the marginal product of capital (MP_k) defines the marginal rate of technical substitution between capital and labour and is the negative of the slope of an isoquant. Unlike indifference curves, isoquants have cardinality. Isoquant $\overline{Q}_x = 60$ is three times as much output as isoquant $\overline{Q}_x = 20$.

Production functions can come in virtually infinite variety (reflecting the virtually infinite variety of technological processes that are in the world). It is likely that modern information and communications technologies (ICT) are making these processes more complex. It is not surprising, therefore, that theoreticians have sought to simplify situations, by classifying production functions in various ways and seeking to work with those that have analytically convenient properties. The justification of the latter choice has to be that the function used is an empirically defensible version of the actual process being modelled – the most popular of these are named after their originators, e.g. the Cobb–Douglas function has proved to be very useful. For thorough treatments of production functions see Heathfield and Wibe (1987), Beattie and Taylor (1985) and Chung (1994). That is not to say that many published journal articles often require a very specific and unusual production function to sustain arguments.

The first distinction made here is between homothetic and non-homothetic production functions. Visually, homothetic production functions involve isoquants that have the same slopes along any ray from the origin, whereas non-homothetic ones have different slopes along any ray from the origin. Figures 3.1(a) and 3.1(b) illustrate this distinction with the ray being 0-R at angle θ. Further, homothetic production functions can be subdivided into homogeneous and non-homogenous ones.

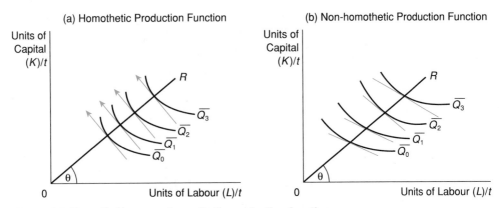

Figure 3.1 **Homothetic v. non-homothetic production functions**

3.2.1.1 Production functions and the long run (returns to scale)

Homogeneity says that, if inputs are all raised a factor 'b', there is a fixed rule to establish what happens to maximum output per period. Therefore, if $Q_x = Q_x(bK, bL)$ and Q_x
can be rewritten as $Q_x = b^r Q_x(K, L)$, then exponent r defines the degree of homogeneity
(returns to scale) of the production function.

If $b = 4$ and $r < 1$ (e.g. 0.5) then, raising all the inputs in proportion 4 times only causes
the output to double as $4^{0.5} = \sqrt{4} = 2$. If $r < 1$ then there are decreasing returns to scale.

If $r = 1$ then constant returns to scale (linear homogeneity) obtains. Raising all the
inputs in proportion 4 times causes the output to rise $4^1 = 4$ times (anything raised to
the power 1 is itself). In the absence of further information, this might be viewed as a
natural assumption to make about a production process.

If $r > 1$ there are increasing returns to scale, e.g. with $b = 4$ and $r = 2$, raising all the
inputs in proportion 4 times causes the output to rise $4^2 = 16$ times. The latter is economic good news but actually presents some theoretical difficulty (as will be seen later).

It should be emphasised that returns to scale is a physical production relationship
that, by definition, must be long-run (as it involves scaling up *all* the inputs in proportion and, by definition, this cannot be done in the short run).

What type of production function might be typical of many production processes?
Figure 3.2 provides a partial two-dimensional representation of a three-dimensional 'production mountain' available from all combinations of two inputs, capital and labour. It
has the typical shape adopted in the neoclassical firm theory. Total output or, more conventionally, total product is recorded on the y-axis with capital and labour units recorded
on the two horizontal axes. It has a peak at point 1, suggesting there is implicitly a fixed
factor somewhere that prevents ever more output from ever more units of capital and
labour inputs being possible. Trying to represent three dimensions on a page, as noted
above, is not easy. Hence, Figure 3.3(a) shows how isoquants are edges, convex to the
origin, of successive horizontal slices through an output mountain.

Figure 3.3(b) provides a picture of the isoquant map consistent with the three-
dimensional diagram. It contains a great deal of information. Units of capital (K) per
period are measured on the y-axis and units of labour (L) per period on the x-axis.
They can be thought of as 'cloned' workers, in that each unit of labour is identical. The
isoquants are labelled 10 to 90 and can be thought of as being 'thousands of units' of
output of good X. In the long run all factors are variable and, therefore, increasing
output is about altering the level of all the inputs into production. An instructive way
to consider doing this is simply to increase the scale of production. As above, this is
looking at what happens to output along a ray from the origin, such as 0-R (as this keeps
the ratio of the two inputs constant and changes in output are reflecting changes in scale

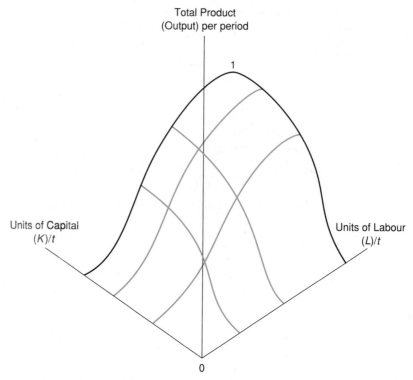

Figure 3.2 A typical total product 'mountain'

only). The fact that the tangents to the isoquants have a different slope as the ray cuts each one in turn (visually compare the tangent t_1 to point 1 with the one t_9 to point 9 in Figure 3.3(b)) indicates that the production function is non-homothetic (ruling out homogeneity). The fixed ratio of capital to labour inputs is given by $\tan \theta$.

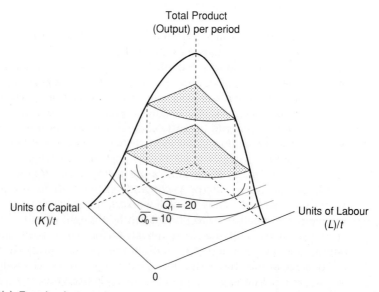

Figure 3.3(a) Forming isoquants

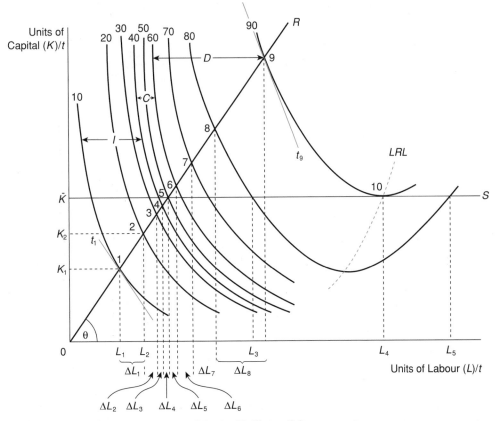

Figure 3.3(b) An isoquant map consistent with Figure 3.2

Figures 3.4(a) and 3.4(b) further illustrate what is going on. Given the original 'shape' in Figure 3.2, total product alters in the way illustrated by the isoquants labelled 10 to 90 (000s) along 0-R in Figure 3.3(b) and the shaded shape above 0-R in Figure 3.4(a) indicates how output is affected. It shows a slice through the 'production mountain', dictated by the ray 0-R in Figure 3.4(a).

Figure 3.4(b) shows the shaded hill of Figure 3.4(a) as a flat surface laid on the page, so that it can be viewed to provide information on returns to scale in this specific production process. Note: the ray chosen does not allow the top of the 'production mountain' to be reached. It is a hill of output labelled $LRTP(\theta)$ to signify it is the long-run total product based on the capital-to-labour ratio captured in the angle θ. For the moment, concentrate on the uphill portion before point A. The x-axis records how the factors are being scaled up, so that, if the ray 0-R dictated a ratio of 2K to 1L as indicated (angle θ would = 64° so that tan 64° = 2), that particular ratio being maintained along the x-axis. It would read 1(2K to 1L), 2(2K to 1), 3(2K to 1L), etc. The curve has a point of inflection (a change of slope but not direction) at A in Figure 3.4(b). Between 0 and A the hill is increasingly steep (slope increasing at an increasing rate), whereas after point A it is decreasingly steep (the slope increasing at a decreasing rate). As inputs are being scaled it is clear that initially $r > 1$, doubling inputs being more than doubling outputs. Or, alternatively, it takes less than double all inputs to double outputs.

Returning to Figure 3.3(b) distance 1-2 / 0-1 on ray 0-R represents the proportionate increase in inputs to raise output from 10,000 to 20,000. If 1-2 / 0-1 is less than 1 output has been doubled without doubling all the inputs – indicating increasing returns to scaling

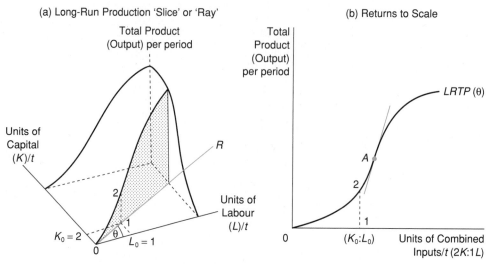

(a) Long-Run Production 'Slice' or 'Ray'

(b) Returns to Scale

Figure 3.4 **Long-run production relationships**

up (marked *I*). Along 0-*R* output increases each time by 10,000 units of good *X* – indicating the returns to scale available. Beyond point 6 scaling up inputs brings a less than proportionate output increase and decreasing returns are now present. In Figure 3.3(b) ratios 6-7 / 0-6 > 7-8 / 0-7 > 8-9 / 0-8 along 0-*R* but output only increases each time by 10,000 units of good *X* – indicating the decreasing returns to scaling up property over this range (marked *D*). In between the two sections of the curve briefly *r* = 1, so that constant returns to scale are observed. In Figure 3.3(b) ratio 4-5 / 0-4 = 5-6 / 0-5 along 0-*R* and output increases both times by 10,000 units of good *X* – indicating the presence of constant returns to scale, albeit briefly (marked *C*). Heathfield and Wibe (1987) describe the density of the isoquant map seeing the map as becoming 'more dense' with increasing returns to scale and the map becoming 'less dense' with decreasing returns to scale.

This is quite a complicated picture but it does yield the most commonly used shapes in microeconomic theory. If 'returns to scale' is the principle that illuminates physical production relationships in the long run, what is the short-run physical equivalent?

3.2.1.2 Production functions and the short run (principle of variable factor proportions)

In the short run at least one factor is fixed (capital is assumed fixed here), so that any desire to increase output in the short run can only be met by increasing the units of variable factor (labour) employed per period in the production process. In the short run, any producer is constrained to a horizontal slice across the production mountain in Figure 3.2 (parallel to the Units of Labour/*t* axis) with the location of the slice set by the existing value of $\bar{K}$.

This can be seen in Figure 3.5(a) and in isoquant form in Figure 3.7, where 0-$\bar{K}$ units of capital represents the existing level of capital employed in the production of good *X*. Figure 3.5(b) shows that the shape of the short-run slice is not unlike the long-run one. Figure 3.5(c) illustrates their interrelationship. The long-run total product curve (LRTP) is the envelope of all short-run total product curves each built around a different (fixed) level of capital stock. Three are illustrated, corresponding to the levels of capital stock picked out on Figure 3.5(a), namely $\bar{K}$, *K'* and *K''*. Each total product curve begins with zero output, so they all have a common origin. In Figure 3.5(c) only one point on each short-run curve is on the long-run curve. The long-run total product curve envelope

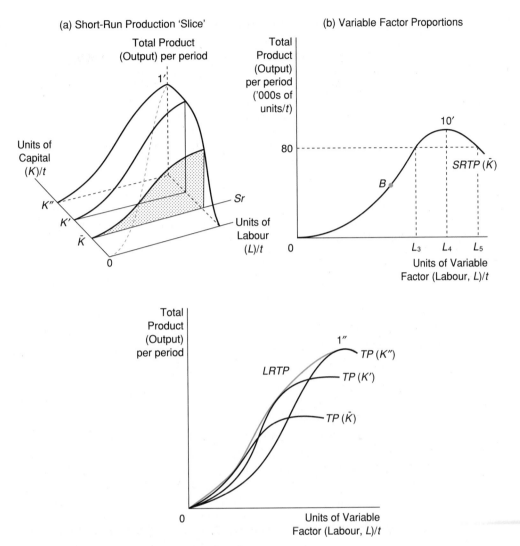

Figure 3.5 **Short-run production relationships**

in 3.5(c) is in effect the dashed 'up the mountain path' line running from 0 to 1' in Figure 3.5(a). Figure 3.5(a) has a role in helping the interpretation of long-run total product curve. The dashed line in Figure 3.5(a) may suggest you can physically expand output along it. Figure 3.5(c) shows that this is not the case, as otherwise the distinction between the short and long run would blur. Economic life is a series of short runs. The sense in which output can be expanded in the long run is by building plants, incorporating a different capital stock, so that the continuous envelope curve is an artefact generated by imagining an infinite number of short-run situations (values for K). The amount of capital K'' is required for the top of the production mountain 1' in Figure 3.5(a) and 1'' in Figure 3.5(c) to be achieved.

The importance of the interpretation of the short-run situation (depicted as Figure 3.5(b)) to understanding post-foundational microeconomics cannot be over-estimated. Observation of 3.5(b) shows the hill of output and that the 'ground' rises initially but later falls. The x-axis records how the units of variable factor labour are being added to the fixed amount of capital, whereas the y-axis records the amount of output. It can be seen that this curve also has a point of inflection (a change of slope but not direction) at point B. Between 0 and B the hill is increasingly steep (slope increasing at an increasing rate), whereas after point B it is decreasingly steep (slope increasing at a decreasing rate). As units of variable factor labour are being added, it is clear that, initially, an additional worker is adding more to output than the previous one (hence the curve is increasing at an increasing rate). Beyond point B, as units of variable factor labour are being added, it is clear that an additional worker is adding less to output than the previous one (hence the curve increasing at a decreasing rate). At point 10′ maximum output is found corresponding to point 10 in Figure 3.3(b). It is clear that additional workers (beyond the 0-L_4 associated with point 10 in Figure 3.3b) are reducing total output. The curve is a decreasing one, so that its slope has become negative (the data from Figure 3.3(b) show that, with 0-$\bar{K}$ units of capital, 0-L_3 workers produce the same output as 0-L_5 workers, namely 80,000 units of good X). Remember, all the units of variable factor, labour, are homogeneous, so that this shape of the short-run total product curve is nothing to do with the quality of workers, or the order they are added to the production process. It is the initial 'production mountain' (the production function) illustrated in Figure 3.2 that is doing all the work in generating these specific shapes.

Rather than use total product curves, it is more convenient to consider the average product of labour and marginal product of labour curves dictated by the shape of the total product curve. This is where the rays of hope and tangential interests of Chapter 1 make things very easy. Figure 3.6(a) reproduces Figure 3.5(b) and can be made to show:

(i) the marginal product of labour (the change in output from a small change in labour input $MP_l = dQ/dL$) and

(ii) the average product of labour (total output divided by the number of units of labour required to produce that output $AP_l = Q/L$) in Figure 3.6(b).

Dealing with the marginal product of labour first involves the tangents to the total product curve in Figure 3.6(a). Below the point of inflection at point B tangents to the curve would form increasingly large angles, so that MP_l must be rising. At point B the tangent to the curve cuts the curve and, therefore, MP_l is at a maximum, as tangents beyond point B would form smaller angles (see B′ in Figure 3.6(b)). At point B, the angle formed by the ray 0-R_1 is θ_1. As this is less than the angle formed by the tangent to the curve at point B on the x-axis (namely θ_2), it is evident that the average value is less than the marginal value at point B (at labour input level 0-L_1). The ray 0-R_2 indicates the maximum value AP_l can take. Given this, the peak of AP_l must be located above labour input level L_2. There is, however, an important piece of further information. The tangent to point 1 is coincident with ray 0-R_1 and they both form the angle θ_3 on the x-axis, indicating a common tan θ value. That is, the MP_l and the maximum AP_l value coincide at labour input L_2. As it has been established that the margin exceeds the average before L_2, the shape of the total product curve means that MP_l cuts AP_l from above at AP_l's maximum value. Note ray 0-R_2 forms the same angle (θ_1) at point B as at point 1 and, therefore, the AP_l must be the same at L_3 as at L_2 (see B″ and 1′ in Figure 3.6(b)). Critical rays from the origin and tangents to the curve define the shape of MP_l and AP_l and their relationship to each other.

Observing Figure 3.6(b) allows the 'principle of variable factor proportions' to be stated: when adding units of variable factor (labour) to a given quantity of the fixed factor (capital) in production the marginal product of the variable factor (MP_l) will eventually decline, if it does not do so everywhere. (Let the name help you – 'variable factor proportions' – given K is fixed, output is expanded by increasing units of labour L, hence factor proportions must be altering – more specifically K/L is falling as output increases.) What then determines whether MP_l will rise initially?

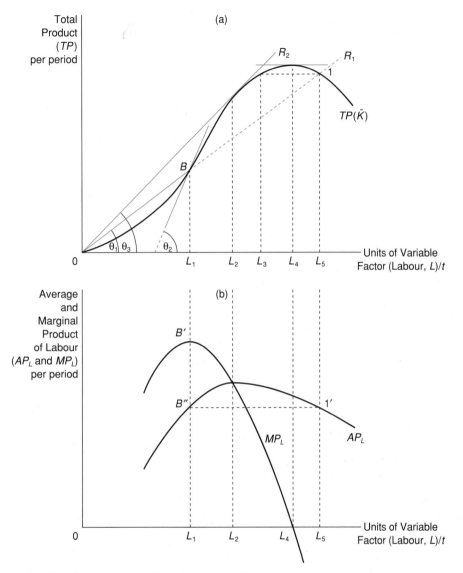

Figure 3.6 Deriving average and marginal product curves

The answer requires a return to the production function, as captured by the isoquant map in Figure 3.3(b). The initial section marked I is designed to correspond to the situation of increasing returns to scale and relates to the section of Figure 3.3(a), which is increasing at an increasing rate, i.e. the section before the point of inflection. In terms of Figure 3.3(b), given ΔQ is always 10,000 units, the value of MP_l turns on the size of ΔL distances 0-1, 1-2, 2-3, etc. These are associated with falling ΔLs, indicating that, in order to increase output proportionally, inputs can be increased less than proportionally and MP_l is rising. In the 'constant returns to scale' section, marked C, ratio 4-5 / 0-4 = 5-6 / 0-5 and distances 4-5 < 5-6 indicate $\Delta L_4 < \Delta L_5$ and, to increase output proportionally, inputs also have to be increased in the same proportion (as $\Delta L_4 < \Delta L_5$, MP_l is falling despite constant returns to scale, as explained below). In the 'decreasing returns to scale' section marked D ratios 6-7 / 0-6 > 7-8 / 0-7 > 8-9 / 0-8 along 0-R but output only increases each time by 10,000 units of good X. Distances 6-7 < 7-8 < 8-9 indicate that,

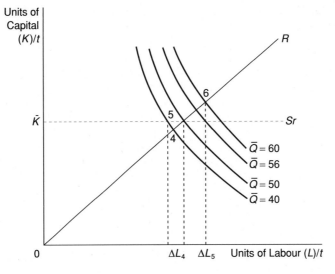

Figure 3.7

Constant returns to scale and falling marginal product in the short run

to increase output proportionally, inputs of labour have to be successively increased, so that $\Delta L_6 < \Delta L_7 < \Delta L_8$ and MP_l must be falling. In symbols:

$$\frac{\Delta Q}{\Delta L_1} > \frac{\Delta Q}{\Delta L_2} > \frac{\Delta Q}{\Delta L_3} > \frac{\Delta Q}{\Delta L_4} < \frac{\Delta Q}{\Delta L_5} < \frac{\Delta Q}{\Delta L_6} < \frac{\Delta Q}{\Delta L_7} < \frac{\Delta Q}{\Delta L_8} \tag{3.8}$$

But the careful reader will realise that it has already been made clear that scaling up is only available in the long run. As indicated above, increasing MP_l, decreasing MP_l and (briefly) constant MP_l cannot be directly associated with increasing, decreasing and constant returns to scale in the production function. To emphasise the reasoning, consider Figure 3.7, which recreates the constant-returns-to-scale section of Figure 3.3(b) (not to scale), although the ΔQs are identical between the isoquants and distance 4-5 < 5-6 because of scale constancy. Despite $\Delta L_5 > \Delta L_4$, it is not sufficient to secure 60,000 units of output per period (as labelled it gives only 56,000 units) in the short run when capital is fixed. Hence, it is clear that the horizontal distances between successive isoquants are not the same as ones along a ray like 0-R. In the short run a producer is constrained to expand output along $\bar{K}$-Sr and it can be seen that $\Delta L_4 < \Delta L_5$ and ΔQ is falling so that $\Delta Q/\Delta L_4 > \Delta Q/\Delta L_5$ and MP_l is falling, i.e. constant returns to scale in the long run is consistent with falling MP_l in the short run. Labour is not working with enough capital to achieve point 6 in Figure 3.7. The implication is that the rising section of MP_l in Figure 3.6(b) must come from a production function with significant increasing returns to scale in its early stages.

These are all physical relationships *specific* to the starting production function 'shape' illustrated as Figure 3.2. If a different shape had been used to describe the production mountain then all the subsequent diagrams would be altered, i.e. it is the production function specification that is fundamental. Working with physical information is often difficult; economists are always anxious to convert physical information into a common numeraire – money – so that addition, subtraction, multiplication, division, etc. can be accomplished.

3.2.2 From production information to cost information

The easiest way to begin this conversion is to recognise that profit maximisers must choose least-cost factor combinations with which to produce any output. To isolate cost information involves the use of an isocost curve (the parallel to the budget constraint in consumer theory)

$$C = rK + wL \tag{3.9}$$

A given total cost outlay C = rental price of capital (r) times the quantity of capital (K) + wage of labour (w) times the quantity of labour (L). Rearranging (3.9),

$$K = C/r - w/r \cdot L \tag{3.10}$$

So the slope of an isocost line is $dK/dL = -(w/r)$ or $-dK/dL = (w/r)$.

Least-cost production occurs when the isocost line is tangential to an isoquant, so that the ratio of the factor prices $w/r = (\partial Q/\partial L)/(\partial Q/\partial K) = -dK/dL = MRTS_{KL}$ = marginal rate of technical substitution between capital and labour.

More formal treatment

The objective is to minimise the cost of producing output $\overline{Q}$. That is, to minimise the cost function given by

$$C = rK + wL \tag{3.11}$$

subject to

$$\overline{Q} = Q(K, L) \tag{3.12}$$

Forming the Lagrangian:

$$\mathcal{L} = rK + wL + \lambda(\overline{Q} - Q(K, L)) \tag{3.13}$$

Setting the partial derivatives = 0,

$$\frac{\partial \mathcal{L}}{\partial L} = w - \lambda \frac{\partial Q}{\partial L} = 0 \tag{3.14}$$

$$\frac{\partial \mathcal{L}}{\partial K} = r - \lambda \frac{\partial Q}{\partial K} = 0 \tag{3.15}$$

$$\frac{\partial \mathcal{L}}{\partial \lambda} = \overline{Q} - Q(K, L) = 0 \tag{3.16}$$

Rearranging (3.14) and (3.15),

$$\frac{w}{\partial Q/\partial L} = \lambda = \frac{r}{\partial Q/\partial K} \tag{3.17}$$

so that

$$-dK/dL = w/r = (\partial Q/\partial L)/(\partial Q/\partial K) \equiv MP_l/MP_k \equiv MRTS_{KL} = \frac{-dK}{dL}\bigg|\overline{Q} \tag{3.18}$$

defines least-cost production.

See Appendix 3 for an illustration of duality theory as applied in the context of production functions and supply relationships.

Figure 3.8 indicates the connection between output level and cost as dictated by the above considerations. To make matters specific it is assumed that 300 units of output are required, so that $\overline{Q}_0 = 300$, the wage rate = £1 per unit per period and the rental price of

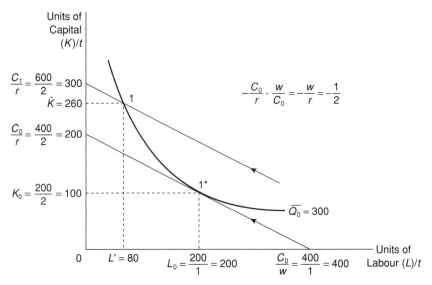

Figure 3.8 **From physical to cost information**

capital = £2 per unit per period. As indicated above and on the diagram, this makes the slope of the isocost line −1/2. The least-cost way to make 300 units of output is found by locating that isocost line with a slope −1/2 that is tangential to the isoquant $\overline{Q}_0$. This tangency occurs at point 1*, indicating that the least-cost solution involves $L_0 = 200$ units of labour per period and 100 units of capital. Hence the required total cost outlay to produce 300 units of output = 100 (= K_0) × £2 + 200 (= L_0) × £1 = £400 = C_0. Note: the intercepts of Figure 3.8 must be consistent with the total cost outlay being £400 everywhere along the isocost line. The *y*-axis intercept shows the maximum units of capital obtainable with a total cost outlay C_0 = £400, i.e. C_0/r = £400/2 = 200 units. The *x*-axis intercept shows the maximum units of labour obtainable with a total cost outlay C_0 = £400, i.e. C_0/w = £400/1 = 400 units. It would seem that all a profit-maximiser has to do is to meet the rule: $w/r = (\partial Q/\partial L)/(\partial Q/\partial K) \equiv MRTS_{KL}$ to choose input quantities for the profit-maximising level of output. However, the distinction between the short run and the long run again exerts influence. In the long run all factors are variable by definition and 100 units of capital and 200 units of labour would be employed per period. However, in the short run it would be fortuitous indeed if the existing fixed capital stock = 100 units.

In Figure 3.8 it happens that $\bar{K} = 260$ units is the existing capital and with the best will in the world the producer cannot adjust to point 1. The best that can be done is to adjust to the isocost line that cuts through the $\overline{Q}_0$ isoquant on the horizontal from K, i.e. point 1. As illustrated, this involves a total cost outlay C_1 = £600 and 260 units of capital and L' = 80 units of labour. The message is that, although in the long run 300 units of output can be made for £400, the least-cost way to make 300 units of output in the short run is £600.

Figure 3.9 allows this picture to be generalised. Although, at first sight, it looks daunting, it only contains information already discussed. The right-hand corner of the figure contains Figure 3.8 except for the illustrative numbers. The 'rugby ball' shape defines the so-called economic region of the production function illustrated by the isoquant map. It was noted above that, after some point, isoquants cease to have a negative slope and have a positive one (see Figure 3.3(a) and point units of labour L_4 and point 10 in Figure 3.3(b)). This means that the marginal product of labour (or the marginal product of capital) has become negative (see section of MP_l below L_4 in Figure 3.6(b)). The upper ridge

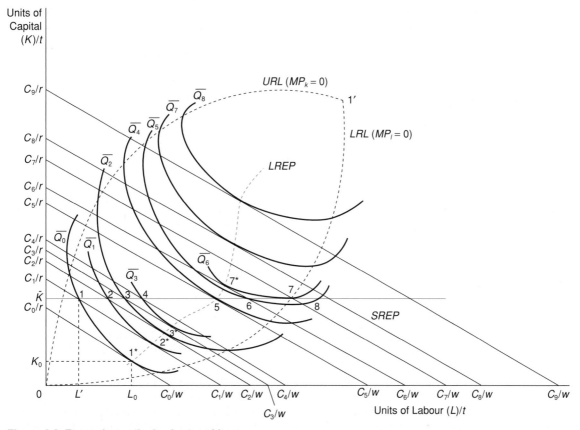

Figure 3.9 Expansion paths in short and long run

line (*URL*) is the locus of points where the marginal product of capital is zero ($MP_k = 0$), whereas the lower ridge line (*LRL*) is the locus of points where the marginal product of labour is zero ($MP_l = 0$). The ridge lines meet at the top of the production mountain, so that point 1 in Figure 3.2 corresponds to 1' in Figure 3.9. Note how everything comes back to Figure 3.2 – the production function really is fundamental. Successively, higher isocost lines involve greater total cost outlays $C_0 < C_1 < C_2 < C_4$ etc. and the factor price ratio (w/r) is captured in the slope of each isocost line. The fact that the factor price ratio (w/r) is assumed constant can be seen from the fact that all isocost lines are parallel to each other.

This is all well and good, but let's cut to the chase. The chase is that the long-run expansion path (labelled *LREP* in Figure 3.9) picks up all least-cost ways to make a given output level (see points 1*, 2*, 3* and 7* associated with output levels $\overline{Q_0}, \overline{Q_1}, \overline{Q_2}$ and $\overline{Q_6}$ and total-cost outlays C_0, C_1, C_2 and C_6). The expansion path is non-linear, indicating that the least-cost way to produce output in the long-run does not involve simply scaling up the inputs, as this would generate a linear long-run expansion path associated with homotheticity (see Figure 3.1). The shape of the long-run cost curve here is about 'economies of size' (not scale). As recognised above, it is only possible to move along the long-run expansion path by enacting a series of short runs. The long-run expansion path is an artefact of the infinite number of short-run situations.

In the short run, capital is fixed at $\bar{K}$ and the short-run expansion path is the horizontal line labelled *SREP*. It picks up all least-cost ways to make given output levels $\overline{Q_0}, \overline{Q_1}, \overline{Q_2}, \overline{Q_3}, \overline{Q_4}, \overline{Q_5}$ and $\overline{Q_6}$ given K at points 1, 2, 3, 4, 5, 6 and 7 and involves the total-cost outlays C_1, C_2, C_3, C_4, C_5, C_6 and C_7. Point 5 is where the long- and short-run expansion paths cross, indicating there is one point on the short-run total-cost curve that is also a point on the long-run total-cost curve. Information contained in figures like Figures 3.8 and 3.9 allows the construction of cost curves (see Equations (3.3) and (3.4)).

Using the information it would be possible to directly plot the long- and short-run total-cost curves from data such as:

Short-run total cost (SRTC)	Quantity of X per period	Long-run total cost (LRTC)
C_1 (£600)	Q_0 (300 units)	C_0 (£400)
C_2	Q_1	C_1
C_3	Q_2	C_2
C_4	Q_3	C_3
C_5	Q_4	C_5 (SRTC and LRTC equal)
C_7	Q_6	C_6

Conventionally, however, analysis is continued in a geometric way, beginning with the short run.

3.2.2.1 Short-run cost curves

In this and the next subsection the original shape in Figure 3.2 remains dominant. A distinction is made between total variable cost, associated with the use of the variable factor, and total fixed cost, associated with the use of the fixed factor (capital). Figure 3.10 shows the derivation of the total variable cost curve. Quadrant (I) plots the total product per period curve of Figure 3.6(a), rotated through 90°. Quadrant (II) contains a 45° line which simply 'throws' data on units of labour employed onto the x-axis of Quadrant (III) (which contains the wage line, where the angle marked w sets the wage per unit of labour input). Initially, the assumption of £1 per unit per period is retained, so that $w = 45°$ and the wage line has a slope of +1.

Quadrant (IV) contains the desired curve, produced by working from Quadrant (I) where total product per period is renamed quantity of X per period (Q_x/t) and becomes the x-axis of Quadrant (IV). The renaming is a matter of convention and does not signify anything fundamental. Moving initially horizontally and then vertically from Quadrant (I) through (II) puts the data on units of labour employed onto the x-axis of Quadrant (III), where the wage line converts the units of physical input to a money sum. That money sum is the total variable cost (TVC) of production per period and is recorded in Quadrant (IV). This cost depends on the level of output per period chosen in the short run. From point B in Figure 3.10 moving north identifies the output of good X per period. Moving west from point B through Quadrant (II) identifies the quantity of labour per period with Quadrant (III) using the wage line to convert that quantity into a money sum $£L_1$, allowing completion of the rectangle at point B′ in Quadrant (IV). Point B′ is one point on the total variable cost curve TVC. Repeating the exercise generates the continuous curve TVC.

The shape in Figure 3.2 has done its work, in that the curve produced is the one that would arise if Quadrant (I) were folded forward around the x-axis through 180°. Note that the negatively sloped section of TVC comes from the section of TP/t associated with a negative marginal product of labour (MP_l) (see Figure 3.6 and compare the connections between C and C′ and D and D′). Raising the wage from w (= £1) to w′ moves B′ north to B″, indicating a higher total variable cost for the associated output level. In general, however, the shape of the curve is preserved as TVC′ and that is what produces the U-shaped average variable-cost and average total-cost curves described below.

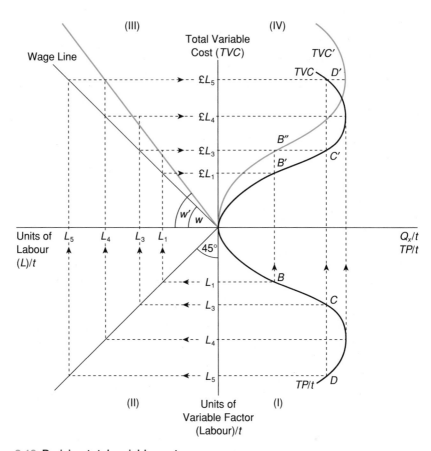

Figure 3.10 Deriving total variable costs

Fortunately, the total fixed cost (*TFC*) curve is easily dealt with, as it is simply a horizontal straight line located by multiplying $\bar{K}$ by the rental price of capital (*r*) (see Figure 3.11). The total fixed cost curve is horizontal because, by definition, it is independent of the level of output per period. This cost is inescapable in the short run.

Figure 3.12(a) puts the total variable cost curve and the total fixed cost together and vertically sums them to provide the Short-Run Total Cost curve, as illustrated. Although it is possible to work with 'total' curves, it is much easier to work with average and marginal

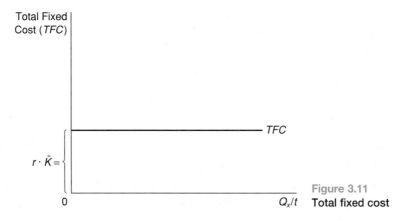

Figure 3.11
Total fixed cost

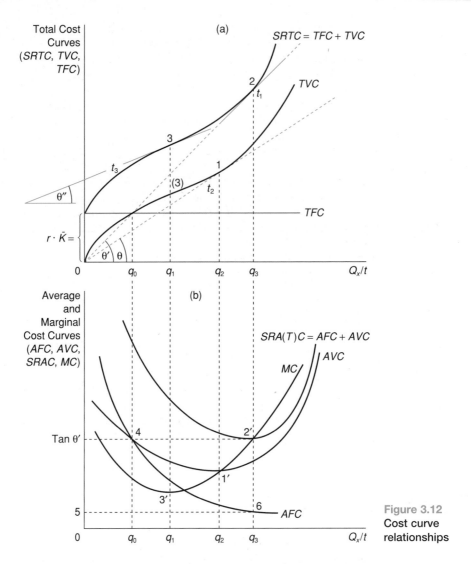

Figure 3.12
Cost curve
relationships

values. Figure 3.12(b) shows the shapes of the average fixed cost curve, the average variable cost curve, the (short-run) average total cost curve and the marginal cost curve. They have precise relationships to each other dictated by the shape of the relevant total curve:

Average fixed cost $AFC = TFC/Q_x/t = r\bar{K}/Q_x/t$

and, therefore, $AFC \times Q_x/t = TFC = r\bar{K}$ (a curve is required that has a constant product under it, i.e. a rectangular hyperbola in Figure 3.12(b) where area 0-5-6-q_3 = area 0-Tanθ'-4-q_0 = $r\bar{K}$).

Average variable cost $AVC = TVC/Q_x/t$.

(Recall, once again, to establish an average value look at the angles formed by rays from the origin to the relevant curve. Here it can be seen that angle θ' is greater than angle θ and AVC is falling to a minimum – point 1' in Figure 3.12(b) associated with level of output q_2 and point 1 in part (a) of the figure. It follows that AVC rises.)

Short-run average total cost ($SRATC$) (shortened to AC below) is $SRTC/Q_x/t$
$= TFC/Q_x/t + TVC/Q_x/t = AFC + AVC$.

(Here, it can be seen that the angle θ' is as low as the angle formed by a ray from the origin to the curve will get. It follows that $SRATC$ is falling to a minimum (point $2'$ in Figure 3.12(b) associated with level of output q_3 and point 2 in part (a) of the figure. Thereafter, $SRATC$ rises. Note how AVC must vertically close on $SRATC$ as AFC is falling throughout its length.)

Marginal cost (MC) is the cost of an additional unit of output per period and is defined by $\Delta TC/\Delta Q_x/t$ and $\Delta TVC/\Delta Q_x/t$, since $SRTC$ and $SRTVC$ are simply vertically displaced by the constant TFC and, at each Q_x/t, the slopes of $SRTC$ and $SRTVC$ are the same. Alternatively, $\Delta TFC/\Delta Q_x/t$ is zero. In terms of 'the quick ways' to establish relationships, it is a question of looking at the tangents (t_1 and t_2) to $SRTC$ or $SRTVC$. These fall everywhere to the point of inflection at point 3 or (3) and therefore MC is falling to a minimum (point $3'$ in Figure 3.12(b) associated with level of output q_1. Thereafter MC rises. Note how MC must cut AVC and $SRATC$ at their lowest points as the tangent to the TVC curve and $SRTC$ curve coincide with the angles formed by the rays namely θ and θ'. That MC is cutting from below can be seen from the point of inflection tangent (t_3) angle θ''. Observation makes it clear that that angle is smaller than the ones formed by the rays to point 3 and (3) from the origin (not drawn) and, therefore, MC must be below $SRATC$ and AVC at that point.

The importance of accuracy of all these points can be seen from the fact that many texts put these diagrams on separate pages! The ray associated with angle θ' in Figure 3.12(a) has been selected to show the need for care in that AFC, AVC and minimum $SRATC$ all have the same monetary value $\tan \theta'$ in Figure 3.12(b). While this may look a little fussy there is no alternative, in that the results discussed below rely on accuracy if they are to be established with minimal appeal to mathematics. The U-shaped cost curves set up here are vital to the neoclassical theory of the firm and can also be used to establish an introduction to the notion of duality in production. In symbols the concepts above are:

$$AFC = TFC/Q_x/t = r \cdot K/Q_x/t = r(K/Q_x/t) = r(1/AP_k);$$

i.e. average fixed cost is determined by the rental price of capital multiplied by the inverse of the average product of the fixed factor (capital);

$$AVC = TVC/Q_x/t = w \cdot L/Q_x/t = w(1/AP_l);$$

i.e. average variable cost is determined by the wage rate multiplied by the inverse of the average product of the variable factor (labour);

$$SRATC = AFC + AVC;$$

$$MC = \Delta T(V)C/\Delta Q_x/t = w \cdot \Delta L/\Delta Q_x/t = w(1/MP_l);$$

i.e. marginal cost is determined by the wage rate multiplied by the inverse of the marginal product of the variable factor (labour).

This, once again, makes it clear that it is the physical world of the production function that is driving these key relationships. Suppose, however, that the production function is unknown. Is there any way forward? The answer that is central to duality theory is 'yes'. If cost data are available and profit-maximising behaviour is assumed then the data imply what the production function must be. For example, from the above $AP_l = w/AVC$ and $MP_l = w/MC$, so that duality says if cost concepts are derived from physical relationships in production then physical relationships in production can, with suitable assumptions, be derived from information on cost concepts.

3.2.2.2 Long-run cost curves
All that remains is to establish the relationship between short- and long-run cost curves. This can be done by recognising, once more, that the long run is an artefact of the

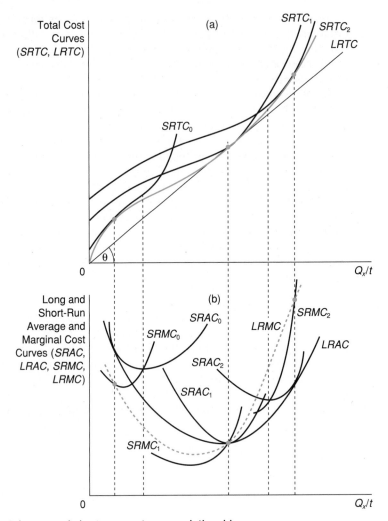

Figure 3.13 Long- and short-run cost curve relationships

infinite number of short-run situations, each built around a different value of short-run capital stock. Figure 3.13(a) shows the long-run total cost (*LRTC*) curve as the envelope of the short-run total-cost curves (three representative ones are illustrated, $SRTC_0$, $SRTC_1$ and $SRTC_2$). The basic shape was determined previously at Figure 3.5(c) and Figure 3.10. The *LRTC* curve has no *y*-axis intercept as, in the long run, all factors are variable and therefore the curve emanates from the origin. The no-intercept effect is achieved by beginning at zero or, if output requires both inputs, a very, very small fixed level of capital stock that can effectively be treated as zero. Other *SRTC* curves have a *y*-axis intercept reflecting the cost of the given quantity of fixed factor.

Figure 3.13(b) records the associated short-run average-cost curves and the relevant short-run marginal-cost curves. The long-run average-cost curve is the envelope of all the short-run average-cost curves with one point on each average-cost curve being one point on the long-run average-cost curve. Only one short-run average-cost curve ($SRAC_1$) has its minimum point on the long-run average-cost curve and that is the minimum point of the long-run average-cost curve. The long-run marginal-cost curve is also a composite from the short-run counterparts. It is made up of the points on the short-run marginal-cost curves that are on a vertical line to the single point on each short-run average-cost curve that is on the long-run average-cost curve.

Overall, the long-run picture is a bigger version of a single short-run picture as set up by the production mountain in Figure 3.2. Up to the base point of *LRAC* economies of size obtain in that the average cost per unit of output is falling. Beyond the base point of *LRAC* diseconomies of size obtain in that the average cost per unit of output is rising. As recognised above, for physical production relationships it is only possible to move along the long-run cost curve by enacting a series of short runs, which involves using different amounts of capital stock that become fixed in the short run. The long-run cost curves are an artefact of the infinite number of short-run situations.

3.2.2.3 Economies of scope

There is another 'economies' term that requires introduction if the standard production/cost ground is to be covered. This is 'economies of scope'. So far, the discussion has been about the production of a single good *X* per period. But it would make sense to consider the production of more than one good by a firm, as this is what is typically observed. For this to be attractive to a profit-maximiser the cost of producing a quantity of good *X* per period in isolation must be more than producing that same quantity alongside a given quantity of good *Y* per period. This situation describes economies of scope and is captured more formally as:

$$C(Q_x, Q_y) < C(Q_x, 0) + C(0, Q_y)$$

where *C* = costs. In short, a bodily shift downwards in cost curves may arise if a firm increases the scope of its operations to include good *Y* as well as good *X* in its production activities (suggesting a cross-product or cross-output effect on costs).

This is likely to arise where there is underlying similarity in the inputs and/or technology in the production of both good *X* and good *Y*, e.g. circuit boards, skilled electronic engineers. For the moment, the presentation continues with the assumption of a single-product firm producing good *X*.

3.2.3 Costs and rules of output choice

Homer Simpson's three phrases to get you through life are – 'cover for me', 'good idea, boss' and 'it was like that when I got here'. The advice of Homer's boss at the nuclear plant, Mr Burns, for those responsible for decision making in a firm would be: 'produce where *MC* = *MR*', 'smile if *P* > *AC*' and 'cry if *P* < *AVC*'. These three golden rules answer three big questions for a decision maker: What output per period shall I choose? Am I making a profit? Should I stay in business? The logic of this advice is as follows.

3.2.3.1 'Produce where *MC* = *MR*'

This is the rule for profit maximisation. Economic profit is the difference between total revenue (*TR*) and total cost (*TC*):

$$\pi = TR - TC \tag{3.19}$$

$TR = P(Q) \cdot Q$, where *P* is product price and *Q* is output quantity per period.

The first-order condition to maximise profit is that the first derivative of profit with respect to output should be zero. So that:

$$\frac{d\pi}{dQ} = P + \frac{QdP}{dQ} - \frac{dTC}{dQ} = 0 \tag{3.20}$$

$$P + \frac{QdP}{dQ} = \frac{dTC}{dQ} \tag{3.21}$$

In Chapter 2 it was established that the first term is marginal revenue (*MR*, the additional revenue that arises from the sale of one more unit of output per period). The second term is marginal cost (*MC*). To profit-maximise the producer must produce where *MR* = *MC*.

There is also the second-order condition to consider in order to guarantee that profit is being maximised and not minimised. It is that the second derivative is negative:

$$\frac{\mathrm{d}MR}{\mathrm{d}Q} - \frac{\mathrm{d}MC}{\mathrm{d}Q} < 0 \qquad (3.22)$$

or

$$\frac{\mathrm{d}MR}{\mathrm{d}Q} < \frac{\mathrm{d}MC}{\mathrm{d}Q} \qquad (3.23)$$

That is, the rate of change of *MR* must be less than the rate of change of *MC*. If *MR* is falling as *Q* increases this condition will be met if *MC* is rising, constant or falling less quickly than *MR*.

What this means is illustrated in Figure 3.14. The total revenue curve is a ray from the origin, so that marginal revenue is a constant value at tan θ in Figure 3.14(b). With the initial total cost curve depicted as *TC*, the first-order conditions *MR* = *MC* are met at both points 1′ and 2′ in Figure 3.14(b), corresponding to points 1 and 2 in Figure 3.14(a) and output levels per period of q_0 and q_5. However, at point 1 the second-order condition is not met. An economic loss is made equal to the vertical distance between *TC* and *TR* (1-3) in panel (a) and rectangle tan θ-4-5-1′ in panel (b) (the slope of *MC* (–ve) is smaller than the slope of *MR* = 0). At point 2 the second-order condition is met and an economic profit is made, equal to the vertical distance between *TC* and *TR* (2-6) in panel (a) and rectangle tan θ-2′-8-7 in panel (b) (the slope of *MC* (+ve) is greater than the slope of *MR* = 0). Therefore, output level q_5 is the profit-maximising one.

3.2.3.2 'Smile if *P* > *AC*'

With *MR* constant it means that each unit of output increases *TR* by the same amount and that amount is the price (*P*) of a unit of good *X*. In Figure 3.14(b), with *P* > *AC* by vertical distance 8-2′, there is reason for a producer (but not a consumer) to smile. Once it is recognised that the cost curve construction involved paying labour a wage (*w*) and capital its rental price (*r*), then all the payments necessary to ensure these factors are supplied to the production of good *X* have been made. It follows that the economic profit described above is a pure surplus – an unnecessary payment paid by consumers and received by producers. To the extent that neoclassical microeconomics is set up to enact the interests of consumers (i.e. consumer sovereignty) they want to wipe the smile off Mr Burns's face. An implication of this reasoning is that if total costs were *TC*′ in Figure 3.14(a), so that *AC*′ in Figure 3.14(b) became relevant, *P* = *AC*′ and, although economic profit would equal zero, capital and labour would still be allocated to good *X*. It is production 'without a smile' that consumers desire.

3.2.3.3 'Cry if *P* < *AVC*'

So far, it has been established that profit-maximisers must choose the level of output where *MR* = *MC* as long as the latter is rising. Are there any further qualifications to this statement? The answer is 'yes'. It must also be the case that *P* > *AVC*.

In Figure 3.14(b) assume *TC* and *AC* still apply and imagine the *MR* = *P* line falling from its position through 2′ and 1′. It has been established at 2′ (and output q_5) that economic profit is made. As *MR* = *P* falls, the decision-maker will choose quantities of output as dictated by the location of *MC* and the economic profit rectangle will be eroded. When *MR* = *P* cuts through point 9 (and output quantity q_4 per period is chosen)

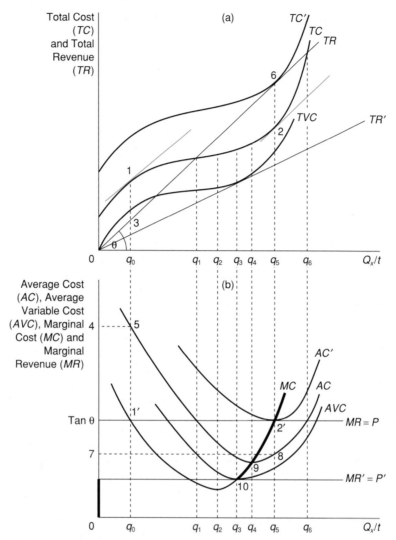

Figure 3.14 **Profit-maximising behaviour**

economic profit is zero. Between points 9 and 10, $P < AC$ indicates that short-run economic losses are made – but $P > AVC$. This means AVC (the escapable costs associated with the variable factor labour) are covered and partial recovery of the inescapable fixed costs rK is possible. It is sensible to keep producing in the short run when, by definition, at least one factor is fixed (losses cannot be sustained period in, period out) as all the associated fixed cost would be lost if output were reduced to zero. Fixed costs provide an upper bound to short-run losses when output is zero.

If $P < AVC$ then escapable variable costs are not being covered and losses are greater than the fixed costs of production. In such circumstances, losses are minimised by producing no output and employing no labour, i.e. shutting down. In short $P' = AVC$ at point 10 with output level q_3 defines the shutdown point for this economic process.

The message is clear, a profit-maximising producer who must accept a given $MR = P$ situation will choose the level of output per period that equates MR with MC as long as $MR = P > AVC$. That is, output supply (the chosen value for Q_x/t) for a price-taking profit-maximiser tracks the y-axis (zero output) up to $MR' = P'$ and then MC above AVC and hence the thickened lines. But what conditions will make a producer a price-taker–quantity-adjuster? The actor 'perfect competition' would say 'this is where I come in'.

3.3 Perfect competition

The set of assumptions commonly employed for perfect competition varies from text to text. For simplicity of exposition, the following list is restricted to seven assumptions:

1) There must be sufficient buyers and sellers of the good X that no individuals think that they have any impact on the market by virtue of their own actions. Contrary to popular claim, this may not require a very large number of actual buyers and sellers. The condition is met by the number at which the individual seller, or the individual supplier, feels powerless, by their own actions, to have impact on the market (i.e. it is not about an objective number of buyers and sellers).

2) The second condition is that of a homogeneous product. One producer's output of units of good X must be indistinguishable from the output of units of good X of other producers. In such circumstances 'brand loyalty' is ruled out. Assumptions 1 and 2 together are sufficient to make an individual producer a so-called price-taker, which means there is a price of a unit of good X which is a given for the individual. It means that a producer can sell as much or as little as is desired at that price. In an earlier terminology, price is said to be parametric, to indicate that price is a parameter of this particular productive context (it is 'given' – something that it is impossible to do anything about). The importance of these two assumptions is that it makes the demand condition that the individual producer faces a simple horizontal straight line. This idea was employed in Figure 3.14 and is illustrated in isolation in Figure 3.15. The two total revenue curves in panel (a) are straight lines emanating from the origin because total revenue is simply price times quantity and price is everywhere a given constant at two illustrated values, $P < P'$. The lines $AR = P \cdot Q/Q = P = dTR/dQ = MR$ and $AR' = P' \cdot Q/Q = P' = dTR'/dQ = MR'$ are two demand conditions rather than the demand curve for good X. The demand curve for good X is the market demand curve for good X and comprises the horizontal sum of all individuals' demand curves for good X. It generally has the 'downward-sloping to the right' characteristic. The demand condition is a construct that each individual producer, or firm, in the perfectly competitive market responds to (e.g. it might be £10 per unit for P and £5 per unit for P').

3) Freedom of entry and exit into the industry. Firms that are not currently in the industry must not find it costly to join in the industry and firms that are currently in the industry must not find it costly to exit the industry.

4) The fourth assumption (which drives the decisions of this skeletal firm) is profit maximisation. The importance of this condition was elaborated above. It immediately locates the point where production will take place, because profit maximisation involves following the rule that $MR = MC$ provided MC is rising.

5) The world is absent of government intervention, so there are no tariffs in operation, no quotas, no subsidies, etc. This assumption helps give the perfectly competitive industry and firms a frictionless world in which to operate.

The assumptions 1–5 are usually sufficient to describe what is called *pure* competition. Two further assumptions are required to translate pure to *perfect* competition.

6) Perfectly mobile factors of production. This condition concerns resources, or inputs, available to firms. It amounts to assuming perfect competition in the markets for the factors, land, labour and capital. These factors of production are assumed to be available

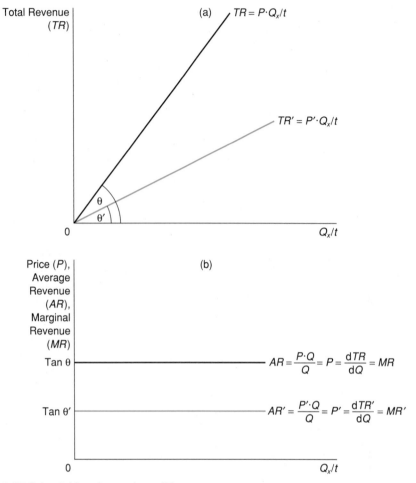

Figure 3.15 **Price-taking demand conditions**

at a price per unit that is the same for all firms. All producers have common access to the same factors on the same terms (offering to pay less than the 'going rate' would cause all factor input to move away from you).

7) The final assumption is a big one, namely perfect knowledge. There is no uncertainty involved in the model, all the relevant prices are known for the current period and in the future. It is difficult to make the idea of an entrepreneur making choices realistic once this assumption has been made (see Wiseman 1989). Indeed, if all future prices are known, then by definition there is nothing that any entrepreneurial decision-maker can do in the current time period that can have an impact on the future. It is a very restrictive assumption and it means that the choice of the best plan and the decisions taken in any firm never results in an unexpected outcome. In later revisions of the theory of the firm, theorists have sought to attack all of the assumptions above, but particularly this one, i.e. perfect knowledge.

As noted above, economic profit is an important term. It differs from accounting profit. In the construction of the average cost curve, labour L received wages (w), and capital K received its reward (r), a rental price, so that any earnings above average cost was a surplus. It follows that economic profit (π) was a payment over and above that necessary to keep that amount of capital and that amount of labour in the industry. Key distinctions in understanding the theory of the perfectly competitive firm are:

- what is happening at the level of the representative firm and what is happening in the industry;
- what is happening in the short run and what is happening in the long run.

3.3.1 The representative firm and industry in the short run

If a representative firm is profit-maximising and a price-taker, its short-run supply curve will be important when identifying the output the producer will choose. Analysis detailed above makes it clear that output is dictated by the condition that MC must exceed AVC.

For clarity this is emphasised in Figure 3.16. Given the U-shaped cost curve structure (developed above), it is possible to trace out the way in which a profit-maximising individual representative firm responds to different prices. At P_1 the firm would face a situation where $P_1 = MR_1$, and would produce at q_1. Given that P_1 is greater than AC_1 at that level of output, the firm would be making economic profit (= distance 1-2). At $P_2 = MR_2$ the profit-maximising firm produces at q_2. Here $P_2 = AC$ at point 3 and no economic profit is being made, as is evident from the location of $\pi(P_2)$ (but, remember, all costs are being covered). At $P_3 = MR_3$ the firm must produce at q_3 and, as P_3 is less than AC (see the vertical distance between points 4 and 5) the firm is making an economic loss.

In Figure 3.16, the price $P_3 = MR_3$ has been strategically chosen to show that average variable cost is being covered. As justified above, the point labelled 4 is the shut-down point of the firm. When profit is maximised with $P_3 = MR_3$ the loss exactly equals the value of the fixed costs as $AC - AVC = AFC$ then TFC = distance 4-5 $\times q_3$ = distance 6-7. In the short run, each firm will equate (whatever the price equals marginal revenue turns

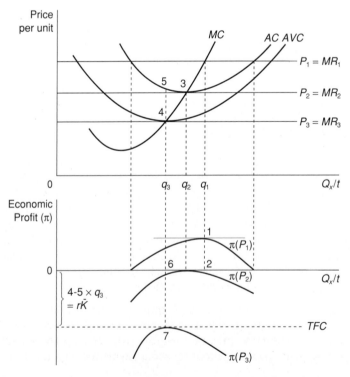

Figure 3.16
Price-taking output
adjusting

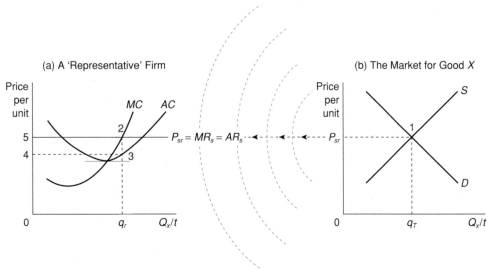

Figure 3.17 **Short-run profit maximisation**

out to be) with its marginal cost curve, as long as that price exceeds the average variable-cost curve. Therefore, it can be said that the individual firm's short-run supply curve is simply a trace-out of its marginal-cost curve above its average variable costs.

The market demand curve for any good X is the horizontal sum of the individual demand curves for good X. The market supply curve in the short-run competitive indus-try is a similar construction. It is the horizontal sum of the individual marginal costs of firms that make up the perfectly competitive industry as long as the marginal cost curve is above the average variable cost curve. The two together (the two horizontal sums) give the industry demand curve and supply curve (labelled D and S in Figure 3.17(b)). It is the intersection of these two curves at point 1 that provide the short-run parametric price P_{sr}.

Because of assumption 1, nobody feels that they have any impact on the location of the market supply or market demand curve and the price to them is as if it comes as an announcement out of the blue, say a radio message from afar. It is, by definition, sufficiently distant from them that they see it as a given and simply react to it. In the short run, the representative profit-maximising firm then simply, as in Figure 3.17(a), equates P_{sr} the parametric price with its marginal cost curve and produces that quantity, q_r in Figure 3.17(a).

Depending on what that price is, it is possible for the firm to be making economic profits, or economic losses, or, by chance, simply breaking even covering all costs. As illustrated, it is economic profits equal to area 2-3-4-5 that are made. The output of the representative firm, q_r, when summed over all the firms in the industry must, by construction, give industry or market output q_T in panel (b). Another illustration could equally well have been chosen. This situation of economic profits being made is not stable – for what will happen in the long run?

3.3.3 The representative firm and industry in the long run

By definition, in the short run there is at least one fixed factor. Here (as usual) this is the quantity of capital K (which may be the size of the factory, the number of machines being employed, etc.). This assumption could equally have related to labour as to capital.

However, as noted above, it is thought more realistic that the assumption applies to capital, rather than labour or land. However, in the long run, by definition all factors are variable. Recall the period of temporal time that the short and the long run concepts refer to varies from production process to production process. It is not an actual amount of time. It is simply that amount of time, which, by definition, is required to make all factors variable. In some industries this may be a matter of weeks and in others it may be a matter of years. It is a reflection of technology.

The outcome in the short run, where the representative firm makes economic profit, is not sustainable in the long run. To profit-maximise, all firms must build a plant (employ an amount of capital) consistent with the base of their long-run average-cost curve (because that way they will make costs of production as low as they can be and increase their chances of making more profit). By the same token, the assumption of freedom of entry and exit into the firm (assumption 3 above) now comes into play. As individuals are knowledgeable, those outside the good-X industry can see economic profit (a surplus) being made, and they will enter that industry. If they enter, their marginal cost curves above average variable costs come in – to be part of the horizontal sum yielding the market supply curve. This process will push the supply curve bodily to the right and, other things equal, the parametric price will fall.

The effect of these two pincer movements (firms adjusting to the base of their long run average cost curve and the effect of entry) is illustrated in Figure 3.18. The price set by the intersection at point 1 in panel (b) to P_e (e for equilibrium) is pushed to the point where it cuts the long-run average-cost curve at its base (see point 1′). At that point short-run average-cost curve will be at its base; long-run marginal-cost curve will run through at the base point, as will the short-run marginal-cost curve.

This dictates a situation for the representative firm such that long-run marginal cost equals short-run marginal cost equals marginal revenue equals price equals average revenue equals short-run average cost equals long-run average cost (for example, they might all be £8 per unit). The first terms relate to conditions that stem from the assumption of profit maximisation, whereas the later set of terms relate to the condition that guarantees that no economic profit will be made, i.e. the entry and exit mechanism. The output of the representative firm, q_e, when summed over all the firms in the industry must, by construction, give industry or market output q_{eT} in panel (b).

Had a firm that was making economic losses in the short run, been illustrated in Figure 3.17, exits would have been taking place. There would have been fewer marginal cost curves in the horizontal sum and supply would shift bodily to the left, raising the price to a point where no profit is being made. The equilibrium illustrated in Figure 3.18 would once again arise.

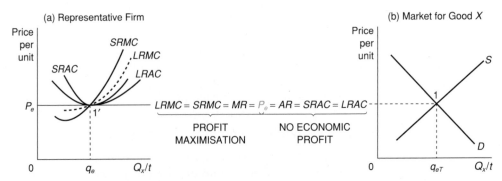

Figure 3.18 **Long-run equilibrium in perfect competition**

The long-run equilibrium has a number of very attractive properties:

(i)   The first is that cost structure for the production of good X is at as low a level as it can possibly be.
(ii) Second, each firm operates with a plant of optimal scale, that is, one whose base point is on the minimum point of the long-run average-cost curve (i.e. plant is being operated at its economic capacity).
(iii) Third, price is as low as it can be, as it covers only the cost of the additional unit of output. Price is set such that it only equals the marginal cost of production of good X.
(iv) Fourth, as has been elaborated above, no economic profit is being made.

In effect, this is the 'ideal' production set-up for the consumer. It is a 'consumer sovereignty' world. In a world in which real resources are scarce, the consumer can expect no more than this with respect to the production of X and hence perfect competition is known as the 'ideal' market form. It is the benchmark market form that allows welfare economics to have purchase as an evaluative device.

3.3.4 Comparative-static responses – long-run industry supply

The comparative statics of this model, which is essentially the mechanics that covers how you move from one equilibrium to the next, are also attractive to consumers. The market economy is a consumer-driven world.

The assumption made in Figure 3.19 is that there has been a change of preference in favour of good X, so that the market demand curve moves to the right (D to D' in panel (b)). The question is, 'what happens now?'

As D increases to D' in the market (or very short-run) period, all the adjustment is price adjustment (because you can, by definition, only trade the existing stock of good X, q_{T0}). Price simply rises from P_0 to P_M (point 1 to 2 in panel (b) associated with 2' in panel (a)). In the short run, existing firms expand their output along their marginal cost curve from 4' to 3' in panel (a) with quantity rising q_0 to q_1. In sum, this represents a movement along the existing market supply curve S, from point 1 to point 3 (where price is now equal to P_1 and quantity has risen to q_{T1} in panel (b)). At point 3 and price P_1 (which is greater than the initial price P_0), existing firms have to be making economic profit (see area 3'-5-6-7 in panel (a)). With freedom of entry this will all be competed away by new entrants, so that when you sum the new set of marginal cost curves it generates a supply

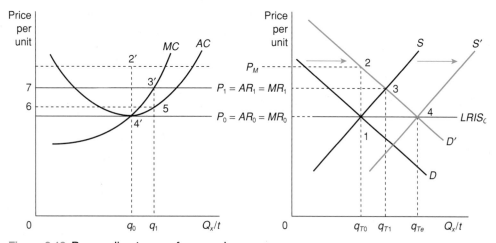

Figure 3.19 Responding to a preference change

curve S' and equilibrium is re-established at 4 in panel (b). Price P_0 results in quantity q_0 for the representative firm and quantity q_{Te} for the industry. As the original price P_0 has been re-established, it is the case that the long-run industry supply curve (*LRISc* derived by joining points 1 and 4 in panel (b)) is horizontal. This is the constant-cost industry case. Intuitively, this is what might be expected to happen. Are there reasons for doubting this?

The shape of the long-run average-cost curve above was dependant on the level of output chosen per period, with technology and factor prices taken as given (see Figure 3.13 and Equation (3.3)). The U-shape that was generated reflected economies of size. More accurately, these were internal economies of size. The word 'internal' is appropriate, because it was about what happens if individual firms expand their output in isolation. However, if all firms expand output together then the fixed technology and fixed factor prices assumptions may no longer be valid.

Given this, it is possible to have the increasing cost industry case where the long-run industry supply curve has a positive slope (see Figure 3.20(a)). If point 4 (and price P_1) is the final equilibrium, it must be the case that cost structures have risen as (by definition) no economic profit can be made in the long run. Why then have cost structures risen? It must be because there were external pecuniary or real (technological) diseconomies of size. These are external to the firms but internal to the good-X industry. A pecuniary diseconomy is one that is monetary and the most obvious candidate is that, in trying to increase the output of good X, demanding greater amounts of labour and capital results in factor prices being driven up. Alternatively, there may be an external real diseconomy of size such that technology is, in some way, adversely affected when all firms try to expand. The production function becomes less 'productive'.

The decreasing-cost industry arises where the long-run industry supply curve has a negative slope (see Figure 3.20(b)). This time the price quantity adjustments result in point 4 and $P_1 < P_0$, a lower price than the initial one. As intimated above, this must indicate either the presence of an external pecuniary economy of size such that, for some reason, factor prices are falling and/or external real economies of size such that, when all firms expand, technology is enhanced.

The punchline is that, in perfect competition, mechanisms exist such that a full long-run equilibrium is always re-established and all the attractive attributes outlined above obtain. The consumer is always in charge. Consumers have had a change of preference and that change of preference has been met in the best way possible as far as consumers are concerned.

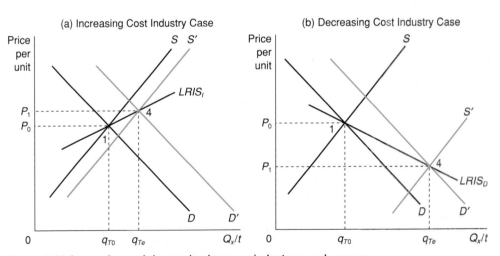

Figure 3.20 **Increasing and decreasing long-run industry supply curves**

A number of important points can now be highlighted:

1) The firm's supply curve is the marginal cost curve above the average variable cost curve;
2) The short-run industry supply curve is the horizontal sum of the marginal cost curves of the incumbent firms (above AVC);
3) The long-run industry supply curve is the horizontal sum of the bases of the long-run average cost curves when all pecuniary and real external economies and diseconomies of size have worked themselves out.

In the next chapter the application of the principles developed here is illustrated. In order to have an understanding of the welfare conclusions drawn a further concept is required.

3.4 Producer surplus and supply

A parallel concept to consumer surplus can be established when analysing the short-run welfare of producers. In Figure 3.21 the supply curve labelled 0-S indicates the minimum price that must be paid to cover the supply cost of successive units of the good per period. (As an exercise use the ray-slope method at, say, point b to confirm to yourself this supply curve has a elasticity of supply equal to 1 and all straight-line supply curves emanating from the origin also have unity elasticity.) In Figure 3.21 the minimum supply price for unit 1 is £2. For the second unit the minimum that is required by the producer is £4, and so on.

For each unit the market price that is paid is £10. Therefore, for the second unit the producer requires £4 but receives £10. For the third unit the producer requires £6 but receives £10. Again, there is a surplus, but this time it is surplus received by the producer. Producer surplus can be estimated by the triangle 0-P_1-b. In the example here, the producer surplus is £25.

To produce 5 units of the good the producer requires a minimum of 0-b-q_1 but receives in revenue 0-P_1-b-q_1 when the market price is P_1. When the market price increases, producer surplus increases. In Figure 3.21 when price increases from P_1 to P_2 the producer receives area α more for the 5 units that are produced. There is also an incentive for the producer to increase output. On these additional units the producer will receive area β more than the costs of production of the additional units per period. It follows that the producer surplus that is received has increased by area P_1-P_2-a-b (i.e. by $\alpha + \beta$).

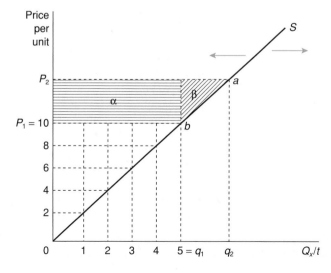

Figure 3.21

Supply and producer surplus

More formal treatment

It is evident that producer surplus is the difference between the market price received by the producer per unit per period and the price per unit the producer would have been willing to supply each unit per period. Putting the supply function in inverse form $P = f(Q)$ and using Figure 3.21, make the relevant price per unit P_2 and quantity per period q_2. So, as described above, triangle $0\text{-}P_2\text{-}a$ corresponds to the definition of producer surplus when output is q_2 per period. In terms of the definite integral with respect to quantity[1] producer surplus (PS) is:

$$PS = \int_0^{q_2} [P_2 - f(Q)] \, dQ = \int_0^{q_2} P_2 dQ - \int_0^{q_2} f(Q) \, dQ = P_2 q_2 - \int_0^{q_2} f(Q) \, dQ \qquad (3.25)$$

This is a more formal way of saying producer's surplus is the area representing payment received by the producer output level q_2 and the area under the supply curve up to q_2. Careful readers will have noticed the use of the words 'analysing the short-run welfare of producers' in the opening sentence to this section. This is because in the long run (in terms of the presentation here) there can be no producer surplus. Units of input are all assumed to be identical and the long-run industry supply curve was defined as the horizontal sum of the bases of the long-run average-cost curves when all pecuniary and real external economies and diseconomies of size have worked themselves out. Given this, the payment received per unit by producer in the long run is the minimum they require to produce that unit and there can be no surplus. In presentations where some producer has access to a superior surplus generating input, e.g. a 'great' manager, to keep that input from going to a competitor, the producer must pay that input an extra amount that reflects the input's superiority. So, whilst the superior input enjoys an extra payment known as 'economic rent', in the long run the producer can have no advantage in that once rent is paid zero economic profit is made. That is, no producer surplus obtains.

3.5 Challenge: Can marginal cost be objective?

'You never know the cost of something until you pay for it' is a common dictum, which has some correspondence with the economist's notion of opportunity cost. In some ways it is illuminating because it captures aspects of the role of cost in choice. First, 'you never know' makes it clear that at the time you make the decision you find yourself in an uncertain situation in which your expectations or imagining about your future guide your actions. Second, implicit in the phrase 'until you pay for it' is a notion that your expectations may not be fulfilled and the costs you bear as a result of your choice may be greater or less than expected. These considerations suggest at least four possible opportunity cost formulations. Table 3.1 contains these possibilities. The 'two by two' framework rests on: (1) the time when opportunity cost is considered (before or after the event); and (2) the agent formulating opportunity cost (the individual decision-taker or another anonymous unspecified observer). The fact of choice, as described above, most closely corresponds to the opportunity cost illustrated in part 4 of the table.

Casual empiricism (i.e. looking at a selection of texts) indicates how economists define opportunity costs in slightly different fashions. The following examples not only provide

---

1. Producer's surplus could also have been established by integrating with respect to price.

Table 3.1 **Notions of opportunity cost formulation**

Time Agent	Ex ante *(contemplating a choice about to be made)*	Ex post *(reflecting on a past choice)*
Individual decision taker (*I*) him- or herself	**1** What is the best anticipated next best alternative should *I* decide to choose activity *X*? Note that the next best alternative (the rejected plan) will never be chosen and therefore never enacted. It must always remain unobservable, a speculation in the individual's mind.	**2** Given that *I* have completed activity *X*, how do *I* now imagine what the next best alternative might have been? Note that the individual may be expected to view the incurred opportunity cost differently because their knowledge and perceptions have been altered by experiencing activity *X*. However, as the text points out, there are reasons to doubt this expectation.
Anonymous individual (economist?)	**3** How would '*I*' as a rational 'economic man' evaluate the next best alternative to committing resource inputs to activity *X*? As we are all human individuals we should have something in common and be able to imagine the relevant alternatives to activity *X*. This is also a 'scenario' that does not take place.	**4** Given that activity *X* took such and such amount of time and other resource inputs, what uses might they have been put to? Only if the outside observer has correctly estimated all the resource inputs etc. will 4 correspond to 3. Possibilities 4 and 3 should approach each other to the extent that past observations improve predictions.

some formal definitions of interest in themselves, but also illustrate some of the distinctions made above:

Earlier vintage:

'the cost of doing or having something is the value of one's best alternative forgone when a choice is made' (McKenzie and Tullock 1981: 11).

'The idea of "opportunity cost" is that in order to have whatever you decide to have you must *give up the opportunity to have the something else you also wanted*' (Bowden 1977: 6).

'The [opportunity cost] concept holds that the cost of a good is measured in terms of the unproduced goods that could have been produced with the inputs used to produce the good in question' (Garb 1981: 111–12).

'Opportunity cost is defined as the highest valued alternative that had to be sacrificed for the option that was chosen' (Miller 1982: 6).

Later vintage:

'Opportunity cost: The cost of using resources, including time, in their best alternative foregone. This benefit foregone does not have to be expressed in money terms' (Allsopp 1995: 430).

'In summary, a cost is a foregone opportunity. The cost of engaging in an activity is the totality of all the opportunities that the activity requires you to forgo' (Landsburg 2002: 37).

'When more of commodity *X* is produced, resources are used up. These resources could have been used to produce alternative commodities. The most highly valued of these foregone alternatives is the opportunity cost of *X*' (Katz and Rosen 1998: 3).

'Opportunity cost the highest valued forsaken alternative' (Eaton, Eaton and Allen 2002: 672).

'The budget constraint also embodies the concept of opportunity cost since if an individual purchases additional units of one good, she must reduce her purchases of the other in order to remain within her budget. We can represent the opportunity cost of one good in terms of the other by the slope of the budget equation, $\Delta Y/\Delta X$' (Mathis and Koscianski 2002: 84).

Of the suggested definitions above, the individual *ex ante* is the relevant one for individual choice but it is not easy to deal with empirically and raises the question: 'is it possible to record a (momentary) conception or plan in a decision-taker's head?'. Hence definitions, textbook examples and research projects concerned with opportunity cost tend to favour definitions along the lines of 3 and 4 in Table 3.1 which tend to give opportunity costs an objective reality. Wiseman (1989), mentioned in the introduction, was a member of the so-called LSE subjectivist cost school and highlighted the type of distinctions that have been copied here. Some selected sentences reveal the strength of his scepticism of the notion of opportunity cost as commonly employed throughout neoclassical economics.

'The "costs" relevant to decisions affecting the allocation of physical resources between uses through time are the (opportunity-)costs of those resources in other uses *as seen by the decision-maker at the point of decision*. . . . It follows there are no "objective" costs: . . . opportunity-cost is a *rejected plan* . . . there is no reason why two individuals deciding on the same ("best") course of action should have the same opportunity-costs' (pp. 144–5). Wiseman argues that typically economists fail to emphasise that forgone alternatives 'have no "objective" manifestation. The examples are frequently "real": the opportunity cost of the cricket bat I buy is the tennis racket I must go without' (p. 146). In keeping with this, he notes 'To prescribe that the products of nationalised industries should be priced at long run marginal cost' – from the analytical model of the perfectly competitive market economy described above – 'is, of itself, of little more practical help than they be priced on the principle that God is Love' (p. 153). Nothing is straightforward, even cost!

3.6 Summary

A good understanding of the notion of costs and therefore supply necessarily involves an appreciation of the often complicated notion of a production function. In the early sections of this chapter the type of production function that provides the U-shaped cost curves of the theory of the firm was analysed in detail (as it is far from an obvious one). Building on a distinction between the long and the short run, it was then possible to build up the relevant cost curves and structure that dominates the neoclassical theory of the firm. The use of isoquants, isocost curves (budget constraints) and the motivation of profit maximisation was central to this construction. The treatment presented here, whilst conforming to the norm, is not without criticism.

Allen (2000) sees the approach as somewhat dated and out of touch with the modern economy:

'The basic standard treatment still follows the outline set forth by Debreu (1959), in which a firm's technological possibilities are specified by a production set.[2] With the

---

2. Note sets are different to functions. For example, the collection of points on a convex production function need not form a convex production set.

exception of consideration of economies of scope, contestability [see Chapter 3] and sustainability, economists haven't made progress in ascertaining which assumptions are appropriate for production sets. For example, microeconomic theory doesn't even recognise Henry Ford's assembly line beyond stories about economies and dis-economies of scale leading to suitable shapes for cost functions. . . . Perhaps our concept of technology needs to be to go beyond standard production sets, or perhaps stronger assumptions are needed. . . . I see vast potential for economists to learn from engineers.' (Allen 2000: 148–9)

Meanwhile Gowdy and Seidl (2004) attack the way convenient utility and production functions assumptions determine serious policy recommendations that seem to be woefully inadequate. They write:

'Nordhaus (1992, 2001) uses a general equilibrium model assuming a CES[3] utility function (implying that market goods are equally substitutable for a stable climate) and a Cobb–Douglas (constant returns to scale) production function to analyze various climate change policies. In this framework, a stable climate is just another commodity on equal footing with a new SUV or a vacation to Disney World. Given the assumptions of the model it is **inevitable** that the "optimal" global warming policy is to make **modest efforts** to insure that the costs and benefits of global warming policies are properly priced.' Gowdy and Seidl (2004: 354, emphasis added)

There is clearly controversy surrounding the standard theory.

Nevertheless, using the standard production and cost function foundations and the demand curve analysis of Chapter 2, allowed the theory of the perfectly competitive firm to be laid out. The role of perfect competition as the benchmark form of economic organisation in the neoclassical world makes familiarity with its assumptions and comparative statics vital to both supporters and critics of neoclassical theory. The concept of producer surplus was introduced as the companion concept of consumer surplus. In the final section a challenge to the notion of the key concept of objective, opportunity cost, was explored by introducing a subjectivist view – which, incidentally, makes the objective market demand curves of Chapter 2 'predictions, existing only in people's heads' (Wiseman 1989: 153). In the next chapter the – not uncontroversial – concepts of this chapter and earlier chapters are put to work in partial equilibrium analysis.

Appendix 3 Production duality

The purpose of this appendix is once more to illustrate the power of duality and it relies on the example developed in Beattie and Taylor (1985: 239–41). When a profit-maximising organisation makes a choice over inputs and outputs it implicitly reveals two things. First, the inputs and associated outputs are part of a feasible production plan and, second, these choices are more profitable than other feasible choices that could have been made. This is the so-called 'weak axiom of profit maximisation' (see Varian 1999). If observed choices are maximum profit choices (and therefore necessarily least-cost) for each set of prices that obtain then it is often possible to derive the form of the production function that generates the observations. Generally the production function underlying a process is mathematically recoverable from the so-called indirect cost function.

Cost Minimisation

$$\text{Min } C = wL + rK \text{ identifies the DIRECT COST FUNCTION} \tag{3a}$$

3. CES stands for constant elasticity of substitution and the CES utility function takes the general form $u = (\Sigma_{i=1}^{n} \beta_i q_i^{-\rho})^{-1/\rho}$ where u is utility, q_i is a commodity, $\beta_i > 0$ and $\rho = (1 - \sigma)/\sigma < 1$.

For a given level of output $\bar{Q}$ subject to a production function

$$Q = Q(L, K) = 2L^{0.5} K^{0.25} \tag{3b}$$

Form the Lagrangian:

$$\mathcal{L} = wL + rK + \lambda(\bar{Q} - 2L^{0.5}K^{0.25}) \tag{3A.1}$$

To isolate the first-order conditions for a minimum set the partial derivatives with respect to L, K and λ equal zero.

$$\frac{\partial \mathcal{L}}{\partial L} = w - \lambda L^{-0.5}K^{0.25} = 0 \tag{3A.2}$$

$$\frac{\partial \mathcal{L}}{\partial K} = r - 0.5 \, \lambda L^{0.5}K^{-0.75} = 0 \tag{3A.3}$$

$$\frac{\partial \mathcal{L}}{\partial \lambda} = \bar{Q} - 2L^{0.5} K^{0.25} = 0 \tag{3A.4}$$

From (3A.2) and (3A.3) obtain the expansion path

$$K = \frac{wL}{2r} \tag{3A.5}$$

Substituting (3A.5) into (3A.4) gives the conditional (meaning holding output constant) demand equation for L:

$$L = 0.5\bar{Q}^{1.33} \, w^{-0.33} \, r^{0.33} \tag{3A.6}$$

Solving the expansion path for (3A.5) as a function of K, w and r and substituting the result into (3A.4) gives the conditional demand equation for K.

$$K = 0.25\bar{Q}^{1.33} \, w^{0.67} \, r^{-0.67} \tag{3A.7}$$

The INDIRECT COST FUNCTION is obtained by substituting the conditional demands for L and K into the direct cost function (3a), yielding

$$C = 0.75\bar{Q}^{1.33} \, w^{0.67} \, r^{0.33} \tag{3A.8}$$

Specification of the indirect cost function is usually the beginning of duality demonstrations involving cost. The application of Shephard's lemma (see Chapter 2) will yield the conditional demand equations (3A.6) and (3A.7), also note that

$$\partial C/\partial Q = \bar{Q}^{0.33} \, w^{0.67} \, r^{0.33} = MC \tag{3A.9}$$

(inverse of the product supply equation when $P = MC$).

DERIVING A PRODUCTION FUNCTION from an indirect cost function is not always possible and can be difficult.

However the 'simple' case here illustrates the process:

With factor demands homogeneous of degree 0 we can replace $w/r = z$ as the input expansion path for a competitive firm in factor markets is a ray line (= constant slope isoquants along a ray and with least cost production $MP_l/MP_k = w/r$).

Therefore the factor demand equations become

$$L = 0.5\bar{Q}^{1.33}z^{-0.33} \tag{3A.10}$$

$$K = 0.25\bar{Q}^{1.33}z^{0.67} \tag{3A.11}$$

Now it is necessary to eliminate $z = w/r$. Squaring each side of (3.10) and rearranging terms in (3A.10) and (3A.11) yields

$$z^{0.67} = 0.25\overline{Q}^{2.67} (L)^{-2} \qquad (3A.12)$$

and

$$z^{0.67} = 4K\overline{Q}^{-1.33} \qquad (3A.13)$$

equating (3A.12) and (3A.13)

$$4K\overline{Q}^{-1.33} = 0.25\overline{Q}^{2.67} (L)^{-2} \qquad (3A.14)$$

rearranging

$$\overline{Q} = 2L^{0.5}K^{0.25} = Q (L, K) \qquad (3A.15)$$

which is the primal problem production function.

References

Allen, B. (2000) The future of microeconomic theory, *Journal of Economic Perspectives*, 14 (1): 143–50.

Allsopp, V. (1995) *Understanding Economics*, London: Routledge.

Beattie, R.B. and Taylor, C.R. (1985) *The Economics of Production*, New York: John Wiley.

Bowden, E.V. (1977) *Economics: the Science of Common Sense*, 2nd edn, Cincinnati: South-Western.

Chung, J.W. (1994) *Utility and Production Functions*, Oxford: Blackwell.

Eaton, B.C., Eaton, D.F. and Allen, D.W. (2002) *Microeconomics*, 5th edn, Toronto: Prentice-Hall.

Garb, G. (1981) *Microeconomic Theory, Applications, Innovations*, New York: Macmillan.

Gowdy, J. and Seidl, I. (2004) Economic man and selfish genes: the implications of group selection for economic valuation and policy, *Journal of Socio-Economics*, 33 (3): 343–59.

Heathfield, D.F. and Wibe, S. (1987) *An Introduction to Cost and Production Functions*, Basingstoke: Macmillan.

Katz, M.L. and Rosen, H.S. (1998) *Microeconomics*, 3rd edn, New York: McGraw-Hill.

Landsburg, S.E. (2002) *Price Theory and Applications*, 5th edn, Cincinnati: South-Western.

McKenzie, R.B. and Tullock, G. (1981) *The New World of Economics*, 3rd edn, Homewood, Ill.: Irwin.

Mathis, S.A. and Koscianski, J. (2002) *Microeconomic Theory: an Integrated Approach*, Upper Saddle River, NJ: Prentice-Hall.

Miller, R.L. (1982) *Economics Today*, 4th edn, New York: Harper and Row.

Varian, H.R. (1999) *Intermediate Microeconomics: a Modern Approach*, New York: W.W. Norton.

Wiseman, J. (1989) *Cost, Choice and Political Economy*, Aldershot: Edward Elgar.

CHAPTER 4

Efficiency, partial equilibrium and prices

4.1 Introduction

In this chapter the first objective is to define 'efficiency'. The focus is on partial equilibrium analysis and on the relevance of perfect competition. If competitive markets prove efficient there are costs associated with rejecting market outcomes. A second objective is to assess the costs of interfering with market outcomes. This chapter changes the focus of analysis, away from the individual and towards markets.

In *The Wealth of Nations* (1776), Adam Smith explained how an 'invisible hand' ensures that, within competitive markets, preferences of consumers are met at least cost. Aping this explanation, the first task is to make the notion of efficiency explicit.

4.2 Efficiency in resource allocation

At the risk of offending those not interested in the 'world game', it is instructive to use a football analogy. Arsène Wenger, the 'economist look-a-like' manager of Arsenal football club, is quoted as saying, what many economists might say, 'For me beauty is efficiency' (*The Guardian* 23 Nov. 1996, p. 10). Whilst Wenger goes on to describe one of his players as efficient, economists focus on the description of efficient economic arrangements. 'Beauty' lies in the attractive properties of an efficient situation – not in the ball being at the back of the net! In order to deem the properties of processes, or outcomes, attractive, a measuring rod for 'attractiveness' has to be devised. Some players have 'vision and passing ability', others 'determination and the knack of scoring'. There are many potential measuring rods. Fortunately, only one measuring rod has assumed importance when defining efficiency in conventional microeconomics. This measuring rod (like all other measuring rods) is founded on value judgements. The key principles that generate the conditions that define efficiency in neoclassical microeconomics stem from the work of an Italian social scientist, Vilfredo Pareto.

A Pareto optimum is attained when it is impossible to reallocate resources so as to make at least one person better off, without at the same time making another person worse off. It ties back to the 'I' in BORING in Chapter 1 because it focuses on the individual. This so-called Pareto criterion avoids one of the formidable problems of welfare economics, i.e. 'interpersonal comparison', or, more simply, comparisons of utility (or welfare) between individuals. Thus, 'better-off', or 'worse-off', are descriptions determined by the individuals themselves. If, *in their own estimation*, an individual is better off as a result of some reallocation, and no one declares themself to be worse off, a Pareto improvement can be achieved.

To employ this criterion, however, is to accept three value judgements. Although often presented in an uncontroversial, matter-of-fact, way, each represents a strong position to take up and to work with. They are that:

1. each individual is the best judge of their own utility or welfare. This is consistent with the view that the only knowledge that an individual can have is of their own feeling, or welfare. You cannot know what is best for other people and they cannot know what is best for you;
2. individuals are the basic and only units of analysis. This, as introduced above, rules out an organic view of society. Margaret Thatcher, as prime minister, was very heavily criticised for saying that there was no such thing as 'society', but this is a commonplace in microeconomics. To recap from earlier material, society is only the sum of individuals and all utility is attached to them as such (and not to some abstract amalgam of individuals);
3. to make someone better off is unambiguously a 'good thing' (a welfare improvement) only if no one else is made worse off. More formally, if it is possible on a reallocation of resources to increase the utility of one individual without decreasing the utility of any other individual, then the welfare of society (conceived of as the sum of all individuals) is increased.

Such value judgements minimise the scope for 'expert' (or other) opinions in directing, or evaluating, choices for others. This is consistent with the view that economists are not invited to express their personal prejudices. They are invited to think in a very specific way. The adoption of such value judgements leads directly to the notion that it would be optimal to seek a set of economic arrangements that reflect consumer sovereignty. The value judgements exclude the notion of maximising the interests of such organisms as: the state, the country, the government, the corporate sector. The significance of these propositions is critical to understanding welfare aspects of microeconomics. If their influence is doubted, consider your views of the following three statements, all of which are consistent with these so-called Paretian value judgements:

1. It is a 'good thing' (there is an efficiency gain) if Bill Gates is made 'better off' while the poorest person in the world is made no worse off;
2. An individual who chooses to be a hard drug abuser is the best judge of their own welfare;
3. Society is no more than the sum of its individual parts.

These issues are provocative in that individuals (including economists) tend to violate all the value judgements in their day-to-day conversations and assessments. To reverse the point, statements such as: 'It makes the rest of us worse off when you see them – "the fat cats" – with all that increased income'; 'It would be good for so and so if such and such happened to them'; 'The mood of the country would be improved if we had more international sporting success'; are everywhere, but are not generally consistent with the value judgements. Whilst it would be wrong to consider the definition of Pareto 'optimality' as in any sense sacrosanct, it is the case that the approach is often attractive and proves the cornerstone of a powerful engine of analysis.

As the value judgements are central to understanding neoclassical microeconomics and are 'strong ones' to accept, some further elaboration is justified. Mishan (1981) points out that the first one can be adopted, either as essentially a belief, or as a moral judgement (we ought to act as if this is the case), or as a political tenet. (In Western democracies, if political decisions are referred to individuals, should not economic ones be also?) But what of individuals themselves? They may not accept that in all situations they are the best judges of their own welfare. For example, (a) they may believe that 'expert' knowledge is available and/or desirable and superior to their own; (b) they may not wish to make a judgement of their own welfare because of lack of experience, ill health, recognised irrationality, etc.; (c) they may not want to take the responsibility for making their own judgements and may prefer to delegate to others (see the concept of merit wants in Chapter 5). As for conceiving of society in a non-organic way, this is obviously at odds with the practice of other disciplines you may be studying. So, for example (as noted above) sociology takes as its unit of analysis society itself (not individuals). Society is the key organism, not the individual.

One way of classifying different disciplines is by their unit of analysis, ranging from physicists' sub-particles and biologists' cells, through subjects that are individually based like economics and psychology, to sociology and cosmology. What seems natural to someone trained as an economist may appear as a very strange set-up to individuals from another discipline. While some may explain this as a methodological distinction, it is based on the value judgement that there are no superior interests to those of the individual.

With regard to the third value judgement, which is sometimes known as 'the' Pareto criterion, this too is far from obvious. As noted, it avoids making interpersonal comparisons of welfare but, in so doing, it can sanction the wealthiest person in the world being made better off as long as no one is made worse off. Many might agree with the statement 'we can say it is a good thing to make one person better off if it contributes to their survival even if it makes another person worse off as long as it does not affect the other person's survival' (Dopfer 1976: 21) but it is not sanctioned in this framework. It is also evident that Paretianism is 'endstate'-orientated, in that it is the utility levels *achieved* by the individuals making up society that alone count. It may be argued that, at least to begin with, the Pareto criterion would be accepted by individuals who start under conditions of fundamental uncertainty, where they neither know the hand of cards they are to be dealt in life, nor the details of the game to be played (see: Sugden and Weale (1979) for an account of the Paretian value judgements along these lines). In so far as individuals are uncertain about the changes to be proposed, and, when the initial income distribution is not specified, there may exist an acceptance of the Paretian criterion when individuals feel that they can veto changes that would make them worse off. In this way, the appeal of the Paretian approach may be explained. It is difficult to over-estimate the importance of this framework for standard literature in microeconomics. The 1986 economics Nobel laureate James Buchanan (1959) noted: 'This Pareto rule is itself an ethical proposition, a value statement, but it is one which requires a minimum of premises and one which should command wide assent' (p. 125). The Paretian value judgements may appear, at this stage, nebulous, so how do they connect to efficiency in resource allocation?

A so-called 'top-level' efficient economy exhausts the possibilities of welfare improvement, as defined in the Pareto criterion, in that it is one in which it is impossible on a reallocation of resources to increase the utility of one individual without decreasing the utility of any other individual. Top-level efficiency requires certain types of low-level efficiency if the Pareto criterion is to be met.

(i) Maximum units of output must be obtained from units of input

A production function (see Chapter 3) is a mathematical relationship that relates the *maximum* quantity of output (Q) that can be obtained from any stated input combination. In symbols:

$$Q_x = Q_x(K, L) \tag{4.1}$$

Typically, as in Chapter 3, the production function is illustrated as an isoquant map. A single isoquant records all combinations of quantities of capital (K) and labour (L) that give a stated amount of output of good X.

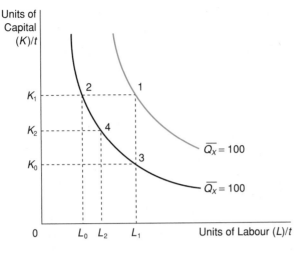

Figure 4.1
Maximising output from inputs

In Figure 4.1 two isoquants are illustrated both labelled $Q_x = 100$ units. It is easy to show that the one to the north-east must be inefficient because it is not consistent with maximum output. Consider point 1 and a move to point 2. The same output of 100 units is being produced but L_1-L_0 units of labour can be released to produce a good elsewhere (allowing at least one person to be better off with no one worse off). Similarly, consider point 1 and a move to point 3. The same output of 100 units is being produced but K_1-K_0 units of capital can be released to produce a good elsewhere (allowing at least one person to be better off with no one worse off). The implication is that, unless the isoquants are as close to the origin as they can conceivably be, the situation is an inefficient one (as labour or capital or a combination of both – e.g. at point 4 K_1-K_2 capital and L_1-L_2 labour – can be released to make output that can at least allow one person to be better off with no one worse off).

(ii) Producers must choose least-cost factor combinations to produce any given output

To recap from Chapter 3, the isolation of cost information involves the use of a budget constraint, or a so-called isocost curve (*iso* means equal):

$$C = rK + wL \tag{4.2}$$

where a given total cost outlay C = rental price of capital (r) times the quantity of capital (K) + wage of labour (w) times the quantity of labour (L).

Rearranging (4.2):

$$K = C/r - (w/r)L \tag{4.3}$$

So the slope of the budget constraint or isocost line is $dK/dL = -w/r$, or equivalently, $-dK/dL = w/r$.

Recalling that least-cost production occurs when the budget constraint is tangential to an isoquant, the ratio of the factor prices implies:

$w/r = MRTS_{KL}$ = marginal rate of technical substitution between capital and labour (= the slope of the isoquant).

The location of the isocost line prevents the producer having output plans that cannot be realised. The best the producer can feasibly do is to be on the constraint. But where? The answer is captured in the two isoquants and isocost lines in Figure 4.2. To settle at points other than point 1 on $Q_x = 100$ (e.g. points 2 and 3) involves lower output ($Q_x = 80$)

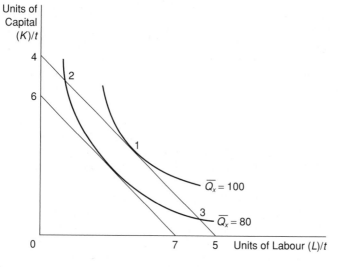

Figure 4.2
Securing least-cost production

than can be feasibly obtained with the stated cost outlay (i.e. points 2 and 3 must be inefficient because it is possible to make 20 units more of output that can at least allow one person to be better off with no one worse off). Conversely, $Q_x = 80$ could be obtained with a lower isocost outlay represented by line 6-7 allowing the purchase of inputs in another output process that can at least allow one person to be better off with no one worse off.

Meeting conditions (i) and (ii) defines what is known as 'X- or technical efficiency' and yields a supply curve reflecting the lowest possible marginal cost of production, where marginal cost by definition is the production cost of an additional unit of output per period.

The third and final condition is allocative efficiency, which states that:

> (iii) the quantity of output per period must be the quantity that consumers would choose when a good is priced at its marginal cost of production

Supply (S) and demand (D) are shown in Figure 4.3; assume the location of S meets X-efficiency. The quantity q_e is described as efficient because it represents the point where it is impossible for consumers of good X to be made better off without someone else

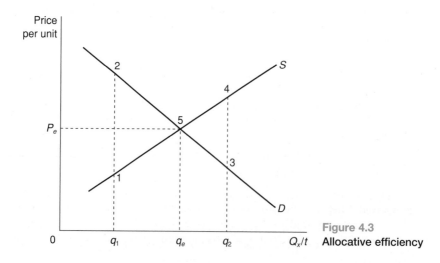

Figure 4.3
Allocative efficiency

being worse off. Consider unit q_1. The producer has been made worse off to the extent of incurring the costs of production equal to q_1-1. Recalling the demand curve indicates willingness to pay, consumers' valuation of the q_1th unit can be read off the demand curve at q_1-2. It follows that a surplus (consumer surplus) 1-2 can be enjoyed after fully compensating the producer by giving the producer the full costs of production q_1-1. The consumer of the q_1th unit is better off and no one is worse off. The trade is an efficient one.

Now consider unit q_2. The producer, once again, has been made worse off, this time to the extent of incurring the costs of production equal to q_2-4. The consumers value the q_2th unit at q_2-3 and, therefore, can only secure a deficit of 3-4 in valuation if they fully compensate the producer by giving q_2-4 in a market trade. The consumers have to make themselves worse off if no one else is to be worse off. Given trade is voluntary this will not happen. Unit q_1 is an 'efficient' purchase, whereas unit q_2 is an 'inefficient' purchase.

The efficient quantity is q_e. The producer has been made worse off to the extent of incurring the costs of production equal to q_e-5 = P_e. The consumer values the q_eth unit at q_e-5 and therefore enjoys no surplus (consumer surplus) or deficit if he or she fully compensates the producer by giving q_e-5 = P_e in a market trade for the q_eth unit. As the consumers are not better off and no one is worse off, the unit q_e is the marginal unit purchased. Units before q_e offer efficiency gain, units beyond q_e are inefficient.

Note that this has all been justified by reference to the Pareto criterion. Units before q_e attract consumer surplus as measured by the gap between the demand curve and the supply curve, whereas units after q_e, which attract a consumer deficit, will never be voluntarily purchased. Hence consumer surplus is maximised at q_e. It can also be noted that the equilibrium combination P_e and q_e has been established by considering demand prices (consumer willingness to pay) and supply prices (producer willingness to supply) at a given Q_x/t on the x-axis. This is the Marshallian approach to equilibrium via quantity adjustment (see Section 4.5 below).

To summarise this section: it is clear that 'efficiency' has different meanings in different minds and different disciplines and is much used in casual conversation, sometimes with cold, calculating, connotations. When using the term, economists have a precise interpretation in mind. Value judgement 3 above, in particular, is vital in that it defines what economists understand by the term 'efficiency'. An efficient economy is one in which the existing allocation of inputs and outputs is such that it is impossible to make one person better off without making someone else worse off by a reallocation. Although this seems an innocuous statement, it can have a strong cutting edge when applied to different economic arrangements.

The question now becomes 'How is perfect competition (as described in Chapter 3) appraised with reference to efficiency criteria?'

4.3 Efficiency and perfect competition

The outcome of a competitive mechanism is illustrated in Figure 4.4 where the equilibrium price is set by the impersonal mechanism of the market for good X at P_e in panel (b). The representative firm reacts to this price by earning zero economic profit at point 1 and producing q units of output of good X in panel (a). The individual consumer reacts to P_e by buying their efficient quantity (at point 1' on their demand curve d), choosing quantity q_e in panel (c). When quantities produced by firms per period and quantities purchased by consumers per period are summed they will equal market output per period Q_e by construction.

It is worth probing this picture a little further. Let S be the long-run industry supply curve. This, by definition, is the horizontal sum of the bases of the firms' long-run average

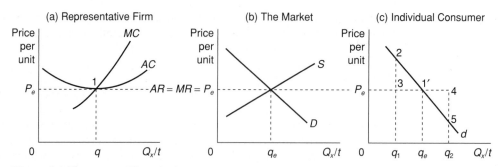

Figure 4.4 The competitive result

cost curves when all external economies and diseconomies of size have worked themselves out and, as such, can involve no kind of surplus to the producer. For panel (c) the quantity q_e was described as efficient because it represents the point where it is impossible for the consumer to make him- or herself better off without some one being worse off. (Unit q_1 will be bought because it offers consumer surplus distance 2-3. Unit q_2 will not be bought because it offers consumer deficit distance 4-5.) An analogous process will apply to all consumers of good X. It is, therefore, evident that, in the long-run equilibrium, when there is no surplus to the producer, perfect competition serves to maximise consumer surplus – truly an ideal market form!

4.4 Market analysis

Given the above, it is not surprising that many economists have great admiration for the workings of the competitive market. But how do market forces (demand and supply) lead to a market equilibrium? Equilibrium is a 'state of balance'. When equilibrium has been reached there will be no further change in the market. Different states of equilibrium are often used as reference points; comparative static analysis as noted in Chapter 3 involves a comparison of one equilibrium with another.[1] When factors affecting demand and supply change, it is likely that the equilibrium price and quantity per period will change as a consequence.

There is nothing normatively attractive about equilibrium *per se* (i.e. it is not necessarily the case that any equilibrium will be deemed 'good' for society in the sense of all individuals). It may be that a particular equilibrium price is far from desirable. To emphasise, equilibrium is simply a state of balance. Having said this, there are many who would commend the equilibrium that emerges in a competitive market. The following sections will demonstrate how, within competitive markets, market forces will lead to an equilibrium that maximises welfare. Yet, despite the attraction of competitive market solutions, even such market outcomes may not be sacrosanct to all. Policy-makers may reject the equilibrium that emerges in a market. However, many economists argue that great care must be taken when attempting to reject an equilibrium market solution.

One reason why 'market economists' question such attempts is that market forces make such action costly. Policy-makers may seek to replace an equilibrium price with an 'administered price' – but the problems of attempting to 'buck' market forces are formidable. The difficulties of rejecting a market equilibrium price are easily illustrated. The examples presented below include: markets for agricultural goods (which feature in many arguments about the EU), rented accommodation and labour. In each case,

---

1. A 'dynamic' analysis considers how the market moves from one equilibrium to another.

policy-makers attempt to reject the equilibrium price and face worrying problems that might have been anticipated by reference to the analysis in this chapter.

4.4.1 Equilibrium in the market: some normative implications

To analyse the workings of the market it is necessary to consider both demand and supply. In Figure 4.5(a) the market is in equilibrium at price P_e being a *state of balance*. At price P_e the quantity of good X that is supplied per period is exactly equal to the quantity of good X that is demanded per period. There is no reason for any change in the market.

In Figure 4.5(a), if the market were not at equilibrium there would be either *excess demand* or *excess supply*. At a price of P_2 there will be excess supply (distance 1-2) as the quantity supplied far exceeds the quantity demand at that price. At a price of P_1 there will be excess demand (distance 3-4) as the quantity demanded far exceeds the quantity supplied at that price. If there is excess supply the market is not in a state of balance and it is likely that the price of the good will fall. Similarly, with excess demand there will be change; it is likely that the price of the good will rise. Such adjustment via price is referred to as *Walrasian*. Above adjustments took place via a change in quantities produced (less at P_2, more at P_1) and this is referred to as *Marshallian*. They represent two

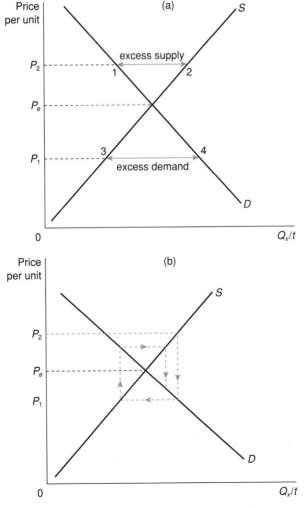

Figure 4.5   Equilibrium in the market

views of the market clearing mechanism devised by two, great, early economists Walras and Marshall. (See Section 4.5 below.)

To show the mechanism by which price changes may bring the market into equilibrium consider Figure 4.5(b). Initially there is excess supply at price P_2. If the price of the good were to fall to P_1 there would be excess demand. At price P_1 excess demand would create pressure for a price rise. Step by step, price will adjust, as can be seen by following the oscillations (directions on the dashed line).

In Figure 4.5, price adjustment will lead ultimately to the equilibrium price P_e. If the market is not at equilibrium there is a tendency for market forces to lead the market back to equilibrium. In such circumstances the equilibrium is referred to as *stable*.

There are circumstances in which any movement from equilibrium may create forces that will push the market away from the equilibrium. In this case, the initial equilibrium is referred to as unstable. The distinction often depends on the time required to adjust and the slopes of the demand and supply curves.[2] In the case shown (in Figure 4.5(b)) the equilibrium illustrated is stable – market forces will return to price and output should any change arise. Pressures of demand and supply lead to an equilibrium price in the market but in the case of a competitive market this equilibrium maximises the sum of consumer surplus and (in the short run) producer surplus. One way to estimate welfare is in terms of social surplus. This is the sum of consumer surplus and producer surplus (concepts introduced in Chapters 2 and 3 respectively). In Figure 4.6, D is the market demand curve and S is the supply curve for the market. Quantity 0-q_e is provided at a price of 0-P_e. This is the quantity at which the sum of consumer surplus (P_e-2-1) and producers surplus (0-P_e-1) is maximised. At this point, as indicated above, 'allocative efficiency' has been achieved. For any other quantity, the sum of consumer surplus and producer surplus must be lower. Take, for example, quantity 0-q_1. Consumer surplus is less by 4-3-1 and producer surplus is less by 5-4-1. If output is less than at q_e there are insufficient resources allocated to the production of this good. 'Allocative inefficiency' can be estimated as the

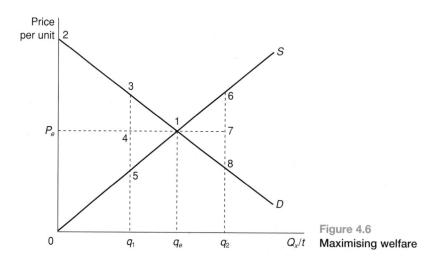

Figure 4.6 Maximising welfare

2. A case in which equilibrium is unstable is illustrated with respect to agricultural products. Supply adjustment may be lagged (an individual farmer may base production plans in any year on the market price the previous autumn). With lagged adjustment it is possible to show that if the slope of the demand curve has a smaller absolute value than the slope of the supply curve the equilibrium is stable. However, if the slope of the demand curve has a greater absolute value than the slope of the supply curve oscillations will increase and the equilibrium is unstable (for a proof see Henderson and Quandt 1971).

deadweight or welfare loss that society experiences (which, in the case just discussed, is triangle 5-3-1). If an output in excess of q_e, like q_2, were produced once again, the sum of consumer surplus and producer surplus is reduced. The additional output (q_2-q_e) is valued at q_e-1-8-q_2 but the additional costs that are required to produce this are shown by the integral under the supply curve over q_e-q_2. The additional costs q_e-1-6-q_2 have been expended in production of something valued at q_e-1-8-q_2. The difference between valuation and cost is a welfare loss triangle 1-6-8. Such welfare loss is described as 'deadweight' because a cost has been incurred that has no offsetting gain elsewhere. There is no other output than q_e at which the sum of consumer surplus and producer surplus is maximised and q_e is the output that will be achieved by the competitive working of market forces (demand and supply). For market economists, this analysis provides a normative defence of the proposition that allocation is best 'left to the market' (and more will be said of this in Chapter 5).

4.5 Market versus administrative prices. Can policy-makers 'buck the market'?

The above discussion illustrates the impact of market forces in bringing about changes in the market. Sometimes, the outcome that emerges within the market will not be the outcome that is thought desirable. Policy-makers then attempt to intervene to resist market forces. The intention is to replace equilibrium prices and outputs with administered prices and outputs. Such intervention may be undertaken with the most noble of intentions. However, how easy is it to resist market forces? For example, if a price other than the equilibrium price is set (with reference to Figure 4.5(a)) there must inevitably be 'excess demand' or 'excess supply' (as illustrated in Figure 4.5(a)). Controlling price only causes an output excess (or deficiency) at the administered price and this requires further policy measures to resist movement from the administered price. Excess supply, or excess demand, will pose problems for policy-makers and any attempt to administer prices will involve a necessary response. This is illustrated in the following examples.

4.5.1 The European Union's Common Agricultural Policy

Article 39 of the Treaty of Rome (1957) states the objectives of a Common Agricultural Policy (CAP). They are: to increase agricultural productivity; to ensure a fair standard of living for the agricultural community; to stabilise markets; to assure availability of supplies; to ensure that supplies reach consumers at reasonable prices.

To understand the European Union's motivation bear in mind that, in 1957, memories of food shortages (as experienced in the Second World War) were still fresh. Moreover, government intervention in the market for agricultural produce was nothing new. Many countries in Europe had engaged in some form of agricultural support since the 1930s.

There are specific reasons why governments are prepared to provide support for agricultural prices. For example:

(i)   Vagaries of climate can sometimes lead to extreme fluctuations of production (leading to scarcity or over-supply). With low price elasticities of demand this generates very marked and undesirable price fluctuations (see Chapter 2).

(ii) Income elasticity of demand for agricultural products is low (relative to that of demand for industrial goods). This means that as the income of individuals grows, demand for agricultural products does not rise by as much as demand for industrial products. The concern is that incomes for the farming community will not increase in line with incomes generally. There is concern for farmers' livelihoods.

(iii) Technological advance is not as rapid in agriculture as in manufacturing. One reason is that there tends to be greater inflexibility (e.g. in terms of farm size) and decreasing returns to scale (see Chapter 3) become relevant at a relatively early stage.

Such concerns have prompted government intervention in many countries. However, for the European Union there were also political concerns (Swann 2000). One such issue was how to balance the national interests of the original six members of the European Union when drafting the Treaty of Rome 1957. It was anticipated that (West) Germany would benefit from the opportunity to sell industrial goods as member states removed their tariffs with one another. In return, France looked for market advantages for its relatively efficient agricultural industry. The politics of integration also motivated the Common Agricultural Policy.

In the 1960s member states set up the European Agricultural Guidance and Guarantee Fund (EAGGF) (or Fonds Européen d'Orientation et Garantie Agricoles) to finance a price support system.[3] An illustrative example of CAP price support is presented in Figure 4.7. The example is based on the market for wheat (W) but it illustrates the different mechanisms that are employed to administer price support.

(i) A *target price* is set above equilibrium price. Target price (P_4) is set on an annual basis. (In this example it is the wholesale price of wheat set at one EU location, Duisburg in Germany, where local supply of wheat is not abundant and price would be above the EU equilibrium price.)

(ii) A *threshold price* is calculated by making an adjustment for transport and distribution costs of moving wheat from the nearest port (Rotterdam). Threshold price is P_3 in Figure 4.7. The intention is that imported wheat will not be available in the EU at a price less than the threshold price. A *variable import tax* is imposed to ensure that imports do not force price below the threshold price. The variable import levy is distance 2-4 (i.e. the difference between the world price, assumed to be P_1, and the threshold price P_3).

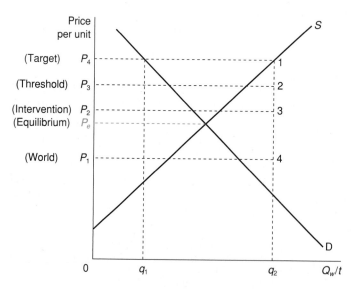

Figure 4.7 The 'CAP' pricing system

3. The Price Guarantee Section operates a series of intervention prices (which varies from product to product). It also funds export subsidies. The Guidance Section of the EAGGF funds improvements and reorganisation in rural infrastructure.

(iii) *An intervention price* is set to deal with excess supply. The target price causes excess supply (q_1-q_2). The intervention price (usually 10 to 15 per cent below the target price) is P_2 in Figure 4.7. If market price falls to P_2 agencies will buy excess supply in order to achieve the target price. The intervention is required to stop excess supply reducing price. However, stocks of agricultural goods are then created. Reports draw attention to the celebrated 'butter mountains', 'wine lakes', etc.

The problem of dealing with excess supply has led the EU to subsidise the export of agricultural goods. One measure that the EU uses is export subsidies. In Figure 4.7 an export subsidy might be set as shown by distance 3-4 so that farmers have an incentive to put excess supply on the world market. The use of *export subsidies* to 'dump' excess supply has brought criticism from other countries that export agricultural goods (and it caused considerable problems for the Uruguay Round of GATT negotiations).

For further discussion of the administrative mechanism in the CAP see Gibbons (1999). The intention here is to illustrate the different ways in which the CAP supports the price of agricultural goods. The objective is to analyse the welfare costs of this policy with respect to stylised accounts of CAP price support.

4.5.1.1 Welfare costs of the Common Agricultural Policy

The objective in this section is to apply analysis of consumer surplus and producer surplus (as described earlier) to comment on the efficiency of this policy. The benchmark is efficiency, as created in a competitive market (i.e. as discussed with respect to Figure 4.6). The approach is one that can (and will) be repeated with reference to other administrative policies. Gains (losses) to producers and consumers are estimated and compared in terms of consumer surplus and producer surplus. After comparing gains and losses, the format will be to focus on the difficulties that are manifest as a result of attempts to maintain an administered price and resist market pressure towards equilibrium.

The impact of price support provided by the CAP depends on the extent to which price is supported. In this section two different forms of price support are considered independently.

(i) The first is case A, where price is supported above world price, i.e. above the price at which imports could be acquired. In this instance, the target price is maintained by a variable import levy.

(ii) The second is case B, where imports are excluded and price is supported above the equilibrium price by intervention burying. In this example (B), world price is above the equilibrium price for the European market.

In both cases it will become clear that there are efficiency losses associated with the policy and in both cases efficiency losses are identified by comparing the welfare effects of the policy.

(A) *Variable import levy*: In this example, to maintain price the CAP makes use of import tariffs and the welfare costs of this form of intervention can be assessed. Focusing on the target price, this administered price is achieved by denying consumers access to imports. In Figure 4.8(a) S is the supply curve for this agricultural good in the EU and D is the demand curve. An import levy keeps the price P_t above the world price, P_W. The price of imports to consumers is P_t and home supply increases from 0-q_1 to 0-q_2. By contrast, demand in the EU is reduced from 0-q_4 to 0-q_3. Imports fall from q_4-q_1 to q_3-q_2.

The increase in price means that producer surplus increases by area a in Figure 4.8(a). With a tax levied on imports, revenue is raised equal to area c. This revenue is paid to the government and is available for expenditure on programmes and it might appear that it

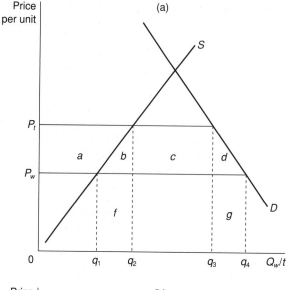

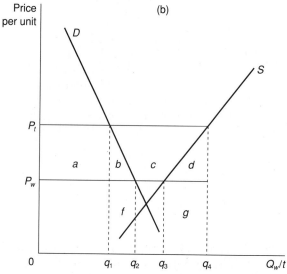

Figure 4.8
Assessing the welfare costs of
CAP

should be counted as a 'gain' (less the administrative and other costs of collection). However, it is the consumer who pays the higher price; consumer surplus is reduced by areas $a + b + c + d$. If the gains to producers (a) and the revenue gains (c) are subtracted from the losses to consumers ($a + b + d + c$) in Table 4.1, the *welfare loss* from the policy is equal to $b + d$.[4] The policy is inefficient and these efficiency losses are referred to as the 'deadweight loss' of the policy.

(B) *Intervention buying*: The second example of intervention via the CAP is one in which the target price has been set so high that there is excess supply in the EU. In Figure 4.8(b) target price (P_t) is so high that EU supply exceeds domestic EU demand (and

---

4. This last result can be confirmed by another interpretation of Figure 4.8(a). Extra resource costs of $b + f$ are stimulated by protection. The additional output might have been acquired by imports which would cost f. Consumers have reduced consumption. They have forgone goods which they value at $g + d$, but which would have only cost them g. In net terms there is an overall reduction of welfare equal to $b + d$.

Table 4.1 The welfare effects of the CAP import levy

Gains to producers	+a			
Gains to taxpayer			+c	
Costs to consumers	−a	−b	−c	−d
Net welfare costs		−b		−d

this has arisen particularly with respect to cereals, beef, dairy products, wine and some fruits). To support this target price there must be intervention buying. In Figure 4.8(b) the export price for the good is P_w (imports are restrained). To maintain price at P_t within the EU, national agencies buy produce at certain times of the year. The welfare effects are shown in Figure 4.8(b).

The higher price increases output (from 0-q_3 to 0-q_4) and this increases producer surplus by area $a + b + c$. Consumer surplus is reduced by areas $a + b$, as demand is reduced from 0-q_2 to 0-q_1. Excess supply (0-$q_4 - 0$-q_1) is purchased by national agencies (to become 'butter mountains', 'wine lakes', etc.). The cost to the EU budget is areas $b + c + d$.[5] (Alternatively, if the surplus (0-$q_4 - 0$-q_1) were disposed of as exports the EU must offer an export subsidy to provide an incentive to producers to export and the cost to the EU budget of this subsidy is equal to area $b + c + d$).[6]

If producer surplus gain $a + b + c$ is added to consumer surplus loss $-(a + b)$, the net gain is c, but when budgetary cost of $b + c + d$ is taken into account, there is a welfare loss for individuals in the community and this is estimated as the deadweight loss of $b + d$ (see Table 4.2).

Table 4.2 The welfare effects of CAP intervention buying

Gains to producers	+a	+b	+c	
Losses to consumers	−a	−b		
Losses to taxpayers		−b	−c	−d
Net welfare costs		−b		−d

Theses two examples identify the welfare loss of government intervention in terms of deadweight loss triangles. They provide a useful introduction to analysis of the forms of intervention that characterise the Common Agricultural Policy.

It is now appropriate to consider a third situation (example C) which combines intervention within the CAP. In this example policy requires intervention via a variable import levy and export subsidy to deal with excess supply. In Figure 4.9 the world price is P_1 but the target price is P_2. The target price is now so high that the equilibrium price exceeds the price that would occur for a closed economy (i.e. at the intersection of S and D). Imports have been excluded; if there were free trade, imports would have increased and the equilibrium would have been at point 3. It is now possible to contrast policy

5. Of course $b + c + d$ underestimates the budgetary cost to the extent that this does not allow for storage costs or for deterioration/wastage of products stored.
6. Once again, there is another way in which the welfare costs of the price support policy can be estimated. If exports were the way to dispose of excess supply, then exports would increase by q_1q_2 and by q_3q_4 as a consequence of policy. The value of q_1q_2 to consumers in Europe is area $b + f$ but the Europeans will only receive area f when this is sold on the world market. The value of q_3q_4 in terms of the costs of production is shown by the area under the supply curve, i.e. area $g + d$ but when these goods are sold on the world market the country will receive only area g. In this way, it is evident that the net loss is area b (on units q_1-q_2) and area d (on units q_3-q_4.).

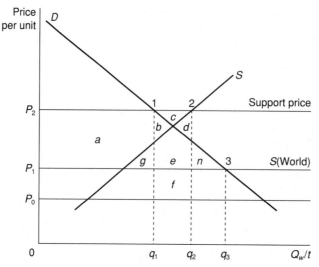

Figure 4.9 Welfare effects of CAP

outcome with such a competitive market outcome. However, in this example policy intervention also includes a subsidy to exports. The intention is that excess supply, q_2-q_1, will be sold on the international market.

Following Swann (2000), a comparison of policy outcome and the competitive market outcome reveals that consumers lose consumers surplus equal to $a + b + e + g + n$. On the other hand, a higher price means that producers enjoy an increase in producer surplus by $a + b + c$. The cost to the Europeans (as taxpayers) of subsidising the sale of excess supply on the international market is the difference between the cost of producing these units (P_2) and the price that will be received on the world market (P_0). In Figure 4.9 this cost is equal to $c + b + d + e + f$. (Of course, if price had not fallen when this production was 'dumped', the cost would only have been $c + b + d + e$).

Applying the same format as described above, the deadweight loss of a policy that now both restrains imports and subsidises exports can now be assessed with reference to Table 4.3. By adding costs and benefits of this form of intervention the net welfare costs of the CAP can be estimated as $-b - d - 2e - f - g - n$.

Table 4.3 The welfare effects of CAP intervention

Gains to producers	+a	+b	+c					
Losses to consumers	−a	−b			−e		−g	−n
Losses to taxpayers		−b	−c	−d	−e	−f		
Net welfare costs		−b		−d	−2e	−f	−g	−n

The common theme is that policy has implications for consumers, producers and taxpayers and that the effect on individuals, taken as a whole, is understood by aggregating these welfare changes. Applied economists convert these 'theoretical' losses into actual money magnitudes. Table 4.4 offers one early example of empirical work on the costs of the CAP. The losses to consumers and to taxpayers in each member state are compared to the gains to producers. The *net* figure is a measure of the deadweight loss. The transfer ratio shows how much it costs, in net terms, to use this price policy to transfer income to the producer. The costs for each member state are evident.

Many other studies have been undertaken to estimate the costs of the CAP. They all focus on the same comparison of consumer surplus, producer surplus and revenue effects. For a survey, see Demekas *et al.* (1995).

Table 4.4 **Welfare effects of the CAP by country in 1980 (US$m)**

Country	Consumers	Taxpayers	Producers	Net	Transfer ratio
EC-9	−34.580	−11,494	30,686	−15,388	1.5
Germany	−12,555	−3,769	9,045	7,279	1.8
France	−7,482	−2,836	7,237	−3,081	1.42
Italy	−5,379	−1,253	3,539	−3,093	1.87
Netherlands	−1,597	−697	3,081	787	0.74
Belgium/Luxembourg	−1,440	−544	1,624	−320	1.22
United Kingdom	−5,174	−1,995	3,461	−3,708	2.07
Ireland	−320	−99	965	546	0.43
Denmark	−635	−302	1,736	799	0.54

Source: Buckwell *et al.* (1982).

4.5.1.2 Can the Common Agricultural Policy be justified?

With such inefficiency, why operate the CAP? To answer this, reconsider the objectives in the Treaty of Rome (discussed in 4.4.1a). While the CAP is vulnerable to criticism in strict efficiency terms, perhaps it performs well with reference to some other objectives?

(a) *Stabilise markets*

One goal listed in the objectives of the Common Agricultural Policy is stability and the CAP uses a variable import levy. Price stability is maintained as the rate of duty rises (falls) when the world price falls (rises). In Figure 4.10 (following Hitiris 1988), D_M is the EU's import demand curve. S_W is the world supply curve of imports to the EU. With no intervention, equilibrium is at 1 and at price P_4 the quantity imported is q_2. The EU wants a price at P_5 and an import duty of distance 2-3 per unit is levied. With this tax consumer demand shifts to the left from D_M to D'_M. EU imports fall to q_1 (and the import price – net of tax – is P_3).

However, when the world supply curve is S'_W the import levy must increase from distance 2-3 to 2-4 per unit if domestic price is to be stabilised at P_5. Within the EU, price will be stabilised at P_5 but what of prices for others? The import price net of tax falls to P_1. Without the policy of the EU the international price would have been P_2 when the world supply curve is S'_W. The use of a *variable* levy on imports stabilises the EU price but amplifies the fall of *world* prices from P_3-P_2 to P_3-P_1 (and increases EU import duty revenue from P_5-2-3-P_3 to P_5-2-4-P_1 at an import level of q_1).

The analysis serves as a reminder that, when assessing welfare, the answer will depend on the cohort whose welfare is under consideration. For citizens in the EU

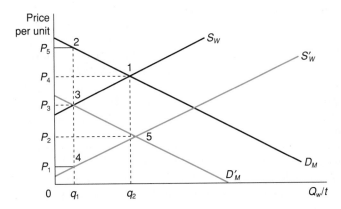

Figure 4.10
The CAP and world prices

there is greater price stability but this may not necessarily be the case for citizens outside the EU. Moreover, in some cases stability is achieved by completely removing imports and relying on self-sufficiency ratios of one (or greater than one). This is a salutary reminder of the costs of price stability in terms of denial of cheaper imports.

(b) *Ensures a fair standard of living for farmers?*

The welfare analysis in Section 4.4.1a revealed that the Common Agricultural Policy increased producer surplus. The impact of this price support on farm incomes is revealed in Table 4.3: producers have gained, even if this is at a cost for consumers and for taxpayers. In net terms, the cost of transferring to producers has been identified as a deadweight efficiency loss. The cost of transfer in each country is estimated in Table 4.3 as the transfer ratio.

However, the question can be raised as to whether this cost could be reduced by relying on other redistribution schemes (taxation and subsidies). Are there other options than reliance on price support? Moreover, are all farmers equally deserving of assistance? If the objective is to redistribute to those farmers who have low income a price support scheme is hardly the appropriate mechanism. It offers most reward to farmers with large farms and fertile ground, i.e. farmers who are least likely to be in need of help. For those farmers with smallholdings and marginal land, such support simply enables them to squeeze a living out of their activity. If the aim is to assist the poor then subsidies and tax relief targeted at farmers on low income might prove more appropriate.

One criticism of the redistribution that price support has yielded is in terms of the argument that different commodities have been given different price support. It has been argued that lower levels of price support have been given to products typically produced by countries of the Mediterranean and it is questionable that, with smaller average holdings such farmers might be in greater need of assistance (see Sloman 1997).

Redistribution via this mechanism has, on some occasions, led to acrimony between member states. Member states' 'gain' is far from equal because countries have very different proportions of their workforce engaged in agriculture. For example, in the UK only 2.1 per cent of the civilian population are employed in agriculture, forestry and fishing. In Belgium the figure is 2.5 per cent, in Germany 3.5 per cent, in the Netherlands 3.9 per cent, in France 5.1 per cent, in Italy 7.3 per cent, in Ireland 13.5 per cent and in Greece 21.3 per cent (Sloman 1997). It is perhaps not so surprising that redistribution via the EU budget has raised concerns particularly on the part of the UK.

(c) *Reasonable prices for consumers?*

Table 4.4 illustrates the losses to consumers because of higher prices. However, there are other concerns:

(i) The impact of higher food prices is *regressive* as the poor spend a larger proportion of their incomes on food than the relatively well off. A system of high prices for food, therefore, directly penalises the poor and increases inequality.

(ii) While consumers are faced with prices higher than those on the world market, they have witnessed excess supply sold at a subsidised price abroad. The EU has attracted notoriety for the subsidies given to surpluses sold abroad. For example, the notorious case of 200,000 tons of butter sold to the Russians in 1973 at a price of 8 pence per pound or 16% of costs was sure to catch the headlines (Scherer 1996).

It is questionable that the policy has delivered reasonable prices to Europeans.

(d) *Implication for the rest of the world?*

The European Union is not alone in supporting its agricultural sector. Almost all countries pursue agricultural policies that lead to distortions in resource allocation.

However, in denying access to EU markets the CAP has generated a strong feeling of resentment among traditional agricultural exporters (Australia, New Zealand, Canada).

The EU is a large consumer of agricultural food and, when it reduces demand for imports of agricultural products, price on the international market will fall (see the discussion of the optimum tariff in Chapter 17). Producers in foreign countries witness adverse terms of trade effects made worse when the EU dumps excess supply on the world market.

Summing up, the case for administered prices is difficult to sustain. The administrative and financial costs of achieving a target price in the EU are well known.[7] The efficiency costs have been identified. Claims that the policy increases equity are spurious. There is little evidence that creating excess supply has had a significant effect on productivity (agricultural productivity increases in the EU have not exceeded the increase of agricultural production outside the EU) and the effects on the environment have been criticised (Sloman 1997).

However, the objective here is not to present an evaluation of the CAP. The objective is to argue that application of market analysis (as described earlier in this chapter) identifies the costs of introducing administered prices. Such analysis yields predictions (emerging as a consequence of excess supply) of the problems of operating administered prices. Policy-makers may pursue administered prices for very laudable reasons but when the equilibrium price is rejected there are likely to be consequences that did not feature as part of the original plan. These arise because of the difficulties of resisting market forces.

4.5.2 Rent control

In this section another illustration is considered. The approach described here is similar to that in the previous section. In the first instance, predictions of the impact of administered prices (and rejection of the equilibrium price) on quantity demanded and quantity supplied per period will be discussed. Second, the welfare costs of administered prices will be assessed (by focusing on consumer surplus and producer surplus). This discussion permits analysis of the welfare (efficiency) costs of policy (as compared with the outcome if provision were left to a competitive market). After considering efficiency equity issues are addressed.

The case of administered pricing in this section is *rent control*. This was first introduced in the UK in 1914. It was introduced as an emergency measure, to prevent profiteering by landlords (in areas of housing shortages, when there were inflows of labour for war production). While successive Housing Acts (e.g. 1923, 1925, 1927, 1933 and 1938) had elements of deregulation, four million houses were subject to control in 1939 (Albon and Stafford 1987). Further deregulation was introduced in 1957 but, in 1965, rent control was imposed again (via an act that embodied the notion of 'fair rents'). In the 1974 Housing Act rent registration and full security of tenure were extended to the previously relatively uncontrolled 'furnished' sector. The 1988 Housing Act saw more moves towards deregulation and in 1989 the British government announced measures to phase out rent control.

---

7. For example, the CAP has sought to set common prices for agricultural goods and when exchange rates were able to move this created difficulty. If a member state devalued this would have the effect of causing its farm prices (in national currency terms) to rise (the contrary would occur if it devalued). The problem necessitated the use of a second exchange rate set for agricultural goods – the 'green exchange rate' – which posed problems.

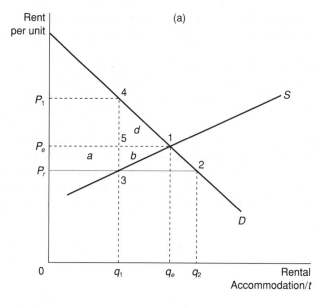

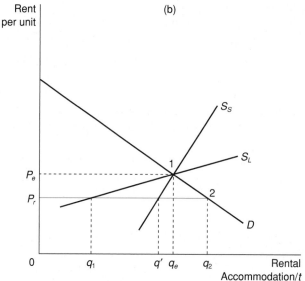

Figure 4.11 Rent control

In Figure 4.11(a) when rent is set lower than the equilibrium, excess demand (q_2-q_1) is created. If maximum rent (P_r) is below equilibrium rent (P_e) there will be excess demand for accommodation. Excess demand may generate economic and social problems (in just the same way as economic, social and political problems were generated when the CAP created excess supply). The following discussion identifies the impact of rent control on the market and the problems that any government will (predictably) face when choosing to replace an equilibrium price with an administered price.

(i)   *The impact of administered pricing on the market: excess demand for accommodation*
In Figure 4.11(a) demand (D) and supply (S) for rental accommodation determines equilibrium price (P_e) and the equilibrium quantity of rental accommodation (q_e). At this point demand for rental accommodation from tenants equals the

amount of accommodation landlords make available. If rent control is introduced, the maximum rent that landlords can charge is P_r. The first observation is that, at this price, equilibrium moves from point 1 to point 2 and demand for rented accommodation (q_2) exceeds the quantity available (q_1). There is a shortage (excess demand), as quantity demanded exceeds quantity supplied.

In Figure 4.11(b) the importance of price elasticity of supply is highlighted. As noted earlier, price elasticity depends on time. The immediate effect of rent control is that demand will increase from q_e to q_2 associated with points 1 and 2. Supply of accommodation falls in the short run (e.g. via non-renewal of contractual agreements) and, with reference to the short-run supply curve S_S, supply of rental accommodation falls from q_e to q'. However, over time more landlords have greater opportunity to respond. Leases on apartments will not be renewed; existing apartments may be removed for rental. In Figure 4.11(b) the elasticity of supply is greater for the long-run supply curve S_L than elasticity for the short-run supply curve S_s. Katz and Rosen (1991) cite a study by Poterba (1984) that, in the USA, long-run price elasticity of supply for rental housing is about 2. This means that rent control policy that keeps the price 10 per cent below the free market level leads to a 20 per cent fall in the total amount of rental housing.

The longer the time period, the greater the impact of policy. In the UK, the market for privately owned unfurnished rental accommodation fell. From 45 per cent of households in privately owned rental accommodation in 1945, the figure fell steadily until by the end of the 1980s it was only 8 per cent (Albon and Stafford 1987). Lipsey and Chrystal (1995) note how a growing shortage put pressure on the state to build accommodation. As private investors would not supply accommodation at controlled rents, UK local authorities assumed this responsibility by supplying 'council housing' at subsidised rents. Financial stringency in the late 1970s and 1980s reduced the ability of local authorities to construct new council housing. Later (in Mrs Thatcher's administration), the policy was to sell 'council houses' to existing tenants.

As is evident by reference to the model of the market, regulated price below equilibrium price leads to excess demand. Albon and Stafford (1987: 33) cite an observation made by George Stigler and Milton Friedman. Referring to reports in the *San Francisco Chronicle*, they observed that in 1906 (after the San Francisco earthquake) there was 1 'wanted to rent' house or apartment for every 10 'houses or apartments for rent'. However, in 1946 when there was rent control there were 375 'wanted to rent' for every 10 available for rent!

(ii) *The welfare costs of administered pricing*

Figure 4.11(a) illustrates the welfare costs of the policy. Landlords lose and the loss is shown by the reduction in producer surplus equal to areas $a + b$ (i.e. P_r-P_e-1-3).

While the objective of the policy might be to increase the welfare of tenants, only some tenants are made better off. There is a gain to existing tenants who retain their tenure. This can be estimated in Figure 4.11(a) as area a (i.e. P_r-P_e-5-3, the difference between the free-market rent P_e and the controlled rent P_r for all remaining tenancies).

What of tenants who lose their tenancy? What of prospective tenants who are unable to find accommodation? In Figure 4.11(a) there are only 0-q_1 tenancies available when there is rent control. At this point, it is easy to see that willingness to pay for rental accommodation (P_1) exceeds the rent that landlords can ask (P_r). If q_1-q_e tenancies were available, then area 3-4-1 is an estimate of the difference between the sum that tenants would pay for accommodation (i.e. q_1-4-1-q_e) and the sum that landlords require for accommodation (i.e. q_1-3-1-q_e). The overall loss, area $b + d$ (triangle 3-4-1) comprises a loss to consumers (triangle 5-4-1) and a loss to producers (triangle 3-5-1), when compared with the market equilibrium outcome (at price P_e).

Once again, the net welfare costs of the policy can be determined by adding gains and losses. Producers lose $a + b$; existing tenants gain a (so that a is simply a transfer); new tenants lose d (as compared with a market price of P_e). The result is that there are net losses of triangles $b + d$ (by triangle 3-4-1). These losses are outright deadweight losses. They are the efficiency (welfare) costs of the policy.

Table 4.5 **The welfare effects of rent control**

Gains to continued tenants	+a		
Loss to discontinued tenants			−d
Loss to landlords	−a	−b	
Net welfare costs		−b	−d

Of course, such efficiency costs may appear worthwhile if the policy succeeds in addressing a distribution objective (note the comparison with the CAP where an attempt was made to justify efficiency costs to assist poor farmers). However, once again, the distribution argument requires careful consideration. Policy-makers restrain price to assist tenants but only some tenants are made better off. Moreover, landlords may not be so obvious a target for redistribution. Browning and Zupata (1996) report that 30 per cent of New York landlords had incomes below $20,000 and half had incomes below $40,000.

(iii) *Costs of generating excess demand and resisting price change*

Just as the CAP is difficult to operate because it continually generates excess supply, so rent control creates many problems because there is excess demand. The following are some unattractive (but predictable) implications:

a) *Deterioration of quality*   Rent control produces incentives for landlords to withdraw accommodation. To induce tenants to leave, landlords have little incentive to maintain quality. Also, landlords who continue to offer accommodation have an incentive to lower maintenance costs to offset (if only in part) the reduction in rent (for an analytical treatment of this, see Barr 1998).[8] Hartley (1977) notes UK government concern (e.g. he cites the report of the Fair Deal on Housing, *Cmnd* 4728, 1971. But, are such results really so surprising?

b) *Harassment of tenants*   The use of administered pricing in the market for domestic accommodation coverage of rent control means that landlords have an incentive to offer their properties for business and commercial rental. The implication of partial rent control is that landlords will prefer to rent their accommodation in markets where there is no constraint. Dobson *et al.* (1998) notes the effect when rent control is applied only to some parts of the market, i.e. to old properties and not to new properties. Landlords evict tenants to demolish buildings (still in good shape) so that they can reconstruct rental units and rent at a higher price. They refer to just such experience in Hong Kong. Hartley (1977) cites the *Francis Report* (Committee on the Rents Act, *Cmnd* 4609 1971) which found that there had been harassment and illegal eviction in the UK. Stiglitz and Driffill (2000: 94) refer to UK experience: 'In the 1950s notorious examples of flagrant exploitation and bullying of relatively poor tenants came to light – it became known as Rachmanism after a particularly egregious practitioner.' Existing tenants were put under considerable pressure as landlords sought to rent their property in an unregulated market.

8. Hills and Mullings (1990) confirm that average quality of housing in the private rented sector in the UK is lower than in other tenures.

Importantly, such examples illustrate the additional measures that government must pursue to administer price. It becomes necessary to set minimum standards of housing quality to safeguard against the more disconcerting aspects of action by landlords. Governments typically pass security of tenure laws that protect the tenant from eviction. Of course, by making it harder to evict undesirable tenants, these laws further reduce the expected return from any given rental price.

(v) *'Black markets'* In Figure 4.11(a) the availability of rental accommodation was reduced to $0\text{-}q_1$ after rent had been controlled. However, at this point the amount that an individual would pay for an apartment is shown as $q_1\text{-}4$ (or $0\text{-}P_1$), well above the rent $q_1\text{-}3$ (or $0\text{-}P_r$) that can be charged. The result is that other mechanisms will exist to ration available accommodation. One way for landlords to appropriate this surplus is to require a lump sum 'entrance' fee (or 'key money') from new tenants. Loopholes may be exploited. As a curious example, Katz and Rosen (1991) refer to a case in Berkley (USA) where one landlord founded the First National German Sebastian Kneipp and Mineral Water Church to ration tenancies to members of the church, membership costing $1200!

Alternatively, the problem of excess demand may be resolved by other non-price means of rationing (which were never envisaged by rent control legislation). Landlords may introduce other criteria to select tenants. For example, non-price rationing might emerge when landlords favour tenants without children, without pets, or of different ethnic origin. If some tenants are able to find accommodation, there may also be a tendency to sublet.

(vi) *Market dislocation – labour immobility* There are implications for other markets. For example, labour mobility is impaired. People are unwilling to move from a controlled house or flat and cannot find accommodation in the areas where there is work (distortions in the housing market spill over as distortions in the labour market).

(vii) *Search costs* A shortage of available accommodation means that prospective tenants will have to expend time and effort searching for accommodation. Parkin *et al.* (2000) refer to experience in San Francisco where specialised agencies (intermediaries) charge fees for clients and undertake the work involved in finding accommodation.

(viii) *Costs of administration* At the same time, if policy is to be effective, it must be enforced. For example, Browning and Zupata (1996) refer to an example in Santa Monica where the Rent Control Board's budget was $5 million in 1994. To pay for this, each tenant was levied an annual fee of $156. Furthermore, since property taxes are the most important source of revenue for many cities and local authorities, rent control erodes cities' tax base. The same authors estimate that rent control reduced property tax revenue by 10 to 20 per cent in Cambridge, Massachusetts.

An overview: The attempt to administer prices imposes welfare losses and turns out to be far more difficult than might have been imagined. Market forces (excess demand) create costs which government must deal with in pursuit of administered prices. Prices may be set but the implications for disequilibria must be taken into account.

4.5.3 Minimum wage legislation

The third example to be considered in this chapter is an administered price in the labour market. A similar format suggests the following analysis.

(i) *The impact of administered pricing on the market: excess supply of labour*
In April 1999 the UK introduced a minimum wage of £3.60 an hour for those aged 22 or more and of £3 for 18-to-21-year-olds. By October 2004 the minimum wage

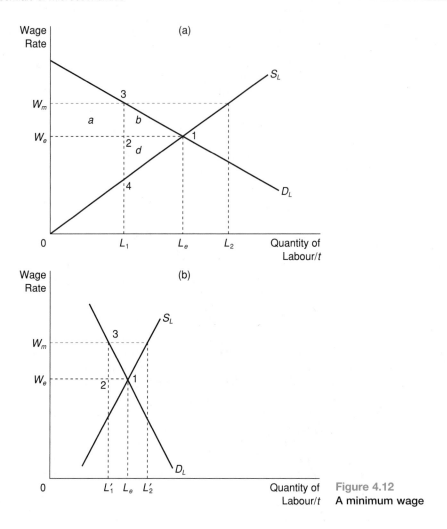

Figure 4.12 A minimum wage

had risen to £4.85 an hour. When the policy was introduced it was estimated that 2 million workers would be affected by this legislation. Critics of a minimum wage policy argued that the introduction of a minimum wage would simply lead to greater unemployment. This prediction can be derived from market analysis described in this chapter. In Figure 4.12(a) D_L is the demand for labour and S_L the supply of labour. W_e is the equilibrium price. If the government introduces regulation an administered price of W_m is set above the equilibrium price. The market analysis suggest that demand for labour will fall from L_e to L_1 and the supply of labour will increase to L_2, leading to unemployment of L_2-L_1.

The effect on the market depends, in large part, on price elasticities of supply. In Figure 4.12(b) both demand and supply elasticities are much lower than in Figure 4.12(a). The result is that, while minimum wage legislation leads to unemployment, the extent of unemployment (L_2'-L_1') is far lower (than L_2-L_1) in Figure 4.12(a).

The effect also depends on coverage. The effect of a minimum wage on employment as shown in Figure 4.12 applies only if *all* workers are covered by minimum wage laws. If there is only partial coverage there may be no increase in unemployment. In Figure 4.13(a) the minimum wage is set for workers in occupation Z. Whereas W_e represents the initial equilibrium wage the minimum wage is set at W_m. The effect of the minimum wage is to reduce the demand for labour from L_e to L_1

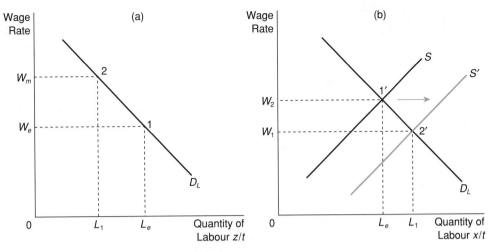

Figure 4.13 **Minimum wage: partial coverage**

associated with points 1 and 2. However, if these workers can move to occupation X, then the effects of the minimum wage are not reflected in increased unemployment but in a fall of the wage paid for labour in the X occupation. As the demand for labour is reduced, unemployed workers in the covered sector switch over to the uncovered sector. The supply of labour in Figure 4.13(b) increases to the right. Thus the minimum wage legislation means that the wage rate in the covered sector rises and the wage rate in the uncovered sector falls. In Figure 4.13(b) the wage falls from W_2 to W_1 associated with points 1′ and 2′.

In the USA minimum wage legislation was introduced in 1938 under the Fair Labor Standards Act. From 1981 to 1989 the minimum wage was $3.35 an hour, though this was raised to $4.25 in 1990, to $4.70 in 1996 and to $5.15 in 1997 (Pindyck and Rubinfeld 1998). Most industries are covered in the USA. While studies have found little evidence of an employment effect on older adults, there is evidence that teenagers (workers aged 16–19) and older adults (aged 20 to 24 years old) have found it more difficult to find employment. For example, Brown (1988) concluded that teenage employment would fall between 1% and 3% as a result of a 10% increase in the minimum wage. There is a debate on this issue. Some studies suggest that minimum wage legislation has led to an *increase* in employment (Card and Krueger 1993) but this proposition is examined in later chapters when other concepts of market structure have been examined. Discussion here is of a competitive market prior to regulation.

In the UK, a report of the Low Pay Commission argued that minimum wage legislation has delivered higher wages for the poor without hurting employment. However the *Economist* (19 Feb. 2000) argued that elasticities are such that, if the minimum wage were increased (to £4 or £5), employment would be affected. The writers argue that apparent success is based on a period in which the economy has shown 'healthy growth' and that had the economy slowed down the effects of wage control on employment would have been more apparent. If the recent legislation in the UK is still under review, it is possible to look back to the Wages Councils that operated in the 1980s. These affected about 2.5 million workers (e.g. in catering, retailing) and they used minimum wage arrangements. They were abolished in 1993. However, empirical work found little effect of adverse employment effects (e.g. Craig *et al.* 1982; Machin and Manning 1992).

(ii) *The welfare costs of administered pricing*

With reference to Figure 4.12(a) it is possible to highlight gains and losses. Those who remain in employment (0-L_1) gain by area *a* (which measures the additional payment area W_e-W_m-3-2 for labour employed). This is an increase in producer surplus for those employed. However, employers lose this area *a* in the additional wage payment that they must pay. They also lose area *b* because their willingness to pay for labour (depending on the marginal product of the unit of labour L_1-L_e – i.e. area L_1-3-1-L_e) exceeds the wages that they would have to pay labour (area L_1-2-1-L_e) if the units of labour L_1-L_e were employed. At the same time, area *d* is a loss to labour. Units L_1-L_e require payment of only L_1-4-1-L_e to supply labour. Prior to the introduction of minimum wage legislation they would have been paid $L_{1.}$2-1-L_e. The difference (the loss) is area *d*. Area *a* is a transfer (from employers to those in work) but there are deadweight costs (triangles $b + d$).

Table 4.6 The welfare effects of minimum wages

Gains to employed workers	+*a*		
Losses to unemployed workers			−*d*
Losses to employers	−*a*	−*b*	
Net welfare costs		−*b*	−*d*

What of equity? Not all workers benefit; only those lucky to remain in employment will benefit. It has been argued that, as employers are likely to dismiss the least productive first, it may be the most disadvantaged and unproductive workers who are most likely to be priced out of the market. The issue of coverage is also important here. It has been shown that, while the wage rate in the covered sector will increase, the wage rate in the uncovered sector will fall. Low-wage earners in uncovered sectors will get lower wages and this may produce income distribution effects that are the opposite of what was intended.

To assess equity it is necessary to identify clearly the groups involved. For example, has labour (as a whole) won or lost? To answer this, price elasticities of demand and supply are relevant. In Figure 4.12(b) the decrease in employment L_e-L_1' is small. In this case, the total wage bill rises (from 0-W_e-1-L_e to 0-W_m-3-L_1'), so, *in principle*, the original employed labour force could redistribute the wage increases so that all workers are better off. In Figure 4.12(a) the decrease in employment L_e-L_1 is large and the overall wage bill falls. In this sense, workers (as a whole) are worse off.

If minimum wage policy is targeted (in equity terms) – as a means of helping poor households – then there are problems. There will be a positive effect on the incomes of some workers. However, not all low-paid workers live in low-income households and, if concern is with the household, minimum wage legislation may not be the best policy. Also, poverty depends on the number of dependants as well as on the wage rate. Moreover, many people who live in poverty do not have jobs and this policy will have nothing to offer this cohort.

All policies to alleviate poverty have shortcomings but, unlike some other methods of helping the poor, a minimum wage increases incentives to find work and to raise work effort. There is more to consider in any comparison of minimum wage legislation and other tax/subsidy arrangements. In practice, the evidence on this issue in the USA is that minimum wage laws have very little effect on income distribution (see Gramlich 1976 for an early study). In the UK, work by the Institute of Fiscal Studies (1998) suggests that more people in the middle-income group will gain more than in the poorest 10%.

(iii) *Costs of generating excess supply and resisting price change*

The cost of administering higher prices has been considered without any possible impact on the productivity of labour. The discussion of Figure 4.12 and Figure 4.13 assumes that there is no effect of higher wages on productivity; there is no change in D_L. Some economists have used an *efficiency wage* argument (associated with Akerlof and Yellen 1986) to argue that higher wages may be desirable. They argue that paying a wage above the market wage may be profitable to a firm if there are costs associated with searching for, selecting and training new workers. Facing these types of costs, a firm may choose to pay higher wages to reduce labour force turnover. Additionally, if there is imperfect information in labour markets and if a higher wage is likely to attract a larger pool of more qualified job applicants, a firm may find it profitable to raise wages above the level needed to attract qualified applicants. Moreover, if hired workers are prone to shirking (i.e. working below their fullest capacity), a wage exceeding the prevailing market level may induce a greater increase in productive effort than the wage premium.

Simpson and Paterson (1992) refer to evidence by Raff and Summers (1987) that an increase in the daily wage from \$3 to \$5 introduced by Henry Ford in 1914 raised productivity and reduced labour turnover for the Ford Motor Company. However, the argument that firms will pay efficiency wages begs the question of why the government is required to legislate a minimum wage in the first place.

There is also an argument (see Simpson and Paterson 1992) that higher wages improve management of firms. The argument is that, while firms relying on cheap labour may survive (despite inefficiencies in the production process), the requirement to pay a minimum wage rate may prove the shock that induces them to use more advanced techniques. But this begs the question of why they would not do this prior to the legislation (as it would be profit-enhancing).

Critics of minimum wage regulation argue that, if there is no consequent increase in productivity, wage increases will be passed on as price increases elsewhere. With a reduction in employment, the output of final goods will be lower and the price of certain goods will increase. The consumer may bear part of the cost of the policy. While it is not obvious that poor consumers will be harder hit than rich consumers, the effect is said to be inflationary for the economy as a whole.

Another aspect of analysis here is that it is comparative static in nature. It compares the outcome that emerges when the market mechanism works with that which would arise when the market is constrained to a minimum wage. What about the impact of policy over time? One dynamic problem associated with the minimum wage is that there is no incentive to invest in skills. If low-skilled workers' wages are held up then the wage differential from investment in human capital is reduced (see, for example, Oi 1997). The existence of the minimum wage may reduce the incentive to invest time in acquiring skills. Lal (1995) argues that it reduces the desire to promote skill accumulation on the part of unskilled workers (particularly the young and females). Some research from the US suggests that minimum wage legislation has encouraged teenagers to leave school and look for work (Neumark and Washer 1995).

Once again, the objective here is not to offer an evaluation of the policy under discussion. The objective is to illustrate the way in which microeconomic analysis of market can be applied, to identify the welfare losses that arise when there is intervention in a competitive market and to highlight the problems that arise when trying to 'buck' the market.

4.5.4 Welfare gains and price uncertainty

As indicated above, much of economic theory throws up surprising (or counter-intuitive) results. As a further simple illustration, consider price uncertainty. In Figure 14.14(a)

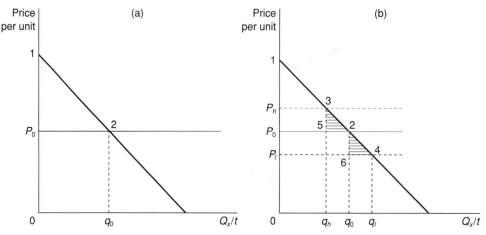

Figure 4.14 **Static welfare gains from price variation**

when price is P_0 and equilibrium quantity q_0 is chosen (at point 2), consumer surplus is triangle P_0-1-2. Now introduce price uncertainty in the form of random price fluctuations of P_h (a higher price) and P_l (a lower price) whose average value is P_0. How is consumer surplus affected? When P_h in panel (b) obtains (which replicates panel (a)), only q_h is purchased per period and the consumer surplus loss compared to P_0 is trapezoid P_0-P_h-3-2. When P_l arises, q_l is purchased per period and the consumer surplus gain compared to P_0 is trapezoid P_l-P_0-2-4. Mentally placing trapezoid P_l-P_0-2-4 on top of trapezoid P_0-P_h-3-2 reveals a net consumer surplus gain equal to triangle 5-3-2 plus triangle 6-2-4. Price uncertainty welfare gains are arising because of quantity adjustment curtailing consumer surplus loss when the price is high and augmenting consumer surplus gain when the price is low.

Considerations of risk discussed in Chapter 7 may modify this result. To the extent individuals are risk-averse they might prefer a certain consumer surplus per period of triangle P_0-1-2 to an expected value of consumer surplus per period that is noticeably higher. That said, risk-neutral and risk-taking consumers will have a preference for price uncertainty, other things equal. This illustration and the profits equivalent are discussed by De Grauwe (1997) in terms of a flexible exchange rate inducing price uncertainty. He concludes that the case for reducing price uncertainty is moot when considered in terms of static welfare analysis.

4.6 Auctions and prices

Above (in Section 4.4) it was noted how the equilibrium price was located in a Walrasian and a Marshallian clearing mechanism in a market:

(i)   In the Walrasian mechanism quantities supplied and demanded at different prices were compared with prices adjusting upwards with excess demands and downwards with excess supply. This is price adjustment.

(ii) In the Marshallian system demand prices and supply prices were compared with excess demand price over supply price signalling increase quantity per period and excess supply price over demand price signalling decrease quantity per period. This is quantity adjustment.

But if both mechanisms get you to equilibrium who cares what the story is? Does it really matter?

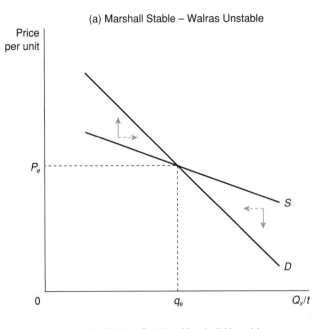

(a) Marshall Stable – Walras Unstable

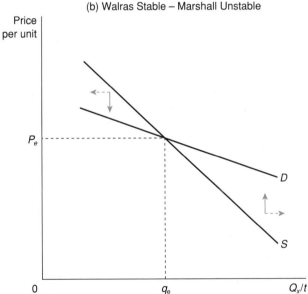

(b) Walras Stable – Marshall Unstable

Figure 4.15
Clearing mechanisms with decreasing costs

Consideration of Figure 4.15 shows that, if supply is downward-sloping, two cases can arise with supply cutting demand from above and supply cutting demand from below. With the solid arrow representing Walrasian adjustment and the dashed arrow Marshallian adjustment, it is clear that where one is stable (pushing towards equilibrium) the other is unstable (pushing away from equilibrium). This is a simple and clear demonstration that the story about how you get to equilibrium matters. In the one mechanism you will not get there and in the other you will.

Walras, in particular, is associated with the story of the auctioneer. The auctioneer announces a set of market prices for each good. Individuals then value their initial endowments of goods at these prices and, in line with their particular preferences, announce quantities of each good that they would like to sell and buy. The auctioneer adds up all the offers to sell and buy for each good to give a market supply and demand picture. If the quantities are matched in each and every market, goods are exchanged at the announced prices and 'everyone goes home' (Katzner 1988: 201) as the job is done. If the quantities do not match, no exchange occurs and the auctioneer announces a new set of prices – higher where there has been excess demand and lower where there has been excess supply. The process is assumed to continue until a full set of competitive prices has been established before any trades actually occur. (There is no trading at non-equilibrium or 'false' prices.) This grope towards equilibrium sounds less sordid when captured in the French word 'tatonnement'.

Having noted that the creation of market prices is an economic process in itself and that it would be desirable if that process had optimising/efficiency characteristics itself, it is worth pursuing the auctions analogy further. This is because in recent decades a large literature has been developed on the properties of actual auctions in themselves. This interest has been driven by the privatisation (selling off nationalised industries) in market economies around the world plus the need to try to establish market prices in the newly democratised transitional economies. There are many forms of auction and types of asset to be auctioned. A first distinction is between private-value auctions, where an asset has a value that is specific to each individual, and common-value auctions, where an asset has an underlying value (or profitability) that is effectively common to all potential owners (bidders). Additionally, auctions can be of single assets or a collection of assets as in multi-object auctions. In this section key issues directed at each of these types are explored.

4.6.1　Common-value auctions and the winner's curse

The 'winner's curse', as the name suggests, relies on the observation that winners of auction have often paid more than the common value of the assets (or, at least, are very disappointed with the actual surplus they receive from the acquisition of an asset) – the winners are losers! How does this paradox arise?

Assume there are i bidders with $i = 1, 2, \ldots, N$ and that the asset for auction has a common underlying value (0.5) and estimates of this value are drawn from an unbiased uniform distribution of values between 0 and 1. The 'unbiasedness' assumption means that the mean value of the number of estimated values will be 0.5. For example, with $N = 3$ sample estimates, the expectation would be that they are at 0.25, 0.5 and 0.75, i.e. evenly distributed across the distribution with a mean value of $1.5/3 = 0.5$. With $N = 4$ sample estimates, the expectation would be that they are at 0.2, 0.4, 0.6 and 0.8, i.e. once again, evenly distributed across the distribution with a mean value of $2/4 = 0.5$.

It is clear that, as the number of estimates (N) increases, it raises the expected highest valuation v_N. With $N = 9$ the expected v_N is 0.9, compared to 0.75 with $N = 3$ (see Figure 4.16). It is also evident that with N estimates, it divides the uniform distribution into $N + 1$ segments with highest estimate being $N/(N + 1)$ times unity in this case. With $N = 3$ it was $3/4 \times 1 = 0.75$ with $N = 4$ it was $4/5 \times 1 = 0.8$ and with $N = 9$ it was $9/10 \times 1 = 0.9$.

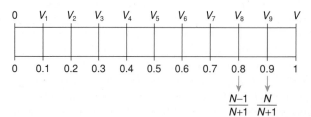

Figure 4.16

Expected valuations when $N = 9$

This can be demonstrated more formally. Taking N estimates from the frequency distribution between 0 and 1 means that the probability that all the estimates are less than a certain value v (e.g. 0.25) is given by v_N. So that if $N = 2$ it would be 0.25^2 (which is 0.0625 or 1/16 as a fraction). If you were asked the question as to what is the probability with one estimate of the highest value being the one located on the x-axis, the curve gives the result, e.g. 0.25 or less (the answer can be taken from the cumulative frequency distribution of v and is 0.25). The probability density function indicates how v_N rises as the chosen value v increases, i.e. $d(v^N)dv$, which is the first derivative of v^N with respect to v and is Nv_{N-1}.

To find the expected value of v_N it is necessary to find the integral (adding up) of all the values v can take multiplied by the probability of their arising That is:

$$\int_0^1 v\, Nv_{N-1}\, dv = N/(N + 1) \tag{4.4}$$

Armed with this information, it is easy to see how the winner's curse of the auction winner paying a value in excess of the common value arises, as the expected highest valuation will always be greater than 0.5 if $N > 1$. Of course, it is reasonable to expect that individuals learn from their mistakes and ask themselves 'Given my valuation is v, how must I optimally adjust (shade) my bid (b) downwards to avoid the winner's curse?'

Suppose there is an auction for a parcel of land and valuations range from 0 to v' and you have $v = £80,000$ and you know there are $N = 100$ bidders. Because of the unbiased distribution assumption, the true value of the parcel is $v/2$ and, given the above, the expected highest valuation will be $(100/101)v$. Now you think – suppose my £80,000 is the highest v, then $(100/101)v = £80,000$ and this implies $v = £80,800$. Therefore, your shaded bid should be $v/2 = £40,400$ which is a large 'correction'. The size of the correction decreases with N. If $N = 1000$, the appropriate bid is £40,040. It is clear that as N increases the highest v approaches v' and $v/2$ approaches $v'/2$, the true valuation.

While this may seem very esoteric, there is a great deal of evidence of the winner's curse. Ashenfelter and Genesove (1992) noted the results of the auction of 83 condominium apartments in New Jersey, which had 2348 bidders. All the units were sold but subsequently 40% of the sales fell through and the properties were then sold in face-to-face negotiations. In the resale, the prices of identical properties to those auctioned fell by 13%, suggesting sub-optimal adjustment to the presence of the winner's curse. The authors also noted the presence of the price decline anomaly, in that the condominiums that had been sold earliest in the auctions but had to be resold face-to-face suffered the biggest price decline (being early is not always good!). Clearly the seller, however, made greater profit via the auction, but would it matter for profitability how the auction was organised? It seems evident that individuals cannot completely 'learn' to compensate for their anomalous behaviour and this will encourage processes like the winner's curse.

Hilton (1998) reports overconfidence effects amongst 'experts'. A common way to assess calibration of predictions is to ask individuals to make a prediction, such that they are certain the actual future value of a variable will fall within the range they specify. In one study 36 foreign exchange traders were asked to make a prediction about the £/€ exchange rate in six months' time such that they were 90% sure the actual rate would be in the range they specified. If calibration is not faulty only 10% of predictions should fail to be in the specified ranges. The miss rate for the exchange rate predictions was actually 71.1% (and was even higher for stock price and general knowledge questions). With this kind of misplaced confidence in your own ability it is not surprising that errors of judgement are made. It is a bit like being asked to set your own exam question and then responding by setting yourself a question you cannot answer!

4.6.2 The revenue equivalence theorem

There are many types of auction but four common ones are:

(i) the English or ascending-bid auction;
(ii) second-price sealed bid (SPSB, where the highest sealed bid gets the asset but the bidder pays the second highest sealed bid);
(iii) Dutch or descending-bid auction; and
(iv) first-price sealed bid (FPSB, where the highest sealed bid gets the asset and the bidder pays the bid made).

It is now assumed the auction is for a private-value asset, so that the valuations are simply those of individuals. The revenue equivalence theorem (RET) is an invariance theorem which states that, in these four private independent-value auctions, the seller's expected price $E(P)$ is the same. 'This fact' is described as 'the biggest result in auction theory' (Rasmusen, 2001: 328). How is the 'fact' established and is the judgement valid?

This section follows a treatment of RET in Molho (1997). At the outset it can be noted that the English and the SPSB auctions are similar, in that the expected price is the second highest valuation (+ a small amount extra in the case of the English auction – an amount ignored as it can be assumed to be very small). Further, both have a truth-telling property, in that there is no incentive to distort your bid. If you overbid and secure the asset when the second price was above your valuation you must penalise yourself as you value the asset less than you pay for it. If you underbid you run the risk of losing an asset that you value greater than the second price that, given your under-bidding, may well gain the asset. Therefore the bid of individual i, b_i, will equal their true valuation v_i.

The Dutch auction and the FPSB have a 'non-truth-telling incentive' in that the bidder needs to trade off two competing incentives. If the individual i shades their bid b_i downwards by applying a factor z_i where $0 < z_i \leq 1$ to their true valuation v_i then $b_i < v_i$ (except when $z_i = 1$) and the expected surplus from the asset, if secured, is increased, but against this the expected probability of failing to secure the asset is raised. Given the incentives of the first two and second two types of auction the theorem will be established if SPSB and FPSB generate the same expected price.

For simplicity, assume again a valuations uniform distribution between 0 and 1. For the FPSB the bidders bid their true valuations v_i and pay the second highest bid, which is known from above to be $(N-1)/(N+1)$ as $N/(N+1)$ is the highest. Revenue will be the second-to-last valuation along the distribution of possible values, e.g. in the 9 bidders case above this give $8/10 = 0.8$ (see Figure 4.16). The RET requires the SPSB auction to offer the same expected revenue.

Things are more complicated for the SPSB auction. However, the key to resolving the trade-off noted above is to determine how to optimally shade your valuation to form your expected surplus-maximising bid. To make the reasoning easier assume that $N = 2$ initially, i.e. there are two bidders and, once again, valuations are drawn from a uniform frequency distribution over the interval 0-1 with the top possible valuation $V = 1$. Bidder 1 secures the asset if $b_1 = z_1 v_1 \geq b_2 = z_2 v_2$ or so that, at the margin, $b_1 = z_2 v_2$ with $v_2 = b_1/z_2$. Given the square probability density function of v_i in Figure 4.17, the probability v_2 is no greater than b_1/z_2 which is the shaded area to the left of the b_1/z_2 value, being $b_1/z_2 \times 1 = b_1/z_2$. Hence, the expected surplus ($E(S)$) for bidder 1 is the surplus v_1-b_1 times this probability of winning the auction:

$$E(S) = (v_1 - b_1)b_1/z_2 \tag{4.5}$$

$$= \frac{v_1 b_1}{z_2} - \frac{b_1^2}{z_2}$$

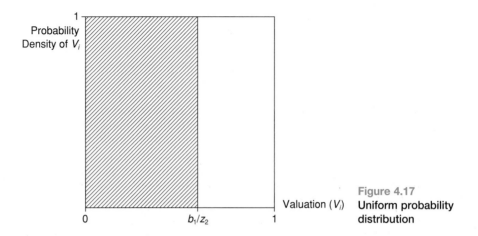

Figure 4.17
Uniform probability
distribution

and the first-order condition for an expected surplus-maximising bid is given by setting the first derivative with respect to b_1 equal to zero:

$$\frac{dE(S)}{db_1} = \frac{v_1}{z_2} - \frac{2b_1}{z_2} = 0 \tag{4.6}$$

so that $b_1 = (1/2)v_1$.

The reasoning has led to the generalisation:

$$b_i = \frac{N-1}{N} v_i \tag{4.7}$$

which has intuitive appeal in that $N = 1$ implies your bid is 0 (more correctly, a tiny amount), with $N = 2$ your bid is $^1/_2\, v_i$ and as $N \to \infty$, $b_i \to v_i$. But what expected payment is generated by this bidding rule? It will be

$$b_H = \frac{N-1}{N} v_H \tag{4.8}$$

where b_H is the highest bid coming from the highest evaluation v_H.

It was established above that with N estimates the expected highest value $v_H = [N/(N+1)]V$ (where here $V = 1$) so that the optimally shaded winning bid is, using (4.8):

$$b_H = \frac{N-1}{N} v_H \tag{4.9}$$

$$= \frac{N-1}{N} \cdot \frac{N}{N+1}$$

$$= \frac{N-1}{N+1} = E(P)$$

so the second highest valuation is the expected revenue and all auctions provide an equivalent revenue. (Q.E.D.)

As with all invariance theorems, great care has to be exercised in understanding their limitations. The RET seems to suggest any auction format will do. But is this really the case?

There are a number of caveats to this 'biggest result'. So far it has been implicitly assumed that both buyers and sellers are risk-neutral and sellers do not put a reservation price on their asset. With the English and SPSB, sellers receive the second highest evaluation. By contrast, in the Dutch and SPSB auctions the seller receives the second highest valuation on average as v_H is the expected highest valuation. Given this, the seller will receive more or less than the second highest valuation on any actual realisation of the auction 'game'. By the same token, the bidders would like to bid their own actual valuation in an English or SPSB auction rather than calculate an expected surplus-maximising bid. Given the variance associated with the Dutch and SPSB options the risk-averse seller and buyer will prefer the English and FPSB to the Dutch and SPSB formats.

So far all formats look efficient in that the asset goes to the bidder with the highest valuation. However, once risk aversity is introduced inefficiency is possible, as risk aversity causes bidders to reduce their bids. It is perfectly possible that a less risk-averse but lower-valuation bidder will outbid a more risk-averse but higher-valuation bidder. If a seller places a significant reservation value on the good when their true valuation is very small, they lose if the reservation value is not bid by either of two assumed bidders but gain if a bid exceeds the reservation value and one does not, as the reservation value effectively becomes the second bid.

Assets like antiques are said to have both a private-value element (e.g. whether you like a painting or not) and a common-value element known as 'affiliation'. In this case being able to observe the actions of other bidders in an open-outcry English auction reveals information about the extent of affiliation as compared with the SPSB. Observed enthusiastic bidding will tend to cause the revenue from the English auction to exceed that of the SPSB. Any mention of antiques raises the question of items being 'ringed out'. This arises when mainly professional dealers collude. If several notice a mis-catalogued item, e.g. something listed as a twentieth-century reproduction when it is a sixteenth-century original then, rather than bid against each other openly and drive the price very high – reducing any (expected) surplus from resale – it is attractive to allow one of the ring to buy the antique cheaply and for those in the ring to re-auction the asset outside with each getting a share of the expected surplus. Here ring members gain at the expense of owners of the assets by colluding.

SB auctions are open in particular to abuse by auctioneers who might illegally look at the bids or put in false second bids. Dutch auctions may be less vulnerable to ring formation as the incentive is for a member of the ring to come in at a price a little higher then the agreed ring bid. However, to be in the ring you need a reputation for colluding 'fairly' so, as with the trust game (see Chapter 8), if the ring is expected to be a regular formation, reneging on your word may prove detrimental in the long run.

These and other arguments blunt the RET and the prediction of auction form indifference. So far the sale of an asset in isolation has been considered, but a further set of problems arise once multi-object auctions come under scrutiny.

4.6.3 Problems with multi-object auctions

With multi-object auctions the objectives of efficiency (allocating the asset to the individual with the highest valuation), revenue maximisation and generating a competitive production environment may well conflict. Jehiel and Moldovanu (2003) provide a very good discussion of the relevant problems and issues when there is interdependence between assets for action and bidders. The concept of auction flexibility is a key matter. Flexibility allows bidders to bid for combinations of assets as opposed to single assets. The problem for flexibility is the downstream effects on winners getting market power in subsequent imperfectly competitive production forms. Jehiel and Moldovanu note four strategic effects that arise with multi-object auctions.

(i) The first effect is a carry-over from the discussions of rings, in that, for ascending bid type formats in particular, tacit collusion becomes a problem. The motivation is to share assets at low prices rather than secure more assets at higher prices. One example of the problem relates to the selling of ten identical blocks of spectrum (wavebands) in a market dominated by two large bidders. Player 1 bids, say, £4000 for blocks one to five and £4400 for identical blocks six to ten and is the round-one top bidder on all blocks. Now the rule for the second-round bidding involves any new bid being 10% higher than the existing bid. Player 2 reads the situation as player 1 bids containing a tacit or implicit invitation to collude with them by bidding £4400 for blocks one to five (adding 10% to the round-one bid) and not bidding on the others. The implicit deal is that players 1 and 2 will have five blocks each at a low price of £4400 a block. The numbers have been altered but this is very close to what happened when ten blocks of spectrum were auctioned in Germany in 1999.

(ii) Deliberately understating the true valuation to you is also part of the second problem of demand reduction. Suppose the auction format is a $(k+1)$th in that all players will make simultaneous bids with the k highest bids securing one unit of the asset each but pay the $(k+1)$th as the common price to all winners. Suppose three bottles of vintage wine are for auction and there are three bidders A, B and C. Bidders B and C only want one bottle each with valuations of 1 and 0.25 respectively. Bidder A, however, is a wine connoisseur and would like all three bottles with valuations of 10, 5 and 2 in order. Here $k=3$ and the valuations are 10, 5, 2, 1, 0.25, so the $(k+1)$th bid is 1. The principle of efficiency says bidder A gets all three bottles at a price of 1, enjoying benefits of $10 + 5 + 2 = 17$ minus costs of $3 \times 1 = 3$, i.e. net benefit is 14. However, if bidder A reduces their demand and bids 15 for bottles 1 and 2, bidder B gets the third bottle as the kth bidder and the $(k+1)$th bid becomes 0.25. The surplus to bidder A from this action is now $15 - 0.5 (2 \times 0.25) = 14.5$, an increase of 0.5. Revenue falls from 3 to 0.75 and the process is inefficient in that bidder B has a valuation of the third bottle of 1 when A has a valuation of 2 and therefore should be allocated the consumption (or investment) benefit.

(iii) The third problem is called the 'exposure problem' and arises where there are complementarities between objects but there is insufficient flexibility to collect them together for auction. Consider two seats on a jumbo jet and two bidders A and B; bidder A weighs 30 stone and requires two seats or none, whereas bidder B is a svelte 11 stone and either seat will serve their purpose. Bidder A has a valuation for two seats at £1000 and £0 for only one. In contrast, bidder B has a valuation of either seat of £750. On efficiency grounds bidder A should get both seats but if flexibility does not allow for the two seats to be sold as a unit then bidder A simply drops out. Bidder A reasons that they will have to outbid bidder B twice at a bid of £750 a time to secure both seats. This involves payment of £1500 when total valuation is only £1000. Insufficient flexibility reduces both revenue (£750 rather than £1000) and causes inefficient allocation to B as opposed to A.

(iv) The final example reported here is the case where the revenue and efficiency criteria are in conflict. There are still only two bidders, A and B, but now there are no complementarities between two objects, 1 and 2, to be auctioned. The objects are assumed to be valued as indicated in Table 4.7.

Table 4.7 **Efficiency versus revenue raising**

	Bidder A	Bidder B
Object 1	12	9
Object 2	7	13
Total valuation {1,2}	19	22

Table 4.8 Muti-object auctions

	Stage 1 *Multi-object auction*	Stage 2 *Downstream market form*
	(i) Efficient	(i′) Competition (ii′) Imperfect competition
Flexibility		
	(ii) Inefficient	(iii′) Competition (iv′) Imperfect competition

With each object auctioned separately on an ascending-bid basis object 1 goes to *A* for £9 (+ a tad) and object 2 to *B* for £7 (+ a tad). If objects 1 and 2 are bundled together then both objects go to *B* at a total revenue of £19 (+ a tad). Total revenue is maximised at £19 as opposed to £16, but object 1 is inefficiently allocated to bidder *B*. In a bigger picture revenue and efficiency characteristics of the multi-object auctions (Stage 1) the subsequent production impact (Stage 2) needs to be included. Table 4.8 indicates a simple taxonomy. Only (i) and (i′) are unambiguously to be recommended. In the remaining cases it is necessary to measure the combination of flexibility and subsequent market form configurations that maximise welfare. The example of implicit collusion above would suggest a thorough assessment of duopoly would be part of an overall evaluation.

Auction theory is a fascinating and difficult area of microeconomic theory that will reward further study (see Klemperer 2004).

4.7 Challenge: Is contestability enough?

As an ideal market form, perfect competition seems rather cumbersome and the question arises as to whether a simpler alternative exists. Some have canvassed contestable market theory as that alternative. The contestable markets approach is associated with Baumol (1982) and Baumol, Panzer and Willig (1982) and could claim unambiguous superiority over perfect competition if it:

1) requires fewer assumptions;
2) assures all the same welfare properties;
3) has additional useful economic implications over and above those of perfect competition;
4) gives more of an everyday feeling to the word 'competition' (there is something of 'handbags at fifty yards' about reacting to a given parametric price!).

Additionally, there is a novelty element. While it is different demand conditions meeting a common set of neoclassical U-shaped cost structures that drives the traditional market forms, the emphasis in contestability is on the cost, and hence supply, side.

With respect to (1) the crucial assumption is that of freedom of entry to and exit from a market. Not only must a potential entrant be able to compete fully on entry, but also, there must be no penalty for exit. A particular issue relating to exit is the existence of sunk costs that are not recoverable. For the moment, let us assume that this entry/exit condition is met and see how, almost unaided, it can generate the same results as perfect competition. If 'hit and run' entry and exit are viable, then existing firms in an industry can only make normal profits or return, as any surplus will be removed by such entry and exit even in the short run. Similarly, if a firm adjusts to other than the base of its short-run average cost (at the lowest point of long-run average cost), it can expect its sales to be displaced by those of lower-cost entrants.

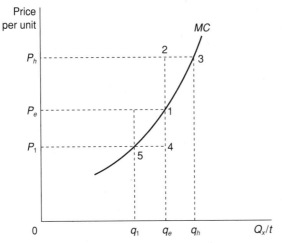

Figure 4.18
Price and marginal cost with contestability

But what of price equalling marginal cost (the very essence of the welfare-maximising property of a competitive equilibrium)? Consider Figure 4.18 which depicts the marginal cost curve of a firm in a contestable market. If output is q_e then marginal cost pricing demands that price $0\text{-}P_e$, be charged, but what happens if you deviate on the high and the low side in a 'contestable' context? If 'too high' a price $0\text{-}P_h$ is charged for $0\text{-}q_e$ an entrant can come in and charge a price very slightly below $0\text{-}P_h$, equating with MC at point 3, and sell $0\text{-}q_h$ – displacing the sales of the greater-than-marginal-cost producer. The entrant raises profits over the incumbent by the difference between additional revenue (q_e-2-3-q_h) and additional costs (q_e-1-3-q_h), which equals triangle 1-2-3. Hence, anyone pricing above MC can expect to be displaced.

But what about producing $0\text{-}q_e$ and selling at a price below MC at, say, $0\text{-}P_l$? Now an entrant can produce $0\text{-}q_l$ at a marginal cost equal to $0\text{-}P_l$ and make more profit than the initial low-cost producer enjoyed by slightly lowering the price. This is because saved costs are q_1-5-1-q_e and lost revenue is only q_1-5-4-q_e, so that additional profit compared with that earned by the initial firm is triangle 1-4-5. In short, anyone pricing either above or below MC, can expect entry to take place, so that they are 'punished' for such actions by losing their sales.

The important point is that this outcome is dependent only on whether existing firms producing good X (which can be very few in number) are open to the threat of entry and exit by potential competitors. In this respect, it is a prime aim of policy to maintain such conditions by preventing the existence of barriers to entry and exit.

Turning to other useful economic implications, the role of the demand curve is in determining the number of firms in the industry. Price is not determined by the Marshallian scissors of supply and demand but rather by the location of the cost structure of firms. Firms must be at the minimum point on their AC curves, so that is where price will be driven. In Figure 4.19 this occurs at 200 units per period and, given the industry demand curve in panel (b), sales per period will be 1000 units and there will be only five firms. Nevertheless, given the above reasoning, they are forced to act as competitors. Recognising that there may be a range of output, once minimum efficient size (MES) is reached that can be produced at minimum AC (as in panel c) prevents any problems if the market size is not divisible by, in this case, 200 units. But, as noted above, 'hit and run' entry and exit are vital to make the model work.

A major determinant of whether 'hit and run' entry and exit is possible is the presence, or absence, of sunk costs. On entry to an industry, an entrepreneur would anticipate the purchase of capital, e.g. machines, factory buildings, and, as with all capital goods,

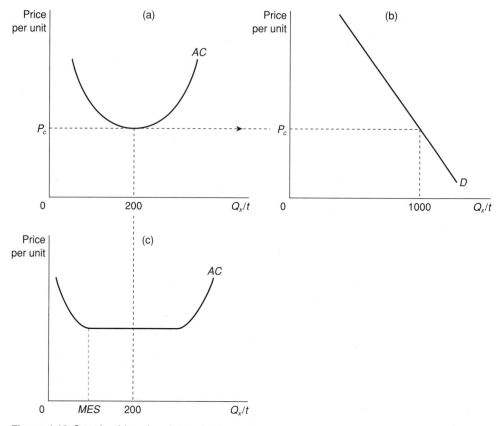

Figure 4.19 **Supply-side price determination**

anticipate their depreciation over successive periods. If on exit from the industry the purchased capital goods have their original value minus depreciation costs alone, then no sunk costs to entry and exit are present. If, on the other hand, with exit, the value of purchased capital equipment is near zero, sunk costs are very large.

The fourth characteristic described above concerned giving an everyday meaning to the notion of competition. Here contestable markets theory does very well. Perfect competition is about quantity adjusting to a parametric price, whereas here you can almost sense a band of marauding entrepreneurs seeking to eradicate profit opportunities through 'hit and run' entry and exit raids!

4.7.1 Evaluating contestable market theory

Whilst this market form is attractive it also has limitations:

(1) it remains a 'black box' market form, in that the firm still has no significant economic content (everything in the model is driven by the external world);

(2) this market form replaces a story about sufficient buyers and sellers within an industry to generate competition with what some commentators have felt is a rather optimistic account of competition from external potentially competing suppliers;

(3) it has also been emphasised that sunk costs – so critical to freedom of entry and exit – are likely to be ubiquitous. Sunk costs may not even take a visible form so, for example, existing firms are almost certainly going to have informational advantages

over any external individuals contemplating entry. If 'learning by doing' is a significant aspect of a production process then it is not possible for entrants to be fully competitive directly on entry. Furthermore, existing firms in the industry have an incentive to create sunk costs for potential entrants. Very large advertising campaigns designed to create brand recognition and loyalty are very costly to undertake and create no tangible asset capable of being resold.

In short, natural and created barriers cast doubt on the validity of the key assumption of contestable markets theory. To date, it has not succeeded in displacing the 'monarch's' role performed by perfect competition and this is the test of any pretender to the throne of economic analysis.

4.8 Summary

In this chapter the concept of efficiency and its relation to a perfectly competitive outcome was explored as a cornerstone to welfare analysis. The importance of market forces (demand and supply) has been considered in determining an equilibrium price and an 'efficient' quantity of output per period. In this way, the admiration which many economists hold for equilibrium in a competitive market, has been explained. This normative analysis has been used as a benchmark when considering other outcomes.

Many economists question the alacrity with which policy-makers attempt to administer prices. The almost intolerable difficulties and costs incurred are predictable by reference to the market analysis described here. Moreover, the costs of such a policy can be estimated with reference to the impact of policy on consumers and producer surplus (and this exercise is repeated in later chapters). A basic format has been applied when appraising policies in the markets for agriculture, accommodation and labour and the reader is encouraged to apply this to other policy initiatives designed to administer price.

However, returning to the common theme in this text, models as abstractions are always dependent on the underlying assumptions. For example:

All cases described here consider policy by reference to the outcome that would have emerged in a competitive market. In later chapters the concepts of monopoly (single-seller) and monopsony (single-buyer) are explained and employed. The opportunity will be taken to show how the conclusions drawn here are dependent on the assumption that markets are competitive; appraisals of the effects of policy depend on how the market is characterised.

A very important theme (which links a great deal of discussion in this text) is that neoclassical microeconomics analysis is premised on the predicted behaviour of a very specific representative individual, i.e. *homo economicus*. However as noted in Chapter 2 a plethora of studies (in experimental economics) in recent years have indicated that individual behaviour differs systematically to that predicted of *homo economicus*. While differences are referred to as anomalies, anomalies are so ubiquitous that they cannot be easily dismissed.

For example, the endowment effect indicates that goods in an individual's endowment, i.e. owned by them, are valued more highly than those not owned by them. The effect suggests that 'willingness to pay' for a good is smaller than the 'willingness to be accept compensation' for giving it up. There are also implications for policy appraisal. For reasons identified above, economists usually disapprove of rent control.[9] Yet Miceli and Minkler (1995) show how recognition of the endowment effect adds a whole new dimension.

---

9. Arnott (1995) reports that in a survey of American Economic Association members 93.5% agreed with the statement that 'a ceiling on rents reduced the quantity and quality of housing available'.

Economists' aversion to an 'administered price' is that it prevents those who value accommodation most (i.e. those with the highest 'willingness to pay') from attaining the good or service (in this case accommodation). If a 'new' entrant into the market displays a willingness to pay (WTP^N) greater than, or equal to, the controlled rent it is 'inefficient' if the good is consumed at a lower 'controlled' price by an existing occupant (with a lower willingness to pay, i.e. WTP^E). However, consider such policy if there is an 'endowment effect'. Existing tenants, already endowed with an entitlement, are very likely (given the results of economic experiments) to exhibit a 'willingness to accept' compensation for the loss of the accommodation (WTA^E) which is in excess of 'willingness to accept' compensation of the potential entrant (WTA^N). It is no longer obvious that the existing tenant should relinquish accommodation if 'willingness to accept' is the basis for valuation.

Rent control may be justified by reference to a 'willingness to accept' criterion if there is a significant difference between willingness to pay and willingness to accept, i.e. if individuals do not always behave as *homo economicus* is predicted to behave[10] and the decision is to value according to 'willingness to accept' rather than 'willingness to pay'.

Enough has been said to demonstrate that the analysis described in this chapter should not be thought of as 'set in stone'. It is open to revision, especially as further insight is gleaned on the decisions individuals make and on individual behaviour. In later chapters this theme will be pursued further.

The analysis presented here was based on the standard perfect competition model. As the theme has been prices and allocation, a natural extension was the consideration of auction theory and the allocation of goods under different auction formats. The winner's curse and the revenue equivalence theorem were rehearsed and some of the limitations of auctions noted. In the final, substantive, section the question was posed as to whether the simpler contestable markets theory was superior to perfect competition. Whilst contestable markets theory has its merits, it has not proved able to dislodge the traditional approach. However, it does raise issues like entry barriers – relevant to the imperfect market forms and non-black-box models of the firm to be discussed later.

After the discussion in this chapter it would be reasonable to ask two questions:

(i) 'Why was the analysis described as partial equilibrium?'
(ii) 'Are there any situations in which the government should intervene in the market?'

The answer to (i) is that the analysis so far looks at a *single market* in isolation – a 'partial' perspective. The answer to (ii) (perhaps surprisingly at this stage) is *yes*. Government intervention may be required when the market 'fails'. Both these answers are elaborated upon in the next two chapters.

References

Akerlof, G. and Yellen, J. (1986) *Efficiency Wage Models of the Labor Market*, Cambridge: Cambridge University Press.

Albon, R. and Stafford, D.C. (1987) *Rent Control*, London: Croom Helm.

Arnott, R. (1995) Time for revisionism on rent control, *Journal of Economic Perspectives*, 9 (1): 99–120.

Ashenfelter, O. and Genesove, D. (1992) Testing for price anomalies in real estate auctions, National Bureau of Economic Research Working Paper No. 4036.

Barr, N. (1998) *The Economics of the Welfare State*, 2nd edn, Oxford: Oxford University Press.

10. The 'endowment effect' has been used to justify the adoption of social policies and constitutional constraints. For example, Knetsch (1990) identifies a list of policy choices (mainly concerned with the environment) that are sensitive (given the 'endowment effect').

Baumol, W.J. (1982) Contestable markets: an uprising in the theory of industry structure, *American Economic Review*, 72 (1): 22–59.

Baumol, W.J., Panzer, J.C. and Willig, R.G. (1982) *Contestable Markets and the Theory of Industrial Structure*, San Diego: Harcourt Brace Jovanovich.

Brown, C. (1988) Minimum wage laws: are they overrated? *Journal of Economic Perspectives*, 2 (3) Summer: 133–45.

Browning, E.K. and Zupata, M. (1996) *Microeconomic Theory and Applications*, 5th edn, New York: HarperCollins.

Buchanan, J.M. (1959) Positive economics, welfare economics, and political economy, *Journal of Law and Economics* 2, October: 124–38.

Buckwell, A.E., Harvey, D.R., Thomson, K.L. and Parton, K.A. (1982) *The Costs of the Common Agricultural Policy*, London: Croom Helm.

Card, D. and Krueger, A. (1993) *Minimum Wages and Employment: a Case Study of the Fast Food Industry in New Jersey and Pennsylvania*, National Bureau of Economic Research Working Paper No. 4509, October.

Craig, C., Rubery, J., Tarling, R. and Wilkinson, F. (1982) *Labour Market Structure, Industrial Organisation and Low Pay*, Cambridge: Cambridge University Press.

De Grauwe, P. (1997) *The Economics of Monetary Integration*, Oxford: Oxford University Press.

Demekas, D.G. *et al.* (1995) The effects of the Common Agricultural Policy of the European Community: a survey of the literature, in M. Uger (ed.) *Policy Issues in the European Union*, London: Greenwich University Press.

Dobson, S. Maddala, G.S. and Miller, E. (1998) *Microeconomics*, London: McGraw-Hill.

Dopfer, K. (1976) *Economics in the Future: Towards a New Paradigm*. London: Macmillan.

Gibbons, J. (1999) The Common Agricultural and Fisheries Policy, pp. 281–301 in F. McDonald and S. Dearden (eds) *European Economic Integration*, Harlow: Longman.

Gramlich, E. (1976) Impact of the minimum wages on other employment and family incomes, *Brookings Papers on Economic Activity*, part 2, pp. 406–51.

Hartley, K. (1977) *Problems of Economic Policy*, London: Allen and Unwin.

Henderson, J.M. and Quandt, R.E. (1971) *Microeconomic Theory: a Mathematical Approach*, New York: McGraw-Hill.

Hills, J. and Mullings, B. (1990) Housing: a decent home for all at a price within their means?, pp. 135–205 in J. Hills (ed.) *The State of Welfare: the Welfare State in Britain since 1974*, Oxford: Oxford University Press.

Hilton, D.J. (1998) *Psychology and the City: Applications to Trading Dealing and Investment Analysis*, April London: The Centre for the Study of Financial Innovation.

Hitiris, T. (1988) *European Community Economics*, 3rd edn, Hemel Hempstead: Harvester Wheatsheaf.

Institute for Fiscal Studies (1998) Press release 6 June cited and discussed in C. Dillow (2000) Minimum wage myths, *Economic Affairs*, 20 (1): 47–53.

Jehiel, P. and Moldovanu, B. (2003) An economic perspective on auctions, *Economic Policy*, April: 269–308.

Katz, M. and Rosen, H. (1991) *Microeconomics*, Homewood, Ill.: Irwin.

Katzner, D.W. (1988) *Walrasian Microeconomics – an Introduction to the Economic Theory of the Market*, New York: Addison-Wesley.

Klemperer, P. (2004) *Auctions: Theory and Practice*, Princeton, NJ and Oxford: Princeton University Press.

Knetsch, J. (1990) Environmental policy implications of disparities between willingness to pay and compensation demanded, *Journal of Environmental Economics and Management*, 18 (3): 227–37.

Lal, D. (1995) *The Minimum Wage: No Way to Help the Poor*, Occasional Paper 95, London: Institute of Economic Affairs.

Lipsey, R.G. and Chrystal, K.A. (1995) *An Introduction to Positive Economics*, 8th edn, Oxford: Oxford University Press.

Machin, S. and Manning, A. (1992) Minimum wages, wage dispersion and employment: evidence from the UK Wages Councils, Discussion Papers in Economics No. 92-05, University College London.

Miceli, T.J. and Minkler, A.P. (1995) Willingness-to-accept versus willingness-to-pay measures of value: implications for rent control, eminent domain and zoning, *Public Finance Quarterly*, 23 (2): 255–70.

Mishan, E.J. (1981) *An Introduction to Normative Economics*, Oxford: Oxford University Press.

Molho, I. (1997) *The Economics of Information*, Oxford: Basil Blackwell.

Neumark, D. and Washer, W. (1995) Minimum wage effects on school and work transitions of teenagers, *American Economic Review Papers and Proceedings*, 85, May: 244–9.

Oi, W.Y. (1997) The consequences of minimum wage, *Economic Affairs*, 17 (2) June: 5–14.

Parkin, M., Powell, M. and Matthews, K. (2000) *Economics*, 4th edn, Harlow: Addison Wesley.

Pindyck, R.S. and Rubinfeld, D.L. (1998) *Microeconomics*, 4th edn, New Jersey: Prentice-Hall.

Poterba, J.M. (1984) Tax subsidies to owner occupied housing: an asset market approach, *Quarterly Journal of Economics*, 99 (4) (Nov.): 729–52.

Raff, D.M.G. and Summers, L.H. (1987) Did Henry Ford pay efficiency wages? *Journal of Labor Economics*, 5 (4): 57–86.

Rasmusen, E. (2001) *Games and Information: an Introduction to Game Theory*, 3rd edn, Oxford: Basil Blackwell.

Scherer, F.M. (1996) *Industry Structure Strategy and Public Policy*, New York: HarperCollins.

Simpson, L. and Paterson, I.A. (1992) A national minimum wage for Britain, *Economics*, Spring: 12–18.

Sloman, J. (1997) *Economics*, 3rd edn, London: Prentice Hall.

Stiglitz, J.E. and Driffill, J. (2000) *Economics*, New York: Norton and Co.

Sugden, R. and Weale, A. (1979) A contractual reformulation of certain aspects of welfare economics, *Economica*, 46 (182) May: 111–23.

Swann, D. (2000) *The Economics of the Common Market*, 9th edn, Harmondsworth: Penguin.

CHAPTER 5

Efficiency, general equilibrium and equity

5.1 Introduction

As promised, this chapter will 'pick up' on the first of two questions posed at the end of Chapter 4. It relates to general equilibrium analysis and perfect competition. As its name suggests, general equilibrium looks beyond the achievement of equilibrium in a single-output (or input) market holding 'other things equal' (*ceteris paribus*). After all, a market economy is a whole series of interconnected markets and, against a fully employed background, if more labour is devoted to the production of good X per period then less must be devoted to the production of some other good. General equilibrium attempts to deal with all markets simultaneously and involves a set of prices for each good at which the demand and supply of each good is in equilibrium. The questions posed in general equilibrium are fundamental; they have attracted the attention of the great names of economics (historically Walras (1874) and more recently the Nobel laureates of 1972, Kenneth Arrow, and of 1983, Gerard Debreu (1959)).

As Starr (1997) points out, the main questions relate to the:

i) *existence* of a general equilibrium. Can all markets simultaneously be in equilibrium? If not, what would be the point of advocating a market economy and studying the properties of equilibrium?

ii) *uniqueness* of a general equilibrium. Is there one, or more, sets of prices for each good at which the demand and supply of each good is in equilibrium? (That is, a multiple or a single solution.)

iii) *stability* of a general equilibrium. Is it the case that a rising price for a good in excess demand and a falling price for a good in excess supply will serve to re-establish a market-clearing equilibrium (see Chapter 4)? If there is no mechanism to re-establish equilibrium once a disturbance to a general equilibrium has occurred, there would be no possibility of a return to equilibrium.

iv) *welfare properties* of a general equilibrium. What are the characteristics of a world in which all input and output markets are simultaneously in equilibrium? Will one of the properties be efficiency? If the properties of a general equilibrium are unattractive then the existence of a general equilibrium may not be of much concern (current, almost universal, pursuit of a competitive market economy would then seem a wildly misplaced objective).

v) properties of *bargaining versus price-taking* in a general equilibrium. Is it the case that a conception of competition as price-taking and a conception of competition as self-interested bargaining are formally equivalent?

Here, the main focus is question (iv) and the Two Fundamental Theorems of Welfare Economics. Dealing with all markets simultaneously and their interactions is clearly a daunting task and the use of sophisticated mathematical theorems is required. Fortunately, following analysis by Bator (1957) it has been common to simplify the depiction of general equilibrium in the so-called 'two-by-two-by-two' model. It is this model that dominates the early sections of this chapter. General equilibrium does not invalidate partial equilibrium analysis but does force the question as to when simpler partial equilibrium analysis will suffice in dealing with any problem or issue. The answer rests on isolating situations when the *ceteris paribus* assumption can be reasonably defended, e.g. when a good that is a very small part of input and output markets with no significant interconnections in an economy is being considered.

5.2 Welfare maximisation: a general equilibrium analysis

Schotter (1990: 2) emphasises that: 'The free market argument assumes that economic and social agents are rational in that they are fully aware of their own preferences and capable of making all of the calculations necessary to pursue their interests efficiently'.[1] In this section the objective is to define a resource allocation that would maximise the welfare of such individuals and then illustrate how competitive markets would deliver such a resource allocation in a general equilibrium context.

To employ a diagrammatic analysis, consider resource allocation for the provision of two goods X and Y. Assume that these goods are produced by two factors of production, capital (K) and labour (L), and that there is a two-person society comprising individuals A and B. For obvious reasons (and as signalled in the introduction), this is called the '$2 \times 2 \times 2$ model'.

If the state of technology is given and constant, a relationship can be defined between the output of any good (e.g. X) and the factors (K and L) required for production. With reference to discussion in Chapter 3, such a relationship (e.g. $Q_x = Q_x(K, L)$) defined a production function and was illustrated in terms of an isoquant map. In Figure 5.1 (containing the now-familiar isoquant construction) the alternative combinations (K_1, L_1, and K_2, L_2) are identified for a given output of $\overline{Q}^x = 100$ units of X. It is clear that K_1-K_2 of capital can be substituted for by L_1-L_2 of labour and the same output can be achieved at points 1 and 2. Hence, recall the slope of the isoquant at any point is the marginal rate of technical substitution of capital for labour in the production of X ($MRTS_{KL}^X$). If an economy has a fixed quantity of capital and labour and the state of technology is given, the first problem that must be confronted is how to allocate capital and labour between the production of goods X and Y. This question of *production efficiency* can be resolved by reference to an 'Edgeworth box diagram'. Figure 5.2 presents such a box. The fixed quantities of capital and labour available determine the dimensions of the sides of the box. From origin 0_X the isoquants for good X are illustrated in the normal way, whereas from 0_Y the isoquants appear inverted to form the box. Initially, assume that of the total capital in the economy: $0\overline{K}$, an amount 0_XK_1 is allocated to the production of good X and of the total labour, $0\overline{L}$, available, 0_XL_1 is allocated to the production of good X.

At point 2, in Figure 5.2, 200 units of X can be produced. If the remaining labour (0_YL_1) and capital (0_YK_1) are allocated to the production of Y, output of Y is similarly 200 units. Now the 'Pareto question' can be posed. Can capital and labour be reallocated so as to increase the output of one good without, at the same time, reducing the output of the

---

1. Schotter notes (p. 2) that this assumption of rationality has 'two components – utility maximization and selfishness'.

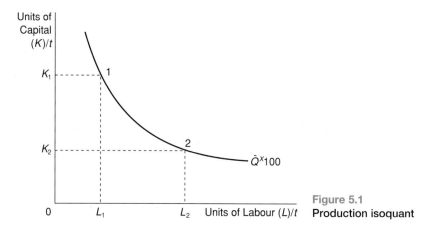

Figure 5.1
Production isoquant

other good? If both goods are valued by the residents of this economy, such a reallocation may be recommended against this Paretian (efficiency) condition. If capital was
switched from X to Y and labour from Y to X, so that a movement from point 2 to point
1 in the Edgeworth box took place, it is clear that output of Y might increase by 20 units
without a reduction in the output of X. At point 1 the essential observation is that the
slopes of the X and Y isoquants are identical (they are tangential, i.e. $MRTS^X_{KL} = MRTS^Y_{KL}$).
At this point, it is impossible to increase the output of one good without a fall in the output of the other.

Whilst it is still not resolved as to how much X and Y should be produced, it is clear
that an efficient range of options is demarcated by the dashed contract curve 0_x0_Y. These
may be illustrated in Figure 5.3 in the form of a *production possibilities frontier* labelled
T-T'. Any point on the frontier (such as $1'$) accords to a point on the contract curve (here
point 1 in Figure 5.2) and indicates that the condition $MRTS^X_{KL} = MRTS^Y_{KL}$ applies. From
any point within the frontier, like point $2'$ ($2'$ corresponds to point 2 in Figure 5.2), it is
possible to increase the output of one good without a fall in the output of the other good
– e.g. the movement from point $2'$ to point $1'$ (from point 2 to point 1 in Figure 5.2) –
or to increase both (e.g. a move to a point like $3'$ in Figure 5.3, reflecting a point like 3
in Figure 5.2). The frontier shows how much X would be gained if resources were
moved from the production of Y and full employment maintained. The slope at any

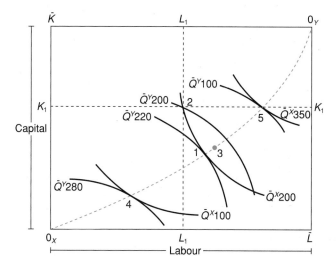

Figure 5.2
Production efficiency

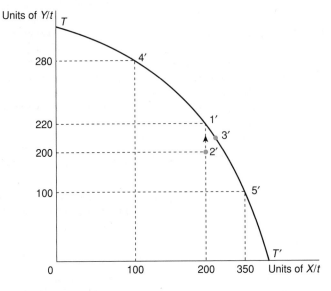

Figure 5.3
The production possibilities
frontier

point on the frontier reflects the marginal rate of transformation of one good into the other, i.e. MRT_{XY}.

In Figure 5.4 we look more closely at the output level 1′ on the production frontier. If this output level were produced, how would the goods be allocated between two individuals, A and B? Considering the origin of the Edgeworth box, $0 = 0_A$, the vertical axis measures units of Y per period and the horizontal axis measures units of X per period. The curve I_A^1 is an indifference curve (recall that it represents a locus of points which stipulates those combinations of X and Y that provide an identical level of utility for individual A). For example, any such curve to the right of I_A^1 will imply consumption of the same amount of one good but more of the other (or more of both), and, hence, will be associated with a higher level of utility. It was established earlier that the slope at any point on an indifference curve indicates the rate (at the margin) that the individual is prepared to substitute one good for another and remain on the same utility level, i.e. the marginal rate of substitution in consumption (MRS_{XY}).

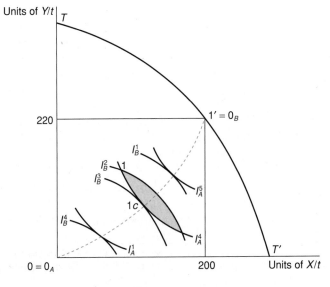

Figure 5.4   Exchange efficiency

Here, in the Edgeworth box, we have placed the origin of B's indifference curves at $1' = 0_B$. At $1'$ on the production frontier, 220 units of Y and 200 units of X are produced. If these were allocated at random between A and B it is unlikely that Pareto optimality would be attained. Following exactly the same reasoning as applied to Figure 5.2, the allocation of X and Y indicated at point 1 in the Edgeworth box is inferior to one such as 1_C (it leaves A no worse off but makes B better off). Indeed, a movement from point 1 to any point within the shaded area reflects a *Pareto improvement*. Once again, only at tangency points on a contract curve will a Pareto improvement be impossible. Thus, for any production level of X and Y, *exchange efficiency* demands that $MRS_{XY}^A = MRS_{XY}^B$.

To determine whether or not $1'$ on the production possibility is the optimal quantity to be produced requires further analysis. If the MRS_{XY} in consumption of X and Y were not equal to the MRT_{XY}, it would be possible to achieve a Pareto improvement. For example, imagine that the MRT_{XY} was two units of X for one unit of Y and the common MRS_{XY} was one for one. It would be possible to move capital and labour to reduce the output of Y (by one unit) and hence increase X (by two units). For any individual who had lost one unit of Y, one unit of X may then be substituted and that individual's welfare would not decline. This would leave one unit of X by which a Pareto improvement might be achieved should it be given to either A or B or shared. Hence, $MRS_{XY}^A = MRT_{XY}$ is a necessary condition for Pareto optimality. It constitutes the third, or *top-level efficiency*, consideration (see Chapter 4). Together with conditions for production efficiency and exchange efficiency, the top-level efficiency condition determines Pareto optimality.

Determining the income distribution at any point along the exchange contract curve in Figure 5.4 implicitly means picking a specific value of the MRS_{XY}. If it transpired that this value was equated to the MRT_{XY} at $1'$, then welfare would be maximised here. It will always be possible to find one point on each possible exchange contract curve pertaining to each point on the production frontier, i.e. where $MRS_{XY}^A = MRS_{XY}^B$ equals MRT_{XY} (it may be possible to find more so there would be non-uniqueness). Thus, the conditions of Pareto optimality can be satisfied for any income distribution.

Choosing the 'appropriate' welfare distribution (or 'equity') implies a specific MRS_{XY} somewhere on the exchange contract curve. When this equals MRT_{XY}, the total output of X and Y is resolved. The use of capital and labour in the production of X and Y is, similarly, uniquely determined once the appropriate point on the production frontier is indicated. For further discussion see Bator (1957).

5.2.1 Mathematical derivation of Pareto-optimal conditions

More formal treatment

This section offers a more precise formulation of the Pareto optimal conditions. It forms a reference point for other derivations discussed in the next chapter when market failure is discussed (e.g. externalities and public goods) and the conditions determined here will then require amendment.

The three conditions for a Pareto-efficient economy described above can be derived via a constrained maximisation process (using the Lagrangian multiplier method).

(i) *Production efficiency:* The production condition requires that:

$$MRTS_{KL}^Y = MRTS_{KL}^X \tag{5.1}$$

The production frontier shows the maximum amount of X that can be produced given the level of output of Y, say $\bar{Y}$, and the endowment of capital and labour (K and L) respectively. Given the resource constraint:

$$\bar{L} = L_X + L_Y \tag{5.2}$$

$$\bar{K} = K_X + K_Y \tag{5.3}$$

and the production functions:

$$X = X(K_X, L_X) \tag{5.4}$$

where X = quantity of good X produced per period (i.e. Q_x/t),

$$Y = Y(K_Y, L_Y) \tag{5.5}$$

and where Y = quantity of good Y produced per period (i.e. Q_y/t).
The object is to maximise $X = X(K_X, L_X)$ subject to

$$\bar{Y} = Y(\bar{L} - L_X, \bar{K} - K_X) \tag{5.6}$$

Form the Lagrangian:

$$\mathcal{L} = X(K_X, L_X) + \lambda[Y - Y(\bar{L} - \bar{L}_X, K - \bar{K}_X)] \tag{5.7}$$

Partially differentiating $\mathcal{L}$ with respect to K_X and L_X and setting equal to zero:

$$\frac{\partial \mathcal{L}}{\partial K_X} = \frac{\partial X}{\partial K_X} - \lambda \frac{\partial Y}{\partial K_X} = 0 \tag{5.8}$$

$$\frac{\partial \mathcal{L}}{\partial L_X} = \frac{\partial X}{\partial L_X} - \lambda \frac{\partial Y}{\partial L_X} = 0 \tag{5.9}$$

so that at a constrained maximum

$$-\frac{\dfrac{\partial X}{\partial K_X}}{\dfrac{\partial Y}{\partial K_X}} = \lambda = -\frac{\dfrac{\partial X}{\partial L_X}}{\dfrac{\partial Y}{\partial L_X}} \tag{5.10}$$

and, with $MRTS_{KL}$ representing the marginal rate of technical substitution,

$$MRTS_{KL}^Y \equiv \frac{MP_l^Y}{MP_k^Y} = \frac{\partial Y/\partial L_X}{\partial Y/\partial K_X} = \frac{\partial X/\partial L_X}{\partial X/\partial K_X} = \frac{MP_l^X}{MP_k^X} \equiv MRTS_{KL}^X \tag{5.11}$$

where MP_l and MP_k are the marginal products of labour and capital respectively.

(ii) *Consumption efficiency:* This states that

$$MRS_{XY}^A = MRS_{XY}^B \tag{5.12}$$

Here the structure of the problem is similar. The objective is to maximise the utility of one individual, say A, while holding the level of utility achieved by B constant at, say, $\bar{U}^B$.
    The individual utility functions are given by:

$$U^A = U^A(X, Y) \tag{5.13}$$

$$U^B = U^B(X, Y) \tag{5.14}$$

where X and Y are, as before, the outputs in the 2-good world. Forming the Lagrangian:

$$\mathcal{L} = U^A(X_A, Y_A) + \lambda[\bar{U}^B - U^B(X_B, Y_B)] \tag{5.15}$$

Partially differentiating $\mathscr{L}$ with respect to X and Y and setting equal to zero yields:

$$\frac{\partial \mathscr{L}}{\partial X} = \frac{\partial U^A}{\partial X_A} - \lambda \frac{\partial U^B}{\partial X_B} = 0 \tag{5.16}$$

$$\frac{\partial \mathscr{L}}{\partial Y} = \frac{\partial U^A}{\partial Y_A} - \lambda \frac{\partial U^B}{\partial Y_B} = 0 \tag{5.17}$$

$$\frac{MU_X^A}{MU_X^B} = \frac{\partial U^A/\partial X_A}{\partial U^B/\partial X_B} = \lambda = \frac{\partial U^A/\partial Y_A}{\partial U^B/\partial Y_B} = \frac{MU^A Y}{MU^B Y} \tag{5.18}$$

and, with MRS_{XY} representing the marginal rate of substitution in consumption,

$$MRS_{XY}^A \equiv \frac{MU_X^A}{MU_Y^A} = \frac{\partial U^A/\partial X_A}{\partial U^A/\partial Y_A} = \frac{\partial U^B/\partial X_B}{\partial U^B/\partial Y_B} = \frac{MU_X^B}{MU_Y^B} \equiv MRS_{XY}^B \tag{5.19}$$

where MU_X and MU_Y are the marginal utilities of good X and good Y respectively.

(iii) *Top-level efficiency* requires that

$$MRS_{XY}^A = MRS_{XY}^B = MRT_{XY} \tag{5.20}$$

This involves adding to efficiency condition (5.15) the production possibilities frontier constraint. The production transformation function can be defined as:

$$T = T(X, Y) \tag{5.21}$$

To be on the frontier

$$T(X, Y) = 0, \tag{5.22}$$

so that

$$-\frac{\partial T}{\partial X} dX + \frac{\partial T}{\partial Y} dY = 0 \tag{5.23}$$

and

$$\frac{dY}{dX} = (-) \frac{\partial T/\partial X}{\partial T/\partial Y} = MRT_{XY} \tag{5.24}$$

Adding the transformation function constraint to the Lagrangian (as in 5.15) yields:

$$\mathscr{L} = U^A(X_A, Y_A) + \lambda [\bar{U}^B - U^B(X_B, Y_B)] + \mu [0 - T(X, Y)] \tag{5.25}$$

Partially differentiating with respect to X_A, Y_A, X_B and Y_B and setting equal to zero:

$$\frac{\partial \mathscr{L}}{\partial X_A} = \frac{\partial U^A}{\partial X_A} - \mu \frac{\partial T}{\partial X} = 0 \tag{5.26}$$

$$\frac{\partial \mathscr{L}}{\partial Y_A} = \frac{\partial U^A}{\partial Y_A} - \mu \frac{\partial T}{\partial Y} = 0 \tag{5.27}$$

$$\frac{\partial \mathscr{L}}{\partial X_B} = -\lambda \frac{\partial U^B}{\partial X_B} - \mu \frac{\partial T}{\partial X} = 0 \tag{5.28}$$

$$\frac{\partial \mathscr{L}}{\partial Y_B} = -\lambda \frac{\partial U^B}{\partial Y_B} - \mu \frac{\partial T}{\partial Y} = 0 \tag{5.29}$$

Rearranging and dividing each of the pairs of equations yields:

$$MRS_{XY}^{A} = \frac{\partial U^{A}/\partial X_{A}}{\partial U^{A}/\partial Y_{A}} = \frac{\partial T/\partial X}{\partial T/\partial Y} \tag{5.30}$$

and

$$MRS_{XY}^{B} = \frac{\partial U^{B}/\partial X_{B}}{\partial U^{B}/\partial Y_{B}} = \frac{\partial T/\partial X}{\partial T/\partial Y} \tag{5.31}$$

Given that the right-hand term in these equations is the marginal rate of transformation and is common, the condition is that

$$MRS_{XY}^{A} = MRS_{XY}^{B} = MRT_{XY} \tag{5.32}$$

Pareto optimality (i.e. 'efficiency') requires that all three conditions are satisfied. If, as long ago as 1776, Adam Smith extolled the virtues of the market, how does the market's invisible hand ensure these efficiency conditions are met?

5.2.2 The normative case for competitive markets

Having defined the conditions that are required to determine a Pareto-optimal allocation of resources it is now possible to show that, when individuals behave as *homo economicus*, a perfectly competitive market will provide incentive structures that cause resources to be allocated in a Pareto-optimal way.

If there is no price discrimination in either factor or product markets, the production and exchange efficiency requirements will apply. Each self-interested, rational producer, striving to maximise profits, will equate $MRTS_{KL}$ to the factor (input) price ratio. With a production function, $Q_x = Q_x(K, L)$ the firm seeking to profit-maximise must produce any output level Q_x^* as cheaply as it can. Total expenditure on inputs equal $rK + wL$ (where r is the price of capital and w the price of labour). This total cost can be minimised by the mathematical procedure of obtaining the Lagrangian expression for a constrained minimisation problem, i.e.

$$\mathcal{L} = rK + wL + \lambda[Q_x(K, L) - Q_x^*] \tag{5.33}$$

Partially differentiating $\mathcal{L}$ with respect to K_X and L_X and setting equal to zero:

$$\partial\mathcal{L}/\partial K = r + \lambda\partial Q_x/\partial K = 0 \tag{5.34}$$

$$\partial\mathcal{L}/\partial L = w + \lambda\partial Q_x/\partial L = 0 \tag{5.35}$$

i.e. to minimise costs for producing Q_x^*

$$r + \lambda\partial Q_x/\partial K = w + \lambda\partial Q_x/\partial L = 0 \tag{5.36}$$

or:

$$w/r = \partial Q_x/\partial L \,/\, \partial Q_x/\partial K \tag{5.37}$$

Hence, the ratio of marginal products of labour and capital in the production of good X ($\partial Q_x/\partial L \,/\, \partial Q_x/\partial K$), or the marginal rate of technical substitution between capital and labour, is equated to the factor price ratio. If the same factor price ratio applies for all producers then marginal rates of technical substitution will necessarily be equated between producers.

Similarly, each consumer equates marginal rate of substitution between good X and good Y (MRS_{XY}) with the commodity (output) price ratio in order to maximise utility. Consumers will maximise a utility function ($U = U(X, Y)$) subject to the budget (or income) they have to allocate on the two goods. This budget or income is $I = p_X X + p_Y Y$ (where p_X is the price of X and p_Y the price of Y so that $I - p_X X - p_Y Y = 0$). The first-order conditions for the constrained maximisation are:

$$\mathcal{L} = U(X, Y) + \lambda(I - p_X X - p_Y Y) \tag{5.38}$$

Partially differentiating $\mathcal{L}$ with respect to X and Y and setting equal to zero:

$$\partial\mathcal{L}/\partial X = \partial U/\partial X - \lambda p_X = 0 \tag{5.39}$$

$$\partial\mathcal{L}/\partial Y = \partial U/\partial Y - \lambda p_Y = 0, \tag{5.40}$$

i.e. to maximise utility

$$\partial U/\partial X \big/ p_X = \lambda = \partial U/\partial Y \big/ p_Y \tag{5.41}$$

or

$$p_X/p_Y = \partial U/\partial X \big/ \partial U/\partial Y \tag{5.42}$$

Hence, to maximise utility $(\partial U/\partial X \big/ \partial U/\partial Y)$ – the marginal rate of substitution between X and Y – is equal to p_X/p_Y – the price ratio. Thus, the marginal rates of substitution in commodities will be equated if all consumers face identical price ratios.

Finally, as the MRT_{XY} is equal to the ratio of marginal costs of production, consider a movement from point 4 to 5 in Figure 5.5. Full employment exists at both points on the frontier. Therefore, with reference to Figure 5.5,

$$\text{4-6 (units of } Y) \times \text{marginal cost } Y = \text{6-5 (units of } X) \times \text{marginal cost of } X \tag{5.43}$$

By substitution, the marginal rate of transformation (in this case distances 4-6/6-5) can be written as:

$$\text{4-6/6-5} = MC_X/MC_Y \tag{5.44}$$

But 4-6/6-5 = slope of the production frontier (i.e. equals the marginal rate of transformation).

As discussed in Chapter 3, at equilibrium the firm in perfect competition will set output such that marginal cost equals price. In perfect competition, total revenue equals price (P) times output sold (Q). Total cost depends upon fixed costs (b) and variable costs that, by definition, depend on the level of output $(f(Q))$. To maximise profits:

$$\pi = PQ - f(Q) - b \tag{5.45}$$

$$\partial\pi/\partial Q = P - f'(Q) = 0 \tag{5.46}$$

$$P = f'(Q), \tag{5.47}$$

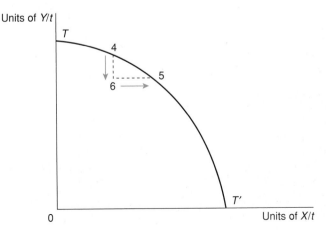

Units of Y/t

Units of X/t

Figure 5.5
Marginal cost and the marginal rate of transformation

Table 5.1 **Perfect competition and Pareto optimality in general equilibrium**

A	B
(a) Marginal condition for factor substitution: $MRTS_{kl}^X = MRTS_{kl}^Y$	For production to be at *minimum* cost, $MRTS_{kl} = (-)w/r$. The latter will be the same for both producers of X and Y, and therefore $MRTS_{kl}^X = MRTS_{kl}^Y = (-)w/r$
(b) Marginal condition for exchange: $MRS_{xy}^A = MRS_{xy}^B$	For consumers to *maximise* utility, $MRS_{xy} = (-)p_x/p_y$ and the latter will be the same for both A and B, so that $MRS_{xy}^A = MRS_{xy}^B = (-)p_x/p_y$
(c) Marginal condition for product substitution: $MRS_{xy}^A = MRS_{xy}^B = MRT_{xy}$	Profit *maximisation* occurs where $P = MC$ (i.e. $p_x = MC_x$ and $p_y = MC_y$), or $MU_x/MU_y = MRS_{xy} = p_x/p_y = MC_x/MC_y = MRT_{xy}$

Source: Cullis and Jones (2009).

i.e. price equals marginal cost (as $f'(Q)$ is the change in total (variable) cost as output is increased by a very small amount – see, for example, Henderson and Quandt 1971).[2]

MRS_{XY} will equal MRT_{XY} when the price ratio equals the marginal cost ratio. As in perfectly competitive markets, profit-maximising firms in equilibrium equate price with marginal cost; perfect competition also satisfies the top-level requirements. The analysis in general equilibrium again shows that a perfectly competitive market will satisfy the resource allocation conditions required for a Pareto-optimal solution. The conditions of perfect competition (e.g. many producers and many consumers, see Chapter 3) offer incentive structures in which decisions will lead to an 'efficient' allocation of resources when efficiency is defined in terms of Pareto optimality).

The achievement of modern welfare economics has been to show how Adam Smith's faith in the 'invisible hand' (operative in a free competitive market) can achieve Pareto optimality. This is stated in terms of the first of the two Fundamental Theorems of Welfare Economics:

> The First Fundamental Theorem *(the Direct Theorem) states*: resource allocation is Pareto optimal if there is perfect competition, no technological externalities and no market failure connected with uncertainty.

This First Fundamental Theorem is, as noted above, achieved in perfect competition because consumers utility-maximise and producers cost-minimise and profit-maximise. In doing this the efficiency conditions are met. The discussion of this section is summarised in Table 5.1.

5.2.3 The Second Fundamental Theorem of Welfare Economics

The first theorem states that every competitive equilibrium is a Pareto optimum. Here, the focus is on what is meant by 'every'.

---

2. This creates an importance for the concept of marginal cost pricing. However, in practice it is difficult to estimate marginal cost. Wiseman (1978) comments: 'The most formal espousal of this perception of (Pareto) efficiency . . . required that nationalised industry products should be sold at prices equal to their long-run marginal cost. I have argued elsewhere that the practical relevance of this prescription is of the same order as would be an injunction to price according to the principle God is Love: the sentiment is difficult to deny, the practical consequences of conformity unidentifiable' (p. 74).

(a) Production Possibility Frontier

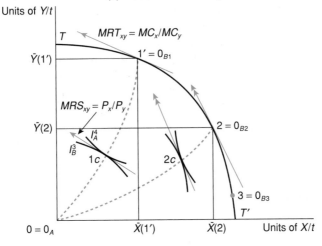

(b) Utility Possibility Frontier

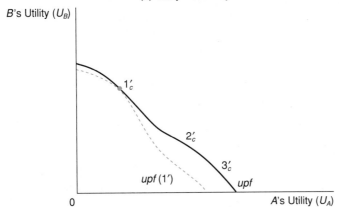

Figure 5.6
Distribution and the utility-possibility frontier

Figure 5.6(a) reproduces the production possibilities or transformation frontier $T\text{-}T'$. This uses the detail from Figure 5.4 point $1' = 0B_1$ and $0 = 0A$ as the relevant origins (for individuals B and A respectively).

Figure 5.6(b) plots the (ordinal) utility level of individual B against the (ordinal) utility level of individual A; the dashed line represents the maximum utility levels of individuals A and B consistent with moving along the exchange contract curve from $0 = 0_A$ to $1' = 0_B$. This curve is the utility possibilities frontier contingent on the outputs of good X and good Y associated with point $1'$ and is labelled $upf(1')$ accordingly. It is evident that there will be a negatively sloping curve like this for each starting point on $T\text{-}T'$. However, there is something special about one point on $upf(1')$.

In Figure 5.4 assuming point 1_c was the efficient point on the exchange contract curve would mean the common marginal rate of substitution between goods X and Y equalled the marginal rate of transformation between goods X and Y so that $MRS^A_{XY} = MRS^B_{XY}$ ($= p_x/p_y = MC_x/MC_y) = MRT_{XY}$. The labelled tangents through points $1' = 0_{B1}$ and 1_c in Figure 5.6(a) make this clear. As noted above, given perfect competition, the relevant price ratio and marginal cost ratio are also described by these tangents (the terms in brackets above). At point 1_c the relevant indifference curves are I^3_B and I^4_A, which can be thought of as identifying point $1'_c$ on $upf(1')$ as a point with respect to the starting point $1'$ on $T\text{-}T'$

where all efficiency conditions are met. As such, it is one point on *UPF* the 'efficient' utility possibilities frontier sometimes called the *grand utility possibilities frontier*.

In Figure 5.6(b) it is possible (by similar construction) to produce a whole series of such points and, therefore, ultimately a continuous curve (the heavier envelope curve) as different points on *T-T'* are selected as the starting endowment. If the production point was at point $2 = 0_{B2}$ the points 2_c and $2'_c$ would be isolated and again for point $3 = 0_{B3}$ and $3'_c$ (the attendant Edgeworth–Bowley trading box is not drawn).

There are a number of important points to note:

i)   If all possible beginning points on *T-T'* were chosen, it is possible to trace out the efficient utility possibilities frontier for this two-person economy drawn as *UPF* in Figure 5.6(b). That is, each point on *T-T'* would generate its own *upf* and contribute one point on *UPF*;

ii) All points on that frontier (*UPF*) meet all efficiency conditions, by construction, so that the efficiency criterion alone cannot serve to distinguish between any points on the frontier: all are equally efficient;

iii) The utility of individual *A* can only be raised in an efficient economy if the utility of individual *B* is simultaneously lowered, i.e. the utility possibilities frontier is negatively sloped (this is also true for component *upf*'s);

iv) *UPF* has been drawn deliberately as a 'wavy' line to repeat the conventional signal that the notion of utility being worked with is ordinal.

As long as *A* and *B* have different preferences, a different point on *UPF* is achieved depending on (1) factor ownership K_A, L_A, K_B and L_B and (2) factor prices (*w* and *r*) which dictates the budget or incomes *A* and *B* enjoy from the market process of supplying factors of production. That is,

$$\bar{L} = L_A + L_B; \quad \bar{K} = K_A + K_B \quad \text{(note also } \bar{X} = X_A + X_B \text{ and } \bar{Y} = Y_A + Y_B) \tag{5.48}$$

$$I_A = wL_A + rK_A, \quad I_B = wL_B + rK_B, \tag{5.49}$$

where *I* = income.

Given that in the utility-maximising process the budget constraint is $I = P_y Y + P_x X$, individuals *A* and *B* must have incomes that match their expenditures on their utility-maximising quantities of *X* and *Y*. That is,

$$P_x X_A + P_y Y_A = wL_A + rK_A \text{ and } P_x X_B + P_y Y_B = wL_B + rK_B \tag{5.50}$$

with all prices and X_A and Y_A given; *A*'s income requirement is met by any combination of ownership L_A and K_A that satisfies the equation.

For the economy as a whole, the value of output will exactly equal the value of inputs. If the 'adding up' problem discussed below is resolved with the presence of constant returns to scale,

$$P_x \bar{X} + P_y \bar{Y} = w\bar{L} + r\bar{K} \tag{5.51}$$

If *A*'s equation is subtracted from this it is clear that the K_A and L_A (which satisfies *A*'s equation) will also satisfy *B*'s.

$$P_x(\bar{X} - X_A) + P_y(\bar{Y} - Y_A) = w(\bar{L} - L_A) + r(\bar{K} - K_A) \tag{5.52}$$

and, therefore,

$$P_x X_B + P_y Y_B = wL_B + rK_B \tag{5.53}$$

from equation (5.48).

These deductions are formalised into the *Second Fundamental Theorem* (the Converse Theorem). This states: *any specified Pareto-optimal resource allocation that is technically feasible can be achieved by establishing competitive markets and an appropriate pattern of factor ownership, if there are no increasing returns, no technological externalities and no market failure connected with uncertainty.*

This is clearly a very powerful result as it raises the possibility that a competitive economy could be efficient and equitable. The second theorem is prescriptive; it indicates that any Pareto-optimum state can be supported by a competitive equilibrium. That is, if the government could assign initial factor ownership, allowing the competitive process to unfold would enable the government to engineer any point on *UPF* deemed equitable. With equity and efficiency achieved there would be no economic problems left to resolve! Fortunately, at least for economists who would play a more active policy role, the world is not that easy.

The analysis raises a number of further issues of both a 'technical' and value judgement kind and these issues in one guise or another largely dominate the remainder of the book.

i)   The fundamental theorems only apply in certain conditions. For example, the Second Fundamental Theorem requires 'no increasing returns, no technological externalities and no market failure connected with uncertainty'. The question naturally arises as to what actually 'goes wrong' if these conditions are not met.

ii) Will the government have the knowledge, ability and indeed desire to establish equity and efficiency?

iii) Are the Pareto value judgements sufficient to be a complete account of an economic Nirvana? With respect to the value judgements, has a fourth value judgement, that 'the distribution of final utilities ought to be equitable', been mistakenly omitted? Is the first value judgement that each individual is the best judge of their own welfare tenable?

The brief answers to these questions are:

i')   Market failure arguments mean that Pareto optima are not a guaranteed outcome of universal perfect competition.

ii') Governments are not all-knowing and, to the extent they pursue equity, they tend to work on the existing distribution of income with taxes and transfers rather than radical reassignments of factor ownership. Such taxes cause welfare (or efficiency) losses of their own (see Chapter 13). Individuals in government are also *homo economicus* and, therefore, seek their own interests, rather than acting as the unbiased judges or 'ethical observers' somehow outside the analysis (see Chapter 14).

iii') There is much dispute as to whether 'equity' is a necessary value judgement to adopt. The issue is complex. Whether individuals are the best judges of their own welfare is highly debatable (as noted at the outset in Chapter 4).

In this chapter only one example of technical market failure is explored, namely the consequences of increasing returns. This is done first in the context of Euler's theorem (see below) and, second, in the context of community indifference curves.

The remaining uncovered issues are all explored later in the text. In this chapter a deliberate attempt is made to build on the general equilibrium framework in the exploration of the issues addressed.

5.2.4 Income shares and factor ownership: Euler's theorem

One major problem that faced early theorists was the issue of 'adding up' mentioned above. The theorising above says that $w/MP_l \, [= r/MP_k] = MC$ and that profit maximisation requires $MC = P$ in perfect competition; so a factor should be paid wage w for labour and r the rental for capital that equals the value of the marginal product of the marginal unit employed ($w/MP_l = MC = P$, so $w = P \cdot MP_l$ which defines the value of the marginal product of labour $VMP_l = P \cdot MP_l$).[3] The question arises whether, when this is done, the sum of the values of the marginal products of all factors (ΣVMP) will be greater than, equal to or less than the value of output produced, $P \cdot Q$. That is, will $PQ > =$ or $< \Sigma VMP$?

The answer turns on the nature of the production function. Beginning with a homogeneous two-factor production function (capital K and labour L) and using b as the scaling factor and r as the degree of homogeneity (see Chapter 3) then, as a matter of definition,

$$Q(bL, bK) = b^r Q(L, K) \tag{5.54}$$

Using the chain rule to take partial derivatives with respect to b on both sides yields

$$\frac{\partial Q}{\partial b} \cdot \frac{\partial bL}{\partial b} + \frac{\partial Q}{\partial b} \cdot \frac{\partial bK}{\partial b} = \frac{\partial(\,b^r Q(K, L)}{\partial b} \tag{5.55}$$

Now b is a positive constant. Let it equal 1 and

$$\partial Q/\partial L\, L + \partial Q/\partial K\, K = rb^{r-1}\, Q(L, K) \tag{5.56}$$

$$\partial Q/\partial L\, L + \partial Q/\partial K\, K = r\, Q(L, K) = rQ \tag{5.57}$$

To turn equation (5.57) into monetary terms it is necessary to multiply both sides by P, yielding

$$L \cdot P \cdot \partial Q/\partial L + K \cdot P \cdot \partial Q/\partial K = rPQ \tag{5.58}$$

It can now be seen that, if $r = 1$, the money value of the marginal product of the factors times their quantities employed will equal the money value of output, and this is what is understood by the 'product exhaustion theorem' or Euler's theorem.

If $r < 1$, there are decreasing returns to scale for the homogeneous production function and, paying all factors the value of their marginal products will less than exhaust the total, i.e. there is a surplus. If $r > 1$, there are increasing returns to scale for the homogeneous production function and paying all factors the value of their marginal products will more than exhaust the total, i.e. there is a deficit.

To gain a clear picture, consider a linearly homogeneous Cobb–Douglas production function, so that:

$$Q = Q(L, K) = L^\alpha K^\beta \quad \text{and} \quad \alpha + \beta = 1 \tag{5.59}$$

Forming the marginal products

$$\partial Q/\partial L = \alpha L^{\alpha-1} K^\beta = MP_l \tag{5.60}$$

$$\partial Q/\partial K = \beta L^\alpha K^{\beta-1} = MP_k \tag{5.61}$$

Multiplying the marginal products by the level of employment of the factors yields:

$$(\partial Q/\partial L)L = \alpha L^\alpha K^\beta = \alpha Q \tag{5.62}$$

$$(\partial Q/\partial K)K = \beta L^\alpha K^\beta = \beta Q \tag{5.63}$$

and total output is given by

$$(\partial Q/\partial L)L + (\partial Q/\partial K)K = (\alpha + \beta)\, L^\alpha K^\beta = Q \tag{5.64}$$

Again, to turn into monetary terms it is necessary to multiply both sides by P, yielding

---

3. An analogous manipulation can be done for capital.

$$L \cdot P \cdot \partial Q / \partial L + K \cdot P \cdot \partial Q / \partial K = (\alpha + \beta) \, P \, L^{\alpha} K^{\beta} = PQ \tag{5.65}$$

$$L \cdot P \cdot MP_l + K \cdot P \cdot MP_k = (\alpha + \beta) \, P \, L^{\alpha} K^{\beta} = PQ \tag{5.66}$$

$$L \cdot VMP_l + K \cdot VMP_k = (\alpha + \beta) \, P \, L^{\alpha} K^{\beta} = PQ \tag{5.67}$$

The money value of the marginal product of the factors multiplied by their quantities employed will equal the money value of output and 'product exhaustion' obtains for a constant-returns-to-scale production function.

This tends to look very restrictive, in that product exhaustion requires constant-return-to-scale production functions that are not ubiquitous. However, a further consideration softens this requirement. Long-run equilibrium in perfect competition requires firms to be at the base of their long-run cost curves, so that any increasing returns to size (scale) are exhausted and any decreasing returns to size (scale) have not yet been met. In short, it must, momentarily, be the case that constant returns to size (scale) apply. That is, 'product exhaustion' is guaranteed for a constant-returns-to-scale production function and long-run equilibrium in perfect competition. Outside these conditions this is not the case. This is, of course, one reason why a constant-returns-to-scale production function is a favourite of much exposition and empirical work. To emphasise this, consider the diagrams that arise with a linearly homogeneous production function. Figure 5.7 shows a particular 'three-dimensional' production surface.

Figure 5.8(a) illustrates the production surface as an isoquant map, whereas panels (b), (c) and (d) illustrate associated product curves contingent on a constant short-run quantity of capital K_0 of capital (so that TP_L in panel (b) corresponds to the short-run product cross-section K_0-S in Figure 5.7). Given that for constant returns

$$Q = L \cdot \partial Q / \partial L + K \cdot \partial Q / \partial K \tag{5.68}$$

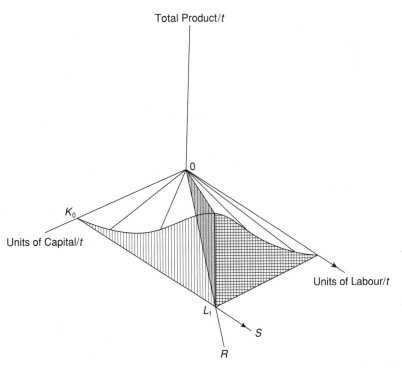

Figure 5.7 'Three-dimensional' production surface with constant returns to scale and changing marginal product curves

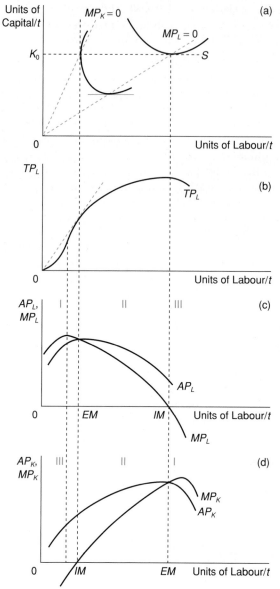

Figure 5.8
The stages of production and product curves

so that, on the upper ridge line in Figure 5.8(a) (where by definition $MP_k = \partial Q/\partial K = 0$),

$$Q/L = \partial Q/\partial L \tag{5.69}$$

$$AP_l = MP_l \tag{5.69a}$$

This neatly anchors the $AP_l = MP_l$ directly below the point where the tangent and ray to the total product curve coincide and AP_l is at a maximum.

Along the lower ridge line in Figure 5.8(a) where, by definition, $MP_l = \partial Q/\partial L = 0$,

$$Q/K = \partial Q/\partial K \tag{5.70}$$

$$AP_k = MP_k \tag{5.70a}$$

Figure 5.8(d) shows what is happening to the productivity of the fixed factor capital, as more and more units of labour are added and the capital-to-labour ratio is falling. Panels (c) and (d) show symmetry in the three stages of production:

(i) stage I, the AP_l is rising (MP_k is negative);

(ii) stage II begins at the so-called extensive margin (EM in panel (c)), where AP_l is at a maximum and extends over the range from the maximum average product of the variable input (labour) to zero marginal product of the variable input ($MP_l = 0$ defines the intensive margin IM in panel (c));

(iii) stage III, TP_l is falling, MP_l is negative and AP_k is falling as capital is used too intensively.

Producing where either MP_k or MP_l is negative makes no sense and connects the economic region of the production function to stage II. Also, note that the extensive margin for the variable factor corresponds to the intensive margin for the fixed factor ($MP_k = 0$) and vice versa; cf. Figure 5.8(c) with 5.8(d).

Figure 5.9 indicates the relevant product and cost structures consistent with the picture painted so far. Panel (c) indicates how, in many textbook examples, a horizontal

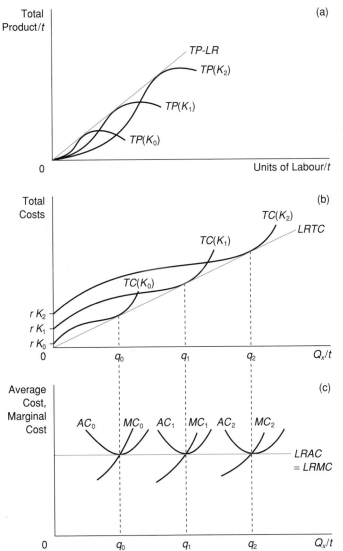

Figure 5.9
Cost curves and constant returns to scale

long-run average and marginal cost curve and U-shaped average and marginal cost curves can legitimately be employed as coming from a constant-returns-to-scale production function. This often seems confusing but it is a useful special case.

As a prelude to the discussion of equity below it is worth emphasising what has been established with respect particularly to labour income generation in a competitive market. The question arises as to the extent to which it can be said that a factor reward is a reflection of the attributes of a particular individual. The neoclassical account of a factor demand, briefly outlined above, depends on the value of marginal product and whilst it appears to say 'you take out what you put in' and sanction the 'justice of a competitive economy' (Okun 1975: 41) this is not the case. All the units of a factor added to the production process are assumed to be identical. Product price depends on the fate of an industry. The size of a marginal product will reflect the nature of the production function a factor 'works' with. Further, it depends on the level of other factors that are part of the input combination. For the discussion here, the amount of capital that labour works with has an important impact on the marginal product of labour. None of these influences is a reflection of the attributes of a particular individual, rather they are about the marginal product of an anonymous individual who could turn out to be anyone. Some claim the amount of human capital (skills and training) a unit of labour contains is not only an important influence on the marginal product of labour but also a matter of individual choice (see Chapter 10). This then may be the basis of a case for arguing that market-determined income distributions are in this sense 'fair' and 'equitable' and therefore should be respected and left alone. At least three observations can be made with respect to this point:

(i)   First, human capital acquisition is powerfully affected by parental choice and not the individuals themselves. For example, the more educated keep their children in education.

(ii) Second, there is the concept of social capital (see Coleman 1988) which describes the quality of an environment where a person grows up and develops.[4] Holding parental time and market inputs into children constant, children exposed to an environment in which their role models and peer groups are educated are differentially more successful in the labour market than those children surrounded by unemployment and the receipt of social security benefits. The concept suggests there is a human capital externality in the production of children's human capital. Independent of the 'internal to the family' effect (parental inputs into children's quality) there is the 'external to the family' effect (this human capital externality affecting the course of human capital acquisition).

(iii) Third, and possibly most important, the idea 'that income *ought* to be based on contribution to output' (Okun 1975: 41) is simply an arbitrary choice, or as Okun calls it, a 'presumption'. The 'punchline' then is that value of marginal product theory tells you that, in a competitive market, an individual will get a reward that equals the *VMP* (value of marginal product) of the marginal unit employed but it is silent as to whether this is in any sense 'fair'; much of government intervention policy is geared to adjusting a market-generated income and ultimately utility distribution.

---

4. Social capital is a feature of one fairly recent strand of economic theorising. The term was coined (see Serageldin and Steer 1994) to cover an amalgam of individual and institutional relationships that determines why one society is more effective than another in transforming a given endowment of assets and resources into sustained well-being.

5.3 Community indifference curves and non-convexities

Community indifference curves show combinations of units of X and units of Y that make it just possible to achieve a particular combination of utilities enjoyed by individuals. The starting point is to choose a pair of indifference curves that you would like individuals A and B to be on. For example, point 1 in Figure 5.10 is uniquely associated with one indifference curve for each individual, I_A^1 and I_B^0, respectively. From these, it is possible to derive a 'community indifference curve' in commodity space, showing the various combinations of goods X and Y that would make it possible for A and B to achieve that pair of utility levels.

In Figure 5.10 the tangential indifference curves I_A^1 and I_B^0 are plotted with respect to origins 0_A and 0_B of the initial Edgeworth–Bowley box, with $0\text{-}Y_2$ and $0\text{-}X_1$ units of Y and X per period. The size of this box is determined by the required units of goods X and Y that just allow the achievement of I_A^1 and I_B^0. Given this, 0_B, taken with reference to A's origin, is a point on CIC_1. Indifference curve I_B^0 can now be moved downwards (or upwards) around I_A^1 from the initial tangency point 1, always maintaining parallel axes and tangent indifference curves. The locus of 0_B (as this operation is performed) traces out curve CIC_1, the coordinates of which (with respect to 0_A) indicate the alternate combinations of good Y and good X required to sustain utility levels associated with I_A^1 and I_B^0. Point $0_B'$, for example, shows that $0\text{-}Y_1$ units of Y and $0\text{-}X_2$ units of X would be just as attractive as $0\text{-}Y_2$ and $0\text{-}X_1$ units of Y and X per period if both were distributed as to establish I_A^1 and $I_B^{0'}$ at point 2. If both A and B's indifference curves are convex the community indifference curve CIC_1 must be convex.

The entire curve CIC_1 of Figure 5.10 is thus derived from point 1. Suppose initial starting point 3 was now chosen (giving a different distribution of utilities between A and B); then it could similarly be translated into curve CIC_2 in Figure 5.10. While both community indifference curves are necessarily downward-sloping and convex there is no reason why they should not intersect. Point $0_B'$ exists on CIC_1 because the box $0_A\text{-}Y_1\text{-}0_B'\text{-}X_2$ accommodates indifference curves I_A^1 and $I_B^{0'}$ tangent at point 2. As $I_B^{0'}$ is moved around I_A^1 to trace out the community indifference curve, its slope at 0_B must be the same as the slope of the common tangent to the indifference curves at point 1. This says that the slope of a community indifference curve is the common marginal rate of substitution between X

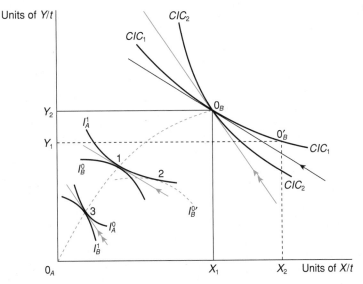

Figure 5.10
Deriving community indifference curves

and Y. Given that the same box might include indifference curves I_A^0 and I_B^1 tangent at point 3, that could also be a starting point in box 0_A-Y_2-0_B-X_1 . . . So point 0_B is also a point on CIC_2 described by moving I_B^1 around I_A^0. The slope of CIC_2 at 0_B would then be the same as the slope of the common tangent to the indifference curves at point 3. In the absence of special assumptions about the indifference maps there is no reason why the slope of the common tangent at point 1 should equal that of the common tangent at point 3 (note that both are on the 'dashed' contract curve). If these slopes differ, then so will the slopes of CIC_1 and CIC_2 at 0_B, which is the point at which the two community indifference curves intersect. An infinite number of other curves through 0_B are clearly possible, depending on the starting tangency on the contract curve in 0_A-Y_2-0_B-X_1. CIC_1 and CIC_2 are Pareto-uncomparable as A is better off on CIC_1 with I_A^1 level of utility than on CIC_2 with I_A^0 level of utility. B is better off on CIC_2 with I_B^1 level of utility than on CIC_1 with I_B^0 level of utility. However, given an arbitrary starting combination of the level of welfare for the two individuals a family of non-intersecting CIC curves can be built up. If CIC_1 is chosen, then a new box anchored at point 0_A that allowed say I_A^1 and I_B^1 to be achieved could be drawn. The box would be bigger, as the initial box 0_A-Y_2-$0_B'$-X_1 cannot accommodate a tangency between indifference curves I_A^1 and I_B^1. The new CIC curve would be to the north-east of CIC_1 and be comparable with CIC_1 in the sense of offering a Pareto improvement in that A is no worse off on welfare level I_A^1 and B is better off in terms of welfare being on I_B^1. In this way a map of CIC curves can be generated that show Pareto-preferred positions (increased community welfare) the further away they are from the origin in a north-east direction. Note, however, that the map is generally not unique as it is perfectly possible to begin with I_A^0 and I_B^1 and hence CIC_2 and build a consistent but different CIC map from there. CIC maps are used as a heuristic rather than an empirical construct. They feature a good deal in international trade theory (see Chapter 17).

The Second Fundamental Theorem makes explicit reference to no increasing returns. The CIC can be used to illustrate the technical form of market failure that arises when this condition is not met. In Figure 5.11 the production possibilities frontier T-T' has the concave shape illustrated earlier but the community indifference curves illustrated are

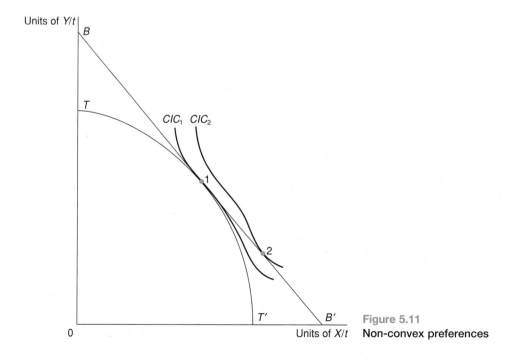

Figure 5.11   Non-convex preferences

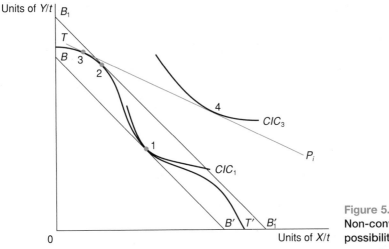

Figure 5.12
Non-convex production possibilities

seen to exhibit non-convexities. Now the Second Fundamental Theorem states that 'any specified Pareto optimal resource allocation that is technically feasible can be achieved by establishing competitive markets and an appropriate pattern of factor ownership'. Suppose point 1 on CIC_1 was the desired Pareto optimum; then the budget line is B-B' with the implied relative price for goods X and Y that would allow its achievement. However, given the shape of the community indifference curve, equilibrium would not be found at point 1 but at point 2 on a higher CIC, namely CIC_2. The implication is that the Pareto-optimal allocation associated with point 1 cannot be a competitive market outcome, contradicting the second theorem.

Similarly, if the production possibilities frontier exhibited non-convexity, as a reflection of increasing returns to scale (as in Figure 5.12), then an attempt to engineer technically feasible point 1 on CIC_1 with budget constraint B-B' would degenerate to point 2 on the higher budget constraint (equals value of output for the economy) B_1-B_1'. Again, the Pareto-optimal allocation associated with point 1 cannot be a competitive market outcome, contradicting the second theorem that any technically feasible outcome can be achieved. Cowell (2006), however, notes that international trade can serve to 'convexify' the production possibilities set. If world trade prices for goods X and Y are captured in P_i in Figure 5.12 then a point like 3 on CIC_3 would be achieved, independent of the shape of the domestic production possibilities. In this case the '*if there are no increasing returns*' phrase can be dropped from the definition of the Second Fundamental Theorem above. The partial equilibrium analogue of this technical form of market failure is discussed in Chapter 6 under the heading of the 'decreasing cost' case.

5.4 An equity value judgement and market failure

Are the Pareto value judgements sufficient to be a complete account of an economic Nirvana? With respect to the value judgements, has a fourth value judgement, that 'the distribution of utilities generated by the economy should be equitable', been mistakenly omitted?

It may be instructive in terms of fixing and linking ideas to return to the construction of community indifference curves. Suppose the initial starting point 3 in Figure 5.10 was deemed a distribution of utilities between A and B that was the equivalent of point 1. Recall, point 1 generates CIC_1 and point 3 generates CIC_2 in Figure 5.10. Since points 1 and 3 offer the same overall welfare, it follows that any point on CIC_1 represents a

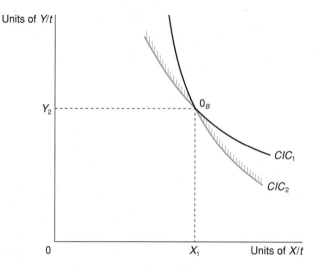

Figure 5.13
Towards a social welfare function

combination of units of Y and X, which, if distributed so as to yield CIC_1, would be just as attractive as any point on CIC_2 so distributed to generate CIC_2. The way 'equity' is traditionally considered in the $2 \times 2 \times 2$ general equilibrium model is via a social welfare function, which depends on individual utility levels and is represented as $W = W(U_A, U_B)$. How might this relate to the community indifference curves?

The welfare function in commodity–goods space will depict the minimum quantities of X and Y that permit the achievement of a given chosen level of welfare, say, SW_0. In Figure 5.13, which reproduces relevant sections of Figure 5.10, the curve CIC_1 (south-east of 0_B) shows combinations of X and Y per period that permit achievement of the utility levels associated with point 1 (namely I_A^1 and I_B^0). However, it does not show minimum combinations that can achieve an equivalent level of welfare to this. The curve CIC_2 shows smaller combinations of X and Y that can achieve utility levels I_A^0 and I_B^1 deemed of equal welfare to I_A^1 and I_B^0. If the community indifference curves deemed welfare equivalents cross, then the portions of curves showing the larger quantities of X and Y would seem redundant. In Figure 5.14 the two utility combinations deemed to offer

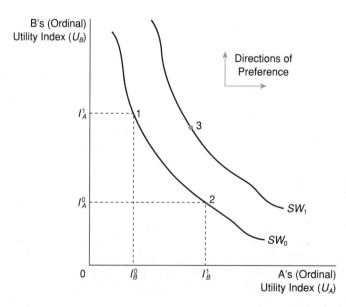

Figure 5.14
A two-person welfare function

equal welfare are plotted on SW_0 at points 1 and 2. The social welfare function SW_1, represents combinations of utility for A and B that offer a higher level of social welfare. The social welfare function briefly introduced here reflects the value judgement of society with respect to the distribution of utilities between A and B that are deemed welfare equivalents. Society is indifferent between points 1 and 2 on SW_0 but prefers any point, e.g. point 3, on SW_1.

The nature of measurement (in the constructions used in this chapter) is worth emphasising. In commodity–goods space the dimensions are tangible or physical, measurable and cardinal. In contrast, in utility space there is only ordinal measurement. Quantitative measurable utility that could be compared across individuals A and B would be very welcome but, as noted in Chapter 1, is never going to be possible. In Figure 5.14 SW_0 and SW_1 are conventionally drawn somewhat 'wavy', to signify this. That said, some form of interpersonal comparability of utility is required to operationalise different concepts of equity and it is the description of such concepts and their mathematical statement that is found in Section 5.4.1. Problems of input allocation and exchange are naturally handled in commodity–goods space, whereas it is clear from the discussion here that issues of equity naturally involve the rather more difficult-to-handle utility space.

5.4.1 Equity and the shape of the social welfare function

Equity is a difficult issue within economic analysis. The Paretian value judgements discussed above define what economists understand by 'efficiency'. One of their strengths is that they avoid taking a specific position on interpersonal comparisons of utility or welfare, which unfortunately is, as noted above, the heart of a definition of equity. Universal perfect competition (in the absence of technical market failure) will generate a top-level efficient economy in which it is impossible to make one person better off with no one else worse off. However, it was evident above that a vast range of allocations meet this condition, one corresponding to each distribution of final utility levels for the individuals that make up society. In short, to determine both an efficient and equitable economy requires the adoption of an additional value judgement about what constitutes equity.

In the above discussion, the development of a social welfare function was mooted. However, discussion does not end with the function illustrated. There are many suggestions about the 'optimal' distribution of income (utilities) but no single principle has found common acceptance. Tresch (1981) points out that 'Economists have all too often assumed away distributional problems in order to analyze more comfortable allocation issues, knowing full well that dichotomizing allocational and distributional policies is not legitimate' (p. 9). Indeed, efficiency and equity issues overlap in a number of fashions. For example, the 'atmosphere' created in society by the existing distribution of income is a non-rival, non-excludable good/bad, i.e. it is a pure public good (see Chapter 6). Additionally, any unilateral attempt by an individual to alter the distribution of income towards the poor creates the knowledge that the poor have been helped. This is non-excludable, raising the spectre of individuals 'free-riding' in redistribution matters, i.e. letting others incur the costs but sharing in the benefit of the knowledge that the poor have been helped. Any attempt by the government to enact redistribution on equity grounds is almost certain to have efficiency costs.

The government does not have the ability to set initial allocations of factors of production to individuals, so that when the competitive process runs its course – and factor prices, etc., are determined – both equity and efficiency are achieved. Instead, the government has to work on the income distribution that arises. Taxes and transfers that are not lump-sum, however, distort the relative prices faced by the individuals and thereby distort their utility-maximising choices. This represents inefficiency and identifying and measuring welfare loss triangles is much of the task of tax theory (to be discussed in Chapter 13).

Efficient allocation may be inequitable, whereas moves towards equity generate inefficiency; hence these twin criteria are typically at odds with one another and cannot be treated in isolation. If, for example, a government wishes to assist one category of individuals, it may reject the market efficiency condition of marginal-cost pricing and provide the goods to these individuals at a lower price. It will seek to pursue an equity goal and hopefully minimise the efficiency losses associated with departure from the efficiency conditions.

Introducing equity as a criterion provides a case for cash, or in-kind, redistribution, through the organising agency of the government. However, there is little consensus on what equity is, or indeed, if actual government policies increase or decrease equity on any given definition. It is generally accepted that equals should be treated equally. This represents so-called horizontal equity. But what defines 'equals'? It is also accepted that unequals should be treated unequally (vertical equity). But how unequally? Furthermore, there is the question as to where to apply the equity principle. Equity may relate to entry conditions – a level start to the economic race. Equity may relate to process conditions – equity of treatment during the economic race. Equity may relate to exit conditions – equity of outcome in the economic race. Such equity-increasing policies as exist are generally identified in Western democracies with the operation of welfare states. A major criticism of welfare states as far as the libertarians are concerned is that such activities are inimical to individual freedom, so a further complex dimension is raised.

Whilst economists (as economists) have no handle on the 'truth' of equity they have, nevertheless, done very considerable work on the topic. The spirit of this work is to identify the consequences of adopting different shapes of social welfare functions and allow others to assess the personal, ethical or democratic appeal of different shapes once the consequences have been articulated. Given the size of the question, it is not surprising that the literature on social welfare functions is both large and complex. The answer to 'the universe and everything' may be '42' but the question of equity has not proved so amenable to a solution. The basic problem is to compare different economic configurations. Given the individualistic nature of neoclassical economic theory, it is not surprising that economists have shied away from reference to an imposed choice in search of a ranking dependent on individual utilities. This so-called 'welfaristic' (from 'welfarism') view has been criticised because it ignores other information, such as the identity and personal characteristics of any individual (see Sen 1977).

Even if it is agreed that it is individual utilities only that are to matter, there is the question of utilities over what? In the broader Arrow-type formulation it is individual utility views over a complete description of all individuals' allocations of each good and service and inputs (X); in the narrower Bergson–Samuelson formulation it is the individuals' utility view of their own consumption bundle that comprises the basic data. Next, there is the question of how to sum and weight them.

For our purposes here, it is convenient to introduce a mathematical form that has the ability under different assumptions to offer many different shapes for 'social indifference curves'. This so-called constant elasticity function is given by

$$W = \sum_{i=1}^{n} \frac{a_i(U_i)^{1-e}}{1 - e} \tag{5.71}$$

where

W = social welfare;
a = parameter;
U = utility;
$1/e$ = constant elasticity of substitution of a social indifference curve.

Boadway and Bruce (1984) indicate what happens as different assumptions are made.

1. If $e = 0$ and $a_i = 1$, then $W = \sum_{i=1}^{n} U_i$, which is the so-called Benthamite or utilitarian social welfare function that maximises the sum of utilities of the individuals and, in the two-person case, gives social indifference curves like those depicted in Figure 5.15(a).
2. If $e = 0$ and $a_i \neq 1$, the so-called generalised utilitarian social welfare function arises, which is a weighted sum of the utilities of the individuals and in the two-person case gives a constant slope of other than minus unity to the social indifference curves (see

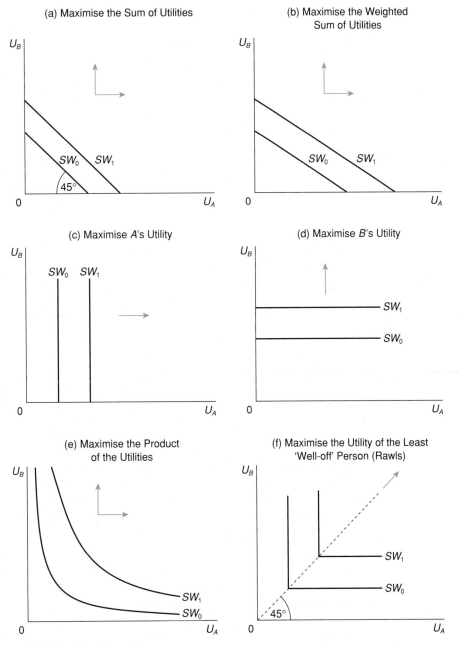

Figure 5.15 Social welfare shapes

Figure 5.15(b)). As a_i approaches 0 for one of the individuals, this amounts to maximising the utility of the other (see Figure 5.15(c) and (d)).

3. If $e \rightarrow 1$ and $a_i = 1$, a social welfare function associated with Nash is derived as $W = \pi_{i=1}^n U_i$, which maximises the product of individual utilities and in the two-person case yields social indifference curves that are rectangular hyperbolas, as illustrated in Figure 5.15(e).

4. If $e \rightarrow \infty$ and $a_i = 1$, the well-known Rawlsian social welfare function is obtained, so that $W = \min(u_1 \ldots, u_n)$ and the choice is to maximise the utility of the least well-off individual in society, dictating, in the two-person case, social indifference curves that are right angles along a 45° ray from the origin, illustrated as Figure 5.15(f).

As noted above, $1/e$ defines σ, the elasticity of substitution of the social indifference curves. The coefficient e can be handily remembered as 'e for equity', so that as e rises (and σ falls) so does concern with equity ($e = 0$ indicates no concern with equity).

For these 'shapes' illustrated by reference to (complete)-type allocations see Varian (1978), and for the n (individual allocation) case see Russell and Wilkinson (1979). The use of majority voting to aggregate individual preferences over (complete)-type allocations is discussed in the context of Arrow's impossibility theorem below. The point here is that it requires the adoption of a social welfare function to establish both an equitable and efficient configuration of an economy.

5.4.2 Equity and concern for others

The above implicitly assumes that individuals gain utility 'selfishly' from their own incomes or goods and services. But as the economist Boulding noted:

> 'The general theory of preference can take care of benevolence and even malevolence just as well as it can deal with selfishness. If we identify the welfare of another as our own, we can take care of this in formal theory by simply supposing that the preference function that governs our behaviour has goods possessed by others in its domain as well as goods that we possess ourselves. If we make a gift, it is presumably because we prefer the distribution in which we have less and another more to the one from which we started. There is nothing irrational in this; indeed, because community is one of the supreme achievements of man, it is highly rational.' Boulding (1967: 69)

There is now a considerable literature recognising the message of the quotation, that your utility will be affected positively or negatively by the utility achieved by others around you. Other individuals' utility, in effect, becomes an externality to you, and if Pareto-relevant this would suggest that you would willingly agree to some redistribution.

The effect of this type of 'everybody gains' argument is to provide positive sections to the utility possibility frontier as illustrated in Figure 5.16(b). The relevant foundations to this curve are found in the Edgeworth–Bowley box of Figure 5.16(a). If individuals A and B embody 'one of the supreme achievements of man' and have some concern about the quantities of goods X and Y per period they each have access to, then the contract curve becomes attenuated. Suppose individuals A and B had a free pick as to where to be in the Edgeworth–Bowley box of Figure 5.16(a) and they chose I_A^* and I_B^* respectively. These two points would now represent the top of each individual's ordinal utility mountain and any movement away from these points would represent a utility decrease on the circular indifference maps illustrated for the relevant individual. The section between I_B^* and I_A^* in Figure 5.16(a) has the interpretation that has been employed elsewhere in the chapter. That is, they are points of efficiency on the exchange contract curve generating the negatively sloped section 1-2 of the utility possibilities frontier (UPF_1) in Figure 5.16(b). Now consider points 4 and 5 in Figure 5.16(a), which are points of tangency. However, the ordinal utility level of I_B^7 is common for individual B whilst individual A enjoys either I_A^3 or I_A^5 ordinal utility levels.

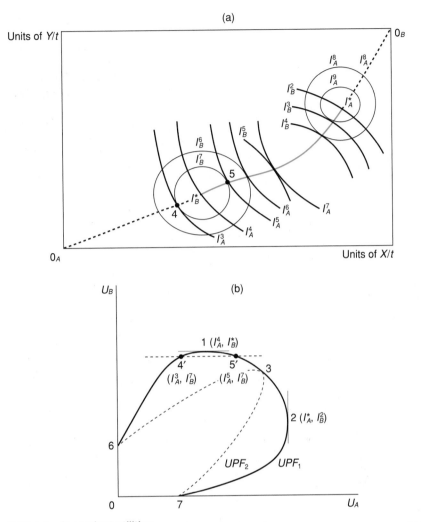

Figure 5.16 Interdependent utilities

Both are plotted in Figure 5.13(b), indicating that *UPF* cannot be monotonic and negatively sloped. Indeed, the dashed section of the contract curve $0A$-I^*_B in Figure 5.16(a) indicates that UPF_1 in Figure 5.16(b) must have a positive slope, in that they are distributions of utility where both *A*'s and *B*'s utility are rising. They form part of a consensus section on the contract curve in that both, via redistribution of the goods *X* and *Y*, would voluntarily move from point 6 on UPF_1 in Figure 5.16(b) to point 1. Beyond point 1 their utilities are in 'conflict'. An identical process of reasoning applied to point I^*_A would generate section 7-2 in Figure 5.16(b).

A recognition of interdependent utilities like this only serves to 'narrow' the efficient area of the frontier UPF_1 to the negatively sloped section between points 1 and 2 and ordinal utility levels (I^4_A, I^*_B) and (I^*_A, I^2_B), respectively. Mishan (1972) explains that a unique result obtains in the unlikely situation of a case like UPF_2 where 3 represents an optimal distribution of income. Note that the construction assumes that *B* is altruistic towards *A* as well as vice versa. The fact that this explanation can be formulated in an externality and utility possibility frontier context makes clear that the effect of interdependent utility functions is to make equity an 'efficiency' matter.

5.4.3 Equity as non-envy

The standard 'utility functions' allow the social valuation of the welfare of individuals to be calculated independently of the utility (income) levels of others. This 'separability' is a weakness if an interdependent view of income distribution is deemed crucial (see Sen 1973). Putting yourself in the position of others is the core idea of fairness or equity, being seen as the absence of envy.

The familiar Edgeworth–Bowley trading box can be used once more to illustrate the argument. In Figure 5.17(a) point 1 is the centre of the box and, unless individuals have identical preference maps, cannot be on the contract curve. Suppose the contract curve is the continuous curved line between 0_A and 0_B and point 2 an efficient allocation of X and Y between A and B along it. Now the question is, does A (B) regard their consumption bundle as attractive as that of B (A)? To find the response, the mirror allocation can

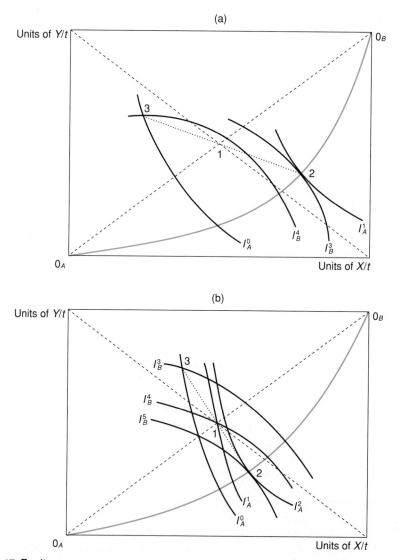

Figure 5.17 Equity as non-envy

be located at point 3 by striking a line from 2 through 1 and extending it for a distance equal to 2-1; i.e. distance 3-1 = distance 1-2. As illustrated, B, but not A, can attain a higher indifference curve at 3 than at 2 and, therefore, B is seen as being envious of A (and therefore point 2 is efficient but unfair in B's terms).

One allocation that would be both efficient and equitable in this sense would be an initial endowment at 1 where both A and B have the same X and Y. Since they face the same budget constraint, each can have what the other has so that any trades away from equal allocation to the contract curve must meet the reverse allocation test illustrated as Figure 5.14(b). A movement to point 2 raises both A's and B's utility, whereas the reverse assignment at point 3 lowers the utility of both – they are not envious of each other. The presence of malice or envy can be a spur to redistribution.

5.4.4 Redistribution and envy of others

The analysis of Section 5.4.3 offered one mechanism whereby individuals would voluntarily redistribute income. There is no requirement, however, for altruism to be the argument causing the interdependence. Redistribution can stem from malice and envy. Brennan (1973) employs a diagram such as Figure 5.18 to demonstrate this point.

For individual A, own income, Y_A, is a good, but the other person's income Y_B is a bad, reflecting the presence of malice towards B. (Envy is increasing marginal disutility of the other person's income.) The shape of B's indifference map reflects the same malicious feelings, being the map between a good and a bad (see Chapter 2). With initial allocations of income at point 1 on I_B^1 for B and I_A^1 for A, there are clearly gains from 'trade' to be had from the lowering of both incomes, as long as adjustment is contained within the usual rugby-ball shape bounded by utility levels I_B^1 for B and I_A^1 for A. The locus of points between 2 and 3 defines the relevant portion of the contract or, more aptly, in this case (in Boulding's terminology), the conflict curve. An outcome such as 4 raises A's utility to I_A^2 and B's to I_B^2.

Intuitively, what is happening is that A's loss of utility from the reduction of own income is more than compensated for by the knowledge that B's income is also falling. But how is the income reduction to be achieved? With many As and Bs, individuals will attempt to allow others to reduce their incomes, gaining in utility from that knowledge, while not lowering their own incomes. Additionally, the process could get out of hand. Not all income reductions raise utility. If the cuts become too deep, both A and B can

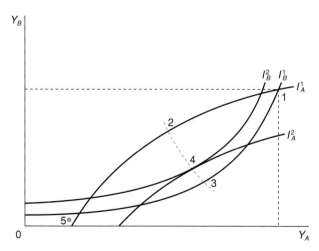

Figure 5.18
Y_A Redistribution from malice

be made worse off, say at point 5. These two observations suggest the need for power of government, to solve the incentive to free-ride on other's income losing actions and to referee the process to keep losses within bounds.

Brennan now introduces a third actor (or set of actors) C, whose income level Y_c is a neutral good as long as $2Y_c < Y_A$ or Y_B, i.e. they are unconcerned about those with less than half their own income level. Government redistribution of income from A and B towards C, within limits, raises the utility in this society of some well-off but malicious and envious individuals!

The impact of the considerations and arguments in the last three subsections is typically to set limits to the extent of inequity but not to resolve the issue uniquely. What precisely constitutes 'equity' in society will always remain a vital matter of individual opinion and be open to debate.

5.4.5 Fairness and the Shapley value

Moulin (2003) offers a modern approach to the question of fairness. The starting point is what are called the four classic, but conflicting, principles of distributive justice.

The first, exogenous rights, is similar to the 'one-person one-vote' rule in a democracy, which gives equal weight to each individual irrespective of the quality of their thinking in the political process.

Second, the principle of compensation is about ensuring equality in the form of access to basic requirements of living, e.g. shelter, food and clothing. Those who do not have wealthy parents could not afford market-priced education, whilst some parents, even with money, might not spend it on education for their children. A rule of education 'free' at the point of use for those who have somehow fallen through the net might then be justified on compensation grounds. Elsewhere, we have noted that being fair in the distribution of education may involve giving more education resources (inequality of inputs) to 'sink estate' areas to compensate for a deprived social and environmental background.

The third principle is that of reward and suggests that those who contribute more to any venture should be differentially rewarded for that greater contribution. It raises the issue that individuals should consider their impact on the costs and benefits others feel because of their actions or contributions (in the next chapter the Clarke tax and public goods preference revelation mechanism has this principle embodied in it).

The fourth principle is that of fitness and it requires that real resources should be in the hands of those who can make most use of them (not easily defined).

In dividing an estate of four valuable antique paintings between four offspring, Moulin suggests:

(i)   exogenous rights would say one painting each;
(ii) compensation says give the paintings to the poorest of the offspring;
(iii) reward to the offspring who helped keep the stately home from ruin; and
(iv) fitness to the offspring who graduated from the Royal College of Art, as philistines are not fit to have good antique paintings.

The author elaborates these principles in a series of examples and exercises but here we concentrate on the use of the Shapley value. The Shapley (1953) value has a role in cooperative game theory whose focus is the set of joint ventures individuals may contribute to. Rasmusen notes, 'The motivation for the Shapley value is that player i receives the average of his marginal contributions to different coalitions that might form' (Rasmusen 2001: 320) and therefore finds its justification in the reward principle above. Moulin provides an example of the joint venture, being the provision of an elevator in a building comprising four identical apartments. The costs are:

Elevator:	Marginal cost
First to second floor alone £5,000	£5,000
First to second and third floors alone £10,000	£5,000
First to second, third and fourth floors £40,000	£30,000

Adding the fourth floor is disproportionately expensive (marginal cost £30,000), perhaps because it is a much bigger engineering job. The question is, how should total costs be fairly shared? Sharing in line with number of floors carried $(1 + 2 + 3 = 6)$ would give sharing proportions of 1/6, 2/6 and 3/6, implying payments of £6667, £13,333 and £20,000. Lower-floor dwellers clearly would be upset, as their shares are greater than the total cost of an elevator that would cover their needs. Basing cost contributions of the 'stand-alone' costs of £5000, £10,000 and £40,000) implies shares of $5/(5 + 10 + 40)$ of £40,000 = £3636 for floor 1 and $10/(5 + 10 + 40)$ of £40,000 = £7272 for floor 2 and $40/(5 + 10 + 40)$ of £40,000 = £29,091 for the top floor, which seems more reasonable, although floor 3 still pays less than the marginal cost they impose.

However, the Shapley value assigns the costs of each extension of the range of the elevator to those who will use it. So there are 3 users of the elevator to the first floor, 2 to the second and 1 to the third and the Shapley value contributions become:

$1/3 \cdot$ £5000 = £1667 for the first-floor dweller,
$1/3 \cdot$ £5000 + $1/2$ £5000 = £4167 for the second-floor dweller,
$1/3 \cdot$ £5000 + $1/2$ £5000 + 1 $\cdot$ £30,000 = £34,167 for the third-floor dweller.

In effect the third-floor dweller has to pay for the use of the first- and second-floor elevators to enjoy access to their third-floor one.

Vega-Redondo (2003: 24) provides the two-person case, where there is now a benefit of £1000 to be shared by any subgroup of individuals $N = \{1, 2, \ldots, n\}$ $n \geq 2$, provided the subgroup is a strict majority (2 in the case $n = 2$) and there is unanimity about the sharing of the £1000. The Shapley value assigns each individual their average marginal contribution in the sequential process of forming what is called the grand coalition N, where every possible order in which this coalition might be formed is given equal weight. With two individuals, 1 and 2, there are only two orders in which the grand coalition can be formed '1-2' or '2-1'. In the first case, the marginal value of individual 1 on entry to the coalition is zero, as they are not a majority in isolation. If they enter second, as in order two, their marginal value is the full £1000, as they are decisive in forming the majority. What is the relevant Shapley value? It is the average (here therefore divide by 2) of the marginal contributions (£0 and £1000) in the two sequences, namely $1/2$ £0 + $1/2$ £1000 = £500. As the approach is fully symmetric, player 2 also receives £500. This is not to suggest the Shapley value is the solution to distributive fairness, as there are other principles than the reward one (exogenous rights, compensation and fitness) and other proposed solution concepts to cooperative games, e.g. the Nash bargaining solution in Chapter 9.

5.5 The 'sovereign individual' value judgement and market failure

In this chapter it has been demonstrated that when individuals behave as *homo economicus* and when there is no market failure the outcome is one whereby competitive markets lead to a Pareto allocation of resources. As emphasised at the outset, Pareto optimality is determined with reference to the individual. It is an outcome in which it is impossible to make any individual better off without making another individual worse off (in terms of *their own estimation* of welfare).

However, scholars have pointed to instances in which government intervention is required *because* it is impossible to rely on the preferences of individuals. For example, Musgrave (1959: 13) defines a *merit want* as one '. . . considered so meritorious that [its] satisfaction is provided for through the public budget, over and above what is provided for through the market and paid for by private buyers'.

The essence of merit wants is that individual preferences are replaced by the preferences of an outside or external decision-taker (e.g. an expert). There are situations in which markets would not be relied upon as the means of provision of goods and services, because individual preferences would not be thought appropriate to guide resource allocation to a welfare maximum. But how can this be justified? Why should the individual be rejected as the best source of information concerning the individual's welfare? Why, would an 'outside' decision-maker know better than the individual what is in that individual's own interests?

One answer to this question is in terms of individuals' access to information. Another is in terms of individual ability to process information (i.e. that they would not act 'rationally' even if they had information).

(i)   *Information access* There are reasons to doubt that receipt of information will be efficient. Information has characteristics that make it subject to 'market failure' arguments. Knowledge (i.e. information) is non-rival, in that its use by one individual does not decrease the total available to other individuals. Indeed, knowledge may be supra-non-rival, in that, if learning or knowledge augmentation takes place with use then more use may actually increase the quantity available. This suggests it is likely to be inefficient to use the market to achieve exclusion (restriction of use).

Furthermore, the nature of information makes exclusion difficult. It is only possible to know the value of information to you once you have it, but then you have an incentive to avoid paying for it. Furthermore, the passing of information from one to another makes it difficult for an originator to maintain a property right (ownership) over its use. These considerations suggest under-provision in the market. In terms of consumer-type goods, it is those whose quality is difficult to inspect that are seldom repeat purchases and which involve harmful consequences, or side effects, that are the most obvious candidates for policy concern. There is then a basis for information provision in some circumstances, but its appropriate production and dissemination method is likely to be open to debate.

(ii) *Rational response.* If access to information was the sole problem then the response of governments might be to subsidise its provision or to provide information directly. For example, if individuals did not consume 'sufficient' medical care because they were unaware of the benefits of appropriately referring to a doctor, or unaware of the dangers of different life-style consumption patterns, medical education programmes might be introduced by the government and, indeed, are (but with disputed consequences). The response here would be to over-ride the individual's decision concerning the merits of investment in acquisition of information. However, something more fundamental occurs if the government takes one step further and rejects an individual's ability to use information advisedly (even if it were made available). For example, market provision of certain drugs might be rejected because it is assumed that, even if warned, individuals would still be inclined to make the wrong decision *vis-à-vis* consumption of such goods.

As emphasised throughout this text, microeconomics is *individualistic* in that it is the decision of the individual that is the focus of analysis. How can such rejection of individual rationality be justified? One way in which economists attempt to 'square the circle' is to assume that individuals rationally decide to relinquish some regulatory decisions to others. In order to suspend individual judgement in some parts of economic analysis, without it smacking of inconsistency and arbitrariness, the explanation is in terms of individual 'deciding not to decide'. Mooney (1979) has an escape route in which individuals choose in their own best interests to delegate their decisions to government – they choose to have what would have been their individual choice 'corrected'. If there is a lack of information the individual may not think they ought to make a decision on such and such. Mental and other limitations may make the individuals feel unable to make decisions so that expert outside knowledge is desirable. Individuals may think some issues are simply 'too big' for them and they may not want to make such decisions.

Despite these 'rationalisations', commentators remain rather sceptical of the concept of merit wants especially if they are justified in terms of dislike of 'outcomes' based on individual preferences. The notion is that individuals' preferences may be sublimated by authority that does not stem from individuals. As noted in Chapter 4, Mishan (1981: 10) explains that the decision to respect the preferences of individuals may be

(i)   a judgement of fact (a belief that individuals generally are the best judge of their own welfare);
(ii) a judgement of morality (it is appropriate to act as if individuals are the best judges of their own welfare); or
(iii) a judgement about political expediency (it is politically expedient, in the Western world, at least, to act on the assumption that individuals are the best judges of their own welfare – democracies rely on individuals each having a single vote). Such arguments are not put aside lightly in economics.

Wiseman and Littlechild (1986) concentrate on restriction of choice. They argue that the market failure approach cannot deal adequately with the idea that, somehow, individual preferences may simply be 'wrong'. The paternalist framework they see as based on the information paucity and spurious decision-making competence on the part of the individual. They also widen the discussion to include consideration of endogenous preferences (people who are the product of a 'faulty' environment or childhood experiences, etc., will have 'faulty' preferences which need not be respected). However, their analysis focuses on a libertarian framework, one that is associated with extensive liberty, *subject to not violating the rights of other individuals*. Here lies a possible rationale for the provision of merit wants. In this context, the authors note any restriction of choice imposed by government on an individual must flow from the social decision-making rule adopted by individuals as being acceptable to justify public policy (e.g. a voting rule of unanimity, see Chapter 12).

The authors recognise different frameworks for the justification of provision of merit wants and they argue that sometimes these will be compatible, albeit for different reasons. However, emphasis is placed on the connections between decision making and institutional settings and the policies that are selected within them, with a view to isolating those collective decision-making processes a majority would be likely to find acceptable. The justification for the provision of merit wants is then found, not so much in the 'undesirability' of certain allocations of resources as in the desirability of certain *collective decision-making processes*. 'If citizens accept that the social decision making processes from which policies emerge are fair, then they will be willing to accept the possibility that, at least some, policies which emerge will be contrary to their best interests. This is the price they must pay to obtain agreement from others on the policies they themselves want' (p. 170). The issue of where individuals are allowed to smoke is a clear example of this type of problem.

Microeconomic theory acknowledges the possibility that 'public policy aims at an allocation of resources which deviates from that reflected by consumers' sovereignty'

(Musgrave 1959: 9). The problem is reconciling this with an approach based on the individual. However, in any discussion of why market solutions may be rejected the merit want argument cannot be ignored.

5.6 Challenge: Are efficiency and equity enough?

So far the focus has been on efficiency and equity as evaluative criteria. For many, these two criteria (despite being quite complex) are not enough; they would claim other criteria are also important for evaluation (especially if government intervention is involved). One criterion with a claim to relevance is individual freedom. The view that individuals take, with regard to the importance of equity, invariably colours the lens through which any loss (or gains) of freedom are assessed. If equity-type policies are unimportant, then any demonstration that they infringe individual freedom is damning. In what follows, an attempt is made to sketch alternative views of the importance of equity with the object of developing a notion of freedoms that may be gained or lost (and to whom they are gained or lost).

5.6.1 Your view of equity

It is readily accepted that equity typically involves making value judgements over and above those embedded in traditional (neoclassical) economic theory and, as such, will always be a cause of controversy. Rather than ask for such value judgements, the question here is why people disagree on the importance of equity as a goal in the first place. The answer seems to be simply that different people view the world differently. In terms of social policy analysis, people can be said to have different 'assumptive worlds' in which they are operating. Table 5.2 outlines a taxonomy of some assumptive worlds that rely on two characteristics which you (the reader) consider individuals do, or do not, possess.

The first is whether you believe people are broadly similar in their abilities, especially in relation to the marketplace. The second is whether you think people have similar tastes or preferences, especially in relation to certain basic commodities. Case 1 is interesting because in a world of broadly similar abilities and tastes there would be little observed inequality, and therefore little need to direct policy towards it.

Case 2 similarly leads to rather little concern about inequality. The different tastes or preferences of people would mean that they would choose different production and consumption patterns. Therefore, there would be observed inequality but, given broadly equal abilities, it would be within everyone's grasp to achieve what others around them have. The main purpose of any equality-motivated policies would be towards establishing equality of opportunity. In short, if you think individuals have broadly similar basic abilities, opportunities in life and you are not really concerned with the fate of others, then a low e value in Equation (5.71) is appropriate for you.

Table 5.2 Assumptive worlds

	People have broadly similar abilities	People have broadly similar tastes	Emphasis
Case 1:	Yes	Yes	Negative freedom
Case 2:	Yes	No	Negative freedom
Case 3:	No	Yes	Positive freedom
Case 4:	No	No	Positive freedom

Case 3 provides grounds for strong welfare-state policies, especially those provided in an in-kind form. Unequal abilities would mean considerable inequality being observed in the economy and would be a rather intractable problem because, for the individuals doing less well, equality of opportunity is not enough; they are fundamentally disadvantaged. However, because tastes or preferences are similar (to the extent, again, that inequality is thought a problem) government in-kind provision is acceptable because there is little efficiency loss from in-kind redistribution where (basic) preferences are not very different and therefore all will tend to choose in the same way.

Case 4 provides similar concern over observed inequality, but suggests that the inefficiency losses from in-kind provision would be large and hence (to the extent inequality is to be tackled) cash transfer payments will invoke less efficiency loss. (Field 1981 seems to broadly hold this view.)

Cases 2, 3 and 4 all involve observed inequality but, depending on your assumptive world, its significance and the appropriate policy response will vary.

The next question is: how, if at all, do different conceptions of freedom relate to this simple taxonomy?

5.6.2 Kinds of freedom

Freedom is an emotive word and is self-evidently a 'good thing'. Hence, any suggestion that the public-policy intervention encroaches on freedom is a powerful criterion in debate. As Stein (1985: ii) puts it, 'In America, and the Western world generally, "freedom" is a good word and "big government" is a bad word.'

Generally speaking, the runway for most take-offs into discussions of freedoms is Isaiah Berlin's distinction between positive and negative freedom (Berlin 1958). Berlin makes the distinction between the freedom from something and the freedom to do something. The first represents negative freedom and the second the positive notion of freedom. Apart from the differential role of the government in establishing positive and/or negative freedoms, Goodin (1982) suggests that negative freedom is about the set of available options, whereas positive freedom is about the capacity or otherwise to exercise these options. Furthermore, there is a constant-sum aspect to negative freedom (an individual's 'freedom from' means another's option has been circumscribed) in contrast with a positive-sum aspect to positive freedom. Here Goodin has in mind that freedoms may have different 'values' so their distribution matters. The loss of some freedoms to some individuals can be overcompensated for by the extension of liberties to others. Table 5.3 outlines the distinctions made in this section between positive and negative freedom and as with Table 5.2 is useful in identifying where your (the reader's) perspective lies.

Green (1982) makes a similar distinction in a review article on Field (1981) when he writes of plain freedom and freedom as power. Plain freedom is associated with the desires of individuals to be protected from the injustice of other individuals and the power of central authorities which in upholding individuals' rights must be given power to enact this task – a power that can be abused. Freedom as power correlates with positive freedom above, in that it concerns the use of the power of central authorities to give the 'have-nots' freedom to do things by essentially compulsory redistributive policies. In short, freedom as power can be identified with the desire to solve inequality problems. It is in this way that Table 5.3 can be linked with the third column of Table 5.2. The argument here suggests that those who have an assumptive world that sees individuals as broadly equal in ability should favour negative freedom and (if they are concerned with equity) equality of opportunity policies, whereas those who see individuals as fundamentally different should favour positive notions of freedom and government in-kind and/or cash transfer policies.

Table 5.3 **Characteristics of negative and positive freedom**

Negative freedom	Positive freedom
1. Involves freedom from the actions of others.	1. Involves a broad constraint that includes social structures and institutions.
2. Is available without any extensive government action.	2. Requires government action to make it exist.
3. Involves the set of available opportunities.	3. Involves the capacity to utilise the set of available opportunities open to individuals.
4. Is essentially constant-sum in nature (one's loss is another's gain).	4. Has a positive-sum aspect (exchanging freedom between individuals can involve the gainers gaining more than the losers lose).

Unless the more esoteric is lost sight of, it is worth noting that Goodin (1982) draws attention to both psychological and moral freedom. The former concerns the subjective capacity to take advantage of opportunities (crudely it appears to be the freedom to 'go for it') and the latter the freedom to conform with individually held principles. Religious debates and conflicts over recent years have brought these concerns to the level of violence.

Perhaps the other end of the definitional scale is represented by the 'University of Chicago economist', Stigler (1978). He equates freedom with wealth and writes: 'A wider domain of choice is another way of saying that a person has more freedom or liberty' (p. 214). Given this, it is the efficiency of public policy that matters. 'Let me ask of any proposed or actual policy: will it increase the wealth of individuals in society? If it does, then on balance it will increase the range of options available to the people in that society' (Stigler 1978: 217). If this is accepted, then the relevant question to ask in this context would appear to be: does intervention in a market economy accelerate the rate of growth of the economy? Perhaps equity and efficiency are sufficient evaluative criteria after all!

5.7 Summary

In this chapter the objective was to consider the way in which market processes serve *homo economicus*. As indicated by reference to Adam Smith's analysis of the 'invisible hand', competitive markets offer an incentive structure that will lead to a Pareto-optimal resource allocation. More specifically, it was established in a general equilibrium context that, in the absence of market failure, perfectly competitive markets achieved a Pareto-optimum allocation of resources (the First Fundamental Theorem). The market mechanism ensured that the first-order conditions were satisfied (and if second-order conditions for a maximum are also sustained the community maximises welfare in Paretian terms).

The Second Fundamental Theorem indicated that any competitive equilibrium generates a Pareto-efficient outcome for some initial pattern of factor ownership. Put another way, it was evident that the top-level efficient economy is an incomplete picture to the extent that the Paretian conditions can be satisfied for *any* distribution of welfare between those in the community. This raised a first value judgement source of market failure, namely, the question of equity of utility distribution. Until the appropriate social welfare function is established the precise allocation of resources that would maximise welfare for the community of all individuals cannot be determined. With respect to equity the general equilibrium framework did, however, prove useful in exploring altruism and envy.

A second 'value judgement' source of market failure was introduced in the form of a discussion of merit wants. It was seen that there are cases in which conforming to the choices of individuals is a questionable value judgement to respect. Individuals may not be the 'best' judges of their own welfare, either because they do not have sufficient information or because they are not able to process the information in a manner deemed appropriate. In such cases it appears to some that government intervention to 'correct' individual choices should depend on expert opinion.

In the challenge section 5.6, the question was posed as to the adequacy of efficiency and equity as the economists' evaluative criteria. In a short section on freedom a simple taxonomy was proposed as a way of the reader identifying where their views with respect to equity and freedom are located. The attraction of intervening in a market economy or not depends, in part, on the assumptive world you hold in your head. However, to complete this view, sources of technical market failure (other than non-convexities met above) requires consideration of other arguments. This is the task of the next chapter.

References

Bator, F.M. (1957) The simple analytics of welfare maximization, *American Economic Review*, 97: 22–59.

Berlin, I. (1958) *Two Concepts of Liberty*, Oxford: Oxford University Press.

Boadway, R.W. and Bruce, N. (1984) *Welfare Economics*, Oxford: Basil Blackwell.

Boulding, K. (1967) The basis of value judgments in economics, in S. Hook (ed.) *Human Values and Economic Policy, a Symposium*, New York: New York University Press.

Brennan, G. (1973) Pareto desirable redistribution – the case of malice and envy, *Journal of Public Economics*, 2 (2): 173–83.

Coleman, J.S. (1988) Social capital in the creation of human capital, *American Journal of Sociology*, 94 Supplement: 95–120.

Cowell, F. (2006) *Microeconomics: Principles and Analysis*, Oxford: Oxford University Press.

Cullis, J.G. and Jones, P.R. (2009) *Public Choice and Public Finance*, 3rd edn, Oxford: Oxford University Press.

Debreu, G. (1959) *Theory of Value*, New York: Wiley.

Field, F. (1981) *Inequality in Britain: Freedom Welfare and the State*, London: Fontana.

Goodin, R.E. (1982) Freedom and the welfare state theoretical foundations, *Journal of Social Policy*, 13 (2) April: 149–76.

Green, D.G. (1982) Freedom and paternalistic collectivism, *Journal of Social Policy*, 11 (2) April: 239–44.

Henderson, J.M. and Quandt, R.E. (1971) *Microeconomic Theory*, New York: McGraw-Hill.

Mishan, E.J. (1972) The futility of Pareto efficient distributions, *American Economic Review*, 62 (5): 971–6.

Mishan, E.J. (1981) *Introduction to Normative Economics*, Oxford: Oxford University Press.

Mooney, G.H. (1979) Values in health care, pp. 23–44 in K. Lee (ed.) *Economics and Planning*, London: Croom Helm.

Moulin, H.J. (2003) *Fair Division and Collective Welfare*, Cambridge, Mass.: MIT Press.

Musgrave, R.A. (1959) *The Theory of Public Finance*, New York: McGraw-Hill.

Okun, A.M. (1975) *Equality and Efficiency – the Big Tradeoff*, Washington: The Brookings Institution.

Rasmusen, E. (2001) *Games and Information – an Introduction to Game Theory*, 3rd edn, Oxford: Blackwell.

Russell, R.R. and Wilkinson, M. (1979) *Microeconomics: a Synthesis of Modern and Neoclassical Theory*, New York: Wiley.

Schotter, A. (1990) *Free Market Economics*, 2nd edn, Oxford: Basil Blackwell.

Sen, A.K. (1973) *On Economic Inequality*, Oxford: Clarendon Press and New York: Norton.

Sen, A.K. (1977) Social choice theory: a re-examination, *Econometrica*, 45: 53–89.

Serageldin, I. and Steer, A. (1994) 'Epilogue: Expanding the capital stock?' in I. Serageldin and A. Steer (eds) *Making Development Sustainable: From Concepts to Action*, Environmentally Sustainable Development Occasional Paper Series No 2, World Bank, Washington.

Shapley, L. (1953) A value for *n*-person games, pp. 307–17 in H. Kuhn and A. Tucker (eds) *Contributions to the Theory of Games, Vol. II*, Annals of Mathematics Studies No. 28, Princeton, NJ: Princeton University Press.

Starr, R.M. (1997) *General Equilibrium Theory – an Introduction*, Cambridge: Cambridge University Press.

Stein, H. (1985) Foreword, to S.E. Plaut, *The Joy of Capitalism*, London and New York: Longman.

Stigler, G. (1978) Wealth and possible liberty, *Journal of Legal Studies*, 7 (2): 213–17.

Tresch, R.W. (1981) *Public Finance: a Normative Theory*, Plano, Tex.: Irwin-Dorsey.

Varian, H.R. (1978) *Microeconomic Analysis*, New York: Norton.

Vega-Redondo, F. (2003) *Economics and the Theory of Games*, Cambridge: Cambridge University Press.

Walras, L. (1874) *Eléments d'Economie Politique Pure*, Lausanne: L. Corbaz.

Wiseman, J. (1978) The political economy of nationalised industry, pp. 73–92 in *The Economics of Politics*, IEA Readings No. 18, London: Institute of Economic Affairs.

Wiseman, J. and Littlechild, S.C. (1986) The political economy restriction of choice, *Public Choice*, 51: 161–72.

CHAPTER (6)

The 'benefits' of market intervention

6.1 Introduction

As promised, this chapter will 'pick up' on the second of the two questions posed at the end of Chapter 5. It relates to technical sources of 'market failure' and, as the chapter heading suggests, the possible benefits from intervention in the market. With respect to this question, self-interested *homo economicus* so far appears to have done very well (at least, in terms of generating efficient outcomes). However, this is to look at the economic world with rose-tinted glasses. The focus of this chapter is on the question of why market failure can arise even when markets are perfectly competitive. Specifically, the focus is on the impact of problems created by externalities, public goods and decreasing costs.

Evidence suggests that there is not only *market failure* but also *individual failure* in that individuals do not behave as *homo economicus* (Jones and Cullis 2000). Here, however, different examples of *market failure* are the focus of this chapter. The assumption that individuals behave as *homo economicus* is retained. Indeed, it is precisely because individuals operate in a rational self-interested way that markets fail. As Schotter (1990: 47) emphasises: 'the very rationality that makes the market work so well often destroys the optimality of its results'. When individuals behave as *homo economicus* and when there are externalities or public goods then, even if perfect competition prevails, this same 'rational' pursuit of self-interest will mean that a Pareto-optimal resource allocation may not be achieved. Thus market failure is often taken as a *prima facie* case for government intervention.

6.2 Externalities

In the following discussion the implications of externalities are discussed. It will become clear that, if there are externalities, then even if the market is perfectly competitive the welfare of the individual and the welfare of the community of all individuals are not reconciled. If individuals act rationally from self-interest (i.e. are concerned only with their own happiness) they respond to *private* costs and *private* benefits, which may be at variance with actions that would prove to be in the best interests of all individuals taken as a whole. It is this analysis of market failure that motivates discussion of government intervention in markets.

6.2.1 Definition

There are two defining characteristics of an externality. Externalities occur if there is *interdependence*, e.g. if the utility of an individual depends on the activities of other individuals. Individual A might derive utility from goods and services $(x_1, x_2, x_3, \ldots, x_n)$ but A's utility might also depend on the activity (Y^B) of individual B. This activity might be smoking, creating litter, playing a radio too loudly. In this case:

$$U^a = U^a(x_1, x_2, x_3, \ldots, x_n, Y^B) \tag{6.1}$$

If A's utility increases as Y^B increases the interdependence is referred to as an *external economy* (or positive externality). If A's utility decreases as Y^B increases there is an *external diseconomy* (or negative externality).

Within a price mechanism the action of one individual may affect others (Mishan 1988). If some consumers switched consumption from tea to coffee, other things equal, the price of coffee would increase and potentially this might reduce the welfare of existing consumers of coffee. However, an externality is quite different because *interdependence is external to the market mechanism*. The activity occurs outside (i.e. is 'external' to) the price mechanism. The definition of an externality requires reference to interdependence *outside the price mechanism* (and is therefore uncompensated) because the implication is then that the affected individual has no way to respond. For example, if individual A suffers from smoking by individual B, individual A has no way of influencing the decision of individual B as far as smoking is concerned. If individual A could persuade (by negotiation, bribes, or the offer of payment) individual B to alter consumption of cigarettes then the activity would be priced. In this case the externality is said to be 'internalised'. (Negotiation would bring the activity within the price mechanism and offer the possibility that both parties could gain as a result of negotiation.)

Externalities may occur between:

- Consumer and consumer (e.g. smoking cigarettes);
- Producer and producer (a chemical firm which issues effluent in an estuary affects the output of a fishing firm);
- producer and employee (an employee produces output but learns a skill at the same time);
- producer and neighbour (the factory that issues smoke that dirties the washing of a neighbour).

Externalities might be *reciprocal* or *unidirectional*. They might be *marginal* $(dU^a/dY^B \neq 0)$ or they might be *infra-marginal* $(dU^a/dY^B = 0)$. For example, if there were pollution in a lake, individuals would find that they could not swim in the lake (the externality is marginal). Compare the situation in which pollution might increase without decreasing utility. After a certain pollution level further pollution might have no effect until eventually levels affect utility derived from boating (to this level pollution was infra-marginal but has now become marginal).

6.2.2 Externalities and welfare effects

Externalities are a matter of concern. Even if markets are perfectly competitive welfare might not be maximised. Consider the case of an external diseconomy. In Figure 6.1 good X is supplied in a perfectly competitive market. However, when X is produced, the production process creates pollution that reduces the welfare of those who live nearby. The marginal external costs (of pollution) are shown in Figure 6.1 by *MEC*.

Profit-maximising firms produce at the output level at which price is equal to marginal private cost (where private cost refers to the costs firms must meet – e.g. labour costs, capital costs). The competitive price is P_c and the competitive output is q_c. However, there is a difference between *private cost* and *social cost*. Marginal social cost (*MSC*) includes the marginal private cost (*MPC*) that firms must meet but it also includes marginal external costs (created by pollution). In Figure 6.1 $MSC = MPC + MEC$.

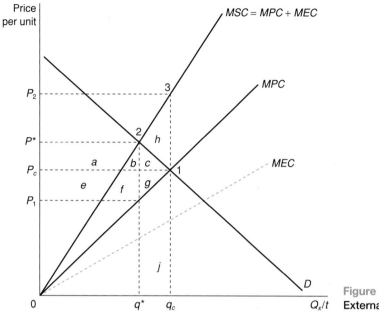

Figure 6.1
External diseconomy

It is now no longer the case that the output level of a perfectly competitive market maximises welfare for the community. Welfare will be maximised at the point at which the marginal social benefit of good X is equal to marginal social cost. Marginal social benefit can be estimated with reference to the demand curve. At any output level, a point on the demand curve reveals the maximum sum that an individual would be prepared to pay for the last unit consumed (see Chapter 2). In this way, marginal social benefit of good X can be estimated with reference to the demand curve D in Figure 6.1. The output level at which *marginal social benefit* is equal to *marginal social cost* is q^*. This output reflects an allocation of resources that is optimal for the community.

Figure 6.1 illustrates the way that the optimal allocation of resources changes if there is an external diseconomy. Now, more generally, consider how the Pareto-optimal conditions (discussed in Section 5.2) change if there is an externality. If there are two individuals, A and B, each consumes a private good X. A's utility depends upon the consumption of good X and also upon an activity (e.g. playing a CD). This activity E creates an external effect which affects the utility of individual B. Individual A maximises utility from consumption of X and E subject to a budget constraint. The budget constraint is:

$$Y_A = X_A P_X + E_A P_E \tag{6.2}$$

where

Y_A = income that might (potentially) be spent on X and on E;
P_X = the price of X;
P_E = the price attached to the externality activity;
X_A = the quantity of good X consumed by A per period;
E_A = the extent of the externality.

It follows that individual A maximises utility $U_A(X_A, E_A)$ subject to the constraint $Y_A = X_A P_X + E_A P_E$ and in the following Lagrangian:

$$\mathcal{L} = U_A(X_A, E_A) + \lambda(Y_A - P_X X_A - P_E E_A) \tag{6.3}$$

Partially differentiating $\mathscr{L}$ with respect to X_A and E_A and setting equal to zero:

$$\partial\mathscr{L}/\partial X_A = \partial U_A/\partial X_A - \lambda P_X = 0 \tag{6.4}$$

$$\partial\mathscr{L}/\partial E_A = \partial U_A/\partial E_A - \lambda P_E = 0 \tag{6.5}$$

i.e. to maximise utility,

$$\partial U_A/\partial X_A \Big/ P_X = \lambda = \partial U_A/\partial E_A \Big/ P_E \tag{6.6}$$

or

$$\partial U_A/\partial E_A \Big/ \partial U_A/\partial X_A = P_E/P_X \tag{6.7}$$

The first-order utility-maximising condition *for individual A* is that MRS_{XE} (which is $\partial U_A/\partial E_A \big/ \partial U_A/\partial X_A$) is equal to the price ratio.

However, it can be shown that for those involved in the community (A and B) this is not the welfare-maximising solution. To achieve a Pareto-optimal solution it is necessary to maximise utility for one individual (in this case individual A) subject to the additional Paretian constraint of holding the utility of another individual (B) constant. This constraint can be described as:

$$\bar{U}_B = U_B(X_B, E_A) \tag{6.8}$$

Now the Lagrangian takes the following form:

$$\mathscr{L} = U_A(X_A, E_A) + \lambda(\bar{U}_B - U_B(X_B, E_A)) + \mu(Y_A + Y_B - P_X X_A - P_X X_B - P_E E_A) \tag{6.9}$$

so that the first-order conditions are:

$$\frac{\partial\mathscr{L}}{\partial X_A} = \frac{\partial U_A}{\partial X_A} - \mu P_X \qquad = 0 \tag{6.10}$$

$$\frac{\partial\mathscr{L}}{\partial X_B} = \lambda\frac{(-\partial U_B)}{\partial X_B} - \mu P_X \qquad = 0 \tag{6.11}$$

$$\frac{\partial\mathscr{L}}{\partial E_A} = \frac{\partial U_A}{\partial E_A} - \lambda\frac{\partial U_B}{\partial E_A} - \mu P_E = 0 \tag{6.12}$$

Divide equation (6.12) by μP_X (which from equations (6.10) and (6.11) is equal to $\partial U_A/\partial X_A$ and $\lambda(-\partial U_B)/\partial X_B$ respectively) and it is possible to obtain the Pareto-optimal conditions:

$$\frac{\partial U_A/\partial E_A}{\partial U_A/\partial X_A} + \frac{\partial U_B/\partial E_A}{\partial U_B/\partial X_B} = \frac{P_E}{P_X} \tag{6.13}$$

and it is clear that the condition reported in equation (6.7) is not the Pareto optimum, The condition in equation (6.13) says that marginal rate of substitution for A (MRS_{XE}) plus the marginal value of the externality to B should be set equal to the price ratio. It follows that if

$$\frac{\partial U_B/\partial E_A}{\partial U_B/\partial X_B} > 0 \tag{6.14}$$

there is an external economy and A 'purchases' too little E (and too much X) if the externality is not internalised. On the other hand, if

$$\frac{\partial U_B/\partial E_A}{\partial U_B/\partial X_B} < 0 \tag{6.15}$$

there is an external diseconomy and a reduction in the E is required.

It should be noted that the Pareto-optimal conditions described in Section 5.2 (in the absence of an externality) are no longer the Pareto-optimal conditions in the presence of an externality.[1]

6.2.3 Public-sector solutions to externality problems

Public-sector intervention may be required to solve problems created by an externality. Alternative instruments are available to governments and the question is which instrument (or combination of instruments) is optimal. The instruments can be illustrated with reference to Figure 6.1:

a) *Taxation.* The objective in a tax solution is to bring the external costs to the attention of the decision-maker. In the example shown, a tax could be set to make the producer aware of the costs that are imposed on others (i.e. to internalise the externality). If tax per unit of output were set equal to marginal external cost (*MEC* in Figure 6.1) the producer would have no incentive to produce at output q_c. At this output the marginal private cost (distance q_c-1) and marginal tax (1-3) would exceed the price that the producer receives (P_c). The cost that others experience is trapezoid ($h + c + g$) = trapezoid *j*. The producer's incentive is to reduce output to q^*. The welfare effects of the tax are presented in Table 6.1.

 Note that the optimal response involves only a reduction in pollution (not a complete curtailment of pollution). The optimal outcome is not one in which there is 'no pollution' but one in which there is 'optimal pollution'.

b) *Regulation.* An alternative instrument that might be introduced is regulation. In Figure 6.1 output might be regulated to q^* (e.g. by standards for noise or for effluent emission that would be breached if output exceeded q^*). The welfare effects that would be evident if there were regulation are shown in Table 6.2.

 Once again, this is not a charter for the ecologist (it does not imply a perfectly 'green' environment). There is no recommendation to strive for a pollution-free

Table 6.1 Welfare effects of taxation

Group affected	Source of welfare change	Welfare change
Producers	decrease in producer surplus	$-e - f - g$
Consumer	decrease in consumer surplus	$-a - b - c$
Those affected by the externality (neighbours)	decrease in cost	$+h + c + g$
Government	increase in tax revenue	$+a + b + f + e$
Net welfare effect	net increase	$+h$

Table 6.2 Welfare effects of regulation

Group affected	Source of welfare change	Welfare change
Producers	increase in producer surplus	$+a + b - g$
Consumers	decrease in consumer surplus	$-a - b - c$
Those affected by the externality (neighbours)	decrease in cost	$+h + c + g$
Net welfare effect		$+h$

1. The reader can pursue this further by reference to an example presented by Henderson and Quandt (1971) that highlights how Pareto-optimal conditions change in the presence of an externality.

environment. With marginal adjustment, there is no reason to stop production. The objective is to bring the externality into the decision calculus (to internalise the externality) and to achieve a Pareto-efficient allocation of resources. If the output were motor cars consumers would not want to live without motor cars. The optimal output is not necessarily zero.

Analysis of the different welfare effects experienced by different groups explains why different groups might have different preferences for the instruments that government can introduce. For example, with reference to Figure 6.1 compare the impact of taxation and regulation on producers. In the case of taxation they lose area $c + f + g$ but in the case of regulation they may be better off if areas $a + b > g$. The implication is that producers may lobby for regulation to deal with pollution (for further discussion see Cullis and Jones 2009).

c) *Subsidies*. The same approach can be applied to examine the use of a price subsidy and to illustrate the impact that is created by an external economy. Figure 6.1 analyses the impact of an external diseconomy. It is now convenient to explore the welfare effects of an external economy.

In Figure 6.2 demand for good X (D) reflects marginal private benefit (MPB). It is willingness to pay by consumers who derive satisfaction from good X. However, it is now the case that others also gain as a consequence of consumption of good X, i.e. there is an external economy. One example (education) is explored in depth in Chapter 12. If demand in Figure 6.2 were demand for education, D would represent the marginal private benefit of education to students (e.g. in terms of an increase in future earning – and in terms of the intrinsic benefit that can be derived when studying is interesting). However, if there are positive externalities, marginal social benefit exceeds marginal private benefit. If, for example, others may gain because an educated worker introduces a new design or a new production process there are positive spillovers (see Chapter 12 for further discussion of these spillover effects).

To ease exposition marginal external benefit (MEB) is assumed constant and equal to distance 0-MEB. It follows that at the output of a competitive market marginal social benefit exceeds marginal private benefit by 0-MEB. If D reflects marginal private benefit (the maximum sum that would be paid for each successive unit), marginal

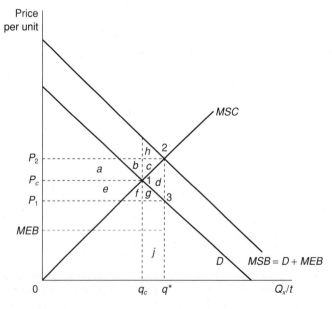

Figure 6.2
External economy

Table 6.3 **Welfare effects of a subsidy**

Group affected	Source of welfare change	Welfare change
Producers	increase in producer surplus	$+a + b + c$
Consumer	increase in consumer surplus	$+e + f + g$
Those affected by the externality (other citizens)	increase in benefit	$+c + d + g$
Government	cost of the subsidy	$-a - b - c - d - e - f - g$
Net welfare effect	net increase	$c + g = h + c$

social benefit in Figure 6.2 is MSB = the vertical sum of $D + MEB$. A competitive market would supply too little (for at q_c marginal social benefit exceeds marginal social cost). The output that maximises welfare is q^*. At q^* the increase in benefit to others is $(c + d + g) = j = h + c + d$.

If government intervenes, the objective is now to increase output. A subsidy equal to the marginal external benefit reduces the price that individuals would pay at output q^* from P_2 to P_1. The demand for this commodity increases from q_c to q^*. The welfare effects are described in Table 6.3.

All of these options may be considered with reference to the different welfare effects experienced when resolving externality problems. It is not always the case that everyone will be better off. However, it is the case that gains to the gainers (the most they would pay for a change) from such intervention outweighs losses to the losers (the most that they would require to accept the change).[2] It follows that this is a *potential Pareto improvement* (see Chapter 12).

If the government intervenes to maximise welfare for the community it should choose the form of intervention that corrects the misallocation of resources at minimum transactions costs. 'Government transactions costs' are based on two issues:

(a) *Information.* How does the government know the 'correct' level of output to aim at? One attractive feature of a perfectly functioning market is that it presents considerable information in terms of the prices that it creates. However, if market prices are unacceptable, because of the problem of externalities, how are social costs and social benefits to be estimated?

b) *Agreement.* How are the various groups to reach agreement? In principle, the gainers may outweigh the losers (in terms of their impact) but, if a majority of losers exist, these policies may not be enacted via the political process (even if they pass the *potential* Pareto improvement criterion). The costs of coming to agreement and of political process will be considered further in Chapters 12 and 14.

It is very often the nature of the transactions costs that dominates the question of whether there should be a public-sector response and how large the public-sector response should be (see Arrow 1971). The identification of market failure is only a *prima facie* case for government intervention. There are still costs of information and of agreement in the political process. It follows that there may be instances in which public-sector responses are not required because the costs of intervening exceed the gains that would be achieved.[3]

---

2. That is the same as saying that the compensating variation of the gainers exceeds the compensating variation of the losers.

3. It is also the case that some externalities may be infra-marginal (because when included they do not affect the efficient quantity). If transaction costs are excessive the externality may also be Pareto-irrelevant.

6.2.4 **The Coase theorem**

If there are externalities, market solutions (in which individuals maximise welfare with respect to private costs and private benefits) will not maximise welfare (even if markets are competitive). While economists (e.g. Pigou 1932) were quick to suggest that there may be a *prima facie* case for government intervention to correct market failure, Coase (1960) (the 1991 Nobel laureate) asked why externality problems persist. Surely, if 'gains to the gainers' exceed 'losses to the losers', the problem could be resolved by negotiation between the affected parties?

Figure 6.3 expands on Figure 6.1 to highlight the welfare effects experienced by those parties who emit externalities and those who suffer as a consequence of externalities. As in Figure 6.1, Figure 6.3(a) focuses on market outcome in a perfectly competitive market. Profit-maximising producers will produce output q_m, i.e. the output at which price equals marginal private cost. With an external diseconomy (e.g. pollution) marginal social cost exceeds marginal social benefit at this output (as in Figure 6.1). There are welfare gains if producers reduce output to q^*.

Figure 6.3(b) is constructed from Figure 6.3(a). *MEC* is the difference between *MSC* and *MPC* and $D - MPC$ is the difference between the price that the producer would set at a

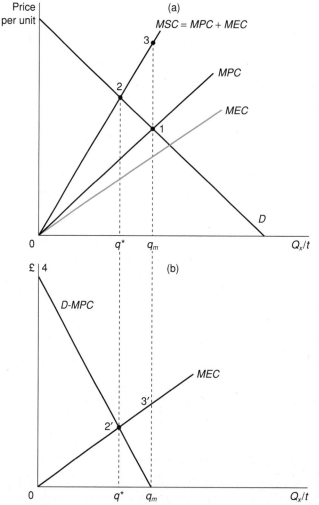

Figure 6.3
The Coase theorem

given output and the marginal private cost that would be experienced at that output (in this case a measure of incremental profit).

Ignoring the external diseconomy, the value of each successive unit of output to the producer is the difference between the price that consumers would pay and the marginal cost of production. The price that consumers would pay is estimated with reference to the demand curve D (because the demand curve reports willingness to pay for each successive unit of the good).

If the external diseconomy is now considered, neighbours experience external costs as product X is produced (e.g. pollution). In Figure 6.3(b) MEC is the maximum sum those affected by the external diseconomy would pay to reduce output by each successive unit. Analysis in Section 6.2.3 focused on instruments (tax, regulation, subsidy) that would achieve the efficient level of output q^*. But, surely, if the 'gains to gainers' exceed the 'losses to the losers' there are incentives to negotiate this output level?

Profit-maximising firms continue to produce to the output at which the price paid equals marginal private cost (i.e. to the point that $D - MPC = 0$). At this output (q_m) it is clear that neighbours (who experience pollution) would be willing to compensate producers to reduce output from q_m to q^*. The sum that neighbours are willing to pay is equal to q^*-2'-3'-q_m and this exceeds the potential gain that producers would experience ($D - MPC$) on units between q_m and q^*. Triangle 2'-3'-q_m represents the 'gains from trade' that are possible if there is negotiation. Coase argued that what is required from government is a clear statement of property rights. If property rights are clearly stated negotiation can take place.

Following this reasoning it also appears that it is irrelevant (in terms of resource allocation) whether neighbours must compensate the producer not to produce, or whether the producer must compensate neighbours to produce. For example, it is equally possible to start from a set of property rights whereby the producer has to compensate neighbours in order to get their permission to set up operations. With reference to Figure 6.3(b), it is evident that neighbours could be persuaded to accept an output level as high as q^* per period. Up to this point, the producer can offer more to increase output by one successive unit (0-4-2'-q^*) than the losers require to put up with the external costs (0-2'-q^*). In either case, negotiation would prove successful.

The proposition is that the parties involved can rectify the problem of externality as long as property rights are clear. While it does not seem to matter who compensates who in terms of *resource allocation* (the same 'optimal' output – q^* – will be achieved), it does matter as far as the *distribution of income* is concerned. As the resource allocation solution is invariant to the assignment of property rights, the allocation of resources is uniquely determined, irrespective of who is legally entitled to compensation, and this is referred to as the *invariance* conclusion (Cooter and Ulen 1997).

6.2.5 Problems with the Coase theorem

The bargaining response to the problem of externalities is quite general. Where there is an external diseconomy, the output of the producer is 'too large' and those affected would attempt to offer compensation to secure a reduction of the activity in question. Where there is an external economy, output would be 'too small' and compensation would be offered to increase the activity. Surely, if all parties perceive 'gains from trade', negotiation will take place? Instead of the government intervening directly (by tax, regulation or subsidy), the government might resolve the problem of externalities simply by clarifying property rights (i.e. by clarifying who is liable to pay compensation).

Coase suggests that the problem of externalities can be resolved by a clear statement of property rights and that resource allocation will be invariant to the manner in which property rights are stipulated but:

(a) *Transactions costs*. Pigou (1932) notes that there are costs of negotiation (in terms of time and effort) when engaging in negotiation. If the costs of negotiation exceed the 'gains from trade' there is no incentive to resolve the problem but if the costs that are incurred when government intervenes (by tax, regulation and subsidy) are lower than the gains from trade that are possible, there is still a case for government to intervene directly.

(b) *'Large' numbers*. If the pollution problem is experienced by a large number of neighbours each individual might prefer to sit quietly in the hope that the others will offer enough compensation to produce a less polluted atmosphere. If numbers are 'large' each individual might hope to 'free-ride' on the actions of others. If all behave in this way, negotiations will not 'get off the ground'.

(c) *Imperfect competition*. One of the attractions of a Coasian solution is that it leads to the efficient use of resources (i.e. to resource allocation illustrated by output q^*) but the starting point in this analysis is that markets are perfectly competitive. The solution in Figure 6.3 is one at which $P - MPC = MEC$ (i.e. the situation that exists when $P = MPC + MEC$) and, at this optimal output, marginal social benefit equals marginal social costs. But what if there is *imperfect competition*?

To illustrate how negotiation might lead to an inefficient allocation consider the same analysis when output is produced by a monopolist. In Figure 6.4(b) output will be set at the point at which $MR - MPC = 0$ (because a monopolist maximises profits when marginal revenue – MR – is equal to marginal private cost). If output is set where marginal private cost, MPC, equals marginal revenue, MR (i.e. the output at the intersection point 3 in panel (a)), negotiation between the producer and neighbours would lead to a solution at which marginal social cost ($MPC + MEC$) is equal to marginal revenue (i.e. the output at the intersection point 4 in panel a). The output of the monopolist falls from $0\text{-}q_2$ to $0\text{-}q_1$ while the optimum output is $0\text{-}q^*$.

Negotiation fails because the interests of consumers are never fully represented. The starting point is the one at which output is inadequate as compared to the socially optimal output q^*. The absence of consumers at the negotiation table means that the socially optimal solution is not at the point that $P = MPC + MEC$. The solution is at the point at which $MR = MPC + MEC$ (Buchanan 1969).

(d) *'Well-behaved functions'*. In Figure 6.3(b), marginal externality cost (MEC) cuts ($D - MPC$) from below. If this were not the case the solution would be unstable. If MEC cuts ($D - MPC$) from above then to the right of the intersection point producers could compensate those affected to accept increases in output and to the left of the intersection point E sufferers could compensate polluters back to a zero output per period (Baumol and Oates 1988).

(e) *Asymmetric information*. Davis and Kamien (1971) argue that there may be situations of asymmetric information, so that one side may have rather more information than the other (see Chapter 7). This may lead to cheating or blackmail. For example, assume that neighbours do not know the producers' profit function. Competitive producers may threaten to produce a greater output level than q_m in Figure 6.3 unless the neighbours offer a larger sum in compensation. In Figure 6.4 the monopolist may threaten to produce an output level of q_4. Focusing on Figure 6.4(b) the producer may ask for as much as area $q_3\text{-}5\text{-}6\text{-}q_4$ extra to reduce output to q^*. In this way neighbours may be blackmailed into offering the additional compensation to the producer.

(f) *Competitive bargaining*. In order to specify property rights monopoly positions may be difficult to avoid. For example, in the case of pollution property rights must be granted to each individual neighbour (e.g. as a quantum of noise-free, pollution-free air). Mishan (1988) notes that it is difficult – if not impossible – to achieve this. Even if it could be done, there would be no market perfectly functioning in pollution-free air as each individual would have property rights to a specific defined quantum. Each individual would then have a monopoly position.

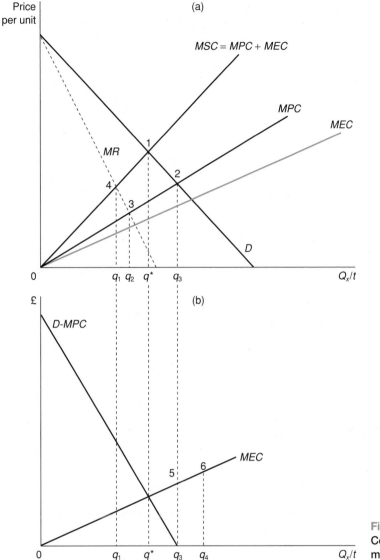

Figure 6.4
Coasian solution with
monopoly

This list of problems is by no means exhaustive (for further discussion see Cullis and Jones 2009). In some instances it is just very difficult to identify the parties that are responsible for external effects. Suppose farmers use chemicals which ultimately pollute streams. Who is culpable? The manufacturers of chemicals, the farmers who use the chemicals, or the government that permits this? Who, in this example, is liable?

In some cases it is impossible to bring all parties to the negotiation table, e.g. when external costs are experience by future generations. Many pollutants are long-lived. They stay in the environment and the people who will be affected may not yet be born. How can negotiation take place?

All of these problems indicate that a market solution may not be readily forthcoming and if one occurred it would involve transactions costs. The list of transaction problems (by no means exhaustive) casts some doubt on the proposition that the unaided market can adequately resolve the problem of externalities.

6.2.6 **Empirical analysis of the Coase theorem**

While there are two aspects to the Coase theorem the focus so far has been on the proposition that property rights will facilitate a resolution of the externality. The second aspect is that resolution is invariant with respect to the actual property rights that are stated. However, in this section the focus falls on the argument that individuals have incentives to negotiate solutions if property rights are clearly specified.

There are different ways in which this proposition might be tested:

(a) Behavioural tests

    (i) *Bees and honey.* Meade (1952) argues that there was a spillover from apple growers to honey-producing beekeepers. Meade refers to the 'case of an unpaid factor, because the situation is due simply and solely to the fact that the apple-farmer cannot charge the beekeeper for the bees' food' (p. 57). If so, is there evidence that the spillover has been internalised by negotiation between producers?

        Cheung (1973) considered production in Washington State. He reported that it appeared that there was a long history of both explicit and implicit contractual arrangements, which provided for beekeepers to be compensated for the beneficial contribution made by their bees to the apple crop. However, Cheung (1978: 61) notes that: 'Contrary to what most of us have thought, apple blossoms yield little or no honey.' The positive external effect was mainly from beekeepers to apple growers. Bees create a positive external effect for apple growers in pollinating apple trees. Cheung illustrates Coase's theorem in action by reporting evidence of payments from apple growers to beekeepers that internalises this spillover (for further discussion see Cullis and Jones 2009). While it is not clear that the outcome was the social optimum nor that this solution was the 'best' means of tackling the externality problem there was evidence that individuals respond to incentives to internalise spillovers.

    (ii) *Law suits.* A second example of a behavioural test of the Coase theorem is research which has been carried out with respect to law suits. Typical of this approach is the work of Galanter (1983). He found that 90% of all law suits in the US were settled before trial. As trials were very expensive, individuals were able to recognise that negotiation and settlement prior to trial could make all parties better off. The cases that went to trial were: (a) those where the costs of cases were lowest, (b) cases which have other high settlement or transactions cost and (c) those which could not otherwise be settled easily.

(b) Experimental tests

    An alternative test is to design experiments to discover individuals' willingness to negotiate when there are gains from trade. The Coasian solution to the externality problem rests on the proposition that rational individuals will find a way to rectify the damage done by an externality if they are allowed to negotiate among themselves. To discover whether this actually happens, Hoffman and Spitzer (1982) performed the following experiment.

    Subjects were brought in pairs into a room (one pair at a time). One of the subjects in the pair was designated 'controller' (by the flip of a coin). The subjects were given a payoff schedule like that shown in Table 6.4. The controller had two options. First, the controller might pick a row unilaterally and the controller and the partner would then receive the payoffs indicated in Table 6.4. Alternatively, the controller and the partner could select a row jointly and bargain over how total payoff (indicated in that row) should be divided. As the controller could affect the payoff received by the partner, the controller's position had the capability of causing an externality.

    With reference to Table 6.4, if the controller unilaterally chose row 7 the controller would receive $11 and the partner would receive nothing (the total payoff

Table 6.4 Payoffs for the Hoffman–Spitzer experiment

Row numbers	Controller	Non-controller
1	$0.00	$12.00
2	$4.00	$10.00
3	$6.00	$6.00
4	$8.00	$4.00
5	$9.00	$2.00
6	$10.00	$1.00
7	$11.00	$0.00

Source: Hoffman and Spitzer 1982.

being $11). However, if the controller chose row 2 the total payoff is $14. Row 2 is the highest possible total payoff. In this way, row 2 is the Pareto-optimal choice. It is the choice that would be predicted by the Coase theorem – within a Coasian solution there would be negotiation between the controller and the partner to appropriate 'gains from trade'. The partner would be expected to offer sufficient compensation to induce the controller to choose row 2.

The experiment revealed support for the Coasian solution. Hoffman and Spitzer report that only one of the 24 pairs of subjects who participated in this experiment failed to choose the Pareto-optimal outcome for both players. However, closer analysis of this behaviour suggests that the actions of participants were not motivated solely by self-interest. Of the 24 subjects acting as controllers all but 7 agreed to an equal division of the payoff.

6.2.7 Property rights and invariance

Turning to the second part of the Coase theorem, is it really the case that outcomes are invariant to the assignment of property rights? When analysing Figure 6.3 it was argued that the same allocation of resources would ensue whether or not producers were entitled to produce good X. If they were entitled to produce good X, neighbours would compensate them to reduce production from q_m to q^*. If they were not entitled to produce without the consent of neighbours there was an incentive to compensate neighbours to produce up to output q^*.

This discussion ignores the impact of transactions costs. How will the outcome differ if there are transaction costs associated with negotiation? The following example (based on Conybeare 1980) focuses on the impact of transactions costs.

Figure 6.5 focuses on the costs of dealing with an external diseconomy (pollution). A producer (P) can incur abatement costs to deal with emissions of pollution. The marginal cost of abatement is A. The marginal benefit to those who would otherwise incur the costs of pollution is B. In the absence of transactions costs there are incentives to agree to a level of pollution abatement equal to x per cent because the gains to those affected exceed the cost that the producer must bear. If property rights are permissive those who suffer (S) must compensate P to reduce pollution up to x (and B is greater than A). If property rights were prohibitive (so that P must persuade S to accept less than 100% abatement) there is an incentive for the producer to compensate S to accept a lower level of abatement to x per cent (as A is greater than B). The outcome appears to be invariant to the question of whether S must compensate P to introduce abatement or whether P must compensate S to accept levels of abatement lower than 100%.

If there are transaction costs the situation is quite different. If those who benefit must incur transactions costs (e.g. when mobilising collective action to reach collective

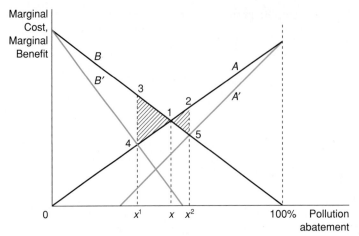

Figure 6.5 **Transactions costs and Coasian solutions**

agreement) the amount that they are able to pay is B' and the solution is x^1. On the other hand, if the producer must incur costs to negotiate the amount that the producer will offer to accept less than 100% abatement is A' and the solution is x^2.

If there are transactions costs the outcome varies with the way that property rights are assigned. It is also the case that the optimal assignment of property rights now also depends on the relative size of the welfare costs created. The efficiency loss of being at x^1, rather than at x, is triangle 1-4-3 and the efficiency loss of being at x^2 rather than x is triangle 1-2-5 (Conybeare 1980).

The choice of property rights might also have an impact on the allocation of resources if analysis also considers the impact of income effects. If there are income effects, there will be a difference between willingness to pay (compensating variation) and willingness to accept (equivalent variation) – see the discussion of consumer surplus in Chapter 2. For further discussion of the impact of income effects on Coasian solutions see Cullis and Jones (2009).

6.2.8 Network externalities: rediscovering Leibenstein and Veblen

In recent decades what was essentially a curiosity set of demands have come to the fore in a different guise. Leibenstein (1950) and Veblen (1934) explored the individual demand for 'bandwagon' and 'snob' goods. These share the feature that demand depends on the number of other individuals who consume the good. They differ in that the inter-dependence is positive in the case of 'bandwagon goods' (B) and negative in the case of 'snob goods' (S).

In Figure 6.6(a) the bandwagon case is illustrated. At point 1 the price is P_1 and the quantity chosen per period by the individual q_1 per period is conditional on the quantity of total sales Q_1. If price falls to P_2 the standard expectation is an expansion of demand point 1 to 2 (q_1 to q_1') as a price effect. But, given the demand curve is conditional on the quantity others purchase, this is not the equilibrium. Lowering the price causes others to consume more, thereby increasing the demand of the depicted individual to $D(Q_2)$; q_2 will now be chosen at point 3. The increase in demand from q_1' to q_2 is the bandwagon effect on demand – 'craze-type' toys might correspond to this, with all wanting what is currently the fashion. If price falls to P_3 the standard expectation is an expansion of demand from point 3 to 4 (q_2 to q_2') as a price effect.

Lowering the price further causes others to consume even more, thereby increasing the demand of the depicted individual to $D(Q_3)$ and q_3 will be chosen at point 5. The

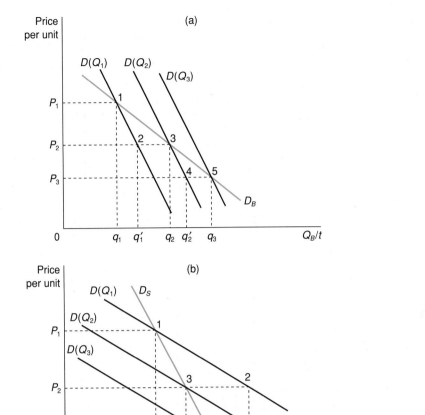

Figure 6.6 Network externalities

increase in demand from q_2' to q_3 is the bandwagon effect on demand. The effect of these adjustments is to make the individual demand curve more elastic, joining points 1, 3 and 5, labelled D_B. If the market demand curve is required then it is the D_B of each individual that has to be horizontally summed.

In Figure 6.6(b) the 'snob' case is illustrated. At point 1 the price is P_1 and the quantity chosen per period by the individual q_1 per period is conditional on the quantity of total sales of Q_1. If price falls to P_2 the standard expectation is an expansion of demand from point 1 to point 2 (q_1 to q_1') as a price effect. But, given the demand curve is conditional on the quantity others purchase, this is not the equilibrium. Lowering the price causes others to consume more, thereby decreasing the demand of the depicted individual to $D(Q_2)$ and q_2 will be chosen at point 3. The decrease in demand from q_1' to q_2 is the snob effect on demand.

A 'snob good' is one you can show off, knowing (by definition) few others have the good. Alternatively, the interdependence can be via price itself. Veblen (1934) noted the price of a good may be an end in itself, showing you are able to afford the high price represents conspicuous consumption of the good. The fact that more individuals might purchase the good at the lower price decreases its attraction. If price falls to P_3 the standard expectation is an expansion of demand point 3 to 4 (q_2 to q_2') as a price effect. Lowering the price further damages the 'you cannot afford this' signal to others, thereby decreasing the demand of the depicted individual to $D(Q_3)$ and q_3 will be chosen at point 5. The decrease in demand from q_2' to q_3 is the snob effect on demand. The effect of these adjustments is to make the individual demand curve the more inelastic one joining points 1, 3 and 5, labelled D_S. If the market demand curve is required then it is the D_S of each individual that has to be horizontally summed. A similar picture arises if price is used as an indicator of quality with high price being interpreted as high quality and vice versa.

Recently, the bandwagon effect has been reintroduced as 'network externalities', whereby initial sales of different types of mobile phone or VCR causes increased later sales as the number of people in the network influences the location of the demand curve as above. As Betamax VCRs lost out in a format struggle with the VHS format, the joke was – Q: 'How do you make sure no one steals your VCR?' – A: 'Buy a Betamax!'.

Network externality indicates the consumer has two sources of utility. The first source is called 'stand-alone utility', which captures utility that the individual enjoys as an isolated single buyer and the second is positively related to the number of other users.

6.3 Public goods

In the same way that analysis focused on the response of *homo economicus* to the existence of externalities, the following sections consider the response of *homo economicus* to the provision of public goods. It will, once again, be evident that when goods are public, rather than private, each individual's self-interest and the interest of the community are difficult to reconcile via market mechanisms. As noted already (see earlier reference to Schotter 1990), the rational pursuit of self-interest will not reconcile individual and community (all individuals) welfare maximisation when there are public goods.

The requirement for government to intervene to provide public goods arises because *homo economicus* is so concerned with pure self-interest that there is no incentive to bear the costs that voluntary provision of public goods would imply. Once again, the assumed rationality of individuals works against the supposition that voluntary action will result in maximisation of the welfare of all individuals. Indeed, even when public-sector intervention is undertaken (to determining tax arrangements to fund such public good provision) the expectation is that special incentives (a Clarke tax) will be required to induce individuals to reveal their demand honestly (the so-called preference revelation problem). In the following sections the intention is to begin with an exposition of the problems posed by public goods for *homo economicus* and then to turn to experimental evidence of how individuals behave when presented with a public good issue.

6.3.1 What are public goods?

Perhaps the defining characteristic of a public good is that if the good is available to one individual it is available to all. The 1970 Nobel laureate Samuelson (1954: 387) referred to a public good as one 'which all enjoy in common in the sense that each individual's consumption of such a good leads to no subtraction from any other individual's consumption of that good'. The difference when comparing a public good with a private good is that a private good 'can be parcelled out among different individuals' (Samuelson 1954: 387).

When focusing on provision of a private good aggregate provision is equal to the sum of each individual's consumption. If good X is a private good (e.g. apples, loaves of bread) and, if there are two individuals A and B, total consumption (X_c) is the sum of each individual's consumption:

$$X_c = X_A + X_B \tag{6.23}$$

When focusing on a public good (G) aggregate provision is the same for every individual, so that

$$G_c = G_A = G_B \tag{6.24}$$

One example is national defence. National defence is an example of a public good in a very specific sense. National defence is a public good when defence capability acts as a deterrent. Each individual enjoys security but consumption of security by one individual does not reduce the availability of security from attack for other citizens. The total available security (G_c) is equal to the amount consumed by individual A (G_A) and equal to the amount that is consumed by individual B. This does not mean that A and B value security equally – simply that the level of security supplied for A is equal to the level of security supplied for B.

(i) *Non-rival consumption and aggregate demand*

When consumption of one individual does not reduce the benefits derived by all other individuals the good is described as non-rival in consumption. One implication of this characteristic is that the aggregate demand for a public good differs systematically from the aggregate demand for a private good. Figure 6.7 compares the familiar demand and supply diagram for private goods with that for public goods.

In Figure 6.7(a), D_a and D_b are the demand curves of individuals A and B for a rival private good X. The aggregate demand curve D_{a+b} is found by adding the quantities each individual demands at each price (see Chapter 2). For example, at price $0P_X$, A demands q_a and B demands q_b. The market demand is q_{a+b}. The addition is clearly horizontal (over quantity at any price). The marginal costs of production are shown by MC_X. In this partial equilibrium context the Pareto optimal quantity of the good is the output that is produced when price is equal to marginal cost. As each individual will consume the good (provided that the marginal benefit from so doing exceeds the price), the 'optimal' quantity of the private good is q_{a+b}. Marginal benefit from the product is estimated with reference to the demand curve. At any output, the marginal benefit (MB) is willingness to pay for the marginal unit. It follows that in the diagram the condition for optimal provision is:

$$MC_X = P_X = MB_a = MB_b \tag{6.25}$$

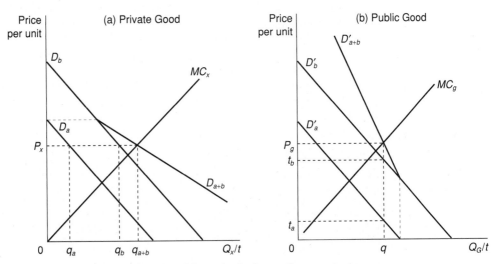

Figure 6.7 **Aggregate demand: public and private goods**

where MB_a and MB_b measures the marginal benefit enjoyed by individuals A and B from successive units of consumption of good X per period. It has been shown (in Chapter 4) that, provided there are no other distortions in the economy, this condition is Pareto optimal (the quantity provided is an efficient one).

Now consider the conditions that are required for Pareto optimality in the case of public good. In Figure 6.7(b), D'_a and D'_b are the demand curves of individuals A and B for a public good G. In order to find the aggregate demand D'_{a+b} it is not sensible to talk about the quantity A consumes as distinct from the quantity that B consumes. By definition, each individual can consume the same quantity of the public good. In this case it becomes more appropriate to ask how much would individual A pay for a given quantity of the good and how much individual B would pay for a given quantity of the good and to add these sums together. At q individual A would pay t_a and individual B would pay t_b for this quantity (the use of t indicates a general association of public goods with tax prices and public-sector provision). The aggregate demand curve is therefore D'_{a+b}; it is established by repeating this addition at every quantity level. It should be clear that now addition is vertical, i.e. addition 'over price' at any quantity per period.

The Pareto-optimal conditions are satisfied when the sum of the marginal benefits or demands of the two individuals equals the marginal cost (MC_g). If taxes are set with reference to the *Benefit Principle of Taxation*, individual A would pay a tax of 0-t_a and individual B would pay a tax of 0-t_b. The *Benefit Principle of Taxation* requires that each individual pays a tax equal to the marginal benefit to them of the good provided via the public sector. It is now the case that

$$MC_g = P_g = MB_a + MB_b \tag{6.26}$$

More formally, the process indicates that, if the 'ceteris paribus' variables are unchanged, the aggregate (n-person) or market demand P_gM for public good G for a given quantity $\bar{Q}_g$ is the sum of the prices from the demand curves of n individual consumers:

$$P_gM = \sum_{i=1}^{n} P_{gi}(\bar{Q}_g) \quad \text{over all } \bar{Q}_g \tag{6.27}$$

To repeat, the underlying logic of vertical summation is that good G is a public good, so that it is non-rival in consumption. That is, one person's consumption of a unit of good G stands in a non-rival relationship to another person's consumption of that same unit, so that each consumer does not need 'own' units of good G if they are to enjoy the consumption benefits. (Note: horizontal and vertical summation do not generate the same construction. It is not a case of being fussy over words.)

Generally, the *Benefit Principle of Taxation*, therefore indicates:
(a) the total optimal amount to produce is that amount where the vertical sum of the marginal benefits of individuals equals the marginal costs of production;
(b) each individual should be taxed according to the marginal benefit derived from the public good (there is no presumption whatsoever that they have equal marginal benefits).

The characteristic of non-rivalness in consumption plays an important part in altering the specification of the Pareto-optimal conditions (which are more formally derived later) when there are public goods. However, it is necessary to have knowledge of the marginal benefits individuals derive from a public good to determine Pareto-optimal provision. The second characteristic of a public good (non-excludability) throws doubt on the likelihood that it is possible to know anything reliable about the demand curves of the individuals. This characteristic suggests that, if anything, preferences for public goods are likely to be under-revealed.

(ii) *Non-excludability*

While non-rivalness in consumption is the first characteristic of a public good, the second characteristic is that consumers cannot be excluded from consumption benefits. While technically it might be possible to exclude (e.g. scrambling devices may be used to exclude those who do not pay for a television signal), a good is deemed non-excludable if the costs of making it excludable are prohibitive (if the costs cannot be justified).

In the case of private goods, there are property rights. Markets operate because consumption of a private good can be made contingent upon payment of a 'price' for it. An individual may be denied consumption of the good unless they are able to establish property rights to the good. However, with public goods, if the good has been provided by one individual, there is no sanction to prohibit or restrict consumption of the good to that individual.

The absence of excludability almost inevitably causes a problem when analysing preference revelation. If individuals anticipate they can consume a good without having to pay for it, the incentive appears to be to 'keep quiet' (let others bear the cost of provision). The incentive is to 'free-ride'. However, it is not a strategy that will succeed if each individual plays this same strategy. If everyone attempts to free-ride nothing will be provided and a free ride is impossible.

Buchanan (1968) illustrates the free rider problem. Assume an individual is one of a 'large' number. In microeconomics a member of a large number has no (or very little) influence on outcome (when markets are perfectly competitive there is a large number of producers – no one producer can influence price). Each individual in the group would benefit to the extent of £10 if a public good were provided. Each individual is asked to contribute only £5 to its provision.

- If the individual contributes (and others also contribute) the good is provided and the payoff matrix illustrated by Table 6.5 reports that the net return to contribution is £5.
- If others attempt to free-ride and hence do not contribute, the individual will have lost their £5 contribution.
- If the individual attempts to free-ride (refuses to contribute) and others cover the costs of provision, the individual cannot be excluded and secures a payoff of £10.
- If the individual does not contribute and others also free-ride, then the individual cannot lose anything.

Each individual faced with the decision to voluntarily contribute to a public good, therefore, chooses the best 'payoff' and attempts to free-ride even though all would gain if everyone contributed. (This same theory is applied in Chapter 15 when assessing the extent to which altruists are able to act collectively to provide assistance to a beneficiary group.)

The theory described here provides the basis of a rationale for government intervention. It is arguable that it is in everyone's interests if they are coerced to pay taxes to finance the production of the good, provided, of course, that taxes are determined

Table 6.5 Voluntary contribution v. free-riding

	OUTCOMES	
STRATEGIES	*others contribute (good provided)*	*others free-ride (good not provided)*
Individual contributes	(£10 – 5) = £5	–£5
Individual free-rides	£10	£0

appropriately (e.g. as illustrated in Figure 6.5(b)). The problem is that the information used in Figure 6.5(b), i.e. an individual's demand curve is not likely to be readily revealed.

The optimal provision of public goods was established in Figure 6.5 given that the demand curves of individuals could be determined. The problem of free-riding is that it calls in question the assumption that preferences for public goods are known. However, if this problem is resolved it is possible to consider a general equilibrium analysis of the 'optimum' provision of public goods.

6.3.2 Pareto-optimum provision of a public good: a general equilibrium approach

In Chapter 5 the 'top-level' condition for Pareto efficiency was determined. In Section 6.2.3 this top-level condition was amended to allow for the existence of externalities. How will the 'top-level' condition for efficiency be determined when one of the goods is a public good. In Chapter 5 it was emphasised that Pareto optimality required that $MRS_{YX} = MRT_{YX}$. How is this condition affected when one of the goods is a public good? The following analysis is based on the same Lagrangian mathematics. However, it is followed (later) by a diagrammatic analysis.

X_A and X_B represent the private levels of consumption of private good X by consumers A and B, R refers to the resources available for consumption, G refers to the output of the public good and $c(G)$ is the cost of the supply of the public good. A Pareto-efficient outcome is where consumer A is as well-off as possible, given B's level of utility subject to their total resource constraint. It follows that the objective is:

$$\text{Max } U^A(X_A, G) \tag{6.28}$$

with respect to X_A and G, subject to

$$U^B(X_B, G) = \bar{U}^* \text{ and } X_A + X_B + c(G) = R \tag{6.29}$$

Form the Lagrangian:

$$\mathcal{L} = U^A(X_A, G) + \lambda((\bar{U}^* - U^B(X_B, G)) + \mu(R - X_A - X_B - c(G)) \tag{6.30}$$

Maximise $\mathcal{L}$ with respect to X_A, X_B and G. The first-order conditions are:

$$\partial\mathcal{L}/\partial X_A = \partial U^A/\partial X_A - \mu = 0 \tag{6.31}$$

$$\partial\mathcal{L}/\partial X_B = -\lambda\partial U^B/\partial X_B - \mu = 0 \tag{6.32}$$

$$\partial\mathcal{L}/\partial G = \partial U^A/\partial G - \lambda\partial U^B/\partial G - \mu\partial c/\partial G = 0 \tag{6.33}$$

Solve (6.31) to find $\mu = \partial U^A/\partial X_A$. Solve (6.32) to find $(\mu/\lambda) = -\partial U^B/\partial X_B$. Divide (6.33) by μ and rearrange:

$$(1/\mu)\partial U^A/\partial G - (\lambda/\mu)\partial U^B/\partial G = \partial c/\partial G \tag{6.34}$$

Now substitute for μ and (μ/λ):

$$(\partial U^A/\partial G)\big/(\partial U^A/\partial X_A) + (\partial U^B/\partial G)\big/(\partial U^B/\partial X_B) = \partial c/\partial G = MRT_{GX} \tag{6.35}$$

Note that $(\partial U/\partial G)\big/(\partial U/\partial X) = MRS_{GX}$; therefore the Pareto-efficient outcome is where

$$MRS_{GX}^A + MRS_{GX}^B = MRT_{GX} \tag{6.36}$$

That is,

$$\Sigma MRS_{GX} = MRT_{GX} \tag{6.37}$$

The 'top-level' optimum condition for the Pareto-efficient provision of private goods is no longer appropriate for provision of public goods. It is now the case that the *sum* of

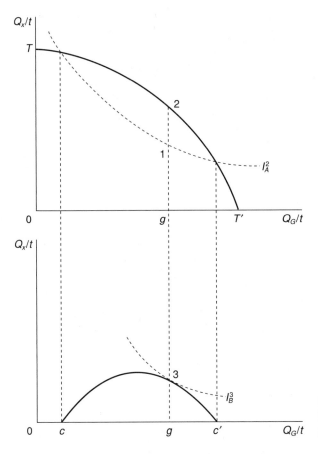

Figure 6.8
Pareto-optimal provision of public goods

marginal rates of substitutions must equal the marginal rate of transformation. This solution is illustrated in Figure 6.8.

In Figure 6.8(a) the transformation curve (T-T') indicates the production possibilities of the economy. Efficiency is achieved when the economy operates on this boundary. The boundary shows the combinations of the two goods (X, a private good, and G, a public good) which can be produced. The question is: 'what combination of private and public goods is Pareto optimal?'

Samuelson (1955) demonstrates the conditions required for Pareto optimality. In Figure 6.8(a) the production possibilities for an economy are shown as T-T'. Capital and labour are used to produce a private good X and a public good G. If there are two individuals A and B the decision is made to determine the income of individual A. Individual A is to be kept on indifference curve I_A^2 as shown for individual A. This indifference curve reveals alternative combinations of good X and good G that keep A at a constant level of welfare.

The locus of points shown by indifference curve I_A^2 stipulates the combination of goods X and G that must be consumed by A if A is to achieve this real income. If A consumes 0-g of the public good, individual B must similarly consume 0-g of the public good. The amount of the private good available to B is equal to distance g-2 minus distance g-1, which is equal to g-3. In part (b) of Figure 6.6 this distance g-3 is recorded as one point on a set of consumption possibilities that are available to B when A's welfare is maintained as I_A^2.

The same process is repeated at every possible output of the public good to produce the curve c-c', and this curve is the set of consumption possibilities that are available to individual B assuming that A is kept on I_A^2. It is derived by deducting I_A^2 from T-T', (bearing in mind that, when units of the public good are provided for one individual, they are also provided for the other).

The optimal provision of a public good is now the output of private and public goods that maximises the welfare of individual B (given that A's welfare is held constant on I_A^2). This is shown by the tangency between I_B^3 and the curve c-c'. It follows that the Pareto-efficient allocation of resources for the economy would be that 0-g public goods were provided and g-2 private goods.

The tangency, point 3, has been found by deducting (at quantity g) MRS_{GX}^A from MRT_{GX} (shown in (a)) and by then equating MRS_{gx}^B to the slope of c-c' (in part (b)) – which, by definition, is $[MRT_{GX} - MRS_{GX}^A]$.

Instead of stating the condition as

$$MRS_{GX}^B = [MRT_{GX} - MRS_{GX}^A] \tag{6.38}$$

This can be written as:

$$\Sigma MRS_{GX} = MRT_{GX} \tag{6.39}$$

which is the equation reported as (6.37). This condition is the 'top-level' condition for Pareto optimality in an economy that produces public and private goods.

Of course, in all of this, the 'free-rider' problem remains. How would preferences of individuals be revealed? Also, the efficiency conditions involve different MRS_{GX}s (or MBs) for individuals, suggesting no single common price or tax–price ratio is appropriate for all. This increases the problem of preference revelation for it suggests discriminatory pricing is appropriate for public goods.

6.3.3 Provision of pure public goods: can the free-rider problem be resolved?

It is clear that while *theoretically* it is possible to determine the Pareto-optimum conditions required for the provision of public goods, it is not possible to implement them if individuals refuse to reveal the marginal benefit that they receive from the provision of a public good. Recent decades have seen much work on so-called 'truth-telling mechanisms' and one of the early examples was designed for public goods problems. The objective in this section is to show that while *homo economicus* will not reveal preferences in large groups, a tax mechanism can be constructed which will induce them to reveal preferences honestly. This tax is known as the *Clarke tax*. Clarke (1971) explains the operation of the tax, while Groves and Ledyard (1977) provide a rigorous analysis of such an incentive mechanism. The intention here is to explain the procedure of the Clarke tax and, with reference to *homo economicus*, show how incentives lead to an honest revelation of preference for a public good.

To begin an analysis of the Clarke tax, assume that there are three individuals (X, Y and Z) who must decide between two options A and B (each option might relate to a different quantity of a public good). The recommended procedure is:

(i)   to ask voters to report the amount they would be prepared to offer for each alternative (A and B);
(ii) to sum the total values recorded for each option (T_a and T_b respectively) and choose to adopt the option which records the highest value;
(iii) to levy a Clarke tax on each voter according to the rule that each voter must pay the absolute difference ($T_a - T_b$) between the sums (calculated without their vote) for the two options.

As an example consider the case in Table 6.6. It is clear that option A would be chosen (as $T_a > T_b$).

Table 6.6 **The Clarke tax**

Voter	Option A	Option B	Clarke tax
X	40	0	30
Y	0	50	0
Z	20	0	10
TOTAL	$T_a = 60$	$T_b = 50$	

Individual X would pay a Clarke tax of 30 (i.e. X reduces net welfare of the 'others' by 30 to the extent that if X did not vote individual Y would be better off by 50 and individual Z would be worse off by 20).

Voter Y pays no tax, as the vote declared did not change the outcome.

Voter Z pays a tax of 10 as Z's vote alters the outcome and the difference between the two sums involved without Z's vote is (50-40).

If individual X had over-estimated preference in order to secure the selection of A, X would either have no effect on the final outcome or else X would run the risk of paying more than the true value of A. For example, suppose that individual X had claimed (falsely) that Option A was worth 80 in order to make sure that Option A succeeded. In the event that Option A wins it does not affect their Clarke tax, as the tax is based on the way in which X's vote changes net welfare (and in this case it is still 50-20).

Suppose exaggeration does alter the outcome. Suppose that individual Y had said that Option B was worth 70 and, in this way, ensured that Option B exceeds Option A, and wins. Now the Clarke tax for individual Y would be based on the change in welfare estimated as a result of a vote and it would now be equal to 60. Remember, the difference is estimated in the absence of the individual's vote. If individual Y had not voted X and Z would have gained 60 from the Option A and there would be no welfare loss (in the absence of Y) from not having Option Y. Therefore, the tax for individual Y would be 60 and this is greater than the 'true' value of having Option B rather than Option A. Clearly, there is no percentage in over-estimating preferences – either it makes no difference or it results in losses.

Suppose, instead, we look at the potential outcome from under-revealing preferences. Suppose that individual X decided to under-reveal preference and claim a benefit of 20 from Option A. In this case, while X would pay no Clarke tax (because their vote does not change the outcome), the individual would also not receive the benefit of the option that is worth most to the individual. Alternatively, if X claimed to offer 35 then the option A would be accepted but under-revealing of preferences would not mean that any different Clarke tax would be due. The Clarke tax is based on the difference in the sums without X's vote and this remains $50 - 20 = 30$. In this way the individual either gains nothing by under-revealing or else stands to lose the option that offers them the most benefit.

(a) *The incentive structure within the Clarke tax*

The essence of this mechanism is to convert the 'large'-number situation into a 'small'-number one. The mechanism is to employ the Clarke tax to induce honesty (Clarke 1971). Here we follow an exposition of this mechanism outlined by Tideman and Tullock (1976). (Further discussion is provided by Groves and Ledyard 1977.)

By converting a 'large'-number situation into a 'small'-number situation, the individual is made to feel that there is some significance associated with *her* action. For this to occur, the individual must be liable directly for the consequences of her revealing (or not revealing) her preference. Assume that a large group of individuals

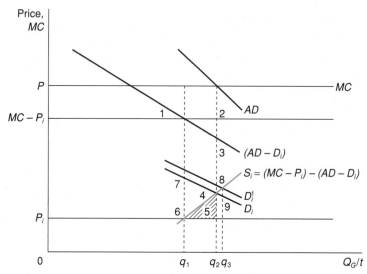

Figure 6.9 The Clarke tax

is considering the collective provision of a pure public good. The marginal costs of providing the good are constant and are shown as MC in Figure 6.9. The aggregate demand function (added vertically) is AD. The problem is to produce an incentive mechanism that will reveal this information. For any representative individual i, we proceed by apportioning the share of MC to be paid by individual i (this is P_i); the remainder of the share $(MC - P_i)$ is paid by the rest of the group. In order to make i reveal her true preference, she must be made conscious of the effect of her vote on the remainder of the group.

The Clarke tax operates in this way. In Figure 6.9 the group would produce $0\text{-}q^1$ of the public good if i paid her share (P_i), but individual i played no role in the decision-making; i.e. $(AD - D_i)$ is equated with $(MC - P_i)$ at output $0\text{-}q^1$. If i votes to increase output of the good beyond this, then her preferences are playing a role. Clearly, output will increase from $0\text{-}q^1$ to $0\text{-}q^2$ if her demand is added to the rest of the community demand. If this happens then individual i imposes costs on the rest of the community equal to triangle 1-2-3. This is the excess burden the rest of the community carries as a consequence of increasing output from $0\text{-}q^1$ to $0\text{-}q^2$. The additional cost to the other individuals is area $1\text{-}2\text{-}q^2\text{-}q^1$ but the additional benefits are $1\text{-}3\text{-}q^2\text{-}q^1$.

The Clarke tax that is applied is an estimate of these costs. Individual i is charged according to the additional costs she imposes on the rest of the community. The line $MC - P_i$ is the marginal costs she imposes on others as she influences output. The line S_i, however, reflects the net marginal costs i imposed on others being constructed as $(MC - P_i) - (AD - D_i)$. It is, in effect, the supply curve of the public good to i.

In the diagram, and in the context of this example, the Clarke tax is triangle 4-5-6. (It is the mirror image of triangle 1-2-3.) It is clearly worthwhile for individual i to record her preference. The additional benefit to her (net of her share of costs of production) for $0\text{-}q^1 - 0\text{-}q^2$ units of the public good is 6-7-4-5, whereas the Clarke tax is only triangle 4-5-6. However, if she dishonestly overestimates her demand as D_i^1 then, on the additional units $q_2\text{-}q_3$, she pays more in tax than the additional net benefits she actually receives, the net loss being triangle 4-8-9. It is, therefore, wise to neither underestimate nor overestimate her preference, but rather to reveal her true preference.

(b) *Problems using the Clarke tax*

While applied microeconomic theory confirms that the Clarke tax has the potential to resolve the free-rider problem, there are obvious problems that question its practical application. It is unlikely that, in practice, a Clarke tax will be viable because:

(i) It is not possible to return tax revenue to voters. If the money were returned it is likely that this would change individuals' demand. This would simply negate the exercise. While the cost involved is disconcerting it has been argued that the tax revenue diminishes as the number of voters increases (see Tideman and Tullock 1976).

(ii) The Clarke tax will not work if individuals are organised to vote in a coalition (for an example of how coalition voting will lead to inefficiency even in the presence of a Clarke tax, see Cullis and Jones 2009).

(iii) A problem arises if the Clarke tax bankrupts the individual concerned. It is not obvious how preferences of voters should be considered if individuals cannot subsequently pay the Clarke tax.

(iv) The Clarke tax will only succeed if individuals participate in the process. But where is the incentive to vote? The whole mechanism may run foul of what has been referred to as 'rational apathy'. (This is discussed in greater detail in Chapter 14.) If the individual is one of many voters, the individual feels that there is little consequence associated with an individual vote (in terms of changing an electoral outcome). There is no incentive to incur costs participating in the vote (see Downs 1957, for a discussion of this argument).

If economic theory offers an incentive structure to induce honesty, there remains a question mark over its viability. The possibility that individuals will free-ride remains a problem. But how 'real' is this prediction that individuals will free-ride?

6.4 Natural monopoly

One reason why the market will not satisfy all the conditions for Pareto optimality is that there are decreasing costs of production. The problem of decreasing costs of production can be seen with reference to Figure 6.10, where long-run average cost is declining and long-run marginal cost is everywhere below average cost well past the point where market demand becomes sated. An industry is a 'natural monopoly' if the production of a particular good, or service, by a single firm minimises costs. If there are decreasing average costs society can benefit from least-cost production if there is a single producer. However, the problem is that society might suffer from monopoly pricing if there is a single producer. With decreasing costs a single firm will eventually win the entire market by expanding output and lowering its costs. Having won the market, it could then set the monopoly price.

In Chapter 5 it was argued that marginal-cost pricing is required for the achievement of a Pareto optimum when there is perfect competition and no other sources of market failure. However, as can be seen with reference to Figure 6.8, marginal cost pricing would lead a firm with decreasing production costs (a reflection of increasing returns to scale) to losses. That is, when demand D is equated with long-run marginal cost ($LRMC$) at point 2, a competitive 'market price' of $0\text{-}P_c$ is set when average cost at the chosen output $0\text{-}q_3$ is distance $q_3\text{-}1$ compared to price distance $q_3\text{-}2$ generating a loss per unit sold of $1\text{-}2 = AC(q_3)\text{-}P_c$. In short, if the firm were to price at marginal cost, the result would be that average cost would exceed average revenue and the firm be out of business in the long run.

What happens if nothing is done? As noted above, exits would take place until a single producer is left with monopoly power. The incentive now will be to profit-maximise,

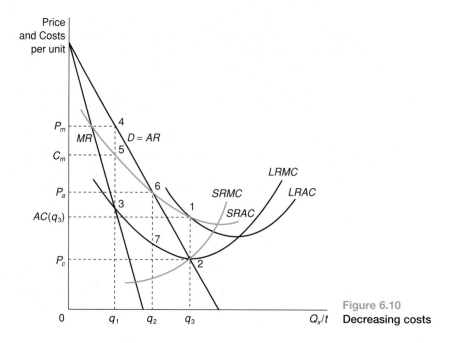

Figure 6.10
Decreasing costs

choosing in the long run output 0-q_1 associated with $MR = LRMC$ at point 3. Monopoly price would be 0-P_m (= q_1-4) and monopoly average cost per unit 0-C_m (= q_1-5). Monopoly profit would be rectangle C_m-P_m-4-5 and output would be inefficiently low, at 0-q_1, compared to 0-q_3. While there is always the option to do nothing if the problem of decreasing costs does not involve high costs, there are policy options open for consideration. Following Viscusi *et al.* (1992), consider:

i) *Subsidy.* A 'natural monopoly' that prices at marginal cost at point 2 (note the firm must operate with the plant characterised by short-run average and marginal costs – *SRAC* and *SRMC*) would make the loss 1-2 per unit as above, with the total loss being P_c-$AC(q_3)$-1-2 in Figure 6.10.[4] One solution would be for the government to offer a subsidy to the firm. The problem is that such a subsidy would require financing and if a tax were used this may create distortions elsewhere. For reasons explained in Chapter 13, a lump sum tax would be preferred to avoid distortions elsewhere in the economy. However, such taxes are difficult to levy in practice. Moreover, even if it were possible to levy a lump sum tax there are other potential problems associated with a subsidy. First, a subsidy would only be justified if total benefit from provision of the good exceeded total costs (in Figure 6.8 total benefit can be estimated by reference to the integral under the demand curve and total cost by reference to the integral under the marginal cost curve). Second, the availability of a subsidy may weaken incentives to keep costs at a minimum. Management may prefer to believe that losses will be subsidised. Third, there are equity considerations. Why should the consumers of this particular product be subsidised by a tax on other individuals in the community?

---

4. Because marginal-cost pricing appears to conform with efficiency, publicly owned industries are sometimes exhorted to price (as far as possible) at marginal cost (e.g. guidelines set for UK nationalised industries in the 1970s). They are then criticised if they should make losses. However, it is clear from Figure 6.8 that, when average cost is falling, losses are predictable if price is set at marginal cost.

ii) *Average cost pricing.* An alternative solution would be to set the price at average cost to avoid a loss. In Figure 6.8 this would mean a price of P_a associated with point 6 and an output of $0\text{-}q_2$. However, the cost of this would be that, with a departure from marginal cost pricing, there would be welfare loss measured as area 6-7-2 as output would still be inefficiently low at $0\text{-}q_2$ compared to $0\text{-}q_3$.

iii) *Two-part tariffs.* A two-part tariff (discussed in Chapter 2) is a solution which consists of a fixed amount or fee (regardless of consumption) and a price per unit. If the loss that would arise from a policy of marginal cost pricing is L (i.e. $P_m\text{-}AC(q_3)$-1-2 in Figure 6.10), a fixed fee could be set to raise revenue to finance L. One option (perhaps the most straightforward) would be to set the fee equal to L/n (where n is number of consumers). However, consumers' demand may very well vary. The result may be that some consumers would no longer benefit sufficiently to continue consuming the good (this would arise if L/n exceeded the consumer surplus that is available when price equals marginal cost). If some consumers are excluded there are efficiency losses (as these consumers would have been willing to pay marginal cost). To avoid excluding consumers it may be appropriate to charge different fixed fees to different consumers. An 'optimal' two-part tariff accounts for two potential sources of welfare loss – if price equalled marginal cost there would be a deficit but if price exceeds marginal cost there are welfare losses when some are excluded.

iv) *Ramsey pricing.* One option may exist if the firm produces more than one product. Ramsey (1927) suggested prices that would ensure that total revenues equal total cost constraint but, at the same time, minimise deadweight welfare losses. It is possible to show that deadweight loss may be minimised when sufficient revenue is raised. Ramsey optimal pricing and the so-called inverse elasticity rule developed from his work on public finance (as discussed in Chapter 13). He suggested the optimal tax was one that minimises the welfare cost of meeting the public-sector revenue requirement.

The following example is based on Viscusi *et al.* (1992). The natural monopoly produces two goods X and Y. Total cost of production is

$$TC = 18 + 2X + 2Y \tag{6.53}$$

The quantities demanded of the two goods depends on prices P_X and P_Y:

$$X = 10 - P_X \tag{6.54}$$

$$Y = 12 - 2P_Y \tag{6.55}$$

It is important to emphasise that the demand for good X is independent of the price of good Y (and vice versa).

The demand function for good X and for good Y is shown in Figure 6.9(a) and marginal cost is assumed constant at £2 per unit in each case. If the marginal costs of X and Y are each £2 (and marginal cost is constant) then it is not possible to cover the fixed cost of £18. However, if price is raised from £2 to £3.63 for both products then while demand falls (for Y from 8 to 4.76, and for X from 8 to 6.36), sufficient revenue can be generated to cover total cost. There is a surplus equal to the shaded area from the sale of Y (i.e. £7.76 = 4.76 × £1.63) and a surplus equal to the shaded plus dashed rectangle from sale of product X (i.e. equal to £10.36 = 6.36 × £1.63). The rectangles (together) cover the £18 fixed cost. However, the deadweight loss triangle for product Y is triangle 1-2-3 and for product X triangle 5-4-3 (whose areas are £2.64 and £1.33 respectively, in total £3.97).

The question that Ramsey asked was whether an alternative pricing would generate the £18 at a lower deadweight welfare cost. The answer is to use a rule that raises prices in inverse proportion to price elasticities (for further insight into the derivation of this rule see Chapter 13).

Ramsey argued that for each (independent[5]) good the following relationship must apply.

$$\frac{P_i - MC_i}{P_i} = \frac{\alpha}{e_i} \tag{6.56}$$

Or equivalently

$$\alpha = \frac{P_i - MC_i}{P_i} e_i \tag{6.57}$$

where

P_i = price of good i;
MC_i = marginal cost of i;
e_i = elasticity of demand of good i;
α = a constant sometimes called the 'Ramsey number'.

To illustrate the effect of this rule consider Figure 6.11(b). The firm now charges £4 for good X and £3 for good Y. The increase in the price of the good X is now twice as great as the increase in the price of good Y. If price elasticities at output 8 are considered it is clear that the price elasticity of X is half that of Y.

One easy way to check this is to apply the formula for price elasticity of demand. If output is q units and the intercept with the x-axis is q_i units then the ratio of distance q-q_i to distance 0-q is price elasticity of demand. In Figure 6.11(b) is (–)0.5 (i.e. = 4/8) for good Y and (–)0.25 (i.e. = 2/8) for good X. As Y has price elasticity greater than X the price mark-up is lower for Y. The same net revenue (£18 = £12 = (6 × £2) from good X plus £6 = (6 × £1) from good Y) is achieved, but deadweight loss is now lower. It is triangle 1-2-3 for good X (area = £2) and triangle 1-4-3 for good Y (area = £1). The total net revenue is covered (= £18) but the total deadweight loss is only £3 (as compared with £3.97 in the previous case).

A Ramsey pricing rule requires an equal proportionate decrease in output for the two goods. That is, $\Delta X/X = \Delta Y/Y$. In Figure 6.9 both outputs are cut by (8 – 6)/8 (i.e. by 25%). A Ramsey rule requires the output of all goods to be reduced by the same proportion, until total revenue just equals total cost.

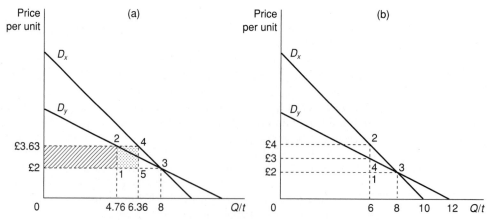

Figure 6.11 Ramsey pricing

5. The formula is more complicated if cross-price elasticities of demand are not zero, i.e. when goods X and Y are complements or substitutes.

(v) *Franchise bidding*. One option that has been considered is that of franchise bidding. Firms bid to supply the market as a natural monopoly. They are awarded the position if they can supply the market at the lowest price (even if this is above marginal cost).

Again, there are a number of possible solutions to a market failure and again a *prima facie* case for government intervention. The market fails and regulation may be required.

6.5 Challenge: Are there really public goods?

A number of concepts have been introduced in this chapter. However, there are challenges that can be made. To illustrate, this section reflects on arguments made about public goods. While analysis has been presented to describe the Pareto-optimal provision of public goods and to deal with the free-rider problem of public goods, just how pervasive are public goods?

One criticism of the concept of public goods is that such goods do not really exist (Margolis 1955). Where is it possible to perceive goods that perfectly satisfy the non-rivalness definition of Samuelson (1954)? Consider the provision of law and order (or medical care). The use by individual A of the law courts (or hospitals) reduces the available consumption by individual B (if they must now wait). Even the classic example, defence, can be called in question (Sandler 1977). If armies are employed in the north, surely this will detract from protection for communities in the south?

A second (and related) criticism of the concept of public goods is that any classification of goods is sensitive to existing technology and legislation (e.g. Peston 1972). Closer inspection of examples quoted by Samuelson (1954) revealed that there were more ways of dealing with non-exclusion than might be imagined. Consider the case of lighthouses (Samuelson 1954). Lighthouses were traditionally provided in the private sector in the UK (Coase 1974; Peacock 1979). With changes in technology exclusion becomes possible. Consider television signals. Television signals can now be scrambled so that access is made excludable. Some goods are assigned property rights; others are made freely available via the legislature (Malkin and Wildavsky 1991). In this way the determination of goods (as public goods or private goods) might also depend on constitutional and political considerations.

So, how important are these challenges? Begin with the criticism that there are no public goods in the 'real world'. Samuelson's (1969) response to this challenge was to emphasise that between *pure* public goods and *pure* private goods there exist *impure* public goods that are more readily observable than either pure public or pure private goods. So how can this spectrum be analysed? Taxonomies have been established with reference to characteristics that describe consumption and characteristics that describe production:

(a) *Excludability and non-rivalness in consumption*
    One approach focuses on characteristics of consumption, i.e. on non-rivalness in consumption and non-excludability (Head 1962; Peston 1972). In Table 6.7, four categories of goods are identified.

Table 6.7 **Characteristics of private and public goods**

	Excludable	Non-excludable
Rival	A	B
Non-Rival	C	D

Goods in category D are non-rival in consumption and non-excludable: they are pure public goods. Those in category A are rival in consumption and excludable: they are pure private goods. Goods that fall in category B are rival but non-excludable. Common resources may prove an example. Consider the case of bees from the hives of different beekeepers that collect the nectar from a nearby orchard of apples (Meade 1952). The blossom is rival: nectar collected for one hive is unavailable to another. Even so, it may be inconceivable to try to deny any particular honey bee access; i.e. the situation is non-excludable. By contrast, goods in category C are non-rival in consumption but excludable. A tollbooth may exclude traffic from roads unless payment is made, yet if the road is not congested one car may utilise it with no loss of benefit even though other cars are also consuming the road service. Similarly, admission to a theatre (circus, swimming pool) has the potential of exclusion, but (below capacity limits) each individual admitted may consume services without subtracting from the benefit of others (and may add benefit if a good-sized audience is required to make an event 'work'). Here the market could be applied, but the existence of at least limited non-rivalness indicates that exclusion would cause inefficiency. (One person could be made better off by the consumption of the good without fully denying consumption to another.)

b) *Consumption sharing*

It is possible to refine this distinction by focusing on the degree to which goods are non-rival in consumption. This can be assessed in terms of consumption sharing possibilities (Buchanan 1968). In Figure 6.12 (drawn on the assumption of a given population and given property rights) a relationship is depicted between the degree of indivisibility and the number of people P consuming the good. At one extreme are purely private goods (category 1), which are fully divisible between single persons (or single households); at the other extreme are goods that remain fully indivisible over large groups, in the sense that each member of the group may consume the same good. An example offered is mosquito-spraying; the benefits from this service are probably indivisible between individuals in one specific suburb. In essence, the key is the extent to which sharing is possible. Category (2) may refer to fire extinguishers that are shared (indivisible) between a small number of neighbours. Category (4) could represent swimming pools, which are uncongested when used by small numbers. By contrast, item (3) may refer to services such as inoculation against disease, which when experienced by any individual provides an additional degree of protection for everyone else with whom that person comes into contact. Of course, item (5) is a pure public good, an example of which is national defence expenditure that deters aggression.

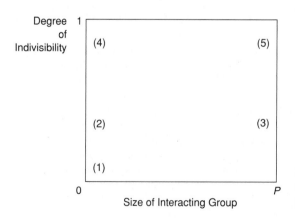

Figure 6.12
Consumption sharing
Source: Buchanan (1968).

It may be argued that goods such as (1) 'should' be left to market provision. Goods in category (2) may be left to voluntary arrangements between the individual members of small groups concerned. Category (4) arguably contains goods that are provided by clubs. 'Clubs' are arrangements in the private sector by which goods that are, to a degree, non-rival in consumption are voluntarily provided. Typically, the good is excludable (i.e. there is a membership fee) but it is by no means private (i.e. below capacity limits consumption is non-rival). Buchanan (1965) developed a theory of clubs and established the conditions for optimum output and membership. Clubs are consumption-sharing arrangements providing goods from which consumption can be excluded but for which consumption by one member may be non-rival with consumption by another member (below capacity limits).

c) *Different aggregation technologies*
    Public goods can also be classified with reference to technology in production, i.e. with reference to aggregation technology (Hirshleifer 1983; Cornes and Sandler 1996). For example:

(i) **Summation technology**. Each unit contributed to a public good adds identically and additively to the overall level available to all. Sandler (2003) cites the example of a public bad. With the accumulation of greenhouse gases, if 200 nations each emit 1000 metric tons of greenhouse gases into the atmosphere, 200,000 metric tons heating the atmosphere result. Each unit contributed has the same effect on the total. Each unit is a perfect substitute for each other.

(ii) **Weighted-sum technology**. In this technology weights are no longer always equal to one. Sandler (2003) notes that with efforts to reduce sulphur deposits falling on a country, the influence of cutbacks abroad depends on wind patterns, the sites of emission sources, and the pollution's airborne time. With weighted-sum technology, provision efforts are no longer perfect substitutes. If some receive a disproportionate share of the benefits then they have stronger incentives to supply the good (for acid rain, geographically larger countries experience a greater portion of the reduction that results from curtailing their emissions and are more motivated to act).

(iii) **Weakest-link and weaker-link technologies**. The smallest contribution determines the quantity of a public good for a group. If a disease is to be contained the weakest-link technology is in that country exercising the fewest precautions. A network is only as strong as its weakest link.

(iv) **Weaker-link technology**. In this case the smallest contribution has the greatest impact on overall provision, followed by the second smallest contribution, and so on. Sandler (2003) points to stability of financial markets: the most unstable market has the most destabilising effect, followed by the second most unstable market, and so on.

(v) **Best-shot technology**. Total quantity of a public good is determined solely by the largest contribution from different possible participants. Contributions below that level add nothing. For example, each country in a group might spend resources researching for a cure for a disease but only one (with sufficient resources and skills) has a chance of discovering a cure.

(vi) **Better-shot technology**. The largest contribution has the greatest impact on overall supply, followed by the second-largest contribution, and so on. Better-shot public goods are likely to have multiple suppliers; even a second-best effort may add to the overall quantity. The treatment regime for a disease may be 'better-shot' technology if a less desirable regime also benefits patients who cannot tolerate the preferred regime.

d) *'Mixed' or joint-supply goods*

Another approach to the question of the mix of privateness and publicness in goods in the 'real world' is to see goods and services as blends of private and public goods. Suppose for instance that *A* derives benefits from being inoculated against polio; they create not only a private benefit but also an external effect in so far as they reduce the chance of infection for all other individuals with whom they come into contact. Recognition of the private–public mix means that goods can be viewed as having private benefits as well as external effects with the characteristic of a public good. This is explored with respect to education in Chapter 10.

This approach to dealing with the blend of privateness and publicness in goods is illustrated in Musgrave (1969). Sandler (1977) extends the concept of joint supply. He considers the example of provision of national defence by a country in a defence alliance. In the first instance, expenditure can be considered a private good (for the country) because resources can be deployed internally (to maintain law and order). However, at the same time there is provision of a good that is not perfectly rival but also not perfectly non-rival. The country's defence expenditure yields a spillover to other countries if there is an alliance. Suppose that there are conventional forces in country *A*, to the north of allies *B* and *C*. These forces in *A* also protect the northern borders for countries *B* and *C*. Of course, the extent of protection (the degree of non-rivalness) is not the same for all three (*A*, *B* and *C*). Finally, if country *A*'s defence expenditure also includes expenditure on nuclear weapons and if the alliance strategy is to deter by threat of a nuclear response to any attack on an ally, there is also provision of a pure public good (i.e. deterrence).

The extent to which optimal resource allocation of joint products is likely depends on the ratio of excludable benefits to total benefits from the public activity. As this ratio approaches one the share of excludable benefits increases, enabling markets and clubs to optimally allocate resources to the good's provision. As the ratio approaches zero, the share of purely public benefits increases, making it likely that the activity will be undersupplied (or oversupplied if public spillovers are negative).

Returning to the challenge that there are no public goods, it is evident that there is a taxonomy of goods and publicness is relevant when considering many goods and services. Moreover, there is continued response to the challenge; new perspectives on the spectrum between private and public goods continue to be developed.

But what of the challenge that concepts are unhelpful because changes in technology and changes in legislation mean that the same good or service might be assigned to one classification in a taxonomy or to another. Classification might well switch at different moments of time and in different societies (Malkin and Wildavsky 1991). Cornes and Sandler (1994) accept that changes in definition are possible. However, they insist that the concept of public goods (and the spectrum of private and public goods) remains important. For, in any society, at any moment, decisions will be made with respect to resource allocation and decisions can be informed by the characteristics that define the goods and services in question.

6.7 Summary

In this chapter the objective was to consider the way in which market processes may fail to serve *homo economicus* in an efficient way. This chapter gave meaning to the conditions required to secure the First and Second Fundamental Theorems of Welfare Economics. As such, they are viewed as technical forms or sources of market failure. The existence of externalities alters the Pareto-optimal conditions and markets (even perfectly competitive markets) fail to achieve an optimum. Similarly, for the case when there are public goods. 'Second-best' responses to situations in which not all the Paretian equivalences can be met were outlined and the complexities of such responses indicated. The existence of decreasing costs – the partial equilibrium equivalent of the increasing returns to scale problem part of the Second Fundamental Theorem (discussed in Chapter 5) – caused market failure because the Pareto-optimal conditions would mean that firms would make losses.

In all these cases there is market failure and the possibility that government intervention might be required. It should be emphasised that this is only a possibility. The existence of market failure indicates that (in Paretian terms) there is likely to be a welfare loss. However, government intervention is by no means costless as Chapter 14 will emphasise. There is no reason, *a priori*, to believe that the costs of each case of market failure will exceed the costs that arise when government directly intervenes.

Observant readers will recall that the First and Second Fundamental Theorems of Welfare Economics also required no market failures connected with uncertainty. It is uncertainty and information issues (partly raised in connection with merit wants in Chapter 5) that are the focus of Chapter 7.

References

Arrow, K.J. (1971) The organization of economic activity: issues pertinent to the choice of market versus non-market allocation, pp. 59–73 in R.H. Haveman and J. Margolis (eds) *Public Expenditure and Policy Analysis*, Chicago: Markham.

Baumol, W.J. and Oates, W.E. (1988) *The Theory of Environmental Policy*, Cambridge: Cambridge University Press.

Buchanan, J. (1965) An economic theory of clubs, *Economica*, 32 (125): 1–14.

Buchanan, J.M. (1968) *The Demand and Supply of Public Goods*, Chicago: Rand McNally.

Buchanan, J.M. (1969) External diseconomies, corrective taxes and market structure, *American Economic Review*, 59 (1): 174–7.

Cheung, S.N.S. (1973) The fable of the bees: an economic investigation, *Journal of Law and Economics*, 16 April: 11–34.

Cheung, S.N.S. (1978) *The Myth of Social Cost*, Hobart Paper 82, London: Institute of Economic Affairs.

Clarke, E.H. (1971) Multi-part pricing of public goods, *Public Choice*, 11 Fall: 17–33.

Coase, R.H. (1960) The problem of social cost, *Journal of Law and Economics*, 3 October: 1–44.

Coase, R. (1974) The lighthouse in economics, *Journal of Law and Economics*, 17: 357–76.

Conybeare, J.A.C. (1980) International organization and the theory of property rights, *International Organization*, 34 (3): 307–34.

Cooter, R. and Ulen, T. (1997) *Law and Economics*, 2nd edn, Reading, Mass.: Addison Wesley.

Cornes, R. and Sandler, T. (1994) Are public goods myths? *Journal of Theoretical Politics*, 6 (3): 369–85.

Cornes, R.C. and Sandler, T. (1996) *The Theory of Externalities, Public Goods and Club Goods*, Cambridge: Cambridge University Press.

Cullis, J.G. and Jones, P.R. (2009) *Public Finance and Public Choice – Analytical Perspectives*, 3rd edn, Oxford: Oxford University Press.

Davis, O.A. and Kamien, M.I. (1971) Externalities, information and alternative collective action, pp. 74–95 in R.H. Haveman and J. Margolis (eds) *Public Expenditure and Policy Analysis*, Chicago: Markham.

Downs, A. (1957) *An Economic Theory of Democracy*, New York: Harper Row.

Galanter, M. (1983) Reading the landscape of disputes: what we know and don't know (and think we know) about our allegedly contentious and litigious society, *UCLA Law Review*, 40: 44–104.

Groves, T. and Ledyard, J. (1977) Optimal allocation of public goods: a solution to the 'free rider' problem, *Econometrica*, 45 May: 783–809.

Head, J.G. (1962) Public goods and public policy, *Public Finance/Finances Publiques*, 17 (3): 197–219.

Henderson, J.M. and Quandt, R.E. (1971) *Microeconomics*, New York, McGraw-Hill.

Hirshleifer, J. (1983) From weakest-link to best-shot: the voluntary provision of public goods, *Public Choice*, 41 (3): 371–86.

Hoffman, E. and Spitzer, M. (1982) The Coase theorem: some experimental tests, *Journal of Law and Economics*, 25: 93–8.

Jones, P.R. and Cullis, J.G. (2000) 'Individual failure' and the analytics of social policy, *Journal of Social Policy*, 29 (1): 73–93.

Leibenstein, H. (1950) Bandwagon, snob and Veblen effects, *Quarterly Journal of Economics*, 64 May: 183–207.

Malkin, J. and Wildavsky, A. (1991) Why the traditional distinction between public and private goods should be abandoned, *Journal of Theoretical Politics*, 3: 355–78.

Margolis, J.A. (1955) Comment on the pure theory of public expenditure, *Review of Economics and Statistics*, 37 (4): 347–9.

Meade, J.E. (1952) External economies and diseconomies in a competitive situation, *Economic Journal*, 62 (245): 54–76.

Mishan, E.J. (1988) *Cost Benefit Analysis*, 4th edn, London: George Allen and Unwin.

Musgrave, R.A. (1969) Provision of social goods, in J. Margolis and M. Guitton (eds) *Public Economics*, New York: St. Martin's Press.

Peacock, A. (1979) *The Economic Analysis of Government and Related Themes*, Oxford: Martin Roberston.

Peston, M. (1972) *Public Goods and the Public Sector*, London: Macmillan.

Pigou, A.C. (1932) *The Economics of Welfare*, 4th edn, London: Macmillan.

Ramsey, F.P. (1927) A contribution to the theory of taxation, *Economic Journal*, 37 (145): 47–61.

Samuelson, P. (1954) The pure theory of public expenditure, *Review of Economics and Statistics*, 36 (4) Nov: 387–9.

Samuelson, P. (1955) Diagrammatic exposition of a theory of public expenditures, *Review of Economics and Statistics*, 37 (4) Nov: 350–6.

Samuelson, P.A. (1969) Pure theory of public expenditure and taxation, pp. 98–123 in J. Margolis and H. Guitton (eds) *Public Economics*, New York: St Martin's Press.

Sandler, T. (1977) Impurity of defense: an application to the economics of alliances, *Kyklos*, 30: 443–60.

Sandler, T. (2003) Assessing the optimal provision of public goods, pp. 131–51 in I. Kaul, P. Coneicao, K. Le Goulven and R. Mendoza, *Providing Global Public Goods*, Oxford, Oxford University Press.

Schotter, A. (1990) *Free Market Economics*, 2nd edn, Oxford: Basil Blackwell.

Tideman, T.N. and Tullock, G. (1976) A new and superior process for making social choices, *Journal of Political Economy*, 84 (6) December: 1145–59.

Veblen, T. (1934) *Theory of the Leisure Class*, New York: Modern Library.

Viscusi, W.K., Vernon, J.M. and Harrington, J.E. (1992) *Economics of Regulation and Antitrust*, Lexington, Mass.: D. C. Heath and Company.

CHAPTER 7

Risk, information, insurance and uncertainty

7.1 Introduction

'Knowledge is of two kinds. We know a subject ourselves, or we know we can find information upon it.' (James Boswell quoted in Hemenway 1988)

'The future is incalculably uncertain.' (John Maynard Keynes)

These two quotations serve to introduce two elements of microeconomics that are both vital and difficult (to the point of seeming semi-mystical at times). If the objective is to predict and analyse what individuals do then it is helpful, if not vital, that they do not act at random or in a capricious way. This is where the notion of rationality introduced in Chapter 1 plays its part. 'What would a rational individual choose in such and such circumstances?' is a question that allows analysis to proceed. Applying a notion of rationality involves a specification of what individuals are assumed to know. Much analysis proceeds as if the actors 'know a subject' themselves, in that they are assumed to have enough information to solve the problem to hand without information becoming part of the problem itself. Many of the more fruitful insights into microeconomics, however, come from the 'finding information' part of the quotation above (broadly defined). Uncertainty can be thought of as a lack of information about the future and is clearly omnipresent. If prediction of behaviour is required, an account of how uncertainty is dealt with is essential. This, however, is a complex matter. This chapter attempts to introduce the ways by which economic theorists have either side-stepped or confronted these very big issues. Key economists in this area of research are George Akerlof, Michael Spence and Joseph Stiglitz who were jointly awarded the 2001 Nobel prize for economics.

7.2 Risk

To this point, the objects of choice have not involved any unknowns but, in what students are wont to call 'the real world', Y and X may be different values of the same good depending on which of a range of possible events turns up (e.g. wheat output with good weather versus wheat output in bad weather). Can preference maps be constructed when situations involve risk? The answer is 'yes' and earlier chapters provide a clue as to how to do it. By employing axioms and the notion of subjective utility it is possible to construct subjective expected utility theory.

This aspect of microeconomic theory is largely due to the insights of John Von Neumann and Oskar Morgenstern[1] (1944) who adopted the axioms listed below. The objects of choice are lotteries, which are simply descriptions of consequences (or outcomes) and their associated probability. For example, the lottery L might be described by: $L = (c_1, c_2 : p, 1 - p)$. That is, there are two possible consequences to choosing the lottery, namely c_1 or c_2, and these consequences arise with a probability p and (logically) $1 - p$. (A more general notation would be $L = (c_1, c_2 \ldots c_s : p_1, p_2 \ldots p_s)$ suggesting s possible consequences or states of the world can arise with associated probabilities $p_1, \ldots, p_s$ which must sum to 1).

Required axioms:

(i)   Individual preferences over lotteries are reflexive, complete and transitive, This is simply axioms (i), (ii) and part of (iv) outlined in Chapter 1 (p. 24) combined; it says that individuals must treat any lottery as being at least as good as itself,[2] can rank all lotteries and conform to transitivity with respect to lotteries they are assumed or actually confronted with in experimental situations.

(ii) The continuity, or measurability, axiom corresponds to axiom (iv) in Chapter 1 and says if there are two uncertain outcomes with x_W the worst, x_B the best and a certain ($p = 1$) intermediate one x_I then there is a unique probability that the individual can state that makes them indifferent between x_I and the lottery $(x_W, x_B : p, 1 - p)$.

(iii) Preference for lotteries with identical outcomes must be such that the individual prefers the one that has the higher probability of the best outcome. Preference increasing with a higher probability of the better outcome is called monotonicity. If L_1 is $[x_1, x_2 : p, 1 - p]$ and L_2 is $[x_1, x_2 : q, 1 - q]$ then, if x_1 is preferred to x_2, it is the case that L_1 is preferred to L_2 if and only if (iff) probability p is greater than probability q.

(iv) Strong separability, strong independence, independence substitution axiom, 'sure thing' principle, substitutability of outcomes and choices and irrelevance of independent alternatives are all phrases that have been used in connection with one axiom. This states: if x_1 and x_2 are equally attractive and x_3 and p are common (the same), then the two lotteries $L_1 = [x_1, x_3 : p, 1 - p]$ and L_2 is $[x_2, x_3 : p, 1 - p]$ must be equally attractive for any values of p and x_3. The series of names for this axiom flags the fact that this has been the most controversial of the axioms. It is an important axiom because it enables a radical simplification of choices involving risk discussed below.

(v)   The final axiom says that individuals should be able to identify when underlying lotteries are identical, even if at first glance they do not seem to be. A so-called compound lottery whose outcome itself is a lottery must be as attractive as the simple lottery it comprises. If L_1 is $[L_{1a}, L_{1b} : p, 1 - p]$ and L_{1a} is $[x_1, x_2, : q, 1 - q]$ and L_{1b} is $[x_3, x_4 : r, 1 - r]$ it can also be expressed as L_2 $[x_1, x_2, x_3, x_4 : pq, p(1 - q); (1 - p)r; (1 - p)(1 - r)]$. Substitution of some simple values for probabilities of p, q and r will allow the reader to establish they are the same underlying lottery and the axiom says the individual must spot them as such.

Armed with the protection of these axioms it is now possible to explain how researchers have derived what are (in the light of Chapter 1) unfortunately called 'cardinal utility functions', directly from individual responses to choices over lotteries. The idea is to build up a relationship between 'utility' on the y-axis and income or wealth levels

---

1. Their famous book published in 1944 is titled *The Theory of Games and Economic Behavior*.
2. If this looks a strange requirement see footnote 6 in Chapter 1 explaining that this guarantees that all lotteries will belong to an indifference set.

on the x-axis. Suppose it is arbitrarily decided to assign zero utility to £0 and 20 utils to = £1000. It is now possible (with the aid of someone willing to reveal their preferences and acting in accordance with the above axioms) to develop a 'utility' function. Suppose they are offered a choice between lottery 1 (L_1) a certain £0 [0 : 1] and lottery 2 (L_2). Suppose the second lottery is [+£1000, –£1000 : p, $1 - p$]. The respondent is now asked to state the value of the probability p that makes them indifferent between L_1 and L_2. Given axiom (ii) the individual must be able to state the value of p such that

$$u(£0) = pu(+£1000) + (1 - p)u(-£1000) \tag{7.1}$$

for them. Suppose, after reflection, they say p is 0.7, then, given the assumptions, it must be the case that

$$u(£0) = 0.7u(£1000) + (1 - 0.7)u(-£1000) = 0 \tag{7.2}$$

Hence:

$$0.3u(-£1000) = -0.7u(+£1000)$$

$$u(-£1000) = -0.7u(+£1000)/0.3$$

With a u value of +£1000 pre-assigned 20 utils then

$$u(-£1000) = -0.7(20)/0.3 = -14/0.3 = -46.7 \text{ utils} \tag{7.3}$$

On Figure 7.1 three points can now be plotted: £0, 0 utils; +£1000, 20 utils; –£1000, –46.7 utils. As only two values are required to determine (with the aid of probability information) a third, the scene is now set for repeated lottery choice questions and the filling in of a continuous total utility of income curve labelled $TU(Y)$. For example, you could now confront the individual with the choice between L_1 above and L_3, where L_3 was [+£2000, –£1000 : p, $1 - p$]. Suppose $p = 0.6$ then

$$u(£0) = 0.6u(£2000) + (1 - 0.6)u(-£1000) = 0 \tag{7.4}$$

Hence:

$$0.6u(+£2000) = -0.4u(-£1000)$$

$$u(+£2000) = -0.4u(-£1000)/0.6$$

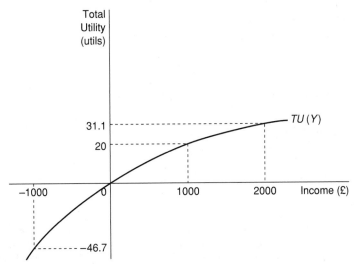

Figure 7.1
Generating a Von Neumann–Morgenstern utility function

with a *u* value of −£1000 derived as −46.7 utils above, then:

$$u(+£2000) = -0.4(-46.7)/0.6 = 18.7/0.6 = 31.1 \text{ utils} \tag{7.5}$$

and another point is established on the utility of income curve and can be plotted. The 'utility' can be called VN-M utility (from Von Neumann and Morgenstern).

7.2.1 Risk aversion, preference and neutrality

The shape finally generated is a reflection of a particular individual's choices with respect to lotteries but is very important in a wide range of contexts. The shape generated is a reflection of an individual's attitude towards risk. Figure 7.2 illustrates four cases and isolates the utility assigned to an expected value compared to a certain one. In each figure the utility assigned to +£500, +£1500 and identical negative values are plotted.

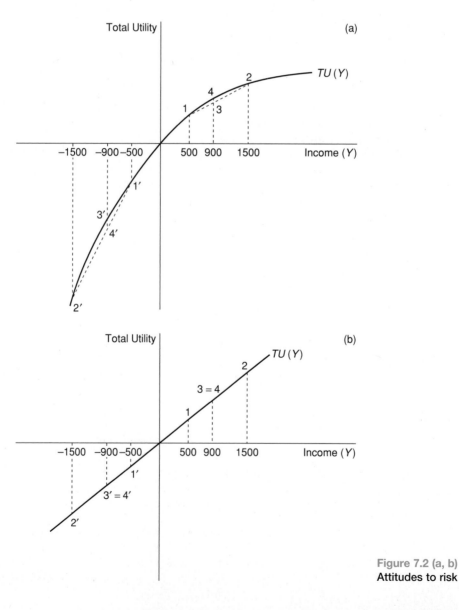

Figure 7.2 (a, b)
Attitudes to risk

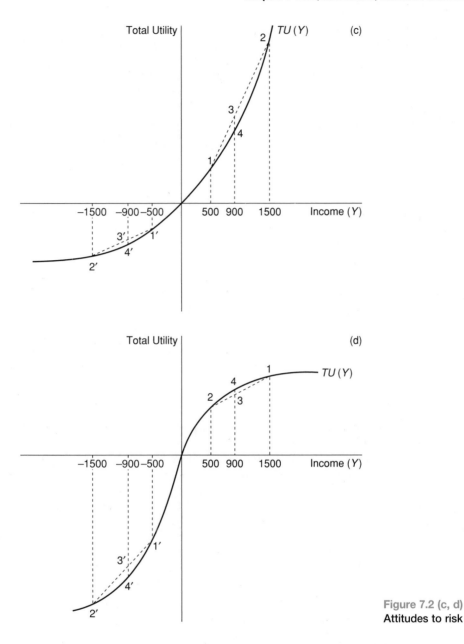

Figure 7.2 (c, d)
Attitudes to risk

Suppose the individuals, whose utility of income curves have been derived, are farmers and the money sums are income with good weather, very good weather, bad weather and very bad weather respectively. Note all prefer more income to less. If it was possible to say with certainty what the weather was going to be then income and VN-M utility would be determined. For the moment, assume it is known only that the weather will be good-ish or bad-ish and concentrate on the good-ish case where income will be positive. The risk is now whether the weather will be good or very good and this makes a difference in income of £1000. Although it is not known whether the weather will be good or very good, suppose probabilistic information is available on the chance it will be good or very good and suppose the chance of very good weather is 0.4 and hence of good weather is 0.6. In these circumstances, each farmer can formulate their expected income as a so-called expected value (*EV*) where *EV* = 0.6 £500 + 0.4 £1500 = £300 + £600 = £900. Suppose £900 is exactly the income that would occur with moderately good weather that, for the sake of the argument, could be guaranteed. Does this suggest that farmers are indifferent to probabalistic weather that offers an income whose expected value is £900 and guaranteed (certain) moderate weather that offers a certain income of £900?

It can be seen, by inspecting Figure 7.2 (a) to (d), that the expected value is recorded on a dashed line segment between the certain income values of £500 and £1500, i.e. joining points 1 and 2. The location of the precise point is determined by the probability of very good weather (the point migrates to the left as this probability increases). The continuous line is the VN-M utility of income curve and, although derived from statements about choices over lotteries, it indicates a VN-M utility at each given (or certain) income level. Comparing the utility of the expected value of income with the certain value of income (the certain moderate weather case here) reveals that in panel (a) the certain income offers a higher VN-M utility level, being at point 4 compared to point 3. This individual is said to be *risk-averse*, preferring the certain £900 to an income whose expected value is £900. (Note actual income will be £500 or £1500 depending on whether good, or very good, weather actually occurs.)

For the individual depicted in panel (b) points 3 and 4 coincide and this individual is indifferent between the certain income and the same expected value of income. The individual is said to be *risk-neutral*.

In panel (c) point 3 is above 4 and the individual prefers the expected value of income to the certain equivalent income. This individual is a *risk-lover* (*risk-taker* or *risk-preferer*).

As depicted, the individual in panel (d) is also risk-averse for this 'positive income' situation (point 4 is above point 3). The panels also illustrate the situation for losses (negative income), where it is known that weather will be bad-ish but not whether it will be bad or very bad weather. The probability of very bad weather is assumed to be 0.4 and hence the expected value of income loss can be located at −£900. *EV* = 0.6 − £500 + 0.4 − £1500 = −£300 − £600 = −£900.

For panels (a) to (c), the individuals have the VN-M utility of the expected value of income (points labelled 3′) inferior (equal, superior) to the certain equivalent income (points labelled 4′) and are risk-averse, risk-neutral and risk-preferring as was the case for gains. Where inferior means more negative, equal means equally negative and superior means less negative – no one here likes losses! In panel (d) the individual who was risk-averse for positive income is risk-loving for losses, preferring an expected income of −£900 to a certain one of −£900. This is a combination of preferences that was typical of the value function of Kahneman and Tversky (1979) employed in Chapter 2.

A number of points need to be made very clear here:

(1) Economists do not dictate the 'shapes' of the VN-M utility functions but can work with the shape the empirical world suggests appropriate, or, more comprehensively, with a large number of possible cases indicating how matters change for different shapes.
(2) The majority of individuals are characterised by risk aversion (ask yourself what you think your VN-M utility curve looks like) and much economic analysis is developed on this assumption.
(3) The shapes have been derived from individual statements about hypothetical lottery choices and are unfortunately said to exhibit 'cardinality'. This statement is the source of much misunderstanding and is discussed next.

7.2.2 VN-M 'cardinality'

Having put actual utility numbers against different income levels in Figure 7.1 it is awfully tempting to use them in a way that cannot be justified. Figure 7.3 illustrates two

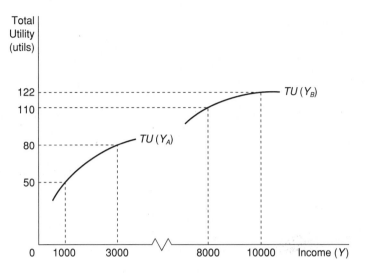

Figure 7.3
Redistributing
income?

VN-M utility curves for two individuals derived from the procedure described above. Individual A has, say, an income of £1000 per period and individual B £10,000 per period. Given the discussion above, both are risk-averse. Suppose you considered redistributing £2000 from individual B to individual A. It is tempting to read the net change in utility as a 12 util loss for B and a 30 util gain for A and therefore the utility of this two-person society has unambiguously been raised. This is what the early economist Francis Edgeworth (1881) had in mind as some day being possible. But recall utility is a subjective experience: we can never know what happiness or sadness means except in ourselves. Each individual may have a scale in their heads but the nature of this scale is unique to them and cannot be conveyed in precise form to others. How then did Figure 7.1 become possible?

The answer is by adopting axioms and making two arbitrary assumptions, one that the utility of £0 was zero and one that the utility of £1000 was 20 utils. This has fortunate and unfortunate implications that are reverse sides of the same coin. The unfortunate implication is that the location of the curve on the utility scale is dependent on the arbitrary starting values. Individuals can be made to have more or less utility from income at the whim of the individual conducting the utility experiment. If $U = U(Y)$ describes the utility function illustrated above, there exists a whole family of curves that would perform the same task. These are so-called positive linear transformations of $U = U(Y)$ so that:

$$V(Y) = a + bU(Y) \tag{7.6}$$

would also do as a representation of the individual's total VN-M utility of income curve where:

$a \gtrless 0$ is a shift parameter that 'shifts' the curve bodily up or down the axis (+ up and – down);
$b > 0$ is the scaling factor. $b < 1$ causes compression of the curve, whereas $b > 1$ causes expansion.

In Chapter 1 the utility function used a number to label every possible commodity bundle and higher numbers were preferred. For uncertain situations, utility over consequences is connected to utility over actions via the expected utility rule. This is the probability weighted average of the utility over consequences functions, the utility over consequences function is 'cardinal' in that only positive linear transforms are permissible.

Table 7.1 Actions and consequences

	States of the world (only one of which will arise but which one is unknown) Consequences or outcomes		
	1	2	3
Probabilities	$p_1 = 0.5$	$p_2 = 0.3$	$p_3 (1 - p_1 - p_2) = 0.2$
Action A or prospect A	a_1 (£80)	a_2 (£200)	a_3 (£400)
Action B or prospect B	b_1 (£40)	b_2 (£380)	b_3 (£370)

If such transformations are legitimate then the net 18 util gain from transferring £2000 from individual B to individual A could be changed into a loss by shifting or scaling individual B's (or A's) VN-M utility function. The point is that having VN-M utility functions for individuals does not permit interpersonal comparisons of utility to be made. What then can this piece of conceptual apparatus do?

This is where the fortunate side of the coin faces up. Table 7.1 allows an illustration to be developed.

Recall, the task is to model economically rational choice in the presence of risk. Faced with the choice over the two actions, or prospects, described in Table 7.1, which one should the individual choose? The answer is to choose the one that maximises their VN-M expected utility ($EU_{v\text{-}nm}$). Suppose Figure 7.4 is this individual's VN-M utility function, constructed as described above, the util values for each money outcome can be read off and the appropriate probabilities attached to form the expected utility value for each action as follows. The curve happens to be $U(Y) = \ln Y$ (the utility of income is equal to the value of its natural log which gives a risk-averse shape) but this is not vital in any way – any shape will do:

$$EU_{v\text{-}nmA} = 0.5 \ln 80 + 0.3 \ln 200 + 0.2 \ln 400$$
$$EU_{v\text{-}nmA} = 0.5 \times 4.38 + 0.3 \times 5.30 + 0.2 \times 5.99$$
$$EU_{v\text{-}nmA} = 2.19 + 1.60 + 1.20 = 4.99 \tag{7.7}$$

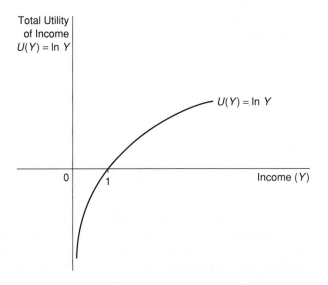

Figure 7.4
Logarithmic utility function

$$EU_{v\text{-}nmB} = 0.5 \ln 40 + 0.3 \ln 380 + 0.2 \ln 370$$
$$EU_{v\text{-}nmB} = 0.5 \times 3.69 + 0.3 \times 5.94 + 0.2 \times 5.91$$
$$EU_{v\text{-}nmB} = 1.84 + 1.78 + 1.18 = 4.80 \tag{7.8}$$

On expected utility grounds, action A will be rationally chosen over action B as it offers higher expected utility. 'Ah! Ah!', people cry, 'this cannot work because it is legitimate to subject the illustrated utility function to any positive linear transformation and this will make the numbers and therefore the choice vary.' At last here is the 'payoff'. Although the numbers will vary, action A will always offer greater expected utility than action B and will therefore always be chosen. The choice is independent of any positive linear transformation of the VN-M utility function and it is said to be 'unique up to any positive linear transform' – and this is what is meant when VN-M utility functions are unfortunately described as cardinal – it does not mean interpersonal comparisons of utility can be made.

This is indeed good news, as now it can be said that individuals can rationally choose between risky options simply by ranking them in order of their expected utility to them. That is :

$$EU_x = \sum_{i=1}^{n} p_i U_i(x_i) \tag{7.9}$$

where

x = any action or prospect;
n = the n possible states of the world following from this action ($n = 3$ above for both actions A and B for ease of illustration only);
x_i = the outcome in each state of the world ($1, \ldots, n$) if it arises;
p_i = the probability that each state of the world will arise;
U_i = utility measured from a VN-M utility function from each state of the world should it arise.

To recap, for any positive linear transformation of the originally derived VN-M utility function adopted in the example, it will always be the case that

$$EU_A = \sum_{i=1}^{3} p_i U_i(a_i) < EU_B = \sum_{i=1}^{3} p_i U_i(b_i) \tag{7.10}$$

Since the utilities of the outcomes weighted by their probabilities are simply being added up to form the expected utility of the action or prospect, the VN-M utility function is said to be additively separable. This very attractive property stems from axiom (iv) whose multiple titles, as suggested, almost shout that there is a worry here. And indeed there is. However, before digging out the foundations that have just been laid, which, as discussed below, may or may not be faulty, it is fruitful to keep building and incorporate information in the discussion.

7.3 Information

Nobel laureate Joseph Stiglitz (1985) writes about economics *and* information, not the economics of information, to emphasise the point that information is central to the propositions of economics and that information is not a sub-discipline within economics that is, or can be, treated as somehow peripheral or exotic. Individuals may range from being fully informed to completely ignorant, depending on what they are assumed to know. Economically rational people with full information are easiest to model and this is typically the implicit case in many textbook situations. To use the opening quote they have information they know themselves. Incomplete information situations trigger theory that is more difficult but much richer in content. In such situations individuals respond with actions that are themselves governed by an economic calculus. In risky situations, in which individuals do not know what will happen, they can make it *as if* they have complete information – a certain world – by buying insurance. In risky situations, in which individuals do not know what will happen, they can buy information messages that allow them to 'Bayesian update' their view of the world and change their course of action. Ng (1977) uses the terms 'information scarcity' and 'information poverty' to describe different informational environments in the context of second-best theory. Fama (1970) describes informational efficiency as the extent to which prices contain available information. Muth (1961), on the other hand, initiated a rich vein of theorising by postulating that people placed information into economic models to form rational expectations. In the presence of informational poverty, individuals may respond by searching for information or by signalling information. In the sections and chapters that follow the significance of these lines of thought are explored in the context of utility maximisation.

7.3.1 Utility maximisation with costless information in a risky world

In this section it is assumed that the context is a risky one in that the assumed risk-averse individual is uncertain as to what 'state of the world' will show up, but does possess information on the probability of each of, say, two states of the world arising. (To illustrate in two dimensions is like having a two-dimensional actor – one that is very good on paper!)

Assume the uncertainty relates to your state of health and your earning in the next period. If you are well, your earnings are Y_w, if you are sick they are Y_s, where $Y_w > Y_s$. This information locates two points (1 and 2) on a VN-M cardinal utility function ($TU(Y)$) in Figure 7.5. If the probability of being sick is 0.2 then the expected value of income is Y_{ev}. As noted above, for risk-averse individuals the utility of the expected value of income $U[Y_{ev}]$ is greater than expected utility of income $E[U(Y_{ev})]$. In these circumstances, the individual can raise their utility if Y_{ev} can be made certain at that value. That is, they would enjoy utility level $U[Y_{ev}]$ as opposed to $E[U(Y_{ev})]$. Note that decreasing the possible spread of income around the same expected value increases expected utility. Witness the

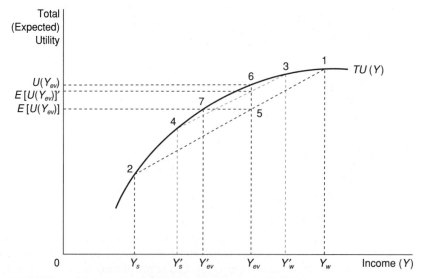

Figure 7.5 Utility and income uncertainty for a risk-averse individual

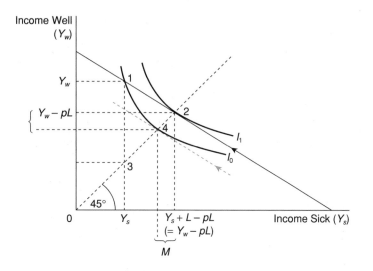

Figure 7.6
Risk aversion and full insurance

expected utility of income associated with an income spread of Y_s and Y_w and points 3 and 4 on the VN-M cardinal utility function in Figure 7.5 is $E[U(Y_{ev})]' > E[U(Y_{ev})]$. This risky income information is recorded as point 1 on Figure 7.6. Such a figure is called a 'state–space diagram' because it shows the value of the same variable – here income – in two states of the world.

Now, in a risky world, if insurance was available could the individual increase their utility? For the illustrated individual, utility depends on income so that $U = U(Y)$ and with two states of the world the utility expected is given by $U = (1 - p)U(Y_w) + p\ U(Y_s)$, where p is the probability of being sick and hence $(1 - p)$ is the probability of being well. Now, point 1 will be on an indifference curve which must have the property that the total differential associated with it is zero, so that

$$dU = (1 - p)\frac{\partial U_w}{\partial Y_w}\,dY_w + p\,\frac{\partial U_s}{\partial Y_s}\,dY_s = 0 \qquad (7.11)$$

so that:

$$\frac{dY_w}{dY_s} = \frac{-p}{1 - p}\frac{\partial U_s / \partial Y_s}{\partial U_w / \partial Y_w} \equiv \frac{-p}{1 - p}\frac{MU_s}{MU_w} \qquad (7.12)$$

This says that the slope of an indifference curve in a state–space diagram is the odds-weighted ratio of the marginal utility of income in the two states of the world. Noting that decreasing income spread in Figure 7.5 raises utility and that on the 45° line in Figure 7.6 income is the same in both states of the world implies that at point 2 income is Y_{ev}. That is, the expected value of income is

$$Y_{ev} = p \cdot Y_s + (1 - p)Y_w \qquad (7.13)$$

$$Y_{ev} = p \cdot Y_s + Y_w - pY_w \qquad (7.14)$$

$$Y_{ev} = Y_w - p(Y_w - Y_s) \qquad (7.15)$$

Now $Y_w - Y_s$ is the income loss when ill (L) and therefore $Y_{ev} = Y_w - pL$. If income is the same sick or well, $MU_s = MU_w$ and utility is raised for a risk-averse individual, so point 2 therefore must be on a higher indifference curve (I_1) than point 1 (I_0). Further, the indifference curve's I_1 slope at point 2 is necessarily $-p/(1 - p)$, given equation (7.12) above (this is true for each indifference curve as it crosses the certainty line).

Clearly, the individual would rather be at point 2 than at point 1. Is this going to be possible? The answer is 'yes' in a frictionless world, i.e. a world in which insurance can be arranged with no administration or profit costs. In such circumstances the fair insurance or premium (*FP*) is available, with the premium being the probability of the loss times the size of the potential loss. Here the income loss (L) from being sick is distance 1-3, so that $FP = pL$. If such insurance is purchased then income would be $Y_w - pL$ if well and $Y_w - L (= Y_s) + L - pL$ if sick, with income lost being covered by the insurance company. Income, whatever happens, will be $Y_w - pL$.

In order to complete the picture it is necessary to establish the slope of the budget constraint in this world. This can be done using the relationships just described.

$$Y_{iw} = Y_w - pL \tag{7.16}$$

$$Y_{is} = Y_w - L + L - pL \tag{7.17}$$

where

Y_{iw} stands for income insured and state of the world well;
Y_{is} stands for income insured and state of the world sick.

From equation (7.16),

$$pL = Y_w - Y_{iw} \tag{7.18}$$

$$L = Y_w/p - Y_{iw}/p \tag{7.19}$$

From equation (7.17),

$$L - pL = Y_{is} - Y_w + L \tag{7.20}$$

$$L(1 - p) = Y_{is} - Y_w + L \tag{7.21}$$

$$L = Y_{is}/(1 - p) - Y_w/(1 - p) + L/(1 - p) \tag{7.22}$$

Substituting for L from (7.19) into (7.22) yields:

$$Y_w/p - Y_{iw}/p = Y_{is}/(1 - p) - Y_w/(1 - p) + L/(1 - p) \tag{7.23}$$

$$Y_{is}/(1 - p) + Y_{iw}/p = Y_w/p + Y_w/(1 - p) - L/(1 - p) \tag{7.24}$$

$$Y_{is}/(1 - p) + Y_{iw}/p = Y_w/p(1 - p) - L/(1 - p) \tag{7.25}$$

Multiplying all terms by $p(1 - p)$ yields:

$$pY_{is} + (1 - p)Y_{iw} = Y_w - pL \tag{7.26}$$

$$Y_{iw} = -p/(1 - p)Y_{is} + Y_w/(1 - p) - p/(1 - p)L \tag{7.27}$$

Hence

$$\frac{dY_{iw}}{dY_{is}} = \frac{-p}{(1 - p)} \tag{7.28}$$

Noting the budget line is a straight line enables a quick way to check this result. The downward vertical movement between points 1 and 2 translated to the *y*-axis is given by $-pL$ whereas the horizontal movement between points 1 and 2 on the *x*-axis is given by $L - pL$ and, dividing the former by the latter to give the slope, yields $-pL/(L - pL) = -pL/(1 - p)L$, which simplifies to $-p/(1 - p)$.

It is clear that the slope of the budget constraint everywhere is the negative of the fair odds ratio. Considering Figure 7.6 the individual begins at point 1 on I_0 with the availability of fair insurance allowing them to adjust along the budget constraint through point 1. It is easy to pick out utility-maximising adjustment, as the slope of the budget constraint is $-p/(1-p)$ and the slope of the indifference curve is $-p/(1-p)$ only when it crosses the 45° certainty line. Hence the individual maximises utility at point 2 on I_1. At point 2 the individual enjoys the expected value of their income (Y_{ev}) with certainty and, because of risk aversion, this increases their utility.

It is easy to establish the size of the utility gain. In Figure 7.5 the effect of being insured and to have Y_{ev} with certainty is to increase utility from point 5 to point 6, i.e. from $E[U(Y_{ev})]$ to $U(Y_{ev})$. Indeed, $U(Y_{ev}) - E[U(Y_{ev})]$ in utility terms, equals Y_{ev}-$Y_{ev'}$ in money terms, could be taken off the individual before they would reject fair insurance as uncertain income Y_{ev} (the world without insurance) offers the same utility at point 5 namely $E[U(Y_{ev})]$, as the certain insured income $Y_{ev'}$ at point 7. Distance Y_{ev}-$Y_{ev'}$ is known as the *Markowitz risk premium*. Note that Figures 7.5 and 7.6 are intimately connected: uninsured utility in Figure 7.5 at point 5 must correspond to point 1 on I_0 in Figure 7.6; the insured utility at point 6 in Figure 7.5 must correspond to point 2 on I_1 in Figure 7.6. The insured utility with the Markowitz risk premium at point 7 in Figure 7.5 must correspond to point 4 on I_0 in Figure 7.6. Given the Markowitz risk premium measures how much you can take off the insured individual in money terms, before they are indifferent to being insured or facing the world uninsured, it is evident that Y_{ev}-$Y_{ev'}$ in Figure 7.5 must equal distances marked M in Figure 7.6 as points 1 and 4 are on the same original indifference curve. For emphasis the complete picture is put together in Figure 7.7 and developed from the data recorded in Table 7.2.

Expected income $E(Y)$ for the individual if uninsured is $0.4 \times £1000 + 0.6 \times £4000 = £2800$ recorded in panel (c) of Figure 7.7 along with the certain income outcome of £1000 and £4000. Full insurance cover at a fair premium would cost in a frictionless world $0.4 \times £3000$ (income loss contingent on sickness) equals £1200. So that, with full insurance cover, the certain income the individual could enjoy is £2800 (= £4000 – £1200). Using the 45° line in panel (b) of Figure 7.7 allows income when well to be translated to the y-axis of panel (a), whereas using the two 45° lines in panels (d) and (e) of Figure 7.7 allows income when sick to be translated to the x-axis of panel (a).

The uncertain endowment point is at point E on I_0 in panel (a) of Figure 7.7, being the utility level assigned to expected income $E(Y) = £2800$ for the individual if uninsured, that is $I_0 = E[U(Y)]$ noted in panel (c). Drawing the fair-odds budget constraint through point E in panel (a) involves noting $E(Y) = pY_s + (1-p)Y_w$ so that:

$$Y_w = \frac{E(Y)}{(1-p)} - \frac{pY_s}{(1-p)} \tag{7.29}$$

The y-axis intercept occurs where $Y_s = 0$ and is therefore £2800/0.6 = 4666.7 and, given the slope dY_w/dY_s is $-p/(1-p)$, its value is $-0.4/0.6 = -0.67$. The purchase of full insurance means income is certain and the same in both states of the world at £2800. Again, this is recorded in panel (c) and using the 45° lines in panels (b), (d) and (e) of Figure 7.7 allows income when well (and sick) to be translated to the y-axis and x-axis of panel (a), documenting the fully insured point as point F. The point F is on I_2 in panel (a) of Figure 7.7, being the utility level assigned to expected income $Y = £2800$ for the individual if insured, that is $I_2 = U[E(Y)]$ noted in panel (c). Given the Markowitz risk premium measures how much you can take off the insured individual in money terms before they are

Table 7.2 **Income in states of the world sick (Y_s) and well (Y_w)**

States of the world	Sick	Well	Income
Probabilities	$p = 0$	$(1-p) = 1$	£4000 (Certain)
	$p = 1$	$(1-p) = 0$	£1000 (Certain)
	$p = 0.4$	$(1-p) = 0.6$	£2800 (Expected)

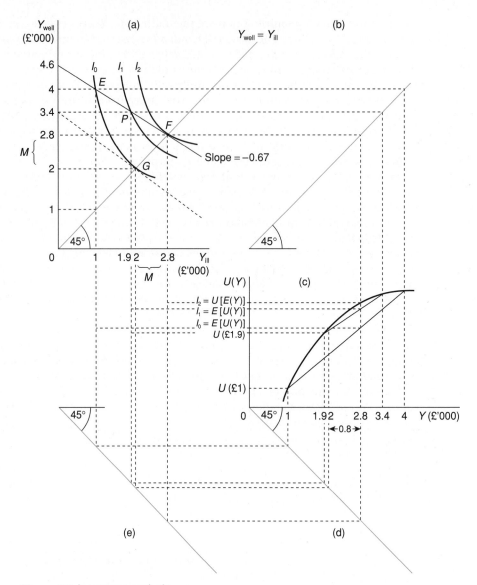

Figure 7.7 Insurance analysis

indifferent to being insured or facing the world uninsured, it is evident that, as drawn, this is £800 in Figure 7.7(c) – and must equal distances marked M in Figure 7.7(a). As points E and G are on the same original indifference curve, this indicates the point where the individual, although risk-averse, faced with a premium of £1200 plus £800 = £2000 would toss a coin to decide whether to insure or go without as required by the definition.

There is a clear proposition here that all risk-averse individuals will buy full insurance at a fair premium. What about the insurance company? Suppose as above the loss $L = £3000$ and $p = 0.4$ then, as far as the insurance company is concerned, $FP = £1200$ as calculated above. If, say, 100 people like the one depicted were insured, premiums would sum to £120,000 and 40 of the insurees would be sick, requesting £3000 each, so that the fund could exactly cover the claims. The role of the frictionless world is important because it rules out administrative cost and profit claims on the pool that would prevent the ability to cover all claims at fair insurance. That is, 'loading' for such costs would otherwise be required. There is, however, a second proposition that all risk-averse individuals will buy full insurance at a fair premium plus a 'loading' that does not exceed the Markowitz risk premium which here is £800. Insurance premiums that allow for administration costs and a profit are therefore possible within limits.

How is the picture amended to deal with partial cover? If the depicted individual wanted partial cover of £1500 the insurance cover at a fair premium would cost in a frictionless world $0.4 \times £1500$ (income loss contingent on sickness) equal to £600. So, with partial insurance cover the income the individual could enjoy is £3400 (= £4000 − £600). Using the 45° line in panel (b) of Figure 7.7 allows income when well to be translated to the y-axis of panel (a), whereas using the two 45° lines in panels (d) and (e) of Figure 7.7 allows income when sick £1900 (= £1000 [income sick] + £1500 [insurance payout] − £600 [premium]) to be translated to the x-axis of panel (a). The uncertain partially covered point is point P on I_1 in panel (a) of Figure 7.7, being the utility level assigned to expected income $E(Y) = £2800$ (= $0.4 \times £1900(Y_s) + 0.6 \times £3400(Y_w)$) for the individual if partially insured, that is $I_1 = E[U(Y)]$ noted in panel (c). It is clear that partial insurance at a fair premium also raises utility for the risk-averse individual, as being on I_1 is superior to being on I_0.

The ubiquitous problems with insurance are called 'moral hazard' and 'adverse selection' and arise in many guises throughout microeconomics. Moral hazard arises when *ex-ante* magnitudes that define a fair premium, the probability p and the size of the loss L, become inflated on insurance, so that p increases to p' and L to L'. Individuals with fire insurance are more careless with matches and it is invariably an antique Turkish carpet that is burnt! Adverse selection arises where insurance policies are not drawn up on an individual basis but on a group-average basis.

More fully:

(i) *Adverse selection* arises where one party to a transaction knows information relevant to the transaction that is unknown by the second party, e.g. in life insurance the insuree may know things about their health status that the company does not. Individuals can sometimes signal who they are by their actions, e.g. only the relatively healthy might buy a policy offering limited benefits in the form of a deductible (in the case of ill health you pay the first £x yourself).

(ii) *Moral hazard:* one party to a transaction may undertake actions that (a) affect the other party's valuation of the transaction but (b) the second party cannot easily monitor or enforce the original conditions of the transaction. For example, as intimated above, those with fire insurance are more likely to be careless with matches and lose an antique Turkish carpet in the fire! The usual response is to offer only partial insurance to preserve some incentive not to have a fire. As these two problems arise in many 'contract' contexts it is worth elaborating on them.

In the presence of full information on every individual in a frictionless world they would each be charged a premium that was fair to them. High-risk individuals would face high premiums and low-risk individuals low ones. However, it is very costly to tailor-make every contract and therefore contracts are written for groups of individuals. If there are 150 individuals assume 100 are well-ish and 50 are sick-ish with probabilities of being ill in the coming period of 0.1 and 0.5 respectively. Further, assume the cost of ill health should it arise is £100. A fair premium for the group can now be formulated which is a probability-weighted average. It is as if there is a representative statistical individual who is one-third sick-ish and two-thirds well-ish.

$$\text{Fair premium } (FP) = [(0.1 \times 100/150) + (0.5 \times 50/150)] \times £100$$
$$= (0.067 + 0.166) \times £100$$
$$= 0.23 \times 100 = £23$$

Now a fair premium for well-ish individuals = $0.1 \times £100 = £10$ and a fair premium for sick-ish individuals = $0.5 \times £100 = £50$.

The outcome depends on what you assume individuals know. If individuals do not know if they are well-ish or sick-ish they will be content to buy full insurance given they are risk-averse. If individuals do know if they are well-ish or sick-ish then the well-ish will realise that their fair premium is £10 and the group premium rate of £23 involves them cross-subsidising the sick-ish. The sick-ish will realise that their fair premium is £50 and the group premium rate of £23 involves them being cross-subsidised by the well-ish. In these circumstances the well-ish will not demand insurance and exit the scheme whilst the sickish are very keen would-be insurees. That is, the presence of bad risks drive out the good risks, causing the insurance company to recalculate the group fair premium upwards. With more classes of individuals it is easy to imagine the final result is the high risk insured with a suitably high premium. This cannot be optimal in that all risk-averse individuals would prefer to be insured and yet in the presence of adverse selection they may well not be.

Moral hazard is a problem that the knowledge you have become insured alters individual behaviour. An *ex-ante* fair premium is given by $FP = p \cdot £L$ where p is the *ex-ante* probability of the event, say illness once more, and £L the costs (losses) of ill health if it arises (see Pauly 1968). Once insured, individuals tend to be less careful about avoiding ill health so that p rises to p' and, once ill, demand increased expenditure so that £L rises to £L'. The *ex-post* fair premium is given by $FP' = p' \cdot £L'$ with $FP' > FP$.

To illustrate further, concentrate on the compensation demanded when ill. Assume there are three states of the world: not ill, demanding (D_0) zero units of medical care (M) per period with a probability of 0.5; moderately ill, demanding (D_m) fifty units of medical care with a probability of 0.25; and seriously ill, demanding (D_s) a hundred units of medical care with a probability of 0.25. In Figure 7.8 the marginal cost of health care is assumed constant at a £1 per unit per period and demand curves D_0, D_m and D_s reflect the (*ex-ante*) information above and indicate a fair premium of

$$FP = 0.5 \times 0 \cdot £1 + 0.25 \times 50 \cdot £1 + 0.25 \times 100 \cdot £1 = £37.50$$

Once insured (the *ex-post* situation), the price of medical care for the insured decreases to zero and, given D_m and D_s are not perfectly inelastic, the individual demands 75 units of medical care when moderately ill and 200 units of medical care when seriously ill. The *ex-post* information indicates that the insurance company will set a fair premium of

$$FP = 0.5 \times 0 \cdot £1 + 0.25 \times 75 \cdot £1 + 0.25 \times 200 \cdot £1 = £68.75$$

An individual who will buy insurance at the *ex-ante* fair premium may well reject insurance at the *ex-post* fair premium (their insured behaviour implies the Markowitz risk premium is less than £31.25).

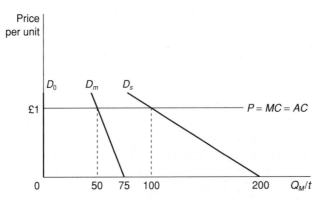

Figure 7.8 Illustrating moral hazard

Given adverse selection and moral hazard, individuals often have less than full insurance: insurance with limited indemnity (you are insured up to £Y); co-insurance (you pay a percentage of the price of each unit you consume); deductible (you pay the first £X yourself); and self-insurance, that is you simply assume your own risks by having no insurance.

7.3.2 Utility maximisation with costly information in a riskless world

In the above analysis the state of the world that would arise was unknown; however, here the situation is one where there is so-called market uncertainty. That is, the information is there to be found but searching for it is costly.

Here the utility-maximising response by the individual, not knowing the lowest price for good X, is considered. It is assumed the potential customer knows the distribution of prices for good X and, in crude terms, it might look like Figure 7.9 where there are only four prices. What is not known is which retail outlet offers which price. Search reduces the expected price you will pay but will increase your cost of obtaining the good. With one search the consumer will pay the expected value of the prices in the distribution, that is, the sum of each possible price multiplied by its relative frequency. In the case illustrated this is £630 (£500 · 0.2 + £600 · 0.4 + £700 · 0.3 + £800 · 0.1). It is assumed that the cost of search (time, trouble, travel, phone or whatever) is constant at c per search. This means that search costs (SC) are a positive straight line, increasing at a constant rate with the number of searches, n as in Figure 7.10. If n is increased to two, the expected minimum price paid can be formed by noting that with four prices there are $4^2 = 16$ possible pair of prices two searches might result in, but the individual does not know which pair of prices will be quoted. In these circumstances, they form the expected lowest price, which involves calculating the probability of each pair and multiplying by the lower price in the pair. For example, for the pair (£600, £700) the probabilities are (0.4, 0.3) and, therefore, one of the 16 sub-calculations is 0.2 times £600, which is £120. Adding the 16 sub-calculations gives the expected price conditional on two searches $E(P_x \mid _2)$. The curve labelled $E(\text{Min } P_x \mid _n)$ shows how the expected price of good X falls as the number of searches rises.

The economically rational person searches the number of times that minimises the expected cost of the good and the cost of the searches combined. In Figure 7.10 the curve labelled TC is the vertical sum of SC and $E(\text{Min } P_x \mid _n)$ and indicates the minimum occurs at n^* searches. The person carries out n^* searches and then accepts the lowest price they have been quoted. Note: the individual *ex ante* only knows the number of searches and the expected price. The actual price depends on how the n^* searches turn out for them as they are effectively sampling the market with replacement, so that some uncertainty remains in this optimal response.

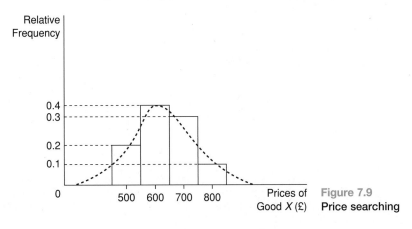

Figure 7.9
Price searching

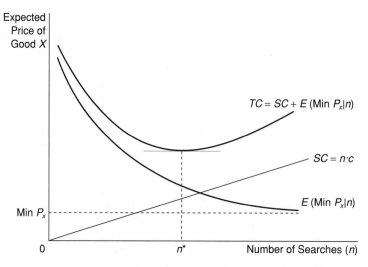

Figure 7.10
Optimal price search

7.3.3 Utility maximisation with costly information in a risky world

Rather than purchase insurance that transforms a risky situation into a certain one, it might only be possible to buy information that will allow you to update probabilities of each state of the world's arising. Here a treatment developed by Hirshleifer and Riley (1992) can be employed. The context is one in which there are three possible actions an individual can choose to take, labelled a_0 to a_2, in a situation where one of two states of the world (S_1 and S_2) will arise.

The vertical axis of Figure 7.11 records levels of VN-M cardinal utility from a risk-averse individual's total utility of income schedule (a schedule like Figure 7.5). As such, equal steps up each axis correspond to successively larger amounts of money income reflecting diminishing marginal utility of income that characterises a total utility of income curve that is concave when viewed from below. The x-axis documents the probability that each state of the world will arise. On the left-side axis, $p_2 = 1$ and $p_1 = 0$ and on the right $p_2 = 0$ and $p_1 = 1$. In between these extremes are the mixed combinations with $p_1 = 0.5$ and $p_2 = 0.5$ in the middle. Consider action a_1, the line labelled accordingly indicates on the axes the utility level enjoyed when each state of the world actually arises

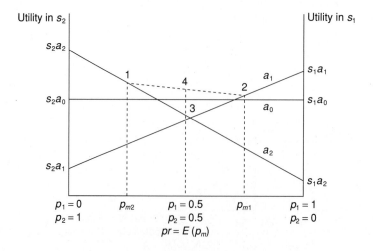

Figure 7.11
Costly information in a risky world

with S_1 offering greater utility than S_2, as can be seen by comparing s_1a_1 with s_2a_1. In the absence of the knowledge that one state of the world is certain to arise, the expected utility of each action will guide choice. The height of a_1 above the midpoint of the x-axis measures this expected utility when there is a fifty–fifty chance of each state of the world, i.e. it is 0.5 times distance 0-s_2a_1 + 0.5 times distance 0-s_1a_1. The remainder of points along a_1 are the probability-weighted sums of 0-s_2a_1 and 0-s_1a_1, with the weight being given to s_1 rising as you move left to right – hence the upward slope (the probabilities must sum to 1 as one of the states of the world will arise). Curves labelled a_0 and a_2 are constructed in a similar fashion and since a_0 offers the same utility in both states of the world it can be considered the certain action.

At different probabilities different actions offer greater expected utility. The rational action to be chosen depends on the prior probabilities of each state of the world arising that the individual holds. With the initial priors at 0.5 for s_1 and s_2, then a_0 is the chosen action and utility given by point 3 but what if further information is available at a price? Further information takes the form of a message that will cause the individual to revise their prior probabilities and, therefore, choice of action. It must be the case that the contents of the message are unknown to the individual before purchase, as otherwise the individual would have no willingness to pay for the message. Suppose, however, the individual does know that only one of two messages can be received. Message m_1, if received, makes s_1 more likely and m_2, if received, s_2 more likely and the likelihood of receiving each message q_1 and q_2. The points p_{m1} and p_{m2} indicate where the posterior (to the message) probabilities would be located once a particular message is received. In the absence of the precise knowledge of the message, it is the expected value of the posterior probabilities that guides choice and, for this, it is the likelihood of receiving each message that is relevant. It is the case that

$$p_r = q_1 \, p_{m1} + q_2 \, p_{m2} = E(p_m) \tag{7.30}$$

That is, the prior probability (p_r) is the same as the expected value of the posterior probability $[E(p_m)]$ when the expected value involves weighting by the likelihood of receiving each message (q_1 for m_1 and q_2 for m_2)(see the numerical example below). This property allows the expected utility gain from the receipt of an unknown message (and therefore the willingness to pay for it) to be isolated. In Figure 7.11 the dashed line 1 to 2 indicates expected utility formed on the basis of action a_2 if m_2 is received and a_1 if m_1 is received. Moving vertically in Figure 7.11 above $p_r = E(p_m)$ shows the expected utility to be gained from the message service as distance 3-4 in utility terms. If the utility price of the message exceeds this the individual increases expected utility by not buying the message and using prior probabilities to choose a_0. The message is that purchasing information in a risky context can raise expected utility when the price is right.

7.3.4 Utility maximisation and asymmetric information (I) signalling

Signalling mechanisms are at the centre of many of the more recent contributions to microeconomic theory. Such problems are associated with unobserved or hidden characteristics. Rather than search for information, or purchase a message service, it is appropriate in some circumstances for an individual to undertake a course of action that signals something about themselves. These situations arise where one party knows something that is relevant to another party who does not know that something. It is not that the information does not exist, rather it is the case that it is asymmetrically distributed. Whilst it is not always socially welfare-increasing to make information available, private incentives can be, and often are, set up in such a way that information is revealed (a classic article here is Spence 1973).

One of the classic examples is education or training as a signal of pre-existing ability. That is, at the outset it is assumed that education/training in itself does not raise your marginal product. This is a strong assumption but less strong is the observation that much modern production takes place in a team context, where it is difficult for an employer to separate the more able members of the, say n-member team from the less able. For interest and for the attraction of 'a play on words', let the team be an n-member apprentice (Youth Training Scheme) football squad. In circumstances where the employer or manager does not have the time to watch their games, they cannot easily separate the very good from the simply good players, so a wage that is a weighted average of the marginal products of all the members of the team is offered. If α is the number of able team members then with wages reflecting marginal products, the team wage will be:

$$W_t = \frac{\alpha MP_p + (n - \alpha)\ MP_c}{n} \tag{7.31}$$

where

p = Premier League performer with MP_p = 2 units;
c = Conference League performer with MP_c = 1 unit.

Assuming a unit is worth £1000 per week and n = 40 and α = 20, W_t will equal

$$\frac{20 \cdot 2 \cdot £1000 + 20 \cdot 1 \cdot £1000}{40} = £1500$$

The manager who wishes to separate out the ps from the cs reasons that the ps can acquire skills in a less costly manner than the cs and offers to pay those who, at the end of the year, can best demonstrate a variety of difficult cooking skills (i.e. skills not directly related to football but related to underlying different abilities).

Suppose the acquisition of the skills involves a payment, equal to sacrificing pay for the time involved and it will take the ps $1/4$ of each week to acquire all the skills and the cs $1/2$ of each week. If the weekly wage for those who can demonstrate the skills is W_s (= £2000) then the ps' incentives are such that the costs of the skills (C_s) are (0.25 times £1500 times 52 =) £19,500 and the potential reward £500 times 52 = £2600 (52 times $W_s - W_t$) and the skills will be acquired. For the cs, C_s = (0.5 times £1500 times 52) = £39,000 and with the same return to skill acquisition ($W_s - W_t$) times 52 they will not acquire the skills.

When test day comes, at the end of the year, the manager lets those without the cooking skills go. A so-called separating equilibrium has been created where some have the signal and others do not. A pooled equilibrium arises if the incentive structure were such that nobody has the cooking skills or all have the cooking skills.

While this particular account is contrived (and not designed to be taken too seriously), there is a principle involved. In circumstances where $C_s < (W_s - W_t) < C_c$ separation is created with the more able having the signal and the less able not. Note that the marginal products of the players have not changed, it is simply the identity of those who are very good that is revealed. A mistake in setting the incentives means all might have the signal or none. These cases correspond to $C_s < C_c < (W_s - W_t)$ and $C_c > C_s > (W_s - W_t)$ and generate a pooled equilibrium where all receive the same weighted average wage. The situations are, however, different in that when all have the signal real resources have been used up in the acquisition process.

7.3.4 Utility maximisation and asymmetric information (II) principal–agent problems

Principal-agent problems are also at the centre of many of the more recent contributions to microeconomic theory. Such problems are associated with unobserved or hidden actions. This is very much an active ('doing') perspective on events. In the principal–agent literature one person (the principal) hires another (the agent) to perform an activity where:

a) the agent has some degree of autonomy over a variable that affects both principal and agent;
b) the principal and agent differ in their preferences over the level of the agent's decision variables, i.e. there is conflict, or incentive incompatibility: e.g. for both principal and agent pecuniary return is a 'good'; however, for the principal, the agent's effort is 'a neutral' whilst for the agent their own effort is 'a bad' (they prefer to work less);
c) outcomes depend on the agent's chosen effort level and uncertainty – the state of the world that arises, e.g. a harvest and good or bad weather.

A basic question is the design of economic arrangements, or contracts, that induce 'incentive compatibility' and participation. The problem is a moral hazard one and Macho-Stadler and Perez-Castrillo (2001) present it as the following structure:

Principal (P)   Agent (A) accepts   Agent supplies   Nature determines   Outcome
   designs $\Rightarrow$ (or rejects) $\Rightarrow$ non-verifiable $\Rightarrow$ state of world (θ) $\Rightarrow$ and
   contract   effort (e)   payoffs

The task is for the principal to maximise surplus, or profit, by setting up the contract, so that it is utility-maximising for the agent to supply effort. There are two constraints to be met. The first is the no-shirking or incentive-compatibility constraint, where the agent must choose to supply effort (e). In the simplest of cases there is either effort or no effort. The second is the no-quitting or participation constraint, as the contract must offer at minimum the reservation utility that the agent can leave and obtain elsewhere (U_r).

Following an example in Bosworth, Dawkins and Stromback (1996) the nature of the contract can be deduced with the aid of Figure 7.12. It is a state-contingent diagram familiar from the discussion of insurance above. The common variable is the wage of the agent, which is high (W_h) when output is high and is low when output is low (W_l). The

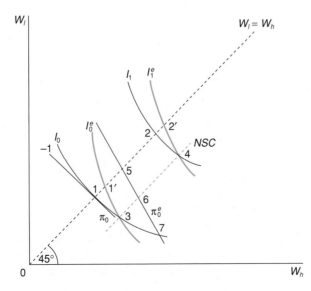

Figure 7.12
Locating the efficient
principal–agent contract

wage only has these two values, as output is either high (Q_h) or low (Q_l). Output depends on effort and nature $Q(e, \theta)$, e.g. a crop depends on the farmer's (agent's) effort and the weather (nature). To keep the example simple assume the probability of high output as determined by nature is 0.5 when $e = 0$ but is greater than 0.5 when $e > 0$ (effort is supplied). In Figure 7.12 points 1 and 2 are on no-effort indifference curves I_0 and I_1. As with the insurance case, their slope as they cross the 45° line is $-p/(1 - p)$. Here $0.5/1 - 0.5 = -1$ and hence the marked slope through point 1. I_0 and I_1 are also symmetrical around the 45° line. If the agent provides effort two changes take place. First, because effort is a source of disutility the expected wage must be higher so that indifference curves that offer the same subjective utility as I_0 and I_1 must be further from the origin here at points 1' and 2'. Second, $e > 0$ increases p so the $-p/(1 - p)$ must become greater in absolute value, so that on the 45° line the indifference curves must be steeper.

This is also captured in Figure 7.12. The two new indifference curves are labelled I_0^e and I_1^e and represent the same utility levels as I_0 and I_1 and hence the use of 1' and 2' to signal this. Where I_0 and I_1 cross I_0^e and I_1^e at points 3 and 4 is important as to the north-west of points 3 and 4 no-effort offers greater utility to the agent than effort as the space involves being above I_0 (I_1) but below I_0^e (I_1^e). Similarly, to the south-east of points 3 and 4, effort offers greater utility to the agent than no-effort as the space involves being above I_0^e (I_1^e) but below I_0 (I_1). In this way, points 3 and 4 are two points on the boundary that cause the agent to choose effort thereby representing the no-shirking constraint (*NSC*) or incentive-compatibility constraint.

What of the second constraint? π_0 is the no effort isoprofit line at point 1 which also changes location and slope (from -1) when wage is increased to induce effort whilst holding profit constant. The higher wage causes point 1 to migrate to a point such as 5 and, given the greater probability of having to pay W_h, a greater fall in W_l is required to hold profit constant. That is, π_0^e must be steeper than π_0 as illustrated. Points to the south of point 6 in area 6-7-3 are attractive to the principal as they offer wage combinations that would place the principal on a higher isoprofit line. It is now evident where an efficient contract would be found. Assuming, for convenience, I_0 is the reservation utility U_r, then a contract at point 3 would induce effort and maximise profit. More generally, the non-shirking constraint is the core of a principal–agent model and the contract is located where the reservation-utility constraint cuts it.

7.3.5 Utility maximisation in forming expectations in a risky world

The adjustments so far indicate that, with incomplete information, it is expected values that can be employed to help make economically rational decisions. The expected values have been formed by applying probability weights to relevant outcomes, or consequences. However, expectations formation involves more complications than this and involves distinct schools of thought.

To give insight to expectations formation in a microeconomic context the familiar cobweb result is rehearsed. It is the stuff of many early economics chapters introducing supply and demand as it was in Chapters 2 and 3 but it is worth rehearsing it again here. The proposition is that agricultural markets are subject to 'hog' cycles of high–low–high–low prices being successively observed. The essence of this story is captured in Figure 7.13 where the supply and demand of an agricultural product (A) is depicted. The idea is that you start out of equilibrium at point 1 where quantity is low at q_l and price is high at P_h. The seemingly myopic farm community expects next period's price to be this period's price, so that, more formally, $E(P_t + 1) = P_t$, where t is time period and E stands for expected. At P_h the appropriate supply decision is at 2 with a high quantity, q_h, being produced at the end of the next growing season, when price in the context of q_h will be a low price set at P_l from point 3 on the demand curve. Myopic farmers will assume P_l for

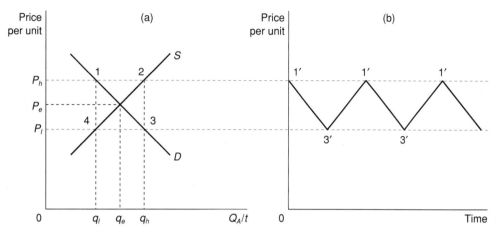

Figure 7.13 **Price cycling**

the next season and produce q_l associated with point 4, so as a consequence, P_h will once more appear. As drawn, the absolute slopes of the demand and supply curves are the same and the cycle will have a constant amplitude for ever (see Figure 7.13 (b)).

This costly result of every price expectation being falsified by the market outcome arises because the 'irrational' farmer uses only one piece of information (the present price) and couples it with the assumption of no other changes apart from their own reaction in making a current forecast. But is this likely behaviour for a utility-maximising actor in this context? Looking at the situation from the outside, the errors in price expectation are perfectly forecastable, as they are systematically repeated.

The notion of adaptive expectation suggests that the individual bases a price forecast on the past and current experience of prices, so that the general function for the expected price (P_{et+1}) would be:

$$P_{et+1} = f(P_t, P_{t-1}, P_{t-2}, P_{t-3}, \ldots) \tag{7.32}$$

An illustration of using this approach might involve the adage that 'we learn from our mistakes' rather than, as above, simply endlessly repeating them. It is the difference between farmers with having, say, twenty years' experience and those who have had the same experience twenty times. Looking backwards just one period would allow the farmer to form an expectation as follows:

$$E(P_{t+1}) = E(P_t) + \theta[P_t - E(P_t)] \tag{7.33}$$
[current forecast] = [previous forecast] + θ [previous forecast error]

where P_t is the actual price in period t. This simply says the expected price next period will be the one expected this period plus a proportion θ ($0 < \theta < 1$) of the error made in forecasting this period's price. For example, if P_t was £10 per unit, $E(P_t)$ was £4 and $\theta = 0.5$ then $E(P_{t+1})$ would be £4 + 0.5(£10 − £4) = £7. In this way, the equilibrium price would be located after a number of periods elapsed and, without an exogenous change, the forecast error approaches zero.

There are a number of criticisms of this adaptive approach. The farmer is only looking backwards and restricting the information used to past values of the variable the individual is trying to forecast. Muth (1961) effectively argued that economic man should be modelled as if the individual formed expectations in an economically rational way. He felt this would involve using all information that was available and that, since the agricultural market is an economic construct, the rational actor would place the information an economic model creates to form a prediction. All profitable information (for which the expected marginal benefit of its use exceeds the marginal cost of its acquisition) and the use of an economic model are the hallmarks of an economically rational expectation – hence the phrase. This concept brings together the three elements of rationality, uncertainty and information.

The economically rational farmer poses the question in a world of uncertainty, what price should I expect, so that, if all others act like me, forming the identical forecast we will, on average, be correct. Expecting P_h and P_l in sequence means the individual's expectation is never realised and that cannot be rational. The economically rational farmer attempts (figuratively, or literally from experience, study, reading, etc.) to approximate the relevant supply and demand functions and feed in all profitable information and, in this way, will forecast the equilibrium value P_e as the price to use in supply decisions – supplying q_e in Figure 7.13. Because of uncertainty – events that cannot be anticipated – the forecast will typically be wrong for any single period but correct on average. On average, the errors will be zero and will contain no pattern as it would indicate information was being ignored, i.e. the information of the pattern if this were not the case. The variance (spread) of the errors will be as small as it can be, as it is the variance of the economic process itself. The farmers will have the best price forecast they can have.

7.3.6 Risk, unprotected sex and the spread of HIV-AIDS

With the exception of rape and contaminated blood transfusions, HIV is largely the outcome of individual choice and, therefore, should be amenable to economic modelling. Philipson and Posner (1993) are among the authors who have taken on this task. Their basic approach involves explaining why unsafe sex can increase expected utility of an individual i and a partner p who are assumed not to be altruistic towards each other.

If for simplicity i and p are assumed risk-neutral, the relevant decision can be cast as an expected value (EV) calculation. The expected value of safe over unsafe sex for an individual is equal to the benefits of unsafe sex over protected sex (B) minus the expected costs:

$$EV_i = B - C[P_{tp}(1 - P_i)P_p] \tag{7.34}$$

where

C = costs of becoming infected with the AIDS virus;
P_i = the probability that the individual, i, is already affected;
P_p = is the probability that partner p is already affected;
P_{tp} = the transmission probability as measured by the fraction of unprotected sexual acts between an infected p and unaffected i that result in infection;
B = the benefit of unsafe sex and is essentially viewed as the disutility of using a condom.

In the simplest version of the model it can be assumed the probability of transmission is unity and condoms are free, so that

$$EV_i = B - C(1 - P_i)P_p \tag{7.35}$$

The costs of becoming affected to i are both pecuniary and non-pecuniary. The pecuniary ones include medical costs and lost earnings net of tax – transfer receipts. The non-pecuniary ones include the disutility of pain and an anticipated earlier death, possible stigma costs and preclusion from certain types of future sexual activity. If $p_i = 1$, so that i is already infected, C goes to zero and a selfish infected person has no incentive to avoid unsafe sex and, in this sense, someone finding out they are HIV-positive may not be helpful. In less extreme circumstances for the virus to spread through voluntarism $EV_i > 0$ and the equivalent equation for the partner must also yield $EV_p > 0$. The boundary value of indifference between safe and unsafe sex occurs where $EV_i = 0$ and the probability value for i with respect to p is derived as

$$EV_i = B - C(1 - P_i)P_p = 0 \tag{7.36}$$

$$P_p = B/[C(1 - P_i)] \tag{7.37}$$

This translates into a boundary in the 'probability box' Figure 7.14 that divides no-risk sex from risky sex. A similar construction can be developed for individual p. When $P_i = 0$ attention is focused on the left-hand upright of the box, unsafe sex will be chosen by i if the benefit–cost ratio exceeds unity. Moving north from 0 this condition is met up to the point labelled $B/CP_p = 1$ for P_p values greater than those implied by this condition i chooses safe sex. The curve labelled i indicates the relevant boundary condition as P_i increases from zero towards 1. A similar construction can be developed for individual p and is labelled p in Figure 7.14. The two boundaries create five areas.

(i)   The north-west area is a no (trade) sex area as i refuses unsafe sex.
(ii) The south-east area is a no (trade) sex area as p refuses unsafe sex.
(iii) The middle horizontal-hatched elipse is a safe-sex zone as both i and p prefer safe sex.
(iv) The two cross-hatched shapes at the south-west and the north-east are the danger areas. The south-west is a low-probabilities unsafe-sex area (*LPUS*), where intuitively the low probabilities weight the costs sufficiently low for the benefit–cost ratio to exceed 1.
(v)   The north-east is a high-probabilities unsafe-sex area (*HPUS*) where intuitively the i and p already have high probabilities of being infected and there is less to gain from safe sex.

The existence of *LPUS* and *HPUS* explains how infection is voluntarily spread, creating a flow of new cases. Only at 0 where $P_i = P_p = 0$ and 0′ where $P_i = P_p = 1$ is this not the case. The authors elaborate this basic model to make it more realistic but the point is clear: unsafe voluntary sex can offer positive net expected utility, thereby facilitating the spread of HIV.

The associated policy issues are very complex but two, pointed out by the authors, deserve mention. First, to the extent there are externalities, chosen unsafe sex acts are too numerous. Such uninternalised externalities might take the pecuniary form – of those

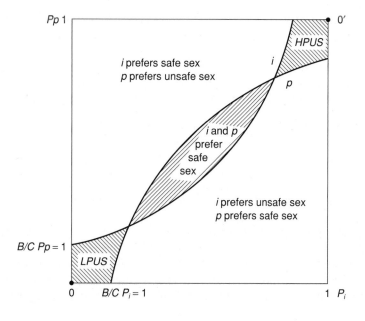

Figure 7.14

Expected values and (un)safe sex

Source: Philipson and Posner (1993).

who get infected not bearing their full medical, or other, costs – or the non-pecuniary form of future partners becoming infected from i or p. Not being infected benefits you and others, whose fate are ignored in the expected value calculation above. If externalities are internalised in the decision there might be less unsafe sex but individuals do enhance their expected *ex-ante* utility by choosing dangerous activities, e.g. mountaineering, and the economic model cannot condemn this. To other disciplines this will look odd, as from an *ex-post* perspective no one wants AIDS and policy should aim to minimise the stock of cases by eradicating the flow of new ones.

Second, implicit in this model is some hope. If individuals are ill-informed and simply set the P_i and P_p probabilities to P – the actual prevalence of the disease (stock of cases) in the population – then

$$EV = B - C(1 - P)P \tag{7.38}$$

$$EV = B - CP + CP^2 \tag{7.39}$$

$$dEV/dP = -C + 2CP \tag{7.40}$$

The derivative in equation (7.40) is negative as long as $P < 1/2$, which suggests as long as the incidence of infection in the population is not already very large, the flow of new infections should fall as the probability of infection increases.

This does not pretend to be an exhaustive discussion of the issues raised by HIV-AIDS but an important illustration of economically rational decision-making in the presence of risk.

7.3.7 Features to look for with asymmetric information problems

Asymmetric information problems come in many guises and it is difficult to summarise them completely; however, there are a number of features to look out for.

(i)   The first is that the nature of equilibrium becomes ambiguous. There is typically a separating and pooling equilibrium.

(ii) Second, sorting, or separating, is mainly achieved by meeting, or not meeting, an exit/entry (participation, no-quitting) constraint and an incentive compatibility (honesty, no-shirking) constraint.

(iii) Third, the need to maintain a reputation is a feature of many models, e.g. second-hand car dealers.

(iv) Finally, for this list the second and third characteristics tend to combine to imply some form of Paretian inefficiency. For the second-hand car dealer with a good reputation there is always the incentive in the short run to increase profits by 'cashing in' your reputation by selling low-quality cars at 'good-reputation prices' until the reputation is lost. Therefore, there needs to be an incentive to keep your reputation for good second-hand cars in the long run and this will take the form of an economic surplus. The implication is that price will exceed marginal cost, which reflects the value of information to the consumer that this will be a good second-hand car. Likewise, employers may need a reputation for honouring their labour contracts (see Section 10.5) when there may be a short-run incentive to renege on them. The signalling approach to education in Section 10.4 involves a negative social rate of return to creating a separating equilibrium.

7.4 Rationality and games

La Manna (2003: footnote 1 in Chapter 1) flags game theory as one of the inherently interesting aspects of economics and there is no doubt that it is an area of research that has attracted the 'beautiful minds' of economics. In the text some of the classic games are rehearsed as they become relevant to a particular topic. Rasmusen (2001) in the preface to his book on games and information lists 49 competitor titles arranged chronologically from 1988 (and there have been many more since 2001). There is clearly no shortage of relevant material.

The core of game theory, built from the work of Von Neumann and Morgenstern introduced at the beginning of this chapter, is interdependence of choices of individuals. Situations where the consequences of your decisions are dependent on the choices made by others are legion and hence the widespread applicability of game theory. Games come in many types and forms (see Hargreaves-Heap and Varoufakis 1995). They may be zero-sum (what one player gains another necessarily loses) or not, they may be cooperative, non-cooperative or some combination, they may be static or dynamic, they may involve complete or incomplete information and, as early as 1970, Shubik (1970) noted as many as 30 to 40 solution concepts to games. Given this, no wonder there are so many books! At their simplest, games have four elements:

(i)   There is a list of players who are going to strategically interact.
(ii) A list of choices or strategies they can adopt.
(iii) The order of play is stated – who goes first or do they move simultaneously.
(iv) There is a list of payoffs – the gains or losses that are at stake.

To solve games, players are assumed to be instrumentally rational (accounting for interdependence of decisions in a way that will suit them 'best' – i.e. they maximise their expected payoff).

To fix ideas and illustrate some basic points in the context of redistribution consider the zero-sum game portrayed in so-called normal or matrix[3] form in Table 7.3. The row player is rich R and the column player is poor C. It is a game of pure conflict in a context in which voting on a 'yes–no' basis will take place to redistribute from rich to the poor. As noted, what R loses C gains and how much will be redistributed will be the solution to the game.

If poor C is instrumentally rational they will realise that they have a dominant strategy in this game, that is, a strategy they should undertake irrespective of the choice of the other player (R). Looking at the possibilities, C can reason:

C plays Yes and R plays Yes $\Rightarrow$ 20;
C plays Yes and R plays No $\Rightarrow$ 15;
C plays No and R plays No $\Rightarrow$ 0;
C plays No and R plays Yes $\Rightarrow$ –10.

Table 7.3 **A redistributive game**

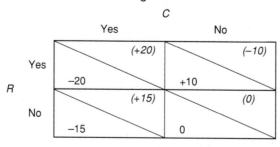

3. In 'normal form' nothing is said about the order of play so that the implication is that players are thinking and choosing in a simultaneous manner. In 'extensive form' games the sequence of play is clear. See Chapter 8 for an example.

C playing Yes dominates as a strategy irrespective of what *R* chooses and therefore it can be concluded that *C* plays Yes. *C* is displaying zero-order common knowledge of rationality in that they do not have to assume anything about *R*'s decision motivation. But rich *R* now displays what is termed 'first-order common knowledge of rationality' in that, by assuming that *C* is instrumentally rationally, *R* can conclude, on the same reasoning as above, that *C* will vote Yes. Given this it can be seen that *R*'s best response is to play No and lose 15 to poor *C*. Game over!

But is the game over? All this looks terribly harmless and obvious but, as highlighted in other sections of this text, there is a powerful implied world behind 'economic' reasoning. First, there are alternatives to instrumental rationality (see Chapter 7). Rich *R* might employ an empathy-type rule and put themselves in *C*'s place and think 'If I was poor *C*, who may be poor for no good reason, I would like *R* to vote yes'. If this empathy rule is followed, 20 would be redistributed in the solution to the game and not instrumentally rational 15. If *C* thinks 'you carry your own pack in this life' and resents being the object of redistributive charity they might vote No and, depending on *R*'s motivation, *C* would receive 0 or lose 10!

Second, *C* might not have the ability to conduct dominance reasoning and set out the outcomes of strategy combinations in the way done above and might fall back on tossing a coin or the like. The limits to cognitive ability in the form of bounded rationality might arise, so that perhaps only two of the four possible pairs of strategies are considered and the better of the two chosen. (People typically have to be taught to play games.)

Third, *R* has to display first-order common knowledge of rationality to locate their best strategy – they have to act on the assumption that *C* is instrumentally rational.

In the context of this particular game these worries may appear 'over-cooked' but in more complex games, with incomplete information, the solution concepts get very difficult and are far from 'obvious'. Note: here the game to be played was taken as a 'given'; however, there is a further literature that goes back a step and poses the question as to what rules of a game or 'mechanism' can be devised to produce a 'best' equilibrium when the 'designed' game is played. This is the mechanism design literature (see Dutta 1999). In Chapter 6 the Clarke–Groves mechanism to elicit truthful individual preference revelation for public goods essentially has this structure.

7.5 Challenge: How limited are the economic conceptions of rationality, risk and information?

This chapter has posed some big questions and outlined some of the answers typical of conventional microeconomic theory. However, nothing is beyond criticism and improvement. Many commentators have been unconvinced about the answers outlined above. It is the work of some of the critical economists that is now introduced.

7.5.1 Forms of rationality

Beginning with the reliance on instrumental rationality employed in the game above, Hargreaves-Heap and Varoufakis (1995) note a number of objections to setting up games in this way.

a) Commentators have questioned instrumental rationality. For example, to prevent bullying it might seem a good idea to physically retaliate; it is an instrumentally rational choice, whereas reason says that you might want to put yourself in their place and appeal to the notion that you would, or should, constrain your behaviour to the way that you would like to be treated. That is, you refrain from physical retaliation because you employ an empathy-type rule. Reflection suggests that instrumental rationality would not be the appropriate solution. The American comedian Emo Phillips used to crack a joke about finding a wallet with many dollars in it and thinking what he ought to do with the wallet. He performs a mental experiment of thinking what would I like to happen if this lost wallet was mine. He feigns thought for a while and concludes 'I would like to be taught a lesson for my carelessness'. In fact, of course, many people are honest and lost wallets are often returned.

b) Immanuel Kant, the philosopher, wrote about the categorical imperative and posed the question, would it be possible for us all to act in this way, and if it is not, then you would not choose that action. Doing the 'right' thing becomes important. For example, you do not evade taxes because you realise that, if all people evade taxes, there would be no public goods and you reject the free-rider preference ('I don't pay taxes all others do' because you can anticipate this secures your third preference, 'no one pays taxes', rather than your second option, 'I and all others pay taxes'). That is the categorical imperative. In contrast, Ludwig Wittgenstein argued that people's actions are part of the practices of society in which they find themselves, so that you are born into and inculcated into the values of that particular society and instrumental rationality really does not come into it.

c) There is also the concept of cognitive dissonance: reasoning used to justify action not to determine it, so that for example if people find themselves smoking as a habit they choose to think it is a safe action in order to justify what they have already chosen.

d) Fehr and Gachter (2000) explore reciprocity as a motivation. 'Reciprocity means that in response to friendly actions, people are frequently much nicer and much more cooperative than predicted by the self interest model: conversely, in response to hostile actions they are frequently much more nasty and even brutal' (p. 159). Individuals take revenge and repay gifts incurring cost that generate neither present nor future material rewards. In public goods experiments the authors have found where there are punishment opportunities reciprocal types can induce selfish types to choose the cooperative action as opposed to free-riding.

As always, there is nothing neutral. Adopting instrumental rationality is one assumption among many that might have been chosen.

More generally, a wide variety of economists, sociologists and other social scientists have explored what is meant by 'rational' behaviour and choice. In order to give meaning to 'rationality', it is necessary to take a view on at least four questions. These questions form the schema below:

Question	Answer		
1. Does the individual have to have perfect information?	Yes	No	Not applicable
2. Does the individual go through a deliberative process, including belief formation that they can *ex ante* (or *ex post*) explain, or are they simply assumed to know their beliefs or preferences?	Yes	No	Not applicable
3. Has the individual the capacity to be unboundedly rational?	Yes	No	Not applicable
4. Is the result of acting rationally the best possible outcome for the individual?	Yes	No	Not applicable

Depending on your answers, different definitions of rationality can be isolated. The material of Section 1.5 in Chapter 1 related to utility maximisation in a riskless world of perfect information and would correspond to perfect unbounded rationality (Tisdell 1975), in that the answers to the four questions would be Q1–Yes, Q2–N/A, Q3–Yes, Q4–Yes.

It is generally recognised that these conditions will not be met but, for many, this does not mean this concept of rationality is rejected. It may be sufficient for accurate prediction. It may be true of actions on average but not true for an isolated individual. It may be possible to soften some of the assumptions without affecting the results. For example, Tisdell notes an intransitive preference ordering for a set of possibilities that are unattainable, or inferior, will not affect choices made.

Further, there is the survival-type argument, which arises in many defences of economic theorising, and claims that individuals that act as postulated will be economically more successful than those who do not and, by a process akin to 'natural selection', come to dominate the economy – good rationalists (perfect and unbounded) will drive out bad ones.

Another favourite line of argument is that people can learn from experience in the long run and get to approximate perfect unbounded rationality in the long run. For example, in the long run in perfect competition all plans are fulfilled and no economic actor has any regrets, in that they would not wish to change any choices they have made with the benefit of hindsight. But, again, as Tisdell points out, this is not foolproof, in that past decisions may have been optimal by chance.

A number of economists have imported ideas from psychology, one of which is the concept of cognitive dissonance. This concept suggests that individuals need to feel their preferences and actions are consistent or make sense (see Akerlof and Dickens 1982), so that something has to change when the preferences the individuals hold and the consequences of their choices are in contradiction. In these circumstances, individuals may revise their conception of their past preferences to fit in with actual current outcomes, confirming they would not wish to change their past choices, as *ex-post* consequences appear to be consistent with their preferences. Once preferences can change it raises the prospect that they are the product of experience, rather than the shapers of experience.

Opposition to the notion of perfect unbounded rationality is associated with authors like Shackle (1949) and Simon (1959). Shackle required perfect unbounded rationality to involve perfect information but notes that the only full information that is obtainable is of the past, but the past is fixed and, paradoxically, cannot be the object of choice. Simon was an Economics Nobel prize winner in 1978 who, amongst other issues, was critical of the notion of rationality in economics. He argued that there were limits to the computational and processing capabilities of the decision-maker, which is a constraint making possible only a limited form or degree of rationality, the so-called 'bounded rationality' noted above.

Two types of model are consistent with the 'bounded' notion:

(1) Where the set of alternatives is reduced to the degree of complication the decision-maker can handle and then those options are ranked and the best chosen. This is a type of optimisation model but is approximately optimal; there may be better but unconsidered options available in the absence of information processing limitations.
(2) Satisficing models begin with an aspiration level of the value of the outcome, which is satisfactory or acceptable (N.B. with a stable environment and repeated choices the aspiration level will be revised upward towards the optimum level). The decision-maker considers a broader set of alternatives than the approximate optimisation model but stops searching when a satisfactory, rather than the best solution, is found.

However, large questions remain:

(i)   How are aspiration levels set?
(ii) Which alternatives are considered?
(iii) In what order are they considered?

It is not obvious that replicating the process of choice-making is useful in *a priori* analysis of the consequences of choice making.

It is a short step from these ideas to the notion of 'rules of thumb', convention and habits in choice-making in a world of incomplete information, i.e. heuristics. Whilst some rules can be shown to approximate optimal decision-making, it does not necessarily imply they are the product of a type of rational choice-making process. The subjective expected utility approach to risky situations softens perfect unbounded rationality to the extent of allowing for less than perfect information about the state of the world will arise in the future, but retains unbounded rationality in the sense that individuals have to conform to the axioms elaborated above which describe a view of consistency etc. This approach is worthy of separate appraisal in that it forms the conventional way to model risk.

7.5.2 Criticisms of the subjective expected utility approach

Criticisms of the Von Neuman–Morgenstern approach to dealing with risk are legion, but here only some of the key issues will be reported (see Machina 1987, for further discussion).

Individuals seem to consistently violate the axioms of the theory. With respect to axiom 1, they are seen to exhibit non-transitive choices in the famous P-bet $-bet experiment. The experiment offers a choice over two lotteries: $L_1 = (\$X, \$x : p, 1 - p)$ and $L_2 = (\$Y, \$y : q, 1 - q)$ where the values are such that $\$X > \$x$; $\$Y > \$y$; $\$Y > \$X$ and probability $p > q$.

L_1 is known as the P-bet because it involves a higher probability of winning, whereas L_2 is known as the $-bet because it offers a larger payoff when winning occurs. When asked, individuals state a preference for the P-bet over the $-bet but offer a higher monetary valuation of the $-bet. This may seem harmless but it is in fact very damaging to the foundations of economics.

Recall the static consumer equilibrium of Section 1.5.2 of Chapter 1. In the depicted equilibrium the solution was chosen by the logic of utility maximisation, so that quantities y^* and x^* could be assumed to be a reflection of the individual's preference map. The economist holds dear the notion that actual choices reveal individual preferences, but in the P-bet $-bet this appears to be violated in that valuation may not reveal preference. For transitivity, the valuation of the $-bet as greater than the valuation of the P-bet should indicate a preference for the $-bet over the P-bet, but in fact individuals typically claim to have a preference for the P-bet over the $-bet, which is inconsistent and very damaging to the idea of valuations (actual choices) revealing individual preferences.

The violation of axiom (iv) has attracted a greater amount of concern as it underpins the additively separable property of the subjective expected utility approach. In particular, the Allais paradox (Allais was a Nobel prize winner in 1988) is thought by some critics to be very damaging. The paradox is usually set up along the following lines with four lotteries and three states of the world. Table 7.4 provides the relevant information.

Note that the lotteries L_1 and L_3 have common S_1 and S_2 payoffs and that lotteries L_2 and L_4 have common S_1 and S_2 payoffs. The S_3 payoffs are identical in L_1 and L_2 and L_3 and L_4. The question posed is how an individual would choose between the pair L_1 and

Table 7.4 The Allais paradox

State of world Probability	S_1 0.01	S_2 0.1	S_3 0.89
L_1	£500,000	£500,000	£500,000
L_2	£0	£1,000,000	£500,000
L_3	£500,000	£500,000	£0
L_4	£0	£1,000,000	£0

L_2 and the pair L_3 and L_4. The answer developed here is that they would be ranked by the expected utilities they generate.

To make matters concrete suppose someone's Von Neumann–Morgenstern utility function was empirically established to be $U = U(Y) = \ln Y$ as in Figure 7.4; then the VN-M utility values of the payoffs are established as the natural log of the payoff value.

Y	U(Y)
0	0
500,000	13.12
1,000,000	13.82

The expected utility rule says that the four lotteries can now be evaluated by the sum of the probability-weighted average of the payoff consequences so that

$$L_1 = (0.01 \times 13.12) + (0.1 \times 13.12) + (0.89 \times 13.12)$$

Because the probabilities sum to 1 and the utility payoffs are all 13.12, the expected utility value of $L_1 = 13.12$. (Note that the first two terms sum to 1.44 and the third is 11.68.)

$$L_2 = (0.01 \times 0) + (0.1 \times 13.82) + (0.89 \times 13.12)$$
$$= 0 + 1.382 + 11.68 = 13.06$$

Given this, L_1 is preferred to L_2 by the individual. What about the second pair?

$$L_3 = (0.01 \times 13.12) + (0.1 \times 13.12) + (0.89 \times 0) = \text{the first two terms of } L_1 \text{ plus zero}$$
$$= 1.44.$$

$$L_4 = (0.01 \times 0) + (0.1 \times 13.82) + (0.89 \times 0) = \text{the first two terms of } L_3 \text{ plus zero}$$
$$= 1.382.$$

Given this, L_3 is preferred to L_4 by the individual. So what is the problem?

The problem is that, confronted with choices of this kind, individuals typically prefer L_1 to L_2, usually rationalised on the grounds that a certain £500,000 (the payoff in all states of the world) is preferred to a 10% chance of a much larger sum (£1,000,000) and a 1% of £0, but prefer L_4 to L_3. This seems reasonable in that in choosing L_4 to L_3 you are exchanging an 11% chance of £500,000 for a 10% chance of £1,000,000. But expected utility theory correctly predicted L_1 is preferred to L_2 and incorrectly predicted L_3 is preferred to L_4. Recall axiom (iv) states: if x_1 and x_2 are equally attractive and x_3 and p are common (the same), then the two lotteries $L_1 = [x_1, x_3 : p, 1 - p]$ and L_2 is $[x_2, x_3 : p, 1 - p]$ must be equally attractive for any values of p and x_3.

Subjective expected utility theory (SEUT) would require:

$$1.0U(\text{£500,000}) > .01U(\text{£0}) + 0.1U(\text{£1,000,000}) + 0.89U(\text{£500,000}), \text{ i.e. } L_1 > L_2$$

subtract $0.89U(\text{£500,000})$ and add $0.89U(\text{£0})$ to both sides

$$0.11U(\text{£500,000}) + 0.89U(\text{£0}) > 0.1U(\text{£1,000,000}) + 0.90U(\text{£0}), \text{ i.e. } L_3 > L_4$$

Here S_1 and S_2 are not equally attractive in L_1 and L_3 and S_1 and S_2 are not equally attractive in L_2 and L_4 and the choice over each pair of lotteries is being influenced by the common-to-each-pair S_3 payoffs. This is what the axiom seeks to rule out because it means that it cannot be the case that the individual is evaluating the risky choices as the simple sum of the probability-weighted payoffs in each state of the world. There may be a rule they are conforming to, but it is not the simple one postulated in SEUT. Before noting responses to criticism of subjective expected utility theory there are others that require introduction.

Individuals violate axiom (v) in that they are susceptible to so-called framing effects (see Chapter 2). That is, even sophisticated respondents answer differently depending on how a choice is presented to them. When offered a single probability they answer differently than if given the same probability represented as the joint occurrence of four probabilities (joint occurrence makes gains more attractive and losses less so). Individuals treat the same expected wealth calculations differently depending on whether they are framed as 'gains' or 'losses'. Further, the same information expressed as a matrix, a decision tree or in words elicits different responses. In the face of this, results appear to be an artefact of the question or problem framing and individuals are not conforming to the axioms of the theory.

Finally, in this brief treatment of issues relating to subjective expected utility theory there are further probability problems. In subjective expected utility theory individuals can be assumed to be using objective observation-based probabilities or personal subjective ones. If personal subjective ones are employed it is not the case that anything will do. Rather, because it is about rationality, it would be desirable that these probabilities be reasonable in the light of the information an individual has (i.e. they can be rationalised by the individual – effectively question 2 in the preceding subsection). This is where another famous paradox can be reported. It is the Ellsberg paradox. An opaque jar contains 90 balls of which 30 are red and 60 are yellow or blue. Individuals are then confronted with two pairs of prospects: L_1 £1000 if they pull out one of the (thirty) red balls and L_2 £1000 if they pull out one of the (unknown number of) blue balls; L_3 £1000 if they pull out one of the (unknown number of) red or yellow balls and L_4 £1000 if they pull out one of the (sixty) blue or yellow balls. Individuals typically choose L_1 over L_2 and L_4 over L_3 but in choosing L_1 they must be assuming there are more red than blue balls in the jar and in choosing L_4 more blue than red (yellow is common to both L_3 and L_4). The clue to what individuals appear to do is provided by the words in brackets. That is, they are attracted by the option with the known probability even if these choices reflect an inconsistent view of probabilities.

Overall then, expected utility theory has been heavily questioned, but before assessing the strength of those questions it is information as a good that is considered.

7.5.3 Problems with information

As introduced in Chapter 5, information is an unusual economic good in that its characteristics exemplify market failure. Once it exists, information is non-rival in use in that one individual's use of a piece of information does not reduce the stock of information, so that the marginal cost of an additional user is zero. Indeed, if enhancement of the information by additional users is allowed for, the stock may actually grow with use and the marginal cost of use is negative! Additionally, it is very difficult to make information excludable in that once it has been passed on, or sold, by the original possessor of information, that person can also pass or sell it on. If this is the case, the original possessor of information will find it very difficult to establish a property right over their information as non-excludability raises the spectre of free-riding. Given all this, it is not surprising there is public policy intervention in the information market with patent laws and the like to preserve some property rights.

These points are not elaborated here but it is worth noting that people may not interpret the same piece of information in the same way, or may not be able to pass on information even if they wish to. Individuals have what is sometimes called 'tacit knowledge' that inheres in them, which they cannot consciously pass on. All sorts of information can be summarised in a recipe book but following the book may not give the desired results. Countries that buy say Western technologies often cannot make them work successfully without the help of experts, because the experts have unconsciously acquired knowledge of how to make a process work that they cannot articulate. Knowledge of economic theory can be gained from a myriad of excellent sources, e.g. textbooks, self-study guides and the Internet. So, why is it attractive to have lectures? It may be good trade union activity on the part of academics but less cynically it is important to see how something is explained live to get pace, emphasis and a guide to the level of understanding some people have. Good lectures can have an impact on your thinking that you may not wholly understand. As is well known, this cannot be guaranteed!

Moving from an almost mystical view of information to a more concrete one raises the question of how an individual is meant to respond to an information message. The answer is they are meant to update their prior probabilities in a Bayesian way to form posterior probabilities. This was the process alluded to in Section 7.3. The following example elaborates Salop (1987). Imagine a witness sees you knocked down and rendered memoryless by a 'hit and run' taxi driver on your holiday in Bath. Bath only has two taxi companies, White Taxies and Black Taxies. The latter have 85% of the total taxis in Bath. The witness is known to be 100% reliable in spotting taxis as such and 80% reliable in distinguishing their colour. You may wish to sue the White Taxi Company as the witness says the taxi that hit you was white. For you to gain compensation a court has to be convinced that there is at least a 50% chance that the eyewitness was correct.

Given the above data, do you expect to win your case or not? Intuitively the answer appears to be 'yes'. After all, the witness is 100% reliable in taxi recognition and 80% reliable in colour identification. However, developing the posterior probabilities in line with Bayes's theorem unfortunately shows that your case will be lost. This counter-intuitive result can be established with the aid of Table 7.5.

The prior probabilities are 15% chance you were hit by a white taxi and 85% you were hit by a black one. The witness can give the court one of two messages. Message 1 says the taxi was white with the likelihood of that being the case being 80% so that there is a 20% chance because of the witnesses error rate that the taxi was black when the witness says it was white. Message 2 says the taxi was black with the likelihood of that being the case being 80% when it was black, so that there is a 20% chance because of the witness's error rate that the taxi was white when the witness says it was black. The joint probability of the state of the world and the receipt of message 1 or 2 is the next step in the calculation. The probabilities are: white taxi witness says white (12%); white taxi witness says black (3%); black taxi witness says white (17%); black taxi witness says black (68%).

The posterior probabilities are formed by dividing through by the overall probabilities of receiving each message, namely 29% (12% + 17%) white and 71% (3% + 68%) black.

Table 7.5 Bayesian updating

State of world (s)	Prior probability (p_s)	Message likelihood in each state of world $(q_m \mid s)$		Joint probability of state of world and message $(j_{s.m} = p_s \times q_m \mid s)$		Posterior probability $(p_{sm} = j_{s.m}) q_m$	
		m_1 (White)	m_2 (Black)	m_1	m_2	m_1	m_2
S_1 (White)	0.15	0.8	0.2	0.12	0.03	0.41 True W	0.04 False B
S_2 (Black)	0.85	0.2	0.8	0.17	0.68	0.59 False W	0.96 True B
			$(q_m = 1)$	0.29 q_{m1}	0.71 q_{m2}	1.0	1.0

The posterior to the message probabilities are: it was truly white taxi, witness says white (41%); it was truly a white taxi, witness falsely says black (4%); it was truly a black taxi, witness falsely says white (59%); it was truly a black taxi, witness says black (96%). When the witness says, in court, it was a white taxi, there is only a 41% chance they are correct – unfortunately not enough to receive compensation. The 41% comes from dividing the probability of being truly white when the message white is received (0.12) by the total probability of receiving the message white (0.29).

It is now possible to demonstrate the prior probabilities are the expected value of the posterior probabilities when the weights are total likelihood of receiving each message (q_{m_1} and q_{m_2} above). In schema form:

white 0.04 | m_2		white 0.15		white 0.41 | m_1
black 0.96 | m_2		black 0.85		black 0.59 | m_1

S_1 (white) 0	posterior	priors	posterior	S_1 (white) 1
S_2 (black) 1	m_2 (black) received		m_1 (white) received	S_2 (black) 0

In the information-buying example, *ex ante* you do not know if you will receive message 1 or 2 but you do know that there is a 0.29 chance of m_1 and a 0.71 chance of m_2. Hence if you form the expected value of the posterior probabilities it will be for

$$S_1 = 0.71 \times 0.04 + 0.29 \times 0.41 = 0.029 + 0.12 = 0.15 \text{ and}$$
$$S_2 = 0.71 \times 0.96 + 0.29 \times 0.59 = 0.68 + 0.17 = 0.85$$

Whilst this is the logical way for amending prior probabilities on the basis of additional information, it seems far from a simple procedure and in experiments individuals seldom do it and for many this is a criticism.

7.5.4 How to respond to criticisms

Nobody likes criticism and most individuals are anxious to respond usually to defend their position. Economic theoreticians are no different. The first line of any defence is the question of what you want theory to do for you, as it can have several purposes. It is then possible to say that the theory was not designed to answer that question. What are plausible roles for theorising? Given the B for boring in Chapter 1 it has already been recognised that building economic models is the central work of microeconomics. However, there are several different tasks that you might wish a good economic model to perform.

First, although involving abstraction, some readers will want models to be descriptive of the processes underlying any question to hand. In this respect, any assumptions and/or axioms adopted need to approximate what people know and the processes they enact.

Second, in a so-called positivistic methodology predictive capacity is all. The world is one in which (if this model applied) the following predictions would arise and these are not resultant from the assumptions of the model itself and are potentially falsifiable by appeal to empirical evidence.

Third, it is possible to want an economic model to serve a postdictive purpose. In this perspective all behaviour will appear to be economically optimal once a situation has been closely examined. *Ex post* apparent anomalous behaviour can be repaired when additional transactions costs and/or constraints are introduced into the analysis.

Whereas this view tends to imply individuals always 'do the right thing', the fourth normative, or prescriptive, approach suggests that individuals do the wrong things. In these circumstances with good theorising it may be possible to tell people how they should, or ought to, make choices under certain circumstances. That is, you may want a theory to be descriptive, predictive, postdictive or prescriptive or some combination of these roles.

Taking subjective expected utility theory as an example, in Section 7.4.2 above, a number of criticisms were elaborated. Given the criticisms, Schoemaker (1982) doubts that the theory can be descriptive, predictive, postdictive or prescriptive. It is not descriptive as individuals do not analyse issues or form probabilities in the way required of the theory. It is not predictive, as individuals do not appear to conform to the predictions, for example in the form of insurance purchase. As for the postdictive role, this may not be all that powerful; after all, with enough ingenuity all theories can be sustained until they go out of fashion when adherents to the theory retire or pass away. Is subjective expected utility prescriptive? Schoemaker suggests that the axioms are too far removed from what actual individuals actually do to indicate a normative role for the theory.

Many others take a different view. They respond to criticisms of this well-accepted theory. The first is to simply pose the question how would the existing theory have to be amended in order to incorporate the observed criticism. This is sometimes called an axiomatic response to criticism (see Frey and Eichenberger 1989). How could the expected utility rule be amended to avoid the Allais paradox is a question that has been explored by some theorists. Those anxious to preserve existing theory can always turn to the issue that the theory is for idealised conditions and anomalies are the product of the frictions of the real world. In this respect, it is usually always possible to find some form of transactions costs, imperfect information, etc. that will repair the theory (the postdictive role of theory). In this perspective, deviant observations are more apparent than real. Hirshleifer and Riley (1992), for example, outline a set of lottery choices that prevent the Allais paradox arising. What might be termed a pragmatic approach recognises that economic theory may well not be able to do everything and it may well be the case that certain things within its bounds have to remain unresolved. Valuations may not always reveal preferences but a psychologist might simply say preference and valuation are different concepts and you are in error if you want them always to be in accord.

The massive criticism of subjective expected utility theory is that it does not deal with real uncertainty, in that it assumes the possible *s* states of the world are capable of being listed when true uncertainty is about states of the world arising that no one can currently conceive of – 'the future is imaginable but is not knowable' (Wiseman 1980: 474). While this is true, it is also true that advocates of this line of reasoning have, as yet, to provide a fully articulated alternative to subjective expected utility theory as a way of dealing with risk that has commanded wide assent.

7.6 Summary

This chapter has covered the basic economic approach to the issues of risk, information and, in later sections, rationality. These crucial concepts show up in all the remaining chapters of the text and, as such, cannot be ignored. It is very easy to become convinced with a line of theorising if the reader is carefully led along the apparently uncontroversial blueprint of its construction. Close up hand magic works by focusing your attention only where the conjuror wants your attention to be. To see how things 'work' it is necessary to raise your head. Metaphorically, this is the case with microeconomic theory. In this chapter it has been suggested that individual economic actors will:

(i) if risk-averse, buy full insurance at a fair premium; also, if risk-averse, buy full insurance at a fair premium plus a 'loading' that does not exceed the Markowitz risk premium;

(ii) purchase information in a risky context if the gain in expected utility exceeds the utility price of the message;

(iii) set incentives for individuals to signal their quality;

(iv) set contracts to induce participation and no-shirking;

(v) use all profitable information (for which the expected marginal benefit exceeds the marginal cost of acquisition) and an economic model if their forecasting is to bear the hallmarks of an economically rational expectation;

(vi) play games.

But, as can be seen from the discussion of criticisms, these propositions are by no means obvious and unassailable. As noted in Chapter 1, it is the task of the reader to constantly question the bases or credentials of what is taken to be knowledge.

References

Akerlof, G.A. and Dickens, W.T. (1982) The economics of cognitive dissonance, *American Economic Review*, 72 (3): 307–19.

Bosworth, D., Dawkins, P. and Stromback, T. (1996) *The Economics of the Labour Market*, Harlow: Addison Wesley Longman.

Dutta, P. (1999) *Strategies and Games – Theory and Practice*, Cambridge, Mass.: The MIT Press.

Edgeworth, F.Y. (1881) *Mathematical Psychics*, London: Kegan Paul.

Fama, E.F. (1970) Efficient capital markets: a review of theory and empirical work, *Journal of Finance*, 25: 383–417.

Fehr, E. and Gachter, S. (2000) Fairness and retaliation: the economics of reciprocity, *Journal of Economic Perspectives*, 14: 158–81.

Frey, B.S. and Eichenberger, R. (1989) Anomalies and institutions, *Journal of Institutional and Theoretical Economics*, 145: 423–37.

Hargreaves-Heap, S.P. and Varoufakis, Y. (1995) *Game Theory: a Critical Introduction*, London and New York: Routledge.

Hemenway, D. (1988) *Prices and Choices – Microeconomic Vignettes*, 2nd edn, Cambridge, Mass.: Ballinger.

Hirshleifer, J. and Riley, J.R. (1992) *The Analytics of Uncertainty and Information*, Cambridge: Cambridge University Press.

Kahneman, D. and Tversky, A. (1979) Prospect theory: an analysis of decision under risk, *Econometrica*, 47 March: 263–91.

La Manna, M. (2003) Letters and opinion, *Times Higher Education Supplement*, 9 May, No. 1588, p. 15.

Machina, M.J. (1987) Choice under uncertainty: problems solved and unsolved, *Journal of Economic Perspectives*, 1 (1) Summer: 121–54.

Macho-Stadler, I. and Perez-Castrillo, J.D. (2001) *An Introduction to the Economics of Information*, 2nd edn, Oxford: Oxford University Press.

Muth, J. (1961) Rational expectations and the theory of price movements, *Econometrica*, 39 July: 315–34.

Ng, Y.K. (1977) Towards a theory of third best, *Public Finance / Finances Publiques*, 32 (1): 1–15.

Pauly, M.V. (1968) The economics of moral hazard: comment, *American Economic Review*, 58 (3) June: 231–7.

Philipson, T.J. and Posner, R.A. (1993) *Private Choices and Public Health: The AIDS Epidemic in an Economic Perspective*, Cambridge, Mass.: Harvard University Press.

Rasmusen, E. (2001) *Games and Information – an Introduction to Game Theory*, 3rd edn, Oxford: Blackwell.

Salop, S.C. (1987) Evaluating uncertain evidence with Sir Thomas Bayes: a note for teachers, *Journal of Economic Perspectives*, 1 (1) Summer: 155–9.

Schoemaker, P.J.H. (1982) The expected utility model, *Journal of Economic Literature*, 20 June: 529–63.

Shackle, G.L.S. (1949) *Expectations in Economics*, Cambridge: Cambridge University Press.

Shubik, M. (1970) A curmudgeon's guide to microeconomics, *Journal of Economic Literature*, 8 June: 405–34.

Simon, H.A. (1959) Theories of decision-making in economics and behavioral science, *American Economic Review*, 49: 253–83.

Spence, M. (1973) Job market signalling, *Quarterly Journal of Economics*, 87 August: 355–74.

Stiglitz, J.E. (1985) Information and economic analysis: a perspective, *Economic Journal*, 95 Conference Papers: 21–41.

Tisdell, C. (1975) Concepts of rationality in economics, *Philosophy of the Social Sciences*, 5: 259–72.

Von Neumann, J. and Morgenstern, O. (1944) *Theory of Games and Economic Behavior*, Princeton, NJ: Princeton University Press.

Wiseman, J. (1980) Costs and decisions, pp. 473–90 in D.A. Currie and W. Peters (eds) *Contemporary Economic Analysis* Vol. 2 London: Croom Helm.

CHAPTER 8

Time, fundamental commodities, discounting and the economic analysis of knowledge creation

8.1 Introduction

Time is the fourth dimension. So far this concept, which in some ways describes existence, has been ignored. Individuals essentially have a block of expected time available to them. Although people often choose to act as if they are going to live for ever, the empirical evidence tends to run counter to this cherished illusion! Once this illusion is set aside, then a crucial question is how to allocate (expected) time over competing uses of it. While dying people seldom say, 'I wish I had spent more time at work', they typically do spend much of their allotted span working (which suggests such a decision is an expected utility-maximising one). The early sections of this chapter consider the decisions people make with respect to work and time allocation in the context of so-called fundamental commodities, which require time as an input. A distinction is made between household (non-market) and market production and an indication of the importance of household production allows some measurement issues to be raised.

In later sections of the chapter, time arises in the context of delay and the economic significance of individuals apparently having a preference for the present over the future is explored. Time and the achievement of efficiency and the nature of time in economic modelling are also topics explored. As a way of capturing a number of themes explored in the first seven core chapters of the text, the process of knowledge creation has been considered.

8.2 Time allocation, production and output

If you ask individuals to think about production, or output, they typically tend to think about:

1) Market production;
2) A small number of people who are entrepreneurs and risk-takers;
3) Market production as being the result of combining market work hours with both raw materials and capital;
4) Capital goods that are physical (machines, factory buildings, etc.), whose construction is what is understood as the 'process of investment'.

However, central to richer accounts of microeconomics are fundamental commodities and human capital theory (developed mainly at the University of Chicago by Nobel prizewinners Theo Schultz and Gary Becker – in 1979 and 1992 respectively).

Their basic insights are that:

1) Non-market (household) production is quantitatively very important.
2) Virtually all people make entrepreneurial-type decisions involving risk.
3) Households are producers, just as much as firms are producers. Households are seen as producing fundamental commodities by combining own-time input with market and possibly public-sector inputs, e.g. combining own time, golf clubs (a market purchase) plus municipal golf course (a public-sector purchase) to produce the fundamental commodity of recreation.
4) Capital goods can be human (in the form of the skills and training individuals embody). Similarly, the process of human capital formation can also be seen as governed by the principles of investment appraisal.

In what follows it is helpful to distinguish between consumption and investment (or capital) goods:

Consumption goods:

1) Offer a direct source of utility or 'psychic benefit';
2) If the benefit lasts one period, the good is called a *non-durable consumption good*;
3) If the benefit lasts many periods the good is called a *durable consumption good*;
4) For non-market (household) production, the return is typically non-pecuniary (non-monetary) and, as such, less easily quantified (but no less valuable for that).

In contrast, for investment goods:

1) The utility they generate comes in an indirect form via a production process.
2) By definition, they are long lived and only partly used up in the current production period and this 'partial using up' is what is understood by the term depreciation.
3) For market production, the return is typically pecuniary (monetary) in form and lends itself to easy qualification.

Non-market (household) production is central to the way people actually live and this crucially involves time allocation. As a starting point, consider Figure 8.1. It shows a transformation curve TT'. At point T all available hours per period (say week or month) are devoted to leisure, whereas at zero leisure hours T' (all available hours per period) are devoted to non-market production. The shape of the frontier TT' indicates how leisure hours can be reduced to raise output in the form of non-market production. That is, the slope of TT' indicates the rate at which leisure reduction can be converted into household output. Suppose the individual begins with an equilibrium at point 1 on indifference curve I_0 where:

HP = household/informal non-market production (as indicated on the x-axis);
L = amount of leisure (as indicated on the y-axis);
HW = distance $0T - 0L$ = amount of household/informal work hours required to generate HP output per period.

The implicit wage is illustrated by the tangent at point 1 (recall from Chapter 1, the actual number would be found on your calculator as inverse tan angle iw). Now imagine a market sector is introduced to this world. The presence of a labour market allows the individual to 'trade' along the line whose angle to the vertical is marked w (for wage rate). Note, angle w is greater than angle iw and therefore the market wage exceeds the implicit wage. Once market production is an option, the individual finds equilibrium at 2 on I_1, dividing the figure, so that informal, market and leisure hours can be

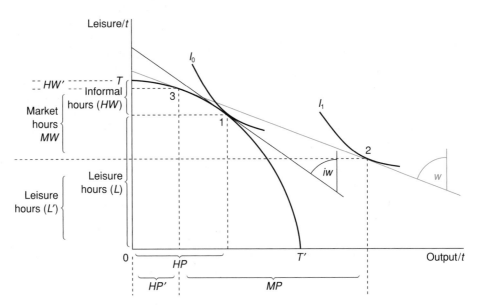

Figure 8.1 Time allocation and different types of production

distinguished as indicated. That is, with equilibrium at 2 on I_1, time is divided into allocations once more – but different ones involving three types of time:

1) HW' = a lower amount of household work hours (see point 3);
2) MW = the new activity of market work hours;
3) L' = revised amount of leisure time;
   and an additional output
4) MP = market production per period.

This can be recognised as a typical picture for household allocation of time for those active in the workforce. It requires elaboration if further insights are to be gained. In particular, the movement from 1 to 2 involves the introduction of market work hours (MW) and market production or output (MP). It is, of course, the latter that is the centre of national income accounting exercises in most countries and the introduction to typical courses in macroeconomics. Simply looking at Figure 8.1 allows the observation that this is a rather narrow conception of output, as it ignores non-market production HP'.

Although it is intuitively easy to understand what market work is (as, by this stage of their lives, most readers will have worked for a wage in the formal labour market), the distinction between leisure and household work is less obvious. This is usually made by references to the 'third-party criterion', an activity is household work if another economic agent could do it for you, e.g. meal preparation, mending the water pipes yourself in your own house are household work, while sleeping, watching TV, playing sport for fun are leisure, as it is difficult to imagine anyone sensibly doing these tasks for you.

8.3 Measuring the household economy

Household production is a major concept in many feminist perspectives (as, for reasons discussed elsewhere (see Chapter 9), it is women who often differentially specialise in this form of work). If it is argued that household production is important, then it is helpful to try to quantify its extent.

Methods of quantification are stock problems for economists and some way forward can usually be found that may be more, or less, perfect. In the present context, two possibilities have been explored as natural measurement approaches (see Chadeau 1992): output-based and input-based. Whilst neither is perfect they are helpful.

The output method involves looking for a market substitute for household production and subtracting the value of intermediate inputs, depreciation of household capital and net indirect taxes to isolate an imputed value of labour in household production (i.e. the value added in the household). The difficulty of this approach is that there may not be a close market substitute to certain types of household production and the valuation derived can look arbitrary.

The input method effectively reverses this process, as it imputes a value to household labour directly (and if a value of non-market production is desired, it is possible to reverse the process of subtraction above). The question is where does the imputed value come from? There are options:

(i)   *The 'global substitute' method* values household work at the wage of general household employees. But, whatever proxy is chosen, you are implicitly assuming that market productivity is equal to the household productivity. Too rough a comparison leads to conservative estimates.

(ii) The 'specialised substitute' method breaks down household production into specialised tasks and values them by reference to each task: if it is plumbing for one hour then a plumber's wage rate is used. If a nail is knocked in, a carpenter's wage rate is sought, and so on. But this is perhaps too fine a classification, as the employment of too many specialists is unlikely to be the realistic alternative production method.

(iii) *The opportunity cost approach* values household production time by reference to the wage that could have been earned on the formal labour market. This is disliked because it carries over male–female wage differentials to the household. The same household task done by a man or a woman will have different opportunity costs. It makes household work of the unemployed look costless. Further, it implies that you can vary the household and market work hours continuously, whereas many people tend to be exclusively specialised in household or market production (see Chapter 9). In general, the value of household production would be different depending on who did it or, conversely, different household products would be given the same value.

The upshot of this is that household production is measured in an imperfect way and, whilst not attaching too much weight, the results imply:

a)   National income accounting significantly underestimates the true value of output and non-market output would have a value of 20–40% of reported GDP.

b)   Measured rates of economic growth, because they refer to gross domestic product or the like (i.e. market conceptions of output), will almost certainly be overestimated (because part of any increases in market output will often come by sacrificing non-market household output as a reflection of increasing market work hours).

c)   Since, as noted above, women are predominantly specialised in household production it is their contribution that is systematically underestimated.

d)   Conventionally measured income inequalities, say between households, are reduced if the value of household production is included.

8.4 Time inputs and fundamental commodities

Having justified an interest in non-market production, it is time to consider the process involved in more detail. Becker (1965) is an economist who analysed, amongst many other issues, household production and bridged a gap in consumer theory accordingly.

His theory is developed in terms of fundamental commodities which, as noted above, are produced by combining own-time input with market and/or public-sector inputs.

To illustrate the theory in a simple way, consider a two-fundamental-commodity world labelled Zs. Individuals are assumed to gain utility from the consumption of both of them, so that the general description of the utility function and standard shape indifference curves can be employed. That is $U = U(Z_1, Z_2)$. These commodities have different input intensities. It is assumed there are two inputs – market goods inputs and own-time inputs. Fundamental commodity Z_1 is assumed to be 'market-goods-intensive'. That is, using relatively more market goods inputs per unit of output than Z_2 which is assumed to be 'own-time-intensive'. Production of Z_1 and Z_2 takes place subject to constraints, which are:

1. A money expenditure constraint that expenditure on the assumed single market input X into Z_1 and Z_2 cannot exceed income. The price of the market input is given at p, whereas earned income is w (the wage rate) multiplied by work t_w (time in hours) and unearned income is given by v. The constraint is therefore:

$$\sum_{i=1}^{2} pX_i = w \cdot t_w + v \tag{8.1}$$

2. A time expenditure constraint, that total time available, T, can only be allocated to market work time, t_w, time input into Z_1 (t_1) and time input into Z_2 (t_2). The constraint is therefore:

$$\sum_{i=1}^{2} t_i + t_w = T = t_1 + t_2 + t_w \tag{8.2}$$

3. The relevant production functions are assumed to be of a Leontief fixed-coefficient kind, i.e. for every unit of Z_1 (Z_2), a_1 (a_2) quantity of the market input X_1 (X_2) is the required amount. Similarly (for time inputs), for every unit of Z_1 (Z_2), b_1 (b_2) quantity of time input t_1 (t_2) is the required amount, so that

$$X_1 = a_1 Z_1 \qquad t_1 = b_1 Z_1$$
$$X_2 = a_2 Z_2 \qquad t_2 = b_2 Z_2$$
$$a_1 > a_2 > 0 \qquad b_2 > b_1 > 0$$

4. The quantitative use of inputs (X_1, X_2, t_1 and t_2) needs to be converted into expenditure outlays by using the price of the market good with the X-quantities and the wage rate with the t-quantities, which allows the construction of a three-column presentation of what is going on (Table 8.1). The third row is the sum of each column and column 3 is the sum of columns 1 and 2.

The rows and columns allow the construction of a figure illustrating the constraints and their relationship to each other.

Table 8.1 Fundamental commodity constraints

Market good input expenditure	Time input expenditure	Total expenditure
Column 1 $pX_1 = a_1 p Z_1$ $+ pX_2 = a_2 p Z_2$	Column 2 $wt_1 = b_1 w Z_1$ $+ wt_2 = b_2 w Z_2$	Column 3 $(a_1 p + b_1 w) Z_1$ $+ (a_2 p + b_2 w) Z_2$
$= \sum_{i=1}^{2} pX_i = w \cdot t_w + v$	$= \sum_{i=1}^{2} t_i w$	$= T \cdot w + v = $ Full income

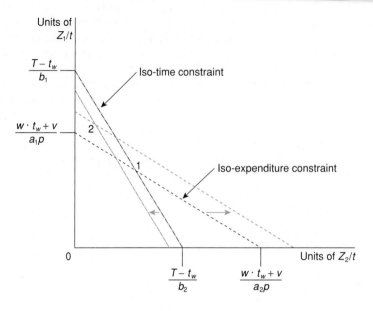

Figure 8.2
Constructing the full income constraint

Column 1 anchors the iso-market good-input expenditure line in Figure 8.2.

$$a_1 p Z_1 + a_2 p Z_2 = w \cdot t_w + v$$

On the y-intercept $Z_2 = 0$ (and therefore $X_2 = 0$),

$$a_1 p Z_1 = w \cdot t_w + v$$

$$Z_1 = w \cdot t_w + v/a_1 p = \text{maximum } Z_1 \text{ if all expenditure was on market good inputs for } Z_1.$$

Similarly, for the x-axis intercept

$$a_1 p Z_1 + a_2 p Z_2 = w \cdot t_w + v$$

On the x-intercept $Z_1 = 0$ (and therefore $X_1 = 0$),

$$a_2 p Z_2 = w \cdot t_w + v$$

$$Z_2 = w \cdot t_w + v/a_2 p = \text{maximum } Z_2 \text{ if all expenditure was on market good inputs for } Z_2.$$

Because of the assumptions about intensities, the y-intercept is smaller than the x-intercept. Column 2 anchors the iso-time expenditure line in Figure 8.2.

$$\sum_{i=1}^{2} wt_i = b_1 w Z_1 + b_2 w Z_2$$

$$wt_1 + wt_2 = b_1 w Z_1 + b_2 w Z_2$$

On the y-intercept $Z_2 = 0$ (and therefore $t_2 = 0$),

$$wt_1 = b_1 w Z_1$$

Now $t_1 = T - t_w$ and

$$w \cdot (T - t_w) = b_1 w Z_1$$

$$Z_1 = w \cdot (T - t_w)/b_1 w = (T - t_w)/b_1 = \text{maximum } Z_1 \text{ if all non-market work time was on time inputs for } Z_1.$$

Similarly, for the x-axis intercept:

$$\sum_{i=1}^{2} wt_i = b_1 w Z_1 + b_2 w Z_2$$

$$wt_1 + wt_2 = b_1 w Z_1 + b_2 w Z_2$$

On the x-intercept, $Z_1 = 0$ (and therefore $t_1 = 0$),

$$wt_2 = b_2 w Z_2$$

Now $t_2 = T - t_w$ and

$$w \cdot (T - t_w) = b_2 w Z_2$$

$$Z_2 = w \cdot (T - t_w)/b_2 w = T - t_w/b_2 = \text{maximum } Z_2 \text{ if all non-market work time was on time inputs for } Z_2.$$

Because of the assumptions about intensities the y-intercept is larger than the x-intercept.

The interpretation of the cross-over point, labelled 1, is central. It is the cross-over point of the iso-market good expenditure constraint and the iso-time expenditure constraint and, as such, it is a point where both constraints are met. Inspection of column 3 (which sums the elements in columns 1 and 2) reveals that 'expenditure' on Z_1 and Z_2 sums to equal all time, T, multiplied by w, the wage rate, plus any unearned income, v. This sum defines what Becker (1971: 46) calls 'full income', which is the income that would be earned if all time were devoted to market work. Notice the 'if'; it is not suggested that people would devote all time to market work but, rather, that this would be their limiting money income. Actual work hours are t_w which do not show in the definition of full income, so that the full-income constraint is unaffected by the actual choice of work hours. Full income defines what is feasible for the individual so that point 1 is feasible, in that it involves expenditure on market inputs given by $w \cdot t_w + v$ (see bottom row of column 1) and sacrificed earnings from market work (to free time for fundamental commodity production) equal to $\Sigma t_i w$ (where, in this simple case, $i = 1, 2$ reflects the assumption of only two fundamental commodities). Together, the two terms sum to full income. To get more points on the full-income constraint involves altering the value of work time, t_w. Increasing t_w will shift the iso-market good expenditure constraint bodily upwards (see the expressions for the y- and x-axis intercepts); simultaneously the iso-time constraint will be moved bodily downwards (see the expressions for the y- and x-axis intercepts) and hence the cross-over point will migrate to the north-west – a point like 2. If this were done for all values of t_w a continuous full-income constraint would be generated.

Column 3 offers the ability to derive the full-income constraint directly. Given that, $(a_1 p + b_1 w) Z_1 + (a_2 p + b_2 w) Z_2 = T \cdot w + v = $ Full income, the relevant intercepts can be found as above by setting Z_2 and Z_1 to equal zero in turn. With $Z_2 = 0$, then $Z_1 = (T \cdot w + v)/(a_1 p + b_1 w)$. When $Z_1 = 0$ then $Z_2 = (T \cdot w + v)/(a_2 p + b_2 w)$. The constraints are collected together and labelled in Figure 8.3. The final step is to impose the indifference curve representation of the utility function on the figure to pick out an equilibrium. This is done in Figure 8.3, where Z_1^* and Z_2^* are the relevant utility-maximising quantities of fundamental commodities Z_1 and Z_2 per period.

Observant readers (and those not much enamoured of economic theory in particular) are likely to note that this is very much like the consumer equilibrium diagram that has already been met – so why all the sweat? Whilst the diagram does indeed look familiar there are important differences in interpretation and in what can be achieved with this formulation. For example, if $a_1 = 1$ and $b_1 = 0$ the good involved would have zero time input and, as such, be a pure market good. If, however, $a_1 = 0$ and $b_1 = 1$ the good would have only time input and be pure leisure. This points up the fact that the formulations of individual choices so far have been in the form of special extreme cases. Those who cry out for things that are more real ought to embrace more readily a framework that

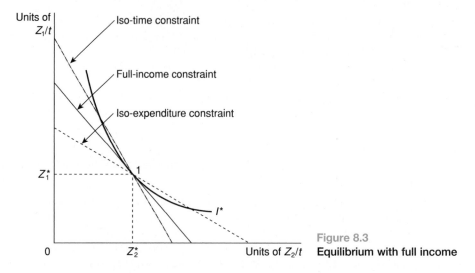

Figure 8.3
Equilibrium with full income

allows the everyday observation of market and time inputs being involved in virtually all individual activities to take centre stage. However, the real payoff is not that the framework fills in consumer theory (by incorporating the vast majority of goods that individuals meet), rather it is in allowing the discussion of topics on which economics might have to otherwise lie silent. This task is reserved for the next chapter where it is assumed the reader is familiar with the concepts raised here.

8.5 Time and analysing investment projects

Investment appraisal, in whatever context it arises, typically involves considering incurring costs now and securing benefits in compensation in the future. As noted above, an investment (or capital good) is long-lived. Further, such capital goods can take the form of physical or human capital and both can arise in the private- or the public-sector context.

Figure 8.4 shows a simple negative–positive axis so that costs are below the axis and benefits above it. It is assumed that, with sufficient ingenuity, the size of the squares accurately measures all costs and benefits to this project converted to money terms. The project could be almost anything – deciding to migrate, attempting to acquire a degree

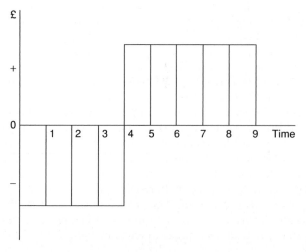

Figure 8.4
A simple investment prospect

in economics, buying a new computer-operated machine for a car plant, laying new water pipes. The figure shows a very simple pattern with four equally sized cost blocks and five equally sized benefit blocks. Does this picture represent a good investment? In other words is it efficient, in that it would make someone better off and no one worse off? The person on the street would be tempted to say 'yes' (in that, if the benefits are used to meet all the costs, there will be one surplus rectangle – so that at least one person will be better off). The economist, as ever, says 'not so fast, things are really more complicated than this'. The simple logic is not appropriate as time is on the x-axis and some allowance must be made for the fact that costs and benefits are being experienced at different points in time (or an explicit decision should be made to treat all points in time as equal to each other).

Individuals are not indifferent between receipt of a certain sum of money today and receipt of the same sum of money in the future. For example, if you were offered £100 today or £100 in one year's time, what advantage would there be in waiting the year? Usually, £100 received today is worth more than £100 in one year's time. The sum of £100 received today could be invested and could earn a rate of interest. Suppose the rate of interest were 8 per cent. In one year's time today's £100 would be worth £108. It follows that £100 today is worth £108 in one year's time. It is not possible to add up benefits that are incurred at different times without allowing for this. As money received today is preferred to the same sum of money received in the future, it is necessary to discount future benefits (and future costs) to make them comparable with each other today.

To add together future costs (or benefits), the future costs (or benefits) have to be discounted to make them equivalent to present costs (or benefits). 'Discounted' simply means they are being made less valuable. From the above example, £108 in one year's time is worth £100 now. It follows that the present value of £108 received in one year's time can be found by applying a discount factor equal to $1 / (1 + r)^n$. The present value of £108 is equal to $108/(1 + r)^n$, where r is the rate of discount and n is the number of years from the present the sum actually arises (in this case $n = 1$). But what is the present value of a sum received in two years' time? As £100 now is worth £100$(1 + r)$ $(= £108)$ in one year's time, it follows that £108 discounted at $1/(1 + r)$ is equal to a present value of £100. It is possible that £100 today might be invested at 8 per cent for two years and, after the additional year, the sum would be worth £116.64 $(= £108 (1 + r))$. By comparison with the original sum, the future value would be $[£100(1 + r)(1 + r) = £100(1 + r)^2]$. To convert a sum of money received in two years' time into present values, it is necessary to discount by $1/(1+ r)^2$.

Suppose that an investment project yields benefits in each year of its expected life. If estimates of the benefit are reported in monetary values $(B_1, B_2, \ldots, B_n)$ experienced in each of n years of the project's life they can be added even though they are experienced at different times. Benefits received in each year can be converted into present values and then added. The present value (PV) of this stream of valuations is:

$$PV = \frac{B_1}{(1 + r)} + \frac{B_2}{(1 + r)^2} + \frac{B_3}{(1 + r)^3} + \ldots + \frac{B_n}{(1 + r)^n} \tag{8.3}$$

As has been established, discounting is required to allow for the fact that the benefits and costs that flow from investment will appear at very different times. The costs of projects are likely to be split between the 'initial' investment (capital) costs (I_0), to be incurred on the project now, i.e. in the present period, and the 'current' costs $(C_1, C_2, C_3, \ldots, C_n)$, which will occur during the lifetime of the project. In this way, a capital project will generate a stream of net benefits. During the lifetime of the project annual net benefits $(B - C)$ must be discounted in order to evaluate the net present value (NPV) of the project. (Figure 8.5 illustrates this more typical pattern of events where the undiscounted net benefit of a project, e.g. the net benefit 'block' in Figure 8.4 would serve to

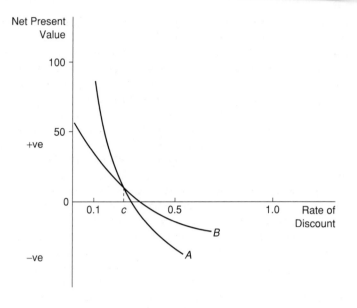

Figure 8.5
NPVs and IRR

provide the y-axis intercept for the project.) This is the difference between the discounted sum of the stream of future net benefits and the initial costs of the project. It can be shown as

$$NPV = -I_0 + \frac{(B-C)_1}{(1+r)^1} + \frac{(B-C)_2}{(1+r)^2} + \frac{(B-C)_3}{(1+r)^3} + \ldots + \frac{(B-C)_n}{(1+r)^n} \qquad (8.4)$$

The net present value of an investment, therefore, may be written as

$$NPV = -I_0 + \sum_{t=1}^{n} \frac{(B-C)_t}{(1+r)^t} \qquad (8.5)$$

Investment projects may be ranked according to their net present value. Projects will be worthy of serious consideration if $NPV > 0$ (unless there are additional capital constraints). The best projects will be those with the highest NPV. Alternatively, projects may be ranked according to their internal rate of return. The internal rate of return of a project is the value of r that makes the stream of discounted net benefits equal to the initial capital cost. Those projects which would record a high net present value will also typically record a high rate of return. However, there are reasons for preferring one form of ranking to another. Generally it is preferable to rank projects by net present value rather than by rate of return, for the following reasons.

First, it is not always the case that there is a unique solution to the internal rate of return. For example, in Table 8.2 (following Webb 1973), as the arithmetic shows there

Table 8.2 **NPV and internal rates of return (IRR)**

	Time	Discounted cash flows	
t_0	−£100	−£100	−£100
t_1	+£230	£230/1.1 = £209.1	£230/1.2 = £191.7
t_2	−£132	−£132/1.21 = −£109.1	−£132/1.44 = −£91.7
Total		£0	£0

IRR = 10% or 20%
Source: Webb (1973): 23.

are two internal rates of return (10 and 20 per cent) when the future net benefits take the values shown.

Second, with mutually exclusive projects, the internal rate of return may select projects that would not be chosen by the net present value criterion. In Figure 8.5 the net present value of two projects *A* and *B* are shown for various rates of discount. The internal rate of return (that rate of discount which makes *NPV* = 0) is seen to be higher for *B* than for *A* (look along the *x*-axis). However, if the *NPV* is considered at discount rates lower than *c* then project *A* has a higher *NPV* than *B*. If the objective were to maximise the *NPV* of the project, then for discount rates below *c* the *NPV* would indicate the correct project, but to rely on the internal rate of return would indicate the wrong project. The conclusion is that using the *NPV* by definition leads to the correct choice. While the internal rate of return test may be modified to allow for this problem, the simple *NPV* test is often regarded as superior. However, whatever approach is chosen the value of the discount rate is important. If projects are tested by reference to the internal rate of return on the project (i.e. the rate of discount that makes the *NPV* zero), there has to be a test rate of discount which serves as a requirement that must be equalled or surpassed. If the *NPV* is used the appropriate value of the discount rate must be selected to compute the *NPV*.

An example from Harvey (1983) will serve to fix ideas introduced so far. Suppose the Aqua Sulis Water Co, is planning to lay new pipes. When in place it is anticipated that the net annual benefit stream, which begins in year 5, will be £3.5 million and will occur for 24 years. The pipes will take a total of £30 million to put in place with a quarter of the cost arising in each of the four construction years. To indicate the impact of discounting, consider the net present value of this project at a discount rate of 12% and 8%. Tables 8.3 and 8.4 are relevant entries from published sets of discount tables.

Table 8.3 Discount factors: the present value of 1 at a future date

	2% ...	8% ...	12% ...	25%
1	0.980	0.926	0.893	0.800
2	0.961	0.857	0.797	0.640
3	0.942	0.794	0.712	0.512
4	0.924	0.735	0.636	0.410
.				
.				
.				
29	0.563	0.107	0.037	0.002

Table 8.4 Sum of the discount factors: the present value of 1 received or paid each year for a number of years

	2% ...	8% ...	12% ...	25%
1	0.980	0.926	0.893	0.800
2	1.942	1.783	1.690	1.440
3	2.884	2.577	2.402	1.952
4	3.808	3.312	3.038	2.362
.				
.				
.				
.				
29	21.844	11.159	8.022	3.994

The structure of the investment appraisal is as follows:

Table 8.5 Investment appraisal

Years	Cash flows	Discount factor (12%)	Net present value (12%)	Discount factor (8%)	Net present value (8%)
1–4	–7.5 (Cost = 30m ÷ 4)	3.038	–22.8	3.312	–24.8
5–29	+3.5	4.984	+17.5 −5.3	7.847	27.4 2.6

The costs occur in years 1 to 4 and could each be discounted using the 12% discount factor for years 1 to 4 which, using Table 8.3, give:

Year			
1	–7.5 × 0.893	=	–6.697
2	–7.5 × 0.797	=	–5.978
3	–7.5 × 0.712	=	–5.34
4	–7.5 × 0.636	=	–4.77
			–22.8

Given the equal sums, it is, however, easier to use the sum of discount factors in Table 8.4 which means all that has to be done is multiply –7.5 by 3.038 = –22.8. The benefit stream can similarly be summarised. As the benefit stream does not begin until year 4 and ends in year 29, to use Table 8.4 involves subtracting the year 4 'sum' from the year 29 'sum', i.e. 8.022 – 3.038 = 4.984. In this way, the calculation becomes very simple. (Enough of the relevant tables are provided for readers to check the arithmetic.)

With a 12% discount rate the project has a negative *NPV* and therefore should be rejected. However, the use of an 8% discount rate makes the *NPV* positive and therefore it should be accepted. Here is a clear indication of the decisive power of the discount rate with respect to a project – rejection can easily turn to acceptance and vice versa. In the UK public sector it has been common to use a standard discount rate. This was 5% in real terms for many years before being raised to 6% in real terms in the late 1980s. Whether this is the 'correct' discount rate involves quite detailed reasoning, reflecting arguments introduced below.

8.6 Time and discounting: the individual calculus

Having described the mechanics of discounting, attention turns to the rationale of discounting. The individual economic actor is seen as a utility-maximiser and this viewpoint carries over to choices over time (intertemporal choice). Individuals must allocate consumption in different periods (labelled C_1 and C_2) to maximise utility.

The logic of discounting begins with the observation that people exhibit impatience in that they require compensation for postponing consumption. This compensation is their rate of pure time preference. It is generally assumed that the same utility function obtains in different time periods. Further, assume the utility from consumption in one period is independent of the utility of consumption in another. Putting this into symbols for a two-period case:

$$U(C_1, C_2) = U(C_1) + \frac{1}{1 + \rho} U(C_2) \tag{8.6}$$

where

U = utility;
C = consumption level;
$\rho > 0$ = the pure rate of time preference.

The budget constraint for a two-period case can be established using Figure 8.6. For simplicity assume income in period 1 (Y_1) equals income in period 2 (Y_2) so that the so-called endowment point is on a 45° line from the origin, here at point E. With a rate of interest r maximum period 1 consumption would be $Y_1 + [1/(1 + r)]Y_2$, i.e. the discounted present value of income over the two periods yields the x-axis intercept. That is, the present value of the income over the two periods and can be represented as:

$$Y = Y_1 + \frac{1}{1 + r}Y_2 \tag{8.7}$$

where

Y = income
r = (single-period) rate of return.

In these circumstances maximum period-2 consumption is $Y_2 + (1 + r)Y_1$, establishing the y-axis intercept. Note: dividing $(1 + r)Y_1$ by Y_1 is sufficient to identify the slope of the (straight-line) intertemporal budget constraint as $-(1 + r)$.

Consumption in periods 1 and 2 is given by:

$$C_1 = Y_1 + \frac{1}{1 + r}Y_2 - \frac{1}{1 + r}C_2 \tag{8.7'}$$

$$C_2 = Y_2 + (1 + r)(Y_1 - C_1) \tag{8.7''}$$

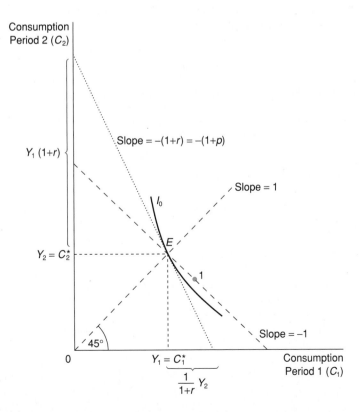

Figure 8.6
The pure time preference rate and consumption

Substituting (8.7) into (8.7') yields:

$$Y = C_1 + \frac{1}{1+r} C_2 \tag{8.7'''}$$

To isolate the first-order conditions for utility maximisation it is necessary to form the Lagrangian function ($\mathcal{L}$) and set the partial derivatives equal to zero.

$$\mathcal{L} = U(C_1, C_2) + \lambda \left(Y - C_1 - \frac{1}{1+r} C_2 \right) \tag{8.8}$$

$$\frac{\partial \mathcal{L}}{\partial C_1} = \frac{\partial U}{\partial C_1} - \lambda = 0 \tag{8.9}$$

$$\frac{\partial \mathcal{L}}{\partial C_2} = \frac{1}{1+\rho} \frac{\partial U}{\partial C_2} - \frac{\lambda}{1+r} = 0 \tag{8.10}$$

$$\frac{\partial \mathcal{L}}{\partial \lambda} = Y - C_1 - \frac{1}{1+r} C_2 = 0 \tag{8.11}$$

Ignoring the partial derivative with respect to λ, but using the others, yields

$$\frac{\partial U}{\partial C_1} = \frac{1+r}{1+\rho} \frac{\partial U}{\partial C_2} \tag{8.12}$$

or

$$(1+\rho)MU_{c_1} = (1+r)MU_{c_2} \tag{8.12'}$$

where $MU_c = \partial U / \partial C$ = marginal utility of consumption.

With a given budget constraint and a given utility function exhibiting diminishing marginal utility of consumption, total utility will be maximised over the two periods by choosing levels of consumption (denoted by *) such that various equilibria might be observed:

(i) $C_1^* = C_2^*$ when $r = \rho$ and the endowment point E (income in the two periods Y_1, Y_2) is on the 45° line: the equal-consumption case (see Figure 8.6);

(ii) C_1^* involves period-1 borrowing ($C_1^* > C_2^*$) when in a figure labelled like Figure 8.6 the equilibrium is to the right of the initial endowment point E on the relevant budget constraint through E;

(iii) C_1^* involves period-1 lending ($C_1^* < C_2^*$) when in a figure labelled like Figure 8.6 the equilibrium is to the left of the initial endowment point E on the relevant budget constraint through E.

To illustrate these possible results more fully, consider Figure 8.6, which illustrates the indifference curve (I_0) for an individual with a positive pure rate of time preference. The total differential of the utility function (equation 8.6) is:

$$dU = \frac{\partial U}{\partial C_1} dC_1 + \frac{1}{1+\rho} \frac{\partial U}{\partial C_2} dC_2 = 0 \tag{8.13}$$

so that the slope of the indifference curve is:

$$\frac{dC_2}{dC_1} = -\frac{-\partial U / \partial C_1}{\dfrac{1}{1+\rho} \partial U / \partial C_2} \tag{8.13'}$$

On the 45° line $C_1^* = C_2^*$, so that with a given utility function $\partial U / \partial C_1 = \partial U / \partial C_2$

$$\frac{dC_2}{dC_1} = -(1 + \rho)$$

This views the pure rate of time preference as the discount rate of the individual, measured by the slope of their indifference curves when intersecting the 45° line (point E) in a two-period diagram like Figure 8.6. Given that $\rho > 0$, this slope necessarily has an absolute value greater than unity. For the equal-consumption case $C_1^* = C_2^*$ to arise, $r = \rho$ and the slope of the budget constraint $-(1 + r)$ through the endowment point E would be coincident with the dotted line labelled Slope $= -(1 + r) = -(1 + \rho)$. If the rate of interest were zero the budget line would be the dashed line marked Slope $= -1$ and the depicted individual would maximise utility by consuming more in period 1 than in period 2 at a point like 1 (relevant indifference curve not drawn) as a reflection of $\rho > 0$.

Other formulations of this type of analysis note that the slope of the indifference curve indicates the change in period-2 consumption (dC_2) required to compensate the individual for a reduction in period-1 consumption (dC_1) whilst leaving utility unchanged, so that at a point on the indifference curve:

$$-\frac{dC_2}{dC_1} = (1 + \delta) \tag{8.14}$$

where δ is now the intertemporal rate of substitution.

Using equation (8.7″) it can be seen that the slope of the budget constraint (dC_2/dC_1) is $-(1 + r)$ and given that equilibrium for an individual is always found where the slope of the indifference curve equals the slope of the budget constraint it is evident that

$$-(1 + r) = -(1 + \delta) \tag{8.15}$$

so that $r = \delta$ in all equilibria. As before, this may involve lending or borrowing in period 1. The value of δ varies at each point on the typical convex-to-the-origin indifference curve. This occurs because of the varying marginal utilities of consumption as the level of consumption in each period changes. That is,

$$(1 + \delta) = (1 + \rho)\frac{MU_{C_1}}{MU_{C_2}} \tag{8.16}$$

Only on the 45° line does $\delta = \rho$. It must be noted that, although this is a typical shape of an individual's indifference curve, it does not imply there are no differences in preferences or income endowments between individuals.

Figures 8.7 (a) and (b) indicate borrowing and lending equilibria respectively. Point E is the endowment point and in panel (a) equilibrium is found at point 1. Noting that consumption in period 1 is increased compared to point E and consumption in period 2 is decreased compared to point E, this is an individual who is borrowing in period 1.

Point E is also the endowment point and in panel (b) equilibrium is found at point 1. Noting that consumption in period 1 is decreased compared to point E and consumption in period 2 is increased compared to point E, this is an individual who is lending in period 1.

It is possible to indicate the consequences for equilibrium from increasing the interest rate. Increasing the interest rate causes the budget constraint to swivel through the endowment point, lowering period 1 consumption opportunities and increasing period 2 consumption opportunities.

It is possible to distinguish the income and substitution effect contributions of the price change indicated by the move from point 1 to point 2 in panels (a) and (b). Beginning in panel (a) the price effect has moved consumption from point 1 on I_1 to point 2 on I_0. To isolate the effect of the income change from the relative price effect, the exercise is one of increasing income at the new price ratio until the initial utility level I_1

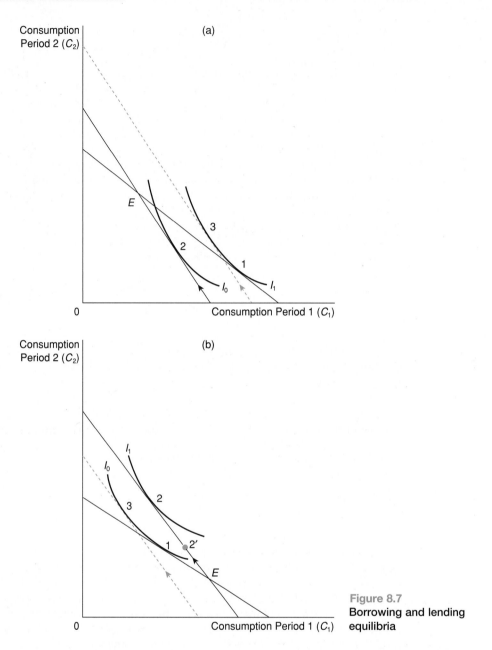

Figure 8.7
Borrowing and lending equilibria

is once again secured. Moving the new budget constraint to the right in a parallel fashion until it is tangential to I_1 (here at point 3 – with the associated consumption pattern) operationalises this experiment. The income effect is negative (having moved period-1 consumption chosen from point 3 to point 2). In this case, period-1 consumption is said to be normal, as the individual chooses less of it as income falls. The substitution effect from point 1 to point 3 is also negative, reflecting a response to a change in relative prices with utility level constant on I_1. With an initial borrowing equilibrium, the price effect of a rate of interest increase (move 1 to 2) is to reduce borrowing. This effect comprises an income effect that reduces borrowing point 3 to point 2 and a substitution effect point 1 to point 3.

Turning to panel (b), the price effect has moved consumption from point 1 on I_0 to point 2 on I_1 (consuming less in period 1 – saving more). To isolate the effect of the income change from the relative price effect, the exercise is to decrease income at the new price ratio until the initial utility level I_0 is once again secured. Move the new budget constraint to the left in a parallel fashion until it is tangential to I_0 (here at point 3). The income effect is positive (having moved period-1 consumption chosen upwards from point 3 to point 2). In this case, period-1 consumption is again said to be normal, as the individual chooses more of it as income rises. The substitution effect from point 1 to point 3 is negative, reflecting a response to a change in relative prices (utility level constant on I_0). With an initial saving equilibrium, the price effect of a rate of interest increase (move 1 to 2) appears to be an increase in saving. This effect comprises an income effect that reduces saving (increasing period-1 consumption) point 3 to point 2 and a substitution effect point 1 to point 3 increasing saving (decreasing period-1 consumption). Unlike the rate of interest increase and a borrowing equilibrium where the income and substitution effects both decrease borrowing, with a saving equilibrium the income and substitution work in opposite directions. The rate of interest increase and a saving equilibrium has an income effect that reduces saving and a substitution effect that increases saving. As illustrated, the latter is greater than the former so that overall saving is increased. However, point 2′ could equally have been the new equilibrium with savings decreased. It is an empirical matter as to which is dominant.

8.6.1 The rationale for ρ and δ

Why should individuals have preference for consumption now over consumption in the future (i.e. impatience)? The first explanation is 'pure myopia' – generally described as an irrational preference for the present over the future. Whilst some will have higher values of ρ than others the presumption is that a positive value is very common. Unless a strong rationale can be provided for this, some have argued that 'pure myopia' does not seem to be a very firm foundation on which to base discounting.

Second, consider the implications of a total utility of income function that is concave from below (indicating diminishing marginal utility of income or consumption). A greater utility gain is attached to an additional £1 of consumption when consumption is £100 per period than an additional £1's consumption when consumption is £1000 per period. If as the result of, say, economic growth, an individual expects to have higher income in period 2, then abstracting from any risk/uncertainty considerations, the marginal utility of a unit of future consumption will then have a lower utility evaluation. That is, more than one unit of future consumption is required to compensate for reducing consumption by one unit in period one.

Risk/uncertainty is a third rationale for time preference. The popular saying 'a bird in the hand is worth two in the bush' captures the idea that a certain smaller sum is more valuable than a larger uncertain one. A total utility of income function that is concave from below reflects risk aversion. In a world of uncertainty individuals do not know if they will be alive in future periods and, if they are, the nature of their world will be different. Technology will have changed and their own preferences may be different. Risk-averse individuals prefer a certain value of C_1 to an uncertain C_2 whose expected value is the *same* as C_1. They will need the promise of additional expected consumption in period two to be indifferent to the certain value of consumption in period one.

Having established a 'logic for discounting' at an individual level, the question is how to translate these considerations to a 'social' level. In short, how can a social discount rate be rationalised and estimated for analysis of investment projects in the public sector? This is discussed in Cullis and Jones (2009).

8.6.2 The impact of discounting is everywhere

The following applications illustrate how widespread are the circumstances in which discounting is crucial to making an economic decision.

(i) *Price changing and exchange rate volatility*

In Chapter 4 it was shown that exchange rate volatility induced static welfare gains. Here the impact of exchange rate changes on price setting is explored for an imperfect competitor who sells output at home and abroad. Figure 8.8 depicts a monopoly pricing situation for the home producer with respect to the foreign demand (D_f) and associated marginal revenue (MR_f) for their output.

Initially, the foreign price is set at P_1 (associated with $MR_f = AC = MC/e_0$ at point 1 where e_0 is the exchange rate £ per $ – so the curve represents the marginal cost of output in the foreign currency ($)). If the £ depreciates to e_1 there will be more £ per $ and the assumed constant average and marginal costs move to $AC = MC/e_1$. This lowers the profit-maximising price to P_2 and increases profit over the range of raised sales q_1-q_2 by the extent to which marginal revenue (MR_f) exceeds MC/e_1 over that range. That is the change in profit $\Delta\pi$ = triangle 1-2-3. But will the export price change occur once it is recognised there are transactions costs (T) in changing prices (often called 'menu costs' – raising the image of having to reprint or otherwise alter price lists)?

The answer depends on whether the exchange rate change is thought transitory or not. If the change is thought permanent the relevant formula to change the price is

$$\sum_{t=0}^{n} \frac{\Delta\pi}{(1+r)^t} > T \tag{8.17}$$

where r is the discount rate. That is, the discounted present value of the raised profits must exceed the transactions costs. If the change is thought transitory, say one period, then the relevant calculation is

$$\Delta\pi + \frac{\Delta\pi}{(1+r)} > T + \frac{T}{(1+r)} \tag{8.18}$$

In the transitory case, the discounted value of transactions cost has to be included because of the need to change prices again in one period's time. The higher T, the higher r, the lower $\Delta\pi$ and the lower n the less likely price adjustments will be observed and trade flows will not be influenced by a volatile exchange rate (see De Grauwe 2007).

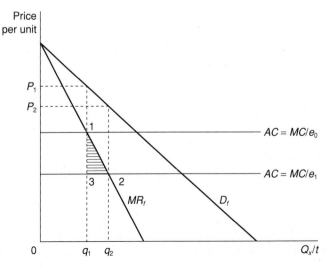

Figure 8.8
Transactions costs and price changing

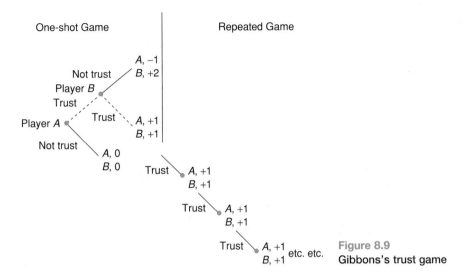

One-shot Game   Repeated Game

Figure 8.9
Gibbons's trust game

(ii) *The trust game*

In Figure 8.9 a trust game discussed in Gibbons (1997) is pictured in extensive form. That is, the order of play is indicated by the figure where player A is seen to have to move first, either trusting player B or not. If A does not trust B the game stops now and A's (and B's) payoff is zero. If, however, A trusts B, the game moves to the decision node for B who can act honourably and receive a payoff of +1, with a similar payoff for A. If, however, B does not trust (reneges), the payoff is to B +2 and −1 for A.

In a one-shot game, with full information, the continuous arms in the figure represent dominant strategies for players A and B. A does not trust because, by backwards induction (working backwards from the final stage), A can expect B to renege because of common knowledge of their rationality (instrumentally rational B prefers 2 to 1). A will therefore not trust, so that A and B get zero each.

How is the game transformed if it becomes a repeated one? Now player B will cooperate if the discounted present value of the payoffs from cooperation over the future (C) (see additional decision nodes offering +1 indefinitely) exceeds the discounted present value of defection payoff (D) and any associated 'punishment' for defection (P), e.g. loss of reputation. That is a discounted present valuation calculation once more becomes relevant.

Given the general formula for calculating a present value (PV) is

$$PV = \frac{R}{r}[1 - 1/(1 + r)^t] \tag{8.19}$$

where R is the relevant annual sum, r the rate of discount and the years are $t = 1, 2, \ldots, n$ as t increases $(1 + r)^t \rightarrow \infty$ and $1/(1 + r)^t \rightarrow 0$ and the formula $\cong R/r$. So, if the game is assumed to be repeated infinitely the relevant calculation is:

$$\{1 + (1/r)\}C \geq D + (1/r)P \tag{8.20}$$

and this can be simplified to:

$$C + (1/r)C \geq D + (1/r)P$$

$$C/r - P/r \geq D - C$$

$$(C - P)/r \geq D - C$$

$$r \leq (C - P)/(D - C)$$

where r is the discount rate. If in Gibbons's case the punishment is zero, then by substitution it can be seen that individual B will cooperate if

$$\{1 + (1/r)\}1 \geq 2 + (1 + r)0 \tag{8.21}$$

or

$$r \leq (1 - 0)/(2 - 1)$$

That is, if $r \leq 1$, B will cooperate.

8.7 What should be discounted and by what method?

While the mechanics of discounting are apparently well established, a number of questions remain unresolved. Should all types of cost and benefit be discounted at the same rate? Should all types of cost and benefit be discounted? Do individuals actually behave in the way described in microeconomic theory? Whilst there is insufficient space to be exhaustive with respect to these questions some examples serve to illustrate their importance.

Goodin (1982) questions both the rationale and the form of discounting. As regards the rationale, he suggests that the psychological approach of individuals having a pure time preference is a frailty that need not be respected. The diminishing marginal utility of income argument is accepted as an argument, with the proviso that it should be reversible if the future generation is poorer than the present generation. At the same time, risk and uncertainty are quite different arguments to discounting for time as such, in that the relationship between risk and uncertainty will vary for different goods and different periods. While discounting on the basis of risk/uncertainty arguments may be justified, it will not take the usual simple form.

Similarly, Goodin reflects that, even accepting the listed approaches, they do not imply the application of a uniform discount rate over time. Psychologically, some periods are more important than others; diminishing marginal utility will not occur at a constant rate because income growth will vary over time and income itself does not translate into utility at a given rate; opportunities sacrificed in one period are greater than those sacrificed in others.

In this way, having questioned the case for discounting at all, Goodin questions the decision to discount at a uniform rate. He argues that to treat all goods in the same fashion would be inappropriate. Some goods are psychologically more important than others, and this is true with respect to the degree of risk and uncertainty associated with them. The conversion of all goods to the common numeraire money, as in the marginal utility/opportunity cost argument, is viewed as running up against the incommensurability-type argument.

Loss of life is one such example. Goodin's argument is that such an event cannot sensibly be reduced *ex ante* to a 'money metric' and that 'non-tradables' can be sacrificed now only if the stock of the non-tradable under discussion can be raised in the future – a life for lives. A restricted form of discounting is applicable to non-tradables on this argument with its form and rate reflecting the form and rate of stock growth of the particular non-tradable. Broome (1987), in his approach to discounting in the health care context, also advocates a special form. He suggests a complicated discounting mechanism, justified by reference to the 'psychological connections' between successive periods in an individual's life, and being weaker the more periods are temporally separated.

Parsonage and Neuburger (1992) suggest that the appropriate discount rate for non-monetary health benefits 'should be at or close to zero' (p. 71). Their argument is that the traditional case for discounting rests on three pillars (noted above): (i) future income growth; (ii) the rate of fall of the marginal utility of an additional £1 as income rises; and (iii) pure time preference; and that these pillars fail to support discounting in non-monetary benefit contexts. The authors argue that the first two pillars crumble, because the marginal utility connected with health improvements are not related to income and the third because empirical and *a-priori* reasoning do not support a positive pure time preference over health improvements.

Cairns (1992) is critical of this stance. He argues that they are fairly selective in the range of empirical studies they quote and that the key to the argument is the lack of an uncontroversial 'shadow price' for health improvements. If there were an uncontroversial 'shadow price' the health improvement would be a monetary sum and look and be treated as any other element in an investment appraisal. Both authors agree that more empirical work is required to resolve some of the arguments involved.

There are many different methods of discounting. In the discussion so far the most common exponential method is employed. In this method the discount rate has a constant positive value over time and the discount factor was given by $1/(1 + r)^t$ with t being the unit of time, so that the discount factor decreases over a range that runs from 1 (at $t = 0$) towards 0 (as t increases towards infinity). This is called 'exponential discounting' because the time path of the discount factor follows an exponential function of the form e^{-rt} where r is the discount rate and t, once more, is the unit of time. This has at least two advantages. The first is simplicity in that there is a constant discount rate. The second is that, because the method discounts net benefits in the future very highly, any error in measuring distant costs and benefits (the most difficult ones to measure) does not matter very much in the final calculation. Both these advantages can be questioned in the light of empirical work.

It has been noted that there are anomalies in the thinking of individuals who are not '*homo economicus*' (see Chapter 2). With respect to discounting, Thaler and Sheffrin (1981) note the problem of preference reversal. With a constant discount rate scheme only the absolute difference between measures of value matters. For example if benefit V_a due next year is preferred to benefit V_b in four years' time that ranking should be preserved if ten years (or any number of years) is added to both time dates, i.e. 11 years' and 14 years' time. However, Thaler and Sheffrin found individuals do not behave like this in that, if $V_a < V_b$, individuals often alter their preference as a function of the time the choice is made, even though the delay between the two sums is held constant as above (3 years). That is, V_b is typically preferred to V_a in the 11 and 14 years' time scenario. To fix ideas, a majority of individuals apparently prefer £50 immediately to £100 in two years' time but almost no one prefers £50 in four years' time to £100 in six years' time. The worry, or anomaly, is that this is the same choice except it is viewed at four years greater distance but preferences have reversed.

Ainslie (1991) also reports that if you conduct experiments with individuals they do not conform to the numbers portrayed in discount tables, i.e. an exponential curve. Rather they conform to a hyperbolic curve that is more bowed to the origin than the exponential curve. Individuals change their choices over the same prospect when the time to the availability of the good is changed. Individuals apparently follow 'Hernstein's matching law'. There are a number of specific hyperbolic forms for discount functions, but for a single good valuation (V) using the following formula is advocated by Ainslie:

$$V = A/\xi + \Gamma(T - t) \tag{8.22a}$$

where A is the amount involved, T is the time at which each amount is available and t is the time of the behaviour that obtains it, so that $(T - t)$ is the delay for A. The term ξ is an empirical constant that determines the value of zero delay and Γ is an empirical constant that modifies the steepness of the delay gradient. Empirically both ξ and $\Gamma \cong 1$ so the formula simplifies to:

$$V = A/1 + 1(T - t) \tag{8.22b}$$

For example, if the delay is 3 units of time and A is 1, then $V = 1/4$.

Table 8.6 **Hyperbolic discounting**

Time to V_a	Value V_a	Time to V_b	Value V_b	Preference
0	$1/(1 + 0) = 1$	3	$2/(1 + 3) = 1/2$	V_a
1	$1/(1 + 1) = 1/2$	4	$2/(1 + 4) = 2/5$	V_a
2	$1/(1 + 2) = 1/3$	5	$2/(1 + 5) = 1/3$	Indifference
3	$1/(1 + 3) = 1/4$	6	$2/(1 + 6) = 2/7$	V_b
4	$1/(1 + 4) = 1/5$	7	$2/(1 + 7) = 1/4$	V_b
5	$1/(1 + 5) = 1/6$	8	$2/(1 + 8) = 2/9$	V_b

Table 8.6 extends an example in Ainslie (1991). $V_a = 1$ and $V_b = 2$ and V_a and V_b are always separated by three units of time. In Table 8.6 equation (8.22b) is employed to show how preference changes as delay time changes from 0 for V_a (implying a 3 time-unit delay for V_b) to 5 units of time for V_a (implying an 8 time-unit delay for V_b).

As time increases, preference for V_a passes through indifference to V_b to a preference for V_b and, once again, the rationality of individuals as compared to *homo economicus* is called into question. Further discussion of hyperbolic and exponential discounting can be found in Van der Pol and Cairns (2000).

There are many methods of discounting and the instruction to look at the 'discounted present value' when costs and benefits are temporally separated is not an obvious one to follow.

How is time incorporated into economic theorising? Neoclassical theory employs what is called 'analytical time'. Analytical time is an abstraction. It is a situation where virtually all information, past, present and future, is available. It is possible to move backwards and forwards in time, so that the sequencing of decisions is not an issue. The essence of the theory is to perform hypothetical exercises of causes leading to consequences. Critics of microeconomics say that this concept of analytical time leads thinking in precisely the wrong directions and that you have to operate with what is called 'perspective time'. This is time as people get to experience it. Often people have limited and ill-defined pieces of information. These pieces of information are open to different types of interpretation, i.e. the message conveyed is individual-specific. Further, sequence matters, it is impossible to re-make past choices and once past choices have been made they often preclude a great deal of current ones. You simply cannot move backwards and forwards in time. Once you have chosen one path you are closing out options in the future and the claim would be that any realistic theory must take account of this so-called path dependency.

A final point here is that decision making is often very stressful and that it is not done in the sort of clear analytical air in which the theory on these pages is presented. Individuals often respond in emotional ways and do not lend themselves easily to the axioms of choice.

8.8 Knowledge creation: 'Is there nothing this good can't illustrate?'

This section draws on Hirshleifer and Riley (1992: Chapter 7). Apart from intrinsic interest the reason for considering the material here is that knowledge creation demonstrates the importance of a large number of the concepts introduced in these first eight chapters of this text, along with the 'symmetricalness' typical of (micro)economic theory. Apart from being of interest in itself, this section can be seen as a kind of examination of the material presented so far.

Knowledge creation is used to include inventions and message creation. The objectives (as elaborated in Chapters 4 and 5) are efficiency and equity. Production efficiency requires concern with the optimal level of knowledge creation in terms of both quantity and quality. Consumption efficiency concerns the optimal use or transmission of newly created knowledge. Equity means concern with the identity of who gains and who loses from knowledge creation.

There are different forms of knowledge creation (KC):

(i)   *Investment (real, technological, production) KC* is the type that lowers a marginal cost of production, or equivalently bodily shifts the production possibilities frontier outwards to the right, by 'improving' the production function;

(ii) *Pecuniary (speculative, redistributive) KC* is the type that simply leads to a *redistribution between individuals, in what is effectively a zero-sum game;*

(iii) *Consumption KC* is knowledge for its own sake, as a direct source of utility, e.g. studying the role of the country house in English literature 1700–1705.

Initially the focus is (i) and (ii) and production efficiency. There is a distinction indicated above between quantitative and qualitative KC. Quantitative KC is seen as routine, or normal, KC, whereas qualitative KC is seen as spectacular, or paradigm shifting. With respect to quantitative KC, there are difficulties that rely on the market-failure-type arguments of Chapter 6.

First, there is the public goods problem. As analysed in Chapter 7, once created, information is non-rival in use (in that one individual's use of a piece of information does not reduce the stock of information), the marginal cost of an additional user is zero. This suggests (from the competitive pricing rule) that, for consumption efficiency, price should be zero. Indeed, if enhancement of the knowledge by additional users is allowed for, the stock may actually grow with use; the marginal cost of use is negative, suggesting a subsidy!

Additionally, it is very difficult to make information excludable in that, once created, it tends to leak in an unintended way. Once it has been passed on from the original creator of information, that person can also pass, or sell, it on. If this is the case for the original possessor, it is very difficult for the originator to establish a property right over their created knowledge, as non-excludability raises the spectre of free-riding. Given all this, it is not surprising that there is public policy intervention in the information market (with patent laws and the like to preserve some property rights). But this also creates difficulties, as it cuts across consumption efficiency.

Property rights are institutional rules that specify what individuals are entitled to do with resources and goods. These rules (which may be formal or informal) govern rights over ownership, use and the disposal of resources and goods. Property rights can be more, or less, clearly defined. Strong private property rights allow an individual to use a resource as they see fit and exchange private property on any terms that is acceptable to them. They are able to own, alter and transfer economic resources.

In the absence of strong property rights in quantitative KC there is likely to be under-provision of the quantity of effort devoted to KC per period (Q_e/t in Figure 8.10) Using Figure 8.10 it can be seen that equating the marginal benefit of individual effort (MB_i) with the marginal cost of effort to an individual (MC_i) at point 1 yields a Q_e/t at q_i. The lack of strong private property rights allowing the creator to capture all gains suggests the marginal benefit to all individuals (marginal social benefit, MSB) is increased, as compared with MB_i, generating an efficient equilibrium at point 2 (yielding a Q_e/t at q_s). Being at q_i (as opposed to q_s) generates a welfare-loss triangle whose area is 1-2-3.

In contrast with strong private property rights, communal property rights exist where individuals own the rights to use a resource in common with others. If no individual can be excluded from the use of a resource, it is by definition communal. The problem that

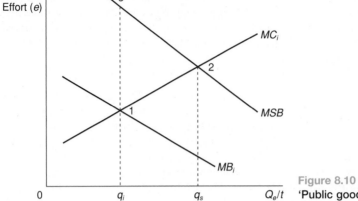

Output
per unit of
Effort (e)

MC_i

MSB

MB_i

0   q_i q_s Q_e/t

Figure 8.10
'Public goods effect' and KC

now arises is the 'commons effect'. This effect relies on the notion of too much effort, as one individual creates a piece of knowledge that another individual would have created. It is the over-grazing, or over-fishing, problem. Using Figure 8.11(b), which is derived from Figure 8.11(a), it can be seen that equating marginal benefit of individual effort

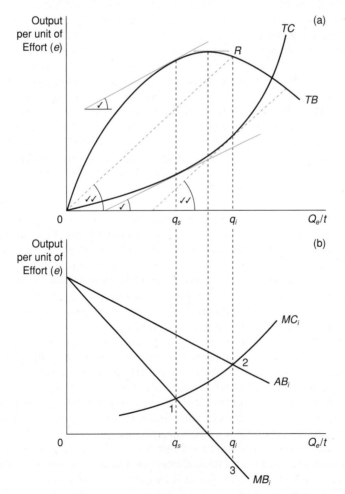

Output
per unit of
Effort (e)

(a)

TC

R

TB

0   q_s q_i Q_e/t

Output
per unit of
Effort (e)

(b)

MC_i

AB_i

MB_i

0   q_s q_i Q_e/t

Figure 8.11
'Commons effect' and
KC

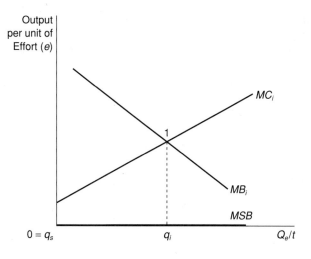

Figure 8.12
'Redistributive' KC

(MB_i) with marginal cost of effort to an individual (MC_i) at point 1 maximises the differ-ence between total cost (TC) and total benefit (TB) in panel (a) and yields a Q_e/t at q_s which is the efficient level of effort. The communal property rights aspect suggests the average benefit to an individual (AB_i) is greater than MB_i, generating an inefficient equi-librium at point 2 (yielding a Q_e/t at q_i). (The reader should look at the tangencies and angles of Figure 8.11(a) to check their understanding of the development of the relevant curves in Figure 8.11(b).) Being at q_i as opposed to q_s generates a welfare loss from over-production, that is a triangle whose area is 1-2-3 in Figure 8.11(b).

Whether the underproduction effect of Figure 8.10 or the overproduction effect of Figure 8.11(b) will dominate (or, fortuitously balance) cannot be determined *a priori*.

Turning to pecuniary, speculative or redistributive KC, it is the type of KC that simply leads to redistribution between individuals, in what is effectively a zero-sum game. In these circumstances the only change is a transfer of purchasing power from one indi-vidual to another and nothing real has changed. In Figure 8.12 it can be seen that equating the marginal benefit of individual effort (MB_i) with the marginal cost of effort to an individual (MC_i) at point 1 maximises the position of the individual and yields a Q_e/t at q_i, which is not the efficient level of effort. Why?

As the 'benefit' of the KC is simply a transfer, the marginal social benefit is zero (as what one gains another loses) so that MSB is the x-axis (as illustrated), making the social optimum level of Q_e/t zero at $0 = q_s$. The creation of a perfect stock-exchange prices-forecasting machine would alter the identity of who gains when stock prices move but would have a zero social rate of return! Such pecuniary, speculative or redistributive KC would be rejected on efficiency grounds but would have an equity role if it was a least-cost method to achieve equity in providing transfers – an unlikely configuration of events.

Qualitative KC is seen as spectacular or paradigm-shifting by Hirshleifer and Riley (1992: Chapter 7). Here, the payoff is for being first to make the discovery or knowledge created. Figures 8.10 to 8.12 all apply but the interpretation of the benefit curves is altered. The MB_i curve now takes the form $G\partial p_i/\partial e_i$, where G is the payoff to being first and $\partial p_i/\partial e_i$ the marginal change in the probability of being 'first' as effort changes (so that the whole term can be interpreted as the expected marginal private benefit). The term $\Sigma G\partial p_i/\partial e_i$ is the 'expected' version of marginal social benefit and, as such, the product of vertical summation. The term AB_i is replaced by Gp_i/e_i, where G is the payoff to being first and p_i/e_i the average probability of being 'first'. Substitution of these terms leaves the analysis unaffected; however, there is a time dimension to be added. Left alone, an iso-lated individual would time the date of KC via the chosen scale of effort to maximise the social benefit from KC.

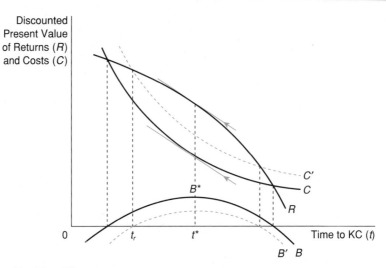

Figure 8.13 'Rush' to KC

In Figure 8.13 the *y*-axis measures the discounted present value of the return to KC labelled *R*, which will fall as the date of KC is postponed. Similarly, the total cost of KC labelled *C* will fall as the date of KC is postponed because of the impact of discounting. There are other reasons why the costs are falling with time. As the time horizon is lengthened fewer processes in KC will be carried out simultaneously, so that the sequencing of the process improves and the right building blocks are in the right place at the right time. Less labour will be assigned simultaneously to the process, so that decreasing marginal products will be encountered in a less severe way. The surplus (or profit-maximising) KC date is given as t^*, the top of the net benefit curve *B* at B^*. This arises as $B(t) = R(t) - C(t)$ and the first-order condition for benefit maximisation is $dC/dt = dR/dt$. In Figure 8.13 this is where the tangents to the *R* and *C* curves have the same slope as illustrated.

Suppose, however, the situation is made competitive by the emergence of a potential but higher cost (C' in Figure 8.13) rival in KC. To defeat the rival, the incumbent must choose a KC date that makes the rival's profit level zero. That is, they must choose t_r ($< t^*$) in Figure 8.13 and surplus or profit-maximising outcome B_r ($< B^*$). In short, the rival induces rushing, by comparison with the isolated solution. As with many economic problems there is an offsetting effect.

The lack of strong private property rights (allowing the creator to capture all gains from KC) suggests the discounted present value of the return to KC (labelled *R*) will fall at each *t* value (not drawn in Figure 8.13). This causes the net benefit 'bubble' to shrink on the *x*-axis and therefore point t_r migrates to the right (i.e. it decreases the incentive to rush). The new location of t^* depends on how the curve *R* shifts downwards. For the case of the pecuniary, speculative, or redistributive, KC the *R* curve is the *x*-axis and the KC is, by definition, always rushed in that it cannot be justified as socially efficient.

The predictions for production efficiency suggest a policy response to correct market failure:

(i)   the public goods problem seems to suggest that enforced patent or copyright protection to knowledge creators is justified, as it allows creators to reap the return to their effort exclusively (at least for a number of years). In addition, as KC is a public good that, once created, is non-rival (suggesting $P = MC = 0$), it might be appropriate for government to give grants to institutions (e.g. universities) to produce basic research that is 'free' to use by anyone (e.g. by reading scientific journals);

(ii) the commons effect of 'over-fishing' for KC suggests dulling the incentives to KC and recourse to management of the process, e.g. restricting an individual to a number of patent registrations per period, offering licences to knowledge creators to try to license the least-cost knowledge creators and offset the incentive to 'rush';

(iii) the redistributive, or speculative, KC has no social payoff and, therefore, should be discouraged by prohibitive taxation of speculative gains and the denial of patent and copyright protection.

As the nature of the good KC is complex, so are the economic policy solutions. For example, if the production of good X is competitive (as indicated in Figure 8.14), with constant cost supply at $MC = S$ and demand $D = AR$, equilibrium will be at point 1 with output q_c per period and price P_c per unit. Real, or investment, KC allows one firm to lower MC to MC_{kc} and therefore undercut competitors at point 2 with output q_{kc} and price P'_c. The firm, because of its KC advantage, may now exercise monopoly power. In the example created monopoly pricing at $MC = MR$ (at point 3) with output unchanged at q_c and price P_c. After KC the picture looks unchanged, although there is a gain to the extent of saved real resources (rectangle P'_c-P_c-1-3) there is a welfare loss from underproduction of good X per period of triangle 1-2-3.

Similarly, consider Figure 8.15: the initial situation is (with constant cost supply at MC and demand D) an equilibrium at point 1 (with output q_c per period and price P_0 per unit). If real, or investment, KC allows one firm to lower MC to MC_{kc} what might the knowledge creator do in the way of setting a fee, or royalty, for the creation? The creator realises the demand curve for the knowledge created is derived from the trapezoid P_1-P_0-1-2 as this is the gain it confirms on the firm illustrated. This is labelled d in Figure 8.15. For the horizontal section of d the associated marginal revenue is mr. They are coincident because implied total revenue curve is a ray from the origin and price equals average revenue equals marginal revenue (see Chapter 1). At the kinked point 3, the negatively sloped section of d is encountered; mr becomes negative and there is a discontinuity from 3 to point 4. Its construction can be seen as the marginal revenue curve if the negatively sloped section of d was made into a whole curve which is illustrated by reference to the dashed lines emanating leftward from point 3 and point 4. (Of course, the curve mr is falling twice as fast as d as in Chapter 2.) Once the knowledge has been created the marginal cost to the inventor is zero and labelled at mc (horizontal with the x-axis).

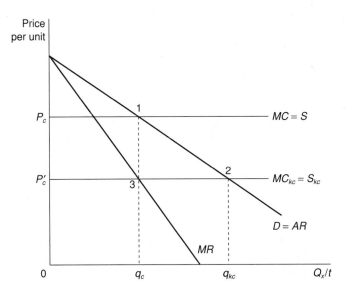

Figure 8.14
KC and competition to monopoly

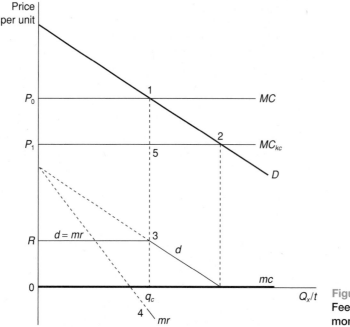

Figure 8.15
Fee setting: competitor v. monopolist

Pricing at $mc = mr$ would direct the focus at the discontinuity and suggest the knowledge creator charge a fee or royalty equal to the rectangle 0-R-3-$q_c = P_1$-P_0-1-5.

After KC the picture looks unchanged to consumers of good X; although there is a gain to the extent of saved real resources (rectangle P_1-P_0-1-5) that is taken as a royalty payment by the knowledge creator; there is a welfare loss from underproduction of good X per period of triangle 1-2-5. The underlying message is that policy design in the knowledge creation process is difficult and that policies that tend to increase production efficiency may well militate against consumption efficiency.

A final point, worth considering in this context, is the theory of second best. If it is accepted that the non-excludability of information reduces the incentive to create knowledge, a policy response to this market failure might be the introduction of property right protection via patent laws. However, such laws grant at least temporary monopoly power. Once there is a monopoly outcome that cannot be made a competitive one then the apparatus of second best seems relevant. However, McKee and West (1984) note that monopoly is the outcome and not the impediment to policy design. They would view distortions like the patent case 'as part of the Paretian solution and their existence constitutes part of the first best allocation' (McKee and West 1984: 250). With KC there is an economic concept to apply and interpret at almost every turn.

8.9 Challenge: What would 'surprise' you about an investment project?

Of course, psychological forces influence individuals and uncertainty is everywhere. One example of a response to these criticisms that also includes these elements is presented here. It involves the work of Shackle (for example, 1952). The subjective expected utility approach to uncertainty and some of its criticism were met in Chapter 7. Shackle's approach can be considered as one of the possible alternative theoretical approaches.

Imagine, with Shackle, the decision under analysis is investment. Individuals are motivated to take actions depending on the feelings they experience when they consider future events and whether the events will be a source of pleasure or pain (gains or losses).

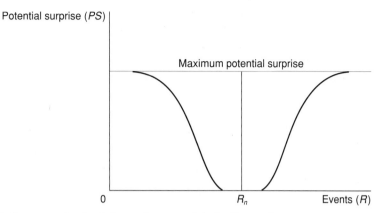

Figure 8.16 Degrees of potential surprise associated with events

Unlike subjective expected utility theorising, the S possible states of the world are not assumed known. Rather, individuals have imaginations and the list of the future events individuals consider, dubbed 'hypotheses', can vary with the arrival of information and therefore do not correspond to S. Shackle notes, also, that the probability of each state of the world arising is also typically unknown, as significant choices relate to unique events where relevant probability distributions are not known. Further, he argues that *ex-post* utility will not be the risk-weighted sum of the *ex-ante* utility associated with the S states of the world but will be the utility of the state of the world that actually arises in the fullness of time – which will be influenced by choices made (models in which the future is assumed to be known contain the implication that no current choice can influence the future).

Armed with these assumptions, return to an individual investment project (IP_0). It has already been suggested that the discounted present value of expected net returns is an appropriate economic guide to its success. Let the discounted present value of expected net returns for the safe, or neutral, context be represented by R_n in Figure 8.16. Individuals are seen as evaluating gains or losses relative to R_n, so that for each possible event/hypothesis considered there is a calculated value for R. Also, for each hypothesis there is a numerical measure of the degree to which each hypothesis is possible. This is its potential surprise value (PS).

Given this potential surprise, hypotheses can be plotted against each other as in Figure 8.16. If all the evidence leads an individual to a belief that a particular outcome will arise then the potential surprise if it arises is zero (the 'I knew that would happen' reaction to events). If, on the other hand, all the evidence leads an individual to totally disbelieve that a particular outcome will arise then the potential surprise if it arises is very great (the 'you could have knocked me down with a feather' reaction). In between, cases fill in the potential surprise scale – hypotheses that are partially believable. Using this apparatus, Shackle plots degrees of potential surprise for values of outcome R for a given investment project (see Figure 8.17).

Again, focusing on the nature of individuals, Shackle develops the ascendancy, or stimulus, function (AS). The ascendancy or stimulus function has two main arguments. First, for the given outcome R it is less stimulating the higher its potential surprise (PS). Second, the degree of ascendancy, or stimulus, is an increasing function of the value of R. Hypotheses involving high potential relative gains or losses that are not easy to disbelieve, catch individuals' attention. Given this, iso-ascendancy/stimulus curves can be drawn on the basis of the above description of the function $AS = AS(R, PS)$. Each iso-ascendancy/stimulus curve to the left or right of R_n offers equal stimulus by construction. The direction of ascendancy/stimulus is indicated by labelling curves to the further left,

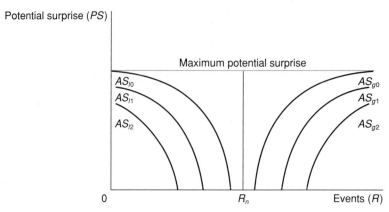

Figure 8.17 **Ascendancy stimulus curves**

or right, offer greater stimulus; that is, $AS_{l0} < AS_{l1} < AS_{l2}$ for losses and $AS_{g0} < AS_{g1} < AS_{g2}$ for gains (as indicted in Figure 8.17).

Putting Figures 8.16 and 8.17 together in Figure 8.18, it is possible to pick out two values for R (hypotheses) at tangency points 1 and 2, which maximise ascendancy/stimulus. Note, at point 1 the value of R is negative at R_l and at point 2 the value of R is positive at R_g with associated potential surprises of PS_1 and PS_2 respectively. These points are known as the 'primary focus loss' and 'primary focus gain' points. It is as if each investment project can be summarised with two pairs of data points (here R_l, PS_1; R_g, PS_2). With different investment projects R's and PS's values would be incomparable, so in order to make the values at points 1 and 2 comparable across investment projects they are standardised to their (ascendancy/stimulus constant) R values when potential surprise is zero. These points are known as the 'standardised focus loss' and 'standardised focus gain' points (here SF_l and SF_g respectively) in Figure 8.18. In principle it would now be possible to locate each investment project ($IP_0, \ldots, IP_n$) by its SF_g and SF_l value in a diagram with those two values recorded as the vertical and horizontal axes respectively (see Figure 8.19). The final step is to be able to pick out the desired investment project to undertake.

This is done with the introduction of the gambler indifference map between SF_g and SF_l. The map is effectively the indifference map between a 'good' (standardised focus gain) and a 'bad' (standardised focus loss). The positive slope indicates, for constant

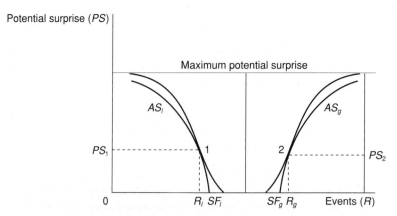

Figure 8.18 **Primary and standardised foci**

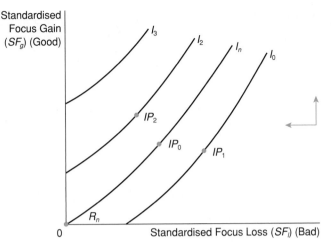

Figure 8.19
Decision-taker's indifference map

utility, standardised focus loss and standardised focus gain must move in the same direction. The increasing positive slope of each indifference curve indicates that, as standardised focus losses increase they generate increasing marginal disutility. The indifference curve labelled I_n, which emanates from the origin, indicates combinations of standardised focus gain and standardised focus loss that offer the same utility as the safe or neutral return R_n. With three investment projects IP_0, IP_1 and IP_2 located in SF_g-SF_l space, the indifference map indicates IP_1 is inferior to R_n, which is indifferent to risk-taking project IP_0, with IP_2 the utility-maximising choice.

As compared to subjective expected utility theory, the approach offers another set of insights into the mental process that might characterise individual decision-making under uncertainty. However, the relevant curves are conjectures and operationalising the theory correspondingly difficult.

8.10 Summary

This chapter has considered five aspects of time: time allocation; time as an input; time as delay, time and efficiency; and time in analysis itself. Time is generally allocated between leisure, home or non-market production and market work hours. Moving beyond the extreme goods of the pure market goods and pure leisure involves the notion of fundamental commodities that involve both 'market' and 'own' time inputs in their production.

As individuals exhibit a pure rate of time preference the process of discounting is involved in comparing costs and benefits that arise at different points in time. Efficient allocation of goods across time involves the implication that a full set of contingent markets exist. However, this is not the case and the presumption is that a market is more efficient in allocating goods in the current period than in future ones.

Knowledge creation was analysed not only in its own right but also as a vehicle to illustrate the economic concepts and reasoning developed in the first eight foundational chapters of this text.

Questions were raised as to the rationale and form of discounting for time that can be justified. The role of time in economic analysis itself is open to debate in that neoclassical economic analysis employs analytical time whereas, for many, decision making should be modelled in the context of perspective time.

References

Ainslie, G. (1991) Derivation of 'rational' economic behavior from hyperbolic discount curves, *American Economic Review*, 81 (2): 334–40.

Becker, G.S. (1965) A theory of the allocation of time, *Economic Journal*, 75: 493–517.

Becker, G.S. (1971) *Economic Theory*, New York: Alfred A. Knopf.

Broome, J. (1987) 'Good, fairness and QALYs', in M. Bell and S. Medus (eds) *The Proceedings of the Royal Institute of Philosophy and Medical Welfare*, Cambridge: Cambridge University Press.

Cairns, J. (1992) Discounting and health benefits: another perspective, *Health Economics*, 1 (1): 76–80.

Chadeau, A. (1992) What is households' non-market production worth? *OECD Economic Studies*, No 18 Spring: 85–103.

Cullis, J.G. and Jones, P.R. (2009) *Public Finance and Public Choice – Analytical Perspectives*, 3rd edn, Oxford: Oxford University Press.

De Grauwe, P. (2007) *Economics of Monetary Union*, 7th edn, Oxford: Oxford University Press.

Gibbons, R.S. (1997) An introduction to applicable game theory, *Journal of Economic Perspectives*, 11 (1): 127–49.

Goodin, R.E. (1982) Discounting discounting, *Journal of Public Policy*, 2 (1): 53–72.

Harvey, C. (1983) *Analysis of Project Finance in Developing Countries*, London: Heinemann.

Hirshleifer, J. and Riley, J.G. (1992) *The Analytics of Uncertainty and Information*, Cambridge: Cambridge University Press.

McKee, M. and West, E.G. (1984) Do second best considerations affect policy decisions, *Public Finance/Finances Publiques*, 42 (1): 246–60.

Parsonage, M. and Neuburger, H. (1992) Discounting and health benefits, *Health Economics*, 1 (1): 71–5.

Shackle, G.L.S. (1952) *Expectation in Economics*, 2nd edn, Cambridge: Cambridge University Press.

Thaler, R. and Sheffrin, H.M. (1981) An economic theory of self control, *Journal of Political Economy*, 89: 392–406.

Van der Pol, M. and Cairns, L. (2000) Valuing future private and social benefits: the discounted utility model versus hyperbolic discounting models, *Journal of Economic Psychology*, 21: 191–205.

Webb, M.G. (1973) *The Economics of Nationalised Industries: a Theoretical Approach*, London: Nelson.

PART II

THE HOUSEHOLD ECONOMY

CHAPTER 9

The economic family

9.1 Introduction

'There is one thing all people of the world have in common: they all belong to a household' (Kooreman and Wunderink 1997: 1). Despite this 'commonness' it is only in the last thirty years or so that family economics known as 'the new Home Economics' (to distinguish it from cooking!) has come to the fore and been integrated into more mainstream economics (see Ermisch 2003; Bryant 1990; Grossbard-Shechtman 2003). This 'lateness' partly reflects:

(i) a mistaken perspective that economics confines itself to market relationships (Swedberg 2003: 264 notes that the term 'economics' comes from the Greek term for the management of a household);
(ii) the lack of a conceptual framework capable of shedding light on the family; and
(iii) the feeling that, somehow, the family is a sacred thing, not to be analysed or questioned.

Ironically, although Mrs Thatcher will be for ever slated for saying 'there is no such thing as society' – a value judgement close to neoclassical economists' hearts – she is unfairly quoted in that she proceeded to emphasise the important role of the family.

In Chapter 1 it was suggested that economics was a mental skill, as opposed to being defined by subject matter, and in Chapter 8 the apparatus of fundamental commodities was explored. This, combined with considerations of rationality, risk and information (introduced in Chapter 7), means that enough material has been covered to develop an analysis of the economic family.

William Shakespeare in *As You Like It* (II, vii) vividly describes the seven ages of man from 'Mewling and puking' to 'second childishness, and mere oblivion' (had he been on a 'student night out'?). Understandably, less ambition is displayed here. The focus is family formation, functioning and potential dissolution.

A final section marshals some of the criticisms levelled at the 'economic family', which, in large measure, are the general criticisms of neoclassical microeconomics itself. Those who hate this subject may find some comfort here – you may not be alone!

9.2 Family formation

The definition of a family is not an easy matter but, here, what is in mind is a consensual and legal arrangement that involves at least two adults. At the risk of taking any romance out of the family, it is viewed from an economic perspective as a production unit. Given the previous chapter it is not surprising that the production unit is seen as producing fundamental commodities by combining own-time inputs with purchased market inputs.

The fundamental commodities produced can be both tangible and intangible. Tangible commodities would be sources of utility like meals, shelter, bringing up children, mutual physical insurance (to help each other in tough times). Intangible ones would be more abstract sources of utility like love, friendship, companionship and mutual mental insurance. The first question that is relevant to the economics of the family is at what stage do people cease to be individuals and become part of a family?

The answer is that it depends upon: (a) when individuals enter the marriage market, so called, and (b) the length of time that individuals choose to search that market. The idea is that this process can be described as being governed by economic principles. In Chapter 8 individuals searched for lower prices by balancing the gain from securing the lower price for the good against the costs of searching the market further. In the same way, it is possible to imagine that individuals search for a marriage partner and consider the benefits of getting a 'better-suited' partner against the costs of searching the market more extensively. In this type of context a partner is simply considered as a bundle of characteristics (see Chapter 2).

The type of characteristics can be divided into two. First, so-called *search characteristics*, which cover attributes like appearance, level of education and religion and, as such, are fairly easily investigated and established. More tricky are the *experience characteristics* individuals possess, e.g. the level of their ambition; their resilience to adversity; their loyalty; their trustworthiness; and the accuracy of their perception of their own ability that they convey. All of these are difficult to establish easily; they are only discovered through the passage of time (especially at times of stress or crisis).

As the process is an economic one, it is a question of balancing costs against benefits and, further, because being part of a marriage relationship is a voluntary process, individuals must do better inside a marriage than outside to be part of a marriage. 'Doing better' is seen in terms of enjoying a level of fundamental commodities that is higher than the level of fundamental commodities they can 'produce' as a single individual. As the length of time of search increases, more productive partner combinations can be found. But, when do you know when to stop searching? Basically, there are two answers that are outlined in the next two subsections.

Some illustrative numbers are calculated from the simple frequency distribution illustrated as Figure 9.1. It shows the frequency distribution (adapted from Fleisher and Kniesner 1980) of the units of additional fundamental composite commodity Z (see Chapter 8) – namely, 50, 60, 70, 80 or 90 units available to an individual if they form a joint partnership (marriage) arrangement with an individual of each 'productive' value-type. It is assumed a searching individual knows the nature of the distribution but not the identity of the actual individuals who have different productive values. It is further assumed, for reasons that will become clear below, that an assumption has been made about how the gains secured in the marriage are to be divided between the partners, so that the 'additional Z' figures incorporate this assumption, e.g. it might be 50–50 sharing.

9.2.1 'Go back and grovel' (Stigler search)

Figure 9.2 helps describe a search procedure developed by Stigler (1961). The curve labelled $E(Z|n)$ indicates how the expected total of a composite fundamental commodity (Z) increases with the number of searches (n = dates with potential partners). As drawn, it indicates that this level of commodities is increasing at a decreasing rate, so that the expected marginal benefit to search in terms of Z declines. Table 9.1 details the relevant arithmetic based on Figure 9.1.

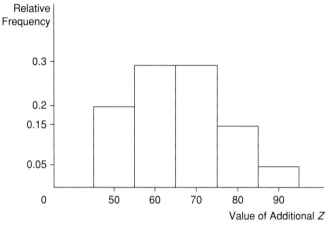

Figure 9.1
Frequency distribution of additional Z

Source: Adapted from Fleisher and Kniesner (1980).

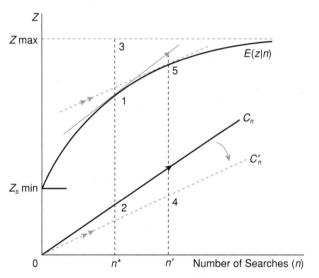

Figure 9.2
Stigler search for a partner

With a single search, the value of $E(Z \mid n = 1)$ is given as:

$$E(Z \mid n = 1) = 0.2 \times 50 + 0.3 \times 60 + 0.3 \times 70 + 0.15 \times 80 + 0.05 \times 90 = 65.5.$$

If n rises to 2 and, given there are 5 productive value types, there are $5^2 = 25$ possible pairs that might be drawn from the distribution. The objective is to form the expected highest payoff. For example, the pair (50, 60) has a probability (0.2, 0.3) so that, if it arose, the maximising choice of partner would be the '60' one, and the chance of having that choice is $0.2 \times 0.3 = 0.06$, so that the contribution to $E(Z \mid n = 2)$ of that particular pair is $0.06 \times 60 = 3.6$ units. The addition of 25 similar calculations yields $E(Z \mid n = 2) = 71.7$. When $n = 3$ the same process is completed for triples, etc. As the number of searches increases $E(Z \mid n \to \infty)$ approaches 90.

The curve labelled $E(Z \mid n)$ in Figure 9.2 can be viewed as the continuous version of the entries in Table 9.1. The y-axis intercept point Z_s min indicates the output of Z available to the individual if they remain single and undertake zero searches (assumed to be 10 units in Table 9.1). The line Z max indicates the total possible level of fundamental commodities if the perfect Z-producing partner is located. If it is assumed search involves a constant cost c per unit (£5 in Table 9.1) and the number of searches is n, then total search costs can be described as a straight line labelled C_n in Figure 9.2 whose slope is c.

Table 9.1 Approximating Stigler search for a partner

(a) No. of searches (n)	(b) Expected highest Z value on n searches $E(Z|n)$	(c) Marginal benefit $\Delta E(Z|n)$	(d) Search costs $(cn = £5 \times n)$ (cn)	(e) Marginal cost $\Delta(cn)$
0	10 (= Z_s min)	–	£0	–
1	65.5	65.5	£5	£5
2	71.7	6.2	£10	£5
3	75.0	3.3	£15	£5
4	77.1	2.1	£20	£5
5	78.7	1.6	£25	£5

As depicted in this figure, the optimal point to stop searching is at n^* 'dates', where the marginal benefit of search (witnessed by the tangent to the total fundamental commodities curve at point 1) is equal to the marginal cost of search (which is the tangent to the curve labelled cn at point 2). The optimal point is where the tangents are parallel.

In this way, the expected gain from search is maximised. (In Table 9.1 it is a question of comparing columns (c) and (e).) Assuming the value of a unit of Z at £1, the optimal number of searches in Table 9.1 is clearly only 2, as marginal benefit exceeds marginal cost for 2 searches but not for 3. Having searched for an optimal number of times, the individual is then conceived of as choosing the partner (from amongst those the individual has met) that will maximise the expected gain of fundamental commodities. This may clearly involve going back to early 'dates' and saying: 'you are the one for me' – hence the grovelling in the subsection title. (This may seem fanciful. However, everyday (and film) representations of love situations involve a line to the effect: 'Since we parted I have found no one to compare with you'. So, when you hear this you may literally be being told the truth, that you are the best of a (possibly very small) bunch considered.)

Note that the process involves being nowhere near the maximum of fundamental commodities. Distance 1-3 in Figure 9.2 is a measure of your optimal level of ignorance of the marriage market in this respect. An optimum involving Z max would only arise as the number of optimal searches grew very large, implying a world in which search was free, so that cn becomes the x-axis. Should the cost of a search fall from c to c' then the cost of search curve $c'n$ would apply and an increased number of searches n' become optimal, so that distance 4-5 measures the expected gain in fundamental commodities to be secured from partner search. Speed-dating schemes are about reducing (considerably) the size of c.

9.2.2 Setting a reservation payoff (sequential search)

The search modelled above presupposes you can go back and pick up on past associations. However, many might view it as more realistic to model the process as one that stops when Mr, or Miss, Right is met. But how do you know who is 'Right'?

The answer is that you form a reservation payoff to marriage and when you meet a partner that offers at least this reservation value of additional Zs you stop the process. This is a sequential search process, which can also be built around the frequency distribution in Figure 9.1.

Table 9.2 shows the data necessary to formulate a reservation value of Zs called Z_r. In column (a) the value of a unit of Z is assumed to be £1, so that the units are all in £s. The idea is to form the marginal benefit associated with increasing Z_r and compare it with the marginal cost in terms of search time of obtaining that Z_r. The optimising Z_r is the one

Table 9.2 Approximating sequential search for a partner

(a) Reservation Z value benefit $(Z_r) \times £1$	(b) Probability (p_r) of Z value at least $(= Z_r)$	(c) Expected Z value $E(Z)$	(d) Expected search cost $(c/p_r\ (Z \geq Z_r)$	(e) Net $(c) - (d)$
50	1.0	65.5	£5 (£5/1.0)	£55.50
60	0.8	69.38	£6.25 (= £5/0.8)	£63.13
70	0.5	75.0	£10 (= £5/0.5)	£65.00
80	0.2	82.5	£25 (= £5/0.2)	£57.50
90	0.05	90.0	£100 (= £5/0.05)	−£10.0

where marginal benefit equals marginal cost ($MBz_r = MCz_r$). The searcher is then assumed to search until that Z_r value at a minimum is met and to accept it.

The actual Z_r value may, in fact, be higher. To see this, suppose 50 is selected as Z_r. This is the minimum value of Z but with one pick (or 'date') from the distribution in Figure 9.1 the expected value of Z is as calculated above, namely

$$E(Z|n = 1) = 0.2 \times 50 + 0.3 \times 60 + 0.3 \times 70 + 0.15 \times 80 + 0.05 \times 90 = 65.5.$$

That is, with luck, you date someone with a Z greater than 50 and accept them, as they exceed your minimum requirements.

What is the expected value of Z if $Z_r = 60$ is chosen? From Figure 9.1 it can be seen the probability of getting 60 is 0.3 but the probability of getting 60 or more is 0.8. Given that you will search until you receive 60 or more, the conditional probability of accepting 60 is 0.3/0.8. Intuitively, there is a 30% of 80% chance of accepting 60. By the same reasoning, there is a 30% of 80% chance of accepting 70, a 15% of 80% chance of accepting 80 and a 5% of 80% chance of accepting 90. Note: the sum of the conditional probabilities is 1 and the expected value of Z when $Z_r = 60$ is the sum of the following terms that are not in parentheses. The numbers in parentheses indicate the derivation of the numbers to be summed. That is, the expected Z value = 22.50(0.375 × 60) + 26.25(0.375 × 70) + 15.0(0.1875 × 80) + 5.63(0.0625 × 90) = 69.38. The remaining entries in column (c) in Table 9.2 are constructed in an analogous fashion.

But what of expected search costs? Suppose $Z_r = 50$ is chosen (given that all the values in the distribution are 50 or greater), one date (or search) will suffice to secure an acceptable partner. The data of column (b) indicate that this is not always the case. When the probability of securing a given Z_r is not 1 the expected searches required to find Z_r at a minimum can be estimated by considering the number of 'searches' (n) required to make the probability of securing $Z_r = 1$. For example, if $Z_r = 70$ is chosen, 0.5 of the distribution has that value or greater. That is $p_r(Z \geq Z_r)$ is 0.5 and what is required is that $p_r n = 1$, so that the unknown $n = 1/p_r$. It is in this way that nc (column (d)) can be constructed as the expected search cost. Recall that c, the cost per search, is assumed constant at £5, so that cn is simply £5 × $1/p_r$. This is an expected value because p_r is a probability and the actual experienced value of n might be higher (or lower) depending on chance. The entries in column (d) are calculated in this way.

Column (e) presents net benefit as Column (c) minus Column (d), where it can be seen that given the nature of the discrete data you would not set Z_r below 70 or above 80. In order to develop further insights it is convenient to look at marginal benefits and marginal costs. Table 9.3 details these values from the data in Table 9.2.

Again, it is evident that Z_r should be set somewhere between 70 and 80, as this is where $MBz_r = MCz_r$. Before 70 $MBz_r > MCz_r$ and above 80 $MBz_r < MCz_r$. With these mechanics in mind, it is easier to work with continuous diagrammatic methods.

Table 9.3 Using marginal benefits and costs to locate Z_r

(a) Z_r	(b) MBz_r	(c) MCz_r
50		
60	3.9	1.25
70	5.6	3.75
80	7.5	15.00
90	7.5	75.00

Figure 9.3 illustrates the typical presentation of the relevant MBz_r and MCz_r curves and are broadly consistent with the data of Table 9.3. The intersection at point 1 determines Z_r^*. A clear reply to someone who says to you 'I have been looking for someone like you all my life' is 'You have almost certainly set Z_r too high!' (which casts doubt on their rationality!). This raises the question of how sequential search for a partner is affected by changes of variables implicitly held constant above.

Stigler (1961), Becker (1991) and other (mainly University of Chicago) economists, who were involved with the development of the majority of the pieces of theory which relate to the family, being logical positivists, were interested not in mimicking the process of marriage formation in economic terms but in deriving a set of testable hypotheses. In this section we continue to assume (to make the theory simple) that there is only one fundamental commodity Z. It is a composite of all other fundamental commodities and it is produced by own-time input t and the level of a single market input (X_1). That is, the individual combines X_1 with own time T to produce $Z[Z = Z(X_1, T)]$. All individuals have the same time available to them per period, so that the x-axis is identical for all individuals. For example, it could be the time in a week or the time in a month or a year. However, people vary in their access to the market input, as this depends on their market wage rate w and their unearned income V (see Chapter 8 for relevant analysis) and the price of the market good p_{x1}. It is assumed that the price of the market good is common to all individuals and $V = 0$, so the only variable to be considered is the wage rate w. The object of the exercise is to establish gains from the marriage trade.

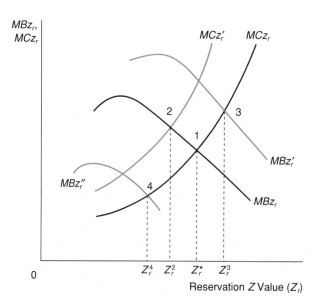

Figure 9.3 Setting Z_r in sequential search

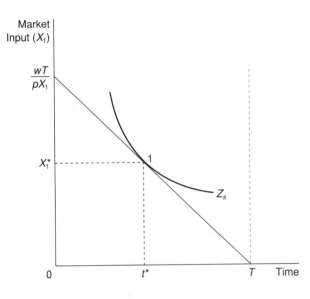

Figure 9.4
Producing a fundamental
commodity alone

This begins with Figure 9.4, which shows the production of Z available to an individual when they are single. The intercept on the y-axis isolates the individual's maximum access to the purchased inputs and is simply the product of their wage and the time they have available divided by p_{x1}. For the moment the wage w is for an individual whose sex is ignored. The x-axis intercept is simply all time available. The straight line joining the two intercepts can be viewed as a simplified full income constraint. The optimum for the individual is to combine X_1^* market input with t^* own time input to produce Z_s at point 1. It can be noted that this is where the Z_s min employed in the search scenarios above (see Table 9.1) comes from. It is the maximum fundamental commodity available to the single individual. However, 'it takes two to make a marriage' and to be an attractive proposition marriage must offer gains or (at minimum) no loss.

If it is assumed the marriage is between heterosexuals, the question is where will *economic* differences arise? Typically people face different wage rates and, as a matter of fact, males tend to face a higher wage rate than females. It is therefore reasonable to associate the high wage rate (w_h) with males and the low wage rate (w_l) with females. The reason for this disparity in wage rates is that men and women differ in their innate abilities, that they contain different human capital investments, there is labour market discrimination, or (as is likely) some combination of all these factors applies. But this is not of great concern here because it is the existence of different wage rates that 'does the work'.

Recall that the object of the exercise is to establish gains from the marriage trade (see Crouch 1979). Turning to Figure 9.5, it shows the production of Z available to an individual when they are single portrayed in an Edgeworth–Bowley box way (see Chapter 5). The intercepts are as before but now a high male wage w_h is involved and a lower female w_l, so that Z_s^m and Z_s^f are the Z isoquants obtainable when the male and female remain single and adjust to their Z-maximising positions at points 1 and 2. Putting two pictures together allows a presentation of the gains from the 'marriage trade' in the same way that the principle of comparative advantage is presented for international trade (see Chapter 17).

Looking at Figure 9.5, it is possible to see that there is a triangular area labelled T_m-T_f-3 that is only obtainable by marriage and specialisation of tasks. As illustrated, the man will specialise in all market input, providing $w_h T/p_{X1}$ units of market input, because he has a comparative advantage there. The woman will provide all time inputs where she has a comparative advantage (so T_f is the amount of time provided by the female). The

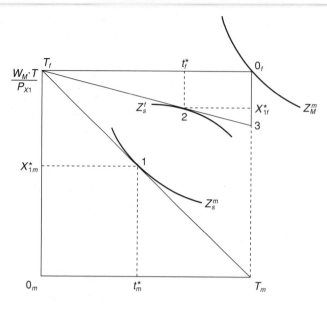

Figure 9.5
Gains from the 'marriage trade'

combination of time (T_f) and market inputs ($w_h T/p_{X1}$), now available, secures an isoquant labelled Z_M^m, where M stands for marriage and m superscript denotes evaluation with respect to the male fundamental commodity production function. Z_M^m through 0_f is considerably further to the north-west than Z_s^m, which is the amount of fundamental commodity that is available to the man alone. However, it must be recognised that the woman previously enjoyed Z_s^f, so that the gain from marriage, as represented via the male isoquant map, is $Z_M^m - (Z_s^m + Z_s^f)$.

A number of testable implications flow from this simple stylisation.

(i) First, if Z_s^f is held constant, then the higher w_h, the greater are the gains from marriage.
(ii) Second, with w_h rising, the opportunity cost of searching increases and therefore it is optimal to search less. This can be seen in Figure 9.3 where it amounts to a rise in c (the cost of a search), so that MCz_r rises to MCz_r' and equilibrium moves from point 1 to 2 and Z_r downwards from Z_r^* to Z_r^2. A shorter search should be required to locate a lowered Z_r.
(iii) Third, if Z_s^m is constant, there are greater gains from trade the lower is w_l.
(iv) Finally, if w_l falls, the opportunity cost of search is lowered and therefore (other things equal) you would expect to search more.

It is intuitive to expect that the third effect dominates the fourth effect. The potentially falsifiable hypotheses that come from this are that:

(1) High-wage males get married sooner than low-wage males;
(2) Low-wage females on balance tend to marry sooner than high-wage females;
(3) Low-wage males and high-wage females have less to gain and, therefore, are less likely to be married (and more often divorced).

In the standard methodology it now becomes a question of looking at the empirical evidence in respect of these hypotheses. Becker can claim that there is a considerable amount of evidence that is consistent with his theorising. Note that the formularisation of the theory suggests the adage that 'opposites attract' is a sound one, in that the maximum gains from the marriage trade are secured by high-wage males marrying low-wage females.

There are a number of other implications that are part of this analysis. Education is a key variable in the framework, in that education and non-market production are both time-intensive activities and therefore 'competitors'. Given the actual pattern of special-isation of females to non-market production, other things equal, it can be anticipated that educated females marry later.

Also, there are considerations about the nature of the environment. Especially the urban/rural split has implications for the frequency distribution of additional Z in Figure 9.1. First, urban environments are more exciting and therefore you would expect individuals to search longer and marry later. Second, urban environments are more heterogeneous and therefore the distribution of additional Z might be expected to have a higher mean and larger variance, so that the payoff to search is likely to be greater than in the more homogeneous rural environment. In terms of Figure 9.3, MBz_r increases to MBz_r' and equilibrium moves from point 1 to 3 and Z_r upwards from Z_r^* to Z_r^3. A longer search should be required to locate a raised Z_r. As for the more homogeneous and less 'rich' rural en-vironment, in terms of Figure 9.3 MBz_r decreases to MBz_r'' and equilibrium moves from point 1 to 4 and Z_r downwards from Z_r^* to Z_r^4. A shorter search should be required to locate a lowered Z_r. Other things equal, urban-dwellers marry later than rural ones.

A third consideration is that part of the demand for family formation is the derived demand for children. In the rural setting the direct costs of children are often lower, market input prices are typically lower in rural, as compared to urban, environments. Furthermore, the indirect costs of children are also likely to be lower. These are the opportunity costs in terms of work opportunities for women in the country, which other things equal, tend to be much less. The upshot is that rural-dwellers marry sooner and this is again a hypothesis that is not inconsistent with the evidence.

It is worth noting two further things about this analysis. The first is that there is no discussion of gains secured because of economies of scale. Although it is true that indi-visibilities may give rise to economies of scale (for example, not needing two cookers, two fridges and meals for two not having twice all the ingredients etc.). This is not part of the analysis because that is a gain that is available to any sharing group, not just those who choose to marry. Public-goods-type arguments may also fall into this category, as all members of a sharing group, not just the married, can enjoy the consumption benefits of, say, a well-laid-out private garden. However, the positive externality of seeing another person enjoy the scent and view of the garden may be more intense if that member is your marriage partner rather than just part of a sharing group.

Those following through the analysis are often somewhat alarmed in that they tend to observe that high-wage males do not marry low-wage females. Here is a genuine need to augment the analysis. So far, negative assortative mating seems to emerge as a conse-quence of traits that are substitutes for each other. Complementarities between the indi-viduals have been ignored. People often prefer to be with people who have the same interests, enjoy the same prejudices, often therefore you get like with like. 'Like with like' choices are known as 'positive assortative mating'. Education level, intelligence, age and religious affiliation are factors associated with positive assortative mating. Adjusting for this tends to blunt the edge of the analysis but widen its application.

9.2.3 The dating game

One of the classic games is called (rather 'datedly') 'battle of the sexes' or 'tender trap' (for this and many other games see Gibbons 1992). In the current context it is useful to illustrate the problem of undertaking a search (or date).

While at separate workplaces the 'searchers' must choose to attend one of two activ-ities. These are full-contact karate and flower arranging. Ron (the row player) has a dif-ferent first choice from that of Cathy (the column player) but both prefer to choose the same activity over being at separate venues all evening, making the date non-existent. There is an element therefore of conflict and the need for coordination to be at the same

Table 9.4 The battle of the sexes game

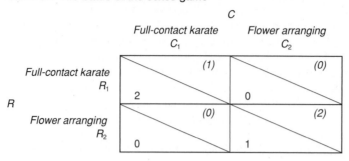

place. Ron prefers full-contact karate while Cathy prefers flower arranging. The payoffs set down in Table 9.4 capture this information.

The question is what should Ron and Cathy choose to attend in the absence of any contact between them. Ron (Cathy) must consider how to maximise their payoff taking into account his (her) first choice differs from Cathy's (Ron's) and knowing that the choice made will affect both of them. John F. Nash, a joint Nobel prize winner in 1994 (who was made famous with the general public in the film *A Beautiful Mind*) argued that, in equilibrium, a player would not wish to alter their strategy on finding out what the other player's strategy is. In this, Nash (1950) argued that Table 9.4 contains two so-called Nash equilibria in pure strategies where there are a pair of strategies (here $R_1:C_1$ and $R_2:C_2$) such that for Ron (Cathy) R_1 (C_1) is the best response to Cathy (Ron) choosing C_1 (R_1) and Ron (Cathy) choosing R_2 (C_2) when Cathy (Ron) chooses C_2 (R_2). Given the 'symmetricalness' of the game, both represent equally compelling equilibria.

In Figure 9.6 these two Nash equilibria in pure strategies are denoted by points 2 and 2′ in the probability box. Point 2′ is where they both go to flower arranging and point 2 is where they both go to full-contact karate. Rather than choose a so-called pure strategy of going to karate or flower arranging, the two might choose a mixed strategy of using a probability device to select which to do. What probabilities should be used? A first suggestion might be for Ron (Cathy) to say what probability of going to karate (flower arranging) would make him (her) indifferent to whether Cathy (Ron) chooses karate or flower arranging. Let p (q) be the relevant probability of karate (flower arranging).

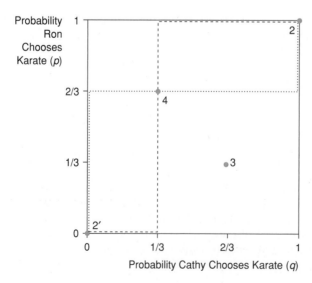

Figure 9.6
Isolating Nash equilibria

Taking Ron's perspective, the question is what p solves

$$R_1:C_1 + R_2:C_1 = R_1:C_2 + R_2:C_2$$

Given the payoffs from Table 9.4 this becomes

$$p \cdot 2 + (1 - p) \cdot 0 = p \cdot 0 + (1 - p) \cdot 1$$

$$2p = 1 - p$$

and

$$p = 1/3$$

That is, the solution is for Ron to roll a three-sided die with one side marked K for karate and two sides marked F for flower arranging and then doing what the roll of the die says. (Readers can check the solution is symmetrical for Cathy.) Point 3 in the probability box of Figure 9.6 represents this solution.

However, Nash argued in a different fashion. Nash suggested a mixed strategy solution as one in which each player's mixed strategy was a best response to the other player's mixed strategy, a natural extension of the description of Nash equilibria described above. How would this affect the solution obtained above?

Let $(q, 1 - q)$ be the mixed strategy for Cathy going to karate with a probability of q and flower-arranging with a probability of $1 - q$. Similarly, let $(p, 1 - p)$ be the mixed strategy for Ron going to karate with a probability of p and flower arranging with a probability of $1 - p$. With Cathy playing $(q, 1 - q)$ Ron's expected payoffs are:

$q \cdot 2 + (1 - q) \cdot 0 = 2q$ for going to karate,

$q \cdot 0 + (1 - q) \cdot 1 = 1 - q$ for flower arranging.

If $q > 1/3$ Ron will choose karate and $p = 1$.
If $q < 1/3$ Ron will choose flower arranging and $p = 0$.
If $q = 1/3$ then any value of p is a best response. This is captured in the dashed line in the probability box of Figure 9.6.

With Ron playing $(p, 1 - p)$ Cathy's expected payoffs are:

$p \cdot 1 + (1 - p) \cdot 0 = p$ for going to karate,

$p \cdot 0 + (1 - p) \cdot 2 = 2(1 - p)$ for flower arranging.

If $p > 2/3$ Cathy will choose karate and $q = 1$.
If $q < 2/3$ Cathy will choose flower arranging and $q = 0$.
If $p = 1/3$ then any value of q is a best response. This is captured in the dotted line in the probability box of Figure 9.6. Where the dotted and dashed lines cross, at point 4, represents the *mixed-strategy Nash equilibrium*. This is with Ron going to karate or flower arranging using a three-sided probability die with two sides marked K and one side marked F and Cathy going to karate or flower arranging using a three-sided probability die with two sides marked F and one side marked K.

It is now evident why point 3 is not a Nash equilibrium, with Cathy choosing karate with a probability of 2/3. The reasoning is that Ron will no longer choose karate with a probability of 1/3; rather, as noted above, with $q > 1/3$ Ron will choose karate and $p = 1$. The fact that Ron will change his choice when Cathy's strategy is revealed violates the notion of a Nash equilibrium. Similarly, with Ron choosing karate with $p = 1$ Cathy's best response is karate with $p = 1$ and Nash equilibrium at point 2 in Figure 9.6 is established.

Having solved the dating game in a Nash fashion what role, if any, will marriage play in Ron and Cathy's future?

9.2.4 **The role of marriage**

If there are economies of scale in groups and/or cohabitation in couples is an option, the question arises as to the role that marriage plays. Rowthorn (1998) adds to the analysis of the economic family by noting that marriage has many features of the modern business partnership, so that the joint enterprise can only secure maximum economic gains if the individuals involved commit themselves both fully and seriously. In turn, full and serious commitment will result in large costs if one partner fails to keep to their commitments or leaves (divorces from) the partnership (marriage) when either preferences change or the opportunity of a better partnership (relationship) presents itself. If the fear of these costs arising cannot be allayed, individuals will not fully commit by keeping their options open and avoiding actions that put them at the mercy of opportunistic behaviour. Opportunistic behaviour arises in particular in the work of Williamson's (e.g. 1985) transactions costs economics and is defined as 'self-seeking behaviour with guile'. If partnerships are to be successful then trust between partners has to be created and hence marriage can be analysed as the institution that fosters the creation of trust – the expectation that a partner will actually do what they explicitly or implicitly promise they will.

The successful marriage involves relationship-specific investments, in which individuals commit their own time and market inputs in a process that is typically costly to terminate. For such investments to take place optimally, each partner must make credible commitments about their experience characteristics in particular. Trust creation involves paying a purchase price, in that an individual's ability to break commitments made is attenuated by compulsion (the set of laws that obtain) or, less drastically, by the requirement to make some form of compensation when a commitment is broken. Rowthorn (1998) lists the way in which marriage can create a trust-fostering environment:

(i) Marriage is a signalling mechanism. One feature a convincing signal has to have is that it is costly to fake, copy or imitate.
(ii) An expensive marriage ceremony is a sunk cost in that it produces no resaleable asset but serves a purpose by indicating sincerity with respect to future joint plans.
(iii) The marriage vows themselves involve very public promises that raise the fear of loss of reputation should they not be kept.
(iv) Divorce laws that ascribe fault (and favour innocent parties) are compensation mechanisms for those subject to opportunistic behaviour. For trust to be fostered the obligations of the married must be more onerous than for those cohabiting. Exit needs to be costly.[1]

Trust fosters specialisation and exposure to risk (e.g. fully specialising in non-market production). Therefore, each partner needs to be assured that they will receive a fair share of the benefit stream created by their joint enterprise should divorce occur. Principles of allocation between ex-partners should be compensation proportionate to contributions made within the marriage, modified upwards or downwards in line with the degree of fault each partner must bear in the context of partnership breakdown.

---

1. As in many other situations there may be a large gap between the actual law and the everyday perceptions of it. One major myth in this context is that a woman who lives with a man for at least seven years without marrying him becomes a so-called common law wife and as such has all the rights of married women. In fact they have few legal rights (*Financial Mail*, Sunday 2 July 2000, p. 30).

9.3 Family functioning: 'How does the economic family work?'[2]

Once a family has formed issues arise as to its functioning. The gains from the marriage trade have to be distributed. The number and quality of any children has to be determined and the family coordinated. Decisions relating to these key areas of family life are explored in a microeconomic way in this section. This is not to say that microeconomic theory can satisfactorily deal with all the relevant aspects of these choices but nevertheless the claim would be that it is insightful.

9.3.1 The distribution of the gains from marriage

Having established that in the presence of trust there are gains from marriage over and above those that are available to single individuals that cohabit, there is the question then of who secures the gains from the institution of marriage. This in effect is a bargaining problem over the distribution of the marriage gains $Z_M^m - (Z_s^m + Z_s^f)$ located from Figure 9.5.

Figure 9.7 illustrates a more generalised picture (see Ermisch 1993). The commodity increment frontier indicates the gain in fundamental commodities that is available inside the marriage. Z availability when single Z_s^m and Z_s^f for the male and female respectively indicates, in bargaining theory, the so-called security, or *status quo*, points in the relationship. These points represent the amounts of fundamental commodity that are available to the man and the woman if they remain single. These are security or *status quo* points because, given the voluntary nature of marriage, no one is voluntarily going to be pushed to a level of enjoyment of fundamental commodities below those points. The area between 1 and 2 represents the relevant part of the frontier where the final contract, if that term can be used, will be found. A number of possible solutions to the bargaining problem have been suggested. In assessing the additional units of Z available in marriage in the search descriptions, the searcher will have necessarily made an explicit, or implicit, assumption on how the total gains to the marriage trade would be divided.

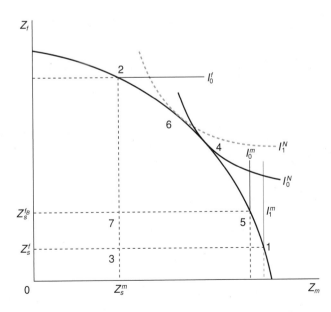

Figure 9.7
Bargaining over the gains from marriage

2. For an authoritative book-length treatment see Ermisch (2003).

A number of possibilities merit consideration. In a dominant male solution then point 1 is likely to be secured because this pushes the woman to her security point and offers all the gains to men. An environment in which there are many marriageable females but few marriageable males encourages this kind of result. Post-war France might well be a context exhibiting this kind of result from marriage. Because it treats the Z_f value as a neutral to the male, the indifference curve I_1^m reflecting this (vertical) is used to isolate point 1 (see Chapter 2).

In contrast, a dominant female solution reverses the roles and occurs at point 2 on (horizontal) I_0^f where Z^m is neutral to the female and where all the gains from marriage are being secured by the female. A world of few marriageable females is one where this type of result is likely to be found.

An interesting result in bargaining theory is associated with the so-called Nash bargaining solution. Nash (1950) argued that a relevant solution in a bargaining context would be one in which you maximise the value of the indifference curves available, where that indifference curve is the product of the gains to each person. In geometric terms, the indifference curve is a rectangular hyperbola with respect to the origin for the commodity increment frontier, i.e. the origin being point 3.

Such a solution is the outcome of theorising that any bargaining solution should have the following attractive properties.

(i)   The first of these is *invariance*. The result should be independent of the units of measurement. It turns out (as we noted in Chapter 1) that a rectangular hyperbola has an elasticity of substitution that is unity. As an elasticity is a real number it has the precise property that it is independent of the units of measurement.

(ii) A second feature is *efficiency*. It must be impossible to make one person better off and no one worse off. If you are maximising the product of the gains this condition must automatically be met because if one could be better off with no one worse off, the product of the gains cannot be as large as possible.

(iii) A further criterion is the *independence of irrelevant alternatives*. In this context this means that if you remove part of the constraint that does not contain this solution it will have no impact on what the solution turns out to be. This condition is also met.

(iv) Finally, Nash thought that the characteristic of *anonymity* should apply to the bargaining solution. That is, re-labelling of the bargainers does not affect the solution.

Adopting the Nash (1950) bargaining solution (not to be confused with Nash equilibrium) the equilibrium is at point 4 with the indifference curve I_0^N (N for Nash) drawn with respect to axes 2-3-1. This depiction of the distribution of the gains from marriage has some further implications. One example relates to how the outside environment can affect the bargaining solution inside a marriage. If, for example, a welfare benefit (B) that is available only to single women and not to married women was introduced, then it would have the effect, if it was binding, of raising the security point of females (raising Z_s^f to $Z_{s'B}^f$). The impact of this is to move the dominant male solution, such that point 5 on I_0^m is picked out, and to move the Nash bargaining solution, such that point 6 on I_1^N is picked out as the relevant axes become 2-7-5. Note that these are gains to females in marriage. It is an interesting point that these gains can be secured for women inside marriage, independent of anyone being actually observed to receive the transfer payment available to single women. The knowledge of its existence affecting the opportunity cost of being single is all that matters to make the implication relevant.

As we are considering marriage as an economic process, it is quite possible that the gains from marriage can be reduced to zero. For example, if the putative transfer payment to single women were raised far enough, it would erode any possible gains from marriage. Females would choose to drop out of the marriage market altogether.

The nature of the divorce laws also matters. Rowthorn (1998) points out with respect to divorce laws that, when guilt (default) can be established, not assigning fault to one or other of the parties weakens the bargaining power of the 'honest' partner who wishes either to end or continue their marriage. The fact that there is little or no penalty to reneging on the marriage partnership strengthens the bargaining position of the dishonest partner, as the opportunity cost of their actions are decreased. If the importance of this is doubted, econometric evidence from American states produced by Brinig and Crafton (1994) found that a switch to 'no-fault' divorce was accompanied by a significant increase in domestic violence. This is consistent both with victims having access to less compensation on divorce and the violent feeling less threatened by divorce action. The apparently more liberal law had changed the bargaining power relationship within marriage to the physical and emotional detriment of one partner.

9.3.2 The quantity and quality of children

What about children? A Church of England bishop caused controversy a few years ago by declaring that it is a Christian duty to have children as part of a marriage. Here a more secular view is adopted.

It has already been noted that children are often part of the derived demand for the institution of marriage. Children are viewed similarly as fundamental commodities that offer utility in the form of a consumption of direct psychic gain (e.g. the 'That's my boy', 'That's my girl' aspects of having children). Also, there is an indirect investment payoff in that you may gain from the non-market, or market, production that your children produce. In many societies children represent an old-age pension scheme.

In order to make matters simple and to work in two dimensions, suppose that there are only two fundamental commodities Z_y, a composite and Z_c children, so that utility depends on the quantities of Z_y and Z_c:

$$U = U(Z_y, Z_c) \tag{9.1}$$

The objective is to consider the potentially falsifiable implications derivable from this set-up. In Figure 9.8 the axes are labelled Z_y and Z_c. The budget constraints are the Becker full-income budget constraints that were derived in Chapter 8. It is a simple matter to

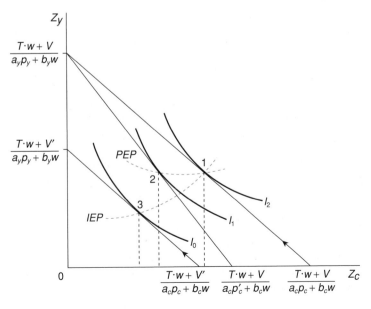

Figure 9.8
Economic factors and the number of births

manipulate this diagram to isolate the consequences of altering the economic incentives to have children. In case readers think that this is in some way frivolous, in essence what you are doing is studying 'population economics'. Given that the world is generally claimed to be over-populated, the arguments discussed are arranged to give the prediction of fewer births.

What determines the number of children people choose to bring into the world? In Figure 9.8 the intercepts of the full-income constraints are as constructed in Chapter 8, that is $T \cdot w + V$ divided by the shadow prices of the fundamental commodities $\pi_y = a_y p_y + b_y w$ and $\pi_c = a_c p_c + b_c w$, where a_y, b_y, a_c and b_c are the Leontief coefficients into the production of fundamental commodities Z_y and Z_c respectively and p_y and p_c can be regarded as the price index for a composite of required market inputs X_y and X_c into Z_y and Z_c respectively (see Chapter 8).

If the price of the market inputs, X_c, into Z_c, is increased (i.e. p_c to p'_c), equilibrium will move from point 1 to point 2, reflecting a movement of tangency with an indifference curve from I_1 to I_2 as the full-income constraint swivels around its y-axis intercept. It is now utility-maximising to choose fewer births. A lowering of the unearned (or property) income, variable (V from V to V') moves equilibrium from 1 to 3. There is a pure negative income effect, as reflected in the parallel backward shift of the full-income constraint. Given that children can be described as a 'normal' good (see Chapter 2), with lower income it would be expected that the optimum combination again involve fewer child births. Equilibrium has moved from point 1 on I_2 to point 3 on I_0. Points 1 and 2 are on the price expansion path (PEP) and 1 and 3 are on the income expansion path (IEP).

If the wage rate is increased from w_0 to w_1 the effect is fairly complicated but it represents a good illustration of the power of 'fundamental commodities analysis'. With wage rate on the numerator and denominator of the construction of the full-income constraint in Chapter 8, a rise in its value must serve to relocate it. A rising wage alters $T \cdot w + V$ as well as $b_y w$ and $b_c w$ (i.e. the shadow prices of time inputs change).

The analysis of the associated income and substitution effects is captured in Figure 9.9(a). Initial equilibrium is found at point 1 on full-income constraint F_0 and indifference curve I_0. This would leave the initial iso-time constraint line through 1 (y-axis intercept $(T-tw_0)/b_y$ and x-axis intercept $(T-tw_0)/b_c$) unchanged (the dashed–dotted line through point 1) where tw_0 is initial market work-time hours. However, the initial iso-money expenditure line (dashed) through point 1 will increase to the right in a parallel fashion as the numerator given by $tw_0 \cdot w_0 + V < tw_0 \cdot w_1 + V$, picking out a single point 2 on a new full-income constraint. As in Chapter 3, the new full-income constraint, labelled F_1, is constructed by allowing work time tw to alter. As Z_c, children, is viewed as the time-intensive fundamental, F_1 is not parallel to F_0. The new equilibrium is found at point 3 on F_1 with utility level I_1 and more of Z_y and Z_c.

To decompose the wage effect it is necessary to pull back the new full-income constraint F_1 in a parallel fashion until it is tangential to I_0 at point 4. Horizontal distance 4-1 is the substitution effect indicating less of the time-intensive good Z_c is chosen as the wage rate rises. Note: the iso-time constraint through point 4 would be to the left of one through point 1 and therefore more market work time is being supplied. As income rises (and children are a 'normal' good) you would expect them to choose more. As illustrated, this substitution effect is dominated by the income effect, as captured by the horizontal distance between 4 and 3 (where less market work time is supplied to free up time for the own-time inputs into Z_c and Z_y).

Figure 9.9(b) is a skeletal version of Figure 9.9(a) and serves to highlight the main consequences of increasing the wage rate. It is worth noting that the non-parallel shift of F_0 to F_1 indicates a lower impact of the wage-rate increase on the ability to produce the relatively time-intensive commodity (children), as compared with the composite commodity which is assumed to be less time-intensive in production. The substitution and

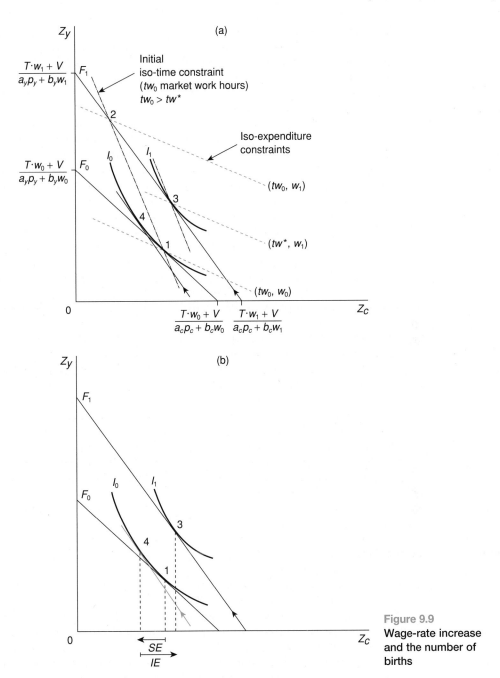

Figure 9.9
Wage-rate increase
and the number of
births

income effects are marked, so their impact on childbirths can be visualised. As yet, there is no solid prediction here as the income effect may not be of a sufficient magnitude to outweigh the substitution effect.

If a further assumption is made a testable prediction can be formed (see Ermisch 1993). Broadly, it is possible to tie the male wage rate to the income effect and, therefore, we would expect a rising male wage to indicate that more children would be chosen. As regards the substitution effect, this can be broadly attached to the female wage rate, as women are differentially specialised in the own-time inputs into children and therefore you expect fewer children to be chosen. The prediction that comes from this casual logic is that the birth rate should vary inversely to the ratio of female to male wage rates and it is this observation that is consistent with the decline in fertility observed in developed economies over the last twenty years or so.

The education level enjoyed by females is also an important variable. Education like children is a time-intensive activity and therefore competes with children. Educated women have fewer years in which to have children and, therefore, other things equal, have fewer births. Also, education shows up in terms of knowledge of contraception and therefore a more educated group of people are less likely to make mistakes with respect to unwanted pregnancies. The more educated are also, generally speaking, better at looking after children and therefore they enjoy a higher survival rate so that less births are required to establish a target number of children in a family. In general, greater education, other things equal, is likely to be associated with fewer births. Furthermore, greater opportunities for market employment for females have led to their participation rate in the formal labour market increasing and it is also associated with more marriage break-ups and therefore fewer children.

Greater investment in public health projects, good water, sanitation etc. has an important impact. It ensures a greater survival rate and again it is easier to reach a target number of children when the public-sector inputs (justified by a public goods argument – see Chapter 6) into children are increased.

Finally, the cost of contraception (broadly defined to include, say, religious attitudes and convenience) is important. The expectation is that, as the cost of contraception falls, fewer children would be part of the optimal consumption bundle of fundamental commodities.

The empirical world tends to be fairly kind to this set of implications. The list of seven factors above provides a short list for those who are interested in population containment, as they have all been phrased in terms of factors derivable from theorising about the economic family.

Children have a quality as well as a quantity dimension. The quality that is in children is important because it is itself a source of utility to parents. That is, the utility from children depends on both their number (N) and their quality (Q):

$$UZ_c = UZ_c(Q, N) \tag{9.2}$$

If constant returns to scale are assumed and utility sources are divided by N, utility per child depends on child quality:

$$UZ_c/N = UZ_c(Q/N, 1) \tag{9.3}$$

The quality of children essentially reflects two things. A nature-type argument in that their genetic make-up, in part, determines their quality and this in turn is part of the reflection of partner choice. Also, nurture has an influence on what people turn out to be like. The impact of the way individuals are brought up is hotly debated, especially in the light of the human genome project, which seems to be locating a gene for everything (microeconomics?). In this subsection here it is assumed that nurture affects quality, at least to some extent, so that the 23 chromosomes inherited from your mother and the 23 inherited from your father do not alone dictate what you are like.

The quality of children then is reflected in the production function for quality and this depends, like the production of all other fundamental commodities on time inputs and market inputs (labelled X_c). The time inputs are those devoted by the father (t_f) alongside those devoted by the mother (t_m), and the market inputs are things like books, imaginative toys, TV and video programmes that are part of most children's growing-up stages:

$$Q/N = Q/N(X_c, t_m, t_f) \tag{9.4}$$

The implication of this argument is that higher-income people are likely to have higher-quality children because they can simply afford more of the market inputs. More time inputs by parents in general (reading, story telling and the like) are suggested to increase quality. The education level of the mother is also very important because, as has been noted, it is females who tend to be time-intensive with children. The more education embodied in that time the greater the quality of the children that eventually grow up. Other children in the family are, unfortunately, potential competitors to any given child. Therefore, the lower you are in the birth order the higher quality you are. The impact of this message is that it is best, in terms of quality, not to be number 15 child in a family of 15! The prediction is that, other things equal, you would be relatively low-quality compared to no.1 – the message is in the number! With respect to these arguments, economists like Becker and others at the University of Chicago indicate that there is considerable supporting evidence.

There is also the external environment. In Chapter 5 the concept of social capital was introduced (Coleman 1988) which describes the quality of an environment where a person grows and develops. Holding parental time and market inputs into children constant, it was claimed that children exposed to an environment in which their role models and peer groups are educated are differentially more successful in the labour market than those children surrounded by unemployment and the receipt of social security benefits. The concept suggests there is a human capital externality in the production of children's human capital. Independent of the parental inputs (internal to the family) into children's quality (noted above) there is, external to the family, a human capital externality affecting the course of human capital acquisition. Negative human capital externalities reside in bad physical and social conditions (e.g. the so-called 'sink estates') and drag down the quality of children living in those areas. Positive human capital externalities reside in good physical and social conditions (e.g. the so-called 'posh' or 'nice' areas) and push up the quality of children living in those areas. Where you live and who you mix with matters for child quality. On this argument parents really are right to isolate children from 'bad influences'.

9.3.3 The 'rotten kid' theorem

Returning to the internal context, the economic family has to be coordinated in some way and, given a general reluctance in microeconomics to look beyond self-interest, it is important that the coordination relies as far as possible on this motivation. The 'rotten kid' theorem is a good illustration of how far self-interest can be adapted to a seemingly alien context and still have the ability to offer insight.

The economic family is described as minimally altruistic, in that there is a family head of household who sets the level of net transfers that take place to all the individuals within the family. It is assumed that the head has interdependent utilities with the family members, so that their utility or income level positively affects their own level of welfare (the reason, or reasons, for the interdependence is not important to the development of the argument).

$$U_h = U_h(Y_h, Y_{m1}, Y_{m2}, Y_{m3}, Y_{m4}, \ldots) \tag{9.5}$$

Here the utility enjoyed by the family head depends on their own income Y_h and the income enjoyed by all the other family members Y_{mi}.

In Figure 9.10, Y_h is recorded on the x-axis and Y_{mi} on the y-axis. The initial distribution point is at 1, which involves an income of Y_{h0} for the head and Y_{m0} for the family member. The head, as the distributor of income, has a budget line with a slope of -1 emanating from point 1 (a costless transfer will increase Y_m's income by £1 as it reduces Y_h's income by £1). The head will redistribute income to maximise their utility and, in the

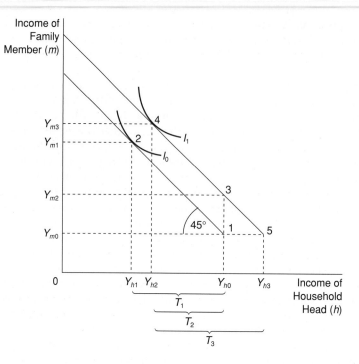

Figure 9.10
Illustrating the 'rotten kid' theorem

case illustrated, this involves moving to point 2 (achieving utility level I_0). The transfer involved is measured as T_1, decreasing Y_{h0} to Y_{h1} and increasing Y_{m0} to Y_{m1}. If the family member enjoys an income increase, the endowment point becomes point 3 (with income Y_{m2}) and the budget constraint is shifted out in a parallel fashion. The family head in responding to the new situation finds equilibrium at point 4 on I_1, reducing the transfer to T_2, so that the family member's gross-of-transfer income rises from Y_{m1} to Y_{m3} (which is less than the income rise which equals vertical distance 1-3). The household head, reducing the size of the transfer, increases the size of own gross of transfer income from Y_{h1} to Y_{h2}.

But what would have happened if the household head had increased income and not the family member? The endowment point would move to point 5 and Y_{h3}, but equilibrium would still be at point 4 on I_1. The distance T_3 (Y_{h2}-Y_{h3}) would now be the appropriate increased transfer from the head to the family member but the gross-of-transfer incomes remain the same, so that they are invariant to the identity of who actually enjoyed the income increase. As long as all income flows through the hands of the household head, the ability to make net transfers places the power to determine the allocation of family income in their hands, regardless of which family member earns it. This power of the last transfer gives rise to the so-called 'rotten kid theorem'. This notes that, if you have two family members, the one will help get the other a job, not for the love of the rotten kid, but because their net of transfer income will be the same as if the job were their own. The 'self-interested' action is to help others raise family income.

In short, the economic family with a 'net transfer maker' can be made to operate along the lines of the market as exemplified in Adam Smith's classic statement:

'It is not from the benevolence of the butcher, the brewer, or the baker that we expect our dinner, but from their regard to their own interest. We address ourselves, not their humanity but to their self-love, and never talk to them of our own necessities but of their advantages. Nobody but a beggar chooses to depend chiefly upon the benevolence of his fellow citizens.' (Smith 1910: 13).

Apart from the 'net transfer maker', the benevolence of other family members, then, is not central to the economic family! With this thought in mind, it is perhaps appropriate that the next section deals with factors that suggest marriage dissolution.

9.4 Marriage dissolution

Nothing is for ever, and this includes many marriages. Given the theory as developed so far, marriages are likely to break up because they offer insufficient gains from trade.[3] A number of relevant arguments are prompted by the way in which the discussion of marriage formation was set up.

First, there was an account of Stigler search, so that individuals searched in such a way that they determined the optimal number of searches (associated with an expected value of fundamental commodities conditional on the optimal number of searches having taken place). Because this is an expected value, it may well be the case that, for some people, the actual value that they get to enjoy is less than the expected value. On the up-side, for some people the actual value they enjoy is greater than the value expected. With sequential search the number of searches is uncertain but the fundamental commodities involved have a minimum reservation level that may, or may not, be exceeded. A happier marriage is likely to be associated with a level of fundamental commodities way in excess of the reservation level. Those enjoying a value of fundamental commodities less than the expected value (or at the reservation level) are likely to find themselves disappointed with the results of their search and therefore more likely to be disappointed with their marriage.

The search process also involves imperfect information in other ways. In considering the additional Z available from each potential partner, an assumption was required about the distribution of gains from marriage. The bargaining solution enacted simply may have been less advantageous than anticipated or, even if it was initially as expected, it may have changed in an adverse way over time because of changes of circumstances. In either event, disappointment and dissatisfaction will set in. It was noted above that experience characteristics like ambition, resilience, loyalty are only identified with events that arise with the passage of time (or in crises) and the passage of time (and crises) may reveal that your partner choice is rather deficient in experience characteristics. You may be disappointed with the amount of loyalty, caring, etc. they display towards you.

Also, given there is a theme here of uncertainty and imperfect information, circumstances change. A decision made at one point in time may look less attractive at a future point in time. Preferences change over time as individuals grow older and, given that cells in the human body replace themselves, individuals after the passage of time are literally not the person they were when they were young.

The external (as well as the internal) environment changes. In particular, market opportunities for women have increased extensively in the post-war world and, for example, women have returned to education. This alters their production possibilities and the shape of the potential gains in trade. Changing circumstances may well be a pre-disposing factor to marriage break-up. Casual empiricism often seems to suggest that women who take up education in later life have difficulty in going back to a situation (or home life) where they were in a role that was associated with household production and uneducated input.

The existing level of divorce causes risk and encourages individuals to be less than fully specialised. If you anticipate that some time down the road you will become

3. For a discussion see Lehrer (2003).

divorced then you will reduce your degree of specialisation so that you remain 'marketable' should divorce arise. This failure to fully specialise partly destroys the basis of the gains from trade, so the gains from specialisation may be lost and, therefore, divorce is more likely to occur. Like any other economic problem it is about maximising utility subject to the constraints you face.

In this respect the nature of the divorce laws themselves is very important. Becker used an application of Coase's theorem (discussed in more depth in Chapter 6) to support an argument that the number of divorces was independent of the divorce laws in existence.

Coase's theorem states that in the presence of externalities and with small bargaining costs, the same efficient level of activity per period will arise independent of the property right structure in place. Mutual-consent divorce on the surface looks more demanding because it requires both parties to choose divorce. However fault-based divorce relies on the notion that one partner chooses to commit a fault and the other chooses to take legal action on the basis of it, i.e. it is chosen by two people also. Becker argued that with a mutual-consent law it either takes place because both are better off with divorce, or the partner wishing to divorce could do so by compensating the other partner, who effectively has veto power, for their consent. This is a willingness to pay/accept approach. Such consent would be efficient to obtain only if the benefits from ending the marriage to the partner wanting to leave exceeded the required bribe/compensation the other partner demands. If the divorce occurs one has received full compensation and the other has voluntarily paid it – at least one party is better off and no one is worse off – describing an efficient transaction. But, what of the no-fault situation? The partner wanting to divorce can apparently walk away as the property right is effectively vested with them. If the other partner wants them to leave both are better off – an actual Pareto improvement occurs. However, if the other partner does not want them to do so they can offer to bribe/compensate them to stay, again establishing a 'willingness to accept/pay' to do so. If the partner pays this amount, then again no one is worse off and one must be better of – voluntarism guarantees this.

Under either assignment of legal rights marriages fail because both partners want that and because it is inefficient to save the marriage. Or, to put it in converse form, efficient marriages are saved under both systems so that the number of divorces is independent of the legal rules or their change.

This argument is subject to the same limitations as the Coase theorem itself. It is common ground that the distributional consequences vary. The non-consenting (consenting) partner is better (worse) off under the mutual-consent rule. Additionally, Becker does not dispute that the divorce law in existence affects the distribution of gains within marriage, as discussed above.

The clue to the weakness of the invariance statement lies in willingness-to-pay or -accept phrase. Clark (1998) explores this issue more fully but a more straightforward account that relies on the definitions of compensating and equivalent variations (*CV*s and *EV*s, see Chapter 2) is offered here. In the conflict case with mutual consent the non-consenting partner has a property right over their utility in marriage, so that they have to receive the compensating variation for a loss to agree to divorce. A willingness-to-accept sum has to be less than the compensating variation of the gain from divorce by the initiating partner – a willingness-to-pay sum. In the conflict case, with the no-fault rule the consenting partner has a property right over their utility in the event of divorce, as does the non-consenting partner. So the non-consenting partner offers the equivalent variation of a loss to preserve a marriage which, in the case of divorce, is less than the equivalent variation for the gain for the initiating partner, i.e. a willingness-to-pay sum has to be less than a willingness-to-accept sum. For equivalent variations and normal goods the equivalent variation of a gain exceeds the compensating variation of the gain while the equivalent variation for a loss is smaller than the compensating variation for a loss.

Other things equal, and assuming marriage to be a normal good, one would expect more offered compensations to fail (divorces to occur) under the no-fault law than the mutual-consent law. As with the compensation criteria (discussed in Chapter 5), a paradox can arise. Gainers from divorce may not be able to compensate losers under one set of rules (under the mutual case the divorce may not occur $CV_g = 6$ and $CV_l = 8$) and losers from divorce may not be able to compensate the gainers (under the no-fault case divorce takes place $EV_l = 6$ and $EV_g = 8$). In this case, it is evident that the intuitive response, that number of divorces is affected by the divorce laws in operation, proves correct.

Generally, the more difficult it is to divorce, the longer people are likely to search the marriage market and the fewer marriages are likely to take place. Until relatively recently the divorce laws were based around the idea of trying to have the partners after the divorce in the same position as if they were married, but here is where economic implications are important. If marriage is based around securing the gains from trade – the increased production of fundamental commodities – then the law that is designed to make people equally as well off outside marriage is impossible to enact. Because of the way the economic process works there are simply fewer fundamental commodities to be allocated once divorce has taken place. The logic of the law makes no sense against the logic of economics. More recently, divorce laws have been built around the notion of a 'clean break', so that it is now less easy for partners to get payments from the other partner. If this is the situation, people are likely to specialise less within marriage (to keep marketable) and, by the same token, the gains from marriage in themselves are reduced. Retaining and changing the divorce laws inevitably set up incentives. Whether you like those incentives or not is essentially a normative judgement. There is no escaping the fact that how the divorce laws are framed actually affects the size of gains from marriage, the number of marriages and (Becker's argument notwithstanding) the number divorces that are observed.

A final consideration that may lead towards divorce is that the distribution of gains within marriage has been modelled in terms of bargaining theory and, as we noted, there are different solutions to various bargaining problems. The minimum amounts of fundamental commodities you enjoy being single were the security points in the bargaining process. If you increase the security points for either, or both, partners then this lowers the opportunity cost of divorce and therefore you would expect more divorces. For example, equal pay legislation, other things equal, should be associated with more divorces taking place because (to the extent that equal pay is effective) it raises the wage rate of women in the marketplace.

Does empirical evidence support the list of the main factors in causing the dissolution of marriages discussed above? Kiernan and Mueller (1988) pose the question 'The divorced and who divorces?'. The reply is framed around data from the Family Resources Survey, the British Household Panel Survey and the National Child Development Study. The divorced tend to differentially be unemployed, in receipt of state benefits and suffer from disability. These same three factors plus financial difficulties were found to be precursors of divorce. Poor economic and somatic (bodily) well-being seems to be both a cause and consequence of divorce.

In the analysis above, low-wage males appeared to have little potential gain from marriage, given the observed wage structure. Men and women with lower psychological well-being are likely to divorce and emotional problems in childhood are a signal that this might happen. Broadly, this might be interpreted as issues surrounding preference formation and stability. Apart from these factors, it seemed that those who embarked on relationships at an early age and those whose own parents were divorced seemed more likely to divorce. The former may reflect sub-optimal search and the latter a preference-affecting experience.

9.4.1 Single-parent families

'Divorce and children' is a very important and topical issue (see Beller and Graham 2003). The biggest source of single-parent families is, in fact, divorce, and there is an important debate about who becomes the custodial parent and the way in which children who are the product of broken homes are left in poverty by the non-custodial parent.

Who should become the custodial parent? A number of principles have been employed and advocated. Should the 'best interests' of the child be met irrespective of how the divorce arose? But who decides the 'best interest' – the child itself (at what age?), one or more parents, the legal system, specialist social workers? Should the arrangements agreed and favoured by the divorcing parents be respected? Should the parent who has been differentially specialised in parenting time inputs be awarded with custody, or the parent who will do most to maintain and foster the child's link with the other parent? While there are pros and cons to each principle, Rowthorn (1998) argues that, given that marriage is an institution that fosters trust, a currently unfashionable case can be made that the child should be in the care of the non-reneging ('innocent') parent where this can be established. In short, there is a public interest in upholding the trust-creating features of marriage, so that protecting an economically advantageous institution is itself an important objective. Child custody should be seen to go to those who kept to their part of the marriage bargain and not to those who default.

The fate of children of divorced parents is a problem. When married, the treatment of children is a collective decision; it is said to be 'unitised'. What is done for the children is a local public good in the sense that the members of the family can all enjoy the benefits without decreasing the quantity of benefits to others. If there is a significant local public good aspect to caring for children inside marriage then, once divorced, these decisions are separated and, therefore, there is an incentive to free-ride.

In Figure 9.11 a demand curve for support to the child per time period is illustrated. It is downward-sloping to the right (like other demand curves) and is assumed common to both parents – one is not more loving of their child or children than the other. Interpreting it as for the custodial parent, the cost of a pound's worth of support is simply a pound and the custodial parent would choose the appropriate quantity, namely 0-q_c, associated with point 1 on the demand curve.

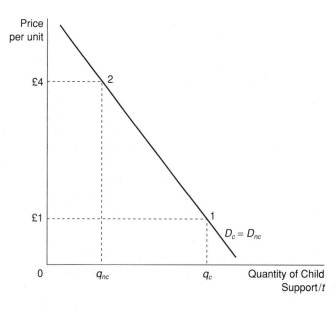

Figure 9.11
Divorced parents and the quantity of child support

For the non-custodial parent the cost of a pound's worth of support is rather different. In fact, it is higher because it is one pound divided by one minus the marginal propensity for personal consumption by the custodial parent. The idea is that if you, as a divorced non-custodial parent, give £4 to the custodial parent to be directed to a child it may well be the case that part of it will simply leak away to expenditure on the custodial parent. So, for example, if you are the custodial parent and the marginal propensity to consume for yourself is 0.75, the non-custodial parent has to give £4 to the family in order to provide £1 worth of child support. Given this, higher price, the non-custodial parent chooses a lower quantity of support at 0-q_{nc} and point 2 on the demand curve.

The implication of this type of argument is that you need a third party to monitor expenditure if you want to help the fate of children. But this is a very difficult process in itself, especially if non-custodial expenditure 'crowds out' custodial expenditure in a disguised way (so that the monitor 'sees' the £4 being spent on the child but, once the custodial parent sees money coming in, there is a reduction in the amount that the custodial parent would otherwise have provided for the child – a 'rotten parent' type argument!).[4] Overall, even if this mechanism works less ruthlessly than presented here, one can expect that in many cases there is a lower expenditure on children that are part of divorced families, other things equal. A decrease in the utility of the non-custodial parent arises at minimum because this parent faces a higher price in order to support their children. The converse of this argument is that it helps explain why families without children divorce more often. The fate of children is often a main concern in this context.

9.5 Challenge: Is applying microeconomics to the family useless?

This section provides a convenient point at which to take stock of what has been discussed and analysed so far. In many ways the 'new' home economics is quintessentially neoclassical economics applied to the family context. People have made a number of criticisms of the new home economics and, in microcosm, they are the type of criticisms that can be levelled at neoclassical economics *per se*. Despite Becker and other Chicago economists firmly putting household production and the role of women in particular at the centre of the stage, they are often very heavily criticised for the nature of their work and the way in which their analysis develops.

In what follows criticisms are divided into four broad categories. The first category are viewed as being largely misplaced or irrelevant – of course, this may not be the readers' view.

9.5.1 Misplaced criticisms

i) The first objection levelled at the theory discussed in this chapter is that it is simply not economics because it is not about the economy, as it does not appear to refer to business life, shares, profits, etc. This problem has already been met in Chapter 1 where it was pointed out that economics is essentially a question of applying a consistent mental skill; it is not to be defined by topics covered.

ii) A second criticism is that the whole approach seems to boil down what is noble in people to something that is base and instrumental. For many, there is simply not

---

4. Note: this is the same debate that accompanies claims that transfers made to developing countries for, say, health and education provision find their way into arms purchases and/or the president's Swiss bank account.

enough love in the economic family. The answer to this type of criticism is that surely everything must be able to stand up to analysis; that no subject is so privileged that you cannot be allowed to criticise, or analyse it in a way that some people find initially unattractive, or even ultimately very unattractive. In some sense, these are criticisms that things are destroyed by discussing them in a certain way. There is clearly a certain element of truth in this and, indeed, a literature on intrinsic motivation (see Chapter 16) deals with this approach. However, something as central as the family is surely robust enough to be discussed in any way people want to discuss it. The strange world, academe, is inhabited by individuals who tend to believe that all ideas deserve to be taken seriously and not summarily dismissed as being somehow inappropriate.

9.5.2 Technical and theoretical criticisms

Most technical and theoretical criticisms are amenable to further analysis. In many ways those who start to make technical criticisms of the sort of approach employed here have 'the hook in their mouth': they have bitten into the story and they are merely discussing how it can be elaborated (e.g. how some assumptions might be replaced by better ones). Adding to the criticisms noted above, the types of points that are made in this kind of context are:

iii) The relevant constraints in the family include elements like legal specifications, social customs, norms, religious precepts. The point is that the economist *per se* simply does not have skills in these areas and that it requires someone with a legal, social anthropological training, etc. in order to deal adequately with the subject. This may be a fair criticism but, as a response, there are many economists around the world who are trained in more than one subject. For example, there are economists that deal with the economics of law who typically have law degrees to start with and who have gone on to study economics. So it may be that things are being missed in the theory but people more adequately trained will be able to repair these weak elements later on.

iv) In similar vein, there is the criticism that says that too much weight is given to linear budget constraints and constant returns to scale and other convenient assumptions. The response to this is simply that these assumptions are made in order to make the theory easier to understand and therefore more helpful. If this is valid, such assumptions are said to be 'simplifying'. The 'stuff' of many journal articles is to elaborate on basic themes and deal with the more complicated situations. Much of a theoretician's work is about isolating the conditions under which a particular proposition, or hypothesis, remains tenable. Here the trick is to differentiate determining assumptions from simplifying ones, as the former really are a worry. Bryant and Zick (1994) provide a relevant example. In the discussion of family specialisation complete specialisation was the prediction of the theory. However, this prediction does not carry over to the case of decreasing returns to scale in household production. In the absence of constant or increasing returns to scale in household production, the partner engaged in household work may also engage in market work. In this case it is empirical evidence on the extent of decreasing returns to scale that is required to throw light on the issue.

v) A further criticism of this type of analysis is that it makes activities discrete. Family activities do not necessarily fall into the discrete categories like reproductive, productive and leisure activities. If you choose to take your child to a football match you are entertaining them on Saturday afternoon, but also socialising them into the way crowds behave and how abusive people can get when upset.

However, with sufficient ingenuity it is possible to deal with this essentially joint output problem.

9.5.3 Empirical criticisms

A third class of criticisms that are made against the new home economics and as intimated above against neoclassical economics as such is that the supportive empirical evidence can be called into doubt.

vi)　Much of the so-called Chicago-positivistic view of economics is that the subject is about developing hypotheses that are potentially falsifiable by reference to empirical evidence. The strength of Becker's economic family (he would claim) is that he can find strong empirical evidence consistent with the hypotheses developed. However, criticisms have been made of the theory in that many of the variables are difficult to proxy in empirical contexts. For example, people's genetic endowments are not easy to observe, or giving a production function to the household requires assumptions about the mathematical nature of the production process when you cannot tell if the assumptions are warranted or not. The econometric and statistical evidence employed by authors like Becker are claimed to be consistent with theory. But some economists have disputed that the evidence is indeed consistent with the theory. Others have claimed that there are simpler, more natural, theories that offer a better account of those statistical, or econometric, regularities.

vii)　A more intuitive criticism is that the economic family does not seem to accord with the casual observation of what families are in fact like. The economic family requires only minimal altruism to make it work (hence the importance of the 'rotten kid theorem'). It employs an enlightened head of household. But this enlightened head of household seems to be very much at odds with a world in which families are often characterised by internal power struggles. Household heads can be destructive people and, indeed, in what seems an increasing number of cases, are oppressive and violent. Joint utility maximisation does not seem to characterise this kind of world. At this stage, it is easy to recall the point that economics, like other subjects, involves the creation and deployment of language and even the most sophisticated of people are moved by the way in which cases are presented. Robert Solow the 1987 the Nobel laureate in Economics, describes the situation:

> 'some of us see the Smithian virtues as a needle in a haystack, as an island of measure zero in a sea of imperfections. Others see all the potential sources of market failures as so many fleas on the thick hide of an ox requiring only an occasional flick of the tail to be brushed away. A hopeless eclectic like me has a terrible time of it. I need only to listen to Milton Friedman talk for a minute and my mind floods with thoughts of increasing returns to scale, oligopolistic interdependance, consumer ignorance, environmental pollution, intergenerational inequity and so on. There is no cure for it except to listen to John Kenneth Galbraith in which case all I can think of are the discipline of competition, the large number of substitutes for any commodity, the stupidities of regulation, the Pareto optimality of Walrasian equilibrium, the importance of decentralising decision making to where the knowledge is and so on and so on.' Solow (1980: 2).

Clearly, If a 'Nobel Prize' sophisticated economist is influenced by who they read and what they listen to, it is not easy to make economic judgements. The important thing for anyone to do is to try to assess the situation as best they can for themselves, to try to judge the arguments and to assess the strength of the empirical evidence. It is always necessary to be sceptical about the results you are offered, or the world you are expected to accept (and, indeed, the things you believe).

9.5.4 **General criticisms of the neoclassical approach**

It is now possible to turn to a fourth class of criticisms. These are ones that really are common to virtually all the applications of neoclassical theory and in this sense are more fundamental.

viii) The first of these is that neoclassical economics has no 'story' about preferences. In virtually all the applications they are treated as exogenous and, as such, are created outside the piece of theory that is being studied. For many instances of situations this may be an acceptable way forward. But here, in the economics of the family, we are actually modelling the institution in which individual preferences are formed. The family context is quite often where people's lives are shaped and therefore you must see preferences as endogenous to the analysis. It is no longer acceptable to believe they are exogenous.

ix) The second criticism of this more general kind is that the neoclassical family (like the neoclassical firm) itself has no significant internal context. The theory that is reported above does not confront, in a very serious way, the internal power structure of the family, the incentive and monetary problems of domestic team production. However, it is easy to push this criticism too far, as there are quite substantial contributions on the distributional problems within families and the sort of mechanisms that involve the discipline and reward of the family team players. Witness the discussion of trust-building mechanisms.

x) In Chapter 3 the way in which time is incorporated into theory was introduced. Neoclassical theory employs what is called *analytical time*. Analytical time is an abstraction. It is a situation where virtually all information, past, present and future, is available. It is possible to move backwards and forwards in time so that the sequencing of decisions is not an issue. The essence of the theory is to perform hypothetical exercises of causes leading to consequences. Critics of family economics say that this concept of analytical time leads thinking in precisely the wrong directions and that you have to operate with what is called *perspective time* (see Winston 1988). This is time as people get to experience it. Often people have limited and ill-defined pieces of information. These pieces of information are open to different types of interpretation, i.e. the message conveyed is 'individual-specific'. Further, sequence matters. It is impossible to re-make past choices and once past choices have been made they often preclude a great deal of current ones. You simply cannot move backwards and forwards in time. Once you have chosen one path you are closing out options in the future and the claim would be that any realistic theory must take account of this. A final point here is that decision-making is often very stressful and that it is not done in the sort of clear analytical air in which the theory on these pages is presented. People often respond in emotional ways and do not lend themselves easily to the axioms of choice.

xi) Neoclassical economics, as the earlier chapters of this book attest and the remaining ones are going to attest, looks best when applied to optimising contexts where rapid adjustment to equilibrium can seem valid. In the current context all the family has to do to survive (as an institution) is not to be in equilibrium; it just has to be better than the alternatives. It does not have to exhibit 'optimum' adjustment and, indeed, typically changes take place very slowly in family contexts. One problem this raises is that the family is typically in disequilibrium all the time, whereas the observations of it are treated as if they are equilibrium ones.

xii) If individuals are modelled as far-seeing optimisers, quickly exhausting all gains from trade to establish efficient solutions then government policy intervention is seldom likely to look helpful and, at worst, will be seen as making a situation more inefficient and/or inequitable.

xiii) Further, neoclassical economics is output (product) end-state-orientated. This is an aspect of so-called consequentialism, where utility is based solely on the consequences of choices under consideration and nothing else. In the family context, there may well be a need to incorporate process utility, so that it is not the utility of the finished adult that may matter but rather the *process utility* associated with the use of your own-time inputs into the production process of bringing up children. This can be done, but in doing so predictions change.

xiv) Penultimately, in this section there is the criticism that the family like neoclassical society is a non-organic concept. That is, the family is simply the sum of the individuals that make it up. There is no synergy (where the whole is bigger than the sum of the individual parts) and, you may at least want to have individuals who can learn from each other, so that they can change their productive capacities and change their preferences in a family context. In short, the description of isolated individuals collected in the family does not represent the 'true' situation. There must be elements of an organism about the family that is entirely missed in a non-organic approach.

xv) The sociologist Max Weber (e.g. 1949) distinguished *formal* from *substantive* rationality. The former is about calculation of the best way of meeting given needs by quantifiable means, whereas the latter involves the use of particular values to determine action. Consider the time in minutes a wife and husband may take to complete two domestic tasks – cleaning the house and mowing the lawn (see Table 9.5).

Formal rationality would say specialise according to comparative advantage: assign the husband to the house cleaning and the wife to lawn mowing, with the tasks taking a total of 200 minutes. *Substantive* rationality might say a family must run on a sharing value and assign the husband and the wife to the house cleaning and to lawn mowing equally. With sharing, the tasks take a total of 280 minutes, which may look *formally* irrational but be *substantively* rational. A final assignment might be random (tossing a fair coin) so that the husband would do X half the time and Y the other half, and similarly for the wife. With this approach the tasks would take an expected time of 280 minutes.

Using instrumentally rationality, the task assignment rules would rank first specialisation (as it is least cost), second sharing and third random assignment as risk-averse individuals would prefer a certain cost of 280 minutes over an expected cost of 280 minutes. In short, as has been noted elsewhere, there are more types of rationality than the one typically conceived of in microeconomic theory.

This final set of more fundamental criticisms goes to the heart of the way neoclassical theory works. If you think these criticisms are valid then you are unlikely ever to be seduced by the clean analytical lines of neoclassical theory. On the other hand, if you think that the criticisms that are presented here are not fundamental, or not as fundamental as people think, then you will find the content of previous and remaining chapters more convincing and more palatable. In all events, microeconomic theory has a great deal to say about what individuals see around them and no pretence here is made that this is in some sense an objective view. Neoclassical theory employs a very specific perspective on the world and life's decisions and, at least at this time, has come to dominate

Table 9.5 **Formal and substantive rationality**

TASK	House cleaning	Mowing the lawn	Opportunity cost
Husband	100	300	1/3 of a lawn
Wife	60	100	3/5 of a lawn

the way in which economics is conducted. Criticisms are made but, as the poem records, 'dogs may bark but the caravan still moves on'. There are many people that criticise neoclassical microeconomic theory from many different directions but, at this stage in history, it carries the day. As the dominant paradigm it has to be the starting point of any serious economics education. There is no objection to being heavily critical of neoclassical theory but to command respect that criticism must come from an informed position. The cost of becoming informed, is the price that must be paid to be listened to.

9.6 Summary

This chapter has attempted to illustrate the impact of microeconomic theorising by talented economists in the relatively recent context of the 'new home economics'. The principles involved are of value in themselves and are of wider application. The search process described has mainly been used to analyse the process of searching the labour market for a job. The gains from specialisation and trade are the basis for international trade theory. Game theory and bargaining solutions are part of any conflict situations. Mechanisms to avoid opportunistic behaviour are central to some theories of the firm. Invariance of final outcomes from institutional detail are the stuff of Ricardian equivalence in macroeconomics, etc.

As for the application of the principles to the family *per se*, some find the approach truly informative and insightful, whilst others view it as an interesting vehicle for approaching 'boring' neoclassical microeconomics and indeed exemplifying its strengths and weaknesses in a stark way.

For other commentators the whole approach is either anathema to them or seriously misleading. Consider Bergmann's (1995: 142) comment:

> The thesis of this paper is that many of the theoretical developments in this field, far from being of aid in coping with our actual problems, are fatally simplistic, and where not irrelevant are misleading. Gary Becker's *A Treatise on the Family* (1991) well exemplifies the state of this dubious art. If a judgment of quality is to be made on the basis of economy of means and utilization of the traditional tools of economic analysis (to say nothing of attracting the world's most prestigious accolades), the Becker model surely must be declared a success. However, if the judgment depends on contribution to a realistic appreciation of actual problems that are being encountered and the policies that might be applied to them, then the Becker approach fails badly.

In lighter tone the philosopher Martin Hollis comments on the 'reservation search' process for finding a partner:

> 'if this is how people look for partners, good luck to them: they need it badly!' (quoted from Varoufakis 1998: 67)

At minimum, the approach discussed in this chapter puts major questions on the map and typically brings them into sharp relief.

References

Becker, G.S. (1991) *A Treatise on the Family*, Cambridge, Mass.: Harvard University Press.

Beller, A.H. and Graham, J.W. (2003) The economics of child support, pp. 153–76 in S.A. Grossbard-Shechtman (ed.) *Marriage and the Economy*, Cambridge: Cambridge University Press.

Bergmann, B.R. (1995) Becker's theory of the family: preposterous conclusions, *Feminist Economics*, 1 (1) Spring: 141–50.

Brinig, M.F. and Crafton, S.M. (1994) Marriage and opportunism, *Journal of Legal Studies*, 23 (2): 869–94.

Bryant, W.K. (1990) *The Economic Organisation of the Household*, Cambridge: Cambridge University Press.

Bryant, W.K. and Zick, C.D. (1994) The economics of housespousery: an essay on household work, *Journal of Family and Economic Issues*, 15 (2): 137–68.

Clark, S.J. (1998) Law, property and marital dissolution, University of Edinburgh Economics Department Discussion Paper Series.

Coleman, J.S. (1988) Social capital in the creation of human capital, *American Journal of Sociology*, 94 Supplement: 95–120.

Crouch, R.L. (1979) *Human Behavior – an Economic Approach*, North Scituate, Mass.: Duxbury Press.

Ermisch, J. (1993) Famila oeconomica: a survey of the economics of the family, *Scottish Journal of Political Economy*, 40 (4) November: 353–74.

Ermisch, J.F. (2003) *An Economic Analysis of the Family*, Princeton, NJ: Princeton University Press.

Fleisher, B.M. and Kniesner, T.J. (1980) *Labor Economics – Theory, Evidence and Policy*, 2nd edn, Englewood-Cliffs, NJ: Prentice-Hall.

Gibbons, R. (1992) *A Primer in Game Theory*, Hemel Hempstead: Harvester.

Grossbard-Shechtman, S.A. (2003) (ed.) *Marriage and the Economy*, Cambridge: Cambridge University Press.

Kiernan K. and Mueller, G. (1988) *The Divorced and Who Divorces?* Centre for Analysis of Social Exclusion LSE CASE paper 7.

Kooreman, P. and Wunderink, S. (1997) *The Economics of Household Behaviour*, Basingstoke: Macmillan.

Lehrer, E.L. (2003) The economics of divorce, pp. 55–74 in S.A. Grossbard-Shechtman (ed.) *Marriage and the Economy*, Cambridge: Cambridge University Press.

Nash, J.F. (1950) The bargaining problem, *Econometrica*, 18 (2): 155–62.

Rowthorn, R. (1998) Marriage and trust: some lessons from business organisation, WP 113 ESRC Centre for Business Research University of Cambridge.

Smith, A. (1910) *An Inquiry into the Nature and Causes of the Wealth of Nations*, New York: Modern Library.

Solow, R. (1980) On theories of unemployment, *American Economic Review*, 70: 1–11.

Stigler, G. (1961) The economics of information, *Journal of Political Economy*, 69 (3): 213–25.

Swedberg, R. (2003) *Principles of Economic Sociology*, Princeton: Princeton University Press.

Varoufakis, Y. (1998) *Foundations of Economics – a Beginner's Companion*, London and New York: Routledge.

Weber, M. (1949) *Essays in the Methodology of the Social Sciences*, New York: Free Press.

Williamson, O.E. (1985) *The Economic Institutions of Capitalism*, New York: Free Press.

Winston, G.C. (1988) Three problems with the treatment of time in economics: perspectives, repetitiveness, and time units, in G.C. Winston and F. Teicgraeber III (eds) *The Boundaries of Economics*, Cambridge: Cambridge University Press.

CHAPTER 10

Growing up and down: investment in human capital and labour supply incentives

10.1 Introduction

Having discussed life's decisions and household production and the economic family it is time to move towards the external world. After all, apart from the early years of life and retirement individuals probably spend the majority of their waking time outside the home. In this chapter the question of schooling and human capital formation is explored. As one of the major elements in the return to human capital comes via the labour market, this is a natural place to discuss labour supply and associated micro-economic theorising. The typical economic life cycle is used as the organising device. Over that cycle individuals literally grow up and grow down as they physically get bigger and later smaller with age, but what is happening from an economic perspective?

10.2 Overview of an economic life cycle

Following Addison and Siebert (1979) it is possible to build an economic picture for the average individual over a typical lifetime. This is done with the aid of Figure 10.1. In the figure, time is on the x-axis in the form of age, whereas money values are recorded on the y-axis. The typical actual earnings profile of the individual is portrayed in panel (b) as Y_0, Y_1, Y_2. Stages I and II of the figure represents the pre-labour-force years, so that actual income steps up from zero at Y_0 to Y_1 on leaving school. The objective is to connect the actual earnings profile to commonly observed patterns of human capital investment with the net human capital stock recorded as K_{h0}, K_{h1}, K_{h2} in panel (a). The shape of this profile dictates the possible capacity earnings profile in panel (b), labelled E_0, E_1, E_2. It is formed on the assumption that earnings at point t are set by multiplying the net capital stock at any point in time (K_{ht}) by an assumed constant rate of return to human capital, (r):

$$E_t = rK_{ht} \tag{10.1}$$

In stage I the pre-schooling years begin with the child inheriting K_{h0} and this stock (the intercept value in panel (a)) growing with time and market inputs into the household production of child quality. The result of this process is school entry with a level of human capital K_{h1}.

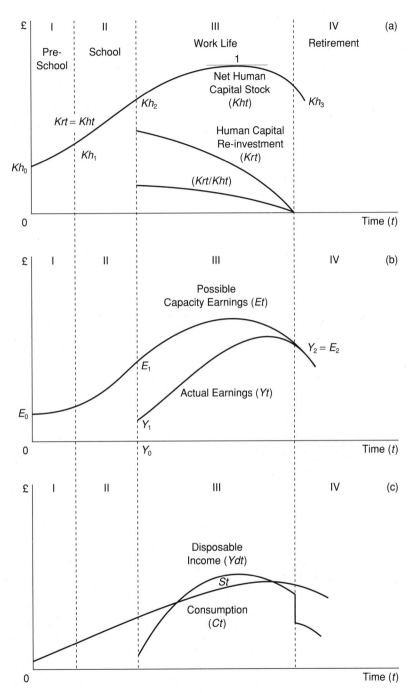

Figure 10.1 Overview of an economic life cycle

Source: Adapted from Addison and Siebert (1979).

In stage II (the schooling years) it is assumed that the individual devotes all the existing capital stock to reinvestment, so that the task is human capital accumulation. Given that *r* is the rate of return to investment, and introducing δ as the human capital depreciation rate, the change in the net stock of human capital is given by:

$$\Delta K_{ht} = I_t - \delta K_{ht} \tag{10.2}$$

where

I_t = is the given output of human capital;
ΔK_{ht} = the change in the net stock of human capital.

The magnitude of I_t is determined by the production function that converts human capital devoted to human capital construction into new human capital, so that $I_t = f(K_{rt})$ where K_{rt} is the amount of capital reinvested. Here $K_{rt} = K_{ht}$. At the end of stage II – leaving school – K_{rt} falls as work begins (as some human capital is devoted to earning income). The path of K_{rt} shows the level of reinvesting falling off steadily to zero at the retirement age. The path of the capital stock follows a similar pattern, increasing at a decreasing rate in stage III, reaching a peak at point 1 when $\Delta K_{ht} = 0$ and hence $I_t = \delta K_{ht}$ (that is, the product of reinvestment equals the amount of human capital depreciation).

The ratio of reinvestment to capital stock is labelled K_{rt}/K_{ht} and, as drawn in panel (a), falls throughout the work-life period of stage III (reflecting the falling payoff to human capital investment as age increases and remaining work-life decreases). Actual earnings are recorded in panel (b) as capacity earnings E_t minus returns forgone (i.e. the opportunity cost) on capital used for reinvestment in human capital. That is,

$$Y_t = E_t - rK_{rt} = r(K_{ht} - K_{rt}) = rK_{ht}(1 - K_{rt}/K_{ht}) = E_t(1 - K_{rt}/K_{ht}) \tag{10.3}$$

In the construction of panel (b) area $0\text{-}E_0\text{-}E_1\text{-}Y_0$ represents net investment in schooling and area $Y_1\text{-}E_1\text{-}Y_2$ net investment in the post-schooling period of stage III.

At retirement, actual earnings from work fall to zero but, of course, consumption cannot fall to zero. Panel (c) illustrates a life-cycle perspective on disposable income (Y_{dt}), that is, actual income Y_t corrected for the payment of direct taxes and receipt of transfers. Here disposable income falls on retirement but not to zero, as private and/or public pension arrangements begin to apply.

In the life-cycle hypothesis the path of consumption is smoothed so that C_t represents that path with the period when $Y_{dt} > C_t$ determining the area labelled S_t to stand for saving. At the beginning and the end of a life-cycle individuals typically dissave.

Whilst this simplified picture may not be accurate for any specific individual it does highlight processes where microeconomic analysis will have relevance. The life-cycle presented in Figure 10.1 is used to structure the remainder of this chapter.

10.3 The early years – stage I

In Chapter 9 the quality and quantity of children were discussed. In that chapter the quality of children reflected the production function for quality and this depended, like the production of all other fundamental commodities, on time inputs and market inputs (labelled X_c). The time inputs were those devoted by father (t_f) alongside those devoted by the mother (t_m) and the market inputs were everyday things like books, toys, TV and video games that are part of most children's growing-up stages. In symbols:

$$Q/N = Q/N(X_c, t_m, t_f) \tag{10.4}$$

The implication of this argument was that higher-income people are likely to have higher-quality children, because they can simply afford more of the market inputs. More time inputs by parents in general, reading, story telling (and the like), are expected to increase quality. The education level of the mother is also very important because, as has been noted, it is females who tend to be time-intensive with children; so, the more education embodied in that time, the greater the quality of the children that eventually grow up. Other children in the family were, unfortunately, potential competitors to any given child. Therefore, the lower you are in the birth order the higher-quality you are, other things equal. But, as critics of economics are always keen to say, other things are not equal. The question arises as to what these other things are. In this chapter these other things are investments in human capital.

Here the distinction between consumption and investment benefits made in Chapter 8 comes into play. To briefly recap:

Consumption benefits are:

1)   a direct source of utility or psychic benefit;
2)   called 'non-durable consumption' if the benefit is for one period;
3)   called 'a durable consumption good' if the benefit lasts many periods;
4)   less easily quantified for non-market (household) production as the return is typically non-pecuniary (non-monetary).

In contrast, investment goods generate benefits that:

1)   come in an indirect form, via a production process;
2)   by definition, are long-lived and only partly used up in the current production period (this is defined as 'depreciation');
3)   lend themselves to easy quantification, as in market production the return is typically pecuniary (monetary) in form.

10.4 The schooling and university years – stage II

In this section compulsory school education and voluntary post-school education are considered and, as indicated above, in economic terms this is the process of human capital formation (and is modelled as an investment decision). The process involves comparing discounted benefits and costs. The questions that arise are 'what will these costs and benefits comprise?' and 'to whom will these costs and benefits accrue?'.

10.4.1 The nature of a physical and human investment decision

Types of benefit that accrue to the individual undergoing education are here described as *internal payoffs* to education. They are:

(a) A non-durable consumption good or bad, where the process of education may be congenial to (use a positive sign) or disliked (use a negative sign) by the child or individual;
(b) A durable consumption good, where there may be an ability to enjoy a 'fuller life', via enhanced appreciation of the nature and workings of the world;
(c) A pecuniary (monetary) investment good, where an increased contribution to market production (increased marginal product) is measured by higher earnings of the educated (rate of return calculations discussed below usually measure this);
(d) A non-pecuniary investment good, where there is enhanced non-market home production generated by an increased marginal product in this sphere of production.

Points (a) to (d) suggest that in isolation individuals will want to acquire education as an investment in themselves, as this generates these considerable 'internalities'.

What then is the rationale for a public policy on education provision? The answer lies in three types of argument that rely on aspects of market failure:

(I) *Financing human capital investment*

Problems may arise as an unaided market may not be forthcoming with sufficient finance to allow this process to take place optimally. That is, there are difficulties in borrowing to finance investment in yourself as:

On the *lender's side:*

(a) It is not possible to take a mortgage out on an individual's ability. With investment in physical capital, if default occurs the lender can repossess it. But this cannot be done with human capital in a non-slave society, as the capital inheres in the individual – in non-slave societies individuals are not bought or sold.

(b) The success of education depends on difficult-to-observe 'experience' characteristics – motivation, determination, etc.

(a) and (b) mean increased risk for lending to finance human as opposed to equivalent physical capital construction.

On the *borrower's side* there is the risk that an individual will not get differentially higher earnings (or other forms of return) for long enough for the investment to pay off. Therefore, the risk may even deter the rich who have funds available for investing in themselves. The poor, if not put off by the risk, may well not be in a position to offer collateral to secure a loan to invest in themselves. It follows that without some form of policy intervention, investment in human capital may be less than optimal and income inequality accentuated by differential access to funds. This suggests a case for state intervention to make loans only on the reasonable prospect of success, and to write off the failures.

(II) *Externalities*

The description of the internal payoffs as internalities allows the contrast with externalities associated with human capital formation, that is, benefits that accrue to other individuals than those who receive the education and remain uncompensated for in the market mechanism. A list of possible educational externalities has been presented by Blaug (1970) and is repeated below:

First-round spillovers

(i)   Income gains to others (i.e. other than those who acquired the education) because of team production, e.g. gains from having an educated team leader and/or the ability of others to learn from observing the educated.

Second-round spillovers

(ii)   Income gains to future generations (because the educated tend to keep their children in education longer – enhancing their marginal products compared to the choice of less education).

(iii) A mechanism for discovering and cultivating talent.

(iv)   A mechanism for fostering occupational flexibility.

(v)   Public goods benefits from stimulating an increase in research/knowledge.

(vi)   Encouragement of law and order and responsibility towards public provision (e.g. via the welfare state).

Societal benefits

(vii) Education fosters political stability via an informed electorate and competent political leadership.

(viii) Social cohesion increased, via the transmission of a common cultural heritage.

(ix)   Widening intellectual horizons for both the educated and the uneducated leads to enhanced enjoyment of leisure (there is always someone in the pub who wants to tell you what Sartre really meant by existentialism!).

To the extent that (i) to (ix) are valid externalities, it suggests subsidies are required because the 'wrong' quantity of education would be chosen (too little) if decisions were premised only on narrow self-interest. Individuals will rationally ignore the external benefits to others. However, Blaug is scathing about most of these external effects, dismissing them as either insignificant or already allowed for ('internalised'). There is also a methodological problem in that most of the assertions about the externalities of education are from those whose preferences have been altered by education. It is the educated who seem keenest on education but, in good measure, they have been 'trained' to that view. It is probably the case that there are externalities to education but it may be the case that compulsory education to a certain age exhausts their Pareto relevance at the margin.

(III) *Parental incompetence*

(1) Merit want arguments (see Chapter 5) question the information and/or rationality of those parents who would not voluntarily send their children to school.

(2) Some parents might lack income to implement their preferences over the education of their children.

(1) and (2) indicate that specific people have to be encouraged to raise the level of education their children acquire via:

(a) information provision;

(b) compulsory schooling to a given age;

(c) subsidies and grants to offset income problems.

It is evident that the arguments collected at (I) to (III) are a long way away from the commonly observed state production of education. Therefore, it appears another argument requires inclusion and that factor is 'equity' (discussed in Chapter 5). There seems to be a consensus that the education system should be equitable but would that entail:

(IV) *Equality of opportunity* – will state production of education make for a more equitable situation by:

(a) increasing social mobility via the breaking down of the correlation between the distribution of education and the income distribution, and

(b) eroding class division and privilege?

Here it has to be asked if the concern is *equality of access*, which might involve

(i) compulsory school,

(ii) tax allowances for children in education and

(iii) maintenance grants.

Or, is it *equality of treatment*? This involves the 'comprehensive' view of education, that individuals are educated up to their ability (meritocracy) with no access to private education, thereby creating the same situation for all.

Finally, and more radically, is it *equality of performance of outcome* that matters? Education to date seems to have patently failed to offset the disadvantages of deprived home backgrounds and may have reinforced them. Therefore, for some, 'equality' inevitably involves the unequal distribution of resources and positive discrimination in favour of the disadvantaged so that when individuals leave education they can compete equally. Whilst the appropriate notion of equality is not agreed, it is generally agreed that equity justifies some form of intervention in the provision of education.

Provision of a good involves both a mechanism of finance and a location of production. For education, a case for policy concern has been made and many would agree with the case for state intervention in finance. But much less consensus exists about the merits, or otherwise, of state production (state-owned and -run educational facilities). The need for intervention in the finance of education has taken place against a background in which economists have measured rates of return to investment in education. After all, if the private return is very high many would argue that education should come much closer to market provision.

Table 10.1 Elements in rate of return calculations

	'SOCIAL' RATE OF RETURN	PRIVATE RATE OF RETURN
(1) Direct costs	1. Wages & salaries of lecturers and other staff 2. Operating and maintenance 3. Capital costs	*Minus* 1. Subsidies that allow fees to be less than costs
(2) Indirect costs	1. Forgone gross earnings 2. Differential feeding, housing costs	*Minus* 1. Grants 2. Tax on forgone earnings 3. Vacation earnings
(3) Benefits	Gross return = Gross earnings with degree minus Gross earnings with A-levels (i.e. before tax)	Net return = Net earnings with degree minus Net earnings with A-levels (i.e. after tax)
(4) Rate of return	Calculate 'social' rate of return from an internal rate of return calculation A measure of how all individuals are affected	Calculate 'private' rate of return from an internal rate of return calculation A measure of how an individual is affected

10.4.2 Rates of return to education

Table 10.1 outlines the main elements in a rate of return calculation. Typically, rate of return calculations to education centre on degree acquisition after the completion of A-levels or the equivalent. They are couched in terms of the traditional 'human capital model', so that an extra layer of education is viewed as raising the marginal product of the individual.

The object of the exercise is essentially a cost–benefit calculation and this has typically been conducted in a narrow way. There are essentially two reasons for this. The first is that if, even on a narrow calculation, it can be shown that the rate of return to education is comparable with other investments, then this is a certain underestimate of the true returns and the real attraction of investment in human capital. The second is a matter of expediency in that data are very easily calculated for the pecuniary aspects of investment in human capital.

Two types of calculation have been typically reported. The first is the so-called private rate of return which attempts to measure the costs and benefits that will be felt by an individual choosing to do a degree on completion of their A-level or equivalent courses. There is also the 'social' rate of return calculation, which unfortunately is a misnomer in that it does not seriously capture the social rate of return (the return to all individuals).

In Table 10.1 the social rate of return and private rate of return elements are noted and a picture illustrating the investment process is provided by Figure 10.2. Costs are usually divided into two types, *direct* costs and *indirect* costs. The *direct* costs in a social context are elements like: (i) the wages and salaries of university lecturers and other workers, (ii) maintenance costs of a university institution, and (iii) capital costs involved in providing degree-level education. These costs are captured as area (1) in Figure 10.2. *Direct* costs from a private viewpoint differ substantially from the social ones as there may be significant subsidies in place that allow fees actually paid by students to be substantially lower than the true direct costs suggest that they ought to be.

Indirect costs are essentially the opportunity costs that arise when an individual undertakes higher education. The main *indirect* cost is simply the forgone earnings net of taxes

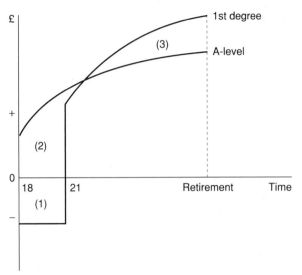

Figure 10.2
Earnings profiles and rates of return

the individual would have obtained had they joined the labour market with A-levels rather than attending university. At the social level it is gross earnings that represent the individual's contribution to output and this is sacrificed by investment in human capital. These costs are captured as area (2) in Figure 10.2. A second element of *indirect* costs arises if there are differential levels of expenditure contingent on the status of being in full-time education. Differential accommodation and living costs incurred by university students as compared to 'A-level' completers who did not go to university would fall into this category. As noted above, the private analogue of these *indirect* costs involves income net of taxation, in that it is assumed that, as far as the individual is concerned, taxes are completely lost to them (i.e. the benefits of public-sector provision are ignored as individuals are not seen as making the 'fiscal connection'). Also, if students receive grants or scholarships then their financial sacrifice is being accordingly reduced. Vacation-time earnings and, increasingly, term-time(!) earnings are also off-sets to the *indirect* costs of education as far as the private individual is concerned.

As for the benefits of degree acquisition, from the *social* point of view these are represented by the difference in earnings stream gross of taxation for those with A-levels as compared to those with a degree. The logic is that this differential reflects the increased marginal product of the individual. For the *private* calculation it is differences in the net income streams that are thought to matter, again justified by the fact that individuals treat their tax contributions as lost causes. These benefits are captured as area (3) in Figure 10.2. Data on these elements are collected for a cross-section situation (data for different individuals at different ages – one group with A-levels the other with a first degree), so that there is no need to wait for groups of individuals to complete their economic life-cycle before a rate of return calculation can be made. Given this, a data point for someone of 33 years of age will come from observing average earnings for someone who is currently 33 with only A-levels and someone who is also 33 but has a first degree. In this way, the cross-section data are necessarily hypothetical but it is only the 'on-average' picture that economists have sought to describe.

Once the data have been collected it is a mechanical matter to work out the implied rate of return. A number of points need to be emphasised:

    (i)   This is a narrow, almost accounting exercise, so that, although the one exercise is described as a social rate of return, it does not include anything that would make it 'social' in the way of measuring externalities.

    (ii)   Additionally, the exercise excludes non-pecuniary investment benefits, that is, it takes no account of increased marginal product in non-market home production.

    (iii) At no point are any *consumption* benefits, or disbenefits (costs), associated with higher education brought into the calculation. As noted above, it is commonly claimed that *consumption* benefits of higher education (in the form of enhanced appreciation of what life has to offer etc.) are claimed to be large.

It has to be recognised that those people who study for a university degree are generally a self-selecting sample of the most able of those that studied A-levels. To allow for this, economists have applied what is called the Dennison (1967) coefficient 'alpha' which suggests that only approximately two-thirds of any earnings differential is attributable to the higher education.

As for the results, the *social rate of return* is typically less than the *private rate of return*, mainly reflecting the historical presence of subsidies for those doing higher education. Even for the, admittedly narrowly conceived, rate of return calculation, the calculated rate of return generally exceeds the rate of interest on personal borrowing, so that investment in higher education typically is an efficient choice. By and large, studies have shown that the rate of return to successive levels of education gets smaller. It is at the early stages of schooling that the highest rates of return are attained and it is at the later stages (e.g. gaining a PhD over a Masters degree) that lower rates of return seem to be secured. As a generalisation, there seems to be (something like) decreasing marginal returns to successively higher levels of education.

10.4.3 Financing university education

Those reading this book as part of a university course would like to minimise the financial cost of that course. Historically, many would have enjoyed grants for higher education. But, in the past twenty to thirty years a considerable change has taken place in the way in which university education has been financed in the UK. This change can be seen as a change of view as to the economic rationale for intervention.

There are several strands of failure identified above: the existence of externalities, concerns reflecting equity, and possible inefficiencies and inequities associated with the market in loans for human capital investment. Views on the major location of failure have changed. In the 1960s, in particular, the idea was that higher education generated significant externalities along the lines described by Blaug (1970), so that if Figure 10.3 is considered, the marginal private benefit (MPB = demand) for higher education (HE) is measured in the location of the MPB curve. It is assumed that there are no problems on the cost side, so that marginal private cost (MPC) equals marginal social cost (MSC). The unaided market will produce an equilibrium at point 1 with quantity 0-q_p per period and price P_0.

If there are significant positive externalities then they should be included in the efficient configuration. The marginal social benefit to higher education is captured in the MSB line, which vertically sums MPB with measured marginal external benefits (MEB) as illustrated. In these circumstances the efficient equilibrium is point 2 with quantity 0-q_s and price P_s. The policy task is how to realise this result.

Even when education is given away 'free' it would be at a sub-optimal level. That is, only 0-q'_p would be chosen. So that the efficiency case for grants would be that grants would move the private demand curve for higher education to the right at MPB' through an income effect (so that, at price equals zero 0-q_s, the optimal level of higher education

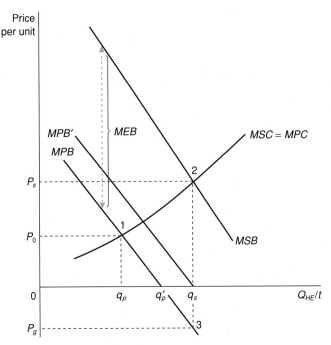

Figure 10.3
The efficiency case for higher education grants

per period, is chosen). It is as if distance 2-3 represents the appropriate corrective subsidy to higher education with a negative price P_g (grant) associated with the initial *MPB* curve.

Reinforcing this efficiency consideration about the quantity of higher education per period is the equity consideration, i.e. that the identity of who received the education matters. The argument has been that university education is the province of the middle and upper classes, so that, in order to secure some type of *equality of access* by individuals from all sections of social spectrum, financial aid in the form of grants is required.

With the passage of time and closer scrutiny of the arguments it became increasingly difficult to sustain the idea of widespread uninternalised externalities to higher education, undercutting the efficiency case for grants. Furthermore, it became apparent that grants represented another illustration of the so-called Director's law (see Chapter 16) where public expenditure serves mainly to help the middle-income classes and does very little for the working and lower classes. The whole system began to look like one that provided financial help to those who came from a background that was comfortable, and whose differentially higher future earnings stream would suggest an attractive private rate of return to any investments made. In these circumstances public policy was directed away from externality correction and equality of access arguments to focusing on imperfections in the human capital investment market listed above. Given this, attractively priced loans would be made available to individuals seeking to invest in themselves. At the moment in the UK most young people are familiar with this system, i.e. one that tries to treat human capital investment very much on a par with physical capital investment, albeit on less than fully commercial terms.

10.4.4 Screening versus the traditional approach

In Chapter 7 the notion of signalling and screening was introduced and a natural question to ask is how it modifies the above discussion. In a signalling, or screening, model of education, the receipt of education (by definition) does not alter the marginal product of the individual but simply signals pre-existing higher marginal product.

Suppose there is a group of n individuals, some of whom are high-ability, the H's and the remainder of whom are low-ability, the L's. The situation is one of asymmetric information; the individual knows if they are high- or low-ability but employers cannot look at individuals and see for themselves if they are high- or low-ability. In this situation the employer will offer a wage consistent with the mean level of ability of the group to all. It will be a weighted average of the marginal products of the high- and low-ability individuals. This is a pooled equilibrium. If high-ability individuals have a marginal product that is twice as high as the low-ability individuals, the wages for the H's should be twice the wages for the L's. That is, $W_h = 2W_l$ if marginal product wages obtained in a separating equilibrium. Employers wishing to create a separating equilibrium can reason that it is cheaper for the high-ability to acquire an education signal than it is for low-ability individuals.

In Figure 10.4, wage is indicated on the y-axis and the quantity of signal (education) on the x-axis. Wage W_h is twice W_l and $C(H)$ is the lower cost of signal acquisition for high-ability individuals compared to $C(L)$ for the low-ability ones. Now, if the employer offers to give W_h to all those with e^* education and W_l to the others, then, in a one-period analysis, for individuals to acquire the signal the net return (R) must be such that:

$$R = W_h - C(e^*) > W_l \qquad (10.5)$$

As illustrated, this is met for high-ability individuals but not for low-ability individuals. A separating equilibrium has been created with all those with e^* being high-ability. Note the importance of setting the signal correctly. If it is set at e_1 all will acquire the signal. As $C(L) = W_l$ at point 2 for the low-ability individual, this is the boundary value in equation (10.5) at which they will acquire the signal. The high-ability individual is inframarginal with signalling costs measured by e_1-3 < e_1-2 = W_l. On the other hand, if the signal is set at e_2 no one will incur the real resource cost of having the signal and all must be treated alike and receive the weighted average mean wage. These are pooled equilibria. As illustrated, the optimal separating signal is marginally to the right of e_1.

The underlying economics of this model are interesting and counter-intuitive. The creation of a separating equilibrium makes the low-ability individuals worse off and has the potential to make the high-ability individuals worse off as well! Assume the number of low-ability individuals in the group is b, then the weighted-average wage is given by

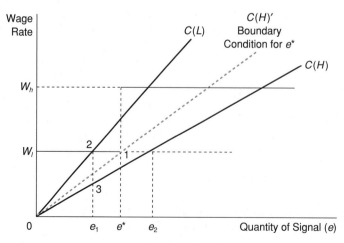

Figure 10.4
A screening perspective on education

$$\bar{W} = \frac{bW_l + (n - b)W_h}{n} \tag{10.6}$$

Given $W_h = 2W_l$ (by assumption),

$$\bar{W} = \frac{bW_l + (n - b)2W_l}{n} \tag{10.7}$$

$$\bar{W} = \frac{(2n - b)W_l}{n} \tag{10.8}$$

$b < n$ means $(2n - b) > n$ and implies $\bar{W} > W_l$, so the low-ability must be worse off.

Now consider the boundary condition $C(H)'$ for acquiring $e*$ education at point 1 in Figure 10.4.

$$R = W_h - C(H)' (= W_l) = W_l < \bar{W} \tag{10.9}$$

Ironically, the high-ability individuals are also worse off, obtaining a post-signal wage less than $\bar{W}$. It is clear from the formula that the lower is b, the number of low-ability individuals in the group, the more likely this is to occur.

Second, if education cannot increase the marginal product of any individual, then the social rate of return to education is unambiguously negative. There has been no increase in output but a considerable use of real resources in providing education.

Third, the private rate of return to education remains unaffected whether education is a signal or whether education enhances the individual's marginal product. In either case the individual is enjoying an increased wage rate, and generally speaking whether this increase reflects pre-existing ability or the acquisition of education is a matter of indifference.

Fourth, there are some less extreme forms of signalling or screening models in which some gains in output can be secured. In these models the increased marginal product arises because individuals are sorted into jobs that suit their characteristics. Round pegs are put in round holes and square pegs in square holes. In these circumstances, the social rate of return would be measured by comparing benefit (which takes the form of the changing output secured by using education as the screening device as compared to the next best alternative) with the differential cost (that is, the difference between the cost of using education as a screening device compared to the next best alternative). The next best screening device might be, for example, intelligence tests, interviews, selection weekends. *A priori* whether this social rate of return is greater or less than the private rate of return is unknown. It would require empirical analysis to resolve this point.

Fifth, it is clear that, in a pure signalling model, an extra layer of education for all is of no value. The individual has to be able to signal something that they have that others do not. This argument is part of Hirsch's (1977) contention in his influential book *Social Limits to Growth*. He notes 'more education for all leaves everyone in the same place' (p. 49). That is, an extra layer of education for all does not allow anyone to alter their position in the labour queue.

The final, and perhaps most surprising, implication of the screening world is that the content of any particular education course is irrelevant. It must simply be that some are seen to pass and others are seen to fail. Those that fail a course are doing others a favour! In this context, courses that students claim have no practical or relevant content can make perfect sense. (For those doing a vocational degree this type of argument obviously does not apply.)

The points above make it clear that the world of screening (signalling) is very different from that envisaged in the traditional human capital approach where the acquisition of education increases your marginal product.

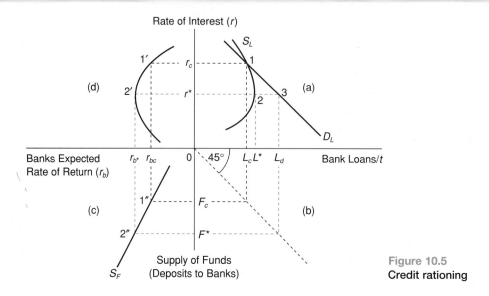

Figure 10.5
Credit rationing

10.4.5 Will borrowing be easy?

The advice so far is that it will be efficient to borrow to invest in human capital if the private rate of return exceeds the rate of interest on funds. It has already been recognised that borrowing to invest in human capital will be harder than borrowing to invest in physical capital. The concept of signalling has also been met. In this section the two come together in the market for borrowing to finance an investment.

This section summarises the contribution of Stiglitz and Weiss (1981) as well as a treatment in Strong and Walker (1987). In Figure 10.5. the market for bank loans is depicted. In panel (a) the supply and demand for loans are represented as S_L and D_L with the number of bank loans per period on the x-axis and the rate of interest on the y-axis. In panel (d) the relationship between the rate of interest and the bank's expected rate of return (r_b) is indicated. Panel (c) shows how the bank will attract a greater supply of funds (S_F) in the form of deposits with them as their expected rate of return (r_b) rises. The 45° line in panel (b) ensures consistency between the supply of funds and loans made. The market clears with interest rate r_c at point 1 with loans 0-L_c in panel (a) associated with expected rate of return r_{bc} at point 1′ and supply of funds F_C at point 1″. But it is clear that the market-clearing rate of interest will not be chosen as the expected rate of return is maximised at point 2′ with non-market-clearing rate of interest r^* causing excess demand for loans distance 2-$3 = L^*$-L_d. This is associated with expected rate of return r^* at point 2′ and supply of funds F^* at point 2″. But why is the banking-sector credit-rationing the maximising strategy?

The answer lies in adverse selection and adverse incentive effects. Assume would-be borrowers each have a single project with the same mean gross return (R). These projects, however, have different degrees of risk. That is, there are differences in the variances around the mean return. The bank, however, cannot distinguish between high-risk (high-variance) and low-risk (low-variance) projects. Bankers, however, recognise that would-be borrowers seek to maximise the net return (π). That is, they act to maximise:

$$\pi = \max(R - (1 + r)B; -C) \tag{10.10}$$

where r is the rate of interest, B the amount borrowed and C the collateral required to secure the amount borrowed.

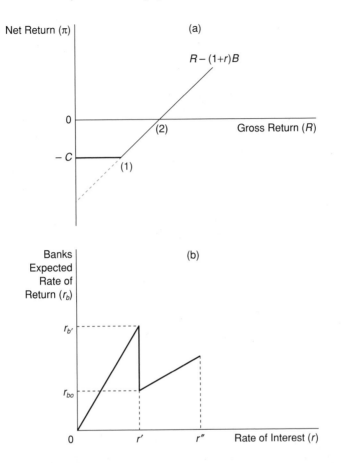

Figure 10.6
An adverse selection
of borrowers

In Figure 10.6(a) the net return profile is illustrated. Initially, up to the kink point labelled (1) $R - (1 + r)B < -C$, that is, the net return is $-C$ the lost collateral. On the incline (1) to (2) $R - (1 + r)B > -C < 0$. A net loss is being made but it is less than $-C$. On the incline above point (2) $R - (1 + r)B > 0$, being 0 at point (2). It is evident that firms with higher-risk projects will always find it more attractive to borrow at any r value. This is because with higher variance of the returns they have a greater probability of a low gross return (R) but this loss is bounded at $-C$. Similarly, they have a higher probability of a high R and high net return (π). Bankers realise that as they push up r it is only borrowers with high-risk projects that find it attractive to apply for loans.

This adverse selection effect is represented in Figure 10.6(b). Between 0 and r' would-be borrowers with both risky and safe projects apply to borrow and the bank's expected rate of return (r_b) rises with the rate of interest. At r' all the safe projects drop out of the market and the bank's rate of return falls r_b' to r_{b0}. As illustrated, there is some recovery of the expected bank rate of return as r rises further towards r''. The message, paradoxically, is to not continually allow r to rise even if there is excess demand for loans, i.e. do not clear the market.

The second effect is the adverse incentive effect. Above, at r' only those individuals with risky projects wish to borrow. In this second effect, as interest rates rise individuals choose a risky project over a safe one. Safe projects are driven out. Beginning with $R_s < R_u$ with s standing for safe and u unsafe and $p_s > p_u$ where p are the probabilities of R_s and R_u. The r for indifference (r_i) between a safe and an unsafe project is given by:

$$[R_u - (1 + r_i)B]p_u = [R_s - (1 + r_i)B]p_s \tag{10.11}$$

so that

$$R_u\,p_u - (1 + r_i)B\,p_u = R_s\,p_s - (1 + r_i)B\,p_s \text{ (condition for equal expected net returns)}$$

$$(1 + r_i)B\,p_s - (1 + r_i)B\,p_u = R_s\,p_s - R_u\,p_u$$

$$(1 + r_i)B\,(p_s - p_u) = R_s\,p_s - R_u\,p_u$$

$$(1 + r_i)B = \frac{R_s\,p_s - R_u\,p_u}{(p_s - p_u)}$$

$$r_i = \frac{R_s\,p_s - R_u\,p_u}{B(p_s - p_u)} - 1$$

If r is raised above r_i (dictated by the terms on the RHS), individuals will choose to have a risky rather than a safe project, i.e. adverse incentives arise. Willingness to offer to borrow at a high r signals to bankers that you have a high-risk project. In these circumstances the rate of interest should not be used to clear the market and credit rationing (excess demand) is the equilibrium as far as rate-of-return-maximising banks are concerned. Traditionally you had to see a bank manager to secure a loan and discuss your investment in solemn terms (with you deferring to the banker). Additionally, it was made clear that borrowing was to be frowned on. This seems ironic when banks make money by lending. However, the analysis here can lend support to this behaviour if bankers have greater demand for loans than the loans they are willing to make at the going rate of interest. The stern interview is to try to (imperfectly) establish the riskiness of a loan. The puritanical 'put-down' from the bank manager reflects that the rate of interest is below market-clearing, so that part of the interest you pay is non-monetary in having to listen to a sermon on your implied fecklessness!

10.5 Worklife – stage III

However long individuals try to delay the awful day, the vast majority eventually arrive at the formal labour market and have in social situations to respond to the question 'and what do you do?'. In a wide spectrum of circumstances, work involves common processes: training; choosing work hours; responding to the tax system; considering migration to another labour market; and, of course, dodging the supervisor! It is these issues that are addressed in turn below.

10.5.1 Training and investment in human capital

Most of the central ideas have already been met when dealing with education above but one of the key early human resources contributions was provided by Becker's (1964) work on training as an investment in human capital. Becker distinguished between two types of training and associated prediction on the location of finance and return:

(i) *general training* is that which raises an individual's marginal product in all firms. (In these circumstances the trainee pays all cost and receives all the return.)

(ii) *specific training* is that which raises an individual's marginal product only in a given firm. (In these circumstances the trainer (employer) pays all costs and receives all returns.)

Referring to Figure 10.5, MP_u is the marginal product of untrained individuals while MP_t is the marginal product of the generally, or specifically, trained (linearity is employed for simplicity). The wage obtained while training is given by

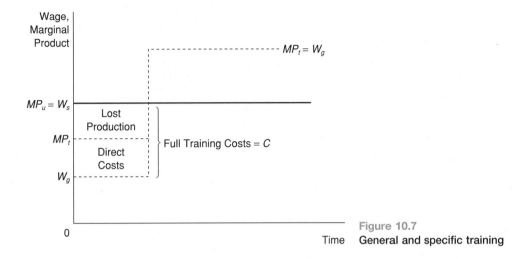

Figure 10.7   General and specific training

$$W = MP_u - (1 - a)C \tag{10.12}$$

with $(1 - a)$ the proportion of the return that goes to employer and C as full training cost. Training costs involve two elements. The direct costs cover the costs of providing a trainer, materials and a location to train. There is also the opportunity cost of lost production from the training phase, that is, the difference between the untrained marginal product (MP_u) and the trained marginal product path (MP_t).

Specific training: $a = 1$ and wage for the specifically trained $W_s = MP_u$. It is as if you have no skill. Employers invest by paying you more than you are worth in training and get a return in the form of paying you less than your worth after training (in Figure 10.7 compare MP_t with W_s).

General training: $a = 0$ and wage while training

$$W_g = MP_u - C \tag{10.13}$$

You are paying the full cost of training by receiving a wage less than you could earn anywhere as an untrained person ($W_g < MP_u$). But the post-training wage is greater than if you were untrained and represents the return to general training ($W_g > MP_u$).

What is the impact of this analysis? Every month or so radio broadcasts tell us that there is insufficient training in the UK because employers wait for other employers to incur training costs and then poach the skilled labour. But this makes little sense in the current context; the specifically trained are not the object of poaching as (by definition) they have no skill valuable elsewhere. Moreover, the generally skilled invested in themselves and are receiving the return; the employer is indifferent whether they go or stay as they incurred none of the costs and are receiving none of the benefits. It is, however, possible to soften these stark results because few training programmes are 100% specific or general. It suggests actors need to share the costs and returns, so that $0 < a < 1$.[1]

Figure 10.8 illustrates this. In Figure 10.8 W_a = alternative wage = marginal product unskilled; s = skilled; MP = marginal product, W_s = wage skilled. Here employers' costs and returns are represented by the darker area, while employees' costs and returns are the unshaded area. By observation, the steeper W_s, the more workers want to train and the

---

1. Furthermore, once labour markets are less than perfectly competitive, incentives alter because $W < MP$, i.e. in monopsonistic and oligopsonistic situations (see Chapter 11).

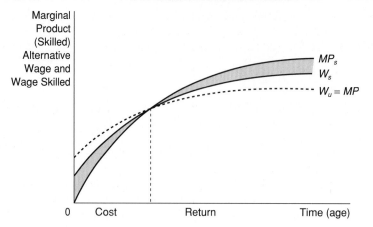

Figure 10.8
Sharing training costs and returns

fewer are likely to quit, as the lower their costs and the higher their return. With a steeper MP_s, the more employers want to train, as the lower their costs and the higher their return. It can also be noted:

I) If employees expect to be sacked or employers expect quits, then, because of the uncertainty, there will be a reduction in training.
II) Towards the end of careers, marginal products are generally falling off (compared to wage received) and in some cases, $W_s > MP_s$. Employers may want people to leave and employees want to stay on. An institutional device for dealing with this conflict is to have a set retirement age, and this sets the last period and allows an introduction to the theory of optimal wage contracts discussed below.

More generally, for the analysis of human capital acquisition:

$$\text{Present value} = (R/r) \; (1 - [1/(1 + r)^n]), \tag{10.14}$$

where

R = annual return,
r = rate of discount,
n = number of years.

An optimising human capital investor will have:

$$C = R/r(1 - [1/(1 + r)^n]) \tag{10.15}$$

where C is the cost of the investment, typically dominated by forgone earnings.
The formula suggests more investment in human capital:

1) the lower is C;
2) the higher is R;
3) the lower is r;
4) the larger is n (period of time over which the return obtains).

As n increases, the negative second term in brackets tends to 0 and for large n values:

$$C = R/r \tag{5.16}$$

This simple formula can be used to illustrate the effect of subsidising education. Assume: (i) the wage of uneducated people = £8000; (ii) it takes 5 years of school to acquire education; (iii) the rate of interest is 10%. Then, for individuals to acquire education $C = R/r$ (so R = £4000). This indicates that the annual income of the educated has to be £12,000 (this is an over-economic calculation). If education is subsidised to the tune of £2000 per annum, $R = £3000$. By subsidising education the wage for the educated has moved from £12,000 to £11,000 per annum and therefore the policy has reduced income inequality.

10.5.2 Supplying hours of work

Labour supply is a multi-dimensional concept. It involves effort, length of working life-time, holidays, human capital acquisition. Here the focus is a narrow one, namely the number of hours of those available per period that are devoted to hours of market work. This has been covered in a general way in Chapter 8 and now it is time to be more specific.

The choice over individual work hours, like other neoclassical choices, is one of maximising utility as represented by a preference map subject to constraints represented in a budget line. Preferences are captured in the utility function

$$U = U(y, L) \tag{10.17}$$

where

L = hours of leisure which can be interpreted as leisure time and time allocated to non-market production;
y = real income = Y/P;
Y = nominal income;
P = the price level (an index).

Both leisure and real income are viewed as 'goods' to the individual but, of course, each individual has their own precise map over the goods. Figure 10.9(a) shows the map of a 'leisure lover' who is willing to sacrifice considerable real income for a modest increase in leisure, whereas Figure 10.9(b) illustrates the map of a 'work lover', willing to sacrifice only a modest amount of real income for a considerable increase in leisure.

It takes all sorts to make a world. Economists cannot dictate the shape of individual preference maps but can work with different shapes. By definition, there can be no change in utility along each indifference curve, so that the total differential is constrained to equal zero. That is,

$$dU = (\partial U/\partial y)\, dy + (\partial U/\partial L)\, dL = 0 \tag{10.18}$$

and the negative of the slope of an indifference map over real income and leisure is:

$$-dy/dL = \partial U/\partial L \big/ \partial U/\partial y = MU_L/MU_y \equiv MRS_{Ly} \tag{10.19}$$

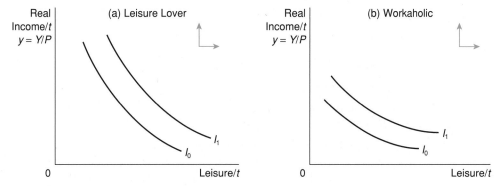

Figure 10.9 **Work–leisure preferences**

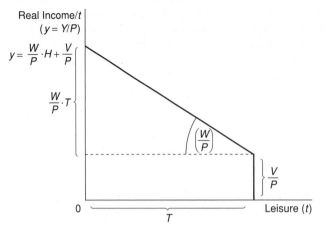

Figure 10.10
Budget constraint over income and leisure

This is the familiar result, i.e. that the marginal rate of substitution between the two goods is the ratio of the marginal utilities.

The budget constraint an individual faces, with respect to hours of work supply, can be quite complicated. To begin, a fairly straightforward budget constraint is represented in Figure 10.10. It involves:

$$y = W/P \cdot H + V/P \tag{10.20}$$

where

W = nominal wage rate
H = hours of work and
V = nominal non-work income

When $L = 0$ then $H = T = $ time available per period. The y-axis intercept is $W/P \cdot T + V/P$ whereas the x-axis intercept is $T = L + H$. As $L = 0$ at the origin, $T = H$ at that point:

$$y = W/P \cdot (T - L) + V/P \tag{10.21}$$

and the negative of its slope is $-dy/dL = W/P$.

Utility maximisation means the individual must pick a point where the indifference curve is tangential to the budget constraint and therefore

$$-dy/dL = \partial U/\partial L \big/ \partial U/\partial y = W/P = -dy/dL \tag{10.22}$$

This result can be obtained more formally using the Lagrangian method where the objective is to

$$\text{maximise } U = U(y, L) \tag{10.23}$$

$$\text{subject to } y = W/P \cdot (T - L) + V/P \tag{10.24}$$

The Lagrangian function becomes:

$$\mathcal{L}(y, L, \lambda) = U(y, L) + \lambda(y - W/P \cdot (T - L) - V/P) = 0 \tag{10.25}$$

Setting the partial derivatives of $\mathcal{L}$ with respect to y, L, λ equal to zero yields the first-order conditions for a maximum:

$$\partial U/\partial y + \lambda = 0 \tag{10.26}$$

$$\partial U/\partial L + \lambda \cdot W/P = 0 \tag{10.27}$$

$$y - W/P \cdot (T - L) - V/P = 0 \tag{10.28}$$

Rearranging:

$$\lambda = -\partial U / \partial y \qquad\qquad (10.29)$$

$$\lambda = -\partial U / \partial L \,\big/\, W/P \qquad\qquad (10.30)$$

so that:

$$-\partial U / \partial y = -\partial U / \partial L \,\big/\, W/P$$

and

$$\partial U / \partial L \,\big/\, \partial U / \partial y = W/P \qquad\qquad (10.31)$$

Given the recipe for a utility-maximising equilibrium, it is now possible to illustrate the main comparative-static results with respect to supplying work hours. Implicit in the literature seems to be the idea that more work hours is a superior outcome. This seems to reflect a Protestant work ethic plus a GNP-maximising transfer-payment-minimising perspective, which as is discussed elsewhere (see Chapter 19) is not the same as a utility-maximising perspective.

In Figure 10.11 it is assumed that $V/P = 0$, so the only source of income is earnings from work. As the real wage rises, equilibrium is found on successively higher indifference curves at points 1, 2, 3 and 4. Joining up points of equilibrium traces out the wage-consumption path, illustrating the fundamental question of hours of labour supply. That question revolves around the strength of the income and substitution effects.

As the real wage rises, an individual's income rises from each work hour and the prediction is that they will buy more of all normal goods, i.e. those with a positive income elasticity including leisure. That is, they will work less hours per period. In opposition to this, as the real wage rises the opportunity cost (in the form of lost earnings from work) also rises with the real wage. This suggests an individual will choose less of a good whose price has risen, so that fewer hours of leisure are predicted to be in the utility-maximising bundle. The prediction as to the number of hours worked is indeterminate (it depends on which effect is stronger).

For the individual depicted in Figure 10.11, the typical prediction is incorporated in the shape of the wage–leisure-consumption curve, i.e. increasing work hours (falling leisure hours) over a range (here 1-2-3) – so that a maximum work hours (WH_{max}) is eventually met (here at point 3) and thereafter work hours decline. It must be the case that,

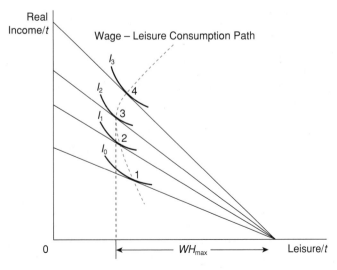

Figure 10.11
Work–leisure hours choice

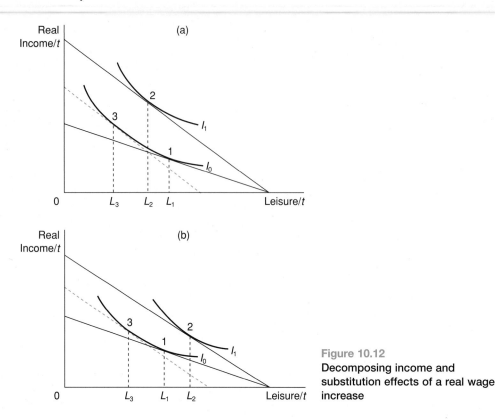

Figure 10.12
Decomposing income and substitution effects of a real wage increase

over the range 1-3, the substitution effect is dominating the income effect but the reverse is true after point 3 is reached.

Figure 10.12 allows the income and substitution effects to be decomposed. The income effect is isolated by picturing what would happen if the opportunity cost of leisure were held constant when income rises. Analogously, the substitution effect stems from the opportunity cost of leisure rising, so that this effect needs to be isolated whilst real income is unchanged. Holding utility constant is one way of defining real income constant. After all, what can be more fundamental than holding your subjective level of utility constant. In Figure 10.12 it is this interpretation of real income constant that is central and it is denoted by $U = U_0$ associated with indifference curve I_0.

The economic change modelled in Figures 10.12 (a) and (b) is a rise in the real wage W_0/P_0 to W_1/P_0. In terms of Figure 10.12(a), with W_0/P_0 in operation point 1 on I_0 is the initial equilibrium, with L_1 the chosen quantity of leisure. Allowing the real wage to rise to W_1/P_0 in Figure 10.12(a) causes point 2 to be the new utility-maximising equilibrium, with L_1 the new quantity of leisure. As discussed above, there is a difference between a 'real income constant' situation and the 'wage effect' move 1 to 2. To isolate the real-income-constant part of the decision a compensating variation in income is required. That is, the exercise is carried out to reduce income at the new real wage until the initial utility level $U = U_0$ is once again secured on I_0. Moving the new budget constraint to the left in a parallel fashion until it is tangential to I_0 (here at point 3, with L_3 the associated leisure quantity) operationalises this experiment. It serves to separate the substitution and income effects. In panel (a) the income effect is positive, having moved quantity chosen from L_3 to L_2. The substitution effect from L_1 to L_3 is negative, reflecting a response to a change in the relative increase in the price of leisure, real income constant

($U = U_0$). Here the negative substitution effect dominates the positive income effect and overall leisure hours are observed to fall as the real wage rises (work hours rise).

In terms of Figure 10.12(b), with W_0/P_0 in operation, point 1 on I_0 is the initial equilibrium with L_1 the chosen quantity of leisure. Allowing the real wage to rise to W_1/P_0 in Figure 10.12(b) causes point 2 to be the new utility-maximising equilibrium with L_2 the new quantity of leisure. The move 1-2 is, once more, the 'wage effect' move. To isolate the 'real income constant' part of the decision, a compensating variation in income is again required. That is, the exercise of reducing income at the new real wage until the initial utility level $U = U_0$ is once again secured on I_0 is carried out. Moving the new budget constraint to the left in a parallel fashion, until it is tangential to I_0, picks out point 3, with L_3 the associated leisure quantity. Once again, it serves to separate the substitution and income effects. In panel (b) the income effect is again positive, having moved quantity chosen from L_3 to L_2. The substitution effect from L_1 to L_3 is again negative, reflecting a response to a change in the relative price of leisure, real income constant ($U = U_0$). Here the negative substitution effect is dominated by the positive income effect and overall leisure hours are observed to rise as the real wage rises (less work hours).

It is an empirical matter if, for an individual, panel (a) or panel (b) is observed. That is, whether work hours rise with real wages for a given individual cannot be predicted *a priori*. Note that this is a picture that is unique for a given individual. Most individuals can have the typical wage leisure-consumption line (see Figure 10.11) and yet the aggregate supply curve can be positively sloped over a wide range of increasing real wages as long as the turning points are different for different individuals.

It was noted in the overview of the economic life-cycle that the difference between earned income and consumption determining disposable income was the presence of direct taxes and transfers. In particular, the impact of taxation on the supply of work hours has been hotly debated. This topic is addressed in the next section where income and substitution effects are more precisely analysed.

10.5.3 Choosing to work

Figure 10.13(a) illustrates non-participation in the labour force. Given the location of the budget constraint, utility maximisation is found at point 1 – a corner solution – on I_1. Utility maximisation involves all time T being devoted to leisure hours per period and the enjoyment of non-labour income V/P. As noted above, implicit in the literature seems to be the idea that more work hours is a superior outcome, reflecting a Protestant work ethic plus a GNP-maximising transfer-payment-minimising perspective. Between the approximate ages of 21 and 60, non-participation seems to meet some disapproval so changes that might encourage participation attract interest.

Panel (b) in Figure 10.13 illustrates the effect of decreasing non-labour income $(V/P)' < (V/P)$. The change causes a pure negative income effect and, given leisure is a normal good, the new equilibrium is at point 2 on I_0, with L_0 leisure and positive work hours equal to L_0-T. Points 1 and 2 are on the income consumption curve (ICC).

Panel (c) in Figure 10.13 illustrates the effect of increasing the real wage rate; in this case by the angle $(W/P) < (W/P)'$. Equilibrium moves from the 'no work hours' equilibrium at point 1 to the L_0-T work hours equilibrium at point 2 on I_2. From the point of view of the individual, the non-market income option decreases utility from I_1 to I_0, whereas increasing the real wage raises utility from I_1 to I_2. It is better to be induced into work than forced into it by reduced circumstances.

The effects of personal income taxation are usually viewed in relation to the aggregate supply of hours of market work and the associated welfare costs. The presence of income tax at high marginal rates should also induce movements into untaxed areas: jobs with

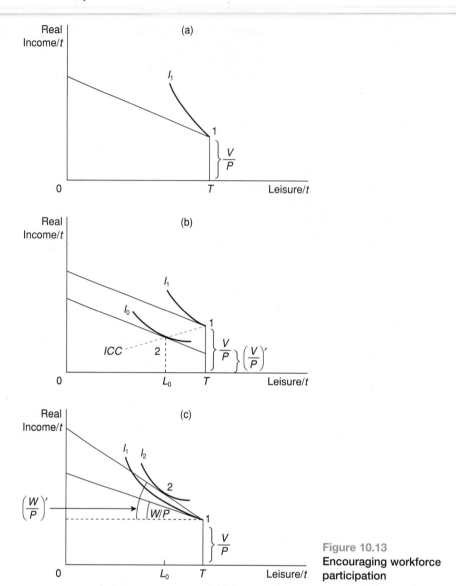

Figure 10.13
Encouraging workforce participation

high non-monetary returns or attributes, fringe benefits as opposed to recorded cash payments, and work in the 'black economy'. One of the most heavily researched areas in economics is the response of labour supply (hours) to income taxation and is reserved for discussion in Chapter 13.

10.5.4 Migration as investment

Migration is another area where the application of the investment in human capital approach found favour. After all, it should reflect private rational decision-making in the form of estimating costs and benefits appropriately discounted. Individuals will move if they can increase the discounted present value of benefits by greater than the costs of moving. The general presumption is that migration is insufficient in efficiently removing income disparities.

Sjaastad (1962) provided an early contribution in this area. As in the rate of return calculation above, this author breaks down the costs into direct and indirect costs. However, in his study they are labelled 'money' and 'non-money' costs. The money costs are out-of-pocket expenses and cover the increased expenditure on food, lodging and transportation for migrants and their belongings necessitated by migration. The non-money – indirect – opportunity costs of migration covers: earning forgone while moving, earnings forgone while searching for work and training for a new job. A measure of these costs would be the difference between forgone earnings in an origin location as compared with earnings in a destination location. The author recognised that there are also non-money psychic costs to migration in that individuals are reluctant to leave familiar surroundings, family and friends. Sjaastad sees psychic costs as different from real resource costs.

The return to migration as investment takes the form of finding a better market for pre-existing skills, upgrading yourself within your occupation or by gaining the opportunity to change occupation acquiring a new skill and thereby increasing earnings. These returns to migration represent higher productivity, whereas any non-monetary psychic returns from location preference represent consumption gains that have a zero real resource cost of production. The author accepts that his framework based only on real resource costs is restrictive but considers that psychic costs and benefits do not lend themselves to ready quantification. Leaving this point aside, in general terms the relevant net present value of migration (NPV_m) calculation is given by:

$$NPV_m = \text{Discounted benefits} - \text{Discounted costs}$$

$$NPV_m = \sum_{t=1}^{n} \frac{(Y_a - Y_h)}{(1 + r)^t} - \sum_{t=1}^{n} \frac{C}{(1 + r)^t} + \sum_{t=1}^{n} \frac{(\psi_a - \psi_h)}{(1 + r)^t} \tag{10.32}$$

where

h = home;
a = away;
Y = net-of-tax earnings;
C = net direct and indirect costs stemming from migration in year t;
ψ = psychic income (enjoyment).

Given equation (10.32) it is easy to list the factors that foster migration. Migration will be greater the

(i)   greater the annual income differential $(Y_a - Y_h)$ (e.g. lower age allows a longer period over which to enjoy increased net earnings);
(ii) smaller direct and indirect migration costs (e.g. lower-age individuals typically have accumulated fewer possessions, implying lower direct migration costs; additionally single individuals need not consider that another family member may have a good job at home, making the opportunity costs of moving high);
(iii) smaller psychic costs (the young have fewer community roots, are less likely to have school-age children and have a less extensive network of friends and acquaintances).

In short, it is young, single individuals with no children that are most likely to have a positive net present value to migration as a human capital investment and to migrate.

10.5.5 Work incentive mechanisms

Keynesian unemployment is associated with the notion of 'sticky' wages, so that workers are seen as resisting any fall in the level of money wages. The rigidity of the wage forces quantity, as opposed to price, adjustment in the labour market, so that unemployment is partly caused by worker-induced, insufficient wage adjustment. In contrast with this picture, the theory of labour market relationships over the last decade or so has emphasised that it may well be employers who wish to pay greater-than-market-clearing wages. They have rediscovered what was once termed 'the economies of high wages'. The basic idea is that an individual's marginal product is not independent of the wage they receive. Higher rates of pay may induce higher marginal products. The newer contributions on the 'economies of high wages' are dubbed 'efficiency wage theories'.

The theory can be set up using a simple production function that makes output, Q, dependent only on one variable, L, the quantity of labour supplied per period. That is:

$$Q = Q(L) \tag{10.33}$$

The L term is broken down into two elements: the number of workers employed per period, N, and the number of effort or efficiency units (e) they are willing to apply at work, which is a function of the wage (W) offered, so that with substitution for L:

$$L = N \cdot e(W) \tag{10.34}$$

and

$$Q = Q(N \cdot e(W)) \tag{10.35}$$

The question posed in this literature is: 'What wage should a profit-maximising employer choose to pay?' Profit (π) is the difference between the revenue received from the sale of output (product price P times the level of output $Q(N \cdot e(W))$) and wage costs (WN). More formally:

$$\pi = P \cdot Q(N \cdot e(W)) - WN \tag{10.36}$$

To make matters simple, product price P is assumed to be a constant, so the first-order conditions for a maximum are found where the derivative of profit with respect to the wage paid and the derivative of profit with respect to the numbers employed are set equal to zero.

$$\partial \pi / \partial W = P \cdot \partial Q / \partial L \cdot N \cdot \partial e / \partial W - N = 0 \tag{10.37}$$

Rearranging yields:

$$P \cdot \partial Q / \partial L \cdot \partial e / \partial W = 1 \tag{10.38}$$

where $P \cdot \partial Q / \partial L$ is simply the marginal revenue product of labour.

$$\partial \pi / \partial N = P \cdot \partial Q / \partial L \cdot e(W) - W = 0 \tag{10.39}$$

Moving W to the right-hand side and dividing the result by equation (10.38) yields:

$$e(W) \big/ \partial e / \partial W = W$$

or

$$e(W) / W = \partial e / \partial W \tag{10.40}$$

That is, the profit-maximising employer must set the average wage-induced effort level equal to the marginal wage-induced effort level.

What this condition looks like depends on how the relationship between effort and the wage level per period can be described. In Figure 10.14 a familiar shape is chosen, so that effort initially increases at an increasing rate with the wage paid and, thereafter (beyond the point of inflection at 1), increases at a decreasing rate. It is evident the ray (0-R) from the origin (the average wage-induced effort level) equals the tangent (T) to the curve (the marginal wage-induced effort level) at point 2, so that this illustrates the 'efficient wage' should be W^* and the efficient level of effort e^*. Although W^* will not be

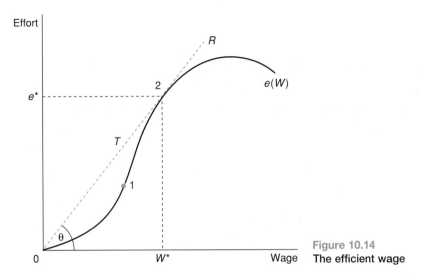

Figure 10.14
The efficient wage

an equilibrium wage with respect to the numbers employed (N), it is an equilibrium with respect to the efficiency wage and employers who profit-maximise would not seek to reduce that wage.

Possible causal links between effort and wages paid can be both physical and mental. In very poor countries, with considerable unemployment, it has often been noted that wages for those who are employed are higher than they need be to attract that quantity of labour. The resolution to this apparent paradox is that, with higher wages, the physical condition of workers is improved as their nutrition improves and hence their marginal product is higher with higher wages. There may also be a simple 'morale effect': even where workers are well nourished because a higher wage will induce greater morale and effort via workers' feeling good about their explicit recognition as important workers, worthy of their hire. This motivation may be especially relevant where the employer finds it very costly to actually monitor what a worker does and fears 'shirking'.

Where wages are greater than market-clearing wages, workers will be fearful of unemployment and work harder. Employers may wish to minimise quits by specifically trained workers and therefore pay apparently 'over the odds'. Further, there will generally be a queue of workers seeking employment, so that should quits occur there is a quickly available choice of would-be replacements (preventing considerable output loss from production disruption).

The existence of a pool of workers who would like to receive the efficiency wage by getting a job raises a problem. How is it they cannot put pressure on the employer to give them a job? The so-called 'bonding critique' (Carmichael 1990) says workers wanting a high-paid efficiency-wage job could post a bond with the employer effectively buying their way in. If, over time, there was no evidence of shirking, the bond plus interest would be returned to the worker on retirement. The value of the required bond would, in a competitive market, settle to the point where workers would be indifferent between high-wage and low-wage industries. This bonding process is seldom observed but, as noted below, an upward-sloping wage-earnings profile may serve a similar role.

Agency theory indicates that it may be important to design earnings systems that prevent self-interested workers from 'shirking'. In the alternative labour market theories discussed below, one characteristic emphasised is the absence of a close connection between marginal product and human capital. One explanation of this is that the deviation is more apparent than real. Lazear (1979) has theorised that workers will wish to signal that they are honest workers and not 'shirkers'. In order to do this they will accept, up to a

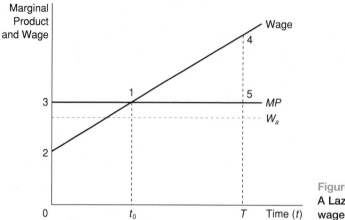

Figure 10.15
A Lazear signalling
wage profile

certain point in their work careers, t_0 in Figure 10.15 – a wage that is less than their marginal product. Once t_0 is past, the workers receive a wage that is greater than their marginal product until retirement takes place at time T.

In Figure 10.15, It is the case that the present value of wage payments would equal the value of the worker's marginal product over their working lifetime. The line W_a is the alternative wage the worker would earn elsewhere and can be viewed as the opportunity-cost wage (it is drawn below MP in deference to arguments introduced above). In the post-signalling stage the worker is receiving a bonus and, therefore, is unlikely to quit; the worker is a 'non-shirker'. To the extent that a signalling mechanism is not a feature of the alternative employment, quits will be greater, as will shirking, and output will be correspondingly lower.

Note, in this framework the marginal product and wage are only matched up completely in a straightforward neoclassical way in period t_0. The worker who has made the signal is, of course, very vulnerable, in that, between time periods t_0 and T, the wage exceeds marginal product (the honesty bonus) and, other things equal, the employer has an incentive to sack the worker. The worker, by the same token, would be anxious to keep working. For the sacking incentive not to be a problem the employer has to feel the need to maintain a good reputation as an employer to continue to attract labour in the future and, therefore, be honest with workers currently employed. For the staying-on incentive not to be a problem the employer has to know that at a certain date the employment relationship can be legitimately ended and, in this respect, statutory retirement age has an efficiency role.

10.6 Retirement – stage IV

In retirement disposable income tends to fall and public and private pension arrangements come into place. In the economic life-cycle it is depicted as a period of dissaving. Currently many public policy issues surround retirement. Individuals are living longer and, because many people rely on unfunded (transfer-based) public pensions, the tax implications for current and future workers look worrying. Longevity is partly secured by advances in health care which are typically expensive and, again, a tax-financed provision in many countries.

For the moment (as promised above) the efficiency role of retirement is further explored in the context of Carmichael's (1989) 'life-cycle incentives' model. Carmichael

(1989) provides a summary of life-time incentives models. Their name derives from the assumption that workers retire at a fixed time in the future time period T. Time period T is special in that neither the worker nor the employer has any expectation of gaining from their relationship beyond that time period. The work context assumed in the model described here involves two key elements. The first is that the worker's performance is monitored only at the end of each time period t. The second is that the effect of the monitoring exercise either establishes workers' honesty with certainty, or detects so-called 'shirking' (or cheating) imperfectly with a probability p.

The theoretical task to hand is to establish the cost-minimising wage structure. This is achieved by a process called 'backward induction' met in an earlier chapter with respect to game theory. As the name suggests, you begin with the final period and once you have located the optimal decision in that period, you work backwards to successive periods, having anchored the final period. In the model the self-enforcing mechanism for the employer is reputation. And, as noted above, this implies the need for the employer to attract and retain workers and further implies that some form of quasi-rents are arising in the productive process. If this is not the case, the employer would be always in the position to renege on agreed arrangements with employees, move location and set up elsewhere.

What will the wage profile look like? The relevant terms involved are Wm_t, which is the minimum wage paid by the firm in period t. W_a is the worker's alternative wage elsewhere. B_t is the bonus paid in period t if the monitoring procedure establishes honesty. C is the net benefit to the worker from shirking/cheating in any period t. Note that in the last period the employer cannot pay a fixed wage, otherwise workers would cheat and the cheating would not be detected until it is too late. This reasoning suggests some sort of bonus- or pension-type scheme has to operate in the final period. Two conditions need to be met.

(i) First, the no 'shirking' (or cheating) condition. If the individual worker shirks then their wage payoff is: $Wm_t + C + (1 - p)B_t$ and, to be indifferent between this and honesty, the bonus must be set so that $Wm_t + C + (1 - p)B_t$ must be equal to the honest payoff $Wm_t + B_t$. That is, the boundary condition is

$$Wm_t + B_t = Wm_t + C + (1 - p)B_t$$

$$Wm_t + B_t = Wm_t + C + B_t - pB_t$$

$$pB_t = C$$

$$B_t = C/p$$

(10.41)

(ii) The second condition is the no-quitting condition, which requires that the worker earns at least W_a. That is, $Wm_t + B_t = W_a$.

Now, consider wage policy in the next-to-last period $(t - 1)$. It is not sufficient to simply promise to fire those found cheating at the end of the period, as they can only expect W_a in the final period and that they can get elsewhere by definition. Therefore, the offer must be W_a if the worker is honest and Wm_t to detected shirkers, who are also sacked. That is $B_{t-1} = Wm_t - W_a = B_t$ and the cost-minimising wage profile is a flat one across periods.

The introduction of an enforced minimum wage W_g such that $Wm_t < W_g < W_a$ causes the last-period wage to be $W_g + B_t (= C/p) > W_a$, so that the individual is earning a premium in the final period compared to the alternative (W_a). This makes it easier to deter cheating in the next-to-last period, as those found cheating at the end of the period could have expected greater than W_a in the final period. Preventing cheating in period $t - 1$ therefore requires only that $B_{t-1} = W_a - W_g < B_t = W_a - Wm_t$. Given this reasoning, the cost-minimising wage profile involves an 'entrance fee' which is offset by the payment of a final-period premium.

Again, as in the Lazear model, reputation is required to stop employers claiming workers cheat and giving them the sack and keeping the entrance fees. A number of other implications are contained in the model.

First, mandatory retirement ages allow honest workers to quit without being accused by employers of being cheats, fearful of detection at the end of the period and fired without their honesty bonus. That is, employers could say the reason that you want to quit your job is that you know that monitoring at the end of the period will detect you as a cheat. If the alternative wage, W_a, rises over time, then so can the associated wage profile. The entrance fee and final-period premium characteristics of this model are robust to many changes in assumptions, but, unfortunately, seem to seldom closely fit actual wage arrangements.

10.7 Challenge: How do labour markets really work?

So far, two views of how the labour market operates have been introduced. For the bulk of this chapter a pure human capital model has been employed. In this, individuals acquire human capital in the form of education and training and this alters their marginal product in a positive direction in the formal labour market or in home production. A second model, assuming asymmetric information, was introduced in the form of signalling and screening. Here, in contrast, the acquisition of an education signal simply signalled that the individual was pre-existingly more able. In the extreme forms of signalling model education has no impact whatsoever on the marginal product of an individual. However, there are a wide variety of alternative views as to how the labour market may work (see Sawyer 1995).

Credentialism is a type of signalling view of the labour market in which employment is rationed by educational qualifications that are not actually required for the job. Employers have a taste (in this view of the world) for educated workers who have done 'the right subjects' at 'the right places'. This approach suggests that there will be economic rents earned by those who manage to find employment in occupations whose entry is restricted in this way. It is the area of the economy where class, family background, accent and school history are viewed as important. This description suggests that credentialism is differentially likely to be found in the non-competitive 'not-for-profit sectors' of any economy, e.g. the civil service.

Many labour economists set great store by a view of the labour market that sees it as a segmented market. In particular, dual-labour-market theorists have divided the labour market into a primary and a secondary sector. The primary sector of the labour market is dominated by so-called 'good jobs'. These are jobs with high wages, access to considerable training, low turnover rates, and firms that are said to have well-structured internal labour markets. Areas of the economy where good jobs are to be found are likely to involve significant technology and high capital intensity. In the secondary sector of the economy there are the so-called 'bad jobs'. Firms in the secondary sector have a very limited or no internal labour market. The wages are low, training is insignificant or minimal and there is chronic job changing. The key question then is what type of individuals get primary-sector jobs and what type get secondary-sector jobs.

As part of the model, it is the disadvantaged groups in society who find themselves condemned to the secondary sector so the sector is dominated by young, black and women workers. It is to be noted that these groups do not necessarily lack the human capital for a primary-sector job, it is just that the labour market has worked against them. As part of the theory, those individuals who get secondary-sector jobs begin to acquire secondary-sector characteristics in the form of high absenteeism, lack of effort and ambition, so that, *ex post*, they are unlikely to ever get primary-sector jobs.

Thurow's (1975) job competition model questions the nature of the 'market' in the labour market. He argues that the labour market does not auction off the services of skilled individuals to the highest bidders but rather allocates individuals to so-called individual 'on-the-job' training slots. The allocation process depends on an individual's position in the labour queue. That position is a function of an individual's background characteristics and includes variables, innate ability, age, sex, psychological test scores. Different employers will use different sets of background characteristics. Within this perspective, the labour market becomes very much a lottery. Individuals with identical human capital characteristics may find themselves with very different earnings and other employment characteristics. The view is a subtle one, in that it argues that marginal products actually reside in jobs rather than in individuals. Recognising that firms often require an institutional framework that will facilitate training in the form of one person teaching another, or in terms of individuals being very ready to adopt new technologies, it is in the interest of employers to: (i) repress wage competition between individuals, (ii) offer individuals tenure in their jobs so that they do not fear being replaced by the people they have trained and (iii) deliberately restrict competition to the entry points of firms.

Finally, in this brief account of alternative perspectives, there is the Marxist position (see Bowles 1985). Whilst Marxism is currently out of favour, there remain a number of theorists who see the labour market as essentially being driven by social class considerations. In their view, income is mainly determined by your social class, so that education is a mechanism that allows the continuation of existing income inequalities. Publicly provided education is perceived as working to the advantage of the capitalist class, in that it emphasises the disciplines of punctuality and deference, whilst, at the same time, stifling individual initiative. In contrast, the private (equals 'public' in the UK) school system caters for the capitalist elite. Here there is no emphasis on the norms of being the fodder for industry, rather individuals are educated for positions they have exclusive access to.

Whilst these 'thumbnail' sketches do not do justice to alternative perspectives, enough has been said to make it clear that the traditional human capital approach and the screening/signalling approach are not alone. Apart from the traditional human capital approach, all the other approaches, at one level or another, question the connection between education and training and an individual's marginal product.

10.8 Summary

On the point of death an individual's life is meant to flash before their eyes. This chapter has created a picture of life that you may not want to see again, as there is emphasis on education, training and work. Whilst these generate compensations, it is leisure time that typically attracts individuals more readily.

Pre-school years set your quality via a 'fundamental commodity process'. In a traditional model, formal schooling and higher education offer investment and consumption payoffs that may generate some positive externalities. The private rate of return to education, even narrowly conceived, suggests that sticking with this economics course will offer a financial return. Externalities, the imperfect nature of the capital market to finance investment in human capital combined with equity and 'merit want' consideration provide the case for public policy intervention of some kind.

In the formal labour market, training is important and, depending on its nature, its costs and returns are shared in different ways between employer and employee. Because individuals are sentient, incentives are important features of labour markets. Taxation affects the choice of work hours. Labour market migration can be viewed as an investment in human capital and the payment of greater-than-market-clearing wages an effort-inducing mechanism. Even the date of retirement has an important efficiency role. Microeconomics is everywhere!

Challenges to the traditional neoclassical view of the labour market come on all fronts. In an asymmetric information context, education is seen as a screening device with a negative social rate of return.

In other views of the labour market, the connection between education and your marginal product is also questioned. 'Credentialism', dual labour markets, job competition and a Marxian perspective all offer insights into what is perhaps the richest and most important market. For most individuals, the main asset they have to trade is their labour and, therefore, the functioning of the labour market is a prime determinant of how people get to live. This consideration helps explain why Labour Economics is a popular option in many degree courses.

References

Addison, J.T. and Siebert, W.S. (1979) *The Market for Labor: an Analytical Treatment*, Santa Monica: Goodyear.

Becker, G.S. (1964) *Human Capital: a Theoretical and Empirical Analysis, with Special Reference to Education*, Princeton, NJ: Princeton University Press.

Blaug, M. (1970) *An Introduction to the Economics of Education*, Harmondsworth: Penguin.

Bowles, S. (1985) The production process in a competitive economy: Walrasian, neo-Hobbsian and Marxian models, *American Economic Review*, 75: 16–36.

Carmichael, L.H. (1989) Self enforcing contracts, shirking and life cycle incentives, *Journal of Economic Perspectives*, 3 (4) Fall: 65–84.

Carmichael, L.H. (1990) Efficiency wage models of unemployment – one view, *Economic Inquiry*, 28 April: 269–95.

Dennison, E.F. (1967) *Why Growth Rates Differ. Postwar Experience in Nine Western Countries*, Washington, DC: Brookings Institution.

Hirsch, F. (1977) *Social Limits to Growth*, London: Routledge and Kegan Paul.

Lazear, E.P. (1979) Why is there mandatory retirement? *Journal of Political Economy*, 87 December: 1261–84.

Sawyer, M. (1995) The operation of labour markets and the economics of equal opportunities, Chapter 2, pp. 35–54 in J. Humphries and J. Rubery (eds) *The Economics of Equal Opportunities*, Manchester: Equal Opportunities Commission.

Sjaastad, L.A. (1962) The costs and returns to human migration, *Journal of Political Economy*, LXX (5) October: 80–93.

Stiglitz, J.E. and Weiss, A. (1981) Credit rationing in markets with imperfect information, *American Economic Review*, 71 (3): 393–410.

Strong, N. and Walker, M. (1987) *Information and Capital Markets*, Oxford: Basil Blackwell.

Thurow, L. (1975) *Generating Inequality*, Basingstoke: Macmillan.

PART III

THE FIRM ECONOMY

CHAPTER 11

The imperfect 'black box' market forms for outputs and inputs

11.1 Introduction

Having discussed the perfectly competitive market form in Chapter 3, it is necessary to complete the picture of the 'black box' market forms, by introducing imperfect competition in both output and input markets. The 'black box' epithet reminds the reader that the firm will have no serious internal content in this chapter. It will remain a set of lines on diagrams and a set of equations that locate outcomes after a certain number of assumptions have been made.

The task of this chapter is to explain and justify this level of abstraction and show why it is important. The theory of the firm as it relates to output generally discusses four major market forms. These are (1) perfect competition, (2) monopoly (3) monopolistic competition and (4) oligopoly. Forms (2), (3) and (4) are all forms of imperfect competition. It was emphasised in Chapter 3 that a good understanding of perfect competition is vital because it is the theoretical benchmark against which economists appraise other economic arrangements. In this chapter it can be used to assess the sense in which the imperfect market forms are 'imperfect'. An essential starting point for all the market forms is an understanding of the analysis of cost structures and where they come from (also developed in Chapter 3). The trick to understanding the theory of the firm is simply to recognise that the U-shaped cost curves apply in all the market forms (with some modification in certain cases). Differences in the implications for the outcomes of different market forms are differences in the demand conditions decision-makers face.

As regards the theory of the firm and inputs, the perfect competition account of demand for a factor was described in Chapter 3. Similar imperfect market forms can be developed for the input market and can be elaborated in the context of models of trade unions which have a similar 'black box' structure and make use of the classic tools of intermediate microeconomic theory.

11.2 Monopoly and an output market

In this section 'un-natural monopoly' contexts are explored. In imperfectly competitive situations firms face a downward-sloping demand curve and in the case of monopoly the firm and the industry are one and the same. It is, therefore, the firm that faces the downward-sloping demand curve for the industry ($D = AR$ in Figure 11.1). In these

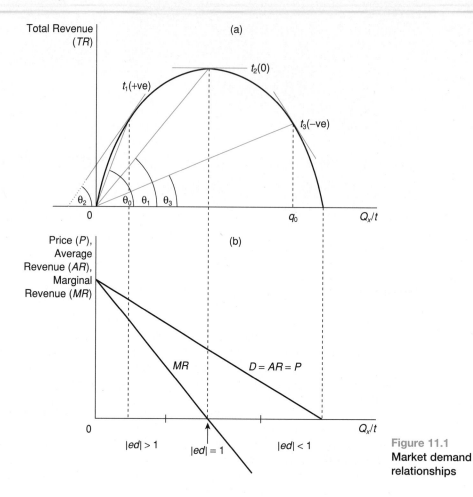

Figure 11.1
Market demand
relationships

circumstances it has to be recognised that the rule for profit maximisation requires the identification of marginal revenue before it can be applied.

If a straight-line market demand curve is adopted, then, in general form,

$$D = P = AR = a - bQ \tag{11.1}$$

$$TR = P \cdot Q = (a - bQ)Q = aQ - bQ^2 \tag{11.2}$$

$$MR = \mathrm{d}TR/\mathrm{d}Q = a - 2bQ \tag{11.3}$$

The manipulation above indicates that, with a straight-line average revenue = demand curve, the associated marginal revenue curve has, in itself, to be a straight line (and has to fall at twice the rate that the demand falls). In the straight-line case, it is certain that the MR curve touches the x-axis equidistant between the origin and the x-axis intercept of the demand curve. Furthermore, it is certain that the point on the demand curve directly above is the point where total revenue is maximised and the absolute value of the own-price elasticity of demand takes a value of unity.

Figure 11.1 illustrates these points and includes tangents and rays for the visual interpretation of marginal and average values from a total value. Once this picture is recognised monopoly output is determined by the cost curve (facing the firm) and the demand curve (facing the industry). The only distinction that needs to be made is between the short and the long run. As monopoly is the case of a single-seller there can

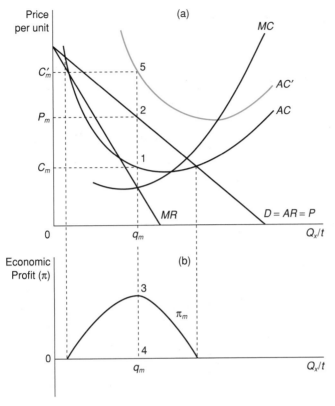

Figure 11.2
Monopoly in the short run

be no distinction between the representative firm and the industry because the firm is the industry.

11.2.1 Monopoly in the short run

In the short run Figure 11.2 depicts the relevant situation. Monopolists, like all profit-maximisers, choose output at q_m per period, where $MC = MR$ (and MC is rising). The monopolist will make an economic profit per unit, indicated by the distance between P_m and C_m. Total profit will be the area P_m-2-1-C_m = distance 3-4 on π_m in panel (b) (not to scale). There is no guarantee that, with monopoly power, economic profit can be made. There is nothing to guarantee that the appropriate average cost curve does not look like the one labelled AC', in which case, even with monopoly power, average cost will be above the profit-maximising price ($C'_m > P_m$) and losses will be made equal to C'_m-5-2-P_m.

11.2.2 Monopoly in the long run

In the long run, the only adjustment the monopolist can make is to the situation of maximum profit. This is determined by reference to the long-run cost curves (*LRMC* and *LRAC* in Figure 11.3). The plant built is consistent with the intersection of long-run marginal cost (equals short-run marginal cost) and marginal revenue. This adjustment may involve a plant that is at a point less than the base of long-run average cost or beyond the base of long-run average cost. Only by chance will that plant be consistent with the base of the long-run average cost curve and, although many textbooks illustrate this case (because it has intuitive attraction), it is nevertheless a misleading one.

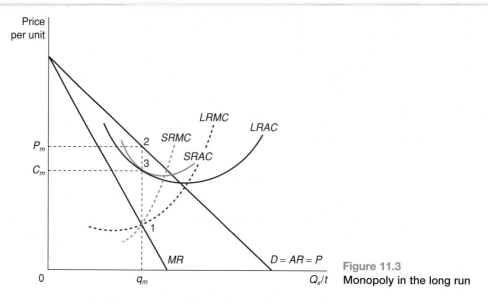

Figure 11.3
Monopoly in the long run

Monopoly is more commonplace than perfect competition. In industrial organisation many firms are seen as having some degree of monopoly power. The question then becomes what to do with monopoly power. Some students believe that if there is only one firm in the industry (so that, by definition, there can be no further entrants to compete away any economic profit), the monopolist will set an infinitely high price for the product and somehow sell an infinitely high quantity. This is clearly false. Where there is monopoly power, profit-maximising still occurs where $MC = MR$, and the point is that MR derived from the demand curve will constrain monopoly power. If price is pushed up, then quantity sold per period will fall. If price is lowered, quantity per period will rise. Price and quantity cannot be pushed up at the same time. However, this is not to say monopolists do not have further impact; there are situations where they can price discriminate.

11.2.3 Monopolies and price discrimination

These situations involve separating markets and the markets must be such that in each one there is a different demand condition operating. Further, it must be the case that it is not expensive to keep the markets separate. The Table 11.1 indicates the different degrees of price discrimination. The taxonomy turns on questions of whether consumers pay the same price for all units of good X and whether they pay the same price for any quantity of good X per period.

If the answer to both is Yes, then you have a zero degree, or no price, discrimination. This would be the outcome that was implicit in our discussion of perfect competition. In the other cases you have first, second and third degree price discrimination.

Table 11.1 **Degrees of price discrimination**

DO YOU	Pay the same price as all other consumers of X? (second answer)	
Pay the same price for all units of X? (first answer)	YES, YES Zero degree NO, YES Second degree	NO, NO First degree YES, NO Third degree

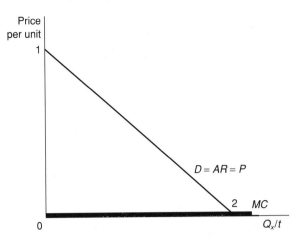

Figure 11.4
First-degree price discrimination

11.2.3.1 First-degree price discrimination

First-degree price discrimination is perfect price discrimination, where consumers receive no consumer surplus (which involves paying for each unit exactly the consumer's valuation).

Figure 11.4 shows the demand curve for an individual for a good whose MC is taken to be zero. Zero MC may not be an inappropriate assumption for goods sold in tourist traps. Imagine you are on a coach trip to Paris. There are many individuals ironically selling plaster of Paris 'ivory' models of the Eiffel Tower. You are invited to bargain for one but the seller is a master of bargaining compared to you. Indeed, once you start to bargain you are almost lost. Some minutes later you have your model tucked under your arm and you return to the coach to find virtually all the other passengers with their models. Discussion quickly reveals that different prices have been paid from very large to very small ones, yet no one seems very pleased with the trophies.

Typically, the sellers open with a ludicrously high price in order to 'anchor' the bargaining process, so that would-be purchasers feel they are being very successful when they have bargained the price away from the hopelessly unrealistic 'anchor' ('I wasn't having that'). In the circumstances described it is virtually impossible for a bargain not to be eventually struck. How can you be certain that purchasers have obtained no consumer surplus from their holiday bargain souvenirs of towers, fluffy donkeys and castanets? The response is another question: Have you ever been to a car-boot sale?

The perfect price discrimination case can be used to underscore an understanding of the difference between average and marginal revenue. Return to Figure 11.1. It can be seen that average revenue is located as the tan of the ray angle for each quantity, e.g. $\tan \theta_0$ for q_0. This makes clear the assumption that all of q_0 units per period are being sold at a single price. Indeed, this is what is making the difference between marginal and average revenue. To sell more, when facing a downward-sloping demand curve, price must be lowered; gaining extra revenue on new sales but losing revenue on all units previously sold at a higher price if all units must be sold at a single price.

In Figure 11.5 the conventional monopoly situation is depicted on the basis that all units are sold at the same price. If perfect price discrimination is possible each unit is sold at a different price that is exactly the height of the demand curve. In these circumstances $P = AR$ is also MR_d. Now, with MR_d, the $MC = MR$ rule takes us from point 1 to point 4. Price has moved from P_m associated with point 2 to P_d associated with point 4. Quantity has moved from q_m to q_d. Profit (additional revenue minus additional costs) is raised (the object of price discrimination), i.e. area P_m-3-2 + q_m-2-4-q_d minus q_m-1-4-q_d.

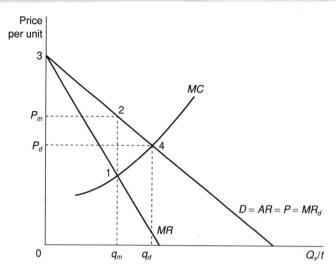

Figure 11.5
Making average and
marginal revenue equal

11.2.3.2 Second-degree price discrimination

Table 11.1 illustrates that second-degree price discrimination is about a common price structure for all, but a structure that exhibits different prices for different quantities. It is the block tariff case, familiar in the nationalised industries and their subsequent replacements.

At its simplest, it is about moving down demand curves in steps. Figure 11.6 illustrates three blocks: q_0 units can be bought at P_3, q_0 to q_1 at P_2, and beyond q_1 at price P_1. Compared to a single price, revenue is raised by rectangles P_1-P_3-1-2 plus 5-3-2-4.

11.2.3.3 Third-degree price discrimination

Table 11.1 reveals that third-degree price discrimination is about situations where a consumer pays a single price for all units but different consumers pay different prices. For this to be profitable different consumers must have different demand elasticities and, for it to be possible, the monopolist must be able to prevent arbitrage. That is, the monopolist must be able to prevent transferability of the good from one market to another at

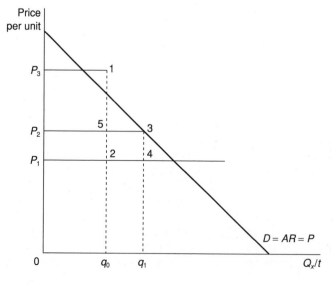

Figure 11.6
Second-degree price
discrimination

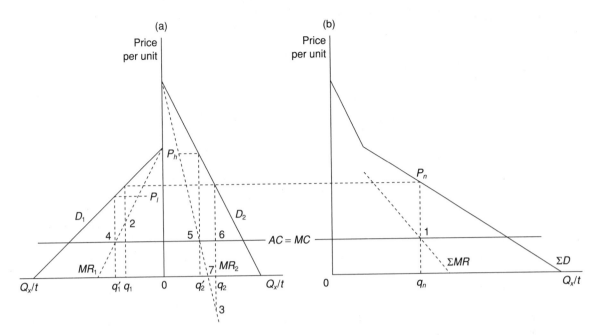

Figure 11.7 Third-degree price discrimination

low cost. It also must not be to the advantage of a consumer with one demand curve to act like one with another demand curve.

Figure 11.7 illustrates the process involved. There are two demand curves in panel (a) with D_2 being more inelastic than D_1. The cost curve is assumed to be horizontal so that $AC = MC$. Panel (b) shows the picture for the horizontal sum of the two markets with no price discrimination $MC = \Sigma MR$ at point 1 yields price P_n and quantity q_n per period. A common price implies $MR_1 > MR_2$ (given as distances q_1-2 and q_2-3 with MR_2 negative). The monopolist can do better than this. Provided the conditions above are met the profit-maximising decision is to equate $MC = MR$ in the two markets. This yields a higher price P_h in the inelastic market and a lower price P_l in the elastic market. Note: now the MRs are equal at distances q'_1-4 and q'_2-5.

That this third-degree price discrimination increases profit is clear. Reducing output in market 2 saves costs equal to the area under the MC curve over that range (which is area q'_2-5-6-q_2). This loses revenue equal to the area under the MR curve when MR is positive minus the area above MR when MR is negative (that is, q'_2-5-7 minus 7-q_2-3). It is more profitable to have single MR values than a single price P_n.

Note that the fact that a higher price is required in the market with the more inelastic demand curve can be deduced from the equation for MR.

$$MR = P[1 - (1/\,|ed|)] \tag{11.4}$$

$$MR = P - P/\,|ed| \tag{11.5}$$

Now, to equate MRs when $|ed_2| < |ed_1|$, $P_1 < P_2$; this is formalised in the elasticity rule: $MR_1 = P_1[1 - (1/|ed_1|)] = MR_2 = P_2[1 - (1/|ed_2|)] = MC$.

There may be some justification for this pricing policy if it is required for the survival of an industry. In Figure 11.8 with a single price P_a and total demand curve ΣD quantity is q_a and total revenue 0-P_a-1-q_a is less than total cost 0-P_a-2-q_d, so that bankruptcy is imminent. Recognising that ΣD is the horizontal sum of D_1 and D_2 allows price discrimination and a higher price P_h (selling q_h) and lower price P_l (selling q_l). Summing the two

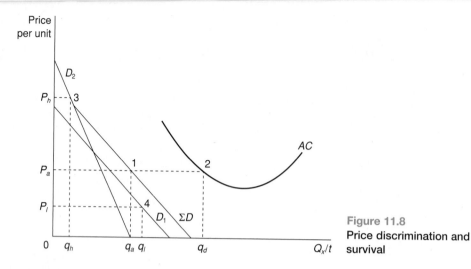

Figure 11.8
Price discrimination and
survival

total revenues $0\text{-}P_h\text{-}3\text{-}q_h$ and $0\text{-}P_l\text{-}4\text{-}q_l$ may well exceed total cost $0\text{-}P_a\text{-}2\text{-}q_d$, making the firm (= industry) viable.

The simplest message of these three subsections is that, if you do not understand the pricing structure you face, then you are almost certainly in a price discrimination context (e.g. rail fares).

11.2.4 Evaluating monopoly

Monopoly is commonly disliked. Why is this? The answer is clear by a comparison of monopoly with perfect competition; it is easy to show that there is an efficiency, or welfare, loss triangle.

In order to make this comparison a strong assumption must be made. As monopoly is the industry it is necessary to compare the monopoly outcome with what would happen if that firm were the perfectly competitive industry. To make this a valid comparison, assume the sum of the marginal cost curves above AVC in perfect competition (ΣMC_c) would turn out to be the marginal cost curve that is exhibited in the monopoly context (MC_m). Figure 11.9 illustrates this assumption.

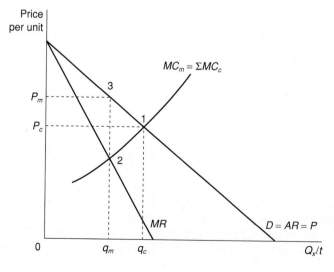

Figure 11.9
Comparing monopoly and
perfect competition (1)

The price and quantity in perfect competition associated with point 1 (P_c and q_c) compares favourably with the price and quantity in monopoly associated with point 2, (P_m and q_m). This is because, over the range q_m to the q_c, the units of output that would be produced in competition but not produced under monopoly are valued at the trapezoid q_m-3-1-q_c, whereas the costs of those units of output is given by the area under the marginal cost curve q_m-2-1-q_c. Therefore, the loss inflicted by not having those units is triangle 1-2-3. This is known as the efficiency, or welfare, loss of monopoly. In short, the monopoly produces too little and this generates the welfare loss.

It is worth noting that monopoly is not about 'good' or 'bad' people. It is simply the logic of profit maximisation in different demand contexts. Anybody running a monopoly would do exactly the same if they maximise profit. Monopoly allows economic profit to be made in the long run and this might be seen as unattractive in the sense that it creates a redistribution from buyers of a monopolised product to the sellers of monopolised products. Now, in principle, this is an unsanctioned redistribution and (in a frictionless world) it would be possible to use a tax-transfer policy to attempt to correct this. In reality it might be cumbersome and costly but, in principle, it would nevertheless be correctable.

Less correctable is the fact that outsiders can see economic profit being made by monopolists in the long run and the lesson they learn is that, if they too can create a monopoly situation, they too will make economic profit. Therefore, it is worthwhile investing real resources to set up their own monopoly. This may take the form of lobbying for parliamentary legislation to make them the only supplier of a good, or erecting entry barriers to an industry. The point is that economic profit, a transfer, is now converted to a real resource loss – that is, a loss to the economy. This process is known as *rent seeking* and is further discussed in Chapter 14. These are the essential reasons why monopolies are considered 'bad'.

Furthermore, once you give monopoly power to someone in any situation, it is very easy for them to abuse you with respect to other dimensions, a 'take it or leave it' attitude with respect to the quality of the good, the way you get treated, etc. You only have to be a customer of a monopoly franchise anywhere to know what this feels like. Having no exits is very unattractive to consumers.

This evaluation tends to make monopoly a 'bad thing' but there are those who have defended monopoly positions because they attack the assumption that the cost curve location will be the same in monopoly as in perfect competition. Their line of argument is that, given monopolies are secure in the fact that their monopoly profit will run into the future and is not going to be competed away, they have incentives to invest in research and development. They will eventually have improved technologies over those that would otherwise exist in competition. If so, monopoly is claimed to have a lower cost structure.

Indeed, it is possible to draw Figure 11.9 in such a way that the cost curves are much lower under monopoly (MC_m) than with perfect competition (ΣMC_c). The price is now lower under monopoly than it is under competition ($P_m < P_c$) and the quantity is higher under monopoly ($q_m > q_c$) than it is under competition. This is illustrated in Figure 11.10, where $D = \Sigma MC_c$ at point 1, yielding P_c and q_c, and $MR = MC_m$ at point 2, yielding P_m ($< P_c$) and q_m ($> q_c$).

It is also possible, of course, to argue the reverse. If you realised that you are competing with no one and you have monopoly profit guaranteed into the future, the incentive is to put your feet up, physically and metaphorically, thereby causing the cost structure to rise. If this is the case then the monopoly will have a higher cost than that which would have obtained under perfect competition. In all events, monopoly is generally not thought of as an attractive model of economic organisation although the great economic historian Joseph Schumpeter (1950) argued that the source of dynamic change in

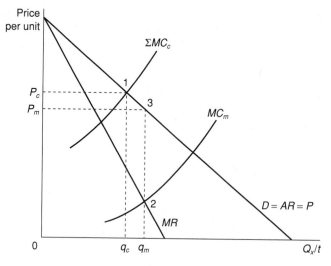

Figure 11.10
Comparing monopoly and
perfect competition (2)

many capitalist economies has been heavy concentrations of monopoly power in certain
key industries.

All of the above relates to a situation in which monopoly is in a sense un-natural in
the context in which perfect competition could obtain. There are, however, relatively
rare situations where so-called natural monopolies tend to arise. This was the situation
where a competitive environment would always degenerate into a monopoly (one was
analysed in Chapter 6).

11.3 Monopolistic competition and an output market

The two further 'black box' market forms that are part of any textbook on economics are
monopolistic competition and oligopoly. Monopolistic competition has in many ways
not been a very successful theoretical construct. In contrast, oligopoly is probably the
most important of the market forms for those interested in industrial organisation but it
is the one that is most complicated; it does not lend itself to easy summary, description
or results.

As regards monopolistic competition, the context is a situation where there are many
firms and the assumption of free entry and exit is retained. In these respects it mimics
competition. The key distinction as compared to perfect competition is that the product
of these many firms is not homogeneous: there are either real or imagined differences
between the output of one firm as compared to another, so that consumers do not treat
output identically. This creates some degree of brand loyalty to each individual firm – a
mini-monopoly element. The demand curve will be inelastic if there is a high degree of
brand loyalty and become more elastic the lower the degree of brand loyalty. (Perfect
competition is the case where there is infinite price elasticity at the level of the representative firm, because there is no brand loyalty whatsoever in a world in which products
are homogeneous.)

In the short run (see Figure 11.11) the picture for the representative firm in a monopolistically competitive industry is identical with that of a monopoly. Output (q_{sr}) is
where $MC = MR$ (at point 1). Price P_{sr} (associated with point 2) is above average cost per
unit for the successful monopolistic competitor. In the short run economic profit can be
made and this is represented by the area P_{sr}-2-3-C_{sr} in panel (a) and as vertical distance 4-
5 in panel (b) of Figure 11.11.

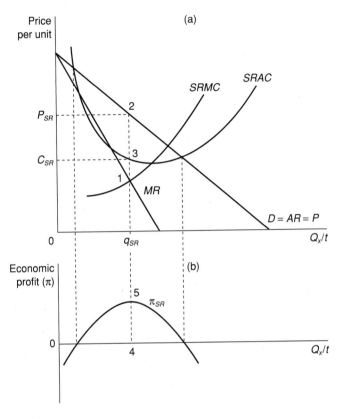

Figure 11.11
The 'representative firm' in monopolistic competition in the short run

In the long run, however, adjustment to the best point on the long-run average cost curve and the discipline of freedom of entry and exit comes into play. Individuals outside the industry can see economic profit being made. Such individuals will enter until all economic profit is competed away. In Figure 11.12, the entry in effect spreads the demand for the product X over many more sellers and the demand curve ($D = AR = P$) is decreased (a leftwards shift to $D' = AR' = P'$). It decreases to the point that MC equates with MR' at point 1. This means that price (P_{LR}) and average cost at point 2 are exactly matched, so that in the long run zero economic profit is made (see panel (b) point 3).

11.3.1 Evaluating monopolistic competition

Since in long-run equilibrium $P_{LR} > MC$ (at point 2) the result, like that of monopoly, is an inefficient one. In these circumstances there is a situation where there are too many firms producing, with a plant that is less than optimal scale. This is not the plant whose base point is at the base of long-run average cost at point 4 in panel (a). Indeed, this representative firm in the long run is using this less-than-optimal scale plant at a sub-optimal level of capacity, so it is producing at point 2 rather than point 5.

The gain from monopolistic competition is claimed to be in terms of a greater variety of products than would otherwise be produced. It is the situation that is meant to correspond to 'branded goods' (many different varieties of the same product with small differences between them). In this sense there seems to be a balance between the sub-optimal plant and scale argument against the gain from greater variety.

However, the real criticism that is made of monopolistic competition as a market form is that no 'real world' situation seems to conform very readily to the description.

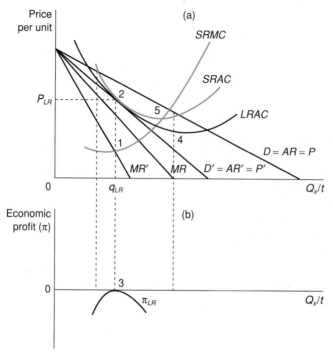

Figure 11.12
The 'representative firm' in
monopolistic competition
in the long run

Examples that apparently fit are petrol stations. They sell the same different grades of petrol but they are not really monopolistic competitors. There are certainly many of them but competition is essentially between a few in any geographical location.

This said, Magenheim (1995) is an author who has relatively recently applied monopolistic competition theory. In a study of the American child-care market the author isolates the main features of monopolistic competition:

1. a large number of producers in local markets;
2. regulations that are lax (so that entry is easy and not costly);
3. slightly differentiated products (types of care);
4. easy entry making the long-run demand curves faced by individual producers more elastic than short-run ones and leading to excess capacity.

Although empirical evidence for the latter prediction seems weak, it is the case that the monopolistic market form is still employed and cannot be ignored.

In general, as intimated above, many apparently monopolistically competitive situations have attributes that better fit an oligopoly situation. Many modern microeconomic theoreticians concerned with the firm have concentrated on oligopoly as the central model to explore.

11.4 Oligopoly and an output market

Oligopoly is a situation where there are said to be a few producers. Like many definitions in economics, 'a few' does not correspond to a definite number. Rather, it corresponds to a situation where each producer thinks (in their decision-making) that they have to take into account others' reaction to what they do. There is interdependence.

Indeed, oligopoly is the only market form where there is any interdependence. In perfect competition and monopolistic competition there are (by definition) so many that you do not need to consider others who have no individual impact on your situation. In monopoly you are on your own so there is no one else to worry about. So what distinguishes oligopoly is *conjectural interdependence*. Concern not about what you do alone but about what your actions (e.g. with respect to price, quantity, advertising) will have on other producers and the impact that their reactions in turn have on you.

Given that modelling interrelationships is complicated and straddles many academic disciplines it is not surprising that there are many oligopoly models. Here some of the most well known are rehearsed, beginning with the most well known.

11.4.1 Sweezy's kinked demand curve model

The title of this model has allowed economists to make vaguely salacious journal titles (suggesting they have a sense of humour) but that is not its only merit. The situation is essentially one where you arrive at work at, say, 9.00 a.m. on a Monday morning and what you know is the current price of your product (P_0 in Figure 11.13) and the current quantity situation (q_0). It is as if you are asked by the boss to consider altering the price at which you sell your product. The scenario you imagine is the one depicted in Figure 11.13.

Aware that you are in an industry where there are a few other producers you reason in the following way. If I raise the price of the product then everybody will let me do that because I will be a high-price seller when the others in the industry will be holding their price at the current level and therefore I will lose all, or virtually all, my sales. I imagine I will track left along a very elastic demand curve D_1 through point 1.

In contrast, if I consider lowering my price then everybody can be anticipated to match that lowering of price because they do not want me to steal their market share by having a lower price while they hold their price constant. So I would then track right along a very inelastic demand curve D_2 through point 1. The relevant portions of D_1 and D_2 form an imagined demand curve with a kink in it at point 1 associated with the current price.

Now once the demand curve has a kink in it, the marginal revenue curve has a discontinuity in it directly below that kink between points 2 and 3. It is as if you are shifting from part of the marginal revenue curve associated with D_1 to the left of point 1 to the marginal revenue curve associated with D_2 to the right of point 1. When that is done the discontinuity appears. To complete this piece of theorising, if the marginal cost curve is in the discontinuity it requires a very big shift in cost structure for a profit-maximiser to receive the signal that they ought to alter their price when employing the rule $MC = MR$.

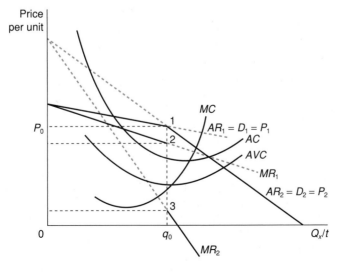

Figure 11.13
Sweezy's kinked demand
curve oligopoly

Your report to the boss is of course to do nothing – always welcome advice – but here there appears to be some justification. The implication is that oligopolistic price structures tend to be stable, as all producers will think in this way.

As regards evaluating this particular form of oligopoly, it has been seen as wanting in a number of respects:

1. First, there is no explanation of how original price P_0 is determined.
2. Second, people have pointed out that, although oligopolistic industries tended to advertise fixed list prices for long periods, trades actually took place at different prices (a claim recently made by UK car-sellers accused of overcharging) so that the prediction of a stable price was not actually borne out in practice. Unfortunately the theory was heavily geared to establishing price stability as a prediction. As such, the theory explained an observation that turned out to be false.
3. Also, the theory tends to be rather weak in other areas, so that it is silent on: (i) advertising policy and (ii) periods of cooperation and retaliation between oligopolists. This is why analysts have turned to game theory. Game theory, as met in earlier chapters, is a theoretical framework that allows interdependence, cooperative and uncooperative strategies to be analysed and predictions made about this particular type of market form.

11.4.2 Duopoly models and Nash equilibrium

In 1838 Augustin Cournot derived a model to explain the action of firms when there is conjectural interdependence (i.e. when the actions of one firm influence the actions of others). The model focuses on quantities. The key assumption is that each firm takes the output of its rival as given and does not expect rivals to change their output as a consequence of any decision that the firm makes.

In this illustration of the Cournot model (see Estrin and Laidler 1995), assume there are two identical rival firms. The 'identicalness' simplifies matters as it allows symmetry. In the duopoly case, the profits of each firm depend on the level of output of both because output price is given by the industry demand curve. The industry demand curve is

$$P = P(Q_X) = P(Q_{X1} + Q_{X2}) \tag{11.6}$$

where Q_X is industry output of good X. The profits of the two firms are then given by

$$\pi_1 = P(Q_{X1} + Q_{X2})Q_{X1} - C(Q_{X1}) \tag{11.7}$$

and

$$\pi_2 = P(Q_{X1} + Q_{X2})Q_{X2} - C(Q_{X2}) \tag{11.8}$$

where $C(.)$ represents each firm's identical cost function.

To be more specific, assume the demand curve is linear (as in 11.9). As elsewhere in the text, assume that costs C have a fixed element F and a constant marginal cost, c per unit of output (as in 11.10).

$$P = a - b(Q_{X1} + Q_{X2}) \tag{11.9}$$

and

$$C(Q_{X1}) = F + cQ_{X1}; \quad C(Q_{X2}) = F + cQ_{X2} \tag{11.10}$$

It is now possible to define the profit functions more specifically

$$\pi_1 = aQ_{X1} - bQ_{X1}^2 - bQ_{X2}Q_{X1} - F - cQ_{X1} \tag{11.11}$$

$$\pi_2 = aQ_{X2} - bQ_{X2}^2 - bQ_{X1}Q_{X2} - F - cQ_{X2} \tag{11.12}$$

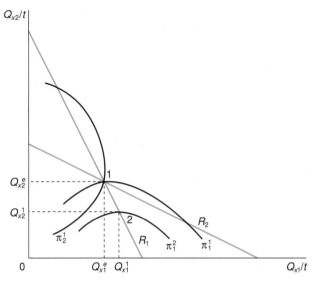

Figure 11.14
Isoprofit curves and reaction curves

In Figure 11.14, it is possible to illustrate these profit functions as *isoprofit curves*. An *isoprofit curve* for firm 1 is the locus of points in $(Q_{X1} \, Q_{X2})$ space defined by different levels of output for both firm 1 and firm 2 which yield the same profit to the firm.

As is evident in Figure 11.14, isoprofit curves are concave to the axis of the firm to which they relate. In the example here, the isoprofit curve for firm 1 is shown as π_1 and that for firm 2 is shown as π_2. The equations which underlie these curves can be derived. Rearrange equation (11.11) and the isoprofit curve can be described as:

$$Q_{X2} = \frac{a - c}{b} - Q_{X1} - \frac{(\pi_1 + F)}{bQ_{X1}} \qquad (11.13)$$

This shows (for each value of π_1) an inverse U-shaped line concave to the X_1-axis as depicted in Figure 11.14. Similarly, for firm 2 the equation of the isoprofit line is

$$Q_{X1} = \frac{a - c}{b} - Q_{X2} - \frac{(\pi_2 + F)}{bQ_{X2}} \qquad (11.14)$$

Note that, in both cases, profit increases with a movement closer to the respective axis, e.g. in Figure 11.14 π_1^2 is a greater profit than π_1^1. A profit-maximising firm will hope to attain the highest isoprofit curve possible.

To analyse how each firm behaves remember that the Cournot assumption is that each firm will choose its output level *taking the output of its rival as given*. In Figure 11.14 if the output of firm 2 is Q_{X2}^1 then firm 1 can sell Q_{X1}^1 and achieve the isoprofit curve π_1^2 (which is a greater profit than π_1^1). However, when firm 2 sells Q_{X2}^e the best that firm one can do is to sell Q_{X1}^e and achieve π_1^1. In this way, firm 1 makes its decision as to how much to produce when it takes into account the output of its rival. Similarly, firm 2 maximises profit on isoprofit curve π_2^1 when firm 1 produces Q_{X1}^e.

Given this, it is possible to describe the reaction of each firm to the output produced by the rival, each firm will attempt to reach the highest possible isoprofit given the quantity produced by a rival firm. Therefore, in Figure 11.14 the output reaction curves can be described. For example, for firm 1 the profit-maximising output is Q_{X1}^1 given that the output of firm 2 is Q_{X2}^1 and the best output is Q_{X1}^e given that firm 2 produces Q_{X2}^e. A locus of such points defines firm 1's reaction curve R_1. In the same way, the reaction curve for firm 2 can be defined as R_2.

Firm 1's reaction function can be determined by maximising π_1 in equation (11.11), taking Q_{X2} as given. Profits are maximised where

$$\frac{\partial \pi_1}{\partial Q_{X1}} = a - 2bQ_{X1} - bQ_{X2} - c = 0 \qquad (11.15)$$

which can be rearranged to yield the relationship between Q_{X1} and Q_{X2} when profits are maximised. The reaction curve for firm 1 can be written as:

$$Q_{X1} = \frac{a-c}{2b} - \frac{Q_{X2}}{2} \qquad (11.16)$$

Similarly, firm 2's reaction function is derived by maximising π_2 in equation (11.12) taking X_1 as given:

$$\frac{\partial \pi_2}{\partial X_2} = a - 2bQ_{X2} - bQ_{X1} - c = 0 \qquad (1.17)$$

and this gives a relationship between Q_{X2} and Q_{X1},

$$Q_{X2} = \frac{a-c}{2b} - \frac{Q_{X1}}{2} \qquad (11.18)$$

This is firm 2's reaction function.[1]

A *Cournot equilibrium* is reached when the expectations of each firm about its rival's output proves to be correct. Consider Figure 11.15. The reaction curves for the two firms are R_1 and R_2 respectively. Assume that firm 2 produces Q_{X2}^1, the best response from firm 1 is to produce Q_{X1}^1 (at point 1 on R_1). However, if this is the case, then firm 2 will change

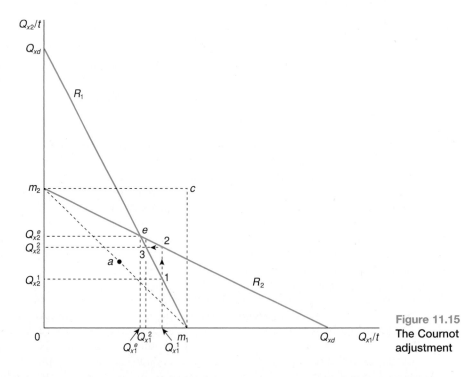

Figure 11.15
The Cournot adjustment

1. The reaction functions are linear when demand and marginal cost curves are linear.

its output. For if firm 1 produces Q_{X1}^1 then the profit-maximising response from firm 2 is to produce Q_{X2}^2 at point 2 on reaction curve R_2. It must be clear, then, that now firm 1 must change output for its profit-maximising output is at point 3 on R_1. This Cournot adjustment leads ultimately to point e at the intersection of the two reaction curves. This is an equilibrium, for now expectations prove correct (e.g. in Figure 11.15 firm 1 expects firm 2 to produce at Q_{X2}^e and so produces Q_{X1}^e and when firm 1 produces Q_{X1}^e then firm 2 will, indeed, produce Q_{X2}^e).[2] Note it is the peak of each isoprofit line that is on the reaction function.

Recall from the dating game in Chapter 9 that John Nash (1951) defined an equilibrium in a similar way. A set of strategies yields a *Nash equilibrium* when (holding the strategies of all other firms constant) no firm can obtain a higher payoff by choosing a different strategy. A Nash equilibrium is one in which no player wants to change its strategy. The equilibrium described in Figure 11.14 is therefore sometimes referred to as a *Cournot–Nash equilibiurm.*

As the Cournot–Nash equilibrium occurs where the two reaction functions intersect it is possible to substitute (11.16) into (11.18) to show that the equilibrium output for firm 2 is:

$$Q_{X2} = \frac{a-c}{2b} - \frac{a-c}{4b} + \frac{Q_{X2}}{4} \tag{11.19}$$

This can be rewritten as:

$$Q_{X2} = \frac{a-c}{3b} \tag{11.20}$$

Substituting back into equation (11.16) gives the equilibrium output for firm 1:

$$Q_{X1} = \frac{a-c}{3b} \tag{11.21}$$

Demand and cost conditions have been assumed identical so that the reaction functions are symmetric. It follows that the firms divide the industry output between themselves equally.

In Figure 11.15 this equilibrium solution can be compared with those which emerge from other market structures. It is useful to note that the competitive market sets demand equal to marginal cost so that $P = a - bQ_x = c$ so that ideally $Q_x = (a - c)/b$. Given duopoly output is $Q_x = (a - c)/3b$ for each firm the total output for this market is 2/3 of the competitive one. In comparison we have:

(i) *Monopoly.* If firm 1 were the only seller then setting $Q_{X2} = 0$ means that output would be 0-m_1. Using equation (11.5) the monopoly industry output is $Q_{X1} = (a - c)/2b$, half the competitive output (conversely if firm 2 were the single seller then output would be at 0-m_2 the monopoly industry output is $Q_{X2} = (a - c)/2b$, again half the competitive output). Hence, output is greater and price lower in the Cournot equilibrium as compared with the pure monopoly outcome and in this sense duopoly is pro-competitive;

(ii) *Cartels.* If both firms were to collude and act as a monopoly (splitting the market between them) the equilibrium would be at point a in Figure 11.15;

(iii) *Competition.* In the model described, the monopolist supplies one-half of that supplied by a competitive market; therefore total output with monopoly would be

2. The equilibrium is stable, because the slope of firm 2's reaction function ($\partial Q_{X2}/\partial Q_{X1} = -1/2$) is less in absolute value than the slope of firm 1's reaction function ($1/(\partial Q_{X1}/\partial Q_{X2}) = -2$). Industry output is $Q_x = Q_{X1} + Q_{X2} = (2(a - c)/3b)$, while price is $(a + 2c)/3$.

at point c (where firm 1 supplies 0-m_1 and firm 2 supplies 0-m_2). Given 0-$m_1 = Q_{X1} = (a - c)/2b$ and 0-$m_2 = Q_{X2} = (a - c)/2b$ and using equations (11.15) and (11.17) and finding the R_1 (R_2), Q_{X2} (Q_{X1}) axis intercept by setting $Q_{X1} = 0$ ($Q_{X2} = 0$) yields $Q_{X2} = (a - c)/b$ ($Q_{X1} = (a - c)/b$), revealing that these intercepts correspond to the competitive market demand/quantity outcome. The labels 0-Q_{Xd} in Figure 11.15 then can be seen to record the competitive output. Hence in the 'symmetrical' example illustrated it will be noted that in the duopoly situation the total output of the two firms is $\frac{1}{3} \times$ 0-Q_{Xd} + $\frac{1}{3} \times$ 0-Q_{Xd} = $\frac{2}{3} \times$ 0-Q_{Xd} (where 0-Q_{Xd} is the market output of good X) whereas the monopoly outcome is $1/2 \times$ 0-Q_{Xd}, and in general, when there are n firms the output in a Cournot model is $n/(n + 1) \times$ 0-Q_{Xd}. According with intuition, as the number of firms increases the competitive output is approached.

Before leaving this discussion of the Cournot equilibrium it is also possible to compare the outcome with a Stackelberg equilibrium. Heinrich von Stackelberg considered how the outcome might change when one of the firms understands the Cournot process by which the other firm operates. For example, in Figure 11.16 firm 1 understands that firm 2 will select that output on its reaction function that maximises its profits for the output that firm 1 selects. In this way firm 1 becomes a 'leader'. In Figure 11.16 it chooses the highest profit possible given its knowledge of the reaction curve of firm 2. This tangency occurs at point 1. By selling Q_{X1}^S the firm acts as a 'Stackelberg leader' and firm 2 becomes a 'Stackelberg follower', choosing output Q_{X2}^S. The advantage that the leader enjoys is clear, for instead of each producing the same output (Q_{X1}^C and Q_{X2}^C at point e) the leader now produces Q_{X1}^S and the follower only sells Q_{X2}^S. (An application of this theory to analysis of export subsidies is provided in Chapter 18.)

The Cournot model is but one model that deals with *conjectural interdependence*. As early as 1883 Joseph Bertrand took issue with Cournot's model. Bertrand argued that competition would take place not by changes in the quantity produced but via changes in the price charged. In Bertrand's model each rival sets its price assuming that the others will hold constant their price. This model yields different reaction curves and a different solution. The reaction curves have positive slopes. In the Cournot–Nash scenario 'quantities' are strategic substitutes as one firm increasing quantity of output reduces the marginal profit of the other firm. In contrast, in the Bertrand (1883) scenario 'prices' are

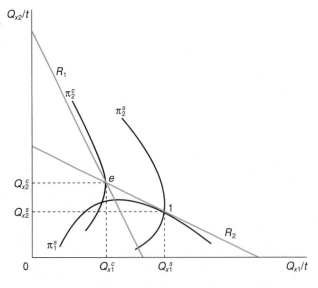

Figure 11.16
Cournot and Stackelberg equilibria

strategic complements as one firm increasing the price of output increases the marginal profit of the other firm (there is a good deal of symmetry in microeconomic theory). The labour market (input) duopoly model outlined in the appendix to this chapter is in effect an elaboration of a Bertrand model of the labour market. However, this is only one example of alternative assumptions that might be introduced to explain the way in which competition in a duopoly (oligopoly) will take place.

Another limitation of the Cournot model is the assumption that each rival continues to assume that the other firm will hold constant its quantity. Each rival sees that when it sets its own quantity the rival then proceeds to change the rival quantity.

11.4.3 The game theory approach

As is clear from earlier chapters, game theory deals with adversarial processes, where rewards, or benefits, depend on what others do. Depending on the particular game you may have to act when you do not know the actions of other players. There is a very wide variety of games but, to recap from Section 7.4, at their hearts, there are three elements:

(i)   there is a set of players, 2, 3 or n;
(ii) there are strategies which amount to a set of rules to select courses of action chosen (either sequentially or simultaneously) by the players;
(iii) there is a description of the payoffs (the numbers that are put in the various boxes are what the players are in effect playing for).

People are modelled as if they are acting in an instrumentally rational way. They are seeking to get the highest of these numbers. There are objections to this, as the reader will recall from Chapter 7, but nevertheless it is the assumption used here.

Games fall into different types and there are a certain number of classic games.

Zero-sum games are ones in which there is pure conflict. The two players modelled here, assumed to be duopolists, are a row player R and a column player C (the payoffs to C are shown in brackets). In a zero-sum game the amount R loses (or gains) C gains (or loses). In the tables labelled 11.2, 11.3 and 11.4 there are payoffs for a no-strategy game, a Von Neumann–Morgenstern strategy (saddle-point solution) and a game that has no saddle point solution but has a mixed strategy solution.

In the *no-strategy game* (Table 11.2) it is simply a game of 'heads and tails' where when the players toss the coins, if they match, R wins and, if they do not match, C wins. The payoffs are such that no strategy is involved. There is no gain to going first, and indeed no gain to knowing what the other player has. In effect you are playing against nature, so this game has no strategy.

In Table 11.3 there are three choices of action for R, labelled R_1–R_3, and three choices of action for C, labelled similarly C_1–C_3. To relate it to oligopoly the choices can be thought of as 'increase the advertising budget', 'lower price' and 'improve product quality'.

Table 11.2 **A no-strategy zero-sum game**

Table 11.3 Von Neumann–Morgenstern strategy and saddle point

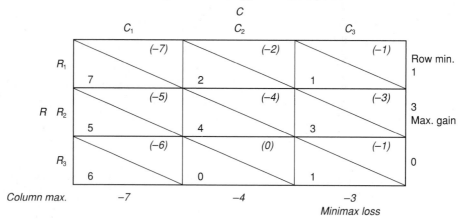

	C_1	C_2	C_3	
R_1	(−7) 7	(−2) 2	(−1) 1	Row min. 1
R R_2	(−5) 5	(−4) 4	(−3) 3	3 Max. gain
R_3	(−6) 6	(0) 0	(−1) 1	0
Column max.	−7	−4	−3 Minimax loss	

Each player must maximise their payoff knowing that an instrumentally rational opponent will be trying to minimise their payoff as they are playing against each other. The Von Neumann–Morgenstern strategy is accused of being a somewhat risk-averse one and involves adopting a so-called mini-max strategy. The idea is that, if you find out for each column the minimum of the maximum loss and for each row the maximum of your minimum gain then the solution of the game can be established. As illustrated, irrespective of C choice, R will never do worse than 3 if R maximises the minimum gain and chooses R_2. C's minimum of the maximum loss occurs when action C_3 is chosen and therefore with R choosing R_2 and C choosing C_3 the solution occurs in that (3, (−3)) box.

Table 11.4 illustrates a *no-saddle-point game* but there is a mixed-strategy solution, where the pure strategies are played with certain probabilities. The column maxima and the row minima are recorded in the table and, outside the game, it seems that R ought to play R_2 and C ought to play C_2. This is not a stable equilibrium because R reasons that C will play C_2 and therefore R will choose to play R_1. Then C reasons that R will play R_1 and therefore C plays C_1. But if C_1 is expected, R plays R_2. But with R_2 expected C plays C_2. The whole process cycles. In order to get a solution to this game it is necessary to consider probabilities. The task is to establish what probability of action R_1 makes the player R indifferent between C choosing C_1 and C choosing C_2. The parallel question for C is to establish what probability of action C_1 makes the player C indifferent between R choosing R_1 and R choosing R_2. If p_r is this probability of R playing R_1 then $1 - p_r$ is the probability of playing R_2. If p_c is the equivalent probability for C_1 then $1 - p_c$ is the probability of C_2.

Table 11.4 No-saddle-point and mixed-strategy solution

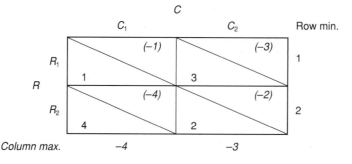

	C_1	C_2	Row min.
R_1	(−1) 1	(−3) 3	1
R R_2	(−4) 4	(−2) 2	2
Column max.	−4	−3	

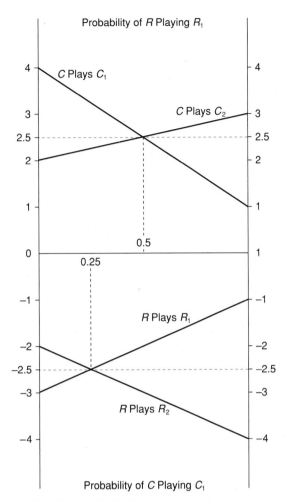

Figure 11.17 **Forming a mixed strategy**

Figure 11.17 illustrates the payoffs from Table 11.4 in relation to the probability of R_1 and C_1. Looking along the diagram, players wish to select the probability where maximum payoff can be expected. Figure 11.17 shows R should play R_1 with the probability of $^1/_2$ and C should play C_1 with the probability of $^1/_4$. The arithmetic of this is as follows.

For R to be indifferent between C playing C_1 and C_2, the expected payoffs must be the same so that:

$$p_r \cdot \text{Payoff } C_1 + (1 - p_r) \cdot \text{Payoff } C_1 = p_r \cdot \text{Payoff } C_2 + (1 - p_r) \cdot \text{Payoff } C_2 \qquad (11.22)$$

substituting the relevant numbers:

$$p_r \cdot 1 + (1 - p_r) \cdot 4 = p_r \cdot 3 + (1 - p_r) \cdot 2 \qquad (11.23)$$

$$p_r + 4 - 4p_r = 3p_r + 2 - 2p_r \qquad (11.24)$$

$$4p_r = 2 \qquad (11.25)$$

$$p_r = 1/2 \qquad (11.26)$$

For C to be indifferent between R playing R_1 and R_2 the expected payoffs must be the same, so:

$$p_c \cdot \text{Payoff } R_1 + (1 - p_c) \cdot \text{Payoff } R_1 = p_c \cdot \text{Payoff } R_2 + (1 - p_c) \cdot \text{Payoff } R_2 \qquad (11.27)$$

substituting the relevant values in

$$p_c \cdot (-1) + (1 - p_c) \cdot (-3) = p_c \cdot (-4) + (1 - p_c) \cdot (-2) \qquad (11.28)$$

$$-p_c - 3 + 3p_c = -4p_c - 2 + 2p_c \qquad (11.29)$$

$$4p_c = 1 \qquad (11.30)$$

$$p_c = 1/4 \qquad (11.31)$$

The idea behind the solution is that the individual will toss a coin each time to decide whether to play R_1 or R_2 and C will throw a 'shape' with three sides labelled Play C_2 and one Play C_1. The expected payoffs to the game or security points are:

for R,

$$R_1{:}C_1 \cdot \text{Payoff} + R_1{:}C_2 \cdot \text{Payoff} + R_2{:}C_1 \cdot \text{Payoff} + R_2{:}C_2 \cdot \text{Payoff} \qquad (11.32)$$

$$\left(\frac{1}{2} \cdot \frac{1}{4} \cdot 1\right) + \left(\frac{1}{2} \cdot \frac{3}{4} \cdot 3\right) + \left(\frac{1}{2} \cdot \frac{1}{4} \cdot 4\right) + \left(\frac{1}{2} \cdot \frac{3}{4} \cdot 2\right) \qquad (11.33)$$

which simplifies to 20/8 = 2.5 = expected payoff, which confirms the evidence of your eyes in Figure 11.17. The equivalent calculation for C must generate –2.5 as this is a *zero-sum game*.

The other games illustrated are so-called *non-zero-sum games* and these involve elements of cooperation. In economics zero-sum games are generally thought to be less applicable than non-zero-sum games which involve elements of cooperation. Tables 11.5 and 11.6 illustrate two further classic games which (taken along with the dating game of Chapter 9) only involve two strategies but exhibit increasingly severe collective action problems. To isolate Nash equilibria in the two games ® indicates a best response by R to

Table 11.5 The hawk–dove or 'chicken' game

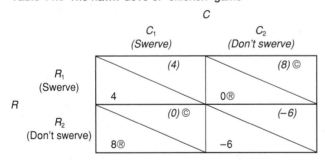

Table 11.6 The prisoner's dilemma game

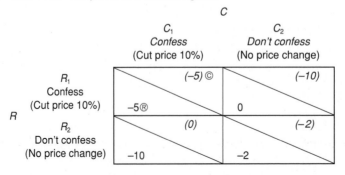

strategy C_1, C_2 whereas © indicates a best response by C to R_1, R_2 being chosen. Where they both occur in the same box that is a Nash equilibrium.

The game depicted in Table 11.5 is the so-called 'chicken game' or 'hawk/dove game' where, like in the dating game, the situation is one where there are two Nash equilibria in pure strategy. The situation is a competitive one so that the preference is to choose opposing actions. It is called the chicken game because it recalls two motorbike riders riding along facing each other and the payoffs turn on actions as the bikes close on each other at speed, that is whether to swerve and look cowardly or not to swerve and look brave. Clearly disaster is only avoided if your action is the opposite of the other rider's choice (complete disaster is R_2 and C_2).

The game in Table 11.6 is the famous 'prisoner's dilemma game'. This features in virtually all texts on economics and every talk on game theory. The scenario is that you and another person have been arrested as suspects for a crime and the authorities indicate the payoffs in terms of punishments reflected in different 'cells' of Table 11.6. It is known that the evidence against both of you is not that strong and non-confessions by both parties mean only mild punishment for both (here 2 months' prison each). Preferences over payoffs for R (C's are identically symmetrical) are:

1) R confesses, C does not: R is released and C is imprisoned for 10 months;
2) R and C both do not confess and get 2 months' prison each;
3) R and C both confess and get 5 months' prison each;
4) C confesses, R does not: C is released and R is imprisoned for 10 months' prison.

The payoffs are such that you (as an outsider) see that it is best for you and the other person arrested not to confess to the crime. It seems as though a dominant strategy would be R_2 and C_2. However, given the way that the payoffs are actually structured, the best response by R to C_1 and C_2 is to confess. If R confesses when C confesses, R gets 5 months instead of 10 months (option 4 would have otherwise been enacted). If R confesses when C does not confess, R gets no prison sentence instead of 2 months (option 2 would have otherwise been enacted). By exactly the same reasoning the best response by C to R_1 and R_2 is confession. With confession the dominant strategy for R and C both will confess and receive 5 months each when, if neither had confessed, they would have had 2 months each. Confession may be 'good for the soul' but it is not good for your freedom. Instead of securing their second-best choice they do in fact secure their third-best choice. It is the attempt to get the first-best choice by both players that is their downfall. It is, in effect, the 'free-rider' strategy. It is this kind of thinking that has application in several areas of economics and was employed in the discussion of public goods in Chapter 6. In oligopoly theory it is about setting prices, advertising budgets, etc. When considering pricing, R_1 and C_1 might be 'no price cuts' and R_2 and C_2 'price cuts' and the numbers in the cells millions of £s of profit.

11.4.4 Evaluating oligopoly theory

As is clear, there is no single oligopoly model to evaluate. It is difficult to develop firm conclusions. The fact that oligopoly is the most complex and frequently observed of the market forms is reflected in the content of industrial economics courses which typically have at their heart situations where each firm's output is large relative to the total demand for that good. Given this, it is clear that the presentation of oligopoly above is very much a partial one.

The Sweezy model is a timeless classic of textbooks but, as noted above, the theory was heavily biased towards the false prediction of price stability in oligopolised markets. The Cournot duopoly model relies on firms' setting output levels whereas critics say they choose prices. The model also assumes simultaneous decision-making, knowledge of rivals' costs and Nash equilibrium, all of which are open to question. Periods of cooperation and retaliation between oligopolists directed attention towards game theory as it allows interdependence and cooperative and uncooperative strategies to be analysed and predictions made about this particular type of market form. In employing games, heavy reliance is placed on the rationality of players and their belief that other players are similarly rational. The type of rationality employed has been criticised (see Section 7.4).

As regards the welfare cost of oligopoly, a lead seems to come from the fact that oligopoly lies between perfect competition and monopoly. It is generally considered that oligopoly is inferior to perfect competition but superior to monopoly. However, given the complexity of actual production contexts, this is open to debate.

11.5 Imperfect competition and an input market

Imperfection can be found in input markets, as well as output markets, and parallel reasoning applies. What happens if there are monopoly and oligopoly elements in the market for labour? Recall the rule for the profit-maximising employment of factors (here labour for illustration). That is, they should be employed up to the point where: $w = MR.MP_l$, where w is wage, MR is marginal revenue and MP_l the marginal product of labour. The product of MR and MP_l defines the marginal revenue product of labour and is the addition to revenue secured from selling one more unit of output. The rule on how many units of labour to employ has intuitive appeal. It says they should be employed up to the point where the addition to costs via the price of an additional unit of factor must be equal to the addition to revenue secured from selling the increased output secured from the employment of an additional unit of factor.

11.5.1 Labour market monopsony and neoclassical exploitation

Monopoly is about single sellers. Monopsony is about single buyers. On the input side this analysis takes the form of the company town, e.g. a bauxite mining town, where you work for the mine owner or you do not work. How will the wage rate and level of employment be set? A numerical example will help to fix the key theorising.

Assume the mine owner has the following data:

(1) Bauxite can always be sold at £20 per tonne (perfect competition in the bauxite output market).
(2) The marginal product of labour is given by $MP_l = 1000 - 0.05L$, where L is number of workers (units of labour).
(3) The town supply of labour (S_l) is given by $S_l = 200 + 0.2L$. This also defines average wage cost (AWC).

The owner must first form the demand for labour (D_l) by establishing the marginal revenue product of labour.

$$D_l = MRP_l = MP_l \times MR \qquad (11.34)$$

From assumption (1)

$$P = AR = MR = £20 \qquad (11.35)$$

so that

$$D_l = MRP_l = (1000 - 0.05L)£20 = 20{,}000 - L \qquad (11.36)$$

Whilst the competitive result is employment where demand equals supply, the monopsonist recognises the supply of labour curve is upward-sloping and, on the assumption that all workers must be paid the same wage rate, realises that the marginal wage cost is greater than the average wage cost. The employment of one more worker involves paying that worker a little more than the previous worker to attract the new marginal employee plus paying all currently employed workers a little bit more.

The owner can readily calculate the marginal wage cost curve (*MWC*) from the data available – it is the first derivative of the expression for total wage cost (*TWC*) which is average wage cost times the number employed.

$$TWC = AWC \times L = (200 + 0.2L)L = 200L + 0.2L^2 \tag{11.37}$$

$$MWC = dTWC/dL = 200 + 0.4L \tag{11.38}$$

(Note the inverted symmetry with (linear) average revenue and marginal revenue – *MR* falls at twice the rate of *AR* from a common *y*-axis intercept whereas *MWC* rises at twice the rate of *AWC* from a common *y*-axis intercept.)

To exploit monopsony power, the rule is to employ where $D_l = MWC$ and then pay that number of workers a wage (*W*) according to the supply curve.

Monopsonistic employment level (L_m) is therefore:

$$D_l = MWC \tag{11.39}$$

$$20{,}000 - L = 200 + 0.4L \tag{11.40}$$

$$1.4L = 19{,}800 \tag{11.41}$$

$$L = 14{,}143 \text{ workers} = L_m \tag{11.42}$$

The monopsonistic wage level is given by:

$$S_l = AWC = 200 + 0.2L = 200 + 0.2(14{,}143) = £3029 \text{ per period} = W_m \tag{11.43}$$

This arithmetic is illustrated in Figure 11.18.

What would have been the benchmark perfect competition employment? It would be where $D_l = S_l$ and, therefore, the competitive employment level (L_c) is:

$$20{,}000 - L = 200 + 0.2L \tag{11.44}$$

$$1.2L = 19{,}800 \tag{11.45}$$

$$L = 16{,}500 \text{ workers} = L_c \tag{11.46}$$

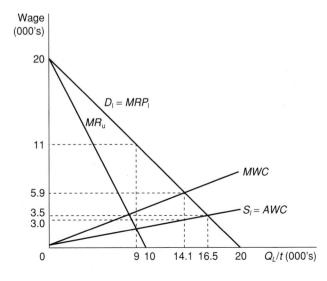

Figure 11.18
Labour market equilibria

The competitive wage level (W_c) is given by:

$$S_l = AWC = 200 + 0.2L = 200 + 0.2(16,500) = £3500 \text{ per period} = W_c$$

The prediction is clear. The mine owner in a company town is the 'happy' individual, while the workers find some 2,357 are unemployed and wages are reduced by £471 per period, compared with what would have been the competitive outcome.

At the monopsonistic employment level, the value of the marginal revenue product of the marginal worker is $D_l = MRP_l = 20,000 - L = 20,000 - 14,143 = £5857$, whereas the wage is £3029. That is, workers are paid less than the marginal revenue product of the marginal worker employed and are, therefore, said to be 'exploited'. It must be noted that this defines neoclassical exploitation.

In a Marxist perspective, all workers (not just those with $W < MRP_l$) in an economy are exploited, as surplus value is taken from them. The mine owner may decide to not fully exploit the possession of monopsonistic power for a number of reasons:

(i)   First, there is the fear of economic migration of workers to another labour market as discussed in Chapter 10.
(ii) Second, as also discussed in Chapter 10, paying higher wages may increase the marginal product of workers.
(iii) A third possibility is that the 'unhappy' and 'exploited' workers may seek to oppose monopsony power with monopoly power by forming a trade union. This bilateral monopoly outcome is discussed below.

11.5.2 Labour market oligopsony

Once again, inverted symmetry can be illustrated. The situation is again one where you arrive at work at, say, 9.00 a.m. on a Monday morning and what you know is that you are one of a few employers of labour. You know your current wage is W_0 (see Figure 11.19) and employment level (l_0). It is as if you are asked by the boss to consider altering the wage and consequent employment level. The scenario you imagine is the one depicted in Figure 11.19 beginning at point 2.

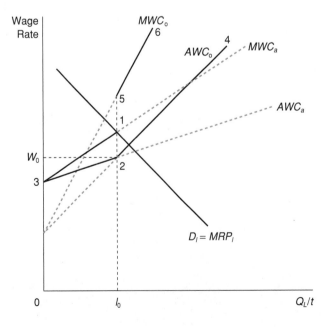

Figure 11.19
Oligopsony in the labour market

Aware that you are one of a few employers, you reason in the following way. If I raise the wage then everybody will follow me, because if I am a high-wage employer when the others are holding their wage at the current level they will lose all, or many of, their employees to me. I imagine, therefore, that will track right along an inelastic supply of labour (average wage cost) curve $S_{lo} = AWC_o$ from point 2, through point 4 (label o for 'others'). The associated section of marginal wage cost is labelled MWC_o and runs through points 5 and 6. The location of MWC_o is anchored by the observation above, i.e. that MWC rises at twice the rate of AWC from a common intercept (here point 3).

In contrast, if I consider lowering my wage then everybody can be anticipated to let me act alone, as I will not be able to attract labour at less than the going rate. So I would then expect to track left along an elastic supply of labour (average wage cost) curve $S_{la} = AWC_a$ from point 2 to point 3 (label a for 'alone'). The associated section of marginal wage cost is labelled MWC_a and runs from point 3 to point 1. The location of MWC_a is located as before. The relevant portions of $S_{la} = AWC_a$ and $S_{lo} = AWC_0$ form an imagined supply of labour with a kink in it at point 2 associated with the current wage.

Now, once the supply curve has a kink in it, the marginal wage cost curve has a discontinuity in it directly above that kink between points 1 and 5. It is as if you are shifting from part of the marginal wage cost curve associated with $S_{lo} = AWC_o$ (the right of point 1) to the marginal wage cost curve associated with $S_{la} = AWC_a$ (the left of point 1). When that is done the discontinuity appears.

To complete this piece of theorising, if the demand for labour ($D_l = MRP_l$) curve is in the discontinuity it requires very big shifts in the demand curve for a profit-maximiser to receive the signal that they ought to alter their price when employing the rule $MWC = D_l(MRP_l)$.

Again, your report to the boss is, of course, to do nothing – and, again, always welcome advice – but here there appears to be some justification. The implication is that, with oligopsonistic input markets, wage structures tend to be stable, as all producers will think in this way. As regards evaluating this somewhat curious piece of theory, it does provide one explanation of why employment does not vary in the face of sizeable demand shifts and labour can be seen as a quasi-fixed factor. Bhaskar, Manning and To (2002) present a very versatile *oligopsony-cum-monopsonisitic* model of labour markets but this is reserved for the appendix to this chapter. For the moment another of life's decisions is considered: should I join the union?

11.6 'Black box' economic models of trade unions

In the monopsony theory above it was suggested that unions might be the countervailing force to monopsony power exercised by an employer and, indeed, trade unions have been prime movers in lobbying for minimum wage legislation. The economic analysis of unions has in the last few decades been an important area of research, much of which uses the tools of microeconomics already met in this text.

A key starting point in discussion of an institution in an economic way concerns the way in which the institution is modelled. To borrow a distinction from health economics, there may be so-called 'organism models', in contrast to 'exchange models'.

Organism models treat an economic institution as an entity in itself with its own objectives and constraints. The organism is treated as an entity, so that it appears to be able to consider choices and take actions.

Exchange models, in contrast, focus the attention on the individuals that are party to decision-making in an institution and pose the questions: 'what are likely to be sources of utility to different individuals?'; 'what constraints do they face in maximising utility?'. As the emphasis is pushed back towards individual actors, these models have a more natural attraction.

However, the application of neoclassical economics has (in the tradition of abstraction, deduction and potentially falsifiable predictions) taken more of an organism approach. A debate that developed in relation to the economic modelling of trade unions became known as the 'Dunlop–Ross debate' and this debate echoes these concerns. Dunlop (1944) argued: 'economic theory of a trade union requires that the organisation be assumed to maximise (or minimise) something'. Ross (1948), on the other hand, viewed unions as containing a heterogeneous set of members with heterogeneous interests and goals. He argued that there was no simple maximising process at work, rather the correct form of analysis was political decision-making where union leaders (given their own objectives), acted to secure those objectives in the face of internal and external constraints. The internal constraints came from the various factions that are likely to be part of any union. The external constraints came from employers, other trade unions and the government. Ross saw the central objective of union leaders as the organisation's survival because their personal and professional ambitions would be inevitably connected to the survival of the union and furthermore, individuals who lead unions would grow to identify very closely with the union.

In order to give this debate a 'cutting edge', it must be the case that unions appear to make decisions that are economically irrational but politically rational. In short, the debate was about how much weight to give to economic, versus political, arguments in union decision-making. More recent contributions to trade union models formalise the mechanism by which union objectives might be satisfied (see Oswald 1985 and Estrin and Laidler 1995).

11.6.1 Elements in an economic model of a trade union

Preferences, as always, can be illustrated with indifference curves. For unions, the relevant sources of utility are taken to be the wage rate (W) and the level of employment (L). Plausible preference maps are illustrated in Figure 11.20, panels (a) to (c). Recalling Chapter 2, the slope of an indifference map in general is:

$$-dY/dX = \partial U/\partial X \Big/ \partial U/\partial Y = MU_x/MU_y \tag{11.47}$$

Replacing good Y with wage and good X with employment then:

$$-dW/dL = \partial U/\partial L \Big/ \partial U/\partial W = MU_l/MU_w \tag{11.48}$$

That is, the negative of the slope of an indifference curve is the marginal rate of substitution between L and W and equates with the ratio of the marginal utility of the level of employment to the marginal utility of the wage rate.

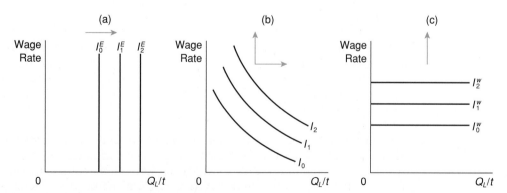

Figure 11.20 Wage–employment preferences

In Figure 11.20(a), the wage rate is a neutral, so that MU_w is zero and

$$-dW/dL = \partial U/\partial L \ / \ \partial U/\partial W = MU_l/MU_w = \infty \qquad (11.49)$$

That is, the indifference curves are vertical and only increases in employment increase utility I_0^E, I_1^E and I_2^E, etc. This preference map represents a union whose decision-takers are only concerned with employment, treating it as the maximand.

In Figure 11.20(c) the wage rate is a neutral, so that MU_l is zero and

$$-dW/dL = \partial U/\partial L \ / \ \partial U/\partial W = MU_l/MU_w = 0 \qquad (11.50)$$

That is, the indifference curves are horizontal and only increases in the wage rate increase utility I_0^W, I_1^W and I_2^W, etc. This preference map represents a union whose decision-takers are only concerned with the wage rate, treating it as the maximand.

Panel (b) represents what might be considered the more typical case, where the employment level and the wage rate are both sources of positive utility, yielding the conventional map between two 'goods'. Increases in either the employment level, or the wage rate, increase utility I_0, I_1 and I_2. The flatter the map, the more the union decision-takers are wage-rate-preferring. The steeper the map the more the union decision-takers are employment-level-preferring.

Whilst unions seek wage rate improvements, or employment level increases, or both, employers are modelled as seeking higher profit levels, so that the isoprofit curve becomes important. It is formulated as follows. By definition profit (π) is

$$\pi = P \cdot Q(L) - W \cdot L \qquad (11.51)$$

where

W = wage rate;
P = price of the output per unit treated as a constant;
Q = output level;
L = level of employment.

Along an isoprofit curve the change in profit $d\pi = 0$ by definition, so that the total differential is constrained to be zero. That is:

$$d\pi = P \ \partial Q/\partial L \ dL - WdL - LdW = 0 \qquad (11.52)$$

and

$$P \ \partial Q/\partial L = \text{the marginal revenue product of labour} = MRP_l.$$

Rearranging:

$$dW/dL = \frac{MRP_l - W}{L} \qquad (11.53)$$

indicating if:

(i) $MRP_l > W$, then dW/dL is positive and the isoprofit line is rising;
(ii) $MRP_l < W$, then dW/dL is negative and the isoprofit line is falling;
(iii) $MRP_l = W$, then dW/dL is zero and the isoprofit line momentarily has a slope of zero (at its peak).

Of course, $MRP_l = W$ is the profit-maximising condition for the employment of labour (see Section 11.5) and, as such, must be a point on the demand curve for labour D_l.

These relationships are depicted in Figure 11.21, where the level of profit understandably falls as the wage rate rises, so that $\pi_0 < \pi_1 < \pi_2$. Putting the pieces together allows different models of unions to be built up.

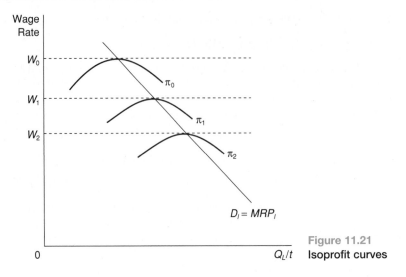

Figure 11.21
Isoprofit curves

11.6.2 Traditional monopoly models of unions

First, some unfinished analysis from above, where it was noted 'unhappy' and 'exploited' workers may seek to oppose monopsony power with monopoly power by forming a trade union. This bilateral monopoly outcome can also be seen in Figure 11.18.

If the union is formed and becomes the only seller of labour to the mine owner, then the labour demand curve $D_l = MRP_l = (1000 - 0.05L)$ £20 $= 20,000 - L$ becomes the average revenue curve as far as the union is concerned (AR_u). For the union to flex its monopoly muscle involves setting employment where the marginal revenue to the union (MR_u) is equated with the supply of labour (average wage cost curve) and wage is set by the labour demand curve $D_l = MRP_l$ at that employment level.

The union can readily calculate the marginal revenue union curve from the data available. It is the first derivative of the expression for total revenue product (TRP), which is average revenue ($= D_l = MRP_l$) times the number employed (L):

$$TRP = MRP_l \times L = (20,000 - L)L = 20,000L - L^2 \tag{11.54}$$

$$MR_u = \mathrm{d}TRP/\mathrm{d}L = 20,000 - 2L \tag{11.55}$$

(Note again the symmetry with (linear) average revenue and marginal revenue – MR_u falls at twice the rate of AR_u from a common y-axis intercept.)

To exploit the monopoly power, the rule is to employ where $MR_u = S_l = AWC$ and to demand wage (W) for that number of workers according to the demand curve. Union monopoly employment (L_u) level is, therefore:

$$MR_u = S_l = AWC \tag{11.56}$$

$$20,000 - 2L = 200 + 0.2L \tag{11.57}$$

$$2.2L = 19,800 \tag{11.58}$$

$$L = 9000 \text{ workers} = L_u \tag{11.59}$$

Union monopoly wage level (W_u) is given by:

$$D_l = MRP_l = 20,000 - L = 20,000 - 9000 = £11,000 \text{ per period} = W_u \tag{11.60}$$

This arithmetic is illustrated as Figure 11.18. This indicates that a monopoly union facing a monopsonistic employer would have wage–employment offers of 9000 employed at

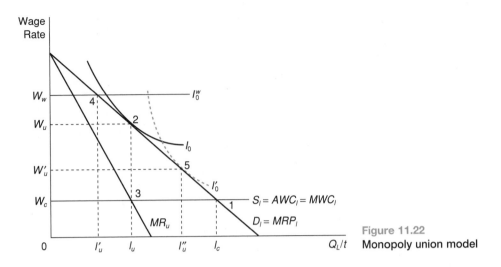

Figure 11.22
Monopoly union model

£11,000 per period and 14,143 employed at £3029 per period respectively. The scene is then set for a bargaining contest of some size, which might take the outcome towards the competitive result of 16,500 workers at £3500 per period.

Moving away from the arithmetic and the bilateral monopoly case, in Figure 11.22 the familiar apparatus for dealing with monopoly situations is pictured. Instead of the demand curve for a final product, however, it is the demand curve for labour that is relevant ($D_l = MRP_l$). So, the marginal revenue curve is the marginal revenue in terms of the increase in the wage bill (MR_u) that would go to union employees as the wage rate is altered and all employees are paid the same wage rate. Given that the supply of labour curve (S_l) is assumed constant (perfectly elastic), the average wage cost of labour (AWC_l) and the marginal wage cost of labour (MWC_l) are identical with it, so that the competitive wage would be W_c and the competitive level of employment l_c (see point 1).

If unions are now assumed to form and use the threat of strike to push up wages, the question becomes, how far will they choose to cause the wage rate to rise. If the union is assumed to be rental-maximising, the level of employment chosen maximises the product of the difference between the union wage (W_u) and the competitive wage multiplied by the number of employees under union presence (l_u). The rental-maximising union therefore equates MR_u with AWC_l, making the wage rate W_u and the employment level l_u (both associated with point 2). Given this, the area W_u-2-3-W_c is the extra reward, over and above the competitive wage secured by those members of the union that are employed (i.e. $W_u - W_c$ per worker). For point 2 to be a utility-maximising solution it is implied that the union decision-maker's indifference curve is that illustrated by I_0. However, as was noted above, the indifference map may take different shapes. For instance, a wage-maximising union would try to maximise the wage subject to some union employment constraint, say l_u'. In this case, the wage would be W_w and the relevant indifference curve I_0^w, with equilibrium at point 4. A union that placed much more emphasis on the employment level of its members would have a much steeper indifference map like I_0', with equilibrium at point 5 (with wage W_u' and employment level l_u'').

Clark and Oswald (1993) devised an empirical experiment-questionnaire to establish the likely shape of the union decision-taker's preference map. The schema is presented in panels (a) to (c) of Figure 11.23. In panel (a) points in wage-employment space 1, 2 and 3 are located. In a questionnaire you are told there is 0% inflation and that you can choose to move to point 2 (a 5% increase in employment) or point 3 (a 5% increase in wages). Of 52 union leaders' responses:

Figure 11.23 **Clark and Oswald's preference experiment questionnaire**

- 34 opted for point 3 (the wage increase), indicating their indifference map was flat (point 3 preferred to point 2) as in panel (b), This suggested they were 'wage-increase' preferring.
- 18 opted for point 2 (the employment increase), indicating their indifference map was steep (point 2 preferred to point 3) as in panel (c), suggesting they were 'employment-increase' preferring.

Whilst the authors suggest that the surveyed leaders may have been responding strategically and might not even know union members' preferences, there are reasons why wage preference might be the predicted response and these reasons arise in the efficient bargaining models of unions considered next.

In general, the versatile Stone–Geary utility function has been employed in this (and other areas (see Chapter 16) of research). It is an extension of Cobb–Douglas preferences and takes the form:

$$U = U(W, L) = (W - \gamma)^\theta (L - \delta)^{1-\theta} \tag{11.61}$$

where γ and δ are so-called reference values for wage (W) and employment (L) respectively. (In consumer theory they are called subsistence levels of consumption of goods.)

Given this, the term ($W - \gamma$) is supernumary wages (i.e. the difference between actual wages and the 'basic' reference level) and the term ($L - \delta$) is supernumary employment (i.e. the difference between actual employment and the 'basic' reference level). In natural logs this becomes:

$$U(W, L) = \theta \ln(W - \gamma) + (1 - \theta) \ln(L - \delta) \tag{11.62}$$

Indifference curves are not defined for values of W below γ and L below δ.

If θ, γ and δ are varied, the function can be used to illustrate a variety of maximands. If γ and $\delta > 0$ and θ is 0.5, the preference map, illustrated in Figure 11.24, is symmetrical and Cobb–Douglas (with respect to the reference value axes).

If γ and $\delta = 0$ and θ is 0.5 the utility function becomes $U = (W)^{0.5} (L)^{0.5} = \sqrt{(WL)}$.

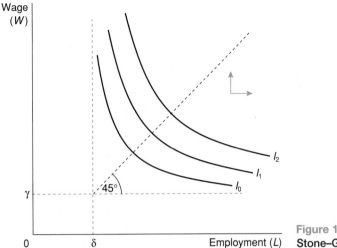

Figure 11.24
Stone–Geary preferences

This is 'wage bill' maximisation. The indifference curves are rectangular hyperbolas with an elasticity of substitution of +1.

If γ and $\delta = 0$ and $\theta = 1$ the utility function becomes $U = (W)$. This is wage maximisation as in Figure 11.20(c).

If γ and $\delta = 0$ and $\theta = 0$ the utility function becomes $U = (L)$. This is employment maximisation as in Figure 11.20(a).

If $\gamma = W_c$ (the competitive wage), $\delta = 0$ and $\theta = 0.5$, the utility function becomes $U = (W - W_c)^{0.5} (L)^{0.5}$. This implies maximisation of the size of surplus or rental earning over that generated by competitive conditions.

11.6.3 Efficiency bargaining models of unions

Looking at Figure 11.25 it is easy to establish that a solution, such as the rental-maximising one, at point 1 with the union on indifference curve I_0 (and wage W_u and

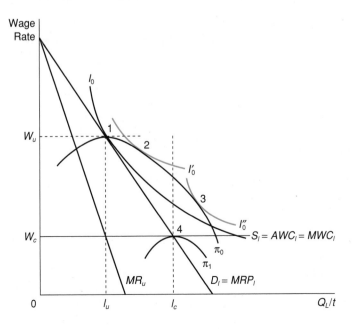

Figure 11.25
Efficient bargaining models

employment level l_u) may not be the highest level of utility obtainable. The isoprofit line through point 1 is labelled π_0 (by definition, everywhere along this, the firm makes exactly the same profit). Looking at the figure, a point such as 2 offers a higher level of utility to the union, I_0', in the form of a somewhat lower wage rate but a higher level of employment, whilst the employer makes exactly the same profit as is achieved at point 1. Indeed, anywhere within the rugby-ball shape formed by the isoprofit curve π_0 and the indifference curve I_0 offers either I_0, or better, to the union, or π_0, or better, to the firm. It follows that one organisation can be better off with the other organisation no worse off, or both are better off than at point 1.

The ellipse contains Pareto-preferred positions. Hence this type of model is called an 'efficiency wage model'.

As drawn, it is clear that if the indifference map for the union is sufficiently steep, the employment level and wage achieved by the union associated with point 3 and indifference curve I_0'' are greater than the wage rate and employment level secured under competitive conditions (wage W_c and employment l_c associated with point 4). If this seems odd, notice the firm is on a lower isoprofit line (π_0) at point 3 as compared to π_1 at point 4. As can be seen from the solutions at point 2 and 3, the equilibrium is off the demand curve; hence these are also often called 'off the demand curve models'.

If a contract curve is drawn, connecting points of tangency between union indifference curves and employer isoprofit curves, its shape could be negative towards point 2 or positive towards point 3. An interesting implication of this is the proposition that, if the competitive wage (or alternative wage) W_c is decreased then point 4 migrates to the right (as does the associated contract curve). It suggests that the alternative wage and the unionised employment level should move in opposite directions. The empirical evidence on this is, however, somewhat mixed.

Whilst these models seem attractive, it has to be noted that the equilibria depicted are inherently unstable. So in Figure 11.26, if initial equilibrium is off the demand curve, say, at point 5 (with wage W_1 and employment l_1) as compared to the demand curve solution at point 1 (with wage W_0 and employment l_0), the solution has attractive properties for both parties compared to point 1. At point 5 on the contract curve the union is on indifference curve I_1, as opposed to I_0 on the demand curve, and the firm is on isoprofit line π_1, as opposed to π_0 at point 1. However, it will always be attractive for the employer to

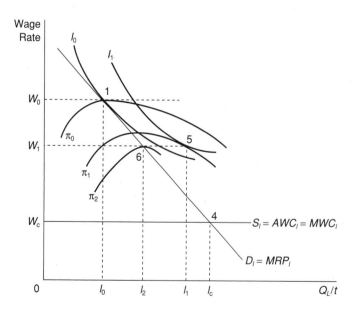

Figure 11.26
Off-the-demand curve and instability

decrease employment from l_1 off the demand curve to l_2 on the demand for labour curve at point 6, where there must be the peak of a higher isoprofit curve than π_1 (here π_2) available to the employer. In short, there is always an incentive for the employer to renege on any deal made that is off the demand curve.

The reasons why a wage-increase preferring preference map may be sensible now emerge. It is recognised that unions, striking a deal over employment levels, face a disciplining problem. It is very difficult to monitor the employment levels in large-scale organisations, or in firms that are multi-plant. This monitoring (and, therefore, enforcement) difficulty may explain why few union contracts in the labour market seem to specify employment levels as opposed to wage rates. Furthermore, as is recognised in Chapter 14 (which deals with the median voter theorem), when decisions are made on a simple majority basis (50% + 1), it is the median voter whose preference is enacted. Given that the union's median voter is likely to have a number of years of seniority, and employment decisions are typically made on a 'last-in first-out' type of rule, the median voter is unconcerned about employment, because any contraction in employment is very unlikely to have any personal affect. Simple majority voting may foster a 'wage-increase-preferring' preference map.

11.6.4 Right-to-manage models

These models are in a somewhat intermediate category, in that they do not make unions 'all-powerful' in terms of the workplace. They typically allow employers to unilaterally adjust employment levels and, given the observation made above, the best profit points are to be found on the demand curve $D_l = MRP_l$, rather than any position off it. In these circumstances an intermediate position like point 6 in Figure 11.26 is regarded as a more plausible impact of a union (as compared to the competitive solution point 4 with W_c and l_c).

11.6.5 Evaluating unions: welfare costs

The impact of unions on wage rates and employment levels is a commonly discussed issue. However, an equally important issue is their welfare costs. The simplest approach to answering this question is captured in Figure 11.27. This adopts the idea of a two-sector

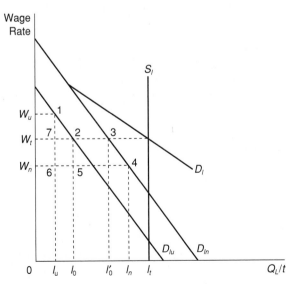

Figure 11.27   The impact of a unionised sector (1)

economy, one of which is to become unionised (u) and the other non-unionised (n). For simplicity of exposition, there are two 'demand for labour' curves that are parallel to each other. These are labelled D_{lu} and D_{ln}.

Summing the two demand curves horizontally produces an overall demand for labour D_l and, given the supply of labour for the economy is assumed perfectly inelastic at S_l, the overall level of employment is l_t (l_0 in one sector and l_0' in the other) with the associated wage rate W_t.

If it is now assumed that the demand curve, D_{lu}, is the demand curve in a unionised sector, the union has used its power to increase wages to W_u, reducing the employment to l_u. So that l_u-l_0 workers are made unemployed by this action. If these workers can gain employment in the non-unionised sector, then for this to take place the non-unionised wage must be reduced to W_n. That is, in the diagram distance l_u-l_0 must equal l_0'-l_n. The effect of the union has been to create a 'non-union–union wage differential' equal to the distance $W_u - W_n$.

It is clear from the construction that the value of lost output in the unionised sector is trapezoid l_u-1-2-l_0. However, this has to be offset with the value of gained output in the unionised sector, namely, trapezoid l_0'-3-4-l_n. Given the assumed parallel nature of the demand curves the difference between these two trapezoids is the rectangle 2-5-6-7. This is a measure of the output, or welfare, loss caused by the union generating a misallocation of labour between the two sectors of this simple economy (the marginal revenue product of labour is greater in the unionised sector than in the non-unionised one).

While this looks fairly damning and hostile to the power of unions, the 'off-the-demand-curve' models can be used to considerably soften this blow. In Figure 11.28 the same demand curves used in Figure 11.27 are reproduced, except that the demand for labour in the unionised sector is now measured from the right-hand vertical axis. Point 1 recreates the initial equilibrium, with W_t being the wage rate and 0-l_0 workers employed in the potentially unionised sector and 0-l_0' in the non-unionised one. If the unions now push up wages in the unionised sector to point 2, the wage and employment

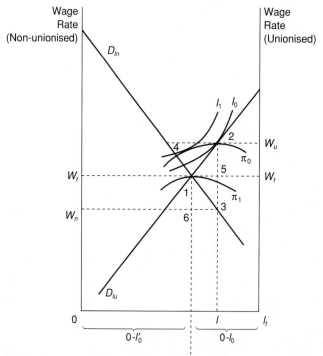

Figure 11.28
The impact of a unionised sector (2)

consequences are as in Figure 11.27. It follows that W_u and W_n obtain and, in Figure 11.28, 0-l (equals 0-l_n in Figure 11.27) and l-l_t (equals 0-l_u in Figure 11.27) are the employment levels in the two sectors. It can be noted that at point 2, profit in the unionised sector has fallen from the isoprofit line π_1 to π_0. The welfare loss rectangle is rectangle 1-5-3-6. This must equal 2-5-6-7 in Figure 11.27 and is identical, by construction, to the triangular area 1-2-3. If an 'off-the-demand-curve' solution is possible, unions can raise their utility from I_0 to I_1 by moving from point 2 to point 4, where a wage less than W_u will arise. The union's power has succeeded in reducing profit from π_1 to π_0; however, point 4, as constructed, is directly above point 1, the initial competitive allocation of labour between the two sectors, so that labour allocation is unchanged. The net result is that unions have increased the wage rates of the employees and not reduced their employment level. This gain occurs in the form of redistribution from profits in the unionised sector to unionised workers leaving the non-unionised sector unaffected. While this is clearly an attractive outcome for all potential trade unionists, the empirical evidence for this particular result is not strong – but the analysis remains instructive.

In this section the basic tools of microeconomic analysis have been used to explore the impact of unionism. As can be seen, much turns upon the shape of the indifference curve that is attributed to decision-makers within the union and the amount of economic power they are assumed to wield. In general, it is argued that unions have a significant wage impact on their formation mainly in the form of setting employer monopsony power (see Section 11.5.1). Thereafter, their impact on wages is not usually thought to be that great, with wage rate increases generally being a reflection of raised marginal products, for example, caused by a technological change, rather than the use of union monopoly power.

11.7 Challenge: What is wrong with the 'black box' forms?

The criticisms of 'black box' market forms were signalled in the introduction to this chapter. They do not contain a rich account of individuals and their role within organisations. Decision-taking and how conflicts between individuals are resolved are not analysed. Uncertainty is not discussed in any significant way.

In many ways Chapter 12 represents the economist's response to these types of criticisms, as it deals with how the 'black box' forms were elaborated upon and how *alternatives* to the 'black box' form of organisation developed. In short, for many commentators what is wrong with the 'black box' forms is that they lack sufficient realism. Some have drawn attention to the two alternative modes of resource allocation that can be observed in a market economy, namely reliance on the price mechanism as opposed to forms of cooperation and coordination within firms. Whilst the former highlights the nature and extent of competition between firms, the latter has as its focus cooperation and suppression of the market mechanism within the boundary of the firm.

The boundary of the firm is defined by answering the question 'which activities should be undertaken within the firm itself and which should be bought in from the market (other firms)?'. The early part of the next chapter focuses on departures from 'black box' forms and indicates how this question has been answered.

11.8 Summary

This chapter has developed the 'black box' market forms on the output and input sides of the economy. Equilibria stem from a profit-maximising motive applied in different demand and supply contexts. Institutional detail is deliberately lost in a positivistic–deductive methodology, so the models must rely on empirically unfalsified predictions as their measure of success. However, the focus here has been the predictions, at the expense of the empirical evidence.

Monopoly and price discrimination were analysed and the effects on welfare assessed. Chamberlain (1933) described monopolistic competition as a blend of monopoly and competition and this is how it appeared. The welfare consequences of monopolistic competition also seemed to be a 'blend'. Three of many possible models of oligopoly were presented, each shedding some light on the oligopolistic market form without being definitive. Monopsony, oligopsony and monopoly in the labour market were also explored and it was clear there was much in common in output and input analysis.

'Organism models' of trade unions were also outlined, not simply because they are interesting in their own right, but because the form of analysis employs many of the concepts of this, and earlier, chapters. The appendix elaborates further on imperfect competition and the labour market in the context of a specific model.

Appendix 11.1 Labour markets once more

Bhaskar, Manning and To (2002) present a versitile *oligopsony-cum-monopsonisitic* model of labour markets. Competition suggests a 'law of one wage', in that equal quality workers would receive an equal wage. However, the authors document much wage dispersion. They note: product differentiation, imperfect information and mobility costs, which means employers face less than perfectly elastic labour supply curves (lowering wage does not cause all employees to leave). In particular, they explore the case of workers having heterogeneous preferences. With an identical marginal product in two jobs, individuals prefer one over another, because of its associated non-wage characteristics (e.g. many workers do not like dealing with meat, or food, in general). This is *horizontal* job differentiation, in that it is not being claimed that one job is inherently superior to another, it is just that there are non-wage differences that attract some workers and repel others.

The device the authors employ is travel costs, as a representation of psychic distances. They assume workers are uniformly distributed along a straight mile with firm A at one end firm B at the other. Travel costs are t per mile. Given this, a location along the mile at point x from firm A has associated travel costs to firm A of tx and $t(1 - x)$ for firm B. All workers at each employment are assumed to be paid the same wage.

Beginning with $W_A = W_B$, and with reference to Figure 11.29, if you live at A (B) and work at A (B) you receive net wage W_A (W_B). If you live at A (B) and work at firm B (A) you receive net of 'travel cost' wage $W_A - t$ ($W_B - t$). The cross-over point at 1 of the W_A line and the W_B line allocates A-x workers to A and $1 - x$ workers to B with the 'thickened' line representing the best net wage at each psychic distance.

Now suppose employer A lowers their wage to W'_A. This causes x'-x workers to move to B associated with the new cross-over point 2. In this way, labour supply to each firm falls with wage in a continuous fashion. The larger t (psychic costs), the steeper the wage lines and the less elastic labour supply. Given labour supply inelasticity and employers with market power, it was clear from above that the rule was to employ where marginal wage cost equals demand for labour ($MRP_l = D_l$) and pay average wage cost ($AWC = S_l$).

In Figure 11.30, that means employing (l_a) at point 1 but paying at point 2, producing a wage (W_a) – marginal revenue product gap (distance 1-2) that grows with the extent of supply inelasticity. That is, wage W is a function of the employment level (L):

$$W = f(L) \tag{11A.1}$$

So total wage cost (TWC) is given by:

$$TWC = L \cdot W = L \cdot f(L) \tag{11A.2}$$

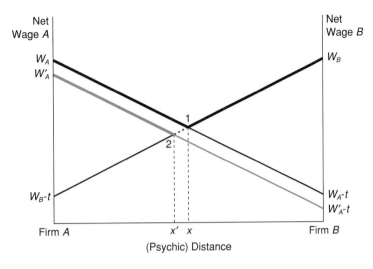

Figure 11.29
Worker location with heterogeneous preferences

Source: Bhaskar, Manning and To (2002).

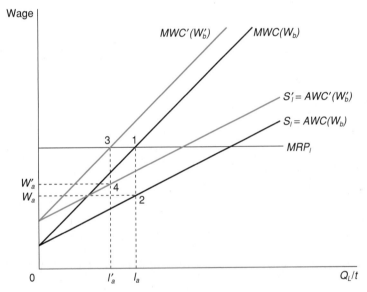

Figure 11.30
Profit maximisation under oligopsony

Source: Bhaskar, Manning and To (2002).

and marginal wage cost (*MWC*) is:

$$MWC = dTWC/dL = f(L) + (dW/dL)L \tag{11A.3}$$

$$= W + (dW/dL)L \tag{11A.4}$$

$$= W\left(1 + \frac{dWL}{dLW}\right) \tag{11A.5}$$

$$= W\left(1 + \frac{1}{E_s}\right) \tag{11A.6}$$

where E_s is the elasticity of labour supply with respect to the wage rate.

Employing where $MRP_l = MWC$ gives:

$$MRP_l = W\left(1 + \frac{1}{E_s}\right) \tag{11A.7}$$

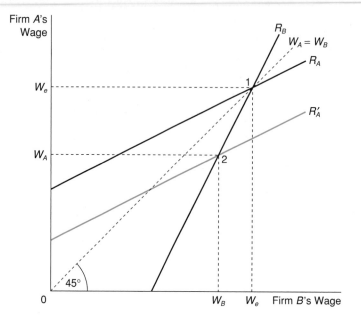

Figure 11.31
Duopsony equilibrium using employer wage reaction functions

Source: Bhaskar, Manning and To (2002)

Rearranging yields:

$$\frac{W}{MP_l} = \frac{E_s}{E_s + 1} \tag{11A.8}$$

This indicates that the higher (lower) E_s (less [greater] inelasticity), the closer (further) is MRP_l to W. Empirically, E_s is about 5, so that W/MP_l is 5/6 and the wage gap is approximately 17%.

Against this background, assume firm B raises its wage W_b to W_b', thereby decreasing labour supply to firm A, which is conditional on the wage paid by firm B. Hence $S_l = AWC(W_b)$ moves to $S_l' = AWC(W_b')$ (reversing the mechanism in Figure 11.19). Firm A (as indicated in Figure 11.30) will now employ (l_a') at point 3 and pay at point 4, raising wage from W_a to W_a'. The wage rise in A is lower than the wage rise in B and the associated employment fall in A is l_a-l_a'.

In this way, a reaction function of A's wage to B's wage can be developed, having a positive slope less than +1. This is labelled R_A in Figure 11.31. Given the symmetry of the model R_B is the equivalent construction for B and Figure 11.31 gives the duopsony equilibrium associated with cross-over point 1 which involves several properties:

(1) equal wages W_e;
(2) wage $< MRP_l$ with the gap increasing with the greater degree of preference heterogeneity (degree of imperfect competition);
(3) as in the monopolistic competition model, economic profits need not obtain. If there is free entry of employers wage will equal average product of labour (i.e. no surplus overall) but be below the marginal product (in monopolistic competition $P = AC > MC$, see above);
(4) The authors do not see workers as being exploited as, presumably, the situation is reflecting their preference heterogeneity, but it does seem to show inefficiency as employment is where $MWC = MRP_l = D_l$ and not $S_l = AWC = MRP_l = D_l$.

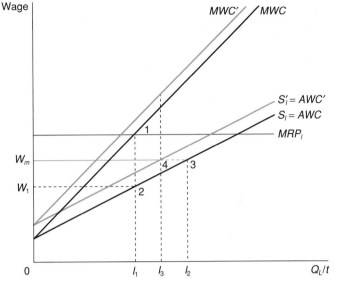

Figure 11.32
Minimum wages and employment under oligopsony

Source: Bhaskar, Manning and To (2002)

This model has a number of valuable implications:

(1) First, employers will wish to wage-discriminate, as in Figure 11.29 employer A (B) would only want to offer workers to the right (left) of x raised wages to attract them.
(2) Second, since wage is less than marginal revenue product firms may well pay even for general training (see Chapter 10).
(3) Third, the main object of the theory was to explain wage dispersion. How is this done? If employer A has a lower MRP_l than B, say, because it uses an outdated technology then the adjustment by A to B's wage illustrated in Figure 11.31 will involve a lower wage in A (imagine wages generated by a lowered MRP_l but the same supply structure in Figure 11.30). In Figure 11.31, with a lower W_A for each W_B value means R_A is shifted downwards to R_A'. The new equilibrium is now at point 2 with $W_A < W_B$, which is wage dispersion in the presence of equal-quality workers.

In the light of this model, it is now possible to reinterpret the discussion of minimum wages in Chapter 2. In Figure 11.32, it is possible to compare the monopsonist and the oligopsonist cases. Initial equilibrium is at point 1 where $MWC = MRP_l$ with wage (W_1), determined at point 2, and employment $0\text{-}l_1$. Imposing a binding minimum wage, W_m, causes the monopsonist to move to point 3, equating W_m with $S_l = AWC$ and employment has increased by $l_1\text{-}l_2$ to $0\text{-}l_2$ overall. Bhaskar, Manning and To (2002), however, argue that oligopsony power with freedom of employer entry and exit is more typical. Given the inter-relatedness of wage rates, an increase in wage for firm B (achieved via the imposition of a minimum wage) moves A's supply condition bodily to the left $(S_l' = AWC'$ and $MWC')$, producing equilibrium at point 4. Here the increased employment is attenuated to $l_1\text{-}l_3$ with overall employment at $0\text{-}l_3$. Intuitively, the higher wage rate is increasing labour force participation. Given that minimum wage reduces profit, some employers will go bankrupt and exit the employment market. The employment consequences now depend on the strength of two opposing forces, namely, oligopsonistic employers increasing firm-level employment and fewer overall employers decreasing employment, making the impact of a moderate minimum wage on the level of employment marginal.

References

Bertrand, J. (1883) Théorie mathematique de la richesse sociale, *Journal de Savants*, 67: 499–508.

Bhaskar V., Manning, A. and To, T. (2002) Oligopsony and monopsonistic competition in labour markets, *Journal of Economic Perspectives*, 16 (2) Spring: 155–74.

Chamberlain, F. (1933) *The Theory of Monopolistic Competition*, Cambridge, Mass.: Harvard University Press.

Clark, A. and Oswald, A. (1993) What shape are trade union indifference curves, *Economic Review*, 11 (2) November: 17–18.

Cournot, A. (1838) *Researches into the Mathematical Principles of the Theory of Wealth*, in French, Paris: L. Hachette.

Dunlop, J.T. (1944) *Wage Determination under Trade Unions*, New York: Macmillan.

Estrin, S. and Laidler, D. (1995) *Introduction to Microeconomics*, 4th edn, Hemel Hempstead: Prentice Hall/Harvester.

Magenheim, E.B. (1995) Information, prices and competition in the child-care market: what role should government play? pp. 269–307 in J.M. Pogodzinski (ed.) *Readings in Public Policy*, Oxford: Basil Blackwell.

Nash, J.F. (1951) Non-cooperative games, *Annals of Mathematics*, 54 (2) July: 286–95.

Oswald, A. (1985) The economic theory of trade unions: an introductory survey, *Scandinavian Journal of Economics*, 87 (2): 160–93.

Ross, A.M. (1948) *Trade Union Wage Policy*, Berkeley, Calif.: University of California Press.

Schumpeter, J.A. (1950) *Capitalism, Socialism and Democracy*, 3rd edn, New York: Harper and Row.

CHAPTER 12

Firms with an institutional content

12.1 Introduction

In Chapters 5 and 11 the familiar 'black box' market forms were rehearsed. In schema form they can be represented as:

$$\textit{Physical Flows}: \text{inputs} \rightarrow \qquad \text{output} \rightarrow$$
$$\text{FIRM}$$
$$\text{(maximising decision rules)}$$
$$\textit{Pecuniary Flows}: \leftarrow\text{costs} \qquad \leftarrow\text{revenue}$$

where the emphasis is on external environment. By and large, no individuals were involved and the firm collapsed to a set of maximising and minimising rules. The firms are institution-free and the emphasis is on comparative-static predictions. Much weight was placed on profit maximisation as a way of 'closing' the model of the firm. Critics argue that there are other, more plausible, objectives for a firm, e.g. sales-revenue maximisation, growth. A minimum profit constraint may have to be met (rather than profits maximised). In the presence of uncertainty and imperfect information it may not be possible for firms to be able to realise a strategy of maximising profits even if they wanted to.

Note that the firm has been talked about as an entity with its own objectives, so that an organism approach has been adopted. This, as noted in Chapter 11, is considered a weakness by those not convinced by an 'as if' approach and the claim that it is only, as yet, non-falsified predictions about behaviour that matters. Once individuals, as such, are brought to the fore, the economic approach is to view them as maximising their utility, or preferences, subject to constraints set by the internal, or external, environment. This is deceptively simple. Content needs to be given to preferences and detailed specification of the relevant constraint (or constraints) is required.

Williamson (1967) and others suggest personal objectives for managers, e.g. salary, status, security, power, prestige, professional excellence and the desire to help others by providing a social service. In this chapter and elsewhere in this text, most of these suggestions are discussed. In more recent work, it is issues surrounding information, incentive mechanisms and uncertainty that have been seen as crucial.

12.2 Principal–agent problems

Principal–agent problems are at the centre of more recent contributions to the theory of the firm. Such problems are associated with unobserved or hidden actions. This is very much an active ('doing') perspective on events. As discussed (Chapter 8), in the principal–agent literature one person (the principal) hires another (the agent) to perform an activity where:

a) the agent has some degree of autonomy over a variable that affects both principal and agent;

b) the principal and agent differ in their preferences over the level of the agent's decision variables, i.e. there is conflict or incentive incompatibility: e.g. for the:
   (i) principal – pecuniary return is a 'good';
   (ii) agent – pecuniary return is a 'good';
   (iii) principal – the agent's effort is a 'neutral';
   (iv) agent – their own effort is a 'bad'.

c) outcomes depend on (i) agents' effort and (ii) uncertainty (the state of the world that arises – e.g. a harvest and good, or bad, weather).

A basic question is the design of economic arrangements, or contracts, that induce 'incentive compatibility' and the basic solution was presented in Chapter 7. The general cost associated with principal–agent problems is moral hazard, which, as noted in Chapter 7, involves post-contractual opportunism. Once a contract has been signed, the agent's position has been guaranteed (or insured) and the incentive for the agent is to alter behaviour (e.g. by taking less care or less effort than is contracted), thereby raising monitoring difficulties for the principal.

To focus on principal–agent problems in a firm means the context must deviate from the neoclassical theory of the firm that is a 'black box' (see below). Furthermore, to focus on the internal structure of firms requires an answer to the question as to why firms exist at all. After all, most, if not all, goods (e.g. a car) could be made by a series of market transactions – you buy in, 'do your bit' and then sell on to whoever is going to carry out the next stage. Therefore the question becomes, given the attractions of market mechanisms, why create an area where you choose to suppress markets as the organising thread?

Two answers, which are not totally unrelated, have been advanced.

12.2.1 Coase: contracting cost approach

Nobel laureate in 1991, Ronald Coase (1937) made an early contribution to thinking about the nature of firms. He argued that, when producing a good, there is always a choice between an internal and an external way of performing a task. Each will have a different set of related costs and a least-cost solution is likely to involve a variety of choices. (Writ large, this is the choice between a market economy and a centrally planned one.)

In Table 12.1 a list is made of the type of costs that are likely to arise with the 'internal/ make/plan' option as compared with the 'external/buy/market' option.

Figure 12.1 assumes there are 1000 decisions to be made and illustrates total internal (TIC) and total external costs (TEC) plotted from opposite origins. Finding the least-cost solution involves equating the marginal cost of the external option with the marginal cost of the internal option. Note: this does not occur where the total curves cross but rather where the absolute values of their slopes are equal (see tangents t_i and t_e in Figure 12.1). As illustrated, 300 decisions will be made within the firm and 700 with the external market. With this reasoning, the boundary of the firm will alter as the relative costs of internal and external decisions alter. Recall the recent increase in outsourcing. The costs of organisation within a firm suggest internal difficulties of organisation so that firms may contain their own internal market failures. This is an insight elaborated especially in the work of Williamson (see Section 12.3.4 below).

Table 12.1 **Sources of transactions costs**

'Make'/ Internal/ Plan/ 'nexus of contracts'	'Buy'/ External/ Market/ 'arm's length' arrangements
Cost rises because: (i) as the boundaries of an organisation are extended greater spatial and conceptual distances are involved which make it more costly to plan; (ii) as scope of plan widens more mistakes are made compared to the market alternative; (iii) the more you plan the greater the demand for scarce planning resources and their price rises.	Cost rises because: (i) buyers must survey prices and characteristics of goods; (ii) sellers must research preferences and requirements of buyers; (iii) contracts, especially long-term ones, are vulnerable to changes, which creates uncertainty. If short-term contracts are adopted large negotiating costs are generated, using the very information decision-takers are trying to economise on. Contracting costs are high, especially for multilateral deals. For example, with 8 individuals there are $n(n-1)/2$ pairs = 28 but only $(n-1)$ pairs in which each agent contracts with one central agent; (iv) there is; (a) greater specificity of physical and human capital; (b) greater frequency of decisions.

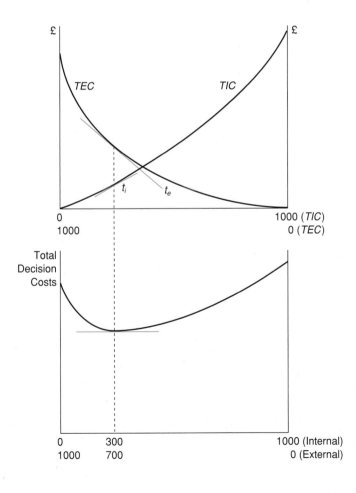

Figure 12.1
The Coasian boundary to the firm

12.2.2 Alchian and Demsetz: team production approach

Alchian and Demsetz (1972) came at the same issue from a different angle. In their approach there is an entrepreneur who monitors and directs production. A necessary but not sufficient condition for this is the efficiency of team production, e.g. more trees are cut down with 2 people and a 2-person saw than 2 people using a 1-person saw each. Team production is not sufficient because it creates a metering problem, as total output does not easily separate into individual contributions. In these circumstances individuals have an incentive to 'shirk' (not work in the expectation that their lack of contribution will not be detected). Team production causes the free-rider preferences to arise in narrowly self-interested individuals: first, I shirk, others work; second, I work, others work (i.e. all work); third, I shirk, others shirk – i.e. all shirk; and fourth, I work and others shirk. This is the 'prisoner's dilemma' motivation when all try to get their first preference, the third preference emerges as the collective result.

Figure 12.2 pictures this motivation. Leisure is on the x-axis and output is on the y-axis. Constraint Y_T-L_T indicates maximum output–leisure combinations when individuals combine as, say an N-person team. It is assumed that each team member receives $1/N$ of the output produced. Utility is maximised at point 1 on I_1, with Y_1 output and L_1 leisure per period.

Reasoning in isolation, the individual thinks, if I shirk and all others work, my reward in output only falls by $1/N$ of my contribution to output. If others stay at L_1 hours of leisure then the constraint to me is altered as, with others working all the time, total output falls from Y_T to Y_O (to set the y-axis intercept) so that the opportunity cost of leisure to an isolated individual runs from Y_O through point 1. Utility maximisation now dictates point 2 is chosen on I_2 with increased leisure level L_2 for the individual. This is a reflection of the decreased opportunity cost of leisure in teams where output is shared.

However, what is the case for the isolated individual is also the case for all, so that all trying to adjust to point 2 results in point 3 on I_0 arising on the team constraint with output falling to Y_2. This is the 'prisoner's dilemma' motivation. When all try to achieve their first preference (point 2 and utility level I_2), the third preference emerges (point 3 and utility level I_0) as the collective result, even though point 1 (utility level I_1) is superior to point 3.

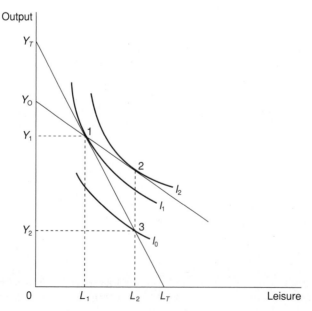

Figure 12.2
The 'representative' shirker

In order to reach an outcome like point 1, workers may well be prepared to hire a monitor. The monitor contracts with each team member what they are expected to do and workers must accept the discipline of the monitor (eventually firing those who do not 'meter-up') if the free-rider result is to be avoided. With the 8 individuals of Table 12.1 there are $n - 1 = 7$ contracts required. But there is the age-old problem of who guards the guard? The monitor also needs an incentive to do this job efficiently (i.e. to maximise the value of the productive team or institution). This incentive is created if the monitor is made a residual claimant, receiving reward only after all contracts have been met. In these circumstances, the monitor maximises the residual and workers realise that future contracts will improve if the residual rises this period.

A further incentive is required to prevent the monitor from maximising their position only over the anticipated tenure as monitor. The role of the stock market is partly to prevent the incentives fostered by an attenuated time horizon. The stock market determines the value of shares (as the anticipated discounted present value of the stream of net benefits from the institution). In these circumstances a bad decision (one that lowers the anticipated discounted present value of the net benefits stream) made by a monitor today will show up today as a lowered share price, making the firm vulnerable to takeover and the monitor open to criticism and displacement. On these issues, non-profit institutions look inefficient – there is no owner with a saleable property right over the discounted net benefit stream associated with the institution (see the discussion of charities in Chapter 15). It is not possible to assign part of the net benefit stream to trustees of non-profit institutions in order to foster managerial efficiency.

The upshot of this discussion (see Lindsay 1984) is that proprietary firms have:

I)   a residual claimant who;
II)   monitors input behaviour;
III) is central and common to all contracts;
IV)   has the power to terminate contracts;
V)   has authority to sell these property rights.

It may seem as if the nature of the firm has now been resolved but a casual look around any economy reveals many types of economic arrangement that coexist. (i) *Proprietorship* involves private property rights (where the owner and the manager are one person). (ii) *Joint stock enterprises* involve the existence of shareholders and a shift from private property rights to more collective property rights (where there are shared rights), and a separation of ownership (shareholders) from control (manager or chief executive officer) where the managers make decisions on behalf of the owners, that is they act as their agents. (iii) *Non-profit firms* (or non-profit organisations) are typical of the charity sector of the economy and have featured in health-care provision analysis. (iv) *Co-operatives* vary in structure but have the characteristic that members control the firm collectively. The model of (v) the *labour-managed firm* developed by Vanek (1970) was popular when centrally planned economies were numerous. Some economists have argued that different models of the firm are relevant within different property right structures, e.g. profit maximisation is the natural candidate for the owner-controlled firm.

Historically, it was the development of large capital requirements that led to the arrangement of shareholders and a management responsible to the board of directors (and ultimately to shareholders). Big firms in a market economy were joint stock companies with salaried managers who were no longer owners; whose fate depended on residual maximisation. Therefore, there was a need for economic discipline. This need for economic discipline is a feature of models of the firm that depart from the 'black box' market forms.

The institutional types, other than proprietorships (noted above), provide the organising thread below. In the various models it is instructive to note:

(i)   which individuals (if any) make decisions;

(ii) the nature of any internal constraints (e.g. factions within organisations);

(iii) external constraints (e.g. the extent of competition) and

(iv) the degree to which predictions now deviate from the competitive outcome.

12.3 Managerial theories of the firm – steps towards reality

Theorists, anxious to add to the realism of the firm, have a number of issues to address. The first relates to *time*. A multi-period analysis is required if concerns about investment and other dynamic questions are to be included. The second, raised in the introduction, relates to *decision-makers' preferences*, as a range of maximands need to be considered. Profit maximisation is one among many assumptions that can be made to provide an equilibrium solution and further specification of decision-makers' utility functions enhances the picture that is painted.

Elaboration of the external environment, as noted above, is required to set up constraints on what decision-makers (however motivated) can achieve. In particular, attention has been related to the stock market, not only as the source of investment finance but as a source of discipline. For publicly quoted (joint stock) companies this discipline could come from the annual general meeting where shareholders, in theory at least, could vote out existing directors if they thought the performance of the firm was poor. More likely, the discipline is the fear of a takeover, as shares are bought by other management teams who think they can make more profit with the firm's resources.

Hence, in earlier models of the firm that departed from the 'black box' market forms it was a minimum profit constraint that could be used to close a model. Baumol (1959) was one of the first economists to question and elaborate on the profit-maximising firm. He noted that managers claimed to be interested in other aspects of the firm than profit. In particular, issues associated with sales revenue maximisation, advertising and growth of the firm were incorporated into models.

12.3.1 Sales revenue maximisation

Figure 12.3 illustrates the total cost curve shape derived in Chapter 3 and a total revenue curve reflecting a downward-sloping demand curve. Profit maximisation would occur where $MR = MC$, that is, when the tangents t_r and t_c to total revenue and total cost curves respectively are of equal slope (at points 1 and 2 respectively) and, as drawn, the profit mountain reaches a peak at point 3 in panel (b) with q_0 units of good X per period sold at a per unit price set by $\tan \theta$ in panel (a).

The unconstrained sales-revenue-maximiser will choose Q_x/t, such that TR is maximised and hence the absolute value of the own-price elasticity of demand equals one. Tangent t_m to the total revenue curve has zero slope at point 4 and therefore $MR = 0$ and q_1 is the appropriate output level per period with the associated profit level at point 5 in Figure 12.3. However, it was noted above that the stock exchange will exert some disciplining pressure; in this case, by having a minimum profit level that is considered satisfactory. In the explanation so far, it is as if a profit constraint like π_1 obtains, i.e. it is non-binding. More likely is the case where the constraint is binding like π_2, where the sales-revenue-maximiser is constrained to meet π_2 at point 6 in panel (b), choosing q_2 output level per period and a price determined by $\tan \theta'$ in panel (a).

12.3.2 Advertising budget

Baumol also explored the determination of the firm's advertising budget. This is analysed in Figure 12.4, where the advertising budget is measured on the x-axis and total revenue

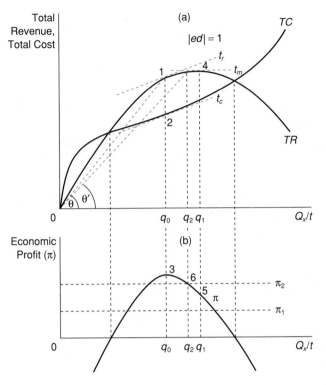

Figure 12.3
Baumol and revenue maximisation

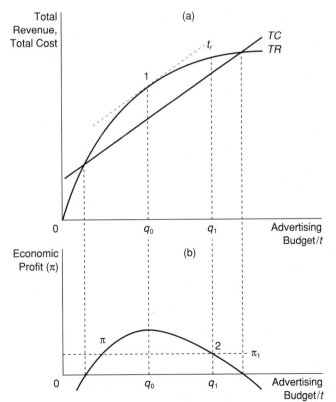

Figure 12.4
Baumol and the advertising budget

and total costs on the *y*-axis of panel (a). Total costs are assumed linear and cover prod-uction, distribution and selling costs along with the advertising costs themselves. Total revenue, as drawn, increases everywhere as the advertising budget is increased (sales quantity/*t* rises) but does so at a decreasing rate. This assumption makes $MR > 0$ and the effect would be the prescription to increase the advertising budget without limit.

In panel (b) the economic profit curve is depicted with the profit-maximising output q_0 under point 1, where MR (measured by tangent t_r) equals MC. The indeterminacy of the model is removed once the stock market's profit constraint π_1 is imposed on panel (b) and the solution is found at point 2 and quantity per period q_1. Note that q_1 is an expenditure sum that is the constrained sales-revenue-maximising advertising budget.

12.3.3 Firm growth as an objective

Maximising the growth rate of the firm involves several stages of reasoning. Profits from the firm (π) can be retained for investment (R) or distributed to shareholders (D), so that

$$\pi = R + D \tag{12.1}$$

Dividing by the amount of capital invested in the firm (K) yields the ratios:

$$\pi/K = R/K + D/K \tag{12.2}$$

The level of investment by the firm (I) is governed by R and access to borrowing (B), i.e.

$$I = R + B \tag{12.3}$$

Dividing by the amount of capital invested in the firm (K) yields the ratios:

$$I/K = R/K + B/K \tag{12.4}$$

In turn, external borrowing is positively influenced by D/K and π/K (attributes of a firm external investors approve of), so that

$$I/K = R/K + B/K(D/K, \pi/K) \tag{12.5}$$

The firm's growth rate (g) is seen to depend on the ratio of investment to capital stock and the ratio of profit to capital stock π/K. The necessary promotional expenses of advert-ising, price concessions and product innovation are costly and will tend to reduce π/K. In symbols:

$$g = g(I/K, \pi/K) \tag{12.6}$$

To increase the growth rate π/K must suffer, as expenses on promotions, etc. increase but a falling π/K damages growth, as B/K and R/K are affected (see equations 12.2 and 12.5). A classic trade-off emerges that can be resolved by appeal to the relevant marginal con-ditions. The maximum value is located where the partial derivatives with respect to the profit and dividend rate are zero:

$$\partial g/\partial \pi/K = \partial g/\partial I\big/K \, (\partial B/K\big/\partial \pi/K + 1) + \partial g/\partial \pi\big/K = 0 \tag{12.7}$$

$$\partial g/\partial D/K = \partial g/\partial I\big/K \, (\partial B/K\big/\partial D/K - 1) = 0 \tag{12.8}$$

Making $B = 0$ means that the possibilities for growth come from two sources related to π/K, and, for simplicity, it is assumed this can be added. These are:

$$g = g_1(I/K(\pi/K)) + g_2(\pi/K) \tag{12.9}$$

In Figure 12.5 a simple version of the growth-maximising firm is depicted. The growth rate is on the *y*-axis and the rate of profit on capital on the *x*-axis. The line g_1 shows how growth depends positively (assumed in a linear way) on investment and investment on

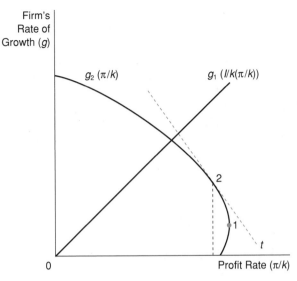

Figure 12.5

Baumol's growth equilibrium

the rate of profit on capital. The curve shows how the rate of profit on capital affects g_2 via the promotional expenses of advertising, price concessions and product innovation costs. At very low growth rates, rate of profit on capital and growth move directly with each other but a point is reached at 1 beyond which the postulated negative relationship is evident. At point 2, the growth rate is maximised where the positive slope of g_1 representing $(\partial g_1/\partial(I/K) \cdot \partial(I/K))/\partial(\pi/K))$ is equal and opposite to the negative slope of g_2, $\partial g_2/\partial(\pi/K)$ located by tangent t.

12.3.4 The Marris–Radice model

This section elaborates on the growth maximising theme by considering the Radice version of one of Marris's models (see Marris 1964).

In Figure 12.6 panel (a) captures the shareholders' perspective and panel (b) that of management. In panel (a), growth of sales volume depends linearly on the profit rate (π), hence $g = g(\pi)$. This is the case as retained profits are the internal source of expenditures required to foster growth. Less directly, a high profit rate will be a prerequisite of funds being sought from external sources, like share and bond issues. In turn, profits will depend on the growth rate $\pi = \pi(g)$. As illustrated in panel (a) of Figure 12.6, the relationship is seen to be positive up to point 1 and thereafter negative. The positive section indicates that, with a growth rate rising from zero, the profit rate will rise up until point 1. However, beyond that point the growth and profit rate are in conflict. This may be because the cost of capital rises, prices may have to be reduced considerably to increase sales and/or increasing costs might take the form of bidding up managerial salaries with growth. All are inimical to the profit rate. Clearly the profit-maximising rate (π_{max}) is at point 1 with growth rate g_{max}. This, however, may not be chosen as shareholders consider the discounted present value of all future returns – the dividends and capital gains associated with shareholding. Current dividends may be maximised with point 1 but capital gains on shareholdings requires a greater growth rate than g_{max}. Given this, both growth and profit rate are positive sources of utility and the utility-maximising choice for shareholders is at point 2 on indifference curve I_s with profit rate π_s. The 'steepish' slope to the curve suggests a closer to profit-maximising (as compared to growth-maximising) preference.

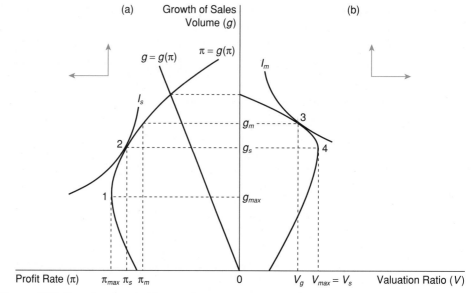

Figure 12.6 **Growth, shareholders and managers**

In panel (b) the management's perspective is summarised. The additional dimension on the x-axis is the valuation ratio (V) which measures the risk of takeover as perceived by the management and, as such, is the ratio of the capital market's valuation of the firm (price of shares times number of shares) to the subjective valuation of the firm (as proxied by the replacement value of the firm's assets or the takeover predator's valuation). The higher the ratio, the lower the risk of takeover and the greater the security of the current management. The indifference curve I_m shows that growth and security are both goods to management. The growth-valuation opportunity set is concave to the origin and yields the utility-maximising combination at point 3 on indifference curve I_m. As point 2 maximises the discounted present value of the firm, it is also the maximum value of the valuation ratio (point 4) and the point shareholders desire. However, as the management has greater interest in growth, 'their' equilibrium involves less security at v_g but more growth at g_m with associated profit rate in panel (a) at π_m.

As can be seen, the range of solutions for the profit rate and valuation ratio are those in the growth range g_s to g_m. A unique solution will reflect the differing bargaining power of the two groups.

12.3.5 Williamson and the theory of the firm

Williamson (1975), following on Baumol, also made major contributions to the understanding of the firm and is more utility-maximising in orientation. Part of Williamson's work revolves around the economics of discretionary behaviour. In the *staff and emoluments model*, management as well as staff has a positive preference for profit. Corporate personal consumption expenditures are sources of utility (U), so that

$$U = U(S, M, \pi_r - \pi_0 - T) \tag{12.8}$$

where

S = staff (in money terms) or approximately general administrative and selling expenses;
M = managerial emoluments (salaries);
π_r = reported profit = $\pi - M$;

π = revenue (TR) – production costs (TC) – S;
π_0 = minimum after-tax profit demanded;
T = taxes, where $\bar{T}$ is lump-sum tax and t the tax rate on reported profit.

The further terms relevant to the definition of the variables in equation (12.8) are:

Y = output;
TR = total revenue = $P \cdot Y$ where P = price;
TC = $TC(Y)$ = total cost.

Using the above, $\pi_r - \pi_0 - T$ defines π_d, the level of discretionary profit, so that the problem is to maximise utility given by $U = U(S, M, \pi_d)$ subject to $\pi_r \geq \pi_0 + T$. Substituting the functional relationships for discretionary profit yields:

$$U = U[S, M, (1 - t)(TR - TC - S - M - \bar{T}) - \pi_0] \tag{12.9}$$

and the first-order conditions for a maximum are found by setting the partial derivatives of U with respect to Y, S and M equal to zero.

The maximum involves:

(i)   the production level being conventionally determined where $MR = MC$ as $\partial TR/\partial Y = \partial TC/\partial Y$;
(ii) the marginal value product of staff less than their marginal cost as

$$\frac{\partial TR}{\partial S} = -\frac{\partial U/\partial S + (1 - t)\partial U/\partial \pi_d}{(1 - t)\partial U/\partial \pi_d} = 1 - \frac{1}{1 - t}\frac{\partial U/\partial S}{\partial U/\partial \pi_d} \tag{12.10}$$

($\partial U/\partial S \,/\, \partial U/\partial \pi_d$ is the marginal rate of substitution between profits and staff);
(iii) dependence on the level of the tax rate, the firm will use some actual profit as emoluments as $\partial U/\partial M = (1 - t)\partial U/\partial \pi_d$.

The managerial utility function recognises salary, status, prestige and power as utility sources (see the 'economics of bureaucracy' in Chapter 14). In a later contribution Williamson (1985) replaced the above with the managers having the directive to maximise the rate of growth of the firm.

However, Williamson's (1975) central contribution concerns the transactions cost perspective on the firm. He identifies sources of transactions costs and seeks organisational forms to minimise them. This approach builds on three concepts:

(i)   Bounded rationality (cognitive and language limits on individuals' ability to process and act on information);
(ii) Asset specificity (specialisation of assets with respect to use or users);
(iii) Opportunism (self-seeking behaviour with guile).

When all three coexist the market mechanism is in trouble but, with any two, the market mechanism is safe and robust:

a) If bounded rationality is not the case, all contingencies can be 'contracted' for, including asset specificity and opportunism;
b) If asset specificity is absent and assets are easily switched, mistakes from boundedness and opportunism are easily corrected;
c) If opportunism is absent, honest individuals can resolve surprises and unexpected problems.

In short, with only one missing element contracts can deal with the situation and markets are secure. But Williamson argues that in many economic situations all three elements are absent and, therefore, the challenge is to organise transactions to economise bounded rationality, while simultaneously safeguarding them against the hazards of opportunism.

The 'transactions costs approach' is a line of thought that is complementary to property rights and agency study. As such, it is sensible to postpone further discussion until these are introduced.

First, for the convenience of the reader, the basics of the term 'bounded rationality' is repeated from Section 7.5.1 where other forms of rationality were also discussed.

12.4 Simon and behavioural theories of the firm

Simon was an Economics Nobel Prize winner in 1978 and, amongst other issues, he made a contribution by being critical of the notion of rationality in economics (Simon 1959). He argued that there were limits to the computational and processing capabilities of the decision-maker, which is a constraint that makes possible only a limited form or degree of rationality, so-called 'bounded rationality'.

Two types of model are consistent with the 'bounded' notion.

(1) Where the set of alternatives is reduced to the degree of complication the decision-maker can handle by ranking options and choosing the best. This is a type of optimisation model but is only approximately optimal, as there may be better (but unconsidered) options available in the absence of information processing limitations.
(2) Satisficing models begin with an aspiration level of the value of the outcome which is 'satisfactory', or acceptable. (N.B. with a stable environment and repeated choices, the aspiration level will be revised upward towards the optimum level.) Here the decision-maker considers a broader set of alternatives than the approximate optimisation model but stops searching when a satisfactory, rather than the best (maximising), solution is found.

However, commentators have noted that important questions remain unanswered:

(i) How are aspiration levels set?
(ii) Which alternatives are considered?
(iii) In what order are they considered? (It is not obvious that replicating the process of decision-making is useful in *a priori* analysis of the outcomes of decision-making.)

Agency theory concentrates on the specific role of contractual provisions leading to a search for contractual institutional forms that minimise the overall cost of the agency. There are two broad traditions:

(i) Principal–agent theory concentrates on formal models of incentive compatibility (met in Chapter 7 and further discussed immediately below).
(ii) Positive theory of agency concentrates less fully on formal models and, as such, is more applied and *ad hoc*.

12.5 Principal–agent theory and sharecropping

Anyone leafing through more recent economics texts would think economists are failed farmers, as there is inevitably a section or a chapter on sharecropping. This picture partly stems from the work of Cheung (1969). The context is one in which you own a parcel of land that you cannot work for yourself. In such circumstances, you (the principal) have to employ someone to work the land (the agent) for you, whilst at the same time you wish to secure the maximum return on your land. There are two constraints to consider (see Chapter 7). The first is a so-called 'participation constraint', or 'no exit condition'.

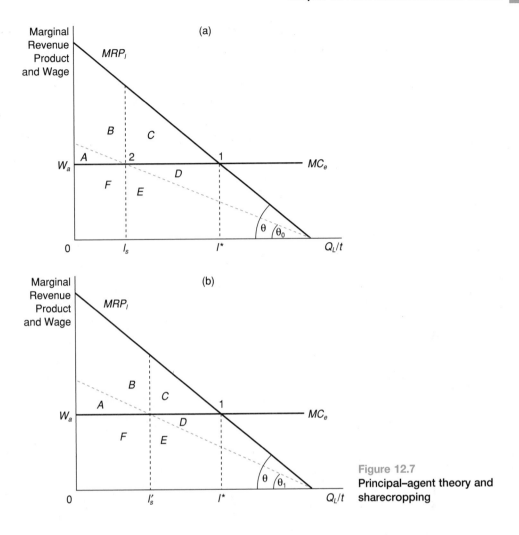

Figure 12.7
Principal–agent theory and sharecropping

For the worker there will be a certain utility level, return, or wage that the worker can obtain by working for another employer. The worker will not work for you if this is not met; the worker will move to the superior alternative. This is expressed as 0-W_a (alternative wage) per unit of labour effort per period in Figure 12.7. It is assumed constant for simplicity. Also, in the figure the marginal cost of effort to the worker (assumed constant) is labelled $MC_e = W_a$. Given that the worker requires $MC_e = W_a$, the best the owner can do is equate this magnitude with the marginal revenue product of labour (MRP_l) at point 1. This secures the return triangle (labelled $A + B + C = R$ under the marginal revenue product curve and above $W_a = MC_e$) with the associated optimal level of labour effort by the agent 0-l^*.

The problem faced by the owner is to develop a payment system that is incentive-compatible with the achievement of R (i.e. that does not lead to shirking, dishonesty or cheating – so that 0-l^* labour offers a higher level of utility than any other choice of labour effort). Formulating such an incentive constraint is relatively easy in the context of perfect information and seems to suggest an invariance theorem. At the outset it can be established that a lump-sum payment in advance to the worker would fail as an incentive constraint, as the worker would accept the lump sum, choose zero labour effort in response, and seek W_a elsewhere.

In the presence of perfect information the owner of the parcel of land can be assumed to face zero monitoring costs to establish the level of effort the worker supplies. The payment system could take a number of equivalent forms:

(i) First, the owner could charge a rent equal to R in advance. The worker is assumed to be able to get area $D + E + F = Z$ elsewhere and can only get it in the owner's employment if the value of output is $R + Z$ (i.e. the worker supplies labour effort $0\text{-}l^*$).

(ii) Second, the owner could offer to pay the wage $0\text{-}W_a$ until $0\text{-}l^*$ is reached, so that, once again, Z is achieved as the product of $0\text{-}W_a$ and $0\text{-}l^*$.

(iii) Third, it is possible to make a 'take it or leave it' offer to the worker of area Z only if $0\text{-}l^*$ is observed to take place. Recall there is perfect information.

(iv) Fourth, there is the sharecropping option. The owner could offer the worker a percentage of the value of the marginal product of labour, i.e. < 1.

Initially, the sharecropping option looks like a sub-optimal solution in Figure 12.7(a), as the worker chooses effort level $0\text{-}l_s$ consistent with point 2 and the 'dashed' share line. The landowner receives $B < R$ and the worker $A + F$ as a sharecropper, earning $D + E$ in the alternative employment. The scheme is incentive-incompatible as $0\text{-}l_s < 0\text{-}l^*$ (the rent-maximising level of effort supply). However, there is a successful sharecropping arrangement, which is to insist on $0\text{-}l^*$ effort and to set the share line such that area $A = D$ (note angle $\theta_1 > \theta_0$). In symbols:

$$A + B + C = B + C + D = R \tag{12.11}$$

$$D + E + F = A + E + F = Z \tag{12.12}$$

It is evident that, in the presence of perfect information, all the solutions look identical, so that the underlying economic outcome is independent of the 'superficial' institutional detail of payment arrangements. This is a victory for abstraction over real-world detail, as this invariance theorem seemed to resolve puzzling observations that:

(i) sophisticated people use sharecropping arrangements;

(ii) they are found on rich and poor soil, geographically side-by-side with other payment arrangements chosen by different owners and geographically side-by-side with other payment arrangements chosen by the same owners.

'Economic Darwinism' suggests that inefficient economic arrangements will be displaced be efficient ones, so the very persistence and ubiquity of sharecropping is testimony to its efficiency. The above theorising explains this persistence and ubiquity.

Can it really be as easy as this? Does it really not matter how you pay your employee? The answer is 'no'. As with many invariance theorems, they are extreme cases set up in frictionless worlds with no information difficulties. Whilst not uninstructive, this is not a very rich economic context. It is in the presence of asymmetric information that the worth of principal–agent theory can be established.

The situation typical of many economic arrangements is one of asymmetric information. In this example, the worker knows the level of labour effort they are supplying but the landowner is typically unable to observe it. It is tempting to use output as the indicator of effort but it has to be remembered that, in principal–agent problems, output is a product not only of agent (worker) labour effort, but also of an uncertain random component. In this context, weather conditions experienced and the quality of other inputs come readily to mind. Whilst the alternative payment methods above were equivalent, this does not carry over to the asymmetric information context. If a rent equal to R is charged in advance, all the risk of being a farmer is borne by the worker who is almost certainly more risk-averse than the landowner – as landowners have more ability to diversify their activities. In these circumstances, the worker would willingly give up

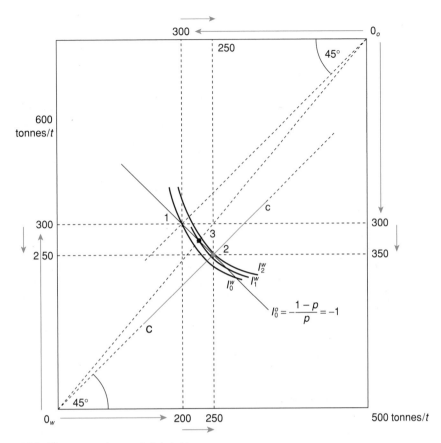

Figure 12.8 **Sharecropping and risk-taking**

some of their residual claim for a more constant income stream and the situation is less than optimal.

Figure 12.8 illustrates the development of this point and applies some of the concepts rehearsed in relation to insurance (see Chapter 7). The situation is one of social risk, in that the output of crops is assumed to be 600 tonnes with good weather and only 500 tonnes with bad weather. Given this, both parties cannot be fully insured in the sense of enjoying the same entitlement to output in both states of the world (there is simply not enough output in bad weather for this to be the case). To make all the arithmetic simple, it is assumed that good weather is equally as likely as bad, i.e. they both have a probability of 0.5. Putting the axes for the worker 'w' with the axes for the owner 'o' produces a vertically elongated box because of the different outputs in different states of the world (the fact that the 'sure thing' 45° lines are not coincident is a further indication that this is a social risk case). Here the strong assumption that the landowner is completely risk-neutral is adopted, illustrating the landowner's indifference curves as straight lines – with a slope of minus $(1 - p)/p$ where p is the probability of bad weather (0.5) and minus $(1 - p)/p$ equals -1. (Remember the slope of an indifference curve in a 'state space' diagram is the ratio of the marginal utilities of income in the two states of the world weighted by minus $p/(1 - p)$. With a straight-line total utility of income curve, required for risk neutrality, marginal utilities of income are constant and therefore cancel out. The probability weight ratio is inverted for the owner because the bad outcome is on the y-axis and the good one on the x-axis.)

Now if R is fixed at 300 tonnes, point 1 in the figure is located with the owner fully insured (as it were) and with the worker taking all the output variation risk of 300 tonnes in good-weather conditions and 200 tonnes in bad-weather ones. That this is an inefficient arrangement can be seen from the fact that point 1 is not on the contract curve c-c. Given the assumptions, point 2 is the efficient solution, where the worker increases utility from I_0^w to I_2^w – moving to the fully insured outcome of 250 tonnes of output irrespective of the state of the world. The risk-averse agent has reduced their 'income' variation in output tonnes (300,200 to 250,250) to zero, a direct implication of the result that risk-averse individuals will always choose full insurance at a fair premium (reflected in the fair odds line). The principal is taking all the risk, increasing 'income' variation in output tonnes (300,300 to 350,250). A reflection of the principal's risk neutrality is that utility is unchanged on I_0^o. They are, therefore, no worse off and the worker is better off. The fixed R of 300 tonnes cannot be efficient.

What of the other options? If the wage option is employed in the asymmetric information context, the owner is unable to monitor hours supplied and even if it was observed, hours of work may not correspond to the level of labour effort. The 'take it or leave it' option fails by the same token, because once effort is unobservable the payment method is similar to the wage option. Note that if Z is made conditional on the output level $R + Z$, with a random bad harvest the worker may have zero income under this option and it is clear that the risk of exposure of the worker is very large. Given these considerations sharecropping is described as something of a happy medium (Varian 1999) in that:

(i) it preserves some work incentives as the level of compensation received by the worker depends on labour effort;
(ii) the risk of output fluctuations as a consequence of the uncontrollable random element is shared between the owner and the worker.

In terms of Figure 12.8 sharecropping is about adjusting to point 3 on the diagonal between 0_w and 0_o. So, a point like 3 is achieved with the owner still on I_0^o but the worker is on I_1^w (the indifference curve through point 3), which is not as good as I_2^w but is an improvement on I_0^w. The shares employed here are 45% to the worker and 55% to the owner; the allocations for the worker are 275 tonnes good weather and 225 tonnes bad weather (risk exposure is reduced – increasing utility for the risk-averse worker). For the owner the allocations are 325 tonnes good weather and 275 tonnes bad weather; risk exposure is increased but utility is unaffected for the assumed risk-neutral owner. A sufficient condition for the picture presented here to obtain is that the owner is less risk-averse than the worker, so the strong assumption of risk neutrality is not necessary. In the world of asymmetric information the invariance theorem disappears.

Barzel (1997) explores the agricultural tenant contract issue much more fully and is distrustful of the above explanation of sharecropping, because of its reliance on the attitudes to risk that drive the explanation, which does not lend itself to refutation. In addition, Barzel wishes to introduce the transactions costs of contracting into the explanation of variety of observed arrangements. The author turns the invariance result introduced above on its head by explaining the observed variety of arrangements with reference to the relevant costs of transacting indifferent contexts.

His starting point is the fact that parcels of land are each unique and workers are also very different in their farming and other characteristics. Contracts cannot specify everything, so that there are always margins for exploitation by both the landowner and the worker. For example, unspecified attributes might be (i) use of nutrients in the soil and (ii) maintenance and improvements on the land. These might be in the control of different parties to the contract. Table 12.2 illustrates Barzel's taxonomy of transactions costs and their predicted associated size for the different contracting arrangements set

Table 12.2 **Source of losses from various contractual forms**

	Policing labor	Policing land	Policing output	Lack of specialising
High losses	FW	FR	SC	SO
Intermediate losses	SC	SC	FW	SC
Low or no losses	FR, SO	FW, SO	SO, FR	FW, FR

SO: Sole owner of land and labor
SC: Share contract
FW: Fixed-wage contract
FR: Fixed-rent contract
Source: Barzel (1997).

out above. Policing labour effort, land use and improvement and output monitoring are easily understood but specialisation losses need elaboration.

Sole ownership of land and labour owning land and working it yourself might appear to reduce all policing costs to zero (as you have the perfect incentives to be efficient – you will not try and exploit yourself!). However, two types of transactions costs arise. The first is that there is unlikely to be a perfect match between the owner's skills (human capital) and the owner's physical capital, so that to maximise total output it would be attractive to exchange land parcels (or portions of them), reintroducing the need for contracting and opportunities for rent capture. The second is that the gains from specialisation are attenuated, in that a worker would specialise in cultivation skills and a landowner in land maintenance work. Having to do both as a sole owner may make the owner a 'Jack of both tasks but master of neither' (i.e. no gains from specialisation).

Two examples illustrate the purchase of this reasoning. Consider a new worker arriving in an area. No landowner will know their skills, work attitudes, etc. and landowners will therefore be reluctant to offer the new worker the current market wage contract. Rather than accept less than the current wage, the worker might well choose to signal that they are a good worker by becoming a fixed-rent tenant, resolving the asymmetric information problem by becoming the residual claimant. Experience will reveal information and, in a future period, a wage contract becomes appropriate.

Now consider the introduction of a new crop. The knowledge of cultivating and profitability of existing crops are likely to be well known by both landowner and worker. However, a landowner with some growing experience and a sharper incentive (in terms of new crop profit incentives) will be likely to have an advantage over workers who, in these circumstances, are unlikely to accept a fixed-rent contract. The landowner can accept all the risk of crop innovation by offering a fixed-wage contract. Again, in the future, a fixed-rent contract may become the least-cost contract.

In Barzel's analysis the variety of coexisting contract arrangements and their pattern of change over time is the product of a heterogeneous world, not one of perfect information (which allows all institutional arrangements to be made identical at the level of incentives).[1]

12.6 Positive theory of agency

The Jensen–Meckling (1976) model is much quoted, as it picks up on many of the issues discussed so far. To begin, there is the recognition of *ex-ante* prospective owner–manager conflict of incentives. Proprietorships, as noted above, have owner–managers but quoted

---

1. For those interested in a detailed treatment of contract theory and incentive mechanisms see Salanie (1997) and Laffont and Martimort (2002).

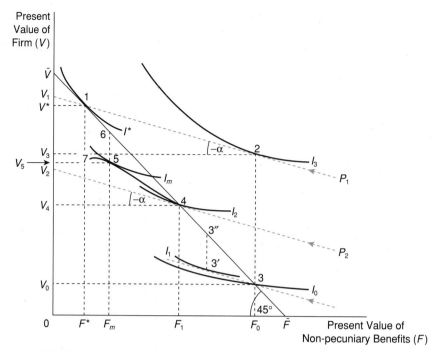

Figure 12.9 The Jensen–Meckling model

joint stock companies are owned by shareholders. Jensen and Meckling explore incentives when managers are less than 100% owners, in a context in which some activities both increase firms' income stream and offer direct utility to the manager.

The relevant variables in this analysis are:

F = present value of non-pecuniary benefits (activity taken beyond the profit-maximising point);

V = present value of firm which is at its maximum when $F = 0$.

As F rises V decreases by same amount; the effect can be captured in Figure 12.9 as a straight-line constraint $\bar{V}$-$\bar{F}$ with slope −1. In Figure 12.9 an owner–manager maximises utility at point 1 on I^* sacrificing $\bar{V}$-V^* firm value for 0-F^* non-pecuniary benefits. If outsiders buy 100% of the firm, retaining the manager and constraining them to 0-F^* its selling price would be V^*. Suppose the owner–manager wishes to retain a proportion α of the shares. With less than complete sale, the price can be anticipated as $(1 - \alpha)$ of total shares for $(1 - \alpha)V^*$. However, once this is done the budget constraint shifts to V_1-P_1 (P for partially owned) and utility-maximisation occurs on I_3 at point 2, with F_0 non-pecuniary benefits and V_3 'firm value'. But this is not feasible because, as F_0-V_3 is not on $\bar{V}$-$\bar{F}$, it is evident that with F_0 the value of firm = V_0. If this is anticipated then the appropriate offer for $(1 - \alpha)$ of the shares is $(1 - \alpha)V_0$ but this is not an equilibrium position, as at point 3 the owner–manager is on I_0 with a slope of the indifference curve not equal to the slope of V_1-P_1. Utility can be raised by decreasing non-pecuniary benefits at point 3' on I_1. However, this is inside the $\bar{V}$-$\bar{F}$ constraint and greater utility can be achieved by moving to another V–F combination, e.g. at 3″.

The equilibrium value of the firm is found at point 4 on I_2 where I_2 is tangent to V_2-P_2, the 'partially owned' budget constraint slope and because it is on $\bar{V}$-$\bar{F}$ it is also feasible. With F_1 non-pecuniary benefits the value of firm is V_4 and, with anticipation, outsiders buying shares force the existing owner to bear the full cost of increasing F from

F^* to F_1, as the utility-maximising response to a changed budget constraint contingent on property right changes.

The introduction of control devices can be modelled in this context. Monitoring (M) and bonding decreases managerial discretion and increases value of the firm. The monitoring budget constraint 4-5-7 in Figure 12.9 decreases F at a decreasing rate. The new equilibrium is on I_m at point 5, with V_5 'firm value' and F_m non-pecuniary benefits. Spending on monitoring is vertical distance 6-5, so that generally $F = F(\alpha, M)$.

The main implications from the above analysis are:

(1) full anticipation of post-sale managerial opportunism leads to the seller bearing all its costs *ex ante*;
(2) control devices are worthwhile until their marginal cost = marginal benefit.

Actual owner–manager conflict may differ from this as:

(1) Shareholders' meetings are generally weak disciplining mechanisms. It is costly for shareholders to be informed and to turn up to vote.
(2) The benefit is $1/n$ of any rise in efficiency secured by your vote, i.e. there is a public good problem leading to all trying to free-ride on others' costly information acquisition and their time and trouble costs of voting.

Clearly, other disciplining mechanisms may be attractive and these include:

(1) Hierarchical monitoring. If information or knowledge impactedness means that you delegate, there is the threat of loss because of delegatee discretion. A response is to ensure a series of 'checks and balances' are created. There is a split between decision management (which is about initiation and implementation) and decision control (which is located one layer further up the hierarchy). Decision control is about ratification (approval and sanctioning) and monitoring power. Effective decision control requires independent and informed individuals but these are difficult to find and employ.
(2) Payment systems might be designed to foster effort, risk-taking and long-term time horizons in decision-taking. These may involve executives being offered as a percentage of profit obtained, share options, insider trading opportunities, or 'golden parachutes' to prevent potential victims of change blocking an efficiency increasing take-over.
(3) Market discipline can work as a threat to the existing management and involves owners staying open to offers from other management teams and recognition of the take-over discipline emanating from the stock exchange.
(4) Debt bonding means issuing debt to increase leverage (the debt–equity ratio). Here management indicates pre-commitment (or bonding) to generate a sufficient cash flow to meet increased interest charges (bond holders enjoy first claim on their interest payments). In effect management is signalling that it will not indulge in agency costs, otherwise with high leverage bankruptcy would quickly follow.

In the context of the Jensen–Meckling model, many of the features of actual corporate life come into focus in a way that is not possible in the 'black box' market forms. But not all institutions have the same property right structures.

12.7 Non-profit institutions

It was noted above that non-profit institutions have an inherent tendency to look inefficient, as there is no owner with a saleable property right over the discounted net benefit stream associated with the institution. Further, it is not possible to assign part of the net benefit stream to trustees of non-profit institutions in order to foster managerial efficiency. The output of non-profit institutions is typically services whose quality is difficult for the consumer to evaluate. The advantage of the non-profit form of organisation is that there is little incentive to cheat on quality, as this cannot be used to increase profit. Indeed, the non-profit model elaborated by Newhouse involved quality as its central novel inclusion.

12.7.1 Newhouse's non-profit hospital

Newhouse (1970) provides a model of the effects of non-profit-making objectives on the provision of medical services. The decision-makers of the hospital are assumed to have two objectives to maximise: (i) the quantity of care delivered, and (ii) its quality.

The first objective is clearly uncontroversial. Since the aim of a charity hospital is to reduce the suffering owing to ill health, it requires only the assumption that more care leads to improved health for the quantity of care to be an objective. Quality of care is assumed to be an objective in addition to quantity because of the key role of quality (technological advances etc.) in medical services. Newhouse links the quality of care to the prestige of hospital staff (which could be both doctors and administrators) which itself replaces profits as a target for the decision-maker. Furthermore, the quality of care is likely to be of great significance to the consumer–patient.

Thus Newhouse assumes that the demand curve for care increases (shifts right) as quality rises. Figure 12.10 shows the possible equilibria for the hospital. Care of increasing quality (q_i, $i = 0, 1, 2, 3$) can be provided at an average cost per unit shown by the associated average cost curve AC_i. (The absence of marginal cost in the figure reflects the non-profit-making motive. Patient payments need only cover average cost so that the hospital breaks even.) For a charitable foundation the costs to be covered by charges may be less than the total cost of provision, the deficiency being made up from the charity's funds.

Associated with each quality level is a demand curve D_i which, together with the cost curve, gives the break-even quantity of care of any given quality level. The curves locate a series of these break-even points, B_i, for each quality level in Figure 12.10(a), so that it is possible to construct a transformation curve showing the possible combinations of quantity and quality that the hospital can attain. A key assumption in its construction is that, beyond some quality level, the cost of further increases in quality rises more rapidly than the demand for care. That is, when quality is high already, consumers attach less importance to a further increase in quality (declining marginal utility) but the cost of raising quality further is increasing (increasing marginal cost of quality). As a result of the assumed behaviour of demand and cost, the transformation curve is backward-bending in Figure 12.10(b).

The decision-maker chooses the optimal levels of quality and quantity by selecting the combination on the possibility frontier P-F that yields the highest level of utility. Graphically, a typical tangency exists between the possibility frontier and highest attainable indifference curve, I_0 at point 1. This shows that, with the indifference map postulated, the decision-maker chooses three-star quality and a quantity of output (i.e. patients treated or patient days of care) q_0 that is lower than the maximum q_1.

Clearly, with the right indifference map, quantity q_1 and two-star quality could be selected at point 2. But, at the point that the transformation curve turns back on itself, its slope is vertical. Thus, an indifference curve will be tangential at that point only if it has a vertical slope like I_0'. Yet this would imply that the marginal utility of quality to the decision-maker is zero, which violates the initial assumption that both quality and quantity yielded utility to the decision-maker (and, by implication from consumer theory, that the decision-maker can never be satiated [marginal utility = 0] with either). Therefore, a

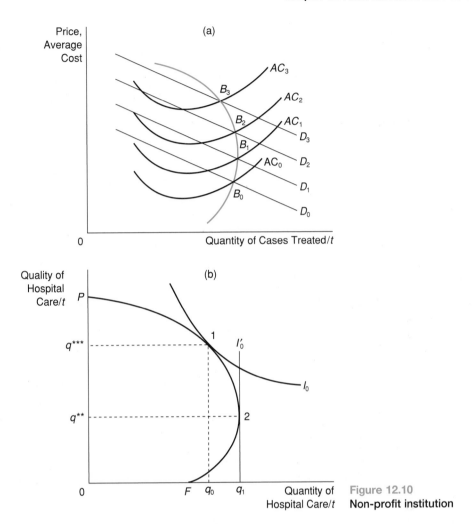

Figure 12.10 **Non-profit institution**

solution to the left of q_1, is inevitable as long as the decision-maker always attaches some positive marginal utility to the quality of care.

Critics have questioned who the decision-maker actually is. By implication, the preference map seems to be some sort of an amalgam of doctors' and administrators' preferences. A further criticism made is that there is no strong account of what quality entails. Does quality relate to inputs or outputs or some weighted sum of the both? Resolving quality issues is difficult.

12.7.2 Limits to survival for non-profit institutions

It has been noted that non-profit institutions may contain the seeds of their own failure, or demise, because of a process of internal asset-stripping that is encouraged by:

(i) Inverse Darwinian selection – successful non-profit institutions may, paradoxically, be quite profitable, accumulating reserves with (by definition) no shareholders with a property right over reserves. Utility-maximising managers will be tempted to appropriate them (opportunistic behaviour).

(ii) The difficulty of choosing an internal organisation structure to prevent opportunism. Members of the controlling instances (trustees) have no share in the profit, leading to a moral hazard problem. They have no incentive to operate against the interests of managers and to protect assets over which they have no claim. Moral hazard means 'non-profit status' alters the behaviour of those whose job is to monitor (compared to 'for-profit' status).

12.8 The labour-managed firm

Given that a hospital was used as the example for the non-profit firm, it is convenient to sustain the topic into discussion of cooperatives. Here we adapt a contribution by Pauly and Redisch (1973) entitled 'The Not-for-Profit Hospital as a Physicians' Cooperative'. The authors note (p. 88): 'Results obtained are similar to those derived from models of producers' cooperatives in Yugoslavia and collective farms in the USSR. The physician plays a role analogous to that of the Yugoslav worker and the Russian peasant.'

The model is one in which staff are income-maximising, with the hospital seen as the vehicle through which the medical staff can maximise their income. Hospital output is denoted by Q and a function of production by physical capital, non-doctor labour and doctor (or medical) staff (M). To simplify the exposition it is assumed that physical capital and non-doctor labour can be aggregated into a factor of non-medical staff inputs (N). That is:

$$Q = Q(N, M) \tag{12.13}$$

It is assumed that the maximand is medical staff income and that the demand for hospital output is given by $P_t = P_t(Q)$, where P_t stands for the total price of hospital care. For simplification, it is assumed that P_t is fixed in the short run, so that $\partial P_t/\partial Q = 0$. Included in P_t are payments for non-medical staff inputs (N), P_n, so that:

$$P_n Q = cN \tag{12.14}$$

where c is the constant cost of a unit of factor N.

A feature met above is that the drive to maximise one aspect of performance requires that other aspects are done in a least-cost manner. Here, because the maximand is medical staff income, the requirement for other costs is simply that they are covered. In the short run the number of doctors is fixed at $M = \bar{M}$ and of hospitals at $H = \bar{H}$. In this context, the solution is to maximise income per staff member (Y_m), where $Y_m = (P_t Q - P_n Q)/M = (P_t Q - cN)/M$. For this to be maximised with M fixed the employment of factor N must be determined. Using the quotient rule and setting the relevant partial derivative equal to zero yields:

$$\frac{\partial Y_m}{\partial N} = \frac{P_t(\partial Q/\partial N) - c}{M} = 0 \tag{12.15}$$

Rearranging:

$$P_t(\partial Q/\partial N) = c \tag{12.16}$$

This gives the standard result that a factor N is employed until its marginal revenue product equals its price. That is, $MRP_n(P_t(\partial Q/\partial N)) = c$. The long run is more interesting in that M now becomes variable for a hospital–firm. For Y_m to be maximised, two results must obtain: the first relates to the employment of factor N (already determined above) and the second to the number of sharing doctors. Again, using the quotient rule and setting the relevant partial derivative equal to zero yields:

$$\frac{\partial Y_m}{\partial M} = \frac{M(P_t \partial Q/\partial M) - P_t Q + cN}{M^2} = 0 \tag{12.17}$$

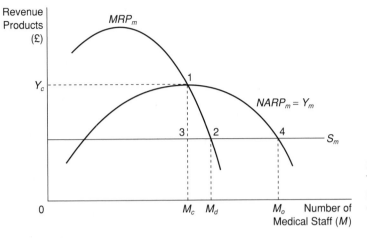

Figure 12.11
The Pauly–Redisch
physicians'
cooperative in the
long run

Rearranging:

$$P_t \partial Q / \partial M = \frac{P_t Q - cN}{M} = Y_m \qquad (12.18)$$

This gives the result to maximise Y_m. The size of M must be that where the marginal revenue product of doctors equals the (net of other input costs) average revenue product of doctors in the co-operative. In Figure 12.11 the typically shaped marginal revenue product curve for medical staff is displayed (MRP_m) with the net average revenue product curve of medical staff ($NARP_m = Y_m$) along with a perfectly elastic supply of medical staff curve (S_m).

Three sharing rules are considered by Pauly and Redisch:

(a) A *Closed Staff Policy* involves equal sharing per member of medical staff and is the result just obtained. In terms of Figure 12.11, point 1 must be chosen where $MRP_m = NARP_m$ at employment level M_c and income level Y_c.

(b) A *Discriminatory Sharing Policy* allows extra staff to join but only on the terms that they receive their individual supply wage S_m. This results in M_c to M_d extra medical doctors being employed and paid S_m. The surplus of MRP_m over S_m from M_c to M_d is area 1-2-3 and is shared equally by the M_c initial employees. Note, doctors M_c to M_d earn less than the M_c group and are likely to be disgruntled. Note also that the competitive employment level is mirrored as $MRP_m = S_m$.

(c) An *Open Staff Policy* allows any number of medical staff to join and this implies employment will occur at point 4, with M_o doctors each receiving a wage equal to S_m.

From the industry viewpoint, the number of hospitals becomes variable in the long run and, at this level, it seems reasonable to relax the constant price assumption introduced above so that $\partial P_t / \partial Q < 0$. With discriminatory sharing and an open policy there are doctors who know they can earn more if they start another co-operative hospital. A long-run process causes the quantity of hospital care (Q) in the market to rise, lowering P_t. Hence, MRP_m and $NARP_m$ are lowered at the same time that those setting up new co-operatives bid up the supply wage of doctors, until the number of hospitals equals that number where each one looks like Figure 12.12 – employing M^* doctors at the point where $S_l = MRP_m = NARP_m$. While this long-run equilibrium is akin to the long-run competitive outcome, the short-run response of a labour-managed firm (co-operative) to a demand increase, or a reduction in non-doctor input costs, is perverse and is known as the Ward–Vanek effect.

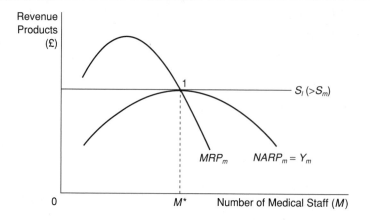

Figure 12.12
Physicians'
cooperative long-run
equilibrium

12.8.1 The Ward–Vanek effect

The perverse result for this type of model is a criticism of this co-operative form of economic organisation. In Chapter 3 the short-run response of the competitive firm to a demand increase was outlined and involved the expansion of output along a firm's marginal cost curve, so that more inputs are employed and more output secured. This seems an economically rational response. Consider what happens in a closed staff cooperative in the short run.

A demand increase that results in a price increase for medical care means equation (12.18) may well be affected asymmetrically, as the RHS may rise proportionately more than the LHS so that equilibrium is lost. The marginal revenue product of doctors $(P_t \partial Q/\partial M)$ is now less than the net (of other input costs) average revenue product of doctors $((P_t Q - cN)/M = Y_m)$ in the cooperative. That is, the contribution of members at the margin is now below Y_m.

This is all illustrated in Figure 12.13 where MRP_m has proportionately increased to MRP'_m and the net average revenue product of doctors has increased from $NARP_m$ to $NARP'_m$ in a skewed fashion. At point 1, with a cooperative membership of M_c, the contribution of the member at the margin at point 2 is now below Y'_m by distance 2-3. The necessary adjustment is clear: the membership of the cooperative must be reduced to raise the income of the remaining members, i.e. a move to point 4, decreasing cooperative membership to $M'_c (< M_c)$ and increasing the income level to $Y'_c (> Y_c)$. A price increase has produced a membership and output reduction!

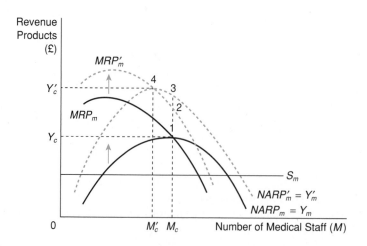

Figure 12.13
The Ward–Vanek
effect

This outcome is the opposite to an economically rational response. Whilst this result is dependent on certain functional forms and is alleviated in the long run, the 'effect' damages the image of cooperative production in the sense of calling its short-run efficiency into doubt.

12.9 What insights are offered?

Given the perspective developed here, a different account of standard pieces of economics can be explored. Here, the focus is on different types of integration.

12.9.1 Different economic rationales for integration

The standard approach in introductory microeconomics is to differentiate horizontal, vertical and conglomerate integration or merger. Horizontal mergers are of firms that are competitors at the same stage of production. Here the comparison of monopoly with competition is generally repeated (see Chapter 11).

Figure 12.14 illustrates the possibility that moving from competition to monopoly, via horizontal mergers, may be welfare-improving. Assuming $MC_m = \Sigma MC_c$, initially perfect competition produces equilibrium at point 1, resulting in price P_c and quantity q_c. While monopoly results in equilibrium at point 2, with price P_m and quantity q_m. This results in an efficiency or welfare loss triangle 1-2-3.

Mergers are viewed as offering the possibility of lower costs as a reflection of economies of size, rationalisation (cutting surplus capacity) and better management. In such circumstances, MC_m will fall, say to MC'_m in Figure 12.14, so that it is a question of comparing cost gains with the welfare loss triangle. The lower-cost monopolist will produce at point 4 with price P'_m and quantity q'_m. As illustrated in Figure 12.14, $P'_m > P_c$ and $q'_m < q_c$ yields a welfare loss triangle that is reduced in area from 1-2-3 to 1-5-6. However, with the area under the two MC curves illustrating cost differences there is a saving under monopoly produced by merger, equal to area 4-7-8-5. Here the benefit of reduced cost exceeds the welfare loss triangle and a horizontal merger looks like a potential Pareto improvement (see Chapter 2) – hence the title of the figure.

Vertical integration is about integrating processes backwards towards input markets or further forward in the production chain towards the output market. In Figure 12.15 a simple non-integrated arrangement is illustrated with the producer in panel (b) having

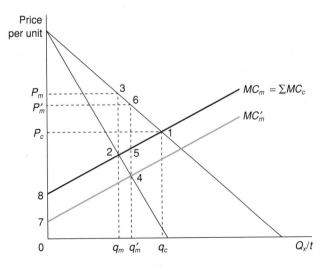

Figure 12.14
'Defending' horizontal integration

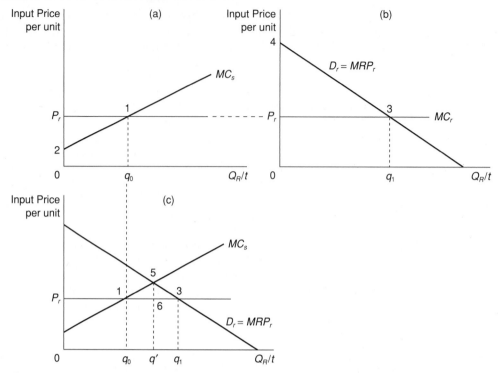

Figure 12.15 'Attacking' vertical integration

access to resource input R at a constant price P_r. Panel (a) illustrates the situation for a given supplier(s) of input resource R. As determined in panel (a) by the intersection of MC_s with P_r at point 1 (price-taking quantity-adjusting competitive behaviour is assumed in the market for R) the supplier illustrated is competitive over the quantity q_0 per period. The market for R has producer surplus equal to P_r-1-2 (the analysis is short-run) over the range of supply q_0. Given the demand equals marginal revenue product curve associated with the employment of R ($D_r = MRP_r$) in panel (b), q_1 ($> q_0$) units per period are purchased at point 3, generating surplus triangle P_r-4-3.

If the firm's source of supply of R is now integrated into the boundaries of the firm, panel (c), which is built up from panels (a) and (b), becomes relevant. If, on vertical integration, the firm must 'buy' resource R internally, the output decision in the face of MC_s is at point 5. This decreases quantity to q', sacrificing surplus equal to triangle 5-3-6 (by reference to q_1), and increases costs by triangle 5-6-1 (by reference to q_0), with the welfare loss being triangle 1-5-3 in total. If R can still be purchased externally the effect on surplus generation is zero, as q_0-q_1 will be bought externally.

This kind of analysis makes vertical integration look economically neutral or unattractive – hence also the title of the figure. To be rationalised, appeal is typically made to: (i) the R purchaser obtaining R supply security, (ii) forestalling monopoly development in the pricing of R in the future, or (iii) entry barrier creation (to be in the market for good X requires entrants to also own a source of input R). The process may also produce price discrimination advantages if, at the next stage of the market, there is monopoly power and market separation that is not obtainable at the current stage of the production process.

There are also conglomerate mergers that feature the creation of diversified firms operating in different industries because, unlike horizontal mergers, this does not raise the possibility of monopoly power. Appeal is generally made to *economies of scope* (see Chapter 3) where it is less costly to produce two or more outputs in a single firm than in separate firms. The costs of two or more outputs from a single firm are less than the sum of the costs of the same outputs being produced by separate firms. The source of economies of scope has to be a shared element of labour skill or capital equipment. The shared elements need not be identical but they do need to be complements.

So far, explanations of integration have been to do with the technology of production and/or the creation of a market form that can exert greater economic power by decreasing external competition. Whilst not wishing to deny these arguments, more modern approaches to integration, once again, rely on the market failures internal to the firm.

It has been argued elsewhere (see Chapters 7 and 8) that information is a crucial and unusual good. Information shares the attributes of a public good, being non-rival in use (you do not degrade the quantity by sharing it with another user), and difficult to make excludable, in that once passed, or sold, on to someone else, the recipient also can pass, or sell, it on, making the protection of your property right difficult (unintended and unsanctioned dissemination of the knowledge). The peculiar features of the new information (inventions) market, e.g. patent laws (guaranteeing you sole use of information for a period) and licensing agreements (intended and sanctioned dissemination of the knowledge), are an institutional response to this. Of course, these set up complex incentives in themselves (see Gallini 2002). In terms of the theory of the firm, the response may be to enlarge the internal market for the information. If the information is product-specific, then expand your product production, i.e. the situation is one of horizontal integration. If the information spills forwards towards product markets or backwards towards factor markets, then vertical integration may be an appropriate response. If new information is relevant over many different production processes, then conglomerate integration may be signalled.

Above, the question of quality was raised when there may be an incentive to pass on shoddy goods if quality is not readily assessed. If resource input, R, is vulnerable to this motivation, then vertical integration is a mechanism to guarantee input R's quality.

In this way, explanations of integration now focus on a different set of motivations, i.e. on information considerations.

12.10 Challenge: Has there been a payoff to greater realism?

This chapter and the previous chapter present discussion of major contributions to the theory of the firm. In this chapter, rationales for the firm have been explored; the firm, as an organisation, has been viewed as the product of economic forces. For example, the firm arises as a least-cost solution to: (i) contracting difficulties (in the case of Coase 1937), or (ii) securing productivity gains from team production (in the case of Alchian and Demsetz 1972). Chapter 11 surveyed the 'black-box – marginal rules – approach' to the firm, in which the existence of the firm was the starting point. By comparison, this chapter presents the work of authors who offer insight on contracts and team effort and, in so doing, inject greater institutional content into the 'firm'.[2]

The time has come to ask what has been gained from the study of the material of this chapter and of the previous chapter. As this is a text about theory, this poses the question: 'what do you expect from "good" theorising?'. Do you want theory to be *descriptive*

---

2. Discussion of firm integration was chosen for this chapter as a topic that, in part, reflected a distinction between a technology world and monopoly pricing advantage world (more in keeping with Chapter 11) and a view of the world in which integration reflects the insight that the firm contains its own market failures (especially with respect to information).

of processes of production within firms? If so, then clearly more realism has been added to the theory of the firm by the material discussed in these chapters. Of course, in large measure this was the intention of the authors; and as such, this conclusion is hardly surprising.

Whilst the logic of the marginalist rules that stand proud in the 'black box' theories is difficult to escape, these theories have always been open to the criticism that they do not reflect what business people actually do. The response to this criticism is twofold (and to some extent contradictory). Some rely on empirical studies that report that many businesses use marginal concepts and that, therefore, the 'marginalist approach' is not totally unrealistic. The 'black box' theories might claim a greater degree of realism than has usually been credited to them. The second response relies on studies that claim that, even if decisions within the firm are not made explicitly in terms of analysis of marginal changes, they are dependent on concepts that are consistent with the application of marginalism. Whatever the rights and wrongs of this debate, it is still difficult to escape the conclusion that theories presented in this chapter offer far more descriptive power.

Yet, while 'good' theorising might require description, there are other considerations. There is the argument that, in a positivistic methodology, all that matters is *predictive power*. For many, description is not everything. Theory is about developing potentially falsifiable hypotheses. If so, comparative static predictions (with respect to impact on price and output) might simply require the *ceteris paribus* assumptions of the 'black box' models (if these are generally accepted). Machlup (1967: 13), a distinguished neoclassical economist, captures this view succinctly:

> 'Frankly, I cannot see what great difference organizational matters are supposed to make in the firm's price reactions to changes in conditions.'

If so, the relevant question is: 'what additional insight – or more precisely – what potentially falsifiable predictions have been achieved by the introduction of descriptive "realism"?'

Chapter 1 warns about the difficulties of taking the empirical ('real') world as the check on the validity of particular theories, as the 'empirical world' is the consequence of the theory individuals hold and work with (as opposed to being independent of theory). In the extreme, this brings a plague on all houses, for theories cease to be falsifiable.

However, Chapter 1 also made reference to the *postdictive* view of theory. The *postdictive* perspective of theory might apply if there are deviations from the rationality prescribed by the neoclassical paradigm, i.e. if something is missed. It offers the 'we can repair theory' view of the world. So, *ex post*, once the missed friction is included, observed action will accord with neoclassical economics. In this context, the 'something being missed' is usually the transaction costs of enacting the appropriate marginal rule.

For some, this tends to look both tautological and self-serving. The empirical relevance of the *postdictive* aspect suggests investigators start to include transactions costs and particular preference specifications in apparently harmless bids to operationalise 'tests' of their, or other, theories. The criticism is that, as so often observed, the theories 'tested' are not very close to the theories postulated. Furthermore, it is a very 'poor' econometrician indeed that cannot find some 'not inconsistent' support for theories in the evidence that is analysed.

Recognition of the empirical world as the product of theory and the effects of postdiction are consistent with the observation that economic theories are seldom refuted but simply go out of fashion. Will this be the fate of the principal–agent property-rights school with its emphasis on incentive structures?

The fourth role of theory is the *prescriptive* one, i.e. theory describes how individuals 'ought' to behave in given situations. If Pareto efficiency is accepted as a central goal, it is clear that the prescriptive role of perfect competition is vital in economics. By contrast, all the other market forms must look inefficient. This pushes the issue back towards the question 'could perfect competition exist everywhere?' In the standard neoclassical approach, decreasing-cost industries provide a rare exception. For the managerial, behavioural and property-rights schools, the question is: 'Are the market forms they analyse the "best" that could arise, given the nature of some goods, some production processes, the stock of information and the extent of risk and uncertainty?' The sharecropping example illustrated that it only approximated a point on the contract curve (an efficient solution) but, in the absence of full information, is this the best that can be done? Is it always the case that, when you unravel situations far enough, the constraint that prevents efficiency can be removed? Debates surrounding the meaning of 'second best' partly address this very issue (see Section 6.4).

Economists who find themselves uncomfortable with inconclusiveness at the heart of their subject typically wish to put things together in a way in which all parties to a debate can have a legitimate perspective. In this respect (and following Zamagni 1987) the presence, or absence, of internal or external conflicts of interest has been seen as the source of different perspectives and an apparent resolution (Phillips 1967). Table 12.3 illustrates a simple two-by-two taxonomy.

Different theories can now be located in different parts of the taxonomy and, therefore, be seen to be addressing different issues or contexts. The owner-managed firm has no internal or external conflict. The managerial theories of the firm, like those of Baumol, are seen as ones of resolved conflict. Oligopoly theory has external conflict that comes to the fore when increased competition and rivalry is observed.

Ultimately, if the importance of different theories becomes a question of which theory is more typical of extant economies, Zamagni (1987: 439) comments: 'when there are large profit margins there is space for all groups to pursue their own goals, but when competition increases and profit levels fall firms adopt the behaviour of survival which is that described by neoclassical theory. Now, the difference between Machlup and Phillips is to be found in the fact that, whereas Machlup argues that the latter describes the general rule, Phillips argues, more realistically, that the opposite is true'. Ironically, at this stage the section has come full circle to its starting point in that an appeal to realism has been made.

But what is 'realism'? Ricketts (1989) questions whether managerialism, behaviourism, etc. has simply replaced one set of 'empty box' concepts (e.g. varieties of homothetic and non-homothetic production functions) with another set of 'empty box' concepts (e.g. impacted information and strategic hold-up possibilities where one party in a contractual relationship exploits the other party's specific relationship with them). Neither these nor other, apparently relevant, concepts may have much purpose beyond creating a sense of comfort in an uncertain world, that someone understands what is going on in the firm. In medicine many reported visits to the doctor end in the outcome: 'The doctor said I had a virus that was going around'. For some, at least, that is enough of an explanation, for others this is an empty statement. Indeed, the word 'syndrome' describes a medical condition in terms of a list of its symptoms, revealing little if anything. In

Table 12.3 Conflict or not

		Internal firm Conflict of interest	
		No	Yes
External firm	No	1	2
Conflict of interest	Yes	3	4

sociology, 'relativism' includes the notion that the closer you get to a subject the greater is the level of uncertainty of its understanding. So that the experts are, in fact, uncertain and 'the person who really knows about this is X who incidentally, in our experience, is always somewhere else'.[3]

12.11 Summary

Developments of the theory of the firm constitute the core material of industrial economics courses. In this respect, the material presented here can only cover some of the relevant issues and models. The models provide an opportunity to rehearse many of the tools of microeconomics as 'maximisation subject to constraints' underlay most approaches. An attempt has been made to highlight key contributors and a variety of models.

Earl (1995: 119) suggests a set of methodological criteria on which competing economic models might be evaluated: logical coherence, mathematical tractibility, assumptive realism, simplicity, philosophical appeal and empirical adequacy (predictive power). In principle, score cards (e.g. with each criterion marked out of ten) for each of the models introduced above could be constructed. However, in different methodological approaches different weights, say summing to one, would then have to be attached to the various criteria. For example, in a positivistic methodology a weight of 1 would be attached to empirical adequacy. It might be possible to agree on the scores, or the weights, but almost certainly not both.

Debates go on and change form. Events make once-prominent models and discussion look flat and uninteresting, e.g. the decline of the centrally planned economy and the Ward–Vanek effect. Academics have an incentive to say something different – we all have to have a stock in trade! – and it is the incentive literature with its emphasis on asymmetric information that is the focus of the more recent discussions of the theory of the firm.

References

Alchian, A. and Demsetz, H. (1972) Production, information costs and economic organisation, *American Economic Review*, 62: 777–95.

Barzel, Y. (1997) *Economic Analysis of Property Rights*, 2nd edn, Cambridge: Cambridge University Press.

Baumol, W. (1959) *Business Behavior, Value and Growth*, New York: Macmillan.

Cheung, S.N.S. (1969) *A Theory of Share Tenancy*, Chicago: University of Chicago Press.

Coase, R.H. (1937) The nature of the firm, *Economica*, 4: 386–405.

Earl, P.E. (1995) *Microeconomics for Business and Marketing*, Cheltenham: Edward Elgar.

Gallini, N.T. (2002) The economics of patents: lessons from recent US patent reform, *Journal of Economic Perspectives*, 16 (2) Spring: 131–54.

Jensen, M.C. and Meckling, W.H. (1976) Theory of the firm: managerial behaviour, agency costs and ownership structure, *Journal of Financial Economics*, 3 (4) October: 305–60.

Laffont, J.-J. and Martimort, D. (2002) *The Theory of Incentives – the Principal–Agent Model*, Princeton, NJ: Princeton University Press.

Lindsay, C.M. (1984) *Applied Price Theory*, New York: Holt-Saunders.

3. In this respect it was always frustrating going to staff seminars on what Staffa meant in his controversial 1960 book *Production of Commodities by Means of Commodities* when in fact he was alive living in Italy and could easily have been consulted. At least one dimension of uncertainty could have been removed in this way, viz. what he thought he was saying.

Machlup, F. (1967) Theories of the firm: marginalist, behavioral, managerial, *American Economic Review*, 52 (1): 1–33.

Marris, R.L. (1964) *The Economic Theory of 'Managerial Capitalism'*, London: Macmillan.

Newhouse, J. (1970) Toward a theory of non-profit institutions: an economic model of a hospital, *American Economic Review*, 60 (1): 64–74.

Pauly, M.V. and Redisch, M. (1973) The not-for-profit hospital as a physicians' cooperative, *American Economic Review*, 63: 87–99.

Phillips, A. (1967) An attempt to synthesize some theories of the firm, in A. Phillips and O.E. Williamson (eds) *Prices: Issues on Theory, Practice and Public Policy*, Philadelphia: University of Pennsylvania Press.

Ricketts, M. (1989) The new institutional economics and the structure of the firm, *Economic Affairs*, 9 (4): 23–6.

Salanie, B. (1997) *The Economics of Contracts – a Primer*, Cambridge, Mass.: MIT Press.

Simon, H.A. (1959) Theories of decision making in economics and behavioral Science, *American Economic Review*, 49: 253–83.

Sraffa, P. (1960) *Production of Commodities by Means of Commodities: Prelude to a Critique of Economic Theory*, Cambridge: Cambridge University Press.

Vanek, J. (1970) *The General Theory of Labor-managed Market Economies*, Ithaca, NY: Cornell University Press.

Varian, H.A. (1999) *Intermediate Microeconomics: a Modern Approach*, 5th edn, New York: Norton.

Williamson, O.E. (1967) *Economics of Discretionary Behaviour: Managerial Objectives in the Theory of the Firm*, London: Kershaw.

Williamson, O.E. (1975) *Markets and Hierarchies: Analysis and Antitrust Implications*, New York: Free Press.

Williamson, O.E. (1985) *The Economic Institutions of Capitalism: Firms, Markets, Relational Contracting*, New York: Free Press.

Zamagni, S. (1987) *Microeconomic Theory: an Introduction*, Oxford: Basil Blackwell.

PART IV

THE PUBLIC ECONOMY

CHAPTER 13

Taxing economics

13.1 Introduction

When applying the principles of neoclassical microeconomics to taxation the question that usually preoccupies analysts is how different taxes and different tax structures can be assessed. A set of criteria for assessment is often based on Adam Smith's 'canons' of taxation. Smith (1776) argued that a good tax should satisfy four criteria. The tax should be equitable (so that consideration of ability to pay and tax progressivity are relevant). The tax should not be expensive to administer and the greatest possible proportion should accrue as net government revenue. The method and frequency of the tax should be convenient to the taxpayer. The tax should be formulated so that taxpayers are certain of how much they have to pay and when they have to pay it.

Subsequently, economists have considered other criteria. For example, it may be deemed important that taxes be regarded as payment for services, i.e. that a 'benefit principle' is introduced. It may be thought important that a tax is flexible, in the sense that revenue rises in line with prices (e.g. value added tax will go up automatically as prices rise whereas specific rates of excise tax do not).

The objective in this chapter, once again, is to illustrate the extent to which analysis can be premised on the assumptions of neoclassical microeconomics. Each section of the chapter considers the use of taxation against a specific criterion. For example, in the following section it is argued that it is likely that taxation will create 'deadweight loss' as individuals generally alter their choice decisions in the presence of taxation. Efficiency requires that taxes be chosen so as to minimise deadweight loss. In a following section in this chapter (dealing with work effort) taxes will be compared in terms of their disincentive effect. Again, later in the chapter the impact of taxes on 'equity' will be considered (should taxes be related to 'ability to pay' and, if so, what implications follow for the structure of taxation?).

Another objective in this chapter is to highlight how neoclassical microeconomics adds new dimensions. It will become clear that what appears 'obvious' when reviewing tax policy is far from 'obvious'. When taxpayers refer to the cost of taxation or when they assess who pays taxes their perspective differs from that of the economist. The 'costs' of taxation differ from the sums that taxpayers transfer to the tax collector. The incidence (and burden) of taxation often differs from the amount that individuals are legally responsible to pay. The consequence is that assessing the burden of taxation is far more involved than it may appear at face value.

Throughout the chapter there will be reference to the extent to which neoclassical economics sheds insight. For example, tax evasion is far less than would be predicted by standard neoclassical economics. Can this dichotomy be reconciled by amendment of the neoclassical microeconomics approach, or does it suggest that analysis should be based on a representative individual more broadly defined than *homo economicus*? A neoclassical microeconomic approach to taxation is consistent with the prediction that individuals become more honest as the rate of tax is increased. This is a prediction that is at odds with intuition and again begs the question of the extent to which neoclassical microeconomics proves informative.

To begin, consider more closely the 'costs' of taxation and the 'burden' of taxation.

13.2 Taxation and efficiency: the costs of taxation

It would not be surprising to discover that taxpayers regarded the costs of taxation simply as the tax payments made to the tax collector. However, application of microeconomic theory reveals that the costs of taxation exceed this sum. An 'excess burden' of taxation relates to the efficiency of the tax. If the government wishes to raise revenue it would be efficient to do so at least cost to the taxpayer. However, in practice, the cost to the taxpayer depends on the way in which the tax is levied. The taxpayer's welfare is often reduced by more than the value of the tax payment. There is an 'excess burden' (or deadweight loss) of taxation which is defined as 'that amount that is lost in excess of what the government collects' (Auerbach 1985: 67).

One measure of consumer surplus is the *equivalent variation* (see Chapter 2). This is the amount of income which could be taken away from the individual *in the absence* of a specific change so as to leave the individual as well off *as if* the change had occurred. In the case of taxation the tax payment is usually less than the equivalent variation. The difference is the *excess burden* of the tax.

The following example illustrates the excess burden of a selective excise tax. A selective excise tax is levied on one particular good (in this case good X). The tax is set as an *ad valorem* tax (so that for every pound that the consumer spends the government keeps the fraction t).[1] It would be possible to consider the selective excise tax as a *specific* or *unit* tax (in this case a specified amount T is collected per unit of output).

In Figure 13.1(a) the individual allocates a fixed budget between two goods, X and Y. The budget line is 1-2. The slope of the budget line is determined by the relative price of the two goods $-P_x/P_y$. Before tax the individual maximises utility at point 3 on indifference curve I_2. At this tangency point the slope of the indifference curve (i.e. the marginal rate of substitution defined as MU_x/MU_y) is equal to the slope of the budget line $(-P_x/P_y)$. Utility is maximised because the marginal utility per pound spent on good X equals the marginal utility per pound spent on Y.

When the excise tax is introduced on good X (at a rate t), the relative price of X rises. The budget line swivels from 1-2 to 1-4. The individual's welfare is reduced to I_1 at the new tangency point, point 5. The more the individual purchases good X the greater the tax that is paid. (If the individual allocated all income to good X, tax equal to 4-2 in units of X would be paid.)

As the price of X has increased, 0-4 units of good X cost 0-1 units of Y (whereas, prior to the tax, 0-2 units of good X cost 0-1 units of good Y – the difference in price is the tax which is paid to the government). The utility-maximising individual chooses that combination of the two goods shown by tangency point 5 in Figure 13.1(a). The ratio $-MU_x/MU_y$ (the slope of indifference curve I_1) now equals $-P_x(1 + t)/P_y$ (the slope of 1-4).

The *equivalent variation* of the tax can be discovered if the budget line 1-2 is shifted backwards in a parallel fashion to 6-7 until a new tangency point, i.e. 8, is identified on

---

1. For any product selling at £100 the government collects 5% × £100 = £5.

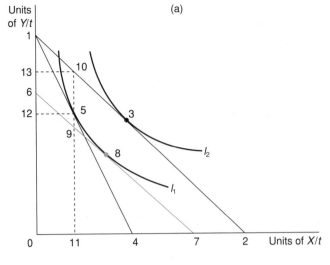

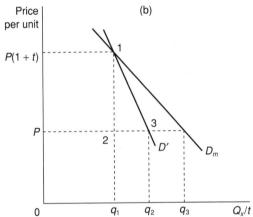

Figure 13.1

Excess burden of a selective excise tax

indifference curve I_1. This sum (equal to distance 1-6) is the amount that can be taken from the individual *in the absence* of a change (i.e. the imposition of the selective excise tax) to leave the individual with exactly the same welfare *as if* the change in question had taken place.

In Figure 13.1(a), the individual chooses 0-11 of good X (at tangency point 5). This will cost 1-12 units of Y after the tax is imposed. Comparing the slopes of the budget lines 1-2 and 1-4, the additional cost of purchasing 0-11 as a consequence of the tax is distance 10-5 (= distance 13-12). Without the tax the individual would have 0-13 units of Y and 0-11 units of X, instead of only 0-12 units of Y and 0-11 units of X.

In Figure 13.1(a) if a total of 1-6 units of Y is taken from the individual, the individual is at exactly the same welfare *as if* the selective excise tax had been imposed. However, by comparison with the tax revenue of 13-12 (units of Y) there is an 'excess burden' of this selective excise tax to the extent of distance 5-9 (in units of Y). This excess burden is a 'deadweight loss'. The tax is a transfer paid by the taxpayer and collected by the tax collector but the excess burden is a (deadweight) loss.

Note that in Figure 13.1(a) that excess burden depends on the 'substitution effect' of the price change brought about by the tax. The important consideration is the 'compensated' response (i.e. the movement around the same indifference curve). Comparing point 5 with point 8 in Figure 13.1(a) the marginal rate of substitution has changed (whereas, comparing 3 and 8, the marginal rate of substitution is the same). The extent of the loss depends on the extent of this substitution effect (created by the change of relative prices). It is this distortion of choice that explains excess burden. If a *lump-sum tax* had been levied the budget line would have moved back in a parallel fashion. A lump-sum tax is a theoretical construction where, by definition, the amount of tax does not depend on any particular activity that the taxpayer undertakes. With a selective excise tax on X the individual pays more tax the greater the consumption of good X per period. However, with a lump-sum tax the slope of the budget line would not change. There is, therefore, no substitution effect as relative prices have not changed. As there is no substitution effect there is no excess burden. The outcome with a lump sum tax is often used as a benchmark against which other taxes can be compared and will be considered more fully in Section 13.2.2.

As excess burden depends on the substitution effect, the welfare loss of the selective tax on X is estimated with reference to the 'compensated' demand curve. In Figure 13.1(b) the line D_m represents the Marshallian (uncompensated) demand curve drawn under the assumption that money income is held constant. D' represents the income-compensated demand curve (see Chapter 2). The income-compensated demand curve shows how much individuals would demand of the good at the same real income. In Figure 13.1(a) it shows the substitution effect associated with a price change. A Marshallian demand curve shows the change in quantity demanded when the price changes, holding money income constant. A compensated demand curve shows the change in quantity demanded holding real income constant, i.e. it shows changes on the same indifference curve.

In Figure 13.1(b) the excise tax (with *ad valorem* rate t) raises the price of good X from P to $P(1 + t)$. In the absence of this tax, the amount of money which it would be possible to take away from the individual to make the individual as well off *as if* the tax were levied (i.e. the *equivalent variation*) is trapezoid $P(1 + t)$-1-3-P. This is a measure of the welfare loss (the consumer surplus loss) that the individual experiences from the imposition of the tax.

When the tax is levied the individual purchases 0-q_1 and pays in taxation an amount equal to the difference between P and $P(1 + t)$ on each unit to the government. In Figure 13.1(b), rectangle $P(1 + t)$-1-2-P is an estimate of the total tax paid. It follows that the tax payment is less than the loss of consumer surplus from taxation $P(1 + t)$-1-3-P (this sum $P(1 + t)$-1-3-P is the amount that could be taken away from the individual in the absence of the tax-induced price rise to leave the individual as well off as if the price had risen). The difference between the tax cost and the total loss of consumer surplus is the 'excess burden' of the tax, i.e. triangle 1-2-3 is a loss over and above the loss of consumer surplus derived from the tax loss (hence the term 'excess burden'). The amount $P(1 + t)$-1-2-P is a transfer; the individual loses this but the government receives the revenue. The triangle 1-2-3 is not a transfer, it is a 'deadweight loss' (as there is no offsetting gain elsewhere).

Excess burden (or deadweight loss) can be estimated by measuring the area of triangle 1-2-3. The area of any triangle is 1/2 the product of the base and the height of the triangle. In this case, the area of the triangle is $(1/2)$ $(dP \cdot dQ)$ where dP is the change in price created by the tax (i.e. the difference between $P(1 + t)$ and P) and dQ is the difference between q_2 and q_1. If the income effect is negligible, because the change in price (tax increase) is small, the Marshallian demand curve approximates the linear compensated demand curve and the perceived change in quantity, q_3-q_1, is similar to q_2-q_1.

The difference between $P(1 + t)$ and P is tP (which is the tax paid per unit of the good). In Figure 13.1(b) triangle 1-2-3 is equal to $(1/2)tP \cdot dQ$. If estimates are required *ex ante*, i.e. before the tax has been imposed, the problem is to estimate dQ (ideally with reference to the income-compensated demand curve). This estimate will depend on the price elasticity of demand, $e_d = (dQ/dP)(P/Q)$. Therefore:

$$dQ = \frac{e_d \, dP \, Q}{P} \qquad\qquad (13.1)$$

and (as tP equals dP) excess burden (EB) can be estimated as:

$$EB = (1/2)(e_d \, t^2 \, PQ) \qquad\qquad (13.2)$$

The argument concerning deadweight loss can be applied to an income tax using the same arguments. In Figure 13.2(a), the individual faces a choice between supplying labour and taking hours of leisure. On the x-axis the total available hours are 0-1 and the rate at which hours can be transformed into income is determined by the wage rate (as illustrated by the slope of budget line 1-2). Again, the individual is at an initial equilibrium at point 3 on indifference curve I_2. A proportional income tax is levied which causes the budget line to swivel to 1-4. The individual now maximises income at tangency point 5 on indifference curve I_1 (now enjoying more hours of leisure equal to 0-11 compared to 0-12). The equivalent variation is the amount of income that can be taken from the individual to leave the individual as well off as if there had been a proportional income tax. Moving the initial budget line towards the origin it is possible to find

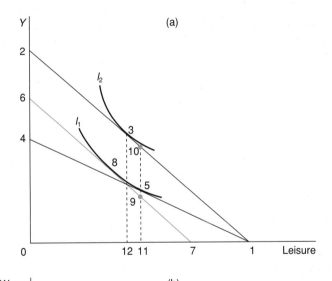

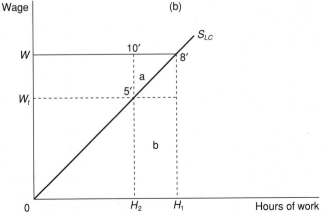

Figure 13.2
Excess burden of a proportional income tax

tangency point 8 (on budget line 6-7) which shows that 2-6 can be taken from the individual to leave the individual as well off as if there had been a proportional income tax levied. When the proportional income tax is levied the tax payment is the difference between what is paid (by reference to budget line 1-2) and what is received by the individual (by reference to budget line 1-4). So, at point 5 on budget line 1-4, the individual is paid 11-10 for sacrificing 1-11 hours of leisure to work but, after tax, receives only 11-5. The tax payment is distance 10-5. Once again, there is an *excess burden* of taxation, measured by distance 5-9. The amount that can be taken from the individual to leave the individual as well off as if there had been a proportional income tax is 2-6 and this distance is 5-9 greater than the tax that is received (i.e. 10-5).

Once again, the deadweight loss, or excess burden, depends on the substitution effect (i.e. the shift from 8 to 5). Therefore, when estimating the deadweight loss of taxation it is important to make estimates by reference to the compensated supply curve of labour (i.e. the supply of labour that would occur holding constant the real income level). In Figure 13.2(b) the excess burden can be estimated by the triangle labelled *a*. If the wage rate were 0-W then 0-H_1 hours of labour would be supplied. When a tax is levied the after-tax income is W_t and the supply of labour is only 0-H_2. If the individual were to work the additional hours then (from the compensated supply curve) the individual would require compensation equal to area *b* (i.e. H_2-5'-8'-H_1). However, if the tax were not levied the individual would have been paid 0-W per unit, i.e. area *a* more than required. The tax imposes an excess burden of area *a*. (When the tax is levied tax revenue is W-10'-5'-W_t but the welfare of the individual is reduced by this plus area *a*).

The excess burden of tax can be estimated by reference to the size of this triangle. The area of the triangle is $\frac{1}{2}$ dWdH (where dW is the change in wage created by the tax and dH is the change in the hours worked). As $e_s = (\mathrm{d}H/\mathrm{d}W)(W/H)$ then

$$\mathrm{d}H = \frac{e_s \mathrm{d}WH}{W} \tag{13.3}$$

and, by substitution:

$$\text{Excess burden} = \frac{1}{2}\,\mathrm{d}W \frac{e_s \mathrm{d}WH}{W} \tag{13.4}$$

As

$$\mathrm{d}W = Wt \tag{13.5}$$

it follows that:

$$\text{Excess burden} = \frac{1}{2}\,e_s t^2 WH \tag{13.6}$$

As governments wish to raise revenue by imposing the least cost on the taxpayer, there is a reason for preferring taxes that minimise excess burden. But does this mean that the tax system should be neutral? This question will be discussed in Section 13.2.3. First, the opportunity is taken to show how the analysis above can help in the selection of different taxes.

13.2.1 Estimates of the marginal excess burden per unit of revenue: the efficiency loss ratio

One objective of tax policy is to be efficient, i.e. to minimise deadweight loss. It is efficient to reduce reliance on taxes with high excess burdens per pound of revenue raised. If revenue can be raised by reliance on taxes with lower excess burdens per pound, so much the better. The objective is to minimise total deadweight loss within the tax system without sacrificing revenue. With knowledge of the efficiency-loss ratio of taxes, greater reliance may be placed on some taxes than on others. If the efficiency loss per

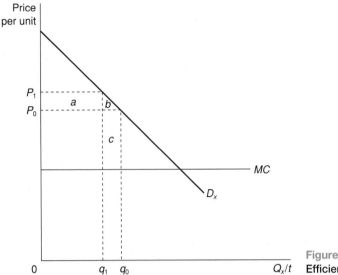

Figure 13.3
Efficiency loss ratio

pound raised by a tax on interest income were estimated as 0.3, while the efficiency-loss ratio per pound raised by a tax on housing were only 0.1 then, on efficiency criteria, the tax on housing would be preferable.

With reference to Figure 13.3, an *ad valorem* tax (equal to t_X) is levied on good X and this increases the price (assumed, initially, to be 1). The price that consumers now face is 0-P_0 $(= 1 + t_X)$. A change in the tax (Δt) is proposed. This change will mean that the price that consumers face will increase to P_1. There will be a decrease in consumer surplus equal in Figure 13.3 to areas $a + b$.

As the proposed tax change is infinitesimally small, the size of triangle b is minuscule and can be ignored in the following analysis. The objective is to consider the *marginal welfare cost* of the tax, i.e. the increase in efficiency loss for an increase in the tax rate. The increase in deadweight loss when the rate of tax is increased is equal to area c. The change in the revenue raised as the rate of tax is increased is equal to area a minus area c.

This increase in tax revenue (area a minus area c) can also be written as $q_1 \cdot \Delta t + t_X \cdot \Delta q$. This must be compared with the marginal loss of consumer surplus associated with the tax increase (area a) and this can be represented as $q_1 \cdot \Delta t$. The marginal burden of taxation (*MBT*) (additional burden of tax *per pound* of revenue raised) is the *efficiency-loss ratio*. Using the areas identified in Figure 13.3 (and following Bruce 1998) the efficiency-loss ratio can be written as:

$$MBT = \frac{a}{a - c} \tag{13.7}$$

and this can be expressed as:

$$MBT = \frac{q_1 \Delta t}{q_1 \cdot \Delta t + t_X \cdot \Delta q} \tag{13.8}$$

As Δq is negative, this, in turn, can be written as:

$$MBT = \frac{1}{\dfrac{(1 + t_X)}{q_1} \cdot \dfrac{\Delta q}{\Delta t}} \tag{13.9}$$

With reference to Figure 13.3 the price elasticity of demand can be written as $e = (\Delta q/\Delta p)$. $(1 + t_X)/q_1$. In equation (13.9), $\Delta q/\Delta t = \Delta q/\Delta p$ (because in the example in Figure 13.3 marginal cost is constant – note that the marginal cost curve is a horizontal line). If, by definition, $\tau = t_X/(1 + t_X)$, then as $[(\Delta q/\Delta p) \cdot (1 + t_X)/q_1] \cdot t_X/(1 + t_X)$ is equal to $\Delta q/\Delta p \cdot t_X/q_1$, the equation (13.9) can be rewritten as:

$$MBT = \frac{1}{(1 - \tau) \cdot e} \qquad (13.10)$$

This formula permits us to estimate the efficiency loss of the tax. Bruce (1997) illustrates the case of a tax on good X. When the tax is £1 then 100 units are consumed. If the tax were increased by 5 pence and consumption falls to 99 units, by substitution in (13.9):

$$MBT = \frac{1}{1 + \dfrac{1}{99} \cdot \dfrac{-1}{0.05}} \sim 1.25 \qquad (13.11)$$

In this particular example, the marginal excess burden (MBT) is 25 pence, i.e. the marginal burden of raising £1 tax revenue is £1.25. The example illustrates that price elasticity of demand and the rate of tax levied is important. (In Section 13.2.2, it will be shown that excess burden increases with the tax rate and – for linear demand and supply curves – increases by the square of the increase of the tax rate).

With knowledge of the efficiency loss of a tax, policy-makers are able to estimate the costs of raising tax and consider how much reliance to place on different taxes. For example, a study by Ballard *et al.* (1985) estimated that the excess burden per dollar of tax revenue in the US tax system ranged from 13 cents to 24 cents per dollar of revenue in the mid-1970s and about 18.5 cents in the mid-1980s. These sums may seem small but, over time, aggregation highlights their importance. For example, if tax laws and tax rates in 1973 are used as a base, the authors reported that the present value of the gain associated with replacing the tax system of 1973 with a system of lump-sum taxes was of the order of $1.86 trillion to $3.36 trillion!

Focusing on US taxation of interest and investment income, the greatest distortion in 1973 occurred with an efficiency-loss ratio for taxes on capital income ranging from 15 to 35 cents per dollar.[2] With an interest elasticity of saving supply of 0.4, savings would have been 80 per cent higher had a lump-sum tax been used to collect the same revenue). Simulations (over 100 years) reveal that higher savings would have increased the ratio of capital to labour in production by 31 per cent; there would have been higher labour productivity and higher wages for workers.

Estimates differ according to the tax and according to elasticities that have been assumed and according to the difficulties associated with estimation (for a discussion see Browning 1987).[3] However, Feldstein (1997) presented a critique which suggests that deadweight losses are, in general, greater than the sums usually reported. The reason is that such a formula looks only at the changes (elasticities) in the markets in which the tax is levied. He argues that excess burden is associated with a wider range of distortion. Feldstein (1997) argues that a more inclusive measure is required. Excess burden arises from a reallocation of resources away from taxed activities to untaxed activities. For example, tax rates may not only affect the number of hours worked, they may also

---

2. Depending on estimates of the elasticity of the supply of savings with respect to the rate of interest.
3. For example, Hansson and Stuart (1983) produced figures varying from 1.05 to 1.29 for a marginal tax on labour of 40% and with the money raised being spent on transfers (though for other parameter values and uses of the taxes raised there was values of 0.67 and 4.51). In the USA, Fullerton (1984) surveys another range of estimates which range from 1.07 to 1.21.

influence occupation choices (discouraging individuals from high-wage occupations). High tax rates on money income encourage the use of fringe benefits (e.g. a motor car, health insurance) to reward workers. High tax rates may encourage individuals to retire earlier.

The distortion arises when individuals substitute towards actions that are not taxed. If on some actions income is tax-deductible, individuals engage in these activities beyond the point at which marginal benefit falls to their marginal cost. For example, if there were a 40 per cent marginal tax rate on income and interest on borrowing money to buy a home were tax-deductible, then an individual has an incentive to borrow until the marginal benefit falls to 60 pence per pound borrowed. The tax creates an incentive to give up a pound for something that is only worth 60 pence. In this way it creates a dead-weight loss of 40 pence on each pound spent.

Feldstein argued that excess burden must be measured by focusing on the elasticity of demand for tax-favoured goods (i.e. the elasticity of demand for activities which reduce an individual's tax bill) with respect to the net of tax price of such activities. Using this elasticity, he reports that the excess burden per additional dollar of tax revenue raised for the US tax system in 1994 was $1.65. With every dollar raised costing a marginal excess burden of $1.65, the total cost of raising a dollar of tax revenue would be $2.65. The implication is that without knowledge of this efficiency cost the size of the public sector will be pushed higher than the 'optimum'.

13.2.2 Tax neutrality and tax efficiency

Tax neutrality is not a concept likely to occur in everyday conversation but is a term that will feature in discussions of tax policy. Neutrality aims to minimise the extent to which taxes distort the choices of households and firms. Tax neutrality arises if the same rate of tax is levied on both goods X and Y. In Section 13.2 it was argued that a lump-sum tax would cause no excess burden because the slope of the budget line would not be altered and there would be no substitution effect. Surely, if the same rate of tax were levied on both commodities (i.e. if there were tax neutrality) then it would be as if there were a lump-sum tax (i.e. as if the budget line had been drawn back in a parallel fashion). Tax neutrality implies the same rate of tax on all goods but when leisure is not taxed tax neutrality is not the same as lump-sum taxation. It is therefore unlikely that tax neutrality (as described) will prove optimal. Indeed, optimal tax may require that different rates of tax are levied on different goods.

In Figure 13.4, prior to the introduction of taxation the individual chooses an allocation of income between X and Y at point 3 on indifference curve I_3. If a selective excise tax were levied the budget line would swivel from 1-2 to 1-4 and the new welfare equilibrium would be at 5 (on I_1). If the government were to introduce a lump-sum tax to raise the same amount of tax then the individual would be liable to make a payment to the government irrespective of how many units of goods X or Y were purchased. The lump-sum tax is quite similar to a poll tax; it must be paid whatever the individual chooses to do. A lump-sum tax reduces the individual's income. In Figure 13.4 the impact of a lump-sum tax can be shown by shifting the budget line (1-2) leftwards (in a parallel fashion). Shifting 1-2 inwards to 6-7, it is clear that the same revenue, distance 8-5 (= distance 1-6), can be raised with no excess burden. The cost to the taxpayer is simply the direct cost of the tax payment. Indeed, if the individual were to choose an allocation of income on the budget line 6-7, a tangency point with an indifference curve higher than I_1 is possible. This is point 9 on I_2.

In this way neutral taxation *appears* to act like a lump-sum tax. The same rate of tax is levied on both goods X and Y; there is no change in the slope of the budget line. Instead of the budget line swivelling from 1-2 to 1-4, it simply shifts inwards in a parallel fashion to 6-7. This argument supports a presumption that broad-based taxes (tax levied

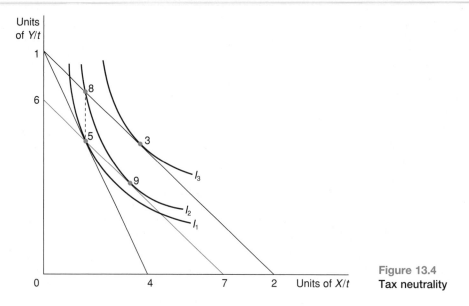

Figure 13.4
Tax neutrality

on all goods and services) is better than narrow-based taxes (taxes levied on only some goods and services).

However, there is a problem if leisure is difficult to tax. Rosen (1999: 329) notes that while neutral taxation is offered as a solution, 'in general, neutral taxation is *not* efficient'. The reason is that while (in Figure 13.4) taxation is neutral between goods X and Y, there are other distortions because leisure is not taxed.

One 'good' which an individual enjoys is leisure time. If goods X and Y are substitutes with leisure time, distortion will arise (even though taxation is neutral between goods X and Y). Individuals forgo leisure time (by working) to earn income to purchase good X and/or good Y. The taxes on goods X and Y make leisure time relatively less expensive. To avoid distortion the same rate of tax must also be levied on leisure time. The problem is that it is difficult in practice to tax leisure time – how can it be identified?

The question is how should tax rates be set if one good (leisure time) cannot be identified and taxed? Assume government must raise revenue and can only levy taxes on X and Y. In Figure 13.5 the horizontal axis measures the amount of revenue that is required (0_X-0_Y). The vertical axis MBT_X records the marginal burden of tax when more revenue is raised from a tax on X. If £1 revenue were raised the marginal burden of tax exceeds one pound because there is an excess burden. Indeed, the more that the tax rate is increased on good X the greater the marginal burden. The vertical axis MBT_Y provides similar information for good Y. The more that revenue is raised by taxing good Y the higher the marginal burden of the tax will be.

To minimise efficiency costs it is necessary to equate marginal burdens. In Figure 13.5 this will occur as 0_X-m^* is raised from taxing X and 0_Y-m^* revenue is raised from a tax on Y. If another outcome were considered (e.g. 0-m^{**}) the burden of taxation would be a greater (e.g. by area 1-2-3). Excess burdens arise as individuals substitute away from the taxed goods, e.g. towards leisure time.

The optimal tax rates to levy are the rates that arise when marginal burden of tax on good X and good Y are equal. From Section 13.2.2 this will occur when:

$$MBT_X = \frac{1}{(1 - \tau_X) \cdot e_X} = MBT_Y = \frac{1}{(1 - \tau_Y) \cdot e_Y} \tag{13.12}$$

or

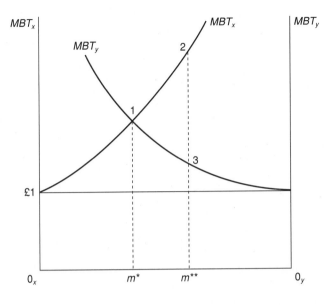

Figure 13.5
Optimal commodity taxation

$$\tau_X = \frac{MBT_X - 1}{MBT_X} \cdot \frac{1}{e_X} = \tau_Y = \frac{MBT_Y - 1}{MBT_Y} \cdot \frac{1}{e_Y} \tag{13.13}$$

Equation (13.13) states that the tax rate will be higher for goods with a low price elasticity of demand. This is referred to as the *Ramsey rule* (or 'inverse elasticity rule'). It is called the Ramsey rule following the analysis of Frank Ramsey (1927). Throughout, it is assumed that the goods are 'independent' (i.e. the cross partial derivatives $\partial q_X / \partial P_Y = 0$). The rule can be expressed as

$$e_X \cdot \tau_X = e_Y \cdot \tau_Y = \frac{MBT - 1}{MBT}. \tag{13.14}$$

and this states that the percentage fall in the amount demanded for each good should be equal. Remember, from Chapter 2, that $e_X = \partial Q_X / Q_X$ divided by $\partial P_X / P_X$. This is multiplied by $\tau_X = \partial P_X / P_X$. Therefore $e_X \cdot \tau_X = \partial Q_X / Q_X$. The same applies in the case of $e_Y \cdot \tau_Y$ which is equal to $\partial Q_Y / Q_Y$. Therefore the optimum tax rates apply when $\partial Q_X / Q_X = \partial Q_Y / Q_Y$. It follows that tax neutrality (uniform tax rates on goods) is not optimal. Optimal tax rates (that minimise excess burden) exist when proportionate change in quantity demanded is equal across goods and services.

13.2.3 Broad-based versus narrow-based taxes

Tax neutrality is not optimal when leisure cannot be taxed. However, an implication that seems implicit in tax neutrality is that broad-based taxation is preferable to narrow-based taxation. Some considerable time ago, Musgrave (1959: 157) observed that 'we are left with the common-sense view that the excess burden of more general taxes tends to be smaller than that of selective taxes'.

One way to demonstrate that broad-based taxation is likely to be a preferable alternative to narrow-based taxation is to return to the marginal welfare costs of taxation. It has been argued that as the tax rate on any good increases the marginal burden of taxation increases more than proportionately. In Figure 13.6(a) demand for good X is shown as D and price (with no taxation) is P_1. Initially, a tax is levied on good X and price with the tax increases to P_1. The deadweight loss (excess burden) is equal to triangle c. Assume

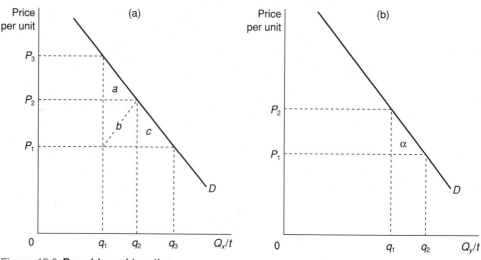

Figure 13.6 **Broad-based taxation**

now that the government doubles the tax so that price increases to P_2. Excess burden now equals areas $a + b + c$.

If, alternatively, the government had put a tax on good Y then in panel (b) of Figure 13.6 there is excess burden of area α. The option of putting a tax on Y (broadening the tax base) as compared with increasing the tax on X (maintaining a narrow-based tax) means that efficiency loss has only increased by α rather than by $a + b$. (If the goods are independent it is possible to add these deadweight losses and report that efficiency loss of broad-based taxation is $c + \alpha$ instead of $a + b + c$.)

When the supply and demand curves are linear the excess burden is proportional to the square of the tax rate (Bruce 1997). Consider Figure 13.6(a) once again. When the tax rate is doubled excess burden increases by a factor of four – two squared (when the tax rate is doubled area $b = 2c$ so that $a + b + c = 4c$).

Tax analysts are conscious of the advantages of broad-based taxation. Consider tax reform in the late 1980s and early 1990s in the UK (Swift 1993):

1. Some goods in the UK were zero-rated for Value Added Tax (e.g. food, gas, electricity, coal, newspapers, books, transport and clothing for young children). In 1993 the Chancellor of the Exchequer announced that VAT at the standard rate would be applied to fuel. This may reflect concern for efficiency (but the attempt to extend taxation was attacked on equity grounds – pensioners spend a much larger fraction of their income on fuel).
2. Tax reform required that 'fringe benefits' (or benefits 'in kind' – the use of a company car and other such 'perks') be taxed. The 1993 budget changed the basis for assessing the benefit to an employee of a company car to set this in terms of the value of the vehicle (rather than its engine capacity) and this reduced the tax advantages of a company car.
3. In the UK, when money was borrowed to buy a house (a mortgage) it attracted tax relief on the interest payments (by contrast, money borrowed for other purpose might not be as generously treated). Steps were taken first to reduce and then to remove this tax benefit.

13.2.4 Other criteria than efficiency

While the discussion so far has placed great emphasis on how microeconomic analysis identifies the costs of taxation, it should be emphasised (as noted at the opening of the chapter) that there are other concerns:

1. Efficiency costs (estimated as excess burden) are not the only costs when raising taxation. For example, there are also administrative costs (i.e. the costs to the government of collecting taxes) and compliance costs (e.g. the costs of time and effort to the taxpayer in terms of filling in forms, etc.). A study by Sandford *et al.* (1989) showed that UK administration and measurable compliance costs were over £5 billion for the tax year 1986–87 and this represented 4 per cent of total tax revenue. In the case of corporation tax, administrative and compliance costs were 0.56 per cent of revenue (see also Hudson and Godwin 2000). Some taxes might perform well in terms of excess burden but may be more costly to administer.

2. Throughout the analysis above there is reason to be concerned about issues of 'second best' (see Chapter 6). Take, for example, the possible existence of an externality. Assume consumption of commodity *X* (e.g. tobacco, leaded petrol) creates an external cost for other individuals. In this case, analysis in Chapter 4 indicates that a tax on the specific ('polluting') product may be required to increase efficiency (economists refer to a double dividend in that revenue is raised when efficiency is increased).

3. Reference has already been made to merit goods (see Chapter 5) and some demerit goods (e.g. alcoholic drink) may be subject to heavier taxation.

4. As already noted, equity concerns are always present. A lump-sum tax was identified as one that would not impose efficiency costs. However, it is difficult to imagine that, on equity grounds, the same tax should be paid by the rich as by the poor!

While more will be said about these issues in other sections, these points are noted here to emphasise that efficiency of tax systems is unlikely to be the only concern.

13.3 Tax incidence: specific and *ad valorem* taxes

Neoclassical economic theory shows that the 'costs of taxation' are not simply the tax payments that are made to the tax collector. The costs of taxation are likely to exceed the tax revenue raised. However, neoclassical microeconomic theory also reveals that the incidence of taxation is also not obvious. The person who pays a tax may not be the person who bears the full burden of the tax. *Legal* incidence (responsibility to pay tax) may differ from *economic* incidence of tax.

The objective in this section is to highlight difficulties that arise when identifying the incidence of tax. In this section the first piece of analysis shows, more formally, the importance of price elasticities of demand and supply in competitive markets. Thereafter, the focus is on the importance of market structure. To deal with the importance of market structure, the question posed is whether the incidence of sales taxation differs as between an *ad valorem* tax and a per-unit (specific) tax. In Section 13.2 it was stated that an *ad valorem* tax is a tax whereby, for every pound that the consumer spends the government keeps a fraction (*t*); while a specific (or unit) tax requires that a specified amount *T* is collected per unit of output.[4] Does it matter whether the tax is levied on the producer or on the consumer?

(a) *Specific taxes: competitive markets*

In Figure 13.7 producers of a good are legally liable to pay a specific per-unit tax on output (i.e. a tax that is set as a fixed amount of payment per unit of tobacco, or per gallon of petrol, etc.). However, if the producer must pay the tax, the producers' costs increase. This is illustrated in part (a) of the figure by the shift of the supply curve from *S* to S_t. (The vertical distance between *S* and S_t measures the tax payment *t* per unit of the good.)

4. For any product, a tax *T* of say 50 pence per unit is charged.

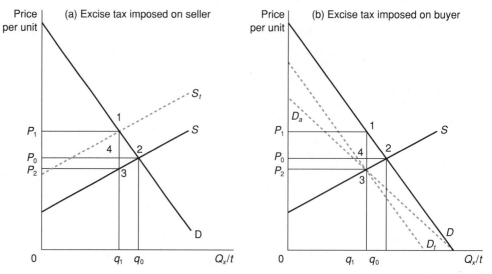

Figure 13.7 Specific taxes and competitive markets

The demand curve D slopes down from left to right, and when S shifts to S_t the price of the good to the consumer will rise. In Figure 13.7(a) the price increases from P_0 to P_1. The deadweight loss of the tax is measured by triangle 1-2-3. The tax revenue raised is P_2-P_1-1-3. However, closer inspection of area P_2-P_1-1-3 reveals that part of the revenue is met by a reduction in consumer surplus of P_1-1-4-P_0. This part of tax revenue has been paid by consumers in the form of higher prices, enabling the producer to raise the money to pay the tax. The remaining part of the tax revenue P_0-4-3-P_2 is a reduction of producer surplus. In legal terms the producer is liable for the tax but part of the cost of the tax has been 'passed on' to consumers.

If demand for the good were perfectly price-inelastic, the price of the good would increase by the full amount of the tax. Legally the producer would be liable for the tax payment but in practice the tax cost would be passed on fully to the consumer. If the price elasticity of demand were infinity, there would be no increase in price created by the shift in the supply curve. However, it is not only the price elasticity of demand that is relevant. For example, if the demand curve slopes down from left to right and the price elasticity of supply were infinite, all of the burden of the tax would be met by the consumer in the form of a higher price for the good.

How do price elasticity of demand and price elasticity of supply interact to determine tax incidence? The price that the consumer (demander) pays (P_1 in Figure 13.7(a)) will be referred to as P_d. The price that the producer (supplier) would require, if there were no tax to pay (P_2 in Figure 13.7(a)), will be referred to as P_s. The difference between P_d and P_s is the tax T per unit. Following Hyman (1999),

$$P_d - P_s = T \tag{13.15}$$

so that:

$$dP_d - dP_s = dT \tag{13.16}$$

In Figure 13.7(a), the distance q_0 to q_1, i.e. the change in quantity demanded, depends upon the change in price to consumers, $P_1 - P_0$ (i.e. dP_d) and the slope of the demand curve, D. Similarly, the distance $q_0 - q_1$ can be estimated as the change in the supply price, $P_0 - P_2$ (i.e. dP_s) multiplied by the slope of the supply curve (i.e. S_p). Therefore:

$$dQ_d = D_p dP_d \tag{13.17}$$

$$dQ_s = S_p dP_s = S_p(dP_d - dT) \tag{13.18}$$

$$dQ_d = dQ_s \tag{13.19}$$

It follows that:

$$D_p dP_d = S_p dP_d - S_p dT \tag{13.20}$$

$$dP_d(S_p - D_p) = S_p\, dT \tag{13.21}$$

$$\frac{dP_d}{dT} = \frac{S_p}{S_p - D_p} \tag{13.22}$$

Starting from an initial, no-tax, position and assuming a small tax rate change, this expression can be rewritten. To express this in terms of price elasticities, it is necessary to divide the numerator and denominator of this expression by P/Q. In this case:

$$\frac{dP_d}{dT} = \frac{e_s}{e_s - e_d} \tag{13.23}$$

where e_s and e_d are the price elasticities of supply and demand, respectively.

If $e_d = 0$ (demand is perfectly inelastic), the rise in price for the consumer is equal to $1(dP_d/dT = 1)$. If $e_d = $ infinity (demand is infinitely elastic), $dP_s/dt = 1$, since by similar manipulation:

$$\frac{dP_s}{dT} = \frac{e_d}{e_s - e_d}. \tag{13.24}$$

The question of who pays the tax cannot then be answered without information about the price elasticity of demand and the price elasticity of supply. The burden of the tax need not fall on the party responsible legally for paying the tax.

The same outcome occurs if tax is imposed on the buyer. In Figure 13.7(b), for the purposes of comparison, suppose that the consumer must pay the tax. Now the demand curve shifts inward to D_t. At the new equilibrium only part of the payment goes to the seller – the rest goes to the Treasury. The share of the tax paid by the consumer and the share paid by the producer are the same in both cases. In Figure 13.7(b), as we assume that the tax falls on the consumer, the after-tax price received by the producer has fallen by the extent of the per-unit tax. An inspection of the relevant areas in this part of the figure confirms that the burden of the tax between consumers and producers is identical to that in part (a).

(b) Ad valorem *taxes: competitive market*

When an *ad valorem* tax is levied the effects are similar. While the impact of the specific tax is easily shown by a shift in demand from D to D_s in Figure 13.7(b) the impact of the *ad valorem* tax can be shown by the shift from D to D_a. The tax collected per unit of output is P multiplied by the number of units sold and in Figure 13.7(b) this will be equal to the tax revenue when a selective tax per unit is levied (i.e. areas P_2-P_1-1-3). The incidence of an *ad valorem* tax is shared between consumers and producers in exactly the same way. The rate of the *ad valorem* tax has been set so that the same tax revenue is raised and the impact on market equilibrium price is identical to that for the specific tax. The deadweight loss (area 1-2-3) is exactly the same.

(c) *Specific taxes: monopoly*

Figure 13.8 compares the effects of a specific tax and an *ad valorem* tax when the producer is a monopoly. Once again, the comparison is one in which the impact of the tax is to reduce output by the same amount (i.e. from 0-q_0 to 0-q_1).

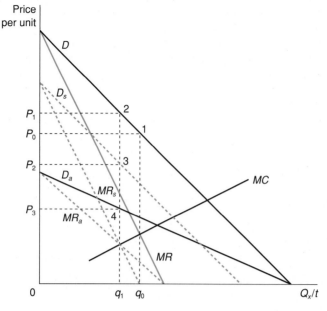

Figure 13.8
Ad valorem v. selective tax and monopoly

Prior to the imposition of a specific tax, the firm maximises profit by equating marginal cost and marginal revenue at output $0\text{-}q_0$ and price $0\text{-}P_0$. When a specific tax (T), equal to $0\text{-}P_1 - 0\text{-}P_2$ per unit, is levied, the demand curve shifts from D to D_s. Output falls to $0\text{-}q_1$ and tax revenue of $P_2\text{-}P_1\text{-}2\text{-}3$ is raised.

(d) Ad valorem *tax: monopoly*

The effects of an *ad valorem* tax can be identified in Figure 13.8 by examining the shift in the demand curve from D to D_a. The profit-maximising output is again $0\text{-}q_1$ and the price charged is $0\text{-}P_1$. However, it is clear that the government raises greater revenue for any reduction in output by using the *ad valorem* tax. The revenue raised is now $P_3\text{-}P_1\text{-}2\text{-}4$ which is $P_3\text{-}P_2\text{-}3\text{-}4$ greater than the revenue raised when the government relied on a specific tax.

In conditions of monopoly there is a difference in the outcome if there is reliance on a specific tax as compared with an *ad valorem* tax. As it is the case that, in practice, governments tend to rely more heavily on *ad valorem* taxes than specific taxes, Perloff (1999) argues that governments can get things right!

In conclusion it can be said that the economic incidence (burden) of taxation may differ from the legal (statutory) incidence of taxation. The difference depends on price elasticity of demand and price elasticity of supply (as indicated in Chapter 7). However, market structure also proves an important consideration when deciding tax policy.[5] Predictions drawn from microeconomic theory depend sensitively on how the problem is modelled.

13.4 Taxation and incentives

One area of the economics of taxation has attracted considerable attention in recent years. This is the impact of taxation on incentives. In recent years supply-side economists have argued that a cut in the rate of income taxation will increase work effort. To many,

---

5. There would be a difference in the effects of a specific tax and an *ad valorem* tax which reduced output by the same amount in any imperfect market structure (e.g. oligopoly).

the relationship seems obvious! If individuals take home more of their income they will be prepared to work longer hours. On both sides of the Atlantic the 1980s saw tax reforms which reduced the basic rate of tax and the higher rates of tax. For example, in 1979 when Margaret Thatcher became Prime Minister the basic rate of income tax in the UK was 33% and the top rate of income tax was 83% (98% if income came from invest-ment). By 1990 the basic rate of tax was 25% and the top rate of income tax was 40%. The government explained that reduced income tax would increase work effort, increase incentives and increase output in the economy. Does microeconomic theory support this proposition?

13.4.1 How much will theory predict?

In Figure 13.9 (which can be compared with Figure 13.2(a)) the budget line is 1-2 and the initial welfare maximum is tangency point 3 on indifference curve I_2. A proportional income tax is levied which means that, after tax, the budget line is 1-4. The new welfare maximum is tangency point 8 on indifference curve I_1. (The curve *PCC* is the price consumption curve.) The tax has caused the individual to work less hard. The individual initially consumed $0\text{-}L_0$ hours of leisure (and therefore worked $1\text{-}L_0$ hours). After tax, the individual prefers to have $0\text{-}L_1$ hours of leisure and to work $1\text{-}L_1$ hours. The tax has acted as a disincentive to work.

However, looking at the analysis more closely it is possible to identify two effects. First, an income effect. The tax reduces the individual's income. This income effect is illus-trated by drawing a budget line parallel to 1-2 at a tangent to indifference curve I_1. At point 8 the individual experiences the same level of welfare as if the tax had been levied. The impact of this reduction in income is seen by reference to the income consumption curve *ICC*. It is clear that leisure is a *normal* good (see Chapter 7). As income falls the indi-vidual consumes less leisure.

Second, there is a substitution effect. The change in the price of leisure creates both an income and a substitution effect. The change in price causes the movement from point

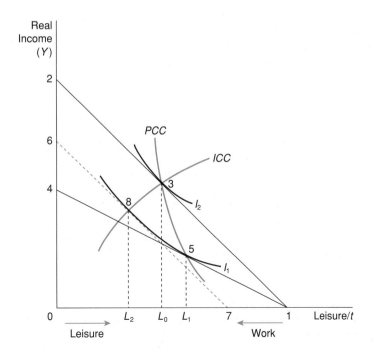

Figure 13.9
Income tax and labour supply

3 to 5 and the income effect is the movement from point 3 to 8. It follows that the movement around the indifference curve I_1 from 8 to 5 is the substitution effect. The substitution effect arises because the income tax alters relative prices. It makes leisure less expensive. Staying away from work is less costly because the tax collector takes part of what would be earned. The substitution effect is always in favour of the cheaper good and hence the movement from point 8 to point 5 (in favour of more leisure).

In the example shown the income effect is more than offset by the substitution effect. The income effect is an incentive effect (to work more hours). The substitution effect acts as a disincentive effect (to work less hours). As the substitution effect is greater there are less hours worked. However, it is a simple matter to move the new tangency point (5) to the left of L_0 and to illustrate a position in which individuals work more hours after the tax. This situation would be one in which the income effect is not offset by the substitution effect. It cannot be said *a priori* that an income tax will reduce the number of hours worked. It may or it may not, depending on the relative strengths of the substitution and income effects. Similarly, it cannot be said *a priori* that a removal (or reduction) of income tax will cause individuals to work harder. It may or it may not, depending on the relative strengths of the income and substitution effects.

The separation of income and substitution effects is possible by looking at the way in which a change in wages W (possibly as a result of taxation) affects hours worked. The change comprises the two effects; a substitution (s) and an income (y) effect. If the only tax is a proportional income tax and changes in a proportional income tax cause changes in the wage (W) that individuals receive, the income effect (y) and the substitution effect (s) can be identified. The change in hours worked, as a consequence of a change in the proportional rate of tax (which causes a change in W) will depend on both effects:

$$\frac{\partial H}{\partial W} = \frac{\partial H_s}{\partial W} + \frac{\partial H_y}{\partial W} \tag{13.25}$$

The term ∂W can be expressed as the change in income (Y) divided by hours worked (H), so that substituting $\partial Y/H$ for ∂W in the final term of (13.25) and multiplying all terms by W/H yields:

$$\frac{\partial H}{\partial W}\frac{W}{H} = \frac{\partial H_s}{\partial W}\frac{W}{H} + \frac{\partial H_y}{(\partial Y/H)}\frac{W}{H} \tag{13.26}$$

Multiplying the top and bottom of the final terms by Y yields:

$$\frac{\partial H}{\partial W}\frac{W}{H} = \frac{\partial H_s}{\partial W}\frac{W}{H} + \frac{\partial H_y}{\partial Y}\frac{Y}{H}\frac{WH}{Y} \tag{13.27}$$

This equation says that the (uncompensated) elasticity of supply of labour with respect to wages is equal to a substitution elasticity (the elasticity of compensated supply) plus an income elasticity weighted by the share of income coming from hours of work.[6]

Analysis of the effects of taxation on incentives is pursued with reference to the way tax affects the budget line. Usually individuals are able to retain a fixed ('tax-free') slice of income without taxation. In Figure 13.10(a) the initial real wage is W_0/P_0 (captured as the tangent of the marked angle) and leisure hours per period are recorded on the *x*-axis with real income on the *y*-axis. With no income taxation, equilibrium is found at point 1 on I_1. There is the introduction of a tax system with a tax-free slice (Y_e) that is exempt income and thereafter a single tax rate t. This is referred to as a *degressive tax*

---

6. See Chapter 8 for further discussion of the uncompensated and compensated supply of labour – it will be noted that the compensated supply of labour depends on the assumption that income is constant so that it reflects the substitution effect.

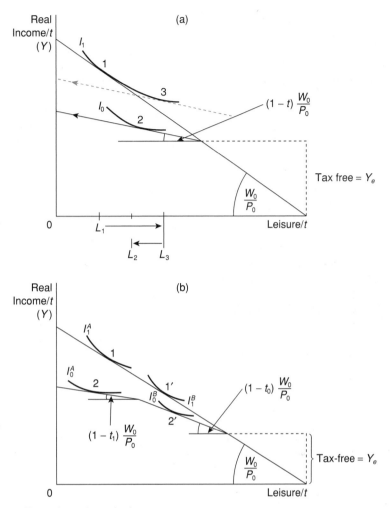

Figure 13.10 Tax reform: introducing tax structures

system. Once Y_e is exceeded, earnings per hour are $(1 - t)W_0/P_0$ and this represents the new lower opportunity cost of leisure. The individual now chooses point 2 on I_0 which, given the discussion above, must be the product of an income and substitution effect. If the pre-tax income level (I_1) were held constant by shifting the segment of the after-tax budget line above Y_e to the right, this picks out point 3 on I_1. With reference to I_1 the substitution effect is the movement from point 1 to point 3. If there were no income effect the individual would choose more leisure (L_1-L_3). However, the tax also creates an income effect (the movement from point 3 to point 2). As leisure is a normal good the reduction in income created by the tax reduces the demand for leisure (from L_3-L_2). The introduction of a degressive tax system (with a slice of tax-free income) might increase individuals' demand for leisure. However, this is only one illustration (it would be easy to locate point 2 to the left of point 1 and the prediction would be more work hours – less leisure hours – as the income effect outweighs the tendency to substitute in favour of leisure).

Figure 13.10(b) illustrates how the budget line changes when the tax arrangement becomes further complicated. The tax structure permits a tax-free slice, Y_e, but now has two tax rates $(t_0 > t_1)$. Here the indifference map for two individuals A and B is illustrated. Individual A moves from point 1 on I_1^A to point 2 on I_0^A choosing less leisure (increasing work hours). Individual B moves from point 1' on I_1^B to point 2' on I_0^B choosing more leisure (decreasing work hours). Again, there is no clear-cut prediction.

For further implications of more complex tax arrangements see Appendix 13.

13.4.2 Can nothing be said?

The following examples consider the application of microeconomics to assess changes in tax arrangements (i.e. an application when a tax system pre-exists). The analysis above highlights the difficulty of making predictions when an income tax is introduced. Can anything more definite be said of analysis when there are changes to income tax arrangements?

In the following example the Chancellor decides to present a tax reduction and chooses to provide this by an increase in tax allowances. Will work effort increase or decrease? Once again, analysis proceeds by tracking the impact of tax reform on the budget line faced by a representative individual. In this case, there will be an increase in the tax-free slice from Y_e to Y_e'. As can be seen from observation of Figure 13.11(a), this change only produces an income effect. Surely if there is only an income effect it will be possible to present unambiguous predictions? If leisure is a 'normal good', more will unambiguously be chosen as the individual depicted moves from a point like 1 to a point like 2 on their income expansion path, involving an increase in utility from I_0 to I_1. Note that the tax rate is unchanged at t_0.

This prediction is clear for full-time workers but there is a caveat. The tax system puts a kink in the budget line, what happens at the kink?

(i)   In Figure 13.11(b) the same tax reform is introduced; however, the individual initially found equilibrium at a 'corner solution' (i.e. at point 1). The tax reform (increasing tax allowances) means that the individual moves to a new corner solution (at point 2). Utility increases from I_0 to I_1. Under both regimes zero tax is paid but, with the new tax threshold, less leisure is chosen (more work hours undertaken). This type of equilibrium is thought typical of part-time workers.

(ii) In Figure 13.11(c) the increase in tax allowances changes the situation for an individual. The individual initially pays tax but after the increase in tax allowances the individual pays no tax. The individual moves from a tax-paying equilibrium at point 1 on I_0 to a non-tax-paying equilibrium at point 2 on I_1.

It follows that the analysis in Figure 13.11(a) focused only on those who pay tax both before and after the tax reform. With this proviso, an increase in tax allowances can be analysed simply in terms of an income effect and it is possible to predict that, for this cohort, the reform will reduce work incentives; leisure will increase when leisure is a normal good.

Turning now to changes in the rate of tax, Figure 13.12(a) illustrates the indifference map for two individuals A and B. Individual A moves from point 1 on I_0^A to point 2 on I_1^A choosing less leisure (increasing work hours). Individual B moves from point 1' on I_0^B to point 2' on I_1^B choosing more leisure (decreasing work hours). Here both income and substitution effects are relevant; there is no clear-cut prediction.

In Figure 13.12(b) there is a tax-free slice of income, followed by a two-tax system. In this example, the first tax rate of a two-tax rate system is reduced (see Figure 13.12(b)). For equilibria that occur on the first changed tax rate segment would involve repeating the analysis of part (a). In the instance where the second tax includes the initial equilibrium like point 1 on I_0, then the posited tax reform produces only an income effect and a new equilibrium like point 2 on I_1 on the individual's income expansion path involving more leisure, and fewer work hours is predicted.

In general, clear predictions from indifference curve analysis of the introduction and reform of tax systems are difficult to achieve, accentuating the interest in empirical

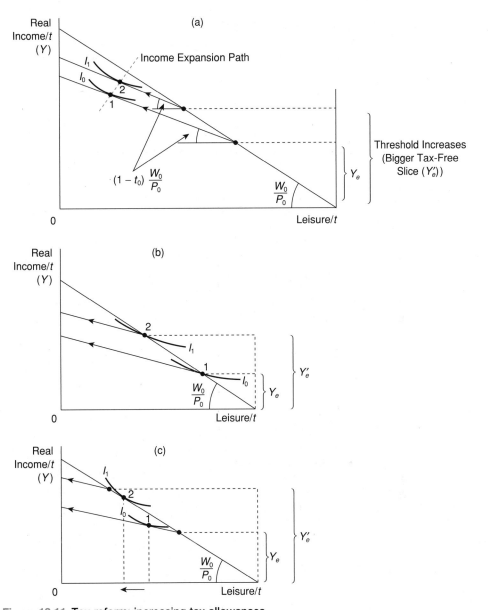

Figure 13.11 **Tax reform: increasing tax allowances**

evidence and intensifying debate in an area where individuals tend to think increasing (reducing) direct taxation reduces (increases) work hours.

An instance in which it is possible to predict the response to a tax reform is when the income and the substitution effect (of a change in tax) work in the same direction. Take the case shown in Figure 13.13. This example considers the impact of the introduction of a negative income tax. Initially, the budget line is shown as 1-2 and the welfare maximum is at the tangency point 3 on I_0. A negative tax proposal is introduced, by which individuals below an income y_i receive a transfer (equal to distance 1-4) from the government and then pay tax on all earned income at a proportional rate t. This negative tax reform alters the budget line to 1-4-5 and the new tangency point is 6 on I_1. The substitution effect is found by drawing a budget line (dashed) with the same slope as 1-2

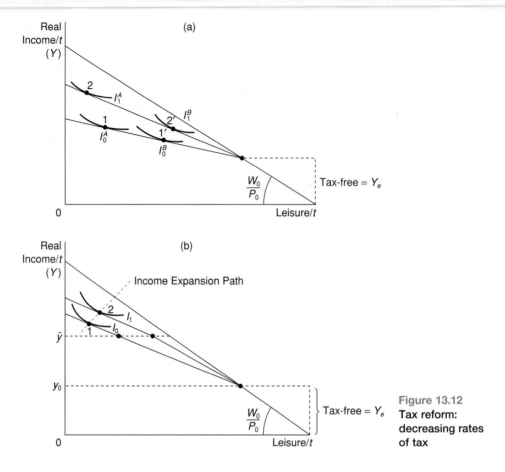

Figure 13.12
Tax reform: decreasing rates of tax

to the right to a tangency with the new indifference curve I_1. The income effect is shown by the shift along the income consumption curve ICC. Thereafter, the substitution effect of the tax reform is shown by the shift between points 7 and 6. As can be seen, the income effect is apparent in terms of an increase in leisure (as this is a normal good).

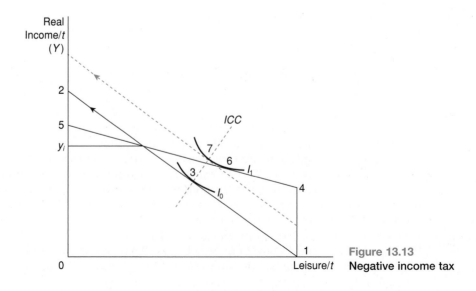

Figure 13.13
Negative income tax

While the substitution effect moves in the same direction (as the price of leisure has fallen, lowered compensation for each hour of work). In this case, it can be shown that the negative income tax will increase the demand for leisure for those who are recipients of the tax. This is an example of a case when microeconomic theory yields a consistent conclusion: both income and substitution effects move in the same direction, indicating more leisure and fewer work hours.

13.4.3 Income taxation and work effort: some empirical issues

If everything usually depends on the evidence, how are empirical studies undertaken? Before considering empirical tests it is important to note that, while the focus has been on work hours, high marginal rates of income tax may also induce other responses (as discussed in Section 13.2.2). For example, there may be a movement into untaxed areas or into jobs with high non-monetary return attributes. There may be career changes. There may be little change in hours worked but changes in the quality of labour supplied.

Atkinson and Stiglitz (1980) survey various empirical approaches:

(i) *Surveys of attitudes.* Individuals are asked their responses to higher taxes on earnings. However, even if couched in sophisticated designs, surveys have weaknesses:
   - They are 'hypothetical' and do not correspond to actual behaviour;
   - Respondents may act 'strategically' or tell the interviewer what they think he or she wants to hear;
   - Results are often open to many interpretations and it is often difficult to extend results to produce a reliable quantitative answer in terms of hours worked.

   With these caveats in mind, Table 13.1 provides examples of the results of surveys of high-income earners. These surveys were targeted on the more sensitive sections of the community. Accountants and lawyers are more likely to have knowledge of tax rates and changes in tax rates and, if self-employed, they are more able to adjust the hours that they work. The striking conclusion is that the net impact of income tax changes is negligible. The incentive effect of taxes (the income effect) almost completely offsets the disincentive effect (the substitution effect). (Note that the findings of Fields and Stanbury (1970) are criticised for flaws in questionnaire design; within the questionnaire, respondents were alerted to the likely disincentive effects of income taxation before they were asked their response to changes in tax rates – Brown (1983)).

   One of the most referenced studies of low-income workers is that of Brown and Levin (1974). Their results confirm that for low-income workers the elasticity of supply of labour with respect to tax changes is low.

(ii) *Experimental work.* The most cited example of experiments is experiments in the USA where matching households were assigned to different groups presented with different tax rates on which to order their lives. Behaviour in the different experimental groups was then compared with that of the households that continued on

Table 13.1 Income tax and labour supply: questionnaire/interview studies

Study	Subjects	% reporting incentive effects of taxes	% reporting disincentive effects
Break (1957)	UK solicitors and accountants	10	13
Fields and Stanbury (1970)	UK solicitors and accountants	11	19
Brown and Sandford (1991)	UK accountants	6	6

Source: Based on Brown and Jackson (1990; Table 17.3, p. 446).

the tax system that currently existed in the US. Experimental evidence is also open to criticisms.

- It is argued that those under study are aware they are part of a short-run experiment and therefore are less likely to act 'naturally' and signal their long-run responses (a 'Hawthorn effect').
- Experimental design in any area of research is always open to criticisms concerning sample size, length of time of the experiment, composition and interpretation of the results. Neuberg (1989) is an author who has considered this type of work in detail.

This said, results are comparable with the conclusions from questionnaire analysis. For example Watts and Horner (1977: 58)[7] report:

'The overall responses to tax rates that (on average) cut net wages in half and to income guarantees that were equal to a substantial fraction of pre-experimental income are barely deducible, and could be interpreted as being so minor that further analysis is unwarranted. Further analysis was, however, carried out and tended to confirm prior hypotheses about the direction of response and to support previous non-experimental findings of low elasticities of labour supply for prime age male breadwinners.'

(iii) *Econometric analysis of observed behaviour* in the form of a time series or a cross-section of individuals, industries or regions, comes not from taxation directly but from hours of work supplied at different wages net of tax – which, of course, is not quite the question at hand. If people act differently in response to changes in tax as compared with changes in earnings *per se* this would be a concern.

One type of regression equation employed to give empirical content to the question of taxation and labour supply hours (*H*) is:

$$H = a_0 + a_1 W + a_2 N + \sum_{i=3}^{n} a_i X_i + u \qquad (13.30)$$

where

$a_0, \ldots, a_n$ = coefficients to be estimated;
W = wage rate;
N = income from non-labour sources;
X_i = a vector of variables introduced to allow for other differences between individuals in the sample apart from their wage and non-labour income;
u = randomly distributed error term.

The estimates of a_1 and a_2 are a source of the substitution and income derivatives in equation (13.30), which, when combined with the mean values for *H*, *W* and *Y* in the sample, can give the three elasticities in (13.27). The use of large data sets and sophisticated econometric techniques is impressive but invariably proceeds only in the face of technical difficulties that weaken confidence in the results.

The study by Kosters (1969) which followed these lines was criticised on two counts:

(i) First, that the equation was incorrectly specified (the value of *W* used was income divided by hours worked and average – rather than marginal – wage was used).

(ii) Second, there was endogeneity bias (as the value of *H* depends on the random error term, *W* was not independent). A number of successive studies (e.g. Brown *et al.* 1976) improved on early work.

Table 13.2 (from Blundell 1992) reviews the results of such studies.

7. As cited in Brown (1983).

Table 13.2 Income tax and labour supply: econometric evidence

	Study	Sample	Own wage elasticity, uncompensated	Own wage elasticity, compensated	Total income elasticity
MEN	Blundell and Walker (1982)	UK	−0.23	0.13	−0.36
	Ashworth and Ulph (1981)	UK	−0.33	0.29	−0.62
	Hausman (1981)	US	0.03	0.95	−0.98
WOMEN	Blundell and Walker				
	Children 0		0.43	0.65	−0.22
	1		0.10	0.32	−0.22
	3		−0.19	0.03	−0.22
	Layard, Baritone and Zabalza		0.44	0.63	−0.19
	Ashworth and Ulph		0.32	0.55	−0.23
	Zabalza		1.59	1.82	−0.23
	Cogan (1981)	US	0.65	0.68	−0.03
	Hausman (1981)	US	0.45	0.9	−0.45
	Arrufat and Zabalza (1986)	UK	0.62	0.68	−0.06
	Blundell and Walker	UK			
	No children		0.43	0.65	−0.22
	One child		0.10	0.32	−0.22
	Arellano and Meghir	UK			
	No children		0.37	0.44	−0.13
	Young Children		0.29	0.50	−0.40
	Old children		0.71	0.82	−0.21

Source: Blundell (1992).

Table 13.2 describes the relevant elasticities for men, married women and lone mothers. The own uncompensated elasticities capture the difference between the total income effect and compensated wage elasticities. The total income elasticities are all negative, indicating that leisure is a 'normal good' (as income rises more leisure is demanded and fewer hours of work supplied). The compensated wage elasticities reflect the substitution effect so that, as increases in taxation induce a higher opportunity cost of leisure, less leisure (and more work hours) are chosen, i.e. a positive elasticity is generated. Given the arrangement of signs it is their relative magnitudes that matter in determining the overall impact of tax changes on work effort.

Most of the studies for married women (with positive uncompensated elasticity) indicate increased work effort if tax rates were lowered. Often, the estimated uncompensated wage elasticities for husbands (males generally) are small and negative, i.e. a mildly backward-bending aggregate labour supply curve. The results for lone mothers suggest relatively large uncompensated elasticities, which are thought to reflect mainly a 'labour force participation' (rather than 'work hour') adjustment effect.[8]

The results of empirical work have always been less dramatic than anticipated. Evidence does not indicate that labour supply is very sensitive to taxation. Of course, as noted at the outset, the supply of labour is a multi-dimensional concept and the effect of taxation on labour supply may show up as: less effort while at work; emigration; longer holidays; shorter working life; different occupational choices; and associated human capital acquisition.

8. Blundell (1992) adds to this by emphasising the importance of microsimulation analysis which (via the use of a very large number of data points) allows the consideration of different individuals with different marginal effective tax rates and other incomes, i.e. associating individual labour supply responses with their corresponding marginal effective tax rates.

However, there are other reasons why labour supply may not be sensitive to changes in tax:

(i) Individuals may not work only for pecuniary rewards. Job satisfaction or prestige associated with a particular occupation may be important and these factors are typically ignored.

(ii) Individuals rarely have the control over their work hours that is typically assumed. Hours of work are set for certain occupations (e.g. 40 hours a week); overtime may or may not be an option. For professional workers like solicitors and accountants, there may be greater discretion, but typically the individual's work/leisure choice may be far more constrained.

(iii) The assumption is that individuals are fully aware of tax rates. Empirical work has long cast doubt on this (see e.g. Brown 1968). Solicitors and accountants may have greater awareness of tax rates, but this is less likely for the man in the street. In Brown's 1968 survey only 3 per cent of workers knew the standard rate of tax and only 6 per cent of managers were able to estimate their marginal rate of tax. While Brown's survey indicated that people overestimated the amount of tax paid, a more recent survey by Lewis (1978) confirmed the misperceptions but indicated a general underestimation. Both studies cast doubt on individuals' awareness of *tax changes* and therefore suggest a low labour response.

13.5 Tax evasion: the incentive to be honest

In neoclassical microeconomics the representative individual is self-interested and amoral. Honest behaviour is induced by an appropriate use of incentives rather than a trait that defines the character of the individual. Individuals are predicted only to act honestly when the incentive structure is such that honest behaviour will maximise self-interest (see the discussion of free-riding and the Clarke tax in Chapter 6).

In the context of tax evasion the only concern of *homo economicus* is to maximise self-interest. Only if the expected utility of acting honestly exceeds the net expected utility of acting dishonestly will honest behaviour characterise actions. In the following example (based on the model of Allingham and Sandmo 1972 – see also Cowell 1985 and Pyle, 1991, 1993), this principle is illustrated by analysis of the relative prices of dishonest and honest behaviour. The question under consideration is the amount of income that an individual chooses to declare for taxation. The critical consideration is the relative price of honest behaviour and the way in which a change in parameters affects the relative price of honest behaviour.

The individual's income is Y and the amount that will be declared for taxation is D. The individual can be completely dishonest and declare nothing ($D = 0$) or be completely honest and declare Y. Alternatively the individual can determine the extent to which they will be honest with $D > 0 < Y$.

A proportional income tax (at rate t) will be levied on income that is declared. However, the probability of detection when income is not declared is equal to p and, if detected, undeclared income will be subject to a fine at rate F. This fine (F) will be levied on all income that has not been declared $[Y - D]$.

With D as the level of income declared, then if evasion is successful (i.e. the individual is not caught) net income N is:

$$N = Y - tD \tag{13.31}$$

By comparison, if the individual is caught and the fine is levied, net income is:

$$C = Y - tD - F[Y - D] \tag{13.32}$$

As the rate of fine, F, is greater than the tax rate, t, the individual is worse off if caught.

The problem that the individual faces is to choose the value of D that maximises expected utility (EU), where

$$EU = (1 - p)U(Y - tD) + pU(Y - tD - F[Y - D]) \qquad (13.33)$$

or,

$$EU = (1 - p)U(N) + pU(C) \qquad (13.34)$$

where N is 'not caught income' and C is 'caught income'.

In Figure 13.14 the individual's income if not caught is shown on the horizontal axis. If the individual is honest and declares all income and the amount of income after tax is $(1 - t)Y$. This axis refers to the situation if the individual is not caught.

If the individual is dishonest and not caught the individual retains Y. The vertical axis compares income if *not caught* with income if the individual is *caught*. At point 2 on the 45° line the individual has acted honestly and has nothing to fear if caught. The 45° line reveals that as long as the individual is honest the individual is left with the same income whether or not they are caught. However, in the case in which the individual is dishonest and caught the income of the individual is $Y - F(Y)$ on the vertical axis. In this case, as $F > t$, the individual is worse off.

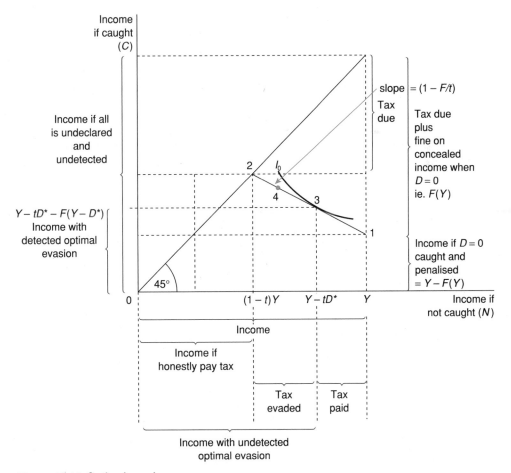

Figure 13.14 Optimal evasion

If the individual is honest and declares all income, then net income is $(1 - t)Y$, i.e. at point 2 in the diagram. If the individual is dishonest, income depends on how much has been declared and on whether the individual is detected. When nothing is declared and the individual is undetected income is recorded as Y on the x-axis of Figure 13.14. However if the individual is detected income will equal $Y - F(Y)$ as recorded on the y-axis. This anchors point 1 (complete dishonesty) as compared with point 2 (complete honesty). The *extent* to which the individual will be honest (the extent to which income will be declared) depends on the options available, as shown by budget line 1-2, and on the utility function of the individual. The individual may choose to declare some optimal level of income (D^*) but less than total income $(Y < D^* > 0)$.

The individual's expected utility function is

$$EU = (1 - p)U(N) + pU(C) \tag{13.35}$$

To find the optimum level of income to declare (D), find the first-order condition of equation (13.35) with respect to D. An interior optimum (i.e. where some income is undeclared) arises for a risk-averse individual when, with reference to equation (13.35):

$$\frac{dEU}{dD} = t(1 - p)\partial U/\partial N - (t - F)p\partial U/\partial C = 0 \tag{13.36}$$

Rewriting this:

$$\frac{-(1 - p)}{p} \frac{\partial U/\partial N}{\partial U/\partial C} = \frac{t - F}{t} \tag{13.37}$$

This condition can be illustrated in Figure 13.14. The slope of line 1-2 in Figure 13.14 is $1 - F/t$ and this illustrates the constrained alternatives open to the individual. At point 2 when everything is declared there is no 'price' to pay for evasion as the individual is honest. At point 1 the individual is completely dishonest and, if caught, the payment is FY to the taxman (instead of tY).

The individual maximises utility at a point of tangency between the indifference curve and the budget line 1-2. If the individual is risk-averse, the indifference curve is convex to the origin. As previously, the slope of the indifference curve can be estimated by setting the total differential to equal zero:

$$dEU = (1 - p)\frac{\partial U}{\partial N} dN + p\frac{\partial U}{\partial C} dC = 0 \tag{13.38}$$

so that:

$$-(1 - p)\frac{\partial U}{\partial N} dN = p\frac{\partial U}{\partial C} dC \tag{13.39}$$

and the slope is

$$\frac{dC}{dN} = \frac{-(1 - p)}{p} \frac{\partial U/\partial N}{\partial U/\partial C} \tag{13.40}$$

Recall N is 'not caught income' and C is 'caught income'.

At a constrained maxima the slope of the indifference curves and the slope of the budget line constraint must be equal, so that

$$\frac{-(1 - p)}{p} \frac{\partial U/\partial N}{\partial U/\partial C} = \frac{t - F}{t}$$

as in equation (13.37). In Figure 13.14 the individual solves the problem of how much to declare at tangency point 3 on I_0. The optimum strategy is to declare D^* and to evade $Y - D^*$ income.

When considering why an individual acts honestly, the answer is that the individual is constrained to act honestly. The extent to which the individual behaves honestly depends on the constraints that the individual faces. If the fine on the individual is increased the individual becomes more honest (declares more) and if the probability of detection increases the individual will act more honestly. However, there are some curious results in this analysis.

(a) *An increase in the fine.* In Figure 13.14 an increase in the fine makes the slope of 1-2 steeper (the slope of line 1-2 equals $1 - F/t$). If the reader draws a diagram such as Figure 13.14 but with a steeper slope, then it must be the case that the amount of income that is declared will increase (i.e. point $Y - tD^*$ will be further to the left). An increase in the slope of the line means that it is more expensive to act dishonestly and so a substitution effect predicts that greater honesty and an income effect (consequent in a price increase) also means a reduction in dishonesty (as risk aversion increases at lower income – see Chapter 7). Both substitution and income effects predict less dishonesty.

(b) *An increase in detection* can be illustrated by a change in the slope of the indifference curve. It is clear from equation (13.38) that the probability of detection affects the slope of the indifference curve. As the probability of detection increases the slope of the indifference curve becomes steeper and the new tangency position would be at say point 4 (rather than 3). Again the prediction runs with intuition.

The taxpayer becomes more honest as the price of dishonesty increases. However, when it comes to consideration of a change in the tax rate the results of this analysis are far more ambiguous.

(c) *The impact of a change in the tax rate.* An increase in the tax rate changes the slope of 1-2 (as the slope is $1 - F/t$). The reader might draw this by anchoring on point 1 and swivelling the budget line anti-clockwise. This would illustrate that the line 1-2 becomes less steep. It might be supposed that this means that less tax will be declared because a substitution effect moves the individual towards dishonesty as the relative price of honesty has increased. However, at the same time an increase in the relative price of honesty has reduced income and if the individual is risk-averse (indifference curves convex to the origin) an income effect may mean that more is declared. As already noted, the individual is likely to become less risk-averse at lower income. The result is that the substitution effect is away from declaration of income but the income effect is towards greater declaration and the net effect cannot be predicted *a priori*. The income effect works in the opposite direction to the substitution effect and the net effect of an increase in the tax rate depends on the strengths of these two effects; *tax evasion may increase or fall.*[9] Once again (as in Section 13.4.3), it is necessary to resort to empirical work. Such work suggests that, on balance, individuals will be more dishonest when the rate of tax increases (see Cullis and Jones 2009 for a review).

---

9. Yitzhaki (1974) argues that in many countries, penalties are levied on evaded tax, i.e. $t[Y - D]$ (not on evaded income, $[Y - D]$). In this case, the penalty paid on undeclared income is Ft (where F is now a surcharge on the tax). When there is an increase in t the 'price line' (1-2) in Figure 13.14 shifts inwards in a parallel way. There is now no substitution effect. The problem of ambiguity is solved but the prediction is counter-intuitive. An increase in the rate of tax makes the individual more honest because an increase in tax reduces the taxpayer's income (as there is only an income effect and decreasing income, the individual is more risk-averse).

(d) It is worth noting that the theory contains, in the language of mechanism design, a 'truth-telling rule'. If s stands for the surcharge rate ($F = t + ts$) on detected undeclared income then the condition to truth-tell about your income is $(1 - p)/p = s$. As can be seen the condition is independent of the tax rate and any consideration of risk aversion. If the parameters so dictate, all individuals should not evade or all evade. The theory should never result in a separating equilibrium, where some individuals evade and others do not as there is a rule connecting the probability of detection and surcharge rate that causes tax evasion to be expected utility-maximising for all – a pooled equilibrium. Whilst this is a strong result that seems contrary to observation – some people tax-evade while many others do not – it relies on p being common to all when in fact it is likely to be very different for different individuals, e.g. the tax authorities tend to look much more closely at the self-employed.

The analysis predicts the behaviour of *homo economicus* but, once again, the extent to which it is helpful depends on how far individual behaviour can be predicted by the behaviour of *homo economicus*. Throughout the analysis the assumption is that individuals are amoral utility-maximisers. Individuals are expected to deal with tax evasion in exactly the same way as they would deal with any gamble. Is this reasonable? Baldry (1984) reports the results of two sets of experiments. In the first, when tax evasion was the decision, some participants never evaded tax (and those who did evade were influenced by the tax schedule). When the experiment was repeated as a gamble (with identical payoffs) the result was everyone gambled (and each made the maximum bet).

Some have attempted to introduce morality by arguing that taxpayers feel badly knowing that they are not discharging their responsibility to the community. For example, Spicer (1986) draws attention to 'norms of compliance' and amends the decision-making analysis to include consideration of psychic costs associated with evasion. Again the question arises as to whether neoclassical microeconomic theory relies too heavily on *homo economicus*.

13.6 Taxation and the distribution of income: the uneasy case for progressive taxation

In Chapter 5 it was stressed that 'equity' is open to a wide range of interpretations. In this section attention focuses on one principle of equity often cited in public finance. This principle is that individuals should make an 'equal sacrifice' according to their ability to pay tax. When considering vertical equity (dealing with individuals in different income groups) this principle is often thought to require progressive income taxation. The argument is that if there is diminishing marginal utility of income: the rich should pay more than the poor in order to ensure an equal sacrifice.

How robust is this argument? In the first instance, what does 'equal sacrifice' mean? Second, when 'equal sacrifice' is defined, will progressive taxation be required?

It is possible to refer to *(i) equal absolute sacrifice, (ii) equal proportional sacrifice and (iii) equal marginal sacrifice*. In Figure 13.15 income is used as the measure of ability to pay. It is assumed that utility from income (for individuals A and B) is measurable in cardinal terms and that A and B have the same marginal utility of income schedules. (Quite strong assumptions to begin!)

Individual A is rich and B is poor; A's income Y_A is greater than B's, Y_B.

(i) Equal absolute sacrifice involves A and B losing the same amount of utility so that, after tax, income will be Y_{Aa} and Y_{Bb} for A and B respectively. Equal absolute sacrifice requires that A loses utility equal to area Y_A-1-2-Y_{Aa} and B loses utility equal

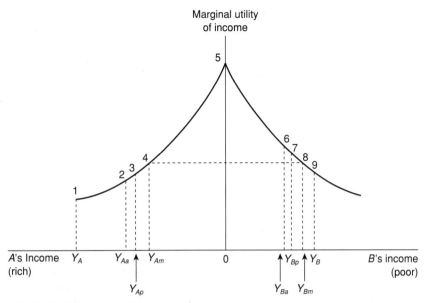

Figure 13.15 **Ability to pay and vertical equity**

to Y_B-9-6-Y_{Ba}. The total tax paid equals $(Y_A$-$Y_{Aa}) + (Y_B$-$Y_{Ba})$. With diminishing marginal utility of income, tax liability increases with income; however, proportionately, progression or regression depends on whether the elasticity of the marginal utility of income schedule with respect to income is equal to, less than or greater than unity.

(ii) Equal proportional sacrifice requires the proportion of total utility lost by A and B to be the same for A and B so that:

$$\frac{Y_A\text{-}1\text{-}3\text{-}Y_{Ap}}{Y_A\text{-}1\text{-}5\text{-}0} = \frac{Y_B\text{-}9\text{-}7\text{-}Y_{Bp}}{Y_B\text{-}9\text{-}5\text{-}0} \tag{13.41}$$

The total tax paid is $(Y_A$-$Y_{Ap}) + (Y_B$-$Y_{Bp})$. A decreasing but straight-line marginal utility of income schedule is sufficient to call for progression.

(iii) Finally, equal marginal sacrifice involves A paying Y_A-Y_{Am} and B paying Y_B-Y_{Bm} so that the marginal utility associated with their post-tax incomes is Y_{Am}-4 = Y_{Bm}-8. In this case any decreasing marginal utility of income schedule implies a progressive income tax schedule. This rule minimises the total loss of utility.

It follows that the case for progressive income taxation based on the requirement that individuals are taxed according to ability to pay requires far greater analysis. It requires far closer specification of the concept of equal sacrifice and of the marginal utility of income function. Are the utilities of individuals easy to measure cardinally and are they comparable? It was explicitly to avoid interpersonal comparisons of welfare that the concept of Pareto optimality was so readily adopted. When comparing utility, will the marginal utility of income to a rich man be lower than that to a poor man? (The rich man may be a miser, the poor man a profligate!)

Of course, the case for progressive taxation must also include other considerations. For example, if there are disincentive effects then tax progression might reduce the rate of economic growth. Other considerations (e.g. economic growth, stabilisation policy) also need also to be taken into account.

13.7 Challenge: Is firing on two 'canons' enough?

As noted in the introduction, tax issues can be appraised by reference to different 'canons' (or criteria). In Section 13.2 the criterion was efficiency. Later, evaluation of tax reform was considered with respect to effects on incentives to work and after this with respect to equity (as defined in terms of ability to pay). Throughout, it has been emphasised that tax reform should be considered with respect to more than one canon (i.e. with reference to a set of criteria). But how can this be achieved?

Literature on 'optimal taxation' illustrates how income-distributional goals can be achieved at least efficiency cost. With reference to a specific social welfare function, the goals of policy are formally articulated. In this section it is possible to illustrate how optimal taxes can be set when concern with income distribution and efficiency cost are both relevant.

A discussion of optimal taxation in terms of minimising efficiency (following Ramsey 1927 in Section 13.2.2) indicated that taxes on goods and services should be set inversely proportional to price elasticity of demand for the commodity. It was noted at the time that this might yield undesirable effects with respect to income distribution. Taxes on some products (e.g. on food) may be efficient because price elasticity of food is low and the excess burden is low. However, such taxes might appear inequitable because (by reference to Section 13.5), the poor spend such a high proportion of their income on food and those with least ability to pay will pay higher taxation. How can the conflict between equity and efficiency be resolved. How can the optimum tax rates be determined when income distribution, as well as efficiency, is a policy target?

Following the derivation of the Ramsey rule in Section 13.2 (as presented by Bruce 1998)[10] assume that there are two individuals A and B. The social welfare function can be defined as $W = W(U_A, U_B)$ (as discussed in Chapter 5). From the social welfare function it is possible to identify equity weights. Assume that the community's social welfare function indicates that when A receives £1 the increase in W is weighted as 1/2. By contrast, when B receives £1 the increase in W is weighted as 3. The difference arises because B is poor by comparison with A. In short, £1 paid by B imposes six times the loss of social welfare as would £1 of tax paid by A.

Within the economy there are two goods X and Y equally priced. Good X is consumed mainly by A and good Y is consumed mainly by B. Assume that 80% of total output of X is consumed by A (20% by B). By comparison, Y is a good consumed mainly by the poor; only 40% of Y is consumed by A (60% by B).

With such information it is possible to estimate the distributional characteristics for each good. The *distributional characteristic* is the weighted value of £1 tax burden on each good. For good X this is estimated as a weighted average $\theta_x = 1/2 \, (0.8) + 3 \, (0.2) = 1$. For Y it would be the weighted average $\theta_y = 1/2 \, (0.4) + 3 \, (0.6) = 2$. The implication is that £1 tax raised on X is a weighted value of £1 whereas £1 tax raised on Y has a weight twice as high (because a larger fraction of the burden is borne by the poor individual, B).

The 'optimal tax' rate on goods X and Y will now be established by equating the 'weighted' marginal burden of tax on each good. If θ_x is the distributional characteristic of good X and θ_y is the distributional characteristic of good Y, the 'optimal' tax system requires that $\theta_x \cdot MBT_x = \theta_y \cdot MBT_y$. In Figure 13.16, as $\theta_x = 1$ and $\theta_y = 2$ the weighted marginal burden is MBT_x and for Y is $2 \cdot MBT_y$. The tax rates that minimise the *weighted* burden of the tax system are found at point m^{**}.

Following this approach it is possible to show how the original Ramsey rule for optimum commodity taxation should be amended to allow for equity considerations. It is

10. For alternative derivations see Cullis and Jones (2009).

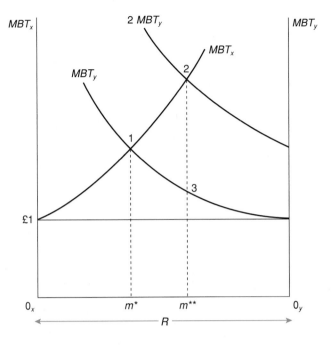

Figure 13.16
Efficiency and equity

possible to solve for the optimal tax rate. As $\theta_x \cdot MBT_x = MBT^{**}$ it is possible to solve for τ_x. It follows (from Section 13.2) that $MBT^{**} = \theta_x/[(1 - \tau_x)\, e_x]$ and therefore

$$\tau_x = \frac{MBT^{**} - \theta_x}{MBT^{**}} \cdot \frac{1}{e_x}$$

In the same way $$\tau_y = \frac{MBT^{**} - \theta_y}{MBT^{**}} \cdot \frac{1}{e_y}$$

It is evident that when both equity and efficiency matter the optimal tax rate on a good is higher when either price elasticity or the distributional characteristic of the good is lower.

The conflict between efficiency and equity is illustrated in Figure 13.16 (which can be compared with Figure 13.5). The optimal outcome for the tax system raising revenue R in terms of *both* efficiency and equity is at point m^{**}. However, this must mean a larger-than-minimum excess burden (as shown at point m^*). On only efficiency criteria, there is additional deadweight loss of triangle 1-2-3. By comparison with the conclusion drawn in Section 13.2.2 with respect to Figure 13.16, it can be seen that the pursuit of equity has a cost (in terms of a higher unweighted excess burden than is absolutely necessary). There may be cases in which it is possible to offer tax reform that delivers improvements in both equity and efficiency. In this case concern only for efficiency and for minimising deadweight loss (i.e. maximising efficiency) may not be consistent with the 'optimal' solution when both efficiency and equity are relevant.

13.8 Summary

The objective in this chapter was to apply neoclassical microeconomic theory to analyse the impact of taxation. Perhaps the most important contribution that such analysis has offered is the realisation that issues that appear so obvious at face value are anything but 'obvious'. The 'costs' of taxation are not simply the amount that individuals pay the tax authorities. The 'incidence' of the tax may not be described by the legal responsibility to pay the taxman. The incentive effects of taxes cannot be taken for granted and require careful analysis of income and substitution effects.

This said, how far does the application of neoclassical microeconomic theory help resolve these issues? As noted in the previous section, the importance of equity considerations stands proud and policy will depend on stronger normative considerations than exist in the Paretian welfare-value judgements made explicit in Chapter 4. When analysis focuses only on Paretian considerations it has also been noted that there are a number of 'second best' situations when theory will not resolve issues.

For some, microeconomics has little to say on very basic questions *per se*. The question of whether a proportional income tax would reduce work effort could not be answered in the absence of empirical work. The conclusion appears to be that 'it all depends'. It is not very helpful to say that it all depends on income and substitution effects in the absence of empirical estimates.

In some cases the application of neoclassical microeconomics conflicts with intuition and defies evidence. In the 1980s the Laffer curve informed policy. This implied that a cut in income tax might increase tax revenues. This seemed intuitive because a cut in income tax might increase work effort and a cut in income tax might lead individuals to report tax more honestly. An application of neoclassical microeconomics indicates that neither is guaranteed – 'it all depends'. These difficulties only increase the more that experiments reveal behaviour that differs systematically from the behaviour of self-interested *homo economicus* (e.g. Baldry 1984).

Before closing this chapter it is perhaps appropriate to note that, for many, the administrative costs of tax are as relevant as 'efficiency' and 'equity' concerns. For some, the relevant 'canon' is administrative and compliance costs. To emphasise the importance that some attach to this canon consider the proposition by Payne (1993a, 1993b) that there is a lower cost alternative to raise public funds'.

Table 13.3 provides an estimate of the cost of raising $100 in tax, which is some $65. The items in the table are:

- compliance costs (the cost of reading detailed instructions, filling in forms and having additional records for tax purposes);
- disincentive costs (reductions in work hours and willingness to invest);
- uncertainty costs (frequent tax code and law changes make it very difficult to plan the efficient use of capital and labour);
- enforcement and litigation costs (individuals can appeal against decisions made by tax authorities and this involves expensive court and other legal procedures);
- evasion and avoidance costs (individuals devote real resources to legally and illegally trying not to pay tax, e.g. using tax havens and working for cash in hand) and the government costs (expenditures on the various agencies that collect taxes).

Table 13.3 Costs of operating the US federal tax system

	Cost to raise $100
Compliance costs	$24.43
Disincentive costs	33.20
Uncertainty costs	1.84
Enforcement and litigation costs	1.97
Evasion and avoidance costs	2.96
Governmental costs (IRS and other agencies)	0.61
Total	$65.01

Source: Payne (1993a).

Inevitably, estimates are far from precise but Payne argues that the cost of raising tax revenue is so high that it would be better to rely on the voluntary sector to provide welfare services. He views charitable giving as zero-cost fund-raising (as workers seek extra hours to contribute to their favourite charity, incur no compliance costs as no records of giving are required and enforcement litigation and avoidance cost also evaporate as there is no code to enforce or avoid). While reliance on the voluntary or charitable sector is typically thought sub-optimal (see Chapter 15 for discussion of the 'free-rider' problem), Payne discounts this problem and argues that the voluntary sector can provide funds for non-private activities.

While estimates of administrative and compliance costs are always open to challenge, the example highlights the criticism that these concerns should not be neglected by analysis focused only on the canons of 'efficiency' and 'equity'.

Appendix 13 Describing more complex income tax arrangements

Progressive tax systems usually involve higher marginal tax rates for higher earnings. This, combined with a level of non-taxable income (Y_e), would generate a budget constraint like 1-2-3 in Figure 13.17(a). In practice the UK tax structure achieves progressivity (a marginal tax rate greater than the average tax rate) by having tax allowances and a wide band of income over which the marginal tax rate is a constant. There is a second, higher, constant marginal tax rate for those who earn more than a certain income level, say Y_h in 13.17(b). This replaces the curvilinear constraint with one that has several flats.

More realistic accounts of the budget constraint allow for a level of unearned income Y_u (see Figure 13.17(c)) and the presence of an overtime premium on the basic wage rate when the 'standard work week' $0'-H_s$, is exceeded. (In the diagram this occurs after the individual involved is liable to tax.) The effect of these is to produce a budget constraint as shown in part (c) of the figure.

As Hausman (1985) notes, the Slutsky equation discussed above must be modified. The presence of non-linearities creates so-called 'virtual incomes' – like those illustrated as Y_1 and Y_2 in Figure 13.17(c). They are established by the extension of any of the budget segments backwards to the right-side vertical axis. Such 'linearisation' establishes an 'as if' budget constraint for an individual. An individual finding a tangency on the segment 1-2 of the Y_u'-1-2-3-4 'kinked' budget constraint would choose the same number of hours of work if they faced the linear budget constraint Y_1-1-2-5. Changes in tax rates generate income and substitution effects by altering the slope of the segments. However, in the non-proportional tax rate case, the 'virtual income' is also altered (except for the first segment), generating a further income effect which will serve to alter labour supply.

A second concern is that, if the tax-transfer system creates a budget constraint that is non-linear and non-convex, it is possible for more than one tangency with an indifference curve to arise. The same indifference curve might have two tangency points, so that small changes in the budget constraint can cause the chosen number of hours to jump from one segment of the constraint to another (e.g. points 6 and 7 in Figure 13.17(c)). The consequences of changes in the budget constraint for hours of work again become generally unpredictable *a priori*. In the case of two tangencies for the same indifference curve illustrated by I_0 in the figure, a 'gap' is created in labour supply as there is no wage at which the individual will choose the number of hours associated with the 'kink' point 2.[11]

---

11. Hausman (1985) explains how specifying a utility function and searching the segments econometrically for the tangency offering highest utility provides an empirical answer to problems posed by non-linearity.

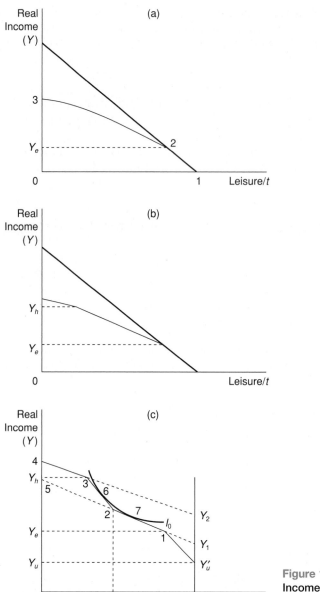

Figure 13.17
Income taxation and budget constraints

References

Allingham, M.G. and Sandmo, A. (1972) Income tax evasion: a theoretical analysis, *Journal of Public Economics*, 1: 323–38.

Atkinson, A.B. and Stiglitz, J.E. (1980) *Lectures on Public Economics*, London: McGraw-Hill.

Auerbach, A.J. (1985) The theory of excess burden and optimal taxation, pp. 61–128 in A.J. Auerbach and M. Feldstein (eds) *Handbook of Public Economics*, Amsterdam: North-Holland.

Baldry, J.C. (1984) The enforcement of income tax laws; efficiency implications, *Economic Record*, 60: 156–9.

Ballard, C., Shoven, J.B. and Whalley, J. (1985) The total welfare cost of the United States tax system: a general equilibrium approach, *National Tax Journal* 38: 125–140.

Blundell, R. (1992) Labour supply and taxation: a survey, *Fiscal Studies* 13 (3): 15–40.

Break, G.F. (1957) Income taxes and incentives to work, *American Economic Review*, 47: 529–49.

Brown, C.V. (1968) Misconceptions about income tax and incentives, *Scottish Journal of Political Economy*, 15: 1–21.

Brown, C.V. (1983) *Taxation and the Incentive to Work*, 2nd edn, Oxford: Oxford University Press.

Brown, C.V. and Jackson, P.M. (1990) *Public Sector Economics*, 4th edn, Oxford: Basil Blackwell.

Brown, C.V. and Levin, E.J. (1974) The effects of income taxation in overtime: the results of a national survey, *Economic Journal*, 84 (336): 833–48.

Brown, C.V. and Sandford, C.T. (1991) *Taxes and Incentives: the Effects of the 1988 Cuts in the Higher Rates of Income Tax*, Economic Study No. 7, Institute for Public Policy Research.

Brown, C.V., Levin, E. and Ulph, D.T. (1976) Estimates of labour hours supplied by married male workers in Great Britain, *Scottish Journal of Political Economy*, 23: 261–77.

Browning, E.K. (1987) On the marginal welfare cost of taxation, *American Economic Review*, 77 (1) (March): 11–23.

Bruce, N. (1997) *Public Finance and the American Economy*, Boston: Addison Wesley.

Cowell, F.A. (1985) The economic analysis of tax evasion, *Bulletin of Economic Research*, 37: 163–193.

Cullis, J. and Jones, P. (2009) *Public Finance and Public Choice*, 3rd edn, Oxford: Oxford University Press.

Feldstein, M. (1997) How big should government be? *National Tax Journal*, 50 (2): 197–213.

Fields, D.B. and Stanbury, W.T. (1970) Incentives, disincentives and the income tax – further empirical evidence, *Public Finance*, 25 (3): 231–42.

Fullerton, D. (1984) Which effective tax rate? *National Tax Journal*, 37: 23–43.

Hansson, I. and Stuart, C. (1983) Tax Revenues and the Marginal Cost of Public Funds in Sweden, mimeo, University of California – Santa Barbara.

Hausman, J.A. (1985) Taxation and labour supply, pp. 216–34 in A.J. Auerbach and M. Feldstein (eds) *Handbook of Public Economics Vol. 1*, Amsterdam: North-Holland.

Hudson, J. and Godwin, M. (2000) The compliance costs of collecting direct tax in the UK: an analysis of PAYE, *Journal of Public Economics*, 77: 29–44.

Hyman, D. (1999) *Public Finance: a Contemporary Application of Theory to Policy*, 6th edn, Chicago: Dryden.

Kosters, M.H. (1969) Effects of an income tax on labour supply, in A.C. Harberger and M.J. Bailey (eds) *The Taxation of Income from Capital*, Washington DC: Brookings Institution.

Lewis, A. (1978) Perception of tax rates, *British Tax Review*, 6: 358–66.

Musgrave, R.A. (1959) *The Theory of Public Finance*, New York: McGraw-Hill.

Neuberg, L.G. (1989) *Conceptual Anomalies in Economics and Statistics: the Negative Income Tax Experiment*, Cambridge: Cambridge University Press.

Payne, J.L. (1993a) The end of taxation? *Public Interest* No. 112 Summer: 110–18.

Payne, J.L. (1993b) *Costly Returns – the Burdens of the US Tax System*, San Francisco: ICS Press.

Perloff, J.M. (1999) *Microeconomics*, Reading, Mass.: Addison Wesley Longman.

Pyle, D.J. (1991) The economics of taxpayer compliance, *Journal of Economic Surveys*, 5 (2): 163–98.

Pyle, D.J. (1993) The economics of taxpayer compliance, pp. 32–57 in P.M. Jackson, *Current Issues in Public Sector Economics*, London: Macmillan.

Ramsey, F.P. (1927) A contribution to the theory of taxation, *Economic Journal* 37, 145: 47–61.

Rosen, H.S. (1999) *Public Finance*, 5th edn, New York: McGraw-Hill.

Sandford, C.T., Godwin, M. and Hardwick, P. (1989) *Administrative and Compliance Costs of Taxation*, Bath: Fiscal Publications.

Smith, A. (1776/1937) *The Wealth of Nations* New York: The Modern Library.

Spicer, M.W. (1986) Civilisation at a discount: the problem of tax evasion, *National Tax Journal*, 39 (1): 13–20.

Swift, S. (1993) Neutrality and UK tax policy, *British Economy Survey*, 23 (1): 9–13.

Yitzhaki, S. (1974) Income tax evasion: a theoretical analysis, *Journal of Public Economics*, 3 (2): 201–2.

CHAPTER 14

Public choice and political markets

14.1 Introduction

The objective in this chapter is to apply neoclassical microeconomic theory to analyse decisions which individuals make when participating in political processes and when dealing with political issues. The 'public choice school' undertake this exercise. They begin by assuming that individuals behave as *homo economicus* (for a discussion see Brennan and Lomasky 1993). The focus of attention is whether decision-making within democratic processes produces outcomes that might be deemed 'efficient'.

In Chapters 4 and 5 it was argued that the incentive structures of competitive markets led self-interested individuals to operate in a way that would maximise welfare for the community (in Paretian terms). The analysis in these chapters illustrates Adam Smith's (*Wealth of Nations*, 1776) discussion of the 'invisible hand'. The 'invisible hand' serves to ensure that additional resources are only allocated to the production of goods and services if individuals are willing to pay sufficient to meet the incremental resource costs involved. Only if individuals value the goods (i.e. are willing to pay for them) by at least as much as the incremental production costs will resources be allocated to increased production. Pareto efficiency is defined as a resource allocation from which resources cannot be reallocated to make one person better off without making another person worse off. As noted, this requires that resources are only allocated to the production of a good (or service) if the marginal value of the good exceeds or equals the marginal cost of the good (or service).

Public choice scholars apply neoclassical microeconomic analysis leads to reach the conclusion that there is no such incentive structure in political processes. Their approach is to consider the political process as a 'political market'. In this 'market', citizens 'demand' legislative change and this is 'supplied' by political representatives and bureaucrats (see, for example, the discussion in Peacock 1992; Tollison 1988). Buchanan (1972) argues that consistency requires that the same motivation be assumed in political processes as is assumed in markets. *Homo economicus* is motivated by self-interest (defined by Brennan and Lomasky 1993 as 'personal wealth maximisation'). However, within the political process there is no 'invisible hand' to ensure that outcomes will maximise the community's welfare (in Paretian terms).

In this chapter the political process is characterised as a 'political market'. On the 'demand side', voters use the ballot box to signal preferences. The voter signals preferred public spending programmes. Intensity of preference is expressed by subscribing to associations that lobby government. Demand is registered by these measures. Legislation is supplied by competing politicians and then administered by bureaucrats.

In just the same way as Chapter 6 identified the possibility of market failure this chapter also identifies sources of 'government failure'. Failures arise on both the demand and supply sides of the political market. It is unlikely that the political market will efficiently reconcile individuals' self-interests to ensure that community welfare is maximised (in Paretian terms).

The implication of government failures almost always point in one direction. Not only are there reasons to expect that resources will not be Pareto-efficiently allocated, there are also endemic reasons to expect that there will be 'excessive' allocation of resources to expand the public sector. Unconstrained, the public sector will exceed the optimum. The prediction of continued growth has led to the conclusion that the public sector is a Leviathan.

Throughout this chapter (as elsewhere in this text) the opportunity is taken to assess the extent to which neoclassical microeconomic theory can be applied. That political processes 'fail' and that the public sector tends towards a Leviathan depends sensitively on the extent to which *homo economicus* is the best description of a 'representative individual' and the extent to which neoclassical microeconomic analysis can be applied to analyse both economic and political markets.

14.2 'Demand' in the political process: why do individuals vote?

The proposition that citizens can be viewed as 'consumer–taxpayers' who express their demand at the ballot box is important when characterising the political process as a 'political market'. However, this proposition immediately runs into difficulty when the inherent assumption is that the representative individual (*homo economicus*) is self-interested. When individuals are assumed to be instrumentally rational, there is no incentive for them to turn out to vote.

Downs (1957) considered the decision to vote in terms of the net expected utility associated with voting. In the first instance, the individual must assess how much better off they will be if one electoral outcome emerges rather than another. Assume the individual will be better off (in utility terms) by B if a preferred outcome were chosen. If the probability that their vote will influence the outcome of the election is p, the expected utility from voting is pB. If there are costs associated with voting, it is not obvious that the net expected utility will be positive. Costs of voting (c) include the costs of gathering information, as well as the costs of registering a vote. They may include costs in terms of time, effort and pecuniary expense. The net expected utility (*NEU*) from voting is therefore:

$$NEU = pB - c \tag{14.1}$$

In a national election it is unlikely that any one individual's vote will be decisive. Indeed, Mueller (2003: 305) writes that: 'Several people have noted that the probability of being run over by a car going to or returning from the polls is similar to the probability of casting the decisive vote. If being run over is worse than having one's preferred candidate lose, then the potential cost of voting alone would exceed the potential gain, and no rational self-interested individual would ever vote.' If p is miniscule, then in equation (14.1) net expected utility from voting is unlikely to be positive (pB is unlikely to exceed the certain costs c).

Mueller (2003) reports that the probability that one vote will make a difference is:

$$P = \frac{3e^{-2(N-1)(q-1/2)^2}}{2\sqrt{2\pi}(N-1)}$$

when

N = the number of voters and
q = the voter's expectation of the proportion of votes each party will get.

P will be high when the election is close ($q = 0.5$) and when the electorate (N) is small. Connolly and Munro (1999) demonstrate how sensitive *P* is to the value of *N*. If *B* (the value of an electoral outcome) is £1000 and *c* (the costs of voting) are £5 the expected value of voting is reported for different-sized electorates. When the probability that any voter votes for or against (q) is $1/2$, the net expected benefit from voting ($pB - c$) is:

- $(0.02 \times 1000) - 5 = £15$ when the number of voters is 1000
- $(0.0027 \times 1000) - 5 = -£2.30$ when the number of voters is 50,000
- $(0.00006 \times 1000) - 5 = -£4.90$ when the number of voters is 100,000,000

Individuals are more likely to abstain if the number of votes is large. However, the prediction that individuals will abstain is refuted by the evidence. Turnout rates, even in national elections, are impressively high (Aldrich 1993). Some empirical tests suggest that the variables identified in Downs's analysis are important in the decision to vote. Mueller (1987) reviews a number of studies which have regressed voter turnout figures on *p* (the expected vote of the leading candidate) and *n* the size of the jurisdiction as a means of testing the Downs formulation. But is it really the case that individuals turn out to vote because they believe that a single vote will change an electoral outcome? If it appears to be the case that turnout increases as *p* declines Aldrich (1997) suggests a different explanation. The value of *p* (the probability of affecting an election outcome) is often proxied in empirical work by the closeness of the election. When elections are close party leaders spend more time mobilising voters (appealing for their support). When allowance is made for the role of political parties, results that suggest that voters act this instrumentally are called in question.

A second reason for questioning the prediction that self-interested individuals participate instrumentally was presented by Frey (1971). Drawing on Lane (1966), he notes that voter turnout at elections is higher for those with high income. This appears incompatible with the opportunity cost theory of voting. It is inconsistent that those with higher income vote in greater numbers, when the cost of giving up time to vote will be greater for high-income individuals.[1] To reconcile behaviour with the expected utility theory, Frey (1971) argues that high-income individuals might be more productive in the use of their time in the political process. While this may be so for such activities as lobbying, it is difficult to apply the argument to the act of voting *per se*.[2]

If it is difficult to explain voter turnout with reference to Downs's analysis of net expected benefit, how can participation be explained? How can the 'paradox of voting' be explained:

(a) The importance of civic duty

Perhaps there are consumption benefits from performing a civic duty? These might be estimated as *d* (in utils) and *d* may well exceed c.[3] If *d* exceeds *c* then the following net expected utility of voting may be positive:

$$pB + d - c > 0 \qquad (14.2)$$

1. Cavanagh (1981), for example, confirms this trend. In the USA, the turnout rate in the 1976 election was 46% for those with an income less than $5000 and 60% for those with an income greater than $25,000.
2. Jones and Cullis (1986) offer an argument to reconcile the rational voter hypothesis with the evidence on turnout by income. They demonstrate that, when individuals are risk-averse, the lower-income individual may be less willing to gamble any certain cost of electoral participation against a given expected gain.
3. Downs recognised that individuals might vote because they regarded this as a civic duty. Downs suggested that individuals recognise that democracy would not survive unless individuals fulfilled this civic duty. Aldrich (1997) more formally regards this as an argument based on long-term utility maximisation for the individual. The initial Downs discussion focused on a single electoral contest but Aldrich argues that it is possible to theorise about 'an essentially infinite stream of elections'. Having said this the idea that voters invest long-term in production of a goal that is essentially public in nature (see Chapter 6) is questionable. The analysis above focuses on the private benefit from fulfilling civic duty.

Riker and Ordeshook (1968) tested the equation $R = pB + d - c$ by reference to 1952, 1956 and 1960 pre-presidential election questionnaires. They suggest that pB and d are important in explaining voter turnout, but a high sense of citizen duty (a higher value of d) has a quantitatively greater impact on voter turnout than does high values of either the probability of affecting the outcome or the benefit derived from the outcome.

(b) The importance of expressive action

Fiorina (1976) and Brennan and Lomasky (1993) argue that individuals derive utility from voting because individuals derive utility from expressing a view. Aldrich (1997: 385) captures the essence of this argument by noting that individuals frequently wish to express a preference by 'applauding a fine symphony performance or . . . cheering the success of the home team . . . But just as symphonies or home teams that perform well receive greater huzzahs, so too should we expect turnout to vary by the characteristics of the election.' This is a consumption benefit of voting that is distinct from performing a civic duty.

Aldrich (1997) offers further analysis of d, in the light of Fiorina's (1976) observation that there is utility from the act of expressing a preference. The d term can be subdivided into $d' + E$ where those with large E terms 'care more about expressing their preferences' and d' includes 'the remaining components of the old d-term' (Aldrich 1997: 385). The relevant expression is now:

$$pB + d' + E - c > 0 \tag{14.3}$$

Lee (1988) suggested that there are issues on which individuals 'consume' the act of supporting ideological goals; the act of voting can be seen as a consumption activity rather than an investment of resources in the hope of gain contingent on outcome. A consumption gain arising simply from the pleasure derived from expressing a view can be distinguished from the d' term that relates to civic duty. Aldrich emphasises that the important consideration when looking at the E term is the difference between electoral options. He comments: 'if there is little difference between the two candidates, as many found to be the case in the 1976 presidential election . . . [this E term] . . . would be relatively small and turnout, even to express one's preferences, will be less likely. If however, many voters see substantial stakes in the outcome, they will be more likely to turn out because of their evaluation of that outcome, even though they are not doing so to affect that outcome.'

Ashenfelter and Kelly (1975) examine survey data on voter attitudes in an attempt to explain the large difference in turnouts in the two presidential elections of 1960 and 1972. Several measures of costs of voting (e.g. the existence of a poll tax and literacy tests) were statistically significant in reducing the probability that an individual would vote. However, the perception of the individual as to whether the election was close run (a proxy for p) did not appear to affect the decision to vote. The importance of the issue (e.g. B) was considered by answers to the question 'How do you think you will vote?' If an individual appeared undecided as to how to vote, the probability that the individual would vote at all was 40 per cent lower. In this study, the obligation to vote was also important. Individuals who felt a strong obligation to vote did so with a 30 per cent higher probability.

But how important are psychic benefits from the act of voting? It has been argued that saying that individuals do things because they like to do things means that Downs's instrumental theory of voting loses its 'cutting edge'. It becomes almost tautological, i.e. individuals vote because they like voting (Barry 1970). However, if the source of psychic gain can be identified then the analysis retains some predictive bite.

Jones and Hudson (2000) argue that analysis of perceptions of the intrinsic value of action (see Chapter 15) can be used to form testable predictions if the determinants of the intrinsic value (consumption benefit) of performing a civic duty can be identified. The important determinant of d' is the element of duty and the intrinsic value of performing a civic duty depends on the extent to which civic virtue is acknowledged (Frey 1992, 1997).[4] Jones and Hudson argue that in a representative democracy the actions of political representatives are likely to signal the esteem in which civic duty is held. If representatives are perceived as deferring self-interest to the 'greater good' (i.e. to the 'public interest'), the value of intrinsic motivation is acknowledged. Conversely, if political representatives (in general) are perceived as pursuing self-interest, voters are likely to reconsider the importance of civic duty. Elster (1989: 80) asks, 'if people feel that they are taken advantage of, why should they not rip off the system in return?'. Jones and Hudson offer evidence that indicates that the intrinsic value of voting depends on perceptions of the actions of representatives and that this explains *why* individuals vote. The importance of expressing allegiance to one policy rather than to another proved statistically significant in explaining *how* individuals vote.

It is also clear that if the decision depends on the net consumption gain from voting, costs of participation may be lower than anticipated. Transactions costs of electoral participation may be reduced by institutional arrangements (Jones and Hudson 1998). Downs argued that political parties reduce voters' information costs by occupying positions on an ideological spectrum. Wittman (1989: 1400) asserted that, as 'parties establish certain reputations regarding policy positions . . . the voter can then vote a party line without knowledge of the particular candidates'. Jones and Hudson (1998) offer evidence that electoral participation increases as party signal becomes more consistent.

(c) A different response to uncertainty; relying on the minimax strategy

An alternative explanation depends on a different analysis of individuals' response to the problem of uncertainty. One possibility is the minimax-regret strategy. In this case the individual wishes to minimise regret and in Table 14.1 the regret that voters would experience is presented for two alternative outcomes (or states of nature) labelled S_1 and S_2. If the outcome is S_1 the individual's vote has no impact on the electoral result. The only source of regret would be costs (c) that the individual would incur if the individual had chosen to vote. These costs were a waste as the individual could not change an electoral outcome.

If outcomes like S_1 are quite likely, it is impossible to discount the possibility that there is an outcome such as S_2 in which the individual's vote might make a difference. If the benefits from voting (U_x) exceed the costs of voting, the individual will now regret nothing if the decision was to vote. However, if the individual does not vote the individual will lose the value of $U_x - c$ (which would have been realised if the decision had been made to participate in the vote).

Table 14.1 The decision to vote

	Alternative states	
	S_1	S_2
Vote	c	0
Abstain	0	$U_x - c$

4. Frey (1997: 8) argues that 'crowding out' of intrinsic motivation occurs when 'reciprocity is violated' and when 'the implicit contract based on mutual acknowledgement of one's engagement is violated'.

If it is assumed that the voter always attempts to minimise the worst of the outcomes that might occur, then, if $B - c > c$, the individual will vote. However, this is an extremely cautious strategy. Ferejohn and Fiorina (1974) use survey data to test this analysis. Under the minimax-regret argument, the value of the benefit to individuals should be related to voter turnout but the probability of the individual's vote being decisive (p) is of little consequence (because, as long as p is positive, i.e. there is even the remotest chance of a state of nature such as S_2, it will result in the individual choosing to vote). In an analysis of pre- and post-election survey results for 1952, 1956, 1960 and 1964, the 'minimax-regret hypothesis' was supported five times and the Downsian hypothesis (relying on p also) was supported only once (1974).

(d) Concern for others: ethical voting

Mueller's response (1987) to the question of why individuals vote is to refer to the objectives of an ethical voter. Individual i, as an ethical voter, is assumed to maximise an objective function of the following form;

$$O_i = U_i + \Theta \Sigma U_j \tag{14.5}$$

where

O_i = the objective of individual i;
U_i = the utility individual i derives from consuming goods and services;
ΣU_j = the sum of the utilities of other individuals in the community;
Θ = a parameter such that $0 \leq \Theta \leq 1$.

When the individual is selfish, $\Theta = 0$, the individual is in the position of Downs's rational voter. However, when $\Theta = 1$ the individual can be deemed altruistic; the individual is concerned with the utilities of others in the community. Individuals vote, not simply because they are concerned with their own welfare, but because individuals are concerned with the welfare of others. The utility from voting is, therefore, likely to be much higher and voting is a rational response for those who look, more broadly, to the effect of a vote on the community at large. With $\Theta > 0$ the individual has far more at stake in any vote than simply the effect on their own utility U_i.

Hudson and Jones (1994) use questionnaire analysis to estimate the weight, Θ, implicit in an individual's objective function. There is evidence that voters are concerned for others. However, the question is whether voters are concerned for others. The question is whether this is the motivation to vote. Plott (1987) points to a problem with this explanation. If you are concerned for the well-being of others you will still only vote if the probability that you can change the outcome, multiplied by the benefit you derive from the difference between the outcomes with and without your vote, exceeds the costs of voting. Assume there are two issues X_1 and X_2 and each affects the community as a whole. The benefits from voting depends on the *difference* in the impact of each on the individual's objective function, i.e. the benefits will be $B = O_i(x_1) - O_i(x_2)$. While the expected benefit is B there is still no incentive to incur costs of participation as p approaches zero.

Downs's original application (1957) of microeconomic analysis predicted that individuals would not incur the costs of voting. But individuals do vote. Successive application of microeconomic analyses has altered the perspective and viewed voting as a 'consumption', rather than a purely 'investment', activity. The argument that individuals enjoy utility from the act of voting is not tautological if the determinants of such utility can be identified. As many of the key decisions in life emerge from the ballot box the importance of such application of microeconomic theory is difficult to ignore.

14.3 Voting rules: how should collective decisions be made?

Individuals turn out to vote in larger numbers than would be predicted if they were only concerned with the impact of their action on outcome. However, if they register their preference at the ballot box, how should their preferences be considered when making a collective decision?

When individuals vote how should collective decisions be made? Is it possible to aggregate votes of individuals (over alternative policy options) to produce a social ordering of alternative options?

Arrow (1963) has shown that there is no constitutional rule that will simultaneously satisfy what might be considered to be a list of 'reasonable' conditions. Given the limitations of traditional welfare economics, the importance of such an analysis should already be evident. In Chapter 5 it was shown that, within the Paretian framework, 'efficiency' could be defined but 'equity' could generally only be considered with reference to a social welfare function. A social welfare function provides information regarding society's preferred income distribution. But while alternative social welfare functions were described in Chapter 5, which social welfare is appropriate?

Each individual has his (her) own social welfare function, i.e. a perception of a just or equitable income distribution. But how can these views by aggregated, so that from individual preferences it is possible to describe the community's social welfare function.

A constitutional rule is a mechanism for aggregating the preferences of individuals to establish a collective social welfare function. Arrow refers to arrangements (for allocation of resources and distribution) as different 'social states'. Consider social states X, Y, Z (within which issues of allocation and distribution are settled in a particular way). While individuals may be able to order these alternatives, is it possible to derive a social ordering? Arrow argues that there are five 'conditions of correspondence' which any constitutional rule must satisfy:

(i) *Collective rationality*: In economics, rationality is defined in terms of consistency. Individuals are consistent if their preference ordering satisfies specific characteristics. The preference ordering must possess the attributes of *connexity* (outcomes must be capable of being compared) and *transitivity*. A transitive ordering of three alternatives X, Y, Z is one in which, if X is preferred to Y and Y is preferred to Z, then X must be preferred to Z.

(ii) *The Pareto principle*: this requires that if all members of the community prefer X to Y, the collective choice which emerges from a constitutional rule must also say that X is preferred to Y.

(iii) *The independence of irrelevant alternatives*: this condition is one of the more controversial conditions. If a choice has to be made between two alternatives X and Y, that choice should not be influenced by the ranking of either X or Y with other alternatives such as Z or V. These latter alternatives are irrelevant, in that they are not part of the decision. The decision is a simple binary choice between X and Y. If, for example, any individual changed his (her) own ranking as between X and Z, this should not alter the collective choice between X and Y.

(iv) *Non-dictatorship*: there should be no one individual whose preferences are automatically the preferences expressed for the community.

(v) *Unrestricted domain*: this stipulates that no individual should be excluded from contributing to the establishment of a collective choice, provided that the individual has a transitive ordering of preferences. There is no way that a 'rational' individual should be disenfranchised within the constitutional rule.

The *Arrow impossibility theorem* demonstrates that there is no constitutional rule that satisfies all these conditions. Consider the simple majority voting rule (50% + 1).

Table 14.2 Majority voting: cyclical

Voters	Options		
	X	Y	Z
A	3	2	1
B	1	3	2
C	2	1	3

Table 14.3 Outcome dependency on agenda setting

Vote between	Vote between	Outcome
Y v X	X v Z	Z
X v Z	Z v Y	Y
Z v Y	Y v X	X

In Table 14.2 three individuals (Voter *A*, Voter *B* and Voter *C*) choose between three alternatives *X, Y, Z*.

In Table 14.2 the ranking of the individuals are shown as 3, 2, 1 (in order of preference). It is clear that each voter has a transitive preference ordering (for example, *A* prefers *X* to *Y*, prefers *Y* to *Z* and also prefers *X* to *Z*). If a collective decision was required as between *X* and *Y*, the majority would choose *X* (Voters *A* and *C*). Between *Y* and *Z*, a majority would opt for *Y* (Voters *A* and *B*). As a consequence, to satisfy the condition of *collective rationality*, majority voting 'should' lead to a preference for *X* rather than *Z*. However, in the example, Voters *B* and *C* constitute a majority in favour of *Z* rather than *X*. This inconsistency was noted by the Marquis de Condorcet in the eighteenth century. As the preference ordering is not transitive this voting rule fails Arrow's condition for collective rationality.

The final winner depends on which vote is taken first. Table 14.3 shows how the sequence of votes possible determines alternative winners. The electoral outcome depends on the way alternatives are presented to the electorate.

The reader may suspect that this specific example has been deliberately contrived. If only the orderings shown in Table 14.3 were different, surely there would be examples in which the preference rankings of individual voters would not lead to a 'cyclical' outcome? However, the point to emphasise is that such a cyclical outcome cannot be ruled out, given the condition of *unrestricted domain*.

The example demonstrates why the simple majority voting rule (50% + 1) would fail to meet the conditions of correspondence that Arrow stipulates, but note that other voting rules also fail Arrow's test (for further discussion see Cullis and Jones 2009). If it is impossible to form a social ordering of alternatives (e.g. *X*, *Y* and *Z*) then neoclassical microeconomic theory must work with the 'weak' value judgements in the Paretian framework (described in Chapter 4). Paretian welfare criteria remain relevant when assessing options within a neoclassical framework.

14.3.1 When will a majority voting rule yield a collective choice?

In Table 14.2 the problem that a 'simple majority voting rule' (50% + 1) will create a cyclical outcome is illustrated. Will this cyclical outcome always emerge?

When the outcome of a 'simple majority voting' (50% + 1) is non-cyclical, the outcome of the vote is the preferred option of the *median voter*. The following example will

Table 14.4 **Majority voting: non-cyclical**

Voters	Options		
	X	Y	Z
A	3	2	1
B	1	3	2
C	1	2	3

illustrate this. Table 14.4 illustrates the preference of three voters with respect to three alternative levels of public spending. Option X refers to a 'high' level of spending, option Y is a 'moderate' level of spending and option Z is a 'low' level of public spending. With a majority voting rule: A and B prefer Y to Z; B and C prefer Z to X and individuals B and C prefer Y to X. The transitive ordering of preferred alternatives reflecting collective choice is: Y preferred to Z; Z preferred to X and Y preferred to X. The community prefers Y and Y is the median level of spending, i.e. the preferred option of the 'median voter'.

Such a result offers another possible application of microeconomic theory. If there are conditions in which majority voting selects the preferences of the median voter then, if the demand function of the median voter can be identified, it is possible to predict the outcome that would emerge as a consequence of a majority vote. If only the outcome proves non-cyclical, microeconomic theory is able to anticipate the outcome of a majority vote. There are conditions in which it will be the option preferred by the median voter.[5]

In Figure 14.1 the tastes and preferences of the median voter are shown and with the constraints faced by the median voter, the choice of the median voter indicates the choices that a community would make. In Figure 14.1 the line 1-2 is the median voter's budget line. For example, it might be thought of as depicting the combinations of G – a government service (e.g. education) – and all other goods available to the median voter, given prices and income with equilibrium found at point 3 with g^* education and y^* all other goods. In just the same way as analysis focused on the individual's indifference

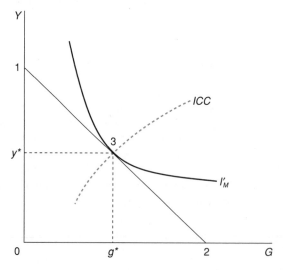

Figure 14.1
The choice of the median voter

5. This median voter model has been explored for some considerable time (e.g. Bowen 1943; Downs 1957; Black 1948).

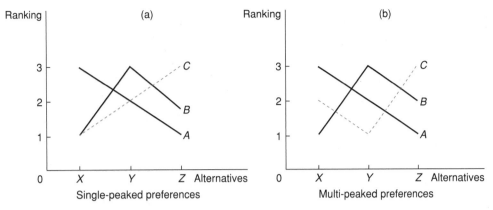

Figure 14.2 **Preferences and outcomes**

curve in Chapter 2, it is now possible, similarly, to predict the community's choices by focusing on the median voter. For example, if the issue was how would a community decide if income increased then, if *ICC* is the income consumption curve of the median voter, economists are able to predict the change in the community's demand. The same standard neoclassical microeconomic individual utility-maximising theory described in Chapter 2 becomes relevant. Changes in relative prices between public- and private-sector goods can be treated in the same way. But what conditions must apply to sustain confidence in the median voter model?

(i) *Single-peaked preferences.* Comparing the outcomes in Table 14.4 with that in Table 14.2 it is easy to show that in Table 14.4 preferences of voters are single-peaked and in Table 14.2 they are multi-peaked. Figure 14.2(a) illustrates the preference of voters as shown in Table 14.4. Figure 14.2(b) illustrates the preferences of voters as shown in Table 14.2. In Figure 14.2(b) there is more than one peak, whereas in Figure 14.2(a) there is a single peak for the preference of each voter. With reference to Table 14.4 the result of a (simple) majority vote is determined and is the option that is preferred by the median voter. Black (1948) demonstrated that this determinate outcome was only possible when there are single-peaked preferences. In neoclassical economics single-peaked preferences are not unusual (see Cullis and Jones 2009). While the possibility of multi-peaked preferences cannot be dismissed, there may be a case for majority voting when preferences are single-peaked.

That individuals may reveal multi-peaked preferences is by no means impossible and cannot be easily dismissed. For example, Hyman (2002) argues that in the US in the 1960s and the early 1970s, multiple-peaked preferences by US citizens were prevalent with respect to the Vietnam War. Many argued that wars, if fought, should be fought to win. The alternative of all-out war (including use of nuclear weapons) or no war at all was preferred to a limited war which simply checked the enemy. (For analysis of the possibility of multi-peaked preferences when expressing demand for education, see Stiglitz 1974).

(ii) *Uni-dimensional issue.* Single-peak preferences are not the only considerations. It is also necessary to assume that the vote is over *uni-dimensional issues*, e.g. higher, medium, lower levels of spending on school education. If issues were not uni-dimensional (e.g. the vote was on different combinations of spending levels for education and for health), McKelvey (1976) shows that, even if there are single-peaked preferences, it is now quite possible for cyclical outcomes if a 'simple majority voting' rule were employed. For a further discussion see Cullis and Jones (2009).

(ii) *Sincere voting*. Throughout it is also important to assume that individuals *vote sincerely*. Voters do not always declare their preferences honestly; sometimes they vote strategically.

14.4 Intensity of preference and lobbying

One problem with expressing 'demand' in the electoral process is that, even if individuals vote, the principle of 'one man, one vote' (so often enshrined in democracy) means that they have no means of expressing intensity of preference. 'One man, one vote' may sound equitable but it means that those who feel very strongly about issues have as much say as those who have no interest at all in the issues that are to be decided. By contrast, in markets intensity of preference is revealed by 'willingness to pay'. If the sums that individuals are willing to pay reveal their valuation, within competitive markets those who are willing to pay more than the opportunity cost are those whose demand will be met.

One aspect of this is that some economists have advocated a case for vote trading (Buchanan and Tullock 1965). Vote trading ('logrolling') is often explicit. This is so when representatives trade policies, in the USA a Congressman from Florida might agree to vote on an issue that is preferred by another from Wyoming and in return the Congressman from Wyoming will vote for an issue of paramount importance to the Congressman from Florida. It is sometimes implicit, e.g. when political parties write manifestos by coupling different issues (so that, if you are particularly keen on policy X you must also vote for policy Y and vice versa). Cullis and Jones (2009) provide a critique of such explicit and implicit logrolling.

An alternative approach to register intensity of preference is to engage in lobbying. For example, if individuals feel strongly about an issue they are able to write to their representatives and to form associations to lobby government. In a pluralistic system 'interest groups' or 'pressure groups' are evident. Surely then there are other mechanisms by which intensity of preference can be revealed? The existence of lobbies, such as the Campaign for Civil Rights, the National Farmers' Union, the British Medical Association indicates that there is an alternative route by which individuals may express intensity of preference.

In line with views expressed by nineteenth-century analysts (such as Alexis de Tocqueville 1835), political scientists such as Arthur Bentley admired the voluntaristic political pluralism of liberal societies (Shepsle and Bonchek 1997). However, when neoclassical microeconomic theory is applied to analyse collective action there are concerns about the way in which individuals express intensity of preference via lobbying government.

Olson's (1965) analysis of group behaviour suggested that the identification of common interests was not enough to motivate group action. The implication was that, far from lobbying allowing intensity of preference to improve resource allocation decisions, the lobbying processes might well reduce the welfare of some groups who faced difficulty in mobilising.

14.4.1 Lobbying in the political process

If participation in the electoral process is difficult to explain, so too is participation in lobbying. Olson's (1965) 'logic' of collective action rejected the supposition that identification of common interests leads naturally to collective action. His logic predicted that an individual member of a 'large' group will not voluntarily support an association, even if the association has the opportunity to advance the group's common interests

Table 14.5 Contribution to lobbying: the large number situation

	Others contribute	Others do not contribute	Net expected benefit
Contribution	10 – 5	–5	$(5 \times 0.5) + (-5 \times 0.5) = 0$
No contribution	10	0	$(10 \times 0.5) + (0 \times 0.5) = 5$

Table 14.6 Contribution to lobbying: the small number situation

	Others contribute	Others do not contribute	Net expected benefit
Contribution	10 – 5	–5	$(5 \times 0.9) + (-5 \times 0.1) = 4$
No contribution	10	0	$(10 \times 0.1) + (0 \times 0.9) = 1$

(e.g. by lobbying for legislative change). Each individual recognises that, if the association were successful, the benefits would be freely available to all (benefits would not be contingent on having offered support). Olson's insight was that contributing to an association is tantamount to revealing demand for a 'public good'.[6] In Chapter 6 it was argued that individuals would try to 'free-ride', rather than contribute to a public good. In the same way, individuals would have an incentive to let others bear the costs of lobbying in an attempt to free-ride on their efforts. If all behave this way, there can be no 'free ride' and the group remains latent.

As in the discussion in Chapter 6, the distinction between 'small' groups and 'large' groups is important. In the following example an individual would be better off by the equivalent of £10 if legislation were introduced and is asked to contribute £5 to an association intent on lobbying for legislation. If others contribute and lobbying is successful the individual will be £(10 – 5) better off. If others do not contribute lobbying will not succeed and the individuals will lose £5 (see Table 14.5). The individual compares the payoffs associated with contribution on the assumption that one contribution will not make a difference to the likelihood that others will participate. The individual assumes that there is 0.5 chance that others will contribute. The net expected payoff from contribution (£0) is lower than the net expected payoff from not contributing (£5).

In a small group the individual feels that personal action is significant. In a 'small' group individuals may be aware of how the individual behaves. The individual now assumes that the likelihood that others will contribute is greater as a consequence of making a contribution. In Table 14.6 the probability that others will contribute is 0.1 if the individual does not contribute but 0.9 if the individual contributes. In a small group the individual contributes (as £4 > £1). The association mobilises support and presses the government for legislation.

The implication of Olson's analysis is that there is likely to be asymmetry when political influence is exerted. Small groups are likely to be at an advantage. When Olson notes that large groups may sometimes be mobilised he emphasises that this is not motivated by the desire to lobby government. Large groups might be mobilised by coercion (e.g. 'closed shop' authority requires membership of an association to secure employment) or via the inducement of a private (excludable) good or service contingent on membership

6. A public good defined in Chapter 6, is a good which is non-rival in consumption and non-excludable (Buchanan 1968). It is non-rival in consumption when the availability of the good to one individual is not reduced by consumption of the good by another individual. It is non-excludable when making the good available to one individual means that it cannot be denied to others in the group.

(e.g. cheap insurance, a journal, an invitation to a social, or gala, occasion). He proposed the 'by-product theory'; large-group associations use private goods (excludable to non-subscribers) to raise revenue to finance public good goals (non-excludable to members of the group) and shows that associations representing 'large' groups rely more heavily on selective incentives.

14.5 Rent-seeking

To this point, the analysis suggests that, in political markets, small groups are likely to be more effective than large groups (consumer groups) in terms of putting pressure on governments. To illustrate the significance of this result, the objective is to consider the gains that lobbying might deliver. Consider once again the costs of monopoly (as discussed in Chapter 11).

Standard microeconomic theory focuses on outcomes. Compare the outcome when there is a monopoly with the outcome if there is a competitive market. In Figure 14.3, D is the demand curve for a product X. The price of the good is P_c and the output of the good is q_c if the good is supplied by a competitive industry (i.e. price set equal to marginal cost). However, if a monopolist were to supply the good then there would be an incentive to equate marginal revenue with marginal cost. In Figure 14.3 a monopolist would sell q_m at a price P_m (i.e. where $MC = MR$). Consumers are denied q_c-q_m of the good to allow the monopolist to increase price. The producer gains a higher price (P_m-P_c) on output (0-q_m). The producer has an incentive to lobby governments to acquire a monopoly position (e.g. sole licence to producer). Of course, if consumers are more difficult to mobilise then resistance to such lobbying may be small.

In Figure 14.3 the monopolist gains P_m-2-3-P_c. However, consumers' loss is estimated by reference to the consumers' surplus that they would have enjoyed on the units q_c-q_m that are no longer supplied (i.e. trapezoid P_m-2-1-P_c). There is a deadweight loss equal to the difference in these two areas, i.e. equal to triangle 3-2-1. The size of the triangle depends on the price elasticity of demand. As Tollison (1982) notes, such triangles are usually small and this implies that the cost of monopoly is usually low. He cites Mundell (1962: 622): 'unless there is a thorough re-examination of the validity of the tools upon which these studies are found, someone will inevitably draw the conclusion that economics has ceased to be important'.

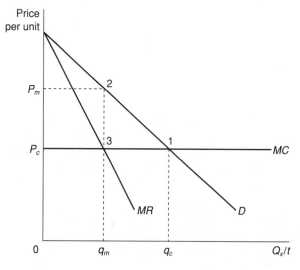

Figure 14.3
The social costs of monopoly

Public choice analysis includes analysis of the process of decision-making and the costs of this process. By looking, not only at outcomes, but also at processes, a different application of microeconomic analysis indicates that resources expended in acquiring and in defending monopoly power may be more important than the deadweight loss. If monopoly power relies on acquiring a licence from government, producers have an incentive to incur costs lobbying government.

Turning to Figure 14.3, Tullock (1967) argued that if there were gains for the monopolist of P_m-2-3-P_c then there is an incentive to spend resources to acquire these rents. Rent-seeking is defined as: 'the expenditure of scarce resources to capture an artificially created transfer' (Tollison 1982: 578). Indeed, it is conceivable that the total P_m-2-3-P_c would be paid to acquire monopoly status (i.e. that individuals would be prepared to pay as much as P_m-2-3-P_c to acquire a monopoly position that would deliver rents equal to P_m-2-3-P_c). The costs of monopoly now exceed triangle 3-2-1. The costs of monopoly equal the trapezoid P_m-2-1-P_c as additional resources (equal to P_m-2-3-P_c) are dissipated in acquiring and maintaining a monopoly position.

How large are such rent-seeking costs likely to be? When considering the *maximum* amount that anyone would invest to acquire a monopoly position the sum involved may be equal to the expected capitalised value of the discounted future income stream from a position of monopoly. The area P_m-2-3-P_c is a transfer of income from the consumer to the producer but a producer may be prepared to pay almost as much as P_m-2-3-P_c to effect this transfer.

If there is *competition for rents* from a monopoly position, when will the dissipation of resources equal the rents? Following Mueller (2003), consider the case in which rent-seekers are risk-neutral (so that utility may be considered in monetary units). The amount used in rent-seeking is S, and the potential rent that might be enjoyed is R. If all rent-seekers have the same initial income (Y) and each chooses to invest the same amount in rent-seeking (S), it is also possible to consider the number who will compete for rents (n). Each rent-seeker will devote resources to rent-seeking to the point at which the expected income of a rent-seeker ($E(Y)$) equals the income (Y) of a non-rent-seeker. If the probability that rent-seeking will prove successful is $1/n$, then this condition holds in equation (14.14):

$$E(Y) = \frac{1}{n}(Y - S + R) + \frac{n-1}{n}(Y - S) = Y \tag{14.14}$$

It follows that, at this equilibrium,

$$Y - S + R + (n-1)(Y - S) = nY \tag{14.15}$$

If so, the total amount spent in rent-seeking (nS) equals R (the rent to be enjoyed). Simplifying equation (14.15):

$$R = nS \tag{14.16}$$

This analysis indicates that resources will be dissipated in rent-seeking to the point at which the number of rent-seekers multiplied by the amount each spends on rent-seeking equals the rents that might be achieved. It should be emphasised, however, that the analysis depends on specific assumptions and, if any of these are relaxed, it is possible that rent-seeking costs may be less than (or greater than) the rents to be earned. In particular it has been assumed that:

(1) rent-seekers are risk-neutral;
(2) they are in symmetric positions;
(3) there is free entry into rent-seeking.

These assumptions are important when predicting the total funds used on rent-seeking.[7]

An alternative analysis of rent-seeking focuses on the contest between producers and consumers. As noted in the previous section of the chapter, producers are well organised to press for legislation and if producers succeed in pressing for legislation that increases price and reduces entry into the industry they are able to set a higher price. In 1776 Adam Smith wrote:

> People of the same trade seldom meet together, even for merriment and diversion, but the conversation ends in conspiracy against the public, or in some contrivance to raise prices.
>
> (Adam Smith, *The Wealth of Nations*, bk I, chap. X, part II, par.27, New York: Modern Library, 1937)

While producers are more likely to prove successful because small groups are more easily mobilised it is possible to demonstrate that the costs of rent-seeking would exceed the rent at stake if consumers also engaged in political lobbying to resist producers. In Figure 14.4 a producer wishes to lobby a regulatory agency to allow a price increase from P_c to P_m. Consumers wish to persuade the regulatory agency to keep the price at P_c. Each party regards the expected price to be equal to $[(P_m + P_c)/2]$, i.e. P_1 in Figure 14.4.

The producer, at maximum, will spend as much as P_C-P_1-1-3 and the consumers will spend at maximum P_C-P_1-1-2 to resist. Total expenditure will then equal P_C-P_m-5-1-2 and this exceeds the value of the uncontested transfer P_C-P_m-4-6. Indeed, rent-seeking now exceeds the value of the original Tullock estimate by area 4-5-1-2-6 (Baysinger and Tollison 1980).

If rent-seeking costs look formidable there are arguments to suggest that rent-seeking is not always welfare-reducing:

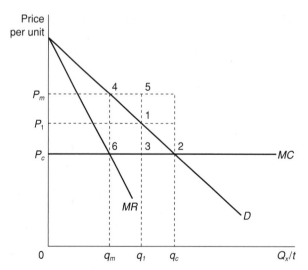

Figure 14.4
Rent-seeking: producers versus consumers

7. Posner (1975) identified such conditions. He argued that if obtaining a monopoly right is a competitive process, that the monopoly right is worth £100,000 and that there are ten risk-neutral bidders, then each rent-seeker would spend £10,000 on attaining the monopoly right. It follows that society would dissipate the £100,000 by the attempt to capture the transfer. Posner notes, more fully, that this result assumed that '(1) obtaining a monopoly is itself a competitive activity, (2) long run supply of all inputs used in rent seeking is perfectly elastic, (3) rent seeking itself creates no externalities, (4) the monopoly privilege is granted for one period only and (5) individual rent seekers are risk neutral' (Brooks and Heijdra 1989: 36).

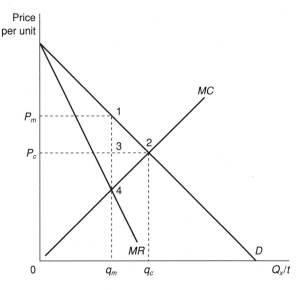

Figure 14.5
Rent-seeking and increasing
marginal costs

(i) *Second-best considerations.* This consideration arises when lobbying helps correct an existing distortion. With reference to Figure 14.5 as a reference point, consider the rent-seeking costs that arise when marginal cost is upward-sloping and firms seek to operate as a monopoly.

The demand curve is shown as D and the marginal cost curve is MC. The output of a perfectly competitive industry would be identified as one where price was set equal to marginal cost, i.e. output q_C. A monopoly producer would restrict output to reap additional profits. If output were reduced to q_m, then consumer surplus would be reduced by P_C-P_m-1-2. However, producers would gain the price difference on all output sold (i.e. area P_C-P_m-1-3 on output 0-q_m) less the producer surplus lost on the output no longer sold (i.e. triangle 3-2-4). The net sum is positive for producers and it will pay them to reduce output on the market until marginal cost (MC) is equal to marginal revenue (MR). The loss to society as a whole includes triangle 3-2-4 and triangle 1-2-3, (i.e. triangle 1-2-4). Area P_C-P_m-1-3 is a transfer from consumers to producers. To effect this transfer, rent-seeking has increased the costs of monopoly from the deadweight triangle loss 1-2-4 to this *plus* the dissipation of resources equal to $[(P_C$-P_m-1-3$) - (3$-2-4$)]$.

Now consider the same analysis with respect to Figure 14.6. The assumption is that there is an external cost associated with the production of the good. This means that the marginal private costs (MPC) are less than the marginal social costs (MSC). If the monopolist lobbies successfully to reduce output, there is an *increase* in welfare (for at the competitive equilibrium q_C there are deadweight losses equal to triangle 1-5-2). The gain to producers from lobbying is P_C-P_m-1-3 on output 0-q_m less the producer surplus lost on the output no longer sold as shown by triangle 3-2-4. However, even if resources equal to this difference are dissipated in the process of rent-seeking these may be less than the gain in welfare from reducing output (i.e. triangle 1-5-2). There has then been a net welfare improvement because rent-seeking costs are outweighed by gains in correcting the allocative inefficiency created by the externality. Once again, 'second best' considerations (see Chapter 6) come into play.

(ii) *Beneficial aspects of rent-seeking expenditure.* Not all expenditure classified as rent-seeking is a complete waste:

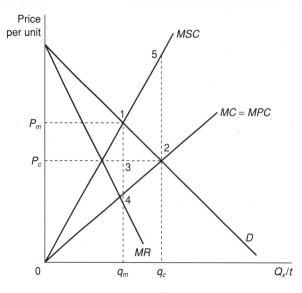

Figure 14.6
Rent-seeking in a second-best world

(a) Not all expenditures are without some social value if lobbying yields additional information as lobbyists make their case (Quibria 1989).

(b) Not all expenditure dissipates resources (e.g. as complete wastes), some reflects income transfer (e.g. to persuade officials by increasing their consumption possibilities). Usually, there is no allowance for this possibility (e.g. the utility gained by politicians taken to pleasant lunches or receptions). These gains reduce costs (Samuels and Mercuro 1984). Congleton (1988) notes that, if the rent-seeker takes the regulator out to dinner, the value that the regulator places on the dinner must be subtracted from the social costs of rent-seeking. Again, bribes are technically not rent-seeking cost; they are a transfer (Tollison 1997).

(iii) *Distinctions between pursuit of profitable opportunities and rents.* One important problem when interpreting rent-seeking costs is how to draw the line between activities which are wasteful and those which increase profit opportunities. Buchanan (1980) made the distinction by emphasising that traditional competitive profit-seeking or entrepreneurship in the competitive model (seeking quasi-rents) does not qualify as rent-seeking. Such profit-seeking is productive; it creates value in the form of new products. In this vein, a strong case has been put by DiLorenzo (1988) that 'the problem of objectively identifying "wasteful" rent seeking is intractable, and that rent-seeking waste can only be identified by introducing one's own subjective standards of value' (p. 318).

14.5.1 Estimating rent-seeking costs

It is difficult to estimate rent-seeking costs (see the review by Tollison 1997). Some estimates focus narrowly on resources dissipated to occupy monopoly status. In other studies attempts are made, more generally, to estimate the extent to which rent-seeking reduces efficiency within the economy as a whole.

Focusing on rent seeking for a monopoly (and with reference to Figure 14.5), Cowling and Mueller (1978) reported rent-seeking and deadweight costs of private monopoly in the USA of 13 per cent of gross corporate product. Posner (1975) estimated social costs of monopolisation through regulation at 3 per cent of USA GNP.

Studies of rent-seeking show there are many ways in which costs are borne. With reference to a range of activities that firms pursue to acquire import licences, Krueger (1974) estimated that 7 per cent of Indian GNP was lost in rent-seeking and 15 per cent of Turkish GNP was dissipated in rent-seeking for import licences. Even more significantly, Ross (1984) estimated that trade-related rent-seeking accounted for 38 per cent of GDP in Kenya.

More generally, rent-seeking costs have been associated with the activity of those most often caught up in the process. The activity of lawyers is often at the centre of empirical analysis. Laband and Sophocleus (1988), Magee, Brock and Young (1989), and Murphy, Shleifer and Vishny (1991) add lawyers in regressions that seek to explain GNP or rates of growth in GNP (for the United States for other countries). The evidence is consistent with the proposition that when there are more lawyers economic growth is lower.[8]

Some have focused on estimates of rent-seeking costs in different sectors. Laband and Sophocleus (1988) focused on expenditures on items such as locks, insurance, police and the military in the US, the argument being that these are required as a result of the rent-seeking or 'rent-protecting'. Focusing on these costs, it appeared that as much as one-half of the US GNP in 1985 was lost on these activities.[9]

In *The Rise and Decline of Nations*, Olson argued that the relative cost of diversionary rent-seeking increases over time in stable societies; resources are moved from growth-producing activities to unproductive rent-seeking. He argued that the relatively strong post-war performance of the German, Italian and Japanese economies indicates that, when political institutions of defeated nations were destroyed, the power of interest groups was reduced. By contrast, lower growth in the USA, Australia, New Zealand and the UK reflected the stable continuity of social structures.

Choi (1983) considered Olson's hypothesis at the macroeconomic level. An index of sclerosis (*IS*) was constructed for eighteen OECD countries depending on: the number of years since last major disruptions; the size and the length of the disruption. The proposition was that income per capita (*Y*) would be lower the higher the index. For the period 1950 to 1973, Choi reports regression equations in which *Y* is lower the higher is *IS*.

At a microeconomic level, Murrell (1983) compared rates of industry growth in the UK and Germany. Following Olson's reasoning, the gap between relative rates of growth in young and old industries should be higher in the UK than in Germany. In the UK, interest groups would have had a longer time to establish themselves in old industries. Murrell reports that for 1969–73 this prediction was supported in over 50% of cases analysed.

Olson's analysis of *The Rise and Decline of Nations* was criticised with the advent of a downturn in the fortunes of countries such as Japan, Germany and France and a relative improvement in growth rates in the USA and the UK. Olson (1982) argued that the power of interest groups may be cyclical. A long period of economic stagnation leads to their entrenched power being challenged by a reforming leader (e.g. Margaret Thatcher in the UK).

Tollison (1997) summarises some of the main empirical results in Table 14.7.

8. Some estimates indicate that aggregate income is lower by as much as 45 per cent as a result of the wastes of lawyers.
9. Categories treated as rent-seeking costs included crime prevention (FBI), police (corrections), restraint of trade (FTC), residential investments (locks), commercial investments (guards), educational investments (library theft), property-rights disputes (tort litigation), and government (defence, lobbyists, political action committees). The approach is to go sector-by-sector to obtain their estimates of rent-seeking costs.

Table 14.7 **Estimates of rent-seeking costs**

Study	Economy	Year	Rent-seeking costs
Krueger	India	1964	7% GNP
Krueger	Turkey	1968	15% GNP (trade sector)
Posner	United States	Various years	3% GNP (regulation)
Cowling & Mueller	United States	1963–6	13% GCP (private monopoly)[a]
Cowling & Mueller	United Kingdom	1968–9	7% GCP (private monopoly)
Ross	Kenya	1980	38% GDP (trade sector)
Mohammand & Whalley	India	1980–1	25–40% GNP
Laband & Sophoeleus	United States	1985	50% GNP
	Various countries	Various years	Up to 45% GNP

[a] Cowling and Mueller (1978) use gross corporate product as the basis of their calculation.
Source: Tollison 1997.

14.6 Rent-seeking through regulation

In Chapter 6, regulation was one policy option used to deal with market failure. The usual application of neoclassical microeconomics focuses on *outcomes*. A static analysis compares welfare in the case of market failure (e.g. an externality) with welfare when government introduces regulation to deal with this. The approach is described as Pigouvian (as it is based on Pigou's *Welfare Economics*). Implicitly, government is perceived as benign; concerned only with the welfare of individuals in the community. Viscusi *et al.* (1992) describe the approach as *normative* in that it prescribes solutions to increase welfare within the community. Consider instances in which regulation might be required.

(i)   *Natural monopoly.* On one hand natural monopoly is desirable (it would be wasteful for a number of firms to incur fixed costs). On the other hand, a sole supplier makes consumers vulnerable to monopoly prices. Regulation offers a way in which a sole supplier might be constrained to produce efficiently – a number of different pricing regulations were considered in Chapter 6.

(ii) *Oligopoly.* When only a few firms exist there is concern that consumers will be exploited if they collude (see Chapter 11). Antitrust legislation is introduced to stop firms colluding and exploiting monopoly power.

(iii) *Externalities* create a divergence between private costs (benefits) and social costs (benefits), see Chapter 6. Government regulation might force individuals to behave *as if* they took social costs (benefits) into account.

(iv) *Common* resources – when several firms extract a common resource (e.g. oil, fish) from the same source, or when farmers graze cattle on common ground, *homo economicus* pursues profit with no account of how private action raises costs for others. Regulation may be capable of increasing welfare.

(v)   *Public good* provision creates difficulties because individuals free-ride. Once again, regulation may be an option. For example, information is a public good (when provided it is difficult to exclude others' access) and, to maintain an incentive to invest in research and development, one regulatory solution is to offer patents (at least for a limited period – see Chapter 8).

(vi) *Asymmetry of information* arises when producers have greater access to information than consumers. For example, consumers of medical care may be unable to distinguish trained doctors from quacks; regulation of medical licences offers consumers a quality standard and redresses asymmetry of information.

Viscusi *et al.* offer a critique of this approach.

(i) *Incomplete theory.* There is no account of the *process* by which government introduces regulation. What motivates legislation?

(ii) *Mixed evidence.* Theory is not always supported by evidence. For example, the theory suggests that industries to be regulated will be natural monopolies or industries plagued by externalities, etc. Yet, economists note that in the USA regulation covers a much wider variety of industries (e.g. in trucking and taxicabs).

(iii) *Industry lobbying.* The theory fails to explain why firms often lobby for regulation. (e.g. railroads in the USA in the late 1880s pressed for regulation). The prediction of Olson is that producers, rather than consumers, will lobby for regulation, and evidence supports this.

(iv) *Regulatory behaviour.* Market failure (normative) theory might suggest that regulation would generally constrain pricing behaviour in consumers' interests but evidence suggests that regulatory agencies favour producers' interests, e.g. Stigler and Friedland (1962).

In this critique, significant attention is paid to the interests of actors who play a role in the political process – e.g. lobbyists, regulatory agencies. This approach is often referred to as a *positive* theory of regulation.

14.6.1 A positive theory of regulation

If a normative account (based on outcomes) fails to explain the existence and character of regulation, perhaps a positive account (based on processes) will have more to say? Stigler (1971) considered why regulation is introduced. The focus is now on rent from regulation and the rent-seeking activity of those who seek regulation. Stigler argued that 'regulation is acquired by the industry and is designed and operated primarily for its benefit' (p. 3). Far from regulation being an imposition on firms, firms demand regulation.

The rent-seeking analysis (explained with reference to Figure 14.3) can, once again, be applied. In Figure 14.7, the advantages of being able to price at P_m, rather than selling at the competitive pricing at P_c, is shown as area α in Figure 14.7. The efficiency loss due to monopoly pricing is β. Stigler (1971) drew attention to the advantages to firms as a consequence of using regulation to acquire α (rather than the market failure – normative – approach which focused on deadweight loss, β).

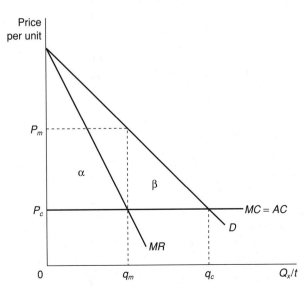

Figure 14.7   Stigler's analysis of regulation

Stigler's analysis emphasised the ability of government to introduce and maintain cartelisation of firms in an industry. Regulation might be used to reduce competitive pressures (if new firms require licences to operate) and this may be the real objective (rather than using regulation as a market corrective). Rents (area α) provide an incentive for producers to call for regulation. Producers are small groups compared with consumers (Olson 1965). Politicians are lobbied by those who want regulation to create rents, rather than by those who would want to regulate to deal with market failure. By focusing on these 'benefits' of state regulation, Stigler argued:

> The central tasks of the theory of economic regulation are to explain who will receive the benefits or burdens of regulation . . . Regulation may be actively sought by an industry, or it may be thrust upon it. A central thesis of this paper is that, as a rule, regulation is acquired by the industry and is designed and operated primarily for its benefit. There are regulations whose net effects upon the regulated industry are undeniably onerous . . . These onerous regulations, however, are exceptional. (Stigler 1971: 3)

Instead of asking (normatively) how welfare for society can be increased, politicians respond to those groups who can most effectively press their case. Government regulation offers producers the ability to appropriate rents that would be unavailable without the authority of the state to control and monitor regulation of industries. Existing firms may find that cartelisation is more cheaply achieved via this route.

Producer groups are more effective lobbyists when considering regulation because they:

(i) are a small group (by comparison with consumers);
(ii) have more at stake financially with respect to any single piece of legislation. (Consumers may be affected by legislation for one good in the basket of goods that they purchase. However, producers of that good recognise that issues of regulation are vital for their livelihood.)

Consumers are more likely to be apathetic (consider, for example, the low proportion membership of the UK Consumers' Association). Producers press for regulation; Stigler comments, 'every industry or occupation that has enough political power to utilise the state will seek to control entry' (1971: 5).

14.6.2 Producers versus consumers: a broader analysis

Stigler's model is supported by evidence (e.g. Crandall and Graham 1984). However, there are criticisms. Can consumer interests be completely overlooked? Consumers may be ineffectual as lobby groups but they have political clout at the ballot box. Politicians who supply regulation in response to pressure from producers will risk vote loss. Also, Stigler's theory (focusing on only producer interest) does not explain all government policy? For example, if producer interests alone dominate, why were there government initiatives to deregulate in the mid-to-late 1970s?

Peltzman (1976) extended Stigler's analysis. The focus is on the incentives faced by politicians. Regulation is supplied by a vote-maximising politician. Following Mueller (2003), V, the number of votes a politician receives, is a function of the impact of regulation on the utility of affected parties. U_P is the utility of producers and U_C is the utility of consumers. V can be written as:

$$V = V(U_P, U_C), \quad \frac{\partial V}{\partial U_P} > 0, \quad \frac{\partial V}{\partial U_C} > 0 \tag{14.17}$$

When a politician–regulator sets a regulated price for a product, the critical question is how will this affect the utility of consumers and producers. Consumer and producer welfare for any regulated price (above the competitive price) depends on areas α and β (as shown in Figure 14.7). For producers:

$$U_P = \alpha \tag{14.18}$$

and, for consumers:

$$U_C = \theta - \alpha - \beta, \tag{14.19}$$

where θ is an arbitrary constant.

A vote-maximising regulator will set price p, so that

$$\frac{dV}{dp} = \frac{\partial V}{\partial U_P}\frac{d\alpha}{dp} - \frac{\partial V}{\partial U_C}\frac{d\alpha}{dp} - \frac{\partial V}{\partial U_C}\frac{d\beta}{dp} = 0 \tag{14.20}$$

or

$$\frac{\partial V}{\partial U_P}\frac{d\alpha}{dp} = \frac{\partial V}{\partial U_C}\left(\frac{d\alpha}{dp} + \frac{d\beta}{dp}\right) \tag{14.21}$$

This vote-maximising condition states that a vote-maximising regulator will set a price so that marginal gain in support from the producers for an increment in monopoly rents is just offset by the loss in consumer votes.

The analysis is illustrated as in Figure 14.8. Panel (a) describes a constant cost market situation for the production of good X. The cost structure, $MC = AC$, means that, initially, there is a competitive price P_c (determined at point 1). The 45° line in panel (b) allows P_c to appear on both the vertical axis and on the horizontal axis of panel (b).

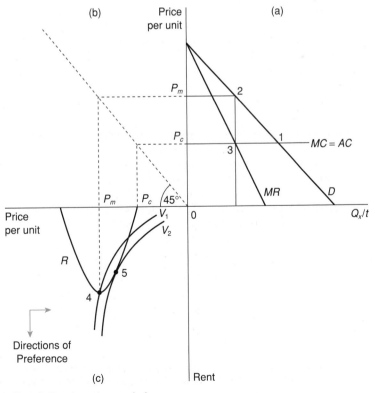

Figure 14.8 Regulation to vote-maximise

In panel (c) V_1 and V_2 are isovote curves. Each isovote curve maps combinations of rent and prices of the good that yield the same votes. The objective of the government is to maximise votes subject to the constraint faced. If government believed that only representing the interests of consumers produced votes, the isovote curve would be a vertical line; any price above P_C would be 'bad' (for it would cost votes). If, however, the government believes that votes (political support) are produced by response to a lobby group and that initially these are greater than vote loss from consumers (because consumers are less aware of this policy), the isovote curve takes the shape illustrated. Lower prices increase votes from consumers. A price above P_C allows producers rent and the politician gains their votes. The direction of vote gains is indicated by the arrows in panel (c). The curvature of the isovote curves indicates that the more the government introduces legislation that permits price increases, the greater the vote loss from consumers; consumers become ever more aware that their interests have been compromised.

When price is P_C, price equals marginal cost (equals average cost) in panel (a); there is no rent (or supernormal profit). Now assume that the politician–regulator considers lobbying by producers, i.e. that there should be procedures by which new firms are restricted entry. New legislation means that existing firms are able to informally reduce output and increase price – there is now no fear that new entrants will enter the industry. In panel (a) price will increase as output is reduced. Of course, the price at which rent is maximised is shown at point 2 as P_m.

In panel (c) rent increases as price increases; the implications for rent are shown by the rent 'valley' (R). This function shows that rent is at a maximum at point 4 in panel (c) – i.e. at point 4 rent is equal to area P_c-P_m-2-3 in panel (a) of Figure 14.8 and deadweight loss is triangle 1-2-3. But at this point the incumbent politician has not maximised votes (the politician's policy is located on isovote curve V_1). It is evident that votes are greater on isovote curve V_2, because on isovote curve V_2 more rent is possible for any increase in price (i.e. V_2 is to the right of V_1).

A vote-maximising government would be at equilibrium on V_2, i.e. at tangency point 5. Votes increase if the politician also takes into account the vote loss that will be experienced in responding only to the producer lobby group. A vote-maximising equilibrium requires a price that is set between P_C and P_m. Producers will gain at the expense of consumers of good X but governments will not set price at the rent-maximising level. With reference to equation (14.21) the vote-maximising outcome is determined by a price which reflects *both* consumer and producer interests. As noted, consumers may be at a disadvantage. They may be ill-informed as to the cause of higher prices (i.e. that this is a result of government regulation). They are difficult to mobilise because the potential gains to any individual of cheaper purchases of just one good are low and the 'free-rider' problem looms large. Moreover, governments are likely to argue that regulation is required for the consumer, e.g. in terms of: 'safety', or that there is a moral case, e.g. in terms of preventing imports from low-quality 'sweatshop' economies.

How helpful is Peltzman's model?

(i) Stigler's model predicts that regulation will be biased toward benefiting a small interest group at the cost of a large group.[10] Of course there is evidence that the strength of producer groups in the decision-making process enhances incomes (e.g. Shepherd 1978; Ulrich, Furtan and Schmitz 1987). But Leffler (1978), and Keeler (1984) present

---

10. It has been argued above that when the numbers involved (n) are large the costs of organisation are high. At the same time, when n is low the share of wealth transfer per person goes up (i.e. the inducement to participate is high).

evidence consistent with the view that both consumer and producer interests receive some weight in the final regulatory outcomes. Also, there is evidence that, in some cases (e.g. the passage of legislation regulating the stock exchanges in the 1930s), consumers have received substantial redistributive gains (Schwert 1977).

Evidence indicates that producers do not always enjoy rent-maximising prices. As long as $\partial V/\partial U_C > 0$ (i.e. as long as there is some loss in votes from reducing consumer utility) the solution will not be one in which there is a rent-maximising price.

(ii) As the legislator chooses action to maximise political support, the regulated price lies between P_C and P_m. This means that the industries most likely to be regulated are those that are either:

1. relatively competitive (so that the unregulated equilibrium price is near P_C), or
2. relatively monopolistic (so that the unregulated equilibrium price is near P_m).

In both cases, there is scope for gain from regulation. Firms will gain in the case of a competitive industry, while consumers will gain in the case of a monopolistic industry. Empirical evidence indicates that it is these two extremes that tend to be subject to regulation (e.g. monopolistic industries include local telephone, electricity producers and railroads, while relatively competitive industries include agriculture, taxicabs and securities). Peltzman's model helps explain the ubiquitous use of regulation of agriculture.

There is then a case for acknowledging the contribution that can be made by this application of microeconomic analysis to the process of decision-making. However, there are also criticisms and unresolved issues:

(i) Theories by Stigler and Peltzman regarding regulation are not the only theories to emerge from the University of Chicago. Gary Becker (1983) offers a theory of competition between interest groups that yields quite different predictions. In Becker's theory the impact of deadweight loss associated with policies plays a critically important role. All interest groups are subject to free-riding and what is important is the *relative* severity of free-riding. When the free-riding problem is less severe in group 1 than in group 2 (perhaps because group 1 has fewer members), group 1 will have a relative advantage over group 2. However, if the deadweight loss from regulation is significant the gains to the group that opposes it will be greater and (notwithstanding differences in free-riding), there will be greater opposition to regulation. Allowing for the deadweight loss suggests that opponents to regulation (in Stigler and Peltzman's approach) will prove relatively more effective. The implication is that regulatory policies that are welfare-improving are more likely to be implemented than policies that are not.

(ii) Following on from this, not all assessment of regulation leads to the conclusion that regulation is consistent with a positive theory (that focuses only on gains and losses to the participants in the decision-making process). For all the criticisms levelled at the normative account of regulation described in Section 14.5 (above), some economists argue that evidence is consistent with the normative (community-welfare-based) theory of regulation. Kelman (1988) reviews a number of examples of regulation. While each might be explained in terms of the interests of the participants in the process of regulation, the overall assessment is that they are consistent with a genuine attempt to enhance the community's welfare. For example:

(a) Peltzman (1975) analyses car safety regulation. The 'naive' hypothesis is that it serves to reduce accidents and increase welfare. A more cynical view is that it results only in risk compensation – leaving an individual exposed to a constant amount of risk. That is to say that there is no advantage in terms of reducing car accidents (if the costs of a potential accident are reduced you increase the probability of an accident by taking more risks).

(b) Viscusi (1985) considers product safety regulation and child-proof medicine caps. The 'naive' hypothesis is that welfare will be increased, as there will be a reduction in accidental poisonings. A more cynical interpretation is that it cannot achieve this goal because (as a consequence of more complicated caps) adults are inclined to take fewer precautions storing medicines away from children.

(c) Bartell and Thomas (1985) analyse occupational safety regulations. The 'naive' hypothesis is that it is designed to reduce workplace accidents. The criticism is that it is ineffective in these terms (because either there is little compliance, reflecting poor enforcement, or the regulations are not closely connected to safety.

(d) Linneman (1980) examines mattress flammability standards. The 'naive' (normative) hypothesis is that the intention is to reduce fires. An approach that considers alternative explanations would note that it has little beneficial impact in reducing fires.

Having reviewed these arguments Kelman (1988) tends to find in favour of 'naive' hypotheses, casting doubt on 'positive' analysis as an alternative explanation of regulation. While he does not doubt elements of truth in the 'regulatory capture' thesis, he argues that empirical evidence is not sufficient for it to dispel a view that well-designed regulation can increase welfare.

(iii) With reference to the discussion of the costs of rent-seeking (discussed in Section 14.3.2), Mueller (2003) criticises the Stigler–Peltzman approach for regarding rent-seeking (in pursuit of regulation) as completely wasteful (the issue of whether such expenditures dissipate resources, or represent a transfer, is not addressed in Stigler's approach).

(iv) Regulation is not necessarily a struggle between producers and consumers. Producers also struggle between one another. McChesney (1997) considers different forms of regulation. One example is a *cost predation* model of regulation. In this case, the emphasis is on the difference between different producers within an industry. The objective of regulation is for one subgroup to achieve regulation to disadvantage another subgroup. For example, capital-intensive firms in an industry may benefit by securing government regulation in the labour market (a minimum wage), which disadvantages more labour-intensive competitors.

In Figure 14.9 producers in an industry have differing amounts of a specific asset. The industry supply curve in the absence of regulation is S_0. The return to the specific assets is paid out of producers' surplus, which is area 0-1-3. These returns are rents (returns to the asset's owner above the returns necessary to induce the owner to keep the asset in its current use). Regulatory measures increase costs for all firms, but proportionately more for some firms than for others. The industry supply curve shifts to S_1.[11] Higher overall costs due to regulation mean higher prices to consumers, and so a lower quantity produced, while reduced quantities mean that rents earned on *some* existing production will be lost. Costs, for capital-intensive producers, rise less than prices. This creates new rents exceeding the old rents lost for capital-intensive producers. In Figure 14.9, area *a* is greater than area *b* (2-3-4-5 > 1-0-5). Firms with high capital investments – and lower marginal (labour) costs – gain. McChesney argues that this *cost predation* model describes many forms of regulation (labour, environmental, broadcasting). This is a variant on Stigler's theory of regulation.

---

11. For example, a regulation increasing the cost of labour affects firms with relatively large capital investments less than those using proportionately more labour than capital in production.

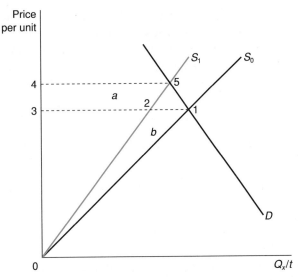

Figure 14.9
Regulation and cost predation

(v)   Another criticism of the Stigler-Peltzman approach is that no role has been attributed
to the politician. In the analysis of Figure 14.8 the politician is a vote-maximiser.
This simply makes the politician a broker between the interests of consumers and
producers. But what if politicians want rent? The goal of politicians might be to
extract rent for themselves. *Rent extraction* may be possible by legislative threats to
use regulation to reduce prices or legislative threats, which would raise costs for firms.
    As an example, consider Figure 14.10. This is similar to Figure 14.9 except that the
demand curve is far more price-elastic. The implication is that regulation would not
increase rents for the industry as area $a < b$. Suppose that the politician threatens to
introduce regulation that would increase per-unit cost for firms, so that the slope
of the supply curve increases and the supply curve swivels from $0\text{-}S_0$ to $0\text{-}S_1$. Firms
would suffer a net loss in producer surplus (equal to area a minus area b). They may
then be motivated to lobby politicians (for example, by way of campaign contributions) to refrain from imposing costs. McChesney (1997: 29) introduces this model
of rent extraction. He notes that '"milker bills" is one term used by politicians to
describe legislative proposals introduced to "milk" producers for payments not to
pass the rent extracting legislation'.

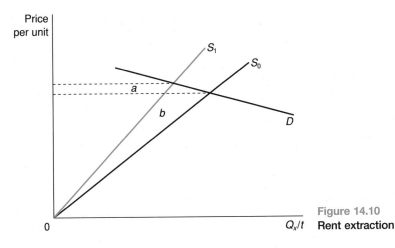

Figure 14.10
Rent extraction

While rent extraction may seem just a transfer to politicians, it can create waste. Action by rent-extracting politicians might affect incentives because it reduces the value of entrepreneurial ability. It might create an incentive for producers to shift investment to socially less valuable (but politically more salvageable) forms (e.g. in the 'underground or hidden economy'). It diverts politicians' time that might be pursued more constructively.

In conclusion,

- the original insight of Stigler's theory of regulation can be modified and expanded in different directions;
- quite different applications of microeconomics theory offer different insights within a positive theory of regulation, premised on the process by which regulation takes place;
- the market failure (normative) application of microeconomics theory is not the only application possible.

14.7 Bureaucracy and the supply of government services: are budgets 'twice' the optimum size?

Turning to agents on the 'supply side' of the political process, microeconomic theory suggests that agents will be unlikely to meet the demands of voters because agents have their own objectives. Once again, the *homo economicus* assumption is important; microeconomists are sceptical of the argument that individuals operate in the 'public interest' rather than in pursuit of their own self-interest. To sociologists, bureaucrats administer public policies benignly and in the 'public interest'. For example, Max Weber saw the bureaucrat as 'an administrative eunuch who dispassionately observes the established set of administrative rules and carries them out unquestioningly' (Brown and Jackson 1991: 196). An application of microeconomic theory offers a different perspective. If bureaucrats pursue self-interest there is concern that any bureau may be able to exploit an asymmetry of information and act as a monopoly supplier.

Niskanen (1968, 1971) assumed that bureaucrats maximise their own utility and that this requires that they maximise the department's budget. If pay, perks, prestige, power and promotion are positive utility sources then, as these are often directly related to the size of the bureaucrat's budget, the bureaucrat has an incentive to ask for as large a budget as possible. The bureaucrat has knowledge of demand for government-provided services and also knowledge of the cost function. Politicians have knowledge of the demand for services but do not have close knowledge of the costs of providing them. As a result, politicians will be prepared to sanction budgets provided only that total benefit of public services to voters (B) does not exceed total cost (TC). In Niskanen's model of bureaucracy this is the only constraint that bureaucrats face when they present their claim for the departmental budget. However, with this informational asymmetry, bureaus are able to present their claim (usually once during a parliamentary year) for an annual budget. In asking for this indivisible sum they are able to exploit their position and achieve the highest budget possible.

In Figure 14.11 the median voter's demand curve is D_m. When marginal cost of the service is MC_0 ($= AC_0$) and price is $0\text{-}P_0$, the consumer–voter would maximise welfare by consuming $0\text{-}q_1^G$ units of the good. However, if offered the choice of agreeing to a budget of $0\text{-}P_0\text{-}1\text{-}q_2^G$ for the provision of $0\text{-}q_2^G$ or having none of the good, the median voter will agree to the large budget. The bureaucrat 'rips off' the consumer surplus (triangle $P_0\text{-}2\text{-}3 = 3\text{-}1\text{-}4$) that the consumer–voter would otherwise enjoy, to facilitate a large budget.

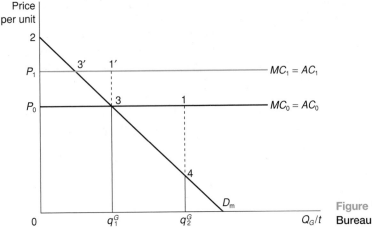

Figure 14.11
Bureaucratic waste

Total benefit is set equal to total cost ($0\text{-}2\text{-}4\text{-}q_2^G = 0\text{-}P_0\text{-}1\text{-}q_2^G$) and the deadweight loss from this form of provision is triangle 3-1-4 (= triangle P_0-2-3).

The example illustrated highlights the welfare costs imposed by bureaucratic provision. When the demand curve is linear and the elasticity of supply is infinite ($AC = MC$) bureaus are likely to be 'twice as large as they should be' (McKenzie and Tullock 1981: 186). It is clear that $0\text{-}q_2^G = 2(0\text{-}q_1^G)$.

That the output of 'Niskanen's bureau' will be twice the output that would arise when marginal cost equals marginal benefit can be demonstrated using the quadratic functions so often employed in microeconomics. Let $B = aQ - bQ^2$ (where Q is quantity of the good provided by the bureau and B is total benefit). It follows that marginal benefit, $MB = a - 2bQ$. Now let the total cost function be described as $TC = cQ + dQ^2$, so that marginal cost $MC = c + 2dQ$.

In Niskanen's model, the bureaucrat will ask for that size budget which equates total cost with total benefit. It follows that the output will then be

$$aQ - bQ^2 = cQ + dQ^2 \qquad (14.21)$$

$$a - bQ = c + dQ \qquad (14.22)$$

$$Q = \frac{a - c}{b + d} \qquad (14.23)$$

By comparison, when the competitive (socially optimal) output Q^* is determined at the point at which marginal benefit (MB) equals marginal cost (MC), then:

$$a - 2bQ = c + 2dQ \qquad (14.24)$$

$$a - c = 2Q(b + d) \qquad (14.25)$$

$$Q = \frac{a - c}{2(b + d)} \qquad (14.26)$$

In this way, the socially optimum output is one-half of the bureau's output. That bureaucrats face an infinitely elastic supply function is an extreme example (Cullis and Jones 1987), but, accepting this extreme position as a starting point, how likely is it that bureaus will produce twice the competitive output? How realistic are the Niskanen assumptions with reference to both the adduced utility sources and the constraint specification?

(a) Is it fair to assume that individuals are always driven by self-interest? Is it possible to argue that individuals who work in the provision of public services are also interested in the pursuit of the public interest? (see Jones and Cullis 2002).

(b) Is it reasonable to assume that the utility of bureaucrats would be dependent on the size of the budget? There are cases in which power and prestige are not so much a function of the size of the budget but of the importance of the tasks of the bureau. For example, Breton and Wintrobe (1975) argue that salaries and other benefits may be greater in small bureaus than in large bureaus (for example, pay, power and prestige may be greater in the Department of Finance of the Canadian government than in much larger bureaus like Health and Welfare).

(c) The proposition that salary and position are dependent on the size of the budget is questionable even in the USA. Sometimes salary and position depend more on budget cutting than on budget expansion. For example, James Schlesinger, the US Secretary of Defense, made his reputation as a budget cutter (Jackson 1982). Moreover, even if self-interest were the sole motivation and this was positively linked to the size of the budget, is it obvious that bureaucrats wish to maximise a budget? (Or might it be argued, instead, that administrators are *satisficers*?)

(d) The proposition that bureaucrats will drive themselves to budget-maximise is questionable when utility might, instead, depend on a more relaxed and comfortable working environment. A fundamental challenge to the assumption that bureaucrats are 'budget-maximisers' comes from Migué and Bélanger (1974). If bureaucrats maximise a more leisurely and comfortable work situation then there must be an element of the budget that finances such extravagances. The bureaucrat now attempts to maximise this net revenue. The outcome is that the bureau produces an output that is identical to the output of a competitive firm. The budget is excessive for this output level but the output is not excessive. If there is 'slack' (or X-inefficiency) in the organisation, costs will be increased to MC_1, $(= AC_1)$ in Figure 14.11 and it is now the case that total benefit equals total cost (triangle P_1-2-3' equal to triangle 3'-1'-3) at 0-q_1^G (the competitive output). Of course, X-inefficiency now simply replaces allocative inefficiency. However, it is only possible to pursue X-inefficiency and budget maximisation in certain well-defined cases (Cullis and Jones 1984).

In the case of the 'X-inefficient bureau' it is as if the bureau is maximising net revenue (which is wasted as 'slack'). A net benefit function $(TB - TC)$ used to finance slack (S) can be described as:

$$S = aQ - bQ^2 - cQ - dQ^2 \tag{14.27}$$

And maximising this function means setting the first derivative equal to zero, so that

$$dS/dQ = a - 2bQ - c - 2dQ = 0 \tag{14.28}$$

so that output (if not the budget) is at the social optimum:

$$Q = \frac{a - c}{2(b + d)} \tag{14.29}$$

(e) Then there are qualifications that arise if the supply curve facing a bureau is upward-sloping and the bureau behaves as a monopsonist. In this case a bureau will produce at twice the output at which marginal cost equals marginal benefit may not imply that this will be twice the output that would emerge in a *competitive market*. Allowance must be made for the fact that a bureau becomes a single purchaser of services (e.g. of soldiers' services in the department of defence, of nurses' services in the department of health) and marginal cost of additional output will exceed the supply price. In Figure 14.12 the supply curve is upward-sloping and the marginal cost curve is everywhere above the supply curve. When there is a competitive market output the

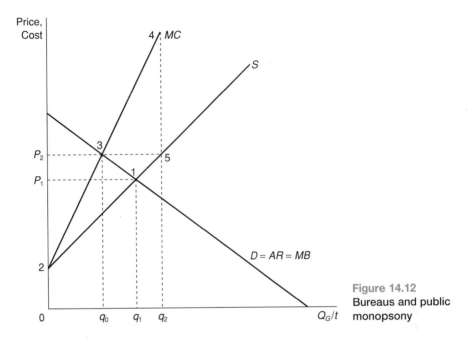

Figure 14.12
Bureaus and public monopsony

equilibrium is at 1 and 0-q_1 (where demand is equal to supply). If a monopsonist *in the market* supplied the good, output would be at 3 and 0-q_0 (where marginal cost equals marginal benefit). If the bureau is a budget-maximising monopsonist the output supplied is at output 0-q_2. At this point total benefit equals total cost (as triangle 2-P_2-3 equals triangle 3-4-5). While this output is above that of a competitive market it is not twice the competitive market output (see Cullis and Jones 1987 for further discussion).

With these objections to assumptions that define the *character* and *goals* of the bureaucrat, there are also questions to raise about the *constraints* that will be faced:

(f) Bohm (1987) points to the existence of a 'free' press, a political opposition in parliament and an electorate that cannot be manipulated all the time as checks on bureaucratic (political) abuse. In the UK there are more checks and accountability for the bureau than was assumed in Niskanen's theory. It is possible to show that, if there is simply the possibility of inquiry, whereby bureaucrats may suffer (for example, in terms of promotion), risk-averse bureaucrats will be far less indulgent (Bendor *et al.* 1985; Mueller 2003). Moreover, if the sponsor conceals his demand from the bureau, the bureaucrat can be forced to reveal true costs (Miller and Moe 1983).

(g) In a principal–agent relationship it is the principal who stipulates what is required, relying upon the agent's concern for their reputation, appropriate incentives and other control mechanisms to secure compliance with the principal's wishes. Legislative principals establish bureaucratic agents – in departments, bureaus, agencies, institutes – to implement policies. The legislature would surely not create an agent able to exploit the legislature in the image of 'Niskanen (1971)'. The legislature wants a compliant agent. Weingast and Moran (1983) employ statistical analysis of data drawn from regulatory policy-making at the Federal Trade Commission in the US to evaluate competing theories. In 1979, Congress appeared to intervene to restrain the Federal Trade Commission (FTC) to curb what were seen as regulatory abuses (policy initiatives were criticised and funds reduced). While a 'Niskanen critique' would suggest that increased restraint was needed because the FTC was a 'runaway' agency (using informational advantage) the change in the composition and preferences of oversight committees explained this increased restraint (liberal members had left these panels in large numbers to be replaced by much more conservative senators). The evidence proved quite consistent with the principal–agent model in which this reflected a change in the principal's preferences.

14.7.1 The economics of bureaucracy: what form of inefficiency?

As with other issues in this text, it is difficult to resolve questions simply by recourse to theory. Is there evidence that Niskanen's predictions have been realised? If so, what form does this inefficiency take?

a) *Budget maximisation.* Early empirical work by Borcherding and Deacon (1972) and McGuire (1981) suggests that the price elasticity of demand for many services provided via bureaus is less than one. This is important because it is difficult to reconcile this observation with the existence of a *budget-maximising* bureaucrat constrained only by the requirement that total budgetary cost may not exceed total benefit. Production beyond the point on the demand curve which has unitary elasticity reduces the budget – a one per cent increase in output soon produces a greater than one per cent fall in average budget revenue.[12]

b) *X-inefficiency ('slack').* On the other hand, some studies that test Migue and Belanger's critique report that per-unit cost is often higher if provision is via a bureau (for comparative studies of the relative efficiency of private- and public-sector provision see Mueller 2003: 374–9). Of course, allowance must be made for the fact that different producers face different levels of competition. Borcherding, Pommerehne and Schneider (1982) surveyed over fifty studies into comparative costs (covering activities from banks to refuse collection, from hospitals to electricity generation) and found only two instances where public production is less costly than private alternatives. In over forty, the private sector supplies equivalent goods at significantly lower cost. The difference could be explained by the degree of competition. This said, Vining and Boardman (1992) surveyed data from the 500 largest non-financial corporations in Canada and they concluded that both state-owned corporations and firms with a mixture of private and public shareholders had significantly lower efficiency compared to private firms, even after allowing for the degree of competition. They conclude that: 'where competition is normatively appropriate, private ownership is preferable from an efficiency perspective' (Vining and Boardman 1992: 226).

c) *Labour intensity.* The debate concerning the wastes of bureaucracy continues. What is evident is that the inefficiency attributed to bureaucracy might take different forms. Orzechowski (1977) argues that bureaus tend to be be biased in favour of labour-intensive production (because senior bureaucrats wish to maximise the patronage value of the budget or because salaries are a function of numbers of employees).

d) *Excessive emphasis on visible output.* Lindsay (1976) identifies costs in terms of bureaucratic provision because of biases that are created by difficulties in monitoring bureaus. Lindsay (1976) explored the mix of outputs produced. In the market the profit motive guides entrepreneurs to produce quantity and quality of goods and services that conform to individual preferences. Government enterprise is characterised by

---

12. For example, in Figure 14.11 if the marginal cost curve cut the demand curve at the midpoint, then price elasticity of demand is equal to 1 (in absolute terms). If marginal cost were below this midpoint the size of the budget would be less than the size of the budget when price elasticity is equal to 1. Even if marginal cost were lower than *MC* the bureau would not operate on the inelastic section of the demand curve. There would be no incentive to operate where price elasticity of demand is less than 1.

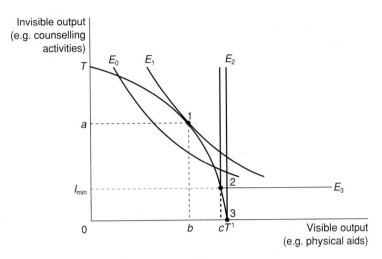

Figure 14.13 **Government enterprise and output bias**

zero-priced output and this means that allocative information comes from a legislative process.

Lindsay focuses on bureaucratic bias towards *visible* outputs. These are capable of easy documentation by the government's monitors. They are easily verified. Consider the example illustrated in Figure 14.13. TT' is a transformation curve. It represents the possible combinations of two outputs produced via a government bureau. One is invisible (e.g. counselling) and the other visible (e.g. physical aids) that an agency concerned with disability policy could choose to produce. The curves labelled E_0 and E_1 are equi-price curves and represent combinations of the visible and invisible outputs that could command the same price on the market. If managers want to maximise revenue for any given outlay (and these curves are treated as managerial indifference curves), the market outcome would be point 1 on E_1 (with 0-a of counselling activities and 0-b of physical aids).

By contrast, when some output is impossible to monitor by government (i.e. some output is invisible), the non-market manager will treat this output as 'neutrals', i.e. the indifference curve will be vertical (e.g. as with E_2). In this case, equilibrium is at point 3. This is a corner solution with the visible output being produced exclusively.

In the case where monitoring costs are discontinuous, it may be sensible for the government to monitor for some threshold level of invisible output (I_{min}). In this case the non-market manager's indifference curve will take the form of E_3 and equilibrium will be found at 2, with I_{min} and 0-c of the invisible and visible outputs respectively. This analysis predicts that there will be inefficiency, as provision by bureaus is skewed towards visible outputs as compared with a market situation in which all output is priced.

14.8 Non-market (government) failure

It is evident that, if there is market failure (Chapter 6), there is also government failure. Just as Bator (1957) offers a taxonomy of market failure, Wolf (1979, 1988) offers a taxonomy of non-market failure. On the *demand side*, he points to an increasing awareness of monopolies, externalities and distributional inequity, which might permit politicians to call for greater-than-optimal government intervention. The reward structure (election to office) makes politicians rationally myopic (optimising over the four- or five-year electoral cycle). The result is inefficiency.

On the *supply side* the non-market sector suffers from the following 'failings':

(i) *Internalities and private goods.* Agencies rely on explicit standards and with the absence of direct-performance indicators (which are available for market organisations, e.g. market shares and profit-and-loss bottom lines), agencies in the public sector develop their own standards. Wolf (1988) refers to these standards as 'internalities'. He defines them as 'goals that apply within non-market organizations to guide, regulate, and evaluate agency performance and the performance of agency personnel' (p. 66). It is these standards, rather than (or in addition to) 'public interest' objectives that are often stipulated for agencies. It is these standards that provide the motivation behind the behaviour of individuals within the agency. Public agencies have 'private' internal goals that form the agency's real agenda, e.g.

(a) *Budget growth ('more is better')* is a goal in the absence of profit.

(b) Technological advance leads to the view that *new and complex is better*. For example, in the military there is sometimes a compulsive tendency towards development of 'next-generation' sophisticated equipment.

(c) *Information acquisition and control ('knowing what others don't know is better')*. In non-market, as well as in market organisations, information is often translated into influence and power (it raises the supply curves of other potential providers). This internality may become the source of activity, irrespective of the usefulness of information for pursuing policy objectives.

Internalities affect non-market activities as externalities affect market activities. In both cases, there is a divergence between outcomes and socially preferable outcomes. Externalities cause some social costs and benefits to be excluded from the calculations of private decision-makers. Internalities mean that a public-sector agency's costs and benefits dominate the calculations of public decision-makers. (In each case *private* costs and *private* benefits determine decision-making.)

(ii) *Redundant and rising costs.* However imperfectly, markets link costs of producing an activity to the income that sustains it; prices paid by consumers provide a vital link. This link is removed if revenues that sustain non-market activities are derived from non-price sources, i.e. taxes paid to government. There is a greater likelihood of misallocation of resources, more resources may be used than necessary to produce a given output and more of a non-market activity may be provided than is warranted. Costs of production are disconnected from revenues that sustain it.

The absence of such linkages means that objectives can become internally inconsistent (e.g. bringing all students' reading scores up to the mean) and objectives may be specified for which no known technology exists (e.g. providing 'dignified' work for people with low IQs). Wolf notes that in the field of disability policy, there might be attempts to seek cures for certain types of handicap as part of an unrealistic short-run research project, e.g. to make individuals with IQs of less than 70 into draughtsmen.

Redundant costs arise when it is difficult to measure the intended purpose of the agency. Goals are removed from the 'internalities' accepted as proxies for non-market objectives. In the absence of competition, X-efficiency may become a common feature of non-market production.

(iii) *Derived externalities.* Government intervention to correct market failure may create unanticipated side effects. Political pressure for non-market intervention may create demand for action before there is adequate knowledge or time to consider potential side effects. Derived externalities are generally likely to occur because of the short time horizon that drives the decisions of politicians (concerned with the next election). The ill-defined nature of quantity and quality of non-market outputs makes it difficult to think seriously about potential unintended side effects. An example of a derived externality is provided by Peacock (1980), who describes how a firm eligible for subsidy will adapt by raising its cost structure by deliberately fostering 'slack'. An example of ill-conceived legislation is provided by complaints against section 504 of the Rehabilitation Act passed in the USA in 1973. Under this section universities and colleges have an obligation to provide handicapped students with expensive special help. (The University of Texas, forced to provide a sign-language interpreter for a deaf student, appealed to the Supreme Court on the grounds that the intention of section 504 was not to impose heavy financial burdens on institutions that drew only a small part of their revenue from federal funds. Whatever the rights and wrongs of the objectives of the legislation, the resistance encountered by its implementation suggests it was less than fully thought through by the legislators.)

(iv) *Distributional inequity.* Public policy action places authority in the hands of some to be exercised over others. Authority is exercised by: the social worker, the welfare-case administrator, the tariff commissioner, the utilities regulator, the securities examiner, or the bank investigator. Power is intentionally lodged with some and denied to others. It might be exercised with compassion and competence; it might also be abused. While there are checks and balances (in law, in administrative procedures, in information generated by the media) these restraints may not be effective. There are opportunities for inequity and abuse. Corrupt practices are one type of abuse; less conspicuous inequities occur when decisions are made by welfare authorities to confer, or withhold, aid to fatherless families with dependent children, or aid to the aged.

Government activity may be a source rather than a remedy for inequality. There are problems created by the exercise of arbitrary power by government servants sustained because regulations and conditions for transfers are complex and elaborate. This makes the achievement of horizontal and vertical equity in treatment in the non-market sector very difficult.

With this list of possible sources of governmental failure, consider the following taxonomy of non-market failings and market failure (as described in Chapter 11).

Despite similarities in terminology, the non-market inadequacies are not the mirror images of those associated with market activities. For example, externalities on the market side of Table 14.8 are related to internalities on the non-market side only because each is a major source of shortcoming (in market and non-market contexts, respectively); externalities in the market sector are conceptually closer to derived externalities.

Table 14.8 **Market and non-market failure**

Market failures	*Non-market failures*
1. Externalities and public goods	1. Disjunction between costs and revenues: redundant and rising costs
2. Increasing returns	2. Internalities and organizational goals
3. Market imperfections	3. Derived externalities
4. Distributional inequity (income and wealth)	4. Distributional inequity (power and privilege)

Source: Wolf 1988.

14.9 Challenge: Are individuals so self-interested?

A key question is whether it is really possible to transfer analysis that has been applied to decision-making processes in markets to assess decision-making in quite different processes.

Some have argued that individuals are less narrowly self-interested when they make decisions in collective decision-making processes (Kelman 1988). Others have argued that individuals employed in the public sector are less self-interested than anticipated (e.g. Auster 1975). Frank (1996) attempts to explain compensated wage differentials with reference to individuals' perceptions of the nature of jobs in different sectors of the economy. First, he reports the results of a questionnaire survey in which occupations were ranked on a social responsibility scale. Of 141 job titles, stockbroker was ranked lowest and teacher ranked highest. Caring professions scored well (e.g. emergency medical technician ranked just below teacher and medical-related occupations, such as nurse's assistant, were well above average). Frank concludes that, *ceteris paribus*, estimates of compensating wage differentials for social responsibility were particularly high, i.e. much lower wages were required if a task was deemed to have a high social responsibility rating.[13] After analysing wage differentials of a cohort of graduates from Cornell University (adjusted for academic profile), Frank reported that 'a person employed by a private for-profit firm earns a salary more than 13 percent larger than she would if she was employed by government'. Individuals have different perceptions of the value of tasks undertaken in different sectors of the economy.

14.10 Summary

This chapter has illustrated how neoclassical microeconomics might be applied to analyse political processes. The approach is to model the democratic process as a 'market' in which 'taxpaying consumers' demand policies and legislation and politicians compete for votes by supplying different policies and different legislation.

Such analysis identifies inefficiencies in political decision-making processes. On the 'demand' side, there is no incentive for individuals to vote, i.e. to express a preference. In large groups, there is no incentive to engage in lobbying, i.e. to express intensity of preference. In a pluralistic society there is a tendency for small groups (more easily mobilised) to exploit large groups. Analysis of government regulation reveals a compromise between pressures by producers (as small groups) and the prospect of vote loss (when the electorate acts as a large group).

On the 'supply' side'. Niskanen's (1968, 1971) analysis of bureaucracy has been very influential. In the extreme, it predicts that bureaucrats will budget-maximise and public expenditure will be twice the 'optimum'. But, of course, criticism of *budget-maximising* is not only a charge levelled at the executive; a plethora of other criticisms of bureaus has been described. Not surprisingly, the chapter has ended with a taxonomy of 'government failures'.

What are the implications of this perspective?

(i) The existence of market failure (Chapter 6) is only a *prima facie* case for government action. There can be no guarantee that intervention by government will be efficient.

---

13. His results were confirmed in similar questionnaires (e.g. Jacobson 1998). Moreover, they are consistent with evidence of wage differentials elsewhere. For example, lawyers employed by public interest groups (e.g. the American Civil Liberties Union) receive far less than lawyers employed by for-profit firms, even though public interest lawyers 'could have had their pick from among the choice entry level jobs in the legal profession' (Frank 1996). See also Goddeeris (1988).

(ii) A distinction has been drawn between 'positive' analysis (based on the objectives and constraints faced by participants in decision-making) and 'normative' analysis (of what 'should' happen to maximise the community's welfare). The distinction was stark when considering analysis of regulation.

References

Aldrich, J. (1993) Rational choice and turnout, *American Journal of Political Science*, 37: 246–78.

Aldrich, J. (1997) When is it rational to vote?, pp. 373–90 in D.C. Mueller (ed.) *Perspectives on Public Choice*, Cambridge: Cambridge University Press.

Arrow, K.J. (1963) *Social Choice and Individual Values*, New York: John Wiley.

Ashenfelter, O. and Kelly, S. Jr (1975) Determinants of participation in presidential elections, *Journal of Law and Economics*, 18: 695–733.

Auster, R.D. (1975) Some economic determinants of the characteristics of public workers, in R.D. Lester and G. Sirkin (eds) *Economics of Public Choice*, New York: Cycero Press, pp. 185–98.

Barry, B. (1970) *Sociologists, Economists and Democracy*, London: Collier-Macmillan.

Bartell, A. and Thomas, L.G. (1985) Direct and indirect effects of regulation: a new look at OSHA's impact, *Journal of Law and Economics*, 28 (1): 1–25.

Bator, F.M. (1957) The simple analytics of welfare maximization, *American Economic Review*, 47 (1): 22–59.

Baysinger, B. and Tollison, R.D. (1980) Evaluating the social cost of monopoly and regulation, *Atlantic Economic Journal*, 8 December: 22–6.

Becker, G.S. (1983) A theory of competition among pressure groups for political influence, *Quarterly Journal of Economics*, 98: 371–99.

Bendor, J., Taylor, S. and Van Gaalen, R. (1985) Bureaucratic expertise versus legislative authority: a model of deception and monitoring in budgeting, *American Political Science Review*, 79: 1041–60.

Black, D. (1948) On the rationale of group decision making, *Journal of Political Economy*, 56 (1): 23–34.

Bohm, P. (1972) Estimating demand for public goods and experiment, *European Economic Review*, 3: 111–30.

Bohm, P. (1987) *Social Efficiency*, 2nd edn, London: Macmillan.

Borcherding, T.E. and Deacon, R. (1972) The demand for services of non-federal governments, *American Economic Review*, 62: 891–901.

Borcherding, T., Pommerehne, W. and Schneider, F. (1982) Comparing the efficiency of private and public production: the evidence from five countries, *Journal of Economics*, 2: 127–56.

Bowen, H.R. (1943) The interpretation of voting in the allocation of economic resources, *Quarterly Journal of Economics*, 58 (1): 27–48.

Brennan, G. and Lomasky, L. (1993) *Democracy and Decision: the Pure Theory of Electoral Preference*, Cambridge: Cambridge University Press.

Breton, A. and Wintrobe, R. (1975) The equilibrium size of a budget-maximising bureau, *Journal of Political Economy*, 83: 195–207.

Brooks, M.A. and Heijdra, B.J. (1989) An exploration of rent seeking, *Economic Record*, 65 (188): 32–50.

Brown, C.V. and Jackson, P.M. (1991) *Public Sector Economics*, 4th edn, Oxford: Basil Blackwell.

Buchanan, J.M. (1968) *The Demand and Supply of Public Goods*, Chicago: Rand McNally.

Buchanan, J.M. (1972) Towards analysis of closed behavioral systems, in J.M. Buchanan and R. Tollison (eds) *Theory of Public Choice, Political Applications of Economics*, Ann Arbor: University of Michigan Press.

Buchanan, J.M. (1980) Reform in the rent seeking society, in J.M. Buchanan, R.D. Tollison and G. Tullock (eds) *Towards a Theory of the Rent Seeking Society*, College Station: Texas A&M University Press, pp. 359–67.

Buchanan, J.M. and Tullock, G. (1965) *The Calculus of Consent*, Ann Arbor: University of Michigan Press.

Cavanagh, T.E. (1981) Changes in American voter turnout 1964–1976, *Political Science Quarterly*, 96: 53–65.

Choi, K. (1983) A statistical test of Olson's model, pp. 57–78 in D.C. Mueller (ed.) *The Political Economy of Growth*, New Haven, Conn.: Yale University Press.

Congleton, R.D. (1988) Evaluating rent seeking losses: do the welfare gains of lobbyists count? *Public Choice*, 56: 181–4.

Connolly, S. and Munro, A. (1999) *Economics of the Public Sector*, London: Prentice Hall.

Cowling, K. and Mueller, D.C. (1978) The social costs of monopoly power, *Economic Journal*, 88: 727–48.

Crandall, R.W. and Graham, J.D. (1984) Automobile safety regulation and offsetting behavior: some new empirical estimates, *American Economic Review*, 74 (2): 328–31.

Cullis, J.G. and Jones, P.R. (1984) X-inefficiency, the economics of bureaucracy and Wagner's law: a note, *Public Finance/Finances Publiques*, 39 (2): 191–201.

Cullis, J.G. and Jones, P.R. (1987) *Microeconomics and the Public Economy: a Defence of Leviathan*, Oxford: Basil Blackwell.

Cullis, J.G. and Jones, P.R. (2009) *Public Finance and Public Choice*. 3rd edn, Oxford: Oxford University Press.

de Tocqueville, A. (1835) *Democracy in America*, reprint edn, Oxford: Oxford University Press.

DiLorenzo, T.J. (1988) Property rights, information costs and the economics of rent seeking, *Journal of Institutional and Theoretical Economics*, 144: 318–32.

Downs, A. (1957) *An Economic Theory of Democracy*, Harper and Row: New York.

Ferejohn, J.A. and Fiorina, M.P. (1974) Closeness counts only in horseshoes and dancing, *American Political Science Review*, 69: 678–90.

Fiorina, M.P. (1976) The voting decision: instrumental and expressive aspects, *Journal of Politics*, 21: 601–25.

Frank, R.H. (1996) What price the moral high ground? *Southern Economic Journal*, 63: 1–17.

Frey, B.S. (1971) Why do high income people participate more in politics? *Public Choice*, 46 (2): 141–61.

Frey, B.S. (1992) Tertium datur: pricing, regulating and intrinsic motivation, *Kyklos*, 45 (2): 161–84.

Frey, B.S. (1997) *Not Just For the Money: an Economic Theory of Personal Motivation*, Cheltenham: Edward Elgar.

Goddeeris, J.H. (1988) Compensating differentials and self-selection: an application to lawyers, *Journal of Political Economy*, 96: 411–28.

Hudson, J. and Jones, P.R. (1994) The importance of the 'ethical voter': an estimate of 'altruism', *European Journal of Political Economy*, 10: 499–509.

Hyman, D.N. (2002) *Public Finance: a Contemporary Application of Theory to Policy*, 7th edn, Fort Worth: Dryden Press/Harcourt Brace.

Jackson, P.M. (1982) *The Political Economy of Bureaucracy*, Oxford: Philip Allan.

Jacobson, J.P. (1998) *The Economics of Gender*, 2nd edn, Oxford: Basil Blackwell.

Jones, P.R. and Cullis, J.G. (1986) Is democracy regressive? A comment on political participation, *Public Choice*, 51 (1): 101–7.

Jones, P. and Hudson, J. (1998) The role of political parties: an analysis based on transaction costs, *Public Choice*, 94: 175–89.

Jones, P. and Hudson, J. (2000) Civic duty and expressive voting: is virtue its own reward? *Kyklos*, 53: 3–16.

Jones, P.R. and Cullis, J.G. (2002) Merit want status and motivation: the knight meets the self-loving butcher, brewer and baker, *Public Finance Review*, 30 (2) March: 83–101.

Keeler, T.E. (1984) Theories of regulation and the deregulation movement, *Public Choice*, 44 (1): 103–45.

Kelman, M. (1988) On democracy bashing, *Virginia Law Review*, 47: 199–227.

Krueger, A.O. (1974) The political economy of the rent-seeking society, *American Economic Review*, 64: 291–303.

Laband, D.N. and Sophocleus, J.P. (1988) The social cost of rent seeking: first estimates, *Public Choice*, 58: 269–75.

Lane, R.E. (1966) Political involvement through voting, in B. Seasholes (ed.) *Voting, Interest Groups and Parties*, Glenview, Ill: Scott, Foresman & Co.

Lee, D.R. (1988) Politics, ideology and the power of public choice, *Virginia Law Review*, 74 (2): 191–9.

Leffler, K.B. (1978) Physician licensure; competition and monopoly in American medicine, *Journal of Law and Economics*, 21: 165–86.

Lindsay, C.M. (1976) A theory of government enterprise, *Journal of Political Economy*, 84: 31–7.

Linneman, P. (1980) The effects of consumer safety standards: the 1973 Mattress Flammability Standard, *Journal of Law and Economics*, 23 (2): 461–78.

McChesney, F.S. (1997) *Money for Nothing: Politicians, Rent Extraction and Political Extortion*, Cambridge, Mass.: Harvard University Press.

McGuire, T.G. (1981) Budget maximising governmental agencies: an empirical test, *Public Choice*, 36: 313–22.

McKelvey, R.D. (1976) Intransitivities in multi-dimensional voting models and some implications for agenda control, *Journal of Economic Theory*, 12 (3): 472–82.

McKenzie, R.B. and Tullock, G. (1981) *The New World of Economics*, Homewood, Ill.: Richard D. Irwin.

Magee, S.P., Brock, W.A. and Young, L. (1989) *Black Hole Tariffs and Endogenous Policy Theory; Political Economy in General Equilibrium*, Cambridge: Cambridge University Press.

Migué, J.L. and Bélanger, G. (1974) Towards a general theory of managerial discretion, *Public Choice*, 12: 27–47.

Miller, J.C. and Moe, T.M. (1983) Bureaucrats, legislators and the size of government, *American Political Science Review*, 77: 297–322.

Mueller, D.C. (1987) The voting paradox, pp. 77–99 in C.K. Rowley (ed.) *Democracy and Public Choice: Essays in Honour of Gordon Tullock*, Oxford: Basil Blackwell.

Mueller, D.C. (2003) *Public Choice III*, Cambridge: Cambridge University Press.

Mundell, R.A. (1962) Review of Jansenn's *Free Trade Protection and Customs Union*, *American Economic Review*, 52 June: 621–2.

Murphy, K.M., Schleifer, A. and Vishney, R.W. (1991) The allocation of talent: implications for growth, *Quarterly Journal of Economics*, 106: 503–31.

Murrell, P. (1983) The cooperative structure of the growth of the West German and British manufacturing industries, pp. 151–71 in D.C. Mueller (ed.) *The Political Economy of Growth*. New Haven, Conn.: Yale University Press.

Niskanen, W.A. (1968) Non-market decision making: the peculiar economics of bureaucracy, *American Economic Review*, 58: 293–305.

Niskanen, W.A. (1971) *Bureaucracy and Representative Government*, Chicago: Aldine Publishing Company.

Olson, M. Jr (1965) *The Logic of Collective Action: Public Goods and the Theory of Groups*, Cambridge, Mass.: Harvard University Press.

Olson, M. (1982) *The Rise and Decline of Nations: Economic Growth and Stagflation and Social Rigidities*, New Haven, Conn.: Yale University Press.

Orzechowski, W. (1977) Economic models of bureaucracy: survey, extensions and evidence, in T.E. Borcherding (ed.) *Budgets and Bureaucrats: the Sources of Government Growth*, Durham, NC: Duke University Press.

Peacock, A. (1980) *The Economic Analysis of Government and Related Theories*, New York: St Martins.

Peacock, A. (1992) *Public Choice Analysis in Historical Perspective*, Cambridge: Cambridge University Press.

Peltzman, S. (1975) The effects of automobile safety regulation, *Journal of Political Economy*, 83 (4): 677–725.

Peltzman, S. (1976) Toward a more general theory of regulation, *Journal of Law and Economics*, 19: 211–40.

Plott, C.R. (1987) The robustness of the voting paradox, pp. 100–2 in C.K. Rowley (ed.) *Democracy and Public Choice: Essays in Honour of Gordon Tullock*, Oxford: Basil Blackwell.

Posner, R.A. (1975) The social costs of monopoly and regulation, *Journal of Political Economy*, 83 (4): 807–27.

Quibria, M.S. (1989) Neoclassical political economy: an application to trade policies, *Journal of Economic Surveys*, 3 (2): 107–131.

Riker, W.H. and Ordeshook, P.C. (1968) A theory of the calculus of voting, *American Political Science Review*, 62 (1): 387–9.

Ross, V.B. (1984) *Rent Seeking in LDC Import Regimes: the Case of Kenya*, Discussion Papers in International Economics no 8408, Graduate Institute of International Studies, Geneva.

Samuels, W.J. and Mercuro, N. (1984) A critique of rent seeking theory, pp. 55–70 in D.C. Colander (ed.) *Neoclassical Political Economy: the Analysis of Rent Seeking and DUP Activities*, Cambridge, Mass.: Ballinger Press.

Schwert, W.G. (1977) Public regulation of national securities exchanges: a test of the capture hypothesis, *Bell Journal of Economics*, 8: 128–50.

Shepherd, L. (1978) Licensing restrictions and the cost of dental care, *Journal of Law and Economics*, 21: 187–201.

Shepsle, K.A. and Bonchek, M.S. (1997) *Analyzing Politics: Rationality, Behaviors and Institutions*, New York: Norton.

Smith, A. (1776/1937) *An Inquiry into the Nature and Causes of the Wealth of Nation*, New York: Modern Library.

Stigler, G.J. (1971) *The Citizen and the State: Essays on Regulation*, Chicago: University of Chicago Press.

Stigler, G.J. (1974) The free riders and collective action: an approach to the theories of economic regulation, *Bell Journal of Economics and Management Science*, 5: 360–72.

Stigler, G.J. and Friedland, C. (1962) What can regulators regulate? The case of electricity, *Journal of Law and Economics*, 5: 1–16.

Stiglitz, J.E. (1974) The demand for education in public and private school systems, *Journal of Public Economics*, 3: 349–85.

Tollison, R.D. (1982) Rent seeking: a survey, *Kyklos*, 35: 575–602.

Tollison, R.D. (1988) Public choice and legislation, *Virginia Law Review*, 74: 339–71.

Tollison, R.D. (1997) Rent seeking, pp. 506–26, in D.C. Mueller (ed.) *Perspectives on Public Choice: a Handbook*, Cambridge: Cambridge University Press.

Tullock, G. (1967) The welfare costs of tariffs, monopolies and theft, *Western Economic Journal*, 5 June: 224–32.

Ulrich, A., Furtan, W.H. and Schmitz, A. (1987) The cost of a licensing system regulation: an example from Canadian prairie agriculture, *Journal of Political Economy*, 95: 160–78.

Vining, A.R. and Boardman, A.E. (1992) Ownership versus competition: the causes of government enterprise inefficiency, *Public Choice*, 73 (2): 205–39.

Viscusi, W.K. (1985) Consumer behaviour and safety effects of product safety regulations, *Journal of Law and Economics*, 28 (3): 527–53.

Viscusi, W.K., Vernon, J.M. and Harrington, J.E. (1992) *Economics of Regulation and Antitrust*, Lexington: D. C. Heath and Co.

Weingast, B.R. and Moran, M.J. (1983) Bureaucratic discretion or congressional control? Regulatory policymaking by the Federal Trade Commission, *Journal of Political Economy*, 91: 765–800.

Wittman, D. (1989) Why democracies produce efficient results, *Journal of Political Economy*, 97: 1395–1424.

Wolf, C. (1979) A theory of non-market failure, *Journal of Law and Economics*, 22 (1): 107–39.

Wolf, C. (1988) *Markets or Governments: Choosing between Imperfect Alternatives*, Cambridge, Mass.: MIT Press.

PART V

THE VOLUNTARY ECONOMY

CHAPTER 15

Self-interest or altruism: a broader framework

15.1 Introduction

The purpose of this chapter is to reconsider the description of the 'representative individual' most often used in neoclassical economics. As noted in Chapter 14, there has been considerable criticism that individuals are really far less self-interested than described (e.g. Kelman 1987; Frank 1997). Can altruism be incorporated in neoclassical microeconomic theory? How would predictions change if individuals were assumed to be benevolent to others? A definition of altruism begs many philosophical questions. It implies self-sacrifice, but if individuals feel better off by helping others, in what sense is there self-sacrifice? This is not the place for a discussion of the different meanings of altruism (for a recent discussion see Khalil 2004). Instead, in order to proceed, 'altruism' is defined in the specific form of utility interdependence. The description of *homo economicus* (as employed elsewhere in this text) is amended by assuming interdependent utility functions. The utility of the representative individual also depends on the well-being of others and, in some more specific cases, on the consumption by others of particular goods and services. What does this imply for the role of markets and for state intervention in markets?

15.2 Altruism: a case of interdependent utility functions?

The neoclassical microeconomist's perception of altruism is based on interdependence of utility functions (Hochman and Rodgers 1969; Becker 1974). For example, in equation (15.1) the utility of individual A (an altruist) depends not only on the consumption of goods and services $(x_1, \ldots, x_n)$ but also on the utility enjoyed by another individual, B:

$$U_a = U(x_1, \ldots, x_n, U_b) \tag{15.1}$$

where

$$\partial U_a / \partial U_b > 0$$

It is easy to demonstrate that, in these circumstances, it is possible for an individual to be better off by giving income to others. In the following example the potential gains from giving are illustrated. The utility of personal consumption $U(x_1, \ldots, x_n)$ is captured in the marginal valuation of income to individual A, whereas the utility from giving income to B (and raising U_b) is estimated in terms of the marginal valuation that individual A places on B's income.

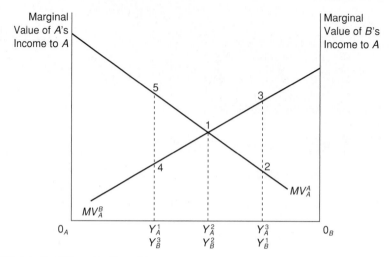

Figure 15.1 An altruist's valuation of income

In Figure 15.1 the horizontal axis measures the income of both individual A and individual B. From the origin 0_A (reading left to right) high-income individual A has an income of Y_A^3 and from the origin 0_B (reading right to left) low-income individual B has an income of Y_B^1. A's marginal valuation of income curve is MV_A^A. This shows the marginal valuation of A's income to A. It is downward-sloping because of the assumption that an addition to income means less the more income that an individual has (i.e. diminishing marginal utility of income). At an income of Y_A^3 the marginal valuation of income to A is shown at point 2 by distance Y_A^3-2.

Individual A's marginal valuation of B's income is shown as MV_A^B. Again, this is downward sloping, indicating that individual A is more concerned about B when B has nothing than when B's income is much higher. With the initial distribution of income, A has Y_A^3 and B has only Y_B^1. A's marginal valuation of B's income of Y_1^B is shown at point 3 by distance Y_B^1-3. The marginal valuation that A derives from personal income (at point 2) is less than A derives from the income of B (at point 3) and it follows that A is made better off by transferring some income to B. While A's utility increases, the act is altruistic as the intention is also to make B better off.

As B gains from receipt of income from A, the transfer may be described as a 'Pareto improvement' (see Chapters 4 and 5). This must be so because both A and B experience an increase in welfare as a result of the redistribution (no one is made worse off). However, the transfer is only a Pareto improvement to point 1 in Figure 15.1. A will continue to feel better off until the welfare-maximising point (point 1) has been reached. At this point individual A is left with Y_A^2 and individual B has Y_B^2. Income has been redistributed from A to B to make both A and B better off. However, if more income were redistributed from A to B, A would be made worse off. If A were left with Y_A^1 and B enjoyed Y_B^3 then MV_A^A exceeds MV_A^B at point 5 and 4 respectively. Position 1, where $MV_A^A = MV_B^A$, might be referred to as Pareto optimal in as much as further redistribution of income from A will not increase A's welfare. It is the welfare-maximising level for A.

However, will A (an altruist on our definition) have the motivation to give? The motivation to give depends on the marginal utility associated with giving ($\partial U^a/\partial U^b$ in equation 15.1) relative to marginal utility from additional expenditure on goods and services (i.e. $\partial U^a/\partial x_i$). However, the act of giving is tantamount to the provision of a public good (see Chapter 6). As each individual feels better off when others contribute to improve B's utility, the implication is that there will be 'under-provision' of altruism.

There will be an incentive for individual *A* to wait for like-minded others to give to charity and it is unlikely that (voluntarily) a Pareto-optimal solution will be achieved.

The Pareto-optimal condition for charitable activity is formally determined in the appendix to this chapter but it is unlikely to be attained if giving is equated to contributing to provision of a public good. The perception that giving is akin to provision of a public good means that even an 'altruist' may not be motivated to give. So *why do* individuals voluntarily give to charities?

15.3 Giving as a 'public good': why do individuals give to charities?

As an extreme example of an application of the public good problem (discussed in Chapter 6), consider the decision of an individual who (in a large-number situation) refuses to act altruistically even though they are an altruist. In Table 15.1 an altruist faces the choice as to whether or not to contribute £5 towards a charitable project (e.g. building a hostel for the homeless).

(i)   If the individual contributes and others contribute to the charity, the hostel will be built and the donor feels the equivalent of £5 net better off to know that the utility of beneficiaries has increased.

(ii)   If others do not contribute to the charity, the individual will simply lose the £5 (as the hostel will not be built).

(iii) If the individual refuses to contribute but others contribute then (as the individual donor is one of a large number of donors) the hostel will be built (in a large-number situation each individual's contribution is of minuscule importance). The individual will be the equivalent of £10 better off as the good is non-excludable (i.e. the individual still feels better off to know that the beneficiaries have a roof over their heads).

(iv)   On the other hand, if others do not contribute, the individual can be no worse off if he, or she, makes no contribution.

By refusing to contribute, the individual will always be better off, no matter what others do (the strategy of not contributing dominates the strategy of contributing in Table 15.1). The payoffs from not contributing are greater than (i.e. dominate) the payoffs from contribution. While the donor might be better off from a contribution (e.g. the possibility of a payoff of £5), there is always the possibility of opting for a preferable strategy which might yield a payoff of £10 or a payoff of £0.

The prediction in this extreme scenario is that well-meaning altruists do not reveal their preferences. Individuals may be kind-hearted but they may never show this. Each individual hopes to free-ride on the contributions of others. But, of course, if all behave in this way there can be no free ride and this means that potential beneficiaries are neglected.

The example highlights the free-rider problem associated with voluntary provision of charity. The project considered is one where there is indivisibility in production (the hostel is either built or not built). The example is extreme for there may be cases in which an individual might exert some influence even when others do not contribute. For example, suppose the £5 transfer will always have some effect, e.g. if only in terms of buying a hot meal for the recipient. In Chapter 14 a distinction was drawn between 'free-riding'

Table 15.1 The donor's dilemma

	Others contribute	*Others do not contribute*
Contribute	(£10 − £5) = £5	−£5
Not contribute	£10	£0

and 'easy-riding'. In the former case no contribution was made but in the latter case a less-than-optimal contribution may be made. When there is divisibility in production a contribution may be made, provided that the marginal benefit for the donor (e.g. from providing a meal) exceeds the marginal cost. However, there is still the same incentive to reduce contributions the more that others provide food and nourishment for the recipient. As discussed in Chapter 14, the 'easy-riding' case is one in which the Cournot–Nash solution is more likely to describe positive contributions.

Andreoni (1988) describes an 'altruistic' Cournot–Nash solution in the following terms:

(i)   only the richest individuals will contribute to charities;
(ii)   the proportion of the community contributing to charity will decrease to zero;
(iii) average giving will fall to zero.

These (pessimistic) predictions follow from an application of analysis explained in Chapter 14. But how well does theory explain evidence? While the 'public good model of charity' does not predict significant altruistic activity, evidence is not perfectly consistent with the 'public good' analysis of charity. For example:

(i)   Surveys in the US indicate that 'individuals differ a lot in how, when and where they give but virtually everyone claims to give' (White 1989: 67).
(ii)   Surveys in the UK indicate that between 1987 and 1990/91 'the proportion donating to charity has remained high and relatively stable . . . ranging from 74 per cent to 80 per cent of respondents (Pettipher and Halfpenny 1993: 14).
(iii) Giving is not the prerogative of the rich (e.g. Jones and Posnett, 1993, report that, in 1984, average donations were £50 per annum for households in the lowest income quintile in the UK).

If the predictions of a public good model are called into question how can altruistic activity be analysed? Sugden (1982) is critical of the public good model. He provides an interesting demonstration that a pure public good theory of philanthropy is spurious. The predictions appear inconsistent with reported income elasticities of giving. If giving to your favourite charity fell by £100 and your income increased by £100, the implication of public good theory is that you would give all your windfall gains to the charity. However, income elasticities of giving (discussed below) are low. Would *you* give all your windfall gains to charity?

With such results, how can microeconomic theory explain the discrepancy? Once again, the basic theory can be amended in the light of evidence. Economists have responded by reassessing incentives and constraints in the public good model. What would induce (or force) individuals to maintain their level of personal donations? Does the source of finance for charity matter? Does it matter whether you, or others, provide the finance? If so, is giving to charity a 'pure' public good?

With these questions in mind consider the following explanations that have been provided:

(i)   There may be a *warm glow* effect associated with the act of giving (donors acquiring utility from the act of giving as well as from the result of donation, e.g. Ireland 1973; Andreoni 1993).
(ii)   Charitable giving may simply be a *response to fund-raising* (donors' objective may be to obtain invitations to gala occasions, ownership of lottery tickets, etc. – Olson 1965 – see Chapter 14).
(iii) Individuals and firms may give to improve their *reputation*; politicians adopt altruistic postures to increase electoral support and prestige.
(iv)   Voluntary work effort may be given with the intention of acquiring 'on-the-job' training experience and/or valuable personal contacts (Knapp *et al.* 1994 refer to *personal investment* gains).

(v) Donations by workers may be offered so as to ease social pressure (*coercion*) from employers and supervisors on workers to contribute to philanthropic schemes (Keating 1981 and Keating *et al.* 1981).

In each case, 'public good' disincentives to act charitably are mitigated by 'private good' considerations (or, alternatively, by coercion). While the list is far from exhaustive, it is clear that the nature of the gift, or donation, means that donors may be constrained to make the gift personally. (Note that, in Chapter 14, the prediction of Olson's *Logic of Collective Action* was that collective action would rely on coercion or on alternative private inducement.)

Before examining the implication of this development, it can be noted that there are other explanations of voluntary giving:

(a) *Small-group giving.* Following a discussion in Chapter 14, it is predictable that in small groups an individual will feel that, if they stopped giving, others in the group would also stop (Buchanan 1968). In small groups the individual is a 'major player'. The individual attaches an importance to giving and believes that the probabilities of the outcomes in Table 15.1 are contingent on whether or not the individual gives. In such circumstances voluntary giving can be predicted.

(b) *Kantian giving.* Some economists argue that individuals behave in a Kantian manner (e.g. Collard 1978). Following the philosopher Immanuel Kant, individuals are assumed to behave in a way in which they would hope others in society would behave. However, the argument has been questioned. With reference to the proposition that people contribute in a way in which they would like others to contribute, Jones and Posnett (1993: 138) comment, 'this sort of rule is unlikely to be accepted if others do not, in practice make the contribution'.

(c) *Team rationality.* With so much academic effort locked into the attempt to reconcile economic theory with evidence, it is hardly surprising that some have questioned the rationality assumption underlying microeconomic theory. Sugden (1993) has argued that an economic approach (even modified as above) is unhelpful because it is founded (like other microeconomic theory) on the argument that altruists are instrumentally rational. He would replace such assumptions of rationality with the concept of 'team rationality'. He notes, '[t]he person who acts as a member of a team evaluates actions as part of a whole that is made up of the actions of all the members of a team: for him or her, an action is rational to the extent that it is part of a set of actions which, taken together, causes good outcomes'. The theory of instrumentally rational choice, as conventionally used in economics, does not provide us with adequate reasons to play out parts in cooperative arrangements that benefit us.[1] By *restricting* attention to instrumental rationality the economic approach to altruism is 'neglecting a potentially significant form of human motivation' (Sugden 1993: 89).

Once again, as so often in this text, the limitations of neoclassical microeconomics have been addressed by two routes. First, theorists have tampered with assumptions in an attempt to reduce the 'wedge' between theoretical prediction and evidence. Second, and more fundamentally, they have raised questions about the defining attributes of rational behaviour, which are assumed in microeconomic theory.

To continue, the intention in the next section is to explore some of the implications that arise from assuming that the 'public good model' is relevant but that there are also 'private' considerations that explain why individuals give to charities.

---

1. Sugden notes Schelling's (1960) analysis of salience. If there is a presumption that some rule is 'best' for both players in a coordination game, then 'it is rational or reasonable for each player to follow this rule and to expect that the other will do so too' (Sugden 1993: 83).

15.4 The charity as a 'firm': responding to different motivations

The previous section uses an application of public good theory to explain why a 'charity market' fails to provide an efficient allocation of resources when the only motive for donations was the public good benefit that would be experienced as a result of giving. If 'giving to charity' is equated with 'contribution to a public good' the prediction is under-provision (by reference to a Pareto-optimal solution). At the same time, it is clear that individuals do contribute to charities and that there are other inducements to give. A distinction was drawn in the previous section between altruism as motivated by other private considerations (e.g. the warm glow from giving, the receipt of inducements to give) and altruism motivated to attain a 'collective good' outcome.

The objective in this section is to apply the theory of the firm (discussed in Chapters 11 and 12) to explain the behaviour of charities (as 'firms') within the charity market. The objective (once again) is to demonstrate that the firm will pursue different objectives according to who has greatest influence on decision-making. With this as a background, there may be a case for regulation of such firms if the objectives of those who control charities are likely to differ from perceptions of the 'public interest'. The case for tax concessions and for regulation depends on an understanding of how the charity (as a firm) is likely to operate.

To apply a market analogy, it is necessary to distinguish between demand and supply. If a voluntary charity is perceived as a firm operating within a market then its role is to raise finance from donors to transfer (as cash or as goods and services) to donees. The objective of the firm, it might be thought, is to maximise the difference between total cost and total benefit. However, when looking at the demand side:

i)   'Consumers' of charities are donors, *not* donees. In neoclassical microeconomics, consumers are those individuals who both need (want, desire) specific goods and *also* have the ability to purchase them (see Chapter 2). Indeed, it is this latter ability that gives consumers influence over the allocation of resources; if producers get it wrong consumers have the sanction to refuse to buy. However, in the charity market this description better fits donors than donees.

ii) If, as argued above, donors often give to charities as a by-product to other pursuits, the interests of consumers and donees may be very different. Fund-raising activities (i.e. private incentives) may be demanded as much for their own sake as for any net revenue they create. If so, what is an 'efficient' charity? Is it one that maximises the output of charitable activity or one that provides the most desirable bundle of selective incentives and charitable activity? Conversely, if the objective is to maximise charitable activity, how can charities compete with private firms that sell similar private goods?

In the theory of the firm, predictions depend on the objectives of decision-makers. In an application of this theory to the behaviour of the charity as a firm, it is possible to distinguish between consumer donors (CDs) and producer donors (PDs) (a distinction akin to that made in Stigler 1970). The distinction depends on whether donors are in receipt of a direct or indirect source of utility when they donate.

CDs are seen as buying 'products' (e.g. tickets for gala outings, or film premieres or prestige) for the direct utility that such 'purchases' generate. Producer donors (PDs) could be seen as supplying finance to charities in the manner in which shareholders supply equity capital but, in contrast, they seek a 'psychic non-pecuniary rate of return' on their investment as compared to a pecuniary one. PDs are concerned with donation for the indirect result, i.e. welfare generated for donees; their rate of return depends on the value of the net revenue transferred to recipients. The PD is, in effect, purchasing the organisational and other activities of the charity in order to enjoy the best psychic rate of return on their investment.

While it is not the case that these stylised caricatures perfectly describe all donors (any one individual may conceivably be a blend of both CD and PD), the distinction facilitates an analogy with decision-making in private-sector firms. If producer donors (shareholders) are considered active in policy-making, they perceive the use of fund-raising and organisational activity purely to maximise net revenue to transfer to donors. They would then set this level of fund-raising and organisational activities (to which consumer donors passively respond in the charity market) so as to maximise the surplus to be transferred to donees. By contrast, if CDs were active in policy-making there might be greater-than-'optimal' fund-raising and organisational activity, (subject to the passive constraint that producer donors enjoyed a minimum rate of psychic return on their investment via the distribution of some surplus).

In discussion of the behaviour of the firm it was noted (in Chapter 12) that it is possible that there exists a divorce of control between shareholders and managers (Marris 1963). While shareholders wish that the firm maximises profit, managers may prefer that the firm maximises growth if manager's salary, power and prestige are growth-related. The management of charities (e.g. trustees or directors) may also have their own objectives, separate from those of donors. On the one hand, these may be genuinely related to maximising the interests of donees. On the other hand, they may be associated with X-inefficiency in production, i.e. they may enjoy 'on-the-job leisure' or working conditions of a higher standard than would be true of a profit-maximising firm (Leibenstein 1966). In the former case, they are identical to producer donors, so that to introduce another set of outcomes it is useful to take the second, more cynical, assumption. In this situation, to the extent that donors are at an informational disadvantage, there will be scope for management to engage in X-inefficiency (Tullock 1966).

With these distinctions in mind, how are charities likely to behave? The objective of the following application of microeconomics is to illustrate how different assumptions concerning the motivation to give and to participate in charitable activity will affect the behaviour of a charity. Later, the question will be raised as to how this discussion might inform the formulation of public policy.

In Figure 15.2(a) contributions to a charity are shown as 0-B. Contributions depend upon the provision of fund-raising and organisational services. The cost function (i.e. expenditure on fund-raising and administrative activity, as distinct from charitable expenditure), is assumed linear and is shown as 0-C. In Figure 15.2(b) the net surplus generated for charitable expenditure is illustrated and shown as 0-π. However, in a discussion of what motivates charitable activity, different perspectives have been offered and these form the basis for discussion of the three alternative situations.

a) *Charity (net revenue) maxima.* Here the assumption is that the objective of PDs is maximised. The charity would choose a total of 0-F_1 units of fund-raising and organisational activity. There is a constraint that CDs must be provided with services if revenue is to be raised (implicit in the 0-B functions) and that management must be paid the minimum required to keep them operative (implicit in the 0-C function). Subject to these constraints the charity maximises its net charitable expenditure, i.e. distance F_1-1 (= distance 2-3).

b) *Fund-raising maxima.* Here assume, instead, that CDs are 'active' in decision-making. The fund-raising maximum is at 0-F_4 (where each unit of revenue raised is devoted to fund-raising). If there is a constraint that it is necessary to spend a certain amount on charitable expenditure (e.g. 0-E) then in Figure 15.2(b), fund-raising and organisational activity will be 0-F_3.

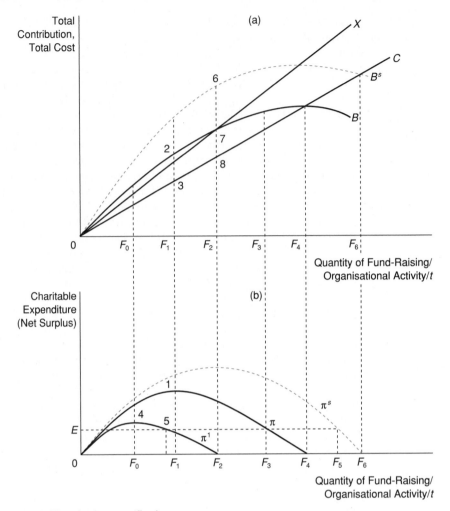

Figure 15.2 **The charity as a 'firm'**

c) *Managerial utility.* The interest of the charity organisers may prove dominant and both PDs and CDs may play a passive role. The question then is what determines utility for the manager? Charity organisers may be committed and dedicated to the avowed objectives of the charity. They may organise the charity to maximise net revenue at $0\text{-}F_1$ (or, if the charity offers a specific service, to maximise the service provided). Alternatively (for reasons discussed in Chapter 14 when discussing the behaviour of bureaucrats), charity organisers may be revenue- (or budget-)maximisers.[2] In this case they will be inclined to devote more than the optimal allocation of resources to fund-raising at $0\text{-}F_4$. In this case fund-raising is acceptable to the extent that it brings in another unit of revenue, whereas for the charity-maximiser fund-raising is only justifiable to the extent that it brings in another unit of *net* revenue. Hewitt and Brown (2000) describe these alternatives and argue that an alternative is a compromise between 'service maximisation' and 'revenue maximisation' (between $0\text{-}F_1$ and $0\text{-}F_4$). However, if management has discretion to enjoy X-inefficiency, then the cost function in Figure 15.2(a) may be inflated (appearing as $0\text{-}X$). The result is

2. Prestige and power may be proportionally related to the size of the budget.

that the pursuit of charitable funds is less than efficient (at $0\text{-}F_0$) and the amount available for charitable expenditure is reduced to distance $F_0\text{-}4$.[3]

The discussion here illustrates how the theory of the firm may be applied to institutions within a 'charity market'. A key finding is that the activities of institutions depend sensitively on *whose* interests are maximised and *what* constraints are relevant. If public policy is concerned to maximise charitable activity there are implications. For example:

(i) If PDs are ineffectual in the organisation of charities (as argued above), public policy may focus on legislative constraints on the proportion of revenue that a charity is able to allocate to fund-raising. Weisbrod (1988) provides examples of legislation in states of the USA to constrain the amount charities allocate to fund-raising. He argues that, without such legislation, donors may be deterred from giving to charity. Moreover, he argues that if there were information that a charity spent a high proportion of income on fund-raising activity, this would deter further donation (from PDs).

(ii) If there is concern that charities might be induced to spend too much on fund-raising then tax/subsidy policy must be amended accordingly. For example, if lump-sum grants were offered to a charity then net surplus would increase by exactly this amount (in Figure 15.2, $0\text{-}B$ would shift up in a parallel fashion). By comparison, tax assistance in the form of tax relief to donations would reduce the price of services to CDs. It would shift $0\text{-}B$ to $0\text{-}B^s$ and the charity maximises net revenue by moving from $0\text{-}F_1$ to $0\text{-}F_2$. Of the surplus now provided, vertical distance 6-7 is the subsidy. Allowing for the increased fund-raising expenditure of the charity the additional surplus from private contributions is reduced (from vertical distance 2-3 to 7-8).

It is impossible to design public policy effectively in the absence of a behavioural model of the charity (as a firm).

15.4.1 Empirical evidence concerning the behaviour of the charity as a firm

A great deal depends on information as to how charities behave. However, the empirical work is mixed. Boyle and Jacobs (1978) implicitly assume that not-for-profit organisations try to maximise net contributions (or, equivalently, services). They concluded that not-for-profits were inefficient, in that there was substantial room to increase net contributions through increased fund-raising efforts. Similarly, having analysed the top two hundred charities in the UK, Cullis *et al.* (1984) argue that too little is spent in the UK on fund-raising.

Weisbrod and Dominguez (1986) estimated the fund-raising productivity of some 300,000 not-for-profit firms (using panel data from IRS tax returns covering the years 1973 to 1976). They modelled current donations as a function of current price and lagged fund-raising expenditures. Their results were consistent with the proposition that charities budget-maximise.

Steinberg (1989) set out to specifically test the proposition that charities budget-maximise. He considered panel data over the period 1974 to 1976, and found that: (i) in some not-for-profit sectors 'charity firms' are service-maximisers (welfare, education and arts), (ii) in other sectors they are budget-maximisers (health), while (iii) there were also cases in which they had mixed motives (research). Hewitt and Brown (2000) argue that this may reflect the specific interests of charity organisers in different sectors.

Posnett and Sandler (1989) studied the 300 largest charities in the UK for 1985/86 and found support for the hypothesis that charities are net-revenue-(service-)maximisers.

---

3. If it were also necessary to meet the demands of CDs and also to provide $0\text{-}E$ for the PDs then the solution would be at point 5 in Figure 15.2.

They used a model similar to that of Weisbrod and Dominguez (1986), but also included sources of income for charities other than contributions (e.g. government grants). However, Khanna, Posnett and Sandler (1995) estimated a model similar to that of Posnett and Sandler (1989) and found results similar to those of Steinberg (1989). In certain sectors, charity firms were revenue-maximisers, in other sectors they were net-revenue-maximisers and there was also evidence in certain cases that charities do not even maximise net revenue.

Evidence appears to challenge the proposition that the same objectives can be attributed to charities in all sectors of the charity market. There is a need for further research to indicate the extent of predictable differences and the way in which public policy might respond.

15.4.2 Further public policy implications

It should be emphasised that, even if the noble PDs dominate (and charities net-revenue-maximise), decisions made in terms of provision of services will still reflect the interests of the donor rather than the donee. While it may be thought that such a difference would be small in the case of a charity transferring revenue, consider the case of a charity that provides an in-kind service. By comparison with equation (15.1) the interdependence may be in terms of donors (A's) concern that donees (B) consume specific goods (e.g. medical care), i.e.

$$U^a = U(x_1, \ldots, x_n, x_m^b) \tag{15.2}$$

where

$$\partial U^a / \partial x_m^b > 0$$

It is unlikely that the preferences of donors and donees (with respect to consumption of a specific good) will match.

However, when PDs dominate, regulation of this market may be required *even if* donor preferences matched those of donees. Donors are not the recipients of the services transferred (by those who manage charities) to the donee recipients. This places them at an informational disadvantage with reference to their position as consumers of other proprietary goods bought in the private sector. While donors are defined as 'consumers' (because they are able to influence the charity), they are not the recipients who actually use the services transferred by the charity. To this extent, the automatic check, which consumers of proprietary goods have on the quality of services of firms, is attenuated. How can the consumers (donors) check on the quality of the good being provided by producers on the supply side of the charity market? Donors may seldom find it worthwhile to invest in the costs of information-gathering and they will be 'rationally ignorant'.

Because of the difficulties which charities face in raising revenue for charitable activity, legislatures have awarded charities legal and fiscal privileges. Such advantages can be rationalised in terms of the need to reduce their costs and thereby enable them to raise more revenue and compete more effectively. The preceding analysis shows how the design of public policy requires an awareness of alternative modes of behaviour of the 'charity as a firm'. (For further discussion, see Jones and Cullis 1990; more will be said of in-kind transfers supplied via the state in Section 15.9).

15.5 Taxation and transfers when utility functions are interdependent

The discussion above illustrates how microeconomic theory can be applied to explain private giving to charity. However, if the objective expected of charities is to maximise assistance given to those in need, the outcome in a 'charity market' may be inefficient.

With reference to public good considerations, there may be under-provision of charitable activity. In this section the objective is to look at ways in which government might respond. As far as tax policy is concerned there are two possibilities to consider. First, the government may use tax expenditures (as noted above) to increase the activity of voluntary charities. Second, the government may take over the role of transferring to the needy, e.g. via a progressive rate of taxation (which implies higher positive payments by the better-off and transfers to the poor). In this section both options are examined.

15.5.1 Tax relief to charitable donations

The problem to be discussed in this section is whether government would be better advised to assist charities by offering tax relief to those who voluntarily give to charities or to use tax revenue to offer grants to charities. At the outset it is assumed that too little is given to charities in the charity market and that intervention is focused on redressing this problem. Once again, microeconomic theory (explained elsewhere in this text) proves useful in resolving the policy problem. In particular, the 'price elasticity of giving' (see Chapter 2 for a discussion of price elasticity) is at the centre of analysis.

An alternative explanation for tax relief to charity-giving relies on the proposition that tax relief would increase charitable giving by more than the cost of the subsidy. In this context, the rule would be to use tax relief provided that giving to charities is 'price'-elastic. The 'price' of giving £1 to a charity might appear to be £1. However, if there is tax relief on that part of income given to a charity then the price of giving £1 is $1 - m$, where m is the marginal rate of tax (it is as if there is a subsidy at rate $s = m$ to giving).

If offering tax relief increased giving to charities by more than the revenue cost of the tax relief, the outcome is referred to as 'treasury-efficient'. If giving to charity was regarded as a 'worthy' activity then the rationale for tax relief would be to maximise charitable transfers.

Why focus on the price elasticity of giving? The critical consideration is whether, by offering tax relief, there will be more funds devoted to charitable activity than had the tax been raised and transfers been provided via grants. If the government did not offer tax relief it could use tax revenue to fund grants to charities. The alternative is to forgo the tax by giving tax relief to encourage private giving.

Let the amount of private giving (private transfer) to charity be T. The cost to the treasury of increasing tax relief (subsidy) on giving to charity can be written as dsT/ds (where s is the rate of tax relief). The question is whether the increase in giving to charity (as a result of an increase in tax relief) is greater than the increase in the cost to the government as a result of increasing the tax relief. That is to say, will dT/ds exceed dsT/ds? If so, it is 'treasury-efficient' to use government finance to increase tax relief (subsidy) than to fund grants (via the public sector) to charities.

With this argument in mind, note that by definition

$$dT/ds = -dT/d(1 - s) \tag{15.3}$$

where $(1 - s)$ is the 'price of giving'. To fulfil the requirements described in the previous paragraph, it must be the case that dT/ds is greater than dsT/ds. This requires that:

$$dT/ds > sdT/ds + T \tag{15.4}$$

Equation (15.4) can be rewritten as:

$$\eta < -1 \tag{15.5}$$

where η is the elasticity of giving with respect to price, i.e. the *absolute* value of η has to be greater than unity.[4]

To say that there is a price elasticity of giving equal to 1 means that for each 1 per cent decrease in the price of giving, giving will increase by 1 per cent (other things equal). As a result of empirical work a consensus has emerged among economists that the 'price elasticity of giving' in absolute terms is just over 1. Income elasticity is between 0.5 and 0.8 (e.g. see Collard 1978; Schiff 1989).

If the price elasticity of giving exceeds 1 then increasing tax relief is *treasury-efficient* because the rise in contributions (£x million) exceeds the revenue cost. In these circumstances Feldstein (1975) suggests that relying on subsidy increases welfare. The analysis assumes that there is no crowding-out associated with government transfers to charities. This will be discussed more fully in Section 15.7. If government giving to charities crowded out private giving (for reasons to be discussed later) it is possible to justify tax relief as treasury-efficient even if the price elasticity was lower than 1 (see Roberts 1984).

The test for public policy is based on empirical estimates of the price elasticity of giving. But how reliable are such estimates likely to be?

(i)   In econometric work there is always a problem that there may be *omitted variables* in regression analysis, so that differences imputed to price and income variation may result from some other unobserved difference, e.g. in education.

(ii) There is a difficulty when using data if those who claim tax relief are really attempting to *evade tax*. Slemrod (1988) noted that, in the US, tax auditors found that giving reported for tax deduction was overestimated by, on average, 7.2 per cent. He therefore argues that a tax subsidy was 'treasury-efficient' if, and only if, the elasticity for reported donations exceeds 1 in absolute value by an amount equal to the elasticity of evasion.

(iii) As with other elasticities (see Chapter 2), it is important to note that the value estimated will be sensitive to the *time period* under consideration. Clotfelter (1980) argues that, in the US, only about half of the long-run change in giving will be realised over the first two years.

(iv) There is also the question of whether such estimates take *full account* of the reaction to tax concessions. Schiff and Weisbrod (1986) found that non-profit agencies would change the emphasis on fund-raising according to the extent of government support available. This possibility was discussed when considering the role of the charity as a firm (in Section 15.4).

So how useful is knowledge that 'price elasticity of giving' exceeds 1?

(i)   Ignoring problems of estimation, this does not enable policy-makers to 'fine-tune' subsidies in line with the extent of the externality. Tax relief on donations to charitable activity can be explained in terms of the perception that there is under-provision in a 'charity market'. If there are externalities associated with the provision of philanthropy, a subsidy might be attached to internalise the externality (see Chapter 6). This does not mean that each charity should necessarily attract the same assistance. Given the extent of the externality, it may be appropriate that different subsidy rates are offered to 'giving' to different charities.

(2)   When considering policy in terms of income distribution, tax relief accepts that the giving that is provided will depend on the preferences of individuals who give

---

4. Equation (15.4) can be written as $(dT/ds)(1 - s) > T$ and, as $dT/ds = -dT/d(1 - s)$, this means that this can be written as $(dT/d(1 - s))(1 - s)/T > 1$. Note that, as $(dT/d(1 - s))(1 - s)/T$ is negative, it is equal to η, the price elasticity of giving, so the necessary condition is that $η < -1$.

(e.g. the wealthier in society tend to give proportionately greater assistance to the arts – opera etc. – than others might wish). Simple tax deduction means that the higher-income (who pay higher tax rates) may gain more from this relief, and there are also equity issues *between donors*.

Having said this, it is an illustration of the way in which government might adopt a simple rule to try to maximise the assistance provided to charities. Once again, policy depends on the effectiveness of empirical work and is always subject to discussion of issues of 'equity'.

15.5.2 Redistribution via 'Pareto-optimal' taxation: progressive income taxation

Rather than relying on a stimulus to the voluntary charitable sector, an alternative (or additional) option is for the state, itself, to adopt a charity role and to redistribute from taxpayer donors to a donee group. Hochman and Rodgers (1969) present a 'first-best' theory of Pareto-optimal taxation. They argue that taxes and transfers for redistribution can be determined in a way that satisfies Pareto-optimal conditions. However, as noted in the previous sections, this willingness of A to give income to B will not be realised fully within a voluntary arrangement because of the free-rider problem. It follows that state intervention may be justified. If so, would this imply progressive taxation? Is it the case that higher-income groups pay a higher average rate of tax? Indeed, in the context of redistribution, is it the case that higher-income individuals pay higher rates of tax and lower-income individuals receive higher transfers?

A closer understanding of the transfers required across income ranges can be achieved by expanding the previous two-person example to consider individuals in three income ranges (Mueller 1989). Begin by assuming that there are three groups in society, Y_a, Y_b and Y_c (as ranked in terms of level of income). Each member of the highest-income group Y_a gains satisfaction when the utility of members of the lower classes increases.

Consider the welfare of an individual i who is a member of group Y_a. This individual maximises the following utility function (which is a weighted sum of the utilities of its own members, and those of members of lower-income groups):

$$U_i = n_a U_a (Y_a - T) + \alpha_b n_b U_b (Y_b + S_b) + \alpha_c n_c U_c (Y_c + S_c), \tag{15.6}$$

where

n_a, n_b and n_c = numbers of individuals in groups Y_a, Y_b and Y_c respectively;

α_b, α_c = the weights that individual i gives to the utility enjoyed by members of groups b and c respectively;

T = tax imposed on the richest group (group a);

S_b and S_c = per-capita subsidies to the other two groups (b and c).

Individual i, as a representative member of the highest-income group a, attaches a weight of 1 to the utility of other members of group a, and lower weights ($\alpha_c < 1$, $\alpha_b < 1$) to members of other groups. The weights capture the degree of altruism. For example, a saint (equating own utility with that of others) places equal weight on own utility with that on others ($\alpha_c = \alpha_b = 1$). Other altruists place more weight on their own utility than on the utilities of others ($0 < \alpha < 1$) and will not favour transfers that are so large that their own incomes are made equal to others.

To focus on the tax T to be raised for redistribution, assume that it is only paid by members of group a. It follows that the tax constraint is:

$$n_a T = n_b S_b + n_c S_c \tag{15.7}$$

To assess the decision of the representative altruist, substituting (15.7) into (15.6) and maximising U_i with respect to S_c and S_b, yields:

$$\frac{dU_i}{dS_c} = -n_a U_a' \left(\frac{n_c}{n_a} \right) + \alpha_c n_c U_c' = 0 \tag{15.8}$$

$$dU_I/dS_b = -n_a U_a'(n_b/n_a) + \alpha_b n_b U_b' = 0 \tag{15.9}$$

If reference is made to the partial derivatives (U'), it follows that utility is maximised when:

$$U_a' = \alpha_b U_b' = \alpha_c U_c' \tag{15.10}$$

It is now possible to consider the tax system that would be preferred by individual i (as representative of the highest-income group). Assume i places the same weight on the utilities of members of classes b and c ($\alpha_c = \alpha_b$), and i expects that representatives of each lower-income group derive the same utility from income. Then i's welfare is maximised when transfers to members of classes c and b equate marginal utilities of income ($U_a' = \alpha_b U_b' = \alpha_c U_c'$). It is usual to assume that when $Y_c < Y_b$, marginal utility of income is lower in income group Y_b than in income group Y_c. Marginal utility of income (U') is assumed to fall with increasing income. It follows that the incomes of the lowest-income group (group c) must be raised to equality with those of group b (to reduce U_c' to U_b') before any transfers are made to group b. Tax contributions would be such that they favoured the least well-off and, to this extent, the tax arrangement that would be preferred would be progressive.

The analysis emphasises the weight given to those in a lower-income group and the extent to which incomes differ. Hochman and Rodgers (1969) offer more general insight in their formulation. In the following analysis the importance of the desire to give to those with a lower income (which will be estimated by the income elasticity of demand for transfers, E) and the importance of the extent of the initial income differential becomes obvious. Both considerations are important ingredients when determining the structure of a tax system that delivers 'Pareto-optimal redistribution'.

Following Hochman and Rodgers, assume a two-person economy. The utility functions for the members are given by:

$$U_A = U(Y_A, Y_B) \tag{15.11}$$

$$U_B = U(Y_B, Y_A) \tag{15.12}$$

where U_A and Y_A are initial values of utility and income for the taxpayer, and U_B and Y_B are initial values for the recipient. Each person is assumed to have a positive marginal utility of income for own consumption (i.e. utility increases with income).

It is assumed that transfers flow from high- to low-income earners. The y-axis of Figure 15.3 records the income differential $Y_A - Y_B$ and the x-axis is A's income. It is assumed that transfers would not be so large as to alter the initial income distribution rank (i.e. they cannot be larger than half of the initial income differential); transfers depend only on the preferences of the taxpayer. In Figure 15.3, this means that budget line that confronts the high-income individual is shown initially as 1-2-3. A welfare maximum is achieved for taxpayer A when there is a tangency between A's indifference curve (I_0^A) and the budget line. The tangency point e_1 determines the size of the transfer (i.e. the reduction in income differential on the y-axis) that the taxpayer would prefer. When income increases the budget line shifts bodily to the right (i.e. to 1'-2'-3'). The line *ICC* is an 'income consumption curve or path' showing how preferred transfers are affected by an increase in income. The shape of the income consumption path reflects the elasticity of transfers with respect to income (i.e. the percentage change in transfer for a percentage change in income – see Chapter 2). In the example, the transfer elasticity, E, is assumed equal to 1).

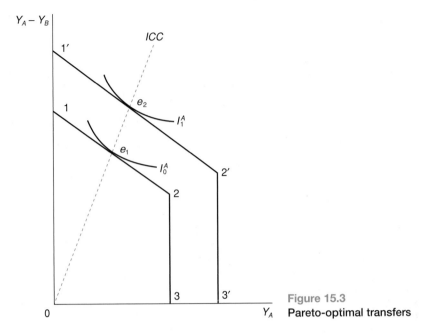

Figure 15.3
Pareto-optimal transfers

The question is, what tax structure is required for Pareto optimality in a multi-person framework? To extend the model to an *n*-person case, Hochman and Rodgers add a number of assumptions. They assume that: (i) there is no free-riding, (ii) individuals have identical tastes and (iii) there is no excess burden (see Chapter 13) from the income tax imposed. It is assumed that each person makes a transfer to everyone with lower income but receives a transfer from all those with higher income.[5] As in the two-person case, optimality depends on the transfer elasticity of the taxpayer (but note that all but the lowest earner is a taxpayer, so all transfer elasticities are relevant). The shape of the initial income distribution is important, as this will determine the number of people to whom an individual will pay a transfer as well as how many transfers an individual receives from others.

Having identified the income elasticity of transfers and the initial income distribution as key considerations, Hochman and Rodgers focus on two values for E:

(i) where the transfer elasticity (E) between all individuals is zero (a case where the income consumption path in Figure 15.3 is vertical and the optimum is a fixed-sum transfer for any income level of A);

(ii) where the transfer elasticity (E) is unity (i.e. transfers proportional to the income differential).

Each case is considered in terms of (i) a rectangular initial income distribution and (ii) a skewed (right) distribution (which more realistically reflected that of the USA in 1960). For a rectangular distribution and a zero transfer elasticity, Pareto optimality requires a degressive tax structure (i.e. a tax exemption band and then a single tax rate – see Chapter 13). However, with a unit elasticity, Pareto optimality requires a more progressive structure.

5. Each individual's net position is given by the sum of the two-person relationships between them and each other member of society.

When the initial income distribution is a skewed distribution and $E = 0$, a complex tax structure is implied.[6] However, with a skewed distribution a uniform progressive structure proves optimal if the transfer elasticity is unitary.

With reference to the argument that *altruism*, therefore, explains the adoption of tax progressivity, Musgrave (1970) makes an important distinction between *primary and secondary redistribution*. It is clear that (regardless of the transfer elasticity) the outcome will differ depending on the initial income distribution. The Pareto-optimal redistribution outlined by Hochman and Rodgers is, therefore, a *secondary redistribution* dependent on factors such as inheritance and education (which determine the initial setting). The resulting *primary redistribution*, may not depend so much on 'giving' as on 'taking' (as it depends on the social structure and the relative bargaining power of income groups).

Musgrave also highlights the importance of the possibility of free-riding in the *n*-person case. Taxpayer *i* may well derive utility from increases in a recipient's income, but may still gain fulfilment by free-riding, letting taxpayer *j* foot the bill. In a small-number case, *i* and *j* will bargain to set the level of the transfers, but amid large numbers *i* may decide that their giving will make little difference to the welfare of the recipient. Government coercion is a vital ingredient.

However, with such qualifications in mind, it should be stressed that the result is important because here there is a quite different explanation for the existence of tax progressivity from that explained in Chapter 13. The underlying rationale is efficiency (i.e. Pareto optimality) and the issue of stronger norms to define equity have not been invoked. Progressivity in the tax system is a matter of revealed preference. It does not rely on the existence of a (difficult to define) social welfare function and the associated (difficult to make) interpersonal utility comparison.

15.5.3 Progressive taxation and 'Pareto-optimal redistribution': empirical evidence

While the previous section explains how, in theory, 'altruism' can explain the adoption of a progressive tax structure, can existing tax structures be explained in this way? Two approaches to this question are considered here. The first predicts the tax structure that would be optimal for a given elasticity of transfer and initial income distribution and the test is to see whether the existing tax arrangements are consistent with those predicted. The second approach identifies those variables that would increase individuals' willingness to redistribute voluntarily. The test is now to examine whether or not they are relevant in explaining the tax arrangements designed to redistribute.

i)   *Tax progressivity.* As explained, the authors (Hochman and Rodgers) argue that the amount that an individual wishes to transfer to another depends on the transfer elasticity (E) and the initial pre-tax income distribution. On the basis of assumptions concerning both of these variables, it is possible to predict the transfers that would be Pareto optimal. The empirical test is to compare the predictions with the actual transfers that take place in any tax system.

Problems arose with the Hochman and Rodgers test to the extent that transfers in the US did not increase monotonically with income (see Table 15.2). How could the transfers that existed in the US be explained in the context of Hochman–Rodgers theory? Hochman and Rodgers found it difficult. They argued that many of the recorded poor were rural poor, whose real incomes were understated by the

---

6. For the US this is progressive up to an income of some $5000; at this point there is a decline in marginal rates because the percentage change in income between this and the next income bracket exceeds the percentage change in eligible recipients.

Table 15.2 Net tax transfers in the US (1960)

Income ($)	Transfer
800	+441
2,500	+1,110
3,500	+648
4,500	−58
6,250	−131
8,750	+148
15,500	−2,046

Source: Hochman and Rodgers 1969: 555.

statistics. In noting that the poor had less political power they accepted that tax systems are not a perfect reflection of altruism. They argued that the very poorest category over-represented single persons, while the categories immediately above over-represented larger families. They recognised that people at around median income (about $5000) did rather badly while those around the lower quartile (about $2750) did quite well (which by reference to discussion of the median voter – in Chapter 14 – is difficult to explain).

Collard (1978) reproduced 'Hochman–Rodgers calculations' for UK data and found a closer match. Once again, the object was to compare the pattern of government transfers with that predicted on the basis of Pareto-optimal redistribution. Following Hochman and Rodgers, he postulated two transfer elasticities, $E = 0$ and $E = 1$. Having calculated a matrix of income differences he derived appropriate transfers by anchoring on the poorest groups. He calculated how much each group received from each of the others and calculated how much it paid to each of the others. The net transfers (in cash and in terms of cash plus in-kind transfers) are illustrated in Figures 15.4(a) and 15.4(b). In these figures the actual transfers are compared with those which would be required when $E = 1$ and when $E = 0$. The amounts transferred do decrease monotonically with income as predicted by the Pareto-optimality assumption. Also, the pattern of actual transfers (if not the actual amounts) accords quite well with those predicted when $E = 1$ (more so than with $E = 0$). Figures 15.4(a) and 15.4(b) indicate that the structure predicted by the Pareto-optimality approach depends both upon transfer elasticity and the pre-tax distribution of income. (In each figure y_m is median income.)

ii) *Support for redistribution.* Orr (1976) and Zimmerman (1975) offer a different test of Pareto optimal redistribution (based on the variables that explain willingness to give). They independently considered payments under the Aid for Dependent Children programme (the largest single welfare programme in the United States at that time). The AFDC operated as a combined state–federal programme. Each state determined the amount of aid and the federal government reimbursed the state for part of the payments. The percentage reimbursement depended on the state's income and the amount of aid given per recipient.

Following Tresch (1981), it is possible to consider the decision of a representative individual member of a high-income group (i.e. individual i) with respect to redistribution. Throughout, it is assumed that there are two sets of people, rich (R) and poor (P). The rich have political influence; they alone decide how much is to be redistributed to the poor. Individual i is a member of the rich set ($i \in R$) and the focus is on the utility-maximising decisions of i. The incomes of the poor appear as vector (Yp) in the utility function of the representative individual. The costs of

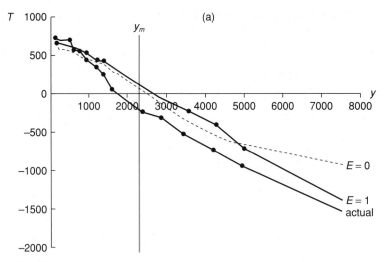

Figure 15.4(a) Cash transfers: actual and Pareto-optimal

Source: Collard (1978).

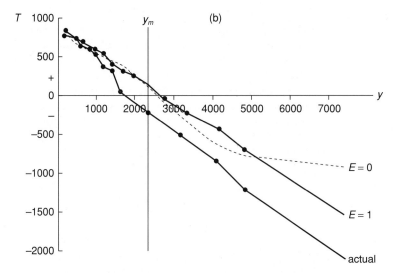

Figure 15.4(b) Cash and kind transfers: actual and Pareto-optimal

Source: Collard (1978).

making the transfer are shared equally amongst the rich and pounds of transfer to the poor are assumed to be distributed equally among all the poor.

It is assumed that each rich person (*i*) has a utility function of the form:

$$U^i = U^i(Y_i, \mathbf{Y}p) \tag{15.13}$$

where

$\mathbf{Y}p$ = the vector of incomes of all the poor people ($p = 1, \dots, P$);
Y_i = the income of rich person *i*.

The objective is to determine the amount of transfer that would be Pareto optimal (as far as a rich person is concerned). If *G* represents a pound of income transferred ('given') to each poor person, tax cost (T) to the rich person increases as G increases (and an increase in T reduces Y_i). If utility of i is maximised, it follows, from (15.13) that for $\partial U^i / \partial G = 0$:

$$\frac{\partial U^i}{\partial G} = \frac{\partial U^i}{\partial Y_i} \frac{\partial Y_i}{\partial T_i} \frac{\partial T_i}{\partial G} + \sum_{p=1}^{P} \frac{\partial U^i}{\partial Y_p} \frac{\partial Y_p}{\partial G} = 0 \qquad (15.14)$$

This is no more than saying that the marginal cost of transfer must equal the marginal benefit:

$$\frac{\partial U^i}{\partial Y_i} \frac{\partial Y_i}{\partial T_i} \frac{\partial T_i}{\partial G} = \sum_{p=1}^{P} \frac{\partial U_i}{\partial Y_p} \frac{\partial Y_p}{\partial G} \qquad (15.15)$$

However, these terms can be simplified when it is recognised that the transfer is in terms of one pound. This means that:

$$\frac{\partial Y_p}{\partial G} \equiv +1 \qquad (15.16)$$

and

$$\frac{\partial Y_i}{\partial T_i} \equiv -1 \qquad (15.17)$$

Moreover, if the tax burden of redistribution is equally shared amongst the rich then for individual i:

$$\frac{\partial T_i}{\partial G} = \frac{P}{R} \qquad (15.18)$$

where

P = number of poor;
R = number of rich.

It follows that, by substitution, (15.8) can be written as:

$$\frac{\partial U^i}{\partial Y_i} \frac{(P)}{R} = \sum_{p=1}^{P} \frac{\partial U^i}{\partial Y_p} \qquad (15.19)$$

The right-hand side of (15.19) is the marginal benefit to taxpayer i of transferring a pound to *each* poor person. The left-hand side is marginal cost (the loss in utility) per pound of income transferred multiplied by the individual's share of the costs.[7]

Once again, giving to the poor is similar to the provision of a non-excludable public good. If any one rich person (i) makes a transfer, all rich people will benefit and so a government programme is required to mitigate the free-rider problem.

The question is, how can a test for Pareto-optimal redistribution be carried out. Orr and Zimmerman utilise the theory described above to propose a number of testable hypotheses. They then undertake tests with respect to state transfers to programmes. The tests depend on identifying those variables that would be expected to influence the 'marginal cost' and 'marginal benefit' of transfers. For example, if this utility interdependence model were actually affecting decisions, then transfer payments per person will be greater the

---

7. It can be seen that each rich person is likely to prefer a government transfer programme in which *all* rich people are required to share the costs to private charity. If the individual acted unilaterally the marginal costs to person i of transferring £1 to all poor people is $-(\partial U'/\partial Y)P$.

i) higher the income of the rich taxpayers (because a higher Y_i implies lower $\partial U'/\partial Y_i$ and this implies a lower marginal cost of transfer);

ii) lower is P/R (because a lower ratio of poor to rich lowers the price of giving);

iii) larger is P (because marginal benefits of giving increase by more than marginal costs when P increases);[8]

iv) more altruistic are the rich (because $\partial U^i/\partial Y_p$ will be higher and the marginal benefits of giving will be greater);

v) higher the federal share of finance on the margin for the programme AFDC (because an increase in the federal share lowers the marginal costs of transfers to the poor within any given state).

Orr analysed a sample of annual observations (from 50 US states and the District of Columbia between 1963 and 1972) with reference to an appropriate set of explanatory variables. Zimmerman had data for 1971 and a reduced set of explanatory variables. Both report findings consistent with the hypothesis that there is Pareto-optimal redistribution. While the Orr–Zimmerman tests support the view that altruism exists and can be modelled as an externality, this does not *prove* that AFDC payments were motivated by altruism. For example:

(i) Each of the preceding five predictions may be compatible with a different explanation of tax transfers. The analysis does not discount the possibility that redistribution can be explained by weights associated with an appropriate social welfare function (see Chapters 5 and 13).

(ii) A second problem arises from a criticism by Mueller (1989). This rests on the underlying theory that guided the test. In the Orr–Zimmerman approach there is no utility to individual i arising from the well-being of individuals within their own group. To explain this criticism in the context of Mueller's discussion (described above), if individual i is a member of the rich group (A) and B is the poor, then for individual i's utility function:

$$U_i = U_a(Y_a - T) + \alpha n_b U_b(Y_b + S) \tag{15.20}$$

and the welfare-maximising value of S is where

$$\frac{n_b}{n_a} U'_a = \alpha n_b U'_b \tag{15.21}$$

It follows that S increases with higher ratios of n_b/n_a and with higher n_b (holding n_b/n_a constant). The implication is that, if the population were to increase (even when n_b/n_a is constant), the rich would impoverish themselves to help the poor! The theoretical underpinning of the test is vulnerable. In the extreme, it assumes that every member of the rich group derives utility from assisting every member of the poor but has no utility implications from a change in the well-being of other individuals in the rich group.

While the empirical tests of the Hochman–Rodgers explanation of state redistribution will always be subject to qualification, the theory opens a new insight when explaining state intervention. Distributions are justified in terms of efficiency. In Chapters 6 and 13 the case for government redistribution was based explicitly on equity and on an assumed

---

8. The marginal benefit of giving to i is $\partial U^i/\partial Y_{P+1}$. It follows that, as P increases, the marginal costs increase by:

$$\frac{\partial (P/R)}{\partial P} = \frac{\partial P/(T-P)}{\partial P} = \frac{(T-P)+P}{(T-P)^2} = \frac{T}{(T-P)^2} \tag{15.1n}$$

where $T = P + R =$ total population (assuming total population constant). If $P < T$, the increase in marginal costs will be small.

social welfare function. In Chapter 16 alternative theories (based on pure self-interest) will be considered when explaining redistribution measures. The problem is to devise empirical tests to assess the extent to which self-interest or altruism can explain existing fiscal measures in order to ascertain the importance of 'altruism'.

15.6 'In-kind' altruism

Interdependent utility functions can be used to analyse altruism and to explain 'giving' to voluntary charities and income transfers via the state. However, transfers via the state are sometimes in terms of cash and sometimes in kind. While cash allowances may be made to certain sections of the community (e.g. the poor, the disabled) it is also the case that goods and services may be provided free to certain recipients (e.g. medical care, education, or, as in the US, food stamps for the poor). The objective in this section is to apply microeconomic theory to explain why redistribution has been in kind.

It is usual for microeconomic texts to illustrate the application of indifference curves with a demonstration that cash transfers are superior to in-kind transfers. If the objective is to increase a recipient's welfare (i.e. a beneficiary, individual B), then it appears more efficient to offer cash transfers than either (i) subsidise goods and services or (ii) offer in-kind services. In Figure 15.5 the indifference curves for individual B are illustrated. In panel (a) the comparison is between subsidising good X and offering a cash transfer sufficient to enable the recipient to increase consumption of good X. Initially, the individual faces a relative price of good X represented by the slope of budget line 1-2. The individual chooses to allocate income as indicated at point 6 on budget line 1-2. If the government offers a price subsidy, the budget line shifts to 1-3. The individual is better off, for it is now possible to reach point 7 on indifference curve I_2. If, instead, the government were to offer a cash transfer to enable the individual to purchase the same quantity of good X (i.e. at point 7) then the budget line must be pushed to the right, to intersect point 7. The required cash transfer is equal to distance 1-4 in Figure 15.5. However, if the individual were in receipt of this cash transfer the individual would be able to increase welfare, at point 8 on indifference curve I_3. The individual would prefer the cash transfer (equal in terms of the required government expenditure to the cost of offering a price subsidy to good X).

In Figure 15.5(b) the choice is between providing a specified quantity of good X free of charge and offering an equivalent cash transfer. Initially, the recipient (individual B) is again on indifference curve I_1 at point 6. If a lump-sum (in-kind) transfer is provided, so that the recipient can enjoy 1-7 units free of charge, the budget line become 1-7-5. The individual is made better off at point 7 on indifference curve I_2. A cash transfer of equivalent value is equal to 1-4 (in units of Y); the new budget line, 4-5, passes through point 7. However, now the recipient can achieve point 8 on indifference curve I_3. Once again, a cash transfer proves superior (at the same cost to the government) to provision of goods and services in kind.

Yet, while application of microeconomic theory demonstrates that cash transfers are superior to provision of goods and services in kind, governments often prefer to provide services (e.g. medical care, education) rather than to provide transfers in the form of cash (Brennan and Pincus, 1983, argue that government budgets in Western democracies are dominated by such expenditures). If governments are concerned with recipients' happiness, surely it would always be preferable to transfer in the form of cash (for this would allow the recipient to choose how best to use the cash)? If taxpayer A is concerned with the well-being of B (so that – following Hochman and Rodgers (1969) – $U_A = u(U_A, U_B)$, then surely governments should provide assistance in cash? For the same expenditure, governments would increase welfare by providing a cash equivalent to services.

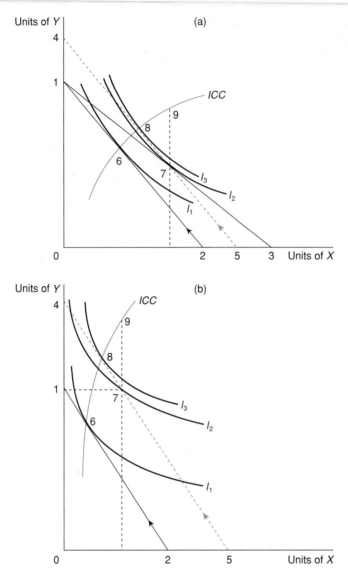

Figure 15.5
Response to in-kind subsidy

One explanation of why transfers are 'in kind' rather than 'in cash' depends on the argument that the government is not solely concerned with the welfare of the recipient. Such transfers reflect a particular form of altruism on the part of *taxpayer–donors*. There is a 'goods-specific externality'. Altruism is not simply described as utility interdependence. If it is reasonable to assume that government is concerned with the welfare of the taxpayer–donor (as well as with assisting the recipient–beneficiary), then publicly financed goods and services may prove a more efficient solution than the provision of cash.

The analysis depends on the assumption that *taxpayer–donors* are not simply concerned with the utility of the individual (as described in equation 15.1). Instead, it is argued that there is a 'goods-specific' externality'. Following Culyer (1971) assume that one high-income individual (*A*) is concerned about the welfare of a poor individual (*B*). Individual *A* is concerned about *B*'s consumption of medical care, i.e. *B*'s consumption of medical care enters *A*'s utility function (there is a 'goods-specific externality'). The individual's utility functions can be written as:

$$U_A = U_A(\,X_1^A,\,X_2^A,\,\ldots\,X_n^A,\,m_A,\,m_B) \tag{15.21}$$

$$U_B = U_B(X_1^B,\,X_2^B,\,\ldots\,X_n^B,\,m_B) \tag{15.22}$$

where

$X_1,\,\ldots,\,X_n$ = a range of goods and services other than medical care;
m = medical care.

A has a *specifically interdependent* utility function; A's utility depends not only on the goods and services A consumes, but also on the *quantity* of one specific good, medical care (m), that individual B consumes.

The analysis employs a triangular Edgeworth–Bowley trading box.[9] To construct this (see Cullis and West 1979) allow Y to act as a *numeraire* commodity (it can be thought of as income). Figure 15.6 (panel a) represents the initial position for B with equilibrium

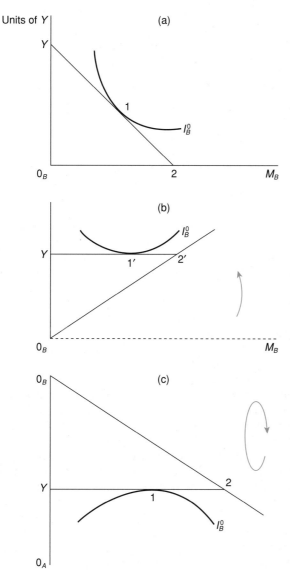

Figure 15.6
Stages towards the triangular Edgeworth–Bowley trading box

9. As constructed by Shibata (1971).

occurring at point 1 and the utility level achieved is I_B^0. The slope of Y-2 represents the rate at which B can substitute income for medical care (as with the normal budget line). In panel (b) the slope of the m_B-axis and B's indifference curve is increased by a constant. This constant is equal to the rate at which society can convert income into B's medical care. For example, suppose the slope of Y-2 in Figure 15.6 (panel a) is (–)3, then 3 units of income must be sacrificed for 1 unit of medical care. If we add to this a constant equal to this ratio (i.e. equal to the slope of Y-2), then the slope of Y-2 (as shown in panel b) must become zero. Similarly, the slope of I_b^0 at 1 (in panel a) is (–)3 and, adding this constant means that (in panel b) the slope of I_B^0 (at point 1′) becomes zero (i.e. again, a horizontal straight line).[10]

The step to panel (c) in Figure 15.6 is straightforward; simply invert B's adjusted indifference map. It follows that, in Figure 15.7, this section (as shown in panel c of Figure 15.6) can be placed on A's 'indifference curve' diagram. The result is that distance 0_A-0_B measures the sum of A's and B's initial endowment of Y (i.e. 0_A-$0_B = 0_A$-$Y + 0_B$-Y).

In Figure 15.7, 0_B-3 represents all possible combinations of Y and B's medical care that are available to this two-person society. With an endowment of income equal to 0_B-Y, it can be seen (left to their own devices), B chooses the welfare-maximising equilibrium 1 (i.e. on the highest attainable utility curve I_B^0).

A is now faced with the question of whether or not this consumption level of B is satisfactory. The triangular Edgeworth–Bowley diagram shows A's utility increases as B's consumption of medical care increases. For example, A can select a welfare maximum point along the budget line Y-4, i.e. at point 5 on I_A^1. Of course, B's purchase of 0_A-6 units of medical care will have the effect of increasing A's welfare and this is shown by the fact that A's consumption possibilities have been pushed to the right (i.e. to budget line Y-1-7) when B consumes to 0_A-6 units. B's purchase of medical care acts as a lump-sum spillover for A (i.e. there is a 'goods-specific externality').[11]

When B consumes Y-1 (= 0_A-6) units of medical care, A's highest attainable utility level is at point 8 on I_A^2. This would mean that A would purchase distance 6-9 units of medical care for B. It follows that A prefers a level of consumption of medical care for B which is above the optimum level that B would choose for himself/herself (0_A-9 > 0_A-6). However, if A purchases medical care for B, B will react by reducing personal demand for medical care (for A would purchase more than B requires, distance 6-9 > 0_A-6).

In this specific case, consider the options open to A. If A transfers cash to individual B then B would increase consumption of medical care. For each income transfer received, B chooses a quantity of medical care that maximises utility and the locus of these points of equilibrium is shown as B-B (i.e. B-B is the income consumption curve). Analogously, A-A is the expansion path for A's purchased care for B (when A's income is not transferred in cash to B). Now if A is deciding on how a transfer should be made, a transfer as cash that maximises A's utility level will occur at point 10 on indifference curve I_A^0 (where I_A^0 is a tangent to B-B). By contrast, if individual A purchases medical care and provides this for B, A can choose point 5 on Y-4 and attain a higher level of welfare on indifference curve I_A^1. It follows that, for individual A, transfer in kind is preferable to transfer in cash. Note that B is also likely to prefer philanthropy in kind in certain cases. For example, if B's indifference curves were drawn at each point along B-B then (with the shape shown by I_B^0) a higher indifference curve for B passes through point 5 than point 10. It follows

---

10. Indeed, the slopes of all B's indifference curves are no longer the marginal rate of substitution between medical care and income but the *difference* between B's marginal rate of substitution and marginal rate of transformation between income and medical care.

11. Williams (1966) offers a similar diagrammatic construction.

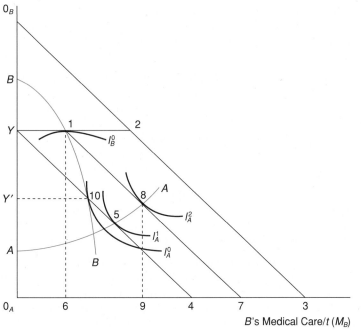

Figure 15.7
In-kind v. cash
transfer

then that both donor and recipient may prefer in-kind transfers (and would vote for this if offered).

The result of this analysis is that, when the taxpayer–donor's preferences are taken into account, in-kind transfer is preferred to cash transfer. Of course, there may be cases in which specific sets of preferences for *A* and for *B* may call this result in question (Culyer 1971). However in usual scenarios, the introduction of concern with the taxpayer–donor explains the pattern of in-kind transfers that can be found in Western democracies. As can be seen in Figure 15.6, the taxpayer–donor is not so keen to provide a cash transfer because individual *B* does not use it to consume sufficient medical care to fully internalise the goods-specific externality. The taxpayer wants *B* to consume a greater quantity of medical care than would ever be chosen if the recipient were offered cash. (Referring back to Figure 15.5(a) if the taxpayer wanted the recipient to consume as much *X* as when a price subsidy is introduced, the cash transfer would have to be much greater – instead of pushing budget line 1-2 to the right to pass through point 7, it would have to be pushed right to pass through point 9 on the income consumption curve, *ICC*. Similarly in Figure 15.5(b), if the taxpayer wanted the recipient to consume 1-7 units of *X*, the budget line would have to be pushed further to the right – instead of pushing budget line 1-2 to pass through point 7, it would have to be pushed through point 9 on the income consumption curve, *ICC*.)

A similar analysis can be applied to explain why, in the USA, assistance is given in terms of food stamps rather than cash. Some argue that if cash were provided then it would be spent on 'undesirables' (e.g. drink or drugs); others simply fear that, while *some* may be spent on 'desirables' (e.g. nutritious food), recipients will get too little nutrition. The question of whether it is wise to let recipients choose what to consume is normative (i.e. a question of values) but if altruism is cast as a 'goods-specific externality' then there is reason to question that the taxpayer–donor will be satisfied with the decision made by the recipient. Experiments in the USA find that cash recipients would prefer receiving cash and that they would consume lower levels of food.[12] Therefore, when explaining why food stamps are provided rather than cash, Perloff (1999: 113) refers to a report by the US Department of Agriculture's Food and Nutrition Service that emphasises the views of taxpayers. This Department administers the Food Stamp Program and explains:

> 'From the perspective of recipient households, cash is more efficient than coupons in that it permits each household to allocate its resources as it sees fit. . . . But in a more general sense, recipients' welfare clearly depends on public support for the program. And what evidence we have suggests that taxpayers are more comfortable providing in-kind, rather than cash, benefits and may consequently be more generous in their support of a coupon-based program. The question of which benefit form best promotes the welfare of financially needy households is thus more complex than it might appear.'

This analysis of altruistic behaviour offers an explanation for the decision of government to provide goods and services, rather than to offer cash to recipients even when there are problems in policing in-kind transfers.[13] However, once again, there are other possible explanations for provision of services in kind. Consider the following:

(i) *Merit good* arguments. In a world of incomplete information, government may provide basic quantities of medical care for *all* because it is assumed that individuals do not have the information and/or ability to choose for themselves (see Chapter 5). *Paternalism* is a justification for providing citizens with goods rather than cash. It reflects a belief that recipients would be incapable of making appropriate consumption decisions if given cash. This runs against the preferences of neo-liberal economists who reject the view that government should distort recipients' decisions (see Rowley and Peacock, 1975).

(ii) *Targeting* arguments. One problem with cash transfers is that they may go to those who are non-deserving. Suppose the government is considering making a transfer either in cash or in the form of low-income housing. All households, needy or not, would like the cash. People may attempt to *masquerade*, that is to claim cash transfers intended for others. The government cannot determine costlessly and unambiguously the intended group. The first consequence of the mimicry is that more non-needy people benefit from the transfer programme. However, few non-needy have an incentive to masquerade to live in very low-income houses (see Cullis and Jones 2009 for further discussion).

(iii) *Agency* problems. In-kind transfers could be preferably used where agency problems may be an issue, that is to say when a cash transfer cannot be made directly to the recipient. This might be the case with medical care for children and education where cash transfers would have to be made via the parents (who might choose to spend such cash in a different fashion). In an attempt to circumvent agency problems associated with providing a cash transfer, the state prefers to provide several commodities at zero (or reduced) prices directly to those who are intended to consume them.

---

12. Perloff (1999) calls on a review of statistical work. An additional dollar of income to low-income households increases, on average, food expenditures by 5–10 cents whereas an additional dollar of food stamps increases food expenditures by 20–45 cents. He notes results from five experiments. In Puerto Rico, giving cash instead of stamps had no detectable influence on food expenditures but a 'black market' in food stamps became widespread. Studies of the nutrition effects of substituting cash for food stamps found no effect in Alabama, a 5% drop in San Diego, and a 6–11% decline in nutrients in Washington State. Recipients in San Diego and Alabama's experiments (4 out of 10) drew attention to the greater choice of goods with cash and recipients noted a feeling of stigma with food stamps.

13. A 1980 experiment of elderly recipients in nine US sites and a 1982 experiment in Puerto Rico indicate that administrative costs could be substantially reduced by switching to cash.

For instance, many countries provide in-kind transfers for the specific needs of particular client groups such as the elderly, the disabled and dependent children.

(iv) *Pecuniary* effects. When a government has limited ability to tax certain groups, the pecuniary effects of in-kind programmes can be used to transfer rents from one group in society to another. By increasing the supply of medical care, the in-kind programme lowers its price and transfers rent from suppliers to consumers. Coate *et al.* (1994) refer to the example of victims of a famine. Cash transfers may have pecuniary effects that hurt the recipient group. By spending extra cash on food, recipients will cause an increase of demand, resulting in a price rise that will end up benefiting those who supply the food rather than intended famine victims. Consequently, it may be more effective to import and deliver food directly to the affected. This pecuniary transfer may have drawbacks. Not only might it exert disincentives for future investment, it may also cause distortion in the economy. For a survey of this literature see Boadway and Bruce (1994).

15.7 Challenge: Does government altruism 'crowd out' private altruism?

As noted in Section 15.2, if the provision of charitable expenditure can be analysed as provision of a public good there are important implications for public policy. If the government takes on responsibility for providing welfare services the implication is that individuals will give less to charities. They are able to free-ride on action taken by the government.

A 'neutrality theorem' concerning the provision of public goods (e.g. Warr 1982) predicts that the total provision of a public good will not differ when income distribution changes. That is to say that if the income distribution changes so that one individual contributes more, then others will respond by contributing less. The implication is that if government (altruistically) provides more to help those in need, it will serve only to decrease the amount of voluntary contributions. The growth of government activity will do little to increase the total amount of welfare provision. The effect will only be on the public–private sector mix of welfare provision.

If direct provision of welfare services via the public sector increases philanthropists' utility equally (by comparison with private giving) then the 'public good theory' of charitable provision predicts that state provision of welfare serves only to 'crowd out' private giving. Policy with respect to the provision of welfare serves only to affect the amount of altruism that surfaces in the public and private sectors, rather than adding to total assistance provided for the poor. The objective here is to question this assertion.

Consider Figure 15.8 where welfare provision to the poor is provided in the public sector and reported as Q_w^G in quadrant II. Welfare provision to the poor is also provided in the voluntary charitable sector and reported as Q_w^m in quadrant I. In both the private and the public sectors welfare provision can be produced at a constant marginal cost $MC (= AC)$. In quadrant I demand in the voluntary charitable sector D_M denotes willingness to transfer welfare provision at different prices. If there were no government involvement, the voluntary charitable sector produces a quantity q_{wo}^m. However if, in quadrant II, the government elects to provide q_{w1}^G, the extent to which voluntary action is affected depends on the extent to which provision of welfare by the government 'crowds out' private charitable provision of welfare.

In quadrant III a 45° line transforms levels of state provision of welfare from the horizontal axis to the vertical axis. This enables a reaction function to be depicted in quadrant IV. The reaction function indicates the extent to which demand for voluntary charitable activity falls as a consequence of state provision of welfare. The case discussed

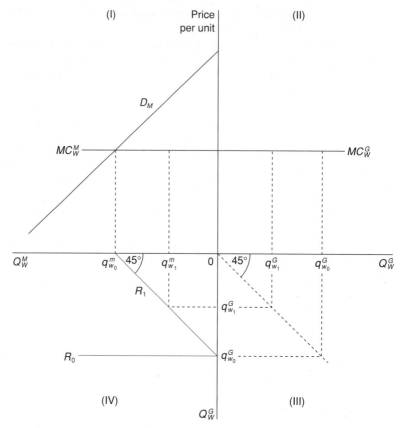

Figure 15.8 'Crowding out' of charitable activity

so far is one in which the reaction function labelled R_1 has a slope of -1 (i.e. the angle involved is 45°). Given D_M and the initial provision of $q_{w_0}^m$ the assumption implicit is that the government takes no responsibility for welfare provision (and this anchors the reaction curve at $q_{w_0}^m$). As government provision increases then voluntary charitable provision is 'crowded out' on a one-for-one basis. Ultimately, if $q_{w_0}^G$ were provided by the government the voluntary charitable sector would be completely crowded out. With a reaction function R_1 market provision is completely 'crowded out'. At any level of state provision between 0 and $q_{w_0}^G$ the impact of action by the state (to relieve the plight of a beneficiary group) serves only to 'crowd out' voluntary charitable action, i.e. government action serves only to affect the public–private mix of charitable provision. It can be noted that total provision of welfare provided remains constant. Government provision has had no significant effect on the total.

Of course, everything depends on the position and the slope of the reaction curve. The other extreme situation illustrated is the case where a 'naive' reaction function indicates that market provision is unaffected by government provision of welfare, i.e. R_0 has a slope of zero. In this case, government provision adds to market provision on a one-for-one basis, so that if the government provides $q_{w_0}^G$ total provision rises from $q_{w_0}^m$ to $q_{w_0}^m + q_{w_0}^G$.

Two considerations are relevant.

(i) The first is the degree to which government provision of charity is regarded as a substitute for private voluntary provision. In Section 15.2 there is a list of reasons to explain why private provision of charitable provision may be considered to offer more utility to donors. The 'warm glow' effect (Andreoni 1988) and the gains in terms of prestige and image to the donor are examples of reasons why the *act* of giving also matters. If the act of giving matters, the individual may find giving via taxation and state provision more remote, less personal and of less utility. In this case, the slope of the reaction curve may 'not be one' but may be less than one.

(ii) A second consideration relates to the issue of whether there are 'income effects' (real or imagined). Holding other things constant, the voluntary provision of welfare W^m will be determined by the initial level of purchase $O\text{-}q_{W1}^m$ minus the consequence of state provision. With state provision there is a substitution effect as described above, so that $0\text{-}q_{W1}^m$ is reduced by $a \cdot q_W^G$ (where q_W^G is the level of state provision and a is the crowd-out parameter which is expected to be positive and equal to or less than 1). However, an income effect arises if provision by the state does not increase costs to donors by an equal amount. For any groups of taxpayer–donors (those in low tax brackets) this income effect may be real. Bergstrom *et al.* (1986) show that if taxes are levied on non-contributors as well as contributors, total provision may be increased by tax-financed spending; 'crowd-out' is partial rather than total because some individuals feel that they are made better off and spend an additional amount on the public good.

The net effect of these two considerations can be explained by reference to equation (15.23). The value of a indicates the extent to which provision by the government can be perceived as a substitute for personal giving. It is 1 for perfect substitutes and 0 for the case where individuals in no way see one unit of government-provided W as a substitute for one unit of market-purchased W. The value of b records the income effect of a perceived income increase ($q_w^G - T_w$). The term q_w^G measures the value of government provision to individuals and T_W the perceived tax or other financial impact of the provision of W^G. The b coefficient represents the marginal propensity to provide good W out of income and can take values 0 to 1 (empirical tests suggest a value less than 1).

$$W^m = 0\text{-}q_{w1}^m - aq_w^G + b(q_w^G - T_w) \tag{15.23}$$

By definition, total provision of charitable welfare provision W is given by:

$$W = W^G + W^m \tag{15.24}$$

Equation (15.23) can be used to give the slope of the reaction function in terms of a and b:

$$\frac{dW^m}{dq_W^G} = -a + b \tag{15.25}$$

While it is possible that reaction functions may take different slopes, the case above consistent with R_1 is $a = 1$ and $b = 0$ and R_0, $a = 0$ and $b = 0$. The first case says that government provides a good W^G which is a perfect substitute to private provision of charitable welfare provision of W and that the marginal propensity to consume W is negligibly small. The second case says that government-provided W is not considered a close substitute for market provision of W and/or the marginal propensity to provide charity is again negligibly small.

Given that these are the two extremes, what does empirical work signify? If giving to charity is a public good (and no income effects for the community as a whole are assumed) government cannot increase the provision of welfare by directly providing welfare to a recipient group. 'The only way that the government can have any (significant) impact on the provision of public goods is to completely crowd out private provision. Joint provision is a veil' (Andreoni 1988: 70).

Table 15.3 **Estimates of 'crowd-out' of voluntary altruism**

Study	Crowd-out parameter[a]	Measure of government spending	Measure of donations
Steinberg (1983)	−0.001 to −0.003 −0.004 to −0.009[c]	Intergovernment grants for recreation. Intergovernment grants for hospitals service (US)	Local United Way allocations to specified service
Amos (1982)	−0.002 to −0.462	Total transfer income; AFDC; public welfare payments	Deductions on US federal income returns
Steinberg (1985)	−0.005[c]	Central and local government spending on social services and housing	Family donations from family expenditure survey (UK)
Reece (1979)	−0.011 to −0.100	AFDC + old age assistance + aid for disabled per recipient	Various, from national survey of philanthropy (US)
Jones (1983)	−0.015 to −0.0016[c]	Central and local government spending on social services and housing	Family donations from family expenditure survey (UK)
Abrams and Schmitz (1978)	−0.236[bc]	Federal expenditure on health, education and welfare	Deductions on US federal income tax returns
Abrams and Schmitz (1984)	−0.30[c]	State and local social welfare payments per $1000 personal income	Deductions on US federal income tax returns
Schiff (1985)	−0.66[c]	Local government expenditures philanthropy	Various from national surveys (US)
	−0.046[c]	State non-cash welfare spending	
	−0.058[c]	State cash assistance	

[a] Change in donations caused by a $1 increase in government spending.
[b] Calculated from reported elasticities and available data.
[c] Reported coefficients different from zero at .05 or better. In some cases, the crowd-out parameter is a non-linear function of reported coefficients and significance tests were not performed for the former.

Source: Adapted from Jones and Posnett (1993).

Andreoni (1988), pursuing a public good analysis of charitable giving, argues that the net effect of government spending, though positive, will be imperceptibly small and therefore the government will only have a significant impact when private provision is completely crowded out. However, this prediction of the public good model is at variance with evidence. While there are problems with the empirical work (Steinberg 1983, 1989) suggests that the 'crowding out' of private contributions by government spending is considerably less than 'one for one'. Table 15.3, adapted from Steinberg (1989: 150) and Jones and Posnett (1993), shows (in order of size) that the crowd-out parameter (i.e. the slope of the reaction curve) varies from −0.001 (Steinberg 1983) to −0.66 (Schiff 1985).

15.8 Summary

The neoclassical approach can be adapted to deal with a 'representative individual' more complex than *homo economicus*. By introducing interdependence of utility functions a particular form of 'altruism' can be analysed. One paradox that emerges is that, with this definition of 'altruism', the adaptation of the self-interested neoclassical model described above suggests 'altruistic' individuals will be motivated to act altruistically. Acting altruistically is tantamount to contributing to a public good and the result is that a 'philanthropy market' will fail to operate in a Pareto-optimal way.

While different motives for giving to charities can be defined, the application of the theory of the firm to charities calls in question the extent to which the actions of charities will always be focused on the needs of their target recipient group. As such, it is important to understand the objectives that charities pursue and to design public policy towards charities accordingly.

More generally, as altruism (characterised by utility interdependence) implies 'market failure', a role for government can be identified by reference to the usual market failure approach of neoclassical microeconomics. Alternative approaches (e.g. tax relief for giving, provision of tax progressivity, provision of specific goods and services in kind) can then be explained.

Two qualifications must be made to the analysis in this chapter. First, it must be emphasised that utility interdependence, as discussed in this chapter, is not the *only* way of modelling altruistic behaviour. In the early 1990s a number of journal articles dealt with a more complicated representative economic actor. Individuals were seen as multifaceted, encompassing a multiplicity of motivations. For example, Chirinko (1990) considered players in a non-cooperative game, who have egoistic and altruistic 'selves' within them. Kuran's (1990) account of multifaceted individuals, contains three sources of utility that broadly correspond to actors that inhabit social science disciplines. These might be interpreted: consumption of private goods = economic actor; decision autonomy = psychological actor; knowledge of the actions of and your reputation with others = socio-economic actor. (Decision autonomy is about the value and ability to choose for oneself whether or not to conform to social pressures that would otherwise guide action.) Different models are possible.

Second, attempts have been made in this chapter to explain how an application of altruistic microeconomic theory can explain behaviour of individuals and of governments. The analysis has shown how well (to a greater or lesser extent) such an application of theory performs. However, actions fail to betray clearly motivation and in the next chapter some of the same *apparently* altruistic actions will be reconsidered. In the following chapter the case will be made that what has been described as altruism can, indeed, be better explained by reference to the self-interest paradigm of neoclassical microeconomic theory.

Appendix 15 Income redistribution as an externality

Pareto-optimal conditions when there is utility interdependence resemble those required for optimality when there is an externality (see Chapter 6). Following the discussion in Tresch (1981), consider the role of government in effecting Pareto-optimal redistribution. Assuming that there is an economy in which each individual, h, has an endowment of two goods Y_h and Z_h. The total supply of Y and Z is assumed fixed, equal to $\sum_{h=1}^{H} Y_h = \mathbf{Y}$ and $\sum_{h=1}^{H} Z_h = \mathbf{Z}$ respectively. Each individual's utility is a function of their consumption of Y and Z, and the *distribution* of Y among members of society. Each individual maximises a utility function:

$$U_h = U_h(Y_h, Z_h, X) \tag{15A.1}$$

where

$X = X(\mathbf{Y})$ represents the distribution of Y among all H individuals,

and the problem is to allocate Y_h and Z_h to maximise social welfare, subject to the total fixed endowment of Y and Z. Focusing only on Pareto-optimal redistribution, this means

$$\max_{(Y_h, Z_h)} \; U_h(Y_h, Z_h, X(Y_1, \ldots, Y_H))] \tag{15A.2}$$

subject to

$$\sum_{h=1}^{H} Y_h = \mathbf{Y}$$

$$\sum_{h=1}^{H} Z_h = \mathbf{Z}$$

The corresponding Lagrangian is:

$$\mathcal{L} = U_h(Y_h, Z_h, X(Y_1, \ldots, Y_H))] + \theta(\mathbf{Y} - \sum_{h=1}^{H} Y_h) + \lambda(\mathbf{Z} - \sum_{h=1}^{H} Z_h) \tag{15A.3}$$

and the first-order conditions with respect to Y_i and Z_i are:

$$\frac{\partial U_i}{\partial Y_i} + \sum_{h=1}^{H} \frac{\partial U_h}{\partial X} \frac{\partial X}{\partial Y_i} - \theta = 0 \qquad\qquad i = 1, \ldots, H \tag{15A.4}$$

$$\frac{\partial U_i}{\partial Z_i} - \lambda = 0 \qquad\qquad i = 1, \ldots, H \tag{15A.5}$$

It follows that the Pareto-optimal condition can be defined as

$$\frac{\dfrac{\partial U_i}{\partial Y_i}}{\dfrac{\partial U_i}{\partial Z_i}} + \sum_{h=1}^{H} \frac{\dfrac{\partial U_h}{\partial X} \dfrac{\partial X}{\partial Y_i}}{\dfrac{\partial U_h}{\partial Z_h}} = \frac{\theta}{\lambda} \tag{15A.6}$$

The relationship between this equation and the standard form for optimisation when there is a consumer externality is clear (see Chapter 6 for the definition of Pareto – optimal conditions when there is an externality). Pareto optimality requires each person's personal consumption marginal rate of substitution between Y and Z, *plus* the sum of everyone's marginal rate of substitution between Z and the distributional parameter X should be set equal to the marginal rate of transformation.

If government were to achieve this via the tax system it would be necessary to set H personalised taxes on good Y,

$$t_i = \sum_{h=1}^{H} \frac{\dfrac{\partial U_h}{\partial X} \dfrac{\partial X}{\partial Y_i}}{\dfrac{\partial U_h}{\partial Z_h}} \tag{15A.7}$$

and the parallel is clear (i.e. a tax set in terms of the benefit *each* individual enjoys from redistribution).

References

Andreoni, J. (1988) Privately provided goods in a large economy: the limits of altruism, *Journal of Public Economics*, 35: 57–73.

Andreoni, J. (1993) An experimental test of the public goods crowding out hypothesis, *American Economic Review*, 83: 1317–27.

Becker, G.S. (1974) A theory of social interactions, *Journal of Political Economy*, 82: 1063–93.

Bergstrom, T., Blume, L. and Varian, H.R. (1986) On the private provision of public goods, *Journal of Public Economics*, 29: 25–49.

Boadway, R. and Bruce, N. (1994) The government provision of 'private' goods in a second best economy, pp. 99–179 in R. Boadway, A. Breton, N. Bruce and R. Musgrave, *Defining the Role of Government: Economic Perspectives on the State Government and Comprehensiveness*, School of Policy Studies, Queen's Unversity, Kingston, Ontario.

Boyle, S.E. and Jacobs, P. (1978) The economics of charitable fund-raising, *Philanthropy Monthly* May, 21–7.

Brennan, G. and Pincus, J.M. (1983) Government expenditure growth and resource allocation, *Oxford Economic Papers*, 35 (3): 351–65.

Buchanan, J.M. (1968) *The Demand and Supply of Public Goods*, Chicago: Rand McNally.

Chirinko, R.S. (1990) Altruism and the role of social capital in the private provision of public goods, *Economics and Politics*, 2: 275–90.

Clotfelter, C.T. (1980) Tax incentives and charitable giving; evidence from a panel of taxpayers, *Journal of Public Economics*, 13: 319–40.

Coate, S., Johnson, S. and Zeckhauser, R. (1994) Pecuniary redistribution through in-kind programs, *Journal of Public Economics*, 55: 19–40.

Collard, D. (1978) *Altruism and Economy*, Oxford: Basil Blackwell.

Cullis, J.G. and Jones, P.R. (2009) *Public Finance and Public Choice*, 3rd edn, Oxford: Oxford University Press.

Cullis, J.G. and West, P.A. (1979) *The Economics of Health: an Introduction*, Oxford: Martin Robertson.

Cullis, J.G., Jones, P.R. and Thanassoulas, C. (1984) Are charities efficient 'firms'? A preliminary test of the UK charitable sector, *Public Choice*, 44: 367–73.

Culyer, A.J. (1971) Medical care and the economics of giving, *Economica*, 38 (151): 295–303.

Feldstein, M.A. (1975) The income tax and charitable contributions: Part 1 – Aggregate and distributional effects, *National Tax Journal*, 28: 81–100.

Frank, R.H. (1997) *Microeconomics and Behavior*, 3rd edn, New York: McGraw-Hill.

Hewitt, J.A. and Brown, D.K. (2000) Agency costs in environmental not-for-profits, *Public Choice*, 103: 163–83.

Hochman, J.M. and Rodgers, J.D. (1969) Pareto optimal redistribution, *American Economic Review*, 59: 542–57.

Ireland, T.R. (1973) The calculus of philanthropy, pp. 63–78 in *The Economics of Charity* (Readings 12), London: Institute of Economic Affairs.

Jones, A.M. and Posnett, J.W. (1993) The economics of charity, pp. 130–52 in N. Barr and D. Whynes, *Current Issues in the Economics of Welfare*, London: Macmillan.

Jones, P.R. and Cullis, J.G. (1990) The charity as a 'firm': implications for public policy, *Policy and Politics*, 18 (4): 289–300.

Keating, B. (1981) United Way contributions: anomalous philanthropy, *Quarterly Review of Economics and Business*, 21: 114–19.

Keating, B., Pitts, R. and Appel, D. (1981) United Way contributions: coercion, charity or economic self interest? *Southern Economic Journal*, 47: 815–23.

Kelman, S. (1987) Public choice and public spirit, *The Public Interest*, no. 87 Spring, pp. 80–94.

Khalil, E.L. (2004) What is altruism? *Journal of Economic Psychology*, 25 (1): 97–124.

Khanna, J., Posnett, J. and Sandler, T. (1995) Charity donations in the UK – new evidence based on panel data, *Journal of Public Economics*, 56: 257–72.

Knapp, M., Koutsogeorgopoulou, V. and Smith, J.D. (1994) The Economics of Volunteering: Examining Participation Patterns and Levels in the UK, Mimeo, University of Kent.

Kuran, T. (1990) Private and public preferences, *Economics and Philosophy*, 6: 1–26.

Leibenstein, H. (1966) Allocative efficiency v. X-inefficiency, *American Economic Review*, 56: 392–415.

Marris, R. (1963) A model of managerial enterprise, *Quarterly Journal of Economics*, 77: 185–209.

Mueller, D. (1989) *Public Choice II*, Cambridge: Cambridge University Press.

Musgrave, R.A. (1970) Pareto optimal redistribution: comment, *American Economic Review* 60: 991–3.

Olson, M. Jr (1965) *The Logic of Collective Action: Public Goods and the Theory of Groups*, Cambridge, Mass: Harvard University Press.

Orr, L. (1976) Income transfers as a public good: an application to AFDC, *American Economic Review*, 66 June: 359–71.

Perloff, J.M. (1999) *Microeconomics*, Reading, Mass.: Addison Wesley.

Pettipher, C. and Halfpenny, P. (1993) The 1990–91 Individual Giving Survey, pp. 11–21 in S.E.C. Saxon-Harrold and J. Kendall (eds) *Researching the Voluntary Sector*, Tonbridge: Charities Aid Foundation.

Posnett, J. and Sandler, T. (1989) Demand for charity donations in private non-profit markets: the case of the UK, *Journal of Public Economics*, 40: 187–200.

Roberts, R. (1984) A positive model of private charity and public transfers, *Journal of Political Economy*, 92: 136–48.

Rowley, C.K. and Peacock, A.T. (1975) *Welfare Economics: a Liberal Restatement*, London: Martin Robertson.

Schelling, I. (1960) *The Strategy of Conflict*, Cambridge, Mass.: Harvard University Press.

Schiff, J. (1985) Does government spending crowd out charitable contributions? *National Tax Journal*, 38: 535–46.

Schiff, J. (1989) Tax policy, charitable giving and the non-profit sector: what do we really know? in R. Magat (ed.) *Philanthropic Giving*, Oxford: Oxford University Press.

Schiff, J. and Weisbrod, B. (1986) Government Social Welfare Spending and the Private Nonprofit Sector: Crowding Out and More. Unpublished manuscript.

Shibata, H. (1971) A bargaining model of the pure public theory of public expenditure, *Journal of Political Economy*, 79 (1): 1–29.

Slemrod, J. (1988) *Are Estimated Tax Elasticities Just Tax Evasion Elasiticities? The Case of Charitable Contributions*, Cambridge, Mass.: National Bureau of Economic Research Working Papers 2733.

Steinberg, R. (1983) Two Essays on the Non-profit Sector, PhD dissertation, University of Pennsylvania.

Steinberg, R. (1989) The theory of crowding-out: donations, local government spending and the new federalism, in R. Magat (ed.) *Philanthropic Giving*, Oxford: Oxford University Press.

Stigler, G.J. (1970) The optimum enforcement of laws, *Journal of Political Economy*, 78 (3): 526–36.

Sugden, R. (1982) On the economics of philanthropy, *Economic Journal*, 92: 341–50.

Sugden, R. (1993) Thinking as a team: towards an explanation of non-selfish behaviour, *Social Philosophy and Policy*, 10: 69–89.

Tresch, R.W. (1981) *Public Finance: a Normative Theory*, Plano, Tex.: Business Publications Inc.

Tullock, G. (1966) Information without profit, in G. Tullock (ed.) *Papers on Non market Decision Making*, Thomas Jefferson Center for Political Economy, University of Virginia.

Warr, P.G. (1982) Pareto optimal redistribution and private charity, *Journal of Public Economics*, 19: 21–41.

Weisbrod, B.A. (1988) *The Nonprofit Economy*, Cambridge, Mass.: Harvard University Press.

Weisbrod, B.A. and Dominguez, N.D. (1986) Demand for collective goods in private non-profit markets: can fundraising expenditures help overcome free rider behavior, *Journal of Public Economics*, 30: 83–95.

White, A.H. (1989) Patterns of giving, pp. 65–71 in R. Magat (ed.) *Philanthropic Giving*, Oxford: Oxford University Press.

Williams, A. (1966) The optimal provision of public goods in a system of local government, *Journal of Political Economy*, 74 (1): 18–33.

Zimmerman, D. (1975) On the relationship between public good theory and expenditure determinant studies, *National Tax Journal*, 28: 227–39.

CHAPTER 16

Do individuals really make 'charitable' decisions?

16.1 Introduction

In Chapter 15 it was argued that neoclassical microeconomic theory is able to incorporate the assumption that individuals choose to behave altruistically. Utility functions can be assumed interdependent, so that one individual, *A*, is better off knowing that another, *B*, enjoys a higher level of welfare (Hochman and Rodgers 1969). For some, this perception of microeconomic theory is a useful development to explain behaviour and (as examples in Chapter 15 illustrate), particularly useful when explaining state intervention. However, it is not always the case that behaviour betrays motivation. There are economists who argue that altruistic state intervention may be motivated by pure self-interest. When, in Chapter 14, microeconomic theory was applied to the political process, it was evident that such decision-making might result in 'government failure' (i.e. decisions did not reflect the interests of all concerned in the collective decision-making process). This critique can be attributed to the 'public choice school' of micro-economics. This school retains the assumption that individuals are purely self-interested. Indeed, Brennan and Lomasky (1993) refer to the assumption that individuals are self-interested as the 'key' premise of public choice analysis. However, if individuals are inherently selfish, why would they *appear* to act altruistically? The explanation offered by public choice scholars is that what passes for philanthropy is really evidence of failure in the political process. It is not that altruistic individuals vote for philanthropic state intervention. It is that self-interested individuals use their position within the political process to effect transfers that were never philanthropically motivated. Individuals may appear to act altruistically but it is a mistake to assume that such action infers motivation.

Once again, there is a distinction to be drawn in the application of microeconomic theory between focusing analysis on outcomes and focusing analysis on processes. The *outcome* may appear altruistic but the process of decision-making that caused the outcome may be anything but altruistic. Why then does the government appear to act altruistically (when introducing regulation, taxation, subsidy, etc.)? In the following the objective is to illustrate how microeconomic theory can often be applied to explain the 'charity of the uncharitable' (Tullock 1971a). In each example the focus of attention is on the way in which legislation, taxation or public expenditure can be used as an instrument to coerce transfers from those with little or no influence in the decision-making process.

The first example (Section 16.2) contrasts the perspectives of social historians and (public choice) neoclassical microeconomists. The example is that of nineteenth-century factory legislation in the UK. This legislation reduced the hours worked by children and women in textile mills. To social historians it represents a milestone in the evolution of philanthropic government responsibility. It is evidence that government can reflect the 'social conscience'. By contrast, an application of neoclassical microeconomics (within a public choice framework) offers a quite different perspective. It reveals that this legislation represented the self-interests of nineteenth-century mill owners. With reference to the discussion of regulation and regulatory capture in Chapter 14, this legislation can be seen as an example of 'cost predation' (see Section 14.3.5). In pursuit of rents, lobbying by one section of the textile industry was undertaken to introduce regulation of a cost-predatory nature for the other section of industry. If economists disagree over this interpretation it is not a disagreement over the issue of whether legislation was motivated by altruism. The existing dispute is whether or not it was rent-seeking on the part of self-interested mill owners or rent-seeking on the part of skilled male workers in the textile mills of nineteenth-century England.

Section 16.3 applies microeconomic theory to the decision to become involved in political processes. This time, the decision is whether to participate in political revolution. Revolutionaries declare that they have made sacrifices for the good of the 'cause'; emphasis is placed on the self-denial of those who resist, or overthrow, oppressive regimes. Action is taken for the good of society. However, is revolutionary action an illustration of selfless behaviour? Closer analysis begs the question of why individuals choose to contribute to the provision of a public good (a 'better' society).

Another example (in Section 16.4) of the 'charity by the uncharitable' focuses on the growth of government as a mechanism to redistribute income. In Chapter 15 government intervention to assist the poor was explained as an 'efficient' way of delivering redistribution on behalf of altruistic taxpayers. In this chapter a different perspective is offered. It is ability of individuals to exert influence in the process of decision-making (rather than utility interdependence) that becomes the focus of analysis. When microeconomics is concerned with outcomes, the objective is to explain why an outcome would favour the least well-off. When microeconomic theory is applied to the process of decision-making, the question is how can the least well-off effect such transfers. The key consideration is the voting rule that is used. If communities rely on a simple majority (50% + 1) rule tax, a poor majority can dictate the tax and welfare structure. Following de Tocqueville (1835), a poor majority may tyrannise a rich minority.

Later sections of this chapter illustrate the proposition that both acts of malevolence and of benevolence can be explained in terms of the pursuit of naked self-interest, i.e. in terms of the motivation of the representative individual *homo economicus*. Historians and sociologists portray racism as outright hatred of one ethnic group for another. Discrimination is introduced because one group in society feels superior to another and wishes to demonstrate this. An application of microeconomic theory questions such stereotyping. Why would any individual bear the costs implied by such discrimination? In the first instance, an application of the theory of markets indicates that there are costs if profit-maximising employers refuse to employ the most productive individuals, or if exchange between different parties is denied. In the second instance, it can be shown that there may be gains (in terms of rents) when discrimination makes markets less competitive.

To some, this chapter may appear a cynical application of microeconomic theory. This is not the objective. The objective is to offer another perspective on the question of how microeconomic theory can be applied. This time, the focus is on an application of theory to the *process* of decision-making. By contrast with discussion in Chapter 15, utility interdependence may not be required (the assumption of altruism may not be required) when explaining 'philanthropic' actions of governments and of individuals.

16.2 Charity and rent-seeking: motives behind humanitarian legislation

In 1833 Lord Althorp's Factory Act regulated employment of children in the textile factories of Great Britain. The act banned employment of children less than 9 years of age and restricted hours and conditions of work for children under the age of 18 years. The regulation was policed by a system of factory inspectors who reported to (and were controlled by) the Home Office. Prosecutions were brought when there was failure to comply with the regulation.

The Act is widely perceived as a milestone in British social history. Roberts (1960: 38) argued that: '(w)henever social distress and local abuses became intolerable and the resulting agitation for reform loud and clamorous, the safe and moderate men in Parliament took some action. . . . Such was the case with child labour in the textile factories.'

The received interpretation is that government action reflected popular demands to redress this social ill. The perception was that the government had grown more responsive to public sentiment and that public sentiment had become more humane. In terms of the Hochman and Rodgers (1969) analysis of altruism, the utility functions of children employed in textile mills were part of the utility function of voters generally.

By contrast, analysis by Marvel (1977) is more akin to the discussion of regulation in Chapter 14 (and, in particular, to analysis of *cost predation*). Marvel begins by focusing on the process by which the Bill was drafted. It was drafted at the behest of *some* of the leading textile manufacturers. Their objective was to bring about an increase in textile prices and to generate rents to textile producers who would be least constrained by the Act. The key in this analysis is the distinction between different textile producers. Large urban manufacturers employed fewer very young children as they relied on steam engines to drive machinery. They were less exposed to interruption of production than were the water-powered textile mills. Water-powered mills relied on full reservoirs and they were often forced to cut production in dry spells. During these periods of drought they relied heavily on child labour. Althorp's Act would have only a modest impact on steam-powered manufacturers by comparison with the impact that it would exert on the costs of water-powered mills.

Water-powered mills would be most affected and water-powered mills were an important segment of the market.[1] Marvel offers the following account of contemporary producers as evidence.[2]

In Figure 16.1, S and D represent market supply and demand for British cotton textile products. S' represents supply *after* the Factory Act. It shows the output reduction resulting from the additional costs imposed by the Act. S'' represents supply from steam-driven mill manufacturers (in Figure 16.1 it is assumed that these producers were not affected by the Act). Point 1 is market equilibrium prior to the Act. Point 2 is the equilibrium after the legislation is enforced. The effect of the legislation is to reduce output from q_1 to q_2

---

1. Marvel (1977) reports that in Manchester, where mills were almost exclusively steam-driven, only 39% of the labour force were children and young persons (under 18). By contrast, in Lancashire, where water power was of greater importance, this figure was 46% and in the West Riding of Yorkshire (which was even more dependent on water power) it was 51%. Marvel used regression analysis to reveal a significant positive relationship between 'source of power' (steam or water) and 'age of labour force'.
2. For example, Marvel (1977: 389) cites Thomas Cook (a Dewsbury manufacturer) that 'the works affected by flood-waters to the extent of fifteen to twenty days (in which children are employed) would be affected' and 'in dry seasons a tithe of time will be lost by deficiency of speed, occasioned by want of water'.

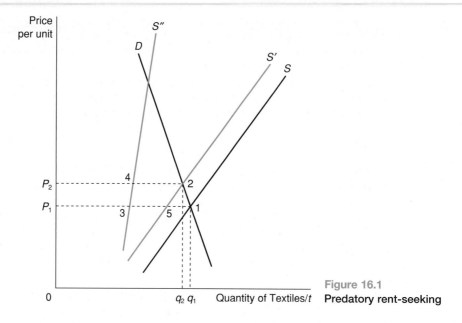

Figure 16.1

Quantity of Textiles/t   **Predatory rent-seeking**

and cause the price to increase from P_1 to P_2. The increase in price created rents (at least quasi-rents, i.e. rents in the short run) for unaffected manufacturers. These quasi-rents are estimated as area P_2-4-3-P_1 for this section of the industry.[3] The example illustrates how one set of producers in an industry will gain from introducing legislation that constrains another section of producers.

Marvel offered a rough estimate of the rents. He argued that, if only water-powered mills experienced output restrictions, about 5 per cent of their output would be lost and this would mean a 1 per cent decline in aggregate production. This measure was based on estimates of supply and demand elasticities with respect to price. If this reduction in output seems small, it should be noted that the demand for textiles was inelastic. If demand and (short-run) supply schedules were both unit-elastic, a 1 per cent shift in the supply curve would raise prices by 0.5 per cent. Marvel estimates that the area P_1-P_2-2-5 (rents for the textile industry as a whole) was approximately £92,000 for 1833–45. If these rents were allocated to mills according to the fraction of labour force accounted for by the mill, Marvel estimates that 5 per cent increase in profits is 'a reasonable approximation for the increase in profitability of the steam powered sector' (p. 392).[4]

In this way, Marvel interprets legislation as a response to a self-interested pursuit of rents. He argues:

(i) The politics of the legislation suggested pursuit of rents. Marvel notes that it is difficult to believe that a more heavily Whig-dominated Parliament would pass a Tory Radical measure to the advantage of the working class (and at the expense of the manufacturers).

(ii) The timing of the legislation makes more sense in the context of a rent-seeking analysis. The 1832 Reform Bill had increased electoral representation of the large textile

---

3. The textile industry was in a process of adjustment as steam-powered technology replaced water. While the supply curve of steam-powered technology was less than perfectly elastic, higher returns would attract new capital investment which would erode rents. Hence, the reference to quasi-rents.

4. Indeed, if anything this was an under-estimate as a full account was not made for increased unit costs of child labour to the water-powered mills.

centres in cities where textile manufacturing was carried out by large steam-powered firms. Water-powered mills were located where water was in plentiful supply and this was generally away from towns. As a consequence, they were less able to take advantage of the new infusion of political strength created by the Reform Bill.

(iii) Marvel comments that many leading manufacturers assisted in the Bill's preparation.

(iv) He draws attention to the reaction of the Scottish textile industry. In Scotland, there was much greater dependence on water than in Lancashire.

Althorp's Act was passed *because* political influence had been exerted in the interests of a distinctive part of the textile industry, not because political power had been exerted (philanthropically) against the interests of the industry. The interpretation of this motivation for this legislation is self-interest, not philanthropy. The case study is an example of regulation premised on 'cost predation'.

When assessing the way in which legislation was executed, Marvel presents quantitative analysis to show that prosecutions resulted in higher fines for water-powered mills than fines levied against steam-powered mills. Factory Inspectors' Reports indicate that owners of mills outside the major urban areas were more heavily penalised than their urban neighbours. Not only were *more* charges of offence levied in water-powered districts but there were *harsher* penalties for those found guilty.

If there has been a challenge to this analysis of regulation, it has come from another set of economists who simply question the source of self-interest. The same microeconomic theory can be applied. There was pressure for regulation to create rents. The issue is who exerted political pressure.

Anderson and Tollison (1984) do not deny the opportunity for quasi-rents, which the legislation presented. They argue that skilled workers would gain rents. In response to the question of who won and who lost as a result of the Factory Acts, they identify two primary groups in the labour market. Male workers, especially skilled male workers, stood to gain because children and women were competitors for their jobs. The idea that child labour could be seen simply as a complement to skilled labour in the process of production is disputed. Children performed functions that might have been carried out by males and, even if they sometimes acted as a complementary input, they would become skilled and become an even closer substitute at a later age. If competing child labour were regulated, the wages to male skilled workers would rise.

Once again, the focus is on self-interest, on gains to those who participate in the process of decision-making:

(i) There is evidence that male workers were agitators for the factory legislation.

(ii) Anderson and Tollison (1984) drew attention to the passage of the 1832 Reform Act. This meant that those who owned houses of rental value of £10 per annum could vote (if skilled operatives spent 20% of their income on housing they could vote).

(iii) Women and children lost jobs and income. Women could not vote and politicians might more easily ignore their interests.

(iv) Anderson and Tollison's approach would be called into question if the women and children employed in the factory mills were the wives and children of skilled male workers. It might be argued that such males would not wish to threaten the joint family income (household income). However, evidence indicates that women employed in the mills were only infrequently the wives of skilled males; infants employed were rarely their children.

Both Marvel (1977) and Anderson and Tollison (1984) illustrate a rent-seeking analysis. Viewed in this light, the Factory Act appears to have been primarily an example of wealth transfer in favour of those with political interest, rather than a philanthropic sacrifice in favour of those without political influence. To emphasise the case against a philanthropic interpretation, there was little concern on the part of legislators about the well-being of those (children and women) who would lose work and payment. There was no attempt to safeguard their livelihood. Many would turn to other low-paid occupations, e.g. domestic service or farm labour. Of course, householders and landowners who had political influence would see an increased supply of domestic help and labourers as a consequence of the factory legislation. There was no conflict with the interest of other groups who had political influence.

16.3 Microeconomic theory and political revolution: self-sacrifice for a better society?

The criticism that legislation has been viewed at face value can be extended to interpretations of social upheavals caused by political revolution. A revolutionary act can be defined as 'an extra-legal act (violent or non-violent) intended by the actor to secure a change in governmental personnel, structure, or policy' (Silver 1974: 63).

When political revolutions are successful, revolutionaries have both the incentive and the opportunity to present themselves as heroes who struggled against oppression. A public choice application of neoclassical microeconomic theory questions the extent to which such historical interpretation explains events. Even if, collectively, individuals might achieve a better society by revolution, there is no incentive to participate. Each individual has an incentive to allow others to make the sacrifice necessary to bring about change. However, if each has an incentive to free-ride, no revolution would ensue. What motivates individuals to undertake the risks inherent in political revolution? How important is self-interest?

Tullock (1971b) questions the interpretation that psychologists, sociologists and historians have given to participation in political revolution, demonstrations and riots. It cannot be the *common cause* that motivates revolutionaries because this is a public good. Tullock shares Olson's (1965) scepticism (see Chapter 14) that individuals will not incur costs to provide a public good unless there is some private inducement. When looking at participation in revolution the focus of attention falls on private payoffs. The argument is that it is the private incentives (or selective incentives) that matter. Individuals who play a part in any political revolution are concerned with the net expected *private* return.

To illustrate, Tullock (1971b) assumes that there is an oppressive regime in Ruritania and that an individual is assessing whether or not to join a group of 'brave heart' revolutionaries. The relevant decisions can be modelled as net expected values of actor calculations. The approach assumes risk neutrality. The individual begins by estimating the *net expected value to inaction* (EV_{In}). This can be defined as:

$$EV_{In} = G \cdot L_V \tag{16.1}$$

where

G = the value of the public good generated by successful revolution (the value placed on replacing the existing regime);
L_V = likelihood of revolutionary victory.

By comparison, the *net expected value of participation* in revolution (EV_r) can be written as:

$$EV_r = G \cdot (L_V + L_i) + R_i \cdot (L_V + L_i) - P_i \cdot (1 - (L_v + L_i)) - L_j I_r + E \tag{16.2}$$

where

L_i = the increase in the probability of success if the individual decides to join;
R_i = the private reward to revolutionaries (e.g. government office);

P_i = the punishment for the individual if the revolution should fail;
L_j = risk of injury;
I_r = the costs of an injury in the revolution;
E = the 'entertainment' value of participation or more broadly the 'psychic income' that is enjoyed from participating in this cause.

The key point is that, for any representative individual, L_i will approach zero. It is hardly likely that the outcome of the revolution will depend on the involvement of any one individual. No individual can expect to play a decisive role. However, if L_i approximates zero then equation (16.2) can be written as:

$$EV_r \simeq GL_v + R_i \cdot L_v - P_i(1 - L_v) - L_jI_r + E \tag{16.3}$$

where EV_r approximates the expression on the right-hand side of (16.3).

The *net expected value of action* (participation in the revolution) rather than inaction, when $L_i = 0$, can be determined by subtracting equation (16.1) from equation (16.3). This can be written as:

$$EV_r \simeq R_i \cdot L_v - P_i(1 - L_v) - L_jI_r + E \tag{16.4}$$

where EV_r approximates the expression on the right-hand side of (16.4). The important conclusion to draw from equation (16.4) is that G (the value of the public good generated by successfully replacing the existing regime – i.e. the 'revolutionary goal') does not motivate the decision to participate.

An alternative decision, which might face the individual, is to join the forces of 'repression' in Ruritania and to oppose the revolutionaries. Once again, concern with the political regime does not motivate the decision. The net expected value of action to oppose the revolution can be written as:

$$EV_d = G(L_v - L_i) + D_i(1 - (L_v - L_i)) - P_p(L_v - L_i) - L_jI_r + E \tag{16.5}$$

where

EV_d = the net expected value of being on the government side;
D_i = the private reward to putting down the revolt;
P_p = the private cost imposed on defenders if the revolt succeeds.

so that, if $L_i \simeq 0$ (i.e. if the increased probability of success as a consequence of individual action approximates to zero), the *net expected value* of joining the government's forces can be written as:

$$EV_d \simeq D_i(1 - L_v) - P_p \cdot L_v - L_jI_r + E \tag{16.6}$$

and G, once again, has no role to play.

The paradox is that the 'public good' aspect of revolution has no (or very little) part to play in an individual's decision to participate in revolution. The decision depends on the *private* gains and *private* losses that might be secured; the risk of injury and the 'entertainment' value (thought to be slight for 'serious' revolutions).

Public good considerations may be relevant for an evaluation of consequences of revolution but they are not relevant to explain the dynamics of revolution. Why then do historians focus on public good issues?

One possible explanation is that these considerations are dominant in historical sources of information (e.g. in memoirs, those who took part are unlikely to present themselves as selfish!). Moreover, in recruitment there will be an appeal to patriotism to ennoble action. Tullock is sceptical, arguing that popular interpretations of revolution (good replacing the bad) is facile; revolutions frequently replace one (not so efficient) despot with another. He notes the rent-seeking costs of revolution. If as many 'good' as 'bad' revolutions occur, the net benefit of revolutions is not high when allowance is made for destruction costs, etc. during the revolution.

The argument that revolution is motivated by a noble pursuit of the 'public good' is disputed. If it were true, G would have to be *very* much larger for it to be relevant (as L_i approximates to zero).

16.3.1 Testing a microeconomic theory of revolution

Tullock's analysis challenges conventional ideas concerning political revolution. Is there any evidence to support this application of microeconomic analysis?

a) A first test is to focus on those who participate. Consider the question, *who is most likely to play an active role in revolutions*? Tullock argues:

   (i) Many revolutions result in small policy changes and are undertaken by those who already hold high office. In particular, *coups d'état* mainly involve a circulation of the top jobs to those already close to the top. A 'public good' motivation theory would suggest that 'outsiders' (i.e. those disadvantaged and removed from the top jobs) should dominate but, historically, this is not so. If outsiders are involved it is usually for direct payment; Tullock reminds us of Lenin's advice that *professional* revolutionaries are of importance because amateurs cannot be trusted.

   (ii) Many revolutionaries are young and well educated. The focus of attention falls on the investment (in time and effort) of participation and the expected return as an annuity. Tullock's theory suggests that revolutionaries will be young (as there will be a longer payoff period) and that they will be educated (as the educated can get the good jobs after the revolution). It is also argued that the educated will be based in the non-industrial sector (because in traditional non-industrial sectors of the economy there are fewer paths to the top). Silver (1974) pointed to the disproportionate participation in nationalist and Marxist revolutionary movements of persons with higher education. Silver suggests this might be tested by correlating fluctuations in the market-equilibrium real wage of educated workers (college graduates, etc.) with the advent of revolutionary movements.

   (iii) Turning to political protest via demonstration (where the risk element is lower than in revolutions), Silver argues that the entertainment aspect of 'revolt' is more relevant and notes the greater participation by students![5]

b) A second test of the microeconomic theory or revolution focuses on the timing of revolutions. In this context, can Tullock's private benefit theory offer the basis for a *taxonomy of revolutions*? Consider the following *typology of revolutions*:

   [α]. *Revolutions following political reform*. It is a paradox that revolutions frequently occur when conditions have improved, or are in the process of improving. Silver notes de Tocqueville's observation that 'history is full of such paradoxes'. With reference to the French Revolution, de Tocqueville notes that 'it is not always when things are going from bad to worse that revolutions break out. On the contrary, it oftener happens that when a people which has put up with an oppressive rule over a long period without protest suddenly finds the government relaxing its pressure, it takes up arms against it.'

   If the public good was the stimulus for revolution then surely greater opposition to an oppressive regime would occur when the regime was at its most oppressive? However, here we see that revolution occurs when the regime is becoming more conciliatory and when oppression is not as harsh.

---

5. Silver (1974) amends the net payoff to participation as $EV_r = R_iL_v - P_i(1 - L_v) - L_jI_r + E - V$, where V = the value of participants' time and other resources (money for lobbying etc.).

Consider the following examples. (i) In 1780 Joseph II of Austria undertook a series of enlightened reforms (with respect to serfdom, religious toleration, occupational choice, and taxation). Yet, in 1789 there was peasant insurrection, followed by demands for democratic reforms and conspiracies in Vienna. (ii) The Prussian Revolution of 1848 was preceded by Frederick William IV decision in 1847 to summon a 'United Diet' and liberalise the press laws. (iii) The Russian's Peasant Emancipation of 1861 was followed by demands for liberalisation, peasant disturbances, student disturbances in St Petersburg and Moscow and insurrection. (iv) Khrushchev's anti-Stalinist speech appeared to pave the way for the abortive revolutions in Hungary and Poland.

These examples can be reconciled with a microeconomic theory because:

(a) Such actions are signs of weakness. In the 'private benefit approach' revolutionary activity is induced because the probability of victory (L_V) is increased. At the same time perceptions of the private penalty if the revolt fails (P_i) is lowered; the probability of injury during participation in revolutionary activity (L_j) is reduced, and perceptions of the injury suffered (I_r) fall. The public good model would, however, search for an impact on L_i, and there is none.

(b) If reforms are introduced this might increase power for those in the inner revolutionary group, e.g. giving them seats in Parliament, coverage in the mass media, and access to financial contributions. Again this serves to raise L_V.

Moreover, when the microeconomic theory of revolution is applied to such cases there are testable predictions.

(i) The private benefit framework explains why governments initiating reform often do so with a 'strong hand'. This signal raises the probability of being apprehended and suggests stiffer penalties (raise P_i and I_r) if there is objection. For example, Lenin (1921–2) ensured that the New Economic Policy was accompanied by a mass purge of the Communist Party and of remaining organised opposition outside the Party.

(ii) Domestic rulers introduce repressive measures if there is a successful revolution in a foreign country that has a similar type of regime. Since L_V might be perceived as relatively higher, they treat dissent with a heavy hand (i.e. P_i and I_r are made relatively high).

Case α of the typology offers these insights.

[β] *Revolutions following defeat in war.* External military defeats followed by revolutions are not unusual. For example: (i) English revolutions in 1204–68 and 1450–87 (the revolt of Jack Cade) followed defeat in war against France. (ii) Bonaparte's defeat led to revolutions in France, Belgium, Poland, Spain, Italy and Portugal between 1815 and 1830. (iii) Prussian victory in 1871 led to insurrection in France. (iv) Defeat predated revolution in Russia, Hungary, Germany and Turkey in 1917–19.

In the context of Tullock's model, defeat in war reveals information and allows individuals to revise upward the probability of a victorious revolution L_V because: (i) rulers are weakened, (ii) many take the defeat as evidence that they had previously overestimated the strength of the regime.

[γ] *Revolutions by attacks on powerful individuals.* When a government fails to adequately reward (or attacks) powerful individuals (e.g. large landowners) it raises R_i for these persons. Often their response is a *coup d'état*. An example is provided by the 1955 revolt against Peron in Argentina.

[δ] *Revolutions as hostility to a regime which focuses on a minority.* Some revolutions (e.g. the 1898–1900 Boxer Rebellion in China) are preceded by increases in racial, ethnic or class solidarity. Such actions increase E. Remember that E includes a sense of duty to class, country, democracy, race. (It is expressive rather than instrumental.)

All of these typologies are consistent with a 'private benefit' (self interest) motivation.

c) A third way of testing Tullock's proposition is via *case study analysis*. Consider street riots. The following case study focuses on individuals' participation. Chalmers and Shelton (1975) apply a similar maximising-calculus, i.e. the decision to participate will depend on the net expected private gain from participation (rather than any pursuit of a public good).

Chalmers and Shelton follow the 'private payoff' explanation to participation. In their research, the question is why will an individual choose to participate in an *existing* riot (i.e. not why does a riot take place). Following Becker (1968), the important consideration is the real and psychic private income that can be derived from participation.

The net expected utility of participation in a riot ($E(U)$) can be written as:

$$E(U) = pU(Y - F) + (1 - p)U(Y) \tag{16.7}$$

where

Y = psychic income (from participation) plus real income from looting;
p = the probability of being caught and convicted;
F = the pecuniary equivalent of any punishment.

From this, the authors predict the number of people taking part in a riot (R) will depend on the value of p and the value of F. It is the case that there will be greater participation the higher the value of p and less participation the lower the value of F.

How then will a rioter's subjective view of 'p' be formed? The argument is that this relies on (i) perceptions of the degree of suppression to be used, (ii) the expected number of the rioters who will participate and (iii) whether or not the riot is during the day or during the night.

$$p = p(C, R, D) \tag{16.8}$$

where

C = degree of suppression (and is positive);
R = expected number of other rioters (and is negative);
D = day (positive) or night (negative).

The value of p will increase as C increases, decrease as R increases and increase if at day (decrease if at night).

The hypothesis is that the intensity of a riot (I_r) can be tested with respect to the following variables:

$$I_r = R(C, R, D, F) \tag{16.9}$$

The empirical work is designed to test the importance of these variables. The attempt is to explain I_r, which is estimated by reference to the 'hour-by-hour' riot intensity profile (i.e. an index ranging from 30 (= fires, looting, etc.) to 1 (= stone throwing etc.). The data source was provided by the US National Advisory Committee on Civil Disorder. The authors report some support for the hypothesis presented. For example, when examining high-intensity riots, the introduction of the National Guard reduced the estimate of intensity. When considering the effect of night-time (a 'darkness' variable) this had a positive coefficient in the pooled regressions. There are clear data limitations and the authors emphasise the need to look at the internal dynamics of the riot. However, with these qualifications, the analysis is consistent with the hypothesis that participation in riots depends on the changing set of opportunities with respect to the present value of income. As suggested by Tullock's analysis of revolution, the 'public good' (*common cause* of the riot) does not provide the motive for participation.

Other case studies also prove consistent with Tullock's 'private benefit' (self-interest) theory. In a survey of Chinese rebellions, Tong (1992) claims that collective action was entirely motivated by private economic gains. Bandits took part because the benefits were excludable (although participation was spurred on by economic hardship).

At the same time, there are criticisms:

(i) Wickham-Jones (1995) draws attention to the interpretation of 'costs' of participating in revolution. Sometimes it is difficult to know if they are 'costs' or (when a different ideology prevails) if they are 'benefits'? For example, Palestinians engaged in the Intifada may not have seen any sacrifice in their actions as a 'cost' but as inherently a benefit to them. Actions of religious revolutionaries may be seen as a glorification and a passport to a glorious afterlife.

(ii) It has been argued that more attention should be given to the role of political entrepreneurs (Wickham-Jones 1995). Just as Olson's analysis was criticised for not giving sufficient emphasis to leadership, Wickham-Jones points to the effectiveness that political entrepreneurs may exert by use of selective incentives and sanctions. They coordinate (assisting communication and information flow) and they break up large tasks, so that the participants are risking less by cooperation. They organise selective incentives (e.g. material resources to win the support of peasants). At the same time, they use coercive measures to ensure complicity from supporters. Referring to a study of Vietnamese peasants by Popkin (1979), he highlights this dual role of political entrepreneurs and emphasises that, once the revolution has begun, there may be external sanctions (if political entrepreneurs remind individuals of the dire consequences should they defect and the revolution fail). Political entrepreneurs have their own private incentives for taking part and their position is less subject to free-riding than other potential revolutionaries'. Leaders receive direct benefits from their participation (e.g. holding office in a post-revolutionary regime).

16.3.2 The economics of terrorism

Analysis of willingness to participate in political revolutions informs policy directed at terrorism. If willingness to engage in terrorism is similarly determined by rational assessment of expected benefits and expected costs, there are important distinctions to make when designing policy to deal with terrorists. While strategy is often premised on the objective of increasing the cost that terrorists incur (e.g. by increasing vigilance to arrest terrorists), policy should encompass a broader perception of costs, i.e. the opportunity costs of terrorism.

(i) *Policy to deal with terrorists*

If terrorists adopt a 'rational' approach (i.e. as associated with *homo economicus*), a terrorist will allocate time between terrorism and other activities in response to perceptions of marginal expected benefits and marginal expected costs. In Figure 16.2(a) the relative expected costs of involvement in terrorism (as compared with other actives is shown by the slope of the budget line 1-2). The costs of terrorism comprise the costs of material resources and collecting information, as well as the time required to prepare attacks. It also includes the costs implied by the inherent dangers of this activity (e.g. the probability of detection and the costs of a prison sentence).

The terrorist derives utility from both legal and terrorist activities. The shape of the indifference curve (in Figure 16.2(a)) depends on marginal utility derived from each form of activity. While the analysis can be presented in terms of instrumental

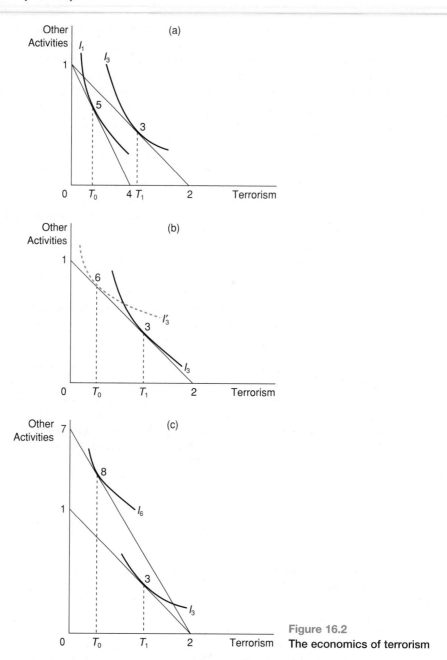

Figure 16.2
The economics of terrorism

rationality (i.e. where benefits depend on the outcomes that are affected by activity), it is also possible to include analysis of utility derived from participation in the process of terrorism (e.g. the excitement etc. of action). If terrorists also derive intrinsic benefit from participation in terrorism, this will affect the slope of the indifference curve. It is predictable that highly intrinsically motivated terrorists ('fanatics') would have an indifference curve that is very steep.

The extent to which the individual participates in terrorism is determined at the initial equilibrium 3 on I_3 associated with T_1 quantity of terrorism in Figure 16.2(a). The utility-maximising individual equates the ratios of expected marginal utilities from this activity and from other activities (that determine the slope of the indifference curve at any point = the marginal rate of substitution) with the relative price of terrorism. The marginal rate of substitution is equated with the slope of the 'budget line' (see Chapter 2).

A typical response to terrorism is to punish offenders and take steps to make repetition of terrorist attacks more difficult in the future. With an increase in the expected costs of terrorism the budget line in Figure 16.2(a) shifts from 1-2 to 1-4. The individual now perceives that terrorist activity is more expensive and (as usual) substitutes in favour of the relatively cheaper activities. The new equilibrium is at tangency point 5 on I_1 (the extent of terrorism falls from T_1 to T_0 per period). But is this response sufficient?

It is evident that policy can also be directed at the benefits of terrorism. Figure 16.2(b) illustrates the impact of policy designed to reduce the marginal benefits of terrorism. If the marginal benefit from terrorist activity is reduced the indifference curve becomes steeper. The initial equilibrium is point 3 on I_3 associated with T_1 quantity of terrorism per period. The new equilibrium is point 6 on I_3'. Again, the policy reduces terrorism from T_1 to T_0. Margaret Thatcher's approach to terrorism in Northern Ireland was to take steps to deny the terrorist IRA (Independent Republican Army) the 'oxygen of publicity'. In the same way, the government authorities might refrain from attributing a terrorist incident to any one terrorist group, to reduce the 'terrorist benefits' from publicity.

Frey and Leuchinger (2003) have argued that greater decentralisation would reduce the benefits from terrorism. If, instead of one centre in the polity, there are a number of key points, a 'terrorist hit' on any point would prove less effective and less symbolic. In this way, decentralisation would reduce the attraction of violent action on the part of terrorists. Political power might be distributed between different political actors (e.g. the division of power between democracy and the rule of law) and political power might be spread across various levels of government (e.g. as in federal arrangements). A market economy is more decentralised and, therefore, less vulnerable to attack than a highly regulated market.

However, in all of this, there is still an important distinction to be made. There is a distinction between the costs of terrorist activity and the opportunity costs of terrorism. The opportunity costs of terrorism are estimated in terms of the utility that terrorists might gain by not engaging in terrorism. An increase in opportunity costs (or a reduction in the costs of 'other activities') will have an impact on decisions. In Figure 16.2(c) this approach to policy focuses on swivelling the budget line from 1-2 to 7-2, which reduces terrorism from T_1 to T_0 and raises utility from point 3 on I_3 to point 8 on I_6.

Frey and Leuchinger suggest that a wider scope of activities outside terrorism must be created. Reminiscent of Tullock's (1971b) analysis of revolution, one option might be to offer better opportunities to individuals, to make it relatively more expensive to commit to terrorism; e.g. investment to increase job opportunities in the economy. The authors also suggest that there should be inducement to existing terrorists to become traitors to their terrorist groups. This would diminish the effectiveness of terrorism by reducing solidarity within terrorist groups. Of course, in the extreme, this approach would imply offering incentives such as money, reduced punishment and a secure life if individuals are prepared to leave the organisation. Ultimately, rewards might be given to terrorists to make it more expensive to maintain their commitment to terrorism. It is notable that after negotiations, leading 'terrorists' often assume important (distinguished) roles in 'peace processes' and in ensuing government. It is argued that the advantage of this approach is to change the nature of the game: to turn the interaction between society and terrorist into a positive sum interaction.

(ii) *Explaining the dynamics of terrorism: the Northern Ireland conflict*

Jennings (1998) uses Tullock's 'private benefit theory of revolution' to analyse paramilitary behaviour in Northern Ireland. There are two issues. First, can an adaptation of the theory explain the dynamics of the conflict? Second, will the theory offer insight when discussing possible solutions to the conflict?

With reference to dynamics, it is argued that Tullock's insight will explain the pattern of violence. Revenue is received by paramilitaries from two sources. (i) Revenue from *gangsterism* (derived from extortion and 'black market' activity). (ii) Revenue from *revolution* is also derived from *voluntary* contributions (from supporters willing to pay for violent protest).

In Figure 16.3(a) the focus is on pure *gangsterism* by two terrorist forces (the IRA and the Protestant militants). The *x*-axis measures 'output' of violence (violence used to extort). The *y*-axis measures the value of violence. Jennings argues that, as violence increases, there will be a decrease of value of violence (because of a fall in the extortion rate). The function is elastic to begin (though the position any 'gang' adopts along this curve between points 1 and E_1 may be constrained by the supply of labour for violence). In the absence of such labour constraint, a Cournot–Nash equilibrium will occur at point E_1 associated with q_{v1} of violence per period. At this point the curve is kinked; the two 'gangs' have exhausted all possible extortion opportunities. To try to increase activities further would be to usurp the other gang.

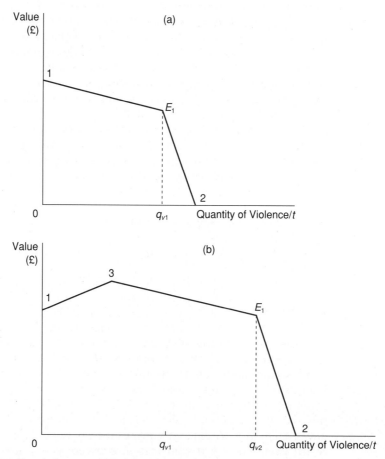

Figure 16.3 Revolutionary conflict

However, in Figure 16.3(b) the value function is also affected by revenue that is received from political associations that support a paramilitary organisation (and which will, in effect, be prepared to pay for political violence). It follows that any equilibrium that has been achieved between two rival groups (gangs) is unstable. In Figure 16.3(b) willingness to support political associations to pay terrorists to pursue their political violence means that, at first, the value of violence (from gangsterism and from payment for political violence) increases (hence the positive slope of segment 1-3). However, the introduction of this revenue source will shift the position of E: shifting E_1 in Figure 16.3(a) further along to the right in Figure 16.3(b) associated with q_{v2} of violence per period. If the initial equilibrium is premised only on competition for 'gangster gains', it will be disturbed if other funds become available (from those who are willing to pay for political violence).

Jennings offers this explanation for instability of conflict in Northern Ireland. For months preceding a ceasefire (in late 1993) there had been some of the worst violence. In late October, nine Protestants were killed in an IRA bomb on the Shankill Road and, in retaliation, the following week saw the deaths of eleven Catholics in three Loyalist attacks. Why was there such instability? With reference to a pure gangster model (Figure 16.3(a)), the inelastic section of the function in Figure 16.3(a) E_1-2 had become relevant and the incentive to gangs to reduce political violence was strong. By calling a ceasefire, the paramilitaries withdrew to point E_1 in Figure 16.3(a) (the Cournot–Nash equilibrium of the pure gangster model). However, when additional revenue from willingness to pay for political violence was more evident there is an explanation for a resumption of political violence (E_1 moved further along the function in Figure 16.3(b) than in Figure 16.3(a)). Jennings concludes that ceasefires are unstable and that instability is due as much to *economic* (i.e. revenue) considerations as to failures of *political* negotiations.

Turning to the second application of Tullock's theory, the supply of labour depends on the same 'private benefit function' (as described in equation (16.4) – i.e. $EV_r \approx R_i L_v - P_i(1 - L_v) - L_j I_r + E$). Any solution to conflict must focus on private issues (possibly even more than on the alleged 'public good' political aims of the Republican and Protestant groups involved). Again, the focus is on the economic incentives to individuals. Application of Tullock's (1971b) model places great emphasis on policies that would reduce the incentive for any individual to engage in paramilitary action (the objective would be to reduce the supply of labour to these organisations). The *opportunity cost* of revolutionary activity is determined by income forgone and if this is taken into account together with the potential cost of being caught and punished:

(i) An economic solution would be to increase the opportunity cost of terrorist activity by *providing other employment* with increased wages – i.e. reduce R_i. (Jennings argues that there is a distinct lack of middle-class support for violence in Northern Ireland.)

(ii) A second strategy would be to increase the costs of supplying labour to the paramilitaries by introducing *stiffer punishment* (notwithstanding the point that stiffer sentences may increase the feeling of alienation of political factions).

Of course, in Jennings's analysis there is also a demand for political violence and, therefore, policy changes that affect this demand are also important.[6] However, policies that impact on the opportunity costs of terrorism are relevant considerations. For a game theory treatment of terrorism see Konrad (2004).

6. 'Demand' for political violence would also be reduced with: increased economic activity; a policy to integrate schooling (despite possible objections from the Catholic Church); a policy (e.g. the Fair Employment (Northern Ireland) Act 1989) to counter the perception of discrimination. While these latter considerations may reduce 'demand for political violence', there is the possibility that paramilitaries will then allocate more time to gangster activity.

16.4 Charity of a minority or tyranny of a majority?

The theme in this chapter is that self-interest might prove sufficient to explain action deemed philanthropic. In this section the focus of attention is on the rules that are employed within the democratic decision-making process. The analysis calls on theory discussed in Chapter 14 that indicated that, when a simple majority voting rule (50% + 1) yields consistent predictions, policy options selected are those preferred by the median voter. In Chapter 15 the provision of welfare services by taxpayer–donors to donees was explained by utility interdependence. However, in the following analysis transfers from taxpayers to recipients are explained when all individuals are motivated by pure self-interest. In the following example redistribution is facilitated by a simple-majority voting rule. The model predicts rich to poor redistribution; all voters with lower than median income favour redistribution, those with income above median income are opposed.

Meltzer and Richard (1981) consider the choices that individuals will make with respect to the tax rate t (set at a proportional rate) to finance a transfer (which takes the form of a per-capita lump-sum grant, g). Throughout, the budget is balanced and the only role for government is to effect redistribution.[7]

Individuals are assumed to have different abilities (measured as x). Ability is randomly distributed across the population. Any individual's income depends on ability (i.e. on a productivity factor x). The fraction of total time worked is w, so that leisure (l) is defined as:

$$l = 1 - w \tag{16.8}$$

If hours worked are w, income (y) is higher the higher is an individual's x factor:

$$y = wx. \tag{16.9}$$

An individual's utility depends on consumption, c, and leisure, l.

$$c = (1 - t)y + g \tag{16.10}$$

For any values of t and g, the individual's decision is how much to work (i.e. w). To maximise $U(c, l)$ with respect to w, given constraints defined in equations (16.8)–(16.10), the first-order condition is:

$$\partial U/\partial c(1 - t)x = \partial U/\partial l \tag{16.11}$$

or

$$\frac{\partial U/\partial l}{\partial U/\partial c} = (1 - t)x \tag{16.12}$$

That is, to maximise utility, the marginal rate of substitution between leisure and consumption is equated to the net-of-tax marginal product of an individual's time.

The intention of Meltzer and Richard is to show how the values of t and g are endogenous. The analysis can be illustrated when there is a Stone–Geary utility function (see Mueller 2003). A Stone–Geary utility function takes a specific form (see Chapter 11). It can be described as:

$$U = \ln(c + \lambda) + a \cdot \ln(l + \theta) \tag{16.13}$$

where ln refers to natural logarithmic values, a is a parameter and λ and θ are 'reservation level' parameters in the function. Substituting (16.8), (16.9) and (16.10) into (16.13)

---

7. With y_m as mean per-capita income, a balanced government budget implies that $g = ty_m$.

and taking the first-order conditions for a maximum, the optimal amount of time to work w can be defined as:

$$w = \frac{(1 - t)(1 + \lambda)x - a(g + \theta)}{(1 - t)(1 + a)x} \qquad (16.14)$$

It becomes clear that w depends on the value of x. Moreover, if x is sufficiently small the value of the numerator might be negative. Of course, w cannot be negative. This means that there is a critical level of ability (defined as x_0) at which optimal $w = 0$. If ability levels were at or below x_0 an individual would not work at all.

Setting $w = 0$ in equation (16.14), it is possible to define this critical level of ability x_0. The level of ability at which individuals would not work can be written as:

$$x_0 = \frac{a(g + \theta)}{(1 - t)(1 + \lambda)} \qquad (16.15)$$

From (16.15) it can be seen that x_0 increases as t increases. As the rate of tax increases there is an increase in the number in the community with an ability level that leads to an optimal choice of work hours of zero. Moreover, substituting the value of w from equation (16.14) back into the individual's utility function, it is clear that utility ultimately depends on g and t.

The implication of this analysis is that, as t increases, more in the community will opt not to work. It is impossible continually to increase t and increase the transfer g. Eventually, the increase in t will cause more in the community to stop working. In Figure 16.4, g increases as t increases but at a decreasing rate (as more individuals are deterred from work by an increase in t). Eventually, mean income y_m falls as the tax rate increases (i.e. $\partial Y_m/\partial t < 0$) because (as is evident from equation 16.14) hours worked fall as a consequence of the disincentive effects of higher taxation. In Figure 16.4, g increases at a decreasing rate until $-dy_m/dt = y_m/t$ and, after this point, it falls.

The function G defines the opportunities available. If g and t are endogenous, how are they chosen? The preferred values (i.e. welfare-maximising values) differ for individuals with different abilities. Suppose individuals are asked to vote on the values of g and t. For voters at work higher taxes mean lower utility (a bad) and increased grants raise utility (a good), so that indifference curves take the shape of I_1. By comparison, individuals who do not work will have utilities unaffected by changes in t (t is a neutral to them). Their indifference curves are horizontal straight lines such as I_2. An individual will choose the combination of t and g that maximises utility. For example, those who choose not to work will prefer the value of t_2 – associated with tangency point 2 – to maximise the

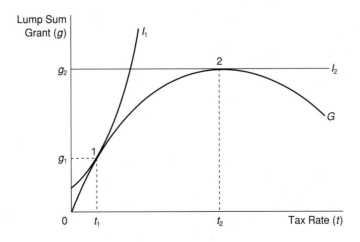

Figure 16.4
Tyranny of a majority

lump-sum transfer at g_2. Those who choose to work (i.e. those with $x > x_0$) will prefer a tax rate lower than t_2, e.g. t_1 dictated by the tangency point 1 between I_1 and 0-G that is associated with a transfer g_1. The final decision that emerges from a simple-majority voting rule depends on the location of the median voter (see Chapter 14 for confirmation).

Two hypotheses can be established. First, with respect to government growth over the past two centuries, the growth of welfare spending can be explained by a gradual extension of suffrage to those with lower incomes within the community. If, as in most Western economies, income distribution is skewed (so that mean income exceeds median income), the prediction is that a majority would redistribute from the richer minority. When suffrage is extended to those with lower incomes (below the income of the existing median voter), the preferences of the new median voter are located nearer to t_2 in Figure 16.4. The median voter becomes more like someone with a flatter indifference map. In Figure 16.4 the relevant tangency (i.e. of the median voter's indifference curve and G) moves further to the right. The growth of government (and further redistribution) occurs as suffrage is extended to the poor.

Consider experience in the UK. In 1790 (i.e. prior to the notable electoral Reform Act of 1832 and subsequent extensions of suffrage) defence and debt interest payments in the UK constituted 63% of public spending and social services only accounted for 9 per cent. In 1998/99 defence and interest payments represented only 15% of spending and social services constituted just over 60 per cent of government spending (Griffiths and Wall 1999).

The second hypothesis refers to a cross-section comparison of different economies (at any moment of time). Differences in government expenditure depend on the income of the median voter relative to mean income. An increase in the difference between median income and mean income will increase pressures for increases in t and g. Meltzer and Richard (1983) offer empirical support for this hypothesis. They reported that:

(i) The ratio of government spending for redistribution to aggregate income, and the share of aggregate income redistributed in cash varied directly with the ratio of mean to median income and with the level of (median) income.
(ii) Redistribution in kind (e.g. education, health care, fire protection) varied directly with the ratio of mean to median income (but was independent of the level of income).

One important conclusion to draw with respect to this research is that redistribution via the public sector is not motivated by altruism but, instead, is the result of the coercive power of a simple-majority voting rule. Behaviour interpreted as altruism can be explained by the self-interested pursuit of income (as expected of *homo economicus*).

However, how successful is the model of Meltzer and Richard in explaining growth of government? As has been the case so many times in this text, many questions are begged when assumptions are scrutinised more carefully.

(a) Meltzer and Richard's analysis depends on the assumption that the role of government is solely to deal with redistribution. This is unrealistic. A significant proportion of government expenditure (exhaustive expenditure) is directed at providing publicly financed goods and services.
(b) The analysis predicts that all voters below the median voter will favour redistribution. Evidence is not always consistent. Surveys suggest that beneficiaries of government growth (e.g. public employees and welfare recipients) register similar preferences for tax limitation proposals to other voters (e.g. Gramlich and Rubenfeld 1982).
(c) Meltzer and Richard's analysis predicts that redistribution will be from rich to poor. The median voter will support the poor as the 'gains' from redistributing from the rich are so great. However, the pivoting median voter may have the option to 'take' from both the rich and the poor (rather than from only the rich). A selfish median

voter will take from both. As the median voter can swing outcomes either in favour of the rich or in favour of the poor, the only predictable outcome is that redistribution will be to those in the middle-income group (an outcome known as Director's law).[8] In the UK there is evidence that government welfare spending favours the middle classes (e.g. see Le Grand 1982).

(d) The analysis assumes that voters are well informed and prepared to incur the costs of voting. However, evidence in Chapter 14 indicates that in many societies (e.g. the USA) there is a difference in turnout between high-income and low-income individuals (with high-income individuals being more ready to vote). It follows that resistance to redistribution from the rich may be relatively greater than predicted.

(e) In similar vein, the analysis makes no allowance for the action of lobby groups. Minorities are able to press for favourable legislation and the majority is often left to pay the tax costs. Mueller and Murrell's (1986) empirical work suggests government size depends on the number of interest groups.

(f) There are difficulties, for it appears that any extension of the suffrage is somehow exogenous. An extension of suffrage that would result in a new median voter of lower income would never be approved under the simple majority voting rule (50% + 1). The decision concerning the size of the tax and the grant is determined endogenously. However, if the majority rule (and the median voter theorem) is employed, how can the extension of suffrage be explained? (Do turkeys vote for Christmas?)

(g) There may be broader considerations to take into account (which limit redistribution via the public sector). As noted in Chapter 12, individuals may be disinclined to increase the value of t because they hold perceptions about an individual's entitlement, or because they anticipate that, one day, their income will be higher (Musgrave 1985).

However, with all of these qualifications it is, nevertheless, the case that microeconomic theory can be applied to the process of decision-making to explain why governments increase the welfare-spending *without* any reference to the assumption that individuals behave altruistically.

16.5 Racism and rent-seeking: racism and income redistribution

Sociologists, psychologists and historians indicate that racism is motivated by an intrinsic ethnic hatred. The explanation for ethnic hatred is sought in past conflicts or in perceptions of race supremacy. The usual assessment is that racism is motivated by irrational malevolence. By contrast, economists explain racism in terms of the rational pursuit of self-interest. It is not a matter of irrational malevolence (happiness experienced from harming someone else). It arises from self-interested income maximisation. Microeconomic theory explains racism via an application of market analysis. Racism can be understood by analysing 'demand' for racism and 'supply' of racism.

How can racism be analysed as the result of forces of 'demand' and 'supply'? To begin, consider the motives that lie behind the demand for racism. Here a distinction can be made between tastes and preferences for harming others and an investment return from introducing racist measures. On one hand, racism may be considered in exactly the same way as any other consumption good. On the other hand, racist measures may represent an investment that will yield a future payoff. The distinction is between racism as a 'consumption' good and racism as an 'investment' good. If individuals are malevolent then they derive utility from the harm experienced by others (and this may be a consumption

8. Named after Aaron Director (see Stigler 1970 and Tullock 1971a).

experience). However, if individuals are motivated only by pure self-interest they are indifferent to the harm caused to others. They are motivated only by the pecuniary gain that might be experienced. (For a similar discussion of 'malevolence', see Brennan 1985.)

Turning to racism as an 'investment', it is not malevolence (in terms of an inherent desire to harm others), it is racism as a means of acquiring rent. In this case, a racist society is introduced because members of one ethnic group are able to increase their financial rewards.

16.5.1 'Demand' for racism

The distinction between consumption and investment motives that explain demand for racism provides the framework for organising microeconomic theories of racist discrimination.

For example:

(1) Becker (1973) explains racism in terms of a taste for discrimination. This can be defined in terms of a willingness on the part of one ethnic group to pay (or to incur costs) to avoid contact with members of another group. However, to what extent will individuals be prepared to incur costs? For example, in a competitive market, tastes for discrimination are unlikely to explain *long-run* wage differentials. In competitive markets for labour (where different workers from different ethnic groups are perfect substitutes in production) employers who discriminate are at a competitive disadvantage. Those who do not discriminate (i.e. non-racist employers) are at a comparative advantage in the ownership of capital (unless, for some reason, consumers are prepared to pay higher prices for goods made by one ethnic group rather than another). The prediction is, therefore, that such racist discrimination will be short-lived (as racist employers suffer higher costs). While the short run and the long run are not specified in calendar months (see Chapter 3), the historical persistency of racism can be used to question this analysis.

Becker's model is an example based on a consumption demand for racism. It implies malevolence. However, it predicts only short-run examples of racism (and calls in question the argument of sociologists and historians that long-run racism can be explained in these terms).

(2) An alternative theory presents racism as a means of acquiring rents. Krueger (1963) focuses on how racism affects the supply of labour. The analysis is similar to that produced in microeconomic trade theory (see the discussion of the optimum tariff in Chapter 17). The argument is that regulation by a white majority of the black community is motivated (not by tastes and preferences) but by an attempt to restrict the supply of labour in certain occupations. By restricting supply it will be possible to create rents for those who are able to work. A white majority may be able to impose restrictions (similar to a quota on imports) on the hiring of black labour. It is now possible to predict long-run wage differentials provided that the regulation can be maintained. For this to be possible there must be a mechanism which forces all employers to enforce the arrangement (e.g. otherwise, white employers might profit by 'smuggling' in black labour – i.e by employing more black labour than is permitted under the quota).

(3) A third approach to explaining racism is via a transactions costs argument. Arrow (1973) applies screening theory to explain demand for racist discrimination. Low-cost signals are able to reduce the costs of those who make decisions in the market. Racism becomes a way of reducing production costs if employers are able to use ethnicity as a signal of relative productivity. Once again, the analysis does not depend on malevolence. However, the analysis does beg the question of why long-run differentials in

the treatment of different ethnic groups persist. The signal will only be used if prior beliefs about racial abilities are confirmed by evidence. If employers are to use the signal they must observe a productivity difference in the workforce they hire. The transactions costs approach requires that groups differ in some relevant characteristic, at least in the initial period (Roback 1989).

In all of this, the issue of the costs of enforcing racism is extremely important. In Becker's analysis it requires that an individual will pay more for something and that they will persist in this, even though others may free-ride. The free-rider problem is once again evident in Krueger's analysis; the prospect of higher rents may mean that in a small group a mechanism for enforcing the 'optimum tariff' and restricting supply will be available. Akerlof (1985) explains racism (in terms of status-based wages) in small markets where every participant is a potential trader and where a social custom to regulate employment is stable. Non-discriminating employers lose profits because a discriminating majority boycott them. However, this mechanism is likely to prove more meaningful in communities in which a small group of people can monitor each other. The issue of how such mechanisms are introduced and maintained is clearly important in this literature. That demand exists is only one consideration.

(4) In the appendix to Chapter 11 the Bhaskar, Manning and To (2002) model of oligopsony in the labour market was discussed. It also has application here as an explanation of persistent racial pay differentials. Return to Figure 11.31. Assume black and white workers are identical in all respects but firm A has a disutility represented by, d, for each black worker employed. Firm B on the other hand does not suffer such disutility, so that the black and white wages are identical and reaction function R_B obtains. With firm A offering lower wages to black workers its reaction function is lowered to R'_A for them but it is R_A for white workers. An equilibrium at point 2 implies lower wages for black workers in both the discriminating A firm and the non-discriminating B firm with $W_B < W_A < W_e$. The lower wage in firm B reflects profit maximisation when the alternative wage for black workers is lowered (as opposed to discrimination by firm B).

Profits are lowered for firm A compared to firm B but paradoxically both could be higher than the non-discrimination case if d is not too large. Discrimination reduces the wage paid by firm B and this raises firm A's profits. This will have an offsetting impact for firm A, which has punished itself by adopting the non-profit-maximising level of black wages. This creates an incentive for persistent discrimination. A profit-maximising firm that is not discriminating has no incentive to buy the discriminating firm A, as a profit-maximiser in the place of firm A would drive up wages of black employees for both, reducing both their profit levels.

16.5.2 An economic theory of apartheid: testing the 'demand/supply' model

Whether demand is motivated by tastes and preferences (Becker 1974) or by an investment demand for an institutional arrangement which will yield rents, microeconomic theory suggests that demand for racism will depend on the price that has to be paid. Is it the case that individuals become more inclined to act in a racist manner when the price of so doing is low?

In Lowenberg's (1989) analysis of racial apartheid in South Africa the focus of attention is on rents that can be enjoyed as a consequence of apartheid. Race discrimination in South Africa is explained in terms of rational self-interest, as opposed to irrational malevolence or as purely prejudicial rationale. The first step in explaining the introduction and maintenance of a 'colour bar' relies on identifying those who earned rents from such legislation. For example, Lowenberg argues that in the case of South Africa:

(i) A colour bar restricting movement of black workers advantaged white unskilled and semi-skilled mine workers. These groups resisted efforts by mine owners to substitute black workers at lower wages (below the 'white wage').

(ii) A colour bar answered the concerns of Afrikaner farmers about depletion of the stock of rural blacks and a consequent rise in farm workers' wages (due to the attraction of the mines and secondary industries in the growing urban centres).

Lowenberg argues that this coalition of interests succeeded in attaining electoral dominance in 1924. The result was a system that restricted property rights for the black community, a system that created a migrant labour force between the 'homelands' (domicile reserves) and white urban areas. Industrial relations legislation was introduced by which racial job reservation prevented wage-undercutting by blacks. The costs of this rent-seeking analysis would be borne, therefore, by capital owners (both foreign and indigenous). If this microeconomic analysis were accurate it would be predictable that this group would oppose regulation in the labour market (as this would prevent the 'best' allocation of labour and 'tax' the returns to capital including human capital). Lowenberg offers evidence in support of this. Moreover, he argues that racism cannot be explained in class terms; it was not a capitalist conspiracy (as radicals and Marxists contended).

The 1948 elections in South Africa revealed that the median white voter favoured Grand Apartheid. This introduced a rigid geographical separation, including the creation of separate sovereign national entities in which blacks would hold citizenship. The objective was to introduce thorough regulation of economic and social interactions between blacks and whites. It was introduced by the new National Party government. The pro-apartheid sections of the community included unskilled and semi-skilled workers and farmers. The anti-apartheid sections of the community included owners of physical and human capital (among the white electorate) and, of course, the black community. Reminiscent of Becker (1983, 1985), the political equilibrium was determined by the relative effectiveness of competing political interests.

In this analysis, apartheid is a pragmatic response by a rational white oligarchy. Racial dogma and jingoistic white nationalism are not the underlying motives. Two tests show that when the costs of racism increased, 'demand' reduced.

(i) The first is a historical interpretation of the eventual relaxation of apartheid. Expansion of the industrial sector of the South African economy increased the demand for highly skilled labour beyond the capacity of the white population to supply. Concessions were made because the economy needed a stable educated (characteristically middle-class) black labour force. Some of the more severe apartheid laws were relaxed in the late 1970s and 1980s. Black unions were given official recognition; pass laws (which regulated the system of 'influx control') were repealed; racial miscegenation was no longer illegal; blacks were granted property rights in some white areas (zoning restrictions, affecting non-whites, were relaxed). In 1986 influx control legislation (i.e. repeal of the pass laws) was aimed at dealing with restraints that increased the costs of hiring black labour. The argument is that, as the economy grew, the demand for black labour increased. There was *an increase in the costs* of administering apartheid and, as a result, a contraction in demand for apartheid (i.e. a 'classic' downward-sloping demand curve for apartheid).

(ii) A second test of the proposition that the demand for apartheid responded to the costs involved empirical estimation. The costs of implementing apartheid included:

  (a) Homelands costs (total real expenditure by South African government institutions in black homelands);

  (b) Defence costs (real per-capita defence expenditure).

There was also evidence that the costs of apartheid were affected by the granting of independence by Portugal to Angola and Mozambique.

Lowenberg shows a statistically significant negative relationship between the quantity of apartheid (as measured by the number of persons presented for offences relating to 'pass law' or influx control regulations per 1000 of the black population) and the *fitted* values of the price of apartheid (Homeland costs). He also reports a statistically significant negative relationship between the level of apartheid and the *fitted* price variable (Defence costs). Once again, demand for apartheid slopes downwards with respect to price.

16.6 Microeconomic theory and trade sanctions

Individuals may *behave* either altruistically, or malevolently, but their motivation might be pure self-interest. Consider the introduction of international trade sanctions (i.e. boycotts of international trade) against regimes that are held in contempt. Obvious examples of trade boycotts include those imposed on South Africa (as a response to the use of apartheid) and, more recently, those imposed on Iraq (as a protest against its dictatorial regime). What makes economic trade sanctions effective? Once again, there are two contrasting microeconomic approaches, one that focuses almost exclusively on *outcomes* and one that recognises the *process* by which policies are introduced.

A usual response to the question of why countries impose trade sanctions would be to argue that the intention is to harm the targeted country and, in this way, to exert pressure on the country to change its policy stance. In these terms, the effectiveness of trade sanctions depends on the harm that they can impose. When other countries disapprove of measures taken by the regime within the targeted country they take steps to register this by a trade boycott. The intention is to harm the targeted country and to 'persuade' it to relinquish its policy option (in order not to relax the trade embargo). A neoclassical microeconomic approach focuses on the comparative outcomes, with and without trade sanctions. Frey (1984) and van Bergeijk (1994) explain how neoclassical microeconomic theory can be applied. However, a second (public choice analysis) focuses (again) on the *process* by which policies are introduced. If lobby groups influence policy in the targeted country, the effectiveness of trade sanctions depends on their impact on those who wield greatest influence.

16.6.1 What factors determine the efficacy of trade sanctions?

Frey (1984) shows how microeconomic trade theory can be applied to establish those factors which are most important in assessing the efficacy of trade boycotts. The focus of attention is on the extent to which a targeted country is exposed to sanctions. What factors affected the extent to which a country can respond to a trade embargo?

In Figure 16.5 point C_1 shows the amounts consumed of two goods (Y and X) per period in the country that will face an embargo. Point P_1 is the production point on the transformation curve T-T'. It shows that the country produces 0-X_1 and 0-Y_1 of the two goods (see Chapter 17). Some of this output is traded internationally. The relative prices at which international trade is possible is shown by the slope of the price line, p^i-p^i. It follows that the country exports X_1-X_3 units of good X to import units Y_1-Y_4 of good Y in order to achieve the highest level of welfare possible (as shown by a community indifference curve CIC_2 – see Chapter 5).

International trade enables the country to consume at a point outside its production constraints. The country's production constraints as noted are shown by the production frontier T-T'. Assuming that there is a given state of technology and fixed supply of capital and labour in this country, this production frontier defines the consumption possibilities open to the country when there is no trade. International trade offers the country

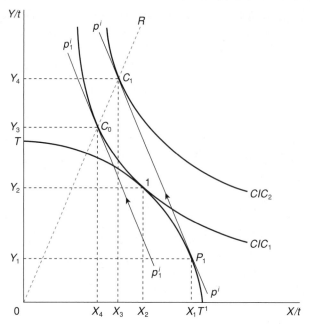

Figure 16.5
Welfare costs of trade sanctions

the opportunity to enhance welfare. The country is able to select a consumption point such as C_1, which is outside the production possibility frontier.

If trading partners were to institute a boycott and cut this targeted country off from international trade, the country would be forced to consume on the transformation curve T-T'. The best it might do is to produce at point 1 on CIC_1 and, as there is no possibility of international trade, point 1 would also be the consumption point. The harm imposed by a trade boycott can now be estimated as the reduction of welfare associated with being on the lower community indifference curve (CIC_1 rather than on the higher community indifference curve CIC_2 consuming X_2 units of good X and units Y_2 of good Y). For ease of exposition, Frey assumes that the indifference curves are homothetic to the origin. This means that the slopes of the indifference curves along a ray 0-R from the origin are equal. The implication is that consumers choose to consume the goods in the same proportion at any given set of relative prices. Consumers are indifferent between the bundle of goods at the no-trade point 1 and at C_0 consuming X_4 units of good X and units Y_3 of good Y. In this case, it follows that the reduction in welfare when trade is not possible can be estimated by the shift of the relative price line from p^i-p^i to p_1^i-p_1^i. The distance between the two relative price lines measures the reduction of real income arising from the introduction of trade sanctions. This can be measured in units of good X as $(X_3 - X_4)/X_3$, or it can be estimated in terms of good Y as $(Y_4 - Y_3)/Y_4$.

Using this neoclassical microeconomic theory, the effectiveness of trade sanctions depends on the harm that trade sanctions impose. The extent to which the targeted country suffers is determined by how easily the country can respond. This means that the gains from international trade are greater the more:

(i)   concave to the origin the production possibility curve;
(ii) convex to the origin the community indifference curve.

It therefore follows that the welfare loss from sanctions (i.e. from a trade boycott) is larger when the economy is not flexible. That is to say that if the country cannot adjust easily to trade sanctions, then the sanctions will impose greater harm. In this way, the extent to which the country is harmed depends on the shapes of the production possibility curve and the shape of the community indifference curve.

(i)   If the production possibility curve T-T' is more concave to the origin, more is gained from engaging in international trade. It is not easy for the country to substitute between the two products and it is likely to be preferable to use the rate of exchange for substitution that is implicit in international prices. (With the slope of the price line p_i at P_1, the consumption possibilities at C_1 are greater than if tangency at P_1 had occurred with a less concave production possibility curve).

(ii) If the community indifference curves are very convex to the origin then it is less easy to substitute consumption between the two goods. In these circumstances the greater availability of the good (at a lower cost via international trade) means far more to the country.

(iii) It should also not be forgotten that, if a boycott were introduced and the country had to reallocate resources from the production point P_1 to point 1, there would be short-run adjustment costs. The country would suffer unemployment as labour is relocated and capital also would need to move from production of X to production of Y. The process of adjustment might involve periods of unemployment and re-training. The path of adjustment would not be around the edges of T-T' (from point P_1 to 1) but inside the production possibility curve from P_1 to 1 (see Chapter 17).

The more concave the production possibility curve and the more convex the indifference curve, the greater the attraction of international trade. The more difficult and the slower the adjustment path, the greater the harm created by trade sanctions.

(i) *Applying a neoclassical theory of the effectiveness of sanctions*

Many studies have concluded that trade sanctions have been largely ineffectual. For example, Knorr (1975) considers 22 cases of economic sanctions (most of which occurred after the Second World War). In this assessment: sanctions failed in 13 cases; they resulted in a compromise settlement in 3 cases; in 2 cases they resulted in an outcome which was considered ambiguous; in only 4 cases were they considered successful. This analysis casts doubt on the use of trade sanctions.

Frey considers the effectiveness of sanctions against Rhodesia (or Zimbabwe as the country is now called). In 1965, after the white Rhodesian government unilaterally declared its country's independence, sanctions were imposed in stages by the UK and supported by the United Nations. They were intended to stop the movement of goods and factors of production to and from Rhodesia. The objective was to force Rhodesia to give up its repressive domestic policy towards the black population. Considering Rhodesia's reliance on trade, the prospects looked good. In 1965 Rhodesian exports were almost 40 per cent of GNP and imports were 30 per cent of GNP. Moreover (with reference to the analysis above), the economy appeared to be inflexible. Production and exports were heavily concentrated on tobacco (and a few minerals) and the consumption tastes of the white Rhodesian population were regarded as inflexible.

In 1966 two-thirds of Rhodesia's former export markets were officially subject to embargo. When Rhodesian exports fell by more than one-third the trade balance worsened. Unemployment increased among the African population. However, in terms of gross domestic product the sanctions were not as effective as might be expected. Gross domestic product increased by 2 per cent in real terms in 1966. Moreover, in the first two years (1966–7) real GDP increased by almost 5 per cent per annum. GDP rose at an average annual growth rate of 7.8 per cent until 1974. Difficulties were experienced but these were because of a bad harvest in 1968 (and OPEC oil price increases in 1973). If there was a burden this was imposed by meeting the costs of anti-terrorist operations. (With a public expenditure burden, real GDP fell by an average annual amount of 2.3 per cent between 1975 and 1979. An independent Mozambique offered a base for terrorism.)

With a new political regime in 1979, trade sanctions were lifted. Perhaps trade sanctions had exerted an effect because, in their absence, things might have been even better in Rhodesia? Perhaps there was an effect? In response, consider changes in economic growth via analysis of the 'residual factor'. In 1955–60 real GDP in Rhodesia rose by 4.4 per cent per annum and it would be possible to attribute part of this change to the productivity of capital and the productivity of labour. The element that is not attributed (the 'residual factor') was 1.9 per cent. If sanctions had the desired effect the residual factor would fall after 1966. However, the residual factor for 1965–70 was 3 per cent and, for 1970, 5.2 per cent per annum. Trade sanctions did not exert the impact anticipated.

This case study is typical of analysis within a literature that suggests that international trade sanctions have a poor success rating. One explanation is that economies are really more flexible than anticipated. With reference to the applications of neoclassical microeconomics (above), the shapes of production possibility curves and community indifference curves do not leave economies so dependent on trade and speeds of adjustment are faster than anticipated. However, it is possible to offer an alternative explanation and illustrate another application of microeconomics. This approach focuses on the *process* by which trade sanctions are introduced and the *motivation* of those who participate. Perhaps trade sanctions are not really simply an expression of outrage against a targeted regime? Perhaps the motivation to introduce trade sanctions is self-interest, rather than philanthropic concern for those subject to a targeted oppressive regime? To explore a different application of microeconomics that (once again) casts doubt on the usual interpretation and offers a different explanation for the failings of trade sanctions, consider a 'rent-seeking' demand for trade sanctions.

16.6.2 Economic sanctions: pursuit of economic rent

The efficacy of trade sanctions is inevitably influenced by political considerations. In particular, efficacy depends on the countries' commitment to sanctions. Seeler (1982) offers three reasons why trade sanctions do not deliver their intended goals. First, when sanctions are introduced there is frequently a time lag between deciding to impose sanctions and implementation. This lag offers the boycotted country an opportunity to reorganise and to adjust production and consumption patterns. Second, sanctions create profitable opportunities for those who break the boycott. Third, countries applying the sanctions find that they also are hurt by a reduction of trade. The question arises as to what determines countries' commitment to introduce and to enforce sanctions? Also, by comparison, what determines the commitment of the targeted country to resist sanctions?

Kaempfer and Lowenberg (1988) apply a rent-seeking model (see Chapter 14). A rent-seeking approach focuses on political decision-making (so often ignored in standard neoclassical microeconomic theory). The implicit assumption above is that the only concern is to use sanctions to produce the greatest harm to the targeted country. Are there other considerations?

With reference to a pure self-interest approach, assume some domestic producers wish to impose trade sanctions to restrain imports from the targeted country. If imports are restrained, domestic producers of competitive goods will earn rents. Begin by assuming that the group that lobbies for sanctions seeks to maximise utility, when utility is a function of income (Y). In this group, individual i seeks to maximise $U_i = U_i(Y_i)$. Sanctions (S) provide import protection and affect utility (via the impact on income Y_i). Individual i's income depends on the level of trade sanctions, i.e. $Y_i = Y_i(S)$, where S is a non-negative continuous variable measuring the level of sanctions. It follows that

$$\partial U_i/\partial S = \partial/U_i/\partial Y_i \cdot \partial Y_i/\partial S \tag{16.16}$$

By comparison, there may be others whose income decreases if there were trade sanctions (e.g. exporters to the targeted country, consumers of imports from the targeted country).

To begin, consider a community comprised of two groups. Individuals in group J gain from trade sanctions and individuals (like j) are prepared to pay to support a political campaign to introduce sanctions. The amount they will pay (P_s) reflects the demand (D_j) for sanctions, so that

$$P_s = D_j(S) = \partial U_j/\partial S = \partial U_j/\partial Y_j \cdot \partial Y_j/\partial S \tag{16.17}$$

However, the other group K (and individuals like k) are willing to pay to support a lobbying campaign to reduce the severity of sanctions. The amount that they will be willing to pay is

$$P_s = D_k(S) = -\partial U_k/\partial S = -\partial U_k/\partial Y_k \cdot \partial Y_k/\partial S \tag{16.18}$$

Kaempfer and Lowenberg (1988) apply Becker's (1983, 1985) analysis of competition between interest groups. It predicts that sanctions emerge if those who press for sanctions are able to commit greater resources to lobby for sanctions than those who do not want sanctions. When imports are restrained, producers of domestic competitive goods will sell at a higher price and earn greater profits. However, domestic consumers pay higher prices. In this way they are a transfer from one group to another. At the same time, there is a *reduction* in demand for imports when their price is increased. Consumers are unable to enjoy these cheaper goods even though they value them more than the import price. This loss is significant; the absence of imports hurts consumers by more than it advantages domestic producers.[9]

Following Becker (1983, 1985), the existence of such loss means that, *ceteris paribus*, the amount individuals are willing to pay to avoid import restriction should exceed the amount that others would pay to introduce sanctions. Rent acquired by the gainers (J) is at a cost to losers (K). As losses are expected to exceed gains, the net political pressure might be against sanctions. It follows that, when utility depends only on income, the amount initially that gainers (J) will pay to lobby government is less than the amount that losers (K) would pay to resist. In Figure 16.6(a) (based on Kaempfer and Lowenberg 1988), J reflects the amount that individuals would pay for successive levels of trade sanctions and K reflects the amount that opponents would pay to avoid successive levels of trade sanctions. At the outset (if income considerations were the only factor) there would be no trade sanctions (point 1).

Becker's analysis of interest group competition allows for the possibility that one group may find it easier than another to mobilise (i.e. in offsetting the free-rider problem discussed in Chapter 14). Kaempfer and Lowenberg (1988) allow for this by assuming that there are shift parameters E^j and E^k, so that

$$P_s = J(S, E^j), \tag{16.19}$$

where the first derivative of J with respect to E is negative ($J_1 < 0$) and the second derivative positive ($J_2 > 0$). At the same time,

$$P_s = K(S, E^k) \tag{16.20}$$

where $K_1 < 0$ and $K_2 > 0$.

9. Sanctions restrain imports and create deadweight loss. See Chapter 17 for a full discussion of the deadweight loss from trade restraint.

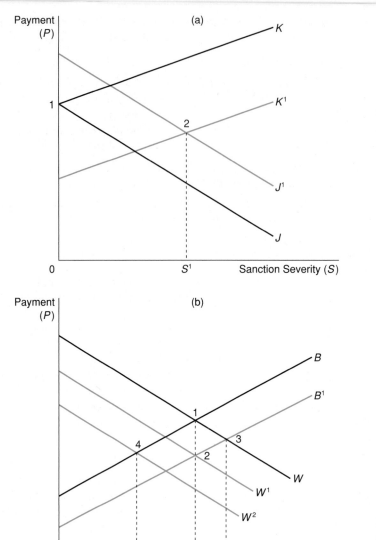

Figure 16.6
A rent-seeking model
of sanctions

However, if these shift parameters are identical in both cases there is no advantage enjoyed by either group. Allowing for the existence of losses to losers that exceed gains to gainers, the amount that J would pay for trade restraint is less than the amount that others would pay to avoid it and in Figure 16.6(a) S (trade sanctions) is 0.

To this point no allowance has been made for the outrage felt against the regime in the targeted country. Trade sanctions may also affect U *directly* (i.e. not simply via Y). Trade sanctions will provide utility in and of themselves (i.e. apart from income-enhancing effects). Some individuals will feel better to be part of a community that registers a protest about the policy adopted in the targeted country. It follows that, for these individuals, $U_i = U_i (S)$. With reference to Figure 16.6(a) this would imply a down-ward shift of K (to K^1) and an upward shift of J to J^1. Now there is sufficient net political pressure; there will be a positive level of sanctions S^1 associated with the intersection at point 2.

With this rent-seeking model in mind, consider the way in which sanctions are likely to be introduced:

(i)   As policy is driven (in large part) by those who have a reason to hope for a payoff, the level of sanctions and the choice of goods for sanctions are not necessarily those required to maximise economic harm on the target country.

(ii) Home producers may be as concerned (if not more concerned) about keeping out foreign competition (as about the issue on which protest is being made). Industries seeking protection from foreign imports have allied themselves with other groups seeking to sanction the exporting country. Kaempfer and Lowenberg argue that it is no coincidence that the package of US sanctions against South Africa (implemented in 1986) included restrictions on import of textiles and steel (given the importance of political pressure for trade protection in these industries). They draw attention to the pressure from sugar producers in the US for sanctions against Cuba.

This analysis questions the way in which sanctions are introduced. They may not, in practice, be designed to maximise harm on the targeted country. But the same analysis also explains why maximising harm *per se* on the targeted country may not be the most effective strategy. Once again, Becker's interest group model forms the basis for analysis (this time of those who form policy in the targeted country). For illustration, consider the case in which a targeted country has introduced apartheid. This policy A consists of regulations that redistribute from one group (B) to another group (W). Figure 16.6(b) reflects the lobbying position of the two groups in that country.

In Figure 16.6(b) comparable willingness-to-pay schedules are shown for advocates (W) and opponents (B) of the policy A. Once again, an analysis of the shift parameters is important. To begin, it is clear that W exceeds B up to intersection point 1 and hence the country adopts the A^1 level of apartheid. Group W is more effective within the political system than group B). The effectiveness of trade sanctions can be analysed, not in terms of the harm imposed on the country as a whole, but in terms of its relative effects on W and on B. Note that:

(i)   If the sanctions reduce income of both factions equally, both functions shift downwards equally. W shifts to W^1 and B shifts to B^1. The result is no change in policy in the affected country as intersection point 2 is directly below intersection point 1. Sanctions have harmed the country but not achieved their objective (A^1 is unchanged).

(ii) Sanctions may be counter-productive (and increase A) if they hurt group B more than group W (it may be noted that, in the case of Rhodesia, it was the Black African population that experienced rising unemployment). In Figure 16.6(b) apartheid policy would increase to A^2 at point 3 if sanctions had no effect on group W but made conditions worse for group B (so that B shifts to B^1).

(iii) Sanctions may be counter-productive if they increase national spirit and identity amongst group W. Sanctions may serve to strengthen the resolve of group W. They may serve to cause a 'rallying around the flag' in defiance of the rest of the world. In this case W in Figure 16.6(b) would shift to the right and apartheid policy might increase beyond A^2 if B has shifted to B^1.

(iv) Conversely, if sanctions signal external support, schedule B^1 may shift to the left for (following the discussion of revolution in the previous section) anything that increases the probability of success may stimulate greater effort and now the sanctions begin to exert an effect.

(v)   If, on balance, pressure against apartheid means that pressure from the B groups remains at B in Figure 16.6(b) but an incremental introduction of sanctions reduces morale for the W pressure group (so that W shifts to W^2), the new equilibrium is at point 4 with a lower level of apartheid at A^3.[10] (Incremental application is used to sap morale as more pressure is anticipated.)

The interest group analysis sheds further insight on the likely effectiveness of international trade. First, if trade sanctions are less effective than might be expected this may reflect the motives of those who press for trade sanctions and the emphasis when choosing how to apply trade sanctions. Second, if trade sanctions are less effective than might be expected, this may reflect a distinction between effectiveness in terms of achieving the greatest economic damage and effectiveness in terms of producing a policy change (i.e. a decrease in A in Figure 16.6(b)). Trade sanctions which have differential impacts on the supporters and opponents of A may more easily be able to produce the desired policy change in the targeted country.

Microeconomic theory offers greater insight when awareness of processes (as well as analysis of outcomes) is part of the analysis.

16.7 Challenge: Is there a 'microeconomic psychology' approach?

To this point, the discussion has been set in terms of whether altruism (or malevolence), as modelled by utility interdependence, must be incorporated in microeconomic theory in order to explain behaviour and assess policies. In this chapter the argument has been that the assumption of self-interest is sufficient. However, in this section the objective is to consider how microeconomic theory might be amended to encapsulate broader motivation. Having outlined what we refer to as a 'microeconomic psychology' approach, this is applied to an issue discussed at the end of the previous chapter. In Section 15.7 the issue of government crowding-out of private giving was considered. The objective here is to offer a different analysis premised on the assumption that individuals' willingness to act altruistically is affected by perceptions of how such action is regarded in the community. The objective is to illustrate different possibilities for broadening the neoclassical assumption of pure self-interest.

Recent results in experimental economics and in cognitive psychology have shed new insights. One important example is the discussion of intrinsic motivation. An individual is said to be 'intrinsically motivated to perform an activity when one receives no apparent reward except the activity itself' (Deci 1971: 105). Intrinsic motivation is based on moral and ethical considerations but it is also affected by external intervention (e.g. Deci and Ryan 1980, 1985). Frey (1992, 1997) illustrates how government intervention (by taxation, regulation, subsidy) will affect intrinsic motivation. An important consideration is whether government intervention carries with it the notion that individual intrinsic motivation is *acknowledged* and esteemed. For example, the act of placing a price on what would otherwise be considered an altruistic gesture debases the gesture. Evidence of this effect is presented in the empirical analysis of Frey *et al.* (1996). In some cases government regulation can 'impair' intrinsic motivation (by debasing an individual's voluntary commitment to community-motivated action). On the other hand, if regulations are astutely framed, they can 'repair' intrinsic motivation (e.g. Frey 1992 cites the example of speed limits in children's play-areas as commendation of socially responsible action). The key is that public policy should *acknowledge* the value of intrinsic motivation.

---

10. It may be noted that in the discussion of the relaxation of apartheid in South Africa it was the increasing costs (as economic growth was experienced and a black middle class was required) that induced relaxation. Sanctions which reduce economic growth in a targeted country may well serve to postpone such change.

Frey's analysis can be applied to explain behaviour that does not fit with predictions based on 'standard' neoclassical microeconomic theory (i.e. based on *homo economicus*). The impact of society's response to demonstration of intrinsic values is important. In the following analysis this is incorporated by allowing for endogeneity of preferences. It is usual in microeconomic theory to attempt to explain behaviour by a change in constraints, rather than by a change in preference (Stigler and Becker 1977).[11] To say that individuals consume more, or less, because of a preference change is to approach tautology. However, there are examples in economic theory of attempts to incorporate preference endogeneity (see Cowen 1989 for a survey). The usual approach (and one described elsewhere throughout this text) to explaining behaviour is to assume that preferences are given and that behaviour is a response to changes in constraints (e.g. price and income). However, here we explore the possibility that the *way* in which constraints change will also impact on preferences to act altruistically. The argument is that this broader approach (inclusive of preference endogeneity) will retain predictive bite if the determinants of preference changes can be identified.

The example relates to the 'Thatcher years' in the UK, when 'markets' were extolled by government and the role of public-sector responsibility for welfare provision was questioned (Jones *et al.* 1998). Individuals were exhorted to take greater responsibility for their own welfare and 'Victorian values' were encouraged (Kavanagh 1990). When the New Right advocated that the public sector should be 'rolled back' in the UK the expectation was that there would be a crowding-in of voluntary philanthropic giving (Bosanquet 1983). The expectation was not realised.

As already noted (in Section 15.9), the one-to-one feature of 'crowding out' is not evident. Most empirical work suggests crowd-out parameters are very low. While explanations were presented in Chapter 15, it is possible to consider another (one that allows a far wider response). The argument emphasises the *way* in which policy was introduced when there was exhortation of markets and individual responsibility. Following Titmuss (1971), greater resort to markets is likely to affect the 'gift relationship' and to damage the intrinsic value of altruistic action.[12]

If social context influences altruistic behaviour, how is this effect incorporated? Following Haines (1981), it is possible to incorporate social context in equation (16.21). U_i represents the total utility of individual i; U_e is the direct egoistic utility an individual gains from their own action; U_b is the utility obtained by others ('beneficiaries') from the same action. α is the weight given by i to U_b and it may be termed a 'coefficient of concern or obligation'. The weight ε given to the individual's own utility (U_e) is an ego or 'self-interest coefficient'.

$$dU_i = f(\varepsilon dU_e + \alpha\, dU_b \mid \bar{M}_i, \bar{M}_a) \tag{16.21}$$

The terms beyond the 'given' line, |, capture social context.

---

11. Frank (1997: 235–6) notes that, for economists, 'the best explanation of behavioral differences . . . is one that assumes that people have the same tastes but face different prices and incomes'.

12. Decision-making in markets is likely to affect individuals' perception of any responsibility to others. Ware (1990) identifies three arguments. First, he notes a 'psychological' argument, that (for example) 'habits, conventions and principles which support aid for others are weakened when cost/benefit calculations of self interest are even contemplated by the actor' (p. 191). Activity in markets causes individuals to place emphasis on costs and benefits and to operate in ways which may be at odds with altruistic behaviour. Second, he refers to a 'territory' argument. For example, by 'opening up' local communities, markets reduce the sense of community spirit. Third, he argues that changes in the 'institutional' structure of society undermine the organisation of altruism. Charities themselves become more 'business'-oriented and this can diminish the contribution of 'participation altruists' (e.g. volunteers). Reliance on markets changes 'social context' and changes attitudes and 'tastes and preferences' for altruism.

(i) $\bar{M}_i$ represents the individual's micro-social context. M_i-type factors relate specifically to each individual. At the micro level it is suggested that tangible micro-social context variables would include an individual's income, specific tax liabilities, relative prices of goods and services consumed by the individual. Intangible micro-social context variables would include the specific location of an altruistic action (workplace, street, home) and the number of witnesses to the action (group size).

(ii) $\bar{M}_a$ is designed to capture the individual's macro-social context. $\bar{M}_a$-type factors are social factors relating to all individuals in the community (and are likely to be more relevant to the longer run than micro-social variables). The macro-social context, like the micro-social context, can be thought of as having tangible and intangible components. Macro-tangible components in this context would be factors like the overall extent of public provision via the state and the rate of economic growth, whereas intangible elements might cover the dominant religion of a country, the general education level, the ambient cultural view of giving, the party in power, international relations. Both micro- and macro-level variables incorporate social context.[13]

The vertical line in equation (16.21) essentially divides an individual's world into an 'internal' and an 'external' part. Initially, holding the external variables constant (hence the bars above the variable names) the equation provides a taxonomy of behaviour. Selfishness means ignoring others, so that $\varepsilon = 1$ and $\alpha = 0$. Egoism means affording others less significance than yourself, so that $\varepsilon = 1 > \alpha > 0$. Altruistic behaviour is about giving others the same weight as yourself, so that $\varepsilon = \alpha = 1$. Self-sacrificing individuals give others more weight than themselves, so that $\alpha > 1 = \varepsilon$. Finally, ignoring oneself – the St Francis case of self-abrogation – yields $\varepsilon = 0$ and $\alpha = 1$ – your only concern is others.[14]

Differing social contexts will elicit different types of behaviour. It is possible to think of individuals being ranked by the ratio of their 'coefficient of concern' to their 'self-interest coefficient' (i.e. by α/ε). The term α/ε effectively represents the relative preferences of individuals over themselves and others' utility *given* the micro- and macro-social contexts. They are weights in a utility function but, by themselves, they are unable to determine the level of charitable giving. They depend on M_i and M_a.

To illustrate this approach, assume the community comprises two groups of which individuals A and B are representative. Equation (16.22) incorporates some of the variables discussed above:

$$U_a = U_a(Y_a, Y_b, G_b \mid \bar{M}_a) \tag{16.22}$$

The utility of A depends on both A's income, Y_a $(\partial U_a/\partial Y_a > 0)$ and the income of B, Y_b $(\partial U_a/\partial Y_b > 0)$. The utility of A also depends on giving to B via the government sector G_b $(\partial U_a/\partial G_b > 0)$. The social context variable $\bar{M}_a$ is a macro variable which refers to the reliance on markets within the economy. A 'rolling back' of the welfare state and greater exhortation of market solutions would affect M_a and, in turn, this would affect the marginal utilities $\partial U_a/\partial Y_b$ and $\partial U_a/\partial G_b$. Both are assumed to be lower the greater the reliance on markets, because, with the withdrawal of government responsibility, individual A becomes more conscious of the virtues of self-reliance.

---

13. The characteristics of the potential beneficiaries (B) may also be important in both the micro and macro contexts. At the micro-social context level, the specific characteristics of donees and your view of them are more likely to be dominant and, whereas α above is envisaged as a general weight (being defined for an anonymous individual), once the anonymity is relaxed α may vary (e.g. being 'spare changed' by a disabled or drunken beggar). At the macro level, information from the political and media arenas set the tone as to whether individuals should see beneficiaries as 'deserving' or as merely feckless.

14. Sadism is $\varepsilon = 1$, $\alpha < 0$ and masochism is $\varepsilon < 0$, $\alpha = 1$.

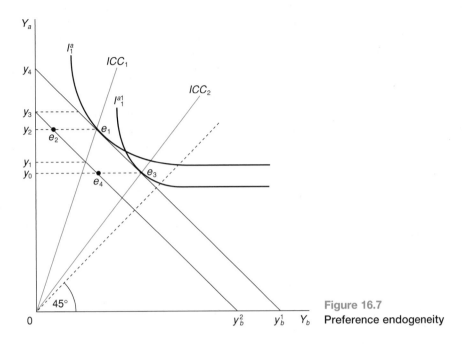

Figure 16.7
Preference endogeneity

To emphasise the endogeneity of tastes, it is possible to illustrate two different effects of changing the public–market sector mix. The vertical and horizontal axes of Figure 16.7 record, respectively, the incomes of individuals A and B. For simplicity, A's indifference curves are assumed homothetic to the origin. Two different sets of indifference curves are illustrated. The first set (tangent to budget lines with a slope of 0-y_4/0-y_b^1) plot an income consumption curve ICC_1. This reflects the relative importance of 'own' and of B's income when government provision of welfare for B is equal to zero ($G_b = 0$). The second set of indifference curves (which reflect a greater concern for B) are tangent to budget lines with the same slope but now tangencies are along the income consumption curve ICC_2 (as government provision of welfare for B (G_b) is assumed to be positive and the intrinsic value of giving is acknowledged).

For both the first and second sets of indifference curves, individual A derives no marginal utility from adding to B's income when B has the same (or greater) income as A. Therefore 'altruism' is evident only in the section of the diagram above the 45° line drawn from the origin.[15] If A's income (before tax) is 0-y_4 a budget line with a slope of (–)1 may be drawn to reflect the cost of giving units of income to B (i.e. transactions costs involved in transferring income have been assumed to be zero). With reference to A's first set of preferences ($G_b = 0$), A's preferred allocation of 0-y_4 income is shown at tangency point e_1 where y_4-y_2 units are given by A to B.

Consider the 'crowding-out/crowding-in' argument as described in 'standard' public good economic theory. When a government undertakes welfare programmes (taxing A to transfer income to B), y_4-y_3 of A's income is taken as tax to provide (via a social security system) income for B. As A considers charity in the public sector to be a perfect substitute for personal charity, A will reduce personal voluntary giving from y_4-y_2 to y_3-y_2 (individual A's equilibrium shifting from point e_1 to e_2 in Figure 16.7). Total giving remains constant but the mix between the government and the private charitable sector

---

15. The indifference curve is a straight horizontal line on the right-hand side of the 45° line.

alters. Government spending 'crowds out' private charitable giving on a 'one for one' basis (the reduction in personal charitable giving is exactly equal to welfare state provision, i.e. to y_4-y_3).[16]

By comparison, assume endogeneity of preferences within an 'economic psychology' approach. In this case A's preferences are conditioned by the kind of society in which A lives; A is more 'altruistic' in a society where the dependence on markets and self-reliance is tempered by provision of public-sector welfare entitlement. When A recognises that the community is concerned to transfer (via the public sector) as much as y_4-y_3 from each person in the same circumstances as those enjoyed by A, then, as an individual, A's 'willingness to give' will increase. At an income level of y_4 the indifference curve (representing the same utility level for A) now takes the shape of curve I_1^{a1}. Such a set of indifference curves would have points of tangency with budget lines of slope 0-y_4/0-y_b^1 (as shown along ICC_2). With the same marginal rate of substitution between 'own' income and 'other's' income, A prefers to give more to B when A's attitudes have been conditioned by this change in macro-social context.

If government spending helps condition 'willingness to give' and if y_4 is 'before-tax income', then there are two effects of government spending. One is to shift preferences so that the individual prefers to give more (e.g. a move from e_1 to e_3). The second is the usual 'substitution' effect associated with public spending (i.e. a move from e_3 to e_4). The full effect of government spending is the move from e_1 to e_4. 'Crowding out' has occurred but would not be recorded in terms of individual giving because crowding out is only one part (the substitution effect) of the full impact of government spending on an individual's propensity to give.[17] By comparison with the conventional case (when ICC_1 is the only relevant income consumption curve) the impact of government spending has had the additional effect of shifting the individual's preferences (i.e. indifference curves shifted to ICC_2). Allowing for this additional effect, the prediction is no change in private giving, i.e. no visible 'crowding out' (total giving is y_4-y_0, government spending is y_4-y_3 and personal giving is y_3-y_0, where y_3-$y_0 = y_4$-y_2).[18]

The example illustrated has been made stark deliberately (i.e. in the first case 'one for one' crowding out and in the second instance no crowding out). However, the less those preferences are affected by the community's reliance on markets, the more likely that the tangency point e_4 is located nearer the initial point e_1. In this way there is some 'crowding out' but not 'one for one' and the results reported by empirical studies are consistent with an explanation based on endogeneity of preferences. Government spending not only acts as a substitute for personal spending, it also affects individuals' willingness to give to charitable concerns. The constraints which individuals perceive are not unrelated or independent of preferences.

In Figure 16.7, when government dismisses responsibility to provide assistance and advocates self-reliance, individual A weights the importance of altruism more lightly. 'Crowding in' is then far less than politicians and policy-makers suggest.[19] If A perceives

---

16. In practice crowding out may not necessarily be 'one for one' if only because of fiscal illusion. If A is unaware of the tax, A would falsely assume an 'income effect' from government spending and personal giving would be cut by less than 'one for one'.

17. In this case e_4 on the after-tax budget line would represent the new equilibrium from which the new level of personal giving would be recorded.

18. Since y_4-$y_2 = y_3$-y_0 no crowding out will be recorded.

19. Saxon-Harrold (1993: 63) cites a statement by Barnett and Saxon-Harrold to the effect: 'If political expectations are out of alignment with public disposition, there could be an unbridgeable chasm: an assumption by government that individuals will fulfil the welfare function, and a continuing assumption by individuals that this is the government's duty.'

that G_b has been completely removed (and markets extolled), individual adjustment in the figure is not from e_4 to e_3 (as the 'crowding-in' school suggests) but from e_4 to e_1, (i.e. back to the preferred position in the absence of government involvement). Cuts in G_b are not accompanied by significant 'crowding in'; individuals' preferences are affected.

The analysis here runs counter to Stigler and Becker's (1977) description of microeconomic theory, i.e. that tastes and preferences are exogenous and that behaviour can be explained by only analysing response to changes in constraints. It opens the discussion of individuals' response to the *way* in which constraints are changed. Increasingly, evidence suggests that the way in which constraints change and the way in which income is received matters (e.g. see Winnett and Lewis 1995).[20] In this section attention has been given to the way in which public policy is introduced (as well as the implications of changes in public policy for shifts in constraints). The analysis retains predictive bite if the relationship between preference changes and independent variables can be identified.

16.8 Summary

The tenor of this chapter is that the assumption of self-interest (attributed to *homo econmicus*) is sufficient to explain behaviour. Pure self-interest is a knife-edge between benevolence and malevolence; individuals neither want to help nor to harm others. It has been argued that, when individuals appear to act with humanitarian concern, they are simply creating rent-seeking opportunities. When governments redistribute to the poor it is because the poor can force individuals to act *as if* they were charitable. By the same token, when individuals seek to exclude others it is because of rent-seeking opportunities. When they engage in racist activity it is because of the existence of profitable opportunities rather than from any ethnic hatred *per se*.

While it may be extreme to argue that individuals will always act as selfless 'knights', it is also extreme to believe that life is lived on such a knife-edge (Kelman 1987). Neither approach offers a complete picture and a broader approach has been suggested, whereby preference endogeneity is introduced. Such analysis would be precluded by neoclassical microeconomics for, in this literature, behavioural changes are explained by changes in constraints holding constant preferences (see also Olson 1967). The difficulty of introducing the idea of preference endogeneity is that analysis may become tautological; individuals do things because they like doing them. The danger with excluding preference endogeneity is that the impact of changing constraints (and the nature in which constraints are changed) is ignored. Frey (1997) provides a host of examples which indicate that individuals are affected by the *way* in which they are paid or the *manner* in which they are regulated. If the behaviour he cites cannot be adequately explained by neoclassical microeconomics there may be greater scope if microeconomic analysis is broadened. A 'microeconomic psychology approach' (see Lewis 2007) might offer insight if the determinants of changes in preferences can be identified and testable hypotheses formed.

---

20. Increasingly, evidence indicates that when individuals receive income it matters *how* income is received and the assumption that money is 'fungible' is not borne out in practice (Sheffrin and Thaler 1988; Thaler 1990; Winnett and Lewis 1995). For example, Winnett and Lewis (1995) identify 'mental accounting schemas'; the use of income depends on the distinction between liquidity, windfall/regular and capital/labour income. In a study of household saving they discovered that 'all income from capital is classified as non-spendable' (p. 441).

References

Akerlof, G.A. (1985) Discriminatory, status-based wages among tradition-oriented stochastically trading coconut producers, *Journal of Political Economy*, 93: 265–76.

Anderson, G.M. and Tollison, R.D. (1984) A rent seeking explanation of the British Factory Acts, in David Colander (ed.) *Neoclassical Political Economy*, Cambridge, Mass.: Ballinger.

Arrow, K.J. (1973) The theory of discrimination, in O. Ashenfelter and A. Rees (eds) *Discrimination in Labor Markets*, Princeton NJ: Princeton University Press.

Becker, G.S. (1968) Crime and punishment: an economic approach, *Journal of Political Economy*, 76 (2): 169–217.

Becker, G.S. (1973) *The Economics of Discrimination*, 2nd edn, Chicago: University of Chicago Press.

Becker, G.S. (1974) A theory of social interactions, *Journal of Political Economy*, 82: 1063–93.

Becker, G.S. (1983) A theory of competition among pressure groups for political influence, *Quarterly Journal of Economics*, 98 August: 371–400.

Becker, G.S. (1985) Public policies, pressure groups and dead weight costs, *Journal of Public Economics*, 28 December: 329–47.

Bhaskar, V., Manning, A. and To, T. (2002) Oligopsony and monopsonistic competition in labour markets, *Journal of Economic Perspectives*, 16 (2) (Spring): 155–74.

Bosanquet, N. (1983) *After the New Right*, London: Heinemann.

Brennan, G. (1985) Pareto optimal redistribution; the case of malice and envy, *Journal of Public Economics*, 2: 173–83.

Brennan, G. and Lomasky, L. (1993) *Democracy and Decision: the Pure Theory of Electoral Preference*, Cambridge: Cambridge University Press.

Chalmers, J.A. and Shelton, R.B. (1975) An economic analysis of riot participation, *Economic Inquiry*, XIII: 322–36.

Cowen, T. (1989) Are all tastes constant and identical? A critique of Stigler and Becker, *Journal of Economic Behavior and Organization*, 11 (1): 127–35.

Deci, E.L. (1971) Effects of externally mediated rewards on intrinsic motivation, *Journal of Personality and Social Psychology*, 18: 105–15.

Deci, E.L. and Ryan, R.M. (1980) The empirical exploration of intrinsic motivational processes, *Advances in Experimental Social Psychology*, 10: 39–80.

Deci, E.L. and Ryan, R.M. (1985) *Intrinsic Motivation and Self Determination in Human Behavior*, New York: Plenum Press.

de Tocqueville, A. (1835) *Democracy in America*, reprint edn, Oxford: Oxford University Press.

Frank, R. (1997) *Microeconomics and Behavior*, New York: McGraw-Hill.

Frey, B.S. (1984) *International Political Economics*, Oxford: Basil Blackwell.

Frey, B.S. (1992) Tertium datur: pricing, regulating and intrinsic motivation, *Kyklos*, 45 (2): 161–84.

Frey, B.S. (1997) *Not Just For the Money: an Economic Theory of Personal Motivation*, Cheltenham: Edward Elgar.

Frey, B.S. and Leuchinger, S. (2003) How to fight terrorism, *Defence and Peace Economics*, 14 (4): 237–49.

Frey, B.S., Oberholzer-Gee, F. and Eichenberger, R. (1996) The old lady visits your backyard: a tale of morals and markets, *Journal of Political Economy*, 104 (6): 1297–1313.

Gramlich, E.M. and Rubinfeld, D.L. (1982) Voting on spending, *Journal of Policy Analysis and Management*, 1: 516–33.

Griffiths, A. and Wall, S. (1999) *Applied Economics*, 8th edn, London: Longman.

Haines, W.W. (1981) The economic consequences of altruism, *International Journal of Social Economics*, 81: 50–69.

Hochman, J.M. and Rodgers, J.D. (1969) Pareto optimal redistribution, *American Economic Review*, 59: 542–57.

Jennings, C.C. (1998) An economistic interpretation of the Northern Ireland conflict, *Scottish Journal of Political Economy*, 45 (3) August: 294–308.

Jones, P.R., Cullis, J.G. and Lewis, A. (1998) Public versus private provision of altruism: can fiscal policy make individuals 'better' people? *Kyklos*, 51 (1): 3–24.

Kaempfer, W.H. and Lowenberg, A. (1988) The theory of international economic sanction; a public choice approach, *American Economic Review*, 78 (4): 786–93.

Kavanagh, D. (1990) *Thatcherism and British Politics*, Oxford: Oxford University Press.

Kelman, S. (1987) Public choice and public spirit, *Public Interest*, 87 (80): 93–4.

Knorr, K. (1975) *The Political Economy of International Relations*, New York: Basic Books.

Konrad, K. (2004) The investment problem in terrorism, *Economica*, 71: 449–59.

Krueger, A. (1963) Economics of discrimination, *Journal of Political Economy*, 71 (5): 481–86.

Le Grand, J. (1982) *The Strategy of Equality: Redistribution and the Social Services*, London: Allen and Unwin.

Lewis, A. (ed.) (2007) *A Handbook of Economic Psychology*, Cambridge: Cambridge University Press.

Lowenberg, A. (1989) An economic theory of apartheid, *Economic Inquiry*, XXVII (1) January: 57–74.

Marvel, H.P. (1977) Factory regulation: a reinterpretation of early English experience, *Journal of Law and Economics*, 20 October: 379–402.

Meltzer, A.H. and Richard, S.F. (1981) A rational theory of the size of government, *Journal of Political Economy*, 89 October: 914–27.

Meltzer, A.H. and Richard, S.F. (1983) Tests of a rational theory of the size of government, *Public Choice*, 41 (3): 403–18.

Mueller, D.C. (2003) *Public Choice III*, Cambridge: Cambridge University Press.

Mueller, D.C. and Murrell, P. (1986) Interest groups and the size of government, *Public Choice*, 48 (2): 125–45.

Musgrave, R.A. (1985) Excess bias and the nature of budget growth, *Journal of Public Economics*, 28: 287–308.

Olson, M. Jr. (1965) *The Logic of Collective Action: Public Goods and the Theory of Groups*, Cambridge, Mass.: Harvard University Press.

Olson, M. (1967) The Relationship of Economics to the Other Social Sciences: the Province of a 'Special Report', paper delivered at the Annual Meeting of the American Political Science Association.

Popkin, S. (1979) *The Rational Peasant*, Berkeley: University of California Press.

Roback, J. (1989) Racism as rent seeking, *Economic Inquiry*, XXVII (4) October: 661–81.

Roberts, D. (1960) *Victorian Origins of the Welfare State*, New Haven, Conn.: Yale University Press.

Saxon-Harrold, S.K.E. (1993) Attitudes to charities, pp. 59–74 in S.E.C. Saxon-Harrold and J. Kendall (eds) *Researching the Voluntary Sector*, Tonbridge: Charities Aid Foundation.

Seeler, H.J. (1982) Wirtschaftssanktionen asl zweifelhaftes Instrument der Aussenpolitik, *Europa-Archiv*, 20: 611–18.

Sheffrin, H.M. and Thaler, R.H. (1988) The behavioral life-cycle hypothesis *Economic Inquiry*, 26 (4): 609–43.

Silver, M. (1974) Political revolution and repression: an economic approach, *Public Choice*, 17: 63–71.

Stigler, G. (1970) Director's law of public redistribution, *Journal of Law and Economics*, 13: 1–10.

Stigler, G. and Becker, G. (1977) 'De gustibus non est disputandum', *American Economic Review*, 67 (2): 76–90.

Thaler, R.H. (1990) Savings, fungibility and mental accounts, *Journal of Economic Perspectives*, 4: 193–205.

Titmuss, R. (1971) *The Gift Relationship*, New York: Pantheon.

Tong, J. (1992) *Disorder under Heaven*, Stanford, Calif.: Stanford University Press.

Tullock, G. (1971a) The charity of the uncharitable, *Western Economic Journal*, 9 December: 379–92.

Tullock, G. (1971b) The paradox of revolution, *Public Choice*, 11: 89–99.

van Bergeijk, P.A.G (1994) *Economic Diplomacy, Trade and Commercial Policy*, Cheltenham: Edward Elgar.

Ware, A. (1990) Meeting need through voluntary action: does market society corrode altruism?, pp. 185–207 in A. Ware and R.E. Goodin, *Needs and Welfare*, London: Sage.

Wickham-Jones, M. (1995) Rationality, revolution and reassurance, in K. Dowding and D. King, *Preferences, Institutions and Rational Choice*, Oxford: Clarendon Press.

Winnett, A. and Lewis, A. (1995) Household accounts, mental accounts and savings behaviour: some old economics rediscovered? *Journal of Economic Psychology*, 16: 431–48.

PART **VI**

THE INTERNATIONAL ECONOMY

CHAPTER 17

Neoclassical microeconomics and international trade

17.1 Introduction

The objective in this chapter is to describe the way in which neoclassical microeconomic theory can be applied to issues of international trade. As elsewhere in this text, a central proposition is that conclusions are sensitive to assumptions adopted when constructing models. International trade policy is an area of great controversy. At the very time political leaders call for free international trade and re-double efforts to remove trade barriers (via international institutions such as the World Trade Organization), no political leader adopts a policy of free trade when deciding open economy issues that have a considerable impact on individuals' lives. The paradox is that, while the virtues of free trade are extolled, no country moves to free trade. Indeed, in recent years there has been even greater political pressure from lobbies to introduce greater protection. Introductory economics texts (and students in economics examinations) rehearse time-tested 'proofs' that free trade increases welfare. Are governments unaware of a basic principle that informs discussion in every introductory economics text? Why would governments prefer to ignore the prescriptions of microeconomic theory?

This chapter focuses on an application of the general equilibrium model (discussed in Chapter 5) to international trade issues. The model appears abstract and esoteric. Is it simply a teaching device, or has it anything to say about recent events and policy choices? The argument here is that, despite its abstract appearance, the model offers insight. The model is able to reconcile the apparent paradox that countries call for free trade but practise protection.

In Section 17.2 the neoclassical 'cornerstone' of international trade theory is described to explain why countries trade. The same analysis can be applied to predict the pattern of trade. In response to initial scepticism by generations of students, the focus of attention is the question of what insight this theory yields. How can such an apparently esoteric model explain the world in which individuals live and choose? Once again, sensitivity of predictions of the model to assumptions employed is a consideration. In Section 17.2 the foundational neoclassical model is adapted to explain responses to trade-liberalising initiatives.

17.2 **The gains from trade**

In the neoclassical general equilibrium model there are three conditions which must be attained before a closed economy may be described as 'efficient' (see Chapter 5). These Paretian conditions are:

(1) *efficiency in production* (which requires that the marginal rate of technical substitution between capital and labour be equal in the production of all goods);
(2) *efficiency in exchange* (which requires that individuals' marginal rates of substitution between goods be equal);
(3) *'top level' efficiency* (which requires that the marginal rate of substitution between goods equal the marginal rate of transformation).

In order to demonstrate that (potentially) there are 'gains from trade', one approach is to compare the welfare of a 'non-trading' (autarchic) economy with the welfare of the same economy *after* it has engaged in free trade. In both cases it is assumed that the economy satisfies the conditions that maximise welfare. It follows that any *increase* in welfare (achieved when the economy is engaged in international trade) must be attributed to access to *international trade* (rather than to any other possible efficiency-enhancing reform that might have been exploited in a closed economy). The economy does everything 'correctly' (with respect to conditions 1 to 3) and still finds the opportunity to increase welfare as a consequence of free trade.

To begin, assume:

1. two goods (X and Y) and two factors of production capital and labour (K and L);[1]
2. markets are perfectly competitive;
3. factors of production are fixed in supply and there is a given state of technology (i.e. this is a 'static' model);
4. mobility of factors of production between different industries *within* the economy.

In Figure 17.1(a) the conditions required for efficiency in the case of a closed economy are satisfied when the economy produces at point 1 on the production possibility frontier $T\text{-}T'$. This is the point at which the economy attains the highest community indifference curve CIC_1. Point 1 indicates the amount of goods X and Y that the economy produces and (as a closed economy is being considered) it also shows the amounts of goods X and Y that are available for consumption. The domestic price ratio is shown by the slope of the line P_d. With given resources and given technology this outcome is the 'best' that can be attained when the economy is autarchic; all three efficiency conditions (listed above) are satisfied.

If the possibility of international trade arises, 'gains from trade' depend on the difference between international prices and domestic prices. In Figure 17.1(a) the slope of P_i (the international set of prices) differs from that of P_d and 'gains from trade' are possible. This indicates that the economy has a comparative advantage in the production of good Y (which is produced at home at a lower price than its international price – as is clear from a comparison of the slopes of P_i and P_d). There are gains from trade and gains are fully exploited when factors of production move into the production of the good in which the economy has a 'comparative advantage'. Resources move from the production of good X to the production of good Y until the marginal cost of producing good Y equals the international price of good Y (i.e. there is a movement from point 1 to point 2 in Figure 17.1).

---

1. This assumption is used simply to facilitate a diagrammatic exposition.

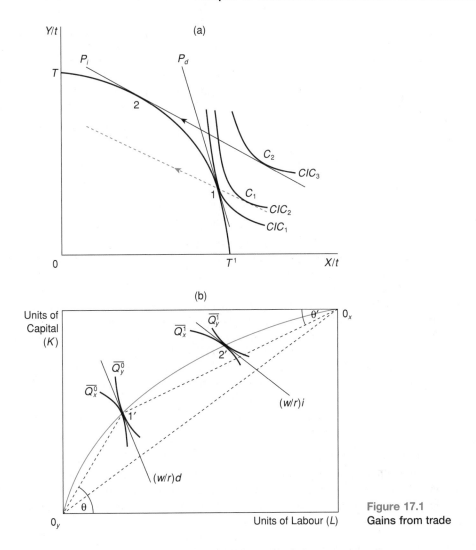

Figure 17.1
Gains from trade

The gains from trade arise when the economy is able to trade at international prices and, in Figure 17.1, this implies that good Y (the good in which the country has a comparative advantage) will be traded (exported) for imports of good X. The new consumption point is at C_2 on CIC_3, where the marginal rate of substitution is equal to the international price ratio (i.e. the marginal rate at which goods can be transformed by international trade). The level of welfare has increased from CIC_1 to CIC_3. The difference between these two levels of welfare (CIC_1 and CIC_3) represents 'gains from trade'.

Note that, to *maximise* the gains from trade, a further 'efficiency' condition is now required. At the free trade equilibrium all three conditions listed above are satisfied. However, inspection of Figure 17.1 shows that there is another requirement. This is that the marginal rate of transformation internationally (as shown by the slope of P_i) is equal to the marginal rate of transformation domestically (as shown by the slope of the production possibility curve). In the case of an open economy a fourth condition for Pareto optimality is:

(4) marginal rate of transformation of goods in trade (MRT_{XY}^f – as shown by the slope of P_i) = marginal rate of transformation in the domestic economy (i.e. $MRT_{XY}^f = MRT_{XY}^d$).

The message seems quite unambiguous – there are gains from focusing production on the good in which the country enjoys a comparative advantage – there are gains from engaging in free international trade. The message is not new – it was understood by classical economists.[2] However, no country engages fully in free trade and, as noted above, in many countries political pressures for trade protection appear as intense as ever. So how helpful is microeconomic theory?

While the classical economists believed that there were unambiguous gains from trade (see Sodersten and Reed 1994), the neoclassical model explains the dichotomy. Alongside the assumption (1–4 already noted) assume that:

5. production functions are linearly homogeneous (i.e. there are constant returns to scale and marginal products of the two factors of production depend only on the ratio in which the two factors are employed – see Chapter 3);
6. the country always produces a quantity of both goods Y and X.

In Figure 17.1(b), the production changes are analysed with reference to the Edgeworth–Bowley input box diagram. To increase the predictive powers of the model the assumption that production functions are linearly homogeneous is helpful. Clearly, production functions are not identical for both X and Y. The shape of the contract curve (to the north-west of a diagonal) indicates that product Y is more capital-intensive in production than is product X (consider the rays from the origins 0_Y and 0_X to say point $1'$ and the angles formed to convince yourself of this – angle θ exceeds angle θ'). If both production functions bear the characteristic that the marginal product of a factor of production depends on the ratio in which factors of production are used (i.e. that production functions are linearly homogeneous, see Chapter 3) it is possible to predict the impact of trade liberalisation on factor prices.

In Figure 17.1(a), when resources move from point 1 to point 2 on the production possibility curve (T-T') they will shift from point $1'$ to point $2'$ on the contract curve in Figure 17.1(b). The implication is that, at point $2'$, both goods have become more labour-intensive in production.[3] If production functions are linearly homogeneous this means that the marginal product of labour (MPP_L) has fallen and the marginal product of capital (MPP_K) will have increased (as the marginal product of factors of production depend only on the ratio in which they are used, see Chapter 3). As markets are perfectly competitive and as payment to factors of production depends on marginal product, the reward paid to capital will have increased and the reward paid to labour will have fallen at point $2'$ (production has become more labour-intensive because cost-minimising producers substitute in favour of the cheaper factor). In Figure 17.1(b) the country with a closed economy produces on isoquants $\overline{Q_x^0}$ and $\overline{Q_y^0}$, indicating the quantity of goods X and Y respectively. The relative factor prices $(w/r)_d$ at point $1'$ are captured by the tangency line to the isoquants. With the opening of the economy $\overline{Q_x^1}$ and $\overline{Q_y^1}$ of goods X and Y respectively are produced at point $2'$ with the relative price of capital raised and that of labour reduced as can been seen in the slope of $(w/r)_i$. Compare the slope of $(w/r)_d$ with $(w/r)_i$. Clearly the output of Y (the capital-intensive 'export' good) is increased and the output of good X (the good now imported) is reduced once trade takes place.

---

2. Adam Smith offered a discussion of the advantages of specialisation and the gains from *absolute advantage* (i.e. when country A is more efficient at the production of Y and B more efficient at the production of X). David Ricardo introduced the gains that arise from *comparative advantage* (even if A is more efficient at production of both goods – but comparatively better at the production of one of the goods – e.g. in Figure 17.1, good Y).
3. Readers may wish to confirm this by drawing lines from 0_X and 0_Y at opposite ends of the Edgeworth–Bowley box to point $2'$. It will be clear from the comparison of the angles formed by the rays that the production of goods uses more labour per unit of capital at point $2'$ than at point $1'$.

The result is quite intuitive. With free trade, the economy moves more resources into production of the good in which it has a comparative advantage (good Y). This means that there is expansion of the capital-intensive sector and decline of the labour-intensive sector of the economy. More capital per unit of labour is demanded than capital per unit of labour released by the declining X industry. The implication is that the price of capital increases and the wage rate declines. As producers profit-maximise, both industries substitute labour for capital, i.e. both industries become more labour-intensive. Hence the well-known Stolper–Samuelson theorem (see Stolper and Samuelson 1941) that:

> an increase in the relative price of a commodity will increase the real return to the factor used intensively in the industry (and reduce the return to the other factor).

The prediction relies on the assumption noted above, e.g. that there are linearly homogeneous production functions, that there is perfect competition, that factors of production are mobile between the industries and that both goods continue to be produced (i.e. that there is not complete specialisation in one product).

However, with this prediction of a change in relative real earnings, the proposition that there are gains from international trade requires qualification! How can it be said that the country has gained when labour is now paid a lower wage and is obviously worse off? In the example considered it would hardly be surprising if labour resisted free international trade. Labourers would argue against the free importation of good X (produced by 'cheap labour' abroad), even though it is precisely because the relative price of the good is lower abroad that the country will gain. The explanation is that not *everyone* in the country need be better off as a result of trade liberalisation.

The conclusion is that there are *potential* gains from trade. It is the case that those who gain from international trade gain by so much that they would be able to compensate the losers and still be better off. In this way, the 'gains from trade' should be seen as a *potential* Pareto improvement (see Chapter 4). Now, as it is extremely unlikely that such redistribution will accompany a movement to free trade, the gains remain *potential* and there will not be a Pareto improvement (i.e. some individuals in the community are likely to be left worse off).

17.2.1 Illustrating the Stolper–Samuelson theorem

To illustrate the impact of the Stolper–Samuelson theorem (and following Appleyard and Field 2001, also see Appleyard, Field and Cobb 2006) consider the debate about income inequality in the USA. Consider the following observations:

(i) From 1973 to 1992, the average real income of the top 20 per cent (the top quintile) of families rose 19 per cent, the average real income of the middle 20 per cent rose 4 per cent; that of the lowest quintile *fell* by 12 per cent.

(ii) The United States is now even more open to international trade. In 1970, the ratio of US exports to US gross domestic product (GDP) was 5.5 per cent, while that of imports to GDP was 5.4 per cent; by 1980 these ratios reached 10.0 per cent for exports and 10.6 per cent for imports; by 1998 the figures rose to 11.3 per cent and 13.0 per cent, respectively.

Following Stolper–Samuelson, if exports from the USA are relatively intensive in the use of skilled labour, the real income of skilled workers (who tend to be in the upper segments of the income distribution) will increase when trade increases. By contrast, as trade expands real incomes of less skilled workers (in the lower segments) will fall.

There is a link between changes in the earnings of skilled labour and changes in income inequality. In 1979 full-time male workers aged 25 years and older who had at least a bachelor's degree earned 49 per cent more than similar workers who had no degree above a high-school diploma. In 1993 this 'premium' was 89 per cent. Relying on a some-what different grouping, in 1997 annual earnings of individuals with a bachelor's degree as the highest degree were 77 per cent above the earnings of those with a high-school diploma but no college attendances.

Many accept that the Stolper–Samuelson theorem is relevant. The debate is over the importance of this explanation. Borjas *et al.* (1992) estimate that between 8 and 15 per cent of the 1980–8 rise in the wage differential between college and high-school gradu-ates in the United States can be attributed to the combined effects of trade and immigration into the United States (with most of the 8 to 15 per cent due to the trade component). Freeman (1995: 25) summarises results of studies to suggest that trade accounts for 10–20 per cent of the overall fall in demand for unskilled labour required to explain rising wage differentials in the United States.

One of the key themes in this text is the difficulty of explaining what actually happens (Chapter 1). The debate continues. Appleyard *et al.* (2006) identify Wood (1991, 1994) as the leading proponent of the Stolper–Samuelson theorem and he argues that the usual estimates of decrease in demand for unskilled labour in the developed countries are significant underestimates. However, the response of critics of the relevance of the Stolper–Samuelson is:

a) If evidence reflects the Stolper–Samuelson theorem the prices of low-skill-intensive goods would also be falling. As illustrated above, the theorem relies on the asso-ciation between changes in factor prices with changes in the prices of the goods that the factors are used to produce. But studies do not find a pronounced decline in the prices of unskilled-labour-intensive goods relative to skilled-labour-intensive goods.
b) The rise in the demand for skilled labour relative to unskilled labour has not been confined to the traded goods industries. The use of skilled labour relative to unskilled labour has risen across industries, whether producing traded goods or non-traded goods. The general rise in demand for skilled labour might reflect technological change (greater use of computers, etc.).
c) There are other explanations for the decline in the relative earnings of unskilled labour in the USA:
    (i)   increased immigration of relatively unskilled labour;
    (ii) a decline in the importance and influence of trade-union-organised labour;
    (iii) a fall in the real minimum wage (the nominal minimum wage has not kept pace with the price level).

If this is 'parry', then further 'thrust' emerges as those who support the importance of Stolper–Samuelson argue:

(a′) the *threat* of imports is also relevant when explaining the reduction in demand for unskilled labour;
(b′) The weakening of unions can also be attributed to new trade pressures.

The difficulty is apportioning the relevance of competing theories. Feenestra and Hanson (1996) suggest that an important consideration when explaining demand for unskilled labour is the rise in 'outsourcing' by US firms. Firms increasingly ship abroad component and intermediate-input production (which is relatively unskilled-labour-intensive in nature), and this plays a role when explaining pressure on wages of US low-skilled labour. But is this a reflection of the importance of 'trade' or 'technology'? The water becomes even more muddy!

To conclude this section, the important consideration is that, if international trade changes income distribution, it is difficult to refer to 'gains from trade' except in the con-text of a *potential* Pareto improvement. The relative importance of the Stolper–Samuelson theorem when explaining changes in income inequality in the USA in recent years remains a matter of debate. However, it would be extreme to conclude that increased international trade does not bring with it some change in incomes for different factors of production.

17.3 How can the determinants of international trade be identified?

The neoclassical model can be applied to shed insight on the pattern of international trade flows. The model is often referred to as the Heckscher–Ohlin model as both Eli Heckscher and Bertil Ohlin (who shared the Nobel Prize for economics with James Meade in 1977) used such analysis to explain the pattern of international trade in terms of the factor endowment of countries.

In this section the model already described has been extended to account for two countries (A and B). If country A is relatively capital-abundant and country B is relatively labour-abundant and if good Y is capital-intensive and good X labour-intensive in production, the analysis can be developed by employing the following assumptions:

1. there are two countries (A and B), two products (X and Y) and two factors of production, capital and labour (K and L);
2. the two factors of production are available in fixed amounts in each of the two countries; they are fully mobile between industries but immobile between countries (country A has relatively more capital);
3. there is a given technology (available to both countries) indicating how capital and labour can be combined to produce output; production functions are linearly homogeneous (i.e. there are constant returns to scale and marginal products of the two factors of production depend only on the ratio in which the two factors are employed – see Chapter 3);
4. perfect competition prevails in all markets (factors of production are paid according to their marginal product) and there is free international trade;
5. 'factor intensity reversals' are excluded (that is to say, goods are either capital-intensive or labour-intensive at any relative price of factors of production – contract curves are everywhere to the north-west or south-east of a straight line joining 0_Y and 0_X);
6. neither country specialises in the production of only one good;
7. consumption preferences in the two countries are identical (and homothetic to the origin). (Remember – Chapter 2 – homothetic indifference curves imply that at a given set of relative prices, consumers will choose commodities in the same ratio irrespective of their income level.)

The problem is to predict the relative quantities of the two goods produced in the two countries. If production of the two goods can be predicted, this can be compared with consumption choices in both countries and it will be possible to determine the way in which each country must rely on international trade.

The two countries are identical in all respects except that one has relatively more capital than labour. In Figure 17.2(b) this is shown for the case in which each country has the same quantity of labour but A has more capital. The Edgeworth–Bowley box diagram is drawn (in solid lines for country B) and is extended (in dashed lines) to show how factor supplies look in country A. To determine how each country allocates resources, begin by assuming that country B produces at point 1. This corresponds to point 1' on the production possibility curve T_B in Figure 17.2(a). If the list of assumptions described above apply, where will country A produce on its production possibility curve?

The assumption that there is free trade is important. It means that in both countries production will occur where the slope of the production possibility curve is identical to

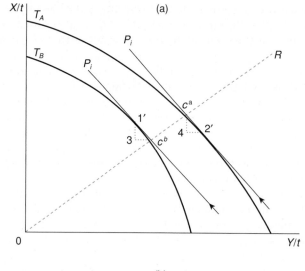

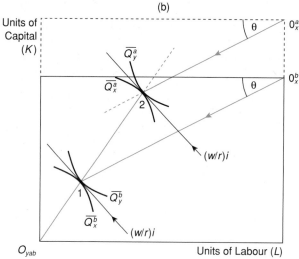

Figure 17.2
Determinants of trade

the slope of the marginal rate of international transformation, i.e. to the set of free trade prices. This means that country A must produce at a point on its production possibility curve that has the same slope as point $1'$ on T_B in Figure 17.2(a).

The marginal rate of transformation is determined by the relative productivity of factors of production in the two industries. The marginal physical product (MPP) of any factor of production is the change in output that results from a small change in the use of the factor. By definition, it is the amount extra that will be available of one good as a result of increasing the input of a factor of production. The marginal rate of transformation shows how output of one good increases and output of another good falls when there is a small reallocation in use of one factor in the production. The domestic marginal rate of transformation is:

$$MRT_{XY} = \frac{MPP_L^X}{MPP_L^Y} = \frac{MPP_K^X}{MPP_K^Y} \tag{17.1}$$

If production functions are linearly homogeneous, the MPP of factors of production depend only on the ratio in which factors of production are used. In Figure 17.2(b) if the ray $0_{Y_{ab}}$-1 is extended and if a line is drawn from 0_X^a parallel to 0_X^b-1, the intersection of these lines at point 2 is significant. At point 2, the *MPP* of labour used in the production of good *Y* in country *A* is the same as the *MPP* of labour in the production of good *Y* in country *B* and the *MPP* of labour used in the production of good *X* in country *A* is the same as the *MPP* of labour used in the production of good *X* in country *B* (as the ratio in which factors are used is identical – see common angle θ).

The implication is that point 2 on the contract curve (not drawn) defines a slope at point 2′ on the production possibility curve for country *A* (in Figure 17.2(a)) that is exactly the same as the slope at point 1′ on the production possibility curve for country *B*. Output levels of each good can be seen from the isoquant maps at point 1 ($\overline{Q_X^b}$ of good *X* for country *B* and $\overline{Q_y^b}$ of good *Y* for country *B*) and at point 2 ($\overline{Q_X^a}$ of good *X* for country *A* and $\overline{Q_y^a}$ of good *Y* for country *A*).

With free trade and competitive markets each country will face the same set of international prices. If the international set of prices are P_i in Figure 17.2(a) consumption preferences (assumed homothetic to the origin) are shown by the ray 0-*R*. This is the ratio which individuals in both countries prefer to consume goods (when the price ratio is P_i).

If production and consumption points for country *B* (1′ and C^b) are compared with production and consumption point for country *A*, with a price ratio P_i:

(i)   country *B* (the relatively labour-abundant country) will export good *X* (the labour-intensive good) for imports of good *Y* (the capital-intensive good);

(ii) country *A* (the relatively capital-abundant country) will export good *Y* (the capital-intensive good) for imports of good *X* (the labour-intensive good).

In Figure 17.2(a) country *B* exports 1′-3 of *X* for 3-c^b of *Y*. Country *A* exports 2′-4 of *Y* for 4-c^a of *X*. The 'trade triangles' are of equal size, so that the market clears at an international price ratio of P_i (sceptics – who believe that this result is 'fudged' by construction – might change the set of international prices to discover that at equilibrium – i.e. when markets clear and 'trade triangles' are equal – *A* will export *Y* and *B* will exports *X*).

In the Heckscher–Ohlin model the pattern of trade is determined by differences in relative factor endowments. Countries that are rich in capital export capital-intensive goods and countries that are relatively well endowed with labour export labour-intensive goods. (For further discussion of this model see Heller 1973 and Chachiolides 1973.)

17.4 Free trade and factor price equalisation

With reference to this neoclassical model of trade flows, it is possible to predict the impact of international trade on factor prices in both countries. If the above assumptions hold, Samuelson (1955) showed that it is possible to predict that free trade will bring about the equalisation of factor prices in both countries. This has already been implicitly illustrated with common relative factor prices (w/r)$_i$ in Figure 17.2(b).

This is an important result, for it means that trade flows can act as a *substitute* for international movement of factors of production. If factor prices are equalised and factors of production are paid according to their marginal productivity then this means that the marginal productivity of labour in industry *X* in country *A* is the same as the marginal product of labour in industry *X* in country *B*. There will be no incentive for labour to move from country *A* to country *B* (or vice versa). Similarly, there will be no incentive for capital to move if the same rate of return applies in each country. The outcome is Pareto optimal. There is a Pareto-efficient allocation of resources; world welfare (in Paretian terms) has been maximised.

To show how factor prices are equalised consider the assumptions in the neoclassical (Heckscher–Ohlin) model: (i) that there is perfect competition and (ii) that there are linearly

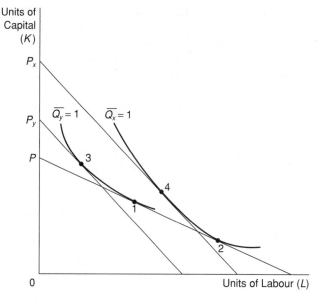

Figure 17.3
Factor intensity and factor prices

homogeneous production functions. Figure 17.3 (sometimes referred to as the Lerner–Pearce diagram[4]) indicates how a unique relationship can be plotted between commodity prices and factor prices. The slope of the isocost line shows the relative price of capital and labour. Initially, the relevant tangencies between the isocost line and isoquants for goods X and Y are at points 1 and 2. If, for simplicity, the isoquants relate to one unit of output for X and one unit for Y, the average cost for both goods is equal to 0-P. As there is perfect competition, price equals marginal cost equals average cost ($P = MC = AC$) and so the prices of the two products are equal. Average cost is equal because total cost, 0-P, in units of capital produces one unit of Y and one unit of X.[5]

To demonstrate the relationship between factor prices and commodity prices, assume that the relative price of labour increases. The slope of the isocost line in Figure 17.3 will increase. There will be a shift to a more capital-intensive form of production and the new tangency points are shown as 3 and 4, respectively. It is now clear that the average cost of producing X (the labour-intensive product) has increased. This is now shown by 0-P_x and is greater than the average cost of producing Y (0-P_y). There is a unique correspondence between commodity prices and factor prices – as the relative price of labour increases so the relative price of the labour-intensive product increases. It is also the case that, as the price of labour increases so both products become more capital-intensive in production.

Both pieces of information can be reported in Figure 17.4. The x-x and y-y rays show that as w/r (the relative price of labour) increases, both goods become more capital-intensive in production (K/L increases). Note that it is also assumed that there is no

4. For a discussion see Layard and Walters (1978).
5. The isocost line (see Chapter 3) refers to the total cost of producing the goods. If output on isoquant y and x respectively are (for argument) equal to 1 then the average cost (at tangencies 1 and 2) is equal to 0-P. In a perfectly competitive market, price equals marginal cost equals average cost (see Chapter 3). The isocost line is given by $C = rK + wL$ where C is a given cost outlay, w and r are the wage rate and rental price of capital respectively and L and K are the quantity of labour and capital respectively. Hence $rK = C - wL$, $K = C/r - w/rL$ and with $L = 0$ on the y-axis $K = C/r = P$. It follows that, at this point, the price of the two goods is identical (and equal to average cost as measured in units of capital K as 0-P).

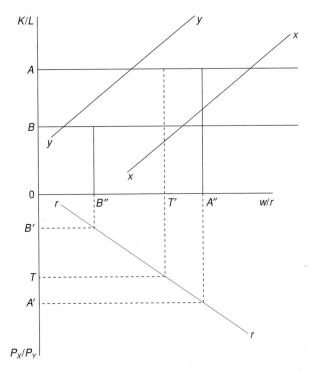

Figure 17.4
Factor price equalisation

factor-price reversal (i.e. good Y is more capital-intensive in production than X at any factor-price ratio). With reference to the lower section of Figure 17.4 the ray r-r shows that as w/r increases so does P_x/P_y (i.e. the labour-intensive good is most affected as the relative price of labour increases).

To discover the impact of international trade on factor prices add information concerning the two countries. In Figure 17.4 the capital-labour ratio for country A is recorded as 0-A and for country B as 0-B. Initially (i.e. prior to trade) commodity prices differ in the two countries with the relative price of the labour-intensive good lower in country B (0-B') than in country A (0-A'). The implication is that factor prices are such that the relative price of the labour-intensive good is lower in the labour-abundant country (0-B') than in the capital-abundant country (0-A').

With free trade, the relative price of commodities will be identical in the two countries (0-T) and the price of the factors of production will equalise (0-T'). The mechanism by which change occurs is straightforward. Country B has a comparative advantage in the production of commodity X but, as more resources are shifted into the production of commodity X, the relative price of labour is bid up (i.e. a shift from 0-B'' to 0-T'). Country A has a comparative advantage in the production of commodity Y but, as more resources are shifted into the production of commodity Y, the relative price of capital is bid up (i.e. a shift from 0-A'' to 0-T').

The assumptions inherent in this model guarantee that there will be Pareto efficiency in the world economy. They ensure that the real marginal product of a given factor is the same in both countries. However, the prediction concerning factor equalisation is very dependent on the preceding assumptions. For example, relax the assumption of no factor-price intensity reversal and there is now no unique relationship between commodity prices and factor price. In Figure 17.4 if good Y were more capital-intensive than commodity X at lower relative factor prices and good X more capital-intensive at higher prices then the y-y and x-x curves would intersect. Up to the intersection point

Table 17.1 Hourly wages in manufacturing in different countries (as a percentage of the US wage)

	1959	1979
Canada	82	95
Japan	11	82
Sweden	39	109
France	27	60
Italy	23	72
West Germany	29	107
United Kingdom	29	76
United States	100	100

Source: International Financial Statistics, United Nations Monthly Bulletin (cited in Ethier 1995).

(the reader might wish to redraw Figure 17.4 accordingly) as the price of labour increases, so the relative price of commodity *X* increases. After this point, an increase in the price of labour means that the relative price of *Y* increases (*Y* is now the labour-intensive good). The implication is that in the lower section of Figure 17.4 the line *r-r* becomes curvilinear. It is now U-shaped (with the minimum point at the intersection of *y-y* and *x-x* in the top section of the figure). If a curvilinear *r-r* function is drawn then the unique relationship between commodity prices and factor prices is lost. International trade may equalise commodity prices but the same relative price of commodities could be related to two sets of factor prices. (The reader can confirm this by making *r-r* U-shaped in Figure 17.4 and reading the factor prices relating to any relative commodity price on the horizontal axis).

What is the evidence on factor price equalisation? It is clear from Table 17.1 that factor prices are not equalised (the assumptions are too demanding). However, with the post-war growth of international trade there has been a reduction in the variance in the distribution of wages (for 1979 as compared to 1959). It cannot be asserted that this is because of the increase in international trade, as over this period there has also been an increase in the international movement of factors of production. Even so, the observation is consistent with (if not proof of) the proposition that international trade leads to a convergence of factor prices.

17.5 Revising assumptions: what if factors of production are specific?

The discussion in the previous sections illustrates how microeconomic theory can be applied to trade issues. The neoclassical model explains the paradox described above (that countries call for free trade, but opt for protection). However, when applied to determine the pattern of trade, the predictions of the Heckscher–Ohlin model may be questioned. It is clear that international trade has not brought about factor price equalisation. It is also clear that countries do not always export the good that uses intensively the factor that is in relative abundance. At the end of the Second World War the USA was unquestionably capital-intensive by comparison with other (exhausted) economies. However, early on, Leontief (1953) reported that the US appeared to import capital-intensive products. The famous 'Leontief paradox' or 'falsification' has attracted a literature in and of itself (concerning the validity of the test). However, is it possible that the neoclassical model (as defined above) is too abstract, too esoteric and too far removed from reality?[6]

One theme of this text is that conclusions depend on assumptions. The list of assumptions described in Section 17.4 seems very demanding and not a little unrealistic. Is it the case that this model should be abandoned in favour of research in a completely different direction? Or, can the assumptions of the model be reconsidered to shed further insight? If so, how much revision would be necessary to enable the model to offer greater insight on current trade issues?

Every model is inevitably an abstraction. The exercise here is to ascertain the sensitivity of models to assumptions. A variation of the factor endowment model is the *specific-factor model* whereby, in contrast to the Heckscher–Ohlin model, some factors of production (for example capital) are no longer considered homogeneous. What if capital was considered specific to a particular industry? A specific-factor model might be seen as a short-run variation of the Heckscher–Ohlin model. Factors which are mobile between industries in the long run may be fixed in the short run.

If capital in each industry (units of M in industry X and units of N in industry Y) is specific to that industry then the production functions for industries X and Y might be described as:

$$X = F_X(M_X, L_X) \tag{17.2}$$

$$Y = F_Y(N_Y, L_Y) \tag{17.3}$$

The total supply of M capital is used in the production of X:

$$M = M_X \tag{17.4}$$

The total supply of N capital is used in the production of Y:

$$N = N_Y \tag{17.5}$$

The total supply of labour is equal to that used in the X industry and in the Y industry:

$$L = L_X + L_Y \tag{17.6}$$

This indicates that capital which is used in the X industry (M) is quite specific to that industry and that all M is used in the production of X. Similarly, N is capital specific to the production of Y. Labour is assumed to be mobile between industries in the short run. If the assumption is made that, in the long run, capital in one industry can be moved to the other industry, then the 'specific factor model' describes short-run responses to changes. It is in this context that the neoclassical model is reassessed here.

To consider the impact of factor specificity, consider one of the 'key' predictions that emerge from the Heckscher–Ohlin model. The objective is to show how the Stolper–Samuelson prediction changes when the assumption is made that factors of production are specific to industries. As explained in Section 17.2, the Stolper–Samuelson theorem uses the basic assumptions of the model to conclude that:

> an increase in the relative price of a commodity will increase the real return to the factor used intensively in the industry (and reduce the return to the other factor).

To illustrate this result (once again), consider the top two panels (a and b) in Figure 17.5. Two goods X and Y are produced and the Y industry is relatively capital-intensive.

6. Theorems emerge from this model but may seem no more that academic curiosa. For, surely, the world cannot be described by the assumptions of the Heckscher–Ohlin model (as listed above)? The description of perfect competition (see Chapter 3) invokes a similar response and, again, there is a tendency to see the Heckscher–Ohlin model simply as a teaching device, with little to say about recent events or policy options.

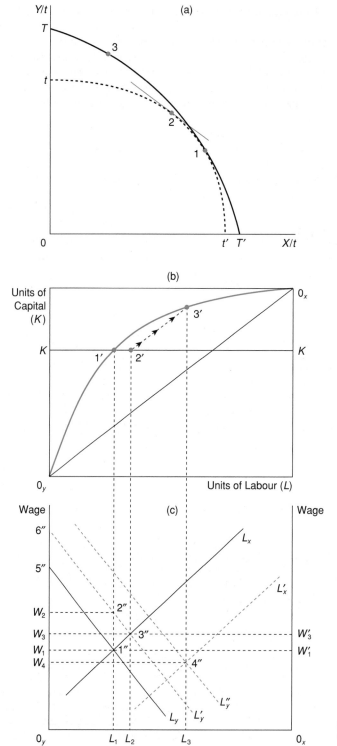

Figure 17.5
The specific factor model

Assume that the initial position is at point 1 on the production possibility curve T-T'. A change (e.g. the advent of international trade) means that the price of good Y increases. As described above, there is now an incentive to increase production of good Y and to shift to a point such as 3 on T-T'. The movement around the contract curve from $1'$ to $3'$ in panel 17.5(b) indicates that both goods become more labour-intensive in production (indicating that the price of capital has increased and the wage rate has fallen). The prediction would be described in the Stolper–Samuelson theorem.

However, now consider the impact of assuming that some factors of production are specific. Assume that capital used in the Y industry (N) cannot be moved to the X industry. The price of good Y increases but the solid line K-K in the Edgeworth–Bowley box (in panel b) indicates that there is no possibility that the amount of capital in the Y industry can be increased. While the neoclassical analysis predicts a move to $3'$, it is only possible to move to $2'$.

In panel (c) of Figure 17.5, the marginal value product is shown for labour in the two industries. (Note that the total supply of labour in the two industries is constant at 0_y-0_x and equal to the labour axis in panel (b).) The value of the marginal product in industry Y is equal to the marginal physical product MPP_y multiplied by the price of the good P_y.

$$VMP_y = P_y \cdot MPP_y \tag{17.7}$$

As the price of good Y increases, L_y (= VMP_y) shifts to the right (L_Y to L'_Y). In Figure 17.5(c) the implication of this is that wages increase from W_1 to W_2 in the Y industry. Wages have increased by a factor identical to the price increase of Y (so enabling workers in the Y industry to purchase as much Y as they once did but to purchase more X if they prefer).

By contrast, the implication for workers in the X industry is that the real wage has fallen. With the increase in the price of Y, workers in the X industry would be unable to purchase as much of good Y as they once could.[7] If the wage rate is lower in the X industry then L_1-L_2 workers will move from the X industry to the Y industry. The wage rate will fall (from W_2 to W_3) in the Y industry and increase (from W'_1 to W'_3) in the X industry (as workers move from X to Y). To retain full employment the wage rate will be W_3. Whether or not labour in both industries is better or worse off is a moot point. The wage rate (in units of Y) has now not increased as much as the price of Y. However, if labourers spend relatively more on good X (whose price has not changed) it is possible that they will yet be better off. Markusen *et al.* (1995) call this the 'neoclassical ambiguity'.

What of the return to capital? The return to capital can be seen in panel (c) by subtracting the payment to labour from the value of the product of labour in each industry. For example, while area 0_y-$5''$-$1''$-L_1 is equal to the value of the product of labour in the Y industry and area 0_y-W_1-$1''$-L_1 is the payment to labour, triangle W_1-$5''$-1 must be the return to capital in this two-factor model. Using this approach, at wage W_3, the return to capital has increased in the Y industry: it is now equal to area W_3-$6''$-$3''$. By the same measure it has fallen in the X industry (by area W'_1-$1''$-$3''$-W'_3).

By contrast with the Stolper–Samuelson theorem, when capital is specific (i.e. a specific-factors model), the prediction is that:

a relative increase in the price of a commodity benefits the specific factor used in that industry, reduces the real income of the other specific factor and has an ambiguous effect on the mobile factor.

If capital were *always* specific this is as far as the comparison goes. However, in the long run it is possible that capital may be transformed and may be relocated. As the rate

---

7. If there were wage inflexibility, so that wages in the X industry were identical to the wage paid in Y, there would be less than full employment (as the value marginal product has not increased in the X industry).

of return on capital is greater in the Y industry than in the X industry there is an incentive for capital to move to the Y industry (the payment to capital has fallen in the X industry even though the same amount of capital is employed in the X industry). In this case the Stolper–Samuelson theorem will describe a long-run equilibrium (by comparison with the short-run equilibrium that emerges in a specific-factor model).

If there were to be movement of capital in the long run then, in panel (b) of Figure 17.5 the path of adjustment may ultimately lead from 1' to 2' to 3' on the contract curve in panel (b). As the rate of return to capital in the Y industry exceeds that in the X industry, there is an incentive for capital to move into the Y industry. As this happens, the marginal product of labour will change in both industries. In panel (c) of Figure 17.5, it is clear that L'_y shifts to the right. With more capital in this industry the marginal product of labour will increase (L'_y shifts to L''_y). Conversely for the X industry, L_x shifts to the right to L'_x (the marginal product of labour falls as labour now has less capital with which to work). Ultimately, the new equilibrium is at the lower wage W_4 associated with the intersection of L'_x and L''_y at point 4" and an allocation of labour 0_y-L_3 to Y production and 0_x-L_3 to X production. At this point, the full long-run equilibrium defined in the Stolper–Samuelson theorem is realised.

With reference to the change in panel (a) of Figure 17.5, when capital is specific the increase in the price of Y causes shifts along t-t' in panel (a). The transformation curve when capital is not specific is T-T'. The shift from 1' to 2' in the Edgeworth–Bowley box represents the movement 1 to 2 around t-t' in panel (a) but, in the long run, there will be a movement to point 3' in panel (b) and to point 3 in panel (a).

Does this more detailed account of the response to a change in the price of Y offer any additional insight? A test by Magee (1980) compares the predictions of the Stolper–Samuelson theorem with those of a specific-factor model when political pressure against trade liberalisation is considered. The Stolper–Samuelson suggests that pressure for protection would come from *either* labour or capital. In the Stolper–Samuelson theorem, one factor gains at the final long-run equilibrium and one factor is worse off. It follows

Table 17.2 Political pressure for protection: testing the specific factor model

| | Position of labour | |
Position of capital	Protectionist	Free trade
Protectionist	Distilling Textiles Apparel Chemicals Plastics Rubber shoes Leather shoes Stone, etc. Iron/steel Cutlery Hardware Bearings Watches	Tobacco
Free trade	Petroleum	Paper Machinery Tractors Trucks Aviation

Source: Magee (1980).

that one factor would prefer trade liberalisation and one would reject it. By contrast, in a specific-factor model political pressure is industry-based. In the previous example (when a movement to free trade caused the relative price of Y to increase) *both* capital and labour employed in the Y industry might gain in the short run (as labour's welfare change depended on its consumption of the two goods).

Magee (1980) tested the proposition that attitudes concerning trade liberalisation would be divided between labour and the owners of capital. He found, instead, that attitudes were related to industry. In Table 17.2 the attitudes of capital and labour to the US trade liberalisation bill are recorded. The strong 'diagonal' distribution in the table indicates that in as many as 19 out of 22 industries *both* labour and the owners of capital shared the same position. The pattern of pressure depended on 'industry lines' rather than on 'factor ownership lines'.

17.6 Trade liberalisation and the costs of adjustment

The theoretical amendment introduced by altering the assumption concerning factor mobility between industries adds insight when dealing with policy issues. For example, an allowance for factor specificity shows that trade liberalisation may be far less easy to achieve than would be implied by the 'standard' neoclassical model. Adjustment does not take place by costless shifts around the production possibility curve (as implied in Section 17.2).

To highlight adjustment costs, Figure 17.6 considers the same adjustment but this time the analysis focuses on the position of workers in the X industry. In Figure 17.5 panel (c) wages were measured in terms of good Y. After the increase in the price of good Y, the wage rate initially increased for those working in the Y industry. It increased by just the same increase as the price (recall that initially these workers were able to buy just as much of Y and more of X, as the price of X had not changed). To highlight the position of those employed in the X industry consider the analysis in terms of the relative fall in the price of good X. With free trade the relative price of good X will fall. In Figure 17.6 the assumption is now that wages are set in terms of good X.

When the relative price of good X (P_X) falls (holding constant the price of Y) the value of marginal product of workers in industry X falls (as the value of the marginal product VMP_L^X equals $P_X \cdot MP_L^X$). Before the advent of free trade the wage was W_1 in both industries

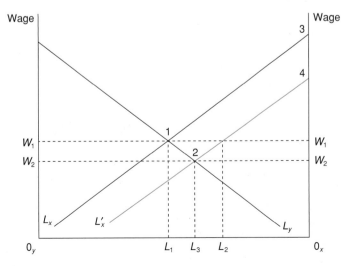

Figure 17.6
Costs of adjustment

(with perfect competition wages must be equal in both industries at long-run equilibrium). The demand for labour in the Y industry is illustrated by the value of marginal product L_y and the value of marginal product in the X industry is shown by the value of marginal product L_x. There is full employment with O_Y-L_1 employed in the Y industry and O_x-L_1 employed in the X industry.

With a fall in the price of good X (as a consequence of cheap imports), L_x to shift to the right (to L'_x). If, in the short run there is no possibility at all of adjustment, this simply creates unemployment for those employed in the X industry (where the value of marginal product has fallen). The unemployment created by the trade liberalisation is equal to L_1-L_2. There are unemployment costs until workers who once were employed in the X industry find jobs in the Y industry. This may mean re-training. It may mean households moving geographically within the country. It takes time and it means that, in the short run, there are costs of adjustment. Wage inflexibility and restrictions in the labour market (e.g. minimum wage legislation) only add to time and costs required for adjustment.

In the medium term, when labour moves, the wage rate will fall (workers made redundant in the X industry seek work in the Y industry). The new equilibrium is at point at 2 in Figure 17.6; with O_Y-L_3 employed in the Y industry and O_x-L_3 employed in the X industry. The economy is still not at a long-run equilibrium, as capital is specific in each industry (only in the long run will capital move). There will be further costs of adjustment to face as capital moves from industry X to industry Y. (The return to capital in the X industry has fallen, as shown by the difference in the triangle W_1-1-3 under L_x and above W_1 and the triangle W_2-2-4 under L'_x and above W_2 – see the previous section).

For estimates of adjustment costs consequent on changes in trade policy see Milner (1996). Adjustment costs are difficult to estimate but if (as the analysis of Figure 17.6 shows) they are relevant, the question arises as to whether government should provide adjustment assistance. In Figure 17.6 factors of production in the declining industry (both capital and labour) lose during the process of adjustment and are likely to resist trade liberalisation. Some have argued that government should take measures to deal with impediments that might exist to the adjustment process (i.e. to ease transition). Surely, it makes sense to ease transition if, at the end of the day, there will be trade liberalisation (and a potential Pareto improvement)?

In the USA a policy was introduced in 1962 by which workers and companies who convince the International Trade Commission that they had been hurt by import competition (consequent on tariff reductions) are eligible for assistance. It was introduced to compensate workers for tariff cuts under the Kennedy Round of multilateral negotiations and, to this extent, appeared to expedite progress towards free trade. From 1962 to 1974 the number of cases helped was small but from 1974 the number of cases receiving assistance rose rapidly.[8] The Trade Act of 1974 increased the generosity of TAA (Trade Adjustment Assistance) benefits and expanded eligibility. By the early 1980s there were concerns about growing costs and, in 1981, a set of amendments to the Trade Act reduced TAA cash benefits. The incoming Reagan administration tightened enforcement of the eligibility rules, so that by 1982 total recipients dropped to 30,000 and costs dropped to $103 million. However, in 1993, as part of the push to secure the passage of the North

8. One objective of this policy appeared to be to win support from labour for the Trade Expansion Act and for the then forthcoming Kennedy Round. It was introduced in 1962 and by 1974 (when it was modified) the International Trade Commission had taken up an average of 22 cases per year. Workers had been certified for benefits in fewer than 40 per cent of those cases. Adjustment assistance compensated workers for the costs of unemployment (incomes of the unemployed were maintained at three-quarters of the levels earned before job loss). However, recipients were unemployed for longer periods than those with unemployment insurance and were more likely to drop out of the labour force (Richardson 1980).

American Free Trade Agreement (NAFTA), Congress created a separate adjustment programme (NAFTA-TAA). This was for workers displaced by trade with, or plant relocation
to, Canada or Mexico. The Clinton administration committed to assisting secondary
workers (upstream and downstream finishers) in 1998. By the early 2000s, trade adjustment assistance had evolved into a programme that provided generous support for a limited number of workers. In 2002 the political climate was favourable for an extension
of the programme. The Bush administration wanted congressional renewal of trade promotion authority. In exchange, Congress demanded substantial expansion of the trade
adjustment programme. This resulted in the Trade Adjustment Assistance reform Act of
2002. The Act was expected to: (i) double the number of TAA recipients and (ii) more
than triple the total cost of the programme to almost $2 billion annually. The 2002 Act
introduced new elements such as wage insurance and health credits.

Is such assistance justified? The following criteria may prove helpful in formulating a
response:

(a) *Equity:* Banks and Tumlir (1986) question the argument that governments should offer
trade adjustment assistance on grounds of equity. Why should only trade-displaced
workers be assisted when other changes (e.g. technological improvement) also causes
unemployment? There is no evidence to suggest that trade-displaced workers are more
economically disadvantaged than non-trade-displaced workers.

(b) *Efficiency:* It is said that there are efficiency gains from the use of trade adjustment
assistance, but how robust are these arguments? Trade adjustment assistance may be
required if wage rigidity and labour market congestion should increase the duration
of job search, resulting in lost output (i.e. a form of externality argument for government intervention). But, set against this, not all job-search is a waste (if it means
that workers are placed where they will be more productive). Government assistance
may shorten job search but make it less 'productive'. The debate demands an empirical response.

Baicker and Rehavi (2004) argue that trade adjustment benefits might increase the
length of time the average worker is unemployed. They refer to empirical evidence
relating to the provision of unemployment benefits and point to 'a well documented
spike in the likelihood of an unemployed worker becoming re-employed at 26 weeks
– that is, when unemployment benefits expire' (p. 248). They also argue that making
benefits more generous may both increase take-up and increase the duration of
unemployment; they refer to empirical evidence of 'an elasticity of take up with
respect to benefit generosity of around 0.5 or higher in the unemployment insurance
program' (p. 248). Moreover, they argue that evidence suggests that a longer spell of
unemployment does not lead to a better job match. Workers unemployed for long
periods can be harmed through stigmatisation. Decker and Corson (1995) found that
the training provided through trade adjustment assistance does not serve to increase
re-employment wages.

One issue that arises when considering efficiency is the possibility that trade
adjustment assistance creates a 'moral hazard' problem if companies who might in
any case go bankrupt hold on to argue that the problem was import competition.
Anderson (1993) reports that firms play the system (through temporary layoff and
recall of workers) when there is unemployment insurance. However, Baicker and
Rehavi (2004) argue that the need for firms to demonstrate a decline in employment
due to trade might mitigate this kind of moral hazard.

There are also rent-seeking issues (see Chapter 14) if there is an incentive for
lobbies to expend further resources lobbying for more help. While it might be argued
that investment in human capital is more risky and government should help bear
insurance costs, it is not clear that trade adjustment assistance is the best option.

Moreover, it follows, inevitably, that if the government does become involved, and tax finance must be raised, there will be distortive costs in raising the finance (see Chapter 13).

(c) *Political expediency:* One argument that has been made for trade adjustment assistance is that it helps facilitate the passage of trade liberalisation legislation. The small size of the TAA programme in the USA prior to 2000 suggests that its role was more of political expediency. However, this argument is spurious. Should groups within the community be bribed to accept legislation that is for the good of community? (Should the community be held to ransom?)

To market economists such intervention is questionable.[9] There would be broader agreement that government policy should help correct for market imperfections which slowed up the adjustment process (e.g. trade union restrictive practices, minimum wage legislation, lack of information). Whatever your view, the existence of adjustment costs is an important consideration when analysing trade liberalisation policies. The point of this example is to show how an amendment to one assumption of the Heckscher–Ohlin model (the neoclassical microeconomic theory of trade) has served to explain the controversy surrounding political initiatives to increase trade liberalisation and shed insight on the associated adjustment costs. Discussion of government intervention to deal with trade adjustment is informed by such theory. To those who find the assumptions of the neoclassical model just too unrealistic, the challenge is to change them and improve the theory so that it does inform life's decisions!

17.7 The costs of protection

The argument so far has been that, while the neoclassical general equilibrium model appears esoteric, by judicious reconsideration of assumptions it can offer significant insight on policy concerns. The example focused on the assumption of factor specificity. In this section the theme is again that the model is useful (in a practical sense); this is shown by reconsidering the general equilibrium model in partial equilibrium terms.

In this section the neoclassical model is applied to consider costs of protection. Returning to the neoclassical model (without factor specificity), the task of identifying the costs of protection is relatively straightforward. Losses are a consequence of denying a country the 'gains from trade'. In effect, the analysis discussed in Section 17.2 (and in Figure 17.1) is simply 'inverted'. To begin this analysis, international trade is restrained by an import tariff (i.e. a tax on imports). At the outset it proves helpful to distinguish between 'small' and 'large' countries:

(a) The *small* country case
A 'small' country is a country unable to influence the terms of trade. With reference to Chapter 3, such a country can be viewed as a 'price-taker'. It has no bargaining power, and no matter how much it imports it will always face the same import price. In Figure 17.7, the initial situation is now the free trade situation. Production is at point 1 on the production possibility curve T-T' and consumption at C on community indifference curve CIC_3. The international terms of trade (i.e. the relative price of imports – good X – to exports – good Y – on the world market) are shown by P_i. It is clear that the country exports good Y and imports good X. If an import tax were introduced (set at a per unit rate of t_1 per unit), the relative prices of the two goods

---

9. The US government has also managed special protection by restricting imports in order to slow adjustment by import-competing industries (Caves *et al.* 1996) – equally questionable!

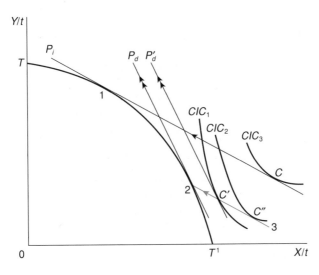

Figure 17.7
Costs of protection: a general equilibrium analysis

(X and Y) differ domestically from the international terms of trade. If on the world market the relative price is π_x/π_y, within the country relative prices are $P_x/P_y = (\pi_x + t_1)/\pi_y$. The domestic set of relative prices is shown in Figure 17.7 as P_d.

Protection increases the domestic price of good X, so that home producers have an incentive to increase output. The production point shifts on the transformation frontier from point 1 to point 2. Consumers equate their marginal rate of substitution to the domestic price ratio, so that consumption shifts from C to C'. From the production point 2 it is possible to trade along the international price ratio – along constraint 2-3 (parallel to P_i). Equilibrium is found along 2-3 at the point where the domestic price ratio (P_d') cuts 2-3 at a tangency with a community indifference curve (here CIC_1 – dictating consumption point C').

The volume of imports falls, but the tariff is not 'prohibitive' (i.e. the tax has not been set so high as to prohibit all imports). The government raises revenue on imports that still come into the country. Consumption in the economy is still outside the production possibility curve T-T'. However, there are welfare losses as a consequence of denying the full 'gains from trade'. The economy is now only able to reach the community indifference curve CIC_1, rather than CIC_3. These losses can be disaggregated:

(i) If there had been a change in production (i.e. production had shifted from point 1 to point 2) but consumers had been able to consume at free trade prices, consumption would be at C''. The only impact of a change in production (i.e. a *production* cost) would be a welfare loss shown by the movement from CIC_3 to CIC_2.

(ii) The further welfare loss occurs because consumers must equate their preferences to the distorted set of prices P_d. This additional welfare loss (i.e. the movement from CIC_2 to CIC_1) can be referred to as a *consumption* cost.

In this analysis students sometimes wonder what 'anchors' the new equilibrium, point C''. If there is a tariff on imports then, surely, the new equilibrium should be on the production possibility curve T-T'? The answer is that this is not a *prohibitive* tariff. The tariff reduces imports but does not eradicate them. There are still some gains from trade but these gains have been reduced. It is still possible to consume outside the domestic production possibility curve T-T'. The extent to which the tariff reduces imports determines the new equilibrium C'. Of course, if in the extreme the tariff was set so high that it removed (prohibited) imports then the new equilibrium would be on the production possibility curve.

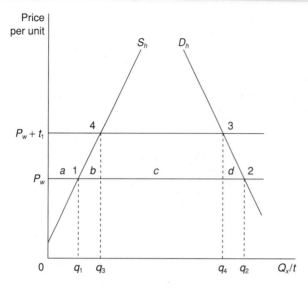

Figure 17.8
Costs of protection: a partial
equilibrium analysis

In all of this it appears, once again, that discussion of a general equilibrium analysis is removed from reality. What does it mean to say that the costs of protection are a reduction in welfare from CIC_3 to CIC_1? If your first appointment was as adviser to a Ministry of Trade, how helpful would it be to report that a proposed import tax would reduce welfare from CIC_3 to CIC_1?

However, the analysis can be reformulated to yield more specific 'answers'. The approach is to consider the same price change but, this time, in terms of a partial equilibrium analysis. In Figure 17.8, with free trade and domestic or home supply and demand curves S_h and D_h imports are $0q_2 - 0q_1$ (associated with points 2 and 1) at a world price of P_w. When the tariff of t_1 per unit is imposed the domestic price is $P_w + t_1$ and imports fall from $0q_2 - 0q_1$ to $0q_4 - 0q_3$ (associated with points 3 and 4). The welfare changes are summarised in Table 17.3.

In Figure 17.8 the effect of trade protection is estimated with reference to welfare changes for consumers, producers and the government. As discussed in Chapter 4, the welfare impact on consumers is estimated by the change in consumer surplus (which arises as a consequence of the price change). When the price to consumers increases from P_w to $P_w + t_1$ the loss of consumer surplus is shown by area P_w-(P_w+t_1)-3-2. The welfare loss to consumers reported in Table 17.3 is therefore the negative sum of areas $a + b + c + d$. Turning to producers, the impact on welfare can be estimated (as in Chapter 3) by reference to a change in producer surplus $(P_w$-(P_w+t_1)-4-1). With a rise in price from P_w to $P_w + t_1$ the gain to producers is area a. Producers are able to charge a higher price for the original ('free trade') production $(0$-$q_1)$ and to increase production from 0-q_1 to 0-q_3. They are not liable to the import tax and are able to charge a higher price as competition from abroad (i.e. imports) is taxed; domestic producers sell at $P_w + t_1$ per unit.

Table 17.3 The welfare effects of an import tax

Consumers	$-a$	$-b$	$-c$	$-d$
Producers	$+a$			
Taxpayers			$+c$	
Net (country) Changes		$-b$		$-d$

There is another impact on welfare. Area c is tariff revenue to the government, on each unit imported a tax of t_1 is levied, so that t_1 multiplied by the volume of imports $0\text{-}q_4 - 0\text{-}q_3$ measures area c. The government gains but in a prescriptive neoclassical approach the government is considered a beneficent decision-maker. Government acts in the 'best' interests of the economy and, while consumers pay the tax (area c), this can be used for government expenditure on behalf of taxpayers (or to reduce taxes elsewhere). Area c is therefore a transfer within the economy.

When considering the net losses to the country it is necessary also to note that, while area a is a loss to consumers, it is a gain to producers. This is also a transfer within the economy. In net terms, the costs of protection are shown by triangles b and d. As there is nothing to offset these losses, they are often referred to as the 'deadweight losses' of protection. In Figure 17.9 it can be seen that triangle d is a 'consumption loss' (shown as the difference between being at point C'' on CIC_2 and point C' on CIC_1 in Figure 17.7) because consumers would pay this much more than the free trade import price for the imports ($q_4\text{-}q_2$) which are no longer available at that price. Triangle b in Figure 17.9 is the production loss (the difference between being at point C on CIC_3 and point C'' on point CIC_2 in Figure 17.7) because ($q_1\text{-}q_3$) would cost only P_w per unit to purchase abroad but costs the integral under S_h between q_1 and q_3 to produce at home.

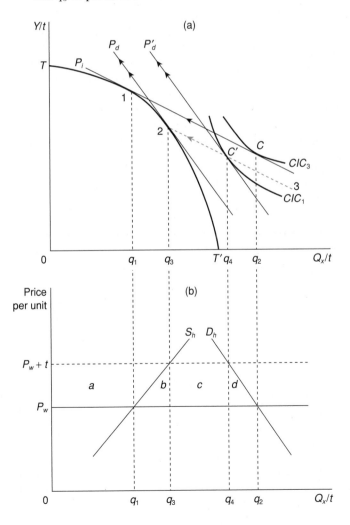

Figure 17.9
Costs of protection

Having identified the welfare changes, the deadweight losses can be estimated as the areas of the triangles b and d. The area of a triangle is $1/2 \times$ base $\times$ height. Therefore the area of $d = \frac{1}{2}t\partial q_s$, where t is the tax rate (so many pounds per unit) and ∂q_s is the change in quantity supplied. The area of $a = \frac{1}{2} \cdot t \cdot \partial q_d$ where ∂q_d is the change in the quantity demanded. While, *ex post* it is possible to ascertain the impact of the tax on the quantity supplied and the quantity demanded, *ex ante* the task is to estimate this impact. The way forward is to use estimates of the price elasticities of supply (η) and demand (ε). The definition of the price elasticity of supply η is $(\partial q_s/\partial p)(p/q_s)$ and for the price elasticity of demand, ε, is $(\partial q_d/\partial p)(p/q_d)$ so that $\partial q_s = \eta \partial p \cdot q_s/p$ and $\partial q_d = \varepsilon \partial p \cdot q_d/p$.

By substitution (and from Figure 17.8):

$$\text{area } b = \frac{1}{2} \cdot t\eta \partial p \cdot q_s/p_w = \frac{1}{2} \cdot t^2\eta \cdot q_s/p_w \tag{17.8}$$

$$\text{area } d = \frac{1}{2} \cdot t\varepsilon \cdot \partial p \cdot q_d/p_w = \frac{1}{2} \cdot t^2\varepsilon \cdot q_d/p_w \tag{17.9}$$

so that the cost of protection is:

$$\text{area } (b + d) = (t^2/2p_w)(\varepsilon q_d + \eta q_s) \tag{17.10}$$

This can also be estimated as $\frac{1}{2}t^2eM_0$ where e is the price elasticity of demand for imports and M_0 the initial (pre-tariff) level of imports. Examples of deadweight losses are reported in Table 17.4.

Hufbauer and Elliot (1994) estimate the welfare effects of some tariffs in the USA. The information in Table 17.4 includes consumer surplus loss $(a + b + c + d)$; producer gain (a) and deadweight loss $(b + d)$. These are estimates of the resource allocation costs of imposing the tariff. They assume no other difficulties in estimation and they are 'static' estimates (computed by a comparison of the outcome without and with protection). The example emphasises the more 'practical' nature of an analysis which, in general equilibrium mode (Figure 17.7), may have appeared somewhat esoteric. When the costs of protection were identified in the general equilibrium model they were estimated as the distances between community indifference curve (between points C-C'' and points C''-C' respectively). What value is there in telling any Minister of Trade that the costs are the differences between CIC_3 and CIC_1? If this appears a limitation then it is important to recognise that a different analysis of this very model will yield more practical insight. Analysing the same change via a partial equilibrium analysis reveals the *same* costs and allows the same costs to be

Table 17.4 Welfare effects of US tariffs (as reported 1994)

Industry	Tariff	Consumer cost (million $)	Producer gain (million $)	Deadweight loss (million $)
Rubber footwear	20	208	55	12
Women's shoes	10	376	70	11
Ceramic tiles	19	139	45	2
Luggage	16.5	211	16	26
Frozen orange juice concentrate	30	281	101	35
Glass and glass ware	11	266	162	9
Chinaware	11	102	18	2
Women's purses	13.5	148	16	13
Costume jewelry	9	103	46	5

Source: Adapted from G.C. Hufbauer and K.A. Elliot *Measuring the Costs of Protection in the United States* (Washington DC Institute for International Economics 1994).

estimated in terms of a *numeraire* (money). Here is resonance with the demands of practical policy decisions! Policy-makers will be impressed to hear that you have estimated the costs of protection at (say) £30 million per annum. (Your position, as adviser to the Minister of Trade, is secure and promotion is on its way!) However, the important point is that this estimate has no meaning except in the context of the general equilibrium model (described in Chapter 11 and applied here).

Figure 17.9 illustrates the relationship between general equilibrium analysis and partial equilibrium analysis. In both cases the introduction of the import tariff reduces import from q_1-q_2 to q_3-q_4. The welfare effects that were highlighted in general equilibrium analysis can be established in the partial equilibrium analysis. From the partial equilibrium analysis, estimates of the effect of the import tariff on welfare are possible. But remember that this analysis is premised on a number of assumptions (as noted in Chapters 3 and 4). There are still a number of qualifications to be borne in mind when reporting these estimates of the costs of protection. For example:

(1) If consumer surplus loss is estimated, it must be measured in terms of constant utility demand curves (see Chapter 3). Note also that demand curves are not always linear as illustrated.

(2) The model assumes that foreign goods are perfect substitutes in demand for domestically produced items (see Husted and Melvin 1998 for analysis when this assumption is relaxed).

(3) Consumer behaviour may also depend on expectations (so that demand curves may shift when a tariff is introduced, if this raised expectations about future price changes).

(4) In practice, estimates of the effects of tariffs are often approximations (based on average tariff rates).

(5) The estimates may require amendment, to the extent that other divergences exist between private and social cost exist (i.e. there may be 'second best' considerations – see Chapter 11).

(6) Balance of payments (and exchange rate) effects have been ignored.

(7) If future costs are to be reported, a discount factor has to be applied to add up costs over time (see Chapter 6). If estimates are required over a period of time, costs in the future will be worth less than costs now and a discount rate will be required to produce estimates in terms of present value (see Chapter 8).

(8) The estimates refer to resource changes in the absence of any dynamic considerations (i.e. they are static estimates). For example, in Figure 17.8 it may be argued that protection will cause the supply curve S_h to shift to the right. The 'infant industry' argument suggests that there is a learning process. If an industry is protected, producers may become more adept at producing the goods and the supply curve will shift downwards. (For an analysis of the effect of such changes see Section 17.8.) However, while the 'infant industry' argument stresses improved efficiency consequent on protection, note that it might be argued that protection 'feather-beds' home producers against competitive forces, so that they become less innovative and less cost-conscious. In this case, the supply curve would shift to the left. In either event, it will be necessary to amend estimates of the welfare costs of protection to allow for such dynamic changes.

Throughout, it should also be remembered that protection will alter the distribution of income between factors of production (capital and labour) (see Section 17.2) and no close account has been taken of this effect when reporting the impact of the introduction of an import tariff in terms of deadweight loss.

To summarise the costs of tariff protection in a single figure is inevitably a difficult task. However, estimates can be provided for policy-makers on the basis of a theory which uses neoclassical microeconomics. While allowance must be made for a large

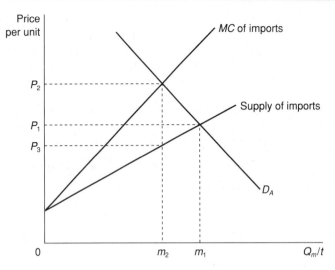

Figure 17.10
Protection in a 'large' country

number of potentially important qualifications, estimates of the costs of introducing a trade tax can be provided. More generally, the costs identified in an abstract general equilibrium model can be given practical relevance, notwithstanding the limitations that apply when using the neoclassical general equilibrium model.

(b) *The large country case*

The analysis so far suggests that policy-makers would be foolish to engage in protection, as there are clear welfare losses. The conclusion rested on many qualifications and, in this section, consideration is given to one assumption. The welfare effects of trade protection are sensitive to the assumption that the country is a 'small' country, i.e. that it is a 'price-taker'. By contrast, a 'large' country is a country that can exert an influence on the terms of trade (e.g. if the country imports less its impact on demand is such that the price on the world market will fall). In Figure 17.10 the implication is the upward-sloping supply curve for imports for the country. The upward-sloping supply curve shows that the price of imports rises as country A imports more. Country A is having an impact on price because it is 'large'.

As discussed in Chapter 11, if the supply curve is upward-sloping (and the purchaser enjoys a monopsony position) the marginal cost of a good exceeds its price. If p_i is the world price of good X, import costs are p_iM (where M is the level of imports). The marginal cost of imports (MC) can be defined as:

$$MC = -\frac{\partial(p_iM)}{\partial M} = p_i + \frac{M\partial p_i}{\partial M} = p_i(1 + 1/\eta) \tag{17.11}$$

where η is the supply elasticity of imports.

For any country, the 'optimum' level of imports is the level at which the marginal benefit of imports equals the marginal costs of imports. In Figure 17.10 this occurs with an import level of 0-m_2, where marginal benefit (measured by willingness to pay) is equal to marginal cost. With free trade the world price is P_1 where demand D_A cuts the supply of imports curve and imports are 0-m_1 and the level of imports is greater than 'optimum'. There is a case for an 'optimum' import tax (t^*) equal to P_2-$P_3/0$-P_3. If this were introduced, price would rise to P_2 and imports would fall to 0-m_2.

In what sense is this an 'optimum tariff'? As already noted, the introduction of a tariff will alter the distribution of income within the country. The introduction of the tariff means that consumers are worse off (imports have been reduced and the price has risen). However, the country has gained as the import price has fallen from P_1 to P_3. The improvement in the terms of trade offsets the welfare loss associated with a reduction in imports. This 'efficiency' gain may cause equity concerns (especially if the imported good is important for low-income consumers). Note also that the gains enjoyed by this country are enjoyed at the expense of those countries that supply the imports. A fall in the import price means a reduction in the price that exporters will receive. It is important to emphasise that the tariff may be Pareto efficient for the country that imposes it but it is not Pareto efficient for the world as a whole. It follows that those countries supplying this good may retaliate by imposing an import tax themselves. Whether or not such retaliation will ultimately reduce welfare for the country that initiates such action is not obvious (see Johnson 1953). However, the possibility of retaliation should be considered in any policy decision to set an 'optimum' tariff.

17.8 'Optimum' trade intervention: the case for export taxes

Once again, how does theory inform policy? How helpful is the optimum tariff theory? The main principle that has been illustrated is that, if a country cannot affect its terms of trade, then protection may reduce welfare (given the set of qualifications noted in Section 17.5) but a 'large' country can enhance national welfare by trade intervention. In this section the objective is to *apply* this principle. The policy question is: 'should countries levy export taxes and, if so, at what rate should they be levied?'

In Figure 17.11 the demand and supply curves of the home country are depicted as D_h and S_h respectively. At a world price of P_w domestic production is 0-q_4, of which 0-q_1 is consumed domestically (so that 0-$q_4 - 0$-q_1 is exported). An export tax (of t_1 per unit) lowers the price producers receive from exported goods to $P_w - t_1$. Domestic production falls to 0-q_3 and domestic consumption increases to 0-q_2. Producers are prepared to sell the good in the 'home' market provided that they achieve the same price $P_w - t_1$ as they would receive had the good been exported. Exports fall to 0-$q_3 - 0$-q_2.

The welfare effects of the export tax can be seen in Table 17.5. Producer surplus is reduced by the sum of areas, a, b, c, d and e. Area d is tax revenue, and the sum of areas

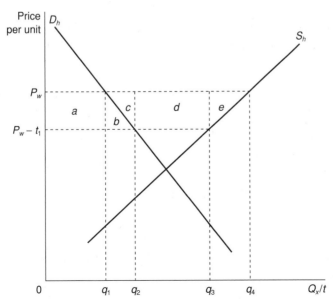

Figure 17.11
Export tax: 'small' country

Table 17.5 The welfare effects of an export tax: small country case

Consumers	+a	+b			
Producers	−a	−b	−c	−d	−e
Taxpayers				+d	
Net changes			−c		−e

a and *b* is additional consumer surplus. Area *b* is the loss due to domestic 'over-consumption' and area *e* is the loss due to domestic 'under-production'. Note that the export tax acts as a subsidy to home consumption and a tax on home production. As can be seen in Table 17.5 the deadweight losses are shown by the triangles *c* and *e*.

In this case, the use of an export tax is questionable. If the country has virtually no impact on world prices there are only deadweight losses. Tanzi (1991) analyses the impact of an export tax on coffee production in Haiti. Haiti's share of world production is almost insignificant. Intuitively, it is unlikely that Haiti would be able to influence the world price of coffee. The export tax levied amounted to a very high proportional tax on the income of coffee producers (equivalent to an average income tax rate of 25–40 per cent) and this made producers (many of whom were the poor of Haiti) the most heavily taxed group in Haiti. As described in Figure 17.11, the tax led to a reduction in coffee production and a shift of production into other crops (an adjustment which took time and which proved costly). The country's resources were used less efficiently (some land being reassigned to the production of subsistence products). Table 17.6 provides a comparison of the periods 1959–64 and 1969–72. It shows that, as predicted in Figure 17.11, home consumption increased while home production fell. Exports declined over the period.

By contrast, consider the case of an export tax when the country is a 'large' country. In the case when the country is a monopoly supplier the terms of trade can be improved by using an export tax to reduce supply. In Figure 17.12 the quantity of exports is shown along the horizontal axis and the price of exports in terms of imports (the terms of trade) along the vertical axis. D_f is the foreign demand curve for exports, MR_d is the marginal revenue curve to the exporting country. MC_d is the domestic marginal cost curve for the production of the exported good. Free trade equilibrium is at point 1 when exports are $0\text{-}q_1$ and price is $0\text{-}P_1$.

At the free trade point, marginal cost equals average revenue (and not marginal revenue). It follows that, for the country, free trade is not optimum. The optimum situation for the country is that export level at which marginal cost equals marginal revenue. This occurs at output $0\text{-}q_2$.

At this output, the price of exports will rise to $0\text{-}P_2$. An optimum export tax rate (t^*) of $P_2\text{-}P_3/0\text{-}P_3$ would cause exports to fall from $0\text{-}q_1$ to $0\text{-}q_2$. The optimum point on the demand curve D_f is point 2. This tax rate can be described as the excess of average over marginal revenue divided by average revenue. In Figure 17.12 the terms of trade have improved (the export price has increased from $0\text{-}P_1$ to $0\text{-}P_2$) so that the total gain is area $P_1\text{-}P_2\text{-}2\text{-}3$ minus triangle 3-1-4.

Table 17.6 The effects of the export tax in Haiti 1959–64 and 1969–72

Years	Coffee Production (average: thousand bags)	Coffee Consumption (average: thousand bags)
1959–64	611	181
1969–72	520	205

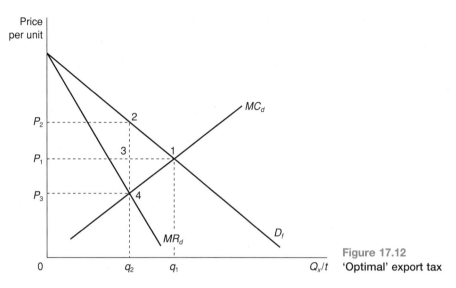

Figure 17.12 'Optimal' export tax

If t^* is the 'optimum' export tax rate and $|e_x|$ = the absolute value of the price elasticity of export demand, it follows that:

$$t_x = 1/|e_x| \tag{17.12}$$

To derive the 'optimum' tax, note (from Chapter 2) that marginal revenue is $P(1 - (1/e_x))$, so

$$\frac{P_2 P_3}{0\text{-}P_2} = \frac{P - P(1 - (1/|e_x|))}{P} \tag{17.13}$$

and, therefore, $t_x^* = 1/|e_x|$,

This outcome can be described as 'optimum' but (as emphasised above) only under certain assumptions. For example, it must be assumed that there is perfect competition in the country and there are no domestic distortions. It is implicit that: (a) the government spends the revenue raised wholly on the importable product; (b) the expenditure of the revenue does not affect the domestic demand for exportables; (c) demand is given, so that foreigners do not alter their taxes on trade in response to the home country's export tax or tariff. Notice, also, that no account is made of the impact of reduced exports on the balance of trade. It is assumed that the desired income distribution is maintained by a costless income distribution policy. The objective is to increase welfare for those in the home country, even if this is at the expense of the welfare of foreign countries. Foreigners have lost consumer surplus equal to P_1-P_2-2-1.

The application is another example of the use of monopoly power (as discussed in Chapter 11). However, it is unlikely that a country will be the sole supplier of any good. Far more likely is the prospect that a country is an 'important' supplier on the world market. To amend the analysis it is necessary to distinguish between the elasticity of demand for the good and the elasticity of demand for the exports of a particular country. To proceed, begin with the identity that the country in question is country i and that country i's exports X_i equal world exports X minus other countries' X_o exports:

$$X_i = X - X_o \tag{17.14}$$

so that:

$$dX_i/dP = dX/dP - dX_o/dP \tag{17.15}$$

or:

$$dX_i/dP \cdot P/X_i \cdot X_i/X = dX/dP \cdot P/X - dX_o/dP \cdot P/X_o \cdot X_o/X \tag{17.16}$$

Table 17.7 Estimates of 'optimum' export tax

	Supply elasticity or the country	Share in world market	Actual duty	High estimated optimal duty	Low estimated optimal duty
Coffee*					
Brazil	0.6	17.9	59.0	47.57	30.85
Colombia	0.6	17.60	13.0	37.59	20.47
Uganda	0.6	2.7	28.0	6.31	3.67
Cocoa**					
Ghana	0.8	23.4	62.0	46.73	43.24

Notes: *demand elasticity is equal to –0.2, or –0.6, supply elasticity for others 0.3.
      **demand elasticity –0.3 or –0.4, supply elasticity for others 0.3.

so:

$$d_i \cdot c = d - s_o(1 - c) \tag{17.17}$$

where d_i is the price elasticity of demand for the country's exports; s_o is the price elasticity of supply for other countries' exports and c is the share of the country's exports in world exports (note that $X_o/X = 1 - c$). Following Pugel (2004):

$$d_i = \frac{d - s_o(1 - c)}{c} \tag{17.18}$$

and, setting the optimum export tax at $t^* = 1/|d_i|$:

$$t^* = \frac{c}{|d - s_o(1 - c)|} \tag{17.19}$$

Once again, the analysis can be applied to appraise the performance of developing countries. Sanchez-Ugarte and Modi (1987) rely on this general approach to estimate the 'optimum' export tax for a number of developing countries. They use long-run supply estimates (as estimated by Askari and Cummings 1977) and demand elasticities (estimated by a number of authors) together with estimates of the share of world exports supplied by particular countries. Table 17.7 provides a sample of their results for the commodities coffee and cocoa. The estimates of 'high' optimum duty and 'low' optimum duty for different products arise because 'high' and 'low' estimates of demand elasticity are used. Having considered different countries and different commodities, Sanchez-Ugarte and Modi (1987: 296) conclude 'most developing countries seem to overtax exports as a result of high "explicit" and "implicit" export taxes. . . . There are 31 cases out of a total of 37 . . . in which export taxes exceed the estimated country optimal level of taxation.'

17.9 Assessing the relative effectiveness of trade protection

Large countries can gain from trade intervention but, in general, if small countries cannot affect the terms of trade, tariffs levied by small countries only impose deadweight losses. Is there a justification for trade intervention by small countries? There are always arguments that can be based on *non-economic* considerations (e.g. tariff protection may be considered of vital strategic or defence importance). However, when utilising the neoclassical trade model perhaps the most robust argument for trade intervention is the optimum tariff argument.

The literature concerning the rationale for trade intervention offers insight into an important distinction that is relevant more generally to other applications of micro-economic theory. It is important to note the distinction between trade intervention increasing welfare and trade intervention being the 'best' policy. The question is whether trade intervention is justified in terms of being the 'best' policy option. Government intervention in trade might increase welfare but this, in itself, is no justification if an alternative policy performs even better. For example, there may be an *equity* case, i.e. that trade intervention will alter the distribution of income in some desirable fashion. However, even if this occurred, trade intervention would not necessarily be the most appropriate form of intervention if there were some alternative policy that would achieve the same income redistribution at lower cost. (For example, in Chapter 4 it was argued that import protection under the Common Agricultural Policy might be defended in terms of the objective of assisting poor farmers. At the same time, it was also argued that there are other tax or subsidy arrangements to consider.)

This distinction can be illustrated by turning, again, to one of the qualifications listed in Section 17.7. Consider the case for trade intervention when there are other distortions in the market, e.g. when there are externalities. In Figure 17.13 the consumption of a particular good (e.g. cigarettes) causes an external diseconomy (see Chapter 6 for a discussion of externalities). Surely, a tariff would reduce consumption and it may be possible that the reduction of the external diseconomy would be so beneficial that the costs of protection would be negative (i.e. the country would be better off)? In Figure 17.13, S_h is the home supply curve and D_h the home demand curve. However, the marginal social benefit (*MSB*) is below the marginal private benefit ($D_h = MPB$) because there is an external diseconomy in consumption. With free trade (at world price of P_W) consumption is $0\text{-}q_4$ at point 1 (of which $q_4\text{-}q_1$ is imported). The negative spillover effect means that there is excess consumption of this good. Marginal social benefit is equal to price (in this case marginal social cost) at point 2 and there are welfare losses equal to triangle 1-2-3. Surely, the trade tax will now increase welfare? The tariff causes the price of imports to rise to $P_W + t_1$ and equilibrium will now be found at point 4 with imports falling to $q_3\text{-}q_2$; consumption is at the 'optimum' level ($0\text{-}q_3$). Certainly, the trade tax has the desired effect of reducing consumption but only at the cost of encouraging inefficient production. As the tax only affects imports, home production expands by $q_1\text{-}q_2$. These

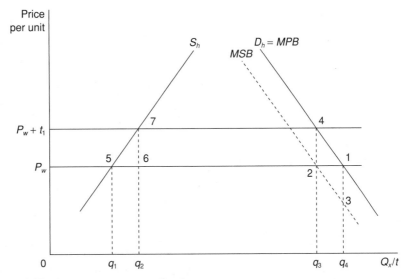

Figure 17.13 Trade taxes v. consumption tax

units can be purchased on the world market for q_1-5-6-q_2 but cost the country q_1-5-7-q_2 to produce.

This inefficient production (with loss equal to triangle 5-7-6) would not arise if a *consumption tax* had been placed on the product because a consumption tax does not discriminate between home-produced goods and imports (see Corden 1997). In this case there is no inefficiency loss from production but the 'optimal' level of home consumption is still achieved. Once again, trade protection may be beneficial but the question is, 'Is there an alternative policy that will prove more beneficial than trade intervention?'

The example illustrates an important principle. While it is possible to make arguments for trade protection, they are only relevant if there is no superior policy that can be introduced. In the next section the intention is to apply this general principle with reference to the, often quoted, *infant industry argument*.

17.10 Assessing the infant industry argument

One of the oldest arguments in favour of protection is the *infant industry argument*. It relies on the proposition that, when goods are produced, two effects are experienced. Of course there is the output that is visible but also there is an increase in human capital; producers learn from experience. These additional gains are referred to as economies of time (Corden 1997). The infant industry argument amounts to the proposition that, if an industry is protected over time, the costs of producing will fall and eventually the industry will be able to compete with those in other countries. Note, however, that the case is for *temporary protection*; at some stage the infant is expected to grow up!

In Figure 17.14, S is the supply curve of the home industry and, as the world price is P_W, the home industry cannot compete with cheap imports (see Hindley 1974). Domestic consumption is 0-q_4 and is entirely supplied by imports at the world price P_W. Tariff protection (with the tax rate, t, defined in *ad valorem* terms) raises the price of imports to $P_W(1 + t)$. This expands domestic production to 0-q_1 and contracts consumption to 0-q_2, the difference being imported. There are welfare losses equal to area P_W-1-2 (the increased cost of supplying 0-q_1 units through home production rather than imports) and area 3-4-5 (the loss of consumer surplus). However, as a result of learning (gained from the establishment of the home industry) as time goes by the home supply curve moves to S'.

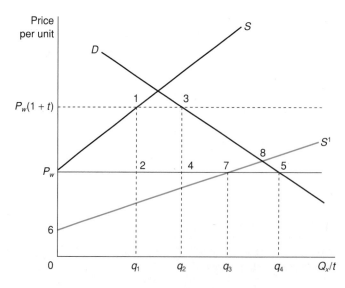

Figure 17.14
Infant industry argument

If the tariff were then removed the community would enjoy a welfare gain of area $6\text{-}P_W\text{-}7$ because a far greater quantity ($0\text{-}q_3$) can be produced at a lower cost at home than by importing.[10] Of course, losses are experienced before gains and it will be necessary to discount both losses and gains to compare them in present value terms (see Chapter 8). However, it is possible that gains will exceed losses, so surely the infant industry argument is robust? To answer this, there are a number of steps in the argument that need further consideration.

(i)   In the first instance, temporary protection benefits those factors employed in the industry. It follows that the industry itself has an incentive to invest and to bear the losses in the first instance in order to enjoy higher profits in the future. Where is the argument for government intervention? If there are *economies of time* then the ultimate beneficiary is the industry. Why should the government be involved?

(ii)   To argue a case for government intervention it is helpful to distinguish between *internal economies of time* and *external economies of time*. In the case of *internal economies of time* the firm is the ultimate beneficiary and the case for tariffs is more difficult to maintain.

(iii) Government intervention might be considered if there are market imperfections. For example, there may be informational asymmetry, which means that the firm is unaware of the future payoff whereas the government is more informed. In these circumstances the government may consider trade protection. But the argument is spurious. Why would the government be better informed? If it were, the best solution might be for the government to provide information to the firm (not tariff protection).

(iv)   Alternatively, the firm may be knowledgeable about the future but unable to finance the initial period in which there are losses. In some countries (e.g. developing countries) capital markets may be weak and there may not be adequate access to finance. However, once again, it begs the question as to whether government policy would be better targeted in terms of providing access to finance, than providing tariff protection.

(v)   The case for government intervention might be considered stronger if it could be argued that there were *external economies of time*. For example, during the learning process a firm might be involved in training its labour force, which ultimately may move to other firms (who will benefit from the investment of the firm). Of course, it might be argued that the labour force itself should bear the cost (e.g. lower wages while the 'apprentice' stage is experienced). However, labourers themselves may find it difficult to finance this investment in human capital and the costs may fall to the firm. In such a case, a market failure argument (see Chapter 10) would suggest a need for government intervention. However, this intervention could take the form of an *industrial subsidy* rather than tariff intervention.

There are, of course, many other examples of such *external economies of time* (e.g. if one firm from a country earns goodwill in an export market, other firms may enjoy an advantage from the goodwill that has been earned). The point, however, is that the case for the infant industry argument is more tenuous than might be expected. It is not argued that tariff protection can never be justified but it is argued that it can only be justified when there is a strong argument for government intervention *and* a reason to believe that alternative forms of government intervention are not to be recommended.

10. It is even possible, in the example shown, that the country would gain if it kept the prohibitive tariff. This would mean that area 7-8-5 would be a welfare loss (a welfare loss arising from consumption of home-produced units $0\text{-}q_4 - 0\text{-}q_3$ rather than importing these units at a price $0\text{-}P_w$). However, overall, welfare may still be higher.

As a 'parting shot', look again at Figure 17.14. Those who would commend tariff protection argue that the home supply curve S shifts to the right. Is this always going to be the case? If home producers are 'feather-bedded' by import tariffs, it is equally possible to argue that they will become less innovative and less competitive and that S will shift to the left. That infant industry protection may not produce higher productivity is quite possible (for empirical evidence see Krueger and Tuncer 1982).

17.11 Challenge: Is a focus on outcomes enough?

As in earlier chapters, the objective has been to assess the insight that is delivered by application of neoclassical microeconomic theory. On the plus side, it is evident that theory that appears very esoteric can be applied in a practical way to deal with policy issues. Estimates of the welfare loss created by protection can be produced. Estimates of the optimal export tax to apply can be provided.

This said, once again, it is clear that predictions are sensitive to assumptions employed. As in previous chapters, neoclassical microeconomic theory is open to challenge. The analysis focuses very heavily on market structures that are competitive. The analysis focuses very heavily on comparisons of outcomes; little is said of processes by which decisions are made. The objective in Chapter 19 is to illustrate how microeconomic theory can be designed to respond to these challenges.

17.12 Summary

This chapter has applied neoclassical microeconomic theory to issues of international trade. The focus of concern is on the usefulness of the general equilibrium model (described in Chapter 5). When applied to elucidate trade issues, is it simply too unrealistic and too abstract?

Economics texts rehearse the argument that there are 'gains from trade' and it is not difficult to understand why students question the relevance of theory when no country practices free trade. However, while classical economists (relying on the labour theory of value) argued forcefully that there are gains from trade, an application of the neoclassical general equilibrium model does not predict that *everyone* will gain as a consequence of trade liberalisation. Instead, the model highlights the implications of free international trade for the payments that are made to factors of production. Closer inspection explains why groups within countries may resist the introduction of free trade even when free trade is a *potential* Pareto improvement (i.e. even when free trade will create gains to the gainers which exceed losses to the losers, see Chapter 4).

The analysis of the neoclassical general equilibrium model means using assumptions (e.g. perfectly competitive markets) which are questionable and, because of this, students are apt to see such discussion as tantamount to simply an intellectual exercise. However, once again, it has been argued that the challenge is to reassess the relevance of the assumptions and to consider how the predictions of the model depend on the assumptions employed. The example discussed here was the assumption of factor specificity. When the assumption that factors of production could move effortlessly between industries is relaxed the 'Heckscher–Ohlin model' (now configured as the 'factor-specific model') sheds insight on problems of adjustment and trade liberalisation.

Analysis of the neoclassical model was 'inverted' when exploring the costs of protection. When the general equilibrium model was re-set in partial equilibrium terms the welfare effects were illustrated in a form which was more readily estimable. As a senior economic consultant in a Department of Trade the advice that trade protection will reduce welfare from CIC_3 to CIC_1 (see Figure 17.7) might appear unhelpful but setting the same analysis in a partial equilibrium framework allows estimates of the costs of protection to be presented in terms of '£x billion' per year. If estimates are open to qualification, qualification arises from an understanding of the limitations of the theoretical model on which they are based.

Considering the case for protection, Johnson (1969: 186) concluded that 'the only valid argument for protection as a means of maximising economic welfare is the optimum tariff argument'. This evaluation is made with reference to the model described in Chapter 11 and the normative (value) judgements that underpin this model.

Yet, for all that it is possible to respond to criticism of neoclassical economic theory it might appear questionable that in this chapter it has relied on analysis of perfectly competitive markets and that little attention is paid to the process of decision-making. What happens if markets are imperfect as far as competition is concerned (as described in Chapter 11)? What happens if the focus of attention falls on the process of decision-making, rather than on outcome (as discussed in Chapter 14)? These questions (challenges) are addressed in Chapter 18. If analysis based on competitive market outcomes offers little reason to restrain international trade, what if market structure is quite different?

References

Anderson, P.M. (1993) Linear adjustment costs and seasonal labor demand: evidence from retail traded firms, *Quarterly Journal of Economics*, 108: 1015–42.

Appleyard, D.R. and Field, A.J. (2001) *International Economics*, 4th edn, New York: McGraw-Hill.

Appleyard, D.R., Field, A.J. and Cobb, S.L. (2006) *International Economics*, 5th edn, New York: McGraw-Hill.

Askari, H. and Cummings, T.J. (1977) Estimating agricultural supply response with the Nerlove model: a survey, *International Economic Review*, 18: 257–92.

Baicker, K. and Rehavi, M.M. (2004) Trade adjustment assistance, *Journal of Economic Perspectives*, 18 (2): 239–55.

Banks, G. and Tumlir, J. (1986) Economic Policy and the Adjustment Problem, Thames Essays No 45, Trade Research Centre.

Borjas, G.J., Freeman, R.B. and Katz, L.F. (1992) On the labor market effects of immigrations and trade, pp. 213–44 in G.J. Borjas and R.B. Freeman (eds) *Immigration and the Work Force; Economic Consequences for the United States and Source Areas*, Chicago: University of Chicago Press.

Caves, R.E., Frenkel, J.A. and Jones, R. (1996) *World Trade and Payments: an Introduction*, 7th edn, New York: HarperCollins.

Chachiolides, M. (1973) *International Trade Theory and Policy*, New York: McGraw-Hill.

Corden, W.M. (1997) *Trade Policy and Economic Welfare*, 2nd edn, Oxford: Oxford University Press.

Decker, P.T. and Corson, W. (1995) International trade and worker displacement: evaluation of the Trade Adjustment Assistance Program, *Industrial and Labor Relations Review*, 38 (4): 758–74.

Ethier, W.J. (1995) *Modern International Economics*, 3rd edn, New York: Norton.

Feenestra, R.C. and Hanson, G.H. (1996) Globalization outsourcing and wage inequality, *American Economic Review*, 86 (2): 240–5.

Freeman, R.B. (1995) Are your wages being set in Beijing? *Journal of Economic Perspectives*, 9 (3): 15–32.

Heller, H.R. (1973) *International Trade: Theory and Empirical Evidence*, Englewood Cliffs, NJ: Prentice-Hall.

Hindley, B. (1974) *Theory of International Trade*, London: Weidenfeld and Nicolson.

Hufbauer, G.C. and Elliot, K.A. (1994) *Measuring the Costs of Protection in the United States*, Washington DC: Institute for International Economics.

Husted, S. and Melvin, M. (1998) *International Economics*, 4th edn, Boston, Mass.: Addison-Wesley-Longman.

Johnson, H.G. (1953) Optimum tariffs and retaliation, *Review of Economic Studies*, 21: 142–53.

Johnson, H.G. (1969) Optimal trade intervention in the presence of domestic distortions, reprinted as pp. 184–217 in J.D. Bhagwati (ed.) *International Trade*, Harmondsworth: Penguin.

Krueger, A.O. and Tuncer, B. (1982) An empirical test of the infant industry argument, *American Economic Review*, 72 (5): 1142–52.

Layard, P.R.G. and Walters, A.A. (1978) *Microeconomic Theory*, New York: McGraw-Hill.

Leontief, W.W. (1953) Domestic production and foreign trade: the American capital position re-examined, *Economia Internazionale*, 7: 3–32.

Magee, S.P. (1980) Three simple tests of the Stolper–Samuelson theorem, pp. 138–53 in P. Oppenheimer (ed.) *Issues in International Economics*, Stocksfield: Oriel Press.

Markusen, J.R., Melvin, J.R., Kaempfer, W.H. and Maskus, K.E. (1995) *International Trade: Theory and Evidence*, New York: McGraw-Hill.

Milner, C. (1996) Empirical analyses of the welfare effects of commercial policy, in D. Greenaway (ed.) *Current Issues in International Trade*, 2nd edn, Basingstoke: Macmillan.

Pugel, T. (2004) *International Economics*, 12th edn, London: McGraw-Hill.

Richardson, J.D. (1980) *Understanding International Economics: Theory and Practice*, Boston: Little, Brown.

Samuelson, P.A. (1955) Prices of factors and goods in general equilibrium, *Review of Economics and Statistics*, 54: 1–20.

Sanchez-Ugarte, F. and Modi, J.R. (1987) Are export duties optimal in developing countries? pp. 279–320 in V.P. Gandhi, *Supply Side Tax Policy: Its Relevance to Developing Countries*, Washington, DC: International Monetary Fund.

Sodersten, B. and Reed, G. (1994) *International Economics*, 3rd edn, London: Macmillan.

Stolper, W.F. and Samuelson, P.A. (1941) Protection and real wages, *Review of Economic Studies*, 9: 50–73.

Tanzi, V. (1991) *Public Finance in Developing Countries*, Aldershot: Edward Elgar.

Wood, A. (1991) The factor content of North–South trade in manufactures reconsidered, *Weltwirtschaftloches Archiv*, 27 (4): 719–43.

Wood, A. (1994) *North–South Trade, Employment and Inequality: Changing Fortunes in a Skill-Driven World*. Oxford: Clarendon Press.

CHAPTER 18

Trade policy: market structure and politics

18.1 Introduction

One of the themes of this text has been the sensitivity of microeconomic theory to assumptions that are employed in the construction of abstract models. In this chapter the objective is to return to the conclusions of Chapter 17 and to illustrate the importance of some of the assumptions that were employed in that analysis.

The analysis of international trade issues in Chapter 17 was undertaken by application of neoclassical trade theory. Once again, theory was constructed with reference to the well-being of a representative individual (defined as *homo economicus*). The focus was on the behaviour of *homo economicus* when faced with incentive structures inherent in competitive markets. In Chapter 17 it was argued that free trade had the potential to be welfare-enhancing. The implication for trade policy is that the best case for trade restraint is as a means of increasing national welfare (when there is the possibility of a 'terms of trade' improvement). The 'optimal tariff' argument proved to be the most robust case for intervention, although even this argument was qualified (e.g. retaliation might reduce welfare). In this chapter the objective is to reconsider this perspective when market structure is not competitive.

Students are inclined to question the relevance of the assumptions of perfect competition (see Chapter 3). When applying this model to analyse trade theory there is one very important concern. The neoclassical microeconomic trade model (the Heckscher–Ohlin model) predicts that trade will take place (and that there will be gains from trade) if there is a difference in relative prices of different goods (as embodied in the *law of comparative advantage*). The implication is that countries will trade one good for another (different) good (e.g. export good Y and import good X). Economists refer to this as *inter-industry trade*. However, a great deal of international trade takes place in what appears to be the same commodity (e.g. Germany both imports and exports motor cars, as do France and the USA). This is referred to as *intra-industry trade*. Yet, if this is the case, how informative is the neoclassical general equilibrium model described in Chapter 17? How can intra-industry trade be explained? While some economists retain the Heckscher–Ohlin model (e.g. viewing one kind of motor car as a different good to another), a relaxation of the assumption of competitive markets offers further insight into explanations of intra-industry trade. It also offers a different perspective on the 'gains from trade'. In the neoclassical model, gains from trade depend on differences in relative prices in different countries but in different market structures it is possible to identify gains from trade even when there is no difference in relative prices in different countries!

Such application of microeconomic theory has implications for trade policy theory. The case for intervention might be broader than implied when analysis of neoclassical general equilibrium model focuses only on competitive markets. In Section 18.3 the case for export subsidies is considered when markets are assumed to be competitive and when market structures are not competitive. This example is chosen to highlight the contrast between trade policy based on a neoclassical (perfect competitive market) model and on 'new' applications of microeconomic theory (when market structure is quite different). If export subsidies are applied and the volume of exports increases, the terms of trade will change – they will deteriorate. If so, it would seem that the country really has no motivation to introduce export subsidies. Why do countries offer export subsidies?

Predictions are dependent on market structure. However, predictions also depend on implicit assumptions underlying the theory of how policy is formed. In Chapter 14 it was argued that microeconomic theory would yield quite different predictions when analysts focused on decision-making processes (rather than on outcomes). If neoclassical analysis concludes that there is little reason to restrain trade (in the absence of the opportunity to improve the terms of trade), the implicit assumption is that the government is operating as a benign omniscient despot. By contrast, Chapter 14 focused on the possibility that politicians pursue self-interest and respond to self-interested pressures from those who exert greatest influence in the political process. If there are gains to vested interests from the introduction of alternative trade restraints, a 'rent-seeking' analysis (as described in Chapter 14) can be applied to explain more about the pattern of trade protection and the trade policies that governments adopt. One example of this is the growth in usage of particular forms of trade restraint (e.g. voluntary export restraints). These trade restraints make little sense when considered in a neoclassical (Heckscher–Ohlin) model but are predictable when microeconomic analysis encompasses the incentive structure that exist in political processes (i.e. when it is applied to analyse the process by which policy is made).

In all of this, the behaviour of self-interested *homo economicus* remains centre stage but, once again, is it the case that trade policy actually reflects the motivation to increase welfare for the community?

18.2 Intra-industry trade

Inter-industry trade refers to a situation in which products from one industry are exchanged for products of a different industry (e.g. a country exports wine and imports wheat). Intra-industry trade refers to trade in goods made within the same industrial classification. Why then has the UK exported cars (Rovers, Jaguars, etc.) only to simultaneously import cars (Mercedes, Audis, etc.)? To some extent the explanation might lie in analysis of market structure and of product differentiation.

Intra-industry trade can be measured by the following index:

$$B = 1.0 - \frac{|X - M|}{X + M} \tag{18.1}$$

where

X = exports;
M = imports and
$|X - M|$ = the absolute value of the difference between imports and exports.

When exports exactly equal imports the ratio in equation (18.1) is zero and the value of B is 1.0 (a maximum value). However, if for any industry, there are exports from the country but no imports (or vice versa) the ratio is 1.0 and the value of B is zero. It is usually the case that this index is higher for consumer goods (e.g. clothing) than for producer goods (e.g. chemicals). For example, the index of intra-industry trade in 1984 for the European Community was: primary commodities 0.58; road vehicles 0.70; household appliances 0.80 textiles 0.91; other consumer goods 0.8 (Begg *et al.* 2000).

It is evident that the pattern of reported estimates of intra-industry trade indices is that intra-industry trade is more likely in consumer goods than in primary products. The possible impact of product differentiation is obvious. With this in mind it is useful (following Grimwade 1989) to distinguish between:

(a) trade in *functionally identical commodities* and
(b) trade in *differentiated commodities*.

In Section 18.2.1 the question is whether microeconomic theory can explain international trade in *identical* goods (countries exporting the very same good that they import!). In Section 18.2.2 attention will be paid to the importance of product differentiation.

18.2.1 Trade in functionally identical products

While it may seem odd that a country should export the very same good that it imports, there is a range of possible explanations:

(i) There may be *aggregation bias* (i.e. the import and export goods are classified in the same commodity category although, in fact, they are really quite different). In this case intra-industry trade would be more apparent than real.

(ii) There may be *cross-border trade* (i.e. high transport costs may mean that country B imports coal from adjacent country A in the northern territory only to export to country A in the southern territory – transport costs are lower moving the good east–west, across national borders, than north–south within the country).

(iii) There may be *entrepôt (warehouse) trade* (whereby the good is imported for re-packaging before export (see Grimwade 1989).

However, an interesting explanation depends on analysis of market structure. The following analysis applies oligopoly (specifically duopoly) theory (discussed in Chapter 11). The following account is an application of the Cournot–Nash model of oligopoly.

To begin, assume there are two countries and that there is a producer of an identical commodity in each country. Each producer behaves in 'Cournot fashion', maximising profit *given the sales of the rival producer*. Each producer chooses the profit-maximising position assuming that the sales level of the rival producer is given and will not change.

The cost function of each producer can be defined as:

$$C(Q) = F + f(Q) \tag{18.2}$$

where

F = fixed costs of production;
$f(Q)$ = variable costs of production.

Demand in each country can be written as an inverse function. In the following equations, regard *superscripts* as referring to *countries* and *subscripts* as referring to *producers*. For example, in equation (18.3), Q_1^1 would refer to the sales in country 1 of the home producer and, in equation (18.4) Q_2^2 would refer to sales in country 2 by the foreign supplier. The inverse demand functions in each country can be described as:

$$p^1 = a - b(Q_1^1 + Q_2^1) \tag{18.3}$$

$$p^2 = c - d(Q_2^2 + Q_1^2) \tag{18.4}$$

It follows that profit (π) for each producer can be defined as:

$$\pi_1 = [a - b(Q_1^1 + Q_2^1)]Q_1^1 + [c - d(Q_2^2 + Q_1^2)]Q_1^2 - f(Q_1^1 + Q_1^2) - F \qquad (18.5)$$

and

$$\pi_2 = [c - d(Q_2^2 + Q_1^2)]Q_2^2 + [a - b(Q_1^1 + Q_2^1)]Q_2^1 - f(Q_2^2 + Q_2^1) - F \qquad (18.6)$$

Consider the market in country 1. As far as sales in that country are concerned, to maximise profit producer 1 must increase sales until the marginal profit from so doing is equal to zero:

$$\frac{\partial \pi_1}{\partial Q_1^1} = -2bQ_1^1 - bQ_2^1 + a - f' = 0 \qquad (18.7)$$

and producer 2 sets

$$\frac{\partial \pi_2}{\partial Q_2^1} = -2bQ_2^1 - bQ_1^1 + a - f' = 0 \qquad (18.8)$$

These equations (see Greenaway and Milner 1986) can be illustrated as the reaction functions R_1 and R_2 respectively in Figure 18.1. Each firm's reaction curve shows the sales that would maximise its own profit *given the sales of its rival*. Equilibrium occurs at the intersection of the reaction curves (see Chapter 11), because only at this point will each firm be doing as well as it can, *given the behaviour of its rival*. At equilibrium *e*, the producer in country 1 sells 0-*S* in country 1 and the producer in country 2 sells (exports) 0-*T* in country 1. Similarly, with reference to country 2 it can be shown that equilibrium will occur when the producer from country 1 supplies the good to the foreign market.

The conclusion that the country exports the very same good that it imports may seem surprising. Krugman (1989) has referred to this as 'reciprocal dumping'. How can it possibly be the case that there are gains from this trade? Would there still be gains if there were costs involved in shipping the good in and out of the country?

To answer these questions, compare the autarky (no trade) solution with the free trade equilibrium. In conditions of autarky, producer 1 would be the only supplier in country 1. As a monopolist this producer would only sell 0-*A*. It can be seen that with free trade total sales (0-*S* + 0-*T*) exceed 0-*A*. Given the inverse demand function (in equation 18.2), this must mean that the price of the good is lower in this country. Consumers must be better off. There is 'pro-competitive trade'. The inefficient monopoly outcome that would

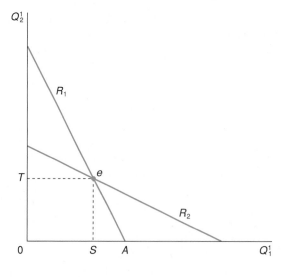

Figure 18.1
Pro-competitive trade

have existed with autarky is no longer tenable. The welfare loss arising from monopoly is reduced.[1] When considering the distortion created by monopoly, the gap between *MRT* and *MRS* in this country has shrunk! Trade has increased quantity in each market and this has reduced the price for consumers and increased the degree of competition.

By beginning with the assumption that markets are not perfectly competitive this analysis has introduced a quite different source of 'gains from trade'. In Chapter 17 'gains from trade' emerged from the difference in relative prices in the trading economies. Here the welfare gains arise as a result of a reduction in inefficiency (which would have been created by monopoly). As in Chapter 17 it is important to note that there may be changes in income distribution as a consequence of trade. Once again, the issue of equity cannot be ignored in any welfare analysis. However, notwithstanding income distribution effects, there are potential gains from free trade, even when this country imports and exports the same good. The gains arise because the transaction is 'pro-competitive'.[2]

To view the gains in terms of consumer surplus and producer surplus (as described in Chapter 7) it is possible to apply an analysis described in Smith (1994). Consider the example shown in Figure 18.2(a). Again, for ease of exposition, suppose that there are two countries with a single firm in each country selling a homogeneous good. Both firms face the same (constant) marginal cost of production (shown in Figure 18.2(a) as *MC*). In conditions of autarky, each firm would be able to act as a monopolist. Focusing on one market (i.e. on one country), the price of the good and output of the producer is shown as $0\text{-}P_2$ and $0\text{-}q_2$ when there is no competition from overseas. If there were international trade then each firm would enter the other's home market. Conditions of 'Cournot competition' apply. With reference to the autarky situation, each firm would identify a 'residual demand' in the foreign market which is defined as the market demand less the sales of the incumbent firm (at autarky output level) in that market. Each firm would increase profit (as defined in equations 18.5 and 18.6) as a consequence of exporting to that market.

The analysis explains why the same good is exported and imported. Where are the gains in welfare? In Figure 18.2 the greater supply of the good has reduced the price of the good to $0\text{-}P_1$ (a reduction that was predicted in Figure 18.1).[3] Consumers enjoy consumer surplus as a result of the reduction in price. The consumer surplus gain is shown by areas *a* and *b* in Figure 18.2(a). Of course, if the price has fallen then the profits of the domestic producer from sales in the domestic market will fall. The home firm loses part of the home market to imports from abroad. Instead of selling $0\text{-}q_2$, the domestic producer sells $0\text{-}q_1$ of a total of $0\text{-}q_3$ supplied to the home market at a price of $0\text{-}P_1$. It follows that the domestic producer finds that profits have fallen by area *a* + *d*. However, the foreign firm picks up profits given by *d* + *e*. Symmetrically, the home firm will make an equal profit gain in the foreign market. Therefore the net impact on the domestic firm is an increase in profit equal to area *e*. It follows that the gains from trade to the home firm and consumers (i.e. the gains to the home country) are shown by *b* + *e*.

But surely this is counter-intuitive? What if costs are incurred in shipping the same good out of the country that is shipped into the country (see Krugman 1989)? Surely, when the transport costs are taken into account there can be no welfare gain? The answer is that welfare gains are still possible provided that transport costs are not so high as to outweigh pro-competitive gains. In Figure 18.2(b) reciprocal dumping occurs and there are international transport costs shown as *t*. Less 'cross-hauling' is carried out in the presence of transport costs and hence $q_1\text{-}q_3$ in panel (a) is smaller than $q_1\text{-}q_3'$ in panel (b).

---

1. The welfare cost of monopoly is explained in Chapter 11.
2. If this duopoly situation were, instead, an oligopoly situation, then countries will export relatively more if their industries are more competitive.
3. For example, if there were a constant price elasticity demand function the price-marginal cost margin would be halved.

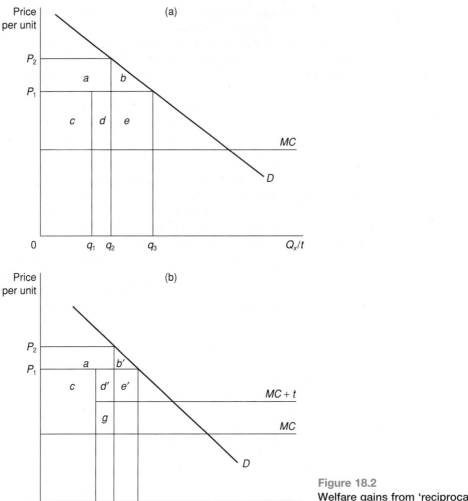

Figure 18.2
Welfare gains from 'reciprocal dumping'

It is still possible that countries are better off as a consequence of international trade. Consumers gain is equal to $a + b'$. The home producer now gains profits in the foreign market equivalent to $d' + e'$ but, as $d = d' + g$, loses the equivalent of g (which would have been enjoyed as profit at home if those units, q_1-q_2, once sold in the home market did not have to be shipped to the foreign country). The net gain to the home economy in the presence of transport costs is $b' + e' - g$. The negative component g is the waste of resources involved in transporting identical goods in opposite directions across frontiers. Of course, if the transport costs t were high enough, this cost (g) can outweigh the pro-competitive gain from reciprocal dumping. However, clearly there is the possibility that, over a range, the pro-competitive gains will outweigh transport costs.

The importance of this explanation of intra-industry trade is that it opens the analysis of welfare gains to arguments that would not be possible if markets were competitive. Of course, there will always be criticism that this reciprocal dumping model is a sufficient explanation of intra-industry trade. For example, the Cournot model relies upon some very specific assumptions concerning conjectural interdependence (see Chapter 11). How realistic is this model of oligopoly behaviour? How sensible is it to assume that each firm takes the output of the rival firm as constant when, each time it sets its output the rival changes output in response? Yet this is the basis of the movement to equilibrium. As noted in Chapter 11, there may be other models of oligopoly (i.e. other than the Cournot–Nash) which are more relevant. Here the importance of this application of theory is not to argue that it *must* explain intra-industry trade, but to illustrate how new assumptions concerning market structure open up a new dimension when considering gains from trade.

18.2.2 Differentiated products

Another way in which intra-industry trade can be explained is to focus on product differentiation. It was argued that intra-industry trade might be greater in consumer goods, where the importance of commodity differentiation is likely to be greater. But how can product differentiation be handled for the purposes of analysis?

Horizontal product differentiation occurs when commodities share core attributes but combine these attributes in different proportions. *Vertical product differentiation* occurs when products have different attributes and where the quality of products can be ranked accordingly. In this section the objective is, once again, to apply microeconomic theory to show how the 'gains from trade' depend on market structure. The market structure under analysis in Section 18.2.2.1 is monopolistic competition (Chamberlain's model), see Chapter 11. Commodities enter utility functions symmetrically. Later, in Section 18.2.2.2 there is horizontal product differentiation but products enter utility functions asymmetrically.

18.2.2.1 Horizontal product differentiation when commodities enter utility functions symmetrically

Following (Krugman 1979) assume that all consumers have the utility function

$$u = \sum_{i=1}^{n} c_i^{\theta} \quad 0 < \theta < 1, \tag{18.9}$$

where c_i is consumption of the ith variety of the good. In this function utility is raised by either increasing any c_i or increasing n (the number of varieties of products). Also it is assumed that if the price and consumption of each good are the same (that is, if $p_i = p$ and $c_i = c$, for all i),[4] then utility will be increased by an x per cent increase in n even if it entails an x per cent reduction in the consumption level of each good. That is, consumers increase their welfare by increasing their variety.

Product differentiation (associated with monopolistic competition) in Krugman's (1979) analysis is referred to as a neo-Chamberlain approach. Assume that each good has an identical production function and relies on a single factor of production, labour:

$$l_i = \alpha + \beta x_i \tag{18.10}$$

where

x_i = output
l_i = labour input.

Given the wage rate, w, the fixed-cost component α ensures that average costs fall as x_i rises (wl_i/x_i falls), but marginal costs are constant at βw. Equation (18.9) gives rise to two equilibrium conditions (explained in Chapter 11).

First, as each firm has some monopoly power (because it produces a unique variety) each firm equates marginal cost (*MC*) and marginal revenue (*MR*), so that

$$MR = p(1 - (1/\varepsilon)) = \beta w = MC \tag{18.11}$$

---

4. The so-called symmetry assumption.

(the subscript has been dropped because of the symmetry assumption, and ε is the elasticity of demand for each individual variety).

Second, as new firms will enter production until there is no more economic profit to be gained, the profit condition for equilibrium of the industry is that total costs (TC) equal total revenues (TR), i.e.

$$TR = px = (\alpha + \beta x)w = lw = TC \tag{18.12}$$

Equations (18.11) and (18.12) define the final equilibrium of the economy. This can be rewritten by deriving the relationships between real prices (p/w) and per-capita consumption (c). From equation (18.11),

$$p/w = \frac{\beta\varepsilon}{\varepsilon - 1} \tag{18.13}$$

This is the 'mark-up' equation indicating that mark-up will rise as the demand elasticity falls.

From equation (18.12) the zero profit condition can be written as:

$$p/w = \frac{\alpha + \beta}{x} = \beta + \frac{\alpha}{Lc} \tag{18.14}$$

where elasticity of demand depends on c (and will fall as c increases) and where output (x) of any variety equals the product of population (L) and per-capita consumption (c). (This is a rectangular hyperbola as the mark-up to cover fixed costs falls as market size (c) increases.) Figure 18.3 plots those two relationships and shows the equilibrium.

If there is full employment,

$$L = \Sigma l_i = nl_i \tag{18.15}$$

so that the number of varieties of products (n) is

$$n = \frac{L}{\alpha + \beta x} = \frac{L}{\alpha + \beta Lc} \tag{18.16}$$

The implication of free trade is that the 'size' of the economy (L) has increased. What happens if L increases to L'? In Figure 18.3 the 'mark-up' curve would be unaffected,

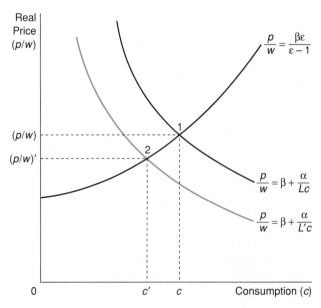

Figure 18.3
Welfare gains from variety

but the zero profit condition would shrink inwards from initial equilibrium at point 1 to a subsequent equilibrium at point 2. It follows that to maintain a given real price, c must fall, here to c', as L rises to L'.

The new equilibrium (point 2) entails lower real prices $(p/w)'$ (with greater elasticity because c is falling the mark-up is lowered) and lower per-capita consumption of each variety, c'. However, because (p/w) has fallen, Lc must have risen (see equation 18.14), so that output of each variety has risen, facilitating lower average costs because of economies of scale. Moreover (from equation 18.16), with a rise in L and a fall in c, this implies a rise in n (the denominator rises less than proportionately to L, first because α is constant and second because c falls). Thus, the increase in L to L' consequent on trade benefits consumers by reducing real prices (p/w) and increasing variety.

In summary, under conditions of autarky, home consumers live in an economy of size L. If this economy trades freely with another economy of size L^* then they now effectively spend their daily lives in an economy of size $(L + L^* = L')$. Each consumer obtains more varieties of commodities. The total number of varieties available will increase and the output of each surviving firm is increased. But the number of home-country firms will decrease; firms have no incentive to produce the same variety of product as other firms. After all, every available variety enters the consumer's utility function symmetrically; and there are falling average costs of production.

Once again, there are gains from intra-industry trade. In this monopolistic market structure a country can simultaneously reduce the number of products it produces and increase the variety of goods available to domestic consumers. By producing fewer varieties, a country can produce each at larger scale and thus at lower average cost, while consumers enjoy an increased range of choice. (There will be some income-distributional effects but, if intra-industry trade is more likely when countries are similar in their relative factor supplies, these are likely to be small).

There are gains from international trade but in this market structure they occur from economies of scale and from the introduction of greater variety. Once again, a different conclusion emerges as compared with that which is derived from neoclassical microeconomic trade theory (which focused on competitive markets). In neoclassical trade theory (Section 17.2) all the emphasis was on gains arising from difference in the relative commodity prices in different countries.

18.2.2.2 Horizontal product differentiation when commodities enter utility functions asymmetrically

In Krugman's analysis of *horizontal product differentiation* it was assumed that different commodities entered utility functions *symmetrically*. However, horizontally differentiated products can enter utility functions *asymmetrically*. The analysis now adopts the form of a *neo-Hotelling approach* (the emphasis being on the spatial location of products on an attribute scale).

In the following analysis (which follows Greenaway 1983), consider again the way in which welfare gains from trade depend on market structure. As if to emphasise the point, Greenaway (1983) reminds readers of the expectation of Aquino (1978) that international trade would not create significant welfare gains in the case of intra-industry trade. Acquino's reasoning was that relative prices of intra-industry goods do not differ significantly and therefore the opportunity for significant welfare gains is reduced (following the logic of a neoclassical trade model).

Greenaway applies a model of product innovation (as presented by Scherer 1979) to show how imports of differentiated products increase welfare irrespective of changes in relative price. Welfare gains are possible now because international trade will mean that the imported good has attributes that better suit the tastes of some individuals in the home country.

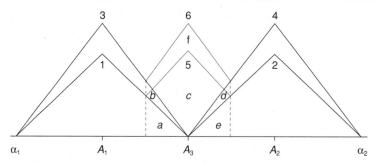

Figure 18.4 **Welfare gains from differentiated goods**

With reference to Figure 18.4 assume that α_1 and α_2 are two attributes of a product (e.g. for a motor car, one attribute may be lower petrol consumption, another might be comfort of seating). Assume that consumers are uniformly located along the horizontal axis (drawn with respect to the two characteristics). Before international trade, the home country produces two goods, A_1 and A_2, which combine the two characteristics in different proportions. Consumers' preferences are diverse, but evenly distributed along 'characteristic space'. It follows that producer surplus and consumer surplus reach maxima at A_1 and A_2 respectively. The peaks at point 1 and 2 relate to the *producer surplus* (i.e. the area below the triangles so formed refer to producer surplus on sales to individuals located along the axis).

The peaks at points 3 and 4 refer to *consumer surplus* (i.e. the area *between* the two triangles refers to consumer surplus from sales to consumers distributed respectively along the axis). Greenaway (1982) provides a discussion of the construction of these triangles. However, intuitively, the two consumers who 'just love' the two products A_1 and A_2 will have a demand curve for these products further to the right than would be the case for any other consumer (because *ceteris paribus* they will be willing to pay more for their 'ideal' product). With demand curves further to the right, greater consumer surplus and producer surplus will be possible (the reader may wish to confirm this by drawing a demand–supply diagram with upward-sloping supply curve).

The pattern of producer surplus and consumer surplus from sales to each individual will therefore take the shape shown here. The further away we move from the consumer who fits the attribute combination of A_1 and A_2 respectively, the lower is producer surplus and (in the inner space) the lower is consumer surplus. Because of the distribution of preferences, consumers between point A_3 (midway between A_1 and A_2) and A_1 will consume A_1 and those between A_3 and A_2 will consume A_2.

In order to identify the gains from intra-industry trade in a differentiated product, the analysis now considers a third good, A_3. It is assumed that A_3 is imported. It follows that consumers from the midpoint between A_1 and A_3 and nearer A_3 will consume A_3, while those from the midpoint between A_3 and A_2 and nearer A_3 will consume A_3. The centre peaks 5 and 6 refer to the producer surplus and consumer surplus that are enjoyed from consumption of the import good.

In assessing gains from trade (as shown in Figure 18.4) the following welfare effects can be identified:

(i)　A gain in consumer surplus equal to area f;
(ii)　A *gross* gain in producer surplus equal to $a + b + c + d + e$;
(iii)　A *net* gain in producer surplus of c (a and e are transfers from producer surplus of A_1 and A_2, and b and d are transfers from consumer surplus of A_1 and A_2).

The producer of the import good offers a product that better suits the tastes of this subset of domestic consumers (e.g. Scandinavian lager for this subset of lager drinkers).

It should be emphasised that the gains outlined here include transfers away from home producers to the foreign producer. However, this example refers to the welfare gains of *importing* a product. The country concerned would also gain producer surplus (symmetrically) when commodities A_1 and A_2 are exported to a foreign country.

The example illustrates Greenaway's criticism of Acquino's assessment (which had been based on neoclassical analysis of trade and competitive market structures). The two examples of horizontal product differentiation provide illustrations of the gains that arise as a consequence of increased product variety. It is possible to explore the implications of trade when there is vertical product differentiation (e.g. see Shaked and Sutton 1984). However, enough has been said to make the case that the application of microeconomic theory will yield quite different predictions and welfare assessments depending on the market structure under consideration. When there is vertical product differentiation it is possible to rank products in terms of quality (e.g. a Rolls-Royce is superior quality to an Austin Metro). Linder's (1961) assessment was that trade patterns would be influenced by quality considerations. As consumers in countries with high average income would be able to consume better-quality goods, he concluded that the potential for trade in manufacturers is greatest between countries at similar per-capita income levels. Empirical evidence supported this prediction (e.g. see Grimwade (1989) and Hocking (1980) but for dissent see Kennedy and McHugh (1983)). In this analysis predictions of the determinants of trade depend on considerations of market structure and product differentiation.

18.3 Market structure and commercial policy

It has been argued that the pattern of international trade is sensitive to assumptions of market structure. The argument has been made that assessment of the welfare gains from trade depend on market structure and that relaxing the analytical assumption of competitive markets opens up this area for further consideration. If so, then trade policy is dependent on the assumption that defines market structure. To highlight the importance of market structure for policy analysis, consider how well the policy conclusions presented in Chapter 17 fare when markets are not perfectly competitive.

The analysis in Chapter 17 suggested that, with the exception of the 'optimal tariff' argument, there was no robust case for the government to intervene in trade issues. However, when the assumption of perfectly competitive markets is relaxed, the case for government intervention must be revised. Here the objective is to illustrate this development with reference to the case for export subsidies. In the first instance, if there is perfect competition, there seems to be no case for export subsidies when the country is 'small'. An application of theory developed in Chapter 17 suggests that export subsidies will simply generate deadweight loss. Perhaps then there is a case if the country is 'large'? The answer is unequivocally 'No'. If there are problems when the country is small, these will only be exacerbated, for an export subsidy will worsen (not improve) the terms of trade. Having explored these arguments the opportunity is then taken to re-appraise the case for export subsidies when markets are less than perfectly competitive. But, to begin, consider the neoclassical analysis of the case for export subsidies (in 'small' and in 'large' countries).

(i) *An export subsidy (competitive markets).* In a 'small' country, for every unit exported, the producer receives the international price *plus* the subsidy. Producers have an incentive to sell in the foreign markets in order to receive the government subsidy and the quantity sold in the domestic market is reduced until the price in the domestic market is equal to the world price plus the subsidy.

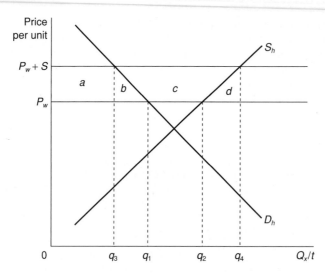

Figure 18.5
Export subsidy: small country case

In Figure 18.5 the home demand and home supply curves are shown as D_h and S_h and (with a world price of P_W) exports are $0\text{-}q_2 - 0\text{-}q_1$. Producers are now offered a subsidy S if they export. They will receive a price equal to $P_W + S$ if they export. It follows that they will require a domestic price which is equal, at least, to $P_W + S$ if they are to sell in the domestic market. This means that there is a reduction in the quantity demanded in the home market from $0\text{-}q_1$ to $0\text{-}q_3$. The export subsidy also acts as an incentive to increase the quantity supplied from $0\text{-}q_2$ to $0\text{-}q_4$. The quantity of exports increases from distance $0\text{-}q_2 - 0\text{-}q_1$ to distance $0\text{-}q_3 - 0\text{-}q_4$. The increase in price reduces consumer surplus by areas a and b. At the same time, producer surplus is increased by area $a + b + c$. The subsidy cost to taxpayers (S multiplied by the volume of exports $0\text{-}q_3 - 0\text{-}q_4$) is equal to area $b + c + d$.[5] The policy is unattractive in terms of a resource allocation analysis as there are simply deadweight losses equal to triangles b and d.

The net social cost of the export subsidy is equal to the two deadweight triangles. Area b represents part of the transfer to producers, which is paid for twice – once by a loss in consumer surplus and once by the cost of the subsidy. Triangle d is a production-efficiency loss that results from the less efficient domestic production (units q_2 to q_4 are cheaper on the world market than they are to produce in this country).

This result seems familiar; in a 'small' country trade intervention can produce deadweight losses (see Section 17.6). As an example (following Appleyard and Field 2001), consider the application of this analysis to the US Export Enhancement Program for Wheat (enacted in December 1985). The act required the Secretary of Agriculture to provide Commodity Credit Commission commodities at no cost to US exporters, users and processors and foreign purchasers.[6] Welfare effects per annum including subsidy costs were estimated as $1000m.[7] In line with Table 18.1, domestic

---

5. In order to finance the expenditure, the government may have to impose taxes on the population equal to the value of area $b + c + d$. As an alternative, government deficit financing could be employed, but this also will have costs.
6. The objective was to combat other countries' subsidies and the high value of the dollar. The expectation was: (i) the subsidy would result in an increase in exports; (ii) the exports should be directed at displacing competing foreign exporters subsidised by their governments; (iii) there should be a gain to the US economy; and (iv) the subsidy cost should be budget-neutral.
7. Although there might later be a reduction to allow for a fall in the cost of price support $350m to $1050m that the government felt it had to provide.

Table 18.1 Welfare costs of an export subsidy: small country

Consumers	$-a$	$-b$		
Producers	$+a$	$+b$	$+c$	
Taxpayers		$-b$	$-c$	$-d$
Net changes		$-b$		$-d$

wheat farmers' gain was between $120m and $300m per annum. The losers were domestic buyers of wheat, including livestock feeders (a loss of $40m to $100m) and domestic consumers' loss (a loss of $200m to $500m). The estimated net welfare costs were between $250m and $770m. As indicated by Table 18.1, the programme appears to have generated a net loss to the US economy.

Problems are worsened when allowance is made for 'terms of trade effects'. To emphasise the detrimental effects of an export subsidy consider how the analysis is amended in a large country case. In Figure 18.6, D is the world demand for the country's export good. The equilibrium price in the export market is P_W and quantity exported is $0\text{-}q_1$. When the government provides an export subsidy, the new price at which the exporter can sell is $P_W + S$ and exports increase from $0\text{-}q_1$ to $0\text{-}q_2$. The country is such an important supplier of the product that, when exports increase, the world price of the product falls to P_1. With price $P_W + S$ received by the exporter but only price P_1 received by the country the costs of the subsidy are S multiplied by the volume of exports, i.e. area $b + c + d + e + f + g$.

As is evident from Table 18.2, the welfare costs to the country are even greater in the case of the large country (i.e. net welfare loss is $b + d + e + f + g$). In the case of a 'large' country there is the additional loss (equal to the price reduction to the foreign buyers) because of the export subsidy. Thus, the export subsidy has a loss which is greater than the deadweight losses noted in the case of the small country.

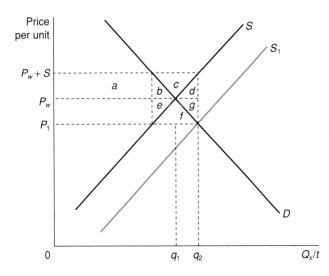

Figure 18.6
Export subsidy: large country case

Table 18.2 Welfare costs of an export subsidy: large country

Consumers	$-a$	$-b$					
Producers	$+a$	$+b$	$+c$				
Taxpayers		$-b$	$-c$	$-d$	$-e$	$-f$	$-g$
Net changes		$-b$		$-d$	$-e$	$-f$	$-g$

(ii) *An export subsidy (international oligopoly).* To highlight the importance of market structure on policy recommendations, consider the case for an export subsidy when markets are not competitive. The following account of Brander and Spencer (1985) assumes that there are two firms (one home-based, one foreign-based) competing in a third market.[8] Throughout the analysis, the number of firms is fixed (there is no entry of new firms no matter how high profits may be) and wages are constant. The model is set up so that all that matters for national welfare are the profits of the national firm. The aim of foreign policy is to shift profits from the foreign firm to the domestic firm. The government of the third country is non-interventionist. Therefore the greater the output of one exporting firm, the less is the profit of the other exporting firm. As in Section 18.2, both firms are assumed to behave in a 'Cournot fashion' (see also Chapter 11).

The domestic firm sets output to maximise profits (π). Profits depend both on demand and costs:

$$\pi(x, x^*, c) = [p(x + x^*) - c]x \tag{18.17}$$

where

$p(.)$ = the inverse demand function;
x = sales of the home firm;
x^* = sales of the foreign firm;
c = marginal cost.

Under Cournot assumptions, each firm assumes that its rival's sales are given and chooses a profit-maximising response by equating marginal cost to marginal revenue. The profit-maximising exports for the home firm are derived as a function of foreign sales and the reaction function is $x = p(x^*, c)$ for the home firm (and $x^* = p^*(x, c^*)$ for the foreign firm).

In Figure 18.7 exports from the home country are estimated on the x-axis and exports from the foreign country are shown on the y-axis (see Helpman and Krugman 1989).

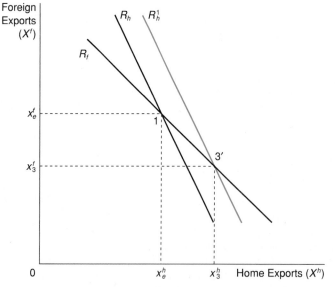

Figure 18.7
Export subsidy:
international oligopoly

8. For purposes of exposition the product is not sold in either of their home markets. In this way the example differs from the 'reciprocal dumping' model described in Section 18.2.

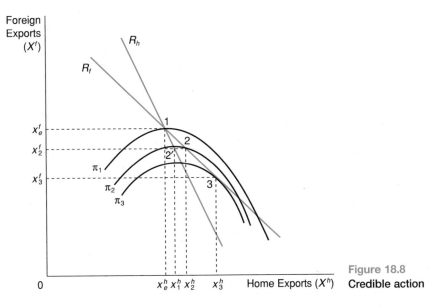

Figure 18.8
Credible action

As in Figure 18.1, the sales of each firm depend on the sales of the other and, in Figure 18.7, reaction functions of the home and foreign firm (R_h and R_f) can be constructed in the same way. A Cournot equilibrium occurs at the intersection point 1 (i.e. where the home firm exports x_e^h and foreign firm exports x_e^f).

The same equilibrium is shown in Figure 18.8. However, this figure also shows the home firm's isoprofit lines (e.g. where $\pi(x, x^*, c) = \pi_i$). At each point on an isoprofit line it is possible to identify exports of the foreign and home firms which will yield the home firm the same profit. The isoprofit curves peak at each point on the reaction function R_h. If the home firm could commit itself to exporting more than x_e^h, it could make more profit than at point 1 provided that the foreign firm reduced its exports accordingly.

Any attempt to increase exports by the home firm may lack credibility. For example, if the home firm committed itself to x_2^h, the foreign firm's best option is to export x_2^f. The problem is that the home firm's commitment needs to be credible, for the foreign firm will see that, when it responds by choosing sales of x_2^f the home firm will find that it can make more profit by moving from point 2 to 2′. After this, the foreign firm finds that it is able to make more profit by moving to a point (vertically above 2′) on its reaction curve (R_f). Step by step, if each firm makes profit-maximising decisions in a Cournot fashion, there is a movement back to the equilibrium point 1.

If a firm could pre-commit itself, it would be at an advantage and this is where export subsidies serve to change the solution in this game from a Cournot solution to a Stackelberg solution (see Chapter 11). It is in the home government's best interest (in pursuit of national welfare) to provide the means by which the home firm can sustain a pre-commitment. The home government has the first-mover advantage by providing a specific export subsidy of s before firms make their choices. In this way the home firm's marginal cost (of export) becomes (c-s) and its profit function becomes (x, x^*, c-s). Its reaction function (R_h^1 in Figure 18.7) is now described by $x = p(x^*, c$-$s)$.

The export subsidy is equivalent to a decline in costs and the reaction function of the home firm shifts away from origin (from R_h [i.e. $x = p(x^*, c)$] to R_h^1 [i.e. $x = p(x^*, c$-$s)$]). That is, a carefully designed subsidy would shift the home firm's reaction function in Figure 18.7 to intersect the foreign firm's reaction function at point 3′.

To see that this is equivalent to a Stackelberg equilibrium, consider Figure 18.8. The solution is shown by point 3, where the home firm's isoprofit curve is tangent to the foreign firm's reaction curve. The home firm now acts as a Stackelberg-leader and the foreign firm as a Stackelberg-follower. The best option for the foreign rival is to export $0\text{-}x_3^f$ and, when the foreign firm selects this option, the home firm's best option is to remain at $0\text{-}x_3^h$. The foreign firm sees that this action is credible (because with the subsidy from the home government the home firm has no incentive to move from this point).

The strategy of export subsidy becomes an attractive option when the market is described as an international oligopoly. The different market structure permits the existence of economic profits (rents) and if these can be captured there are gains from trade. In perfectly competitive markets there are only normal profits. However, in the case of oligopoly, profits can be captured by the use of an export subsidy. There is a quite different case for trade intervention.

Krugman and Obstfeld (2003) illustrate the argument in terms of Table 18.3. This again considers a duopoly situation in which there is competition between two aircraft manufacturers (Airbus and Boeing). Each aircraft manufacturer produces a 200-seat aircraft and each makes decisions knowing that profits depend also on the sales of the rival producer. If Boeing produces and Airbus produces, the profits of each will be negative (–5). However, if Boeing does not produce and only Airbus produced the profits for Airbus are 100. Conversely, if Airbus does not produce and only Boeing produces, the profits for Boeing are 100. Of course, if neither produces neither makes profit.

In this situation assume that governments offer Airbus a subsidy. If Airbus enjoys a subsidy of 25 (whatever happens), the payoffs change as shown in Table 18.4. In this case, Boeing realises that Airbus will produce whatever happens and, if Boeing produces, it will simply make losses. Boeing adopts its best option; it adopts the posture of a Stackelberg follower. Airbus makes profits equal to 125 (of which 25 is a subsidy). The subsidy is a transfer (from taxpayer to producer) and is not a loss for the country.[9] The subsidy has enabled the European producer to capture profits (100) that might otherwise have been enjoyed by the rival.

Table 18.3 Equilibrium in a duopoly

		AIRBUS			
		Produce		Not produce	
BOEING	Produce	–5	–5	100	0
	Not produce	0	100	0	0

Table 18.4 Export subsidy when there is duopoly

		AIRBUS			
		Produce		Not produce	
BOEING	Produce	–5	20	100	0
	Not produce	0	125	0	0

9. Of course, in saying this, we are ignoring costs of collecting the tax to finance the subsidy (see Chapter 13).

The change in market structure opens up new possibilities as far as trade policy is concerned. Strategic trade policy is now an option. However, this does not mean to say that the Brander–Spencer (1985) analysis indicates that government intervention will always prove desirable. There are many criticisms and, as ever, the starting point is to question the underlying assumptions. For example:

(i)   Why should a government know so much about the potential of cost functions of the two firms? It seems odd that in the example discussed, government knows all about the behaviour of the two firms, whereas the firms themselves play a Cournot game. With reference to the last example, suppose that there is an asymmetry in the costs of Airbus and Boeing such that Boeing (with a different technology) can produce at lower costs. In this case, even if Airbus produces, Boeing may also produce and the subsidy may fail to create a market advantage for Airbus.

(ii)   The analysis depends on the assumption that firms play a Cournot game. Firms playing a Cournot game have conjectured responses which are zero (they assume that the rival will not alter their position). It has been shown that export subsidy only raises the country's welfare if 'the home firm conjectures a more aggressive foreign response to its action than the foreign firm actually undertakes' (Baldwin and Richardson 1986: 100).

(iii) What if another model of oligopoly is relevant? Eaton and Grossman (1986) consider the use of export subsidy in oligopoly situations where firms engage in Bertrand price competition. In this case each firm is assumed to choose its own price to maximise its profits taking the other firm's *price* as given. A rise in one firm's price increases its opponent's profits and also makes a rise in its opponent's price marginally more profitable (or less costly). Therefore the reaction curves are positively sloped. An export subsidy would lower the home firm's reaction function towards the origin (it lowers marginal cost). If there is a 'Bertrand duopoly', the export subsidy hurts the firm. In this market structure an export tax on the home firm's exports proves the appropriate strategy.

(iv)   What of the reaction by the government in the rival producer's country? The situation poses a 'prisoners dilemma' in which both countries would be better off not to subsidise but in which each country feels that it has an incentive to subsidise.

(v)   The assumption (noted above) that the number of firms remains constant is important. Dixit (1984) modified the original model by considering the impact of more than two firms. As the number of domestic exporters grows the efficacy of an export subsidy diminishes. An export subsidy may now no longer increase national welfare. Eventually, the best strategy to increase national welfare is for government to tax exports.

(vi)   The analysis described above is a partial equilibrium analysis, No account is taken of the impact of the subsidy on resources available to producers in other sectors of the economy (e.g. the availability of skilled personnel elsewhere if the aircraft industry expands).

(vii) The Brander–Spencer analysis assumes that firms compete in a foreign export market. What if they also sell in the home markets? In this case an export subsidy will encourage the domestic firm to divert sales to the overseas market. Consumers in the home country will lose welfare and it is far less obvious that the country will gain by using an export subsidy. By comparison, a production subsidy will avoid this additional distortion (as a lower price will be available in *both* the domestic and the international market).

It is clear that the model is open to further analysis. The world is a far more complicated place than the description provided above. For example, further complications arise if firms are not uniquely related to a particular country, i.e. if firms are transnationally owned. Moreover, the issues of income distribution always apply. Would the policy seem 'equitable' if the profits of the owners of capital in one industry were increased and nothing else?

This is not the place for further, in-depth, analysis of the Brander–Spencer model. Enough has been said to illustrate that policy conclusions drawn in Chapter 17 are sensitive to the assumptions of market structure. While it is impossible to argue that trade restraint will inevitably prove successful in different market structures (e.g. as the criticisms of the Brander–Spencer model would imply), it is possible to offer a completely different argument for trade intervention when markets are less than perfectly competitive.

But does this explain trade policy? When looking at the decision to intervene it is impossible (once again) to ignore the process of political decision and the application of microeconomics that was described in Chapter 14.

18.4 Rent-seeking and trade policy

In Chapter 17 Johnson's (1969: 186) conclusion was cited; 'the only valid argument for protection as a means of maximising economic welfare is the optimum tariff argument'. However, in Chapter 14 it was predictable that policies adopted often differ from those that are Pareto-efficient when microeconomic analysis was focused on the political decision-making process. In this section one example of this argument is presented. If countries intervene in trade, perhaps this is better explained by the pursuit of rent on the part of a small subset of the economy, rather than in terms of what is optimum for the community as a whole?

In Chapter 14 it was argued that policies that are chosen are likely to be those that yield rent to producer groups. It will be recalled that there are distinct reasons for expecting that producer groups exert greater influence than consumer groups.

(i) Olson (1971) argued that 'large' groups find difficulty in organising because of the 'free-rider' problem. If an association were established to advance the interests of groups, any member of the group would have an incentive to allow others to bear the costs and to attempt to free ride (see Chapter 12). By contrast, in small groups individuals' actions would be more obvious and the action of any individual to contribute may increase the likelihood that others will contribute. It follows that large groups (e.g. consumers) will not be easily mobilised. By contrast, producers, as 'small groups', will be more effectively mobilised.

(ii) A second consideration, which explains why producers are more easily mobilised, is that, for producers, trade policy has a very important impact on their livelihood. For consumers, trade policy with respect to any one commodity will inevitably have less of an effect, as consumers purchase a wide range of goods. In terms of Downs's (1957) analysis (see Chapter 14) they are 'rationally ignorant' (they have no incentive to be fully informed on trade policy). Producer groups are more motivated than consumer groups when considering import tax arrangements with respect to any particular product.

Following on from this, return to the analysis of trade protection discussed in Chapter 17. It is possible to identify the gains to producer groups. In Figure 18.9 D_h and S_h are the home demand and supply curves respectively. The world price is P_W and an import tax (of *ad valorem* rate t) reduces imports from $q_2 - q_1$ to $q_4 - q_3$. As explained in Chapter 17, the producer group gains area a. Consumers are worse off by area $a + b + c + d$. Tax revenue of c is raised but there is nothing to offset the deadweight loss of b and d for the

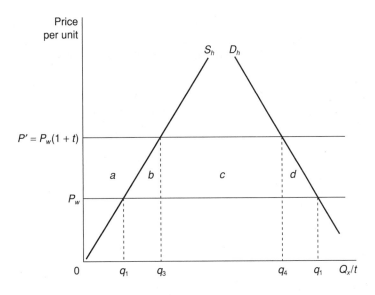

Price per unit

S_h D_h

$P' = P_w(1 + t)$

a b c d

P_w

0 q_1 q_3 q_4 q_1 Q_x/t

Figure 18.9
Rent-seeking and trade protection

country as a whole. So why would a government introduce a tax which had an outcome that reduced welfare?

A public choice explanation focuses on the strength of influence of producer groups in the political decision-making process. If politicians are primarily concerned with electoral success then, as vote-maximisers, they have an incentive to respond to producers. Producers are more politically aware of trade policy than are consumers. Votes and financial support for electoral campaign funds might be won if politicians supply the policies demanded by producer groups. Votes from consumers will not be lost if consumers are unaware of the decisions that have been taken in the interests of producers and at the expense of consumers.

This analysis of the 'political market' suggests that producer groups will exert greater impact on the legislative process than will consumers. Returning to the analysis of Figure 18.9, the producer group stands to gain area a if a tariff is levied and therefore they may spend as much as area a in resources to lobby government to introduce and levy this tax. If so, consider how this analysis affects the discussion of the costs of protection as outlined in Chapter 17. Instead of the costs of protection being captured only by triangles b and d there is an additional cost of protection equal to area a. The costs of protection are now area $a + b + d$.

The question arises as to the use of tax revenue (c). Some have argued that 'revenue-seeking' activity takes place when groups in the economy vie over the allocation of tax revenue to their own specific expenditure programmes (see Bhagwati and Srinivason 1980, 1982). If so, resources are dissipated that might equal the value of the tariff revenue (i.e. area c) and in this case the costs of protection escalate to $a + b + c + d$.

But what if protection is introduced in a different form? Consider the introduction of trade restraint in the form of an import quota. Assume that the quota of imports is set at q_4-q_3. The analysis suggests that the deadweight costs would be equal to triangles b and d. The price of the good would rise to $P'(= P_w(1 + t))$ in Figure 18.9 and there would be the same gain in producer surplus and loss of consumer surplus as if a tariff of *ad valorem* rate t were levied. However, now import licences are required and importers may dissipate resources to acquire such licences. The rent to be acquired from an import licence is the difference in the price at which goods can be purchased on the world market and the price at which they can be sold in the home market. If an import *quota* is used, rather than an import *tax*, then the importer can buy on the world market at 0-P_w and sell at a higher price, 0-P', in the domestic market. The result is that rents are available for importers equal to area c. In this case, importers may dissipate almost as much as area c trying to win the licences (which are equal in value to area c). If protection is via a quota the costs of protection are equal to area $a + b + c + d$. Rent-seeking increases substantially the costs of protection!

Rent-seeking analysis explains why a policy that delivers deadweight loss for the country as a whole emerges from the political process as government policy. It also changes the estimate of the costs of protection – they are far greater than would be predicted by a neoclassical analysis. But how can the importance of this public choice interpretation be assessed? How is it possible to ascertain whether the decision was made in the interests of vested groups, rather than in the 'public interest'? To distinguish between these explanations is not easy but consider answers to the following questions:

1. *How can the pattern of protection be explained?* Why are some goods more heavily protected than others? The optimum tariff argument would suggest that the more heavily protected goods would be those where the elasticity of supply of imports was lowest. The rent-seeking approach would suggest that protected goods are produced by only a few producers (an oligopoly). The ease with which producers can mobilise is the key consideration, and close geographical proximity might also prove important. Marvel and Ray (1983) and Pincus (1975) report that tariffs are higher in more concentrated industries (where producers are easily able to communicate and coordinate). Having compared competing hypotheses, Caves (1976) reports that the 'interest group' model best explains the pattern of tariffs in Canada in 1963.

2. *How can we explain voting in favour of trade restraint?* Turning to the decision-making process, a public choice explanation would suggest that a politician's own interests would supersede the public interest. Baldwin (1976) examined how congressmen voted with respect to the 1973 trade-liberalising bill in the USA. He reported on statistically significant variables that explained whether or not congressmen voted against the bill. The variables were political (public choice), not economic (import price elasticity). They included: (i) the proportion of import-sensitive industries in the congressman's constituency; (ii) the financial contribution to the congressman's campaign made by the three major trade unions opposing the bill; (iii) the party affiliation of the congressman (the bill was introduced by a Republican president and Republicans were more likely to support it).

3. *Why was there a growth in distinct forms of trade protection throughout the 1980s and 1990s?* There was a growing reliance on trade restraints that are less visible. This period (sometimes referred to as the period of 'new protectionism' – Grimwade 1989) saw an increase in usage of instruments of protection that are less visible to voters. One instrument, which has persistently grown in importance, is the voluntary export restraint (VER). As will be explained in the following section, the selection of this instrument of trade policy makes no sense against the criteria used in neoclassical microeconomic theory. Yet it serves well the interests of vote-seeking politicians, conscious of the need to supply protection in response to pressure from producer groups.

4. *How can the pattern of political pressure for protection be explained?* The pattern of pressure for protection predicted by a rent-seeking analysis differs from that expected by reference to a neoclassical analysis of the distributional effects of trade protection. As explained in Chapter 17, in the neoclassical (Heckscher–Ohlin) model, the introduction of a tariff on product Y (which increases the price Y) will increase the reward paid to the factor of production used intensively in industry Y. The expectation of the Stolper–Samuelson theorem is that one factor of production (e.g. capital) will gain from protection while others (e.g. labour) lose. The evidence of Magee (see Chapter 17) did not confirm this neoclassical prediction. In any industry, both factors of production

(capital and labour) either preferred protection or trade liberalisation; there was no difference of view. While this prediction is at odds with the neoclassical model it is quite consistent with a rent-seeking analysis. As implied by the discussion in Chapter 17, it is quite possible for *both* factors of production to enjoy quasi-rent in a protected industry in the short run (i.e. before capital moves from one industry to another). If individuals' views are dominated by the possibility of economic rents in the short run then both factors of production in any industry would be predicted to prefer protection.

The answers to these questions would appear to support the argument that when considering trade policy it is the application of microeconomic theory to the decision-making process, rather than an application of a neoclassical model to assessment of outcomes, that sheds the greatest insight. Estimates of rent-seeking cost were reported in Chapter 14. They can be sizeable. When considering the mechanisms by which producers seek rents from the acquisition of import licences, Krueger (1974) exemplifies some of the forms in which wastes appear. For example:

(i)   Rent-seeking costs would include lobbying efforts as well as bribes (in the form of hiring relatives of customs officials who are less productive than their earnings) to obtain import licences.
(ii) There may be wasteful competition among those in the government who occupy positions to receive the bribes.
(iii) Firms may be involved in the construction of excess plant capacity when import licences are awarded in proportion to firm's plant capacities.
(iv) There may be 'excessive' entry (and, therefore, less-than-optimal-sized firms) when licences are allocated on a *per rata* to applicants.

For several categories of licences, the largest of which was imports, Krueger estimated rents in India in 1964 as 7.3 per cent of national income and her estimate for Turkey in 1968 (with respect to import licences) was equivalent to 15 per cent of GNP. Mohammed and Whalley (1984) estimated total contestable rents associated with pre-existing government policies in India as between 30 and 45 per cent of GNP. (For a survey see Quibria 1989.)

All of these arguments are formidable but the qualifications discussed in Chapter 14 must also be taken into account. One example, illustrated here, is the caveat that, in a second-best world, it is impossible *a priori* to assess whether welfare is lower with rent-seeking. It is too early to assume that costs of protection are greater if there are rent-seeking costs than in the absence of rent-seeking costs. As resources are used up in the process of rent-seeking, the overall losses may be reduced if those resources might have been used even more inefficiently. In this way, the resource cost associated with rent-seeking might be offset.

Bhagwati and Srinivason (1980, 1982) identify cases in which rent-seeking may not always prove a loss. In Figure 18.10, point 1 is the production point on the production possibility curve T if there is free trade and price ratio P_i is relevant. Point 2 is the production point if a tariff creates a distortion and price ratio P_t is relevant. If there is rent-seeking, resources are dissipated which causes the production possibility curve to move to the left to T_1. The free trade position is now at 3 and, if there were a tariff, the production point would be at 4. It is possible to compare the welfare at point 2 and point 4 to see whether costs of protection are greater with than without rent-seeking. One way to proceed is to compare welfare at point 4 with that at point 2, by measuring consumption possibilities in terms of units of X at world prices. Welfare with rent-seeking $(0\text{-}q_{x1})$ is greater than that without rent-seeking $(0\text{-}q_{x0})$. The reason is that, without rent-seeking, even more resources are allocated to the production of good Y which is already over-provided as a consequence of the tariff distortion.

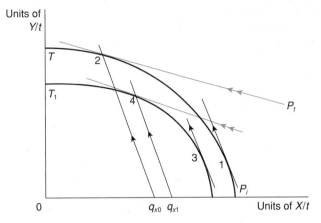

Figure 18.10 Rent-seeking increases welfare

By returning to Chapter 14 it is possible to raise other qualifications to the proposition that rent-seeking, with respect to trade policy, represents an unmitigated waste of resources.

18.5 Choosing instruments of protection: why are VERs preferred to tariffs?

The rent-seeking analysis of the previous section offered a different perspective on international trade policy. In this section a rent-seeking analysis is compared to the neo-classical microeconomic analysis (in Chapter 17) when tackling the question of why there has been a growth in the use of voluntary export restraint as a means of reducing imports. Why would voluntary export restraints be preferred to import tariffs as a mechanism for restraining trade?

A voluntary export restraint (VER) is the result of negotiation between an importing and an exporting country.[10] The agreement requires the exporting country to restrain exports to the importing country. This form of trade restraint has been used as an instrument of trade restraint since 1936.[11] However, in recent years its usage has become far more prevalent. It is reported that in 1957 the only VER applied to Japanese textile exports to the USA but, by 1986, there were about 130 VERs, covering about 10 per cent of world trade (see Hamilton and Reed 1995 for a review).

This form of trade restraint has been concentrated in certain sectors (particularly textiles and clothing, footwear, steel and steel products, automobiles, consumer electronics). It is a feature particularly of bilateral trading relationships between certain countries (notably between the USA, the EU and Japan). The use of such trade restraint in steel is more recent (e.g. from 1968 to 1974 the USA imposed VERs on imports of Japanese and European steel). Similarly, its use to restrain trade in motor cars is more recent; the USA introduced VERs on imports of cars from Japan in 1981.

The growth in the use of VERs is difficult to explain using neoclassical microeconomic theory. It can be shown that tariff protection will prove a 'more efficient' mechanism to reduce imports. Figure 18.11 can be used to illustrate the welfare losses and welfare gains for those affected by the introduction of a VER. In panel (a) S_A is country A's (the home

---

10. Sometimes referred to as voluntary restraint agreements (VRAs) and orderly marketing arrangements (OMAs).

11. They were used as to restrict Japanese exports of certain textiles to the USA from 1936 to 1940, and by France for a variety of products.

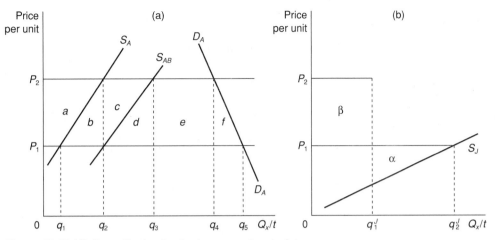

Figure 18.11 Welfare effects of voluntary export restraint

country's) supply curve and D_A is the home country demand curve. With free trade the world price is $0\text{-}P_1$ and $0\text{-}q_1$ is produced domestically. With free trade $q_1\text{-}q_5$ is imported. There are two countries from which country A imports. Of $q_1\text{-}q_5$, $q_1\text{-}q_2$ is imported from country B and $q_2\text{-}q_5$ is imported from country J (Japan ?). Imports are mainly from one supplier (country J).

The supply of home-produced goods and supply of goods from B is shown by S_{AB}. The government decides to reduce imports (the intention being to increase domestic production from $0\text{-}q_1$ to $0\text{-}q_2$). If an import tariff (t) were levied the price of imports would increase to $0\text{-}P_2$. Following the analysis in Chapter 17, there would be gains to home producers equal to area a and there would be tariff revenue equal to $c + d + e$. The deadweight loss would equal triangles b and f. As in Chapter 17, import protection would reduce the level of welfare of the country, although producer groups would be better off.

Suppose, instead, that the intention is to reduce the level of imports by seeking an agreement from J, whereby exports from J will be reduced from $q_2\text{-}q_5$ to $q_3\text{-}q_4$ The right-hand panel of Figure 18.11 (panel b) illustrates the supply curve of exports from J (as S_J). The voluntary export restraint would reduce exports from $0\text{-}q_2^J$ to $0\text{-}q_1^J$.

If J agreed to introduce this VER then, in panel (a), the volume of imports from J is reduced from $q_2\text{-}q_5$ ($= 0\text{-}q_2^J$) to $q_3\text{-}q_4$ ($= 0\text{-}q_1^J$). Home production increases by $q_1\text{-}q_2$ and imports from country B increase (from $q_1\text{-}q_2$ to $q_2\text{-}q_3$). However, with a total volume of imports of $q_2\text{-}q_4$, price in the home market increases to $0\text{-}P_2$ (exactly the same price as if there were an import tariff t). Moreover, the same total quantity of goods are imported ($q_2\text{-}q_4$) as if there were an import tariff t.

Comparing the welfare effects of voluntary export restraint with those that occur if there is an import tariff, it is evident that producers in the home country will gain area a with a VER and that the deadweight losses are, again, triangles b and f. However, there is no tariff revenue! The home country has achieved its goal by relying on a trade instrument that is inferior to simply levying an import tariff (with no need to incur costs of negotiation with the supplier country). Why opt for an instrument that loses the home country the tariff revenue that might otherwise have been enjoyed? Tarr (1989) estimated the loss to US consumers from VERs at $21 billion, $14 billion of which was a direct transfer to foreign exporter profitability and a loss of US government revenue.

The answer to this question is better understood by reference to a rent-seeking analysis and by an understanding of the political pressures which politicians face. While it is difficult to see any economic advantage to be enjoyed by an importing country from the agreement of exporters to introduce a VER (as compared with the use of a tariff that would reduce imports to the same volume), it is possible to show why this option might be preferred by those involved in the political decision-making process. In this reconsideration, remember that the most effective lobbyists are likely to be producer groups. How do they fare in all of this?

Producer surplus for home producers increases by area a (and home production increases, $0q_1$-$0q_2$). Producer surplus for producers in country B increases by area c; their share of this market increases, not only in relative terms (because imports from J decline), but also in absolute terms (imports from B are now q_2-$q_3 > q_1$-q_2). The question arises as to the welfare of producers in J, whose access to this market has been reduced. It might be imagined that they would be worse off. However, the price of the import good has increased and there are rents earned on these exports from J. These are equal to area e. Of course, producers in J are selling less. To see the net effect on their welfare, consider Figure 18.11(b). To ascertain whether or not they have gained, it is necessary to compare the loss of producer surplus on the goods that are no longer sold with the increased rent on the goods that still enter the country. In the left-hand side of Figure 18.11(b), the producer surplus lost is equal to area α but the rent on the exports that are still sold in the home country is area β. If $\beta > \alpha$ it is possible that *all* producer groups (producers in all countries) gain if a VER is employed. Import-competing producers are able to increase the price of their goods and also expand output. Exporters in the restraining country gain because, with a higher price, the gain on existing exports is greater than the loss from restraint. Exporters from other countries gain because the market for their goods has expanded in the home country and they also enjoy a higher price.

So who are the losers? The losers are consumers in the importing country. They suffer from the higher price of the good; there is a loss of consumer surplus equal to area a + $b + c + d + e + f$. Citizens of the home country lose differentially if the same reduction of imports is achieved by a VER rather than by a tariff. Had a tariff equal to P_2-P_1 been levied, imports would have reduced from q_1-q_5 to q_2-q_4 but there would have been tariff revenue of area $c + d + e$. All of this revenue is lost; exporters in country J have appropriated rent.

If producer groups are politically more effective, a rent-seeking analysis predicts that, while VERs make little sense against the criteria of neoclassical microeconomic theory, VERs will be preferred by vote-maximising politicians. This policy option reflects the interests of groups who are most effective in applying political pressure and enables politicians to satisfy their demand at least cost (in terms of vote loss). While the welfare of consumers at home is reduced, consumers constitute a large group and are difficult to mobilise. To each consumer the protected good is only one among many goods in the consumption basket and to the typical consumer the cost increase caused by a VER is perceived (if at all) to constitute a fairly small part of their income. Consumers are 'rationally ignorant': for each consumer there is no incentive to be fully informed about trade protection on each product consumed.

The emphasis throughout has been on political considerations. In this context consider other 'merits' to politicians of VERs:

(i) For politicians, the potential vote loss from VERs is lower because they are less visible than tariffs. Jones (1984: 87) notes: 'While direct import restrictions such as tariffs and quotas must be implemented through legislative (US) or highly visible administrative (EC) channels, a VER can be negotiated in secret, unhindered by open political process and public scrutiny.'

(ii) Internationally, there are political advantages in opting for VERs, rather than for tariffs. For politicians, potential political costs are reduced because VERs were permitted within the Articles of the General Agreement of Tariffs and Trade (GATT). GATT had articles to prohibit the use of quantitative restrictions (Article XI) and to stop discriminatory barriers (Articles II and XIII) but VERs were permitted (VERs circumvent these constraints). Members of GATT agreed not to use quantitative import restrictions and discriminatory quotas and tariffs. By having the restraint via a VER, members of GATT did not infringe the letter of GATT rules (even if they were at odds with the 'spirit' of GATT agreement). The World Trade Organization (WTO) replaced GATT in January 1995 but it pursues the same approach to implement principles described in the GATT agreement.

It is political considerations that dominate in this assessment. Moreover, a rent-seeking analysis also explains the acquiescence of those countries that agree to reduce their exports. There are rents that can be enjoyed as a consequence of introducing voluntary export restraint. Here again, considerations of market structure come into play. If a rent-seeking analysis is correct, it is predictable that exporting countries will enjoy greater rents if withholding exports allows domestic producers in the importing country to enjoy monopoly profits and to set monopoly prices (Pomfret 1989). With this theory in mind, Pomfret argues that 'the monopoly case is what puts "voluntary" in VERs' (Pomfret 1989: 64). He notes that when the 1981 VER on Japanese automobile exports to the USA expired, the US government decided not to request renewal of the VER and in 1985 it was Japanese firms that successfully pressed their government to continue administering a VER (at higher levels). Similarly, the 1983 VER on Japanese exports of video cassette-recorders to the European Community began amid bitter dispute but after 1985 the VER was maintained by Japan apparently without European prompting.

18.6 Challenge: Is more complexity required?

This chapter shows how alternative applications of microeconomics offer explanations for trade protection beyond those prescribed by neoclassical microeconomic theory. However, in the context of this text it would be a mistake to think that these developments have closed the door to further theoretical developments. Far from it! For many, there are still challenges to be met.

With reference to the rent-seeking model, Destler and Odell (1987) regard the model as over-simplistic – domestic producers that are easily mobilised, consumers who are politically disabled. What of producers of export goods, who would fear that tariff protection would create retaliation? Why do they not resist? What of producers who rely on imports of intermediate goods? Are voters so easily discounted?

Similar theories of the political choice of instrument have been based on the *strength* (rather than the weakness) of consumer–taxpayers. For example, in Chapter 4 analysis of the Common Agricultural Policy suggested that production subsidy was preferable to tariff protection to increase output of domestic producers. Why then would tariff protection be chosen? One interpretation is that tariffs are borne by a wider spectrum of the community, whereas, if there is progressive taxation, the burden of alternative tax sources would fall on those with highest income. Perhaps (following Mayer and Riezman 1990) it is the relative political effectiveness of *this* section of the electorate (those with high income) that distorts policy choice?

In Chapter 14 it was argued that policy is not always the output of a bilateral political contest between producers and consumers (consumers who prove so difficult to mobilise). Policy can also reflect contests between different producer groups. Perhaps this is nowhere more evident than in recent struggles over import tariffs on steel in the USA.

The steel industry in the USA had long struggled with competition when, in 2000, the presidential candidate George W. Bush promised to assist. In 2001, 18 steel producers declared bankruptcy and the venerable Bethleham Steel Company was also moving in this direction. In June 2001 the US International Trade Commission was lobbied to determine whether US steel producers were seriously injured by competition. It ruled that

16 product categories were seriously harmed and, in March 2002, President Bush imposed tariffs on 14 of the 16 product categories. The tariffs were scheduled to decline gradually over three years (to be eliminated in March 2005). The policy was deemed 'good politics': 'to position Bush to carry three important steel-producing states Ohio, Indiana and West Virginia that he had won in the 2000 election' (Besanko and Braeutigam 2005: 397).

Resistance to this trade intervention came from other producer groups. In the first instance the Consuming Industries Trade Action Coalition (CITAC) reported that the deadweight loss of the steel tariffs ranged between $500 million and $1.4 billion. It also estimated a loss of between 21,000 and 44,000 jobs in steel-consuming sectors; steel-consuming firms were going out of business. This was particularly disconcerting because the estimates it presented for saved jobs in the steel-producing industry were only between 4400 and 8900.

Outside the USA it was also producer groups who lobbied. Producers in steel-exporting countries registered protest. The European Union took the case to the World Trade Organization and, in late 2003, the WTO ruled that European and Asian nations would be permitted to impose retaliatory tariffs. The EU threatened to target textile and agricultural products. This would be detrimental for significant Southern and Midwestern states in the USA; the potential political costs were obvious.

In December 2003 the Bush administration rescinded the steel tariffs. This was 21 months early. On one hand, steel prices were now high; the political costs of removing the tariffs at this time were lower because the steel industry's plight seemed less acute. On the other hand, the lobbying of producers hurt by the steel tariffs had proved successful.

Once again, the 'real world' proves more complex than the simplifying abstractions that describe microeconomic models. However, in all of this it is impossible to dismiss the view that political costs and benefits prove more important than economic assessment of 'optimum' tariffs when considering trade policy.

18.7 Summary

The objective in this chapter was to illustrate how different applications of microeconomic theory would yield different perspectives on the gains from international trade and shed new insight on the formation of trade policy. Intra-industry trade is not well explained by theories based on the neoclassical (Heckscher–Ohlin) trade model. However, when the assumption of perfect competition is replaced with assumptions of different market structures, there is a new perspective on intra-industry trade. When reference is made to oligopoly (described in Chapter 11) it is possible to explain why the same good is both exported and imported ('reciprocal dumping'). When reference is made to Chamberlain's monopolistic competition (also see Chapter 11) it is possible to show how product differentiation creates an incentive for international trade. These theories offer new motivation for international trade – motivation that, by construction, is absent in the neoclassical model. Trade may be 'pro-competitive' or gains may arise simply from an increase in variety. For those wedded to the neoclassical model the focus of concern is differences in relative prices. However, as demonstrated here, gains from international trade encompass many other considerations.

Recognition of other market structures offers new insight on trade policy. Export subsidies appear an inefficient mechanism for providing 'gifts' to other countries when

---

12. This does not discount the argument that export subsidies are intended as a short-run loss for long-run profits. That is, by exporting subsidies to country *A*, country *A*'s indigenous producers would find it impossible to compete and hence go out of business. Ultimately the export country would enjoy a monopoly position and, in the long run, enjoy higher profits.

analysed by reference to static neoclassical trade theory.[12] However, when the export subsidies are analysed as a strategic trade policy, in a market defined as an international oligopoly, there is a new *prima facie* case for trade intervention. The rationale depends on 'profit-shifting' (or 'rent capture'), which would not be possible in a perfectly competitive market scenario. Such developments led Krugman (1987: 131) to assert that 'the case for free trade is currently more in doubt than at any time since the 1817 publication of Ricardo's *Principles of Political Economy'*.

However, when explaining the 'new protectionism' that characterises the 1980s and 1990s another microeconomic perspective is possible. This theoretical structure applied microeconomic theory to the *process* of decision-making. Empirical analysis supports the proposition that the pattern of trade protection is biased in favour of goods produced by small, well-organised, oligopolies, precisely as predicted by the rent-seeking model discussed in Chapter 14. Inevitably, in this analysis, there is concern, not only that trade protection is in the best interests of all individuals in a country, but also that there is a dissipation of resource by rent-seeking.

Throughout, the message of this text is that the door is always open to further theoretical development. Moreover, the relevance of self-interest in analytical models is always open to question. Baldwin (1976) admits the possibility that trade protection may be biased in favour of industries which favour those with lower levels of skill. In this case, tariff policy may be a reflection of altruism on the part of actors who are concerned about the welfare of individuals who may be adversely affected by import competition, rather than the pursuit of naked self-interest.

References

Appleyard, D.R. and Field, A.J. (2001) *International Economics*, 4th edn, New York: McGraw-Hill.

Aquino, A. (1978) Intra-industry trade and inter-industry trade specialisation as concurrent sources of international trade in manufacturers, *Weltwirtshaftliches Archiv*, CXIV: 275–95.

Baldwin, R.E. (1976) The Political Economy of US Postwar Trade Policy, Bulletin no. 4, Centre for the Study of Financial Institutions, Graduate School of Business Administration, New York: New York University.

Baldwin, R.E. and Richardson, J.D. (1986) *International Trade and Finance: Readings*, 3rd edn, Boston: Little, Brown.

Begg, D., Fischer, S. and Dornbush, R. (2000) *Economics*, 6th edn, Maidenhead: McGraw-Hill.

Besanko, D.A. and Braeutigam, R.R. (2005) *Microeconomics*, 2nd edn, Hoboken, NJ: John Wiley & Sons.

Bhagwati, J.N. and Srinivason, T.N. (1980) Revenue seeking: a generalisation of the theory of tariffs, *Journal of Political Economy*, 88 (6): 1069–87.

Bhagwati, J.N. and Srinivason, T.N. (1982) Revenue seeking: a generalisation of the theory of tariffs – a correction, *Journal of Political Economy*, 90 (1): 188–90.

Brander, J.A. and Spencer, B.J. (1985) Export subsidies and international market share rivalry, *Journal of International Economics*, 18: 83–100.

Caves, R.E. (1976) Economic models of political choice: Canada's tariff structure, *Canadian Journal of Economics*, 9 May: 278–300.

Destler, I.M. and Odell, J. (1987) *Anti-Protection: Changing Forces in United States Trade Politics*, Washington DC: Institute for International Economics.

Dixit, A.K. (1984) International trade policy for oligopolistic industries, *Economic Journal*, supplement 94: 1–16.

Downs, A. (1957) *An Economic Theory of Democracy*, New York: Harper & Row.

Eaton, J. and Grossman, G.M. (1986) Targeted export promotion with several oligopolistic industries, *Quarterly Journal of Economics*, 101: 383–406.

Greenaway, D. (1982) Identifying the gains from pure intra-industry exchange, *Journal of Economic Studies*, 9: 40–54.

Greenaway, D. (1983) *International Trade Policy: from Tariffs to the New Protectionism*, London: Macmillan.

Greenaway, D. and Milner, C. (1986) *Economics of Intra Industry Trade*, Oxford: Basil Blackwell.

Grimwade, N. (1989) *International Trade*, London: Routledge.

Hamilton, C. and Reed, G.V. (1995) Economic aspects of voluntary export restraints, pp. 100–23 in D. Greenaway (ed.) *Current Issues in International Trade*, London: Macmilllan.

Helpman, E. and Krugman, P. (1989) *Trade Policy and Market Structure*, Cambridge, Mass.: MIT Press.

Hocking, R.D. (1980) Trade in motor cars between the major European producers, *Economic Journal*, 90 (359): 504–19.

Johnson, H.G. (1969) Optimal trade intervention in the presence of domestic distortions, reprinted in J.N. Bhagwati (ed.) *International Trade*, Harmondsworth: Penguin, pp. 184–217.

Jones, K. (1984) The political economy of voluntary export restraint arguments, *Kyklos*, 37: 82–101.

Kennedy, T.E. and McHugh, R. (1983) Taste similarity and trade intensity: a test of the Linder hypothesis for US exports, *Weltwirtschaftliches Archiv*, 119: 84–96.

Krueger, A.O. (1974) The political economy of the rent-seeking society, *American Economic Review*, 64: 291–303.

Krugman, P.R. (1979) Increasing returns, monopolistic competition and international trade, *Journal of International Economics*, 9: 469–79.

Krugman, P.R. (1987) Is free trade passé? *Journal of Economic Perspectives*, 1: 131–44.

Krugman, P.R. (1989) Industrial organization and international trade, in R. Schmalensee and R.D. Willig (eds) *Handbook of Industrial Organization*, vol III, New York: North-Holland.

Krugman, P.R. and Obstfeld, M. (2003) *International Economics: Theory and Policy*, 6th edn, Boston, Mass.: Addison Wesley.

Linder, S. (1961) *An Essay on Trade and Transformation*, New York: Wiley.

Marvel, H.P. and Ray, E.J. (1983) The Kennedy Round evidence on the regulation of international trade in the United States, *American Economic Review*, 75 March: 190–7.

Mayer, W. and Riezman, R. (1990) Voter preference for trade policy instruments, *Economics and Politics*, 2 November: 259–74.

Mohammed, S. and Whalley, J. (1984) Rent seeking in India: its cost and policy significance, *Kyklos*, 37: 387–413.

Olson, M. Jr (1971) *The Logic of Collective Action*, Cambridge, Mass.: Harvard University Press.

Pincus, J.P. (1975) Pressure groups and the pattern of tariffs, *Journal of Political Economy*, 83 July/August: 757–78.

Pomfret, R. (1989) Voluntary export restraints in the presence of monopoly power, *Kyklos*, 42: 61–72.

Quibria, M.G. (1989) Neoclassical political economy: an application to trade policies, *Journal of Economic Surveys*, 3 (2): 107–36.

Scherer, F.M. (1979) The welfare economics of product variety: an application to the ready to eat cereals industry, *Journal of Industrial Economics*, XXVIII: 113–34.

Shaked, A. and Sutton, J. (1984) Natural oligopolies and international trade, in H. Kierzkowski (ed.) *Monopolistic Competition in International Trade*, Oxford: Oxford University Press.

Smith, A. (1994) Imperfect competition and international trade, pp. 43–65 in D. Greenaway and A.L. Winters, *Surveys in International Trade*, Oxford: Basil Blackwell.

Tarr, D. (1989) *A General Equilibrium Analysis of the Welfare and Employment Effects of US Quotas in Textiles, Autos and Steel*. Washington: Federal Trade Commission.

PART **VII**

TOWARDS 'THE BIG SLEEP'

CHAPTER (19)

Microeconomics, life and death ('or more serious than that'?)

19.1 Introduction

In 1789 Benjamin Franklin wrote in a letter, 'In this world nothing can be said to be certain, except death and taxes'. Chapter 13 dealt with taxes, so now it is time to face the real certainty – death.

The chapter title refers to the response of the legendary, now deceased, Liverpool football manager, Bill Shankley, to a reporter's question concerning retaining First Division (now Premiership) status for the club. The reporter suggested: 'It must be like life or death to you', to which Shankley responded: 'No, it's more serious than that'. In similar tone the economist, Thomas Schelling, wrote in an article entitled '*The life you save may be your own*', 'Death is an awesome and indivisible event that goes but once to a customer in a single large size' (Schelling 1968: 158). This quotation has both a somewhat amusing and somewhat chilling aspect. It is somewhat amusing in that the language of commerce is being used to describe the, daunting to most, inevitability that all of us will die. It is somewhat chilling in that, for some, the language of commerce as applied in economics ought not to be applied in this context.

Many of the problems met in this book revolve around the notion of uncertainty. For virtually everyone, although death is certain there is uncertainty as to its form, its timing and its anticipated consequences. Will there be any future life or not? If so, what form might that take? How will those left behind be affected?

Economists, armed with the power of theorising, have not been slow to take on the big questions of life and death – sometimes in the face of ridicule. In this final chapter a number of problems that have death in common are explored. Clearly, a suitable way to end!

The first problem deals with heart transplants, the second suicide and the third the choice of your length of life. A later section also deals with the way in which the saving of life is evaluated in cost–benefit analysis. There is also a short section devoted to recent work that connects economic decision-making to the workings of the brain.

To keep the tone light, it is worth recording the remark of our former colleague Professor David Collard, who posed the rhetorical question: 'Would you *want* to live beyond the time where you could read and make a useful contribution to economics?'

19.2 Heart transplants – an actuarial scientist does economics

In this section the prospect of 'being more Catholic than the Pope' is considered, in that non-economists seem to garner exactly the wrong idea about what economics involves. An article by Haberman (1980) was an attempt to apply cost–benefit analysis (or what the, presumably more optimistic, Americans call 'benefit–cost analysis') to the question of the economics of heart transplants. The article was concerned to demonstrate that heart transplants were a 'sound economic investment' (p. 877). Unfortunately, the author (then a lecturer in actuarial science) succeeds in providing a guide as to why everything containing the words 'costs', 'benefits' and '£ sign' symbols is not economics.

To illustrate the cost–benefit technique, the cost of a man (X) aged 25, suffering a critical cardiac condition, is considered in Haberman's study. He is married with two children, with gross earnings of £5000 per annum prior to his illness. Haberman compares the costs and benefits to the state of three alternatives for X:

a) X receives a heart transplant now and then is subject to the same chances of survival and of complete recovery as in the, so called, Stanford series of survival statistics;

b) X does not receive a heart transplant and lives as an invalid with his family for two years before dying;

c) X dies now.

The costs and benefits of each alternative are described in Tables 19.1 (a), (b) and (c). On the basis of these costs and benefits, the analyst recommends provision of transplant treatment as the least-cost way to deal with the expected ill health.

Although this has superficial plausibility, virtually everything about this study fails to correspond to neoclassical microeconomics. The author claims any debate on the value of heart transplant to the nation should make reference to calculations used in this article. The heading to the article makes the assertion 'heart transplants actually save the

Table 19.1(a) Receiving transplant treatment

	£s
(a) Cost of operation	14,600
(b) Cost of dependents' benefits for those patients who die, averaged over all patients in the series	3,760
(c) Cost of dependents' benefits during survival as an invalid, similarly averaged	3,380
(d) Cost of lost earnings during survival as an invalid, similarly averaged	3,160
Total four-year average cost	24,900
Average net of tax earnings as the benefit of the individual returning to work	6,840
Total net cost	18,060

N.B.
(b), (c) and (d) were calculated to allow for the then current survival and recovery rates expressed for individual X.

Table 19.1(b) Care and survival for two years before dying

Cost of nursing care	8,000
On death costs of dependents' benefits	5,010
During survival as an invalid, cost of dependents' benefits	5,870
Cost of loss of earnings	20,000
Total	38,880
Value of benefit of return to work	Zero
Total net cost	38,880

Table 19.1(c) No treatment and immediate death: widow and children receive social security benefits

Cost of dependents' benefits	9,740
Cost of loss of earnings	20,000
Total	29,740
Value of benefit of return to work	Zero
Total net cost	29,740

country money'. The general technique (namely cost–benefit analysis, CBA) attempts to quantify the cost to the state of a particular mode of treatment or therapy.

It is evident from these statements that the author is working with an organic view of the state and not a framework that is built in a non-organic way around individuals. The country or nation is not an actor in economics. Unfortunately, the technique, cost–benefit analysis, is nothing to do with quantifying costs to the state. It is about summing individual compensating variations in income (see Chapter 2). Ignoring the overstated and wrong interpretation of cost–benefit and cost-effectiveness analysis there are a number of other very serious reservations.

(1) It deals with a particular hypothetical individual, so that any claims about what would be the outcome must be treated with caution.
(2) Confusion about what question is being asked:
   ● Should transplants be carried out at all? In which case the concern is with total costs and benefits.
   ● Should we expand transplants as a life-saving technique? In which case the concern is with marginal costs and marginal benefits.
   Confusion is apparent in calculation (a) where the marginal cost of an operation is being compared with the author's view of average total benefits.
(3) Are the costs used a reasonable reflection of opportunity costs. As presented, they look like unadjusted NHS accounting data that may bear no relation to social opportunity costs.
(4) CBA is about allowing or facilitating interpersonal comparisons of utility by reference to individual compensating variations. To the extent this 'study' has a rhyme or reason it appears to be GNP maximisation. Even accepting this wrong interpretation of CBA, the author fails to distinguish between transfers and real resource costs. Social security payments are an example of the former and nursing resources an example of the latter. The author also fails to discuss whether a gross or net output approach is appropriate, i.e. should the patient's own consumption be netted out from any GNP contribution?
(5) The author does not understand that discounting is a reflection of time preference (see Chapter 8).
(6) From an NHS policy viewpoint, the article fails to justify transplants by comparison with other methods of saving life. Possible projects have to be ranked. Given a limited budget a cost-effectiveness table is required to allocate the budget to where mortality can be reduced in a least-cost fashion. Other evidence, e.g. child-proof drugs containers, suggested at the time that a life could be saved many times more cheaply than this estimate of the cost of a heart transplant route.

Doing heart transplants may be a 'good thing', i.e. 'efficient'. Heart transplants may be a cost-effective way to save a life. Unfortunately, this work answers neither of these questions. The only conclusion to draw from the article is that the author knows little about CBA and its Paretian welfare economics foundations. (For analysis premised on Paretian welfare economics see Cullis and Jones 2009).

This is not to say the author is not a sophisticated thinker but rather that, as far as economics goes, his thinking is virtually totally misplaced. There seems to be a case for economists promising not to do actuarial science and actuarial scientists promising not to do economics. For a recent discussion of the difficulties surrounding cost–benefit analysis see Cohn (2003).

19.3 Suicide and microeconomic analysis – economists do sociology!

In the previous section an outsider to economics undertook a small amount of intellectual imperialism; in this section the process is reversed as the focus falls on economists' invasion of (apparently) others' intellectual space.

While analysis of suicide is an important topic in itself, the analysis also illustrates issues raised in Chapter 1. In particular, consider the argument that perceptions of the 'world' are invoked by the theory that is presented and by the nature of 'facts'. What are the 'facts' when considering suicide? Recorded statistics may seem to have a hard reality but their fragility in this area of study is evident (and indeed is a topic of study in itself). Statistics are the product of incentives and chance. The incentive, for example, in Catholic countries where suicide is a sin is not to record death as a suicide if at all possible. By contrast, presumably the last thing any relatives of a kamikaze pilot would want is the death recorded as a flying accident. Everything is a matter of interpretation. Michael Hutchence, the rock star, apparently killed himself whilst indulging in an auto-erotic act. Is that suicide? If a driver kills themself whilst driving drunk, is that suicide? Suppose someone kills themself whilst consciously trying to be an 'attempted suicide' – as a cry for help. Is that suicide? Coroners will record some deaths as suicide if they fit into their notion of what 'suicide' entails and who commits it. It is a matter of subjective judgement that will vary from individual official to individual official, i.e. a chance element.

It follows, as always, that great care has to be taken with the apparent factual material theorists are seeking to explain. It may be more reasonable to see social scientists as comparing a theory of the causes of suicide with a theory of suicide measurement.

With these caveats in mind, using years of life lost under the age of 65 to measure the significance of suicide mortality, it is the third most important contributor after heart disease and cancer. This is a measure that will rise with rising suicide rates among youths around the world. An economic approach to suicide is valuable for a number of reasons (Yang and Lester 2006):

1. it involves individual decision-making, e.g. choice of method, location;
2. economic factors affect the number of suicides, e.g. poverty, bankruptcy;
3. suicides impose costs, e.g. medical and medico-legal costs, lost contribution to GNP;
4. economic policies, e.g. employment, social security and pension arrangements, can have intended and unintended impacts on suicide rates.

Attempted suicides are more prevalent than completed suicides and raise similar concerns with three times more attempts being made by females than males (see McIntosh 2003). Before focusing on economic analysis, the work of one of the founding fathers of sociology deserves recognition.

19.3.1 Durkheim's sociological theory of suicide

In 2000 the suicide rates per 100,000 per year were 44.1 in Lithuania, 39.4 in Russia, 34.9 in Belarus, but only 10.8 in the USA. (See World Health Organization's *World Health Statistics* on-line at www.who.int.) How is it possible to account for the (apparent) fact that suicide rate in one country is vastly different from that of another country and they are typically independent of the apparent 'attractiveness' of the various countries?

A similar question occurred to Frenchman Emile Durkheim (1958–1917) while studying in Paris in the late nineteenth century. The fact that different groups of people had widely differing suicide rates led to his belief that, although suicide might seem to be a highly personal (individual choice) act, it was not simply explained in terms of individual personalities. For Durkheim, to live in a certain society meant you lived under the domination of the logic of that society. Individuals were seen to be guided by this logic even though they might well be completely unaware of its influence (Berger 1963). Given this, in his famous research into suicide it was appropriate to ignore the intentions of suicidal individuals themselves in order to concentrate on their social characteristics. He set out to collect all available statistics on the subject of suicide and to identify those people who were likely to commit suicide and isolate the circumstances under which suicide was most likely to take place.

Durkheim found that divorced people had a higher suicide rate than married people, childless people had a higher suicide rate than those with children. Protestants had a higher rate than Catholics, city-dwellers higher than rural-dwellers, army conscripts had a higher rate than those who volunteered to join the army. Businessmen had a higher suicide rate than people working in other jobs, and socially mobile people a higher rate than people who stayed in their original social class. In 1897 Durkheim published his findings in *Suicide: a Study in Sociology*. In keeping with the perspective sketched above he argued that suicide was not simply an individual act but a product of social forces external to the individual. Clearly, he was not adopting the neoclassical choice framework in which society is non-organic (see Chapter 1).

In suggesting that the causes of suicide were to be found within society, Durkheim was laying the basis of the new science of sociology. Suicide was viewed as the product of social factors: 'real, living, active, forces which because of the way they determine the individual, prove their independence of him' (Durkheim 1897/1951: 38–9). In this view, the individual is the product of societal forces. Durkheim also had a policy dimension in mind, arguing that, if you want to do something about the suicide rate, you have to look at the society as a whole – as an organism.

A great deal of research into suicide has taken place since Durkheim's day. However, his main finding remains relevant: the greater a person's integration into social groups, the less the likelihood that the person will commit suicide. Durkheim suggested it was possible to divide suicide into three general types: *anomic, altruistic* and *egoistic* suicide. He said that each type was the product of a specific social situation:

(1) *Anomic* suicide happens when a person is not properly integrated into society and, instead, is thrown back on their own resources. For example, with respect to religion, Protestant societies had a higher suicide rate than Catholic ones because Catholicism, with its emphasis on rituals and doctrines, involved people in a more collective religious life than Protestantism where there is greater emphasis on free will.

   Anomic suicide also happens when society is so unstable that people cannot find suitable 'anchors' in times of moral uncertainty. The rise of science, for example, caused people to question previously held beliefs in the way that the world was created and to question the very nature or existence of a God. This was accompanied by a rise in the suicide rate as the product of too much angst. Here there is insufficient social integration.

(2) *Altruistic* suicide is the opposite of *anomic* suicide. *Altruistic* suicide happens when the individual is so very closely integrated, or absorbed, into a group that they are unable to distinguish the goals and the identity of the group from their own. A typical example of an individual being prepared to sacrifice their own life for their

peers would be the *kamikaze* pilots of the Japanese air force, who during the Second World War dive-bombed enemy ships, killing themselves in the attack. This kind of suicide can be related to so-called 'herd immunity'. Members of a particular African tribe were never taken as slaves as once any one of them was captured they *always* committed suicide, making capture valueless. Whilst disastrous at the level of the individual called upon to make the ultimate sacrifice it protected the organism – the tribe – from exploitation. Here there is too much social integration.

In recent years the presence of terrorist suicide-bombers has been felt frequently in many parts of the world. While this is partly discussed in Chapter 16, the picture here is complicated by the apparent promise of great tangible rewards to holy war bombers on reaching 'the other side'. The opportunity cost of this form of suicide may appear negative for these individuals. For many 'outside observers' these individuals are over-identifying with their religion.

(3) *Egoistic* suicide is the result of a change in a person's social position, which comes about so suddenly that they are unable to cope with the new situation. This might arise from an unexpected, substantial rise in wealth or fall into poverty, from the death of a close friend (or love – the 'Romeo and Juliet' effect) or from a divorce. Many wealthy Americans committed suicide in 1929 following the Wall Street Crash when they saw their great fortunes disappear overnight; however, Durkheim believed it was not so much the loss of their wealth that led them to commit suicide but the stress caused by having to make an adjustment to a new life – a disturbance in the collective order. Here social regulation (the extent to which society controls emotions and motivations) seems to be too low. Fatalistic suicide occurs where social regulation is too great.

Several empirical trends experienced in England and Wales over the century since Durkheim developed his theory lend some support to his work. The suicide rate dropped sharply during the two World Wars in the twentieth century. It has often been said that social integration was at a particular high level, as people worked together for the war effort – notice how older people reminiscing about the war often describe them as 'hard but good times'. The lowest rate last century for suicide amongst women was in 1915. This was also a very low year for the rate of male suicides.

Again, Durkeim's theorising seems to be supported by the fact that one of the highest suicide rates in the twentieth century for men in England and Wales was 1932. In that year 4045 men committed suicide. In 1933, a then unprecedented 1760 females took their own lives. This figure was exceeded for a very short time in the late 1950s and the early 1960s. The early 1930s were a time of very severe economic depression; in 1932 some 22% of the total insured workforce was unemployed. That the suicide rate peaked during those years backs up the theory of *egoistic* suicide during changes in prosperity – here in a downward direction.

Research since Durkheim reveals:

1. The old are more likely to commit suicide than the young.
2. Males commit suicide more frequently than females.
3. Suicide rates are higher in the highest and lowest socio-economic groups than in the middle groups.
4. Divorced individuals have a higher suicide rate than married people.
5. Those recently bereaved have a higher suicide rate.
6. There is a higher rate of suicide among city-dwellers than amongst rural-dwellers (however, recording procedures are very different in country and urban settings – in country contexts a record of suicide emerges less frequently).
7. Those with a history of mental illness, or chronic alcoholism, have higher rates of suicide than do those without these conditions.

19.3.2 **Hamermesh and Soss's economic theory of suicide**

Hamermesh and Soss (1974), recognised that the majority of suicides can best be explained by non-economic considerations but wished to establish the economic influences on the pattern of suicide. At the outset, it can be noted that economic variables are included in the discussion in the above subsection. The authors begin, in contrast to Durkeim, with the recognition of suicide as an individual decision. It is the location and nature of explanation that differs between the economist and the sociologist. 'Suicide being the only truly independent act' is a perspective suggestive of individual calculation at once at odds with Durkheim's starting point that made no one independent of the forces of society. The Schopenhauer quote at the head of Hamermesh and Soss's article, 'as soon as the terrors of life reach the point at which they outweigh the terrors of death, a man will put an end to his life' is evocative of a cost–benefit calculation. Given this, the task of economists lies in modelling costs and benefits.

As for benefit from life, Hamermesh and Soss argue that the utility function (U_m) for the average individual, age m, in a group can be represented by:

$$U_m = U\left[C(m, Y_p) - K(m)\right] > 0 \tag{19.1}$$

where

C = gross consumption;
m = age;
Y_p = permanent income;
K = per-period cost of subsistence living.

Given this, the present value of expected utility (Z) for this individual is simply the sum of each period's utility determined by net consumption, as the individual moves from age, α, to the maximum possible age ω (omega – the end age). It is the definite integral over that period (the area under the utility function) given by:

$$Z(\alpha, Y_p) = \int_{\alpha}^{\omega} e^{-r(m-a)} U_m P(m) \, dm \tag{19.2}$$

where $P(m)$ is the probability of survival to age m, given that the individual has attained age α and r is the private rate of discount used to form the present value. This formulation indicates that the benefit from remaining life is dependent on the number of expected years left (i.e. it lowers as age increases) and the positive impact of permanent income (life is better the higher your permanent income).

As for costs, they are represented as the term b_i, the 'distaste' for suicide defined for the group at birth. The term b_i is derived from a distribution $b_i \sim N(0, \sigma^2)$, i.e. a distribution that is normal (bell-shaped) with a constant variance. This term captures vital information such as sex and white/non-white status. For non-economists, this cost term is not well specified, in the sense that everything can be claimed to be in it apart from the terms in the utility function. Given this cost–benefit condition, the boundary condition for suicide is where costs equal benefits, i.e. where for individual i:

$$Z(\alpha, Y_p) = b_i \tag{19.3}$$

Suicides have an expected value of lifetime utility that is less than the distaste of death at the time they commit the act. If this is not to be an empty tautology, the empirical work the authors carry out must save the day. Their empirical prediction is that the age-specific suicide rates depend upon the distribution of permanent incomes and the distribution of tastes against suicide. For a given group, the suicide rate depends on (i) discounted real permanent income remaining at time t and (ii) the age of the group.

Using both cross-section and time series data the authors' predictions are largely borne out:

(i) The unemployed and the elderly are more prone to suicide;

(ii) Increased permanent income decreases suicide rates (although this result did not obtain for the youngest age group).

The use of permanent income might be questioned. It is based on the assumption that the individual maximises utility over an extended number of periods – tending to ignore transitory events – seeing things more in the round (e.g. perhaps expecting a stock market crash to be followed by recovery).

Since 1974 there have been other attempts to build economic models of suicide and attempted suicide and these are briefly considered below based on a list provided in Yang and Lester (2006).

19.3.3 Other economic theories of suicide

Given the neutral or amoral stance of economics, suicide is not judged as 'good' or 'bad' but is explored from the perspective of rational behaviour (the N and R of BORING in Chapter 1). However, below, two exceptions to this perspective (that involve, at least in part, irrationality) are the starting point.

19.3.3.1 Irrationality

The notion of rationality in economics has been met in Chapters 1 and 7. Becker (1962), whose notion of rationality was used in Chapter 1, notes two types of irrational behaviour. First, random, erratic, impulsive or whimsical behaviour and, second, preservative choices in which a person chooses, by and large, what they always chose in the past. There is too much habit and inertia about decisions for them to exhibit rationality. The first type of irrationality seems to lack a longer-run dimension and the second a shorter-run dimension. Lester and Yang (1991) match these with a typology of suicidal behaviour. In the first type suicide is the outcome of an impulsive acute episode. The young, for example, tend to apparently 'over-react' to issues that to older heads and eyes look relatively unimportant. In the second type suicide is the outcome of a long-term struggle with deep-seated psychological problems. This irrationality approach leaves economics out in the cold: 'Much suicidal behavior is due to psychiatric illness, for which the individual's reasoning and behaviour is not tractable within the context of economic theory, which requires rationality. However, economic analysis can still illuminate suicide behaviour' (Marcotte 2003: 629). Lester and Yang note that the suicides of those, say, suffering from an incurable painful illness or facing social and economic isolation or psychological hurt may well lend themselves to a cost–benefit approach and thereby reinstate a role for economics in the analysis of suicide and attempted suicide. These suicides at the end of a long painful process may well have involved previous failed suicide attempts.

19.3.3.2 An impulse-filtering model of suicide

In McCain (1990) a random stream of impulses generated in the brain are filtered through a set of motivational filters to see if the impulse should be acted upon, suppressed or transformed. The filtering process is the deterministic aspect of choice. Filters are unique to an individual, active to different degrees in different circumstances and vary over their lifetime. These filters can be focused on incremental utility, cognition, emotion, ethicalness, social conformity and the like. The cognitive filter can transform the action of other filters. Suicide may be prevented by one or more filters and hence the removal of one or more filters, say caused by psychological depression, may trigger suicide. The incremental utility filter might suggest 'My life is good – why would I commit suicide?' whereas the ethical filter might suggest 'It's not right to commit suicide'. In particular, the filter of social conformity is argued to be important for a theory of suicide with the operation of this filter being expressed in the refection: 'People like me just don't do things like that'. The base rate of suicides is not seen as 'rational' but rather the result of failures in the cognitive filter and/or its inactivity (perhaps reflecting mood changes induced by consumption of alcohol or drugs). However, economic variables like expected lifetime utility are, as above, seen as playing a role in explaining deviations from the base rate. Other influences include the knowledge that others with whom the individual identifies have themselves committed suicide, possibly suggesting suicide 'epidemics'. In January 2008 a young woman committed suicide in Bridgend, South Wales; she was the latest of seven apparent copycat suicides in that town within the previous 12 months. Social networking websites were alleged to have played a role in these tragic deaths. An officer in the South Wales Police commented: 'They may think it's cool to have a memorial website. It may even be a way of achieving prestige among their peer group.' Whatever the precise connections in this case, there is evidence of connections between media reports of suicide and copycat deaths.

19.3.3.3 Suicide: a cost–benefit approach

It was noted that the Schopenhauer quote above is evocative of a cost–benefit calculation. Yeh and Lester (1987) pick up on such a cue and offer the following possibilities for valuation.

Benefits	*Costs*
1. Release from physical and/or psychological pain	1'. Costs of physically organising the act and purchasing the means
2. Anticipation of impact, e.g. punishing survivors by making them feel guilty	2'. Costs of psychologically organising the act and fear of death
3. Restoration of public image, e.g. having let down 'the regiment', the empty room with the bottle of whisky and loaded revolver, was in many films the road to redemption	3'. Pain costs
	4'. Possible post-suicide punishment in another 'world' predicted by many religions
	5'. The lost opportunities in the form of net anticipated benefits from living on

Whilst quantifying some of these effects may be difficult, the implication is clear in that reducing benefits and/or increasing costs will reduce the number of suicides. Lester and Yang extend these types of considerations to a demand and supply model of suicide. The demand side (D_s in Figure 19.1) of the 'market' reflects benefits and mainly comprises a relief from tremendous distress. A scale of distress would determine the potential benefit from suicide, giving an upward-sloping demand curve as the greater the distress the greater the probability of committing suicide (plotted on the x-axis of Figure 19.1 with an upper limit at unity). Where D_s meets the vertical line above point 1 the probability of suicide has become 1. The considerations labelled 1' to 5' on the costs side of list comprise the elements in the supply curve (S_s). The lower these costs are the higher the suicide probability and hence the rightwards downward slope of S_s. The intersection of these unconventional D_s and S_s curves at point 2 gives the probability the individual will commit suicide, P_s, with the associated price/cost equalling benefits (B_s). To the right and left of P_s the outcome is unstable. To the left at P_{sL}, a low non-equilibrium value of the probability of suicide, marginal cost P_{sL}-3 exceeds marginal benefit P_{sL}-4 and a reduction in 'output' (the probability of suicide) would be predicted – a lowered suicidal tendency.

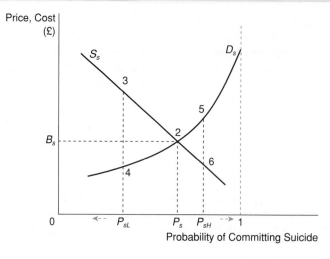

Figure 19.1
A supply and demand approach to suicide

To the right at P_{sH}, a high non-equilibrium value of the probability of suicide, marginal benefit P_{sH}-5 exceeds marginal cost P_{sH}-6 and an increase in 'output' (the probability of suicide) would be predicted – a raised suicidal tendency. Given this crisis, intervention that moves demand (D_s to the left) or moves supply (S_s to the left) or both should be successful. The demand curve may be relatively stable in that it reflects elements such as psychiatric disturbance, age, sex and a dysfunctional family background which might be seen as 'givens', so that it is generally 'shocks' that will shift the demand curve. This suggests that policies of working on the supply side, shifting the S_s to the left, is the most promising policy method to influence the number of suicides (e.g. reducing gun ownership or emphasising permanently lost opportunities in the future).

19.3.3.4 Labour force to 'life force' analogy

Huang (1997) views suicide as the decision to enter or leave the 'life market'. As a labour economist he picks up on the framework used in Chapter 10 to model labour force participation. Adapting the theory, it is recognised that utility sources need to be defined more broadly than simply income. Utility is seen as derived from income, love, health, fame, beauty, prestige, adventure, respect, security, fun, etc. However, these desirable attributes only come at the cost of labouring for them (L). The opposite of labouring in a tough world is leisure or relaxation (R) from labour, the ultimate 'relaxation' being permanent rest as in death. L therefore represents the effort of living and R measures its absence. The higher the expected wage (W) the bigger the reward to a unit of 'life' effort. Whilst most people find an interior solution with some L and some R, others find an (irreversible) corner solution (see Figure 10.13(a)) with all R and no L (committing suicide). This is in effect the 'discouraged worker' who exits the labour market when W falls below a minimally acceptable level to live and participate, perhaps reflecting ill health (physical and/or mental), business failure or public humiliation. The perceived market wage is below the reservation wage for 'life force' participation. Other labour market analogies can be drawn that fit with this.

Referring to Figure 10.13(b) and reversing the causality, an increase in the reservation wage for living captured in the slope of I_1 at point 1 can move the individual from a 'living' interior equilibrium at point 2 with some L and R to a corner solution and suicide at point 1 with all R. The rationale here is that of a very wealthy individual who may need more and more to keep life exciting and challenging, implying a very high reservation wage that may not be attainable. Individuals who expect too much of life may commit suicide.

Whilst the choice of 'complete rest' is seen as the outcome of balancing benefits and costs, the analysis involves the perceived expected wage and if this is mistaken (because of incomplete and imperfect information) the choice of suicide will not be the correct one sometimes (depression and severe emotional disturbances will tend to encourage pessimistic expectations or perceptions). Mistaken choices to commit suicide suggest a public policy that involves information provision, e.g. counselling that forecasts a 'silver lining' beyond the current 'black cloud'.

19.3.4 Economic theories of attempted suicide

19.3.4.1 Suicide attempts as investment in future utility

Marcotte (2003), building on Hamermesh and Soss (1974), has a lifetime utility-maximising model in which an attempted suicide, with currently a negative expected utility in future periods, can affect future expected utility in two ways – one a cost, the other a benefit. First, future health and maintenance costs will be raised if the attempt results in physical injury and disability. There will, however, be a benefit if the suicide attempt is used as an avenue of improving future consumption via inducing more attention and care for oneself. Additionally, there is the cost of the attempted suicide event itself – the distaste for the act itself. As always, when expected benefits exceed expected costs the attempt will take place. The model predicts: (i) that those with higher expected future income will be less likely to attempt suicide; (ii) if attempted suicide induces sympathy or resources from others the more likely it is to take place. If the latter effect is present, other things equal, those who attempt suicide will fare better than those who simply contemplate it because of the subsequent income effect. Using individual-level data[1] the author does indeed find that attempted suicides who survive report higher incomes than those who contemplate but never attempt suicide. The income gain is especially marked close to the attempt and is mainly focused on those investing in the most credible signal in the form of the most severe suicide attempts.

19.3.4.2 Suicide attempts as investment under uncertainty

Dixit and Pindyck (1994) note that a suicide attempt is like an ordinary investment under uncertainty involving an irreversible decision: uncertainty over future payoffs and the need to make a decision over timing. They argue that Hamermesh and Soss ignore the possibility of staying alive. In the language of information economics rather than take an irreversible terminal decision now, it might be better to increase flexibility by waiting and seeing if, in an uncertain future, events unfold to raise your utility. In this sense attempted suicide can be thought of as a holding action. Those that commit suicide predict the current 'blackness' in their lives will be reproduced in all future periods (extrapolative expectations – here negatives following negatives), failing to rationally recognise that the future is uncertain and that unexpected states of the world will arise that may not be so 'black' (adopting regressive-type expectations with positives following negatives – good times may be just around the corner!). Suicide attempters tend to think along rigid 'black' and 'white' lines with polarised views about, for example, the hopelessness of life. The task of regular therapy might then be to get patients to think more flexibly and see life in a more 'grey' way with some good things and some bad things. The authors note that religious and moral proscriptions against suicide can in part serve to repair this failing of rationality, by increasing the perceived cost of suicide and lowering the quality of life that will serve to trigger a suicide response.

---

1. Data on attempted suicides are even more fragile than those for suicides so extreme caution is required in their interpretation.

19.3.4.3 Suicide attempts as a signalling game

Rosenthal (1993) argues that in suicide attempts of moderate severity the individual is gambling over the outcome of surviving the attempt. The attempt is a message to others intended to signal hurt and induce a response from others (doctors, family, friends, etc.) in a way favourable to the sender. In the game, nature makes you a type 'normal' or 'depressed' and you know this as the message-sender but this is not known to the message-receiver. Information is asymmetric. The message-receiver wants to respond empathetically to the honestly depressed but unsympathetically to the dishonest 'normal' person who sends an 'I am a potential suicide' message. The sender wants a sympathetic response but values that response more highly if they are honestly depressed.

The game in extensive form is represented in Figure 19.2. Nature (N) makes the first move, assigning the sender's type depressed with a probability of p and normal with a probability of $1 - p$. On knowing their type the sender selects a strength of suicide attempt msp (standing for message strength probability) with $0 \leq msp \leq 1$ with 0 indicating no chance of death and 1 its certainty. Nature (S_n) now enacts the chosen msp value with $1 - msp$ being the survival rate. The R nodes connected by the vertical dashed line indicate the receiver has observed msp and whether the sender is alive but does not know whether to respond empathetically (e) if they think the type is depressed (node R_d) or unsympathetically (u) if the type is normal (node R_n). In each pair of payoffs (which are Von Neumann–Morgenstern utility numbers (see Chapter 7)), the first relates to the sender S and the second to receiver R. (Note that death offers zero payoff.) Their relative magnitudes for S are $a > b > 0$ and $c > d$ and $c > 0$. These magnitudes ensure S prefers e, an empathetic response, to u, an unsympathetic one. A 'normal' person prefers life to death and the depressed type prefers life with e to death as the payoff $c > 0$. R's payoffs are such that $x > w > 0$ and $y > z > 0$ so that R prefers e to u if the type is depressed but u to e otherwise; however, R always prefers S to live rather than die. R can be assumed to have beliefs about two values of msp contingent on the type information S has – one triggers e and the other u.

As has been met elsewhere for signalling games there are separating and pooling equilibria (within this case the pooling equilibria being no gambling-type suicide attempts). In the separating equilibrium S sets $msp = (a - b)/a$ when depressed and $msp = 0$ when normal and R responds with e when $msp \geq (a - b)/a$ and u otherwise. This is a gambling-type suicide. Normal would not send the message strength $msp = (a - b)/a$ to induce e, as the payoff cannot exceed $ba/a = b =$ payoff when msp is 0. The outcome is that if R observes $msp = (a - b)/a$, they believe S is depressed and enact e, offering a payoff of c to S and y to themselves.

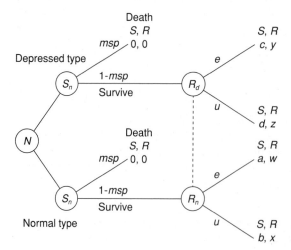

Figure 19.2
Modelling gambling-type suicide attempts as a game

By adopting a refined Nash equilibrium concept Rosenthal is able to draw two conclusions. First, gambling-type suicidal behaviour would be less common if it is relatively unlikely the depressed individual strongly desires an empathetic response (e.g. they might already be receiving care). Second, if the message-receiver's aversion to being empathetic to a normal type $(x - w)$ is greater relative to the receiver's preference for an empathetic response to a depressed type $(y - z)$, then senders are less likely to engage in gambling-type suicidal behaviour.

Generally public policy is directed at suicide prevention and the models presented above offer insights that were briefly reported. Factors involved in preventing suicides are: raising economic well-being; long-term medication and therapy; crisis centres; restricting access to the means of suicide; education and information provision. Yaniv (2001) provides a game-theoretic model of crisis intervention. In this brief excursion into the 'microeconomics of suicide' it is evident that the individual chooses the length of their life. Ironically, the standard economic approach to the demand for health extends this perspective to all individuals.

19.4　Investing in a timely death: do we all commit suicide?

The human body is a complex general equilibrium system (economy). In this system, if one vital organ (market) fails, the whole system (de)ceases. There are clearly incentives to keep the system healthy. There is the non-durable consumption good of feeling well now. There is a durable consumption good in the form of enhanced leisure time in the future.

The investment side can also be dichotomised. Other things equal, greater heath will raise an individual's marginal product in market production and have a pecuniary investment payoff in the form of an increased wage. Other things equal, greater health will raise marginal product in non-market production and have a non- pecuniary investment payoff, in the form of an increased non-market or household production (see Chapter 8).

Following Grossman (1972a, 1972b), health is a fundamental commodity (see Chapter 8), produced by combining own time with market and public-sector inputs. The beneficial market inputs (BI) are elements like good housing, diet, exercise equipment and, one amongst many other inputs, health care. The ability to produce health will vary from individual to individual, depending on:

(1) income, which determines access to market inputs;
(2) access to information and education on how to efficiently combine inputs;
(3) the characteristics of your body production function, which seems to be largely genetically determined.

Many inputs (labelled DI) like smoking, over-eating, fast driving, excessive drinking, over-working have a detrimental impact on health but, nevertheless, offer positive utility to many individuals. The implication is that individuals are utility-maximisers not longevity-maximisers. The insight that health is a fundamental commodity produced in households by individuals not in hospitals by doctors and nurses[2] is in itself fundamental.

Grossman sets these observations into a formal model whose structure is easy to grasp as follows:

(i)　in any time period i individuals have a health stock H_s^i with the initial stock inherited at birth;

---

2. It is wise not to assume hospitals are always helping. Hospital-acquired illnesses appear to be rampant in the UK with the popular press (*Sunday Mirror*, 29 August 2004) claiming the so-called super-bug MRSA is killing 20,000 patients a year!

(ii) the stock faces a depreciation rate (δ^i) in each period, reflecting the biological process of ageing;

(iii) gross investment in the health stock in period i takes place when $BI^i - DI^i > 0$;

(iv) net investment occurs when $BI^i - DI^i > \delta^i$ and H_s^i rises;

(v) net disinvestment occurs when $BI^i - DI^i < \delta^i$ and H_s^i falls;

(vi) death occurs when an individual's health stock falls below the survival minimum (H_s^i min).

The analogy is clearly 'individuals as depreciating capital goods'. Given their full income constraint and the prices of market inputs, individuals choose the level of investment they undertake and within the biological limits that set the maximum possible age, ω, individuals are seen as 'choosing' the length of their own lives (i.e. your length of life is endogenous to your investment choices, as generally in the economics of suicide models). The individual is viewed as having the capacity and information to choose their state of health at all times.

19.4.1 How healthy do you want to be?

A diagrammatic version of Grossman's model developed by Wagstaff (1986) makes clear what is at stake. In Figure 19.3 panel (a) in the south-west corner illustrates the individual's budget constraint with respect to a composite input called health inputs (HI) and a composite consumption good (C). As elsewhere, the location of this constraint depends on income and the prices of these (composite) goods. Moving north to panel (b) a production ray is found that connects heath inputs to health (H), holding the technology of health production (T_h) and social capital (S_c) constant. Social capital describes the quality of an environment where a person lives, grows up and develops and affects the ability, in this case, to produce health. Other things equal, it is more difficult to produce health in poor slums than in more affluent locations.

The slope of the ray is the marginal product of health inputs ($MP_{HI} = \partial H / \partial HI$), which can be seen to fall as health inputs increase. That production function in general form is:

$$H = f(HI \mid \bar{T}_c, \bar{S}_c) \tag{19.4}$$

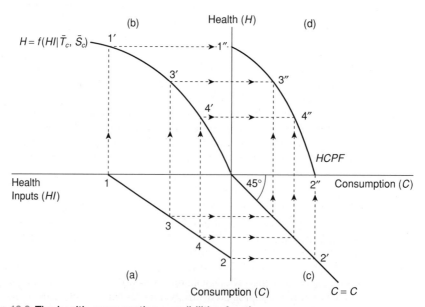

Figure 19.3 The health-consumption possibilities frontier

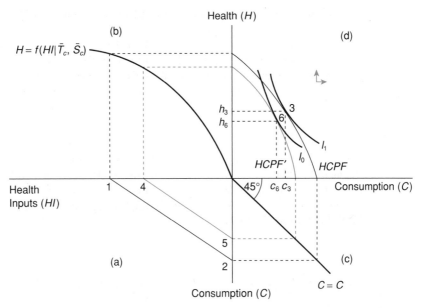

Figure 19.4 The utility-maximising health state

Devoting all income to health inputs gives maximum health at point 1″ on the y-axis in panel (d) associated with input level 1 in panel (a) and point 1′ on the production ray in panel (b).

Moving east from panel (a) is a 45° line (panel (c)) which translates consumption levels in panel (a) to identical consumption levels in panel (d). Devoting all income to consumption gives minimum health at point 2″ on the x-axis in panel (d) associated with consumption level 2 in panel (a) and point 2′ on the 45° line in panel (c). In panel (a), taking all possible intermediate starting points on the budget constraint, e.g. points 3 and 4, generates a continuous health-consumption possibilities frontier (HCPF in panel (d)) for the individual with 3″ and 4″ points on it.

The shape of the health-consumption possibilities frontier is determined by the specific functional form given to the health production function.

Figure 19.4 repeats the salient features of Figure 19.3 and closes the model by introducing the individual's indifference map over health and consumption. With HCPF operative (associated with budget constraint 1-2 in panel (a)) the utility-maximising choice is at point 3 on indifference curve I_1 in panel (d) of Figure 19.4 with health level h_3 and consumption level c_3. (In the extreme, the longevity-maximiser would be represented as someone with a horizontal indifference map in panel (d).)

What are the predictions of Grossman's model? Consider the following.

19.4.1.1 A fall in income

A fall in income for the individual would move the budget constraint in panel (a) of Figure 19.4 to the right in a parallel fashion from 1-2 to 4-5, shifting HCPF to HCPF′ in panel (d) of Figure 19.4. With HCPF′ operative (associated with budget constraint 4-5 in panel (a)) the utility-maximising choice is at point 6 on indifference curve I_0 in panel (d) of Figure 19.4, with health level h_6 ($< h_3$) and a lowered consumption level c_6 ($< c_3$) (with a lower-income individual buy less of all normal goods). Other things equal, health falls with an income fall for an individual. As an exercise the reader may want to amend Figure 19.3 to provide predictions for (a) a fall in the price of health inputs and (b) changes in technology that serve to increase the efficiency of heath production. The results can be checked against Wagstaff (1986).

19.4.1.2 Extending the analysis

It is worth elaborating the Grossman analysis to give a more dynamic perspective. In common with the usual theoretical framework for investment decisions, individuals are assumed to maximise an inter-temporal utility function made up of the flow of services from health and consumption of other goods in each year of life. Maximisation leads the individual to equate the marginal return on the asset health with its marginal cost. The return to the jth individual is made up of the marginal psychic return (a_j) and the marginal monetary return (y_j). The cost of health capital is the rate of interest forgone on other assets (r_j) plus the rate of depreciation (δ_j) (less any saving from purchase of 'health' now, rather than in the future, owing to future increases in the marginal cost of health improvement). Thus,

$$y_j + a_j = r_j + \delta_j \tag{19.5}$$

for a given consumer in time period i.

Grossman examined the consumption and pecuniary investment aspects separately. For simplicity, we concentrate on the investment part of the model only. The pecuniary return (y_j) depends on three components:

(i) the daily wage rate of the representative individual in the ith year (W_j^i),
(ii) the marginal product of health, measured in terms of the number of days of good health generated by a unit of health stock (G_j^i), and
(iii) the marginal cost of gross investment in health (C_j^{i-1}) purchased in the previous period and including both time and money costs.

These three elements combine to give the rate of return:

$$\frac{W_j^i \, G_j^i}{C_j^{i-1}} = y_j^i = r_j^i + \delta_j^i \tag{19.6}$$

For any given individual with a given health state there will be an associated marginal product of health G. Thus a marginal efficiency of health capital (*MEHC*) schedule could be plotted out for the jth individual showing the return to each level of health ($W_j^i \, G_j^i / C_j^{i-1}$). If it can be assumed that the marginal product of health declines asymptotically to zero as health increases; this curve will have the shape familiar in macroeconomics. Grossman supports such an assumption by pointing out that the return to health, measured in healthy days, has a limit of 365 days per year. This copes with the reduction in disability but not with debility. The latter may affect wage rates but this problem is explicitly not pursued in the model.

Given the optimal stock of health capital, defined by equation (19.6), it is possible to examine the separate effects of age and wage-rate increases on the optimal stock. Considering age first, assume that wage rates, the marginal product of health stock and the marginal cost of gross investment are independent of age. The assumed effect of increased age is an increase in the rate of depreciation of health (δ_j). This is not to suggest that all aged individuals are necessarily less healthy than all young ones, but that, for a given individual, the annual rate of depreciation of health is greater in old age. The implication of Grossman's assumptions is that, from equation (19.2), increased depreciation leads the consumer to choose a lower stock of health in order to increase the marginal product of health and equate the marginal return with the higher cost. (Recall the assumption that the marginal product of health is lower the higher the health stock.) Thus, when faced with known and increasing rates of health depreciation, Grossman's model suggests that the individual will *choose* a lower health state in each successive year.

This leads the individual to choose their length of life as the optimal health stock will ultimately decline below the necessary life-supporting minimum and death will occur.

The demand for health care is derived from the demand for an optimal health stock in each period, with current health stock, depreciation and investment in health care being the determinants of future health stock. But the health stock and the flow of gross investment are not simply related. Declining health stock over time is not necessarily associated with declining consumption of health care in each year. The increasing depreciation rate reduces the net increase in health from a unit of gross investment through health care. That is, the additional health created is subject to the same higher depreciation rate as the existing stock and so less net investment is produced per unit of gross investment.

The precise relationship between age and health-care consumption depends on the elasticity of the demand for health. This will be highly inelastic if the marginal product of health rises rapidly as health state falls; e.g. if a small reduction in a particular individual's health state owing to depreciation prevents them working at all when previously they worked full-time, then the marginal product of a small increase in health will be very large.

Thus, in the face of a higher cost of health owing to increased depreciation, the individual will purchase additional health care to offset the depreciation. The new health state will thus be close to the original state (see Figure 19.5(a)). Conversely, if a reduction in health has a smaller effect on the marginal product of health, then the individual will not seek to offset a great deal of the natural depreciation in their state of health. Therefore, when their health state falls they may seek less health care (see Figure 19.5(b)).

The two figures together make this point more simply. Both individuals start at point 1. Over a year their health state depreciates by the same proportion and the rate of depreciation increases to put them at point 2. Both respond according to their demand curves – the marginal efficiency of health capital – to the new higher marginal cost of health. In Figure 19.5(a) a large part of the depreciation is offset by health care while in panel (b) it is not. Both arrive at point 3. In subsequent periods, as depreciation rates increase, an individual behaving as in Figure 19.5(a) suffers bigger losses of health stock, as their absolute level is higher, and invests more in health care to offset the fall, as the amount of health produced per unit of health care falls with rising depreciation. It should be clear that the opposite outcome occurs if the individual's demand for health is elastic as in Figure 19.5(b).

The effect of wage rates on the stock of health and the demand for care is made up from two elements. The marginal product of health, measured in healthy days, is clearly

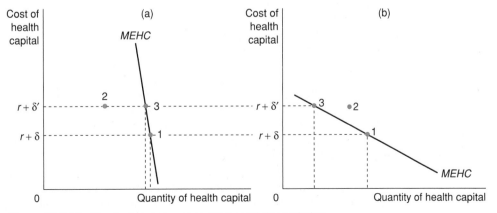

Figure 19.5 **Health stock responses to increased depreciation**

worth more at higher wage rates. But the consumer's time is also an input into health care, and so, if the wage rate increases by Z per cent, then the cost of care will increase by

$$\frac{Wt}{Wt + P_h} \cdot Z < Z \qquad (19.7)$$

where

W = wage rate;
t = time input per unit health care;
P_h = price per unit of other inputs to health care.

Assuming that own time is not the only health care input, the percentage increase in wages will exceed the increase in unit cost and the return to health will increase at all levels of health stock. That is, the marginal efficiency schedule or demand for health will increase (shift rightwards), causing higher levels of health to be demanded at any given interest and depreciation rates. The precise impact of higher wages depends on the elasticity of the demand for health and the share of time costs in total unit cost of health care. However, since the increment of health obtained from a unit of gross investment in health care is not affected by the increase in wages, the demand for health care will increase (or, in the extreme, remain constant) with rising wage rates.

19.4.2 Policy implications of the health capital model

The health capital model has a number of implications for public policy to improve the efficiency, or equity, of the provision of health care. With respect to efficiency it is worth emphasising, as Dowie (1975) has, that perhaps the major public policy role to be filled by government in a Grossman-type world is the provision of health information on the effects of detrimental health inputs and on efficiency in combining favourable inputs rather than the provision of health services *per se*. An indicator of a successful human capital 'chosen' lifespan is a 'tumultuous exit' with all major organs collapsing simultaneously as a consequence of depreciating at consistent rates. Unless you have planned to be a liver donor, 'a liver in good order is useless if the heart goes first' (McKenzie and Tullock 1975: 124) – recall the general equilibrium point above. The objective is 'to die with zero bank balance (above that which is planned) and no surplus capacity in bodily organs (above that which is planned)' (McKenzie and Tullock 1975: 124). In this respect, Napoleon who, on his death, was reported to be suffering from many very serious illnesses may have got it right when many others have got it wrong – as far as is known there are no prizes for the fittest of the dead.

This emphasis on information provision and health education follows from the individual (and not doctors, hospitals and the like) being the 'producer' of the fundamental commodity health. While health-care service inputs will generally (but not always) have a positive impact on health, their contribution may be swamped by the impact of detrimental impacts. (When you next visit a hospital notice how many nurses smoke and how many inpatients in pyjamas are collected at entrances smoking.) The evidence seems clear: individuals are not health-maximisers and are apparently risk-takers with respect to health!

This observation aside, consumers are assumed to be capable of making efficient choices that maximise their utility. Health-care consumption as an input is likely to increase with income, and so, since consumer choice is efficient, income support measures will achieve the desired degree of equity. A further implication relates to longevity data. In health and other social policy debates longevity data are often used as implicit, or explicit, success indicators but the perspective offered here is that you should die when you planned to. Longevity data records what is happening to lifespans may not be a good indicator of what was chosen *ex ante*. Keith Moon, the 'legendary' hell-raising rock drummer, died in his early thirties. Was this his chosen lifespan, or did he die too soon compared to his investment plan (or indeed too late!)?

19.4.3 Criticisms of the model

Key problems with the model (of which Grossman was fully aware) relate to the fact that it is cast in terms that make it subject to the problem areas discussed in Chapter 7, namely information and uncertainty:

(i)   Individuals are assumed to have knowledge of their own health state but neither they, nor a doctor, can establish that piece of information with certainty;

(ii)   Individuals are assumed to know the rate of depreciation and, again, this can only be roughly gauged;

(iii) Perhaps the major uncertainty is the precise production function relating your particular health improvement to any net investment you choose. Some individuals seem to be able to combine smoking with other inputs and not suffer much, whilst others die at a young age. Grossman does introduce a probability distribution to cover deprecation rates but, as Dowie (1975) notes, this is perhaps the best (intuitively) understood parameter.

Against this background, the claim that individuals choose the length of their own lives looks overstated. That said, the approach has very strong economic foundations being consistent with the 'utility-maximising subject to constraints' perspective of the neoclassical world.

19.5 Human life valuation (value of a prevented fatality)

The discussion on heart transplants above partly centred on the failure to identify compensating variations in income as relevant economic measures of cost and benefit (Section 19.2). In Section 19.4 a perspective in which the length of your life is chosen by you was elaborated. In this section the two are combined to the extent that the role of compensating variation measures in your untimely death is explored. The Grossman model does not address the risk of being killed faced daily by all and what, if anything, should be done to reduce that risk.

One of the key considerations in cost–benefit studies of investment in medical care, road safety, etc. is the valuation of human life or value of a prevented fatality. While cost-effectiveness analysis (effectively, searching for the least-cost method to achieve a stated objective) may be sufficient to choose between alternative projects that save the same number (and quality) of life-years, ultimately the decision must be made regarding how much investment to undertake. To answer this question it is necessary, either implicitly or explicitly, to weigh the costs of the investment against the benefits. To estimate the benefits, the value of human life is a key consideration. For our purposes, the literature that has emerged concerning the estimation of the value of human life is important in so far as it illustrates the main questions that a cost–benefit analyst must have in mind when searching for the 'appropriate' shadow price. For a discussion of different methods and their rationale see Cullis and Jones (2009); here the focus is willingness to pay as this reflects consumer sovereignty. The principle that economists recognise in a cost–benefit study is the one related to potential Pareto improvement. If a cost–benefit study yields a net present value and if shadow prices have been accurately estimated, this will mean that the gainers from the project could compensate the losers (who forgo the use of the resources) and remain better off if there were costless redistribution. This means that shadow prices should reflect the values that individuals themselves place on the goods and resources. In any investment in medical care or road safety, the question is how much any individual would pay for a reduction in the probability of the loss of life. Following Jones-Lee (1974), assume that an individual begins with wealth W and a probability of loss of life p (where $0 < p < 1$). The expected utility ($E(U)$) is contingent on the chances that the individual will live to consume wealth or die. That is to say,

$$E(U) = (1 - p)L(W) + pD(W) \qquad (19.10)$$

where $L(W)$ and $D(W)$ are the utility of wealth conditional on survival and death respectively.

Imagine that the individual is offered the opportunity to reduce the probability of their death from p to $p'(< p)$. It is usual to assume that $dL(W)/dW > 0$. It may be that $dD(W)/dW > 0$ (for in calculating expected utility, utility might be derived from assets that can be left as a bequest) – however, it would be reasonable to assume that $L(W) > D(W)$, i.e. that the individual prefers to be alive! In such circumstances the individual will pay money to reduce the chances of a loss of life. Therefore, a reduction in the probability of loss of life means that there is a maximum sum V that the individual can give up which leaves their expected utility identical to the position prior to the reduction in the loss of life:

$$(1 - p')L(W - V) + p'D(W - V) = (1 - p)L(W) + pD(W) \qquad (19.11)$$

The sum V is the compensating variation, i.e. the maximum sum that the individual will be prepared to give up for a reduction in the probability of a loss of life. Under the above assumptions, it is reasonable to suppose that the individual will trade off wealth, as in Figure 19.6, to pay for a reduction in the probability of death from p^*, or will require payment for an increase in the probability of death above p^* (a negative V being the minimum an individual will accept to put up with an increase in p). If an investment in health care, or road safety, alters the probability of a loss of life, dV/dp at $p^* = £x$ and this is the marginal valuation of a decrease in risk from p^*.

Summing this for those at risk will provide a first estimate of the benefits of the investment. There are at least two ways of estimating this value for use in a cost–benefit study:

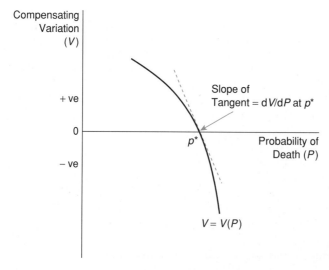

Figure 19.6
Compensating variations and life valuation

(i)   The first explicit way is to use a questionnaire approach. Jones-Lee (1976) attempts this approach, asking respondents what discount (additional) price they would accept to fly with an airline (*B*) which has a stipulated worse (better) accident record than an alternative airline (*A*). On the basis of a survey of some 90 individuals, of whom 31 replied, the evidence suggested that the value of life is £3 million. However, it may be questioned whether individuals can cope with questionnaire studies where the probabilities they are invited to consider are small. Of course, with questionnaire studies there is always the issue of whether or not those involved will respond honestly or prefer to respond strategically or try to second-guess the answer they think the investigator wants.

(iii) A second approach is to consider how much individuals actually pay for additional safety. That is to look at actual behaviour as opposed to hypothetical behaviour. Jones-Lee (1977) examined the implicit valuation that individuals attach to safety according to the frequency with which they incur the costs of changing tyres on their cars.

Within this second approach, the most popular method of obtaining an implicit willingness to pay is an appeal to information contained in labour market decisions. The labour market offers a vast range of jobs with different characteristics. Borjas (2000) (also see Oi 1974) develops the argument in the following manner. In this analysis the two key labour market characteristics are the wage rate (W) and the risk of being hurt in your job (P_h) so that utility to a worker can be given as:

$$U = U(W, P_h) \tag{19.12}$$

with $\partial U/\partial W > 0$ and $\partial U/\partial P_h < 0$.

That is, wage rate is a good and the injury probability a bad. As such, a worker's preference map will take the general shape depicted in Figure 19.7.

In Figure 19.7(a), holding utility constant say on I_1, the slope of the indifference curve shows how the wage rate must increase to compensate for an increase in P_h as indicated by the relevant $+\Delta W$. Of course, a key aspect to economics is that individuals differ and panel (b) shows two individuals *A* and *B* who have different risk aversities. It is clear the steeper the curve the greater the risk aversity.[3] With $+\Delta P_h$ common, *A* requires $+\Delta W_A$ to hold them on the same indifference curve, whereas *B* requires only $+\Delta W_B$ and, hence, *A* can be seen to be more risk-averse than *B*. Employers know that higher wages are required to compensate workers for an increased risk of injury and they have an incentive to produce a safe work environment. However, devoting real resources to producing a safe environment is costly.

Figure 19.8(a) captures this classic trade-off with respect to isoprofit curves increasing at a decreasing rate. The intuition is that to successively lower the probability of injury by similar decrements becomes increasingly costly when the probability is already reasonably low, so that a bigger wage decrement is required to keep profit constant. Witness the relevant Δs. With equal $-\Delta P_h$, the ΔW at the pre-existing lower level of P_h is increased, i.e. $-\Delta W < -\Delta W'$ in absolute size. For any given probability P_{h1}, when wages are lower ($W_1 < W_0$) profits are higher and, hence, $\pi_1 > \pi_0$. The location of isoprofit curves are likely to vary with the nature of the employment, so that in Figure 19.8(b) Firm 1 (starting from a common P_h) finds it less costly to produce $-\Delta P_h$ than does Firm 2 ($\Delta W_1 < \Delta W_2$). It is clear the steeper the curve the greater the marginal cost of decreasing P_h. If perfect competition is assumed there will be no economic profit for any firms and π_0 for each firm is the relevant isoprofit curve.

---

3. Here we are ignoring the risk-loving preference with $\partial U/\partial P_h > 0$.

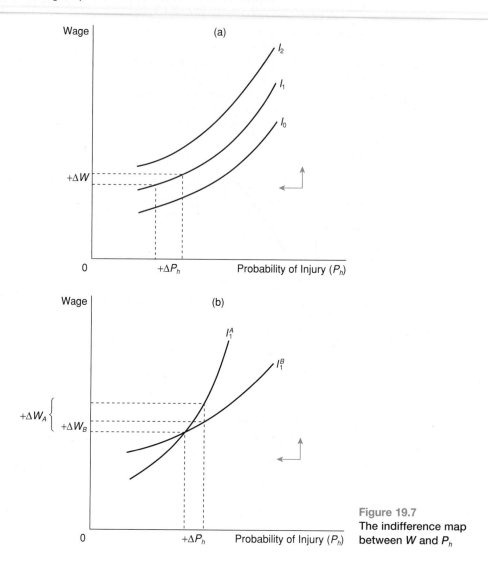

Figure 19.7
The indifference map
between W and P_h

Getting to the heart of the argument involves Figure 19.9, where the indifference curves for three individuals are depicted with individual A more risk-averse than B and B more risk-averse than C. The π_0 line for each of three firms are also illustrated with Firm 1 finding it less costly to produce a safe environment than Firm 2 and Firm 2 less costly than Firm 3. Firm 1 might provide office services, Firm 2 building services and Firm 3 test pilot services. The punchline is that given the shapes of the indifference curves and isoprofit curves, workers should self-sort with the risk-averse individual A working with the firm that finds it low-cost to be safe, namely Firm 1. Similarly, B will be with Firm 2 and C with Firm 3 and self-sorting equilibrium points are points 1, 2 and 3.

If individual A was at Firm 2 at point 4 on I_0^A they could increase utility to I_*^A by moving to point 1. The locus of points like 1, 2 and 3 provides the hedonic wage line or function showing how wages, even in the presence of heterogeneous preferences, have to increase to compensate workers for an increased probability of injury at work.

As regards actual empirical work, Viscusi and Aldy (2003) survey the literature that infers the value of life from individuals' everyday life decisions. Studies focus on the trade-off individuals make when accepting a risky job, or when consuming products that

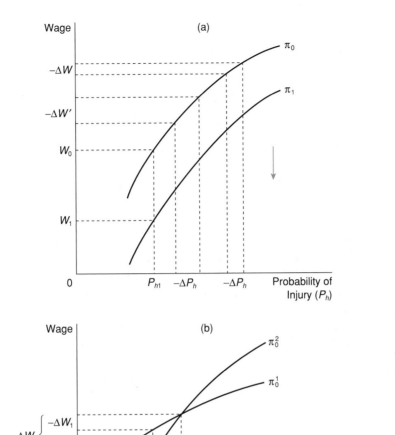

Figure 19.8
The isoprofit curve between W and P_h

involve a risk of loss of life (e.g. driving an automobile, smoking a cigarette). With evidence based on market choices, economists estimate the value of a statistical life.

Focusing on hedonic wage methodology, it is possible to disentangle the wage–risk trade-off from other factors that affect wages. Observed values of p (i.e. the probability of loss of life) and w (the wage paid) reflect the joint influence of supply and demand on market equilibrium. The value of statistical life can be estimated by focusing on the variables that explain the wage that is paid. For example:

$$w_i = \alpha + \beta_1 p_i + \beta_2 q_i + \beta_3 H_i + \beta_4 X_i + \beta_5 C_i + \varepsilon_i \tag{19.13}$$

where

w_i = worker i's wage rate;
α = the constant term;
p_i = the fatality risk associated with i's job;
q_i = the non-fatal injury risk associated with i's job;

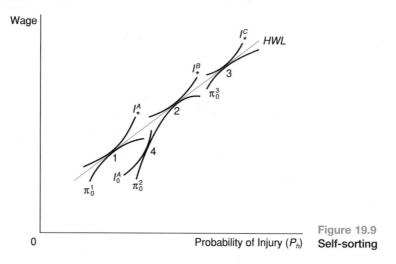

Figure 19.9
Self-sorting

H_i = a vector of personal characteristics for worker i;
X_i = a vector of job characteristics for worker i;
C_i = the worker's compensation benefits payable for a job injury suffered by worker i;
ε_i = the random error term reflecting unmeasured factors influencing i's wage rate.

H is a vector that will include a variety of personal characteristics (e.g. education, job experience, age). **X** is a vector that will include indicators of job (e.g. blue collar; white collar; management position; the worker's industry). The coefficient β_1 indicates how wage is affected by an increase in the risk of death. If the risk were 1.0 then β_1 would indicate the change in wage required to face one expected death (β_1 is then the value of the statistical life estimate).

Housing and product market decisions also reflect a trade-off between mortality risk and money. The same underlying theory is relevant but now the task is to estimate a hedonic price equation (rather than a hedonic wage equation).

19.5.1 Framing public policy from human life valuations

Public policy debates can be brought into sharp relief in this type of analysis. One public policy intervention is to regulate workplace safety. But will this be welfare-enhancing in a labour market that generates compensating wage differentials? In Figure 19.10 suppose the outset is point 1 with wage W^* and probability of injury P_h^* if P_{hg} was imposed by government regulation, then equilibrium would move from point 1 to point 2. The results look welfare-decreasing, as the worker moves to a lower level of utility from I^* to I_g. The firm moves from a normal profit level of π_0 to a lower loss-making one of π_g and must expect bankruptcy! It looks like a recipe of how not to help.

However, critics of this type of 'the market does everything' reasoning do not accept that well-designed policy intervention cannot be welfare-enhancing and doubt these behavioural-based studies. They point out that, if you start from a position of efficiency, then, of course, any policy interference will at best be neutral and typically induce inefficiency. They can provide a number of reasons why they would like their analysis to begin elsewhere. If the labour market is imperfectly competitive, e.g. monopsonised, it is likely that the compensating wage differentials will not be appropriate. They note the analysis assumes that individuals are fully informed about the risks involved when they make job choices and that the information is 'rationally' assessed. However, all sorts of problems can arise here. Some jobs, initially thought not risky, may, with the passage of

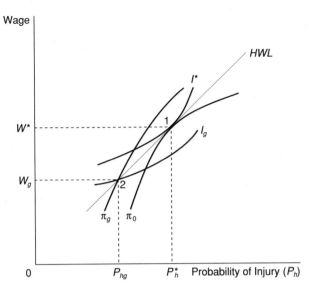

Figure 19.10
Welfare-decreasing regulation

time, be shown to be extremely risky, e.g. working with asbestos, so that the initial probability information is wrong.

Further, there are many criticisms that stem from how individuals think about probabilities. Kahneman and Tversky (1979) developed prospect theory around the s-shaped value function illustrated in Chapter 2 and the use of decision weights to replace probabilities.

For a 'regular prospect', value is given by:

$$v = \pi(p)\, v(x) + \pi(q)\, v(y) \tag{19.14}$$

where p and q are the probabilities and sum to less than 1 and payoffs x and y are of mixed signs. If $p + q = 1$ and x and y are of the same sign then value is assigned as:

$$v = v(y) + \pi(p)\, [v(x) - v(y)] \tag{19.15}$$

where $v(y)$ is the minimum gain, or loss, and the second term is the assessment of the likelihood of further gain or loss. The focus here, however, is the terms $\pi(p)$ and $\pi(q)$ which are the decision weights.

Figure 19.11 shows how people attach decision weights or their subjective evaluation of probabilities to probabilities. While $\pi(0) = 0$ and $\pi(1) = 1$ the function is not well behaved near the end points and sags below the 45° degree line in the middle. Individuals appear to ignore altogether very low probabilities (the range VL) but attach disproportionate significance to low probabilities (say, 1 in 25) (the range L). Differences between very high probabilities and certainty are either ignored or exaggerated (the VH range). Over the whole range $\pi(p) + \pi(1 - p) < 1$, representing sub-certainty as the sum of the weights associated with complementary events is typically less than the weight associated with the certain event. Note how $\pi(0.5) < 0.5$. For the current context, if P_h was in the VL range, it suggests workers would ignore it and require no compensation for a very low probability of injury.

There are other doubts about probabilities. The notion of cognitive dissonance suggests individuals are unhappy if their actions do not correspond with their beliefs. It implies that, in the labour market, you would think:

> 'Only idiots would work in high-P_h jobs but I seem to have a high-P_h job, making me an idiot. But I am not an idiot, therefore P_h must actually be low for my choice of job to be sensible.'

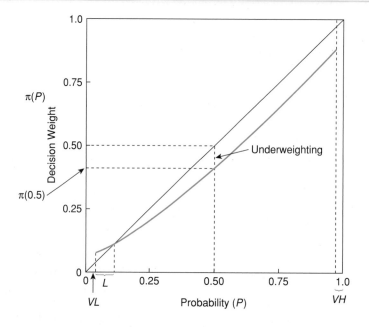

Figure 19.11
Decision weights expressing the subjective evaluation of probabilities

Individuals are said to 'manage' the risk down by choosing a low belief about P_h. (For example, test pilots will think it is a safer occupation than it is.) Here reasoning is being used to justify choices made and not to make the choice. However, the upshot is that the compensating wage differential may be too low.

There is also a merit want dimension in that you might take the view that some individuals accept, in your view, an irrationally small compensating wage differential for the known risk, such that their choices should not be respected (see Chapter 5). Slovic (e.g. 2000), the author who has done most on the social psychology of risk in a joint publication found males perceived risks as much smaller than females for a set of 25 different hazards. If accepted, it would tend to suggest, other things equal, a lower value of life for males than females would be found in behavioural-based studies.

In terms of the public policy debate, consider Figure 19.12. A worker with optimistic probability perceptions may think they are on I_2 at point 2 with wage 0-W exposed to P_{h2} risk when in fact they are at point 1 on I_0 with wage 0-W with much higher risk P_{h0}. In these circumstances, imposing P_{hg} creates an equilibrium at point 3 on a higher indifference curve I_1. Welfare has now been increased. Once again, analysis turns on the assumptions you are prepared to adopt.

Leaving probabilities aside, perhaps the most contentious criticism, however, is that aimed at the underlying conceptual basis of this form of shadow pricing that deceptively involves a 'statistical' life. Broome (1978) argues that, in the case of human life, compensating variations (CVs) are unacceptable because they rely on ignorance to make the approach operational. In the words of Varoufakis (1998: 74) 'The trick that prised this valuation from us was that we were not informed in advance of which one of us will die.' The *ex ante* calculation will not approximate the *ex post* outcome and will, therefore, not be a good policy guide; i.e. those that die would, by and large, require infinite compensation and the net present value of the project could not remain positive. Broome does not suggest a replacement technique, just that some beneficial projects may involve known deaths.

Table 19.2 serves to summarise the above discussion and, moreover, outlines the basis of the principles that may be applied to provide a shadow price in a cost–benefit analysis. It will be clear that, at root, the differences between these approaches depend upon

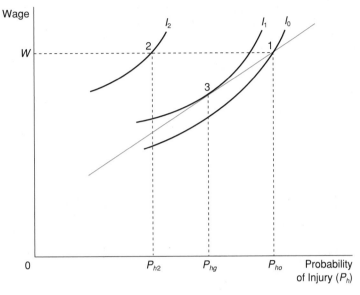

Figure 19.12
Welfare-increasing
regulation

Table 19.2 Sources of life valuations and implied worlds

View of World (a)	Approach (b)	Sources of information (c)
Maximising Gross National Product	Livelihood/(narrow) human capital	Lost market output as measured by (gross) labour earnings
Government sovereignty – government 'merit want' view of world in which 'others' may be a better judge of an individual's welfare (or individuals delegate their choice)	(a) Implicit politico – administrative decisions (b) Explicit politico – administrative decisions	Analysis of past decisions of government Statements of government policy on life valuation
Producer sovereignty – the experts who produce health care are best judges of individual welfare in health care	(a) Implicit medical decisions (b) Explicit medical decisions	Analysis of medical decisions Statements of medical professionals
Consumer Sovereignty – the individual is the best judge of their own welfare (and income distribution not inequitable)	(a) Implicit willingness to pay (b) Explicit willingness to pay	Analysis of individual behaviour Statements of individuals in questionnaires or experiments to elicit their valuations

Source: Adapted from Cullis (1993).

the objective function implied by the analysis. This is a normative decision. However, it would be reasonable to argue that, if a particular shadow price is used, this price should be consistent with the pursuit of a chosen objective function. It might be noted that, in the context of the application of cost–benefit analysis to select a potential Pareto improvement, the relevant shadow price would be that which is based on the compensating variation ('willingness to pay').

19.6 Economics: 'I can't get you out of my head'?

One recent area of economic research is called neuroeconomics (see Camerer, Lowenstein and Prelec (2005) and Montague (2007)). As its name suggests, it connects economics to the functioning of the brain. In much of this work functional magnetic resonance imaging (fMRI) is used to study the functioning of the brain when economic decisions are made with a view to connecting brain behaviour and choices. An important book on this area of study is Glimcher (2003). It attempts to demonstrate that deductive game theory amongst other parts of economic theory cannot only help explain human decisions, but, indeed, how decisions are made in the neurological circuits of the brain. Throughout this text great emphasis has been placed on economics as a mental skill, i.e. as a specific way of applying certain principles to all problems. The question here is what happens if those principles are applied to the brain itself and effectively poses the question as to whether brain functioning itself 'works as if' it conforms to the predictions of economic theory – econoneurology!

If this could be established then economics literally would be everywhere. Neurons located in the lateral intraparietal area of the posterior parietal cortex of the brain, so-called LIP neurons, in expected utility experiments act as if they are Bayesian optimisers in a game theory setting (see Ortmann 2004).

In the example explored here decisions over life and death are used to illustrate the framing effects noted in Prospect Theory (see Chapter 2) and, in the simple presentation here, the brain acting to minimise the cost of making a good decision i.e. least-cost decision-making subject to a utility, or outcome, constraint **within** the brain. Are brain inputs guided by an efficiency calculus? The version presented here is perhaps made more vivid than the original authors would wish to defend, the authors being Gonzalez, Dana, Koshino and Just (2005) who used fMRI to reconsider the irrational decision-making over risky choices apparently induced by framing. They used the well-known 'Asian Disease Problem' first presented by Tversky and Kahneman (1981).

Participants in an experiment are asked to make choices over a certain or probabilistic option to save lives (this is the positive frame) and a certain or probabilistic option to minimise deaths (this is the negative frame). The relevant question (in **bold**) runs as follows (commentary in *italics*):

Imagine the United States is preparing for an outbreak of an unusual Asian disease that is expected to kill 600 people. Two alternative programmes to combat the disease are proposed. Scientific estimates of the consequences of the programmes are as follows:

Positive Frame encouraging coding on the north-east 'gain-risk-averse' arm of the value function in Chapter 2.

If Programme A is adopted, exactly 200 people will be saved.

If Programme B is adopted, there is a 1 in 3 probability that all 600 people will be saved and a 2 in 3 probability that no people will be saved.

That is, Programme A offers a certain 200 saved lives whereas Programme B offers a probabilistic 200 lives saved (= 1/3 × 600 + 2/3 × 0).

Negative frame encouraging coding on the south-west 'loss-risk-taking' arm of the value function in Chapter 2.

If Programme C is adopted, exactly 400 people will die.

If Programme D is adopted, there is a 1 in 3 probability that nobody will die and a 2 in 3 probability that all 600 will die.

That is, Programme C offers a certain 400 deaths, whereas Programme D offers a probabilistic 400 deaths (= 1/3 × 0 + 2/3 × 600).

Of course, these two choices are formally identical: it is just that the same information is cast in different frames.

Respondents to these questions typically display irrationality in that they prefer A to B and D to C; however, A is formally equivalent to C (and B to D) and therefore should be preferred to D by those choosing A over B (the majority). The Prospect Theory explanation for this (indicated in italics) is that individuals tend to be risk-averse for positively framed options, that are hedonically coded as gains, and risk-taking for negatively framed options that are hedonically coded as losses (Gonzalez, Dana, Koshino and Just (2005) review other explanations). Following their exploration, suppose decisions involve two costs. These are emotional costs that depend on the outcome of the decision and cognitive costs (which are the mental processing costs of coming to a decision). Emotion and cognition tend to integrate in the prefrontal cortex (PFC) of the brain and activity in different areas of the brain can be detected by fMRI scans of individuals in the process of making decisions.

Using 10 subjects responding to decision choices in an fMRI scanner allows the authors to shed light on the Asian Disease Problem. They postulate that emotional costs are high for what are deemed 'bad' outcomes (here 'deaths' as opposed to 'saves') and induce greater PFC activity, other things equal. Further risky alternatives require an, albeit simple, expected value calculation producing higher PFC activity, other things equal.

The results of the scans for the relative costs of the Asian Disease Problem seem consistent with the schema in Table 19.3.

Relative costs suggest:

(i)   Certain gains are preferred to risky gains;
(ii) Risky losses are preferred to certain losses;
(iii) Cognitive costs are lower for certain gains as compared to risky gains;
(iv) Cognitive costs for certain losses are equal to cognitive costs for risky losses.

Thus 'least-cost decision-making' ranks the programmes A preferred to B, B to C and D, and D to C and explains the observed decision choices.

Whilst Economic Psychology to date has been about applying psychology to economics, this research effectively reverses the process and applies economics to the psychology of the brain. Currently, a very large amount of research is being carried out in this area and appears to have great potential. In some instances it is clear that implications for taxation and public expenditure lurk behind some research. For example, it will be possible to locate a brain pattern justification for 'merit want' policy when, and if, satisfactory answers can be delivered for questions such as:

Are hard drug abusers' thought patterns very different from non-abusers – they evaluate 'wrongly'?

Table 19.3 Least-cost decisions and the brain

	Emotional costs	*Cognitive costs*
Certain gain (Option A)	LOW	LOW
Risky gain (Option B)	LOW	HIGH
Certain loss (Option C)	HIGH	HIGH
Risky loss (Option D)	HIGHISH	HIGH

Do criminals neurologically make decisions in noticeably different ways – again evaluating 'wrongly'?

How do the brains of the morbidly obese appear to function?

However, caution needs to be exercised. Like the economy, the workings of the brain are still relatively ill-understood (when the brain is young the function carried out by different cells can change as cells adapt; individuals who physically lose a good part of their brain when young appear to function perfectly well, etc.) and rushing down the road to strong policy prescriptions is fraught with difficulties. There is always the problem of cause and effect. Is brain activity being used to rationalise choices, or are choices being used to rationalise brain activity? The now-discredited phrenology used the shape and size of the cranium as an indication of the character and mental faculties of individuals. A major potential pitfall would be to use fMRI scans in the same way so that 'Your fMRI scan defines what you are'.

19.7 Challenge: Is a worked-out paradigm being mined?

Thomas Kuhn (1962) wrote a very influential book, entitled *The Structure of Scientific Resolutions*. As the title suggests, it is about science. Kuhn argued that 'normal' science was built around a paradigm (an underlying framework or conception of reality), which initially enables you to ask big questions and analyse important issues, but after this initial period the paradigm becomes a set of blinkers. The sorts of questions that can be asked become increasingly trivial (decreasing marginal product of the paradigm?) and this ultimately leads to a breakdown as new individuals, often from outside the discipline, and who do not share the paradigm, enter and create a new paradigm and another period of normal science begins. Knowledge, from this perspective, grows not cumulatively but rather changes stepwise with discrete shifts of paradigm. As a casual illustration, this text has noted when a cited author has received the Nobel Prize for economics, a prediction consistent with the Kuhnian perspective, is that they will often not be straightforwardly trained economists. There is some evidence for this in that some of the recipients named were trained as engineers, mathematicians or physicists or drew their inspiration and/or techniques from elsewhere (e.g. psychology and the use of laboratory experiments by Vernon Smith the 2002 Nobel Prize winner who shared with Daniel Kahneman). In a reverse example, the section above notes how neuroscientists are importing some of the content and language of economics. Whilst Kuhn himself doubted his contribution had application to social sciences, the insight is a powerful one.

The neoclassical paradigm that has been the heart of each chapter involves an underlying view of the world in which:

(1) the *status quo* is dominant (and implicitly is capitalism) and is assumed to be the normal form of economic organisation that will always continue;
(2) individuals' conflicting interests can be reconciled with one another in market exchanges as long as property rights are well defined and enforced;
(3) equilibrium forces exist and in the long run, at least, tend to exert themselves;
(4) any changes conceived of are always marginal and of a gradual and adaptive kind. Life is effectively a progression from one equilibrium to the next.

Sweezy (1970) shows how the above provides two lines of attack to those who wish to depart from what for some has become the hegemony of the neoclassical view.

(i) The neoclassical paradigm is exhausted and the questions you can ask within it have long since been asked. Is modern microeconomics left with the minute, elegant and unimportant curiosities? For some, the answer is yes and they might for example, glance at the *Journal of Economic Theory* and see how far professional academic economics is from everyday life's concerns.

(ii) The paradigm, even if it did exist, clearly is not the world you see about you in which there are disruptive forces, conflicts of interests, violent revolution, terrorism and suicide bombers. These are all current observations that could be documented but despite the attention given to them in this text, critics of neoclassical economics can claim that it never has anything fundamental to say about them because it implies a different underlying world from the one described above.

Following this thought leads to other perspectives. Marxists would argue that conflict must be placed at the centre of analysis. Others desire a move from individualism to a 'holistic' approach, where theorists might be encouraged to look at the changing shape of the forest rather than just analyse individual trees – the interrelatedness of components and structures (see Dopfer 1976).

Currently the neoclassical paradigm seems to be largely dominant but that is not to say there are no current critics and the purpose of many of the challenge sections in each chapter was to illustrate this. Those wishing to hone their criticisms might look at Keen's (2001) book *Debunking Economics – the Naked Emperor of the Social Sciences* and Fullbrook (2004), *A Guide to What's Wrong with Economics*. Fullbrook's 'Introduction' notes recent evidence of dissatisfaction with what he calls 'narrowband economics' (the bulk of this text). This is summarised below. In June 2000 a small number of economics students in Paris asked for reform of their economics teaching towards the empirical world of facts accusing neoclassical teaching of exhibiting 'disregard for concrete realities' (Fullbrook 2004: 2). They also called for a more pluralistic approach so that something more than neoclassical economics met their ears in lectures. This is a more 'broadband approach'. In June 2001, 27 PhD students at Cambridge wanted an 'Opening up of Economics' focusing on how neoclassical economics harmfully dominates the research, publications and policy analysis process.

In August 2001 students from 27 countries met in Kansas City and released their 'International Open Letter' to economics departments to take note of broadband concerns. These included: a wider definition of economic actors as a product of their biological and social environment; recognition that individuals are part of a culture that restricts the decision choices and activities that are valid or acceptable; recognition that economic thinking cannot be independent of the personal characteristics of the thinker; greater emphasis on empirical evidence; more use of qualitative techniques (case studies, participant observation, etc.) as opposed to the 'de rigueur' 'formal model, data set, econometric results' of currently published economics articles; greater interdiscipliniarity and awareness of historical processes at work. This is a tall and conflicting order and raises all sorts of large debates in themselves some of which were introduced earlier in this text (see Sections 1.6 and 9.5). It is the 'completeness' of neoclassical economics as opposed to other ways of thinking that is perhaps its greatest strength. Sawyer's (1995: 41) comment on neoclassical labour market economics:

> 'While there is probably no fully coherent alternative model, there are plenty of ideas, some of which may in future be fused together to provide one or more coherent alternatives.'

seems to reflect the state of the debate in general. The type of criticisms listed above are not new (see Dopfer 1976) and some responses have been made. The flavour of this text has been how broad 'narrowband' economics can be. However, it is hoped by now the reader is 'well informed' and will be on the way to taking their own critical view as to the strengths and weaknesses of standard presentations in intermediate microeconomics.

As to the future path of microeconomics, if Kuhn is correct there is no point in asking current (big name) economists what microeconomics will look like in years from now as the 'paradigm-shifters' are in other academic disciplines.

19.8 Summary

As this is the 'end of life's decision line', some general summary discussion is offered alongside material directly relating to this chapter. The idea of liberal democracy seems to have won the day as far as political organisation is concerned and with the collapse of the centrally planned economies the idea of a market (neoclassical) economy seems to have won the day as far as economic organisation is concerned. This does not signal the end of economics – times change. The neoclassical world described in the bulk of this text is peopled by *homo* or *femina economicus*. This caricature is described by three axioms or characteristics: (a) the individual is 'rational'; (b) the individual is egoistic; (c) egoism takes the form of economic self-interest in narrowly defined terms (i.e. *homo economicus* is a personal wealth-maximiser) (Brennan and Lomasky 1993). There are many who would regard *homo economicus* as unrepresentative (see Kelman 1988 for a survey). However, *homo economicus* behaves consistently; behavioural responses to changed constraints are predictable (Stigler and Becker 1977). Moreover, it is possible to evaluate welfare changes by reference to individuals' preferences and, thereby, satisfy a normative underpinning of the Paretian criteria.

Applying Occam's razor, problems in this world are solved, or arise, depending on the extent to which economic man or woman confronts exclusion. On the production or supply side, with no exclusion (freedom of entry and exit) perfect competition can be invoked. If there is exclusion (barriers to entry) then imperfect competition is observed and inefficient quantities produced. On the consumption or demand side, the implications are of a reverse kind. With exclusion, markets can generally work efficiently (private goods). However, without 'appropriate' exclusion, problems of market failure arise (public goods, club goods, quasi-public goods and common-pool goods) and inefficient quantities are consumed. In this way, the vast majority of production and consumption configurations are covered.

Critics, on the other hand, want to supplant *homo economicus* with a more limited and more real character and lay emphasis on bounded rationality, satisficing behaviour, interrelatedness, reference points and the framing of decisions. Research in experimental economics and in cognitive psychology over the past two decades has shed light on 'irrationalities' (see Thaler 1994 for an early survey; also see Wilkinson 2008 on behavioural economics). For example, anomalous behaviour has been identified when behaviour, at variance with the predicted behaviour of *homo economicus*, is systematic and predictable.[4] *Homo realitus*, like *homo economicus*, can also be thought of as embodying three axioms or characteristics: (a) individuals exhibit some form of bounded (or limited) rationality (which may apply to the workings of the brain in itself); (b) individuals are not narrowly self-interested, so that utility derives from many sources; (c) individual behaviour is endogenous to the context, or reference frame, in which it takes place.

Elsewhere this has been dubbed 'individual failure' to provide a parallel concept to market failure (see Jones and Cullis 2000). Whereas the above discussion ascribes market failure to *homo economicus* being confronted with non-exclusion, elaborating individual failure lays emphasis on *homo realitus* and his reaction to different consumption and

---

4. Some argue they can be dismissed as 'mistakes' (Wittman 1995) but such 'mistakes' are not random. They are repeated time after time in experiments and do not 'wash out' of policy analysis.

production contexts or reference frames. As witnessed at various points in this text, this approach to individual decision-taking has enjoyed some exposure but not to the extent of the neoclassical perspective and whether this imbalance is sustained into the future remains to be seen.

As for this chapter, it was clear that non-economists' attempts to proxy economic reasoning and application can go dramatically awry. Attempts to analyse suicide in a neoclassical way offered some insight into that 'tragic choice'. The human being as a depreciating capital good offered a rich set of insights including the one that not only suicide cases choose the length of their own lives. A successful health service allows individuals to efficiently and equitably enact their utility-maximising health investment plan that may, or may not, involve a long life. Human life valuation in cost–benefit exercises provided a convenient way to illustrate the scope of the standard economic calculus. As for the very small excursion into neuroeconomics, it suggests economic theory may have a wider application than even the most ambitious of early economists would have dreamed.

Life and death has been the focus of this chapter. If, like Jack Wiseman, on the anticipated news of a fatal cancer diagnosis, you can courageously write to a colleague:

'I am fairly certain the problem is not trivial. All this must make our plans less certain (**the unknowability of the future!**). But we should simply adapt to it, and press ahead until prevented.' (Quoted by Hartley 2000: F453)

(the highlighted words referring to your central critical contribution to the study of economics) then it is evident economics has permeated your soul. For the rest of us, perhaps, the more limited understanding presented in these chapters will do!

References

Becker, G.S. (1962) Irrational behavior and economic theory, *Journal of Political Economy*, 70: 1–13.

Berger, P.L. (1963) *Invitation to Sociology*, Harmondsworth: Penguin.

Borjas, G.J. (2000) *Labour Economics*, 2nd edn, New York: McGraw-Hill.

Brennan, G. and Lomasky, L. (1993) *Democracy and Decision: the Pure Theory of Electoral Preference*, Cambridge: Cambridge University Press.

Broome, J. (1978) Trying to value a life, *Journal of Public Economics*, 9 (1): 91–100.

Camerer, C., Lowenstein, G. and Prelec, D. (2005) Neuroeconomics: how can neuroscience inform economics, *Journal of Economic Literature*, 53: 9–64.

Cohn, E. (2003) Benefit-cost analysis: a pedagogical note, *Public Finance Review*, 31 (5) 534–49.

Cullis, J.G. (1993) Waiting Lists and Health Policy Chapter 2, in Frankel, S.J. and West R.R. (eds) *Tackling Waiting Lists in the NHS*, London: Macmillan.

Cullis, J.G. and Jones, P.R. (2009) *Public Finance and Public Choice*, 3rd edn, Oxford: Oxford University Press.

Dixit, A.K. and Pindyck, R.S. (1994) *Investment under Uncertainty*, Princeton, NJ: Princeton University Press.

Dopfer, K. (1976) Introduction: Towards a new paradigm, pp. 3–35 in K. Dopfer *et al.* (eds) *Economics in the Future*, London: Macmillan.

Dowie, J. (1975) The portfolio approach to health behaviour, *Social Science and Medicine*, 9 (11/12): 619–31.

Durkheim, E. (1897/1951) *Suicide: a Study in Sociology*, trans. J.A. Spaulding and G. Simpson, New York: Free Press.

Fullbrook, E. (ed.) (2004) *A Guide to What's Wrong with Economics*, London: Anthem Press.

Glimcher, P.W. (2003) *Decisions, Uncertainty and the Brain. The Science of Neuroeconomics*, Cambridge, Mass.: The MIT Press.

Gonzalez, C., Dana, J., Koshino, H. and Just, M. (2005) The framing effect and risky decisions: examining cognitive functions with fMRI, *Journal of Economic Psychology*, 26: 1–20.

Grossman, M. (1972a) *The Demand for Health; a Theoretical and Empirical Investigation*, New York and London: Columbia University Press.

Grossman, M. (1972b) On the concept of health capital and the demand for health, *Journal of Political Economy*, 80 (2): 223–55.

Haberman, S. (1980) Putting a price on life, *Health and Social Service Journal*, 4 July, 877–9.

Hamermesh, D.S. and Soss, N.M. (1974) An economic theory of suicide, *Journal of Political Economy*, 82 (1) January/February: 83–8.

Hartley, K. (2000) Jack Wiseman, 1919–1991 Obituary, *Economic Journal*, 110 (464): F445–54.

Huang, W. (1997) Life force participation perspective on suicide, pp. 81–9 in D. Lester and B. Yang (eds) *The Economy and Suicide: Economic Perspectives on Suicide*, Commack, NY: Nova Science.

Jones, P.R. and Cullis, J.G. (2000) Individual failure and the analytics of social policy, *Journal of Social Policy*, 29 (1): 73–93.

Jones-Lee, M.W. (1974) The value of changes in the probability of death or injury, *Journal of Political Economy*, 82: 835–49.

Jones-Lee, M.W. (1976) *The Value of Life: an Economic Analysis*, London: Martin Robertson.

Jones-Lee, M.W. (1977) An empirical procedure for estimating the value for life from tyre replacement data, Paper presented to the Health Economics Study Group Conference, Newcastle.

Kahneman, D. and Tversky, A. (1979) Prospect theory: an analysis of decision under risk, *Econometrica*, 47: 313–27.

Keen, S. (2001) *Debunking Economics – the Naked Emperor of the Social Sciences*, London: Zed Books.

Kelman, M. (1988) On democracy bashing, *Virginia Law Review*, 47: 199–27.

Kuhn, T.S. (1962) *The Structure of Scientific Revolutions*, Chicago: University of Chicago Press.

Lester, D. and Yang, B. (1991) Suicide behavior and Becker's definition of irrationality, *Psychological Reports*, 68: 655–6.

McCain, R.A. (1990) Impulse filtering: a new model of freely willed economic choice, *Review of Social Economy*, 48: 125–71.

McIntosh, J.L. (2003) 'Fact Sheet', American Association of Suicidology www.suicidology.org.

McKenzie, R.B. and Tullock, G. (1975) *The New World of Economics*, Homewood, Ill.: Richard D. Irwin.

Marcotte, D.E. (2003) The economics of suicide, revisited, *Southern Economic Journal*, 69 (3): 628–43.

Montague, R.P. (2007) Neuroeconomics: a view from neuroscience, *Functional Neurology*, 24 (4): 219–34.

Oi, W. (1974) On the economics of industrial safety, *Law and Contemporary Problems*, 38 Summer-Autumn: 669–99.

Ortmann, A. (2004) Review of Glimcher (2003) cited above, *Journal of Economic Psychology*, 25: 891–4.

Rosenthal, R.W. (1993) Suicide attempts and signalling games, *Mathematical Social Sciences*, 26: 25–33.

Sawyer, M. (1995) The operation of labour markets and the economics of equal opportunities, Chapter 2 pp. 35–86 in J. Humphries and J. Rubery (eds) *The Economics of Equal Opportunities*, Manchester: Equal Opportunities Commission.

Schelling, T.C. (1968) The life you save may be your own, pp. 127–62 in S.B. Chase Jr (ed.) *Problems in Public Expenditure Analysis*, Washington, DC: Brookings Institution.

Slovic, P. (2000) *The Perception of Risk*, London: Earthscan.

Stigler, G. and Becker, G. (1977) De gustibus non est disputandum, *American Economic Review*, 67: 76–90.

Sweezy, P.M. (1970) Toward a critique of economics, *Monthly Review*, January, pp. 1–9.

Thaler, R.H. (1994) *Quasi Rational Economics*, New York: Russell Sage Foundation.

Tversky, A. and Kahneman, D. (1981) The framing of decisions and the psychology of choice, *Science*, 211: 453–8.

Varoufakis, Y. (1998) *Foundations of Economics – a Beginner's Companion*, London: Routledge.

Viscusi, W.K. and Aldy, J.E. (2003) The value of a statistical life: a critical review of market estimates throughout the world, *Journal of Risk and Uncertainty*, 27 (1): 5–76.

Wagstaff, A. (1986) The demand for health: theory and applications, *Journal of Epidemiology and Community Medicine*, 40: 1–11.

Wilkinson, N. (2008) *An Introduction to Behavioral Economics*, Basingstoke: Palgrave Macmillan.

Wittman, D.A. (1995) *The Myth of Democratic Failure: Why Political Institutions Are Efficient*, Chicago and London: University of Chicago Press.

Yang, B. and Lester, D. (2006) A prolegomenon to behavioral economic studies of suicide, Chapter 27 in M. Altman (ed.) *Handbook of Contemporary Behavioral Economics Foundations and Developments*, Armonk, NY: M.E. Sharpe.

Yaniv, G. (2001) Suicide intention and suicide prevention: an economic perspective, *Journal of Socio-Economics*, 30: 453–68.

Yeh, B.Y. and Lester, D. (1987) An economic model for suicide, in D. Lester (ed.) *Suicide as a Learned Behavior*, pp. 51–7, Springfield, Ill: Charles Thomas.

INDEX